READER AND REVIEWER COMMENTS

"I received your book in good shape. It is the Best Book on Stars ever written!...

Your book is the most complete of all books. It covers everybody. If I were a star, I couldn't wait to die just to get in your book!"
— Robert Allen Gray
(ELK VALLEY TIMES, Fayetteville, TN)

"This is a curious book.... In that 'The International Film Necrology' (published by Garland in 1981) does not provide information on causes of death, this book does have value, and it is, in a rather weird way, a fun book through which to browse."
— Anthony Slide
(CLASSIC IMAGES, Davenport, IA)

"As a film necrologist I want to say I found your book interesting and very informative; I would like to say also enjoyable reading, but how can one say they enjoy reading about deaths?"
— Billy H. Doyle (Valley Station, KY)

"I received the wonderful book 'Deaths of Noted Movie and TV Personalities' and it was exactly what I have been looking for for so many years....

The feature I like best, (yet so many chapters are great) is the feature telling how the stars died, such as with cancer, murder, heart attack. I have noticed over the years so many stars have died so young and I wondered just why.... I think they must lead a very fast life."
— James S. Harris (Dayton, OH)

"I correspond with a fellow N.E.A.S. member in Birmingham, England and he keeps quoting from (your book) so much that I think it must be very valuable, and so would like to have a copy...."
— Jane Fritz (Wheeling, WV)

"I have been waiting a very long time for someone to come out with this book! I truly love those old movie stars....

We can truly say that we had our heroes back there. I will never forget the fond memories that I have of them."
— T. Campbell (Washington, D.C.)

"I just today got your book...and enjoyed it very much. My dad called it a 'Dead' book; I thought that was kind of funny.

Keep up the good work with your movie books. I sure do enjoy this first book I have bought of yours."
— Jesse Wayne Barker (Richmond, KY)

"Your revised edition of 'Deaths of Noted Movie and TV Personalities' has really impressed several members of my family and some friends. So far, I have given three copies as gifts. Enclosed is a check...for an additional copy."
— Ann Michalik (Dover, DE)

"I have received all of your editions of 'Deaths of Noted Movie & TV Personalities' and I've enjoyed them very much."
— Mrs. Lucy Jones (Sterling Heights, MI)

"I am in receipt of the 5th edition of your 'Deaths of Noted Movie and TV Personalities.' It is a wonderful book and most

certainly reflects the enormous amount of research you put into the project.

As an author of movie-related books, I most certainly understand what goes into such a project. I have already found it to be a valuable tool in research and will recommend it to others.

I wish you well and urge (strongly) to keep up the good work."
— Leon Smith (Bonsall, CA)

"I must tell you how much I appreciate the 5th edition of your 1991 book of stars, etc. It's beautiful and most informative;... I appreciate the work you put into it and I thank you."
— Frances Lucania (Woodhaven, NY)

"The latest 'Deaths of the Stars' arrived today — you've 'outdid' yourself with this one! It's well worth the money, and I'm going to recommend it to others I know...."
— Lucille Kaplan (Jackson Heights, NY)

"I recently purchased a copy of the 1992 'Final Curtain' and find it to be one of the most fascinating books of its kind...."
— Robert R. Young (Lansdale, PA)

"I just wanted to write and tell you how much I appreciate your book.... It has to be the most informative book in my library, and has helped me in my research.

I have obituaries on the stars going back to 1961, and have often wondered where they were laid to rest....

Thanks again for all the work and time spent on this book. I have looked for a long time to find this kind of book with the information I have been wanting."
— Rosalie Gunderson (Salt Lake City, UT)

"First of all, I think your book 'Final Curtain' is the most accurate and most interesting. It's about time a book like this came out. I refer to this as the 'cemetery bible'....

I am an actress, so hopefully someday I can be mentioned in your book, when that time comes."
— Michele Devulder (Orange, CA)

"Boy, am I glad to hear about you. I am also a movie and film buff....

I wrote to Bob Dorian—host of American Movie Classics— and guess what? I got your name and book title; called up and got your book within three days. Boy, was I surprised. I love the book and everything in it....

Mr. Jarvis, I wish you would print the photos of the deceased right next to the names, so that way I (would) know who they are....

I'm having a ball with your book 'Final Curtain.' If this book had been in any of my book stores, like Walden's or Books-a-Million, I would have gotten it a long time ago."
— Cathy Smith (Richmond, VA)

"I received my copy of 'Final Curtain' just this past week, and I must say that I am extremely pleased with your accomplishment. You are to be congratulated for the great amount of effort and research this work must have entailed. As an avid movie fan, especially of those who were stars during Hollywood's Golden Age, I will treasure this book....

I, for one, will be in the market for your next update!"
— Roger L. Belton (Longview, WA)

"I just bought your book 'Final Curtain' and I have to say it is the best reference book I have read in years. There is certainly nothing like it.

Many times you watch movies and you really wonder whatever happened to that person. Why don't we see them in any other movies? Your book tells you why. And more important, (it) tells you of the person's demise and age.

I was surprised to see that some of my favorite actors and actresses died tragically...

Please keep this book updated through the years. If Leonard Maltin can do it with home videos, you can, too...."
— Renee Grentus (Rochester Hills, MI)

"I commend you for your excellent book—so aptly titled! That picture on the front cover is so original! What a timely and interesting guide. Anyone who has written a book that includes David Hoffman and Maria Ouspenskaya gets an A+ from me.

I work at a military school and I am buying another copy of your book for the school library! My God, the research that you have done is unreal!...

Your book is worth $50. or more and I would have gladly paid (that) for it."
— Jim Dolce (Old Westbury, NY)

"About six weeks ago, I went into a Movie Bookstore here in Burbank (where I live). Looking around on a top shelf I saw two copies of 'Final Curtain.' I enjoyed it so much I told friends. They went in book stores in Glendale and Hollywood, but, believe it or not, the book was not in the stores there; ...they had to send away for it.

I am 87 years old and have lived in California since 1926. Have met many stars and have talked with them personally....
P.S. Get ready to write another book. We need you...."
— Anna Davis (Burbank, CA)

"A thousand thanks for your invaluable works! You see them on the screen (or tube), forever in their prime—you've grown up with them—they are somehow, friends!

And you wonder, are they still with us? What happened to them? Now, we are able to know....

Again—myriad thanks! Swell (monumental) job!"
— Tom Wolf (Phoenix, AZ)

"Thank you for your wonderful book, 'Final Curtain.' I am an actress in New York City....I visited Los Angeles for the first time last year and I found your book a wonderful tool for finding people.

I recently got interested in Ernie Kovacs and Susan Peters movies, and I never would have known what happened to them if it wasn't for your book. It enabled me to visit these people's graves, pray for them and honor them...."
— Sally Diumond Quine (New York, NY)

"I purchased the 1992 edition of your book and I must say I find it very helpful in locating graves of entertainment personalities. What the book lacks in biographical data is more than made up by your inclusion of specific grave locations. Most of the major books on the subject...fail to provide grave location. They stop at the cemetery name.

I hope you will be able to expand your specific interment locations in later issues....

Keep up the good work. I refer to your book often."
— David Lotz (Plano, TX)

"Thank you, thank you, thank you, thank you, and thank you again! It's not very often that a person who is as busy as you must be, will actually take the time to sit down and personally answer an inquiry. And I just want you to know I really appreciate it. (I'm the guy who writes articles on schlocker films.)...

As a matter of interest, I have been telling everyone I know, both writers and editors, of the wealth of information that can be found in 'Final Curtain.' My compliments; and once again, my thanks."
— Edward L. Mitchell (Oceanside, CA)

"What a great surprise and pleasure to find your book 'Final Curtain' under my Christmas tree!

I have been collecting autographs of movie/tv stars since I was 13 (I am 32 now) and have a collection of over 3,000. Because of this collection, I have also collected the obituary of every star since 1973. I have about 6,000 cut out of newspapers, magazines, Variety, and other sources. Your wonderful book has helped me in going back and dating many I didn't do when I was younger."
— Frankie Cifaldi (Memphis, TN)

"Bought your book 'Final Curtain' and I and my family and friends use it constantly. In fact, we use it so much, the poor book is starting to lose its pages."
— Stephen Pisha (Cedar Rapids, IA)

"I would like to thank you for your most informative book 'Final Curtain.' I purchased a copy for myself and a friend and have found it most useful. We 'collect' grave photos as a hobby. It is also good exercise and gets us out in the fresh air!

Recently, my husband and I spent three days in California 'cemetery hopping' with your book."
— Ginny Michaels (Spring Valley, NY)

"I finally was able to purchase your revised and updated book, 'Final Curtain.' I must tell you how pleased I am with your book. Do not stop writing these books, they are really great. I noted that this book had many more pictures of the stars, which was great to see. Also your remembering Jeanette MacDonald was wonderful. I think you should write a book on some of the stars, remembering them as you did Jeanette. I truly enjoyed this.

I am now a member of the Jeanette MacDonald (fan) club, all due to you, as you advised me to get in touch with Clara Rhoades. I went to their Clanclave last June and had a grand time."
— Theresa Dombrowski (Cranford, NJ)

"We visited Los Angeles in July 1995 armed with your very interesting book "Final Curtain.""
— Russell and Doris Anderson (Madison Hts., MI)

"I just picked up the latest edition of FINAL CURTAIN, and I wanted to congratulate you on a job well done. Such a project is obviously a labor of love and it shows in the meticulousness of your research. Every movie lover, film historian and cemetery buff should own a copy of this remarkable book."
— Robert Edwards (Burbank, CA)

[Many thanks to all who have written! — EGJ]

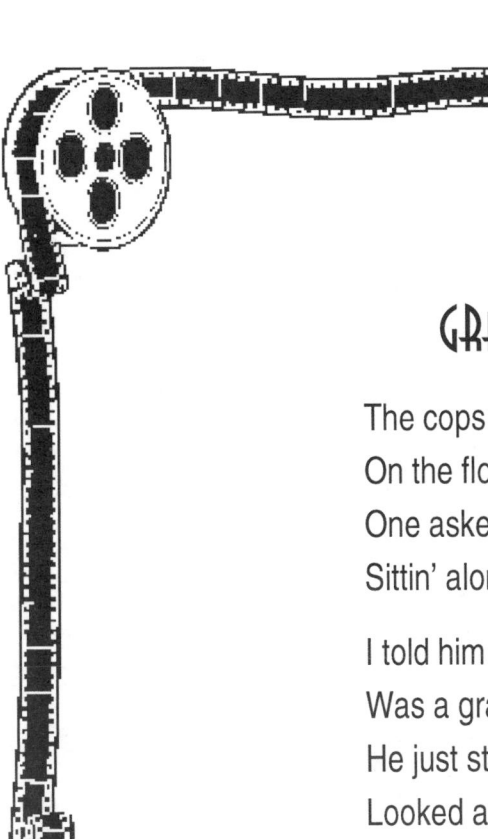

GRAVEYARD GROUPIE

The cops found me sitting
On the floor of the tomb.
One asked me, "Whatcha doin'
Sittin' alone in this gloom?"

I told him that I
Was a graveyard groupie.
He just stood there and
Looked at me as though I was loopy.

I'm a Graveyard Groupie.
It's bigger than me.
I'm just looking for the graves
Of stars of stage, film and TV.

Clark Gable, Curly
And Lon Chaney, too;
Mel Blanc, Gracie Allen
And even Sabu.

— Scott L. Spencer
Austin, Texas

GONE...

CHARLES LAUGHTON

JOSEPH COTTEN

HENRY FONDA

TYRONE POWER

BILL WILLIAMS

GEORGE MURPHY

DANA ANDREWS

WILL ROGERS

Eighth Edition

FINAL CURTAIN

DEATHS OF NOTED MOVIE AND TELEVISION PERSONALITIES

1912 - 1996

By Everett Grant Jarvis

A CITADEL PRESS BOOK • PUBLISHED BY CAROL PUBLISHING GROUP

Carol Publishing Group Edition, 1996

A Citadel Press Book
Published by Carol Publishing Group
Citadel Press is a registered trademark of Carol Communications, Inc.

Editorial, sales and distribution, rights and permissions inquiries should be addressed to
Carol Publishing Group, 120 Enterprise Avenue, Secaucus, N.J. 07094

In Canada: Canadian Manda Group, One Atlantic Avenue, Suite 105, Toronto, Ontario M6K 3E7

Carol Publishing Group books may be purchased in bulk at special discounts for sales promotion,
fund-raising, or educational purposes. Special editions can be created to specifications.
For details, contact: Special Sales Department, Carol Publishing Group, 120 Enterprise Avenue, Secaucus, N.J. 07094

Letters to the author should be sent to
Carol Publishing Group, 120 Enterprise Avenue, Secaucus, N.J. 07094.
If a reply is requested, please enclose a stamped, self-addressed envelope, and allow 2 to 4 weeks.

Manufactured in the United States of America
10 9 8 7 6 5 4 3 2 1

Library of Congress Cataloging-in-Publication Data

Jarvis, Everett Grant.
    Final curtain : deaths of noted movie and television personalities /
    by Everett Grant Jarvis. Eighth edition.
        p. cm.
    "A Citadel Press book."
    ISBN 0-8065-1646-1 (pbk.)
    1. Motion picture actors and actresses — Death.
    2. Television personalities — Death. I. Title.
PN1998.2.J37   1996
791.4'092'2—dc20   94-46368
[B]   CIP

This book was produced on an Apple Power Macintosh 7100/80av computer system
utilizing Adobe Systems PageMaker and Microsoft Excel software.
Fonts were selected from the Adobe Type Library,
and clip art was supplied by T/Maker's Click Art products.

Pictured on the title page: Gene Kelly

DEDICATION

To two dear friends— *Lucy and Perry Pickering*[*]

who share my joy in viewing and reminiscing about unforgettable classic films and the many talented individuals who made them so.

ACKNOWLEDGMENTS

Besides the many librarians and cemetery employees who have assisted with this eleven-year research effort, there are many others who deserve special thanks for their most welcome contributions to this continuum:

Russell and Doris Anderson
    (*Madison Hts., MI*)
Michael R. Bahr (*Baltimore, MD*)
Roger L. Belton (*Longview, WA*)
Paul and Joy Bennett (*Stanley, VA*)
Matt Bohn (*Hemlock, MI*)
Hal J. Bonney, Jr. (*Norfolk, VA*)
Eileen F. Calabrese (*Bedford Hills, NY*)
Art and Willetta Carrington
    (*Huntington Beach, CA*)
John J. Cashman (*Brooklyn, NY*)
Frankie Cifaldi (*Memphis, TN*)
Ed Colbert (*Los Angeles, CA*)
Donald F. Deluccie (*Highland, CA*)
Michele Devulder (*Orange, CA*)
Daniel Timothy Dey (*Medford, NY*)
Carl Dolente (*Camden, NJ*)
Robert Edwards (*Burbank, CA*)
Vivien Field (*Prescott, AZ*)
Frank Fife (*Elmira, NY*)
Sharon George (*Richmond, VA*)
Ann MacGregor Gibb (*New York, NY*)
David L. Graham (*Mt. Pleasant, TX*)
Robert Allen Gray (*Fayetteville, TN*)
Renee Grentus (*Rochester Hills, MI*)
Donald Hammarstrom (*Denver, CO*)
Harry B. Haymes (*Amherst, NH*)
Urwin E. Hendrix (*Lansing, MI*)
Lynn Hereford (*Austin, TX*)
Robert E. Herring (*Los Angeles, CA*)
Mark Holden (*Luton, Bedfordshire, U.K.*)
Jeff Holmes (*Euclid, OH*)

Terry Jeanson (*San Antonio, TX*)
Bernard Johnson (*Santa Monica, CA*)
Lucille Kaplan (*Jackson Heights, NY*)
Jennifer Katz (*Berkeley, CA*)
Bill and LaVonne Lee (*Arlington, TX*)
David N. Lotz (*Plano, TX*)
Celia Lunn (*London, England*)
Peter W. Many, Jr. (*New Orleans, LA*)
Ginny Michaels (*Spring Valley, NY*)
Gerald Morales (*New Orleans, LA*)
Chuck Moran (*Whittier, CA*)
Joseph Morgan Neblett (*Brooklyn, NY*)
Glen Muir (*Bowie, MD*)
James Robert Parish (*Studio City, CA*)
Barry A. Patraw (*Schaumburg, IL*)
Nicholas Patterson (*Pasadena, CA*)
Lucy and Perry Pickering (*Baltimore, MD*)
Charles Pierce (*N. Hollywood, CA*)
Mark H. Rowe (*Whittier, CA*)
Eleanor M. Rude (*New Haven, CT*)
Tom Hughes Sand (*Los Angeles, CA*)
Cindy Shank (*Hagerstown, MD*)
Anita Silverman (*Chesterland, OH*)
André Siscot (*Bruxelles, Belgium*)
Bryan Smith (*N. Hollywood, CA*)
Greg Smith (*Hollywood, CA*)
Scott L. Spencer (*Austin, TX*)
Mildred I. State (*Oceanside, CA*)
George Sweeney (*Boone, NC*)
Stephen Urbaniak (*Roseville, MI*)
B. Scott Wilson (*Richmond, IN*)
Tom Wolf (*Phoenix, AZ*)

[*] Perry is co-president of the Nelson Eddy Appreciation Society, 1106 McAdoo Ave., Baltimore, MD 21207.

...BUT...

ANNE REVERE

SONJA HENIE

EVE ARDEN

ESTHER RALSTON

DAME MAY WHITTY

RITA HAYWORTH

GRACIE FIELDS

PIER ANGELI

JOAN DAVIS

GAIL RUSSELL

FOREWORD

This new eighth edition of *FINAL CURTAIN: Deaths of Noted Movie and Television Personalities* includes deaths reported through May 3, 1996.

Thanks to you, the thousands of enthusiastic readers and owners of one or more of the seven previous editions of this work, the saga of this much-treasured memorial album continues with yet another update.

Having survived a humble beginning—the first edition contained the names of just 400 deceased movie stars and had only three sections and no photos—this newest update now lists in excess of 8,000 obituaries of both film and television personalities—plus lots of related information that many of you requested, in a total of ten cross-referenced sections.

Determining who is still alive and what happened to those who are gone, have always been two of the most important objectives for compiling the data and statistics in this book. A third, and perhaps even more important goal, was to create an up-to-date, "all-inclusive" memorial record that endeavors to honor the memory of not only the more famous stars of film and television, but also the many lesser known supporting actors and actresses, directors, producers, screenwriters, stuntmen, musicians, studio heads, etc.

Regretfully, no single book of this type can ever be truly all-inclusive, for it would take many volumes to list every deceased person who ever worked in the film and/or television industry.

Several readers have suggested that maps of all the cemeteries be included in a future edition. To make this possible, the author requests your help; and asks that you forward unblemished, professionally drawn and printed cemetery maps from your state or area, if they are available.

Once again, the author and publisher would like to thank each of you for your continued interest in, and support of, this on-going research effort. Without your participation, purchases and word-of-mouth advertising, no further updates would be possible. Do write and let us know if any of your favorites have been overlooked. The author would be especially grateful to hear from a family member who may be willing to make known the exact location of a final resting place, not already published herein. Send all such correspondence to the address below. If a reply is requested, please enclose a stamped, self-addressed envelope.

Out of respect for the honored dead and their families, this author would like to remind every reader to display their very best behavior while visiting any of the final resting places identified herein.

— *Everett Grant Jarvis*

...NEVER FORGOTTEN!

BILL BOYD

PETER LAWFORD

GORDON MacRAE

ROBERT RYAN

ALAN LADD

HELMUT DANTINE

CORNEL WILDE

KEEFE BRASSELLE

RALPH BYRD

FEATURES

- ▨ Parts 1 and 2 each list more than 8,000 names of deceased movie and television personalities—first chronologically by Year of Death, then alphabetically by Last Name—*for easy reference.*

- ▨ Key to Death List Symbols and Section Cross-Referencing:
  - • a Bullet symbol in the left margin denotes new entries;
  - + a Plus symbol on the left of the name indicates that a Specific Interment Location is identified in Parts 5 and 6;
  - \# a Pound symbol on the left of the name indicates that an Original or Former Name is provided in Part 7;
  - ★ a Black Star symbol following the name denotes a major Academy Award *winner* (see Part 10 for details);
  - ☆ a White Star symbol following the name denotes a major Academy Award *nominee* (again, see Part 10 for details).

- ▨ A Statistical Summary of Deaths (tabulated by Sex, Year, Age, and all major Causes of death) appears in Part 3.

- ▨ A Directory of 232 Star Cemeteries—with addresses and current telephone numbers is provided in Part 4.

- ▨ Dual listings of exact Interment Locations (now for more than 1,245 stars), arranged first by Last Name and then, as requested, by Interment Sites within each Cemetery, are provided in Parts 5 and 6.

- ▨ Over 2,600 Original Birth (or Former) Names, for both living and deceased movie and television personalities, are identified in Part 7.

- ▨ "Who is Related to Whom—Off Screen?" (in Part 8) identifies 1,850 spouses, children, siblings, and other relatives of film and television personalities *who are also in show-biz.*

- ▨ Hollywood studio affiliations of 400 popular film stars of the mid-1930s are listed in Part 9.

- ▨ A chronological listing of Academy Award winners in six major categories, plus an alphabetical listing of all major Oscar winners and nominees, appears in Part 10.

CORNEL WILDE

CONTENTS

GUY MADISON

COLUMBIA PICTURES PRESENTS

Sidney Buchman's

A Song to Remember

Starring

Paul	Merle	Cornel
MUNI	OBERON	WILDE

with

Nina Foch • George Coulouris • Howard Freeman • Stephen Bekassy

Musical Director **Morris W. Stoloff**   Screenplay by **Sidney Buchman**
Produced by **Louis F. Edelman**   Directed by **Charles Vidor**
Piano Score played by **José Iturbi**

Filmed in

TECHNICOLOR

112 Minutes   © 1945

—Now available on LaserDisc and Video Cassette—

It was late summer—1945. World War II had just ended in both Europe and Asia. I was 14 at the time, in my second year at the Baltimore Polytechnic Institute (one of the ten best public high schools in America), and was also studying piano at the Peabody Conservatory of Music (Preparatory Department)—looking forward to graduation from both educational institutions in the spring of 1948.

As I recall, my dad's favorite actor was Paul Muni, and a new film: "A Song to Remember" (in which Mr. Muni had a starring role), had just opened at the plush Metropolitan Theatre on the corner of West North and Pennsylvania Avenues in Baltimore.

I remember wanting to see another movie instead, but my parents insisted (doing all they could to further my appreciation for good music). At age 14, love stories and Hollywood musicals were not my first choice of entertainment. Besides, there was a long line at the box office that extended halfway down the block, which would mean at least a half-hour wait before we could even get inside.

At least the theatre was air-conditioned (a real luxury in those days), the film was in color (another plus), and I could hope for no less than one two-reel comedy, a cartoon, newsreel and coming attractions before the feature started (I remember thinking to myself as I grudgingly waited in line for one of the few remaining seats in the crowded auditorium). A few moments after opening my 5-cent box of Nibs licorice candy, the feature film began. The background music, played as the opening credits appeared, was, to my youthful ears, the most beautiful I had ever heard. (As I look back, one must recall that there were no hi-fi record players or FM radio stations in those days. At that time, the best recorded sound was to be heard only from movie soundtracks, to be relished in cavernous, ornately decorated movie houses like the "Met.")

As the inspiring and deeply moving account of Chopin's brief life began to unfold on the screen, this young teen was so stirred by the magnificence of the music, acting and story that I insisted on the three of us sitting through a second showing—even though that would get us home way past my usual bedtime.

After finally leaving the theatre, I couldn't wait to get to a music store the following day to purchase the souvenir record album from the film and also the souvenir sheet music album that contained all of Chopin's glorious piano scores that I had never heard or played before. Nothing, before or since, has ever inspired or encouraged me more than did the viewing of this extraordinary film! In fact, the movie was seen a total of twenty-two times at various theatres all over the Baltimore metropolitan area before its initial release had ended. Since the movie is now available on home video, it has been seen in the company of family and friends at least thirty times more. Although Cornel Wilde was nominated for Best Actor of 1945—for this, his first starring role—the Academy of Motion Picture Arts and Sciences apparently thought that Ray Milland's portrayal of a drunk in "The Lost Weekend" was the superior performance—a decision this author has never been able to accept. When Cornel Wilde died in 1989, it was as if the great composer and pianist—Chopin himself—had just passed away. To me, Cornel and Frederic were one and the same person!

I have great hopes that the executives at Columbia Pictures will soon favor the world with a restored, all-digital version of this cinematic masterpiece on home video. Meanwhile, if you have never seen this marvelous film, dear friend, RUN—don't walk—to your nearest video store and rent or purchase it without delay!

A Song to Remember

CREDITS

Producer	Louis F. Edelman
Director	Charles Vidor
From a Story By	Ernst Marischka
Screenplay	Sidney Buchman
Art Directors	Lionel Banks and Van Nest Polglase
Musical Supervisor	Mario Silva
Musical Director	M.W. Stoloff
Piano Score Played By	José Iturbi
Cameramen	Tony Gaudio and Allen M. Davey
Film Editor	Charles Nelson
Technicolor Director	Natalie Kalmus

CAST
[IN ORDER OF APPEARANCE]

Professor Joseph Elsner	Paul Muni
Monsieur Chopin (father)	Ivan Triesault
Madame Chopin (mother)	Fay Helm
Isabelle Chopin (sister, age 9)	Dawn Bender
Frederic Chopin (age 10)	Maurice Tauzin
Frederic Chopin (adult)	Cornel Wilde
Isabelle Chopin (adult)	Sybil Merritt
Major Domo	Walter Bonn
Paganini	Roxy Roth
Polish Count	Henry Sharp
Russian Governor	Michael Visaroff
Constantia	Nina Foch
Titus	William Challee
Jan	William Richardson
Pleyel's Clerk	Ian Wolfe
Henri Dupont	Sig Arno
Louis Pleyel	George Coulouris
Franz Liszt	Stephen Bekassy
Balzac	Peter Cusanelli
Kalkbrenner	Howard Freeman
Madame George Sand	Merle Oberon
Alfred DeMusset	George Macready
Madame Mercier	Claire Dubrey
Postman	Charles LaTorre
Duchess of Orleans	Norma Drury
Duke of Orleans	Eugene Borden
Albert	Earl Easton
Madame Lambert	Fern Emmett
Monsieur Jollet	Frank Puglia
Monsieur De La Croux	Al Luttringer

A SONG TO REMEMBER
IN MEMORIAM

- Fern Emmett *(Madame Lambert)*
  ...died in 1946 at age 50
- Michael Visaroff *(Russian Governor)*
  ...died in 1951 at age 58, of pneumonia
- Walter Bonn *(Major Domo)*
  ...died in 1953 at age 64
- Al Luttringer *(Monsieur De La Croux)*
  ...died in 1953 at age 74
- Charles Vidor *(Director)*
  ...died in 1959 at age 58, apparent heart attack
- Henry Sharp *(Polish Count)*
  ...died in 1964 at age 76
- Howard Freeman *(Kalkbrenner)*
  ...died in 1967 at age 68
- Paul Muni *(Professor Elsner)*
  ...died in 1967 at age 71, of heart trouble
- Eugene Borden *(Duke of Orleans)*
  ...died in 1972 at age 75
- George Macready *(Alfred DeMusset)*
  ...died in 1973 at age 63, of emphysema
- Sig Arno *(Henri Dupont)*
  ...died in 1975 at age 80, of Parkinson's disease
- Sidney Buchman *(Screenplay)*
  ...died in 1975 at age 73, of cancer
- Frank Puglia *(Monsieur Jollet)*
  ...died in 1975, at age 83
- Norma Drury *(Duchess of Orleans)*
  ...died in 1978, age unreported
- Merle Oberon *(Madame George Sand)*
  ...died in 1979 at age 68, of a stroke
- José Iturbi *(Played piano score)*
  ...died in 1980 at age 84, of a heart attack
- Mario Silva *(Musical Supervisor)*
  ...died in 1980 at age 79
- Morris W. Stoloff *(Musical Director)*
  ...died in 1980, age 85
- Ivan Triesault *(Monsieur Chopin)*
  ...died in 1980 at age 79, of heart failure
- William Challee *(Titus)*
  ...died in 1989 at age 84, of Alzheimer's disease
- George Coulouris *(Louis Pleyel)*
  ...died in 1989 at age 85, of a heart attack
- Cornel Wilde *(Frederic Chopin, adult)*
  ...died in 1989 at age 74, of leukemia
- Ian Wolfe *(Pleyel's Clerk)*
  ...died in 1992 at age 95, of natural causes

CORNEL WILDE, MERLE OBERON, PAUL MUNI

Frédéric François Chopin
(1810-1849)

According to his birth certificate, Chopin was born on February 22, 1810, in Zelazowa-Wola, six miles from Warsaw, Poland. His father, Nicholas, was French, and his mother, Justina Krzyzanowska, was Polish. Of their four children, Frederic was the only boy. Nicholas was a tutor and later, professor at the Warsaw Lyceum. The mother was an ideal mother, and, as George Sand declared, Chopin's "only love."

Frederic exhibited an early love for music. His first piano teacher was Adalbert Zwyny, and later he studied composition with Joseph Elsner. For Elsner, Chopin held an abiding love and reverence.

Frederic was 21 years old when he left Warsaw for Paris, where, in 1831, culture and the arts flourished. It was here that he was to spend most of the remaining years of his life and do most of his music writing. His most famous and often-played works for the piano include: the 24 preludes, 27 etudes (studies), 3 sonatas, 21 nocturnes, 4 impromptus, 4 ballades, 19 waltzes, 41 mazurkas, 15 polonaises, 4 rondos, 4 scherzos, 2 fantaisies, and 2 piano concertos. It was also in Paris that Frederic met the "polyandrous George Sand, a trampler on all the social and ethical conventions, albeit a woman of great gifts." Repelled, at first, he finally gave way to the ardent passion she manifested toward him.

By 1839, Chopin's health was a constant source of alarm to himself and his friends. One of his sisters had died of consumption and it was apparent that he was suffering from the same disease.

On his death bed he was quoted as having said, *"I love God and man. I am happy so to die."* His untimely death came on October 17, 1849 (at age 39) between three and four in the morning. On October 30, with a ceremony befitting a man of genius, he was buried in Père Lachaise Cemetery in Paris, France.

—From "Chopin: The Man And His Music" by James Huneker

ERROL FLYNN

1

DEATHS OF MOVIE AND TELEVISION PERSONALITIES – BY YEAR

DEATHS OF MOVIE AND TELEVISION PERSONALITIES — BY YEAR

	YEAR	NAME	AGE	CAUSE AND/OR PLACE OF DEATH
•	1912	BOGGS, Francis	?	Murdered (shot at the Selig film studio by a disgruntled employee)
•	1913	GRAYBILL, Joseph	26	Spinal meningitis (in New York, NY)
•	1915	BOOTH, Elmer	32	Automobile accident (in Los Angeles, CA)
	1915	+ BUNNY, John	51	Bright's disease (in Brooklyn, NY)
	1915	KAUFMAN, Joseph	35	Pneumonia
	1915	# PHILLIPS, Edwin R.	?	Died in the hospital of a complication of diseases
	1915	RUSSELL, William	?	(Do not confuse with William Russell, d. 1929)
	1915	WILDER, Marshall P.	56	Heart disease, aggravated by pneumonia
•	1916	AYRES, Sydney	?	Died in Oakland, CA
•	1916	BRADLEY, Amanda	?	Automobile accident (in New York, NY)
	1916	COTTON, Richard	?	Run over by an automobile
	1916	JOHNSON, Arthur V.	39	Died in Philadelphia, PA
•	1916	PETERS, Page E.	?	Drowned (at Hermosa Beach, CA)
	1917	BERGMAN, Henri	?	Died in New York (Do not confuse with Henry Bergman, d. 1946)
	1917	CAMPBELL, Eric	37	Automobile accident (in Los Angeles, CA)
•	1917	CHAMBERLIN, Riley C.	62	Died in New Rochelle, NY
	1917	FLOOD, Pauline "Baby Sunshine"	1	Run over by a truck (in Los Angeles, CA)
	1917	LaBADIE, Florence	29	Blood poisoning after being crushed when her car overturned (in NY)
	1917	# MACE, Fred	38	Apoplexy (found dead in his room at the Hotel Astor in NYC)
•	1917	STANDING, Jack	31	Died in Los Angeles, CA
•	1917	# SUNSHINE, Baby		(See Pauline Flood, d. 1917)
	1918	BASSETT, Russell	71	Brain hemorrhage (in New York, NY)
	1918	BINNS, George H.	?	Double pneumonia induced by influenza
	1918	# BOARDMAN, True	36	Following a nervous breakdown (in Norwalk, CA)
	1918	BREEN, Harry	?	Drowned in Lake Elsinore
	1918	+ CASTLE, Vernon	30	Airplane crash (in Houston, TX)
	1918	COLLINS, John Hancock	28	Pleural pneumonia following influenza
•	1918	COURTLEIGH, William Jr.	25	Pneumonia (in Philadelphia, PA)
	1918	DEVERE, Margaret	22	Pneumonia
	1918	FRANKLIN, Ruth Darling	22	Crushed by auto while waiting for a street car
•	1918	GONZALEZ, Myrtle	27	Heart disease and pneumonia (in Los Angeles, CA)
•	1918	GUNN, Charles E.	35	Spanish influenza (in Los Angeles, CA)
	1918	# HARRON, Tessie	22	Spanish Influenza (in Los Angeles, CA)
	1918	+ HELD, Anna	45	Pernicious anemia and bronchial pneumonia
	1918	HILL, Dale P.	?	Spanish influenza
	1918	L'ESTRANGE, Julian	38	Spanish influenza (in New York, NY)
	1918	LOCKWOOD, Harold A.	29	Spanish influenza (in New York, NY)
•	1918	# MAURICE, Mary "Mother"	73	
•	1918	PEACOCK, Lillian	27	From previous filming injuries (in Los Angeles, CA)
	1918	PEYTON, Lawrence R. "Larry"	?	Killed in action in France during World War I
	1918	RITCHIE, Franklin	?	Crushed beneath his overturned automobile (in Los Angeles, CA)
	1918	RITCHIE, Perry V.	?	Suicide
	1918	RYCKMAN, Chester	21	Spanish influenza
	1918	SEELOS, Annette	27	Spanish influenza
•	1918	# SHEA, William	?	Died in Brooklyn, NY
•	1918	TRASK, Wayland	31	Spanish influenza (in Los Angeles, CA)
	1918	TURNER, Otis "Daddy"	?	
•	1918	VALE, Louise	?	Died in Madison, WI
•	1918	# WEBER, Rex	29	Spanish influenza
•	1918	WEST, William	?	Injuries from a fall (in New York, NY)
	1918	WILLIAMS, John J.	62	Heart failure (Do not confuse with John Williams, d. 1983)
•	1919	ABELES, Edward	49	Pneumonia (in New York, NY)
	1919	DECKER, Kathryn Browne	?	Died in Columbo, Ceylon, while on a tour of the Orient
	1919	DREW, Sidney	54	Uremic poisoning and heart disease (in New York, NY)
•	1919	GEBHARDT, George M.	39	Tuberculosis
•	1919	GILFETHER, Daniel	65	Kidney disease (in Long Beach, CA)
	1919	GRIFFIN, Gerald	65	Died in Venice, CA
•	1919	LAMPTON, Dee	21	Appendicitis (in New York, NY)
	1919	McCAULEY, Edna	?	Typhoid fever

...DEATHS OF MOVIE AND TELEVISION PERSONALITIES — BY YEAR...

YEAR	NAME	AGE	CAUSE AND/OR PLACE OF DEATH
•	1919	MONTAGUE, Frederick	55	Acute intestinal obstruction (in Los Angeles, CA)
	1919	QUINN, James	35	Accidental (?) asphyxiation (gas) Do not confuse with Jimmie Quinn
•	1919	ROCK, Charles	53	Died in London, England
	1919	ROGERS, Eugene	51	Found dead in bed of myocarditis and alcoholism (in Los Angeles)
	1919	STOWELL, William H.	34	Killed in a train wreck (in Elizabethville, South Africa)
	1919	WASHINGTON, Jesse	?	Drowned during a filming accident
	1920	FINLEY, Ned	50	Suicide (strychnine) in New York, NY
	1920	# HARRON, Bobby	27	Accidentally shot (in New York, NY)
	1920	+ LOCKLEAR, Omer	28	A plane crash filming accident
•	1920	REID, Hal	46	
•	1920	SALTER, Harry	?	Natural causes (in a New Jersey hospital)
	1920	SEYMOUR, Clarine	19	Surgical complications (in New York, NY)
	1920	THOMAS, Olive	35	Suicide (mercury poisoning) in Paris, France
	1921	# BROOKE, Van Dyke	62	Died in Saratoga Springs, NY
	1921	+ CARUSO, Enrico	48	Peritonitis
	1921	# GRIFFITH, Katherine	45	Died in Los Angeles, CA
	1921	LAMBERT, Clara	?	
	1921	# LYONS, Fred	?	After his car skidded and overturned
	1921	+ RAPPE, Virginia	25	Ruptured bladder (in San Francisco, CA)
	1921	RITCHIE, Billie	42	After a 2-yr. illness caused by a filming injury
	1921	# SEARLE, Kamuela	33	From injuries while filming "The Son of Tarzan"
	1921	# TUCKER, George Loane	49	After a years' illness (in Los Angeles, CA)
	1922	# AINSWORTH, Sidney	50	After an illness of several months (in Madison, WI)
•	1922	# CLIFTON, Emma Bell	47	Heart attack (in Los Angeles, CA)
	1922	# CONNELLY, Bobby	13	Bronchitis and an enlarged heart (in Lynbrook, NY)
•	1922	CROCKETT, John	?	Died in Los Angeles, CA
•	1922	HERNANDEZ, George F.	59	Died in Los Angeles, CA
•	1922	# MILLER, W. Christy	79	Died in Staten Island, NY
	1922	#+ RUSSELL, Lillian	61	Complications after a fall onboard ship
	1922	#+ TAYLOR, William Desmond	45	Murdered (shot) in Los Angeles, CA
	1922	# WILLIAMS, Bert	49	Pneumonia (in New York, NY)
	1923	#+ BERNHARDT, Sarah	78	Uremic poisoning/weak heart (in Paris, France)
	1923	KENT, Charles	70	After being hospitalized (in Brooklyn, NY)
•	1923	LONSDALE, Harry G.	?	
	1923	# MANSFIELD, Martha	23	Burns when her dress accidentally ignited on location (San Antonio)
•	1923	PATRICK, Jerome	40	Heart disease (in New York)
•	1923	# RALEIGH, Saba	57	
	1923	+ REID, Wallace	31	Drug addiction (in Los Angeles, CA)
	1923	STEVENS, Edwin	?	Pleurisy
	1923	STRONG, Porter	44	Died in New York City
	1923	TOWNSEND, Anna	39	Died in Los Angeles, CA
	1923	TURNER, Fred A.	?	
•	1924	ARMSTRONG, Billy	32	
•	1924	BRANDT, Charles	60	Died in Philadelphia, PA
•	1924	BROCK, Tony	?	Auto accident while filming stunt in "The Great Circus Mystery" (NY)
	1924	+ HERBERT, Victor	65	Heart attack
	1924	INCE, Thomas H.	42	Heart failure (in Beverly Hills, CA)
	1924	# LESTER, Kate	65	Burned as studio dressing room gas stove exploded
•	1924	LYTTON, L. Rogers	57	
•	1924	MUNRO, Douglas	?	Double pneumonia (in Birmingham, England)
	1924	MOORE, Carlyle Sr.	?	Suicide (in his Milford, NJ, home)
	1925	BARROWS, James O.	72	Heart attack
	1925	CULLINGTON, Margaret	34	After a 6-month illness
	1925	CUNEO, Lester	37	Suicide (gunshot) after his wife filed for divorce
•	1925	EDWARDS, J. Gordon	57	
	1925	FARRAR, Margaret	24	After swallowing poison
•	1925	FIELD, George	46	Tuberculosis (in CA)
	1925	HAMILTON, Jack "Shorty"	37	Crushed after his car hit a steam shovel
	1925	JAMES, Horace B.	72	After a long illness

...DEATHS OF MOVIE AND TELEVISION PERSONALITIES — BY YEAR...

YEAR	NAME	AGE	CAUSE AND/OR PLACE OF DEATH
1925	# LINDER, Max	45	Suicided with his wife (cut wrists and took poison)
• 1925	LYELL, Lottie	33	Died in Sydney, Australia
• 1925	# MARSH, Marguerite	33	Bronchial pneumonia (in New York, NY)
1925	McCABE, Harry	44	After two operations
1925	# McVEY, Lucille	35	Died at her home in Hollywood, CA
1925	PAGET, Alfred	?	
1925	POWELL, David	39	Pneumonia after a nervous breakdown (in a NY Sanitarium)
1925	# RATTENBERRY, Harry	65	Died at his home in Hollywood, CA
1925	SANDOW, Eugene	58	After a blood vessel in his brain burst
1925	Teddy (dog)	14	(In Mack Sennett comedies)
1925	THOMPSON, Frederick A.	55	Heart disease
1925	THURMAN, Mary	31	Pneumonia (in New York, NY)
1925	VOGEL, Henry	60	Heart disease
1925	WUNDERLEE, Frank	50	Apoplexy attack (while dining at the Green Room Club in NYC)
• 1926	# AVERY, Charles	53	Died in Hollywood, CA
1926	FORMAN, Tom	33	Suicide (shot himself through the heart) in Venice, CA
1926	# GRIFFITH, Harry	59	Died in Pasadena, CA
1926	HOLLINGSWORTH, Alfred	52	After a brief illness
1926	#+ HOUDINI, Harry	52	Peritonitis from a ruptured appendix (in Detroit, MI)
1926	HUMPHREY, Paul	22	Premature explosion of dynamite while filming
1926	#+ LaMARR, Barbara	29	Over-dieting (in Altadena, CA)
1926	+ LAWRENCE, Lillian	66	Died at the home of her daughter in Beverly Hills, CA
1926	LOUIS, Willard	40	After being ill with typhoid fever and pneumonia (in Glendale, CA)
• 1926	LYONS, Eddie	39	Died in Pasadena, CA
1926	NEWTON, Charles	?	
1926	QUIRK, William "Billy"	45	Died at a Hollywood rest home after a 2-yr. illness
• 1926	SHAW, Harold M.	47	Automobile accident
• 1926	#+ VALENTINO, Rudolph	31	Peritonitis from a perforated ulcer and ruptured appendix (in N.Y.)
• 1926	# WARD, Carrie	63	Died in Hollywood, CA
• 1927	AUSTIN, Jere	51	Cancer (in Hollywood, CA)
1927	+ DUNCAN, Isadora	49	Strangled in her car by a scarf that caught in rear wheel (in France)
1927	HERBERT, Sidney	?	
1927	+ LEWIS, Tom	63	Following an operation for cancer
1927	+ LOEW, Marcus	57	Died in his sleep of heart failure
1927	MACK, Charles Emmett	27	When another car struck and overturned his car (in Riverside, CA)
• 1927	# MACK, Hughie	42	Heart disease (in Santa Monica, CA)
1927	+ MACK, Rose	61	Died in the Lenox Hill hospital in New York
1927	McKIM, Robert	39	Cerebral hemorrhage (in Hollywood, CA)
1927	NICHOLS, George Sr.	62	Died at his home in Hollywood, CA
1927	+ REYNOLDS, Lynn	37	Suicide (gunshot) during a cocktail party
1927	+ WARNER, Sam	40	Sinus infection/brain abscess/pneumonia
1927	WILLIAMS, Cora	56	Heart trouble (in Los Angeles, CA)
1927	#+ WILLIAMS, Earle	47	Bronchial pneumonia (in Los Angeles, CA)
• 1928	BLINN, Holbrook	56	After falling from a horse (in Crota, NY)
• 1928	CARROLL, William A.	51	Cancer (in Glendale, CA)
• 1928	CLAIRE, Gertrude	75	Died in Los Angeles, CA
• 1928	CONNELLY, Edward J.	73	Influenza (in Hollywood, CA)
1928	CRANE, Ward	37	Pneumonia (in Saranac Lake, NY)
1928	CURRIER, Frank	71	Blood poisoning after car door was shut on a finger (in Hollywood)
1928	DOWLING, Joseph J.	80	After a 2-year illness
1928	#+ FOY, Eddie Sr.	71	Heart disease (in Kansas City, MO)
• 1928	LINDSAY, James	59	
1928	McNAMARA, Ted	?	Pneumonia (in Ventura, CA)
• 1928	PLUMER, Lincoln	51	Heart disease (in Hollywood, CA)
1928	+ ROBERTS, Theodore	67	Uremic poisoning after a flu attack (in Los Angeles, CA)
1928	SEMON, Larry	39	Pneumonia (near Victorville, CA)
1928	SIEGMANN, George	45	Pernicious anemia (in Hollywood, CA)
1928	SIPPERLY, Ralph	37	Died in Bangor, Maine
1928	STILLER, Mauritz	?	Pleurisy
1928	THOMSON, Fred	38	After an operation for gall stones (in Los Angeles, CA)
• 1928	WHITNEY, Ralph	54	Injuries from a fall (in Los Angeles, CA)
1928	WILLIAMS, Clara	?	Following an operation (at her home in Los Angeles, CA)

YEAR	NAME		AGE	CAUSE AND/OR PLACE OF DEATH
1928	YEARSLEY, Ralph		31	Suicide (at his home in Hollywood, CA)
1929	BROCKWELL, Gladys		35	Peritonitis from car accident injuries (in Hollywood, CA)
1929	# BUTLER, Fred		64	Kidney trouble (in Los Angeles, CA)
1929	CAMP, Sheppard		47	From injuries during filming of "Song of Flame"
• 1929	CORRIGAN, James		57	Died in Los Angeles, CA
1929	+ EAGELS, Jeanne	☆	35	Alcohol and sleeping pills overdose (in New York, NY)
1929	FARNUM, Dustin		53	Kidney trouble (in New York, NY)
1929	# HARVEY, Hank		?	Died at his home in Culver City, CA
1929	HITCHCOCK, Raymond		58	Heart trouble
• 1929	HOLDING, Thomas		49	Heart disease (in New York, NY)
1929	LENI, Paul		44	Blood poisoning from a neglected ulcerated tooth
• 1929	MAITLAND, Lauderdale		51	
1929	MALONEY, Leo D.		41	Heart disease aggravated by alcoholism (in New York, NY)
1929	# MASON, Dan		76	Following an attack of pneumonia (in Baersville, NY)
1929	McDERMOTT, Marc		47	During gall bladder surgery (in Glendale, CA)
• 1929	# RAMSEY, John Nelson		65	Heart disease (in London, England)
• 1929	# RICKARD, Tex		59	Peritonitis following appendectomy (in Miami Beach, FL)
1929	RUSSELL, Albert		37	Pneumonia (in Los Angeles, CA)
1929	RUSSELL, William		42	Pneumonia (in Beverly Hills) Do not confuse with W. Russell d. 1915
• 1929	STEINRUCK, Albert		57	Died in Berlin, Germany
1929	TITUS, Lydia Yeamans		63	2 yrs. after a paralytic stroke (in a hospital in Glendale, CA)
1929	WASHBURN, Alice		68	After an illness of several years (in Oshkosh, WI)
1930	BLAISDELL, Charles "Big Bill"		56	Died in Hollywood, CA
1930	#+ CHANEY, Lon Sr.		47	Lung and throat cancer (in Los Angeles, CA)
• 1930	COURTLEIGH, William Sr.		61	Died in Rye, NY
1930	ELLIS, Diane		20	Died in Madras, India on her honeymoon
• 1930	HENDRICKS, Ben Sr.		67	Died in Hollywood, CA
• 1930	JONES, F. Richard "Dick"		36	Heart disease
1930	MELLISH, Fuller Jr.		35	Cerebral hemorrhage (in Forest Hills, NY)
1930	#+ NORMAND, Mabel		35	Tuberculosis (in Monrovia, CA)
• 1930	PENWARDEN, Duncan		50	Died in Jackson Heights, NY
• 1930	Petey ("Our Gang" dog)		7	Arsenic poisoning (in Los Angeles, CA)
• 1930	PHILLIPS, Tubby		45	Automobile accident (in London, England)
1930	# RANDOLPH, Anders		60	Following a relapse after a recent operation (in Hollywood, CA)
1930	SCHILDKRAUT, Rudolf		65	Heart disease (in Los Angeles, CA)
1930	SILLS, Milton		48	Heart disease (in Santa Monica, CA)
1930	TAYLOR, William H. "Billy"		101	
1930	WILSON, Benjamin F.		54	Heart ailment (in Glendale, CA)
1931	+ ACORD, Art		39	Suicide (arsenic) in Chihuahua, Mexico
1931	AMES, Robert		33	Bladder hemorrhage (in New York)
1931	ARBUCKLE, Maclyn		68	Died at his home in Waddington, NY
1931	ARNOLD, Cecile		?	Influenza
1931	# BARRY, Tom		47	Heart trouble
1931	#+ BEIDERBECKE, "Bix"		28	Lobar pneumonia and edema of the brain
1931	# BENNETT, Joe		35	Heart attack
• 1931	BLAISDELL, William		?	Died in Brooklyn, NY
• 1931	CLARY, Charles		58	Died in Los Angeles, CA
• 1931	CONNELLY, Erwin		57	Automobile accident (in Los Angeles, CA)
1931	+ DePUTTI, Lya		31	Pneumonia after operation to remove chicken bone from her throat
1931	EDESON, Robert		63	Hardening of the arteries (in Hollywood, CA)
• 1931	+ FRANKLIN, Sidney (actor)		61	After a long illness (Do not confuse with director, d. 1972)
• 1931	HATTON, Richard "Dick"		40	Traffic accident (in Los Angeles, CA)
1931	HAUPT, Ullrich		43	Accidentally shot on a deer hunting trip (near Santa Maria, CA)
• 1931	KUWA, George K.		46	
• 1931	LAWRENCE, Eddy		?	Suicide (gas) in San Diego, CA
• 1931	McRAE, Duncan		49	Died in London, England (Do not confuse with Duncan Macrae)
1931	MILLARDE, Harry		45	Heart attack (in Queens, NY)
1931	MURNAU, F. W.		42	Automobile accident
1931	+ NEILL, James		70	Heart trouble (in Glendale, CA)
• 1931	PAVLOVA, Anna		46	Died in The Hague, Netherlands
• 1931	PENROD, Alexander G.		?	Killed in a ship explosion while on location in the Antarctic
• 1931	PHILLIPS, Norman Sr.		38	Heart attack (in Culver City, CA)

...DEATHS OF MOVIE AND TELEVISION PERSONALITIES — BY YEAR...

YEAR	NAME	AGE	CAUSE AND/OR PLACE OF DEATH
• 1931	PICK, Lupu	45	Food poisoning
1931	# POWER, F. Tyrone	62	Heart attack
• 1931	# ROCKNE, Knute	43	Airplane crash (near Bazaar, KS)
1931	# RUBENS, Alma	33	Pneumonia (in Los Angeles, CA)
1931	SANTSCHI, Tom	51	High blood pressure (in Hollywood, CA)
1931	TERRY, Ethel Grey	48	After a year's illness (in Hollywood, CA)
1931	WILLIAMS, Robert	31	Peritonitis after an operation for appendicitis
1931	WOLHEIM, Louis	50	Stomach cancer (in Los Angeles, CA)
1932	BENNETT, Belle	41	Following a long illness (in Los Angeles, CA)
1932	+ BERN, Paul	42	Suicide (gunshot)
• 1932	CROWELL, Josephine	?	Died in Amityville, NY
1932	# ENTWISTLE, Peg	24	Suicide (jumped off the "Hollywood" Hills sign)
1932	+ GILLETT, King	77	
1932	GRAN, Albert	70	Injuries from an automobile accident (in Los Angeles, CA)
1932	JEFFERSON, Thomas	76	Following a brief illness (in Hollywood, CA)
1932	# JENNINGS, S. E.	51	
• 1932	LEWIS, Walter P.	60	
• 1932	MATIESEN, Otto	58	Died in Safford, AZ
• 1932	MIDGELY, Fannie	54	
1932	NEVILLE, George	66	Died in New York, NY
• 1932	O'CONNER, Edward	70	Died in New York, NY
1932	OLIVER, Guy	54	After a long illness (in the Hollywood Hospital, CA)
1932	# OSBOURNE, Jefferson	61	Stroke (in Hondo, CA)
1932	Rin Tin Tin (original dog)	16	
1932	+ SOUSA, John Philip	77	Heart attack
1932	STEPPLING, John C.	62	After an extended illness (in Hollywood, CA)
• 1932	VALLIS, Robert "Bob"	?	Died in Brighton, England
• 1932	WALLING, William "Will"	59	
1932	+ ZIEGFELD, Florenz	63	Pleurisy and pneumonia
• 1933	# ADAMS, Jimmy	43	Heart attack (in Glendale, CA)
1933	ADOLFI, John G.	45	Cerebral hemorrhage (while on a hunting trip in Canada)
1933	#+ ADOREE, Renée	35	Tuberculosis (in Tujunga, CA)
1933	AITKEN, Frank "Spottiswoode"	64	After a lingering illness (in Los Angeles, CA)
• 1933	AMES, Gerald	51	Injuries from a fall (in London, England)
1933	#+ ARBUCKLE, Roscoe "Fatty"	46	Heart attack
• 1933	BELL, Ruth	26	Suicide (poison) in Los Angeles, CA
1933	BIGGERS, Earl Derr	48	Heart attack
• 1933	BURTON, Clarence	51	Heart attack (in Hollywood, CA)
1933	CORBETT, James J.	65	Cancer of the liver
• 1933	COURTRIGHT, William "Uncle Billy"	84	Died in Ione, CA
1933	# CRAIG, Richy Jr.	31	Heart failure after a lengthy illness
1933	DALY, James L.	81	Heart trouble (in Philadelphia, PA)
1933	DILLON, Edward "Eddie"	53	Heart attack (in Hollywood, CA)
• 1933	DUNBAR, Helen	65	Died in Los Angeles, CA
• 1933	DYER, William J. "Billy"	52	
1933	# FREDERICI, Blanche	55	Heart attack enroute to a Christmas church service (in Visalia, CA)
1933	GORDON, Julia Swayne	54	After a long illness (in Columbus, OH)
1933	#+ GUINAN, Mary "Texas"	48	After an operation for colitis (in Vancouver, B.C., Canada)
1933	HALE, Louise Closser	60	Following an accident (in Los Angeles, CA)
• 1933	HALL-DAVIS, Lilian	32	Suicide (gas) in London, England
1933	HIERS, Walter	39	Pneumonia (in Los Angeles, CA)
1933	JARVIS, Jean	30	After a lingering illness
1933	JARVIS, Laura E.	67	Injuries from hit-and-run driver
• 1933	KELLY, James T.	79	(Do not confuse with James "Tiny" Kelly, d. 1964)
1933	# MARX, Samuel "Frenchie"	72	Heart and kidney failure (in Hollywood, CA)
1933	MATTOX, Martha	54	Heart ailment (in Sidney, NY)
• 1933	McKEEN, Snookums	8	Blood poisoning (in Los Angeles, CA)
• 1933	MORRIS, Lee	69	Died in California
• 1933	PASHA, Kalla	56	Died in Talmage, CA
• 1933	PAULIG, Albert	?	Heart trouble
1933	#+ PICKFORD, Jack	36	Multiple neuritis (in Paris, France)
1933	ROBBINS, Roy "Skeeter Bill"	?	Killed by a truck while wiping snow from his car
1933	# ROSCOE, Alan	45	After a lingering illness (in a Hollywood hospital)

...DEATHS OF MOVIE AND TELEVISION PERSONALITIES — BY YEAR...

	YEAR	NAME		AGE	CAUSE AND/OR PLACE OF DEATH
	1933	STEWART, Roy		43	Heart attack (in Los Angeles, Ca.)
•	1933	SULLIVAN, Pat		46	Pneumonia brought on by alcoholism
	1933	#+ TORRENCE, Ernest		54	After an operation for gall stones (in New York, NY)
	1933	TREVOR, Hugh		30	Three-weeks after an appendectomy (in Los Angeles, CA)
	1934	ALLEN, Sam		73	Died in Los Angeles, CA
•	1934	BEAL, Frank		70	Died in Hollywood, CA
	1934	BESSERER, Eugenie		64	While planning her golden wedding anniversary
	1934	BILLINGS, George A.		63	Died in West Los Angeles, CA
	1934	BROUGH, Mary		71	Heart ailment (in London, England)
	1934	CHAUTARD, Emile		69	Organic trouble (in Westwood, CA)
	1934	# CODY, Lew		50	Heart disease (in Beverly Hills, CA)
	1934	#+ COLUMBO, Russ		26	Accidentally shot by a friend while examining a pistol (in Hollywood)
•	1934	CROCKETT, Charles B.		62	Died in Los Angeles, CA
	1934	+ DANE, Karl		47	Suicide (gunshot) in Los Angeles, CA
	1934	DELL, Dorothy		19	Automobile accident (in Pasadena, CA)
	1934	+ DILLON, John Francis		50	After suffering a heart attack at a dinner party (in Beverly Hills, CA)
	1934	#+ DRESSLER, Marie	★	65	Cancer (in Santa Barbara, CA)
	1934	FRANCIS, Alec B.		65	Following an emergency operation (in Hollywood, CA)
	1934	# GREY, Robert H.		42	Died in Los Angeles, CA
	1934	# HILL, George W.		40	Suicide (gunshot)
	1934	# LORRAINE, Harry		54	
	1934	#+ MACK, Charles E.		46	Automobile accident (near Mesa, AZ) d.n.c. with C. Emmett Mack
•	1934	# MATTO, Sesto		39	Automobile accident (in Los Angeles, CA)
•	1934	PALLENBERG, Max		57	Airplane crash (near Karlovy Vary, Czechoslovakia)
	1934	# PERCIVAL, Walter C.		46	Died of complications (in Hollywood, CA)
•	1934	PINERO, Arthur Wing		79	Died in London, England
•	1934	PLAYFAIR, Nigel		60	Died in London, England
	1934	+ POLLARD, Harry		55	After several weeks illness (Do not confuse with Harry "Snub" P.)
•	1934	ROCCARDI, Albert		70	
	1934	+ SHERMAN, Lowell		49	Pneumonia (in Hollywood, CA)
	1934	SHOTWELL, Marie		?	Died in L.I., NY
	1934	# SKELLY, Hal		42	Killed by a train in a grade crossing accident (in West Cornwall, CT)
	1934	SUTHERLAND, Dick		51	Died in Hollywood, CA
	1934	TASHMAN, Lilyan		33	Tumorous condition and/or cancer (in New York, NY)
	1934	# TELLEGEN, Lou		52	Suicide (stabbed himself with a pair of scissors) in Los Angeles
•	1934	VIGO, Jean		29	Rheumatic septicemia
•	1934	# YORKE, Edith		?	
	1934	+ YOUNG, Mary		77	Following a 3-month illness
	1935	BOLAND, Eddie		51	Heart attack (in Santa Monica, CA)
	1935	BUNSTON, Herbert		61	Heart attack
•	1935	# COOGAN, Jack Sr.		55	Automobile accident (nr. San Diego, CA)
	1935	DICKSON, W. K. Laurie		75	
	1935	#+ DURKIN, Junior		19	Automobile accident (near San Diego, CA)
•	1935	GELDERT, Clarence		67	Heart attack (in Calabasas, CA)
•	1935	GRAHAM, Julia Ann		20	Suicide (gunshot) in Los Angeles, CA
	1935	GRIEVES, Jack		33	Died in Burbank, CA
	1935	HAMILTON, Lloyd		43	Following an operation for a stomach disorder (in Hollywood, CA)
	1935	+ HARDY, Sam		52	Intestinal problems (in Los Angeles, CA)
	1935	# HOPPER, De Wolf		77	Shortly after a radio broadcast (in Kansas City, MO)
	1935	LANDAU, David		57	After a lingering illness
	1935	MURRAY, Tom		60	After a 1-year illness (in Hollywood, CA)
	1935	NORTH, Wilfrid		82	After a brief illness (in Hollywood, CA)
	1935	POST, Wiley		50	Airplane crash (near Barrow, Alaska)
	1935	# ROBERTS, Edith		36	Died following the birth of a son (in Los Angeles, CA)
	1935	#+ ROGERS, Will		55	Airplane crash (near Barrow, Alaska)
	1935	RUSSELL, J. Gordon		52	Heart attack (in Los Angeles, CA)
•	1935	SALISBURY, Monroe		59	Skull fracture from a fall (in San Bernardino, CA)
•	1935	# SAXE, Templar		69	Died in Cincinnati, OH
	1935	# SCHULTZ, Harry		52	After a lengthy illness (in Hollywood, CA)
•	1935	STANHOPE, Adeline		82	Died in Los Angeles, CA
	1935	SWAIN, Mack		59	Apparent heart attack (in Tacoma, WA)
	1935	+ TODD, Thelma		30	Suicide? Murder? Accident? (carbon monoxide) in Santa Monica, CA
	1935	TRAVERS, Richard C.		45	Pneumonia (in San Pedro, CA)

• New entry. # Original name (Pt. 7). + Interment (Pt. 5).   8   ☆ Oscar nominee, ★ Oscar winner (Pt. 10)

YEAR	NAME	AGE	CAUSE AND/OR PLACE OF DEATH
1935	WEBB, Millard	42	Intestinal ailment (in Los Angeles, CA)
1935	WESTCOTT, Gordon	31	After falling from his horse in a polo game (in Hollywood, CA)
1935	WHITE, Marjorie	27	Automobile accident
1936	ADAMS, Howard	27	Airplane crash (in Chicago, IL)
1936	ASHTON, Dorrit	63	Died in Los Angeles, CA
1936	BELL, Ralph W.	53	Pneumonia (in San Francisco, CA)
• 1936	BLOOD, Adele	50	Suicide (gunshot) in Yonkers, NY
1936	BOWERS, John	36	Suicide (walked into the surf off Malibu Beach)
• 1936	BRADBURY, James Jr.	41	Suicide (burns) in Los Angeles, CA
1936	+ BREESE, Edmund	64	Peritonitis (in New York, NY)
1936	BUCKLER, Hugh	64	Drowned with his son in a car accident
1936	BUCKLER, John (Jack)	30	Drowned with his father in a car accident
1936	# CHANEY, Norman "Chubby"	18	After an operation for a glandular ailment (in Baltimore, MD)
1936	CROSLAND, Alan	42	Injuries after a car wreck
• 1936	DARLING, Ida	60	Died in Hollywood, CA
1936	#+ DAVENPORT, Alice	82	Died in Los Angeles, CA
• 1936	DAVIS, Edwards	64	Died in Hollywood, CA
• 1936	DIONE, Rose	60	Died in Los Angeles, CA
1936	#+ GILBERT, John	38	Heart attack (in Los Angeles, CA)
1936	# HEGGIE, O. P.	59	Pneumonia (in Los Angeles, CA)
1936	HOWARD, Booth	47	Run down by a car (in Los Angeles, CA)
1936	+ HOWLAND, Jobyna	56	Heart attack (in Los Angeles, CA)
1936	INGERSOLL, William	75	Acute indigestion (in Los Angeles, CA)
• 1936	LAIDLAW, Roy	52	Heart attack (in Hollywood, CA)
1936	LARKIN, John	62	Pneumonia (in Los Angeles, CA)
1936	LIVESEY, Sam	63	Following surgery (in London, England)
1936	MEIGHAN, Thomas	57	Cancer (in Great Neck, NY)
1936	MELLISH, Fuller Sr.	71	Heart attack (in New York, NY)
1936	#+ MILLER, Marilyn	37	Toxemia from a sinus infection (in New York, NY)
• 1936	MILLS, John Jr.	25	Tuberculosis (in Bellefontaine, OH)
1936	MURRAY, James	35	Drowned when he fell off a N.Y.C. pier
• 1936	NORTHRUP, Harry S.	58	Died in Los Angeles, CA
1936	PAWLE, Lennox	63	Cerebral hemorrhage (at a hospital in Hollywood, CA)
1936	#+ PICKFORD, Lottie	?	Heart attack
• 1936	# RICE, Frank	43	Nephritis and hepatitis (in Los Angeles, CA)
1936	ROBERTS, Stephen	41	Heart attack
1936	#+ SALE, Chic	51	Pneumonia (in Los Angeles, CA)
• 1936	SCHRECK, Max	57	Died in Munich, Germany
1936	+ SCHUMANN-HEINK, Ernestine	75	Leukemia
1936	STUART, Iris	33	
1936	#+ THALBERG, Irving	37	Lobar pneumonia
1936	+ WALTHALL, Henry B.	58	Chronic illness (near Monrovia, CA)
1936	# WALTON, Fred	71	Pneumonia (in Los Angeles, CA)
1936	WYNN, Hugh	46	
1936	YOUNG, Tammany	49	Died in his sleep of a heart attack (in Hollywood, CA)
• 1937	ABBOTT, Marion	69	Pneumonia (in Philadelphia, PA)
• 1937	ABEL, Alfred	57	
1937	+ ALEXANDER, Ross	29	Suicide (gunshot) in Los Angeles, CA
1937	# BARRIE, James	77	Pneumonia complicated by heart trouble
1937	BEAUMONT, Lucy	63	Died in New York, NY
• 1937	BLACKFORD, Mary	23	Results of an automobile accident (in Santa Monica, CA)
• 1937	BOLDER, Robert "Bobbie"	78	Died in Beverly Hills, CA
1937	+ BOLESLAWSKI, Richard	47	Apparent heart attack
• 1937	BOOTH, Sydney Barton	60	Cerebral hemorrhage (in Stanford, CT)
1937	+ BURGESS, Helen	19	Lobar pneumonia (in Beverly Hills, CA)
1937	CAREWE, Arthur Edmund	42	Suicide (gunshot)
• 1937	CARR, William (actor/director)	69	Do not confuse with other actors of the same name
• 1937	# CHASE, Colin	50	Paralysis attack (in Los Angeles, CA)
1937	#+ CLIVE, Colin	37	Tuberculosis complicated by alcoholism
1937	# DILLON, Jack	61	Pneumonia (in Los Angeles, CA)
• 1937	DONNELLY, James	71	Died in Hollywood, CA
• 1937	DUNN, Robert "Bobby"	45	Heart attack (in Hollywood, CA)
1937	+ EDWARDS, Snitz	75	Arthritis after a long illness (in Los Angeles, CA)

YEAR	NAME	AGE	CAUSE AND/OR PLACE OF DEATH
1937	#+ GERSHWIN, George	38	Brain tumor (in Los Angeles, CA)
• 1937	GLENDON, Jonathan Frank	49	Died in Hollywood, CA
1937	#+ HARLOW, Jean	26	Cerebral edema following uremic poisoning (in Los Angeles, CA)
• 1937	HASSELL, George	55	Heart attack (in Chatsworth, CA)
1937	#+ HEALY, Ted	41	Heart attack (in Los Angeles, CA)
• 1937	HEATHERLEY, Clifford	48	Died in London, England
1937	# INCE, Ralph W.	49	Automobile accident (in London, England)
1937	JENNINGS, De Witt	57	Died in Hollywood, CA
1937	JOHNSON, Martin	52	Airplane crash (in Los Angeles, CA)
1937	LEWIS, Ralph	65	Injuries from an automobile accident (in Los Angeles, CA)
1937	LOSEE, Frank	81	Pulmonary embolism after an attack of arthritis (in Yonkers, NY)
1937	LOWELL, Helen	71	After a lingering illness
1937	# MAILES, Charles H.	66	Died in Los Angeles, CA
1937	MARCUS, James A.	69	Heart attack (in Hollywood, CA)
1937	McCOY, Harry	43	Heart attack (in Hollywood, CA)
• 1937	# MULLER, Renate	30	Died in Berlin, Germany
• 1937	NEWALL, Guy	51	Died in London, England
• 1937	+ OWSLEY, Monroe	35	Heart attack (in Belmont, CA)
• 1937	PANZER, Paul	70	Heart trouble (in NYC) Do not confuse with Paul Wolfgang Panzer
1937	PERKINS, Osgood	45	Apparent heart attack after tonsilitis (in Washington, D.C.)
• 1937	PLAYTER, Wellington	57	Died in Oakland, CA
1937	+ POWELL, Richard	39	Fractured skull from auto accident
1937	# PREVOST, Marie	38	Acute alcoholism (in Los Angeles, CA)
1937	+ ROLAND, Ruth	45	Cancer (in Los Angeles, CA)
1937	ROSLEY, Adrian	47	Following a heart attack (in Hollywood, CA)
• 1937	SANDROCK, Adele	73	Died in Berlin, Germany
1937	SELLON, Charles	58	After a long illness (in La Crescenta, CA)
1937	SHUBERT, Eddie	38	After being stricken watching a golf tournament (in Los Angeles)
1937	SMITH, Clifford S.	51	Peritonitis following a ruptured appendix
1937	STANDING, Guy	63	Following a heart attack
1937	# TREE, Lady	72	After an operation from which she did not rally
1937	WATSON, Roy	61	
• 1938	ACKERMAN, Walter	57	Died in Hollywood, CA
1938	APFEL, Oscar	?	Heart attack
1938	# BETZ, Matthew	56	After a long illness (in Los Angeles, CA)
• 1938	BLACK, Maurice	46	Died in Hollywood, CA
1938	BLYSTONE, John G.	45	Heart attack (in Beverly Hills, CA)
• 1938	+ CHALIAPIN, Feodor Sr. "Felix"	65	
• 1938	CLARK, Harvey	52	Following a heart attack (in Hollywood, CA)
• 1938	COHL, Emil	81	Burns (after his beard caught fire from a candle)
• 1938	CRITTENDEN, Throckwood Dwight	59	Murdered (gunshot) in Los Angeles, CA
• 1938	DOUGHERTY, Virgil Jack	42	Suicide (carbon monoxide) in Hollywood, CA
• 1938	+ FACTOR, Max	61	Kidney and liver ailment (at his home in Beverly Hills, CA)
1938	#+ FREDERICK, Pauline (actress)	54	Asthma (in Los Angeles, CA) — Do not confuse with TV reporter
• 1938	FUREY, Barney	49	Liver ailment (in Los Angeles, CA)
• 1938	GARCIA, Allan	51	Died in Los Angeles, CA
1938	HENDRICKS, Ben Jr.	44	Died in Los Angeles, CA
1938	HILL, Thelma	32	Following a 3-month illness
1938	INCE, Richard	23	Died in Oakland, CA
1938	IRWIN, May	76	Bronchial pneumonia
1938	JANNEY, William "Bill"	34	After a short, serious setback while hospitalized
• 1938	KIMBALL, Edward M.	78	Died in Hollywood, CA
1938	KOHLER, Fred	49	Heart attack (in Los Angeles, CA)
1938	+ LAWRENCE, Florence	50	Suicide (mixture of cough syrup and ant paste) in Beverly Hills, CA
1938	LLOYD, Rollo	55	Died in Los Angeles, CA
• 1938	LONG, Jack	?	Motorcycle accident (in Los Angeles, CA)
1938	McCALL, William	58	Died in Hollywood, CA
1938	McWADE, Robert Jr.	55	Heart attack (in Culver City, CA)
• 1938	MELIES, Georges	77	Died in Paris, France
• 1938	# MONCRIES, Edward	78	Heart attack (in Hollywood, CA)
• 1938	MORENO, Thomas "Sky Ball"	43	Died in West Los Angeles, CA
1938	MYERS, Harry	52	Pneumonia (in Los Angeles, CA)
1938	#+ OLAND, Warner	57	Bronchial pneumonia (in Stockholm, Sweden)
1938	PINCHOT, Rosamond	33	Suicide (carbon monoxide poisoning)

YEAR		NAME	AGE	CAUSE AND/OR PLACE OF DEATH
	1938	ROBERTI, Lyda	29	Heart ailment (in Los Angeles, CA)
•	1938	RORKE, Mary	80	Died in London, England
	1938	STEDMAN, Myrtle	48	Heart trouble (in Los Angeles, CA)
	1938	STEWART, Richard	?	
	1938	STRICKLAND, Helen	74	Died at Mt. Sinai Hospital in New York, NY
	1938 #	TEARLE, Conway	60	Heart attack (in Los Angeles, CA)
•	1938 #	Toto the Clown	50	Died in New York, NY (Do not confuse with Toto, d. 1967)
	1938 #	WALLACE, May	61	Heart disease (in Los Angeles, Ca.)
	1938	WHITE, Pearl	49	Liver ailment (in Paris, France)
•	1938	WIENE, Robert	57	Cancer (in Paris, France)
	1938 +	WOOLSEY, Robert	48	Kidney ailment
•	1939	ANDERSON, Lawrence	45	Pneumonia (in London, England)
•	1939	ARBUCKLE, Andrew	55	Died in Los Angeles, CA
	1939	BACKUS, George	81	
•	1939	BORGATO, Agostino	67	Heart attack (in Hollywood, CA)
	1939 +	BRADY, Alice ★	46	Cancer (in New York, NY)
•	1939	BROWN, Raymond "Ray"	58	Died in Los Angeles, CA
•	1939	BRUNDAGE, Mathilde	67	
•	1939	BURTIS, James	46	Died in California
	1939 #+	FAIRBANKS, Douglas Sr.	56	Heart attack
	1939	FAWCETT, George D.	77	Heart trouble
	1939 +	FRANKLIN, Rupert	77	Died in Los Angeles, CA
	1939	FRAZIN, Gladys	37	Suicide (jumped from her apartment window) in New York, NY
	1939	GILLINGWATER, Claude	69	Suicide (gunshot) in Beverly Hills, CA
	1939	GIRARDOT, Etienne	83	After a brief illness (in Hollywood, CA)
	1939	GLECKLER, Robert P.	49	Uremic poisoning (in Los Angeles, CA)
•	1939	GREET, Clare	67	Died in London, England
	1939	GREY, Zane	64	Died at his home in Altadena, CA
	1939	HARRON, John	36	Died in Seattle, WA
	1939	JARVIS, Sydney	58	Died in Hollywood, CA
	1939 +	LAEMMLE, Carl Sr.	72	Heart attack
	1939 #	LEONARD, Gus	83	After a long illness (in Los Angeles, CA)
•	1939 #	MARSON, Aileen	26	Childbirth (in London, England)
	1939 +	MERCER, Beryl	56	Following a major operation (in Santa Monica, CA)
•	1939	MEYERHOLD, Vsevolod	65	Tortured by Stalin's secret police on false charges of treason
•	1939	MILLER, Ranger Bill	61	Died in Los Angeles, CA
	1939	MOORE, Owen	52	Died in Beverly Hills, CA
	1939	MUNDIN, Herbert	40	Fractured skull from auto accident (in Van Nuys, CA)
•	1939 #	MURDOCK, Ann	48	Died in Lucerne, Switzerland
	1939 +	NICHOLS, George Jr.	42	Automobile accident
	1939 #+	PARROTT, James	46	Heart attack (in Hollywood, CA)
•	1939	RICKETTS, Thomas "Tom"	85	Pneumonia (in Hollywood, CA)
•	1939 #	SELTEN, Morton	79	Died in London, England
	1939	SHELBY, Margaret	39	
•	1939	SHINE, Wilfred	75	Died in Kingston, England
	1939 #+	SMALLEY, Phillips	63	Died in Hollywood, CA
•	1939	SMITH, Albert J.	44	Died in Hollywood, CA
	1939 #	STERLING, Ford	58	Thrombosis of veins and heart attack (in Los Angeles, CA)
	1939 +	TEMPLETON, Fay	74	
	1939	THOMAS, Jameson	49	Tuberculosis (in Sierra Madre, CA)
	1939 +	VERNON, Bobby	42	Heart attack (in Hollywood, CA)
•	1939	VIBART, Henry	75	
	1939	WARE, Helen	61	Throat infection (in Carmel, CA)
	1939	WEBER, Lois	56	After a long illness (in Los Angeles, CA)
	1940	ADAIR, Jack	46	Died in Hollywood, CA
	1940	ARNOLD, William R.	56	Streptococcus infection
	1940	ASHTON, Sylvia	60	
	1940	ASKAM, Earl	41	After a heart attack while playing golf
	1940 #+	AYRES, Agnes	42	Cerebral hemorrhage (while in a sanitarium for depression)
	1940 +	BATES, Granville	58	Heart attack (in Hollywood, CA)
•	1940	BRADBURY, James Sr.	83	Died in Clifton, Staten Island, NY
•	1940	BURR, Eugene "Gene"	?	Pulmonary edema (in Los Angeles, CA)
	1940	CALTHROP, Donald	52	After a heart attack (in England)

• New entry.   # Original name (Pt. 7).   + Interment (Pt. 5).   11   ☆ Oscar nominee, ★ Oscar winner (Pt. 10)

	YEAR	NAME	AGE	CAUSE AND/OR PLACE OF DEATH
	1940	# CAREWE, Edwin	56	Heart attack (in Los Angeles, CA)
•	1940	CECIL, Edward	52	Died in Los Angeles, CA
	1940	CHADWICK, Helene	42	From injuries after a fall (in Los Angeles, CA)
	1940	#+ CHASE, Charley	47	Heart attack (in Hollywood, CA)
	1940	CHURCHILL, Berton	63	Uremic poisoning (in New York, NY)
	1940	+ CLARK, Marguerite	53	Pneumonia after a cerebral hemorrhage (in New York, NY)
	1940	# CLIVE, E. E.	60	Heart attack (in North Hollywood, CA)
	1940	CONNOLLY, Walter	53	Stroke (in Beverly Hills, CA)
•	1940	# CRAIG, Blanche	74	Died in Los Angeles, CA
	1940	DeGRASSE, Joseph	67	Heart attack (in Eagle Rock, CA)
•	1940	DWIRE, Earl	55	Died in Carmichael, CA
	1940	+ FINCH, Flora	71	Streptococcus infection (in Los Angeles, CA)
	1940	+ FITZMAURICE, George	45	After a 2-month streptococcus infection (in Los Angeles, CA)
	1940	# FRANEY, Billy	55	Influenza (in Hollywood, CA)
	1940	# GORDON, C. Henry	57	Result of leg amputation (in Los Angeles, CA)
•	1940	GORDON, Maude Turner	71	Pneumonia (in Los Angeles, CA)
	1940	GREEN, Fred E.	50	
	1940	# GRIFFIN, Carlton E.	47	Heart attack
	1940	HACKATHORNE, George	44	After a long illness (in Los Angeles, CA)
	1940	# HALL, James	39	Liver ailment
	1940	HARLAN, Otis	75	Stroke (in Martinsville, IN)
•	1940	HART, Albert	65	Died in Hollywood, CA
•	1940	JAUBERT, Maurice	40	Killed in action during World War 2
	1940	KEMP, Hal	36	Pneumonia after auto injuries
	1940	LAW, Walter	64	Died in Hollywood, CA
•	1940	LAWFORD, Ernest	69	Died in New York, NY
	1940	LeSAINT, Edward J.	69	After a long illness (in Hollywood, CA)
•	1940	LESLIE, Lilie "Lila"	48	Died in Los Angeles, CA
	1940	LUCAS, Wilfred	69	After an illness of 6-weeks (in Los Angeles, CA)
	1940	MACKAYE, Dorothy	41	Injuries from an automobile accident (in San Fernando Valley, CA)
•	1940	McPHERSON, Quinton	68	Died in London, England
	1940	# MEINS, Gus	45	Suicide (after arrest on morals charges)
	1940	# MILLER, Walter C.	48	After collapsing on a Republic Pictures set (in Los Angeles, CA)
	1940	#+ MIX, Tom	60	A broken neck after his car overturned (in Florence, AZ)
	1940	MONG, William V.	65	After a 2-years' illness (in Studio City, CA)
	1940	# MORGAN, Gene	48	Heart attack (in Santa Monica, CA)
	1940	# MOSCOVITCH, Maurice	68	Following abdominal surgery (in Los Angeles, CA)
	1940	MURRAY, J. Harold	49	After treatment for a kidney ailment
•	1940	# OGLE, Charles	75	Died in Long Beach, CA
	1940	# PEARCE, George C.	75	Died in Los Angeles, CA
	1940	PERIOLAT, George	63	Suicide (arsenic) at his home in Los Angeles, CA
•	1940	RAND, John F.	67	Died in Hollywood, CA
	1940	REGAS, George	50	Following an operation for a throat infection (in Los Angeles, CA)
	1940	RICHMAN, Charles	75	After a brief illness (in a Bronx, NY nursing home)
	1940	+ ROBERTS, Florence	79	After a long illness (in Hollywood) Do not confuse with F.R., d. 1927
•	1940	ROBERTS, Ralph Arthur	55	Died in Berlin, Germany
	1940	SELBY, Norman "Kid McCoy"	66	Suicide (in a downtown hotel in Detroit, MI)
•	1940	# SIEGEL, Bernard	72	Heart attack (in Los Angeles, CA)
	1940	SPACEY, John Graham	44	Suddenly, after attending a party (in Hollywood, CA)
	1940	#+ STEVENS, Landers	63	Heart attack following appendectomy (in Hollywood, CA)
•	1940	STEWART, Athole	61	Died in Buckinghamshire, England
	1940	STONE, Arthur	56	After a brief illness (in Hollywood, CA)
	1940	SWICKARD, Joseph	74	After a long illness (in Hollywood, CA)
	1940	+ TRAINOR, Leonard	61	Heart attack
	1940	#+ TURPIN, Ben	65	Heart disease (in Santa Monica, CA)
	1940	VANE, Denton	50	Heart attack (while walking in Union Hill, N.J.)
	1940	WALTERS, Hal	48	Killed by a German bomb during a WW2 air raid (in England)
	1940	WARREN, E. Alyn	64	Died in Los Angeles, CA
•	1940	WARREN, Fred H.	60	Ruptured ulcer (in Hollywood, CA)
	1940	WESTMORE, Monte	39	Heart condition after a tonsilectomy
•	1940	# WONG, Mary	25	Suicide (hanging) in Los Angeles, CA
	1940	# WRAY, John	52	After a long illness (in Los Angeles, CA)
•	1940	WRIGHT, Hugh E.	60	Died in Windsor, England
•	1940	YOUNG, Olive	33	Internal hemorrhages (in Bayonne, NJ)

. YEAR	NAME		AGE	CAUSE AND/OR PLACE OF DEATH
• 1941	BACH, Reginald		54	Pneumonia (in New York, NY)
1941	+ BERGERE, Ramona		39	Died in Glendale, CA
1941	# BLACKTON, James Stuart Sr.		66	Fractured skull after being struck by a car (in Hollywood, CA)
• 1941	BLINN, Benjamin F.		68	Died in Hollywood, CA
1941	# CALVERT, E. H.		78	Died in Hollywood, CA
1941	# CARLE, Richard		69	Heart attack
• 1941	CAVEN, Allan		60	Died in Hollywood, CA
• 1941	CURRAN, Thomas A.		60	Pneumonia (in Hollywood, CA)
• 1941	# DeGREY, Sydney		55	
1941	DEXTER, Elliott		71	After several weeks illness (in Amityville, NY)
1941	#+ DOLLY, Jenny		48	Suicide (hanging) in Hollywood, CA
1941	# FAIRBROTHER, Sydney		69	Died in London, England
1941	# FIELDS, Stanley		57	Heart attack (in Los Angeles, CA)
1941	FITZGERALD, Cissy		68	Died in Ovingdean, England
• 1941	FORREST, Alan		51	Died in Detroit, MI
1941	#+ GEHRIG, Lou		37	Amyotrophic lateral sclerosis (in New York)
1941	GORDON, James		60	After an emergency operation (in Hollywood, CA)
• 1941	HARBEN, Hubert		63	Died in London, England
1941	HERSHELL, Mayall		78	Cerebral hemorrhage
1941	HOWARD, David		45	Heart ailment
• 1941	KALIZ, Armand		48	Heart attack (in Beverly Hills, CA)
1941	# KING, Claude E.		62	Died in Los Angeles, CA
• 1941	LANG, Howard		64	Died in Hollywood, CA
• 1941	LEE, Auriol		?	Automobile accident (in Hutchison, KS)
• 1941	LLEWELLYN, Fewlass		55	
1941	MacDOWELL, Melbourne		84	Blood clot on the brain (in Decoto, CA)
• 1941	MANN, Margaret		72	Cancer (in Los Angeles, CA)
1941	MASON, William C. "Smiling Billy"		52	After a lengthy illness (in Orange, NJ)
1941	MAYALL, Hershell		78	Cerebral hemorrhage (in Detroit, MI)
1941	MEADE, Bill		?	Fell from a horse onto his sword while filming
1941	+ MORGAN, Helen		41	Kidney and liver ailments (in Chicago, IL)
1941	MORRIS, Adrian		38	Died in Los Angeles, CA
1941	MURRAY, Charlie		69	Pneumonia (in Hollywood, CA)
1941	+ PADEREWSKI, Ignace		80	Pneumonia
• 1941	# PARKER, Barnett		54	Died in Los Angeles, CA
1941	#+ PENNER, Joe		35	Heart attack (in Philadelphia, PA)
1941	+ PORTER, Edwin S.		71	
1941	PRATT, Purnell B.		54	Died in Hollywood, CA
• 1941	RAYNER, Minnie		72	Died in London, England
1941	ROBERTSHAW, Jerrold		74	
• 1941	RUTTMAN, Walther		54	Killed while filming a newsreel of the Eastern Front during W.W.2
1941	+ SCHERTZINGER, Victor	☆	52	Died in Hollywood, CA
1941	#+ SHANNON, Peggy		32	Acute alcoholism (in North Hollywood, CA)
1941	+ STEPHENSON, James	☆	53	Heart attack (in Pacific Palisades, CA)
1941	STONEHOUSE, Ruth		47	Died in Hollywood, CA
• 1941	TRUESDALE, Howard		80	Heart attack (in Los Angeles, CA)
1941	WALKER, Stuart		53	After a heart attack (at his Hollywood home)
1941	# WILSON, Clarence H.		64	Died in Hollywood, CA
• 1941	WORTHINGTON, William J.		68	Died in Beverly Hills, CA
1942	#+ BARRYMORE, John		60	Cardiac condition and other ailments (in Los Angeles, CA)
1942	BRACEY, Sidney		64	After a brief illness (in Hollywood, CA)
• 1942	BRADY, Edward J.		53	Heart attack (in Hollywood, CA)
• 1942	CARLYLE, Richard		63	Died in San Fernando, CA
1942	+ COHAN, George M.		64	Cancer of the lower intestine (in New York, NY)
• 1942	CORBIN, Virginia Lee		31	Heart disease (in Winfield, IL)
• 1942	COWL, George		64	
1942	+ CREWS, Laura Hope		62	After a month's illness (in New York, NY)
1942	#+ CRUZE, James		58	Heart ailment (in Hollywood, CA)
• 1942	CULLEY, Frederick		63	
1942	ELLSLER, Effie		87	Following a heart attack
1942	FOWLER, Brenda		59	Following a short illness (in Los Angeles, CA)
1942	HAINES, Donald		24	
• 1942	HALLARD, C. M.		75	Died in Surrey, England
1942	+ HAMILTON, Hale R.		62	Cerebral hemorrhage

...DEATHS OF MOVIE AND TELEVISION PERSONALITIES — BY YEAR...

	YEAR	NAME		AGE	CAUSE AND/OR PLACE OF DEATH
•	1942	HAWTHORNE, David		54	
	1942	HOLMES, Phillips		33	Air collision of two RCAF planes (near Armstrong, Ont., Canada)
	1942	HORNE, James W.		60	Cerebral hemorrhage
	1942	#+ HOUSMAN, Arthur		52	Pneumonia (in Los Angeles, CA)
•	1942	# HUMPHREY, William		68	Coronary thrombosis (in West Hollywood, CA)
	1942	#+ JONES, Buck		52	Burned to death while trying to save others in a fire (in Boston, MA)
	1942	#+ LOMBARD, Carole	☆	33	Airplane crash (southeast of Las Vegas, NV)
•	1942	LORD, Marion		59	Died in Hollywood, CA
•	1942	LUPINO, Stanley		48	Died in London, England
	1942	MacQUARRIE, Murdock		63	Died in Los Angeles, CA
	1942	McFADDEN, Charles Ivor		55	Cerebral hemorrhage (in Los Angeles, CA)
	1942	McINTOSH, Burr		79	Following a heart attack (in Hollywood, CA)
•	1942	MOFFAT, Margaret		49	Pneumonia (in Los Angeles, CA)
	1942	MORTON, James C.		58	After a long illness (in Reseda, CA)
	1942	NATHEAUX, Louis		44	Died in Los Angeles, CA
	1942	#+ OLIVER, Edna May	☆	59	Intestinal disorder (in Hollywood, CA)
	1942	OTTIANO, Rafaela		48	Heart attack (in Boston, MA)
	1942	#+ ROBSON, May	☆	84	Neuritis (in Beverly Hills, CA)
	1942	#+ ROSING, Bodil		63	Heart attack (in Hollywood, CA)
	1942	RUBEN, J. Walter		43	Heart ailment
	1942	SEARS, Allan		55	After a long illness (in Los Angeles, CA)
	1942	SKINNER, Otis		83	Died at his home in New York
•	1942	# TEMPEST, Marie		78	Died in London, England
•	1942	# THATCHER, Eva		80	Died in Los Angeles, CA
•	1942	# Tony (Tom Mix's horse)		33	
•	1942	TUCKER, Richard (actor)		58	Heart attack (in Woodland Hills, CA) Do not confuse with singer
	1942	VOGEDING, Fredrik		52	Following a heart attack (in Los Angeles, CA)
	1942	#+ WEBER, Joe		74	After an illness of 2-months (in Los Angeles, CA)
	1942	# WESTLEY, Helen		67	
•	1942	WOODS, Arthur		38	Killed in action during World War 2
	1943	ATCHLEY, Hooper		56	Suicide (gunshot)
	1943	# BACON, David		29	Stab wounds (in Los Angeles, CA)
	1943	BARLOW, Reginald		76	Died in Hollywood, CA
•	1943	BAUR, Harry		63	Died mysteriously after being interrogated by the Gestapo in Paris
•	1943	BELCHER, Charles M.		71	Died in Hollywood, CA
•	1943	BENNETT, Charles J.		51	Died in Hollywood (Do not confuse with Charles Bennett, d. 1995)
	1943	BERNIE, Ben		52	After a lingering illness
•	1943	BLEDSOE, Jules		44	Died in Hollywood, CA
	1943	+ BOSWORTH, Hobart		76	Pneumonia (in Glendale, CA)
	1943	BOTELER, Wade		52	Heart attack (in Hollywood, CA)
•	1943	BREAMER, Sylvia		40	Died in New York, NY
	1943	# BROOKE, Tyler		52	Suicide (carbon monoxide in his car) in North Hollywood, CA
•	1943	BRUNETTE, Fritzi		53	Died in Hollywood, CA
	1943	+ BYRON, Arthur		71	After a long illness (in Hollywood, CA)
	1943	CAMPEAU, Frank		79	Died in Woodland Hills, CA
	1943	+ CHARTERS, Spencer		68	Suicide (pills and carbon monoxide) in Hollywood, CA
	1943	COWLES, Jules		65	Died in Hollywood, CA
•	1943	# CUNNINGHAM, Joe		52	Coronary occlusion (in Los Angeles, CA)
	1943	DeLEATH, Vaughn		42	Uremic poisoning and a heart condition
	1943	ETHIER, Alphonse		68	After a long illness
	1943	+ FRYE, Dwight		44	Heart attack (in Los Angeles, CA)
	1943	GUHL, George		?	Died in Los Angeles, CA
	1943	+ HART, Lorenz		47	Pneumonia
	1943	#+ HOWARD, Leslie	☆	50	In a passenger plane shot down by a Nazi fighter (in Bay of Biscay)
	1943	IRVING, William J.		50	Died in Los Angeles, CA
	1943	+ JULIAN, Rupert		54	Stroke
•	1943	JUNKERMANN, Hans		70	Died in Berlin, Germany
	1943	LANGDON, Lillian		?	Died in Santa Monica, CA
	1943	LOFTUS, Cecilia "Cissie"		66	Heart attack (in her New York City hotel room)
	1943	# LOVE, Montagu		62	Died in Beverly Hills, CA
	1943	#+ MARSHALL, Tully		78	Heart and lung ailment (in Encino, CA)
	1943	McWADE, Edward		?	After a brief illness
•	1943	# NARES, Owen		54	Died in Brecon, Wales
	1943	O'CONNELL, Hugh		44	After a heart attack (in Hollywood, CA)

...DEATHS OF MOVIE AND TELEVISION PERSONALITIES – BY YEAR...

YEAR	NAME	AGE	CAUSE AND/OR PLACE OF DEATH
1943	OVERMAN, Lynne	55	Following two heart attacks (in Santa Monica, CA)
• 1943	PADDOCK, Charles	42	Airplane crash (near Sitaka, Alaska)
1943	# PRICE, Kate	70	After a long illness (in Woodland Hills, CA)
1943	+ RACHMANINOFF, Sergei	69	Cancer and pneumonia
1943	#+ RAY, Charles	52	Throat infection from an infected tooth (in Los Angeles, CA)
1943	+ REINHARDT, Max	70	Pneumonia following paralysis
1943	ROQUEMORE, Henry	55	Died at his home in Beverly Hills, CA
1943	SAUM, Clifford	60	Died in Glendale, CA
1943	SHERIDAN, Frank	74	Died in Hollywood, CA
• 1943	# STANMORE, Frank	65	
1943	STRAUSS, William H.	58	After a heart attack (in Hollywood, Ca.)
1943	SWOR, Bert	65	Found dead in his Tulsa, Oklahoma hotel room
• 1943	# Tamara	?	Airplane crash (near Lisbon, Portugal)
1943	+ VEIDT, Conrad	50	Heart attack (in Los Angeles, CA)
1943	VEILLER, Bayard	74	After an illness of 2-months
1943	VonSEYFFERTITZ, Gustav	80	Died in Woodland Hills, CA
1943	+ WALLER, Thomas "Fats"	39	Influenza and bronchial pneumonia (in Kansas City, MO)
1943	WEST, Charles H.	57	
1943	WEST, Claudine	59	
1943	WOOLLCOTT, Alexander	56	Heart attack (while broadcasting at CBS in New York, NY)
• 1943	WRIGHT, Haidee	44	Died in London, England
• 1944	BELLAMY, George	78	
1944	+ BENNETT, Richard	71	Heart attack (in Los Angeles, CA)
1944	BERESFORD, Harry	80	After a long illness
• 1944	# BRODY, Ann	59	Died in New York, NY
• 1944	BROOKS, Jesse Lee	50	Heart attack (in Hollywood, CA)
1944	#+ CARR, Nat	57	Died in Hollywood, CA
1944	+ COBB, Irvin S.	67	Died in New York, NY
1944	+ COLLIER, William Sr.	77	Pneumonia (in Beverly Hills, CA)
1944	#+ CREGAR, Laird	28	Following two heart attacks (in Los Angeles, CA)
1944	CROSMAN, Henrietta	83	Died in Pelham Manor, NY
1944	DILSON, John	53	
1944	#+ DINEHART, Alan Sr.	54	Heart attack (in Hollywood, CA)
• 1944	# EMERTON, Roy	51	Died in England
1944	FERGUSON, George S.	60	Died in Hollywood, CA
1944	# FISKE, Richard	29	Killed in action (in World War 2)
• 1944	FISKE, Robert L.	54	Congestive heart failure (in Sunland, CA)
1944	FRAZER, Robert W.	53	Died in Los Angeles, CA
• 1944	# GERRON, Kurt	?	Executed (in Auschwitz, Germany)
• 1944	GOTT, Barbara	?	
1944	GOTTSCHALK, Ferdinand	75	Died in London, England
• 1944	HALLOR, Ray	44	Automobile accident (near Palm Springs, CA)
1944	HARRIS, Marion	38	Burns in bed from a cigarette fire
1944	HARRIS, Mildred	42	Pneumonia after an abdominal operation (in Los Angeles, CA)
• 1944	# HOFFMAN, Otto	65	Lung cancer (in Woodland Hills, CA)
1944	HOUSTON, George F.	46	Heart attack
1944	# JAMISON, Bud	50	Died in Hollywood, CA
1944	KELLY, Lew	65	Died in Los Angeles, CA
1944	KENNEDY, Merna	35	Following a heart attack
1944	KING, Charles	54	Pneumonia (in London) Do not confuse with Chas. L. King, d. 1957
1944	KORFF, Arnold	73	Heart ailment
1944	LANGDON, Harry	60	Cerebral hemorrhage (in Los Angeles, CA)
1944	MacPHERSON, Aimee Semple	53	Heart attack in her sleep
1944	McNAMARA, Edward C.	57	Heart attack (on a Hollywood-bound train near Boston)
1944	McPHAIL, Douglas	30	From the effects of poison
1944	McRAE, Henry	68	Heart attack
1944	# MILLER, Glenn	40	Lost when his RAF plane, bound for Paris, disappeared
• 1944	# MORRISSEY, Betty	?	Died in New York, NY
• 1944	PAPE, Edward Lionel	77	Died in Woodland Hills, CA
• 1944	PARSONS, Percy	66	
1944	PATON, Stuart	59	
1944	#+ POWELL, Lee B.	36	Killed in action in the S. Pacific, during W.W.II
1944	PURCELL, Richard "Dick"	35	Heart attack after a car crash (in Los Angeles, CA)
1944	# RALPH, Jessie	79	After a lingering illness (in Gloucester, MA)

• New entry. # Original name (Pt. 7). + Interment (Pt. 5).   15   ☆ Oscar nominee, ★ Oscar winner (Pt. 10)

	YEAR	NAME		AGE	CAUSE AND/OR PLACE OF DEATH
	1944	ROWLANDS, Art		46	Died in Hollywood, CA
•	1944	RYAN, Joe		57	
	1944	SEITZ, George B.		56	Died in Hollywood, CA
	1944	SELWYN, Edgar		68	After a cerebral hemorrhage
	1944	+ SELZNICK, Myron		45	Following an attack of portal thrombosis
	1944	SHARLAND, Reginald		57	Died in Loma Linda, CA
	1944	# SHERRY, J. Barney		71	Died in Philadelphia, PA
	1944	STANLEY, Edwin		64	Died in Hollywood, CA
	1944	STUART, Donald		45	Following a heart attack (in Hollywood, CA)
	1944	USHER, Guy		69	After a brief illness (at his ranch in San Diego, CA)
	1944	#+ VanDYKE, W. S. "Woody" ☆		53	After a 6-months' illness
	1944	#+ VELEZ, Lupe		36	Suicide (sleeping pills) in Beverly Hills, CA
	1944	# WEST, Pat		55	Died in Hollywood, CA
•	1944	YARDE, Margaret		65	Died in London, England
	1945	AINLEY, Henry H.		66	Died in London, England
	1945	+ ARMETTA, Henry		57	Heart attack
	1945	BARBIER, George		83	Heart attack (in Los Angeles, CA)
	1945	BARKER, Reginald		59	Following a heart attack (in Los Angeles, CA)
•	1945	BARROWS, Henry A.		69	
	1945	BENCHLEY, Robert ★		56	Cerebral hemorrhage (in New York, NY)
•	1945	BLUM, Sammy		56	Heart attack (in Hollywood, CA)
•	1945	BRECKNER, Gary		49	Automobile accident (in Redlands, CA)
	1945	# CASEY, Dolores		28	Died in Hollywood, CA
	1945	CLYDE, David		60	Died in San Fernando Valley, CA
•	1945	CORRIGAN, D'Arcy		75	
	1945	COSTELLO, Don		44	Died in his sleep (in Hollywood, CA)
	1945	CRAIG, Alec		60	After a long illness (in Glendale, CA)
•	1945	+ CRAVEN, Frank		70	Heart ailment (in Beverly Hills, CA)
•	1945	# CRIMMONS, Daniel "Dan"		82	
	1945	DICKSON, Gloria		28	Asphyxiation from a fire
	1945	# DOUGLAS, Donald "Don"		40	Complications after appendectomy (in Los Angeles, CA)
•	1945	# EDWARDS, Gus		64	Died in Los Angeles, CA
	1945	# ELMER, Billy		75	After a long illness (in Hollywood, CA)
	1945	# EMERY, Gilbert		70	
	1945	EVANS, Charles		88	
•	1945	FAIRBANKS, William		50	Lobar pneumonia (in Los Angeles, CA)
	1945	FIELDING, Edward		65	Heart attack (while mowing his lawn in Beverly Hills, CA)
	1945	FUNG, Willie		49	Coronary occlusion (in Los Angeles, CA)
	1945	GRANACH, Alexander		54	After a brief illness (in New York, NY)
	1945	GREENE, Harrison		61	After a lingering illness (in Hollywood, CA)
	1945	HARVEY, Forrester		65	Stroke (in Laguna Beach, CA)
•	1945	# HERNANDEZ, Anna		77	Pneumonia (in Los Angeles, CA)
•	1945	HOLMES, Ralph		56	Natural causes (in New York, NY)
	1945	# HOPTON, Russell "Russ"		45	Found dead of an overdose of sleeping pills (in N. Hollywood, CA)
•	1945	HUTCHINS, Robert "Wheezer"		20	Killed in an Army training camp accident during World War 2
•	1945	KAYSSLER, Friedrich		71	Died in Leinmachnow, Germany
	1945	#+ KERN, Jerome		60	Cerebral hemorrhage
	1945	# LANE, Charles		76	Cancer
•	1945	LaRENO, Richard "Dick"		71	Died in Hollywood, CA
	1945	#+ LAVERNE, Lucille		72	After being hospitalized for a broken hip (in Culver City, CA)
•	1945	LIEDTKE, Harry		64	Died in Germany
•	1945	LUCY, Arnold		80	
	1945	MANDY, Jerry		52	Following a heart attack (in Hollywood, CA)
	1945	MARION, George F. Sr.		85	Following a heart attack (in Carmel, CA)
	1945	+ McCORMACK, John		61	Died at his home in County Kildare, Ireland
	1945	# McGREGOR, Malcolm		52	Burns (in Los Angeles, CA)
	1945	# McKAY, George W. "Red"		60	Died in Hollywood, CA
	1945	MUNIER, Ferdinand		55	After a heart attack (in Hollywood, CA)
	1945	#+ NAZIMOVA, Alla		66	Coronary thrombosis (in Los Angeles, CA)
	1945	# NORTH, Joe		71	
	1945	O'NEILL, Peggy		21	Suicide after a lover's quarrel (sleeping pills) in Beverly Hills, CA
	1945	#+ RANDALL, Addison "Jack"		38	Fell to his death from a horse, while filming (in Canoga Park, CA)
	1945	SANDRICH, Mark		44	Heart disease (at his home in Hollywood, CA)
	1945	SAXON, Hugh A.		76	Died at his home in Beverly Hills, CA

• New entry.   # Original name (Pt. 7).   + Interment (Pt. 5).   16   ☆ Oscar nominee, ★ Oscar winner (Pt. 10)

...DEATHS OF MOVIE AND TELEVISION PERSONALITIES – BY YEAR...

YEAR	NAME		AGE	CAUSE AND/OR PLACE OF DEATH
1945	# SCHLETTOW, Hans Adelbert		57	Died in Berlin, Germany
1945	SHEEHAN, Winfield		62	Following abdominal surgery
1945	SHY, Gus		51	After a long illness
1945	# SIDNEY, George (actor)		69	After a long illness (in Los Angeles, CA)
1945	SMILEY, Joseph W.		64	Died in New York
1945	VICTOR, Henry		46	Brain tumor (in Hollywood, CA)
1945	WALDMULLER, Lizzi		41	Killed during an air raid (in Vienna, Austria)
1945	# WESSELHOEFT, Eleanor		72	
1945	WHITE, J. Fisher		79	
1945	WU, Honorable		42	Died in Hollywood, CA
1945	# YOST, Herbert A.		65	Died in New York, NY
1946	# ALDEN, Mary		63	Died in Woodland Hills, CA
1946	# ARLISS, George	★	77	Bronchial trouble
1946	+ ATWILL, Lionel		61	Bronchial cancer and pneumonia
1946	AYLESWORTH, Arthur		61	
1946	+ BEERY, Noah Sr.		60	Heart attack (in Los Angeles, CA)
1946	BERGMAN, Henry		76	Heart attack (Do not confuse with actor Henri Bergman, d. 1917)
1946	+ BOWES, Major Edward		71	Died at his summer home in Rumson, N.J.
1946	BRECHER, Egon		66	After a heart attack (in Hollywood, CA)
1946	BROWER, Otto		50	Heart failure (in Hollywood, CA)
1946	BRUCE, Kate		87	
1946	BUCQUET, Harold S.		54	
1946	+ BUSCH, Mae		55	After a 5-mo. illness (in a San Fernando Valley sanitarium)
1946	BUTTERWORTH, Charles		49	Automobile accident (Suicide?) in Los Angeles, CA
1946	CARR, Trem		54	After a heart attack (while vacationing in San Diego, CA)
1946	CARTER, Ben F.		35	(Do not confuse with musician Benny Carter)
1946	+ EMMETT, Fern (Roquemore)		50	Died in Hollywood, CA
1946	#+ FIELDS, W. C.		66	Violent hemorrhage, dropsy and other ailments (in Pasadena, CA)
1946	# GEARY, Bud		47	Injuries from an automobile crash (in Hollywood, CA)
1946	# GEORGE, Heinrich		53	Died in a Soviet internment camp
1946	GLEASON, Russell		37	Accidental fall from a 4th floor hotel window (in New York, NY)
1946	GORDON, Hal		52	
1946	#+ HART, William S.		83	Stroke (in Los Angeles, CA)
1946	+ HATTON, Rondo		51	Heart attack (in Beverly Hills, CA)
1946	HOPKINS, Sis			(See Rose Melville)
1946	HOWARD, Sydney		61	
1946	+ HURT, Marlin		40	Heart attack
1946	JAMES, Walter		60	Heart attack (in Gardena, CA)
1946	KEATON, Joseph Sr.		78	Died in Hollywood, CA
1946	KELSO, Mayme		79	Heart attack (in South Pasadena, CA)
1946	LARKIN, George		57	
1946	+ LEHRMAN, Henry		60	Following a heart attack
1946	MacPHERSON, Jeanie		59	After a long illness (in Hollywood, CA)
1946	# MANDER, Miles		57	Heart attack (in Hollywood, CA)
1946	MANNING, Aileen		60	Died in Hollywood, CA
1946	MARIAN, Ferdinand		44	Automobile accident (near Durneck, Germany)
1946	MATTRAW, Scott		61	Died in Hollywood, CA
1946	McDANIEL, Etta		55	
1946	+ MEEK, Donald		66	Acute leukemia and heart attack (in Los Angeles, CA)
1946	MELVILLE, Rose "Sis Hopkins"		73	Died at her home in Lake George, NY
1946	MERIVALE, Philip		65	Heart ailment (in Los Angeles, CA)
1946	MORRISON, Louis "Lou"		80	Died in CA
1946	NEILL, Roy William		59	After a heart attack, in London
1946	# OLDFIELD, Barney		68	Cerebral hemorrhage
1946	# O'ROURKE, Brefni		57	
1946	# PERRY, Antoinette		58	Heart attack (in New York, NY)
1946	PORCASI, Paul		66	After a long illness (in Hollywood, CA)
1946	# RAGLAND, John "Rags"		40	Uremia (in Los Angeles, CA)
1946	# RAIMU, Jules		62	Heart attack (in Paris, France)
1946	RANKIN, Doris		66	Died in Washington, D.C.
1946	# ROYCE, Julian		76	
1946	ROYCE, Lionel		55	Heart attack in Manilla while entertaining troops with the U.S.O.
1946	# RUNYON, Damon		62	After a long bout with cancer (in New York, NY)
1946	SEMELS, Harry		58	Died in Los Angeles, CA

	YEAR	NAME		AGE	CAUSE AND/OR PLACE OF DEATH
•	1946	SLEZAK, Leo		71	*Died in Bavaria, Germany*
•	1946	STAMP-TAYLOR, Enid		41	*Injuries from a fall (in London, England)*
•	1946	# ST. POLIS, John		72	
•	1946	SULLIVAN, William A. "Billy"		54	*Died in Great Neck, NY*
	1946	# SUMMERVILLE, Slim		53	*Stroke (in Laguna Beach, CA)*
	1946	#+ TAYLOR, Laurette (Cooney)		62	*Coronary thrombosis after several weeks of illness*
	1946	TURNER, Florence		61	*After a long illness (in Woodland Hills, CA)*
	1946	VanTASSELL, Marie		72	*Died in Oakland, CA*
	1946	# VonBRINCKEN, Wilhelm		54	*Following a ruptured artery (in Los Angeles, CA)*
	1946	+ WALDRON, Charles D.		71	*Died in Hollywood, CA*
	1946	WELLESLEY, Charles		71	*Died at the Brunswick Home, Amityville, L.I., NY*
•	1946	WELLS, H. G.		80	*Died in London, England*
	1946	# WELSH, William		76	*Died in Los Angeles, CA*
	1946	YOUMANS, Vincent		47	*Tuberculosis*
	1947	ADAMS, Ernest S.		62	*After a long illness (in Hollywood, CA)*
	1947	ADLON, Louis		40	*Heart attack (in Los Angeles, CA)*
•	1947	ALLEN, Alfred		80	
	1947	#+ AMES, Adrienne		43	*Cancer (in New York, NY)*
	1947	# ARLEDGE, John		41	
	1947	ASHE, Warren		44	*Automobile accident*
•	1947	BAIRD, Stewart		66	*Heart attack (in New York, NY)*
•	1947	BARNETT, Chester A.		62	*Pneumonia (in Jefferson City, MO)*
	1947	+ BING, Herman		57	*Suicide (gunshot) in Los Angeles, CA*
	1947	#+ BORDEN, Olive		40	*Stomach ailment (in Los Angeles, CA)*
•	1947	BOWKER, Aldrich		71	*Arteriosclerosis (in Los Angeles, CA)*
•	1947	BRADLEY, Harry C.		78	*Heart attack (in Hollywood, CA)*
•	1947	BRAHAM, Lionel		68	*Heart attack (in Hollywood, CA)*
	1947	+ CAREY, Harry	☆	67	*Coronary thrombosis, attributed to a bee sting (in Brentwood, CA)*
	1947	+ CARLETON, William P.		73	*Automobile accident (in Hollywood, CA)*
	1947	CARNEY, George		60	
•	1947	CLARK, John J.		69	*Died in Hollywood, CA*
	1947	+ CORTHELL, Herbert		69	*After a year's illness (in Hollywood, CA)*
	1947	DAVIDSON, William B.		59	*Following an operation (in Santa Monica, CA)*
	1947	DEMPSEY, Thomas		79	*After a long illness (in Hollywood, CA)*
	1947	+ DIGGES, Dudley		68	*Stroke (in New York, NY)*
	1947	# FARLEY, Jim		65	*After a long illness (in a Pacoima, CA, sanitarium)*
•	1947	FYFFE, Will		36	*Fall from his hotel window (in St. Andrews, Scotland)*
	1947	GILBERT, Walter		60	*Heart attack*
	1947	# GLEASON, Lucille		59	*Heart attack (in Brentwood, CA)*
•	1947	GREY, Gloria		38	*Died in Hollywood, CA*
•	1947	HALL, Winter		68	
	1947	HALLIDAY, John		67	*Heart ailment*
•	1947	HANRAY, Lawrence		73	
	1947	+ HELLINGER, Mark		44	*Heart attack*
•	1947	# HEWSTON, Alfred H.		66	
	1947	HILLIARD, Ernest		57	*Following a heart attack (in Santa Monica, CA)*
	1947	HILYARD, Norman		74	
	1947	HOLMAN, Harry		73	*After a heart attack (in his Hollywood, CA, home)*
	1947	HOMANS, Robert E.		72	*Heart attack (in Los Angeles, CA)*
	1947	HURST, Brandon		80	*Arteriosclerosis (in Burbank, CA)*
	1947	# INCE, John E.		68	*Pneumonia (in Hollywood, CA)*
	1947	KELLY, John		46	
	1947	#+ KERRIGAN, J. Warren		67	*Bronchial pneumonia (1 of several actors with this name)*
	1947	KING, Leslie		71	
	1947	+ KOLKER, Henry		72	*Injuries from a fall (in Los Angeles, CA)*
	1947	#+ LAWRENCE, William E. "Babe"		51	*Died in Hollywood, CA*
•	1947	LESSEY, George A.		?	*Died in Westbrook, CT*
	1947	+ LOFT, Arthur		49	*Died in Los Angeles, CA*
	1947	LORCH, Theodore A.		74	*After a long illness (in Hollywood, CA)*
	1947	+ LUBITSCH, Ernst	☆	55	*Heart attack (in Los Angeles, CA)*
•	1947	# LUNCEFORD, Jimmy		45	*Died in Seaside, OR*
	1947	MASON, LeRoy		44	*After a heart attack (while filming "California Firebrand") in L.A.*
	1947	MAYNE, Eric		80	*Died in Hollywood, CA*
•	1947	# MERSON, Billy		66	*Died in London, England*

• New entry.   # Original name (Pt. 7).   + Interment (Pt. 5).　　　18　　　☆ Oscar nominee, ★ Oscar winner (Pt. 10)

YEAR	NAME	AGE	CAUSE AND/OR PLACE OF DEATH
1947	MOORE, Grace ☆	45	Airplane crash
1947	+ NEGIN, Koliz	60	
1947	NUGENT, J. C.	72	Coronary thrombosis (at the Lambs Club in New York City)
1947	#+ O'BRIEN, Tom	55	Died in Los Angeles, CA
1947	POTEL, Victor "Vic"	57	Died in Hollywood, CA
1947	# RANKIN, Arthur	46	After a cerebral hemorrhage (in Hollywood, CA)
1947	RAWLINS, Herbert	?	
1947	ROSS, Betty	67	Died at her home in Hollywood, CA
1947	SCHABLE, Robert	74	Died in Hollywood, CA
1947	# SOTHERN, Hugh	65	After an illness of 2 years (in Hollywood, CA)
• 1947	# STURGIS, Eddie	66	Heart disease (in Los Angeles, CA)
• 1947	TAGGART, Ben L.	58	Died in Santa Monica, CA
1947	+ TANGUAY, Eva	68	Heart attack and cerebral hemorrhage (in Los Angeles, CA)
1947	TOLER, Sidney	73	Died at his home in Beverly Hills, CA
1947	VanBUREN, Mabel	69	After a short illness (in Hollywood, CA)
1947	VonTRAPP, Baron Georg	57	
1947	WEBSTER, Ben	82	Following an operation (in Hollywood, CA)
1947	WELLS, Ted	48	Heart attack
1947	ZAHLER, Lee	53	
1948	AGAR, Jane	59	Died in Lakewood, OH
1948	AINSLEY, Norman	67	After a year's illness (at a private sanitarium in Hollywood, CA)
• 1948	ARTAUD, Antonin	52	Colon cancer (in Paris, France)
1948	BACON, Rod	33	
1948	BAGGOTT, King	68	Stroke (in Los Angeles, CA)
1948	# BANJAMIN, Gladys	?	
1948	BASKETT, James	44	Heart ailment
• 1948	BORLAND, Barlowe	71	Died in Woodland Hills, CA
• 1948	BRAITHWAITE, Lilian	75	Heart attack (in London, England)
• 1948	# BRITTON, Milt	53	Heart attack (in New York, NY)
1948	BROWN, Charles D.	60	Heart ailment (in Hollywood, CA)
• 1948	BROWNLEE, Frank	73	
1948	BRYANT, Charles	67	
1948	BURNS, Harry	63	Following a heart attack (in Santa Monica, CA)
1948	+ CARROLL, Earl	56	Airplane crash (in Mt. Carmel, PA)
• 1948	CHANDLER, Eddie	54	(Do not confuse with actor Edward S. Chandler)
1948	CHAPMAN, Edythe	85	Died in Glendale, CA
1948	# CODY, Bill Sr.	57	After an illness of several months (in Santa Monica, CA)
1948	COOLEY, James R.	68	Died in Hollywood, CA
• 1948	# D'ALBROOK, Sidney	62	Heart attack (in Los Angeles, CA)
1948	DeBRULIER, Nigel	69	
1948	EATON, Mary	46	After a heart attack (in Hollywood, CA)
1948	EISENSTEIN, Sergei	50	Died in Moscow, Russia
1948	EVERTON, Paul	79	Following a heart attack (in Woodland Hills, CA)
• 1948	FAIR, Virginia	49	Died in Hollywood, CA
1948	FEYDER, Jacques	54	
• 1948	FULLER, Leslie	58	Died in Margate, England
1948	GALE, Marguerite H.	63	
1948	GORDON, Vera	61	Died in Beverly Hills, CA
1948	#+ GRIFFITH, D. W.	73	Massive cerebral hemorrhage (in Los Angeles, CA)
1948	GRIFFITH, Linda Arvidson	65	(See Linda Arvidson)
1948	# HACKETT, Karl	55	After a long illness (in Sawtelle, CA)
1948	HAMMERSTEIN, Elaine	50	Automobile collision
1948	HINDS, Samuel S.	73	After a brief illness (in Pasadena, CA)
1948	HOLLIDAY, Frank Jr.	35	Suicide (hanged himself with a belt while in jail)
1948	HYMER, Warren	42	After a long illness (alcoholism) in Los Angeles, CA
1948	JAMES, Gladden	56	Leukemia (in Hollywood, CA)
1948	+ KENNEDY, Edgar	58	Throat cancer (in Woodland Hills, CA)
• 1948	KIRK, Jack "Pappy"	53	Died in Alaska
1948	KIRK, John	86	After a heart attack
1948	# LANDI, Elissa	43	Cancer (in Kingston, NY)
1948	#+ LANDIS, Carole	29	Suicide (sleeping pills) in Brentwood Heights, CA
• 1948	LANG, Matheson	68	Died in Bridgeton, Barbados
1948	#+ LAUGHLIN, Billy "Froggy"	16	Motor scooter—truck accident (in Corvina, CA)
1948	LEHAR, Franz	78	Stomach cancer

	YEAR	NAME		AGE	CAUSE AND/OR PLACE OF DEATH
•	1948	LEIGH, Frank		?	Died in Hollywood, CA
•	1948	LEYTON, George		84	Died in London, England
	1948	LLOYD, Charles M.		78	Heart attack
	1948	LOUDEN, Thomas		73	After a stroke (in Hollywood, CA)
	1948	LOVE, Robert		34	Suicide (5-story leap from his doctor's office)
	1948	MacGREGOR, Harman		70	
	1948	MACK, James T.		77	
	1948	MALLALIEU, Aubrey		74	
	1948	MAXWELL, Edwin		62	Cerebral hemorrhage (in Falmouth, MA)
•	1948	MAYER, Ray		47	Heart attack (in Salt Lake City, UT)
	1948	McCAREY, Ray		50	Died alone in his apartment
•	1948	MIKHOELS, Solomon		58	Murdered (run over by a truck) presumably on Stalin's orders
	1948	MILLER, Edward G.		65	
•	1948	MORENO, Marguerite		77	Died in France
	1948	MOROSCO, Walter		49	Stroke
	1948	NELSON, Anne		37	
	1948	#+ NIBLO, Fred Sr.		74	Pneumonia (in New Orleans, Louisiana)
	1948	#+ NOLAN, Mary		42	Found dead at home (in Los Angeles, CA)
•	1948	# NORWOOD, Eille		87	
	1948	# ORTES, Armand F.		68	
•	1948	# OSWALDA, Ossi		49	Died in Prague, Czechoslovakia
	1948	# PETRIE, Hay		53	
•	1948	# RATCLIFFE, E. J.		85	Died in Los Angeles, CA
•	1948	# RAZETTO, Stella		67	Died in Malibu, CA
	1948	RICHMOND, Warner		53	Coronary thrombosis (in Los Angeles, CA)
	1948	ROBERTSON, Willard		62	
	1948	#+ RUTH, Babe		53	Cancerous tumor
•	1948	# SCHINDELL, Cy		41	Died in Van Nuys, CA
	1948	# SELIG, William N.		84	
	1948	# SELWYN, Clarissa		62	Died in West Hollywood, CA
	1948	# SMITH, C. Aubrey		85	Double pneumonia (in Beverly Hills, CA)
	1948	SODERLING, Walter		75	Died in Los Angeles, CA
	1948	SOREL, George S.		48	Died in Hollywood, CA
	1948	STEDMAN, Lincoln		41	Died in Los Angeles, CA
	1948	#+ TAUBER, Richard		56	After an illness of several months (in a nursing home in London)
	1948	TOLAND, Gregg		44	Coronary thrombosis
•	1948	WEGENER, Paul		74	Died in Berlin, Germany
	1948	WHITE, Leo		68	Died in Hollywood, CA
	1948	WHITTY, May	☆	82	Died in Beverly Hills, CA
•	1948	# WILLIAM, Warren		52	Multiple myeloma and blood disease (in Encino, CA)
•	1948	WILSON, Charles Cahill		53	Esophagal hemorrhage
	1949	ALLEN, Lester		58	Struck and killed by an automobile (in Hollywood, CA)
	1949	# ARVIDSON, Linda		65	Died in New York
	1949	BARNES, George		59	Following an operation for cancer
	1949	+ BEERY, Wallace	★	64	Heart attack (in Los Angeles, CA)
	1949	BEERY, William C.		70	
•	1949	BOHNEN, Roman		54	Heart attack (in Hollywood, CA)
	1949	+ BRESSART, Felix		69	Leukemia (in Los Angeles, CA)
	1949	BURNABY, Davy		68	Heart attack
	1949	CAWTHORNE, Joseph		81	Stroke (in Beverly Hills, CA)
•	1949	CHESNEY, Arthur		67	Died in London, England
	1949	CHRISTY, Ivan		61	After a heart attack (in Burbank, CA)
	1949	#+ CLARK, Buddy		38	Airplane crash (in Beverly Hills, CA)
	1949	+ CLIFTON, Elmer		59	Cerebral hemorrhage (in Los Angeles, CA)
•	1949	COSGRAVE, Luke		86	Died in Woodland Hills, CA
	1949	DAVENPORT, Harry		83	Heart attack (in Los Angeles, CA)
	1949	DAVIS, Owen Jr.		42	Drowned after falling overboard from a sloop (in L.I. South, NY)
	1949	DESMOND, William		71	Heart attack (in Los Angeles, CA)
	1949	#+ DIX, Richard	☆	55	Acute cardiac collapse (in Los Angeles, CA)
	1949	DRAYTON, Alfred		68	
	1949	+ FLEMING, Victor	★	64	After a heart attack
	1949	# GIRARD, Joe		78	
•	1949	# GRAHAM, Morland		57	Heart attack (in London, England)
	1949	# HART, Neal		70	Died in Woodland Hills, CA

...DEATHS OF MOVIE AND TELEVISION PERSONALITIES — BY YEAR...

	YEAR	NAME		AGE	CAUSE AND/OR PLACE OF DEATH
	1949	HAY, Will		60	Died in London, England
	1949	# HODGSON, Leland		55	Heart attack (at his home in Hollywood, CA)
	1949	#+ HOWARD, Willie		61	After a brief illness (in New York, NY)
	1949	+ LEDBETTER, Huddie "Leadbelly"		60	Amyotrophic lateral sclerosis
	1949	+ LEIBER, Fritz		67	Heart attack (in Pacific Palisades, CA)
•	1949	LLOYD, Frederick W.		69	Died in Hove, England
•	1949	LONG, Nick Jr.		43	Results of an automobile accident (in New York, NY)
•	1949	# MARRIOTT, Moore		64	
	1949	McKENZIE, Robert B.		65	Heart attack (in Rhode Island)
	1949	# MELESH, Alex		58	Died in Hollywood, CA
•	1949	MIDDLEMASS, Robert M.		64	Died in Los Angeles, CA
	1949	MIDDLETON, Charles B.		69	Heart attack (in Los Angeles, CA)
	1949	MIDGLEY, Florence		59	Died in Hollywood, CA
	1949	MITCHELL, Geneva		42	Died in California
	1949	+ MITCHELL, Margaret		46	Struck by a speeding automobile
	1949	# MORAN, George		67	After suffering a stroke (in Oakland, CA)
	1949	#+ MORGAN, Frank	☆	59	Died at his home in Beverly Hills, CA
	1949	# MORRIS, Philip		56	Died in Los Angeles, CA
•	1949	NORDEN, Cliff		26	Suicide (pills) in Hollywood, CA
	1949	OAKMAN, Wheeler		59	Died in Van Nuys, CA
	1949	OLCOTT, Sidney		76	After a long illness
	1949	+ OUSPENSKAYA, Maria	☆	73	Burned to death from a cigarette fire (in her L.A. apartment)
•	1949	+ RAPF, Harry		67	Heart attack
•	1949	# RAYMOND, Royal		33	Cancer (in Van Nuys, CA)
	1949	# REYNOLDS, Craig		42	Motorcycle/car crash (in Los Angeles, CA)
	1949	# RIPLEY, Robert L.		55	Heart attack (in New York, NY)
	1949	+ ROBINSON, Bill "Bojangles"		71	Heart ailment (in New York)
	1949	+ SCHLESINGER, Leon		66	Viral infection
	1949	# SHEAN, Al		81	Died in New York, NY
•	1949	SPENCE, Ralph		60	Heart attack (in Woodland Hills, CA)
	1949	STOTHART, Herbert		64	After an illness of several months
•	1949	# TUCKER, Harland		?	Heart attack (in CA)
•	1949	TYRELL, John E.		46	Died in CA
•	1949	# VANBRUGH, Irene		76	Died in London, England
•	1949	# WAITE, Malcolm		56	Died in Los Angeles, CA
	1949	WALKER, Johnnie		53	Coronary thrombosis (in New York, NY)
•	1949	WALLS, Tom		66	Died in Edwell, England
•	1949	WELLS, Marie		55	Suicide (sleeping pills) in Hollywood, CA
	1949	# WHITE, Lee Roy "Lasses"		61	Died in Hollywood, CA
	1949	+ WOOD, Sam	☆	66	Heart attack
	1949	WRIGHT, William		37	Cancer (in Ensenada, Mex.) Do not confuse with Will Wright d. 1962
	1950	+ ALLGOOD, Sara	☆	66	Heart attack (in Woodland Hills, CA)
	1950	APPLEBY, William C.		27	Coronary thrombosis
	1950	ARLISS, Florence		?	Died in London, England
	1950	# BANKS, Monty		52	Heart attack
	1950	BELL, Henry "Hank"		58	Following a heart attack (in Hollywood, CA)
•	1950	BENNETT, Mickey		35	Heart attack (in Hollywood, CA)
•	1950	BENNETT, Hugh		57	Coronary thrombosis (at his home in Malibu, CA)
•	1950	BONIFACE, Symona		56	Died in Woodland Hills, CA
•	1950	# BORDEAUX, Joe		56	Died in Hollywood, CA
	1950	BRISCOE, Lottie		69	Died in New York, NY
	1950	BUCK, Frank		62	Lung ailment (in Houston, TX)
	1950	+ BURROUGHS, Edgar Rice		74	Heart ailment
	1950	# CABANNE, William C.		62	Heart attack (in Philadelphia, PA)
	1950	CARLETON, George		65	Heart attack (in Hollywood, CA)
	1950	CARTER, Monte		66	
	1950	CAVANAUGH, Hobart		53	Following major surgery (in Woodland Hills, CA)
•	1950	CLAYTON, Gilbert		89	
	1950	# CLAYTON, Marguerite B.		50	Injuries from an automobile accident
	1950	# CLEMENTO, Steve		64	Cerebral hemorrhage (in Los Angeles, CA)
	1950	COSTELLO, Maurice		73	Heart ailment (in Hollywood, CA)
	1950	+ COWL, Jane		62	Cancer (in Santa Monica, CA)
	1950	CULLINANI, Ralph		68	
•	1950	DAMROSCH, Walter		88	Died in New York, NY

• New entry. # Original name (Pt. 7). + Interment (Pt. 5).   21   ☆ Oscar nominee, ★ Oscar winner (Pt. 10)

YEAR	NAME	AGE	CAUSE AND/OR PLACE OF DEATH
1950	DAVIDSON, Max	75	After a long illness (in Woodland Hills, CA)
1950	DAWSON, Dorice	56	
1950	+ DeCORDOBA, Pedro	68	Found dead of a heart attack (at his home in Sunland, CA)
1950	DeLaMOTTE, Marguerite	47	Cerebral thrombosis (in San Francisco, CA)
1950	DYALL, Franklin	76	Died in Worthing, England
1950	ELDRIDGE, Anna Mae	56	
1950	EVANS, Jack	57	Heart attack (in Hollywood, CA)
1950	FELLOWES, Rockcliffe	65	Heart attack (in Los Angeles, CA)
1950	FRANCISCO, Betty	50	Heart attack (at her ranch in El Cerito, CA)
1950	+ FULTON, Maude	69	Died at the Motion Picture Country Home, CA
1950	GARWOOD, William	66	Coronary occlusion (in Los Angeles, CA)
1950	# GERRARD, Douglas	69	After being found unconscious on the street (in Hollywood, CA)
1950	#+ HALE, Alan Sr.	57	Liver ailment — virus infection (in Hollywood, CA)
1950	HICKMAN, Howard C.	69	Following a heart attack (in Los Angeles, CA)
• 1950	# HOLLES, Antony	49	
1950	HOLMES, Helen	58	Heart attack (in Burbank, CA)
1950	HOPKINS, Arthur	71	Heart ailment
1950	#+ HUSTON, Walter ★	66	Aneurysm (in Beverly Hills, CA)
1950	#+ INGRAM, Rex (Hitchcock)	57	Cerebral hemorrhage (in North Hollywood, CA)
1950	JACKSON, Warren	57	After his car collided with a truck
1950	# JANNINGS, Emil ★	63	Cancer (in Austria)
1950	#+ JOLSON, Al	64	Heart attack (in San Francisco, CA)
• 1950	KAMPERS, Fritz	59	Died in Germany
1950	KEMPER, Charles	49	Injuries from an automobile crash
• 1950	KLOEPFER, Eugen	64	Died in Wiesbaden, Germany
• 1950	# KRAHLY, Hanns	65	Died in Los Angeles, CA
1950	# LAMBERTI, Professor	58	After a long illness
• 1950	LAUDER, Harry	79	Kidney ailment (in Lenarkshire, Scotland)
1950	LEHR, Lew	54	Died at a sanitarium in Brookline, MA
1950	LINGHAM, Thomas J.	75	Died in Woodland Hills, CA
1950	LIPATTI, Dinu	33	
1950	+ LORD, Pauline	60	Heart trouble (in Alamogordo, NM)
1950	MARSHALL, Boyd	65	Died in Jackson Heights, NY
1950	METAXA, Georges	51	Heart ailment (in Monroe, LA)
1950	# MONTANA, Lewis "Bull"	62	Coronary thrombosis (in Los Angeles, CA)
1950	MORRISON, Arthur	71	Died in Los Angeles, CA
1950	NASH, Florence	60	Heart ailment
1950	+ NIJINSKY, Vaslav	62	Nephritis (in London, England)
1950	OBER, Robert	68	Died in New York
1950	OVERMAN, Jack	34	Following a heart attack (in Hollywood, CA)
1950	PATON, Charles	64	
1950	PATRICOLA, Tom	55	Following brain surgery (in Pasadena, CA)
1950	PEMBERTON, Brock	64	After a heart attack at his home (in New York, NY)
1950	PINE, Ed	46	Died at the Motion Picture Country Home, CA
• 1950	# POWELL, Russ	75	Arteriosclerosis (in Woodland Hills, CA)
1950	ROBINSON, Dewey	52	After a heart attack (in Las Vegas, Nevada)
1950	SELBIE, Evelyn	68	Heart ailment (in Hollywood, CA)
• 1950	SHAW, George Bernard	94	Bladder ailment and injuries from a fall (in Ayot St. Lawrence, Eng.)
1950	SMITH, "Whispering" Jack	51	Heart attack (in New York) Do not confuse with Jack Smith, d. 1989
1950	+ STAHL, John M.	63	Heart attack
1950	STARR, Muriel	62	Heart attack
• 1950	# STOOPNAGLE, Col. Lemuel Q.	52	
• 1950	# STUBBS, Harry	75	Heart attack (in Woodland Hills, CA)
1950	SWEENEY, Jack	61	
1950	TILBURY, Zeffie	86	Died in Los Angeles, CA
1950	WADSWORTH, William	77	Died at Queens General Hospital in New York
1950	# WINTHROP, Joy	86	
1950	WRAY, Ted	41	Following a heart attack
1950	+ YULE, Joe	55	Heart attack (in Hollywood, CA)
• 1951	ALLEN, Harry R.	68	
1951	# ARTHUR, Johnny	68	Heart disease (in Woodland Hills, CA)
• 1951	ASH, Samuel Howard	67	Died in Hollywood, CA
1951	# AULT, Marie	81	
1951	AUSTIN, William	66	Stroke

• New entry.   # Original name (Pt. 7).   + Interment (Pt. 5).

☆ Oscar nominee,   ★ Oscar winner (Pt. 10)

...DEATHS OF MOVIE AND TELEVISION PERSONALITIES — BY YEAR...

YEAR	NAME		AGE	CAUSE AND/OR PLACE OF DEATH
1951	# AYE, Maryon		45	Suicide (poison) in Hollywood, CA
1951	BARKER, Bradley		68	Died in New York, NY
1951	+ BAXTER, Warner	★	58	Pneumonia after lobotomy to ease pain (in Beverly Hills, CA)
1951	BENEDICT, Kingsley		69	Died in Woodland Hills, CA
1951	# BENNETT, Billie		75	Cerebral hemorrhage (in Los Angeles, CA)
1951	# BERKES, John "Johnny"		54	Died in Hollywood, CA
1951	BOROS, Ferike		70	Died in Hollywood, CA
1951	#+ BRICE, Fanny		59	Cerebral hemorrhage (in Beverly Hills, CA)
1951	BROMBERG, J. Edward		47	Natural causes (in London, England)
1951	BROOKE, Clifford		79	After being struck by a car (in Santa Monica, CA)
1951	+ CHRISTIANS, Mady		51	Cerebral hemorrhage (in South Norwalk, CT)
1951	CHRISTIE, Al		69	Heart attack
1951	COLEMAN, Charles		65	Stroke (in Woodland Hills, CA)
1951	# COLLINS, Monty		52	Heart attack (in North Hollywood, CA)
1951	CONWAY, Jack (comedian/actor)		?	(Do not confuse with actor/director Jack Conway, d. 1952)
1951	COSSART, Ernest		74	Died in New York, NY
1951	+ DUCHIN, Eddie		41	Leukemia (in New York, NY)
1951	DUNN, Edward F. "Eddie"		55	Died in Hollywood, CA
1951	ELLIOTT, Robert		72	
1951	+ ERROL, Leon		70	Heart attack (in Los Angeles, CA)
1951	FLAHERTY, Robert		67	
1951	# FORBES, Ralph		54	Died at Montefiore Hospital in New York, NY
1951	GOWLAND, Gibson		79	Died in London, England
1951	HARCOURT, James		77	
1951	HART, Richard		35	Heart attack
1951	# HARTIGAN, Pat		69	Coronary attack (in Los Angeles, CA)
1951	HEYBURN, Weldon		46	
1951	#+ HOLT, Jack		62	Coronary thrombosis (in Los Angeles, CA)
1951	JOUVET, Louis		63	Heart attack (in Paris, France)
1951	KING, Joe		68	Died in Woodland Hills, CA
1951	LISTER, Francis		52	Died in London, England
1951	MacDONALD, Edmund		43	Cerebral hemorrhage (in Los Angeles, CA)
1951	MARIN, Edwin L.		50	After a 3-week illness
1951	MAUDE, Cyril		88	Died in Torquay, England
1951	McGLYNN, Frank		84	Died in Newburgh, NY
1951	MELTON, Frank		43	After a heart attack (in Hollywood, CA)
1951	METHOT, Mayo		47	Died in Portland, OR
1951	# MONTEZ, Maria		33	Heart seizure while bathing in her home (in France)
1951	# NORMAN, Josephine		46	Died in Roslyn, NY
1951	# NOVELLO, Ivor		58	Coronary thrombosis (in London, England)
1951	O'MADIGAN, Isabel		78	Died in Los Angeles, CA
1951	OVEY, George		80	Died in Hollywood, CA
1951	OWEN, Garry		48	Heart attack (in Hollywood, CA)
1951	PATTON, William "Bill"		57	
1951	# RAYMOND, Jack		49	Heart attack (in Santa Monica, CA) Do not confuse with British actor
1951	# RIDGES, Stanley		59	Died in Westbrook, CT
1951	# RIGBY, Edward		71	Died in London, England
1951	RODGERS, Walter		64	Following a stroke (in Los Angeles, CA)
1951	+ ROMBERG, Sigmund		64	Cerebral hemorrhage
1951	# ROSEN, Phil		63	Died in Hollywood, CA
1951	SHANNON, Ethel		53	
1951	+ SIMON, S. Sylvan		41	Heart attack
1951	SIMPSON, Ivan		76	Died in New York, NY
1951	# SINCLAIR, Arthur		68	Died in Belfast, Northern Ireland
1951	# STEERS, Larry		69	Died in Woodland Hills, CA
1951	TELL, Olive		56	Died in New York, NY
1951	# TORRENCE, David		87	
1951	VISAROFF, Michael		58	Pneumonia (in Hollywood, CA)
1951	WAKEFIELD, Douglas		51	
1951	WALKER, Robert		32	Respiratory failure (Do not confuse with R. "Bob" Walker, d. 1954)
1951	WALLACE, Richard		57	
1951	+ WARFIELD, David		84	Died in New York
1951	WEIGEL, Paul		83	
1951	WILLS, Drusilla		66	Died in London, England
1951	YARBOROUGH, Barton		51	Died in Hollywood, CA

• New entry. # Original name (Pt. 7). + Interment (Pt. 5). 23 ☆ Oscar nominee, ★ Oscar winner (Pt. 10)

YEAR	NAME		AGE	CAUSE AND/OR PLACE OF DEATH
1951	YOUNG, Clifton		34	Asphyxiation after falling asleep while smoking (in Los Angeles, CA)
• 1952	ABBOTT, Gypsy		57	Died in Hollywood, CA
• 1952	ABBEY, May		80	Fell or jumped from a building (in New York, NY)
1952	ADAIR, John		66	Died in New York
• 1952	ADAMS, Lionel		86	Died in New York, NY
1952	BANKS, Leslie		61	Died in London, England
1952	BASSERMAN, Albert	☆	86	Heart attack (in Zurich, Switzerland)
• 1952	# BOND, Jack		52	Died in Hollywood, CA
1952	BRIGGS, Harlan		72	After a brief illness
1952	+ BYRD, Ralph M. "Dick Tracy"		43	Heart attack (in Tarzana, CA)
1952	COLCORD, Mabel		80	
1952	CONWAY, Jack (actor/director)		65	(Do not confuse with comedian/film actor Jack Conway, d. 1951)
1952	#+ CROSBY, Dixie Lee		40	Cancer
1952	CURTIS, Dick		49	Died in Hollywood, CA
1952	DEAN, Julia		74	Died in Hollywood, CA
1952	# DeROACH, Charles		72	
1952	DUFKIN, Sam		61	
• 1952	EDWARDS, Henry		70	Died in Chobham, England
1952	ELLIS, Edward		80	Died in Hollywood, CA
• 1952	EVANS, Herbert		68	Died in San Gabriel, CA
1952	FOX, William		73	
• 1952	FRANCIS, Olin		59	Died in Hollywood, CA
1952	FRENCH, Charles K.		92	After a heart attack (in Hollywood, CA)
1952	#+ GARFIELD, John	☆	39	Heart attack (in New York, NY)
1952	GRANT, Lawrence		82	Died in Santa Barbara, CA
1952	# HARDING, Lyn		85	
1952	# HENDERSON, Fletch		54	Stroke
1952	+ HERBERT, Hugh		64	Heart attack (in North Hollywood, CA)
1952	#+ HOWARD, Jerome "Curly"		48	Following several strokes (in San Gabriel, CA)
1952	LaCAVA, Gregory	☆	59	Died at his home in Malibu Beach, CA
• 1952	LAUGHTON, Edward "Eddie"		49	Pneumonia (in Hollywood, CA)
1952	#+ LAWRENCE, Gertrude		54	Cancer of the liver (in New York, NY)
1952	#+ LEE, Canada		45	Heart attack (in New York, NY)
1952	# LEE, Dixie		40	Cancer (in Holmby Hills, CA)
1952	#+ LINCOLN, Elmo		63	Heart attack (in Hollywood, CA)
• 1952	# LITTLE, Bozo		45	Heart ailment (in Los Angeles, CA)
1952	LONG, Walter		73	Heart attack (in Los Angeles, CA)
• 1952	# LUFKIN, Sam		59	Uremia (in Los Angeles, CA)
1952	#+ MacDONALD, J. Farrell		77	Died in Hollywood, CA
1952	MAGRILL, George		52	Died in Los Angeles, CA
1952	MALA, Ray		46	Heart attack (in Hollywood, CA)
1952	MALATESTA, Fred		62	After a surgical operation (in Burbank, CA)
• 1952	MARKS, Willis		87	Died in Los Angeles, CA
1952	+ McDANIEL, Hattie	★	57	Breast cancer (in San Fernando Valley, CA)
1952	# McGOWAN, John P.		72	(Silent star/producer) Died in Hollywood, CA
1952	MITCHELL, Bruce		68	Anemia (in Hollywood, CA)
1952	# MORAN, Polly		68	Heart ailment (in Los Angeles, CA)
1952	MORLEY, Robert	☆	60	(Do not confuse with Robert Morley, d. 1992)
1952	PAWLEY, William		46	Died in New York
1952	#+ PETERS, Susan	☆	31	Bronchial pneumonia and chronic kidney infection (in Visalia, CA)
• 1952	# POFF, Lon		82	
• 1952	POST, Charles A. "Buddy"		55	Died in CA
1952	PROSSER, Hugh		46	Automobile crash (near Gallup, NM)
1952	RADFORD, Basil		55	Heart attack (in London, England)
1952	REED, Barbara		85	
1952	# REED, George H.		85	Arteriosclerosis (in Woodland Hills, CA)
1952	RENOIR, Pierre		67	Died in Paris, France
1952	ROBER, Richard		46	Killed when his car went down an embankment due to fog
1952	ROCHE, John		56	Stroke (in Los Angeles, CA)
1952	SHEEHAN, John J., Jr.		61	Died in Hollywood, CA
1952	SHERMAN, Harry		67	After two surgical operations
1952	# SKIPWORTH, Alison		88	Died in New York, NY
1952	ST. CLAIR, Malcolm		55	Died in Pasadena, CA.
• 1952	STEWART, Blanche		?	

YEAR	NAME	AGE	CAUSE AND/OR PLACE OF DEATH
1952	STRANGE, Robert	70	Died in Hollywood, CA
1952	TAYLOR, Ray	63	Died in Hollywood, CA
• 1952	WALDRON, Charles K.	37	Airplane crash (in Los Angeles, CA)
1952	WALES, Ethel	71	Died in Hollywood, CA
1952	WARD, Fannie	80	After suffering a cerebral hemorrhage
1952	WARD, Lucille	72	Died in Dayton, Ohio
1952	WEST, Roland	65	Heart ailment (in Santa Monica, Ca.)
1952	YORK, Duke	49	Suicide (found shot to death in his Hollywood home)
1952	# ZEARS, Marjorie	41	
1953	ADAIR, Jean	80	Died in New York
1953	#+ ADAMS, Maude	80	Heart attack (in Tannersville, NY)
1953	AUSTIN, Albert	71	After a long illness
1953	BARNARD, Ivor	66	
1953	BELMORE, Lionel	85	Died in Woodland Hills, CA
1953	BONN, Walter	64	Died in Hollywood, CA
1953	BORDONI, Irene	59	Died in New York, NY
1953	BRENEMAN, Mark L.	54	Heart attack
1953	#+ BRUCE, Nigel	58	Heart attack (in Santa Monica, CA)
1953	CLARK, Cliff	59	Heart attack (in Hollywood, CA)
1953	COOKE, Baldwin G. "Baldy"	65	Died in Los Angeles, CA
• 1953	# CRIPPS, Kernan	67	
1953	# CURTIS, Alan	43	Following a kidney operation
• 1953	DAWSON, Frank	83	Died in Hollywood, CA
1953	DeGRASSE, Sam	78	Heart attack (in Hollywood, CA)
• 1953	DUNBAR, David	60	Died in Woodland Hills, CA
1953	DUNDEE, Jimmie	52	Leukemia (in Woodland Hills, CA)
1953	+ FARNUM, William	76	Cancer (in Los Angeles, CA)
1953	# FINLAYSON, James	66	Heart attack (in Los Angeles, CA)
1953	FOO, Wing	43	Heart attack
1953	# FORD, Francis	71	After a long illness (in Los Angeles, CA)
• 1953	GALLAGHER, Raymond "Ray"	67	Heart attack (in Camarillo, CA)
• 1953	GRASSBY, Bertram	72	Died in Scottsdale, AZ
1953	GRIFFIN, Frank L.	63	Heart attack (in Hollywood, CA)
1953	# HALL, Porter	65	Heart attack (in Los Angeles, CA)
• 1953	HEPWORTH, Cecil M.	78	Died in Greenford, Middlesex, England
1953	HOYT, Arthur	79	After a long illness (in Woodland Hills, CA)
1953	HURST, Paul C.	64	Suicide (in Hollywood, CA)
1953	JOHNSON, Osa	58	Heart attack (in New York, NY)
1953	KEMP, Paul	54	Died in Bad Godesberg, West Germany
1953	# KENDALL, Cy	55	Died in Woodland Hills, CA
1953	KENT, Craufurd	72	After a short illness (in Los Angeles, CA)
• 1953	#+ Kiki	52	Natural causes (in Paris, France)
1953	LANE, Pat	53	Heart attack
1953	+ LEBEDEFF, Ivan	53	Heart attack (in Hollywood, CA)
• 1953	# LESLIE, Gene	48	Died in Los Angeles, CA
1953	LOGAN, Stanley	67	Died in New York
1953	LOVELL, Raymond	53	Died in London, England
1953	# LUTTRINGER, Al	74	Died in Hollywood, CA
1953	MANKIEWICZ, Herman J.	55	Uremic poisoning
1953	# MARTIN, Chris-Pin	59	Heart attack (in Montebello, CA)
1953	McCORMACK, William M.	62	Following a heart attack (in Hollywood, CA)
• 1953	# McCORMICK, Merrill	61	Heart attack (in Hollywood, CA)
1953	# McINTYRE, Leila	70	After a long illness (in Los Angeles, CA)
1953	MITCHELL, Millard	53	Lung cancer (in Santa Monica, CA)
• 1953	NORTON, Edgar	84	Died in Woodland Hills, CA
• 1953	PAYNE, Edna	61	Liver ailment (in Los Angeles, CA)
1953	# PAYNE, Lou	77	Died in Woodland Hills, CA
1953	PHELPS, Lee	58	Died in Culver City, CA
• 1953	+ PROKOFIEV, Sergei	62	Cerebral hemorrhage
• 1953	PUDOVKIN, Vsevolod	60	Natural causes (in Moscow, Russia)
1953	# PURDELL, Reginald	56	Died in London, England
1953	RAWLINSON, Herbert	67	Lung cancer (in Woodland Hills, CA)
• 1953	# RAYMOND, Jack	66	Died in London, England (Do not confuse with U.S. actor)
1953	REIS, Irving	47	Following a cancer operation

YEAR	NAME		AGE	CAUSE AND/OR PLACE OF DEATH
1953	# ROSE, Blanche		74	*Died at her home in Hollywood, CA*
1953	ROSENTHAL, Harry		52	*Heart attack (in Hollywood, CA)*
1953	+ ROSSON, Richard "Dick"		60	*Suicide (carbon monoxide poisoning) in Los Angeles, CA*
1953	SALTER, Thelma		?	*After a lingering illness (in Hollywood, CA)*
1953	# SANTLEY, Fred		64	*Died in Hollywood, CA*
1953	SARNO, Hector V.		73	*After a long illness (in Pasadena, CA)*
1953	SEDGWICK, Edward Jr.		60	*Following a heart attack (in North Hollywood, CA)*
• 1953	# SHEA, Mervin		52	*Died in Sacramento, CA*
1953	SPOOR, George K.		81	
1953	STEVENSON, Houseley		74	*Died at City of Hope Sanitarium, near Los Angeles, CA*
• 1953	# STOCKDALE, Carl		79	*Heart attack (in Woodland Hills, CA)*
1953	# STONE, Lewis	☆	74	*Heart attack (while chasing 3 teen-aged vandals) in Los Angeles*
• 1953	SYLVANI, Gladys		68	*Died in Alexandria, VA*
1953	# TABLER, P. Dempsey		79	*Died in San Francisco, CA*
1953	TEARLE, Godfrey		68	*Died in London, England*
1953	THORPE, Jim		64	*Heart attack (in Los Angeles, CA)*
1953	VIERTEL, Berthold		68	*Heart ailment (in Vienna, Austria)*
1953	VIGNOLA, Robert G.		71	*Died in Hollywood, CA*
1953	WALLACE, Morgan		65	*Died in Tarzana, CA*
1953	+ WILLIAMS, Hank Sr.		29	*Heart attack from excessive drinking (in Oak Hill, WV)*
1953	WILSON, Dooley		59	*Died in Los Angeles, CA*
1953	YOUNG, Roland	☆	65	*Died at his home in New York, NY*
1954	ADAIR, Robert		54	*Died in London, England*
1954	AHLM, Philip E.		49	*Murdered (shot) in Hollywood, CA*
• 1954	BAGNI, John		42	*Heart attack (in Hollywood, CA)*
1954	#+ BARRYMORE, Lionel	★	76	*Heart attack (in Van Nuys, CA)*
1954	# BATES, Florence		65	*Heart attack (in Burbank, CA)*
1954	CAIN, Robert		67	*Died in New York, NY*
• 1954	# CARDWELL, James		32	*Suicide (gunshot) in Hollywood, CA*
• 1954	CARR, Geraldine		37	*Automobile accident (in Hollywood, CA)*
1954	CASS, Maurice		69	*Heart attack (in Hollywood, CA)*
1954	CLARK, Eddie		75	*Heart attack (in Hollywood, CA)*
1954	COLLINS, Lewis D.		55	*Heart attack*
• 1954	CORDING, Harry		63	*Died in Sun Valley, CA*
• 1954	COXEN, Edward Albert		70	*Died in Hollywood, CA*
• 1954	# DEMAIN, Gordon		56	
• 1954	DIONNE, Emelie		20	*Epileptic seizure*
• 1954	DOWLING, Joan		26	*Found dead in a gas-filled room (in London, England)*
1954	EVANS, Evan		53	
• 1954	GEBUEHR, Otto		76	*Died in Wiesbaden, West Germany*
• 1954	# GEORGE, Gladys	☆	54	*Brain hemorrhage (in Los Angeles, CA)*
• 1954	GLYNNE, Mary		56	*Died in London, England*
• 1954	GRAVINA, Cesare		96	*Died in Italy*
1954	#+ GREENSTREET, Sydney	☆	74	*After a long illness (in Los Angeles, CA)*
1954	HACKETT, Florence		72	*Died in New York City*
1954	HAMPTON, Louise		72	*Bronchial trouble (in London, England)*
1954	HAYS, Will H.		74	
• 1954	HILL, Al		62	*(Do not confuse with stage actor of same name)*
1954	HILTON, James		54	*Cancer of the liver*
• 1954	HOTELY, Mae		81	*Died in Coronado, CA*
1954	HOWARD, William K.		54	*Throat cancer*
1954	# KEY, Kathleen		47	
1954	KINNELL, Murray		65	
• 1954	LLOYD, Art		58	*Paralytic stroke (after filming the Bikini Atoll atom bomb test)*
• 1954	LOOS, Theodor		70	*Died in Stuttgart, West Germany*
• 1954	# LUCAN, Arthur		67	*Died in Hull, England*
1954	LYTELL, Bert		69	*Following surgery (in New York, NY)*
1954	LYTELL, Wilfred		62	*After an illness of several weeks (in Salem, NY)*
1954	MacMILLAN, Violet		66	
1954	MAY, Joe		73	*After a long illness*
1954	McGUIRE, Tom		80	*Died in Hollywood, CA*
• 1954	MITCHELL, Julien		65	
• 1954	NESBITT, Miriam		80	*Died in Hollywood, CA*
1954	+ OLSEN, Moroni		65	*Natural causes (in Los Angeles, CA)*

• New entry. # Original name (Pt. 7). + Interment (Pt. 5). 26 ☆ Oscar nominee, ★ Oscar winner (Pt. 10)

YEAR	NAME		AGE	CAUSE AND/OR PLACE OF DEATH
1954	PAIGE, Mabel		74	Died in Van Nuys, CA
1954	PALLETTE, Eugene		65	After a long illness (in Los Angeles, CA)
1954	PASCAL, Gabriel		60	
• 1954	PAULSEN, Harald		59	Heart attack (in Hamburg, Germany)
• 1954	PERRY, Walter		85	Died in CA
1954	PICHEL, Irving		63	Following a heart attack (in Hollywood, CA)
• 1954	# PRIOR, Herbert		87	
1954	RICE, Grantland	★	73	Following a heart attack (in New York)
1954	RICH, Lillian		53	Died at the Motion Picture Country Home, in Woodland Hills, CA
1954	ROBERTS, Leona		73	Died in Santa Monica, CA
1954	# ROBEY, George		85	Died in Saltdean, Sussex, England
1954	SAUNDERS, Jackie		61	Died in Palm Springs, CA
1954	SCARDON, Paul		75	Heart attack (in Fontana, CA)
• 1954	SCHUNZEL, Reinhold		68	Heart ailment (in Munich, Germany)
1954	#+ SELWYN, Ruth		49	After a long illness (in Hollywood, CA)
1954	SHANNON, Effie		87	Died in Bay Shore, L.I., NY
• 1954	SISSON, Vera		63	Died in Carmel, CA
1954	# Sojin		63	Died in Tokyo, Japan
1954	TRIMBLE, Lawrence		69	Died at the Motion Picture Country House in Ca.
1954	# TYLER, Tom		50	Heart attack after suffering crippling arthritis (in Hamtramck, MI)
1954	VAJDA, Ernest		67	Heart attack
• 1954	WALKER, Robert "Bob"		65	(Do not confuse with actor Robert Walker, d. 1951)
1954	WEEKS, Barbara		47	
1954	WHITMAN, Ernest		61	Following a heart attack
• 1955	AGEE, James		45	Heart attack (in New York, NY)
1955	AKED, Muriel		68	Died in Settle, England
1955	ARNHEIM, Gus		55	Heart attack
1955	+ BACON, Lloyd		65	Cerebral hemorrhage (in Burbank, CA)
1955	#+ BALL, Suzan (Long)		22	Cancer after knee surgery while filming in Sumatra
1955	#+ BARA, Theda (Brabin)		69	Abdominal cancer (in Los Angeles, CA)
1955	# BEECHER, Janet		70	Died in Washington, CT
• 1955	BENGE, Wilson		80	Died in Hollywood, CA
1955	+ BERTRAND, Mary		73	
• 1955	# BLACKLEY, Douglas		46	(See Robert Kent)
1955	BLACKWELL, Carlyle Sr.		71	
• 1955	BORDEN, Eddie		67	Died in Hollywood, CA
1955	+ BRUCKMAN, Clyde		60	Suicide (gunshot)
1955	BRYANT, Nana		67	Died in Hollywood, CA
• 1955	BURTON, George H.		55	Heart attack (in Los Angeles, CA)
• 1955	BUSSE, Henry		61	Heart attack (in Memphis, TN)
1955	CAMERON, Donald		66	Died in West Cornwall, CT
1955	# CAREWE, Ora		62	Died in Los Angeles, CA
1955	# CARVER, Lynn		45	Suicide (in New York, NY)
1955	CHEKHOV, Michael	☆	64	Died in Beverly Hills, CA
1955	# CLARENCE, O. B.		85	
1955	# COLLIER, Constance		77	Died in New York, NY
1955	# DAMPIER, Claude		75	Pneumonia (in London, England)
1955	#+ DANIELS, Victor		66	Cancer (in Ventura, CA)
1955	DARIEN, Frank Jr.		?	Died in Hollywood, CA
1955	DAVIES, Betty Ann		44	Complications after appendectomy (in Manchester, England)
1955	#+ DEAN, James	☆	24	Automobile accident (near Paso Robles, CA)
1955	+ DeMILLE, William C.		76	Died in Playa del Rey, CA
1955	DUDLEY, Robert Y.		80	Died in San Clemente, CA
1955	+ FRANCIS, Robert		25	Airplane crash (in Burbank, CA)
1955	FRIGANZA, Trixie		84	After being bedridden with arthritis (in Flintridge, CA)
1955	# GALLAGHER, Skeets		64	Following a heart attack (in Santa Monica, CA)
1955	GAYE, Howard		?	Died in London, England
• 1955	GILL, Basil		77	Died in Hove, England
• 1955	GODDEN, Jimmy		75	
• 1955	GOLDNER, Charles		54	Died in London, England
1955	GORCEY, Bernard		67	Injuries from an auto accident (in Hollywood, CA)
• 1955	GROVES, Frederick "Fred"		74	
1955	#+ HAMPDEN, Walter		75	Stroke (in Hollywood, CA)
1955	+ HARVEY, Paul (actor)		72	Coronary thrombosis (Do not confuse with radio commentator)

	YEAR	NAME		AGE	CAUSE AND/OR PLACE OF DEATH
	1955	+ HAYDEN, Harry		72	Died in Los Angeles, CA
	1955	+ HODIAK, John		41	Coronary thrombosis (in Tarzana, CA)
•	1955	HONEGGER, Arthur		63	Heart disease
	1955	#+ HOWARD, Shemp		55	Coronary occlusion (in Hollywood, CA)
	1955	HYTTEN, Olaf		67	After a heart attack (on the set of "Sir Walter Raleigh") in L.A.
•	1955	# JERROLD, Mary		77	Died in London, England
	1955	JOYCE, Alice "Vitagraph Girl"		65	Heart ailment (in Hollywood, CA)
•	1955	KEATON, Myra		?	
•	1955	# KENT, Robert		46	
•	1955	KNOTT, Lydia		88	Died in Woodland Hills, CA
	1955	LEDERER, Gretchen		64	
•	1955	LETONDAL, Henri		52	Heart attack (in Burbank, CA)
•	1955	LEVEY, Ethel		73	Heart attack (in New York, NY)
	1955	# LORRAINE, Lillian		63	Died in New York, NY
	1955	MARTINDEL, Edward B.		78	Heart attack (in Woodland Hills, CA)
	1955	McGOWAN, Robert F.		72	
•	1955	McNAUGHTON, Charles		77	
	1955	MILLER, Charles B.		64	Suicide (gunshot) due to unemployment and ill health (Hollywood)
	1955	MILLICAN, James		45	Died in Los Angeles, CA
	1955	#+ MIRANDA, Carmen		51	Heart attack (in Beverly Hills, CA)
•	1955	# Miroslava		29	Suicide (poison) in Mexico City, Mexico
•	1955	MOORE, Eva		85	
	1955	MOORE, Tom		70	Cancer (in Santa Monica, CA)
	1955	MORRELL, George		82	After a long illness (in Hollywood, CA)
	1955	#+ MUNSON, Ona		51	Suicide (sleeping pills) in New York, NY
•	1955	ODEMAR, Fritz		65	Died in Munich, Germany
•	1955	PARDAVE, Joaquin		54	Died in Mexico City, Mexico
	1955	+ PARKER, Charlie "Bird"		34	Heart attack (in the NY apartment of a female friend)
•	1955	# PAYTON, Claude		72	Died in Los Angeles, CA
	1955	+ PIERLOT, Francis		78	Heart ailment (in Hollywood, CA)
	1955	POWERS, Tom		65	Heart ailment (in Hollywood, CA)
	1955	PRICE, Stanley L.		55	Heart attack (in Hollywood, CA)
	1955	RAY, Barbara		40	Leukemia
	1955	RISKIN, Robert		58	After a long illness
	1955	ROSS, Anthony		46	Died in New York
	1955	#+ SAKALL, S. Z. "Cuddles"		71	Heart attack (in Los Angeles, CA)
•	1955	SCHMITZ, Sybille		42	Suicide (pills) in Munich, Germany
	1955	STANDING, Herbert Jr.		71	Died in New York, NY
	1955	STANTON, Paul		70	
	1955	STEELE, Vernon		72	Heart attack (in Los Angeles, Ca.)
•	1955	TATE, Reginald		58	Died in London, England
	1955	#+ THUNDERCLOUD, Chief (1st)		66	Cancer (Do not confuse with 2nd Chief Thundercloud, d. 1967)
	1955	VAUGHAN, Dorothy		65	Cerebral hemorrhage (in Hollywood, CA)
•	1955	WHITE, Lew		52	Died in New York
	1955	WILCOX, Robert		45	Heart attack (on a train near Rochester, NY)
	1956	ACUFF, Eddie		48	Heart attack (in Hollywood, CA)
•	1956	# ADAMSON, James		59	Heart attack (in Los Angeles, CA)
	1956	#+ ALLEN, Fred		62	Heart attack (in New York, NY)
	1956	#+ ARNOLD, Edward		66	Cerebral hemorrhage
	1956	BALLIN, Hugo		76	
	1956	+ BANCROFT, George ☆		74	After a brief illness (in Santa Monica, CA)
•	1956	BLINN, Genevieve		?	Died in Ross, CA
	1956	# BLYSTONE, Stanley		61	Heart attack (in Hollywood, CA)
	1956	BOURNE, Hazel (Imboden)		?	After a 2-yr. illness (in Kansas City)
	1956	BROWN, Clifford		25	Automobile accident
	1956	+ BURNS, Bob "Bazooka"		64	After a 3-yr. illness (at his home in San Fernando Valley, CA)
	1956	#+ CALHERN, Louis ☆		61	Heart attack, brought on by alcohol and medicine (in Tokyo, Japan)
	1956	# CARVER, Louise		86	Died in Hollywood, CA
•	1956	CHARLOT, Andre		73	Died in Woodland Hills, CA
•	1956	# CLIFFORD, Jack		76	
	1956	CLUTE, Chester		64	Heart attack (in Woodland Hills, CA)
•	1956	# CRAWFORD, Anne		35	Died in London, England
•	1956	CURTIS, Jack		75	(Do not confuse with the child actor or Jack B. Curtis)
	1956	DINGLE, Charles W.		68	After an illness of several months (in Worcester, MA)

	YEAR	NAME		AGE	CAUSE AND/OR PLACE OF DEATH
	1956	# DORO, Marie		74	Heart ailment (in New York, NY)
	1956	#+ DORSEY, Tommy		51	Choked while asleep (in Greenwich, CT)
•	1956	DOVZHENKO, Alexander		62	Heart attack
	1956	DRAPER, Ruth		72	Apparent heart attack (in New York)
	1956	DUPONT, E. A.		64	After a long bout with cancer
	1956	EASON, Reeves "Breezy"		69	Heart attack (in Sherman Oaks, CA)
•	1956	ELLIOTT, John H.		80	Heart attack (in Los Angeles, CA)
	1956	# EMERSON, John		84	After a long illness
	1956	+ GANZHORN, John W.		75	
	1956	+ GORDON, Huntly		59	Heart attack (in Hollywood, CA)
	1956	#+ GRAPEWIN, Charley		80	After a long illness (in Corona, CA)
	1956	GRAY, Jack		76	After a long illness (in Woodland Hills, CA)
	1956	GRIFFIN, Charles		67	Died in Hollywood, CA
	1956	# HENDERSON, Del		73	Died in Hollywood, CA
	1956	#+ HERBERT, Holmes		74	Died in Hollywood, CA
	1956	+ HERSHOLT, Jean ★		69	Cancer (in Beverly Hills, CA)
•	1956	# HOEFLICH, Lucie		73	Heart attack (in Berlin, Germany)
	1956	HOWARD, Kathleen		75	Died in Hollywood, CA
	1956	INGRAHAM, Lloyd		81	Pneumonia (in Woodland Hills, CA)
	1956	IRWIN, Bobby		42	Died in Los Angeles, CA
	1956	KEARNS, Allen B.		61	
	1956	#+ KELLY, Paul		57	Heart attack (in Los Angeles, CA)
	1956	# KERRY, Norman		66	Died in Hollywood, CA
	1956	#+ KIBBEE, Guy		70	Parkinson's disease (in East Islip, NY)
	1956	KORDA, Alexander		62	Heart attack
	1956	KOSLOFF, Theodore		74	Died in Los Angeles, CA
	1956	LEIGHTON, Lillian		81	Died in Woodland Hills, CA
	1956	# LeMOYNE, Charles		76	Died in Hollywood, CA
•	1956	LEONARD, Marion		75	Died in Woodland Hills, CA
	1956	+ LEWIS, Mitchell J.		76	Died in Woodland Hills, CA
	1956	LEWIS, Vera		72	Died at the Motion Picture Country Hospital near Los Angeles, CA
	1956	#+ LUGOSI, Bela		73	Heart attack (in Hollywood, CA)
	1956	MacARTHUR, Charles		60	
	1956	MacDONALD, Katherine		62	After a 30-month illness
•	1956	MACY, Jack		70	Heart attack (in Wyoming)
	1956	MAKEHAM, Eliot		73	Died in London, England
•	1956	McWADE, Margaret		83	
•	1956	# MENJOU, Henri		64	Died in West Los Angeles, CA
	1956	MILTON, Robert D.		70	After a long illness and hospitalization
	1956	#+ MORGAN, Ralph		72	After a 3-yr. illness (in New York)
	1956	# NORTON, Barry		51	Heart attack (in Hollywood, CA)
	1956	ORZAZEWSKI, Kasia		67	Rheumatic heart disease
	1956	PROUTY, Jed		77	After a brief illness (in New York)
	1956	RASUMNY, Mikhail		65	
•	1956	RICH, Freddie		58	Died in Beverly Hills, CA
•	1956	RUB, Christian		69	
	1956	RYAN, Tim		57	Heart attack (in Hollywood, CA)
	1956	# SEYMOUR, Jane		56	Died in New York, NY
•	1956	SHADE, Jamesson		60	Heart attack (in Hollywood, CA)
•	1956	# SLAUGHTER, Tod		70	
	1956	#+ STEPHENSON, Henry		85	After a brief illness (in San Francisco, CA)
	1956	# SULLIVAN, Francis L.		53	Died in New York, NY
	1956	TAPLEY, Rose		72	Died at the Motion Picture Country Hospital in Woodland Hills, CA
	1956	+ TATUM, Art		46	Uremia
	1956	TURNBULL, John		75	
	1956	# VALK, Frederick		55	Died in London, England
•	1956	# VonMETER, Harry		85	Died in CA
	1956	WALKER, Hal		60	
	1956	# WERBISECK, Gisela		81	After a 3-year illness
	1956	WIX, Florence E.		73	Cancer (in Woodland Hills, CA)
	1956	WOOD, Freeman N.		59	After a short illness (in Hollywood, CA)
•	1956	WORTH, Peggy		64	Died in New York, NY
	1956	+ WYCHERLY, Margaret ☆		74	Died in New York
•	1956	+ YOUNG, Victor ★		55	Cancer

	YEAR	NAME		AGE	CAUSE AND/OR PLACE OF DEATH
•	1957	ABBOTT, Frank		77	Died in Los Angeles, CA
	1957	ALDERSON, Erville		74	Died in Glendale, CA
	1957	ASHER, Max		76	
	1957	AUERBACK, Arthur "Mr. Kitzel"		54	Heart attack
•	1957	AUSTIN, Lois		47	Cachexia (in Hollywood, CA)
	1957	BAKER, Belle		60	Heart attack
	1957	BEDOYA, Alfonso (Indio)		53	Died in Mexico City
•	1957	BENNETT, Ray		62	Heart attack (in Hollywood, CA)
	1957	# BEVAN, William "Billy"		60	Died in Escondido, CA
•	1957	BINNEY, Faire		57	Pneumonia
	1957	#+ BOGART, Humphrey	★	57	Cancer of the esophagus (in Los Angeles, CA)
	1957	+ BRABIN, Charles J.		75	Heart attack (in Santa Monica, CA)
•	1957	BRIDGE, Alan "Al"		66	
	1957	+ BROWN, John H. "Digger O'Dell"		53	Following a heart attack
	1957	BUCHANAN, Jack		66	Spinal arthritis (in London, England)
	1957	BURTON, Frederick		86	After being hospitalized (in Woodland Hills, CA)
•	1957	# CARR, Jane		48	
	1957	CARTER, Louise		82	After a 4-month illness (in Hollywood, CA)
	1957	# CLARKE, Robert "Buddy"		61	
	1957	+ CLEVELAND, George		74	Heart attack (in Burbank, CA)
	1957	COSTELLO, Helene		53	Pneumonia, tuberculosis, narcotics (in Los Angeles, CA)
	1957	DALE, Dorothy (Hyman)		74	Burned to death in her shack
	1957	DALY, Mark		70	
	1957	D'AMBRICOURT, Adrienne		69	Heart attack after her car struck another car (in Hollywood, CA)
•	1957	DEPP, Harry		70	Died in Hollywood, CA
	1957	#+ DORSEY, Jimmy		53	Cancer (in New York, NY)
	1957	# EYTHE, William		38	Acute hepatitis (in Los Angeles, CA)
•	1957	FAIR, Elinor		53	Died in Seattle, WA
	1957	# FENTON, Frank		51	After a brief illness (in Los Angeles, CA)
	1957	FORD, Harrison		63	Died in Woodland Hills, CA (Do not confuse with the younger actor)
	1957	GERSON, Paul		86	
	1957	GRIFFITH, Raymond		67	Heart attack (while dining in Hollywood, CA)
	1957	HALLIGAN, William		72	After a lingering illness (in Woodland Hills, CA)
	1957	#+ HARDY, Oliver		65	Following a paralytic stroke (in North Hollywood, CA)
	1957	HAY, Mary		55	Prolonged heart ailment
•	1957	HAYE, Helen		83	Died in London, England
	1957	# HICKS, Russell		61	Heart attack after a traffic accident (in Hollywood, CA)
	1957	#+ HULL, Josephine	★	71	Cerebral hemorrhage (in New York, NY)
	1957	IRWIN, Boyd		76	Died in Woodland Hills, CA
	1957	# JOHNSON, Katie		79	
	1957	JOYCE, Peggy Hopkins		63	
	1957	KING, Charles L. Sr.		58	Died in Hollywood, CA (Do not confuse with Charles King d. 1944)
	1957	+ KORNGOLD, Erich Wolfgang		60	The aftermath of a cerebral thrombosis suffered a year earlier
•	1957	LAWRENCE, Gerald		84	Died in England
•	1957	LINDER, Alfred		?	Died in Hollywood, CA
	1957	#+ LOCKHART, Gene	☆	65	Coronary thrombosis (in Santa Monica, CA)
•	1957	LOFGREN, Marianne		47	Died in Sweden
	1957	+ LYMAN, Abe		59	Died in Los Angeles, CA
	1957	MacBRIDE, Donald		67	After a long illness (in Los Angeles, CA)
	1957	#+ MAYER, Louis B.		72	Leukemia (in Los Angeles, CA)
	1957	# MENZIES, William C.	★	60	
	1957	MITCHELL, Grant		82	Following a stroke (in Los Angeles, CA)
	1957	MITCHELL, Rhea "Ginger"		52	Found strangled to death (at her home in Los Angeles, CA)
	1957	MURRAY, John T.		71	Following a stroke (in Woodland Hills, CA)
•	1957	# Musidora		68	Died in Paris, France
	1957	O'NEILL, Jack		74	
	1957	# OPHULS, Max		54	2-months after a heart attack (in Hamburg, Germany)
•	1957	ORLAMOND, William		89	
	1957	PATHE, Charles		93	Died in Monte Carlo
	1957	# PERCY, Esme		69	Died in Brighton, England
	1957	#+ PINZA, Ezio		65	Following a series of strokes (in Stamford, CT)
•	1957	PONTO, Erich		71	Died in Stuttgart, Germany
	1957	RAE, Jack		58	Heart attack
•	1957	RAHM, Knute		81	Heart disease (in Los Angeles, CA)
•	1957	RICH, Vivian		64	Automobile accident (in Hollywood, CA)

	YEAR	NAME		AGE	CAUSE AND/OR PLACE OF DEATH
	1957	ROBINSON, Inez Buck		67	
•	1957	ROLF, Erik		?	
•	1957	SCHAEFER, Ann		87	*Died in Los Angeles, CA*
	1957	# SCHILLING, Gus		48	*Heart attack (in Hollywood, CA)*
	1957	SEARS, Fred		44	*Heart attack (in Hollywood, CA)*
	1957	+ SEBASTIAN, Dorothy		54	*Died in Woodland Hills, CA*
•	1957	SHANNON, Cora		88	*Cancer (in Woodland Hills, CA)*
•	1957	# SHEFFIELD, Reginald		56	*Died in Pacific Palisades, CA*
	1957	SHORES, Byron L.		50	*Multiple sclerosis (in Kansas City, MO)*
•	1957	SILVA, Simone		29	*Natural causes (in London, England)*
	1957	# SPARKS, Ned		73	*Intestinal block (in Apple Valley, CA)*
	1957	ST. JOHN, Jane Lee		45	*After a long illness*
•	1957	SULKY, Leo		82	*Died in CA*
	1957	SWASEY, Bill		29	*Automobile accident*
	1957	TABER, Richard		72	*Died in New York*
	1957	+ TALMADGE, Norma		64	*Cerebral stroke and pneumonia (in Las Vegas, NV)*
•	1957	# TERRY, Sheila		46	
•	1957	TOREN, Marta		30	*Rare brain disease (in Stockholm, Sweden)*
	1957	+ TOSCANINI, Arturo		89	*Following a stroke*
	1957	# TWITCHELL, A. R. "Archie"		50	*Killed in a midair collision over Pacoima, CA*
	1957	# TYLER, Judy		24	*Killed in an automobile crash*
	1957	VAUGHN, Hilda		60	
	1957	VINCENT, James		74	*After a long illness (in New York)*
	1957	# VonSTROHEIM, Erich Sr.	☆	71	*Spinal cancer (in Paris, France)*
	1957	WALDRIGE, Harold		50	
	1957	+ WHALE, James		60	*Died in Hollywood, CA*
	1957	WHELAN, Tim		63	*Died in Beverly Hills, CA*
•	1957	WILLIAMS, Harcourt		77	
	1957	WILTON, Eric		73	
	1957	WING, Paul R.		65	*Following a heart attack*
	1957	WITHERSPOON, Cora		67	*Died in Las Crusas, NM*
	1957	YOUNG, Walter		79	*After a brief illness*
•	1958	ADAMS, Sam		86	
•	1958	ANALLA, Isabel		37	*Cancer (in San Francisco, CA)*
•	1958	ARNAUD, Yvonne		65	*Died in London, England*
	1958	BALLIN, Mabel		73	
	1958	BARNETT, Griff		72	*Heart condition and pneumonia*
	1958	BEECROFT, Victor R.		71	*Died in Newport News, VA*
	1958	+ BELL, Monta		66	*After a lengthy illness (in Hollywood, CA)*
	1958	BENNETT, Barbara		52	
	1958	BENTLEY, Robert		63	*Died in Benton Harbor, MI*
	1958	BERKE, William		54	
	1958	BOSWELL, Martha (Lloyd)		53	*After a long illness (in Peekskill, NY)*
	1958	BRENON, Herbert	☆	78	
	1958	# BRISSON, Carl		64	*Jaundice (in Copenhagen, Denmark)*
•	1958	CAMERON, Rudolph "Rudy"		63	*Hemorrhage (in Los Angeles, CA)*
	1958	CHAMBERS, J. Wheaton		69	*Died in Hollywood, CA*
	1958	+ COHN, Harry		66	*Heart attack*
	1958	COLLEANO, Bonar		34	*Automobile accident (in Liverpool, England)*
	1958	+ COLMAN, Ronald	★	67	*Following operation for a lung infection (in Santa Barbara, CA)*
•	1958	CROCKER, Harry		64	
	1958	DEBUCOURT, Jean		64	*Leukemia (in Paris, France)*
	1958	DEVEREAUX, Jack		76	
	1958	DONAT, Robert	★	53	*Asthma (in London, England)*
	1958	DOONAN, Patric		33	*Suicide (by gassing himself) in London, England*
•	1958	DOUCET, Catherine		82	*Died in New York, NY*
	1958	# DUGAN, Tom		69	*Automobile accident (in Redlands, CA)*
	1958	EARLE, Dorothy		?	
	1958	+ FOX, Wallace		63	
	1958	# FRISCO, Joe		68	*After a long illness*
	1958	GENTLE, Alice		69	
	1958	#+ GOODWIN, Bill		47	*Heart attack (in Palm Springs, CA)*
	1958	# GREEN, Harry		66	*Heart attack (in London, England)*
	1958	GREIG, Robert		77	*Died in Hollywood, CA*

...Deaths of Movie and Television Personalities — By Year...

YEAR	NAME	AGE	CAUSE AND/OR PLACE OF DEATH
1958	GRIFFITH, Gordon	51	Heart attack
1958	HACKETT, Raymond	55	Died in Hollywood, CA
1958	HAGEN, Charles F.	96	Died in Hollywood, CA
1958	HALL, Thurston	75	Heart attack (in Beverly Hills, CA)
1958	HAMILTON, John	71	Heart condition (in Hollywood) Do not confuse with J. H., d. 1985
1958	HARMON, Pat	70	Died in Riverside, CA
1958	HARTMAN, Don	57	Died in his sleep of apparent heart attack
1958	# HAYES, Sam	53	Heart attack preparing his morning news program (in San Diego)
1958	HEYES, Herbert	68	Died in North Hollywood, CA
1958	HINTON, Ed	30	Airplane crash (on Catalina Island, CA)
1958	HOLMES, Burton	88	Died in Hollywood, CA
1958	+ HUGHES, Lloyd	60	Died in Los Angeles, CA
1958	IMHOF, Roger	83	Died in Hollywood, CA
1958	# JAQUET, Frank	73	Heart attack (in Los Angeles, CA)
1958	# KATCH, Kurt	62	During surgery for cancer (in Los Angeles, CA)
1958	# KENNEDY, Fred	48	A broken neck (after falling from his horse during filming)
1958	KINGSFORD, Walter	75	Heart attack (in North Hollywood, CA)
1958	+ LASKY, Jesse L. Sr.	77	Died in Beverly Hills, CA
1958	LEWIS, Sheldon	89	Died in San Gabriel, CA
1958	LOW, Jack	60	After a 2-year illness
1958	LYNN, Emmett	61	Heart attack (in Hollywood, CA)
1958	MALLORY, Boots	45	
1958	MANKIEWICZ, Rose Stradner	45	Found dead at the family summer home
1958	MATHER, Aubrey	72	Died in London, England
1958	McKENNA, Henry T.	64	Heart attack
1968	MORAN, Percy	?	
1958	NEILAN, Marshall	67	Cancer (in Woodland Hills, CA)
1958	+ NEUMANN, Kurt	50	After emergency hospitalization in Hollywood
1958	# NORTON, Jack	69	Respiratory ailment (in Saranac Lake, NY)
1958	# OAKLAND, Vivien	63	Died in Hollywood, CA
1958	#+ OSBORN, Lyn	32	Following brain surgery
1958	+ PANGBORN, Franklin	65	Died in Santa Monica, CA
1958	#+ PANZER, Paul Wolfgang	86	Died in Hollywood, CA (Do not confuse with Paul Panzer, d. 1937)
1958	# Parkyakarkus	54	Heart attack (in Los Angeles, CA)
1958	PEARSON, Virginia	70	Uremic poisoning (in Los Angeles, CA)
1958	# PEIL, Edward Sr.	70	Died in Hollywood, CA
1958	#+ POWER, Tyrone	44	Heart attack (in Madrid, Spain)
1958	# PRATHER, Lee	67	During surgery (in Los Angeles, CA)
1958	+ PURVIANCE, Edna	63	After a long illness (in Woodland Hills, CA)
1958	QUARTERMAINE, Charles	80	
1958	RICKSON, Joe	77	Died in CA
1958	RISDON, Elisabeth	71	Brain hemorrhage (in Santa Monica, CA)
1958	RODZINSKI, Artur	64	Heart ailment
1958	ROOKE, Irene	?	Died in England
1958	SCHUMANN-HEINK, Ferdinand	65	Heart attack (in Los Angeles, CA)
1958	SHORT, Lewis W.	83	
1958	SNOW, Marguerite	68	Kidney complications (in Hollywood, CA)
1958	# SQUIRE, Ronald	72	Died in London, England
1958	STERLING, Larry	23	A water-skiing accident
1958	STRADNER, Rose	45	
1958	TAYLOR, Estelle	58	Cancer (in Los Angeles, CA)
1958	TAYLOR, Sam	62	Heart attack
1958	#+ TODD, Mike	49	Airplane crash
1958	# TWELVETREES, Helen	49	Overdose of sleeping pills (in Harrisburg, PA)
1958	VanZANDT, Philip	53	Overdose of sleeping pills (in Hollywood, CA)
1958	VARDEN, Evelyn	65	Died in New York, NY
1958	VERMILYEA, Harold	68	
1958	VILLARREAL, Julio	73	Died in Mexico City, Mexico
1958	# VonTWARDOWSKI, Hans	60	Died in New York, NY
1958	WALKER, Charlotte	80	Died in Kerville, Texas
1958	#+ WARNER, H. B. ☆	82	Died in Los Angeles, CA
1958	+ WARNER, Harry M.	76	Cerebral occlusion
1958	# WHITLEY, Crane	?	
1958	#+ WHITMAN, Gayne	68	Heart attack (in Hollywood, CA)
1958	WILLIAMS, Charles B.	59	After a long illness (in Hollywood, CA)

• New entry. # Original name (Pt. 7). + Interment (Pt. 5).   32   ☆ Oscar nominee, ★ Oscar winner (Pt. 10)

YEAR	NAME		AGE	CAUSE AND/OR PLACE OF DEATH
•	1958	WINTON, Jane	51	*Died in New York*
•	1958	WOOD, Victor	44	*Died in London, England*
•	1958	WUEST, Ida	74	*Died in Berlin, Germany*
	1958	YOUNG, Noah	?	
	1958	ZIMBALIST, Sam	57	*Heart attack*
	1959	ADAMS, Kathryn	64	*Heart attack (in Hollywood, CA)*
	1959	#+ Adrian	56	*Suicide (in New York)*
	1959	AMBLER, Joss	59	*Died in England*
	1959	#+ ANDRE, Gwili	51	*Burned to death when fire swept her apartment*
	1959	APPLEGATE, Hazel	73	
	1959	ARCHAINBAUD, George	68	*Heart attack*
	1959	BAER, Max	50	*Heart attack*
	1959	#+ BARRYMORE, Ethel ★	79	*Heart condition (in Beverly Hills, CA)*
	1959	# BIRCH, Wyrley	75	
	1959	BISHOP, William	42	*Cancer (in Malibu, CA)*
•	1959	BLAKENEY, Olive	56	*Died in Hollywood, CA*
	1959	BLORE, Eric	71	*Heart attack (in Hollywood, CA)*
	1959	BRODERICK, Helen	68	*Died in Beverly Hills, CA*
•	1959	BRYAN, Arthur Q.	60	*Died in Hollywood, CA*
	1959	BYRON, Paul	68	*Heart attack (in San Diego, CA)*
	1959	CARHART, Georgiana	93	
	1959	CASTLE, Lillian	94	*After a brief illness (in Los Angeles, CA)*
	1959	# CHESEBRO, George	70	*Arteriosclerosis (in Hermosa Beach, CA)*
	1959	# CLARKE-SMITH, D. A.	71	
	1959	COLLINS, G. Pat	64	*Cancer (in Los Angeles, CA)*
	1959	COMPTON, Walter	47	*After a long illness*
	1959	CONKLIN, Charles "Heinie"	79	*Died in Hollywood, CA*
	1959	# COOK, Joe	69	*Died in Clinton Hollows, NY*
	1959	#+ COSTELLO, Lou	52	*Heart attack (in Los Angeles, CA)*
	1959	CREWS, Kay C.	58	
	1959	CUMMINGS, Irving Sr. ☆	70	*Heart attack (in Hollywood, CA)*
	1959	CUNNINGHAM, Cecil	70	*Arteriosclerosis (in Woodland Hills, CA)*
	1959	# DAUBE, Belle	71	*Died in Hollywood, CA*
	1959	DELANEY, Charles	67	*Died in Hollywood, CA*
•	1959	# DEL MAR, Claire	57	*Murdered (head and knife wounds) in her Carmel, CA home*
	1959	#+ DeMILLE, Cecil B. ☆	77	*Heart disease (in Los Angeles, CA)*
	1959	+ DOUGLAS, Paul	52	*Heart attack (in Hollywood, CA)*
	1959	+ DUNCAN, Rosetta "Topsy"	58	*Automobile accident (in Acero, IL)*
	1959	# EAGLE, Jimmy	52	*Cirrhosis of the liver (in Los Angeles, CA)*
	1959	ELLIOTT, Lillian	83	*Stroke (in Hollywood, CA)*
	1959	#+ FLYNN, Errol	50	*Heart attack (in Vancouver, B.C., Canada)*
•	1959	# FOX, Harry	77	*Died in Woodland Hills, CA*
•	1959	FRANCIS, Noel	48	*Died in Los Angeles, CA*
	1959	GAN, Chester	50	*Died in San Francisco, CA*
	1959	GARAT, Henri	57	*Died in Toulon, France*
	1959	GILBERT, Joe	56	
	1959	#+ GLEASON, James ☆	76	*Asthma (in Woodland Hills, CA)*
	1959	GOULDING, Edmund	68	
	1959	# GRANT, Tiny	45	
	1959	#+ GRAY, Gilda	61	*Found dead after food poisoning (in Hollywood, CA)*
	1959	GREGG, Everley	60	*Died in Beaconsfield, England*
	1959	#+ GWENN, Edmund ★	83	*Died in Woodland Hills, CA*
	1959	HACKEL, A. W.	76	*Heart attack (in Hollywood, CA)*
	1959	# HALE, Sonnie	57	*Myelofibrosis (a blood disease) in London, England*
	1959	#+ HALL, Charlie	60	*Died in North Hollywood, CA*
	1959	+ HALTON, Charles	83	*Hepatitis (in Los Angeles, CA)*
	1959	#+ HOLIDAY, Billie	44	*Liver ailment and cardiac failure (in New York, NY)*
	1959	#+ HOLLY, Buddy	22	*Airplane crash (northwest of Mason City, IA)*
	1959	HOLMES, Taylor	87	*Died in Hollywood, CA*
	1959	# HOWLIN, Olin	63	*Died in Hollywood, CA*
	1959	HUBER, Harold	49	*Died in New York, NY*
	1959	IVAN, Rosalind	75	
•	1959	KEANE, Edward	75	
	1959	KELLY, Joe	57	*Heart attack*

...DEATHS OF MOVIE AND TELEVISION PERSONALITIES — BY YEAR...

YEAR	NAME	AGE	CAUSE AND/OR PLACE OF DEATH
1959	#+ KENDALL, Kay (Harrison)	32	Leukemia (in London, England)
1959	KRAUSS, Werner	75	Died in Vienna, Austria
1959	LANDOWSKA, Wanda	80	Died at her home in Lakeville, CT
1959	# LANE, Lupino "Nipper"	67	Died in London, England
1959	#+ LANZA, Mario	38	Heart attack after suffering pneumonia and phlebitis (in Rome, Italy)
1959	Lassie (original dog)	18	
1959	LEE, Duke R.	78	Died in Los Angeles, CA
1959	+ LITTLEFIELD, Lucien	64	Died in Hollywood, CA
1959	LONERGAN, Lester Jr.	65	After a long illness
1959	MacDONALD, Donald	61	
1959	MARTIN, Lock	?	
1959	MASON, Louis	71	After a long illness
1959	McCOMB, Kate	87	
1959	McDONALD, Ray	34	
1959	McINTYRE, Hal	44	Burns after falling asleep while smoking
• 1959	# McKEE, Lafe	87	Arteriosclerosis (in Temple City, CA)
1959	+ McLAGLEN, Victor ★	72	Congestive heart failure (in Newport Beach, CA)
1959	# MERTON, John	58	Heart attack (in Los Angeles, CA)
1959	# MONTAGUE, Walter "Monte"	67	Died in Burbank, CA
1959	# MOORE, Clara	?	Murdered
1959	#+ MORRIS, Wayne	45	Heart attack (aboard an aircraft carrier in the Pacific Ocean)
1959	NORWORTH, Jack	80	Stroke and heart ailment (in Laguna Beach, CA)
1959	O'CONNOR, Frank (director/actor)	71	After a long illness (in Hollywood, CA)
1959	+ O'CONNOR, Una	78	After a long illness (in New York, NY)
1959	OSMOND, Hal	40	
• 1959	# PARIS, Manuel	65	Congestive heart failure (in Woodland Hills, CA)
1959	PARRISH, Helen	34	After a long illness (in Hollywood, CA)
1959	+ PECKHAM, Francis Miles	66	
• 1959	PETERS, Ralph	56	Died in Hollywood, CA
1959	PHILIPPE, Gerard	36	Heart attack (in Paris, France)
1959	PICKARD, Helena	59	
• 1959	# RAKER, Lorin	68	Cancer (in Woodland Hills, CA)
1959	REED, J. Theodore "Ted"	72	Died in San Diego, CA
1959	#+ REEVES, George "Superman"	45	Apparent suicide (gunshot) in Beverly Hills, CA
• 1959	#+ RICHARDSON, Jiles "Big Bopper"	28	Airplane crash (along with Buddy Holly, near Mason City, IA)
• 1959	RIEMANN, Johannes	72	Died in Konstanz, West Germany
1959	ROSS, Thomas W.	86	Died in Torrington, CT
1959	SHANNON, Frank Connolly	83	Died in Hollywood, CA
1959	# SHUMWAY, Lee	74	
1959	SIMPSON, Russell	79	Died in Hollywood, CA
1959	SMITH, G. Albert	61	After a brief illness (in New York, NY)
1959	STERLING, Richard	78	Heart attack
• 1959	ST. MAUR, Adele	70	Leukemia (in Sunnydale, CA)
• 1959	STOECKEL, Joe	65	Circulatory ailment (in Munich, Germany)
1959	+ STONE, Fred	85	After a 2-year illness (in North Hollywood, CA)
1959	#+ STURGES, Preston	60	Heart attack
• 1959	# SUNDMARK, Betty	45	Died in New York
1959	+ SWITZER, Carl "Alfalfa"	32	Murdered (shot over a $50. debt) in Sepulveda, CA
1959	#+ VALENS, Ritchie	17	Airplane crash (along with Buddy Holly, near Mason City, IA)
• 1959	VIDAL, Henri	40	Heart attack (in Paris, France)
1959	VIDOR, Charles	58	Apparent heart attack
1959	WAYNE, Robert "Duke"	55	Following a heart attack
1959	WEBB, Harry	63	Heart attack
1959	#+ WITHERS, Grant	54	Suicide (sleeping pills) in Hollywood, CA
• 1960	+ ADAMS, Constance (DeMille)	67	Died in Hollywood, CA
1960	#+ ADLER, Buddy	51	Lung cancer (in Hollywood, CA)
1960	ALBERS, Hans	67	Died in Munchen, Germany
• 1960	BAGGETT, Lynne	31	Overdose of barbiturates (in Hollywood, CA)
1960	#+ BARRYMORE, Diana	38	Natural causes (in New York, NY)
1960	# BAUM, Vicki	64	After a brief illness
1960	BJOERLING, Jussi	49	Heart attack
1960	+ BOND, Ward	57	Heart attack (in Dallas, TX)
1960	#+ BROPHY, Ed	65	Died in Los Angeles, CA
1960	CATLETT, Walter	71	Stroke (in Woodland Hills, CA)

	YEAR	NAME		AGE	CAUSE AND/OR PLACE OF DEATH
•	1960	CAVENDISH, David		69	*Heart attack (in Hollywood, CA)*
	1960	#+ CLARK, Bobby		72	*Heart attack (in New York, NY)*
	1960	# CLIVE, Henry		77	*Lung cancer (in Hollywood, CA)*
	1960	+ COCHRAN, Eddie (singer)		21	*Killed in a taxi crash at Bath, England*
	1960	# CODY, Emmett		40	
	1960	CORBETT, Leonora		52	*Died in Vleuten, Holland*
	1960	# CRAMER, Rychard		71	*Laennec's cirrhosis (in Los Angeles, CA)*
•	1960	CRAVAT, Noel		49	*After surgery (in Hollywood, CA)*
	1960	#+ CROMWELL, Richard		50	*Died in Hollywood, CA*
	1960	CROSSLEY, Syd		75	*Died in Troon, England*
•	1960	CURLEY, Leo		82	*Arteriosclerosis (in Woodland Hills, CA)*
	1960	+ DASTAGIR, Sheik		47	
	1960	DUNCAN, Bud		77	*Circulatory failure (in Los Angeles, CA)*
	1960	EBURNE, Maude		85	*Died in Hollywood, CA*
	1960	+ EMERSON, Hope	☆	61	*Liver ailment*
	1960	+ FOWLER, Gene		70	
	1960	#+ GABLE, Clark	★	59	*Heart attack (in Los Angeles, CA)*
•	1960	# GALVANI, Dino		69	*Died in London, England*
	1960	GAUGE, Alexander		46	*Heart attack (in Woking, Surrey, England)*
	1960	+ GORDON, Leon		66	*Heart ailment*
	1960	+ GREEN, Alfred E.		71	*After a long illness*
	1960	GRIFFITH, William M.		62	*Died in Hollywood, CA*
•	1960	HAMILTON, Mahlon		77	*Cancer (in Woodland Hills, CA)*
	1960	+ HAMMERSTEIN II, Oscar		65	*Stomach cancer*
•	1960	HARBAUGH, Carl		73	*Died in Hollywood, CA*
	1960	HAVER, Phyllis		61	*Suicide (despondent over Mack Sennett's death) in Falls Village, CT*
	1960	HEYDT, Louis Jean		54	*Heart attack (in Boston, MA)*
	1960	# HOEY, Dennis		67	*Died in Palm Beach, FL*
	1960	JOHNSON, Emory		66	*Critically burned when his bed caught fire*
	1960	# KEITH, Ian		61	*Died in New York, NY*
	1960	KRUGER, Alma		91	*Died in Seattle, WA*
	1960	# LaRUE, Frank H.		81	*Died in Woodland Hills, CA*
	1960	LAWFORD, Betty		50	*After a long illness (in NY)*
	1960	+ LLOYD, Frank	★	74	*Died in Santa Monica, CA*
•	1960	LUND, Richard		75	*Died in Sweden*
	1960	# LUTHER, Ann		67	*Heart condition (in Hollywood, CA)*
•	1960	LUTHER, Johnny		51	*Drowned in a boating accident (in San Pedro, CA)*
	1960	# MATTHEWS, A. E. "Matty"		90	*Died in Bushey Heath, England*
	1960	McLAUGHLIN, Gibb		76	
	1960	METCALFE, James J.		53	
	1960	MILJAN, John		66	*Died in Hollywood, CA*
	1960	MOORE, Matt		72	*Died in Hollywood, CA*
•	1960	# MUELLER, Wolfgang		36	*Airplane crash (in Lostallo, Switzerland)*
	1960	NESBITT, John		49	
	1960	NICHOLS, Dudley		64	*While hospitalized (in Hollywood) for cancer*
	1960	O'SHEA, Oscar		78	*Died in Hollywood, CA*
•	1960	PARKE, Macdonald		68	*Died in London, England*
•	1960	PARKER, Edwin		59	*Heart attack (in Sherman Oaks, CA)*
•	1960	# PLUMB, E. Hay		77	
•	1960	PORTEN, Henny		70	*Died in Berlin, Germany*
	1960	PURDY, Constance		75	*Arteriosclerosis (in Los Angeles, CA)*
	1960	RATOFF, Gregory		63	*Died in Solothurn, Switzerland*
	1960	RELPH, George		72	
	1960	ROSSON, Arthur H.		73	
	1960	RUYSDAEL, Basil		72	*Died in Hollywood, CA*
	1960	+ SCHWARTZ, Maurice		69	*Heart attack (near Tel Aviv, Israel)*
•	1960	SCOTT, Mark		45	*Heart attack (in Burbank, CA)*
	1960	# SEASTROM, Victor		80	
	1960	#+ SENNETT, Mack		80	*Died in Hollywood, CA*
	1960	SMART, J. Scott		57	*Died in Springfield, IL*
	1960	SPENCER, Douglas		50	*Diabetic condition (in Hollywood, Ca.)*
	1960	#+ SULLAVAN, Margaret	☆	48	*Suicide (sleeping pills) in New Haven, CT*
•	1960	# TENBROOK, Harry		72	*Lung cancer (in Woodland Hills, CA)*
	1960	THOMAS, John Charles		68	*Intestinal cancer (in Apple Valley, CA)*
	1960	+ TIBBETT, Lawrence	☆	63	*Following surgery for an old head injury (in New York, NY)*

YEAR	NAME		AGE	CAUSE AND/OR PLACE OF DEATH
•	1960	TIEDTKE, Jakob	85	Died in Berlin, Germany
	1960	TREADWELL, Laura	81	Died in Hollywood, CA
•	1960	VENESS, Amy	84	Died in Saltdean, England
	1960	WASHBURN, Bryant Jr.	?	
	1960	WATKIN, Pierre	70	Died in Hollywood, CA
	1960	WELCH, Joseph L.	69	
	1960	WESTON, Doris	42	Cancer (in New York, NY)
•	1960	WHITAKER, Charles "Slim"	66	Heart attack
	1960	WILLIAMS, Kathlyn	72	Died in Hollywood, CA
	1960	WINDUST, Bretaigne	54	Died in New York
•	1960	WONTNER, Arthur	85	Died in London, England
	1960	YOUNG, Clara Kimball	69	Died in Woodland Hills, CA
	1960	+ ZUCCO, George	74	Pneumonia (at Monterey Sanitarium, S. San Gabriel, CA)
•	1961	ADAMS, Stella	?	
•	1961	AOKI, Tsuru	69	Acute peritonitis (in Tokyo, Japan)
	1961	BANNISTER, Harry	71	
•	1961	# BRADY, Fred	49	Heart failure (in Los Angeles, CA)
	1961	BROWN, Wally	57	Died in Los Angeles, CA
•	1961	BURGESS, Dorothy	54	
	1961	+ CARRILLO, Leo	80	Cancer (in Santa Monica, CA)
•	1961	CASON, John L.	?	
•	1961	#+ CHANDLER, Jeff ☆	42	Blood poisoning after spinal surgery (in Culver City, CA)
•	1961	CHARLESON, Mary	68	Died in Woodland Hills, CA
	1961	+ CHATTERTON, Ruth ☆	67	Died in Norwalk, CT
•	1961	CLARK, Wallis	71	
	1961	CLIFT, Denison	76	Heart ailment
	1961	# CLINE, Eddie	68	Died in Hollywood, CA
•	1961	# COBB, Ty	74	Died in Atlanta, GA
	1961	#+ COBURN, Charles ★	84	Heart ailment (in New York)
	1961	CODEE, Ann	70	Heart attack (in Hollywood, CA)
	1961	COOK, Donald	60	Heart attack (in New Haven, CT)
	1961	#+ COOPER, Gary ★	60	Cancer (in Hollywood, CA)
	1961	CORBETT, Ben	69	Died in Hollywood, CA
	1961	DALE, Esther	75	Died in Hollywood, CA
	1961	#+ DAVIES, Marion	64	Cancer (in Hollywood, CA)
	1961	+ DAVIS, Joan (Williams)	53	Heart attack (in Palm Springs, CA)
	1961	DEL RUTH, Roy	66	Heart attack
	1961	DUNCAN, William A.	80	Died in Hollywood, CA
	1961	# ELDRIDGE, John	57	Heart attack (in Laguna Beach, CA)
	1961	# ELLIOTT, Dick	75	
	1961	+ FARNUM, Franklyn	85	Cancer (in Hollywood, CA)
	1961	+ FAY, Frank	63	Died in Santa Monica, CA
	1961	FERGUSON, Elsie	78	Died in New London, CT
	1961	# FITZGERALD, Barry ★	72	Died in Dublin, Ireland
	1961	# FORMBY, George	56	Died in Preston, Lancashire, England
	1961	+ FRENCH, George B.	78	Heart attack (in Hollywood, CA)
	1961	FREY, Arno	60	Blood clot (in Los Angeles, CA)
	1961	FULLER, Clem	52	Cancer
	1961	# GOODWIN, Ruby	?	
•	1961	GREENWOOD, Winifred L.	69	Died in Los Angeles, CA
	1961	GRIBBON, Harry	76	After a long illness (in Los Angeles, CA)
	1961	# GUARD, Kit	67	Cancer (in Hollywood, CA)
	1961	GUILFOYLE, Paul	59	
•	1961	HANSEN, Juanita	64	Heart attack (in Hollywood, CA)
	1961	+ HART, Moss	57	
	1961	HODGES, William C.	85	
	1961	HOFFMAN, David	57	
	1961	HOUSE, Billy	71	Heart attack
•	1961	HOWELL, Alice	72	Died in Los Angeles, CA
	1961	IRVING. George	87	Heart attack (in Hollywood, CA)
	1961	JENNINGS, Al	97	Died in Tarzana, CA
	1961	#+ JORDAN, Marion "Molly McGee"	64	Cancer (in Encino, CA)
	1961	KEATING, Fred	64	Heart attack
	1961	KELSEY, Fred A.	77	Died in Hollywood, CA

...DEATHS OF MOVIE AND TELEVISION PERSONALITIES — BY YEAR...

YEAR	NAME	AGE	CAUSE AND/OR PLACE OF DEATH
1961	KORDA, Zoltan	66	
• 1961	+ LAWRENCE, Walter Smith	59	*Died in Palm Dale, CA*
1961	LEE, Belinda	25	*Automobile accident (in San Bernardino, CA)*
1961	# LEE, Gwen	55	
1961	LIVESEY, Jack	60	*Aneurysm (in Burbank, CA)*
1961	LOMAS, Herbert	73	*Died in Devonshire, England*
• 1961	# LUPINO, Wallace	63	*Died in Ashford, England*
• 1961	LYON, Frank	59	*Died in Gardner, MA*
• 1961	# MAITLAND, Ruth	81	*Died in Dorking, England*
1961	# MALYON, Eily	81	*Died in South Pasadena, CA*
1961	MARSHAL, Alan	52	*Heart attack during live performance of "Sextette" (in Chicago, IL)*
1961	#+ MARX, "Chico"	74	*Heart attack (in Beverly Hills, CA)*
1961	McLEOD, Gordon	71	
• 1961	McTURK, Joe	62	*Heart attack (in Hollywood, CA)*
1961	MELFORD, George	84	*Heart attack (in Hollywood, CA)*
1961	MELTON, James	57	*Pneumonia*
1961	MORAN, Lee	70	*Heart ailment (in Woodland Hills, CA)*
1961	MURPHY, Joseph J.	84	*Died in San Jose, CA*
1961	#+ NALDI, Nita	61	*Died in New York, NY*
1961	O'NEILL, Henry	69	*Died in Hollywood, CA*
1961	OSBORNE, Vivienne	64	
1961	PARNELL, James	38	*Found dead in his automobile (in Hollywood, CA)*
1961	# POLO, Eddie	86	*Heart attack (in Hollywood, CA)*
1961	RAYMOND, Frances "Frankie"	92	*Died in Hollywood, CA*
1961	REED, Luther	73	*After a long illness*
1961	REYNOLDS, Adeline De Walt	98	*Died in Los Angeles, CA*
• 1961	RICHTER, Paul	65	*Died in Vienna, Austria*
1961	RING, Blanche	84	*Died in Santa Monica, CA*
1961	RIPLEY, Arthur	66	
• 1961	ROBERTS, John H.	76	*Died in London, England*
1961	ROOPE, Fay	68	*Died in Port Jefferson, L.I., NY*
1961	+ RUSSELL, Gail (Moseley)	36	*Found dead from alcohol overindulgence (in Los Angeles, CA)*
• 1961	# SANDFORD, Tiny	67	
1961	SCHOFIELD, Johnnie	71	
1961	# SHEPLEY, Michael	53	*Died in London, England*
• 1961	SOLER, Domingo Jr.	59	*Heart attack (in Acapulco, Mexico)*
• 1961	STAINTON, Philip	53	
1961	+ STEWART, Anita	66	*Died in Beverly Hills, CA*
1961	TAYLOR, Ferris	68	*Heart attack (in Hollywood, Ca.)*
1961	THESIGER, Ernest	81	*Died in London, England*
1961	# TOURNEUR, Maurice	85	
1961	TYLER, Harry	73	*Cancer (in Hollywood, CA)*
1961	VIVIAN, Percival	70	*Arteriosclerosis*
• 1961	VonWINTERSTEIN, Eduard	90	*Died in East Berlin, Germany*
1961	+ WALLING, Effie B.	81	
1961	# WALTON, Douglas	52	*Died in New York*
1961	WHITING, Jack	59	*Died in New York*
1961	WHITTELL, Josephine	?	*Died in Hollywood, CA*
• 1961	WILLIAMS, Bramsby	91	*Died in London, England*
1961	#+ WONG, Anna May	54	*Heart attack (in Santa Monica, CA)*
1962	ALBERNI, Luis	74	*Died in Hollywood, CA*
• 1962	ALLEN, Joseph Jr.	44	*Died in Patchogue, NY*
1962	+ ATES, Roscoe	70	*Lung cancer*
• 1962	AUER, Florence	81	*Died in New York, NY*
1962	BAILEY, William Norton	76	*Died in Hollywood, CA (Do not confuse with Bill Bailey, d. 1978)*
1962	+ BARRIS, Harry	57	*Cancer (in Burbank, CA)*
1962	+ BARTON, James	72	*Heart attack*
1962	BEAVERS, Louise "Beulah"	64	*Heart attack (in Hollywood, CA)*
1962	#+ BELL, Rex	58	*Coronary occlusion (in Las Vegas, NV)*
1962	BEST, Willie	45	*Cancer (in Woodland Hills, CA)*
1962	+ BLANDICK, Clara	81	*Suicide (took pills and pulled a plastic bag over her head)*
1962	+ BORZAGE, Frank ★	72	*Cancer (in Hollywood, CA)*
• 1962	BOULTON, Matthew	69	
1962	BRIGGS, Matt	79	

...DEATHS OF MOVIE AND TELEVISION PERSONALITIES – BY YEAR...

YEAR	NAME		AGE	CAUSE AND/OR PLACE OF DEATH
1962	BROOK-JONES, Elwyn		51	
1962	+ BROWNING, Tod		82	*Following an operation for cancer (in Hollywood, CA)*
1962	# CANTOR, Ida		70	*Heart attack (in Beverly Hills, CA)*
1962	CAVENDER, Glen W.		77	*Died in Hollywood, CA*
1962	# CAVENS, Fred		79	*Uremia (in Woodland Hills, CA)*
1962	CHRISTY, Ken		67	*Died in Hollywood, CA*
1962	CLIFFORD, Kathleen		74	*Died in Hollywood, CA*
1962	CLYDE, Jean		73	*Died in Helensburgh, Scotland*
1962	CONLIN, Jimmy		77	*Cancer (in Encino, CA)*
1962	+ CRAWFORD, Jesse		66	*Stroke (in Los Angeles, CA)*
1962	#+ CURTIZ, Michael	★	73	*Cancer*
1962	DAMON, Les		53	
1962	# DANIEL, Billy		49	*Coronary attack (in Beverly Hills, CA)*
1962	# DILLON, Tom		66	*Died in Hollywood, CA*
1962	+ FAZENDA, Louise		66	*Cerebral hemorrhage (in Beverly Hills, CA)*
1962	FLAGSTAD, Kirsten		67	
1962	GAWTHORNE, Peter		77	*Died in London, England*
1962	#+ GIBSON, Hoot		70	*Cancer (in Woodland Hills, CA)*
1962	HARDTMUTH, Paul		72	*Fall from his apartment building (in London, England)*
1962	HOBBES, Halliwell		84	*Heart attack (in Santa Monica, CA)*
1962	JENKS, Frank		60	*Cancer (in Hollywood, CA)*
1962	#+ JOHNSON, Chic		70	*Kidney ailment*
1962	KEARNS, Joseph		54	
1962	+ KOVACS, Ernie		42	*Automobile accident (in Beverly Hills, CA)*
1962	+ KREISLER, Fritz		86	*Following a heart attack*
1962	LANDERS, Lew		61	*Heart attack*
1962	+ LAUGHTON, Charles	★	63	*Following surgery for spinal cancer (in Los Angeles, CA)*
1962	LEE, Florence		74	*Died in Hollywood, CA*
1962	+ LOVEJOY, Frank		48	*Heart attack (in New York, NY)*
1962	LUTHER, Lester		73	*Stroke (in Hollywood, CA)*
1962	LYNN, Ralph		81	*Died in London, England*
1962	# MACK, Cactus		62	*Heart attack (in Hollywood, CA)*
1962	# MacKENNA, Kenneth		63	*After a long bout with cancer*
1962	MARRIOTT, Sandee		63	*Heart attack (in Hollywood, CA)*
1962	MASON, Reginald		80	
1962	McCARTHY, John P.		78	*Coronary thrombosis*
1962	McCONNELL, Lulu		80	*Cancer (in Hollywood, CA)*
1962	McCORMICK, Myron		54	*Cancer (in New York, NY)*
1962	# McDANIEL, Sam "Deacon"		76	*Throat cancer (in Woodland Hills, CA)*
1962	MELLER, Raquel		74	
1962	MINCIOTTI, Esther		74	
1962	+ MITCHELL, Thomas	★	70	*Cancer (in Beverly Hills, CA)*
1962	#+ MONROE, Marilyn		36	*Suicide? (drug overdose) in Brentwood, CA*
1962	+ MOORE, Victor		86	*Heart attack (in Long Island, NY)*
1962	O'CONNOR, Robert Emmett		77	*Burns after his cigarette ignited his clothing (in Hollywood, CA)*
1962	ORTH, Frank		82	*Died in Hollywood, CA*
1962	PALANGE, Inez		73	*Died in CA*
1962	# PARKER, Frank "Pinky"		70	*Heart attack (in Hollywood, CA)*
1962	PAUL, Val		75	*Died in Hollywood, CA*
1962	# PEIL, Edward Jr.		54	*After a 2-year illness*
1962	PERRINS, Leslie		60	*Died in Esher, England*
1962	PERRY, Robert E. "Bob"		82	*Died in Hollywood, CA*
1962	PIGOTT, Tempe		78	*Died in Hollywood, CA*
1962	#+ POLLARD, Harry "Snub"		75	*Died in Burbank, CA (Do not confuse with Harry Pollard, d. 1934)*
1962	REECE, Brian		48	*Bone disease*
1962	REISNER, Charles F. "Chuck"		75	*Following a heart attack*
1962	# REYNOLDS, Vera		62	*Died in Woodland Hills, CA*
1962	RICHARDSON, Frankie		63	*Following a heart attack (in Philadelphia, PA)*
1962	RIDGELY, Cleo		68	*Died in Glendale, CA*
1962	ROBERTS, Evelyn		76	
1962	ROBINSON, Gertrude R.		70	*Died in Hollywood, CA*
1962	ROONEY, Pat, II		82	*Died in New York, NY*
1962	# SEGAR, Lucia		77	*Died in New York, NY*
1962	SHELDON, Jerome		71	*(Do not confuse with Jerry Sheldon)*
1962	# SHELDON, Jerry		60	*(Do not confuse with Jerome Sheldon)*

• New entry. # Original name (Pt. 7). + Interment (Pt. 5).   38   ☆ Oscar nominee, ★ Oscar winner (Pt. 10)

YEAR		NAME		AGE	CAUSE AND/OR PLACE OF DEATH
•	1962		SHIELD, Leroy	68	Died in Fort Lauderdale, FL
•	1962		SINCLAIR, Hugh	59	Died in Slapton, England
	1962		SOKOLOFF, Vladimir	72	Stroke (in Hollywood, CA)
	1962		SURATT, Valeska	79	
	1962	#+	TOMACK, Sid	55	Heart ailment (in Palm Springs, CA)
	1962		VAL, Paul	75	
	1962		VonBLOCK, Bela	73	
	1962		WALD, Jerry	51	
	1962		WATSON, Lucile ☆	83	Died in New York, NY
	1962		WHITEHEAD, John	89	
	1962		WILLIAMS, Guinn "Big Boy"	63	Uremic poisoning (in Hollywood, CA)
	1962		WREN, Sam	65	
	1962		WRIGHT, Will	71	Cancer (in Hollywood) Do not confuse with William Wright d. 1949
•	1962	+	ZUCCO, Frances	?	Throat cancer following an overdose of radiation therapy
	1963		ARMENDARIZ, Pedro	51	Suicide (gunshot) after suffering with lymph cancer
	1963		ATKINSON, Frank	69	
	1963		BAKER, Phil	67	After a long illness (in Copenhagen, Denmark)
	1963	+	BARTHELMESS, Richard ☆	66	Cancer (in Southampton, NY)
	1963	#	BEVANS, Clem	83	Died in Woodland Hills, CA
	1963	+	BLUE, Monte	73	Coronary attack (in Milwaukee, WI)
	1963	+	BOLEY, May	81	Cancer (in Hollywood, CA)
•	1963	#	BROOKE, Ralph	43	Died in Hollywood, CA
	1963		BROWN, Rowland	62	Heart attack
	1963		CAHN, Edward L.	64	
	1963		CAMPBELL, Alan	58	Died in West Hollywood, CA
	1963	+	CARSON, Jack	53	Cancer (in Encino, CA)
	1963		CASTIGLIONI, Iphigene	62	Died in Hollywood, CA
	1963		CAVANNA, Elise	61	Cancer (in Hollywood, CA)
	1963	#+	CLINE, Patsy	30	Airplane crash (in a forest near the Tennessee River)
	1963	+	COCTEAU, Jean	74	Heart attack (in Milly-la-Foret, France)
	1963	#	DANIELL, Henry	69	Died in Santa Monica, CA
	1963		DARMOND, Grace	65	Lung ailment (in Los Angeles, CA)
	1963	+	DASTAGIR, Sabu		(See under Sabu, below)
	1963		DAVIS, Boyd	77	Died in Hollywood, CA
	1963		DENT, Vernon	63	Died in Hollywood, CA
	1963		DeSOTO, Henry	75	
•	1963		DOLENZ, George	55	Heart attack (in Hollywood, CA)
	1963	#	DURYEA, George	67	(See Tom Keene)
	1963	+	FARROW, John ☆	56	Apparent heart attack
	1963		GASNIER, Louis	87	
	1963		GAXTON, William	70	
	1963	#+	GEORGE, Gorgeous	48	Heart attack (in Los Angeles, CA)
	1963		GORDON, Mary	81	Died in Pasadena, CA
	1963	#	GRAY, Glen	63	Died in Plymouth, MA
	1963		GREEN, Dorothy	71	
	1963		GREENLEAF, Raymond	71	
•	1963		GRUNDGENS, Gustav	63	Suicide (in Manila, Philippine Islands)
•	1963	#	HAMPTON, Grace	87	Died in Woodland Hills, CA
	1963		HARVEY, Don C.	51	Apparent heart attack (in Studio City, CA)
•	1963	#	HAWLEY, Wanda	67	Died in Los Angeles, CA
•	1963		HAYLE, Grace	73	Died in Los Angeles, CA
	1963	#	HEARN, Edward "Eddie"	74	
•	1963		HOPE, Vida	45	Automobile accident (in Chelmsford, England)
•	1963		HUDD, Walter	64	Died in London, England
	1963		HUMBERT, George	81	
	1963		JEAVES, Allan	78	Heart attack (in London, England)
•	1963		JONES, Gordon	52	Heart attack (in Tarzana, CA)
	1963	#	KEENE, Tom	64	Died in Woodland Hills, CA
	1963		KING, Anita	74	Heart attack
•	1963		KIRKWOOD, James Sr.	80	Died in Woodland Hills, CA
	1963		KUPCINET, Karyn	22	Murdered (bound and strangled)
•	1963		LAIDLAW, Ethan	63	
	1963	#	L'ESTRANGE, Dick	73	Died in Burbank, CA
	1963	#+	LONDON, Tom	70	Died in North Hollywood, CA

YEAR	NAME		AGE	CAUSE AND/OR PLACE OF DEATH
1963	# LYNN, Sharon		58	Died in Hollywood, CA
1963	MACHATY, Gustav		63	After a lengthy illness (in Munich, Germany)
1963	# MALTBY, H. F.		82	Died in London, England
1963	MAXEY, Paul		54	Heart attack (in Pasadena, CA)
1963	+ MAXWELL, Elsa		80	Died in New York, NY
1963	+ MAYO, Frank		77	Heart attack (in Laguna Beach, CA)
• 1963	MEADER, George		75	
1963	MENAHAN, Jean		?	
1963	+ MENJOU, Adolphe	☆	73	Chronic hepatitis (in Beverly Hills, CA)
• 1963	# MILLER, Max		68	Died in Brighton, England
1963	+ ODETS, Clifford		57	Cancer
1963	OFFERMAN, George Jr.		45	Died in New York, NY
1963	#+ OLSEN, Ole		71	Kidney ailment
• 1963	PHILLIPS, Mina		77	Heart ailment (in New Orleans, LA)
1963	#+ PIAF, Edith		47	Internal hemorrhage (in Plascassier, France)
• 1963	PIEL, Harry		71	Died in Munich, Germany
• 1963	PILOTTO, Camillo		?	
1963	+ PITTS, Zazu (Woodall)		65	Cancer (in Hollywood, CA)
1963	#+ POWELL, Dick		58	Cancer (in Hollywood, CA)
• 1963	READ, Barbara		45	
1963	RICHARDS, Grant		47	Leukemia (in Hollywood, CA)
• 1963	RIETTI, Victor		75	Heart ailment (in London, England)
1963	+ ROBARDS, Jason Sr.		70	Heart attack (in Sherman Oaks, CA)
1963	RUSSELL, Byron		79	After a brief illness (in New York)
1963	#+ Sabu		39	Heart attack (in Chatsworth, CA)
• 1963	SAMSON, Ivan		67	Died in London, England
1963	SANFORD, Ralph		64	Heart ailment (in Van Nuys, CA)
1963	# SAYLOR, Syd		67	Heart attack (in Hollywood, CA)
• 1963	# SCHARF, Herman "Boo-Boo"		61	Heart attack (in Hollywood, CA)
1963	# SHERIDAN, Dan		46	Suicide (overdose of barbiturates)
1963	SIERRA, Margarita		27	Following heart surgery (in Hollywood, CA)
1963	SLOANE, Olive		66	Died in London, England
• 1963	SMITH, Cyril		70	Died in London, England
• 1963	# STANDING, Wyndham		82	Died in Los Angeles, CA
1963	# ST. JOHN, Al "Fuzzy"		69	Heart attack (in Vidalia, GA)
• 1963	STRANDMARK, Erik		44	Died in Sweden
1963	# SUNSHINE, Marion		65	Died in New York, NY
1963	SUTTON, John		54	
1963	#+ TUTTLE, Frank		70	
1963	# VINTON, Arthur		?	Died in Guadalajara, Mexico
1963	+ WAGNER, "Gorgeous" George		48	Heart attack
1963	WASHBURN, Bryant Sr.		74	Heart attack (in Hollywood, CA)
• 1963	# WASHINGTON, Dinah		39	Overdose of sleeping pills (in Detroit, MI)
1963	WEEMS, Ted		62	Emphysema (in Tulsa, OK)
• 1963	# WHEAT, Lawrence "Larry"		87	
1963	WILLS, Beverly		29	Killed in a fire (in Palm Springs, CA)
1963	#+ WOOLLEY, Monty	☆	74	Kidney and heart ailment (in Albany, NY)
• 1963	# WORTH, Constance		48	
1964	+ ALBERTSON, Frank		55	Died in Santa Monica, CA
1964	#+ ALLEN, Gracie		58	Heart attack (in Los Angeles, CA)
1964	# ANDERSON, Claire		68	
1964	# ANKRUM, Morris		67	Trichinosis
1964	AUGUST, Edwin		81	
1964	AYLMER, David		31	Suicide
1964	BADGER, Clarence		84	Following surgery
1964	+ BARRIER, Edgar		57	Heart attack (in Hollywood, CA)
1964	+ BENDIX, William	☆	58	Lobar pneumonia and cancer (in Los Angeles, CA)
1964	# BRENDEL, El		74	Heart attack (in Hollywood, CA)
1964	BROWN, Russ		72	Died in Englewood, N.J.
1964	BURTON, Robert		69	Lung cancer (in Woodland Hills, CA)
1964	CAINE, Georgia		88	Died in Hollywood, CA
1964	#+ CANTOR, Eddie		72	Heart attack (in Beverly Hills, CA)
• 1964	CARD, Kathryn		70	Heart attack (in Costa Mesa, CA)
• 1964	CARPENTER, Paul		42	Died in London, England

...DEATHS OF MOVIE AND TELEVISION PERSONALITIES — BY YEAR...

YEAR	NAME	AGE	CAUSE AND/OR PLACE OF DEATH
1964	CAVANAGH, Paul	68	Heart attack
1964	CHILDERS, Naomi	70	After a long illness (in Hollywood, CA)
1964	#+ COLE, Buddy	48	Heart attack
• 1964	COMPTON, Francis	79	Died in Noroton, CT
1964	CONROY, Frank	73	Heart ailment (in Paramus, NY)
1964	+ COOKE, Sam	29	Shot by motel manager while the actor was pursuing a girl (in L.A.)
1964	DODD, Jimmie	54	Heart ailment (in Honolulu, Hawaii)
• 1964	# DODSWORTH, John	53	Suicide (asphyxiation) in Los Angeles, CA
1964	DUMKE, Ralph	64	Died in Sherman Oaks, CA
1964	EMERY, John	59	Died in New York, NY
1964	FILAURI, Antonio	74	Emphysema (in San Gabriel, CA)
1964	FORBES, Mary	84	Heart attack (in Beaumont, CA)
1964	GARGAN, Edward	63	Died in New York, NY
• 1964	GOETZKE, Bernhard	79	Died in Berlin, Germany
1964	GOSFIELD, Maurice	51	After being hospitalized for diabetes
1964	# GUILFOYLE, James	72	Heart attack (in Woodland Hills, CA)
1964	HAINES, Rhea	69	
1964	HANEY, Carol	30	Pneumonia and diabetes (in Saddle River, NJ)
1964	HARDWICKE, Cedric	71	Lung ailment (in New York, NY)
1964	HARE, F. Lumsden	89	Died in Hollywood, CA
1964	+ HEARN, Sam	75	Heart attack (in Los Angeles, CA)
1964	HECHT, Ben	70	Heart attack
1964	HENLEY, Hobart	72	After a long illness (in Los Angeles, CA)
• 1964	HEYWOOD, Herbert	83	Coronary thrombosis (in Van Nuys, CA)
1964	HODGINS, Earle	65	Heart attack (in Hollywood, CA)
1964	HOHL, Arthur	74	Died in CA
1964	# HOWES, Reed	64	Died in Woodland Hills, CA
• 1964	HUDMAN, Wesley	47	Murdered (in Williams, AZ)
• 1964	HULBERT, Claude	63	Died in Sydney, Australia
1964	JOY, Nicholas	79	
1964	KEATING, Larry	67	Leukemia (in Hollywood, CA)
• 1964	KELLY, James "Tiny"	49	Heart ailment (in Hollywood) Do not confuse with James T. Kelly
1964	KERRIGAN, Joseph M.	76	Died in Hollywood, CA
1964	+ KILBRIDE, Percy	76	Brain injury from auto accident (in Los Angeles, CA)
1964	KOLB, Clarence	89	Stroke (in Los Angeles, CA)
1964	+ LADD, Alan	50	Accidental death (alcohol/drug mix) in Palm Springs, CA
1964	#+ LORRE, Peter	59	Stroke (in Hollywood, CA)
1964	MACK, Wilbur	91	Died in Hollywood, CA
1964	MADISON, Cleo	81	Heart attack (in Burbank, CA)
1964	MARLOWE, Frank	60	Heart attack (in Hollywood, CA)
1964	MARTIN, Edie	83	Died in London, England
1964	#+ MARX, "Harpo"	75	During heart surgery (in Los Angeles, CA)
1964	MATE, Rudolph	66	Following several heart attacks
1964	MAUR, Meinhart	73	
1964	# McLEOD, Norman Z.	65	After suffering a stroke
• 1964	McSHANE, Kitty	65	Died in London, England
1964	+ MEREDITH, Charles	70	Died in Los Angeles, CA
• 1964	MEREDITH, Cheerio	74	Died in Woodland Hills, CA
1964	MICHAEL, Gertrude	53	Died in Beverly Hills, CA
• 1964	MING, Moy Luke	101	Died in Grenada Hills, CA
1964	MONTEUX, Pierre	89	
1964	MOORE, Dennis	49	
1964	MOORE, Ida	81	
• 1964	MORANTE, Milburn	76	Heart disease (in Pacoima, CA)
• 1964	# MORLAY, Gaby	67	Died in Nice, France
• 1964	MORTIMER, Charles	78	Died in London, England
• 1964	# MOSER, Hans	83	Cancer (in Vienna, Austria)
• 1964	MULCASTER, George H.	72	Died in England
1964	NEWFIELD, Sam	64	Cancer
1964	# OLIVER, Vic	66	
1964	# OSBOURNE, Lennie "Bud"	82	Died in Hollywood, CA
• 1964	# PALMER, Patricia	69	Died in Hollywood, CA
1964	PAYSON, Blanche	83	Died in Hollywood, CA
• 1964	# PEARCE, Peggy	69	Died in Hollywood, CA
1964	PENNICK, Jack	68	After a year's illness (in Hollywood, CA)

• New entry.   # Original name (Pt. 7).   + Interment (Pt. 5).   41   ☆ Oscar nominee, ★ Oscar winner (Pt. 10)

YEAR	NAME		AGE	CAUSE AND/OR PLACE OF DEATH
1964	+ PORTER, Cole		71	*Following surgery for a kidney stone*
• 1964	PRICE, Hal		77	
1964	QUIGLEY, Charles		58	*Cirrhosis of the liver (in Los Angeles, CA)*
1964	#+ REEVES, Jim		40	*Airplane crash (near Nashville, TN)*
1964	#+ RICHARDS, Addison		61	*Heart attack (in Los Angeles, CA)*
1964	RICHARDS, Gordon		70	*Died in Hollywood, CA*
1964	ROBERTSON, John Stuart		86	*Died in Escondida, CA*
• 1964	SADO, Keiji		38	*Automobile accident (in Japan)*
1964	+ SCHILDKRAUT, Joseph	★	67	*Heart attack (in New York, NY)*
• 1964	SCOTT, Harold		72	*Died in London, England*
1964	SEITER, William A.		72	*Heart attack (in his Beverly Hills home)*
1964	SHANNON, Harry		74	*Died in Hollywood, CA*
1964	# SHARP, Henry		76	
1964	SILETTI, Mario G.		59	*Automobile accident (in Los Angeles, CA)*
• 1964	SILVANI, Aldo		73	*Died in Milan, Italy*
• 1964	STEVENS, Bert		59	*Heart attack (in Hollywood, CA)*
1964	STEVENS, Charles		71	*Died in Hollywood, CA*
1964	STRAYER, Frank R.		72	
1964	+ TEAGARDEN, Jack		57	*Pneumonia (in New Orleans, LA)*
1964	TONG, Sammee		63	*Suicide at his home (in Culver City, CA)*
1964	TRAVERSE, Madlaine		88	*Died in Cleveland, Ohio*
1964	VanSLOAN, Edward		81	*Died in San Francisco, CA*
1964	VonELTZ, Theodore		70	*After a long illness (in Woodland Hills, CA)*
1964	WAGNER, William		79	*Died in Hollywood, CA*
1964	# WARWICK, Robert		85	*Following a brief illness (in Los Angeles, CA)*
1964	WILCOX, Fred M.		59	*Died at his Beverly Hills, Ca. home*
1964	WILSON, Whip		49	*Heart attack (in Hollywood, CA)*
1964	# WYNYARD, Diana	☆	58	*Kidney ailment (in London, England)*
• 1965	AMES, Jimmy		50	*Heart attack (in Hollywood, CA)*
1965	+ BACON, Irving		71	*Died in Hollywood, CA*
• 1965	# BARBOUR, Dave		53	*Hemorrhaged ulcer*
• 1965	BARNET, Boris		63	*Suicide (despondent over his faltering career) in Moscow*
1965	BARRISCALE, Bessie		81	*Died in Kentfield, CA*
1965	+ BEATTY, Clyde		62	*Cancer of the esophagus (in Ventura, CA)*
1965	BECKWITH, Reginald		56	*Died in Bourne End, England*
1965	+ BENNETT, Constance		59	*Cerebral hemorrhage (at Ft. Dix, N.J.)*
1965	# BENTLEY, Irene		61	*Heart attack (in Palm Beach, FL)*
1965	BERLIN, Abby		58	*Died in his sleep*
1965	+ BOLAND, Mary		83	*Died in New York, NY*
1965	+ BOW, Clara		60	*Heart attack while watching a movie on TV (in Los Angeles, CA)*
1965	BROWNE, Irene		72	*Cancer (in London, England)*
• 1965	# BUSTER, Budd		74	*Heart attack (in Los Angeles, CA)*
1965	# CARROLL, Nancy	☆	59	*Natural causes (in New York, NY)*
1965	CASEY, Kenneth		66	*Heart ailment (in Newburg, NY)*
1965	CHANDET, Louis W.		81	*After an illness of several years*
1965	+ CHANDLER, Helen		59	*After surgery for a bleeding ulcer (in Hollywood, CA)*
1965	# CHAPLIN, Sydney		80	*Died in Nice, France*
1965	# COCHRAN, Steve		48	*Acute infectious edema of lung (off coast of Guatemala)*
1965	#+ COLE, Nat "King"		45	*Lung cancer (in Santa Monica, CA)*
1965	+ COLLINS, Ray		75	*Emphysema (in Santa Monica, CA)*
1965	COLLINS, Russell		68	*Heart attack (in West Hollywood, CA)*
• 1965	# CORDY, Henry		57	*Heart ailment (in New York, NY)*
1965	CRAIG, Nell		73	*Died in Hollywood, CA*
1965	CRUZE, Mae		74	*After a long illness (in Hollywood, CA)*
1965	+ DANDRIDGE, Dorothy	☆	42	*Overdose of Tofranil, an anti-depressant (in West Hollywood, CA)*
1965	#+ DARNELL, Linda		43	*Fire burns (in Chicago, IL)*
• 1965	DAVIS, George		75	*Cancer (in Woodland Hills, CA)*
• 1965	DILLON, Tim		77	*Died in Burbank, CA*
1965	# DRESSER, Louise	☆	86	*Intestinal obstruction (in Woodland Hills, CA)*
1965	#+ DUMONT, Margaret		75	*Heart attack (in Los Angeles, CA)*
• 1965	# EDWARDS, Neely		75	*Died in Woodland Hills, CA*
1965	EDWARDS, Sarah		81	*Died in Hollywood, CA*
1965	# ELLIOTT, William "Wild Bill"		61	*Cancer (in Las Vegas, NV)*
1965	ENRIGHT, Ray		69	*Heart attack after a long illness*

YEAR	NAME	AGE	CAUSE AND/OR PLACE OF DEATH
1965	ERWIN, June	47	Found dead in her home (in Carmichael, CA)
1965	FEIST, Felix E.	55	Cancer
• 1965	# FETHERSTON, Eddie	?	Heart attack (in Yucca Valley, CA)
• 1965	# GARON, Pauline	63	
1965	GEORGE, Muriel	82	Died in England
1965	GEST, Inna	43	Hepatitis
1965	GLASS, Gaston J.	66	Died in Santa Monica, CA
1965	GRANBY, Joseph	80	Cerebral hemorrhage (in Hollywood, CA)
1965	# GRIBBON, Eddie	75	Cancer (in North Hollywood, CA)
1965	# HALE, Creighton	83	Died in South Pasadena, CA
1965	HANSON, Lars	78	Died in Stockholm, Sweden
• 1965	HARTE, Betty	81	Died in Sunland, CA
• 1965	HENDRIKSON, Anders	69	Died in Sweden
1965	#+ HOLLIDAY, Judy ★	41	Throat cancer (in New York, NY)
1965	HOOD, Joseph B. Sr.	69	
1965	HOWARD, Esther	72	Heart attack (in Hollywood, CA)
1965	HOWARD, Eugene	84	
1965	HOXIE, Jack	75	Died in Keyes, OK
1965	HUGHES, Gareth	71	Died in Woodland Hills, CA
1965	JOHNSON, Rita	52	Brain hemorrhage (in Los Angeles, CA)
1965	#+ JONES, Spike	53	Emphysema (in Beverly Hills, CA)
1965	JORDAN, Robert "Bobby"	42	Liver ailment (in Los Angeles, CA)
1965	+ KASSEL, Art	69	
1965	KENNEDY, Tom	81	Bone cancer (in Woodland Hills, CA)
1965	+ KILGALLEN, Dorothy	52	Accidental death? (Seconal and alcohol)
1965	# KULKY, Henry "Hank"	53	Heart attack (in Oceanside, CA)
1965	#+ LAUREL, Stan	74	Heart attack (in Santa Monica, CA)
1965	# LEE, Johnny "Calhoun"	67	Heart attack (in Los Angeles, CA)
• 1965	# LIGON, Grover G.	79	Died in Hollywood, CA
1965	#+ LITTLE, Malcolm "Malcolm X"	39	Assassinated (shot) in the Audubon Ballroom in Harlem, NY
• 1965	LYNCH, Helen	64	Died in Miami Beach, FL
1965	+ MacDONALD, Jeanette	57	Heart attack (in Houston, TX)
1965	# MANTZ, Paul	61	When a makeshift aircraft crashed enroute to film set (in CA)
1965	MARION, Sid	65	Heart attack
• 1965	# MAUGHAM, W. Somerset	91	Died in Nice, France
1965	#+ McDONALD, Marie	41	Accidental drug overdose (in Hidden Hills, CA)
1965	# MESSENGER, Buddy	55	Died in Hollywood, CA
• 1965	MEYER, Greta	82	
1965	MOFFATT, Graham	46	Heart attack (in Bath, England)
1965	MOWER, Jack	74	Died in Hollywood, CA
1965	# MUDIE, Leonard	81	Heart ailment (in Hollywood, CA)
1965	#+ MURRAY, Mae	75	Heart condition (in North Hollywood, CA)
1965	+ MURROW, Edward R.	57	Lung cancer
1965	+ NEWTON, Robert	50	Heart attack (in Beverly Hills, CA)
1965	#+ NICHOLS, Red	60	Heart attack (in Las Vegas, NV)
1965	OWEN, Catherine Dale	62	
• 1965	PAYNE, Douglas	90	Died in England
1965	PERINAL, Georges	68	
• 1965	PETERS, Ann	45	Heart attack (in Paris, France)
1965	PHILLIPS, Edward N.	65	Killed by a car while crossing the street (in North Hollywood, CA)
1965	REICHER, Frank	89	Died in Playa del Rey, CA
• 1965	REID, Trevor	55	Died in London, England
1965	RENNIE, James	76	Died in New York, NY
1965	REYNOLDS, Quentin	62	Cancer
1965	#+ RITZ, Al	64	Heart attack (in New Orleans, LA)
1965	# ROME, Stewart	79	Died in Newbury, England
• 1965	SCHIPA, Tito	76	Heart attack (in New York, NY)
1965	#+ SCOTT, Zachary	51	Brain tumor (in Austin, TX)
1965	#+ SELZNICK, David O.	63	Acute coronary
• 1965	SERDA, Julia	90	Died in Dresden, East Germany
• 1965	# SHUMWAY, Walter	80	Heart disease (in Woodland Hills, CA)
• 1965	SLACK, Freddie	55	Natural causes (in Hollywood, CA)
1965	SLOANE, Everett	55	Suicide (sleeping pills) in Brentwood, CA
• 1965	STEINER, Elio	60	Died in Rome, Italy
1965	SWOR, John	82	Died in Dallas, Texas

• New entry. # Original name (Pt. 7). + Interment (Pt. 5).　　　43　　　☆ Oscar nominee, ★ Oscar winner (Pt. 10)

YEAR	NAME		AGE	CAUSE AND/OR PLACE OF DEATH
1965	TANNEN, Julius		84	After suffering a stroke (in Hollywood, CA)
• 1965	TAYLOR, Forrest		80	
1965	#+ TRAVERS, Henry	☆	91	Arteriosclerosis (in Los Angeles, CA)
1965	+ Trigger (Roy Rogers' horse)		33	Natural causes
1965	# VICTOR, Charles		69	Died in London, England
1965	WAGNER, Jack		68	Died in Hollywood, CA
1965	# WATSON, Bobby		77	Died in Hollywood, CA
1965	WATSON, Minor		75	Died in Alton, IL
• 1965	WERNICKE, Otto		72	Died in Munich, Germany
1965	# WESSEL, Dick		51	Heart attack (in Studio City, CA)
1965	WILLIAMS, Mack		58	Heart attack (in Hollywood, CA)
• 1965	WILSON, Tom		84	Died in California
1965	WOOD, Britt		70	After a 6-month illness (in Hollywood, CA)
1965	WRIGHT, Mack V.		69	Died in Boulder City, Nevada
1965	#+ X, Malcolm		39	(See Malcolm Little)
1965	YACONELLI, Frank		67	Lung cancer (in Los Angeles, CA)
1966	ALLENBY, Peggy		65	After a brief illness (in New York)
1966	ARLEN, Betty		62	
1966	+ BAKER, Art		68	Heart attack (in Los Angeles, CA)
1966	BEAUMONT, Harry	☆	78	Died in Santa Monica, CA
1966	+ BERG, Gertrude		66	Heart failure
• 1966	# BLAKE, Al		89	Heart attack (in Los Angeles, CA)
• 1966	# BOYNE, Sunny		83	Died in Van Nuys, CA
• 1966	BRICE, Lew		72	Heart attack (in Hollywood, CA)
1966	#+ BRUCE, Lenny		40	Overdose of narcotics (in Hollywood, CA)
1966	BUNKER, Ralph		77	Stroke
1966	+ BUSHMAN, Francis X.		83	Heart attack due to fall (in Pacific Palisades, CA)
1966	# CALHOUN, Alice		65	Cancer (in Los Angeles, CA)
1966	CAMPBELL, Colin		83	Died in Woodland Hills, CA
1966	CASTLE, Don		47	Found dead from overdose of medication (in Hollywood, CA)
1966	CHALMERS, Thomas		82	Died in Greenwich, CT
1966	CHATTON, Sydney		48	Coronary attack (in Berkeley, CA)
• 1966	CLAYTON, Ethel		82	Died in Oxnard, CA
1966	+ CLIFT, Montgomery	☆	45	Occlusive coronary artery disease (in New York, NY)
1966	# COOMBE, Carol		55	Died in London, England
1966	CREHAN, Joseph		79	Stroke (in Hollywood, CA)
1966	DAWN, Isabel		62	Pulmonary infection (in Woodland Hills, CA)
1966	# DeCASALIS, Jeanne		70	
1966	#+ DISNEY, Walt		65	Circulatory collapse after lung surgery
1966	DODD, (Rev.) Neal		88	After a long illness
1966	# DOUGLASS, Kent		58	
1966	# DUNN, Bobby		74	Heart attack
1966	DUNN, Emma		91	Died in Los Angeles, CA
• 1966	ENGLE, Billy		77	Heart attack (in Hollywood, CA)
1966	FAYE, Julia		72	Cancer (in Santa Monica, CA)
1966	FELTON, Verna		76	Stroke (in North Hollywood, CA)
1966	+ FLEMING, Eric		41	Drowned in a river while filming in Peru
1966	# FORD, Wallace		68	Heart ailment (in Woodland Hills, CA)
1966	+ FRAWLEY, William		79	Heart attack (in Los Angeles, CA)
1966	FURTHMAN, Jules		78	Stroke (while vacationing in Oxford, England)
1966	GERAGHTY, Carmelita		65	Died in New York, NY
• 1966	GLASS, Everett		74	Died in Los Angeles, CA
• 1966	GLORI, Enrico		64	Died in Rome, Italy
1966	GORSS, Saul		58	Heart attack
1966	HAADE, William		63	
1966	# HALE, Jonathan		74	Suicide (gunshot) in Woodland Hills, CA
1966	HALLIDAY, Gardner		56	Suicide (sleeping pills) after suffering with cancer
1966	+ HARRIGAN, William		72	Following surgery
1966	HAYNES, Arthur		52	Heart attack
1966	HILL, Robert F.		79	After a long illness
1966	HILLIARD, Harry S.		?	Complications after a fall (in St. Petersburg, FL)
1966	#+ HOPPER, Hedda		75	Double pneumonia and heart complications (in Los Angeles, CA)
1966	JIMINEZ, Solodad		92	Following a stroke
1966	JOHNSTON, Oliver		78	

	YEAR	NAME		AGE	CAUSE AND/OR PLACE OF DEATH
	1966	+ KANE, Helen		58	After a 10-year bout with cancer (in Jackson Heights, NY)
	1966	#+ KEATON, Buster		70	Lung cancer (in Woodland Hills, CA)
	1966	KEITH, Robert		68	Died in Los Angeles, CA
	1966	# KELLY, Dorothy		51	Died in a fire at her home in La Jolla, CA
	1966	KERN, James V.		57	Pneumonia, after a short illness
•	1966	KIEPURA, Jan		64	Heart ailment (in Harrison, NY)
•	1966	# LAWSON, Wilfrid		66	Heart attack (in London, England)
	1966	LEASE, Rex		64	Found dead (at his home in Hollywood, CA)
•	1966	MacKENZIE, Mary		44	Automobile accident (in London, England)
	1966	MARSHALL, Herbert		75	Heart attack (in Beverly Hills, CA)
•	1966	MASON, Haddon		68	Died in London, England
	1966	MATHER, Jack		58	Heart attack (in Wauconda, IL)
	1966	# McDOWELL, Claire		88	After a long illness (in Woodland Hills, CA)
•	1966	MENKEN, Helen		63	Heart attack (in New York, NY)
	1966	MERRILL, Frank		71	Died in Hollywood, CA
	1966	MILLAR, Marjie		?	
•	1966	# MILOS, Milos		24	Suicide (gunshot) in Los Angeles, CA
	1966	# MONTGOMERY, Douglass		57	Died in Ridgefield, CT
•	1966	MORTON, Charles S.		59	Heart disease (in North Hollywood, CA)
	1966	# NAGEL, Anne		53	Cancer (in Los Angeles, CA)
	1966	O'BRIEN, Eugene		83	Bronchial pneumonia (in Los Angeles, CA)
	1966	# O'MALLEY, Pat		75	Died while eating dinner at home (in Van Nuys, CA)
	1966	# OWEN, Seena		70	After a brief illness (in Hollywood, CA)
	1966	PAIVA, Nestor		61	Died in Sherman Oaks, CA
	1966	PATTERSON, Elizabeth		91	Died in Los Angeles, CA
•	1966	PEACOCK, Kim		65	Heart attack (in Emsworth, England)
	1966	PEARCE, Alice		46	Cancer (in Los Angeles, CA)
•	1966	PEARCE, Vera		69	Died in London, England
	1966	PEARSON, Lloyd		68	Died in London, England
	1966	PETTINGELL, Frank		75	Died in London, England
	1966	POMMER, Erich		77	
	1966	POWER, Hartley		71	After a long illness (in London, England)
•	1966	# RAMBOVA, Natacha		69	Dietary complications (in Pasadena, CA)
	1966	REEVE, Ada		91	
•	1966	RODRIGUEZ, Estelita		52	
•	1966	ROGERS, Rena		64	Died in Santa Monica, CA
	1966	#+ ROPER, Jack		62	Throat cancer (in Woodland Hills, CA)
	1966	+ ROSE, Billy		67	
	1966	ROSEMOND, Clinton C.		82	Pneumonia and stroke (in Los Angeles, CA)
	1966	ROSSEN, Robert	☆	57	
	1966	ROWAN, Donald W.		60	Cerebral hemorrhage (in Rocky Hill, CT)
•	1966	SHINER, Ronald		63	Died in London, England
•	1966	Shooting Star		76	Stroke (in Hollywood, CA)
•	1966	STEADMAN, Vera		66	Died in Long Beach, CA
•	1966	STEELE, William "Bill"		76	Died in Los Angeles, CA
•	1966	STEWART, Donald		54	Died in Chertsey, England
•	1966	STEWART, Jack		51	Died in London, England
•	1966	# STOCKFIELD, Betty		61	Cancer (in London, England)
•	1966	# STOKER, H. G.		81	Died in England
	1966	TAYLOR, Deems		67	Stroke
	1966	TAYLOR, Donald F.		47	Found dead at home from an overdose of seconal
•	1966	#+ TERRELL, Kenneth		61	
•	1966	#+ TUCKER, Sophie		82	Lung and kidney ailment (in New York, NY)
•	1966	UNDERWOOD, Loyal		73	
	1966	# URECAL, Minerva		71	Heart attack (in Glendale, CA)
•	1966	# VINCENT, Sailor Billy		70	Heart attack (in Toluca Lake, CA)
	1966	+ WALKER, June		61	
	1966	# WATSON, Wylie		67	
	1966	WATTS, Charles		?	After a long illness (in Nashville, TN)
	1966	#+ WEBB, Clifton	☆	72	Heart attack (in Beverly Hills, CA)
•	1966	# WHEATCROFT, Stanhope		77	Heart attack (in Woodland Hills, CA)
•	1966	WHITLOCK, T. Lloyd		75	
	1966	WHORF, Richard		60	Heart attack after hospitalization for an ulcer (in Santa Monica, CA)
•	1966	WILSON, Jack		49	Cerebral hemorrhage (in Los Angeles, CA)
	1966	WOOD, Douglas		85	Died in Woodland Hills, CA

...DEATHS OF MOVIE AND TELEVISION PERSONALITIES – BY YEAR...

YEAR	NAME		AGE	CAUSE AND/OR PLACE OF DEATH
1966	#+ WYNN, Ed	☆	79	Cancer (in Los Angeles, CA)
1966	# YOWLACHIE, Chief		74	Pneumonia
1967	# AINLEY, Richard		56	Died in London, England
1967	# ALVARADO, Don		62	Cancer (in Los Angeles, CA)
1967	+ ANDREWS, LaVerne		51	Cancer
1967	ANTRIM, Harry		71	Heart attack
1967	# AUER, Mischa	☆	61	Heart attack
1967	+ BICKFORD, Charles	☆	78	Emphysema (in Los Angeles, CA)
1967	# BIG TREE, Chief John		92	
• 1967	BROOKS, Pauline		54	Cancer (in Glendale, CA)
• 1967	BRUGGEMAN, George		62	Died in North Hollywood, CA
1967	#+ BURNETTE, Smiley		55	Leukemia (in Los Angeles, CA)
1967	BURNS, Paul E.		86	Heart attack (in Van Nuys, CA)
1967	CADELL, Jean		83	Died in London, England
1967	CARNERA, Primo		60	Liver ailment (in Sequals, Italy)
1967	# CHANEY, Frances		78	Cerebral hemorrhage (in Sierra Madre, CA)
1967	CIOLLI, Augusta		65	
1967	CLARK, Ivan-John		?	
• 1967	CLARK, Johnny		50	Heart attack (in Hollywood, CA)
1967	+ CLYDE, Andy		75	Died in Los Angeles, CA
1967	# CONTI, Albert		79	Stroke (in Hollywood, CA)
1967	#+ CONWAY, Tom		63	Liver ailment (in Culver City, CA)
1967	COOLIDGE, Philip		58	Cancer (in Hollywood, CA)
1967	# CUNARD, Grace		73	After a long bout with cancer (in Woodland Hills, CA)
1967	CUNNINGHAM, Zamah		74	
1967	#+ DARWELL, Jane	★	87	Heart attack (in Woodland Hills, CA)
1967	#+ DENNY, Reginald		75	Stroke (in Surrey, England)
1967	DONATH, Ludwig		67	Leukemia (in New York, NY)
• 1967	DORLEAC, Francoise		25	After car skidded on wet road and burst into flames (Nice, France)
1967	#+ DUNN, James	★	65	Died in Santa Monica, CA
1967	DUVIVIER, Julien		71	After his car hit another car and tree (in Paris, France)
1967	#+ EDDY, Nelson		65	After suffering a stroke (while performing on stage in Miami Beach)
1967	EDWARDS, Edna Park		72	Died in Burbank, CA
• 1967	ELMAN, Mischa		76	Heart attack (in New York, NY)
1967	+ ERWIN, Stuart	☆	65	Heart attack (in Beverly Hills, CA)
1967	EVELYN, Judith		54	Cancer
1967	FARRAR, Geraldine		85	
1967	FLINT, Helen		69	Struck by a car while crossing the street (in Washington, D.C.)
1967	# FORTE, Joe		71	After a heart attack (in Hollywood, CA)
1967	# FREEMAN, Howard		68	
1967	GARDEN, Mary		92	
• 1967	GLENNON, Bert	☆	72	
1967	GRAF, Louis C.		77	Heart attack
1967	#+ GUTHRIE, Woody		55	After a 13-yr. bout with Huntington's chorea
1967	HACK, Herman		68	Heart attack (in Hollywood, CA)
1967	HACKETT, Hal		44	After a long illness
1967	HALLS, Ethel May		85	
1967	HARKER, Gordon		81	Died in London, England
1967	HARLAN, Kenneth		71	Aneurysm (in Sacramento, CA)
• 1967	HENCKLES, Paul		81	Died in Dusseldorf, Germany
• 1967	HESTERBERG, Trude		70	Died in Munich, Germany
1967	HINES, Harry		78	After suffering from emphysema (in Hollywood, CA)
1967	HOPPER, E. Mason		82	
1967	HUME, Benita		61	Died in Egerton, England
1967	HUTH, Harold		75	Died in London, England
• 1967	JACKSON, Thomas		81	Heart attack (in Hollywood, CA)
1967	KINGSTON, Winifred		?	
• 1967	KORTMAN, Robert F.		79	Cancer (in Long Beach, CA)
1967	#+ LAHR, Bert		72	Internal hemorrhage (in New York, NY)
1967	LAKE, Alice		71	Heart attack (in Paradise, CA)
1967	# LATELL, Lyle		62	Heart attack (in Hollywood, CA)
1967	# LEIGH, Vivien	★	53	Tuberculosis (in London, England)
• 1967	# LITTLE, Billy		72	Stroke (in Hollywood, CA)
1967	LYNN, George M.		?	

• New entry.   # Original name (Pt. 7).   + Interment (Pt. 5).   46   ☆ Oscar nominee, ★ Oscar winner (Pt. 10)

...DEATHS OF MOVIE AND TELEVISION PERSONALITIES — BY YEAR...

	YEAR	NAME		AGE	CAUSE AND/OR PLACE OF DEATH
	1967	MacFADDEN, Gertrude "Mickey"		67	Heart attack
	1967	MacLEAN, Douglas		70	Stroke (in Beverly Hills, CA)
•	1967	# MACRAE, Duncan		61	Died in Glasgow, Scotland (Do not confuse with Duncan McRae)
•	1967	MAERTENS, Willy		74	Died in Hamburg, Germany
	1967	# MANN, Anthony		60	Heart attack
	1967	#+ MANSFIELD, Jayne		35	Automobile accident (in New Orleans, LA)
	1967	MARCUSE, Theodore		47	When his car struck a truck on a Hollywood freeway
	1967	# McCOY, Gertrude		63	Died in Atlanta, GA
	1967	McGRATH, Frank		64	Heart attack (in Beverly Hills, CA)
•	1967	McKEEVER, Mike		27	Brain injuries from an automobile accident (in Hollywood, CA)
	1967	McKENZIE, Eva B.		78	
	1967	McKINNEY, Nina Mae		54	
	1967	McNAUGHTON, Harry		70	
•	1967	MILLS, John Sr.		78	Died in Ohio
•	1967	MOON, George		80	Died in London, England
•	1967	# MORAN, Frank		80	Heart attack (in Hollywood, CA)
	1967	MORENO, Antonio		78	After a long illness (in Beverly Hills, CA)
•	1967	# MORGAN, Lee		64	Heart disease (in Los Angeles, CA)
	1967	#+ MUNI, Paul	★	71	Heart trouble (in Montecito, CA)
	1967	+ NEWELL, William "Billy"		72	Died in Hollywood, CA
•	1967	NIELSEN, Hans		56	Died in Berlin, Germany
	1967	OVERTON, Frank		49	Heart attack (in Pacific Palisades, CA)
•	1967	PADDEN, Sarah		?	
•	1967	# PADULA, Vincent		66	Peritonitis (in Glendale, CA)
	1967	PAYTON, Barbara		39	Natural causes (in San Diego, CA)
	1967	PENDLETON, Nat		68	Heart attack (in San Diego, CA)
	1967	PERRIN, Jack		71	Heart attack (in Hollywood, CA)
	1967	# PETERS, House Sr.		87	Died at M.P.C. Hospital, Woodland Hills, CA
	1967	PRUD'HOMME, Cameron		75	After a long illness (in a New Jersey hospital)
	1967	QUINN, Tony		67	Died in London, England (Do not confuse with Anthony Quinn)
	1967	+ RAINS, Claude	☆	77	Intestinal hemorrhage (in Laconia, NH)
	1967	RALSTON, Jobyna		62	Died in Woodland Hills, CA
	1967	# RAMBO, Dirk		25	Burned to death in a car accident
	1967	+ RANDOLPH, Amanda		65	Stroke (in Durate, CA)
	1967	#+ RATHBONE, Basil	☆	75	Heart attack (in New York, NY)
	1967	REDDING, Otis		26	Airplane crash (near Madison, WI)
	1967	+ REED, Florence		86	
	1967	#+ REEVES, Richard J.		54	Cirrhosis of the liver (in Northridge, CA)
•	1967	REMY, Albert		54	Died in Paris, France
	1967	RHODES, Billy "Little Billy"		72	Stroke
	1967	RING, Cyril		74	Died in Hollywood, CA
	1967	# RUMANN, Sig		82	Heart attack (in Julian, CA)
	1967	SCHAEFER, Armand L.		69	Died in Bridgeport, CA
	1967	SCHNEIDER, James		85	
	1967	SEYMOUR, Harry		77	Heart attack (in Hollywood, CA)
	1967	# SHAIFFER, Howard "Tiny"		48	Died in Burbank, CA
	1967	#+ SHERIDAN, Ann		51	Cancer (in Hollywood, CA)
	1967	# STONE, George E.		63	Following a paralytic stroke (in Woodland Hills, CA)
•	1967	+ TATUM, Reese "Goose"		45	
	1967	THAW, Evelyn Nesbit		82	Died in a Santa Monica, Ca. nursing home
	1967	THOMSON, Kenneth		68	Pulmonary emphysema and fibrosis (in Los Angeles, CA)
•	1967	THORBURN, June		36	Airplane crash (in Fernhurst, Sussex, England)
	1967	# THUNDERCLOUD, Chief (2nd)		68	(Do not confuse with 1st Chief Thundercloud, d. 1955)
•	1967	# Toto		69	Died in Rome, Italy (Do not confuse with Toto the Clown, d. 1938)
	1967	+ TRACY, Spencer	★	67	Heart attack (in Beverly Hills, CA)
	1967	TRACY, William		49	Died in Hollywood, CA
•	1967	TREACY, Emerson		61	Died in Woodland Hills, CA
	1967	+ TROWBRIDGE, Charles		85	
	1967	TYNAN, Brandon		91	Died at Lynwood Nursing Home in New York, NY
	1967	# VERNE, Kaaren		49	Died in Hollywood, CA
•	1967	VOGEL, Rudolf		67	Died in Munich, Germany
•	1967	# WARD, Warwick		76	
	1967	#+ WAXMAN, Franz		60	Cancer
	1967	WEISBART, David		52	Stroke (while playing golf)
	1967	+ WESTMORE, Ernest		63	After a heart attack

• New entry. # Original name (Pt. 7). + Interment (Pt. 5).　　　　47　　　　☆ Oscar nominee, ★ Oscar winner (Pt. 10)

...DEATHS OF MOVIE AND TELEVISION PERSONALITIES — BY YEAR...

	YEAR	NAME		AGE	CAUSE AND/OR PLACE OF DEATH
	1967	WHITEMAN, Paul		77	Heart attack
•	1968	ABBOTT, Dorothy		?	
	1968	#+ ADAMS, Nick	☆	35	Drug overdose (in Beverly Hills, CA)
	1968	# ANDREWS, Lois		44	
•	1968	ANSON, Laura		76	Died in Woodland Hills, CA
	1968	ARNOLD, Phil		58	
	1968	AYRES, Robert		54	Heart attack
	1968	+ BAINTER, Fay	★	76	Died in Los Angeles, CA
	1968	# BAKER, Eddie		70	Died in Hollywood, CA
	1968	#+ BANKHEAD, Tallulah		66	Double pneumonia complicated by emphysema (in New York, NY)
	1968	# BECKETT, Scotty		38	Following a serious beating (in Los Angeles, CA)
•	1968	BELL, Rodney		52	
	1968	+ BENADARET, Bea		62	Cancer
•	1968	BENEDICT, Brooks		?	
•	1968	BLACKTON, James Stuart Jr.		71	
	1968	# BURKE, James		81	Died in Los Angeles, CA
	1968	CASSIDY, Ed		74	Died in Woodland Hills, CA
	1968	#+ CASTLE, Nick		58	Heart attack (in Los Angeles, CA)
	1968	CHAPLIN, Charles Jr.		42	Blood clot (in Hollywood, CA)
	1968	+ CHESHIRE, Harry "Pappy"		76	
	1968	#+ CLARK, Fred		54	Liver ailment (in Santa Monica, CA)
•	1968	COATES, Paul		47	Heart attack (in West Hollywood, CA)
	1968	# COLLYER, June		60	Bronchial pneumonia (in Los Angeles, CA)
	1968	+ COREY, Wendell		54	Liver ailment (in Woodland Hills, CA)
	1968	COX, Morgan		68	
	1968	# CURRIE, Finlay		90	Died in Gerrads Cross, England
	1968	D'ARRAST, Harry		71	
	1968	DAVIDSON, John		81	Heart failure (in Los Angeles, CA) — Do not confuse with the singer
	1968	DAVIS, Jack		?	
	1968	# DEKKER, Albert		63	Found dead (with S. and M. trappings) in his bath tub (in H'wood)
•	1968	# DICKERSON, Henry		61	Cerebral thrombosis (in Lynwood, CA)
	1968	DRISCOLL, Bobby		31	Hardening of the arteries (in New York, NY)
•	1968	DUNN, Ralph		65	
	1968	+ DURYEA, Dan		61	Cancer (in Los Angeles, CA)
	1968	EVANS, Douglas		64	
	1968	EVEREST, Barbara		77	Died in London, England
	1968	+ FARRELL, Virginia		72	
	1968	#+ FOLEY, Red		58	Acute pulmonary edema (in Fort Wayne, IN)
	1968	# FRANCIS, Kay		65	Cancer (in New York, NY)
	1968	# GARDNER, Helen		83	Died in Orlando, FL
•	1968	GEORGE, John		70	Emphysema (in Los Angeles, CA)
	1968	#+ GISH, Dorothy		70	Bronchial pneumonia (in Rapallo, Italy)
	1968	GOUGH, John		70	Cancer (in Hollywood, CA)
	1968	GRANVILLE, Louise		73	Contracted Hong Kong flu after being hospitalized for asthma
•	1968	GUY-BLANCHE, Alice		95	Natural causes (at her daughter's home in Mahwah, NJ)
	1968	HAAS, Hugo		65	Asthmatic attack (in Vienna, Austria)
	1968	HALL, Alexander	☆	74	Stroke
	1968	HALL, Juanita		66	Diabetic complications
	1968	# HANCOCK, Tony		44	Suicide (overdose of sleeping pills) in Sydney, Australia
	1968	# HARVEY, Lilian		61	Died in Antibes, France
	1968	HEMSLEY, Estelle		70	After a brief illness
•	1968	HOBBS, Jack		74	Died in Brighton, England
	1968	INDRISANO, John "Johnny"		62	Apparent suicide (hanged himself in his San Fernando Valley home)
	1968	KAHANAMOKU, Duke		77	After a heart attack (at the Waikiki Yacht Club in Honolulu, Hawaii)
•	1968	KELLER, Helen		86	Died in Westport, CT
	1968	KELLY, Kitty		66	Cancer
	1968	KELTON, Pert		60	Stroke
	1968	KERR, Lorence "Larry"		?	
	1968	KING, Martin Luther Jr.		39	Murdered (shot)
	1968	LACKTEEN, Frank		73	Cerebral and respiratory illness (in Woodland Hills, CA)
	1968	#+ LEONARD, Robert Z.	☆	78	Aneurysm (in Beverly Hills, CA)
	1968	LEWIN, Albert		73	Pneumonia
	1968	LEWIS, Cathy		50	Cancer (in Hollywood Hills, CA)
•	1968	LINDO, Olga		68	Died in London, England

YEAR	NAME	AGE	CAUSE AND/OR PLACE OF DEATH
1968	LINDSAY, Howard	78	
1968	LLOYD, Doris	68	"Strained" heart (in Santa Barbara, CA)
1968	# LORNE, Marion	80	Heart attack (in New York, NY)
1968	MacKAYE, Norman	62	After a brief illness
1968	# MARSH, Mae	72	Heart attack (in Hermosa Beach, CA)
• 1968	MASKELL, Virginia	31	Exposure and overdose of drugs (in Stoke Mandeville, England)
1968	+ MAYO, Archie	77	Cancer
1968	McDONALD, Francis J.	77	After a lengthy illness (in Hollywood, CA)
1968	# MEADE, Claire	84	Pneumonia (in Encino, CA)
• 1968	MEHAFFEY, Blanche	60	Died in Los Angeles, CA
1968	MOHR, Gerald	54	Heart attack (in Stockholm, Sweden)
1968	MORAN, Patsy	63	Died in Hollywood, CA
• 1968	MORENO, Dario	47	Died in Istanbul, Turkey
• 1968	MORRIS, Margaret	64	(Do not confuse with choreographer of same name)
1968	# MORROW, Doretta	41	Cancer
• 1968	MURAT, Jean	79	Coronary thrombosis (in Aix-en-Provence, France)
1968	# NOONAN, Tommy	45	After an operation for a malignant brain tumor (in Woodland Hills)
1968	#+ NOVARRO, Ramon	69	Murdered (bludgeoned) in his Hollywood Hills home
1968	#+ O'KEEFE, Dennis	60	Lung cancer (in Santa Monica, CA)
1968	# O'NEIL, Sally	57	Pneumonia
1968	PETRIE, Howard A.	61	After a long illness (at a hospital in Keene, NH)
1968	+ PIERCE, Jack P.	79	
1968	POST, Guy Bates	92	Died in Hollywood, CA
• 1968	# POWER, Paul	65	Died in Hollywood, CA
• 1968	PUIG, Eva G.	74	Diabetes and heart failure (in Panorama City, CA)
• 1968	REA, Mabel Lillian	36	Automobile accident (in Charlotte, NC)
• 1968	# RICE, Jack	75	Cancer (in Woodland Hills, CA)
1968	# RIDGELY, John	58	Heart ailment (in New York, NY)
1968	RIGA, Nadine	59	Cerebral hemorrhage
• 1968	SALMONOVA, Lyda	79	Died in Prague, Czeckoslovakia
• 1968	SCARFIOTTI, Lodovico	34	Automobile crash (in Berchtesgaden, Germany)
1968	SCOBIE, James	?	
1968	SEATON, Scott	90	After a lengthy illness (in Hollywood, CA)
1968	#+ SEDDON, Margaret	95	Died in Philadelphia, PA
1968	SERVOSS, Mary	80	Heart ailment (at her home in Los Angeles, CA)
• 1968	SHAW, C. Montague	83	Died in Woodland Hills, CA
1968	SHORT, Gertrude	66	After a brief illness (in Hollywood, CA)
1968	SKINNER, Frank	69	Cancer
1968	SMITH, Howard I.	74	Heart attack (in Hollywood, Ca.)
1968	#+ STAFFORD, Hanley	69	Heart attack (in Hollywood, Ca.)
1968	#+ ST. DENIS, Ruth	90	Heart attack (in Hollywood, CA)
1968	+ STROMBERG, Hunt	74	Massive stroke
1968	SUTHERLAND, Victor	79	Died in Los Angeles, CA
• 1968	SWANWICK, Peter	56	Died in London, England
• 1968	SYDNEY, Basil	73	Died in London, England
1968	+ TALMAN, William	53	Cancer (in Encino, CA)
1968	# TONE, Franchot ☆	63	Lung cancer (in New York, NY)
1968	# TRACY, Lee ☆	70	Cancer of the liver (in Santa Monica, CA)
1968	#+ VALLI, Virginia (Farrell)	68	Following a stroke (in Palm Springs, CA)
1968	VAN, Gus	80	After two brain operations when hit by a car in Miami Beach, FL
1968	VonSTROHEIM, Erich Jr.	52	Cancer
1968	WALKER, Helen	47	Cancer (in North Hollywood, CA)
1968	WATSON, Benjamin T. "Ben"	?	
1968	WEEKS, Marion	81	Died in New York
1968	WEIDLER, Virginia	41	Heart attack
1968	#+ WHEELER, Bert	72	Emphysema (in New York, NY)
• 1968	WIFSTRAND, Naima	78	Died in Sweden
• 1968	WILLARD, Jess	86	Cerebral hemorrhage (in Los Angeles, CA)
• 1968	WITHERS, Isabel	72	Died in Hollywood, CA
1968	# WOODS, Harry L. Sr.	79	Uremia (in Los Angeles, CA)
• 1968	WRAY, Aloha	39	Died in Hollywood, CA
1969	AHEARNE, Tom	63	Influenza (in New York)
1969	# ALEXANDER, Ben	58	Natural causes (in Westchester, CA)
• 1969	ANDERSON, James "Jim"	48	Died in Billings, MT

YEAR	NAME		AGE	CAUSE AND/OR PLACE OF DEATH
1969	ANDREWS, Stanley		77	
1969	BACCALONI, Salvatore		69	Following deterioration of a number of organs
• 1969	# BANCROFT, Charles		57	Cancer (in Woodland Hills, CA)
1969	# BARCROFT, Roy		67	Cancer (in Woodland Hills, CA)
1969	BARZELL, Wolfe		71	Heart attack
1969	#+ BATES, Barbara		43	Suicide (in Denver, CO)
1969	BEAL, Royal		68	Cancer (in Keene, N.H.)
1969	BELGADO, Maria		63	After a 3-week illness
1969	# BENDER, Russell		59	Died in Woodland Hills, CA
• 1969	BENHAM, Harry		83	Died in Sarasota, FL
1969	BENNETT, Enid		74	Heart attack (in Malibu, CA)
1969	BERGER, Ludwig		77	Heart failure
1969	BIRCH, Paul		61	
1969	BLAKE, Madge		68	Heart attack
1969	+ BOLES, John		73	Heart attack (in San Angelo, TX)
• 1969	# BOLGER, Robert "Bo"		32	Killed while skydiving (in Oceanside, CA)
1969	BONANOVA, Fortunio		73	Cerebral hemorrhage
• 1969	BONUCCI, Alberto		49	Heart attack (in Rome, Italy)
1969	BRETHERTON, Howard		73	
• 1969	BUSH, Pauline		83	Pneumonia (in San Diego, CA)
1969	#+ CASTLE, Irene		75	Died in Eureka Springs, Arkansas
1969	CIANNELLI, Eduardo		81	Cancer (in Rome, Italy)
1969	+ COLLYER, Bud		61	
1969	# COOLEY, Spade		58	Massive heart attack (in Oakland, CA)
1969	CORRIGAN, Lloyd		69	Died in Woodland Hills, CA
• 1969	# COTTON, Billy		68	Heart attack (in London, England)
1969	+ CRANE, Richard O.		51	Heart attack (in San Fernando Valley, CA)
1969	# CRAWFORD, Howard Marion		55	An overdose of sleeping pills (in London, England)
1969	DALBY, Amy		81	
1969	# D'ARCY, Roy		75	Died in Redlands, CA
1969	DAVIS, Mildred		68	Heart attack (in Santa Monica, CA)
1969	DeAUBRY, Diane		79	Heart attack
• 1969	DELGADO, Maria		60	Died in Hollywood, CA
1969	DEUTSCH, Ernst		78	Heart attack (in Berlin, West Germany)
1969	+ DOWLING, Constance		49	Cardiac arrest (in Los Angeles, CA)
1969	# ENGLISH, John W.		66	
1969	EVANS, Rex		66	Following surgery (in Glendale, CA)
1969	# FLEMING, Ian (actor)		80	Died in London, England (Do not confuse with the writer)
• 1969	+ FREEMAN, Young Frank		78	
1969	FREUND, Karl		79	
1969	#+ GARLAND, Judy	☆	47	Accidental drug overdose (in London, England)
• 1969	+ GOETZ, William		66	
1969	#+ GORCEY, Leo		53	Liver ailment (in Oakland, CA)
1969	GRAFF, Wilton		65	Died in Pacific Palisades, CA
1969	GREEN, Kenneth		61	Heart attack while operating heavy equipment
1969	# GREEN, Mitzi		48	Cancer (in Huntington Harbor, CA)
1969	# GURIE, Sigrid		58	Pulmonary embolism (in Mexico City, Mexico)
1969	+ HAYES, George "Gabby"		83	Heart ailment (in Burbank, CA)
1969	+ HENIE, Sonja		57	Leukemia (on a private plane bound for Oslo, Norway)
1969	HENNECKE, Clarence R.		74	After a brief illness
1969	HOLLIDAY, Marjorie		49	Brain hemorrhage
1969	HUNT, Martita		68	Died in London, England
1969	#+ HUNTER, Jeffrey		42	Head injuries from a fall in his home (Van Nuys, CA)
1969	INGRAM, Jack		66	Heart attack (in Canoga Park, CA)
1969	+ INGRAM, Rex		73	Heart attack (in L.A.) — Do not confuse with Rex Ingram (Hitchcock)
1969	# IRWIN, Charles W.		81	Cancer (in Woodland Hills, CA)
1969	ITURBI, Amparo		70	
1969	#+ JONES, Brian		25	Drowned while under the influence of liquor and drugs (in England)
• 1969	JUDEL, Charles		86	
1969	KANE, Eddie		79	Heart attack (in Hollywood, CA)
1969	# KARLOFF, Boris		81	Respiratory ailment (in London, England)
1969	#+ LaROCQUE, Rod		70	Died in Beverly Hills, CA
1969	# LAWTON, Frank		64	Died in London, England
1969	#+ LOCHER, Felix		86	Died in Sherman Oaks, CA
1969	+ LOESSER, Frank		59	Lung cancer (in New York, NY)

YEAR	NAME		AGE	CAUSE AND/OR PLACE OF DEATH
1969	+ LOGAN, Ella		56	Died in San Mateo, CA
1969	LYDECKER, Howard		58	
1969	+ MacLANE, Barton		68	Double pneumonia (in Santa Monica, CA)
1969	MALLESON, Miles		80	Died in London, England
1969	#+ MARCIANO, Rocky		44	Airplane crash (near Des Moines, IA)
1969	# MASCHWITZ, Eric		68	
1969	MASTERS, Ruth		75	
1969	+ McCAREY, Leo	★	70	
• 1969	McHUGH, Jimmy		74	Heart attack (in Beverly Hills, CA)
1969	# McNAUGHTON, Gus		85	Died in Castor, England
1969	+ McNEAR, Howard		63	After a long illness (in San Fernando Valley, CA)
• 1969	# MEREDYTH, Bess		?	Died in Woodland Hills, CA
1969	MEYERS, Sidney		63	
• 1969	# MILLER, Martin		70	Heart attack (in Austria)
1969	MINNER, Kathryn		77	Heart attack
1969	+ MORGAN, Russ		65	Cerebral hemorrhage (in Las Vegas, NV)
1969	# MORRIS, Johnny		83	Died in Hollywood, CA
1969	MORTON, Charles J.		70	Heart attack
1969	+ MOWBRAY, Alan		72	Heart attack (in Hollywood, CA)
1969	NEWBURG, Frank		83	Died at Motion Picture Country Hospital, CA
• 1969	# O'BRIEN, David "Dave"		57	Heart attack (on Catalina Island, CA)
1969	# OSCAR, Henry		78	Died in London, England
• 1969	# PEARSON, Drew		71	Died in Washington, D.C.
1969	PEPPER, Barbara		53	Coronary (in Panorama City, CA)
1969	PORTMAN, Eric		66	Heart ailment (in St. Veep, England)
• 1969	REEVES, Michael		25	Suicide (sleeping pills)
1969	RENEVANT, George		74	After a long illness (in Guadalajara, Mexico)
1969	RITTER, Thelma	☆	63	Heart attack (in New York, NY)
1969	RYAN, Dick		72	After a long illness (in Burbank, CA)
• 1969	SANGER, Bert		75	Died in Blackpool, England
• 1969	# SEBRING, Jay		35	Murdered (in Los Angeles, CA)
1969	SETON, Bruce		60	Died in London, England
• 1969	SHEA, Donald J. "Shorty"		?	Murdered (in Chatsworth, CA)
1969	SHERMAN, Fred E.		64	After suffering a stroke in 1962
• 1969	SIMON, Abe		56	Died in Queens, NY
1969	#+ SINGLETON, Catherine		65	Died in Ft. Worth, Texas
1969	SPEAR, Harry		47	Died in Hollywood, CA
• 1969	STANLEY, Forrest		80	Results of a fall (in Los Angeles, CA)
1969	# STANTON, Will		84	Bronchial pneumonia (in Santa Monica, CA)
• 1969	STEPPAT, Ilse		52	Died in West Berlin, Germany
• 1969	# SULLIVAN, Brian		49	Died in Lake Geneva, Switzerland
1969	SWARTHOUT, Gladys		64	Died in Florence, Italy
1969	+ TALMADGE, Natalie		70	Died in Santa Monica, CA
1969	+ TATE, Sharon (Polanski)		26	Murdered by members of the Charles Manson cult
1969	#+ TAYLOR, Robert		57	Lung cancer (in Santa Monica, CA)
1969	TONG, Kam		62	Died in Costa Mesa, CA
1969	VanEYCK, Peter		55	Died in Zurich, Switzerland
1969	VARLEY, Beatrice		73	
• 1969	# VOGAN, Emmett		76	Septicemia and pneumonia (in Woodland Hills, CA)
1969	#+ VonSTERNBERG, Josef	☆	75	Heart attack
1969	WALBURN, Raymond		81	Died in New York, NY
1969	WHITE, Ruth		55	Cancer (in Perth Amboy, NJ)
1969	WHITNEY, Claire		79	Died in Sylmar, CA
1969	# WILLIAMS, Hugh		65	Died in London, England
1969	+ WILLIAMS, Rhys		76	Died in Santa Monica, CA
1969	WILLIAMS, Spencer "Andy"		76	Kidney ailment (in Los Angeles, CA)
• 1969	WING, Dan		46	Heart attack (in Fresno, CA)
1969	# WINNINGER, Charles		84	Died in Palm Springs, CA
1969	YORK, Chick		83	
1970	AGUGLIA, Mimi		85	Died in Woodland Hills, CA
1970	AHERNE, Patrick		69	Cancer (in Hollywood, CA)
1970	# Aladdin		57	Found dead at home of apparent heart attack (in Van Nuys, CA)
1970	ALLEN, A. A.		?	Found dead in a San Francisco hotel room
• 1970	ALLEN, Dorothy		74	Died in New York

• New entry.   # Original name (Pt. 7).   + Interment (Pt. 5).   51   ☆ Oscar nominee, ★ Oscar winner (Pt. 10)

YEAR	NAME		AGE	CAUSE AND/OR PLACE OF DEATH
1970	# ALLISTER, Claud		76	Cancer (in Santa Barbara, CA)
1970	BARRAT, Robert		78	Died in Hollywood, CA
1970	+ BEAUDINE, William Sr.		78	Complications of uremic poisoning (in Canoga Park, CA)
1970	+ BEGLEY, Ed	★	69	Heart attack (in Hollywood, CA)
1970	BLANCHARD, Mari		43	Cancer (in Woodland Hills, CA)
1970	#+ BURKE, Billie	☆	84	Died in Los Angeles, CA
1970	CLARE, Mary		76	Died in London, England
1970	CRAIG, Carolyn		?	
1970	CURTIS, Willa Pearl		74	Cerebral arteriosclerosis and diabetes
1970	+ DARRELL, J. Stevan		65	Died in Hollywood, CA
1970	# DAW, Evelyn		58	
1970	DIONNE, Marie		35	
1970	DIX, Dorothy		77	
1970	#+ DOLLY, Rosie		77	Heart failure (in New York, NY)
1970	# DOMINGUEZ, Joe		76	Died in Woodland Hills, CA
1970	DUNLAP, Scott		77	
1970	EATON, Jay		70	Heart attack (in Hollywood, CA)
1970	+ EDENS, Roger	★	64	Cancer
1970	EDWARDS, James		58	Heart attack (in San Diego, CA)
1970	# ELLIS, Patricia		49	Cancer (in Kansas City, MO)
1970	+ FARMER, Frances		55	Cancer (in Indianapolis, IN)
1970	FLAHERTY, Pat J. Sr.		67	Heart attack (in New York)
1970	# FLYNN, Sean		29	Missing in Cambodia (presumed dead)
1970	+ FOSTER, Preston		69	Died in La Jolla, CA
1970	FOULGER, Byron K.		69	Heart condition (in Hollywood, CA)
1970	FREDERICKS, Charles		50	Heart attack
1970	GARCIA, Henry		66	After a long illness (in a hospital in San Antonio, TX)
1970	# GERSTLE, Frank		54	Cancer (in Santa Monica, CA)
1970	GLAUM, Louise		70	Pneumonia
1970	GODFREY, Peter		70	After a long illness
1970	+ GRANT, Earl		39	Automobile accident (near Lordsburg, N.M.)
1970	# GRAVET, Fernand		64	Myocardial infarction (in Paris, France)
1970	GRAY, Lawrence		71	Died in Mexico City, Mexico
1970	GREENE, William		43	Heart attack (in Cleveland Heights, OH)
1970	GREENWOOD, Ethel		82	Heart attack (in Hollywood, CA)
1970	HALL, Geraldine		65	Heart attack while hospitalized
1970	HANLEY, Jimmy		51	Cancer (in England)
1970	#+ HENDRIX, Jimi		27	Inhalation of vomit after barbiturate intoxication (in London, Eng.)
1970	HERNANDEZ, Juan "Juano"		74	Cerebral hemorrhage (in San Juan, Puerto Rico)
1970	HINES, Johnny		73	Heart attack (in Los Angeles, CA)
1970	#+ HOPPER, William		55	Pneumonia (in Palm Springs, CA)
1970	HORNE, David		71	Died in London, England
1970	+ HORTON, Edward Everett		84	Cancer (in Encino, CA)
1970	HUGHES, Joseph Anthony		65	Acute alcohol and barbiturate mixture (in Pasadena, CA)
1970	JARVIS, Al		60	Heart attack
1970	# JENKS, Si		93	Heart disease (in Woodland Hills, CA)
1970	+ JOPLIN, Janis		27	Accidental drug overdose (heroin morphine) in Hollywood, CA
1970	+ KARNS, Roscoe		76	Died in Los Angeles, CA
1970	KEEN, Malcolm		82	Died in England
1970	KIBBEE, Milton		73	Died in Simi Valley, CA
1970	KORTNER, Fritz		78	Leukemia (in Munich, Germany)
1970	#+ LEE, Gypsy Rose		56	Cancer (in Los Angeles, CA)
1970	# LISTON, Sonny		38	Died in Las Vegas, NV
1970	# LOMBARDI, Vince		57	Cancer
1970	#+ LOUISE, Anita		55	Massive stroke (in West Los Angeles, CA)
1970	LULLI, Folco		58	Heart attack (in Rome, Italy)
1970	+ MARCH, Hal		49	Pneumonia and lung cancer (in Los Angeles, CA)
1970	MARLE, Arnold		81	Died in London, England
1970	MAYO, Edna		76	Died in San Francisco, CA
1970	McGRAIL, Walter B.		70	
1970	MODOT, Gaston		82	
1970	MONTOYA, Alex P.		62	Congestive heart failure (in Los Angeles, CA)
1970	MOORE, Del		53	Apparent heart attack (at his home in Encino, CA)
1970	# MORRIS, Chester	☆	69	Overdose of barbiturates (in New Hope, PA)
1970	MUNSHIN, Jules		54	Heart attack

YEAR	NAME		AGE	CAUSE AND/OR PLACE OF DEATH
1970	NAGEL, Conrad		72	*Died in New York, NY*
1970	NEILL, Richard R.		94	*Died at Motion Picture Country Hospital, Woodland Hills, CA*
1970	+ NEWMAN, Alfred ★		68	*Emphysema and complications*
1970	# O'DONNELL, Cathy		44	*Following a long illness (in Los Angeles, CA)*
1970	# PATCH, Wally		82	*Died in London, England*
1970	PEABODY, Eddie		58	*Stroke (in Covington, KY)*
• 1970	# PRICE, Nancy		90	*Died in Worthing, England*
1970	PYNE, Joe		45	*Lung cancer (in Los Angeles, CA)*
1970	+ RAMBEAU, Marjorie ☆		80	*Died in Palm Springs, CA*
1970	# REED, Carol		44	*Cancer (Do not confuse with Carol Reed, d. 1976)*
1970	REMARQUE, Erich Maria		72	*Heart collapse*
• 1970	# RINDT, Jochen		28	*Injuries from automobile crash (near Monza, Italy)*
1970	RISS, Dan		60	*Heart attack (at his home in Hollywood, CA)*
1970	ROBLES, Rudy		60	*Died in Manila, Philippine Islands*
1970	+ RUGGLES, Charles		84	*Cancer (in Santa Monica, CA)*
1970	SAWYER, Laura		85	*Died in a Matawan, N.J., nursing home*
1970	SHIELDS, Arthur		74	*Emphysema (in Santa Barbara, CA)*
1970	# SHRINER, Herb		51	*Killed with his wife in a car crash (in Delray Beach, FL)*
1970	SILVERA, Frank		56	*Accidentally electrocuted in his home (in Pasadena, CA)*
1970	SINCLAIR, Robert B.		65	*Stabbed to death by a burglar (in his California home)*
1970	SPITALNY, Phil		80	*Cancer (in Miami Beach, FL)*
• 1970	# STARR, Randy		39	*Died in Los Angeles, CA*
1970	# STEVENS, Inger		35	*After an overdose of barbiturates (enroute to a Hollywood hospital)*
1970	STEWART, Fred		63	*Died at the Actors Studio in New York*
1970	STRATTON, Chester		57	*Died at his Los Angeles home*
1970	SUDLOW, Joan		78	*Results of a fall (in back of her Calif. hillside home)*
1970	SUTTON, Paul		58	*Muscular dystrophy (in Ferndale, MI)*
• 1970	# Sylvie		87	*Died in Paris, France*
• 1970	TRYON, Glenn		70	
1970	# TUFTS, Sonny		57	*Pneumonia (in Santa Monica, CA)*
• 1970	# VERNON, Dorothy		94	*Heart disease (in Grenada Hills, CA)*
1970	VERNON, Wally		65	*Killed by a hit-and-run driver (at a crosswalk in Van Nuys, CA)*
• 1970	WAYNE, Naunton		69	*Died in Subiton, England*
1970	WESTMAN, Nydia		68	*Cancer (in Burbank, CA)*
1970	#+ WESTMORE, Perc		65	*Coronary occlusion*
1970	+ WIERE, Sylvester		60	*Kidney ailment (in Hidden Hills, CA)*
• 1970	+ WYMARK, Patrick		44	*Found dead in his hotel room of natural causes (in Australia)*
1971	# ALBRIGHT, Hardie		67	*Heart failure and pneumonia (in Mission Viejo, CA)*
1971	ALLMAN, Duane		24	*Motorcycle accident (in Macon, GA)*
1971	#+ ANDERSON, G. M. "Broncho Billy"		88	
1971	# ANGELI, Pier		39	*Suicide (overdose of barbiturates)*
1971	ANGOLD, Edit		76	*After an illness of several years*
1971	#+ ARMSTRONG, Louis "Satchmo"		71	*Heart ailment*
• 1971	# ARNOLD, Jessie		93	*Heart attack (in Los Angeles, CA)*
1971	BAIRD, Leah		88	*Anemia, after a long illness (in Hollywood, CA)*
1971	BIBERMAN, Herbert		71	*Bone cancer*
1971	BLAGOI, George		73	
1971	# BOARDMAN, Virginia True		81	*Heart attack (in Hollywood, CA)*
• 1971	BOOTH, Helen		?	*Died in England*
• 1971	BOYD, Betty		63	
• 1971	BRADFORD, Marshall		74	*Heart attack (in Hollywood, CA)*
1971	# BRONSON, Betty		63	*Died in Pasadena, CA*
1971	BURNS, David		67	*Heart attack (while performing on stage in Philadelphia, PA)*
1971	+ BYINGTON, Spring ☆		84	*Died in Hollywood, CA*
1971	# CARMINATI, Tullio		77	*Stroke (in Rome, Italy)*
• 1971	CARR, Georgia		46	*Stroke (in Los Angeles, CA)*
1971	+ CERF, Bennett		73	*Heart attack*
• 1971	# CHEATHAM, Jack		76	*Heart failure (in La Mirada, CA)*
1971	CONKLIN, Chester		83	*Died in Woodland Hills, CA*
1971	+ COOPER, Gladys ☆		82	*Died in her sleep from pneumonia (in England)*
• 1971	COSTELLO, William A.		73	*Died in San José, CA*
1971	# DALE, Charlie		90	*Died in a Teaneck, N.J., nursing home*
1971	# DALL, John ☆		52	*Heart attack (in Beverly Hills, CA)*
1971	#+ DANIELS, Bebe		70	*Cerebral hemorrhage (in London, England)*

...DEATHS OF MOVIE AND TELEVISION PERSONALITIES — BY YEAR...

YEAR	NAME	AGE	CAUSE AND/OR PLACE OF DEATH
• 1971	DARK, Christopher	?	Heart attack (in Hollywood, CA)
1971	# DARVI, Bella	42	Suicide (opened the gas jets on her apartment stove) in Monaco
1971	DILLON, Josephine	87	Died in Verdugo City, CA
• 1971	+ DISNEY, Roy	77	
1971	# DUEL, Peter	31	Apparent suicide (gunshot) in Hollywood, CA
1971	# EAMES, Virginia	81	(See Virginia True Boardman)
1971	+ EDWARDS, Cliff "Ukelele Ike"	76	Died in Hollywood, CA
• 1971	# FARLEY, Dot	90	Died in South Pasadena, CA
1971	+ FARRELL, Glenda	66	Died in New York, NY
1971	FEALY, Maude	90	After being hospitalized (in Woodland Hills, CA)
• 1971	FERGUSON, Al	83	
1971	#+ Fernandel	67	Lung cancer (in Paris, France)
1971	FioRITO, Ted	70	Heart attack (in Scottsdale, AZ)
1971	+ FLIPPEN, Jay C.	72	Aneurysm (in Hollywood, CA)
• 1971	FUQUA, Charles	60	Died in New Haven, CT
1971	+ GILBERT, Billy	77	Stroke (in North Hollywood, CA)
• 1971	GILL, Tom	54	
1971	GLENN, Roy Sr.	56	Apparent heart attack (in Los Angeles, CA)
• 1971	# GOLDIN, Pat	68	Heart attack (in Los Angeles, CA)
1971	+ GOMEZ, Thomas ☆	65	Died in Santa Monica, CA
1971	# GOODE, Jack	63	Acute infectious hepatitis
1971	# GORDON, Robert	76	
1971	GREENE, Victor Hugo	76	Died in Los Angeles, CA
1971	# HATTON, Raymond	84	Heart attack (in Palmdale, CA)
1971	#+ HEFLIN, Van ★	60	After a massive stroke while swimming (in Hollywood, CA)
1971	+ HELTON, Percy	76	Died in Hollywood, CA
• 1971	HENRY, Robert "Buzz"	40	Motorcycle accident (in Los Angeles, CA)
1971	# HOLMAN, Libby "Peaches"	65	Died in North Stamford, CT
1971	HOLMES, Stuart	84	Ruptured abdominal aortic (in Hollywood, CA)
1971	# JACKSON, Selmer	82	Heart disease (in Burbank, CA)
1971	JARVIS, Robert C.	79	
1971	#+ JOHNSON, Tor	67	Heart condition (in San Fernando, CA)
• 1971	# JONES, Bobby	69	Died in Atlanta, GA
1971	# JONES, T. C.	50	Cancer (in Duarte, CA)
1971	KEENE, Richard	80	
1971	# KING, Dennis Sr.	73	Heart condition (in New York, NY)
1971	KIRKLAND, Muriel	68	Emphysema and complications
1971	LAVA, William B.	59	
• 1971	LEWIS, Joe E.	69	Liver and kidney ailments (in NYC) Do not confuse with the boxer
1971	#+ LEWIS, Ted	80	Heart attack (in New York, NY)
1971	LIGHTNER, Winnie	69	Heart attack (in Sherman Oaks, CA)
• 1971	LLOYD, Gladys	74	Stroke (in Culver City, CA)
1971	LLOYD, Harold Jr. "Duke"	39	Died in a sanitarium in North Hollywood, CA
1971	#+ LLOYD, Harold Sr.	77	Cancer (in Beverly Hills, CA)
1971	LOCKWOOD, King	73	Massive stroke (in Hollywood, CA)
• 1971	LOMBARDO, Carmen	67	Cancer (in North Miami, FL)
• 1971	LONGDEN, John	70	
1971	+ LOWE, Edmund	81	Lung ailment (in Woodland Hills, CA)
1971	# LOWERY, Robert	57	Heart attack (in Hollywood, CA)
1971	# LUKAS, Paul ★	76	Heart attack (in Tangier, Morocco)
1971	#+ LYNN, Diana	45	Brain hemorrhage (in Los Angeles, CA)
1971	# MANN, Hank	84	Died in South Pasadena, CA
1971	MAYNARD, Kermit	68	Heart attack (in Hollywood, CA)
1971	McGOWAN, Oliver F.	64	Died in his sleep
1971	McGUINN, Joseph Ford "Joe"	67	Heart attack one week after surgery (in Hollywood, CA)
1971	# McHUGH, Matt	76	Heart attack (in Northridge, CA)
1971	McMAHON, Horace	65	Heart ailment
• 1971	MIDDLETON, Josephine	87	Died in England
• 1971	MILLER, Flournoy E.	82	Heart failure (in Hollywood, CA)
1971	MOODY, Ralph	83	Heart attack following surgery (in Burbank, CA)
1971	+ MORRISON, Jim	27	Heart attack in his bath tub (after heavy drinking) in Paris, France
1971	#+ MURPHY, Audie	46	Airplane crash (near Roanoke, VA)
1971	O'CONNOR, Harry M.	98	Pneumonia, complicated by cardiac trouble
1971	# O'NEAL, Anne	77	Pancreatitis (in Woodland Hills, CA)
1971	# PARKER, Cecil	73	Died in Brighton, England

• New entry. # Original name (Pt. 7). + Interment (Pt. 5).   54   ☆ Oscar nominee, ★ Oscar winner (Pt. 10)

YEAR	NAME		AGE	CAUSE AND/OR PLACE OF DEATH
	1971	PENNINGTON, Ann	78	*Died in New York*
•	1971	PETERS, Werner	51	*Died in Wiesbaden, West Germany*
	1971	POLLACK, Ben	67	*Suicide (hanged himself in his bathroom) in Palm Springs, CA*
	1971	# RAFFERTY, Chips	62	*Heart attack (in Sydney, Australia)*
	1971	# REDWING, Rodd	66	*Heart attack (while enroute by plane from London to Los Angeles)*
	1971	REEVES, Kynaston	78	*Died in London, England*
	1971	RENNIE, Michael	61	*Died in Harrogate, Yorkshire, England*
	1971	RIANO, Renie	71	*After a long illness (in Woodland Hills, CA)*
	1971	ROACH, Bert	79	
•	1971	# ROBINSON, Frances	55	*Heart attack (in Hollywood, CA)*
	1971	# ROMANOFF, Michael	78	*Heart failure (in Los Angeles, CA)*
•	1971	# ROSMER, Milton	90	*Died in Chesham, England*
•	1971	ROWLAND, Adele	?	
	1971	ROYCE, Ruth	78	
•	1971	SAIS, Marin	81	*Cerebral arteriosclerosis (in CA)*
	1971	# SANTLEY, Joseph	81	*Died in his West Los Angeles home*
	1971	#+ SEDGWICK, Edie	28	*Acute barbitural intoxication (in Santa Barbara, CA)*
	1971	SHAW, Denis	49	*Heart attack (in London, England)*
	1971	SHEARER, Douglas	71	
	1971	SHELTON, George	86	*Burns*
	1971	SKOURAS, Spyros	78	
	1971	# Spivy	64	*Died at the Motion Picture Country Home, CA*
	1971	+ STEINER, Max	83	
	1971	STERN, Bill	64	*Heart attack (in Rye, NY)*
•	1971	STREET, David	54	*Died in Los Angeles, CA*
•	1971	# TERRISS, Ellaine	100	*Died in London, England*
	1971	TSIANG, H. T.	71	
	1971	ULRIC, Lenore	78	*After several years of hospitalization*
	1971	# VICKERS, Martha	46	*After a long illness (in Van Nuys, CA)*
	1971	WAKEFIELD, Hugh	83	*Died in London, England*
	1971	WALKER, Cheryl	49	
	1971	WALKER, Nella	85	*Heart disease (in Los Angeles, CA)*
•	1971	#+ WALTHALL, Wallace	89	
	1971	# WARREN, C. Denier	82	*Died in Torquay, England*
	1971	WESTERFIELD, James	59	*Heart attack*
	1971	WILKERSON, Guy	72	*Cancer (in Hollywood, CA)*
	1971	# WOLFF, Frank	43	*Suicide (slashed his throat with a safety razor)*
	1971	WYNN, Nan	55	*Cancer (in Santa Monica, CA)*
	1971	YOUNG, Carleton G.	64	*Cancer (in Hollywood, CA)*
•	1972	ADAMS, William Perry	85	*Died in New York*
	1972	# ADAMSON, Victor	82	*Died in Hollywood, CA*
	1972	ANDREWS, Tod	52	*Heart attack*
	1972	#+ AUSTIN, Gene	71	*Cancer (in Palm Springs, CA)*
	1972	# BAGDASARIAN, Ross	52	*Natural causes (in Beverly Hills, CA)*
	1972	BARLOW, Howard	80	*Heart attack*
	1972	+ BLOCKER, Dan	43	*Pulmonary embolus (in Hollywood, CA)*
	1972	# BLYTHE, Betty ★	78	*Died in Woodland Hills, CA*
•	1972	BOESEN, William	47	
•	1972	BOND, Lyle	54	*Heart attack (in San Diego, CA)*
	1972	BORDEN, Eugene	75	
•	1972	BOURNE, William Payne	36	*Suicide (gunshot) in Hollywood, CA*
	1972	+ BOYD, William "Hopalong Cassidy"	77	*Parkinson's disease and heart failure (in South Laguna, CA)*
	1972	BRADY, Pat	57	*Died while visiting friends in Green Mountain Falls, Colorado*
•	1972	# BRITT, Elton	59	*Died in Connellsville, PA*
	1972	BROWN, Harry Joe	78	*Apparent heart attack (Do not confuse with Harry Brown, d. 1986)*
	1972	#+ CABOT, Bruce	68	*Lung and throat cancer*
	1972	# CAMPBELL, Webster	79	
	1972	CANNON, Esma	76	
	1972	CARROLL, Leo G.	79	*Died in Hollywood, CA*
	1972	# CHANDLER, Lane	73	*Cardiovascular disease (in Hollywood, CA)*
	1972	#+ CHEVALIER, Maurice ☆	83	*Heart attack after kidney surgery (in Paris, France)*
	1972	CLARKE, Gordon B.	65	*After a heart attack (in New York, NY)*
•	1972	# CLEMENTE, Roberto	38	*Airplane crash (in San Juan, Puerto Rico)*
	1972	# COMINGORE, Dorothy	58	*Died in Stonington, CT*

YEAR	NAME		AGE	CAUSE AND/OR PLACE OF DEATH
• 1972	# COREY, Joseph		45	Heart attack (in Los Angeles, CA)
1972	+ CORRELL, Charles J. "Andy"		82	Heart attack (in Chicago, IL)
1972	#+ COWAN, Jerome		74	Died in Encino, CA
1972	CRAIG, May		82	Died in Dublin, Ireland
• 1972	# CUTTING, Dick		59	Kidney disease and uremia (in Woodland Hills, CA)
1972	DALE, Margaret		92	
1972	DALTON, Dorothy		78	Died in Scarsdale, NY
1972	# DeWILDE, Brandon	☆	30	After his car skidded on wet pavement and hit a truck (in Denver)
1972	# DIETERLE, William	☆	79	Died in Ottobrunn, West Germany
1972	# DIXON, Denver		82	Heart attack
1972	+ DONLEVY, Brian	☆	73	Throat cancer (in Woodland Hills, CA)
• 1972	DUNCAN, Evelyn		79	Died in Bellflower, CA
1972	# DUNCAN, Kenne		69	Stroke (in Hollywood, CA)
• 1972	# DUNHAM, Phil		87	Died in Los Angeles, CA
• 1972	EARLE, Edward		90	Died in Woodland Hills, CA
1972	FELDMAN, Andrea		?	Suicide (jumped from the 14th floor of 51 Fifth Ave, NY)
1972	#+ FRANKLIN, Sidney (director)	☆	79	(Do not confuse with silent film actor of same name, d. 1931)
1972	#+ FRIML, Rudolph		92	Brain hemorrhage
1972	# GAAL, Franceska		68	
1972	GALLIAN, Ketti		?	
• 1972	GORDON, Colin		61	Died in Haslemere, England
1972	GOULDING, Alfred		76	Pneumonia
1972	GREEN, Nigel		48	Found dead at his home (in Brighton, England)
1972	GURIN, Ellen		24	Suicide, after a nervous depression
1972	HAMMOND, Virginia		78	
• 1972	HANNEN, Nicholas		91	Died in London, England
1972	HEATTER, Gabriel		82	Pneumonia
• 1972	HEINZ, Gerard		68	
• 1972	# HOOVER, J. Edgar		77	Heart disease (in Washington, D.C.)
1972	# HOPKINS, Miriam	☆	69	Heart attack (in New York, NY)
1972	HUDSON, Rochelle		57	Died in Palm Desert, CA
1972	+ IHNAT, Steve		37	Heart attack (in Cannes, France)
1972	+ JACKSON, Mahalia		60	Heart disease (in Evergreen Park, IL)
1972	JEWELL, Isabel		61	Natural causes (in Hollywood, CA)
1972	# JONES, Emrys		57	Heart attack
1972	KIKUME, Al		78	
1972	LANDIS, Jessie Royce		67	Cancer (in Danbury, CT)
1972	+ LANFIELD, Sidney		74	Heart attack
1972	LANG, Walter	☆	73	Kidney failure
1972	LANGLEY, Faith		43	Died in New York, NY
1972	# LANSING, Joi		42	Cancer (in Santa Monica, CA)
• 1972	# LAWFORD, (Lady) May		?	Died in Monterey Park, CA
1972	LEDERMAN, D. Ross		76	Kidney and heart condition
1972	LEISEN, Mitchell		74	Coronary complications
1972	+ LEVANT, Oscar		65	Heart attack (in Beverly Hills, CA)
1972	# LITEL, John		77	Died in Woodland Hills, CA
• 1972	LYEL, Viola		71	
1972	MACK, Russell		79	Stroke
1972	#+ MAXWELL, Marilyn		49	High blood pressure and pulmonary ailment (in Beverly Hills, CA)
• 1972	McDERMOTT, Hugh		63	Died in London, England
• 1972	MOORE, Patti		71	Cancer (in Los Angeles, CA)
1972	MUIR, Gavin		64	Died in Fort Lauderdale, FL
1972	MUNRO, Janet		38	Choked to death while drinking tea (in London, England)
1972	NEAL, Tom		58	Natural causes (in North Hollywood, CA)
1972	# NEDELL, Bernard		74	Died in Hollywood, CA
1972	NESMITH, Ottola		83	Died in Hollywood, CA
• 1972	# NIELSEN, Asta		89	Died in Copenhagen, Denmark
1972	#+ OWEN, Reginald		85	Heart attack (in Boise, ID)
1972	PARKER, Lew		64	Cancer (in New York, NY)
1972	#+ PARSONS, Louella (Martin)		91	Arteriosclerosis (in Santa Monica, CA)
• 1972	PENA, Julio		60	Heart attack (in Marbella, Spain)
1972	PRAGER, Stanley		55	While on a business trip (in Hollywood, CA)
• 1972	# PRUD'HOMME, George		71	Brain tumor (in Los Angeles, CA)
1972	PURCELL, Irene		70	Died at her home in Racine, WI
1972	RANK, (Lord) J. Arthur		83	

YEAR	NAME		AGE	CAUSE AND/OR PLACE OF DEATH
• 1972	+ RICHMAN, Harry		77	
1972	+ ROACH, Hal Jr.		53	Pneumonia
• 1972	# ROBINSON, Jackie		53	Heart disease (in Stamford, CT)
1972	+ RUGGLES, Wesley	☆	82	After a stroke (in Santa Monica, CA)
1972	RUTHERFORD, Margaret	★	80	After breaking a hip in a fall (in Buckinghamshire, England)
1972	SANDE, Walter		65	Heart attack (while waiting for cab at O'Hare Airport in Chicago, IL)
1972	SANDERS, George	★	65	Suicide (overdose of barbiturates) in Casteldelfels, Spain
1972	#+ SCALA, Gia		38	Overdose of alcohol and medication (in Hollywood, CA)
• 1972	SCHULZ, Fritz		75	Died in Zurich, Switzerland
1972	SHELTON, John		54	Natural causes (in Ceylon)
1972	SHORT, Antrim		72	Emphysema (in Woodland Hills, CA)
• 1972	SLOMAN, Edward "Ted"		87	Died in Woodland Hills, CA
1972	TAMIROFF, Akim	☆	72	Died in Palm Springs, CA
1972	TASHLIN, Frank		59	Heart attack
• 1972	THORNDIKE, Russell		?	Died in London, England
1972	TOZERE, Frederic		71	Died in his New York apartment
1972	+ TRAUBEL, Helen		69	Heart attack (in Santa Monica, CA)
1972	ULMER, Edgar G.		68	After a long illness
1972	# WARWICK, John		67	Heart attack
1972	# WEEDE, Robert		69	After several months in a hospital
1972	# WHITNEY, Peter		55	Heart attack (in Santa Barbara, CA)
1972	#+ WILSON, Marie		56	Cancer (in Hollywood Hills, CA)
1972	+ WINCHELL, Walter		74	Died in Los Angeles, CA
1972	# WINDSOR, Claire		75	Heart attack (in Los Angeles, CA)
1972	WOODWARD, Robert "Bob"		63	Heart attack (in Hollywood, CA)
1973	# ADRIAN, Max		70	Died in Wilford, England
1973	+ AKEMAN, David "Stringbean"		57	Shot to death by burglars in his home
1973	+ ARMSTRONG, Robert		76	
1973	AVERY, Patricia		71	
• 1973	AVERY, Tol		58	Heart attack (in CA)
1973	# BANNER, John		62	Intestinal hemorrhage (in Vienna, Austria)
1973	# BARKER, Lex		53	Heart attack (in New York, NY)
• 1973	+ BAYLIS, Peter		63	
1973	BEAL, Scott		83	Cancer (in Hollywood, CA)
• 1973	BELL, James		81	
1973	BLACKMER, Sidney		79	Cancer
• 1973	# BLACKTON, Violet		60	
• 1973	BLAKE, Anne		?	
1973	BORG, Veda Ann		58	Died in Hollywood, CA
• 1973	#+ BOYD, Jim		77	
1973	BRADFORD, Lane		50	Following a massive cerebral hemorrhage (in Honolulu, Hawaii)
1973	BRADSHAW, Eunice		80	
1973	BREAKSTON, George P.		53	Died in Paris, France
1973	#+ BROWN, Joe E.		80	After a long illness (in Brentwood, CA)
1973	BUCK, Pearl S.		80	
1973	# BUTLER, Royal "Roy"		80	Died in Desert Hot Springs, CA
• 1973	CANE, Charles		74	Died in Woodland Hills, CA
1973	# CARNEY, Alan		63	Heart attack (at the Hollywood Park racetrack)
1973	# CARR, Mary K.		98	Died in Woodland Hills, CA
1973	CASTLE, Peggy		46	Cirrhosis of the liver and heart condition (in Hollywood, CA)
1973	# CHANEY, Lon Jr.		67	Heart attack, throat cancer, liver ailment (in San Clemente, CA)
1973	+ COOPER, Melville G.		76	Cancer (in Woodland Hills, CA)
1973	COOPER, Merian C.		79	Cancer (in Coronado, CA)
1973	#+ COWARD, Noel	★	73	Heart attack (in Port Maria, Jamaica)
1973	#+ COX, Wally		48	Heart attack (in Los Angeles, CA)
• 1973	COYNE, Jeanne		50	
1973	#+ CRANE, Norma		42	Cancer (in West Los Angeles, CA)
1973	+ CROCE, Jim		30	Airplane crash (on takeoff from Natchitoches Municipal airport, LA)
1973	DALLIMORE, Maurice		72	Laennec's cirrhosis (in Los Angeles, CA)
1973	#+ DARIN, Bobby	☆	37	After heart surgery (in Hollywood, CA)
1973	# DeCORDOVA, Arturo		66	Died in Mexico City, Mexico
1973	DeCORSIA, Ted		69	Natural causes (in Encino, CA)
• 1973	DELGADO, Roger		53	Automobile accident (in Turkey)
1973	DODD, Claire		64	Cancer (in Beverly Hills, CA)

YEAR	NAME		AGE	CAUSE AND/OR PLACE OF DEATH
1973	DOYLE, Maxine		58	Cancer (in Studio City, CA)
1973	# DUNN, Michael	☆	39	Congenital chondrodystrophy (dwarfism) in London, England
1973	ELLIS, Robert "Bobby"		40	Kidney failure following an operation (in Los Angeles, CA)
1973	ESSLER, Fred		77	After a long illness
1973	FIELD, Betty		55	Stroke (in Hyannis, MA)
1973	#+ FORD, John	★	78	Cancer (in Palm Desert, CA)
1973	FOSTER, Dudley		47	Suicide (in London, England)
• 1973	FOXE, Earle A.		84	Died in Los Angeles, CA
• 1973	FRANCIS, Coleman		53	Arteriosclerosis (in Hollywood, CA)
1973	#+ FREED, Arthur		78	Heart attack
• 1973	FRITSCH, Willy		72	Heart attack (in Hamburg, Germany)
1973	+ FULLER, Mary		85	Massive pulmonary embolism
1973	# GERAY, Steven		75	
1973	#+ GOLDWYN, Samuel		91	Cancer
1973	GOMBELL, Minna		80	Died in Santa Monica, CA
1973	#+ GRABLE, Betty		56	Lung cancer (in Santa Monica, CA)
1973	# GREAZA, Walter		76	
• 1973	GREEN, Abel		72	Died in New York
• 1973	GREENE, Billy M.		76	Heart attack (in Los Angeles, CA)
• 1973	# GREY, Olga		75	Died in Los Angeles, CA
1973	HACK, Signe		73	Leukemia (in Hollywood, CA)
1973	HACKETT, Lillian		76	Cerebral hemorrhage (in Hollywood, CA)
• 1973	# HAGNEY, Frank S.		79	Died in Los Angeles, CA
1973	+ HAINES, William		73	Cancer (in Santa Monica, CA)
1973	HARDIE, Russell		69	After an illness of several years (in Clarence, NY)
• 1973	HARRIS, Stacy B.		54	Heart attack (in Los Angeles, CA)
1973	HARTMAN, Paul		69	Heart attack (in Los Angeles, CA)
1973	# HARVEY, Laurence	☆	45	Cancer (in London, England)
1973	HAWKINS, Jack		62	Cancer (in London, England)
1973	# HAYAKAWA, Sessue	☆	84	Cerebral thrombosis and pneumonia (in Tokyo, Japan)
1973	HENNING, Pat		62	
1973	#+ HOLDEN, Fay		77	Cancer (in Woodland Hills, CA)
• 1973	HOLLISTER, Alice		86	Died in Costa Mesa, CA
1973	# HOLT, Tim		54	Brain cancer (in Shawnee, OK)
1973	HUFF, Louise		77	
1973	# INGE, William		60	Suicide (in Hollywood, CA)
1973	JACOBS, Arthur P.		51	Massive heart attack in his sleep
1973	# JEANS, Ursula		66	Died near London, England
1973	+ KELLAWAY, Cecil	☆	79	Died in West Los Angeles, CA
1973	# KENNEDY, Douglas		58	Cancer (in Kailua, Hawaii)
1973	KLEMPERER, Otto		88	Died in his sleep
1973	KORNMAN, Mary		56	Cancer (in Glendale, CA)
1973	+ KRUPA, Gene		64	Heart problems and leukemia (in Yonkers, NY)
1973	#+ LAKE, Veronica		51	Acute hepatitis (in Burlington, VT)
1973	LANDIN, Hope		79	
1973	#+ LANE, Allan "Rocky"		69	Bone marrow cancer (in Woodland Hills, CA)
1973	#+ LEE, Bruce		32	Acute cerebral edema after taking prescribed pain-killer (Hong Kong)
1973	# LEE, Lila		71	Stroke (in Saranac Lake, NY)
1973	# LEONARD, Jack E.		62	Diabetic complications (in New York, NY)
• 1973	LORDE, Athena		58	Cancer (in Van Nuys, CA)
1973	MacGOWRAN, Jack		54	After a bout with the flu (in his New York hotel room)
• 1973	MACKIN, Clara		?	Died in Santa Monica, CA
1973	+ MACREADY, George		63	Emphysema (in Los Angeles, CA)
1973	MAGNANI, Anna	★	64	Cancer (in Rome, Italy)
1973	MARION, Frances		85	Died in Los Angeles, CA
1973	+ MAYNARD, Ken		77	Died alone in his trailer of malnutrition (in Woodland Hills, CA)
• 1973	# McLEOD, Tex		76	Heart attack (in Brighton, England)
1973	McVEY, Patrick		63	After being hospitalized (in New York, NY)
1973	# MELCHIOR, Lauritz		82	After gall bladder operation (in Santa Monica, CA)
1973	# MIDDLETON, Guy		64	Died near London, England
• 1973	MILLS, Frank		82	Arteriosclerosis (in Los Angeles, CA)
• 1973	MISHIMA, Masao		67	Heart ailment (in Tokyo, Japan)
1973	+ MONROE, Vaughn		62	
1973	MOORE, Cleo		44	Died in Inglewood, CA
1973	+ MORELAND, Mantan		72	Died in Hollywood, CA

...DEATHS OF MOVIE AND TELEVISION PERSONALITIES — BY YEAR...

YEAR	NAME		AGE	CAUSE AND/OR PLACE OF DEATH
1973	MORRISON, George "Pete"		81	Died in Los Angeles, CA
1973	#+ NAISH, J. Carrol	☆	73	Died in La Jolla, CA
1973	# O'SHEA, Michael		67	Heart attack (in Dallas, TX)
1973	# PAXINOU, Katina	★	72	Cancer (in Athens, Greece)
1973	PERCY, Eileen		72	After an illness of many years (in Beverly Hills, CA)
1973	PICASSO, Pablo		91	Died in Mougins, France
• 1973	# PRICE, Dennis		58	Died in Guernsey, Channel Islands
1973	RANDOLPH, Isabel		82	Died in Burbank, CA
1973	RAYMOND, Cyril		76	
• 1973	REED, Donald		70	
1973	+ REID, Carl Benton		79	Died in Studio City, CA
• 1973	# RICHMOND, Kane		66	
1973	#+ ROBINSON, Edward G.	★	79	Cancer (in Hollywood, CA)
• 1973	# ROOSEVELT, Buddy		75	Died in Meeker, CO
• 1973	ROQUEVERT, Noel		81	Died in Paris, France
1973	#+ RYAN, Irene		70	Stroke (in Santa Monica, CA)
1973	RYAN, Robert	☆	63	Lymphatic cancer (in New York, NY)
1973	+ SANDS, Diana		39	Cancer (in New York, NY)
1973	SEABURY, Ynez		64	Internal complications (at her home in Sherman Oaks, CA)
1973	SEDGWICK, Josie		75	Stroke (in Santa Monica, CA)
• 1973	+ SHERMAN, Allan		49	
1973	+ SHUMAN, Roy		49	
1973	# SIODMAK, Robert	☆	73	Heart attack (in Switzerland)
1973	# SMITH, Art		73	Heart attack (in West Babylon, NY)
1973	STOSSEL, Ludwig		89	Died in Beverly Hills, CA
1973	#+ STRANGE, Glenn		74	Cancer (in Burbank, CA)
1973	# STUART, Nick		68	Cancer (in Biloxi, MS)
1973	# SUTHERLAND, Eddie		78	Following a long illness (in Palm Springs, CA)
• 1973	TAFT, Sara		?	Heart attack (in Los Angeles, CA)
1973	+ TALMADGE, Constance		75	Pneumonia (in Los Angeles, CA)
1973	TERHUNE, Max "Abibe"		82	Heart attack and stroke (in Cottonwood, AZ)
1973	+ TINDALL, Loren		51	Heart attack
• 1973	TISSIER, Jean		76	Died in Paris, France
1973	+ TRUEX, Ernest		83	Heart attack (in Fallbrook, CA)
1973	VanROOTEN, Luis		66	Died in Chatham, MA
1973	# WESTMORE, Bud		55	Heart attack
1973	# WESTMORE, Wally		67	Stroke
1973	WILBUR, Crane		83	Following a stroke (in North Hollywood, CA)
• 1973	WILLIAMS, Paul		34	Suicide (sang with "The Temptations")
1973	WOODBRIDGE, George		66	
1973	WORLOCK, Frederick		87	Cerebral ischemia after a long illness (in Woodland Hills, CA)
1974	#+ ABBOTT, Bud		78	Cancer (in Woodland Hills, CA)
• 1974	ACE, Jane		74	
1974	ACOSTA, Rudolfo		53	Cancer (in Woodland Hills, CA)
1974	ALLEN, Barbara Jo "Vera Vague"		70	Died in Santa Barbara, CA
1974	#+ ARQUETTE, Cliff		69	Heart attack
• 1974	# ASH, Russell		63	Cancer (in Los Angeles, CA)
• 1974	AUSTIN, Richard		33	Automobile accident (in Hawthorne, CA)
1974	BACLANOVA, Olga		75	
1974	BARD, Ben		81	Cerebral thrombosis (in Los Angeles, CA)
1974	#+ BENNY, Jack		80	Pancreatic cancer (in Holmby Hills, CA)
1974	BERGERE, Ouida		88	
1974	# BEST, Edna		74	Died in Geneva, Switzerland
1974	BLACKWELL, Carlyle Jr.		61	After a 6-month illness
• 1974	# BLOOM, Bobby		27	Murdered or suicide? (shot) in West Hollywood, CA
1974	+ BRADLEY, Truman		69	Died in Los Angeles, CA
1974	+ BRENNAN, Walter	★	80	Emphysema (in Oxnard, CA)
1974	+ BRITTON, Pamela		51	Brain tumor (in Arlington Heights, IL)
1974	# BROOK, Clive		87	Died in London, England
• 1974	BROWN, Helen "Mina"		58	Cancer (in CA)
1974	+ BROWN, Johnny Mack		70	Cardiac condition (in Woodland Hills, CA)
1974	BRUCE, Betty		54	Cancer
1974	CAMPEAU, June Harrison		48	Cirrhosis of the liver
1974	CERVI, Gino		72	Pulmonary stroke

YEAR	NAME		AGE	CAUSE AND/OR PLACE OF DEATH
• 1974	CLAIRE, Helen		67	*Died in Birmingham, AL*
1974	COBB, Edmund F.		82	*Heart attack (in Woodland Hills, CA)*
1974	COLLINGE, Patricia	☆	81	*Heart attack (in New York, NY)*
1974	COMPSON, Betty		77	*Died in Glendale, CA*
1974	CONWAY, Curt		59	*After suffering a massive heart attack*
• 1974	CORBETT, Mary		47	
1974	+ CORNELL, Katharine		81	*After a long illness (in Vineyard Haven, MA)*
1974	COX, Robert		79	*Died in Phoenix, AZ*
• 1974	COY, Walter		68	
1974	+ CRISP, Donald	★	93	*After a series of strokes (in Van Nuys, CA)*
1974	# CUSTER, Bob		76	*Natural causes*
1974	CUTTS, Patricia		48	*Found dead at home from an overdose of pills*
• 1974	# DARLING, Candy		25	*Cancer and pneumonia (in New York)*
1974	DARVAS, Lili		72	*Died at her Manhattan home*
1974	# DASH, Pauly		55	*After cancer treatment (at a hospital in Miami, FL)*
1974	# DAVIS, Rufe		66	*Died in Torrance, CA*
1974	DEARING, Edgar		81	*Lung cancer (in Woodland Hills, CA)*
1974	DeSICA, Vittorio	☆	73	*Died in Paris, France*
1974	#+ DeWOLFE, Billy		67	*Cancer (in Los Angeles, CA)*
1974	DREW, Ann		83	*Died in a Miami nursing home*
1974	DUMBRILLE, Douglas		85	*Heart attack (in Woodland Hills, CA)*
1974	#+ ELLINGTON, Duke		75	*Lung cancer and pneumonia (in New York, NY)*
1974	#+ ELLIOT, Cass		32	*Heart attack, chronic obesity and exhaustion (in London, England)*
• 1974	ELLIS, Robert Reel		82	*Cardiac arrest (in Santa Monica, CA)*
1974	#+ FLYNN, Joe		49	*Accidental drowning (in Beverly Hills, CA)*
1974	+ FONTANE, Tony		47	*Cancer (in Canoga Park, CA)*
1974	FOSTER, Lewis R.		75	*Heart attack*
• 1974	FRASER, Harry		84	*Died in Pamona, CA*
1974	GAUGUIN, Lorraine		50	*Died when fire destroyed her Los Angeles home*
1974	# GLENN, Raymond		76	*Natural causes*
1974	GORDON, Bert		76	*After a long bout with cancer*
1974	GORDON, Kitty		96	*Died at a Brentwood, NY nursing home*
1974	# HADLEY, Reed		63	*Heart attack (in Los Angeles, CA)*
1974	HARLAN, Russell B.		70	*Died in Newport Beach, CA*
1974	# HAROLDE, Ralf		75	*Pneumonia (in Santa Monica, CA)*
• 1974	# HARRIS, Morris		59	
• 1974	# HOLDREN, Judd		58	*Suicide (gunshot) in West Los Angeles, CA*
1974	#+ HUDSON, William		49	*Laennec's cirrhosis (in Woodland Hills, CA)*
1974	HUGO, Mauritz		65	*Heart ailment (in Woodland Hills, CA)*
1974	# HULL, Warren		71	*Heart failure (in Waterbury, CT)*
1974	+ HUNTLEY, Chet		61	*Lung cancer (in Bozeman, MT)*
1974	#+ HUROK, Sol		85	*Apparent heart attack*
1974	IMBODEN, David C.		87	*Died in Kansas City, Missouri*
• 1974	JAFFE, Carl		71	*Died in London, England*
1974	# JENKINS, Allen		74	*Complications following surgery (in Santa Monica, CA)*
• 1974	# JOHNSON, Chubby		71	*Died in Hollywood, CA*
1974	JUDGE, Arlene		62	*Natural causes (in West Hollywood, CA)*
1974	KINSOLVING, Lee		36	
• 1974	KNOX, Teddy		78	*Died in England*
1974	+ KRUGER, Otto		89	*Stroke and cerebral vascular complications (in Woodland Hills, CA)*
1974	#+ LANE, Rosemary		60	*Diabetes and pulmonary obstruction (in Woodland Hills, CA)*
1974	LARGAY, Raymond J. "Ray"		88	*Stroke (in Woodland Hills, CA)*
1974	LEE, Raymond		64	*Died in a Los Angeles suburban hospital*
• 1974	# LESLEY, Carole		38	*Died in New Barnet, England*
1974	# LITVAK, Anatole	☆	72	
1974	+ LONG, Richard		47	*Heart ailment (in Los Angeles, CA)*
• 1974	LONTOC, Leon		64	*Died in Los Angeles, CA*
• 1974	# LYONS, Cliff "Tex"		71	*Died in Los Angeles, CA*
• 1974	# MANN, Billy		?	*Died in New York, NY*
• 1974	MARCH, Eve		?	*Cancer (in Hollywood, CA)*
1974	#+ MASSEY, Ilona		63	*Cancer (in Bethesda, MD)*
1974	MOJICA, Don José		75	*Heart ailment (in Lima, Peru)*
1974	#+ MOOREHEAD, Agnes	☆	67	*Lung cancer (in Rochester, MN)*
1974	MORRIS, Glenn		62	*After a long illness*
• 1974	# MORRISON, James		86	*Died in New York, NY*

YEAR	NAME	AGE	CAUSE AND/OR PLACE OF DEATH
• 1974	MUMBY, Diana	51	Died in Westlake, CA
• 1974	# MURPHY, Edna	69	Died in Santa Monica, CA
1974	NAPIER, Russell	64	Died in England
1974	# NILSSON, Anna Q.	85	Natural causes (in Hemet, CA)
1974	NYE, Carroll	72	Heart attack and kidney failure (in North Hollywood, CA)
1974	# PAGE, Paul	70	Heart attack (in Hermosa Beach, CA)
1974	PARKER, Albert	87	(Do not confuse with Al Parker, d. 1992)
1974	PLATT, Edward C. "Ed"	58	Heart attack (in Santa Monica, CA)
• 1974	PROHASKA, Janos	52	Airplane crash (in Inyo County, CA)
1974	PRYOR, Roger	72	Heart attack (while visiting in Puerta Vallarta, Mexico)
• 1974	# RABAGLIATI, Alberto	67	Cerebral thrombosis (in Rome, Italy)
• 1974	REED, Billy	59	Heart attack (in New York, NY)
• 1974	REED, Maxwell	55	Died in England
1974	# REGAS, Pedro	92	Died in Hollywood, CA
1974	# REPP, Stafford	56	Heart attack (in Inglewood, CA)
1974	RICE, Florence	63	Lung cancer (in Honolulu, Hawaii)
1974	RICHARDS, Paul	50	Cancer
1974	#+ RITTER, Tex	67	Heart attack (in Nashville, TN)
1974	+ ROBINSON, Edward G. Jr.	40	Natural causes (found unconscious in his West Hollywood home)
• 1974	# ROSAY, Françoise	82	Died in Paris, France
1974	# ROUNESVILLE, Robert	60	Heart attack (in New York City)
1974	RUICK, Barbara	41	Natural causes (in Reno, NV)
• 1974	# SAGE, Willard	51	Died in Sherman Oaks, CA
• 1974	SAYRE, Jeffrey	73	Murdered (shot) in Los Angeles, CA
1974	SESSIONS, Almira	86	Died in Los Angeles, CA
1974	# SMITH, Gerald	77	After a short illness (in Woodland Hills, CA)
1974	SNEGOFF, Leonid	90	Heart failure and arteriosclerosis (in Los Angeles, CA)
• 1974	# SOMERSET, Pat	77	Arterial hemorrhage (in Apple Valley, CA)
• 1974	ST. CYR, Lillian "Red Wing"	100	Died in New York, NY
1974	ST. JOHN, Howard	68	Heart attack (in New York, NY)
• 1974	STRASSBERG, Morris	75	Died in South Laguna Beach, CA
1974	STRIKER, Joseph	74	Died in St. Barnabas Hospital, Livingston, NJ
1974	#+ SULLIVAN, Ed	72	Cancer of the esophagus (in New York, NY)
1974	SULLIVAN, Elliott (Elliot)	66	Heart attack (while visiting in Los Angeles, CA)
1974	SUTTON, Frank	50	Heart attack (in Shreveport, LA)
1974	TABBERT, William	53	Apparent heart attack
• 1974	TAYLOR, Alma	79	Died in London, England
1974	# VAGUE, Vera	70	Died in Santa Barbara, CA
• 1974	VAN, Wally	93	Died in Englewood, NJ
1974	VENABLE, Reginald	48	Heart attack (in Hollywood, Ca.)
1974	WADSWORTH, Henry	72	
1974	WALDIS, Otto	68	Heart attack
1974	# WENGRAF, John E.	76	
1974	# WENTWORTH, Martha	?	Died in Sherman Oaks, CA
1974	# WHALEN, Michael	72	Bronchial pneumonia (in Woodland Hills, CA)
• 1974	WILCOX, Frank	66	Died in Northridge, CA
1974	# WING, Red	90	
1974	YOUNGSON, Robert	56	Died at St. Vincent's Hospital in New York
1974	#+ YURKA, Blanche	87	Arteriosclerosis
1975	# ARNO, Sig	80	Parkinson's disease
1975	# BAKER, Bob	74	Stroke (in Prescott, AZ)
1975	BARAGREY, John	57	Cerebral hemorrhage
1975	# BARCLAY, Don	83	Died in Palm Springs, CA
1975	BARHARD, Lawrence "Slim"	71	Apparent heart failure
1975	BELLINI, Laura	73	
1975	#+ BLUE, Ben	73	Died in Los Angeles, CA
1975	# BLYDEN, Larry	49	Automobile accident (while vacationing in Agadir, Morocco)
• 1975	BORZAGE, Daniel "Danny"	78	Died in Los Angeles, CA
1975	# BRENT, Evelyn	75	Heart attack (in Los Angeles, CA)
• 1975	BROKAW, Charles	77	Died in New York City
1975	BROWN, Barbara	68	
1975	BUCHMAN, Sidney	73	Cancer (in Cannes, France)
1975	# CALLEIA, Joseph	78	Died in Malta
1975	#+ CALVIN, Henry	57	

...DEATHS OF MOVIE AND TELEVISION PERSONALITIES — BY YEAR...

YEAR	NAME	AGE	CAUSE AND/OR PLACE OF DEATH
• 1975	# CHEFEE, Jack	81	Died in Hollywood, CA
• 1975	COLMAN, Irene	60	Leukemia (in Santa Monica, CA)
1975	#+ CONTE, Richard	59	Heart attack and stroke (in Los Angeles, CA)
1975	COOPER, Clancy	68	Heart attack while driving his car near his home (in Hollywood, CA)
1975	COURTNEY, Inez	67	Died in Neptune, NJ
1975	CROSBY, Wade	70	After a grand mal seizure aboard a yacht (in Newport Beach, CA)
1975	CROSS, Milton	77	Apparent heart attack (in New York, NY)
1975	#+ DALEY, Cass	59	Neck pierced by glass in a fall at home (in Hollywood, CA)
1975	DELEVANTI, Cyril	88	Lung cancer (in Hollywood, CA)
• 1975	# DEL VAL, Jean	82	Heart attack (in Pacific Palisades, CA)
1975	DIERKES, John	69	Emphysema
1975	#+ DORN, Philip	69	Heart attack (in Woodland Hills, CA)
• 1975	DOYLE, Patricia	60	Cancer (in Los Angeles, CA)
1975	+ DURFEE, Minta (Arbuckle)	85	Congestive heart failure (in Woodland Hills, CA)
1975	#+ FINE, Larry	73	Stroke (in Woodland Hills, CA)
1975	FRECHETTE, Mark	27	Crushed to death by a barbell while in jail
1975	# FRESNAY, Pierre	77	Respiratory ailment (in Neuilly-sur-Seine, France)
1975	#+ FRIZZELL, Lefty	47	After suffering a stroke
1975	GAINES, Richard H.	70	Heart attack (in North Hollywood, CA)
1975	+ GODOWSKY, Dagmar	78	
1975	GRAY, Alexander	73	
1975	# GREEN, Martyn	75	Blood infection (in Hollywood, CA)
1975	GREGSON, John	55	Apparent heart attack on a woodland stroll (in Porlock Weir, Eng.)
1975	# GRIFFIES, Ethel	97	Stroke (in London, England)
1975	GRIFFITH, Edward H.	86	
1975	HANSEN, William	64	After a lengthy illness
• 1975	HARTNELL, William "Billy"	67	Died in London, England
1975	#+ HAYWARD, Susan ★	57	Brain tumor (in Beverly Hills, CA)
1975	HERRMANN, Bernard	64	Heart attack
1975	#+ HOWARD, Moe	77	Cancer (in Hollywood, CA)
1975	HUNTER, Ian	75	Died in England
1975	# JOHNSON, Kay	71	
1975	JUSTICE, James Robertson	70	Found dead in bed (in Winchester, Hampshire, England)
• 1975	KALICH, Jacob	82	Cancer (in Lake Mahopac, NY)
1975	KANE, Joseph	81	Heart attack
1975	KELLERMAN, Annette	87	
1975	LACHMAN, Harry	88	Heart attack
1975	LANDIS, Cullen	77	Died in Bloomfield Hills, MI
1975	LARRIMORE, Francine	77	Pneumonia
1975	LEE, Rowland V.	84	Apparent heart attack (at his home)
1975	# LEE, Ruth	79	After a long illness (in Woodland Hills, CA)
1975	LETTIERI, Al	47	After being hospitalized
1975	LEVEY, Jules	78	Apparent heart attack (on a Manhattan street)
1975	LOHR, Marie	84	Died in London, England
1975	#+ LOPEZ, Vincent	76	Liver and pancreas failure (in Miami Beach, FL)
1975	# LOSCH, Tilly	70	Cancer
• 1975	LUEDERS, Guenther	69	Cancer (in Duesseldorf, Germany)
1975	+ LUNDIGAN, William "Bill"	61	Lung and heart congestion (in Duarte, CA)
1975	#+ MABLEY, Jackie "Moms"	78	Died in White Plains, NY
1975	# MADISON, Noel	77	Died in Fort Lauderdale, FL
1975	#+ MAIN, Marjorie ☆	85	Cancer (in Los Angeles, CA)
1975	#+ MARCH, Fredric ★	77	Cancer (in Los Angeles, CA)
1975	MARK, Michael	85	Heart failure (in Woodland Hills, CA)
1975	MARLOWE, Alan	40	Airplane crash
1975	+ MARSHALL, George E.	84	
• 1975	MASON, Buddy	71	Died in Woodland Hills, CA
• 1975	MATHIESON, Muir	64	Died in Oxford, England
1975	MATTHEWS, Lester	74	
1975	McFARLAND, Nan	58	Cancer
1975	# McGILL, Moyna	80	
1975	# McGIVER, John	61	Heart attack (in West Fulton, NY)
1975	McKINNEY, Florine	62	
1975	# MERANDE, Doro	?	Following a massive stroke (in Miami, FL)
1975	MEYER, Torben	90	Bronchial pneumonia (in Hollywood, CA)
1975	MORGAN, Ray	?	Cancer

...DEATHS OF MOVIE AND TELEVISION PERSONALITIES — BY YEAR...

YEAR	NAME		AGE	CAUSE AND/OR PLACE OF DEATH
• 1975	MORRISON, Chester A.		52	*Died in Portland, OR*
1975	MORTON, Clive		71	*Died in London, England*
1975	MYLONG, John		82	*After a long illness*
1975	#+ NELSON, Ozzie		69	*Cancer (in Hollywood, CA)*
• 1975	# NERVO, Jimmy		85	*Died in London, England*
1975	NIESEN, Gertrude		62	*Died in Kaiser-Permanente Hospital, Glendale, CA*
1975	# OLMSTEAD, Gertrude		70	*Died at her Beverly Hills (Ca.) home*
1975	#+ PARKS, Larry	☆	60	*Heart attack (in Studio City, CA)*
• 1975	PASOLINI, Pier Paolo		53	*Murdered (beaten) near Ostia, Italy*
1975	# PATTERSON, Hank		86	*Bronchial pneumonia (in Woodland Hills, CA)*
• 1975	PEERS, Joan		64	
• 1975	# PENN, Leonard		68	*Heart attack (in Los Angeles, CA)*
1975	PHILIPS, Mary		74	*Cancer (in Santa Monica, CA)*
1975	PIERSON, Arthur		73	*Died at St. John's Hospital in Santa Monica, CA*
1975	PUGLIA, Frank		83	*Died in South Pasadena, CA*
1975	RAY, Jack		58	*Died in Montclair, CA*
• 1975	REYNOLDS, Peter		48	*Died in Australia*
1975	+ ROBERTS, Roy (actor)		69	*Died suddenly in Los Angeles after complaining of back pain*
1975	# ROSS, Shirley		62	*Cancer (at a hospital in Menlo Park, CA)*
1975	# RYAN, Sheila		54	*Lung ailment (in Woodland Hills, CA)*
1975	SCHNEIDER, Stanley		45	*Died in his hotel room*
1975	+ SERLING, Rod		50	*Complications after heart surgery (in Rochester, NY)*
1975	# SHIELDS, Frank		64	
• 1975	+ SHOSTAKOVICH, Dmitri		68	*After a 9-yr. battle with heart disease*
• 1975	# SIMON, Michel		80	*Heart failure (near Paris, France)*
• 1975	SISSLE, Noble		86	*Died in Tampa, FL*
1975	SLATER, John		58	*Heart attack (in London, England)*
1975	SOUSSANIN, Nicholas		66	*Cardiac arrest (in New York, NY)*
1975	+ STEVENS, George Sr.	★	70	*Heart attack (in Lancaster, CA)*
1975	STRAUSS, Robert	☆	61	*Complications following a stroke (in New York, NY)*
1975	# SULLY, Frank		67	*Died in Woodland Hills, CA*
1975	# TETLEY, Walter		60	
1975	# THIELE, William J.		85	*Died at the Motion Picture Country Home, CA*
1975	# TREACHER, Arthur		81	*Heart ailment (in Manhasset, NY)*
1975	+ TROTTER, John Scott		67	*Cancer*
1975	+ TUCKER, Richard (singer)		60	*Heart attack (Do not confuse with actor, d. 1942)*
1975	URE, Mary	☆	42	*Accidental mix of alcohol and tranquilizers (in London, England)*
1975	VERNO, Jerry		79	
• 1975	WAGNER, Max		73	*Heart attack (in West Los Angeles, CA)*
1975	WALKER, Lillian "Dimples"		87	*Died in Trinidad, West Indies (where she had a home)*
1975	WALKER, Walter "Wally"		74	*Stroke*
1975	WARDE, Anthony		66	*Died in Hollywood, CA*
1975	WATTIS, Richard		62	*Heart attack (in London, England)*
1975	WEED, Leland T.		74	*Stroke (in Prescott, Arizona)*
1975	#+ WELLMAN, William A.	☆	79	*Leukemia*
1975	# WEST, Billy		82	*Heart attack (leaving Hollywood Park racetrack, CA)*
1975	WHIPPER, Leigh		97	
1975	WILLS, Bob		70	*Bronchial pneumonia (in Ft. Worth, TX)*
1975	# ZIMBALIST, Al		59	*Heart attack*
1976	ALLYN, Alyce		?	*While hospitalized (in Santa Monica, CA)*
1976	ANDERSON, Warner		65	
1976	#+ ARLEN, Richard		75	*Emphysema*
1976	# BADDELEY, Angela		71	*Flu and bronchitis (in London, England)*
1976	BAKER, Stanley		48	*Complications after a lung cancer operation (in Malaga, Spain)*
1976	BALLARD, Flo		33	*Cardiac arrest from pills and alcohol (in Detroit, MI)*
1976	BAXTER, Alan		67	*Cancer (in Woodland Hills, CA)*
1976	#+ BERKELEY, Busby		80	
1976	+ BOSWELL, Connee		68	*Stomach cancer (in New York, NY)*
1976	# BRENT, Romney		74	
1976	BROWNE, Lucile		69	
1976	BRUCE, David		60	*Heart attack (in Hollywood, CA)*
1976	BURTON, Martin		71	*After a lengthy illness*
1976	+ CAMBRIDGE, Godfrey		43	*Heart attack (in Burbank, CA)*
1976	#+ CASSIDY, Jack		49	*Burned to death (in West Hollywood, CA)*

• New entry.　# Original name (Pt. 7).　+ Interment (Pt. 5).　　63　　☆ Oscar nominee,　★ Oscar winner (Pt. 10)

...DEATHS OF MOVIE AND TELEVISION PERSONALITIES — BY YEAR...

YEAR		NAME		AGE	CAUSE AND/OR PLACE OF DEATH
•	1976	CAVENDISH, June		?	Leukemia (in Los Angeles, CA)
	1976	#+ COBB, Lee J.	☆	64	Heart attack (in Woodland Hills, CA)
	1976	COOPER, Miriam		83	Stroke
	1976	# CORRIGAN, Ray "Crash"		74	Heart attack (in Brookings Harbor, OR)
	1976	COUGHLIN, Kevin		29	Hit-and-run accident while cleaning his car windshield (in L.A., CA)
•	1976	CURZON, George		79	Died in London, England
	1976	# DARRO, Frankie		58	Heart attack (in Huntington Beach, CA)
	1976	DAVIES, Rupert		60	Cancer (in London, England)
	1976	# DEVORE, Dorothy		77	Died in Woodland Hills, CA
•	1976	DEWITT, Alan "Boomie"		52	Heart attack (in Los Angeles, CA)
	1976	# DOWLING, Eddie		81	Died in Smithfield, RI
	1976	DUNN, Liam		59	Emphysema and other medical complications
	1976	EVANS, Edith	☆	88	After a brief illness (in Cranbrook, Kent, England)
	1976	+ FAITH, Percy		67	Cancer
	1976	FIELD, Walter		100	Died in Hollywood, CA
	1976	# FITZGERALD, Walter		80	Died in London, England
	1976	FLAVIN, James		69	Ruptured aorta (in Los Angeles, CA)
	1976	#+ FORD, Paul		74	Died in Mineola, NY
	1976	# FOSTER, Norman		76	Cancer (in Santa Monica, CA)
	1976	FRANKLIN, Alberta		79	
	1976	# GABIN, Jean		72	Heart attack (in Neuilly, France)
	1976	#+ GOLDWYN, Frances Howard		73	(See Frances Howard)
	1976	GOODLIFFE, Michael		61	Suicide leap while in a hospital (in London, England)
•	1976	GWYNN, Michael		59	Heart attack (in London, England)
	1976	# HACKETT, Bobby		61	
	1976	#+ HALOP, Billy		56	Died in Brentwood, CA
	1976	HENABERY, Joseph E.		88	
•	1976	# HILDEBRAND, Hilde		78	
	1976	HOWARD, Frances		73	After a lengthy illness
•	1976	#+ HOWE, James Wong		76	Cancer
	1976	+ HUGHES, Howard		70	Stroke (on a chartered airplane from Acapulco to Texas)
	1976	HUTCHESON, David		71	
	1976	# INESCORT, Frieda		74	Multiple sclerosis (in Woodland Hills, CA)
	1976	JAMES, Sidney "Sid"		62	Died in Sunderland, England
	1976	JONES, Anissa "Buffy"		18	Lethal mix of Quaaludes and alcohol (in Oceanside, CA)
	1976	KELLOGG, Ray		70	Cancer
	1976	# KNIGHT, Fuzzy		74	Died in Hollywood, CA
	1976	+ KUHLMAN, Kathryn		63	Pulmonary hypertension after open-heart surgery
	1976	+ LANG, Fritz		85	
	1976	LEDERER, Charles		65	After a long illness (at UCLA Med. Ctr., CA)
	1976	LEIBERT, Richard "Dick"		73	
	1976	LEIGHTON, Margaret	☆	53	Multiple sclerosis (in Chichester, England)
	1976	LERNER, Irving		67	Heart attack
•	1976	LESLIE, Gladys		77	Died in Boynton Beach, FL
	1976	LIVESEY, Roger		69	Died in Watford, England
	1976	# LOWRY, Judith		86	Apparent heart attack (in New York, NY)
	1976	MACK, Ted		71	
	1976	MADDEN, Peter		71	
	1976	MANNHEIM, Lucie		81	Died in Braunlage, West Germany
•	1976	MARTEL, Alphonse		85	
	1976	MARTINI, Nino		72	Heart attack
	1976	MASON, Sydney		70	Heart attack (in Los Angeles, CA)
	1976	McBRIDE, Mary Margaret		77	
•	1976	McCALLUM, Neil		45	Brain hemorrhage (in Reading, England)
	1976	# McDEVITT, Ruth		80	Died in Hollywood, CA
	1976	#+ MERCER, Johnny		66	After surgery for a brain tumor (in Bel Air, CA)
•	1976	MERLO, Anthony "Tony"		88	Died in Woodland Hills, CA
	1976	# MERVYN, William		64	Died in London, England
•	1976	MILLER, Ruby		86	Died in Chichester, England
	1976	#+ MINEO, Sal	☆	37	Murdered (stabbed to death) in West Hollywood, CA
	1976	# NASH, Mary		91	Died in Brentwood, CA
•	1976	NAUGHTON, Charlie		88	Died in London, England
	1976	# NICHOLS, Barbara		47	Liver ailment
	1976	O'MALLEY, Rex		75	Died at the Mary Manning Walsh Home, NY
	1976	+ PIATIGORSKY, Gregor		73	

• New entry. # Original name (Pt. 7). + Interment (Pt. 5).   64   ☆ Oscar nominee, ★ Oscar winner (Pt. 10)

	YEAR	NAME		AGE	CAUSE AND/OR PLACE OF DEATH
•	1976	PISU, Mario		66	Cerebral hemorrhage (in Castelli Romani, Italy)
•	1976	POLANSKI, Goury		83	Cancer (in Hollywood, CA)
	1976	# PONS, Lily		77	Cancer (in Dallas, TX)
•	1976	PRICKETT, Maudie		60	Uremic poisoning (in Pasadena, CA)
•	1976	RADD, Ronald		47	Brain hemorrhage (in Toronto, Canada)
•	1976	# RAEBURN, Frances		?	Heart failure (in CA)
•	1976	# RAMSEY-HILL, C. S.		84	Died in Van Nuys, CA
•	1976	# RASP, Fritz		85	Died in Graefelfing, Germany
	1976	REDFIELD, William "Billy"		49	Respiratory ailment complicated by leukemia (in New York, NY)
	1976	REED, Carol	★	69	Heart attack (Do not confuse with Carol Reed, d. 1970)
•	1976	RICCI, Nora		50	Liver ailment (in Rome, Italy)
•	1976	RICHTER, Hans		87	Died in Locarno, Switzerland
	1976	RIVERO, Julian		84	Died in Hollywood, CA
	1976	#+ ROBESON, Paul		77	Cerebral vascular disorder (stroke) in Philadelphia, PA
	1976	#+ ROSENBLOOM, "Slapsie" Maxie		71	Paget's disease (in South Pasadena, CA)
	1976	# ROSS, Lenny		71	Cancer
•	1976	# ROTH, Gene		73	Struck by a car (in Los Angeles, CA)
•	1976	RUSKIN, Shimen		69	Cancer (in Los Angeles, CA)
	1976	+ RUSSELL, Rosalind (Brisson)	☆	65	Cancer complicated by arthritis (in Beverly Hills, CA)
	1976	SCOTT, Mabel Julienne		82	Died at the Burlington Convalescent Hospital in Los Angeles, CA
•	1976	SERVAIS, Jean		65	Heart failure following surgery (in Paris, France)
	1976	SHELTON, Don		64	Died in Los Angeles, CA
	1976	SHUTTA, Ethel		79	Died at St. Clare's Hospital in New York
	1976	SIEBER, Rudolf		77	Following a long illness
•	1976	SILVA, David		58	Thrombosis (in Mexico City, Mexico)
	1976	SILVERS, Sid		72	
	1976	SIM, Alastair		75	Cancer (in London, England)
•	1976	# SKELTON, Georgia		54	Suicide (gunshot) in Rancho Mirage, CA
•	1976	# STUEWE, Hans		75	Died in Berlin, Germany
•	1976	# SUNBEAUTY, Olga		78	
	1976	TANNEN, William		65	Died in Woodland Hills, CA
	1976	TEAL, Ray		74	After a long illness (in Santa Monica, CA)
•	1976	THOR, Larry		58	Heart attack (in Santa Monica, CA)
	1976	THORNDIKE, Sybil		93	Heart attack (in London, England)
	1976	# VARCONI, Victor		85	Heart attack (in Santa Barbara, CA)
•	1976	# VESOTA, Bruno		54	Heart attack (in Culver City, CA)
	1976	VISCONTI, Luchino		69	Influenza/cardiac ailment
	1976	# VYE, Murvyn		62	Natural causes (while vacationing in Pompano Beach, FL)
	1976	WELCH, Niles		81	Died in Laguna Nigel, CA
	1976	ZUKOR, Adolph		103	
•	1977	ABBOTT, Merriel		84	Died in Chicago, IL
	1977	ADAMS, Stanley		62	Suicide (gunshot) in Santa Monica, CA
	1977	ADDINSELL, Richard		73	Died in London, England
	1977	+ ANDERSON, Eddie "Rochester"		71	Heart attack
	1977	# ASHLEY, Sylvia		73	Cancer
	1977	ASTOR, Gertrude		90	Stroke
	1977	BALDWIN, Walter		89	Pneumonia (in Santa Monica, CA)
	1977	BARDETTE, Trevor		75	
	1977	# BARNETT, Vince		75	Heart ailment (in Encino, CA)
	1977	BARRETT, Edith		64	Heart attack at a nursing home (in Albuquerque, N.M.)
	1977	BIBERMAN, Abner		68	Died in San Diego, CA
	1977	# BOLES, Jim		63	Apparent heart attack (in Sherman Oaks, CA)
	1977	BOUCHEY, Willis "Bill"		82	Died in Burbank, CA
	1977	#+ BOYD, Stephen		48	Heart attack (in Northridge, CA)
•	1977	BREEDEN, John Norton		73	Died in San Francisco, CA
•	1977	BRENNEN, Claire		43	Cancer (in Hollywood, CA)
	1977	# BROOKS, Geraldine		52	Cancer (in Riverhead, NY)
	1977	+ CABOT, Sebastian		59	Stroke (in Victoria, B.C., Canada)
	1977	#+ CALLAS, Maria		53	Heart attack
	1977	+ CARLSON, Richard		65	Cerebral hemorrhage (in Encino, CA)
	1977	CARSON, Charles		91	
•	1977	# CASTLE, William		63	Heart attack (in Los Angeles, CA)
	1977	#+ CHAPLIN, Charlie	☆	88	Blood clot (in Corsiersur-vevey, Switzerland)
	1977	CHAPMAN, Edward		76	Heart attack (in Brighton, England)

YEAR	NAME	AGE	CAUSE AND/OR PLACE OF DEATH
1977	CHITTY, Erik	70	
1977	CLOUZOT, Henri Charles	70	
1977	CONDON, Jackie	59	Cancer (in Inglewood, CA)
1977	# CORTEZ, Ricardo	77	Died in New York, NY
1977	#+ CRAWFORD, Joan ★	71	Cancer and acute coronary occlusion (in New York, NY)
1977	#+ CROSBY, Bing ★	73	Heart attack (in Madrid, Spain)
1977	DAVENPORT, Dorothy	81	Died in Woodland Hills, CA
1977	#+ DAVES, Delmar	73	
1977	DECKERS, Eugene	60	
1977	DeHAVEN, Carter Sr.	90	Died in Woodland Hills, CA
1977	DELL, Claudia	67	Died in Hollywood, CA
1977	#+ DEVINE, Andy	71	Leukemia (in Orange, CA)
1977	DUGGAN, Jan	?	Died in Los Angeles, CA
1977	FERGUSON, Helen	76	Died in Clearwater, FL
1977	#+ FINCH, Peter ★	60	Heart attack (in Beverly Hills, CA)
1977	#+ FORD, Mary	52	Complications of diabetes and pneumonia (in Arcadia, CA)
1977	+ FOY, Bryon	82	Following a series of heart attacks
1977	# FRANCEN, Victor	89	Died in Aix-en-Provence, France
1977	FREND, Charles	68	
1977	GARBER, Jan	82	Died in Shreveport, LA
1977	GARDNER, Jack	77	After a short illness
1977	GARNER, Erroll	53	
1977	GARNETT, Tay	83	Leukemia
1977	GATESON, Marjorie	86	Pneumonia (in New York, NY)
1977	GERING, Marion	73	
1977	# GIBSON, Helen	85	Stroke and heart attack (in Roseburg, OR)
1977	GRAVES, Ralph	77	Heart attack (in Santa Barbara, CA)
1977	GRIES, Tom	54	Heart attack
1977	# HAGEN, Jean ☆	54	Cancer (in Woodland Hills, CA)
1977	+ HAWKS, Howard ☆	81	Died in his sleep following a fall and concussion
1977	# HAYES, Allison	47	Blood poisoning (in La Jolla, CA)
1977	# HAYES, Margaret	61	Cancer complicated by hepatitis (in Miami Beach, FL)
1977	HULL, Henry	86	Died in Cornwall, England
1977	HYAMS, Leila	72	
1977	HYLAND, Diana	41	Cancer
1977	+ JOHNSON, Nunnally	80	
1977	LEWIS, Forrest	77	Heart attack (in Burbank, CA)
1977	LOCHARY, David	30	Drug overdose
1977	#+ LOMBARDO, Guy	75	Respiratory, kidney and heart failure (in Houston, TX)
1977	+ LUNT, Alfred ☆	84	Cancer (in Chicago, IL)
1977	MANN, George Kline	72	Cancer
1977	MARLOWE, Nora	?	After a long illness (in Los Angeles, CA)
1977	MARMONT, Percy	93	Died in Denville Hall, England
1977	#+ MARX, "Groucho"	86	Pneumonia (in West Hollywood, CA)
1977	#+ MARX, "Gummo"	79	Lung cancer
1977	+ MATTHEWS, Dorothy	54	Stroke
1977	McGANN, William H.	84	Died in his sleep
1977	McGINN, Walter	38	After his car crashed into a parked truck (in Los Angeles, CA)
1977	# McGOWAN, J. P. "Jack"	81	(Screenplay writer)
1977	MELL, Joseph "Joe"	62	Heart condition (in Los Angeles, CA)
1977	MERRITT, George	86	Died in London, England
1977	# MIDDLETON, Robert	66	Heart failure
1977	MOORE, Carlyle Jr.	67	Died in Sun Valley, ID
1977	# MOSTEL, Zero	62	Cardiac disorder (in Philadelphia, PA)
1977	+ MUSTIN, Burt	94	Died in Glendale, CA
1977	NICHOLLS, Anthony	69	Died in London, England
1977	PELT, Timothy "Tim"	39	Automobile accident (in Pacific Palisades, CA)
1977	PERKINS, Voltaire	80	Apparent heart attack (in Los Angeles, CA)
1977	# PETROVA, Olga	91	Died in Clearwater, FL
1977	# POTTER, H. C.	73	After a brief illness (in New York, NY)
1977	#+ PRESLEY, Elvis	42	Cardiac arrhythmia (possibly due to drug abuse) in Memphis, TN
1977	# PRINTEMPS, Yvonne	81	Died in Paris, France
1977	#+ PRINZE, Freddie	22	Suicide (gunshot) in Los Angeles, CA
1977	RATTIGAN, Terence	66	Bone marrow cancer
1977	# RAY, Ted	67	Died in London, England

YEAR		NAME		AGE	CAUSE AND/OR PLACE OF DEATH
	1977	#	REED, Alan	69	After a long illness (in St. Vincent's hosp., West Los Angeles, CA)
•	1977		RISSONI, Giuditta	80	Died in Rome, Italy
	1977	#+	RITCHARD, Cyril	80	Cardiac arrest (in Chicago, IL)
•	1977		RIVERS, Victor	29	Injuries from performing a stunt (in Los Angeles, CA)
	1977		ROSSELLINI, Roberto	71	
•	1977		SHINDO, Eitaro	78	Heart failure (in Tokyo, Japan)
•	1977	#	STARK, Pauline	76	Died in Santa Monica, CA
	1977	#	STEVENS, Onslow	74	Murdered (while in a convalescent home) in Van Nuys, CA
•	1977		STEWART, Sophie	69	Died in London, England
	1977	#+	STOKOWSKI, Leopold	95	Coronary attack (in Nether Wallop, Hampshire, England)
•	1977		TANAKA, Kinuyo	67	Cerebral tumor
	1977		TETZEL, Joan	56	Cancer
	1977		THURSBY, David	88	Died in Hollywood, CA
	1977		TOURNEUR, Jacques	73	
	1977		TRUMAN, Ralph	77	Died in Ipswich, England
•	1977		VALLIN, Richard "Rick"	57	
	1977		VanSICKEL, Dale	69	After a lengthy illness (at his home in Newport Beach, CA)
	1977		VanZANT, Ronnie	28	
	1977	#	VIDOR, Florence	82	Died in Pacific Palisades, CA
	1977	+	WALLER, Eddy C.	88	Stroke (in Los Angeles, CA)
	1977	+	WATERS, Ethel ☆	80	Heart ailment (in Chatsworth, CA)
	1977		WILCOX, Herbert	85	Following a long illness
	1978	+	ACKER, Jean (Valentino)	85	Died in Los Angeles, CA
	1978		ADAMS, Claire	78	Died in Melbourne, Australia
	1978		ADLER, Jay	82	After a long illness (in Woodland Hills, CA)
	1978		AHN, Philip	66	Lung cancer (in Los Angeles, CA)
	1978	+	ALLWYN, Astrid	68	Cancer (in Los Angeles, CA)
•	1978		BACCHIOCCHI, Norman	34	
	1978		BAILEY, Bill	66	(Do not confuse with any of the 3 William Bailey's)
	1978		BARCENA, Catalina	82	Died in Spain
	1978	#+	BARRIE, Wendy	65	After a long illness (in Englewood, N.J.)
•	1978		BATES, Michael	57	Cancer (in London, England)
	1978	#+	BERGEN, Edgar	75	Heart attack (in Las Vegas, NV)
	1978		BETZ, Carl	56	Lung cancer (in Los Angeles, CA)
	1978		BINYON, Claude	72	
	1978	#	BLAKE, Marie	81	
•	1978		BOHN, Merritt F.	73	Pneumonia following a stroke (in Torrence, CA)
•	1978		BOND, Johnny	63	Died in Burbank, CA
	1978		BONOMO, Joe	75	Kidney ailment and pneumonia (in Hollywood, CA)
•	1978		BOURBON, Diana	77	Cancer (in Los Angeles, CA)
	1978	+	BOYER, Charles ☆	78	Suicide (overdose of Seconal) 2 days after his wife died (in AZ)
	1978		BROWN, Barry	27	Suicide at home (self-inflicted wounds)
•	1978		BRYANT, Marie	58	Cancer (in Los Angeles, CA)
	1978	#	BUSHMAN, Ralph	74	Respiratory failure (in Los Angeles, CA)
	1978	+	CARTER, Maybelle	69	
	1978		CAZALE, John	42	Cancer (in New York, NY)
	1978		CHASE, Ilka	72	Internal hemorrhage from a fall (in Mexico City, Mexico)
•	1978		CLARK, Roger W.	69	Stroke (in Los Angeles, CA)
	1978		COMPTON, Fay	84	Died in England
	1978		COOGAN, Robert	53	
	1978	+	CRANE, Bob	48	Murdered (skull crushed by a blow while sleeping) in Scottsdale, AZ
	1978	+	DAILEY, Dan ☆	62	Anemia (in Hollywood, CA)
	1978		DALY, James	59	Heart attack (in Nyack, NY) — Do not confuse with James L. Daly
	1978	#	DAUPHIN, Claude	75	Intestinal occlusion
	1978	#	DAVID, Thayer	51	Heart attack (in New York, NY)
	1978		DAY, Josette	63	
	1978		DOUGLAS, Tom	82	Heart attack (in Cuernavaca, Mexico)
	1978		DOWNS, Cathy	52	
	1978		DRURY, Norma	?	
	1978	#+	EILERS, Sally	69	Heart attack (in Woodland Hills, CA)
	1978	+	ETTING, Ruth	81	Died in Colorado Springs, CO
	1978	#	FENTON, Leslie C.	76	Died in Montecito, CA
	1978		FERGUSON, Frank	78	Cancer (in Los Angeles, CA)
	1978	#+	FIELDS, Totie	48	Apparent heart failure

YEAR	NAME		AGE	CAUSE AND/OR PLACE OF DEATH
1978	+ FONTAINE, Frank		58	Heart attack
• 1978	GAGE, Ben		62	Died in Los Angeles, CA
1978	GARMES, Lee	★	80	
1978	#+ GEER, Will		76	Respiratory arrest (in Los Angeles, CA)
1978	+ GELLER, Bruce		47	Airplane crash
1978	GENN, Leo	☆	72	Died in London, England
1978	GILBERT, Lou		69	Apparent heart attack
1978	GIRDLER, William		30	Helicopter crash (in the Philippines)
1978	GIVNEY, Kathryn		80	
1978	GRAVERS, Steve		56	Lung cancer
1978	GREENE, Angela		55	Stroke (in Los Angeles, CA)
1978	# GREENWOOD, Charlotte		84	Died in Beverly Hills, CA
• 1978	# HANDWORTH, Octavia		90	Died in Hemet, CA
1978	HARRINGTON, Kate		74	Following a stroke
1978	# HASSE, O. E.		75	Died in a hospital (in West Berlin, Germany)
• 1978	HENDERSON, Douglas "Doug"		58	Suicide (carbon monoxide) in Studio City, CA
1978	HOMOLKA, Oscar	☆	79	Died in Sussex, England
1978	# HORVATH, Charles		57	Died in Woodland Hills, CA
• 1978	HULBERT, Jack		69	Died in London, England
1978	JOLLEY, L. Stanford		78	Died in Woodland Hills, CA
1978	L'HERBIER, Marcel		91	
• 1978	# LINGEN, Theo		75	
1978	# LOCKHART, Kathleen		83	Died in Los Angeles, CA
1978	MacDONALD, Wallace		87	Died in Santa Barbara, CA
• 1978	MALONEY, James J. "Jim"		63	
1978	MARDEN, Adrienne		69	Massive heart attack (in Los Angeles, CA)
1978	# MARLY, Florence		59	Heart attack (in Glendale, CA)
1978	MATRAY, Ernst		87	Heart attack (in Los Angeles, CA)
1978	#+ McCOY, Tim		86	Died in Huachuca, AZ
1978	McGRATH, Paul		74	Died in his sleep (in London, England)
1978	McGUIRE, Kathryn		73	Pancreatic cancer (in Los Angeles, CA)
• 1978	McKINNEY, Mira		?	
• 1978	McLAGLEN, Clifford		86	Died in Huddersfield, Yorkshire, England
1978	McNAMARA, Maggie		48	Overdose of pills
• 1978	# MILLER, Lorraine		49	
1978	MONTGOMERY, Goodee		72	After a brief illness (in Hollywood, CA)
1978	MOON, Keith		31	Found dead from an overdose of heminevrin (in London, England)
1978	# MORELL, André		69	Died in London, England
1978	Morris (the original TV cat)		17	
1978	MORRISON, Ann		62	After a lengthy illness
1978	MURPHY, Maurice		65	Died in Los Angeles, CA
1978	MYRTILE, Odette		80	Stroke (in a hospital in Doylestown, PA)
1978	# NEWMAN, Scott		28	Apparent accidental overdose of Valium and alcohol
• 1978	NOBLE, Ray		70	Cancer (in London, England)
1978	#+ OAKIE, Jack	☆	74	Aortic aneurysm (in Northridge, CA)
1978	+ PATERSON, Pat		67	Cancer (in Phoenix, AZ)
1978	+ PERFECT, Rose		82	
1978	# PHIPPS, Sally		67	Died at Long Island College Hospital, NY
• 1978	PICKLES, Wilfrid		73	Died in Brighton, England
• 1978	# POLLARD, Daphne		87	Died in Los Angeles, CA
• 1978	PORTER, Dick		45	Heart attack (in Sedalia, MO)
• 1978	PRETTY, Arline		84	Died in Hollywood, CA
1978	+ PRIMA, Louis		66	Pneumonia (in New Orleans, LA)
1978	RICHARDS, Cully		68	Cancer (in Los Angeles, CA)
1978	ROBERTS, Lenore		47	Cancer (in Los Angeles, CA)
1978	#+ ROBERTS, Lynne (Mary Hart)		58	An intracranial hemorrhage
1978	ROBSON, Mark		64	Heart attack
• 1978	SANO, Shuji		66	
• 1978	SCHOENHALS, Albrecht		90	Died in Baden-Baden, West Germany
1978	SHAW, Robert	☆	53	Heart attack (near Tourmakeady, Ireland)
• 1978	# SHAW, Susan		49	Died in Middlesex, England
1978	#+ SHAY, Dorothy		57	Following a massive stroke (in Santa Monica, CA)
1978	SHOEMAKER, Ann		87	Cancer (in Los Angeles, CA)
1978	SMITH, Queenie		70	Cancer (in Burbank, CA)
• 1978	# STANTON, Harry		76	Heart disease (in Los Angeles, CA)

YEAR	NAME		AGE	CAUSE AND/OR PLACE OF DEATH
1978	# STUART, John		81	*Died in London, England*
1978	SWENSON, Karl		70	*Apparent heart attack (while visiting relatives in Torrington, CT)*
1978	THORDSEN, Kelly		61	*Cancer*
• 1978	TOZZI, Fausto		57	*Emphysema (in Rome, Italy)*
1978	# TREVOR, Austin		80	*Died in London, England*
• 1978	# TUNNEY, Gene		80	*Blood poisoning (in Greenwich, CT)*
1978	UNSWORTH, Geoffrey	★	64	*Heart attack*
1978	VENUTI, Joe		81	*Died in Seattle, WA*
1978	# WALLACE, Regina		86	*Stroke (in Englewood, N.J.)*
1978	WARNER, Jack L.		86	
1978	WILLS, Chill	☆	75	*Died in Encino, CA*
• 1978	WONG, Joe		75	*Heart condition*
• 1978	#+ WOOD, Ed		54	*Heart attack brought on by acute alcoholism*
1978	WOOD, Peggy	☆	86	*Died in Stamford, CT*
1978	#+ YOUNG, Gig	★	64	*Suicide (gunshot) after shooting his 5th wife (in New York, NY)*
1979	ADAM, Ronald		83	*Died in London, England*
• 1979	# ADLER, Celia		88	*Died in The Bronx, NY*
1979	ALLBRITTON, Louise		58	*Cancer*
1979	ARVAN, Jan		66	*Heart attack*
1979	ARZNER, Dorothy		82	
1979	# AYLMER, Felix		90	*Died in a nursing home in England*
1979	# BLETCHER, Billy		84	*After a long illness*
1979	#+ BLONDELL, Joan	☆	73	*Leukemia (in Santa Monica, CA)*
1979	BOURNEUF, Philip		71	*Found dead in his Santa Monica apartment*
1979	BOWMAN, Lee		64	*Heart attack (in Brentwood, CA)*
1979	# BRENT, George		75	*Natural causes (in Solana Beach, CA)*
1979	#+ BUCHANAN, Edgar		76	*Died in Palm Desert, CA*
1979	# BUTLER, David		84	*Ruptured diverticulum, peritonitis and heart failure (in Arcadia, CA)*
1979	BUTTERWORTH, Peter		60	*Heart attack (in Coventry, England)*
1979	CARLETON, Claire		66	*Cancer (in Northridge, CA)*
• 1979	# CARR, Joe "Fingers"		69	*Automobile accident (in Camarillo, CA)*
1979	+ CARROLL, John		71	*Leukemia (in Hollywood, CA)*
1979	CARSON, Robert		69	*Stroke (in Atascadero, CA)*
1979	+ CASSIDY, Ted "Lurch"		46	*During heart surgery (in Los Angeles, CA)*
1979	CHANDLER, Joan		55	
• 1979	CHARLES, Lewis		63	*Cancer (in Los Angeles, CA)*
1979	COSTELLO, Delores		73	*Died in Fallbrook, CA*
1979	CRAIG, Edith		71	*After a long illness (Do not confuse with the English actress)*
• 1979	# CROCKETT, Dick		63	*Cancer (in Los Angeles, CA)*
1979	# CROMWELL, John		91	*Pulmonary embolism (in Santa Barbara, CA)*
• 1979	DAVIS, Karl "Killer"		72	*Died in Chicago, IL*
1979	DeHAVEN, Carter Jr.		68	*After a brief illness (in Encino, CA)*
1979	DIGNAM, Basil		74	*Died in England*
• 1979	DIONNE, Oliva		71	*Died in North Bay, Ontario, Canada*
1979	#+ DVORAK, Ann		67	*Died in Honolulu, Hawaii*
1979	EBERLE, Ray		60	*Heart attack*
1979	+ FIEDLER, Arthur		84	*Heart failure*
1979	# FIELDS, Gracie		81	*After a hospital stay for bronchial pneumonia (in Capri, Italy)*
1979	#+ FLATT, Lester		64	*Heart attack (in Nashville, TN)*
1979	FLEISCHER, Dave		84	*Stroke (in Woodland Hills, CA)*
1979	# FORAN, Dick		69	*Died in Panorama City, CA*
1979	GALENTO, Tony "Twoton"		69	*Heart attack*
1979	GARGAN, William	☆	73	*Heart attack (in San Diego, CA)*
1979	GILBERT, Jody		62	*Following an automobile accident (in Sherman Oaks, CA)*
1979	GRAHAM, Fred		61	*Died in Scottsdale, AZ*
1979	# GRENFELL, Joyce		69	*Cancer (in London, England)*
1979	# GRIFFITH, Corinne		84	*Cardiac arrest (in Santa Monica, CA)*
1979	#+ HALEY, Jack		80	*Heart attack (in Los Angeles, CA)*
1979	#+ HALL, Jon		64	*Suicide after bladder cancer surgery (gunshot) in Sherman Oaks, CA*
1979	HARE, J. Robertson		87	*Died in London, England*
1979	+ HEISLER, Stuart R.		82	
1979	# Hilo Hattie		78	*Cancer following a stroke (in Honolulu, Hawaii)*
1979	HOCH, Winton C.		73	*Effects of a stroke*
1979	HODGE, Al		66	*Heart failure from chronic bronchitis and emphysema*

YEAR	NAME		AGE	CAUSE AND/OR PLACE OF DEATH
1979	#+ HOOD, Darla		47	Died in North Hollywood, CA
1979	HUNNICUTT, Arthur	☆	68	Cancer (in Woodland Hills, CA)
1979	#+ HUTTON, Jim		45	Cancer of the liver (in Los Angeles, CA)
1979	# JASON, Leigh		74	After a long illness
1979	# JENNINGS, Claudia		29	Head-on collision with a truck (on Pacific Coast Hwy, CA)
1979	KADAR, Jan		61	After being hospitalized (in Los Angeles, CA)
1979	KARNES, Robert		62	Heart failure (in Sherman Oaks, CA)
1979	# KASZNAR, Kurt		65	Cancer (in Santa Monica, CA)
1979	+ KELLY, Emmett		80	Heart attack
1979	#+ KENTON, Stan		66	Stroke
1979	KENYON, Doris		81	Died in Beverly Hills, CA
1979	+ KILIAN, Victor		81	Killed by burglars (in his Hollywood apartment)
• 1979	LACEY, Catherine		75	Died in London, England
1979	LAEMMLE, Carl Jr.		71	Stroke (after a 16-yr. battle with multiple sclerosis)
• 1979	LaPLANCHE, Rosemary		54	Died in Glendale, CA
1979	LEHMANN, Beatrix		76	
• 1979	# LEONETTI, Tommy		50	Cancer (in Houston, TX)
1979	+ LYON, Ben		78	Heart attack (aboard a ship in the Pacific Ocean)
• 1979	MANNI, Ettore		52	Accidental gun shot (in Rome, Italy)
• 1979	MARQUET, Mary		84	Results of a fall (in Paris, France)
1979	#+ MARX, "Zeppo"		78	Cancer (in Palm Springs, CA)
1979	#+ MASON, Shirley (Lanfield)		78	Cancer (in Los Angeles, CA)
1979	MAUDE, Margery		90	
• 1979	McCONNELL, Gladys		71	
• 1979	# MILLER, Carl		85	Died in Honolulu, Hawaii
1979	MITCHELL, Belle		90	After a long illness (in Woodland Hills, CA)
1979	MITCHELL, Yvonne		53	Cancer
1979	MULHALL, Jack		87	Congestive heart failure (in Woodland Hills, CA)
• 1979	MULLEN, Barbara		64	Heart attack (in London, England)
• 1979	# MURRAY, Bobby		80	Died in Nashua, NH
1979	MUSE, Clarence		90	Cerebral hemorrhage (in Perris, CA)
1979	NASH, June		68	Died in Hampton Bays, L.I., NY
• 1979	# NAZZARI, Amedeo		71	Cardiac arrest (in Rome, Italy)
1979	NELSON, Billy		75	Following a heart attack
1979	NOVAES, Guiomar		84	
1979	#+ OBERON, Merle	☆	68	Stroke (in Los Angeles, CA)
1979	O'BRIEN-MOORE, Erin		77	Cancer (in Los Angeles, CA)
• 1979	+ O'HARA, Barry J.		53	
1979	# O'HARA, Shirley		68	Cancer
1979	ORCHARD, Julian		49	Died in London, England
1979	PARNELL, Emory		85	Heart attack (in Woodland Hills, CA)
• 1979	PETERSON, Dorothy		?	
1979	#+ PICKFORD, Mary	★	86	Cerebral hemorrhage (in Santa Monica, CA)
• 1979	PIOUS, Minerva		75	
1979	PIPER, Frederick		77	
1979	# POHLMANN, Eric		66	
1979	PREJEAN, Albert		85	Died in Paris, France
• 1979	PRENTISS, Eleanor		67	Died in New York, NY
1979	RAINE, Jack		82	Died in South Laguna, CA
1979	#+ RAND, Sally		75	Heart failure (in Glendora, CA)
1979	# RAY, Nicholas		67	Lung cancer (in New York, NY)
1979	RENOIR, Jean	☆	84	Parkinson's disease (in Beverly Hills, CA)
1979	RHODES, Marjorie		76	Died in Hove, Sussex, England
• 1979	+ RIPPERTON, Minnie		31	Cancer
1979	+ RODGERS, Richard		77	
• 1979	ROONEY, Pat, III		70	Died in Lake Blaisdell, NH
1979	ROSE, Jane		66	Cancer
1979	ROTA, Nino		68	Blood clot
1979	SAVILLE, Victor		82	Died in London, England
1979	SEATON, George	☆	68	Cancer
1979	#+ SEBERG, Jean		40	Suicide (drug overdose) found dead in her car in Paris, France
1979	SHEAR, Barry		?	Cancer
1979	+ SHEEN, (Bishop) Fulton J.		84	Heart trouble (in New York, NY)
1979	SHUMLIN, Herman E.		80	Heart failure complicated by emphysema
1979	SKINNER, Cornelia Otis		78	Cerebral hemorrhage (in New York, NY)

YEAR	NAME		AGE	CAUSE AND/OR PLACE OF DEATH
1979	SMITH, Pete	★	86	Suicide (jumped from the roof of a nursing home) in Santa Monica
1979	#+ SOO, Jack		63	Cancer of the esophagus (in Los Angeles, CA)
• 1979	STANDING, Joan		75	Cancer (in Houston, TX)
1979	SUMMERS, Hope		78	Heart failure (in Woodland Hills, CA)
1979	TAFLER, Sydney		63	Cancer (in London, England)
1979	TALIAFERRO, Mabel		89	Died in Honolulu, Hawaii
1979	TEMPLETON, Olive		96	
1979	+ TIOMKIN, Dimitri	★	80	Natural causes
• 1979	URZI, Saro		66	Heart attack (in San Giuseppe Vesuviano, Italy)
1979	+ VANCE, Vivian		66	Cancer (in Belvedere, CA)
1979	VICIOUS, Sid		21	Overdose of heroin
1979	+ WAGENHEIM, Charles		83	Murdered (bludgeoned) in Hollywood, CA
1979	#+ WAYNE, John	★	72	Lung and stomach cancer (in Los Angeles, CA)
1979	# WESSON, Dick		59	Suicide (gunshot) in Costa Mesa, CA
1979	WHITLEY, Ray		77	While on a fishing trip (in Mexico)
1979	WILDING, Michael		66	Injuries from a fall (at his home in Chichester, England)
1979	#+ ZANUCK, Darryl F.		77	Pulmonary embolism aggravated by pneumonia
1980	# ALDERSON, Floyd Taliaferro		84	Pneumonia after suffering a stroke (in Mt. Sheridan, WY)
• 1980	#+ AVERY, Tex		71	Cancer (in Burbank, CA)
1980	BAILEY, Raymond		75	Heart attack (in Irvine, CA)
1980	BAKER, Frank		86	Died in Woodland Hills, CA
1980	# BARR, Leonard		77	After suffering a stroke
• 1980	BARRIE, John		62	Died in York, England
1980	#+ BARRY, Don "Red"		69	Suicide (gunshot) after a scuffle with his estranged wife
1980	BAVA, Mario		66	Heart attack
1980	BEATON, Cecil		78	
1980	BECKLEY, Tony		50	Cancer
• 1980	BELL, David Scott		22	Murdered (shot) in North Hollywood, CA
• 1980	BLISS, Lela		84	Died in Woodland Hills, CA
• 1980	# BONELLI, Richard		91	Died in Los Angeles, CA
1980	BONHAM, John		32	Choked to death after drinking 40 shots of vodka
1980	#+ BRASSELLE, Keefe		57	Cirrhosis of the liver
1980	# BRITTON, Barbara		59	Cancer
1980	BURKE, Kathleen		66	
1980	# CARROLL, Dee		54	Following corrective surgery after a stroke
1980	CHAMPION, Gower		60	Waldenstrom's disease
1980	COURTNEIDGE, Cicely		87	Died in London, England
• 1980	CRAWFORD, Kathryn		72	Cancer (in Pasadena, CA)
1980	# DAGOVER, Lil		82	Died in West Germany
1980	+ DASSIN, Joseph "Joe"		42	Heart attack (in Papeete, Tahiti)
1980	DEUTSCH, Adolph	★	82	
• 1980	# DORR, Harry		87	Pneumonia (in Los Angeles, CA)
1980	DRAGONETTE, Jessica		75	Heart attack (in New York City)
1980	#+ DURANTE, Jimmy		86	Pneumonitis (in Santa Monica, CA)
1980	EMERY, Katherine		73	Pulmonary illnesses (in Portland, Maine)
1980	EMNEY, Fred		79	
1980	FADDEN, Tom		84	
1980	# FAIRE, Virginia Brown		75	Died in a hospital in Laguna Beach, CA
1980	FAYE, Herbie		81	Died in Las Vegas, NV
1980	FITZPATRICK, James A.		78	Stroke (in Cathedral City, CA)
• 1980	FLINT, Sam		98	Died in Woodland Hills, CA
1980	FOX, Virgil		68	Cancer
1980	FROMAN, Jane		71	Natural causes
1980	FULLER, Frances		73	
1980	+ GARDINER, Reginald		77	Heart attack
1980	GOOLDEN, Richard		86	
1980	GRIFFITH, Hugh	★	67	Died in London, England
1980	# HAMMOND, Kay		71	
1980	#+ HAYMES, Dick		64	Lung cancer (in Los Angeles, CA)
1980	# HENRY, Charlotte		65	Brain tumor (in La Jolla, CA)
• 1980	# HENRY, Tom		?	Died in CA
1980	+ HITCHCOCK, Alfred	☆	80	Heart attack (in Los Angeles, CA)
1980	HOLTZ, Lou		87	Following open-heart surgery
1980	# HOSKINS, Allen "Farina"		59	Cancer (in Oakland, CA)

• New entry.   # Original name (Pt. 7).   + Interment (Pt. 5).

☆ Oscar nominee, ★ Oscar winner (Pt. 10)

...DEATHS OF MOVIE AND TELEVISION PERSONALITIES — BY YEAR...

YEAR	NAME		AGE	CAUSE AND/OR PLACE OF DEATH
1980	# HOUSTON, Renée		77	Died in London, England
1980	HOYOS, Rudolfo Sr.		83	Results of a fall (in Los Angeles, CA)
1980	+ ITURBI, José		84	Heart attack (in Los Angeles, CA)
1980	# JACQUES, Hattie		56	Heart attack (in London, England)
1980	JANNEY, Leon		63	Cancer (in Guadalajara, Mexico)
1980	#+ JANSSEN, David		48	Died of a massive heart attack (at his home in Malibu, CA)
1980	JOYCE, Yootha		53	Cirrhosis of the liver (in London, England)
1980	# KALLMAN, Dick		46	Murdered (in his Manhattan apartment)
1980	KAMINSKA, Ida	☆	80	
1980	KENTON, Erle C.		83	Parkinson's disease & emphysema
1980	+ KORJUS, Miliza	☆	73	Heart attack
1980	+ KOSTELANETZ, Andre		79	
1980	LAKE, Florence		75	Died in Woodland Hills, CA
1980	LANGTON, Paul		66	Heart attack (in Burbank, CA)
1980	LAUCK, Chester H. "Lum"		79	After a brief illness (in Hot Springs, AR)
1980	LAURIE, John		83	Emphysema & a lung ailment (in Chalfont St. Peter, England)
1980	LEE, Chingwah		78	
1980	+ LENNON, John		40	Murdered (shot) in New York, NY
1980	LESSER, Sol	★	90	
1980	# LEVENE, Sam		74	Heart attack (in New York, NY)
1980	# LEVENSON, Sam		68	
1980	LEVIN, Henry		70	Heart attack on the final day of filming
1980	LODEN, Barbara		48	Cancer (in New York, NY)
1980	LONDON, Jean "Babe"		79	
1980	# LOVELY, Louise		83	Died in Hobart, Australia
1980	MANNING, Knox		76	
1980	+ MARTIN, Strother		61	Heart attack
1980	# MASON, Mary		69	Cancer (in New York, NY)
1980	MAX, Edwin "Ed"		71	
1980	MAY, Alyce		65	Heart attack (in Rosa Rito Beach, Baja, Mexico)
1980	MAY, Mia		96	Died in Los Angeles, CA
1980	McCARTY, Mary		56	
1980	McDONALD, Frank		80	
1980	# McGRAW, Charles		66	After falling thru a glass shower door at home (in Studio City, CA)
1980	#+ McQUEEN, Steve	☆	50	Heart attack after cancer surgery
1980	# MEDFORD, Kay	☆	59	
1980	# MEREDITH, Iris		64	Died in Los Angeles, CA
1980	#+ MILESTONE, Lewis	★	84	Following abdominal surgery
1980	MONTOVANI, Annunzio		75	
1980	+ MYERS, Carmel		79	After a heart attack (in Los Angeles, CA)
1980	NEWELL, David (actor)		75	
1980	+ NOLAN, Bob		72	Heart attack (in Newport Beach, CA)
1980	NUGENT, Elliott		80	Died in his sleep (in New York, NY)
1980	O'NEIL, Barbara	☆	69	
1980	O'SHEA, Daniel T.		75	
1980	OWEN, Malcolm		24	Overdose of heroin
1980	# OWENS, Jesse		66	Lung cancer (in Tucson, AZ)
1980	# PAGLIERO, Marcello		73	Died in Paris, France
1980	+ PAL, George		72	Heart attack
1980	PARSONS, Milton		75	
1980	# PATRICK, Gail		69	Leukemia (in Hollywood, CA)
1980	PHILLIPS, Dorothy		90	Pneumonia (in Woodland Hills, CA)
1980	PHILLPOTTS, Ambrosine		68	Died in Ascot, England
1980	PHIPPS, Nicholas		66	Died in London, England
1980	POE, James	★	58	Heart attack (at his home in Malibu, CA)
1980	#+ RAFT, George		85	Leukemia (in Los Angeles, CA)
1980	+ RANDOLPH, Lillian		65	Cancer (in Los Angeles, CA)
1980	REED, Marshall J.		62	Massive hemorrhage after suffering a brain tumor (in Los Angeles)
1980	# RENALDO, Duncan "Cisco Kid"		76	Lung cancer (in Goleta, CA)
1980	ROBBINS, Gale		57	Lung cancer (in Tarzana, CA)
1980	ROBERTS, Rachel	☆	53	Suicide (acute barbiturate intoxication) in Los Angeles, CA
1980	#+ ROTH, Lillian		69	Stroke (in New York, NY)
1980	SANDERS, (Col.) Harland		90	Leukemia and pneumonia (in Louisville, KY)
1980	SANDRINI, Luis "Felipe"		75	Cerebral hemorrhage (in Buenos Aires, Argentina)
1980	# SAPPINGTON, Fay		82	Died in Englewood, NJ

• New entry. # Original name (Pt. 7). + Interment (Pt. 5).

☆ Oscar nominee, ★ Oscar winner (Pt. 10)

YEAR	NAME		AGE	CAUSE AND/OR PLACE OF DEATH
1980	SCHARY, Dore		74	
1980	SCHRAMM, Karla		88	Died in Los Angeles, CA
1980	SELBY, Sarah		73	Died in Los Angeles, CA
1980	+ SELLERS, Peter	☆	54	Heart attack (in London, England)
1980	SELTZER, Daniel		47	Heart attack
1980	SEN YUNG, Victor		65	Apparent victim of a gas leak at his home in North Hollywood, CA
1980	+ SHARPE, David H.		70	Parkinson's disease (in Altadena, CA)
1980	# SHERMAN, Mary		93	
1980	# SILVA, Mario		79	
1980	#+ SILVERHEELS, Jay "Tonto"		62	Complications from pneumonia (in Woodland Hills, CA)
• 1980	# SINATRA, Ray		76	Died in Las Vegas, NV
1980	STEPANEK, Karel		80	
1980	STOLOFF, Morris W.	★	85	
1980	+ STONE, Milburn		75	Heart attack (in La Jolla, CA)
1980	#+ STRATTEN, Dorothy		20	Murdered (shot by her husband) in West Los Angeles, CA
1980	# STRONG, Leonard		71	Died in Glendale, CA
• 1980	STRONG, Michael		?	Cancer (in Los Angeles, CA)
• 1980	SYLVIA, Gaby		60	Heart attack (in France)
• 1980	TAMBERLANI, Carlo		81	Died in Subiaco, Italy
1980	TANNEN, Charles D.		65	Heart attack (while vacationing in San Bernardino, CA)
1980	#+ THOMAS, Billy "Buckwheat"		49	Heart attack (in Los Angeles, CA)
1980	TOBIAS, George		78	Cancer (in Los Angeles, CA)
1980	TRIESAULT, Ivan		79	Heart failure (in Los Angeles, CA)
• 1980	# TSCHECHOWA, Olga		83	
• 1980	VALLI, Romolo		54	Automobile accident (in Rome, Italy)
1980	#+ VAN, Bobby		49	After surgery to remove a brain tumor (in Los Angeles, CA)
1980	# WALES, Wally		83	Pneumonia, after suffering a stroke (in Sheridan, WY)
1980	WALKER, Ray W.		76	Heart failure (in Los Angeles, CA)
• 1980	WARDE, Harlan		?	
• 1980	WATTS, Queenie		52	Cancer (in London, England)
1980	#+ WEST, Mae		88	Complications following a stroke (in Hollywood, CA)
1980	WINTLE, Julian		67	
1980	WOODRUFF, Eleanor		89	
1981	+ ALBERTSON, Jack	★	74	Cancer (in Hollywood Hills, CA)
1981	ALEXANDER, Katherine		79	Died in Florida
1981	+ ANDERS, Glenn		92	Died in Englewood, NJ
1981	#+ ASTAIRE, Adele		82	Stroke
1981	ASTHER, Nils		84	
1981	BARTON, Charles T.		79	After two heart attacks
1981	+ BEARD, Matthew "Stymie" Jr.		56	Stroke (in Los Angeles, CA)
1981	BERNHARDT, Curtis (Kurt)		81	
1981	# BONDI, Beulah	☆	88	Pulmonary complications
1981	+ BOONE, Richard		63	Cancer
• 1981	#+ BOWLING, Alice		54	
1981	BYRNE, Eddie		70	
1981	#+ CARMICHAEL, Hoagy		82	Heart attack
• 1981	CASTLETON, Barbara		85	
1981	#+ CHAYEFSKY, Paddy		58	Cancer
1981	# CLAIR, René		82	
1981	CLEMENTS, Stanley		55	Emphysema
1981	CONWAY, Morgan		81	
1981	COOK, Billy Boy		?	
1981	COOPER, Dulcie		77	After a lengthy illness
1981	#+ DAVIS, Jim		65	Following surgery for a perforated ulcer (in Northridge, CA)
1981	DeBANZIE, Brenda		66	Following surgery on a non-malignant tumor (in Sussex, England)
1981	DeKOVA, Frank		71	Found dead in his home (in Sepulveda, CA)
1981	DIXON, Jean (actress)		84	After a long illness (in New York, NY)
1981	# DOUGLAS, Melvyn	★	80	Pneumonia and cardiac complications (in New York, NY)
1981	DRAYTON, Noel		68	
1981	#+ DWAN, Alan		96	Heart failure (in Woodland Hills, CA)
1981	EBERLY, Bob		65	After 4 heart attacks from cancer chemotherapy
1981	# ELSOM, Isobel		87	Died in Woodland Hills, CA
1981	ENGEL, Roy		67	Meningitis (in Burbank, CA)
1981	FORAN, Mary		61	Died in Los Angeles, CA

YEAR	NAME		AGE	CAUSE AND/OR PLACE OF DEATH
• 1981	# FRANCIS, Sandra		47	Results of a motorcycle accident (in Santa Monica, CA)
1981	FRIEDHOFER, Hugo	★	80	While hospitalized after a fall in his home
• 1981	GAFNI, Miklos		57	Massive heart attack (at Kennedy Airport, NY)
1981	GANCE, Abel		92	Lung ailment
1981	# GARRALAGA, Martin		85	
1981	# GEORGE "Chief" Dan	☆	82	
• 1981	GODDARD, Alf		83	
1981	# GRAHAME, Gloria	★	57	Cancer
1981	GRAY, Mack		75	Following a prolonged illness
1981	GREENE, Stanley		70	After a long illness (in New York City)
1981	# HADEN, Sara		82	Died in Woodland Hills, CA
1981	HALE, Richard		87	Natural causes
• 1981	HALL, Ella		85	Died in Canoga Park, CA
1981	HARBURG, E. Y.		84	Killed in an automobile crash
1981	#+ HARDING, Ann	☆	79	After an illness of several months (in Sherman Oaks, CA)
1981	HARRIS, Robert H.		72	Died in Los Angeles, CA (Do not confuse with British actor)
1981	#+ HAYDEN, Russell "Lucky"		68	Viral pneumonia (in Palm Springs, Ca.)
1981	+ HEAD, Edith		82	Died in Los Angeles, CA
1981	# HEMING, Violet		86	Died in New York, NY
1981	#+ HENDRIX, Wanda		52	Double pneumonia (in Burbank, CA)
1981	HOERBIGER, Paul		87	Died in Vienna, Austria
1981	#+ HOLDEN, William	★	63	Blood loss after head was cut in a fall (in Santa Monica, CA)
1981	HOVEN, Adrian		57	Heart attack (in West Germany)
1981	+ JESSEL, George		83	Heart attack (in Los Angeles, CA)
1981	JOHNSON, Brad		56	
1981	JONES, Barry		87	
1981	JOSLYN, Allyn		75	Cardiac failure (in Woodland Hills, CA)
1981	KEANE, Robert Emmett		96	Died in Hollywood, CA
• 1981	KEATON, Louise		78	Cancer (in Van Nuys, CA)
1981	#+ KELLY, Patsy		71	Cancer (in Woodland Hills, CA)
• 1981	KNAPP, Evelyn		72	Died in West Hollywood, CA
1981	KNOPF, Edwin H.		82	After a long illness
1981	KRASKER, Robert		67	
1981	#+ LANE, Lola		75	Inflammation of the arteries (in Santa Barbara, CA)
• 1981	# LEANDER, Zarah		74	Died near Stockholm, Sweden
1981	LEE, Bernard		73	Cancer (in London, England)
1981	# LENYA, Lotte	☆	83	Died in New York, NY
1981	#+ LINDSAY, Margaret		70	Emphysema (in Los Angeles, CA)
1981	LOOS, Anita		93	Died in Manhattan, NY
1981	# LORRAINE, Louise		79	After a long illness (in New York, NY)
1981	#+ LOUIS, Joe "Brown Bomber"		66	Cardiac arrest (in Las Vegas, NV)
1981	LUDDEN, Allen		63	Cancer (in Los Angeles, CA)
1981	MARKEY, Enid		83	Natural causes
1981	MARKHAM, Dewey "Pigmeat"		77	Stroke
• 1981	# MARSH, Garry		78	Natural causes (in London, England)
1981	#+ MARTIN, Ross		61	Heart attack
1981	MATTHEWS, Jessie		74	Cancer
1981	MAXWELL, Jenny		39	Shot to death outside her condo by possible robbers
1981	McCULLOUGH, Philo		90	Died in Burbank, CA
1981	McHUGH, Frank		82	Died in Greenwich, CT
• 1981	# MEGOWAN, Don		59	Throat cancer (in Panorama City, CA)
1981	MILLER, Ruth		78	
1981	#+ MONTGOMERY, Robert	☆	77	Cancer (in New York, NY)
• 1981	MORE, Unity		86	Died in London, England
1981	# NEY, Marie		86	
1981	O'CONNELL, Arthur	☆	73	Alzheimer's disease (in Woodland Hills, CA)
1981	PALMER, Maria		57	Cancer (in Los Angeles, CA)
1981	# PATRICK, Nigel		68	Cancer (at a hospital in London, England)
1981	PONSELLE, Rosa		84	
• 1981	PRACK, Rudolf		77	Died in Vienna, Austria
• 1981	RIGON, Paolo		22	Injuries from a filming accident (in Cortina d'Ampezzo, Italy)
1981	ROCHELLE, Claire		72	Cancer (in La Jolla, CA)
• 1981	ROULEAU, Raymond		77	Died in Paris, France
1981	# RUSSELL, Don		54	Heart attack
• 1981	+ SAGAL, Boris		58	Automobile accident

YEAR	NAME		AGE	· CAUSE AND/OR PLACE OF DEATH
1981	# SANTELL, Alfred		86	After a lengthy illness & several strokes
1981	#+ SCOTT, Hazel		61	Cancer
• 1981	# SHERWOOD, Bobby		65	Cancer (in Auburn, MA)
• 1981	SHIMODA, Yuki		58	Died in Los Angeles, CA
1981	# SMITH, Joseph		96	
• 1981	SPADARO, Umberto		77	Cancer (in Rome, Italy)
1981	# TALMADGE, Richard		88	Cancer (in Carmel, CA)
1981	TAUROG, Norman	★	82	
1981	# THATCHER, Torin		76	Cancer (in Thousand Oaks, CA)
1981	THOMAS, David		73	
1981	THOMAS, Lowell		89	Heart attack
1981	# Vera-Ellen		55	Cancer (in Los Angeles, CA)
1981	VonZELL, Harry		75	Cancer (in Woodland Hills, CA)
1981	VOSKOVEC, George		76	
1981	WALSH, George		92	Complications from pneumonia (in Pamona, CA)
1981	# WALSH, Raoul		93	Apparent heart attack (in Simi Valley, CA)
1981	WARBURTON, John		78	Cancer
1981	#+ WARREN, Harry (songwriter)	★	87	Died at Cedars-Sinai Med. Ctr., Los Angeles, CA
1981	# WILSON, Edith		83	Cerebral hemorrhage (in Chcago, IL)
1981	#+ WOOD, Natalie	☆	43	Accidental drowning (off Catalina Island, CA)
1981	+ WYLER, William	★	79	
• 1982	ACE, Goodman		83	
1982	ALBERTSON, Mabel		81	Complications from numerous illnesses (in Santa Monica, CA)
1982	+ ALEXANDER, John		85	
1982	ASKEY, Arthur		82	
1982	# ASLAN, Gregoire		74	Heart attack
1982	# BADEL, Alan		58	
1982	BAKER, Lenny		37	Cancer
1982	BAKER, Russell F.		66	After a brief illness
1982	BAKER, Sam		56	Heart attack
1982	BALDWIN, Bill		69	Cancer
1982	BAYNE, Beverly		87	Natural causes
1982	BEAUMONT, Hugh		72	Apparent heart attack
1982	+ BELUSHI, John		33	After speedballing a mix of cocaine & heroin (in Hollywood, CA)
1982	BENET, Brenda		36	Suicide (gunshot)
1982	BENNETT, Marjorie		87	Cancer
1982	+ BERGMAN, Ingrid	★	67	Cancer
1982	BISHOP, Ronald		59	
1982	BLAKE, Larry J.		68	
1982	+ BLOCH, Ray		79	Heart attack
1982	BLUE, David		41	Heart attack while jogging
1982	BOND, Rudy		66	Heart attack
1982	BRAHM, John		89	Died in his sleep at home
1982	BREEDING, Larry		36	Killed when his car struck a pole in Hollywood
1982	+ BRODERICK, James		55	Cancer
1982	BROWN, Joseph		59	
1982	# BRUCE, Virginia		72	After a long illness
1982	BRUCK, Bella		70	Heart attack
1982	+ BUONO, Victor		44	
1982	CALVE, Olga		82	Bronchial pneumonia
1982	CAROL, Sue		73	(See Sue Carol Ladd)
1982	CARSON, Wayne		55	
1982	CAVALCANTI, Alberto		85	
1982	CHEN, Renee Shinn		6	Killed by helicopter rotor while filming
1982	CHRISTI, Frank		52	Shot to death at his home
1982	CHURCHILL, Sarah		67	Following a long illness
1982	# CONRIED, Hans		64	Heart ailment
1982	COOTE, Robert		73	
1982	CORBETT, Harry H.		57	Heart attack
1982	CULLEN, Fred		48	Heart attack
1982	# CUMMINGS, Sandy		68	Pneumonia while hospitalized for another illness
1982	+ DANTINE, Helmut		63	Massive coronary
1982	DAVIS, Herbert H.		52	
1982	# DEVEAU, Jack		47	Cancer

...DEATHS OF MOVIE AND TELEVISION PERSONALITIES — BY YEAR...

YEAR	NAME		AGE	CAUSE AND/OR PLACE OF DEATH
1982	DILLAWAY, Donald P.		78	*After a long illness*
1982	DIX, Constance		60	
1982	DONNELLY, Ruth		86	
1982	#+ DRAKE, Tom		64	*Lung cancer*
1982	DUKE, E. L. Tony		48	*Heart attack*
1982	+ DUNNE, Dominique		23	*Strangled by her boyfriend*
1982	ETHRIDGE, Ella		88	
1982	FASSBINDER, Rainer Werner		36	*Lethal combination of cocaine & sleeping pills*
1982	+ FELDMAN, Marty		48	*Heart attack*
1982	FITZGERALD, Neil		90	
1982	#+ FONDA, Henry	★	77	*Heart failure*
1982	FORMAN, Joey		53	*Complications from pulmonary fibrosis*
1982	FORSTER, Peter		62	
1982	FOX, Virginia (Zanuck)		79	*Complications from stroke & emphysema*
1982	GARROWAY, Dave		69	*Apparent suicide (gunshot)*
1982	GORDON, Steve		44	*Heart attack*
1982	GORIN, Igor		80	
1982	+ GOSDEN, Freeman "Amos"		83	*Heart failure*
1982	+ GOULD, Glenn		50	*Massive stroke*
1982	GRAHAME, Margot		70	*Respiratory failure from chronic bronchitis*
1982	HAMPTON, Hope		84	*Heart attack*
1982	HESSEL, Edith Bell		58	*Alzheimer's disease & exposure*
1982	HOLLOWAY, Stanley	☆	91	
1982	HOWELL, Lottice		84	
1982	HOXIE, Al		80	
1982	JOHNSON, Celia		73	*Stroke*
1982	JOHNSON, Dan		38	
1982	+ JORY, Victor		79	*Apparent heart attack*
1982	JURGENS, Curt		69	*Heart failure*
1982	# KELLJAN, Robert		52	*After a long bout with cancer*
1982	+ KELLY, Grace	★	52	*Brain hemorrhage after a car crash*
1982	+ KING, Henry	☆	86	*Died in his sleep at home*
1982	KING, Mollie		86	*Following a stroke*
1982	KLINGER, Ruth S.		59	*Died in her sleep*
1982	KYDD, Sam		67	*Respiratory ailment*
1982	+ LADD, Sue Carol		73	*Complications of heart attack*
1982	+ LAMAS, Fernando		67	*Cancer*
1982	LANE, Richard		83	
1982	LEE, My-ca Dinh		7	*Killed by helicopter rotor while filming*
1982	LEE, Will		74	*Heart attack*
1982	+ LEMBECK, Harvey		59	*Heart attack*
1982	LEWIS, Ronald		54	*Suicide (sleeping pills) Do not confuse with R. "Raan" L., d. 1995*
1982	LITTLER, Susan		33	*Cancer*
1982	LOWE, Arthur		67	*Following a stroke*
1982	LUCAS, Nick		84	*Following a stroke*
1982	LUDWIG, Edward		83	*Stroke while hospitalized*
1982	+ LYNDE, Paul		55	
1982	MAGEE, Patrick		58	*Natural causes*
1982	#+ MARLOWE, Hugh		71	*Heart attack*
1982	MERCHANT, Vivien	☆	53	*Jaundice & hemorrhage caused by alcoholism*
1982	+ MILLS, Harry F.		68	*Following a tumor operation*
1982	# MINER, Tony		82	*After being hospitalized the previous day*
1982	MIRANDA, Isa		77	*Infected bone fracture*
1982	+ MONK, Thelonius		64	*Following a stroke*
1982	MORAN, Dolores		56	
1982	MORE, Kenneth		67	*Parkinson's disease*
1982	+ MORROW, Vic		50	*Killed in a filming accident*
1982	MULLANEY, Jack		51	*Stroke*
1982	NESBITT, Cathleen		93	
1982	NOVELLO, Jay		78	
1982	NUTT, Rev. Grady		47	*Airplane crash*
1982	OATES, Warren		53	*Heart attack*
1982	+ OBER, Philip		80	*Heart failure*
1982	+ PATRICK, Lee (Wood)		76	*Heart seizure*
1982	PATTON, Mary		66	*Cancer*

• New entry. # Original name (Pt. 7). + Interment (Pt. 5).   76   ☆ Oscar nominee, ★ Oscar winner (Pt. 10)

YEAR	NAME		AGE	CAUSE AND/OR PLACE OF DEATH
1982	PHILBROOK, James		58	
1982	# PHILLIPS, Barney		68	After a brief illness
1982	PICKMAN, Kathryn		60	Cancer
1982	+ POWELL, Eleanor		69	Cancer
1982	PURSELL, Robert		26	Apparent suicide (hung himself from a tree) in Levittown, PA
1982	REVILLE, Alma (Hitchcock)		82	
1982	+ ROBBINS, Marty		57	
1982	+ ROSS, Joe E.		67	Apparent heart attack
1982	+ RUBENSTEIN, Artur		95	Natural causes
1982	RUTHERFORD, Jack "Buffalo Bill"		89	
1982	SAKATA, Harold		56	Cancer
1982	# SAWYER, Joe		80	Liver cancer
1982	#+ SCHNEIDER, Romy		43	Found dead of cardiac arrest (at her apartment in Paris, France)
1982	SEDAN, Rolfe		86	
1982	SEKA, Ron		48	Heart attack
1982	+ SHAW, Reta		69	
1982	# SHAW, Wini		72	
1982	SHDANOFF, Elsa Schreiber		81	Heart failure
1982	SHELDON, Gene		75	Heart attack
1982	SHIMURA, Takashi		76	Emphysema
1982	SNOWDEN, Leigh		51	Cancer
1982	STANLEY, Louise		?	
1982	#+ STRASBERG, Lee	☆	80	Heart attack
1982	# TATI, Jacques		74	Pulmonary embolism
1982	TAYLOR, John		61	Heart attack
1982	THEARD, Sam		78	
1982	THOMA, Michael		55	Cancer
1982	TOBIN, Dan		72	
1982	TULLY, Tom	☆	74	Complications after a long illness
1982	VARELA, Nina		83	
1982	VESTOFF, Virginia		42	
1982	VIDOR, King	☆	88	Heart ailment
1982	WAKELY, Jimmy		68	Heart failure
1982	WALKER, Betty		54	
1982	WALTERS, Charles	☆	70	Lung cancer
1982	WEBB, Alan		75	
1982	+ WEBB, Jack		62	Heart attack
1982	WEBB, Roy		94	Heart attack
1982	WHITNEY, John Hay "Jock"		77	After a long illness
1982	WILSON, Don		81	Stroke
1982	+ ZANUCK, Virginia Fox		83	
1983	ALDRICH, Robert		65	Kidney failure (in Los Angeles, CA)
1983	ALEXANDROV, Grigori		80	Died in Moscow, Russia
1983	# ARNE, Peter		62	Murdered (battered to death)
1983	AURIC, Georges		84	
1983	BAILEY, Robert		70	
1983	+ BALANCHINE, George		79	Creutzfeld-Jakob disease
1983	BIERNE, Michael		46	
1983	BILON, Michael "E. T."		35	Complications from pneumonia
1983	# BLAIR, Randy		32	Cardiac and respiratory arrest while playing a charity basketball game
1983	# BLAKE, Eubie		100	
1983	BRANDON, Peter		57	Apparent heart attack after jogging
1983	BRAY, Robert		65	Natural causes
1983	BRENGEL, George		69	Cancer
1983	BRYANT, Hazel		44	Heart attack
1983	BUNUEL, Luis		83	Cirrhosis of the liver
1983	CAINE, Joan-Ellen		57	Cancer
1983	# CAMERON, Rod		73	Following a long illness
1983	#+ CANOVA, Judy		66	Cancer
1983	+ CARPENTER, Karen		32	Heart attack caused by anorexia nervosa (in Downey, CA)
1983	CHECCO, Jessie		85	
1983	CHRISTIAN, Robert		42	Cancer
1983	CHRISTOPHER, Richard		37	Cancer
1983	CLARK, Kendall		70	

...DEATHS OF MOVIE AND TELEVISION PERSONALITIES — BY YEAR...

YEAR	NAME		AGE	CAUSE AND/OR PLACE OF DEATH
1983	CLAYTON, Jan		66	Cancer
1983	COFFIELD, Peter		37	
1983	CONRAD, Michael		58	Stomach cancer
1983	COSTELLO, Anthony		42	
1983	# CRABBE, Larry "Buster"		75	Heart attack
1983	+ CUKOR, George	★	83	Heart failure
1983	# CUMMINS, Dorothy		80	
1983	# DALIO, Marcel		83	
1983	DANA, Leora		60	Cancer
1983	DARNAY, Toni		61	Lung cancer
1983	DAVIS, Johnny "Scat"		73	Heart attack
1983	deFUNES, Louis		68	Heart attack
1983	# DEL RIO, Dolores		77	Natural causes
1983	DEMAREST, William	☆	91	
1983	DEMPSEY, Jack		87	After an illness of several years
1983	DIETZ, Howard		86	
1983	+ D'ORSAY, Fifi		79	Cancer
1983	DRISCOLL, Robert Miller		55	
1983	DUNN, Josephine		76	Cancer
1983	# ELLIOTT, William D.		49	(Do not confuse with William "Wild Bill" Elliott, d. 1965)
1983	EMERSON, Faye		65	Stomach cancer
1983	EMERY, Dick		65	
1983	EVANS, Madge		73	Cancer (in Oakland, NJ)
1983	FARMER, Richard		67	Cancer
1983	#+ FIX, Paul		82	Kidney failure
1983	#+ FONTANNE, Lynn	☆	95	Pneumonia
1983	# FOY, Eddie Jr.		78	Cancer of the pancreas
1983	FRANZ, Eduard		81	
1983	FUJIKAWA, Jerry		71	Heart disease
1983	GARGAN, Mary Elizabeth		76	Lung cancer
1983	+ GEORGE, Christopher		54	Heart attack
1983	+ GERSHWIN, Ira		86	
1983	GODFREY, Arthur		79	Pneumonia & emphysema
1983	GOODWIN, Robert L.		55	
1983	GORDON, Gavin		82	
1983	GUFFEY, Burnett		78	
1983	#+ HACKETT, Joan		49	Cancer (in Encino, CA)
1983	HAYTER, James		75	
1983	HENDERSON, Jack E.		88	
1983	HOYOS, Rudolfo Jr.		68	Cerebral hemorrhage
1983	HUGHES, Arthur		89	Pneumonia
1983	JAMES, Harry		67	Lymphatic cancer
1983	JONAH, Dolly		53	
1983	+ JONES, Carolyn	☆	54	Cancer
1983	KAPER, Bronislau		81	Cancer
1983	KELLIN, Mike		61	Lung cancer
1983	KINSER, Patrick		30	Pulmonary failure
1983	KLEIN, Adelaide		82	Brain tumor
1983	KULLMAN, Charles		80	
1983	LANCASTER, Robert		70	
1983	LeBOUVIER, Jean		62	
1983	LeMESURIER, John		71	Abdominal illness
1983	+ LIBERACE, George		71	Leukemia and heart disease
1983	#+ LIVINGSTONE, Mary		77	Heart ailment
1983	LLEWELLYN, Richard		76	Heart attack
1983	LOGAN, Jacqueline		78	
1983	LOO, Richard		80	
1983	MACE, Paul		33	Killed in a traffic accident
1983	MADDEN, Donald		49	
1983	MANULIS, Katherine Bard		66	
1983	MARTIN, Freddy		76	After a series of strokes
1983	MASSENGALE, Joseph		66	Suicide (gunshot)
1983	+ MASSEY, Raymond	☆	86	Pneumonia
1983	# McHUGH, Jack		69	Heart attack
1983	MICHAELS, Loretta R.		45	Cancer

• New entry. # Original name (Pt. 7). + Interment (Pt. 5).

78

☆ Oscar nominee, ★ Oscar winner (Pt. 10)

YEAR	NAME		AGE	CAUSE AND/OR PLACE OF DEATH
1983	MOORE, Kathryn		96	
1983	MOSQUINI, Marie		84	
1983	+ NIVEN, David	★	73	Amyotrophic lateral sclerosis
1983	NIXON, Marion		78	Complications following open-heart surgery
1983	NORRIS, Kenneth		34	Injuries from a fall
1983	OAKLAND, Simon		61	
1983	#+ O'BRIEN, Pat		83	Massive heart attack
1983	O'BRIEN, Richard		65	Cancer
1983	O'MOORE, Patrick		74	Following surgery
1983	# PAGE, Gale		72	Lung cancer
1983	PELISH, Thelma		55	
1983	+ PEREIRA, Hal		?	
1983	# PICKENS, Slim		64	Pneumonia
1983	+ PULEO, Johnny		75	Respiratory failure
1983	RAPHAELSON, Samson		87	
1983	+ REYNOLDS, Frank		59	Viral hepatitis
1983	RICHARDSON, James G.		37	Injuries from a fall while skiing
1983	+ RICHARDSON, Ralph	☆	80	
1983	RONET, Maurice		55	After a long illness
1983	ROUNDS, David		40	Cancer
1983	ROYLE, Selena		78	After a brief illness
1983	RUTTENBERG, Joseph		93	
1983	SAMPLES, Junior		56	Heart attack
1983	SAVITCH, Jessica		35	Automobile accident
1983	SHAYNE, Tamara		80	Following a heart attack
1983	#+ SHEARER, Norma	★	82	Bronchial pneumonia
1983	SKOLSKY, Sidney		78	Parkinson's disease
1983	SLEEPER, Martha		72	Heart attack
1983	SLEZAK, Walter		80	Suicide (gunshot)
1983	SOMACK, Jack		64	Heart attack
1983	SPACE, Arthur		74	Cancer
1983	SPAIN, Fay		50	Cancer
1983	STEEN, Malcolm H.		55	
1983	STRUDWICK, Shepperd		75	Cancer
1983	# SWANSON, Gloria	☆	84	Following heart surgery
1983	TAYLOR, Vaughn		72	Massive cerebral hemorrhage
1983	+ TINCHER, Fay		99	Natural causes
1983	TORS, Ivan		67	Massive heart attack
1983	TRAUBE, Shepard		76	Cancer
1983	VALERIE, Joan		68	Automobile accident
1983	VICTOR, Dee		?	After a long illness
1983	# VITTE, Ray		33	Stopped breathing after forcible police arrest
1983	+ VIVYAN, John		67	Heart failure
1983	WALLGREN, Gunn		69	After a long illness
1983	WARREN, Flip		69	
1983	# WEAVER, Doodles		71	Apparent suicide (gunshot)
1983	WHITE, Alice		78	Stroke
1983	WHITNEY, Michael		52	After a heart attack in a restaurant
1983	WILDER, Marie		53	
1983	WILLIAMS, John		80	Following an aneurysm (Do not confuse with John J. Williams)
1983	+ WILLIAMS, Tennessee		71	After choking on a plastic bottle cap
1983	WILSON, Dennis		39	Drowned
1983	WOOD, Cindi		52	
1983	WOODS, Maurice		45	Cancer
1984	ADLER, Luther		81	Died in Kutztown, PA
1984	AGNEW, Robert "Bobby"		84	Kidney failure (in Palm Springs, CA)
1984	ALLEN, Chet		44	Suicide (in Columbus, OH)
1984	ANDRE, E. J.		76	Cancer
1984	AUERBACH, Leon		48	
1984	BARRY, Jack		66	Heart attack while jogging
1984	+ BASEHART, Richard		70	Stroke
1984	#+ BASIE, William "Count"		79	Pancreatic cancer
1984	BENEDICT, Richard		64	Heart attack
1984	BENSON, Lucille		69	Cancer

YEAR	NAME		AGE	CAUSE AND/OR PLACE OF DEATH
1984	BOND, Sudie		56	Respiratory ailment
1984	BONNEY, Gail		83	
1984	BOYLAN, Mary		70	
1984	+ BRISSON, Frederick		71	After suffering a stroke
1984	BULL, Peter		72	Heart attack
1984	BURKE, Walter		75	Emphysema
1984	BURTON, Margaret		60	Heart attack
1984	#+ BURTON, Richard	☆	58	Cerebral hemorrhage
1984	CAGNEY, Jeanne		65	Lung cancer
1984	+ CAPOTE, Truman		59	Died in his sleep (drug & alcohol mix)
1984	+ CARPENTER, Ken		84	After a brief illness (in Santa Monica, CA)
1984	CHAMBERLIN, Howland		73	Complications of lung & liver disease
1984	+ COOGAN, Jackie		69	Heart ailment
1984	COOK, Clyde		92	Died in his sleep
1984	COOPER, Edwin		89	
1984	CULVER, Roland		83	Heart attack
1984	CUMMINGS, Ruth Sinclair		90	
1984	DALTON, Doris		82	Cardiac arrest
1984	DAWSON, Ronald		81	Pneumonia
1984	DEACON, Richard		62	Heart attack
1984	+ DELMAR, Kenny		73	Died in a Stamford, CT hospital
1984	DEXTER, Alan		65	Heart attack
1984	DORS, Diana		52	After two operations for ovarian cancer
1984	DUPREZ, June		66	
1984	DURANT, Jack		78	Cancer
1984	EARLE, Merie		95	Uremic poisoning after colon cancer surgery
1984	FLOWERS, Bess		85	
1984	FOREMAN, Carl		69	Brain cancer
1984	FOX, John		60	
1984	GALLO, Mario		61	
1984	GARNER, Peggy Ann		52	Cancer
1984	#+ GAYE, Marvin		44	Murdered (shot by his father) in Los Angeles, CA
1984	#+ GAYNOR, Janet	★	77	Pneumonia
1984	GIVOT, George		81	
1984	GLASS, Ned		78	
1984	GOODRICH, Frances		93	
1984	GORCEY, David		63	Diabetic coma
1984	GOUGH, Lloyd		77	Aortic aneurysm
1984	# GRANT, Shauna		20	Suicide? Murdered? (gunshot)
1984	GREEN, Gilbert		68	Died in Tarzana, CA
1984	GUNEY, Yilmaz		47	Cancer
1984	# HAMILTON, Neil		85	Complications from asthma
1984	HARGREAVES, Christine		43	Brain hemorrhage
1984	HARPER, Cecilia DeMille		75	
1984	HARTFORD, Karen Kadler		50	Cancer
1984	HASKIN, Byron	☆	84	Cancer
1984	+ HELLMAN, Lillian		79	Heart disease
1984	HENDRY, Ian		53	
1984	HEXUM, Jon-Erik		26	Accidentally shot himself
1984	HOLLANDER, Adam		19	Struck by car while riding a bicycle
1984	HOLLIDAY, Bill		49	Apparent heart attack
1984	HOLMES, Billy		56	Cancer
1984	HOWLETT, Noel		82	
1984	+ HUMBERSTONE, Bruce H.		80	Stomach cancer & pneumonia
1984	HUTTON, Ina Ray		65	
1984	+ JAFFE, Sam	☆	93	Cancer
1984	JENKINS, Gordon		73	Amyotrophic lateral sclerosis
1984	JOHNSON, E. Lamont		29	
1984	JOHNSON, Sunny		30	Cerebral hemorrhage
1984	JORDAN, John Duffield		81	
1984	KARAS, Anton		78	
1984	KAST, Pierre		63	
1984	+ KAUFMAN, Andy		35	Lung cancer (in Los Angeles, CA)
1984	+ KEIGHLEY, William		94	Stroke
1984	KING, Walter Woolf		84	Heart attack

...DEATHS OF MOVIE AND TELEVISION PERSONALITIES — BY YEAR...

YEAR	NAME		AGE	CAUSE AND/OR PLACE OF DEATH
1984	KINGSLEY, Susan		37	Died when her car was struck head-on by another
1984	KRASNA, Norman	★	74	Heart attack
1984	#+ LaRUE, Jack		83	Heart attack
1984	LAU, Wesley		63	Heart failure
1984	+ LAWFORD, Peter		61	Cardiac arrest, liver & kidney disease
1984	LeCLAIR, Lucille		62	Diabetic infection
1984	# LEEDS, Andrea	☆	70	
1984	LITTLE, Ann		93	
1984	LOEB, Tony		76	Cancer
1984	LONG, Avon		73	Cancer
1984	# LOSEY, Joseph		75	
1984	MAPES, Ted		82	
1984	MARLEY, John	☆	77	Following open-heart surgery
1984	MARLOWE, June		81	
1984	MARTIN, D'urville		45	Heart attack
1984	MASON, James	☆	75	Massive heart attack
1984	+ MASSEY, Edith		65	Cancer
1984	MATTHEWS, George		73	Heart disease
1984	MAY, Doris		82	Heart failure
1984	McAVOY, May		82	
1984	McINTYRE, Christine		69	
1984	McMURRAY, Richard		68	Lung cancer
1984	MERCER, Jack		74	
1984	# MERMAN, Ethel		75	Results of a brain tumor
1984	MIDDLETON, Ray		77	Heart attack
1984	#+ MINTER, Mary Miles		82	Heart failure
1984	MOORE, Robert (director)		56	After a brief illness
1984	# MORECAMBE, Eric		58	Heart disease
1984	MYLES, Mary		93	Congestive heart failure
1984	PARFREY, Woodrow		61	Heart attack
1984	PEARCE, Muriel		85	After a long illness
1984	PECKINPAH, Sam		59	Following several heart attacks
1984	PEEPLES, Dennis		50	Heart attack
1984	PEERCE, Jan		80	Pneumonia and coma
1984	+ PIDGEON, Walter	☆	87	Series of strokes
1984	+ POWELL, William	☆	91	Natural causes
1984	PREISSER, June		61	Automobile collision
1984	RAISCH, William		79	Lung cancer
1984	RANDALL, Sue		49	Cancer of the lungs & larynx
1984	RENICK, Ruth		91	
1984	+ RIORDAN, Marjorie (Schlaff)		63	
1984	+ ROBSON, Flora	☆	82	
1984	ROCK, Joe		93	
1984	ROSSITER, Leonard		57	Apparent heart attack
1984	ROTHA, Paul		76	
1984	ROWLAND, Henry		70	
1984	RYAN, Edmond		79	Heart attack
1984	SALVIO, Robert		45	Complications from A.I.D.S.
1984	+ SANDS, Billy		73	Lung cancer
1984	SHARP, Anthony		69	
1984	SHIELDS, John Webster		34	Cancer
1984	STAUDTE, Wolfgang		77	
1984	TAYLOR, Lance Sr.		69	Heart attack
1984	+ TRUFFAUT, François		52	Brain cancer
1984	TUBB, Ernest		70	Emphysema
1984	VanDYKE, Truman		86	Heart failure
1984	VEAZIE, Carol Eberts		89	
1984	VERNAC, Denise		66	
• 1984	#+ VonERICH, David		25	
1984	WAGGNER, George		90	Natural causes
1984	WARING, Fred		84	Stroke
1984	WEBSTER, Paul Francis		77	
1984	#+ WEISSMULLER, Johnny		79	Heart disease
1984	# WERNER, Oskar	☆	61	Heart attack
1984	+ WEST, Brooks		67	Cerebral hemorrhage

• New entry. # Original name (Pt. 7). + Interment (Pt. 5).   81   ☆ Oscar nominee, ★ Oscar winner (Pt. 10)

YEAR	NAME		AGE	CAUSE AND/OR PLACE OF DEATH
1984	WHITING, Napoleon		75	Heart attack
1984	WILCOXON, Henry		78	Congestive heart failure
1984	# WILLSON, Meredith		82	Heart failure
1984	#+ WINWOOD, Estelle		101	Heart failure
1985	ADDAMS, Dawn		55	Cancer
1985	ANDEN, Matthew		42	After a lengthy illness (in New York)
1985	ANDERSON, Edward		70	
1985	#+ ANDREWS, Edward		70	Heart attack
1985	ANKERS, Evelyn		67	Cancer
1985	#+ BAKER, Kenny		72	Heart attack
1985	BARNEY, Jay		72	Cancer
1985	BARR, Patrick		77	
1985	BATE, Tom		85	
1985	BAUER, Charita		62	Following a long illness
1985	BAXTER, Anne	★	62	Stroke
1985	BERLE, Jack		80	
1985	BLACK, Dorothy		85	
1985	# BLAKE, Arthur		70	Heart attack
1985	BOULTING, John		71	
1985	#+ BRADY, Scott		60	Respiratory failure
1985	BRAMBELL, Wilfrid		72	Cancer
1985	BRIGGS, Charles		53	
1985	BROOKS, Louise		78	Heart attack
1985	# BRYNNER, Yul	★	65	Lung cancer
1985	BULOFF, Joseph		85	After a long illness
1985	BURGE, James C.		41	Respiratory failure (pneumonia)
1985	# BURROWS, Abe		74	After a long illness
1985	# BUZZELL, Eddie		89	
1985	CAMPBELL, Kay		80	Injuries from automobile accident
1985	CAMPOS, Rafael		49	Stomach cancer
1985	CARIDEO, Eddie		72	
1985	CARTER, Lynne		60	Pneumonia complicated by A.I.D.S.
1985	CHANDLER, George		82	Alzheimer's disease
1985	# CLAIRE, Ina		95	Lingering effects of a stroke
1985	CLARKE, Philip Norman		81	
1985	CLUTE, Sidney		69	Cancer
1985	COLASANTO, Nicholas "Coach"		61	Heart ailment
1985	COLE, Lester		81	
1985	#+ CRAIG, James		73	Lung cancer
1985	CROTHERS, Joel		44	Cancer
1985	# CURTIS, Jackie		38	Drug overdose
1985	DAVIS, Rick		71	Heart failure
1985	DAWSON, Kurt		43	Complications from cancer
1985	+ DESMOND, Johnny		65	Cancer
1985	+ DIAMOND, Selma		64	Cancer
1985	DOWNEY, Morton Sr.		83	Effects of a stroke
1985	DYALL, Valentine		75	
1985	# EARLES, Harry		83	
1985	ELLSWORTH, Stephen R.		77	Heart failure
1985	ENGLE, Darleen		48	Cancer
1985	ERVIN, (Senator) Sam		88	Kidney failure after gall bladder surgery
1985	EVANS, Clifford		73	
1985	#+ FAYLEN, Frank		79	After a long illness
1985	# FETCHIT, Stepin		83	Pneumonia & heart failure
1985	FEURY, Peggy		?	Automobile accident
1985	FLEISCHER, Louis		94	
1985	FOSTER, Alan		80	Cancer
1985	# FOSTER, Phil		71	Heart attack
1985	# FRAZEE, Jane		67	Pneumonia (following a stroke)
1985	GANTRY, Donald		52	Cancer
1985	GERASIMOV, Sergei		79	
1985	GILMAN, Sam		70	Cancer
1985	GORDON, Noele		61	Cancer
1985	# GORDON, Ruth	★	88	Stroke

YEAR	NAME		AGE	CAUSE AND/OR PLACE OF DEATH
1985	GOUDAL, Jetta		86	
1985	# GRANT, Kirby		74	Automobile accident
1985	GREENE, Richard		66	Cardiac arrest after a fall (in Norfolk, England)
1985	GREENFIELD, Calvin "Rusty"		58	Lung cancer (in Santa Monica, CA)
1985	GREENWAY, Tom		75	Heart attack (in Los Angeles, CA)
1985	# HALE, Georgia		79	
1985	HALL, Grayson	☆	58	Cancer
1985	HAMILTON, John		?	Heart attack (Do not confuse with John Hamilton, d. 1958)
1985	HAMILTON, Margaret		83	Heart attack
1985	HANEY, David		44	Heart attack
1985	HARVEY, Harry Sr.		84	
1985	+ HATHAWAY, Henry	☆	86	Heart attack
1985	HAUSER, Gayelord		89	Complications from pneumonia
1985	HAYDN, Richard		80	
1985	# HAYWARD, Louis		76	Lung cancer
1985	HECHT, Howard		77	
1985	# HENDERSON, Dickie		62	Cancer
1985	HIBBS, Jesse		79	Alzheimer's disease
1985	HILLPOT, William A.		79	Pneumonia
1985	#+ HUDSON, Rock	☆	59	Complications from A.I.D.S.
1985	HUFFMAN, David		40	Murdered (stabbed to death)
1985	JEANS, Isabel		93	
1985	JONES, Tyrone		29	Automobile accident
1985	# JOY, Leatrice		91	
1985	# KARLSON, Phil		77	Cancer
1985	+ KATZ, Mickey		75	Natural causes
1985	KENIN, Alexa		23	
1985	KEYSER, Andy		33	Cancer
1985	KING, Wayne		84	
1985	+ KYSER, Kay		79	Heart attack
1985	LALLY, Michael Sr.		82	
1985	LATCHAW, Paul		38	Complications from A.I.D.S.
1985	# LeROY, Hal		71	Following heart surgery
1985	LEWIS, Jarma		54	Natural causes
1985	LINTON, Mark		28	Heart failure & pneumonia
1985	LIST, Eugene		66	Found dead at home
1985	LIVINGSTON, Margaret		89	
1985	LODGE, John Davis		82	Heart attack
1985	LONDON, George		64	Following a heart attack
1985	MacLAREN, Mary		85	Respiratory problems
1985	MacVEIGH, Earle		74	Cancer
1985	#+ Margo (Margo Albert)		68	
1985	MARIS, Roger		51	
1985	+ MARTIN, Marion		76	Natural causes
1985	MASONER, Gene		41	A.I.D.S.
1985	MATHESON, Murray		73	Heart failure
1985	MAYER, Kenneth M. "Ken"		66	
1985	MEMMOLI, George T.		46	Heart failure
1985	MICHAELIDES, George		66	Complications after heart surgery
1985	+ MILLER, Marvin		72	
1985	NASH, Clarence "Donald Duck"		80	Leukemia
1985	#+ NELSON, Rick		45	Airplane crash (near DeKalb, TX) traces of cocaine found in his body
1985	NOLAN, James		69	Lung cancer
1985	+ NOLAN, Lloyd		83	Lung cancer
1985	+ O'BRIEN, Edmond	★	69	Alzheimer's disease, after suffering heart problems
1985	O'BRIEN, George		85	Following a stroke
1985	O'BRIEN, Kenneth		49	Cancer
1985	OLSON, Johnny ("Come on down")		75	Brain hemorrhage
1985	O'MALLEY, J. Pat		80	Heart condition (Do not confuse with Pat O'Malley, d. 1966)
1985	ORMANDY, Eugene		85	
1985	PARKER, Dennis		38	
1985	PARRY, Harvey		85	Heart attack
1985	PEARY, Harold "Gildersleeve"		76	Heart attack
1985	PURCELL, Noel		84	
1985	READICK, Robert		59	Automobile accident

YEAR	NAME		AGE	CAUSE AND/OR PLACE OF DEATH
1985	REDGRAVE, Michael	☆	77	Parkinson's disease
1985	REESE, Sammy Pharr		55	Massive stroke
1985	+ RIDDLE, Nelson		64	Cardiac & kidney failure
1985	+ RITZ, Jimmy		81	Heart failure
1985	ROBBINS, Randall		45	
1985	ROSS, Jane		50	During surgery for cancer
1985	RYAN, Kathleen		63	
1985	RYSKIND, Morrie		89	Apparent stroke
1985	# SARONY, Leslie		88	
1985	+ SAVALAS, George		60	Leukemia
1985	SAVILLE, Ruth		92	
1985	SCOURBY, Alexander		71	
1985	# SHAUGHNESSY, Mickey		64	Lung cancer
1985	SHERMAN, Ransom		87	
1985	SHUE, Larry		38	Airplane crash
1985	# SIGNORET, Simone	★	64	Cancer
1985	#+ SILVERS, Phil		73	Natural causes
1985	SIMPSON, Mickey		72	Heart attack
1985	SMITH, Kent		78	Congestive heart failure
1985	SMITH, Muriel		61	
1985	SMITH, Samantha		13	Airplane crash after filming in England
1985	SOLON, Ewen		62	
1985	# SONDERGAARD, Gale	★	86	
1985	SPIEGEL, Sam		84	While vacationing in the Caribbean
1985	SPOLIANSKY, Mischa		86	
1985	STOLL, George		79	
1985	STORER, Conrad L.		55	Cancer
1985	STRETTON, Ellen		71	Pneumonia
1985	STROUD, Claude		78	Throat cancer
1985	SWEET, Dolph		64	Cancer
1985	# TERRY, Tex		82	
1985	TRUBSHAWE, Michael		80	
1985	WAYNE, Carol		42	Drowned
1985	# WELLES, Orson	☆	70	Heart attack
1985	WELSH, John		70	Cancer
1985	WEST, Madge		93	
1985	WESTMORE, Frank		62	After treatment for a cardiac condition
1985	WESTON, Steve		45	Results of a fall from the roof of his home
1985	WHITE, Jules J.		84	Alzheimer's disease
1985	WILLIAMS, Grant		54	Peritonitis
1985	WILLIAMS, Tex		68	Cancer
1985	WORMS, Robert A. III		52	Heart failure
1985	ZIMBALIST, Efrem Sr.		95	
1986	# ACKLES, Kenneth		70	Stroke (in Pasadena, TX)
1986	AHERNE, Brian	☆	83	Heart failure (in Venice, FL)
1986	#+ ALDA, Robert		72	Effects of a stroke (in Los Angeles, CA)
1986	AMY, George J.		86	After a long illness (in Los Angeles, CA)
1986	ANDREWS, Ann		95	
1986	+ ANGEL, Heather		76	
1986	ARLEN, Harold		81	
1986	+ ARMSTRONG, Herbert W.		93	Died in his sleep
1986	#+ ARNAZ, Desi		69	Lung cancer
1986	ATWATER, Edith		74	Cancer
1986	BADDELEY, Hermione	☆	79	Stroke
1986	+ BAER, Jacob "Buddy"		71	
1986	BAKER-BERGEN, Stuart		40	Complications from A.I.D.S. (in New Orleans, LA)
1986	BAKER, Hylda		78	
1986	BANDY, Way		45	A.I.D.S.
1986	BASELEON, Michael		61	
1986	BECHER, John C.		71	Cancer
1986	BERGNER, Elizabeth	☆	85	
1986	+ BERNARDI, Herschel		62	Heart attack
1986	# BJORNSTRAND, Gunnar		77	
1986	BONNELL, Lee		67	Heart attack (in Santa Monica, CA)

YEAR	NAME		AGE	CAUSE AND/OR PLACE OF DEATH
1986	BREMEN, Lennie		71	
1986	BRIGGS, Donald P.		75	Cancer
1986	BRODUS, Tex		81	Massive stroke
1986	BROOKE, Walter		71	Emphysema
1986	BROWN, Harry		69	(Do not confuse with Harry Joe Brown, d. 1972)
1986	BRYAN, Ken		32	An A.I.D.S.-related illness
1986	# BUBBLES, John W.		84	Died in Los Angeles, CA
1986	CABOT, Susan		59	Beaten to death in her home
1986	CAESAR, Adolph		52	Heart attack
1986	+ CAGNEY, James	★	86	Diabetes, heart & lung problems
1986	CALDWELL, Don		51	A.I.D.S.
1986	CAMPBELL, Muriel		75	
1986	CANTY, Marietta		80	
1986	# CANUTT, Yakima		90	Natural causes
1986	CAREY, Denis		77	
1986	CARMEL, Roger		53	Drug overdose
1986	CASE, Allen		51	Heart attack
1986	CHAPMAN, Ted		63	Natural causes
1986	CHILDRESS, Alvin		78	Parkinson's disease, diabetes, pneumonia
1986	CLARK, Mamo		72	Cancer
1986	COHEN, Myron		83	
1986	COLERIDGE, Sylvia		76	
1986	# COLONNA, Jerry		82	Kidney failure
1986	COOPER, Edna Mae		85	
1986	COURTOT, Marguerite		88	
1986	CRAIG, Helen		74	Cardiac arrest
1986	#+ CRAWFORD, Broderick	★	74	Series of strokes
1986	+ CROTHERS, Benjamin "Scatman"		76	Lung cancer
1986	CUNNINGHAM, Sarah		67	Asthmatic attack
1986	# DAINTY, Billy		59	
1986	DaSILVA, Howard		76	
1986	DEERING, Olive		67	Cancer
1986	DeRUE, Carmen		78	Heart attack
1986	DOMINIQUE, Laurien		29	Embolism
1986	DRIVAS, Robert		50	
1986	+ DUNCAN, Vivian "Little Eva"		84	Alzheimer's disease
1986	ECCLES, Donald		77	Automobile crash
1986	EDWARDS, Guy		51	Heart attack
1986	# ERICKSON, Leif		72	
1986	FARR, Derek		74	
1986	FERNANDEZ, Emilio		82	Heart attack
1986	FRANCIS, Ivor		68	
1986	+ FREDERICK, Freddie Burke		65	Ventricular arrhythmia due to myocardial infarction
1986	GABEL, Martin		73	
1986	GIBNEY, Louise		90	
1986	GILLMORE, Margalo		88	
1986	GILMORE, Virginia		66	Emphysema
1986	+ GOODMAN, Benny		77	Heart attack
1986	#+ GRANT, Cary	☆	82	Massive stroke
1986	GREGG, Virginia		70	Cancer (in Encino, CA)
1986	HALOP, Florence		63	Cancer
1986	HAMILTON, Murray		63	Cancer
1986	# HAYDEN, Sterling		70	Cancer
1986	HAYNES, Hilda		72	
1986	+ HEIDT, Horace		85	Pneumonia & heart trouble
1986	HELPMANN, Robert		76	
1986	HERBERT, Tim		71	Heart attack
1986	HEWITT, Alan		71	Cancer
1986	HICKMAN, Bill		65	Cancer
1986	HIGBE, Mary Jane		70	Stroke
1986	HOFFMAN, Beth Webb		89	
1986	HURST, B. D.		91	
1986	JAMES, Claire		65	
1986	# JEROME, Suzie		26	Cut wrists & exposure
1986	JONES, Darby		76	Cancer

...DEATHS OF MOVIE AND TELEVISION PERSONALITIES — BY YEAR...

YEAR	NAME		AGE	CAUSE AND/OR PLACE OF DEATH
1986	JOYCE, Anna		74	
1986	# KAY, Beatrice		79	After suffering several strokes
1986	KEAN, Betty		69	After a brief illness
1986	KEENAN, Paul		30	A.I.D.S.
1986	KING, Dennis Jr.		?	Heart attack
1986	#+ KNIGHT, Ted		62	After surgery for a urinary tract growth
1986	LAMBERT, Douglas		50	A.I.D.S.
1986	#+ LANCHESTER, Elsa	☆	84	Bronchial pneumonia
1986	LANDIS, Joseph P.		67	Cancer
1986	LEE, Carl		52	
1986	LEONE, Johnny		71	Stroke
1986	LERNER, Alan Jay		67	Lung cancer
1986	LEWIS, Buddy		62	Apparent heart attack
1986	LOOS, Anne		70	
1986	LOPEZ, J. Victor		39	A.I.D.S.
1986	LORMER, Jon		80	
1986	# LOVE, Bessie	☆	87	
1986	# LYS, Lya		78	Heart ailment
1986	# MACK, Helen		72	Cancer
1986	MacLAUGHLIN, Don		79	
1986	MacRAE, Gordon		65	Cancer of the mouth & jaw
1986	McCARTHY, Frank		74	
1986	McINTIRE, Tim		42	Heart failure
1986	McKENNA, Siobhan		63	
1986	McKENZIE, Ida Mae		?	
1986	McLAUGHLIN, Don		79	After a brief illness
1986	MEARS, Martha		78	Complications from Alzheimer's disease
1986	MERKEL, Una	☆	82	
1986	# MILLAND, Ray	★	81	Cancer
1986	MILLER, Court		34	Complications from A.I.D.S.
1986	+ MINNELLI, Vincente	★	83	
1986	MOLLISON, Clifford		89	
1986	MORRIS, Rolland "Rusty"		63	Cancer
1986	NAZARRO, Ray		83	
1986	# NEAGLE, Anna		81	
1986	+ NELSON, Frank		75	Cancer
1986	# NICHOLS, Dandy		78	
1986	#+ PALMER, Lilli		71	Cancer
1986	PALMER, Norman		65	
1986	PARIS, Jerry		60	Complications from a brain tumor
1986	PENDER, Stephen		35	Complications from A.I.D.S.
1986	# PERKINS, Marlin		81	Lymphatic cancer
1986	# PHOENIX, Pat		62	Lung cancer
1986	POOLE, Roy		62	
1986	PREMINGER, Otto	☆	79	Cancer
1986	PROACH, Henry		66	
1986	#+ REED, Donna	★	64	Pancreatic cancer
1986	+ RITZ, Harry		78	Cancer
1986	ROBINS, Barry		41	
1986	ROBINSON, Bartlett "Bart"		73	After a long bout with cancer
1986	RUBIN, Benny		86	
1986	SCHUSTER, Harold		83	
1986	SCOTT, Ken		58	Emphysema & heart failure
1986	# SIMPSON, Bill		54	
1986	SMITH, Justin		66	Complications from A.I.D.S.
1986	#+ SMITH, Kate		79	After a long bout with diabetes & heart problems
1986	STARRETT, Charles		82	Cancer
1986	STEPHENS, Harvey		85	
1986	STEVENS, Paul		65	Pneumonia
1986	STEVENSON, Robert (director)		81	After a long illness
1986	STEWART, Paul		77	Heart attack
1986	STOCK, Nigel		66	Heart attack
1986	STONE, Sidney		83	Heart failure
1986	STUCKER, Stephen		36	Complications from A.I.D.S.
1986	SWEET, Blanche		90	Stroke

• New entry.   # Original name (Pt. 7).   + Interment (Pt. 5).

☆ Oscar nominee, ★ Oscar winner (Pt. 10)

YEAR	NAME	AGE	CAUSE AND/OR PLACE OF DEATH
1986	TARKOVSKY, Andrei	54	Cancer
1986	TEITEL, Carol	62	Complications after a car accident
1986	TRACY, Steve	34	Complications from A.I.D.S.
1986	+ TUCKER, Forrest	71	Throat cancer
1986	TUCKER, Lorenzo	79	Cancer
1986	+ TUTTLE, Lurene	79	
1986	#+ VALLEE, Rudy	84	Heart attack
1986	VanDYKE, Willard	79	Heart attack (while driving from New Mexico to Mass.)
1986	VIGRAN, Herbert	76	Cancer
1986	+ WALLIS, Hal	88	Died in his sleep
1986	WARNER, Gertrude	68	Cancer
1986	WARNERS, Robert	29	
1986	WHEEL, Patricia	61	
1986	WIECK, Dorothea	78	
1986	WILSON, Margery	89	
1986	WILSON, Teddy	73	Following intestinal surgery
1986	WINDSOR, Marie	64	
1986	#+ WYNN, Keenan	70	Cancer
1986	YALE, Joseph	36	Complications from A.I.D.S.
1986	# ZAREMBA, Jack	77	Heart attack
1987	ABEL, Walter	88	Heart attack (in Essex, CT)
1987	ADAMS, Peter	69	Cancer (in Beverly Hills, CA)
1987	ALDERMAN, John	53	Apparent heart attack (in Hollywood, CA)
1987	ALLEGRET, Yves	79	Heart attack (in France)
1987	ALLEN, Irving	82	After a long illness (in Encino, CA)
1987	ALLEN, Vera	89	Heart failure (at a retirement home in Croton-on-Hudson, NY)
1987	ARLISS, Leslie	86	
1987	# ARNAUD, Georges	69	
1987	#+ ASTAIRE, Fred ☆	88	Pneumonia
1987	#+ ASTOR, Mary ★	81	Emphysema
1987	ATTAWAY, Ruth	77	Injuries from a fire in her apartment
1987	BAILEY, Sherwood "Spud"	64	Cancer
1987	BAIRD, Bil	82	
1987	# BASS, Alfie	66	Heart attack
1987	BAUERSMITH, Paula	78	Cancer
1987	BELLIN, Olga	54	Cancer
1987	BENNET, Spencer Gordon	94	
1987	BERMAN, Dr. Edgar	68	
1987	BISSELL, Patrick	30	Overdose of cocaine, codeine, methadone
1987	# BLAKELY, Colin	56	Leukemia
1987	BLAKELY, Gene	66	Bone cancer
1987	BLASETTI, Alessandro	86	
1987	BOLAND, Joseph S.	83	
1987	#+ BOLGER, Ray	83	Cancer
1987	BOOKER, Bernice Ingalls	91	
1987	BRANNUM, Hugh	77	Cancer
1987	BRESSAN, Arthur J. Jr.	44	A.I.D.S.
1987	+ BROWN, Clarence ☆	97	Kidney failure
1987	BRUCK, Karl	81	Cancer
1987	BURNELL, Peter	44	
1987	BUTTERFIELD, Paul	44	
1987	CAMERON, Donald A.	61	
1987	CAMPBELL, Archie	72	Renal & heart failure
1987	CARROLL, Madeleine	81	Following a long illness
1987	# CARUSO, Enrico Jr.	82	Following a heart attack
1987	CASPARY, Vera	87	
1987	CHARLES, Anthony	42	Heart attack
1987	CHRISTY, Ann	82	Heart attack
1987	CLARKE, Raymond	47	A.I.D.S.
1987	COCO, James	56	Heart attack
1987	COE, Peter	58	Killed when his car collided with a van
1987	# COLLIER, Patience	76	
1987	COLLIER, William "Buster" Jr.	86	Cardiac arrest
1987	COOPER, Olive	94	Pneumonia

...DEATHS OF MOVIE AND TELEVISION PERSONALITIES — BY YEAR...

YEAR	NAME		AGE	CAUSE AND/OR PLACE OF DEATH
1987	COSTELLO, Carole		48	Stroke
1987	# CULVER, Calvin		43	Pulmonary infection
1987	DAMON, Cathryn		56	Cancer
1987	# DANA, Viola		90	Heart failure
1987	DANDRIDGE, Ruby		87	
1987	DAWSON, Hal K.		90	Stroke
1987	DEMPSTER, Hugh		86	Heart failure
1987	DOBSON, James		67	Heart attack
1987	# DONOVAN, Casey		43	Pulmonary infection
1987	DONOVAN, King		69	Cancer
1987	DUNN, Clara Whips		90	Congestive heart failure
1987	DuPRE, Jacqueline		42	Multiple sclerosis
1987	+ EGAN, Richard		65	Prostate cancer
1987	EVANS, Wilbur W.		81	
1987	FAULKNER, Ralph B.		95	After a brief illness
1987	FONG, Benson		70	Following a stroke
1987	# FOSSE, Bob	★	60	Massive heart attack
1987	FRANCIS, Raymond		76	
1987	FRANJU, Georges		75	
1987	# FRASER, Bill		79	
1987	FREGONESE, Hugo		78	Heart attack
1987	FROHLICH, Gustav		85	Following surgery
1987	GEARY, John		47	Apparent heart attack (while driving)
1987	GERAGHTY, Maurice		78	
1987	GESSNER, Adrienne		90	
1987	GIBSON, Wynne		82	Stroke
1987	+ GINGOLD, Hermione		89	Pneumonia & cardiac disease
1987	+ GLEASON, Jackie	☆	71	Cancer of the liver & colon
1987	+ GREENE, Lorne		72	Pneumonia following ulcer surgery (in Santa Monica, CA)
1987	GREENWOOD, Joan		65	Heart attack (in London, England)
1987	HAMMER, Irene Wicker		86	
1987	HANDL, Irene		85	
1987	HARTMAN, Elizabeth	☆	45	Suicide (jumped from her 5th-floor apartment)
1987	HAYES, Bernadine		75	Heart attack
1987	HAYNES, Lloyd		52	Lung cancer
1987	#+ HAYWORTH, Rita		68	Alzheimer's disease
1987	HEIFETZ, Jascha		86	Following brain surgery (after a fall)
1987	#+ HERMAN, Woody		74	Congestive heart failure & emphysema
1987	HOLCOMBE, Harry		80	
1987	HONRI, Baynham		83	
1987	+ HUSTON, John	★	81	Complications from emphysema
1987	# HUTTON, Marion		67	Cancer
1987	ILINSKY, Igor		85	
1987	JAMESON, Joyce		55	
1987	# JARRETT, Art		81	Pneumonia
1987	JEFFRIES, Lang		55	Cancer
1987	#+ KAYE, Danny		74	Heart failure due to hepatitis
1987	+ KAYE, Nora (Ross)		67	Cancer
1987	KAYE, Sammy		77	
1987	KELLER, Harry		73	Heart complications
1987	KENNEDY, Madge		96	Respiratory failure
1987	KEZER, Glenn B.		63	Cancer
1987	KIDD, Jonathan (Kurt Richards)		73	After surgery for an aorta aneurysm
1987	KNIGHT, Esmond		80	
1987	# KNIGHT, June		74	Complications after a stroke
1987	#+ LAKE, Arthur "Dagwood"		81	Heart attack
1987	LEARN, Betsy		98	
1987	+ LeROY, Mervyn	☆	86	Heart failure
1987	LESCOULIE, Jack		75	Colon cancer
1987	LEVINE, Joseph E.		81	
1987	#+ LIBERACE, Walter "Lee"		67	Complications from A.I.D.S.
1987	LONERGAN, Lenore		59	Cancer
1987	LUBOFF, Norman		70	Cancer
1987	# LUCE, Clare Boothe		84	Cancer (Do not confuse with Claire Luce, d. 1989)
1987	LUDLAM, Charles		44	Pneumonia complicated by A.I.D.S.

• New entry. # Original name (Pt. 7). + Interment (Pt. 5).　　88　　☆ Oscar nominee, ★ Oscar winner (Pt. 10)

YEAR	NAME		AGE	CAUSE AND/OR PLACE OF DEATH
1987	MacGIBBON, Harriet		81	After suffering from pulmonary & heart problems
1987	MACKAY, Fulton		64	
1987	MAGNOTTA, Vic		43	Drowned during filming of a car stunt
1987	+ MAMOULIAN, Rouben		90	Natural causes
1987	MANGER, Winifred Brison		94	Following a long illness
1987	MANN, Jerry		77	After a series of strokes that left him an invalid
1987	MARQUAND, Richard		49	Stroke
1987	+ MARTIN, Dean Paul Jr.		35	Crash of his F-4C Phantom-II jet on a training flight
1987	MARTIN, Vivian		95	After a long illness
1987	+ MARVIN, Lee	★	63	Heart attack
1987	McKAY, Scott		71	Kidney failure
1987	McKENZIE, Ella		?	
1987	MEYER, Dorothy		62	Cancer
1987	+ MEYER, Emile G.		76	Alzheimer's disease
1987	MINOR, Michael		46	A.I.D.S.
1987	MONTGOMERY, Earl		65	Cancer
1987	MORGAN, Elizabeth		84	After a stroke
1987	#+ NEGRI, Pola		87	Brain tumor, complicated by pneumonia
1987	NELSON, Ralph		71	Cancer
1987	OBOLER, Arch		78	Stroke
1987	O'BRIEN, Eloise Taylor		84	
1987	# O'DAY, Molly		64	Cancer
1987	ONDRA, Anny		84	
1987	O'PHELAN, Sean		33	Cancer
1987	# ORLANDO, Don		75	Heart attack (while playing golf in Glendale, CA)
1987	PAGE, Geraldine	★	62	Heart attack
1987	# PAIGE, Robert		76	
• 1987	#+ PAM, Anita		77	
1987	PATRICK, Dorothy		65	Cancer
1987	PELLER, Clara		86	Died in her sleep (at her home in Chicago, IL)
1987	POLK, David		55	Cancer
1987	# PRESTON, Robert		68	Lung cancer
• 1987	PRICE, Kenny		?	
1987	# QUALEN, John		87	Heart failure
1987	REED, T. Michael		42	Complications from A.I.D.S.
1987	+ REY, Alejandro		57	Cancer
1987	RHODES, Grandon		82	After a long illness
1987	+ RICE, Adnia		64	Cancer
1987	#+ RICH, Buddy		69	Heart attack (during brain tumor surgery)
1987	+ RORKE, Hayden		76	Cancer
1987	ROSE, William		67	
1987	ROUSE, Russell		74	Heart failure
1987	ROWAN, Dan		65	Lymphatic cancer
1987	SALT, Waldo		72	
1987	SAMPSON, Will		53	Following a heart-lung transplant
1987	SANDERS, Denis		58	Died in his sleep
1987	SANTORO, Dean		49	
1987	# SCOTT, Randolph		89	Natural causes
1987	SECREST, James		51	Lymphoma of the brain
1987	SEGOVIA, Andres		94	Heart failure
1987	# SHAWLEE, Joan		61	Cancer
1987	#+ SHAWN, Dick		63	Apparent heart attack (while appearing on stage)
1987	# SIRK, Douglas		86	Cancer
1987	SLATER, Patrick Scott		42	A.I.D.S.
1987	STRYKER, Christopher		27	A.I.D.S.
1987	SULLIVAN, Maxine		75	A seizure brought on by pneumonia
1987	SUNDBERG, Clinton		81	Heart failure
1987	SUSSKIND, David		66	Natural causes (heart attack?)
1987	SUTHERLAND, Esther		54	Heart attack
1987	#+ TAYLOR, Kent		80	Following several heart operations
1987	TEASDALE, Verree		80	
1987	# TERRY, Alice (Alice Ingram)		88	
1987	THATCHER, Heather		90	
1987	TOMLIN, Pinky		80	Heart attack
1987	+ TORRES, Raquel		78	Heart attack

YEAR	NAME		AGE	CAUSE AND/OR PLACE OF DEATH
1987	TRAEGER, Kim Patrick		36	Heart attack
1987	# TRAEGER, Rick		74	Apparent heart attack two days after his son died
1987	TROUGHTON, Patrick		67	
1987	TURNER, Jerry		60	Throat cancer (in Baltimore, MD)
1987	VALENTY, Lili		86	
1987	VERNON, Jackie		62	Apparent heart attack
1987	#+ VonERICH, Michael		23	
1987	VonTRAPP, Marie Augusta		82	Congestive heart failure
1987	+ WARHOL, Andy		59	Cardiac arrest (gall bladder surgery)
1987	WATT, Harry		80	
1987	WEISENBORN, Gordon		64	
1987	WHITE, Ward		60	Cancer
1987	WIARD, William		59	Lung cancer
1987	WILLIAMS, Emlyn		81	Following cancer surgery
1987	WILSON, Earl		79	After a long illness
1988	AAMES, Angela		32	Died in West Hills, CA
1988	ADAMS, Dorothy		88	Died in Woodland Hills, CA
1988	ARAGON, Jesse		32	Motorcycle accident
1988	ARUNDELL, Dennis		90	
1988	ASHBY, Hal	★	59	Liver cancer (in Malibu, CA)
1988	ASHCROFT, Ronnie		65	After a long illness
1988	AUCLAIR, Michel		65	
1988	# BAKER, Chet		59	Fall from a 2nd floor window (in Amsterdam)
1988	BALLARD, Lucien		84	Bicycle accident
1988	BARNETT, Nate		48	Heart attack
1988	BARNETT, Sanford H.	★	79	Following a stroke (in Oxnard, CA)
1988	+ BARSI, Judith		10	Murdered (shot by her father)
1988	BELASCO, Leon		86	Complications after a stroke
1988	+ BESSER, Joe		80	Found dead in his home
1988	BONNER, Margerie		83	Following a stroke
1988	# BOSWELL, Vet		77	
1988	BOW, Simmy		65	Complications after a stroke
1988	BROADBENT, George		83	
1988	BROWN, Alfredine "Alfie"		56	Heart failure from kidney disease
1988	BROX, Patricia (Gerstenzang)		?	
1988	BRYANT, Margot		90	
1988	BUTTERFIELD, Billy		71	
1988	CAGNEY, William J.		82	Heart attack
1988	CAMP, Wilson		74	Cancer
1988	CAPPELLANO, Francesca (Piazza)		92	Pneumonia
1988	CAREY, Olive (Golden)		92	
1988	#+ CARRADINE, John		82	Heart attack after strenuous stair climbing (in Italy)
1988	CASTELLANO, Richard	☆	55	Heart failure
1988	# CHANDLER, Chick		83	
1988	CHANDLER, Jim		65	Lung cancer
1988	CHODOROV, Edward		84	
1988	CLEMENTS, John		77	
1988	CLEWES, Howard		75	
1988	CODY, William "Wild Bill"		75	
1988	COHEN, Nat		82	
1988	COLLINS, Brent		46	Apparent heart attack
1988	COLMAN, Ben		81	Septicemia
1988	CONDOS, Nick		73	
1988	CONNELLY, Christopher		47	Cancer
1988	CONNOR, Whitfield		71	Complications following surgery
1988	COOK, Nathan		38	Allergic reaction to penicillin
1988	COOPER, Dorothy Jordan		82	
1988	CORTLAND, Nicholas		47	A.I.D.S.
1988	CRUICKSHANK, Andrew		80	
1988	CURTIS, Billy		79	Heart attack
1988	CUTHBERTSON, Allan		67	
1988	DANIELS, William "Billy"		73	Stomach cancer
1988	DAWN, Hazel		98	
1988	#+ DAY, Dennis		71	Amyotrophic lateral sclerosis

...DEATHS OF MOVIE AND TELEVISION PERSONALITIES — BY YEAR...

YEAR	NAME		AGE	CAUSE AND/OR PLACE OF DEATH
1988	DEAN, Priscilla		91	*As a result of a fall*
1988	DEENE, Lally		68	
1988	DeKOVEN, Roger		81	*Cancer*
1988	DELL, Gabriel		68	*Leukemia*
1988	DELVANDO, Amapola		78	
1988	DENTLER, Mary Ann		96	*Stroke*
1988	dePAUL, Gene Vincent		68	
1988	DEPEW, Joseph D.		76	
1988	DeSALES, Francis		76	*Cancer*
1988	# DIAMOND, I. A. L.		67	*Multiple myeloma (a form of cancer)*
1988	#+ Divine		42	*Heart disease*
1988	DOHERTY, Charla		41	*Natural causes*
1988	# DONNELL, Jeff		66	*Apparent heart attack*
1988	DONOVAN, Warde		72	
1988	DRU, Jason		58	*Emphysema-induced heart failure (in Van Nuys, CA)*
1988	DUGGAN, Andrew		64	*Cancer (in Westwood, CA)*
1988	EDWARDS, Gloria		43	*Cancer*
1988	# EDWARDS, Jimmy		68	*Bronchial pneumonia*
1988	EGOROV, Youri		33	*Complications of A.I.D.S.*
1988	# ELDRIDGE, Florence		86	*Natural causes*
1988	EMERY, Mary		91	
1988	FARLEY, Morgan		90	
1988	# FARMER, Virginia		90	
1988	FARRELL, Jack		52	*Cancer*
1988	FENNELLY, Parker		96	
1988	FIDLER, Jimmie		89	
1988	FLETCHER, Bramwell		84	
1988	# FLOWERS, Wayland		48	*Cancer*
1988	FOLSEY, George		90	
1988	FORD, Ross		65	*Cardiac arrest*
1988	FOULGER, Dorothy Adams		88	
1988	FRANK, Melvin		75	*Complications following open-heart surgery*
1988	FREY, Leonard	☆	49	*A.I.D.S.*
1988	FRIEBUS, Florida		79	
1988	# FROEBE, Gert		75	*Heart attack*
1988	GAUTHIER, Suzanne		61	*Cancer*
1988	GEISE, Tanya "Sugar"		71	*After a brief illness*
1988	+ GIBB, Andy		30	*Heart inflammation caused by a virus*
1988	GIBBS, Alan R.		47	*Cancer*
1988	GOODMAN, Lee		64	*Tuberculosis*
1988	GORMAN, Bobby		59	*Following a long illness*
1988	GRAHAM, Sheilah		84	*Congestive heart failure*
1988	GRANDIN, Ethel		94	
1988	+ GRANVILLE, Bonita (Wrather)	☆	65	
1988	HAHN, Paul		67	*After a short illness*
1988	HARRIS, Fox		52	*Lung cancer*
1988	HAWTREY, Charles		72	*Arterial disease*
1988	HAYES, William S.		29	*A.I.D.S.*
1988	HENDERSON, Jo		54	*Automobile accident*
1988	HENDLEY, Janet Stover		55	*Cancer*
1988	HIGGINS, Colin		47	*A.I.D.S.*
1988	HILLAIRE, Marcel		79	*Complications following surgery*
1988	HINTERMANN, Carlo		64	*Automobile accident*
1988	HOLLAND, Anthony		60	*Suicide (after suffering from A.I.D.S.)*
1988	HOLMES, John C.		43	*Encephalitis as a result of A.I.D.S.*
1988	HOPE, Harry		62	*Heart attack after playing in a basketball game*
1988	HOPPER, Jerry		81	*After suffering from heart problems*
1988	# HOUSEMAN, John	★	86	*Spinal cancer*
1988	HOWARD, Trevor	☆	71	*Influenza, bronchitis & jaundice*
1988	HUBBARD, John		65	
1988	JACOBSON, Henrietta		82	
1988	JEFFREY, Howard		53	*A.I.D.S.*
1988	JONES, Duane		51	
1988	JORDAN, Dorothy (Cooper)		82	
1988	+ JORDAN, Jim "Fibber McGee"		91	*Blood clot in brain (from a fall)*

YEAR	NAME		AGE	CAUSE AND/OR PLACE OF DEATH
1988	KINNEAR, Roy		54	After falling from his horse during filming
1988	KJELLIN, Alf		68	Heart attack
1988	KOSTER, Henry		83	
1988	LARSON, Eric		83	
1988	LASKY, Jesse L. Jr.		77	
1988	# LATZ, Elaine		71	
1988	LEIGH, George		78	Heart disease & diabetes
1988	LIGHT, Ann Rork		79	
1988	LINDSAY, Phillip		64	Pneumonia
1988	# LIVINGSTON, Robert (Bob)		79	Emphysema
1988	LLOYD, Paul Francis (Jimmy)		69	Liver disease
1988	# LODER, John		90	
1988	LOEWE, Frederick		86	Heart failure
1988	LOGAN, Joshua	☆	79	Supranuclear palsy
1988	LOW, Carl		71	Cancer
1988	LOWRY, Margerie Bonner		83	After suffering a stroke
1988	LUMMIS, Dayton		84	
1988	LYNN, Mara		60	Cancer
1988	MANSFIELD, Marian		83	Emphysema
1988	MARAVICH, Pete		40	
1988	MARICLE, Leona		81	Apparent heart attack
1988	MARTIN-HARVEY, Muriel		97	
1988	MAURA, Luis		38	A.I.D.S.
1988	McCRACKEN, James		61	Following two strokes
1988	McGUIRE, Tucker		75	
1988	# MEEKER, Ralph		67	Heart attack
1988	MEGLIN, Ethel		98	
1988	MILLER, Joan		78	
1988	# MINTZ, Eli		83	Pneumonia
1988	MITCHELL, Ewing Young		77	Following a stroke
1988	MITRY, Jean		80	
1988	MOBERLY, Robert		49	A.I.D.S.
1988	# MOORE, Colleen		85	Following a long illness
1988	MORGAN, Boyd F. "Red"		72	
1988	MORRIS, Mary		72	
1988	MURPHY, Timothy Patrick		29	A.I.D.S.
1988	MURRAY, Ken		85	
1988	# NAPIER, Alan		85	Natural causes
1988	NELSON, Christine		60	Lung cancer
1988	#+ Nico		49	Cerebral hemorrhage from bicycle fall
1988	NILES, Ken		82	
1988	NISSEN, Greta		82	Parkinson's disease
1988	NORDEN, Christine		63	Chest infection after heart surgery
1988	NOVAK, Eva		90	Pneumonia
1988	# OLIVER, Sy		77	
1988	OLIVER, Virgil		72	
1988	+ ORBISON, Roy		52	Heart attack
1988	+ O'ROURKE, Heather		12	Septic shock, congenital bowel narrowing
1988	OSBORN, Paul		86	Died in New York, NY
1988	PAWLEY, Edward		84	
1988	PINERO, Miguel		41	Cirrhosis of the liver
1988	PRESSBURGER, Emeric		85	
1988	QUINN, Louis		73	After a brief illness
1988	RAAB, Kurt		46	A.I.D.S.
1988	RAINES, Ella		66	Throat cancer
1988	# RAMAGE, Cecil		93	
1988	RAMSEY, Anne	☆	59	Throat cancer
1988	RAWLINS, Lester		63	Heart attack
1988	REARDON, John		58	Pneumonia
1988	# RHODES, Billie		93	Died in Los Angeles, CA
1988	# RICH, Irene		96	Heart failure
1988	RILEY, Jay Flash		72	
1988	+ ROBERSON, Chuck		69	Cancer
1988	ROBERTSON, Hugh A.		55	Cancer
1988	+ ROBINSON, Dar Allen		39	Motorcycle accident

...DEATHS OF MOVIE AND TELEVISION PERSONALITIES – BY YEAR...

YEAR	NAME	AGE	CAUSE AND/OR PLACE OF DEATH
1988	ROBINSON, Max	49	A.I.D.S.
1988	ROGELL, Albert S.	86	Cancer & diabetes
1988	ROSE, George	68	Automobile accident
1988	# ROSS, Lanny	82	Following two strokes
1988	ROSSON, Harold "Hal"	93	Natural causes
1988	# ROWE, Fanny	75	Died in London, England
1988	SCOTT, Timothy	32	Complications from A.I.D.S. (Do not confuse with T. Scott, d. 1995)
1988	SEYMOUR, Anne	79	Heart failure
1988	# SHAW, Victoria	53	Asthma
1988	SHER, Jack	75	After a brief illness
1988	SHOLOMIR, Jack	57	Heart attack
1988	SILVA, Trinidad Jr.	38	Traffic accident
1988	SMITH, Charles "Dizzy"	67	Apparent heart attack
1988	SMITH, Tucker	52	Cancer of the neck and jaw
1988	SOFAER, Abraham	91	Congestive heart failure
1988	+ SPERLING, Milton	76	
1988	ST. JOHN, Adela Rogers	94	
1988	STAVRIDIS, Nicos	77	Heart failure
1988	#+ STEELE, Bob	82	Heart failure after a long illness (in Burbank, CA)
1988	STOPPA, Paolo	81	
1988	# TERRY, Don	86	Stroke
1988	THOMPKINS, Toney	33	A.I.D.S.
1988	TREVELYAN, John	83	
1988	VEHR, Bill	48	A.I.D.S.
1988	VonSTROHEIM, Valerie	91	
1988	WARREN, Jerry	65	Lung cancer
1988	WASHBOURNE, Mona	84	
1988	WASHINGTON, Vernon	64	
1988	WHITE, John Sylvester	68	Pancreatic cancer
1988	WILLES, Jean	65	Liver cancer
1988	WILLIAMS, Kenneth	62	Heart attack
1988	WILLMAN, Noel	70	Heart attack
1988	WILSON, Lois	93	Pneumonia
1988	WYCKOFF, Michael	69	After a stroke
1989	AILEY, Alvin	58	Dyscrasia (a blood disorder) in New York
1989	ALEXANDER, Richard	86	Pulmonary edema (in Woodland Hills, CA)
1989	ALLISON, Fran	81	Complications of a blood disorder (in Sherman Oaks, CA)
1989	ALLISON, May	98	Respiratory failure (in Bratenahl, OH)
1989	ANDREWS, Harry	77	Viral infection complicated by asthma
1989	ANDREWS, Nancy	68	Heart attack
1989	# ANTHONY, Rick	60	
1989	ARLEN, Roxanne (Shafer)	57	Cancer
1989	ARTHUR, Lee	49	Cancer
1989	+ BACKUS, Jim "Mr. Magoo"	76	Pneumonia & Parkinson's disease
1989	BAILEY, John	73	
1989	#+ BALL, Lucille	77	Ruptured aorta (after heart surgery)
1989	BANZHAF, Peter G.	57	Arrhythmia
1989	# BARI, Lynn	73	After a long illness
1989	BARRIER, Ernestine	81	
1989	BARRY, Joan	87	
1989	BASTIN, Charles A.	68	Cardiopulmonary arrest
1989	BAUM, Bobby	62	Following a brief illness
1989	BAVIER, Frances	86	Heart problems
1989	BAZLEN, Brigid	44	
1989	BEAM, Alvin	61	Cardiopulmonary arrest
1989	BENSON, Joe	73	Cancer
1989	#+ BERLIN, Irving	101	Died in his sleep
1989	BERNAU, Christopher	49	
1989	# BLAKE, Amanda "Miss Kitty"	60	A.I.D.S.-related complications
1989	#+ BLANC, Mel	81	Heart disease
1989	BLEYER, Archie	79	
1989	BLIER, Bernard	73	
1989	BLOOM, George	95	
1989	BOND, Raleigh	54	Lymphoma

YEAR	NAME		AGE	CAUSE AND/OR PLACE OF DEATH
1989	BOUISE, Jean		60	Cancer
1989	BRIGHT, John		81	Stroke
1989	BRISTER, John Tyler		38	A.I.D.S.
1989	BROCK, Heinie		89	Emphysema
1989	BROOKNER, Howard		34	A.I.D.S.
1989	BROTHERSON, Eric		78	
1989	BROWN, Tally		64	After suffering a stroke
1989	BRUMER, Martin		28	Automobile accident
1989	BRYANT, John		72	Cancer
1989	BUCK, David		53	Cancer
1989	BUETEL, Jack		74	After a long illness
1989	BURKS, Rick		26	Automobile accident
1989	BUTRICK, Merritt		29	A.I.D.S.
1989	CARMINE, Michael		30	Heart failure
1989	+ CASSAVETES, John	☆	59	Cirrhosis of the liver
1989	CAVALLARO, Carmen		76	Cancer
1989	CAYATTE, André		80	
1989	CHALLEE, William		84	Alzheimer's disease
1989	CHANDLER, Marjorie Grossel		71	Cancer
1989	CHAPMAN, Graham		48	Spinal cancer
1989	CHERRILL, Christine		71	
1989	CHIARI, Mario		79	
1989	CHING, William		75	Congestive heart failure
1989	CHRISTIE, Audrey		79	Emphysema
1989	CIRO, Steve		46	
1989	CLARK, Dort		71	Diabetes and cancer
1989	CLARKE, T. E. B.		81	
1989	COLEY, Thomas		75	Heart attack
1989	COLIN, Jean		83	
1989	COONAN, Sheila M.		66	Liver disease
1989	CORTEZ, Mildred		72	Cardiac arrest
1989	COSTA, Bob		66	
1989	COULOURIS, George		85	Heart attack
1989	COVAN, Willie		92	
1989	CROSBY, Lindsay		51	Suicide (gunshot)
1989	CUMMINGS, Jack		84	Heart attack
1989	DaCOSTA, Morton		74	Heart failure
1989	DALI, Salvador		84	Heart failure & pneumonia
1989	DALRYMPLE, Ian		85	
1989	D'AMICO, Teresa Tirelli		81	Brain tumor
1989	#+ DAVIS, Bette	★	81	Breast cancer
1989	DeCARLO, Vinnie		54	Heart attack
1989	DeSANTIS, Joe		80	Congestive heart failure
1989	DIFFRING, Anton		70	
1989	DIGNAM, Mark		80	
1989	DITTMAN, Dean Gus		57	Heart failure
1989	DRAKE, Dona		69	Cancer
1989	DRANE, Gary		46	
1989	DRINKWATER, Terry		53	Cancer
1989	DRYHURST, Edward		84	
1989	DuMAURIER, Daphne		81	After a brief illness
1989	DURANTE, Vito		64	A.I.D.S.
1989	EAMES, John Matthew		64	
1989	EVANS, Maurice		87	
1989	EVANS, Peter		38	Complications of A.I.D.S.
1989	FAIN, Sammy		87	
1989	FARRELL, Timothy (Sperl)		66	Heart condition
1989	FIELD, Ron		55	Neurological impairment due to brain lesions
1989	FINLEY, Evelyn		73	Heart attack
1989	FORREST, William H.		86	Natural causes
1989	FRENCH, Norma		47	Lymphoma
1989	FRENCH, Victor		54	Lung cancer
1989	FROME, Milton		78	Heart failure
1989	GARDE, Betty		84	
1989	GARDNER, Hy		80	Pneumonia

YEAR	NAME	AGE	CAUSE AND/OR PLACE OF DEATH
1989	GEER, Lenny	75	Heart failure
1989	GENTRY, Britt Nilsson	46	Cancer
1989	GERRINGER, Robert	63	After a series of strokes
1989	GIFFORD, Alan	78	
1989	GIMPEL, Jakob	82	
1989	# GLAUDI, Hap	77	Cancer
1989	GREEN, John	80	
1989	GRIFFIN, Bessie	67	Cancer
1989	GUIGLEY, Robert	76	Died in Los Angeles, CA
1989	HAIG, Jack	76	Cancer
1989	HALLIWELL, Leslie	59	Abdominal cancer
1989	HALSTED, Fred	47	Overdose of barbiturates
1989	HAMBLEN, Stuart	80	Brain cancer
1989	HARRIGAN, Nedda	89	Lung cancer
1989	HAYES, Grace	93	
1989	HAYMER, Johnny	69	Cancer
1989	HENSHAW, Wandalie	54	Parkinson's disease
1989	HERBERT, Pitt	74	Amyotrophic lateral sclerosis
1989	HESLER, G. Christian	33	A.I.D.S.
1989	HEYWOOD, Eddie	73	Parkinson's & Alzheimer's disease
1989	HOFFMAN, Abbie	52	Suicide (massive drug overdose)
1989	HOLT, Jason	39	A.I.D.S.
1989	HORNEZ, André	84	
1989	#+ HOROWITZ, Vladimir	85	Heart attack
1989	HOULE, Daniel	41	A.I.D.S.
1989	# HOWARD, Mary	76	After a brief illness
1989	# IMMEDIATO, Al	72	Cancer
1989	INGRAM, Bill	69	
1989	IVENS, Joris	90	
1989	JAFFE, Allen	60	After a long illness
1989	JONES, Reed	35	Liver cancer
1989	JORGENSEN, Christine (George)	62	Cancer of the bladder
1989	KAYE-MARTIN, Edward	50	Lymphoma
1989	KENNER, Warren	64	Heart attack
1989	KIRKWOOD, James Jr.	64	Cancer
1989	KRAMER, Mandel J.	72	
1989	KREEL, Kenneth	48	A.I.D.S.
1989	LAMPKIN, Charles	76	Natural causes
1989	LeBORG, Reginald	86	Heart attack
1989	# LEE, Billy	60	Heart failure
1989	LEE, Brian	36	Pneumonia
1989	LEONE, Sergio	60	Heart attack
1989	+ LERNER, Sam	86	
1989	LeVEQUE, Edward	92	
1989	LEVINE, Nathan	89	
1989	# LILLIE, Beatrice	94	
1989	LION, Margo	90	
1989	LOW, Warren	83	Following a long illness
1989	LUCE, Claire	88	(Do not confuse with Clare Booth Luce, d. 1987)
1989	LUCKHAM, Cyril	81	
1989	MACCARI, Ruggero	70	
1989	# MACK, Marion	86	Heart failure
1989	MADDEN, Jeanne	73	Heart trouble
1989	MAGUIRE, Kathleen	64	Cancer
1989	# MAHONEY, Jock	70	Stroke following an auto accident
1989	MANES, Gina	94	
1989	MANGANO, Silvano	59	Heart attack following a tumor operation
1989	MARCH, Alex	68	Heart failure
1989	MARQUISS, Ralph E. Jr.	34	Adrenal cancer
1989	# MARSH, Tiger Joe	78	
1989	MARSHALL, Andrew 3rd	52	Cancer
1989	MATSUDA, Yusaku	40	Bladder cancer
1989	MATUSZAK, John	38	Heart failure from drug overdose
1989	McANALLY, Ray	63	
1989	McGUIRE, Jon Brandon	34	Liver failure

YEAR	NAME		AGE	CAUSE AND/OR PLACE OF DEATH
1989	McMILLAN, Kenneth		56	Liver disease
1989	MEILLON, John		55	
1989	MELVILLE, Sam		52	Heart attack
1989	MEYERS, Timothy		44	A.I.D.S.
1989	MILANOV, Zinka		83	Stroke
1989	MILLS, Herbert		77	
1989	MILTON, Billy		83	
1989	MORGAN, Mary		81	
1989	MORGAN, Rex		67	Parkinson's disease
1989	MORIN, Alberto		86	Stroke
1989	# MORRISON, Ernie		76	Cancer
1989	MOSS, Arnold		80	Lung cancer
1989	MOWER, Margaret		93	
1989	# MUELLER, Cookie		40	A.I.D.S.
1989	# MURRAY-MAZWI, Mark		52	Heart attack
1989	NEIDORF, Ross Lee		34	A.I.D.S.
1989	+ NEWMAN, Lionel		73	Cardiac arrest
1989	NIGHTINGALE, Earl		68	After heart surgery
1989	O'DAVOREN, Vesey		100	
1989	O'DAY, Nell		79	Cardiac arrest
1989	# O'HANLON, George		76	Stroke
1989	+ OLIVIER, Laurence	★	82	Died in his sleep (in London, England)
1989	OSTRICHE, Muriel		93	
1989	OSWALD, Gerd		72	Cancer
1989	OZERAY, Madeleine		78	
1989	PASS, Lenny		37	
1989	PAULSON, Al		67	Heart failure
1989	PAYNE, John		77	Congestive heart failure
1989	PERRIN, Vic		73	Cancer
1989	POMPEII, James S.		51	After a long illness
1989	POST, William Jr.		88	Pulmonary disease
1989	# PRINGLE, Aileen		94	
1989	QUAYLE, Anthony	☆	76	Cancer
1989	QUERTERMOUS, Charlie		41	Cancer
1989	QUINE, Richard		68	Suicide (shot himself) in his California home
1989	+ RADNER, Gilda		42	Ovarian cancer (in Los Angeles, CA)
1989	REID, Vivian		95	Natural causes
1989	+ ROBINSON, Sugar Ray		67	Heart & Alzheimer's disease & diabetes
1989	ROOS, Joanna		88	Ruptured aorta
1989	ROUD, Richard		59	Heart attack
1989	ROZAKIS, Gregory		46	A.I.D.S.
1989	SAUERS, Patricia		49	Complications from diabetes
1989	SAYER, Philip		42	Abdominal cancer
1989	+ SCHAEFFER, Rebecca		21	Murdered (shot)
1989	+ SCHAFFNER, Franklin J.	★	69	Cancer
1989	SCHAKNE, Robert		63	Cancer
1989	SCHORR, William		88	Respiratory failure
1989	# SERATO, Massimo		73	Heart attack
1989	SHELLEY, Dave		58	Lung complications after heart surgery
1989	SHENAR, Paul		53	A.I.D.S.
1989	SHERMAN, Connie		72	Respiratory failure
1989	SHERMAN, Hiram		81	Following a stroke
1989	SHERWOOD, Lydia		82	
1989	SHERWOOD, Madeline Hurlock		89	
1989	SHIRLEY, Bill		68	Lung cancer
1989	SILVER, Joe		66	Liver cancer
1989	SILVERMAN, Mark		36	A.I.D.S.
1989	SLATE, Jack		80	Heart attack
1989	SMITH, Jack		57	A.I.D.S. (Do not confuse with "Whispering" Jack Smith, d. 1950)
1989	SORM, Evald		57	
1989	SPINELL, Joe		51	Heart attack
1989	SPITZ, Hank		84	
1989	SQUIRE, William		72	
1989	STARRETT, Jack		52	Kidney failure
1989	STEVENS, Robert		68	Heart attack

YEAR	NAME		AGE	CAUSE AND/OR PLACE OF DEATH
1989	STOUT, Bill		62	Cardiac arrest
1989	SUNDIN, Michael		28	
1989	SYDNOR, Earl		81	Lung cancer
1989	TAFOYA, Alfonso		60	Massive heart attack
1989	TERRIS, Norma		87	After a brief illness
1989	THOMAS, Ann		75	Lung cancer
1989	THOMAS, Frank M.		100	
1989	THOMAS, Madoline		99	Natural causes
1989	THOR, Dan		34	A.I.D.S.
1989	THORPE-BATES, Peggy		75	
1989	TIRELLI, Teresa		81	Brain tumor
1989	TRAVIS, Richard		76	
1989	TRAYLOR, William		60	After a long illness
1989	TREEN, Mary		82	Cancer
1989	TREGOE, William		67	Cardiac arrest
1989	TUCKER, Julius L.		92	
1989	TUCKER, Tommy		86	
1989	+ VanCLEEF, Lee		64	Heart attack
1989	VANEL, Charles		96	
1989	VARDEN, Norma		90	Heart failure
1989	VAUGHAN, Skeeter		66	Heart attack
1989	+ VINCENT, Romo		80	
1989	VonCZIFFRA, Geza		88	
1989	VonKARAJAN, Herbert		81	Heart failure
1989	VOORHEES, Donald		85	Pneumonia
1989	WATSON, Douglass		68	Heart attack
1989	WEAVER, Carl Earl		36	A.I.D.S.
1989	WEBBER, Robert		64	Amyotrophic lateral sclerosis
1989	WEST, Lockwood		83	Cancer
1989	WETMORE, Joan		77	Cancer
1989	WHITE, Chrissie		94	
1989	WHITLEY, Keith		33	Alcohol poisoning
1989	#+ WILDE, Cornel ☆		74	Leukemia
1989	WILLIAMS, Clark		83	
1989	# WILLIAMS, Guy		65	Heart attack
1989	WILLINGER, Laszlo		80	
1989	# WILLIS, Matt		75	
1989	WILSON, Trey		40	Cerebral hemorrhage
1989	WINCKLER, Robert		62	Stomach cancer
1989	WINTERS, Roland		84	Stroke
1989	WONG, Iris		68	
1989	WOODBURY, Joan		73	Respiratory failure
1989	WOOLAND, Norman		83	Following several strokes
1989	WRIGHT, Ben		74	Heart failure after heart surgery
1989	ZAVATTINA, Cesare		86	
1989	ZEMAN, Karel		78	
1990	ABERNATHY, Ralph		64	
1990	ALEX, Robert		30	Gunshot wounds during a robbery at his home (in Silver Lake, CA)
1990	ALINDER, Dallas		58	Heart failure following a liver transplant
1990	ALLAN, Elizabeth		80	Died in London, England
1990	APPLEBY, Dorothy		84	
1990	#+ ARDEN, Eve ☆		83	Heart failure & cancer
1990	+ BAILEY, Pearl		72	Heart failure following surgery to replace a knee
1990	BAILEY, William H.		72	(Do not confuse with actor Bill Bailey, d. 1978)
1990	BALFOUR, Katharine		69	
1990	BALIN, Ina		52	Pulmonary hypertension
1990	BANEY, Joan Blazer		55	Brain tumor
1990	BARA, Nina		66	Cancer
1990	BARKER, Eric L.		78	
1990	BARRY, J. J.		58	Bronchial complications
1990	BARTLETT, Scott		47	Complications from a kidney & liver transplant
1990	BARTON, Larry		80	Following a stroke
1990	# BATORS, Stiv		40	After being hit by a car
1990	BAXLEY, Barbara		63	Apparent heart attack

YEAR	NAME	AGE	CAUSE AND/OR PLACE OF DEATH
1990	BEAGLE, Edward H.	46	Natural causes
1990	BELL, David	53	After a long illness (Do not confuse with David Scott Bell, d. 1980)
1990	BELLAMY, Madge	89	Heart failure
1990	BENNER, Richard	47	A.I.D.S.
1990	BENNETT, Jill	59	Suicide
1990	BENNETT, Joan	80	Cardiac arrest
1990	BERGHOF, Herbert	81	Heart ailment
1990	+ BERNSTEIN, Leonard	72	Complications from lung cancer & emphysema
1990	BERTO, Juliet	42	Cancer
1990	BINGO, Joe	65	Complications from a staph infection
1990	BINNS, Edward	74	Heart attack
1990	BLAKEY, Art	71	Lung cancer
1990	BLOCK, Eva Sully	88	Heart failure
1990	+ BOCK-LEADER, Deborah Lyn	38	
1990	BRADDELL, Maurice	89	
1990	BRANDON, Henry	77	Apparent heart attack
1990	# BRAUER, Tiny	82	Heart condition
1990	BRAUNBERGER, Pierre	85	
1990	BRAY, Stephen	33	
1990	BREM, Beppo	84	Heart failure
1990	BRIGGS, Richard R.	71	After a short illness
1990	BRODKIN, Herbert	77	Aneurysm
1990	BROWN, Karl	93	
1990	# BROWN, Tom	75	Cancer
1990	BUNNAGE, Avis	67	
1990	BURNS, Stephan	35	A.I.D.S.
1990	BURRUD, Bill	65	Heart attack (while swimming in the ocean)
1990	CALLOWAY, Northern J.	41	After being taken to a psychiatric hospital
1990	# Capucine	57	Suicide plunge from her 8th floor apartment (in Lausanne, Switz.)
1990	CAREY, Mary Jane	66	
1990	CARISTI, Vincent	42	Cancer
1990	CARPENTER, Charles	77	Heart attack
1990	CARRERAS, James	81	
1990	# CARSON, Sunset "Kit"	67	Heart attack
1990	CASSON, Ann	74	
1990	CASTLE, Lee	?	Heart attack
1990	CATHEY, Dalton	44	A.I.D.S.
1990	CHAFFEY, Don	72	Heart disease
1990	# CHAMPLIN, Irene	59	After a long illness
1990	CHARLESON, Ian	40	A.I.D.S. (Septicemia)
1990	CHENAL, Pierre	86	
1990	# CHRISTY, June	64	Complications of kidney failure
1990	# CHRYSIS, International	38	Cancer
1990	CLAIRE, Ludi	70	After a long illness
1990	CLANCY, Tom	67	Stomach cancer
1990	CLARK, Dee	52	
1990	CLEMENT, Marc R.	39	Automobile accident
1990	CLOCHE, Maurice	82	Parkinson's disease
1990	COFFIN, Tristram "Tris"	80	Lung cancer
1990	CONDOS, Steve	71	Heart attack
1990	CONIGLIARO, Tony	45	
1990	COOK, Roderick	58	
1990	COPLAND, Aaron ★	90	Complications of 2 strokes & respiratory problems
1990	CORBUCCI, Sergio	62	Heart attack
1990	CUGAT, Xavier	90	Heart failure due to arterial sclerosis
1990	# CULLEN, Bill	70	Heart failure from lung cancer
1990	+ CUMMINGS, Robert "Bob"	80	Parkinson's disease, kidney failure & pneumonia
1990	CURRIN, Jay C.	34	Injuries from a 55-foot fall while filming
1990	DAVIS, Patrick "Grampy"	87	Heart attack
1990	+ DAVIS, Sammy Jr.	64	Throat cancer
1990	# DEANE, Palmer	56	A.I.D.S.
1990	DeGRUNWALD, Dimitri	76	
1990	DEMY, Jacques	59	Leukemia
1990	DENNY, Joe	61	Respiratory failure
1990	DeTREAUX, Tamara "E.T."	31	Respiratory & heart problems

YEAR	NAME		AGE	CAUSE AND/OR PLACE OF DEATH
1990	DeVEGA, José Jr.		56	*A.I.D.S.*
1990	DeVITO, Julia		85	
1990	DeWITT, Lew		53	*Intestinal disorder*
1990	DRAKE, Fabia		86	
1990	DRAPER, Don		62	*A.I.D.S.*
1990	DUFF, Howard		72	*Heart attack*
1990	DUNN, Patricia		60	*Lung cancer*
1990	DUNN, Peter		68	*Heart attack*
1990	#+ DUNNE, Irene	☆	88	*Heart failure*
1990	d'USSEAU, Arnaud		73	*After surgery*
1990	DUX, Pierre		82	
1990	EASTERLING, Gary Lamont		38	
1990	EDDY, Helen Jerome		92	*Heart failure*
1990	EDWARDS, Douglas		73	*Cancer of the bladder*
1990	# EICHELBERGER, Ethyl		45	*Suicide (cut wrists)*
1990	EMERSON, Elsie Mae		86	*Complications from strokes*
1990	ENRIQUEZ, Rene		58	*Pancreatic cancer*
1990	Erté		97	
1990	ESMOND, Jill		82	
1990	FABRIZI, Aldo		84	*Heart attack*
1990	#+ FARRELL, Charles		89	*Cardiac arrest*
1990	FIELD, Irene		59	
1990	FLAUM, Mayer		89	*Pneumonia*
1990	FLETCHER, Jack		68	*Heart failure*
1990	FLUELLEN, Joel		82	*Apparent suicide (gunshot)*
1990	FOGERTY, Tom		48	
1990	FONTANA, Arlene		54	*Cancer*
1990	FRANCHI, Sergio		64	*Brain cancer*
1990	FRANCK, Edward A.		70	*Pneumonia*
1990	FRANK, Ben		56	*Heart attack*
1990	FREDERICK, Pauline (TV news)		84	*Heart attack (Do not confuse with actress Pauline Frederick, d. 1938)*
1990	FRENCH, Valerie		59	*Leukemia*
1990	GAMBARELLI, Maria		89	*Cerebral hemorrhage*
1990	#+ GARBO, Greta	☆	84	
1990	#+ GARDNER, Ava	☆	67	*Pneumonia*
1990	GATLIFF, Frank		62	
1990	# GILFORD, Jack	☆	81	*Stomach cancer*
1990	GLIDDON, John		92	
1990	# GODDARD, Paulette	☆	84	*Heart failure*
1990	GODSELL, Vanda		70	
1990	GORDON, Dexter	☆	67	*Kidney failure*
1990	GOULDING, Ray		68	*Kidney failure*
1990	# GRAZIANO, Rocky		68	*Cardiopulmonary failure*
1990	GREGORY, Charles "Mr. Music"		89	*Pneumonia*
1990	HAINES, Richard		43	*After surgery for a brain tumor*
1990	HAKINS, Dick		87	
1990	HALE, Alan Jr.		71	*Cancer*
1990	HALL, Stuart		86	*Complications from lung surgery*
1990	# HAMER, Rusty		42	*Suicide (gunshot)*
1990	+ HAMMER, Armand		92	
1990	HARDY, Ian Dudley		79	*Killed in a storm*
1990	HARDY, Joseph		71	
1990	HARMON, Tom		70	*Heart attack*
1990	+ HARRIS, Robin		36	*Found dead in his hotel room*
1990	HARRISON, Rex		82	*Pancreatic cancer*
1990	HARVUOT, Clifford		77	*Pancreatic cancer*
1990	HENSON, Basil		71	*Stroke*
1990	HENSON, Jim		53	*Streptococcus pneumonia*
1990	# HERNDON, Bill		54	*A.I.D.S.*
1990	HILL, Ken		49	*A.I.D.S.*
1990	HOLE, William J. Jr.		71	*Respiratory failure*
1990	HUNTLEY, Raymond		86	
1990	IBBS, Ronald		74	*Cancer*
1990	IDEN, Rosalind		82	
1990	+ IRELAND, Jill		54	*Breast & lung cancer*

YEAR	NAME	AGE	CAUSE AND/OR PLACE OF DEATH
1990	IRVING, Richard	73	After heart surgery
1990	JACKSON, Freda	82	
1990	JACKSON, Gordon	66	Cancer
1990	JAMES, Jessica	60	Cancer
1990	JANSSEN, Werner	91	
1990	JARAY, Hans	83	Heart failure
1990	JARVIS, Scott	48	A.I.D.S.
1990	# JONES, Candy	64	Cancer
1990	KASHA, Lawrence	57	Brain cancer
1990	KATZKA, Gabriel	58	Heart attack
1990	KENDRICK, Henry	56	Emphysema and pneumonia
1990	KENNEDY, Arthur ☆	75	Brain tumor
1990	# KERMACK, Paul	57	Heart attack
1990	KIELY, Pat	59	After a long illness
1990	KIRK, Lisa	62	Lung cancer
1990	KRUEGER, Michael	39	Cancer
1990	KULUVA, Will	78	Embolism
1990	LAMONT, Estelle	82	Respiratory failure
1990	LANSON, Snooky	76	
1990	LaRUE, Bart	57	Heart failure
1990	LAUTER, Harry	76	Heart failure
1990	LAWRENCE, Keith	39	Pneumonia
1990	LEACOCK, Philip	73	Collapsed lungs
1990	LEBERMAN, Joseph	85	Cancer
1990	LEE, Larry	48	A.I.D.S.
1990	LEGATT, Alison	86	
1990	LEHMANN, Carla	73	
1990	LEIGH, Megan	26	Apparent suicide
1990	LEWIS, Elliott	73	Cardiac arrest
1990	+ LOCKER, Frances	79	
1990	# LOCKWOOD, Alexander	88	
1990	LOCKWOOD, Margaret	73	
1990	LOCKWOOD, Paul	51	Heart disease
1990	# LOSS, Joe	80	Kidney failure
1990	LUCAS, Gail	37	Viral hemorrhagic pneumonia
1990	LUND, Art	75	Liver cancer
1990	LYNCH, Ken	79	Viral infection
1990	MACKAILL, Dorothy	87	Kidney failure
1990	MARGLISS, Frances	76	Heart attack
1990	MARQUARD, Yvonne Peattie	73	Natural causes
1990	MARR, Alice	89	
1990	MARSH, Lois R.	74	After a long illness
1990	MARSTON, Merlin	45	Non-Hodgkins lymphoma
1990	MARTIN, Kiel	46	Cardiovascular collapse caused by lung cancer
1990	+ MARTIN, Mary	76	Cancer
1990	MAXWELL, James	33	A.I.D.S.
1990	# MAZURKI, Mike	82	
1990	McBEAN, Angus	86	
1990	# McCRAY, Helen Mary "Honey"	83	
1990	McCREA, Joel	84	Pulmonary complications
1990	McGIVENEY, Maura	51	Liver disease
1990	McPHILLIPS, Hugh	70	Injuries from an automobile accident
1990	MENDENHALL, Jim	62	Brain cancer
1990	MERIVALE, John	72	Pneumonia
1990	MERRILL, Gary	74	Cancer
1990	METCALFE, Gordon	43	A.I.D.S.
1990	MILLER, Barbara	68	After a brain tumor operation
1990	MINOTIS, Alexis	90	Stroke
1990	# MORAN, Jackie	67	Cancer
1990	# MORAN, Lois	81	Cancer
1990	MORRIS, Jack Julius	87	Natural causes
1990	MULLINS, Ted	50	Heart attack
1990	MURDOCH, Richard B.	83	Apparent heart attack
1990	MURRAY, Mary Phillips	68	Cancer
1990	MYDLAND, Brent	37	Overdose of morphine & cocaine

• New entry.   # Original name (Pt. 7).   + Interment (Pt. 5).   ☆ Oscar nominee, ★ Oscar winner (Pt. 10)

YEAR	NAME		AGE	CAUSE AND/OR PLACE OF DEATH
1990	NADEL, Arthur H.		68	Diabetes
1990	NAPOLEAN, Phil		89	
1990	NATWICK, Grim		100	Pneumonia & heart disease
1990	NELSON, Herbert		76	
1990	# NESBITT, Frank M.		48	Cancer
1990	NORTH, Edmund		79	
1990	NOVAK, Jane		94	Complications caused by a stroke
1990	NOVELLI, Santo Alex		73	
1990	# OLIVER, Susan		53	Cancer
1990	# PAGE, Jean		95	
1990	PALEY, William S.		89	Apparent heart attack brought on by pneumonia
1990	PALK, Anna		48	Cancer
1990	PAN, Hermes		80	Apparent stroke
1990	PARADJANOV, Sergei		66	
1990	PARKER, Ed		59	Following a heart attack
1990	PIPPIN, Nick		35	A.I.D.S.
1990	PITOEFF, Sacha		70	Heart failure
1990	POND, Barbara		?	Lung cancer
1990	POWELL, Michael		84	
1990	QUILLAN, Eddie		83	Cancer
1990	# RAFFETTO, Michael		91	Natural causes
1990	RAPPAPORT, David		38	Apparent suicide (gunshot)
1990	RAY, Johnnie (pop singer)		63	Liver failure (Do not confuse with actor Johnny Ray, d. 1927)
1990	REED, Gavin		59	Respiratory failure
1990	REEVE, Scott		38	A.I.D.S.
1990	REVERE, Anne	★	87	Pneumonia
1990	REYNOLDS, Helen Fortescu		65	
1990	REYNOLDS, Jack		83	Natural causes
1990	+ RHODES, Erik		84	Pneumonia
1990	RICE, Felix		46	A.I.D.S.
1990	RITT, Martin	☆	76	Cardiac disease
1990	ROLFING, Tom		40	An A.I.D.S.-related illness
1990	+ ROSE, David (pianist/composer)		80	Heart disease (Do not confuse with David E. Rose, d. 1992)
1990	ROSEN, Al		80	
1990	ROSS, Betsy King		66	
1990	ROSS, Frank		85	After brain surgery
1990	ROSSIF, Frédéric		67	
1990	RUSINOW, Irving		75	Cancer
1990	RUSSELL, Craig		42	A.I.D.S.
1990	SACHS, Leonard		82	Kidney failure
1990	SALCIDO, Michael A.		39	Liver failure
1990	SALMI, Albert		62	Apparent suicide (gunshot)
1990	Sandy (original "Annie" dog)		16	Died in his sleep
1990	SANSBERRY, Hope		94	Natural causes
1990	SCHNUR, Jerome		66	Melanoma (skin cancer)
1990	SCHUMM, Hans		93	Heart failure
1990	SEALES, Franklyn		37	A.I.D.S.
1990	SEEGAR, Sara		76	Cerebral hemorrhage
1990	SELZNICK, Irene		83	Breast cancer
1990	SEYLER, Athene		101	
1990	SEYRIG, Delphine		58	Lung disease
1990	SHANNON, Del		50	Suicide
1990	SHANNON, Paul		80	Cancer
1990	SHAW, Steve		25	Injuries from an automobile accident
1990	SHAWLEY, Robert		63	Pneumonia
• 1990	SHERWOOD, Bill		?	A.I.D.S.
1990	SLOANE, Doreen		56	Cancer
1990	SOMMER, Bert		42	Liver failure
1990	SOUTHARD, Stephen		30	A.I.D.S.
1990	SPEWACK, Bella		91	
1990	# SPITALNY, Evelyn		79	
1990	STALKER, John		67	
1990	# STANLEY, Helene		62	
1990	#+ STANWYCK, Barbara	☆	82	Congestive heart failure
1990	STARR, Jimmy		86	

YEAR	NAME		AGE	CAUSE AND/OR PLACE OF DEATH
1990	STEBER, Eleanor		76	Congestive heart failure
1990	# ST. JACQUES, Raymond		60	Lymphatic cancer
1990	STUSSY, Jan		68	Cancer
1990	TARRON, Elsie		87	Heart failure
1990	+ TAYBACK, Vic "Mel"		60	Heart attack
1990	# Terry-Thomas		78	Parkinson's disease
1990	TESSIER, Robert		56	Cancer
1990	# THOMPSON, Carlos		67	Suicide (gunshot)
1990	TOGNAZZI, Ugo		68	Cerebral hemorrhage
1990	TRAUBERG, Leonid		88	
1990	TRENKER, Luis		97	
1990	TUPPER, Loretta		84	Cancer
1990	UNGER, Bertil		69	Liver disease
1990	VanHEUSEN, Jimmy		77	
1990	VAUGHAN, Sarah		66	Lung cancer
1990	+ VAUGHAN, Stevie Ray		35	Helicopter crash
1990	VEJAR, Rudolph		57	Respiratory failure
1990	WALL, Max		82	
1990	# WALLACE, Jean		66	After an internal hemorrhage
1990	WARREN, Betty		83	
1990	WARREN, Charles Marquis		77	Following surgery for a heart aneurysm
1990	WATERS, Elsie		95	
1990	WATTS, Jr., Leroy		72	
1990	WAYNE, Johnny		72	Cancer
1990	WEBB, Robert D.		87	Following a long illness
1990	WEBER, Karl		74	Congestive feart failure
1990	WHEELER, Jerry B.		44	A.I.D.S.
1990	WHITE, David		74	Run over by an automobile
1990	WHITE, Larry		74	Heart attack
1990	WILLIAMS, Brenda		43	Cancer
1990	WILLOCK, Dave		81	Complications following a stroke
1990	WILSON, Josephine		86	Heart attack
1990	WITTENBERG, Marguerite N.		77	Cancer
1990	WITTENBERG, Paul B.		63	Cancer
1990	WOOD, George		56	Diabetes
1990	WURSCHMIDT, Sigrid		37	Metastasized breast cancer
1990	WYNNE, Paul		47	A.I.D.S.
1991	+ ACKERMAN, Harry		78	Pulmonary failure (in Burbank, CA)
1991	ACKERMAN, Jack		59	Brain tumor (in Los Angeles, CA)
1991	# ADRIAN, Louis		93	Died in Lakeport, CA
1991	AGMON, Ami		43	After a long bout with cancer
1991	+ ALLEN, Irwin	★	75	After suffering a heart attack (in Santa Monica, CA)
1991	ALLEN, Ronald		56	Lung cancer (in Reading, England)
1991	# ANDOR, Lotte Palfi		87	After an illness
1991	# ANDOR, Paul		90	After a long illness
1991	ARAVINDAM, Govindan		55	
1991	ARKIN, David		49	
1991	ARNOLD, Monroe		64	After a heart attack
1991	ARRAU, Claudio		88	Complications after surgery for intestinal blockage
1991	#+ ARTHUR, Jean	☆	89	Heart failure, following a paralyzing stroke
1991	# ASHCROFT, Peggy	★	83	After suffering a stroke
1991	ASHE, Martin		80	Respiratory failure
1991	ASHMAN, Howard	★	40	Complications from A.I.D.S.
1991	AUBUCHON, Jacques		67	Heart failure
1991	AUDLEY, Eleanor		86	Respiratory failure
1991	AXTHELM, Pete		47	Liver failure
1991	BAKER, Terence		52	
1991	BALL, William		60	
1991	#+ BANKY, Vilma		90	Died in a L.A. nursing home after a 10-yr. illness
1991	BAREFIELD, Eddie		81	Heart attack
1991	BARNET, Charlie		77	Alzheimer's disease & pneumonia
1991	BARTELL, Eddie		83	Aneurysm
1991	BARTELME, Joe		61	Cancer
1991	BARUCH, André		83	

...DEATHS OF MOVIE AND TELEVISION PERSONALITIES — BY YEAR...

YEAR	NAME		AGE	CAUSE AND/OR PLACE OF DEATH
1991	BATCHELOR, Joy		77	
1991	BATES, Ralph		50	Cancer
1991	BEDDOE, Don		102	
1991	BELL, Hal		65	After suffering a stroke
1991	+ BELLAMY, Ralph	★	87	Respiratory infection
1991	BENNETT, Matt		52	Brain tumor
1991	BERNSTEIN, Sam		80	
1991	BERTI, Dehl		70	Heart attack
1991	BINDER, Maurice		72	
1991	BLAKE, Katharine		62	
1991	BLATT, Edward A.		88	Heart attack
1991	BOARDMAN, Eleanor		93	Died in Santa Barbara, CA
1991	BOIS, Curt		90	Died in Berlin, Germany
1991	BOND, Lilian		83	
1991	# BOOTH, Edwina		86	Died of heart failure, in Long Beach, CA
1991	# BOSTWICK, Dorothy Davis		?	Cardiac arrest
1991	BOTTCHER, Ron		50	A.I.D.S.
1991	BOVASSO, Julie		61	Cancer
1991	BOWEN, Joe		56	Heart attack
1991	BOX, Muriel		85	
1991	BROCK, Stanley		59	Heart attack
1991	BROIDY, Steve		86	Following a heart attack
1991	# BROWN, Reno		70	Cancer
1991	+ BROWNE, Coral		77	Breast cancer
1991	BRUNNER, Howard		51	A.I.D.S.
1991	BUSCH, Niven		88	Heart failure
1991	BUSH, Warren V.		65	Cardiac arrest
1991	BUTLER, Tim		36	A.I.D.S.
1991	CAHAN, George M.		72	Pneumonia
1991	CANTOR, Michael (Max)		32	
1991	+ CAPRA, Frank	★	94	Died in his sleep of natural causes
1991	CARLIN, Thomas A.		62	Heart failure
1991	CARR, Eric		41	Complications from cancer
1991	CASSIDY, Tom		41	A.I.D.S.
1991	+ CAULFIELD, Joan		69	After surgery for cancer
1991	CHABEAU, Ray Edgar		49	
1991	CHAMBERS, Kathy L.		41	Cancer
1991	CHAPLIN, Oona		66	Following cancer surgery
1991	CHAPMAN, Ben		83	Heart & kidney failure
1991	CHIARI, Walter		67	Heart attack
1991	CHRISTMAS, Jason		49	Killed outside a NY comedy club by robbers
1991	CHURCHILL, Donald		60	Apparent heart attack
1991	# CLAYTON, Buck		80	
1991	CLEVELAND, James		59	Respiratory problems & heart failure
1991	COBB, Dita		68	After a long illness
1991	CODY, Iron Eyes		?	
1991	COLVIG, Vance		72	Cancer
1991	COLVIN, Michael		41	After suffering a head injury on a film set
1991	+ CONVY, Bert		56	Cancer (brain tumor)
1991	# COOK, Cookie		77	Kidney failure
1991	COPPOLA, Carmine	★	80	After suffering a stroke
1991	COSTON, Ann Sorg		62	After a short illness
1991	# CRAVEN, Eddie		?	After an illness
1991	CRAVENS, Kathryn		92	Cancer
1991	+ CROSBY, Dennis		56	Suicide (gunshot)
1991	# CURTIS, Ken		74	
1991	# DALE, Bobby		92	Myocardial infarction
1991	# DALY, John		77	Cardiac arrest
1991	+ DAVIS, Brad		41	Complications from A.I.D.S.
1991	DAVIS, Jerome L.		73	Stroke
1991	#+ DAVIS, Miles		65	Pneumonia, respiratory failure & a stroke
1991	DeACUTIS, William		33	Brain lymphoma
1991	DEMPSTER, Carol		89	After a long illness
1991	DEUTSCH, David		65	Kidney failure
1991	# DEVLIN, J. G.		84	

YEAR	NAME		AGE	CAUSE AND/OR PLACE OF DEATH
1991	DEWHURST, Colleen		67	Cancer
1991	DHIEGH, Khigh		75	Kidney & heart disease
1991	DONN, Lee		96	Stroke
1991	DOYLE, Roz		49	Breast cancer
1991	DOZIER, William		83	Stroke
1991	DRAKE, Oliver		88	After a long illness
1991	# DUNBAR, Dixie		72	After a series of heart attacks
1991	DUNNOCK, Mildred	☆	90	Died in Oak Bluffs, Martha's Vineyard, MA
1991	+ DUROCHER, Leo		86	Natural causes (in Palm Springs, CA)
1991	DYER-BENNETT, Richard		73	
1991	ECKHARDT, John		82	Heart failure
1991	EDWARDS, George		67	Cancer
1991	ELKINS, Lenore		77	Heart failure
1991	ELLIS, Karl		41	A.I.D.S.
1991	EMR, Roland Jon		45	Murdered (shot)
1991	# EPSTEIN, Jerry		69	Causes unreported (in London, England)
1991	EVANS, John Morgan		49	After a long illness
1991	FALAT, Stephen J.		34	After a long illness
1991	FAYE, Frances		?	Following a series of strokes
1991	FELDMAN, Phil		69	Cancer
1991	FIELD, Filip J.		67	Heart failure
1991	FISHELSON, Stanley		66	Natural causes
1991	FLORANCE, Sheila		75	Cancer
1991	# FONTEYN, Margot		71	Cancer
1991	# FORD, "Tennessee" Ernie		72	Liver disease
1991	FORD, Lloyd		79	Ventricular fibrillation
1991	# FOXX, Redd		68	Heart attack during rehearsal for new TV show
1991	FRANCESCATTI, Zino		89	
1991	# FRANCIS, Wilma		73	Complications after lung surgery
1991	# FRANCISCUS, James		57	Emphysema
1991	FREEMAN, Everett		79	Renal failure
1991	# FURST, Anton	★	47	Suicide (jumped from 8th level of parking garage)
1991	GAILLARD, Slim		74	Cancer
1991	GAINSBOURG, Serge		62	Heart trouble
1991	GERRY, Toni		65	Cancer
1991	GETZ, Stan		64	After a 5-year battle with liver cancer
1991	GIBSON, Marc		51	Apparent heart attack after a workout
1991	GILBERT, Joan		84	
1991	GILLIES, Carol		50	Cancer
1991	GOBEL, George		71	Complications after arterial leg surgery
1991	GOLDEN, Murray		79	Complications after a stroke
1991	GOLDRICH, Bert		84	
1991	# GRAHAM, Bill		60	Helicopter crash
1991	GRAHAM, Martha		96	Pneumonia & cardiac arrest
1991	GRANGE, Red		87	
1991	GREEN, Lee		72	Automobile accident
1991	GREENE, Graham		86	Leukemia
1991	GREENSPAN, David		68	Lung cancer
1991	GUTHRIE, A. B. Jr.		90	
1991	GUZMAN, Pato		57	After a brief illness
1991	HAGERTY, Michael		39	A.I.D.S.
1991	HALL, Ed		60	Cancer
1991	HALL, Kevin Peter		35	Pneumonia
1991	HAMILTON, Frank		66	Prostate cancer
1991	HARDIN, Ken		62	Cancer
1991	HARRIS, Cassandra		39	Ovarian cancer
1991	HARRIS, Lou		85	Natural causes
1991	HARRIS, Ted		52	Cancer
1991	HAULMAN, Bob		49	Apparent heart attack
1991	HAYDON, Tom		53	Cancer
1991	HAYES, Christopher		?	Heart attack
1991	HEATH, Gordon		72	
1991	HORRALL, Craig		?	A.I.D.S.
1991	HOUSTON, Donald		67	
1991	HOWDEN, Victoria		27	Suicide (gunshot)

...DEATHS OF MOVIE AND TELEVISION PERSONALITIES — BY YEAR...

YEAR	NAME		AGE	CAUSE AND/OR PLACE OF DEATH
1991	# HOYT, John		86	Lung cancer
1991	HUDDLESTON, Floyd	☆	73	Following a heart attack
1991	HURWITZ, Leo		81	
1991	HUTCHENRIDER, C. B.		83	
1991	HYDE-WHITE, Wilfrid		87	Congestive heart failure
1991	IMAI, Tadashi		79	
1991	#+ JACKSON, Mary Ann		68	
1991	JAFFA, Max		79	
1991	JAGGER, Dean	★	87	Influenza
1991	JEFFRIES, Peter		62	Following open-heart surgery
1991	JOHANSEN, Gunnar		85	Liver cancer
1991	JORDAN, Gerry		45	A.I.D.S.
1991	KAUFMAN, Robert	☆	60	Heart attack
1991	KAYE, Sylvia Fine		78	Emphysema
1991	KELLEY, Edward (Barry)		82	Congestive heart failure
1991	KEMPFF, Wilhelm		95	Parkinson's disease
1991	KERMAN, Sheppard		62	Lung cancer
1991	+ KERT, Larry		60	A.I.D.S.
1991	KIKER, Douglas		61	Heart attack
1991	# KILIAN, Pauline		83	Complications from diabetes
1991	KINGHAM, Bernard		65	A stroke related to spinal cancer
1991	KINSKI, Klaus		65	Found dead, apparently of natural causes
1991	KOBAL, John		51	Pneumonia
1991	KOLB, Glenn		39	A.I.D.S.
1991	KREBS, Nita		85	Apparent heart attack
1991	KROEGER, Berry		78	Kidney failure
1991	KULP, Nancy		69	Cancer of the jaw
1991	LACEY, Ronald		55	Cancer
1991	+ LAIRD, Jack		69	Cancer
1991	LAMONT, Deni		59	Lung cancer
1991	LANDERS, Hal		63	After being hospitalized for cancer treatment
1991	#+ LANDON, Michael		54	Cancer of the liver & pancreas
1991	LANGAN, Glenn		73	Complications from cancer
1991	LANHAM, Roy		68	Cancer
1991	LANIN, Howard		93	Pneumonia
1991	LaVERE, Jane		87	Heart problems
1991	LAWRENCE, Mark (producer)		70	Prostate cancer (Do not confuse with actor Marc Lawrence)
1991	LAWRENCE, Mary		73	Respiratory failure following pneumonia
1991	LEAMING, Jim		72	After a long illness
1991	LEAN, David		83	After a long illness
1991	LEFEVRE, René		93	
1991	LeGALLIENNE, Eva		92	Heart failure
1991	LEIGHTON, Merrill		51	Automobile accident
1991	LENSKY, Leib		82	Liver cancer
1991	LESLIE, Bob		64	
1991	# LEWIS, Robert Q.		71	Emphysema
1991	LOMBARDI, Paul Michael		31	A.I.D.S.
1991	LOTT, Lawrence		40	A.I.D.S.
1991	LOURIE, Eugene		89	Heart failure & complications from strokes
1991	LOVE, Edward M.		43	A.I.D.S.
1991	LOVE, Geoff		73	
1991	LOWENSTEIN, Lynn Gendron		30	An inoperable brain tumor
1991	+ LUKE, Keye		86	After a stroke
1991	MacDONALD, James		84	Heart failure
1991	MacMAHON, Aline	☆	92	Pneumonia
1991	#+ MacMURRAY, Fred		83	Pneumonia
1991	MAIBAUM, Richard		81	After a short illness
1991	# MANN, Daniel		79	Heart failure
1991	MARKHAM, Marcella		68	Breast cancer
1991	MARKLE, Fletcher		70	Heart failure
1991	MARLOWE, Louis J.		85	Kidney failure
1991	MAROFF, Robert		57	
1991	MARRERO, Ralph		33	Automobile accident
1991	MARSHALL, Robert H.		67	After a brief illness
1991	+ MASSEY, Curt		81	

YEAR		NAME		AGE	CAUSE AND/OR PLACE OF DEATH
1991		McCALLION, James		72	Heart attack
1991		McCOY, Jack		72	
1991		McCULLOUGH, Stephen N.		48	Pulmonary hypertension
1991		McINTIRE, John Herrick		83	Emphysema & cancer
1991		McLAUGHLIN, Emily		61	Cancer
1991	#	MERCURY, Freddie		45	A.I.D.S.
1991		MILES, Bernard		83	
1991	#	MILFORD, Gene	★	89	Pneumonia
1991		MILLIGAN, Andy		62	A.I.D.S.
1991		MITCHELL, Frank		?	Cardiac arrest
1991		MONDO, Peggy		50	Heart attack
1991		MONICA, Maria A. G.		92	
1991		MONTALBAN, Carlos		87	Heart failure
1991	#+	MONTAND, Yves		70	Stroke
1991		MOORCROFT, Judy		58	
1991	#	MOORE, Eleanor		84	Complications from emphysema
1991		MORALI, Jacques		44	A.I.D.S.
1991		MORGAN, George J.		77	Cancer
1991	#	MURRAY, Arthur		95	Pneumonia
1991		MUSILLI, John		55	Cancer
1991	#	NALDER, Reggie		80	Bone cancer
1991		NEWMAN, Thomas		60	Heart attack
1991		NICHOLSON, Thomas D.		68	Cancer
1991		NORTH, Alex	☆	81	Pancreatic cancer
1991		NUTE, Don		56	A.I.D.S.
1991		OCKO, Daniel		78	Respiratory failure
1991		O'CONNOR, Kevin		56	Cancer
1991		PADILLA, Ruben Dario Sr.		81	Cancer
1991		PAGANO, Ronald F.		37	After a long illness
1991		PALMER, John		75	After a short illness
1991	#	PARIS, Freddie		63	Cancer
1991		PASTERNAK, Joe		89	Parkinson's disease and other ailments (in Beverly Hills, CA)
1991		PATTISON, Arthur		60	Cancer
1991		PERTWEE, Michael		74	
1991		PIAZZA, Ben		58	Cancer
1991		PIERCE, Webb		69	Pancreatic cancer
1991		POPKIN, Harry M.		85	Cancer
1991		POWERS, Tim		34	A.I.D.S.
1991		PRATT, James C.		86	Pneumonia
1991		PRICE, Gilbert		48	Found dead in Vienna
1991		PRIM, Suzy		95	
1991	#	PROVENZA, Sal		45	Lymphoma
1991		RAGNI, Gerome		48	Cancer
1991		RAPF, Matthew		71	After an attack of the flu
1991		RASCEL, Renato		78	Heart failure
1991		RASULALA, Thalmus		55	Heart attack after suffering from leukemia
1991	#	RAY, Aldo		64	Complications from throat cancer & pneumonia
1991		READING, Bertice		58	Stroke
1991		REASONER, Harry		68	Complications and pneumonia after brain clot surgery
1991		REILLY, Howard		79	After a coronary bypass operation
1991		Rellys		85	
1991		REMICK, Lee		55	Kidney & lung cancer
1991		RENICK, Ralph		62	Hepatitis & liver cancer
1991		RICHARDSON, Tony	★	63	A.I.D.S.
1991		RODDENBERRY, Gene		70	Cardiac arrest from a massive blood clot
1991	#	ROGERS, Jean		74	Following surgery
1991		ROGOT, Peter		37	Apparent heart attack
1991		ROMAN, Paul Reid		55	Cancer
1991		ROMANCE, Viviane		82	
1991		ROOSEVELT, James		83	Complications from a stroke & Parkinson's disease
1991		ROSENBLATT, Martin		74	Heart attack
1991		ROSQUI, Tom		62	Cancer
1991	#	ROSSITTO, Angelo		83	Complications from surgery
1991		RUDOLPH, Oscar		79	Following a stroke
1991		RUFFIN, David		50	Apparent drug overdose

YEAR	NAME		AGE	CAUSE AND/OR PLACE OF DEATH
1991	RUSSELL, John		70	
1991	SCHAEFFER, Elizabeth		42	Cerebral hemorrhage
1991	SCHAFER, Natalie		90	Cancer
1991	# SCOTT, Daniel Simon		71	Alzheimer's disease
1991	SCOTT, Dennis		51	After a long illness
1991	SEDGWICK, Eileen		93	
1991	SERKIN, Rudolph		88	Cancer
1991	# SEUSS, Dr.		87	Respiratory & kidney problems
1991	SHERMAN, George		82	Heart & kidney failure
1991	SHUMAN, Mort		52	
1991	SIEGEL, Don		78	After a long illness
1991	SILVER, Dave		72	Heart attack
1991	SMITH, Burleigh		70	Cancer
1991	SMITH, Ray		55	
1991	SOBEK, Allan		46	A.I.D.S.
1991	SONNTAG, Jack		77	After a long illness
1991	# SOUTHERN, Jeri		64	Pneumonia
1991	STEIN, Robert M.		40	Lung cancer
1991	STEVENS, Fran		72	Cancer
1991	STEVENS, Mort		62	Pancreatic cancer
1991	STIERLE, Edward		23	A.I.D.S.
1991	STROHM, Walter Clarence		86	Heart failure
1991	SUBOTSKY, Milton		70	Heart disease
1991	SULLIVAN, Marie Madeline		80	After a brief illness
1991	TALLICHET, Margaret (Wyler)		77	Cancer
1991	# THOMAS, Danny		79	After a heart attack
1991	THOMAS, Wilfrid		87	
1991	# THORPE, Richard		95	
1991	TIERNEY, Gene	☆	70	Emphysema
1991	TOOMEY, Regis		93	
1991	# TRYON, Tom		65	Stomach cancer
1991	TUCKER, Lem		52	Liver failure
1991	TULLY, Lee		?	Cancer
1991	VANOFF, Nick		61	Cardiac arrest
1991	+ VAUGHN, Billy		72	Cancer
1991	# VINCENT, Chuck		51	Heart attack after a bout with pneumonia
1991	# VITTO, G. L.		69	Heart attack
1991	#+ VonERICH, Chris		21	
1991	WALTERS, Casey		75	After an illness brought on by a stroke
1991	WALTERS, Thorley		78	
1991	# WARFIELD, Marjorie		88	Pneumonia
1991	WEBSTER, Byron		58	A.I.D.S.
1991	WEIST, Dwight		81	Heart attack
1991	# WEST, Dottie		58	Complications after an automobile accident
1991	WHEATLEY, Alan		84	Heart attack
1991	WHEDON, John Ogden		86	Pneumonia
1991	WHITE, Carol		47	
1991	WILSHIN, Sunday		86	
1991	WILSON, Richard		75	Pancreatic cancer
1991	WILSON, Stu		87	
1991	WILSON, Theodore		47	Stroke
1991	WINSLOW, Dick		75	Complications from diabetes
1991	WINTERS, Bernie		58	Cancer
1991	WORSLEY, Wallace Jr.		82	Heart failure
1991	YATES, Sterling		65	Cerebral hemorrhage
1991	YELLEN, Jack		98	
1991	ZAMPA, Luigi		86	After a long illness
1991	ZORNOW, Edith		72	Cancer
1991	ZWICKLER, Phil		36	Complications from A.I.D.S.
1992	ABRAHAMS, Gary		48	A.I.D.S.
1992	+ ACUFF, Roy		89	Congestive heart failure
1992	ADES, Daniel		59	Causes unreported (in Los Angeles, CA)
1992	ADLER, Stella		91	Died in her sleep of heart failure (in Los Angeles, CA)
1992	# AHERNE, Gladys		?	After a brief illness

YEAR	NAME		AGE	CAUSE AND/OR PLACE OF DEATH
1992	AIKEN, Bill		34	After a 1-year bout with cancer
1992	ALEXANDER, Tom		29	A.I.D.S. (in Hollywood, CA)
1992	ALISON, Dorothy		66	Causes unreported (in London, England)
1992	ALLEN, Peter	★	48	An A.I.D.S.-related illness (in San Diego, CA)
1992	ALLMAN, Elvia		87	Pneumonia (in Santa Monica, CA)
1992	ALMENDROS, Nestor	★	61	Lymphoma (in New York)
1992	ALZADO, Lyle		43	After suffering brain cancer (in Portland, OR)
1992	AMYES, Julian		74	Causes unreported (in London, England)
1992	# ANDERS, Laurie		70	Cancer (in Tarzana, CA)
1992	# ANDERSON, Judith	☆	93	Pneumonia after suffering a brain tumor
1992	ANDERSON, John		69	Heart attack
1992	# ANDREWS, Dana		83	Congestive heart failure & pneumonia
1992	ANDREWS, Thomas		37	A.I.D.S.
1992	ARDENT, Keith		38	A.I.D.S.
1992	# Arletty		94	Died in Paris, France
1992	ARNOLD, Jack		75	Arteriosclerosis
1992	ASIMOV, Isaac		72	Heart and kidney failure
1992	ATTERBURY, Malcolm		85	Died in Beverly Hills, CA
1992	AUDLEY, Maxine		69	Heart attack
1992	# BABBITT, Art		85	Kidney failure
1992	BABIN, Vitya Vronsky		82	After a long illness
1992	BAIR, Ron		62	Cancer
1992	BAKER, Dorothy Helen		78	Died in Los Angeles, CA
1992	# BARBER, Red		84	Intestinal disorder
1992	# BARTHOLOMEW, Freddie		67	Emphysema & heart failure
1992	BEATTY, Robert		82	Pneumonia
1992	BEAUCHAMP, Clem		94	Natural causes
1992	BENEDEK, Laslo		87	After a lengthy hospital stay
1992	BERKELEY, George		70	Heart attack
1992	BEYERS, Bill		37	A.I.D.S.
1992	BLACKWOOD, Christian		50	Lung cancer
1992	# BLAIRE, Sallie		68	Liver failure
1992	BLATTNER, Robert		40	Airplane crash
1992	BLETCHER, Arline		99	Natural causes
1992	# BOOTH, Shirley	★	94	Natural causes
1992	BOTAS, Juan Suarez		34	A.I.D.S.
1992	BOXER, Warren Neal		34	A.I.D.S.
1992	+ BRAND, Neville		71	Emphysema
1992	BRENNER, Glenn		44	Cerebral hemorrhage from a malignant brain tumor
1992	BRIGHT, David		49	Automobile accident
1992	BRODIE, Steve		72	Cancer
1992	# BROOKS, Beverley		63	Stroke
1992	BROOKS, Richard	☆	79	Congestive heart failure
1992	# BROWN, Georgia		57	Infection after surgery for an intestinal blockage
1992	BROWN, James		72	Lung cancer
1992	# BROWN, Lucille E.		74	After a long illness
1992	BRUNI, Peter		60	Heart failure
1992	BRYAN, William Donald Sr.		74	Cancer
1992	BURKE, Alan		69	Emphysema
1992	CADY, Frank		74	Complications following heart surgery
1992	# CALLENDER, Red		76	Thyroid cancer
1992	CARISI, Johnny		70	Complications from heart surgery
1992	CARNOVSKY, Morris		94	Natural causes
1992	# CARROL, Regina		49	Cancer
1992	CARROLL, David		41	A.I.D.S.
1992	CARTER, Beverly		51	Cancer
1992	CASCELLA, John J.		45	Found dead in his car of apparent heart attack
1992	CASSELL, W. Barry Jr.		74	Pneumonia
1992	CATTANI, Rico		64	Respiratory disease from a chronic heart condition
1992	CHALIAPIN, Feodor Jr.		87	After a brief illness
1992	CHRISTI, Panos		54	Complications from A.I.D.S.
1992	CHRISTY, Howard		79	After a long illness
1992	# CLARKE, Mae		81	Cancer
1992	CLATWORTHY, William	☆	80	After a brief illness
1992	CLORE, Leon		73	Cancer

YEAR	NAME		AGE	CAUSE AND/OR PLACE OF DEATH
1992	# COLBY, Anita		77	Lung disease
1992	COLES, Charles "Honi"		81	Died in his sleep of lung cancer
1992	COLLOFF, Roger		46	Cancer
1992	COMBS, Frederick		57	A.I.D.S.
1992	#+ CONNORS, Chuck		71	Lung cancer
1992	COOPER, Ralph		?	Cancer
1992	# CORDAY, Rita		68	Complications of diabetes after gall bladder surgery (in CA)
1992	COTTLE, Graham D.		51	Congestive heart failure
1992	CRISTALDI, Franco	★	68	Heart attack
1992	CRONIN, Laurel		53	Cancer
1992	# CUEVAS, Joey		34	A.I.D.S.
1992	DANOVA, Cesare		66	Heart attack
1992	DANTON, Ray		61	After suffering from kidney disease
1992	+ DARBY, Ken	★	82	Died in Sherman Oaks, CA
1992	# DAVIS, Jackie		78	Respiratory failure
1992	DEA, Marie		72	
1992	# DEHNER, John		76	Emphysema & diabetes
1992	DELAUDER, Doug		38	A.I.D.S.
1992	DeLAURENTIIS, Luigi		75	After a 3-year illness
1992	DELERUE, Georges	★	67	After a brief illness
1992	DEMAZIS, Orane		87	
1992	# DENNIS, Sandy	★	54	Ovarian cancer
1992	DERR, Richard		74	Pancreatic cancer & heart failure
1992	DEUTSCH, Helen		85	Natural causes
1992	#+ DIETRICH, Marlene	☆	90	Died in Paris, France
1992	DINEHART, Alan Jr.		74	Emphysema
1992	DIXON, Adèle		83	Bronchial pneumonia
1992	DIXON, Joan		61	Heart disease
1992	DOWELL, Clifton		44	A.I.D.S.
1992	# DRAKE, Alfred		77	Heart failure after a long bout with cancer
1992	DUBMAN, Laura		69	Kidney failure (in New York)
1992	DUELL, Randall	☆	89	Stroke
1992	DUFINE, Herbert		61	Heart condition
1992	DUNBAR, Dorothy		90	
1992	DUNNE, Philip		84	Cancer
1992	EISLER, David		36	Pneumonia
1992	ELLERBE, Harry		91	Died in Atlanta, GA
1992	ELLIOTT, Denholm	☆	70	AIDS-related tuberculosis
1992	ENRIGHT, Dan		74	After a brief illness
1992	EPHRON, Henry		81	
1992	EPPER, John		86	Prostate cancer
1992	# EPSTEIN, David S.		73	Heart attack
1992	# Esmeralda		65	Diabetes & complications
1992	FAYE, Marty		70	Heart attack
1992	FELLOWS, Arthur		74	Cancer
1992	FENNELL, Willie		72	Apparent heart attack
1992	# FERRER, José	★	80	After a brief illness
1992	# FIELD, Virginia		74	Cancer
1992	FIELDING, Sol Baer		83	Following a long illness
1992	FOREMAN, John		67	Heart attack
1992	# FRANCHI, Franco		70	Hemorrhage (in a hospital in Rome, Italy)
1992	# FRANKOVICH, Mike	★	82	Pneumonia & Alzheimer's disease
1992	FRASER, June Joyce Lewis		75	Complications of pneumonia
1992	FRASER, Tom		60	Heart failure after exercising at his gym
1992	FROMMER, Ben		78	
1992	# GARDENIA, Vincent	☆	71	Found dead in his hotel room of a heart attack
1992	# GAUDIO, Joe		79	Cancer
1992	GEIL, Joe "Corky"		64	After an illness
1992	GEORGE, Joseph L.		65	Cancer
1992	# GERSON, Jeanne		87	Cancer & pneumonia
1992	GILL, Ray		42	A.I.D.S.
1992	# GIOVALE, Franco		44	After a car accident
1992	GIOVANNITTI, Len		71	Heart disease
1992	GLIONA, Michael		45	Liver failure
1992	+ GOODSON, Mark		77	Cancer

• New entry. # Original name (Pt. 7). + Interment (Pt. 5).

☆ Oscar nominee, ★ Oscar winner (Pt. 10)

YEAR	NAME		AGE	CAUSE AND/OR PLACE OF DEATH
1992	GOODWIN, Thomas Jr.		51	Prostate cancer
1992	GREGORY, Mercedes		56	Cancer
1992	GRIFFIN, Rodney		46	A.I.D.S.
1992	HALEY, Alex		70	Heart attack
1992	HAMMOND, Ruth		96	Died in her sleep
1992	+ HANCOCK, John		51	Found dead of a heart attack
1992	HANNES, Art		72	Respiratory failure
1992	HARRIS, William E.		37	Stabbed when he interrupted a burglary
1992	HARTOG, Simon		52	Leukemia
1992	HARVEY, Rudy		60	Kidney failure after a series of strokes
1992	HAYS, Mickey		20	Progeria (a rare aging disorder)
1992	HEIDER, Frederick		75	
1992	HELD, Martin		83	
1992	# HENREID, Paul		84	Pneumonia after a stroke
1992	HERBERT, Percy		72	Heart attack
1992	HERZBERGER, Jack L.		75	Following heart surgery
1992	#+ HILL, Benny		67	Heart ailment
1992	HOFF, Louise		69	After an illness
1992	HOLLOWAY, Sterling		87	Cardiac arrest
1992	HOVING, Jane Pickens		83	Heart failure
1992	HOWERD, Frankie		70	Apparent heart attack
1992	#+ HUDNET, Bill		47	Liver disease
1992	HUNT, Richard		40	A.I.D.S.
1992	HYDE, Jacquelyn		61	
1992	IRELAND, John ☆		78	Leukemia
1992	ISING, Rudolf "Rudy" ★		88	
1992	JABARA, Paul ★		44	Lymphoma from A.I.D.S.
1992	JACKSON, Felix		90	Congestive heart failure
1992	JACOBS, Everett "Jake"		68	Cancer
1992	JAFFE, Henry		85	Died in Beverly Hills, CA
1992	JAMES, Ralph		67	
1992	JONES, Allan		84	Lung cancer
1992	# JONES, Charlotte		76	Heart disease
1992	JONSON, Kevin Joe		74	Cancer
1992	KANE, Dennis		69	Cancer
1992	KANE, Paul		?	Heart attack
1992	KELLY, Jack		65	After suffering a stroke
1992	KELLY, Paula		72	After a long illness
1992	KENDRICKS, Eddie		52	Lung cancer
1992	#+ KENNY, Herbert C.		77	Cancer
1992	# KING, Michael		69	
1992	KINISON, Sam		38	Internal injuries following a car crash
1992	KINNEY, Jack		82	
1992	KIRSTEN, Dorothy		82	Complications from a stroke
1992	KOPLIN, Merton Y.		71	
1992	KRAMER, Sy		59	Cancer
1992	KRAMER, Tim		34	A.I.D.S.
1992	KRUGMAN, Lou		78	Cancer
1992	KUSELL, Maurice L.		89	Pneumonia
1992	# LANDIS, David		42	A.I.D.S.
1992	LANDIS, Walter James		65	After a long illness
1992	# LANTZ, Gracie		88	Spinal cancer
1992	LAWRENCE, John		60	Apparent heart failure
1992	LEAMING, Chet		66	After a brief illness
1992	LECLERC, Ginette		79	
1992	LEDERMAN, Victoria Kellem		52	Amyloidosis
1992	LEE, Irving Allen		43	A.I.D.S.
1992	# LEE, Vanessa		71	Causes unreported (in London, England)
1992	+ LEHRMAN, Oscar S.		73	Prostate cancer
1992	LEVY, Franklin R.		43	Pulmonary embolism
1992	LEWIS, David		83	After a short illness
1992	LIDDELL, Laura		83	Following a series of heart problems
1992	LISS, Ted		72	Heart attack
1992	LITTLE, Cleavon		53	Colon cancer
1992	LORENTZ, Pare		86	Heart failure

• New entry. # Original name (Pt. 7). + Interment (Pt. 5).   ☆ Oscar nominee, ★ Oscar winner (Pt. 10)

YEAR	NAME		AGE	CAUSE AND/OR PLACE OF DEATH
1992	LOWENSTEIN, Cary Scott		30	A.I.D.S.
1992	LUND, John		81	Found dead in his home; heart trouble
1992	MacGRATH, Leueen		77	Complications after a stroke
1992	MAGERMAN, Les		46	A.I.D.S.
1992	# MARSHALL, Brenda		77	Throat cancer (in Palm Springs, CA)
1992	# MARTON, Andrew		87	Pneumonia
1992	+ MARX, Samuel		90	Congestive heart failure (Do not confuse with Samuel Marx, d. 1933)
1992	MAXWELL, Paul		70	
1992	MAYS, Wendell		72	Cancer
1992	McBATH, James H.		69	Heart attack
1992	McCARTHY, Julia		64	Cancer
1992	McCULLERS, Edward		64	Heart attack
1992	McEDWARD, Jack		94	
1992	McGILL, Shaun		30	A.I.D.S.
1992	# MELL, Marisa		53	Cancer
1992	MERRILL, Joan		74	Stroke & Alzheimer's disease
1992	MILLER, David		82	Cancer
1992	MILLER, Hope		63	Breast cancer
1992	MILLER, Roger		56	Cancer
1992	MILSTEIN, Nathan		88	Heart attack
1992	MITCHELL, Chuck		64	Cirrhosis of the liver
1992	MITCHELL, Coleman		48	After a sudden illness
1992	MOLINARI, Antoinette		63	Kidney failure
1992	MOORE, Brian		59	Congestive heart failure
1992	MORLEY, Robert		84	After suffering a stroke (Do not confuse with Robert Morley, d. 1952)
1992	MORRISON, Barbara		84	Heart failure
1992	MUELLER, William A.	☆	92	Natural causes
1992	MUNRO, Nan		87	
1992	MURPHY, George		89	Leukemia
1992	MYHERS, John		70	Pneumonia
1992	NABBIE, Jim		72	After double bypass heart surgery
1992	# NAISMITH, Laurence		83	After a short illness
1992	NAUGHTON, Bill		81	
1992	NELSON, Ruth		87	Cancer complicated by a stroke & pneumonia
1992	NIGRO, Robert		45	A.I.D.S.
1992	NOVELLO, Roselle		95	
1992	O'DONNELL, Gene		81	Lung cancer
1992	OGAWA, Shinsuke		56	
1992	OLIVER, David		30	A.I.D.S.
1992	# O'NEAL, Frederick		86	After a long illness
1992	# ORLOFF, Thelma		76	Kidney failure
1992	O'TOOLE, Ollie		79	After a long illness
1992	OULTON, Brian		84	
1992	PARKER, Al		40	A.I.D.S. (Do not confuse with Albert Parker, d. 1974)
1992	PARKS, Bert		77	Lung cancer (in La Jolla, CA)
1992	PARSONS, Lindsley Sr.		87	Heart failure
1992	PASCAL, Jean-Claude		64	Following surgery
1992	PASTOR, Guy		55	Heart attack
1992	PECK, Ed		75	Heart attack
1992	PENDRELL, Ernest		?	Cancer
1992	PERKINS, Anthony	☆	60	Complications from A.I.D.S. (at his home in Hollywood, CA)
1992	PETERS, Lennie		59	
1992	# PETTYJOHN, Angelique		48	Cancer
1992	PEYTON, Rev. Patrick		83	Renal failure
1992	PICON, Molly		94	Died in her sleep following Alzheimer's disease (in Lancaster, PA)
1992	POIRET, Jean		65	Heart attack
1992	+ PORCARO, Jeff		38	After an apparent allergic reaction to pesticides
1992	PRENTICE, Keith		52	Cancer
1992	PRESTON, Wayde		62	Cancer
1992	RACKMIL, Milton R.		89	Stroke
1992	RALSTON, Howard		?	After an illness
1992	RAMOS, Lou		51	After a brief illness
1992	RAWLINGS, Richard Sr.		75	After a brief illness
1992	RAY, Harry Milton		45	Stroke
1992	RAY, Satyajit	★	70	Heart ailment

...DEATHS OF MOVIE AND TELEVISION PERSONALITIES — BY YEAR...

YEAR	NAME		AGE	CAUSE AND/OR PLACE OF DEATH
1992	READE, Charles A.		82	After a 2-year hospitalization for a stroke
1992	# REED, Robert		59	Colon lymphoma & A.I.D.S.
1992	REED, Vernon William Sr.		73	After a long illness
1992	REESE, Robert		66	Natural causes
1992	REMME, John		56	A.I.D.S.
1992	# Renie	★	90	Natural causes
1992	RICHARDS, Lloyd		89	Pneumonia
1992	RILEY, Alice Mary		51	Cancer
1992	RILEY, Larry		39	A.I.D.S.
1992	# RINALDO, Fred		78	Complications after an operation for a broken hip
1992	RINI, David		40	Brain cancer
1992	RIO, Joan Maloney		57	Cancer
1992	+ ROACH, Hal Sr.	★	100	Pneumonia
1992	ROBBINS, Duke		71	Pneumonia
1992	+ ROBBINS, Fred		73	Lymphoma
1992	ROBBINS, Michael		62	
1992	ROBERTS, Howard		62	Prostate cancer
1992	ROBERTS, Meade		61	Congestive heart failure
1992	ROBINSON, Cardew		75	Following a bowel infection
1992	ROSE, David E. (producer)		96	Died in Phoenix, AZ (Do not confuse with the pianist/composer)
1992	ROSENBERG, Mark		44	Heart attack
1992	ROSENBERGER, James		84	Pneumonia
1992	RUBENSTEIN, Phil		51	Heart attack
1992	# RUSSELL, Andy		72	Complications from a stroke
1992	SACHA, Kenny		39	A.I.D.S.
1992	SACHS, Scotty		39	Murdered (multiple gunshot wounds)
1992	SALE-WREN, Virginia		92	Heart failure
1992	SAMUEL, Andrew		82	
1992	SANDERSON, Joan		79	After a lengthy illness
1992	SATZ, Wayne		47	Found dead in his home
1992	SCHWARTZ, Sammy		86	Heart attack
1992	SEAY, James		78	Died in Capitol Beach, CA
1992	SEGAL, Vivienne		95	Heart failure
1992	SERPE, Ralph B.		81	Cancer
1992	SEVAREID, Eric		79	Stomach cancer
1992	# SHAYNE, Robert		92	Lung cancer
1992	SHELDON, Richard		59	Cancer
1992	SHORR, Lester	★	85	Cancer
1992	SIMON, Robert F.		83	Heart attack
1992	SINCLAIR, Ronald		68	Respiratory failure
1992	SLYTER, Fred		56	After a long illness
1992	SMITH, Jacqueline		?	After a lengthy illness
1992	# SOUEZ, Ina		89	Stroke
1992	SPENCER, Herbert	☆	87	
1992	STAFFORD, Grace		88	
1992	STEEL, Pippa		44	Cancer
1992	STEPHENSON, Skip		54	Following an apparent heart attack
1992	# STOREY, June		73	Cancer
1992	STRAIT, Ralph		56	Heart attack
1992	STRANGE, Bill		62	Cancer
1992	STURGES, John	☆	82	Heart attack and emphysema (at his home in San Luis Obispo, CA)
1992	SULLIVAN, Larry		46	Stroke
1992	# Superman		54	Slain in combat with "Doomsday"
1992	SWEENEY, Bob		73	Cancer
1992	SYMS, Sylvia		74	Apparent heart attack (while performing on stage in London, Eng.)
1992	TALTON, Alix		72	After a long battle with lung cancer (in Burbank, CA)
1992	TARLOW, Florence		70	Cancer (in New York)
1992	TAVARES, Albert		39	A.I.D.S.
1992	THACKER, Jim		64	Stroke
1992	THOM, Ruth Corbett		78	After a long illness
1992	# THOMAS, Ted		88	Heart attack (in Van Nuys, CA)
1992	# THOMPSON, Marshall		66	Congestive heart failure (in Royal Oak, MI)
1992	TINDALL, Hilary		54	Cancer (in Selbourne, England)
1992	TIPPET, Clark		37	A.I.D.S.
1992	# TODD, Christopher		30	A.I.D.S. (in New York, NY)

• New entry.   # Original name (Pt. 7).   + Interment (Pt. 5).   112   ☆ Oscar nominee, ★ Oscar winner (Pt. 10)

YEAR	NAME		AGE	CAUSE AND/OR PLACE OF DEATH
1992	TOUCHSTONE, John		59	Cirrhosis of the liver (in Sherman Oaks, CA)
1992	TRACE, Christopher		59	Cancer
1992	# TREE, Dorothy		85	Heart failure (in Englewood, NJ)
1992	TROP, Jack Dunn		92	Respiratory infection (in Miami, FL)
1992	TUNBERG, Karl		83	
1992	TURNER, Teddy		75	Died in Horsforth, England
1992	VARSI, Diane	☆	54	Respiratory problems and Lyme disease (in Los Angeles, CA)
1992	VENTURA, Charlie		75	Lung cancer
1992	VINE, Sam		69	Cancer
1992	VonZERNECK, Peter		84	Complications after surgery (in Burbank, CA)
1992	WAGNER, Roger		78	Cancer
1992	WALKER, Bill		95	Cancer (in Woodland Hills, CA)
1992	# WALKER, Nancy		69	Following a 2-year battle with lung cancer (in Studio City, CA)
1992	WALKER, William Arlen		74	Died in Lancaster, CA
1992	WALLACK, Roy Homer		64	Pneumonia (in Van Nuys, CA)
1992	WEAVER, Jackson		72	Heart & kidney failure
1992	+ WELK, Lawrence		89	Pneumonia
1992	+ WELLS, Mary		49	After a long bout with cancer
1992	WHALEY, Jim		44	Heart attack
1992	WHITE, Glenn		42	A.I.D.S.
1992	# WILLIAMS, Bill		77	Complications of a brain tumor (in Burbank, CA)
1992	WILLIAMS, Tony		64	
1992	WOLFE, Ian		95	Natural causes (in Los Angeles, CA)
1992	# WOOLERY, Ade		82	Cancer (in Santa Monica, CA)
1992	#+ WORDEN, Hank		91	Died in his sleep of natural causes (at his Brentwood, CA, home)
1992	WYATT, Allan Sr.		72	Cancer (in Burbank, CA)
1992	WYLER, Jorie		61	After a brief illness (in New York, NY)
1992	YARMY, Dick		59	Lung cancer (in Studio City, CA)
1992	YEVSTIGNEEV, Yevgeny		66	Cardio-vascular problems (in London, England)
1992	YORK, Dick		63	Emphysema and degenerative spinal condition (Grand Rapids, MI)
1992	YOUNG, Jack Haydn		81	Neurological illness
1993	ADLER, Clyde		67	After a long illness (in Petasky, Michigan)
1993	AGUILAR, Thomas J.		41	A.I.D.S. (in Honolulu, Hawaii)
1993	+ AIDMAN, Charles		68	Cancer (in Beverly Hills, CA)
1993	ALLEN, Adrianne		86	After suffering from cancer (in Montreux, Switzerland)
1993	# ALLEY, Paul		87	Died in Winter Park, Florida
1993	#+ AMECHE, Don	★	85	Prostate cancer (at his son's home in Scottsdale, AZ)
1993	+ AMES, Leon		91	Complications after a stroke (Laguna Beach, CA)
1993	ANDERSON, Marian		96	Congestive heart failure following a stroke
1993	ANTHONY, Joseph		80	Died in Hyannis, MA
1993	ARDOLINO, Emile	★	50	Complications from A.I.D.S. (in Bel-Air, CA)
1993	+ ASHE, Arthur		49	A.I.D.S.-related pneumonia
1993	BAKER, Howard		61	Cancer (in Hale, Cheshire, England)
1993	BAKEWELL, Billy		85	Leukemia (in Los Angeles, CA)
1993	BALLARD, Lucinda	☆	87	Cancer
1993	BARCLIFT, Edgar Nelson		76	After a lengthy illness (in Los Angeles, CA)
1993	BARRON, Lee		78	Respiratory failure (in Omaha, Nebraska)
1993	BARROW, Bernard		65	Lung cancer (at Lennox Hill Hospital in NY)
1993	BATTLE, Edwin Louis		33	Stroke (in Toronto, Canada)
1993	BECK, John		83	Cancer (in Woodland Hills, CA)
1993	BECKER, Robert		47	Car accident (in Santa Clarita, CA)
1993	BELLAVER, Harry		88	Pneumonia (in a Nyack, NY, hospital)
1993	BERRY, Eric		80	Cancer (in Laguna Beach, CA)
1993	BERTHELSON, Larry		60	Died in Santa Barbara, CA
1993	BISHOP, Wesdon		60	Liver ailment (in Nashville, TN)
1993	BISSELL, Jennifer Raine		60	Heart ailment (in Los Angeles, CA)
1993	BITTNER, Jack		76	Heart attack (in New York)
1993	+ BIXBY, Bill		59	Prostate cancer (in his Century City, CA, home)
1993	BJORLING, Rolf		64	
1993	# BOOTS, Tubby		59	After a blood clot traveled to his lungs
1993	BOZYK, Reizl		79	Died at St. Vincent's Hosp. Med. Ctr., NYC
1993	BRADEN, Bernard		76	Heart attack (in London, England)
1993	BRAFA, Tony		72	Heart attack (in Los Angeles, CA)
1993	BRANDA, Richard		57	Colon cancer (in Los Angeles, CA)

YEAR	NAME		AGE	CAUSE AND/OR PLACE OF DEATH
1993	# BRANDT, Buzz		60	Heart failure
1993	BRIAN, David		82	Cancer & heart failure (in Sherman Oaks, CA)
1993	BRIDGES, James	☆	57	Intestinal cancer (in Los Angeles, CA)
1993	BROCCO, Peter		89	Heart attack (in Los Angeles, CA)
1993	BROWN, Richard "Dick"		68	Cancer (in Los Angeles, CA)
1993	BROX, Lorayne (Hall)		94	Unreported causes (in Los Angeles, CA)
1993	BRUSATI, Franco		66	Leukemia (in Rome, Italy)
1993	BULLOCK, Burdette III		38	Cancer
1993	BURDETT, Winston		79	After a long illness (in Rome, Italy)
1993	BURKS, Stephen		36	Undisclosed causes (in Los Angeles, CA)
1993	#+ BURR, Raymond		76	Cancer of the liver (in Sonoma County, CA)
1993	BUTLER, John		74	Cancer (in New York)
1993	BYRD, William D.		27	Heart failure (in Inglewood, CA)
1993	#+ CAHN, Sammy	★	79	Congestive heart failure
1993	CAINE, Howard		67	Heart attack (in Los Angeles, CA)
1993	CALLEN, Michael		38	A.I.D.S. (in Los Angeles, CA)
1993	+ CAMPANELLA, Roy		71	After a heart attack (in Woodland Hills, CA)
1993	# Cantinflas		81	Lung cancer (died in Mexico City)
1993	CARLON, Fran		80	Cancer (at her home in Manhattan)
1993	CARROLL, Janice		61	Cancer (in San Fernando Valley, CA)
1993	CHECCHI, Robert J.		67	After suffering a stroke (in Los Angeles, CA)
1993	CINCOTTA, Carmine		41	Hodgkin's disease (in New York)
1993	CLAYWORTH, June		80	Lymphoma (in Calabasas, CA)
1993	COLLARD, Cyril		35	A.I.D.S. (in Paris, France)
1993	CONN, Billy		75	Pneumonia (in Pittsburgh, PA)
1993	CONNOR, Kenneth		77	Cancer (in London, England)
1993	CONSTANTINE, Eddie		75	Heart attack (in Wiesbaden, Germany)
1993	CORBETT, Glenn		59	Lung cancer (in San Antonio, TX)
1993	# CORDAY, Josephine Rich		79	Heart & kidney failure (in Los Angeles, CA)
1993	COREY, Dorian		56	A.I.D.S. (in a New York hospital)
1993	CORT, William		53	Cancer (in Los Angeles, CA)
1993	CORY, Ken		51	A.I.D.S.
1993	COVINGTON, Fred		65	Cancer (in a Marietta, GA, hospital)
1993	CROSBY, Bob		79	Cancer (in La Jolla, CA)
1993	CUSACK, Cyril		82	Motor neuron disease (at his home in London)
1993	DAUGHERTY, Herschel		82	Pneumonia
1993	DAVENPORT, John		62	Diabetes
1993	DAVID, Mack		81	Died in a hospital in Rancho Mirage, CA
1993	DAVIS, Robert		76	Emphysema
1993	+ DeFORE, Don		80	Cardiac arrest (in Santa Monica, CA)
1993	DeGROOT, Katherine Hynes		88	Complications from a stroke (in Englewood, NJ)
1993	DeMILLE, Agnes		88	Stroke & heart failure in her sleep (at home in NY)
1993	+ DeRITA, Joe		83	Pneumonia (in Woodland Hills, CA)
1993	# DESMOND, Florence		87	Unreported causes (in Guildford, England)
1993	DONALD, James		76	Stomach cancer (at his home in Wiltshire, England)
1993	DORR, John		48	A.I.D.S.
1993	D'ORSA, Lonnie		96	Died in Beverly Hills, CA
1993	DOUGLAS, Gordon		85	Cancer (in Los Angeles, CA)
1993	DOUGLAS, Hugh		78	Heart attack (in Los Angeles, CA)
1993	# DOUGLAS, Steve		55	Heart attack (during a studio recording session)
1993	DREIFUSS, Arthur		85	After a bout with the flu (in Studio City, CA)
1993	DREW, Larry		73	After a long illness (in London, England)
1993	DUFFY, John Paul		42	Apparent suicide (in W. Hollywood, CA)
1993	DUNCAN, Mary (Sanford)		98	Natural causes
1993	EARLE, Don (TV sportscaster)		64	
1993	ECKSTINE, Billy		78	Cardiac arrest after suffering a stroke
1993	# ELLISON, James		83	After breaking his neck in a fall (in Montecito, CA)
1993	ENGLUND, Kenneth		78	A recurring illness (in Woodland Hills, CA)
1993	FALCO, Louis		50	A.I.D.S. (in New York)
1993	FELD, Fritz		93	After a lengthy illness (in Santa Monica, CA)
1993	+ FELLINI, Federico	★	73	After suffering a stroke & heart attack (in Rome)
1993	FITZSIMMONS, Bob		53	Heart attack (after collapsing in a NY restaurant)
1993	FORD, Constance		69	Cancer (in New York)
1993	FOX, William J.		95	Died in Fillmore, CA
1993	FROST, Terry		86	Heart failure (in Los Angeles, Ca)

...DEATHS OF MOVIE AND TELEVISION PERSONALITIES – BY YEAR...

YEAR	NAME		AGE	CAUSE AND/OR PLACE OF DEATH
1993	FUCCELLO, Tom		55	A.I.D.S. (in a Van Nuys, CA, convalescent home)
1993	FUCHS, Daniel	★	84	Heart failure (in Los Angeles, CA)
1993	GARRETT, Joy		47	Liver failure (in Los Angeles, CA)
1993	GARVARENTZ, George		61	Heart failure (in Aubagne, France)
1993	GENTRY, Minnie L.		77	Lung cancer (in New York)
1993	GEORGE, George L.	★	85	Heart failure (in New York)
1993	GIBBINS, Duncan		41	Burns (while trying to rescue a cat in a Malibu, CA, fire)
1993	# GILLESPIE, Dizzy		75	Died in his sleep of pancreatic cancer (in Englewood, CA)
1993	GISH, Lillian	☆	99	Cerebral hemorrhage and heart failure (in New York, NY)
1993	GOLDSTEIN, Elayne		59	Cancer
1993	GORDON, Michael		83	Natural causes (at a hospital in Century City, CA)
1993	GORI, Mario Cecchi		73	Apparent heart attack (in Rome)
1993	GRANGER, John		69	Cerebral hemmorage (in Doylestown, PA)
1993	# GRANGER, Stewart		80	Prostate and bone cancer (in Santa Monica, CA)
1993	GREGORY, Dennis		40	Pneumonia (in East Meadow, NY)
1993	# GREY, Nan		75	Heart failure (in her San Diego, CA, home)
1993	GRUNDY, Bill		69	Died in Cheshire, England
1993	GUNN, Moses		64	Complications of asthma (in Guilford, CT)
1993	# GWYNNE, Fred "Herman Munster"		66	Pancreatic cancer (in Taneytown, MD)
1993	HAMMER, Alvin		78	Died in New York
1993	HAMMER, Peter		54	Cancer (in New York)
1993	HARVEY, Rick		43	Kidney failure (died in Memphis, TN)
1993	HAWORTH, Ted	★	76	Heart failure
1993	+ HAYES, Helen	★	92	Congestive heart failure (in Nyack, NY)
1993	HEARST, William Randolph Jr.		85	Heart attack (in New York)
1993	#+ HEPBURN, Audrey	★	63	Colon cancer (in Tolochenaz, Switzerland)
1993	HEYES, Douglas		73	Congestive heart failure (in Beverly Hills, CA)
1993	HIBBERT, Dora		77	Following an illness (in New York)
1993	HILL, Jacqueline		68	Cancer (in London, England)
1993	HILL, Martin		80	Cancer (in Sherman Oaks, CA)
1993	HOGAN, Paul (of WMAQ-TV)		48	Apparent heart attack (Do not confuse with the actor)
1993	HOLLAND, John		85	Respiratory failure and pneumonia (in Woodland Hills, CA)
1993	HONDA, Ishiro		81	Died in Tokyo, Japan
1993	HOPKINS, Speed	☆	44	Viral infection (in Sparks, MD)
1993	HOUSTON, David		57	Brain aneurysm
1993	HOWARD, Cy		77	Heart failure (in Los Angeles, CA)
1993	# HOWELL, Wayne		72	Unreported causes (in Pompano Beach, FL)
1993	HUBER, Gusti		78	Heart failure (in Mount Kisco, NY)
1993	HUNT, Frances		77	Complications following a stroke
1993	INGLIS, Brian		76	Died in London, England
1993	INNOCENT, Harold		60	After a short illness (in London)
1993	JACOBSON, Arthur		92	Died in Woodland Hills, CA
1993	JARVIS, Patience		56	Melanoma
1993	JENSEN, Lenore Kingston		79	Cancer (in Van Nuys, CA)
1993	JOHANN, Zita		89	Pneumonia (in Nyack Hospital, Nyack, NY)
1993	+ JONES, Ken		54	Cancer (in Los Angeles, CA)
1993	# JORDAN, Richard		56	Brain tumor (at his home in Los Angles, CA)
1993	JURIST, Ed		76	Died in Los Angeles, CA
1993	KANIN, Michael		83	Died in Los Angeles, CA
1993	KARAS, Barry		49	Leukemia (in Boston, MA)
1993	KARIN, Rita		73	Following a bout with pneumonia (in New York)
1993	KEANE, Joe		69	Cancer (in Woodland Hills, CA)
1993	KEEGAN, Terry		59	Suicide (near Kingman, Arizona)
1993	+ KEELER, Ruby		83	Cancer (in Rancho Mirage, CA)
1993	KIBBEE, Lois		71	Brain tumor (at Sloane-Kettering Cancer Ctr., NY)
1993	KING, Jean		76	Heart attack (in North Hollywood, CA)
1993	KINGSTON, Lenore (Jensen)		79	Cancer (in Van Nuys, CA)
1993	KLOS, Elmar	★	83	Cause unreported (in Prague, Czechoslovakia)
1993	# KNIGHT, Bob		72	Heart attack (in New York)
1993	KRAFT, David		35	Crohn's disease (in Los Angeles, CA)
1993	KULLER, Sid Charles		83	Colon cancer (in Sherman Oaks, CA)
1993	LAMONT, Charles		98	Pneumonia (in Woodland Hills, CA)
1993	LANDAU, Ely A.		73	Complications following a stroke (in Los Angeles, CA)
1993	LANDAU, Richard		79	Complications after surgery (in Century City, CA)
1993	LANE, David T.		52	Brain cancer (in Dallas, Texas)

• New entry. # Original name (Pt. 7). + Interment (Pt. 5).   115   ☆ Oscar nominee, ★ Oscar winner (Pt. 10)

YEAR	NAME		AGE	CAUSE AND/OR PLACE OF DEATH
1993	# LANTEAU, William		70	Complications after heart surgery (in Los Angeles)
1993	LAZARUS, Irma		80	Cancer (in Cincinnati, Ohio)
1993	LEDOUX, Fernand		96	Unreported causes (in Vilerville, France)
1993	+ LEE, Brandon		27	Hit with a .44-caliber bullet in a filming accident (Wilmington, NC)
1993	# LEE, Pinky		85	Heart attack (in CA)
1993	LEETCH, Thomas		60	Leukemia (in Sherman Oaks, CA)
1993	LEHMAN, Gladys Collins		101	Pneumonia (in Newport Beach, CA)
1993	LeMASSENA, William		76	Lung cancer
1993	LEONTOVICH, Eugenie		93	Cardiac arrest and pneumonia (in Los Angeles, CA)
1993	LEOPOLD, Douglas		49	A.I.D.S.
1993	# LEWIS, Edwina		42	Heart attack (in Augusta, Michigan)
1993	LEWIS, Marlo		77	Heart failure (in Los Angeles, CA)
1993	LINDQUIST, Dan		65	Pneumonia (in Burbank, CA)
1993	LOMBARDO, Lebert J.		88	Emphysema (in Fort Meyers, FL)
1993	LONDON, Roy		50	Lymphoma (in Los Angeles, CA)
1993	#+ LOY, Myrna ★		88	During surgery, after a lengthy illness (in New York)
1993	LYNN, Jack		67	Leukemia (in Albuquerque, NM)
1993	MACK, Wayne		68	Cancer (in New Orleans, LA)
1993	MACKENDRICK, Alexander		81	Pneumonia (in Los Angeles, CA)
1993	MAGALOFF, Nikita		80	After a long illness
1993	MALVERN, Paul		91	Died in Los Angeles, CA
1993	MANKIEWICZ, Francis		69	Cancer (in Montreal, Canada)
1993	# MANKIEWICZ, Joseph L. ★		83	Heart failure (in Bedford, NY)
1993	MANOS, Gloria		69	Cancer (in Reno, Nevada)
1993	MARGOLIN, Janet		50	Ovarian cancer (in Los Angeles, CA)
1993	MARLAND, Douglas		58	Complications following abdominal surgery (in Norwalk, CT)
1993	MARTINEZ, José "Tun Tun"		61	Following surgery for intestinal blockage (Mexico)
1993	McBEE, Keith W.		66	Cancer complicated by other illnesses
1993	McCLEOD, Mercer		86	Heart failure (in New York)
1993	+ McFARLAND, George "Spanky"		64	Unknown causes (in a Grapevine, TX, hospital)
1993	McNEIL, Claudia		77	Complications from diabetes (in Englewood, NJ)
1993	MEISER, Edith		95	Heart attack (at Roosevelt Hospital in New York)
1993	MILLHOLLIN, James		77	Cancer (in Biloxi, Mississippi)
1993	MONTI, Carlotta		86	After a long illness (in Woodland Hills, CA)
1993	# MOORE, Garry		78	Emphysema (at his home on Hilton Head Island)
1993	MOORE, Irving		74	Heart attack (in Sherman Oaks, CA)
1993	MORGAN, Edward P.		82	Cancer
1993	MORK, Erik		67	Died in Copenhagen, Denmark
1993	MORRISON, Harold		62	Died in Springfield, Missouri
1993	MORRISON, Michael D.		33	Accidental overdose of alcohol & illegal drugs
1993	MORROW, Jeff		86	After a long illness (in Canoga Park, CA)
1993	MORSE, Carleton		91	Died in Sacramento, CA
1993	MURPHY, Richard		81	Stroke (in Los Angeles, CA)
1993	MYERS, Stanley		63	Cancer (in London, England)
1993	+ NEGULESCO, Jean		93	Heart failure (in Marbella, Spain)
1993	NELSON, Kenneth		60	An A.I.D.S.-related illness (in London)
1993	NEWMAN, Walter Brown ☆		77	Cancer (at his home in Sherman Oaks, CA)
1993	NIGH, Jane		68	Stroke (in Los Angeles, CA)
1993	#+ NIXON, Pat		81	Lung cancer
1993	NORMAN, Lester		81	Heart failure
1993	+ NUREYEV, Rudolph		54	Cardiac complications from A.I.D.S. (in Paris, France)
1993	NUSSBAUM, Raphael		61	Cancer (in Burbank, CA)
1993	NYBY, Christian ☆		80	Natural causes (in Temecula, CA)
1993	OCHS, Saul P.		82	Unreported causes (in N. Hollywood, CA)
1993	+ O'CONNELL, Helen (Devol)		73	Cancer (at a hospice in San Diego, CA)
1993	O'HARA, Patrick J.		55	After a lengthy illness (in Burbank, CA)
1993	PALEY, Irving		77	Heart attack (in Los Angeles, CA)
1993	# PARHAM, Ernie		64	After a long illness (in Glen Falls, NY)
1993	PARKER, Cecilia		79	Died in Ventura, CA
1993	PARKIN, Leonard		64	Cancer of the spine (in England)
1993	PEALE, (Rev.) Norman Vincent		95	Following a stroke (at his farm in Pawling, NY)
1993	PEARDON, Patricia		69	Pneumonia (at St. Luke's Hospital in Manhattan, NY)
1993	# PEPPER, Buddy		70	Heart failure
1993	+ PEPPLE, Sydney Chester		83	Died at Scripps Ocean View Hospital, Encinitas, CA
1993	PEREDES, Daniel		46	A.I.D.S. (in Los Angeles, CA)

• New entry. # Original name (Pt. 7). + Interment (Pt. 5).

116

☆ Oscar nominee, ★ Oscar winner (Pt. 10)

YEAR	NAME		AGE	CAUSE AND/OR PLACE OF DEATH
1993	PHELPS, Donald		61	A.I.D.S. (in West Hollywood, CA)
1993	PHILBIN, Mary		90	Complications from Alzheimer's disease (in Huntington Beach, CA)
1993	PHILLIPS, Linn III		45	Heart attack (in Denver, Colorado)
1993	+ PHOENIX, River		23	Acute multiple drug intoxication (at a niteclub in West Hollywood)
1993	PIERCE, Edward		77	Natural causes (in Jamesport, NY)
1993	PLAGE, Dieter		57	Died in a filming accident in the Sumatra rain forest
1993	POLK, Lee		69	Leukemia
1993	PREVIN, Steve		68	Unreported causes (in Palm Desert, CA)
1993	+ PRICE, Vincent		82	Lung cancer (at his home in Hollywood Hills, CA)
1993	PRIESTLY, Jack		66	Unreported causes (at his home in Los Angeles, CA)
1993	# RA, Sun		79	Circulatory problems after a series of strokes
1993	RAMSEY, Gordon		63	Cancer (at his home in New York City)
1993	RANDOLPH, Donald		87	Pneumonia (in Los Angeles, CA)
1993	# RAY, René		81	Unreported causes (in Jersey, the Channel Islands)
1993	REED, Taylor		60	Heart attack (in New York)
1993	REID, Kate		62	Cancer (in Stratford, Ontario)
1993	REINHEART, Alice		83	Died in Avon, CT
1993	REVIER, Dorothy		89	Died at Queen of Angels–Hollywood Pres. Med. Ctr., CA
1993	RIVERS, Al		65	Cancer
1993	ROBERTS, Davis		76	Emphysema (in Chicago, IL)
1993	ROGERS, Will Jr.		81	Apparent suicide (gunshot) in Tubac, AZ
1993	ROLFE, Sam	☆	69	Heart attack while playing tennis (in Los Angeles)
1993	RYU, Chishu		88	Cancer (in Yokohama, Japan)
1993	SABATINO, Anthony		48	A.I.D.S. (in Los Angeles, CA)
1993	SALANT, Richard "Dick"		78	Heart failure (while giving a speech)
1993	SALE, Richard		80	After suffering two strokes (in Los Angeles, CA)
1993	SALKIN, Leo	☆	80	Congestive heart failure (in Burbank, CA)
1993	SALMON, Scott		51	After an auto accident (in Northridge, CA)
1993	SARGENT, Thornton		90	Died in Rancho Palos Verdes, CA
1993	SAUTER, Carl		44	Undisclosed causes (in Los Angeles, CA)
1993	SCHAFFEL, Hal		78	Undisclosed causes
1993	SCHMIECHEN, Richard		45	A.I.D.S. (died in Los Angeles, CA)
1993	SCHNEIDER, Abe		87	Pneumonia & Alzheimer's disease complications
1993	SCHNEIDER, Alexander		84	Heart disease (in New York)
1993	SCHOENBRUN, Michael		54	Pancreatic cancer (in Tarzana, CA)
1993	SCORSESE, Luciano Charles		80	After a long illness (in New York)
1993	+ SEYMOUR, Dan		78	Following a stroke (in Santa Monica, CA)
1993	SHARAFF, Irene	★	83	Congestive heart failure (in New York)
1993	SHARITS, Paul		50	Heart attack (in Buffalo, NY)
1993	SHARKEY, Ray		40	A.I.D.S. (in a Brooklyn, NY hospital)
1993	SHEARER, Jacqueline		46	Colon cancer (at her home in Cambridge, MA)
1993	SHEPARD, Bob		76	Heart attack (on a visit to Manhattan)
1993	SHIELDS, Pat		70	Found dead in his car (in Death Valley)
1993	# SHIRLEY, Anne	☆	74	Lung cancer after a long illness (in Los Angeles)
1993	SIDNEY, Sid		?	Parkinson's disease
1993	SIEGRIST, Jeremy		20	Killed in a hiking accident in the Calif. mountains
1993	SMANEY, June		71	An apparent suicide (in Los Angeles, CA)
1993	# SMITH, Alexis		72	Cancer (at Cedars-Sinai Med. Ctr. in Los Angeles)
1993	ST. JOSEPH, Ellis		82	Cancer (in Beverly Hills, CA)
1993	STEADMAN, John		83	Pneumonia (in Montrose, CA)
1993	# STEN, Anna		85	Cardiac arrest (at her home in Manhattan)
1993	STEVENS, Dudley		57	A.I.D.S. (in Hove, England)
1993	STEWART, Bill		67	Heart attack (at a London airport, after filming in Madeira)
1993	STORRS, Tim		43	Found dead in his apartment after a fall
1993	STRIVELLI, Jerry		61	Heart attack (in New York)
1993	STRONG, Robert B.		87	Natural causes (in Burbank, CA)
1993	SULLIVAN, Jeremiah		58	An A.I.D.S.-related illness (in Hollywood, CA)
1993	SYRON, Brian		58	Leukemia (in Sydney, Australia)
1993	TARLETON, Diane R.		51	Breast cancer (at her home in Manhattan)
1993	THOMAS, Gerald		72	Died in Beaconsfield, England
1993	THOR, Jerome		69	Cardiac arrest (in Westwood, CA)
1993	TIPPING, Tim "Tip"		34	While re-enacting a sky-diving accident for TV (in Alnwick, England)
1993	TODD, Ann		82	After a stroke (in a London hospital)
1993	TOMLINSON, Kate		96	Died in New Jersey, cause unreported
1993	TRUSCOTT, John	★	57	During emergency heart surgery (in Melbourne)

...DEATHS OF MOVIE AND TELEVISION PERSONALITIES – BY YEAR...

YEAR	NAME	AGE	CAUSE AND/OR PLACE OF DEATH
1993	# TWITTY, Conway	59	Surgery complications after a stomach aneurysm (Springfield, MO)
1993	VALLI, June	64	Cancer
1993	VALVANO, Jim	45	After a 1-year bout with cancer (in Durham, NC)
1993	VENABLE, Evelyn	80	Cancer (in Post Falls, Idaho)
1993	VILLECHAIZE, Herve "Tatoo"	50	Suicide (gunshot) in his North Hollywood home
1993	#+ VonERICH, Kerry	33	
1993	WALTON, Gladys (Herbel)	90	Cancer (at a nursing home in Morro Bay, CA)
1993	WANAMAKER, Sam	74	After a 5-yr. bout with cancer (in London)
1993	WARING, Richard	82	Natural causes
1993	WARREN, Joseph	77	Respiratory failure (at Village Nursing Home, NY)
1993	WARRISS, Ben	83	
1993	WATERS, Chuck	70	Died in Saginaw, Michigan
1993	WEBB, Richard	77	Suicide (gunshot) after suffering a long illness (in Van Nuys, CA)
1993	WEEDIN, Harfield	77	Died in Boise, Idaho, of undisclosed causes
1993	WELLES, Gwen	42	Cancer (at her home in Santa Monica, CA)
1993	WELLINGTON, Valerie	33	Brain aneurysm (in Maywood, IL)
1993	# WELSH, Ronnie	52	Brain cancer (in New York)
1993	+ WHELAN, Arleen (Cagney)	78	Following a stroke (in Orange County, CA)
1993	WHELAN, Kenneth	72	Died in New York
1993	WILBERN, George E.	77	Emphysema (in Los Angeles, CA)
1993	WILEY, Jan (Greene)	83	Cancer (in Rancho Palos Verdes, CA)
1993	WILKINSON, Kate	76	Bone cancer (in New York)
1993	WILSON, Lester	51	Heart attack (in Los Angeles, CA)
1993	WOLF, Harry L.	85	Died at Cedars-Sinai Hospital, CA
1993	WONDER, Tommy	78	Complications from an ulcer (in New York City)
1993	WRIGHTSON, Earl	77	Heart failure (in E. Norwich, CT)
1993	YOUNG, Marvin	90	Natural causes (in Los Angeles, CA)
1993	# YOUNG, Skip "Wally"	63	Found dead at his CA home of natural causes
1993	#+ ZAPPA, Frank	52	Prostate cancer (in Los Angeles, CA)
1994	# ADRIAN, Iris	81	Complications from earthquake injuries (in Northridge, CA)
1994	+ AKINS, Claude	67	Cancer (in Altadena, CA)
1994	ALBIN, Andy	86	After a long illness (in Woodland Hills, CA)
1994	ALDRIDGE, Michael	73	Died in London, England
1994	ANDERSON, Herbert	77	Died in his sleep 2-months after a stroke (in Palm Springs, CA)
1994	ANDERSON, Lindsay	71	Heart attack (after swimming at a friend's pool in Nice, France)
1994	AUBREY, James T.	75	Heart attack (at UCLA Med. Ctr. emergency room)
1994	BAKER, Benny	87	Died at MPTF Hospital in Woodland Hills, CA
1994	BARRAULT, Jean-Louis	83	Died in his sleep of apparent heart attack (in Paris, France)
1994	# BARTLETT, Richard	70	Complications of diabetes (in Havre de Grace, MD)
1994	# BASQUETTE, Lina	87	Cancer (at her home in Wheeling, W. Va.)
1994	BEERY, Noah Jr.	81	After surgery for bleeding in his brain (nr. Tehachapi, CA)
1994	BELLIN, Steve	43	A.I.D.S. complications
1994	BERNARDI, Jack	85	Heart attack
1994	BLACKBURN, Royce	69	Cancer (in New Ipswich, NH)
1994	BLACKTON, Jay	84	Heart attack (in Los Angeles, CA)
1994	BONDARCHUK, Sergei	74	Cardio-vascular disease (in Moscow, Russia)
1994	+ BOOKE, Sorrell "Boss Hogg"	64	Colon cancer (in Sherman Oaks, CA)
1994	BOOTH, Jim	48	Cancer (in Wellington, New Zealand)
1994	BORLAND, Carroll	79	Pneumonia (in Arlington, VA)
1994	BOYLAN, John	82	Lung cancer & pneumonia (at his home in Bellevue, Wash.)
1994	BRAZZI, Rossano	78	Viral infection (in Rome, Italy)
1994	BRONSTON, Samuel	85	After a brief illness (in Sacramento, CA)
1994	BULGAKOVA, Maya	62	Automobile accident (in Russia)
1994	BUTLER, Chris ☆	42	A.I.D.S. complications (in Los Angeles, CA)
1994	BUTTRAM, Pat	78	Kidney failure (at UCLA Medical Center)
1994	# CALLOWAY, Cab	86	Pneumonia following a stroke (in Hockessin, DE)
1994	#+ CANDY, John	43	Heart attack in his sleep (on location in Durango, Mexico)
1994	+ CAREY, Macdonald	81	Cancer (in his Beverly Hills, CA, home)
1994	+ CAREY, Timothy	65	After suffering a stroke (at Cedars-Sinai Med. Ctr. in L.A.)
1994	CARMET, Jean	73	Heart failure (at his home in Sèvres, France)
1994	CARROLL, Bob	76	After a long illness (at a hospital in Manhasset, L.I., NY)
1994	CARSON, Ken	79	Amyotrophic lateral sclerosis (in Jacksonville, FL)
1994	CARTER, Janis	80	Heart attack (in Durham, NC)
1994	CARTIER, Rudolph	90	Died in his sleep (in London, England)

YEAR	NAME	AGE	CAUSE AND/OR PLACE OF DEATH
1994	# CHANDLER, Janet	78	Heart failure after a stroke (at UCLA Med. Ctr., CA)
1994	# Christian-Jaque	89	Heart attack (in Boulogne-Billancourt, France)
1994	CLAVELL, James	69	Stroke after suffering from cancer (at home in Switzerland)
1994	+ COBAIN, Kurt	27	Suicide (gunshot) while high on heroin & valium
1994	COCHRAN, Ron	81	After a short illness (in Florida)
1994	COLLINS, Christopher	44	After a brief illness (in Ventura, CA)
1994	# COLLINS, Dorothy	67	Heart failure (at her home in Watervliet, NY)
1994	+ CONRAD, William	73	Heart attack (at the Medical Center of N. Hollywood)
1994	CONWELL, John	72	Cancer (at his home in Santa Barbara, CA)
1994	CORVO, Phil	67	After a long illness (in Los Angeles, CA)
1994	+ COTTEN, Joseph	88	Pneumonia (at his Los Angeles home)
1994	CRAVAT, Nick	82	Lung cancer (in Woodland Hills, CA)
1994	CUNY, Alain	85	Died at the Cochin Hospital in Paris, France
1994	CURRY, John	44	A.I.D.S.-related heart attack (at his home in England)
1994	CUSHING, Peter	81	Cancer (in a Canterbury hospice, England)
1994	# DALE, Virginia	77	Complications of emphysema (in Burbank, CA)
1994	#+ DAMITA, Lili	92	Alzheimer's disease (in Palm Beach, FL)
1994	DANO, Royal "Ted" Jr.	47	Liver failure (in Santa Monica, CA)
1994	DANO, Royal Sr.	71	Pulmonary fibrosis (at his home in Santa Monica, CA)
1994	DAVIES, Richard	80	Heart attack (in Weaverville, CA)
1994	# DAVIS, Battle	42	Non-Hodgkins lymphoma
1994	DENGEL, Jake	61	Cancer (at Group One Hospice in Sherman Oaks, CA)
1994	DENNY, C. Patterson	46	Cancer (in Glenbrook, IL)
1994	DEVINE, Jerry	85	Died in Santa Barbara, CA)
1994	DODSON, Jack	63	Heart failure after a year of failing health (in Encino, CA)
1994	DONALDSON, Norma	68	Cancer (at Cedars-Sinai Med. Ctr. in Los Angeles, CA)
1994	DOUCETTE, John	73	Cancer (at his home in Cabazon, CA)
1994	DOUGLAS, Jack	72	Cancer (in Los Angeles, CA)
1994	DOWNS, Johnny "Our Gang"	80	Cancer (at his home in Coronado, CA)
1994	DRAKE, Charles	79	After a lengthy illness (at his home in East Lyme, CT)
1994	# DUFF-GRIFFIN, William	54	Prostate cancer (at the Manhattan home of his companion)
1994	DUKE, Edward	50	Cancer (in London, England)
1994	DULO, Jane	75	After cardiac surgery (at Cedars-Sinai Med. Ctr. in Los Angeles)
• 1994	# DUNFEE, Nora	78	After a brief illness (in Manhattan, NY)
• 1994	EMHARDT, Robert	80	Died at his home in Ojai, CA
1994	EWART, John	66	Cancer (in Sydney, Australia)
1994	# EWELL, Tom	85	After a long series of illnesses (in Woodland Hills, CA)
1994	FABRI, Zoltan	77	Heart attack (at his home in Budapest, Hungary)
1994	FEDDERSON, Donald	81	After a series of heart problems (at Cedars-Sinai Hosp. in L.A.)
1994	FINK, Agnes	74	Died in Germany
1994	FIRKUSNY, Rudolf	82	Cancer (in New York)
1994	FOX, George S.	89	Congestive heart failure (in Los Angeles, CA)
1994	FRANKEL, Daniel	91	Natural causes (in Winchester, N.H.)
1994	FREDERICK, Lynne	39	Found dead in bed, apparently of natural causes (in Los Angeles)
1994	FREED, Bert	74	Heart attack (while on vacation in British Columbia)
1994	FRYD, Joseph	89	Following a stroke (in Rome, Italy)
1994	# FURNESS, Betty	78	Stomach cancer (at Sloan-Kettering Memorial Hospital, NY)
1994	FUSCO, Nelly	85	Cancer (at St. Francis Hosp. in Poughkeepsie, NY)
• 1994	GARFIELD, David	51	Heart attack
1994	GIBBERSON, William	74	Effects of a stroke (in New York)
1994	GIFFORD, Frances	72	Emphysema (in Pasadena, CA)
1994	GILLETTE, Ruth	89	Cancer (in Los Angeles, CA)
1994	GILLIAT, Sidney	85	Died at his home in Wiltshire, England)
1994	GRAF, William	82	Heart failure complicated by pneumonia (in Los Angeles, CA)
1994	GRAY, Nadia	70	Stroke (at New York Hospital in Manhattan)
1994	GRIGAS, John	71	Heart attack
1994	HACKES, Peter	69	Heart attack (in Washington, D.C.)
1994	HARP, Bill	70	Heart attack (in Hollywood, CA)
1994	HARPER, Pat (TV anchor)	59	Heart attack (at her home in Capiliera, Spain)
• 1994	HARRIS, Chris	51	Apparent heart attack (at his home in Newbury Park, CA)
1994	HARRISON, Joan	83	Died in London, England
• 1994	HARTLEY, Neil	78	Heart failure (at his home in Los Angeles, CA)
1994	HAWKINS, Corwin	29	Pneumonia (in Los Angeles, CA)
1994	HAYDON, Julie	84	Abdominal cancer (in LaCrosse, WI)
1994	HAYMAN, Lillian	72	Heart attack (at her home in Hollis, NY)

YEAR	NAME		AGE	CAUSE AND/OR PLACE OF DEATH
1994	HAYNES, Tiger		79	Cardiac arrest (at St. Vincent's Hospital in New York City)
1994	HAZEN, Joseph		96	Died in his sleep (at home in Boca Raton, FL)
1994	HEFLIN, Frances		71	Lung cancer (in New York, NY)
1994	# HIATT, Ruth		88	Congestive heart failure (in Montrose, CA)
1994	HICKS, Bill		32	Pancreatic cancer (in Little Rock, Ark.)
1994	HILL, James		75	Died in London, England
• 1994	HOLLAND, Joseph		84	Heart failure (in Santa Fe, N.M.)
1994	HOREN, Robert		68	Cancer (in New York)
1994	HORNER, Harry	★	84	Pneumonia (at his home in Pacific Palisades, CA)
1994	HUGO, Laurence		76	Alzheimer's disease (in Charlottesville, VA)
1994	+ HUMANN, Helena Enize		52	After a long illness (in Dallas, Texas)
1994	HURST, Margaret		75	Heart failure (at Sherman Oaks Med. Ctr., CA)
1994	# HUTTON, Robert		73	Died in Kingston, NY)
1994	JARMAN, Derek		52	Complications of A.I.D.S. (in London, England)
1994	JOBIM, Antonio Carlos		67	Heart failure after minor surgery (in New York City)
1994	#+ JULIA, Raul		54	Complications of a stroke (at a hospital in Manhasset, NY)
1994	# KABIBBLE, Ish		86	Respiratory failure due to emphysema (Joshua Tree, CA)
1994	KEATS, Steven		48	Suicide (found dead in his Manhattan apartment)
1994	# KERR, Stu		66	After 8-yr. battle with bone marrow cancer (in Balt., MD)
1994	KOSCINA, Sylva		61	After a long illness complicated by heart problems (in Rome)
1994	KOSLECK, Martin		89	After abdominal surgery (in Santa Monica, CA)
1994	KOSTAL, Irwin	★	83	Heart attack (in Studio City, CA)
1994	KRIM, Arthur		84	After a long illness (at his home in New York City)
1994	# LANCASTER, Burt		80	Heart attack after suffering a stroke (at his condo in L.A.)
1994	LANGTON, David		82	Heart attack (at Stratford-on-Avon, England)
1994	# LANSING, Robert		66	Cancer (at Calgary Hospice in the Bronx, NY)
1994	+ LANTZ, Walter	★	93	Heart attack (in Burbank, CA)
1994	LAYTON, Joe		64	After an extended illness (in Key West, FL)
1994	LEONARD, Bill		78	Stroke (at Laurel Regional Hospital in Laurel, MD)
• 1994	LIVINGSTON, Valerie Cossart		87	Pneumonia (in New York)
1994	LOCCHI, Pino		69	After suffering two strokes (in Rome, Italy)
1994	LUXFORD, Nola (Dolberg)		99	Died at a convalescent home in Pasadena, CA
1994	LYNCH, Christopher		73	Heart attack (at his home in Worchestershire, England)
1994	LYNN, Donald		54	A.I.D.S. complications (at his home in Manhattan)
1994	MANCINI, Henry	★	70	Complications from liver and pancreatic cancer (in Los Angeles)
1994	MARTIN, Richard		75	Leukemia (at Hoag Mem. Hospital, Newport Beach, CA)
1994	+ MASINA, Giulietta (Fellini)		74	Lung cancer (at the Columbus Clinic in Rome, Italy)
1994	MAYS, Joe		45	A.I.D.S. complications (in Little Rock, Ark.)
1994	McCALL, Barbara "Bobbie"		50	After a 3-yr. bout with cancer (in Beverly Hills, CA)
1994	McHUGH, Burke		77	Heart failure & pneumonia (at Falmouth Hosp., MA)
1994	McLIAM, John		76	Chronic bronchitis, Parkinson's disease and melanoma (in L.A.)
1994	McMANUS, Mark		59	Pneumonia (in Glasgow, Scotland)
1994	#+ McNALLY, Stephen		82	Heart failure (at his home in Beverly Hills, CA)
1994	McRAE, Carmen		74	Following a stroke (at her home in Beverly Hills, CA)
• 1994	MEISNER, Gunter		66	Heart failure (in Berlin, Germany)
1994	# MERCOURI, Melina		68	Complications of lung cancer (at a New York hospital)
1994	MITCHELL, Cameron		75	Lung cancer (at his home in Pacific Palisades, CA)
1994	MITTY, Nomi		54	Cancer (at her home in Los Angeles, CA)
1994	MONKS, James		81	Cancer (at St. Luke's-Roosevelt Hospital in New York City)
1994	# MORGAN, Dennis		85	Heart failure (at a hospital in Fresno, CA)
1994	# MORGAN, Henry		79	Lung cancer (at his home in Manhattan, NY)
1994	MORRILL, Priscilla		67	Kidney infection (in Los Angeles, CA)
1994	MORRIS, Anita		50	Cancer (at her home in Los Angeles, CA)
1994	+ NATWICK, Mildred	☆	89	Cancer (at her home in New York City)
1994	#+ NELSON, Harriet		85	Congestive heart failure (at her home in Laguna Beach, CA)
1994	NEWINGTON, Peter		71	
1994	#+ NILSSON, Harry		52	Following a heart attack (in Agoura Hills, CA)
1994	NOBLE, Leighton		82	Died in Victoria, Canada
1994	NOVOTNA, Jarmila		86	Natural causes (at her home in Manhattan, NY)
1994	# O'HARE, Brad		43	Complications of A.I.D.S. (in Manhattan, NY)
1994	O'NEAL, Patrick		66	Respiratory failure, tuberculosis & cancer (in Manhattan, NY)
1994	ORMONT, David		79	Heart attack (at his W. Hollywood, CA, home)
1994	# OSBORNE, John	★	65	Heart attack (in a hospital in Shropshire, England)
1994	OSIRIS, Wanda "Wandissima"		89	Cardiac arrest (at her home in Milan, Italy)
1994	OTT, Dennis		36	A.I.D.S. (in Los Angeles, CA)

• New entry. # Original name (Pt. 7). + Interment (Pt. 5). 120 ☆ Oscar nominee, ★ Oscar winner (Pt. 10)

YEAR	NAME		AGE	CAUSE AND/OR PLACE OF DEATH
1994	+ PEPPARD, George		65	Pneumonia (at UCLA Medical Center, CA)
1994	PERILLI, Ivo		92	After suffering a stroke (in Rome, Italy)
1994	PETERKOCH, Lydia		29	Automobile accident (in Los Angeles, CA)
1994	PETERS, Michael		46	Complications from A.I.D.S. (in Los Angeles, CA)
1994	# POTAMKIN, Luba		73	Alzheimer's disease (at her home in Miami, FL)
1994	POTTER, Dennis		59	Pancreatic & liver cancer (in Gloucestershire, England)
1994	POZZI, Moana		33	Liver cancer (in Lyon, France)
1994	RALSTON, Esther		91	After a short illness (in Ventura, CA)
1994	RAMBO, Dack		53	A.I.D.S. (in Delano, CA)
1994	RAWSON, Ron		76	Cancer (at his home in Cohasset, Mass.)
1994	#+ RAYE, Martha		78	After a stroke and circulatory problems (in Los Angeles, CA)
1994	RECTOR, Richard		69	After a brief illness (in San Rafael, CA)
1994	REINHARDT, Gottfried		80	Pancreatic cancer (in Los Angeles, CA)
1994	# REY, Fernando		76	Bladder cancer (in Madrid, Spain)
1994	RIGGS, Marlon		37	A.I.D.S. complications (in Oakland, CA)
1994	RODNEY, Red		66	Lung cancer (in Boynton Beach, FL)
1994	ROEBLING, Paul		60	While vacationing on a Navajo Indian reservation in Arizona
1994	ROGERS, Milton "Shorty"		70	Died in Van Nuys, CA
1994	# ROLAND, Gilbert "Cisco Kid"		88	Cancer (at his Beverly Hills, CA, home)
1994	+ ROMERO, Cesar		86	Complications from bronchitis and pneumonia (Santa Monica, CA)
1994	RUEHMANN, Heinz		92	Died in Berg, Germany
1994	SABLON, Jean		87	After a 3-yr. illness (at Clinica Hosp. in Cannes-la-Bocca, France)
1994	SACKS, Amy Jill		39	Complications from lupus (in Philadelphia, PA)
1994	SADOFF, Fred		68	A.I.D.S. complications (in Los Angeles, CA)
1994	SALTER, Hans J.		98	Heart attack (in Los Angeles, CA)
1994	SALTZMAN, Harry		78	Died at the American Hospital in Neuilly-sur-Seine, France
1994	# SARGENT, Dick		64	Prostate cancer (at Cedars-Sinai Med. Ctr. in Los Angeles)
1994	#+ SAVALAS, Telly "Kojak"	☆	70	Died in his sleep of prostate cancer (Universal City, CA)
1994	SCANLAN, John		73	Congestive heart failure (at his home in Closter, NJ)
1994	SCARFIOTTI, Ferdinando	★	53	After a brief illness (in Los Angeles, CA)
1994	SCHNEIDER, Harold		55	Heart attack
1994	SCOTT, Terry		67	Cancer (in Godalming, England)
1994	# SHARKEY, Jack		91	Respiratory arrest (at the Beverly, Mass., Hospital)
1994	SHELTON, Anne		66	Apparent heart attack (at her home in Herstmonceux, Eng.)
1994	SHILTS, Randy		42	A.I.D.S. (in Guerneville, CA)
1994	#+ SHORE, Dinah		76	Cancer (in her Beverly Hills, CA, home)
1994	SILVANI, Jole		84	Died in her hometown of Trieste, Italy
1994	SIMEK, Vasek		66	Collapsed while playing at the Croatian Nat. Theatre (in Zagreb)
1994	SIMMS, Ginny		81	Heart attack (at Desert Hosp. in Palm Springs, CA)
1994	# SIMMS, Hilda		75	Pancreatic cancer (in Buffalo, NY)
1994	SKALA, Lilia	☆	90s	Died at her home in Bay Shore, NY
1994	+ SMITH, Hal		77	Apparent heart attack (at his Santa Monica, CA, home)
1994	SOMES, Michael		77	Brain tumor (in London, England)
1994	SOULE, Olan		84	Lung cancer (at his daughter's home in Corona, CA)
1994	SPIVAK, Laurence		93	Congestive heart failure (in Washington, D.C.)
1994	ST. JUST, Maria		?	Heart failure from severe rheumatoid arthritis (in London)
• 1994	+ STANDER, Lionel		86	Lung cancer (at his home in Brentwood, CA)
1994	STANLEY, Anita		88	
1994	# STEVENS, K. T.		74	Lung cancer (at her home in Brentwood, CA)
1994	STEWART, Dennis		46	Heart problems & swelling of the brain
1994	STONE, Ezra "Henry Aldrich"		76	Automobile accident (near Perth Amboy, NJ)
1994	STRODE, Woody		80	Died in his sleep after long bout with cancer (Glendora, CA)
1994	STYNE, Jule		88	After open-heart surgery (at Mt. Sinai Med. Ctr., CA)
1994	SULLIVAN, Barry		81	After a chronic respiratory ailment (Sherman Oaks, CA)
1994	SWACKHAMER, E. W.		67	Ruptured aortic aneurysm (in Berlin, Germany)
1994	+ SWIFT, Paul "Eggman"		60	A.I.D.S. (at Francis Scott Key Med. Ctr., Baltimore, MD)
1994	TANDY, Jessica	★	85	Ovarian cancer (at her home in Easton, CT)
1994	# TAYLOR, Dub		87	Congestive heart failure (at Westlake Med. Ctr., L.A., CA)
1994	TEALE, Leonard		72	Heart attack (in Sydney, Australia)
1994	TEAS, William Ellis		80	Died at Fort Miley Veterans Hospital in San Francisco, CA
1994	TESSARI, Duccio		67	Cancer (in Rome, Italy)
• 1994	THRING, Frank Jr.		68	Cancer (in Melbourne, Australia)
1994	THURSTON, Ted		77	Stomach cancer (in East Hampton, NY)
1994	TRAVERS, Bill		72	Died in his sleep (at his home in Dorking, England)
1994	TROISI, Massimo		41	Heart attack (in Ostia, near Rome, Italy)

• New entry. # Original name (Pt. 7). + Interment (Pt. 5).   ☆ Oscar nominee, ★ Oscar winner (Pt. 10)

YEAR	NAME		AGE	CAUSE AND/OR PLACE OF DEATH
1994	TROY, Louise		60	Breast cancer (at her home in Manhattan)
1994	TRUEMAN, Paula		96	Died in New York Hospital
1994	VANCE, Danitra		35	Breast cancer (at her grandfather's home in Markham, IL)
1994	VAWTER, Ron		45	A.I.D.S.-related heart attack (on a plane bound to NY)
1994	VILLARD, Tom		40	Pneumonia complicated by A.I.D.S. (at a L.A. hospital)
1994	VOLONTE, Gian Maria		61	Heart attack (in Florina, Greece)
1994	WALKER, Sydney		73	After a brief bout with cancer (in San Francisco, CA)
1994	WASHINGTON, Fredi		91	
1994	WELLS, Frank		62	Helicopter crash (in central Nevada)
1994	WICKS, Mark Randall		43	A.I.D.S. complications (in Los Angeles, CA)
1994	WIGGINS, James		30	A.I.D.S. (in Goldsboro, NC)
1994	WILLIAMS, Marion		66	Vascular disease (in Philadelphia, PA)
1994	WILSON, Billy		59	Complications from A.I.D.S. (in New York)
1994	WOLFBERG, Dennis		48	After a 2-yr. battle with melanoma (in Culver City, CA)
1994	WOOLF, Charles		67	Cancer (in Sherman Oaks, CA)
1994	YOUNG, Terence		79	Heart attack (at a hospital in Cannes, France)
1994	ZAMORA, Pedro		22	Neurological complications from A.I.D.S. (in Miami, FL)
1994	# ZANE, Bartine		96	Heart attack (in Burbank, CA)
1994	# ZETTERLING, Mai		68	Cancer (in London, England)
1994	ZUKOR, Eugene		97	Died at his home in Beverly Hills, CA
• 1995	ABBOTT, George		107	Stroke (at his home in Miami Beach, FL)
• 1995	ADAMSON, Al		66	Found murdered and buried under his house (in Indio, CA)
• 1995	ALDRIDGE, Kay (Tucker)		77	Died in Camden, Maine
• 1995	ALLEN, Dennis		55	Lung cancer (in Kansas City, Missouri)
• 1995	ALLEN, Randy		38	A.I.D.S.
• 1995	ANDREWS, Maxine		79	Heart attack (while vacationing in Hyannis, Cape Cod, MA)
• 1995	ARNOLD, Danny		70	Heart failure (in Los Angeles, CA)
• 1995	# AUDLEY, Michael		82	Died at his home in New Orleans, LA
• 1995	AVILES, Rick		41	Heart failure (in Los Angeles, CA)
• 1995	BAILEY, William		84	Died in San Francisco, CA (Do not confuse with Bill Bailey, d. 1978)
• 1995	BAKER, Tommie		70	
• 1995	BEGELMAN, David		73	Apparent suicide (gunshot) in a Los Angeles hotel room
• 1995	BENNETT, Charles		95	Natural causes (Do not confuse with Charles J. Bennett, d. 1943)
• 1995	# BENSON, Court		80	Heart failure (in Mount Kisco, NY)
• 1995	BERNSTEIN, Rick		51	Pancreatic cancer (at his home in Los Angeles, CA)
• 1995	BLACKBURN, Clarice		74	Cancer
• 1995	BLACKWELL, Charles		65	Cancer
• 1995	BLAINE, Vivian		74	Congestive heart failure and pneumonia (at a NYC hospital)
• 1995	BLAIR, Frank		79	Died on Hilton Head Island, S.C.
• 1995	BLANE, Ralph	☆	81	After battling Parkinson's disease (in Broken Arrow, OK)
• 1995	BLASI, Silverio		73	Undisclosed causes (in Rome, Italy)
• 1995	BLAUSTEIN, Julian		82	Cancer (in Beverly Hills, CA)
• 1995	# BOLT, Robert	★	70	Heart problems (at home nr. Petersfield, Hampshire, Eng.)
• 1995	BORBONI, Paola		95	After suffering a stroke (in Bodio Lomnago, Varese)
• 1995	BORSOS, Phillip		41	Leukemia (in Vancouver, B.C.)
• 1995	BRESLO, Robert Paul		37	Complications of A.I.D.S. (at New York Hosp. in Manhattan)
• 1995	BRETT, Jeremy		59	Died in his sleep of heart failure (at his London home)
• 1995	BRIGGS, Fred		63	Cancer (in Boston, MA)
• 1995	BRINEGAR, Paul		77	Emphysema (in Los Angeles, CA)
• 1995	BROCK, Alan		85	Died at his home in Hastings-On-Hudson, NY
• 1995	BROCKETT, Don		65	Apparent heart attack (in Pittsburgh, PA)
• 1995	BROOKS, Phyllis (Macdonald)		80	Died in Cape Neddick, Maine
• 1995	CALLAGHAN, Jack		64	Heart attack (in Charlotte, N.C.)
• 1995	CAMPBELL, Mifflin James		89	Cancer (in Indianapolis, IN)
• 1995	CAREW, Peter		73	Heart attack (at his home in Paramus, NJ)
• 1995	CARRARO, Tino		84	Cardiac arrest (in a Milan, Italy, hospital)
• 1995	CASH, Rosalind		56	Cancer (at Cedars-Sinai Med. Ctr. in Los Angeles, CA)
• 1995	CHERKASSKY, Shura		84	Respiratory complications (in London, England)
• 1995	CHEROT, Lewis		26	Automobile accident (in Los Angeles, CA)
• 1995	CLAYTON, Jack		73	After a short illness (at a hosp. in Slough, Berkshire, Eng.)
• 1995	COLON, Alex		53	After an extended illness
• 1995	COOK, Elisha Jr.		91	After suffering a stroke (in Big Pine, CA)
• 1995	COOK, Peter		57	Gastro-intestinal hemorrhage (in a London hospital)
• 1995	CORRIGAN, Douglas "Wrong Way"		88	Died in Orange, CA

YEAR	NAME	AGE	CAUSE AND/OR PLACE OF DEATH
• 1995	CORSAUT, Aneta	62	*Cancer (in Studio City, CA)*
• 1995	# COSELL, Howard	77	*A heart embolism (at NYU Hospital in New York)*
• 1995	CRAVEN, John	79	*Following a brief illness (in Salt Point, NY)*
• 1995	#+ CROGHAN, Joe	74	*Cancer (at Manor Care Ruxton, Baltimore, MD)*
• 1995	CROSBY, Gary	62	*Complications of lung cancer (at St. Jos. Med Ctr, Burbank, CA)*
• 1995	CULLINGHAM, Mark	53	*Complications of A.I.D.S. (in Los Angeles, CA)*
• 1995	DARDEN, Severn	65	*Heart failure (at his home in Santa Fe, N.M.)*
• 1995	DELANEY, Bessie	104	*Died in her sleep*
• 1995	DeMILLE, Katherine (Quinn)	83	*Alzheimer's disease (in Tucson, AZ)*
• 1995	DENNER, Charles	69	*Cancer (in Dreux, France)*
• 1995	DILLARD, William	83	*Complications from lupus & pneumonia (in Manhattan)*
• 1995	DOYLE, Mary	63	*Lung cancer (in New York)*
• 1995	EAGLE, White	43	*A.I.D.S. (in Sioux Falls, S.D.)*
• 1995	EDDINGTON, Paul	68	*After suffering a rare form of skin cancer (in London, Eng.)*
• 1995	EGAN, Eddie	65	*Cancer*
• 1995	EISENSTAEDT, Alfred	96	*Natural causes*
• 1995	+ ELGART, Les	77	*Heart attack (in Dallas, TX)*
• 1995	# ENDFIELD, Cy	80	*Died in London, England*
• 1995	# ERGAS, Joseph	72	*Diabetes (in New York)*
• 1995	ESTABROOK, Ted	76	*Died in New York*
• 1995	FABRIZI, Franco	79	*Cancer (in Cortemaggiore, Italy)*
• 1995	FARRAR, David	87	*Died in South Africa*
• 1995	FINCH, Nigel	45	*An A.I.D.S.-related illness (at his home in London, Eng.)*
• 1995	FINNEY, Jack	84	*Pneumonia*
• 1995	FLACK, Tim	?	*After a long battle with A.I.D.S. (in Los Angeles, CA)*
• 1995	FLANDERS, Ed	60	*Suicide (shot himself in the head) in Denny, CA*
• 1995	FLEETWOOD, Susan	51	*After a 10-yr. bout with cancer (in Salisbury, England)*
• 1995	FORD, Derek	62	*Heart attack (in Bromly, Kent, England)*
• 1995	FORRISTAL, John	37	*Automobile accident (in Colorado)*
• 1995	FRANK, Richard Edward	42	*Complications of A.I.D.S. (in Los Angeles, CA)*
• 1995	# FRANKLIN, Melvin	52	*Heart failure after a series of seizures (in Los Angeles, CA)*
• 1995	#+ FRELENG, Friz	89	*Natural causes*
• 1995	+ GABOR, Eva	74	*Complications of pneumonia (at Cedars-Sinai Med. Ctr. in L.A.)*
• 1995	#+ GARCIA, Jerry	53	*Heart attack (at Serenity Knolls drug treatment center in CA)*
• 1995	# GAZZO, Michael V. ☆	71	*Complications from a stroke (in Los Angeles, CA)*
• 1995	GEE, Kevin John	40	*Pneumonia (in New York City)*
• 1995	GIANNETI, Alfredo	71	*After suffering a stroke (in Rome, Italy)*
• 1995	GIBBENS, Vince	46	*Apparent heart attack (in Milwaukee, WI)*
• 1995	GODUNOV, Alexander	45	*Natural causes (found dead in his West Hollywood, CA, home)*
• 1995	GONZALES, Pancho	67	
• 1995	GORDON, Gale	89	*Cancer (at Redwood Terrace Health Ctr. in Escondido, CA)*
• 1995	+ GOTTLIEB, Conrad I.	77	*Congestive heart failure (at J. Hopkins Hosp. in Balt., MD)*
• 1995	GRANGER, Dorothy	83	*Cancer (at her home in Los Angeles, CA)*
• 1995	GRAYSON, Arlene	45	*Bone cancer (at her home in Los Angeles, CA)*
• 1995	GREENE, John L.	82	*Died at UCLA Med. Ctr. in Los Angeles, CA*
• 1995	GRIMSBY, Roger	66	*Lung cancer (at Lenox Hill Hospital, NYC)*
• 1995	+ GRINKOV, Sergei	28	*Massive heart attack while ice skating (in Lake Placid, NY)*
• 1995	GRUENBERG, Leonard S.	83	*Natural causes (at his home in Rancho Mirage, CA)*
• 1995	GUARDINO, Harry	69	*Lung cancer (in Palm Springs, CA)*
• 1995	HACKETT, Albert	95	*Pneumonia (at St. Lukes-Roosevelt Hosp. in Manhattan)*
• 1995	HAMILTON, Anthony	42	*A.I.D.S. pneumonia*
• 1995	HARRIS, Phil	91	*Heart failure (at his home in Rancho Mirage, CA)*
• 1995	HARRIS, Robert	95	*After a brief illness*
• 1995	HARRISON, Henry M. Jr. (Rev.)	67	*Stroke (in Pineville, N.C.)*
• 1995	HEALY, David	64	*Following a heart operation (in London, England)*
• 1995	HELMORE, Tom	91	*Died in Longboat Key, FL*
• 1995	# HERRIOT, James	78	*Prostate cancer (at his home in Thirsk, England)*
• 1995	HERSHMAN, Robert	41	*A.I.D.S. (in Santa Monica, CA)*
• 1995	HIVELY, Jack B.	85	*After a brief illness (at his home in Hollywood, CA)*
• 1995	HODGES, Gill	80	
• 1995	# HOON, Shannon	28	*Drug overdose (on a tour bus in New Orleans, LA)*
• 1995	HORDERN, Michael	83	*After a long illness (at an Oxford, England, hospital)*
• 1995	HORNUNG, Richard	45	*Complications from A.I.D.S. (in Los Angeles, CA)*
• 1995	HOWARD, John	82	*Heart failure (at his home in Santa Rosa, CA)*
• 1995	HUGHES, Lillian H.	73	*Cancer (at her Charlestown Retire. Ctr. home in Balt., MD)*

YEAR	NAME		AGE	CAUSE AND/OR PLACE OF DEATH
• 1995	HURD, Hugh		70	*Complications of hypertension and kidney failure (in NY)*
• 1995	HURWITZ, Harry		57	*Heart failure (in Los Angeles, CA)*
• 1995	+ HYMAN, Phyllis		45	*Suicide (pills) found unconscious in her NYC apt.*
• 1995	IPPOLITO, Joseph A.		39	*Kidney failure (in Santa Monica, CA)*
• 1995	IVES, Burl		85	*Mouth cancer & congestive heart failure (in Anacortes, WA)*
• 1995	# JACK, Wolfman		57	*Heart attack (at his home in Belvidere, N.C.)*
• 1995	JAMES, Edward		86	*Heart failure (in Escondido, CA)*
• 1995	JEAKINS, Dorothy	☆	81	*Alzheimer's and Parkinson's diseases (in Santa Barbara, CA)*
• 1995	JURGENS, Dick		85	*Cancer (in Sacramento, CA)*
• 1995	KAIDANOVSKY, Alexander		49	*Heart attack (in Moscow)*
• 1995	KALKIN, Gary		44	*Complications from A.I.D.S. (at his home in L.A., CA)*
• 1995	KAROL, Darcie		37	*Breast cancer (in Boston, MA)*
• 1995	KAYE, Toni		49	*Cancer (in Los Angeles, CA)*
• 1995	KELLIN, Sally Moffet		63	*Lung cancer (in Nyack, NY)*
• 1995	KELLY, Nancy	☆	73	*Complications of diabetes (at her home in Bel Air, CA)*
• 1995	KETCHUM, Larry		49	*Heart attack (in Sierra Vista, AZ)*
• 1995	KHEIFITS, Iosif		89	*Died in St. Petersburg, Russia*
• 1995	# KINGSLEY, Sidney		88	*Stroke (at his home in Oakland, N.J.)*
• 1995	KIRBY, George		71	*Parkinson's disease (at a nursing home in Las Vegas, NV)*
• 1995	# KNOWLES, Patric		84	*Cerebral hemorrhage (in Los Angeles, CA)*
• 1995	KNOX, Alexander		88	*Bone cancer (at an infirmary in Northumberland, Eng.)*
• 1995	KOCH, Howard	★	93	*Pneumonia (in Kingston, NY) Do not confuse with producer*
• 1995	KRAMEROV, Savelly		60	*Cancer (in San Francisco, CA)*
• 1995	# LANE, Priscilla		76	*After a brief illness (in an Andover, MA, nursing home)*
• 1995	LANE, Ziggy		75	*Congestive heart failure (at his home in Miami, FL)*
• 1995	LAWRENCE, Bruno		54	*Lung cancer (at his home on New Zealand's North Island)*
• 1995	LAWRENCE, Rodha		71	*Pulmonary fibrosis (in Sherman Oaks, CA)*
• 1995	LESTER, Jerry		85	*Complications of Alzheimer's disease (in Miami, FL)*
• 1995	#+ LEWIS, Ronald "Raan"		39	*Complications from A.I.D.S. (Do not confuse with R. L., d. 1982)*
• 1995	LINDFORS, Viveca		74	*Complications from rheumatoid arthritis (in Uppsala, Sweden)*
• 1995	LISTYEV, Vladislav		?	*Assassinated (at his home in Moscow)*
• 1995	LOCKE, Katherine		85	*Brain tumor (at her home in Thousand Oaks, CA)*
• 1995	LORIMER, Louise		97	*Following an extended illness (in Newton, MA)*
• 1995	LOY, Nanni		69	*Heart attack (while vacationing in Fregene nr. Rome, Italy)*
• 1995	LUBIN, Arthur		96	*Six months after a stroke (in a Glendale, CA, nursing home)*
• 1995	LUKAS, Karl		75	*Died in Agoura Hills, CA*
• 1995	LUPINO, Ida		77	*Colon cancer following a stroke (at her home in Burbank, CA)*
• 1995	# LYNN, Jeffrey		89	*Died at St. Joseph's Hospital in Burbank, CA*
• 1995	LYON, Milton		72	*Natural causes (at his home in Princeton, NJ)*
• 1995	MALEY, Alan	★	64	*Heart attack (at his Belvedere, CA, home)*
• 1995	MALLE, Louis		63	*Lymphoma complications (at his home in Beverly Hills, CA)*
• 1995	+ MANTLE, Mickey		63	*Cancer following a liver transplant (in Dallas, TX)*
• 1995	MARCH, Donald		53	*Complications from A.I.D.S.*
• 1995	#+ MARTIN, Dean		78	*Acute respiratory failure (at his home in Beverly Hills, CA)*
• 1995	# MARTIN, Ernest H.		75	*Liver cancer (at his home in Los Angeles, CA)*
• 1995	MATHEWS, Carmen Sylva		84	*Natural causes (at her farm in W. Redding, CT)*
• 1995	MAYA, Frank		45	*Heart failure due to complications of A.I.D.S. (in NYC)*
• 1995	MAYER, Seymour R.		86	*Heart failure (in New York City)*
• 1995	McCLURE, Doug		59	*Lung cancer (at his home in Sherman Oaks, CA)*
• 1995	McCOY, Dan		37	*Complications of A.I.D.S. (at Roosevelt Hosp. in Manhattan)*
• 1995	McDANIEL, Keith		38	*Complications of A.I.D.S. (in Los Angeles, CA)*
• 1995	McHUGH, Dorothy		87	*Stroke*
• 1995	McLEAN, David		73	*Lung cancer (at UCLA Med. Ctr. in Los Angeles, CA)*
• 1995	#+ McQUEEN, "Butterfly"		84	*Burns (while lighting a kerosene heater in her home in GA)*
• 1995	MEGNA, John		42	*A.I.D.S. (in Los Angeles, CA)*
• 1995	MEIGHAN, Howard S.		88	*Cardiac arrest (at New York Hospital in Manhattan)*
• 1995	MELTZER, Lewis		84	*Pneumonia (at his home in Albuquerque, N.M.)*
• 1995	MILLER, Patsy Ruth		91	*Heart failure (at her home in Palm Desert, CA)*
• 1995	MOFFET, Sally		63	*Lung cancer*
• 1995	MONTGOMERY, Elizabeth		62	*Cancer after surgery to remove a tumor (Beverly Hills, CA)*
• 1995	MORRIS, Charlotte		75	*Multiple medical problems (at NY Hosp.–Cornell Med. Ctr.)*
• 1995	MOSES, Gilbert		52	*Multiple myeloma (in New York)*
• 1995	MUIR, Esther		92	*Natural causes (in Mount Kisco, NY)*
• 1995	MYERS, William		74	*Pneumonia (in New York City)*
• 1995	NEVAREZ, Aramando		44	*Complications of A.I.D.S. (in Los Angeles, CA)*

• New entry. # Original name (Pt. 7). + Interment (Pt. 5).   124   ☆ Oscar nominee, ★ Oscar winner (Pt. 10)

YEAR	NAME		AGE	CAUSE AND/OR PLACE OF DEATH
• 1995	NEWMAN, Joseph		82	Lymphoma (in Washington, D.C.)
• 1995	NIJHOFF, Loudi		94	Died in Amsterdam, Holland
• 1995	O'CONNOR, Hugh		33	Suicide (gunshot) after 16 yrs. of drug abuse (in Los Angeles)
• 1995	O'SHEA, Tessie		82	Died in Leesburg, Florida
• 1995	OKADA, Eiji		75	Died in Japan
• 1995	OLIVER, Gordon		84	Emphysema (at Cedars-Sinai Med. Ctr. in Los Angeles)
• 1995	OLLE, Andrew		47	Brain tumor (after collapsing in his Sydney, Australia home)
• 1995	PAICH, Martin "Marty" Louis		70	Cancer (at his Santa Ynez, CA, home)
• 1995	PARRISH, Robert	★	79	Died at Southampton Hospital on Long Island, NY
• 1995	PERRY, Frank		65	Prostate cancer (at Mem. Sloan-Kettering Cancer Ctr. in NY)
• 1995	PETTIT, Tom		64	Complications after surgery to repair a ruptured aorta (in NYC)
• 1995	PLEASENCE, Donald		75	After surgery to replace a heart valve (at home in France)
• 1995	PORTER, Eric		67	Colon cancer (at a hospital in north London, England)
• 1995	POTTER, Allan M.		75	Cancer (in Stuart, FL)
• 1995	PRECHT, Andrew		34	Cause unreported (in Grenada)
• 1995	REDENBACHER, Orville		88	Drowned in his whirlpool spa after heart attack (Coronado, CA)
• 1995	RICH, Charlie		62	Acute pulmonary embolism
• 1995	RICHARDSON, Ron		43	Complications from A.I.D.S. (in a Bronxville, NY, hospital)
• 1995	RIGGS, Bobby		77	Prostate cancer (at his home in Leucadia, CA)
• 1995	ROBIN, Dany		68	Died in a fire (at her home in Paris, France)
• 1995	ROBINSON, Darren		28	
• 1995	ROCCA, Daniela		57	Heart failure (at a rest home in Milo, Sicily)
• 1995	#+ ROGERS, Ginger		83	Natural causes (at her home in Rancho Mirage, CA)
• 1995	ROKER, Roxie		66	Undisclosed causes
• 1995	# ROMAGNOLI, Margaret		73	Died in Mount Auburn hospital in Cambridge, MA
• 1995	ROSENBLUM, Ralph		69	Heart failure (at his home in Manhattan)
• 1995	ROSS, Bob		52	Cancer (at his home in Orlando, FL)
• 1995	ROSS, Gordon		65	Cancer (at his home in Studio City, CA)
• 1995	ROTH, David		72	Leukemia (in Leonia, NJ)
• 1995	ROZSA, Miklos	★	88	Pneumonia following a stroke (at Good Sam. Hosp. in L.A.)
• 1995	RUSHTON, Donald		70	Died in Indianapolis, IN
• 1995	RUSHTON, Matthew		43	Complications of A.I.D.S. (in Los Angeles, CA)
• 1995	#+ SANDERS, Al		54	Lung cancer (at Johns Hopkins Hosp., Baltimore, MD)
• 1995	SANTI, Lionello "Nello"		77	After a long illness (in Rome, Italy)
• 1995	SCALI, John A.		77	Heart failure (in Washington, D.C.)
• 1995	SCHULMAN, Edward L.		79	Heart disease (at his daughter's home in Detroit, MI)
• 1995	SCOTT, Timothy		57	Lung cancer (in Los Angeles) Do not confuse with T. Scott, d. 1988
• 1995	SHULMAN, Irving		82	Alzheimer's disease (in Sherman Oaks, CA)
• 1995	SINCLAIR, Madge		57	Leukemia (in Los Angeles, CA)
• 1995	# SMITH, John		63	Cirrhosis & heart problems (at his home in L.A., CA)
• 1995	SMITH, Michael C.		34	Died in Stoughton, MA
• 1995	SONBERT, Warren		46	Complications of A.I.D.S.
• 1995	SOUTHERN, Terry		71	
• 1995	SPENCE, Irven "Irv"		86	Natural causes (in Dallas, TX)
• 1995	STARK, Wilbur		83	Cancer (at New York Hospital in Manhattan)
• 1995	STEPHENS, Robert		64	After a liver and kidney transplant (in London, England)
• 1995	STEWART, Samuel Douglas		75	Parkinson's disease (at the Motion Picture Hospital)
• 1995	STONE, Christopher		55	Heart attack
• 1995	STONEBURNER, Sam		66	Esophageal cancer (at his Manhattan home)
• 1995	SUGHRUE, John		67	Lung cancer (in New York)
• 1995	SULLIVAN, Joseph H.		67	After suffering a heart attack (at his Baltimore, MD, home)
• 1995	SUTTER, Linda		54	Brain cancer (in Cambridge, MA)
• 1995	# SUTTON, Grady		89	Natural causes (in Woodland Hills, CA)
• 1995	SWAYZE, John Cameron		89	Natural causes (at his home in Sarasota, FL)
• 1995	TAGLIAVINI, Ferruccio		81	Respiratory problems after a long illness (in Reggio, Italy)
• 1995	THOMAS, Rachel		90	After a fall & long illness (at Cardiff Hosp. in London, Eng.)
• 1995	TOBIN, Genevieve		93	Died at Las Encinas Hospital in Pasadena, CA
• 1995	TORNBERG, Jeff		43	Complications of A.I.D.S. (in Los Angeles, CA)
• 1995	TOTTEN, Robert		57	Heart attack (at his home in Sherman Oaks, CA)
• 1995	TOWNSEND, Claire		43	Cancer (at her parents' home in Los Angeles, CA)
• 1995	TOWNSEND, Dallas		76	Injuries from a fall (at Montclair, N.J., Community Hospital)
• 1995	# TURNER, Lana		75	After a long battle with throat cancer
• 1995	VanEYSSEN, John		73	Cancer (at a hospital in London, England)
• 1995	VENUTA, Benay		84	Lung cancer (at her home in Manhattan)
• 1995	WALKER, Junior		57	Cancer

YEAR	NAME		AGE	CAUSE AND/OR PLACE OF DEATH
• 1995	WALLACH, Ira	☆	83	Complications following a stroke (in New York City)
• 1995	WARD, Janet		70	Comp. from a heart attack (at Mt. Sinai Med. Ctr. in NYC)
• 1995	+ WARNER, Jack M.		79	Cancer (at Cedars-Sinai Med. Ctr. in Los Angeles, CA)
• 1995	WARRILOW, David		60	Complications of A.I.D.S. (in New York City)
• 1995	WATERMAN, Willard		80	Bone marrow disease (at his home in Burlingame, CA)
• 1995	# WAYNE, David		81	After a long bout with lung cancer (in Los Angeles, CA)
• 1995	WELSH, Patricia		79	Pneumonia (in Green Valley, AZ)
• 1995	# WHITE, Slappy		74	Heart attack (at his home in Brigantine, N.J.)
• 1995	# WICKES, Mary		85	Complications from surgery (at UCLA Med. Ctr. in Los Angeles)
• 1995	# WILDER, Honeychile		76	Cancer (at Mem. Sloan-Kettering Cancer Ctr., NY)
• 1995	WILLIAMS, Frances E.		89	Complications from a stroke (in Los Angeles, CA)
• 1995	WILLINGHAM, Calder		72	Lung cancer (at a hospital in Laconia, N.H.)
• 1995	WOODMAN, William		63	Cardiac arrest (in New York)
• 1995	WRIGHT, Eric "Easy-E"		31	A.I.D.S.
• 1995	YOUNG, Donald Jr.		63	Coronary artery disease (at his home in Los Angeles, CA)
• 1995	YOUNGERMAN, Joseph C.		89	Complications from a stroke (at Cedars-Sinai Med. Ctr. in L.A.)
• 1996	ALEA, Tomas Gutierrez		69	Lung cancer (in Havana, Cuba)
• 1996	AMOS, Beth		80	Died in Toronto, Canada while attending a theatre
• 1996	ANDERSON, Thomas Charles		90	After a long illness following a stroke (in Englewood, NJ)
• 1996	ANGUS, Robert		74	Pneumonia (in Fountain Valley, CA)
• 1996	BALSAM, Martin	★	76	Heart attack (found dead in a hotel room in Rome, Italy)
• 1996	BASS, Saul	★	75	Non-Hodgkin's lymphoma (at Cedars-Sinai Med. Ctr. in L.A., CA)
• 1996	BAXTER, Les		73	Heart attack due to kidney failure (in Newport Beach, CA)
• 1996	BEACH, Scott		65	Died in San Francisco, CA
• 1996	BECKER, Sandy		74	Heart attack
• 1996	# BISSELL, Whit		86	Died in Los Angeles, CA
• 1996	BLACKWOOD, Caroline		64	Cancer (in New York)
• 1996	BOMBECK, Erma		69	Complications from a kidney transplant (in San Francisco, CA)
• 1996	BONNER, Priscilla		97	Died in Los Angeles, CA
• 1996	BOWEN, Roger		63	Heart attack (while vacationing in Florida)
• 1996	BREMER, Lucille		79	Heart attack (in San Diego, CA)
• 1996	BROWN, Terry James		48	Lupus (in Los Angeles, CA)
• 1996	#+ BURNS, George		100	Died at his home in Beverly Hills, CA
• 1996	CAMMELL, Donald		57	Suicide (gunshot) at his home in Hollywood Hills, CA
• 1996	CLEMENT, Rene	★	82	Following heart trouble (in Monte Carlo, France)
• 1996	COHN, Joseph Judson		100	Died in his sleep (at his home in Beverly Hills, CA)
• 1996	CULHANE, Shamus		87	Congestive heart failure (in New York)
• 1996	CUMMINGS, Irving Jr.		77	Cancer (in Van Nuys, CA)
• 1996	D'ARCY, Alexander		87	Heart failure (in West Hollywood, CA)
• 1996	DECKARD, James		58	Brain cancer (in Garden Grove, CA)
• 1996	#+ EDWARDS, Vince		67	Pancreatic cancer (in Los Angeles, CA)
• 1996	EVERSON, William K.		67	Prostate cancer (in New York)
• 1996	FABREGAS, Manolo		75	After suffering a heart attack (in Mexico City)
• 1996	FOREMAN, Jack P.		71	Heart attack (at his home in Brentwood, CA)
• 1996	FULCI, Lucio		68	After a long battle with diabetes (at his home in Rome, Italy)
• 1996	GARSON, Greer	★	92	Heart failure (at Presbyterian Hospital in Dallas, TX)
• 1996	GOULD, Morton		82	Died in Orlando, FL
• 1996	GRANGIER, Gilles		85	Died in Paris, France
• 1996	GREY, Denise		99	Died in Paris, France
• 1996	GROVES, William "Bill"		74	Lung cancer (at his home in Morongo Valley, CA)
• 1996	HAREN, Christian		61	A.I.D.S. (in San Francisco, CA)
• 1996	HARGREAVES, John		50	After a long illness (in Sydney, Australia)
• 1996	HARVEY, Harold A. "Herk"		71	Died in Lawrence, Kansas
• 1996	# HUNTER, Ross	☆	75	Cancer (in Los Angeles, CA)
• 1996	JOHNSON, Ben	★	77	Apparent heart attack (in Mesa, AZ)
• 1996	JOHNSTON, Johnny		80	Heart failure (in Cape Coral, FL)
• 1996	KATZ, Oscar		82	After a bout with pneumonia (at his home in Los Angeles, CA)
• 1996	# KELLY, Gene	★	83	Died in his sleep after suffering 2 strokes in 2 yrs. (in Beverly Hills, CA)
• 1996	KIESLOWSKI, Krzysztof	☆	54	Heart attack
• 1996	KINDLE, Tom		47	Complications of A.I.D.S. (in Los Angeles, CA)
• 1996	LEVIN, Irving H.		74	Cancer (at his home in Brentwood, CA)
• 1996	# LEWIS, Henry		63	Heart attack (at his home in Manhattan)
• 1996	LUDMIR, Joseph (Pepe)		64	Heart attack (in Woodland Hills, CA)
• 1996	# MADISON, Guy		74	Emphysema (at Desert Hospital Hospice in Palm Springs, CA)

• New entry.   # Original name (Pt. 7).   + Interment (Pt. 5).

☆ Oscar nominee,   ★ Oscar winner (Pt. 10)

...DEATHS OF MOVIE AND TELEVISION PERSONALITIES — BY YEAR...

YEAR	NAME		AGE	CAUSE AND/OR PLACE OF DEATH
• 1996	MANLEY, Walter		?	Apparent asthma attack (in New York)
• 1996	MAXWELL, Larry		43	Leukemia (at his home in Laurelville, OH)
• 1996	McCREA, Dusty Iron Wing		55	Diabetes (in Hondo, N.M.)
• 1996	McDERMOTT, Tom		83	Complications of prostate cancer (at Beth Israel hosp. in NY)
• 1996	McLEAN, Barbara	★	92	Died in Newport Beach, CA
• 1996	+ MEADOWS, Audrey		71	Lung cancer (at Cedars-Sinai Med. Ctr. in Los Angeles, CA)
• 1996	MORRIS, Richard		72	Cancer (in Los Angeles, CA)
• 1996	MUSTARD, Jim		51	Bone cancer and A.I.D.S. (in Baltimore, MD)
• 1996	NGOR, Dr. Haing S.	★	55	Murdered (shot) outside his home in Los Angeles, CA
• 1996	O'BRIEN, Liam	☆	83	Heart failure (at his home in Los Angeles, CA)
• 1996	O'CONNELL, David J.		79	Chronic lung disease (in Santa Monica, CA)
• 1996	O'DONNELL, Lynn		43	Ovarian cancer (in San Francisco, CA)
• 1996	OPATOSHU, David		78	After a long illness (in Los Angeles, CA)
• 1996	PATTEN, Luana		57	Respiratory failure (in Long Beach, CA)
• 1996	# PEARL, Minnie		83	Following a stroke (in Nashville, TN)
• 1996	PISTILLI, Luigi		66	Suicide at his home before appearing on stage (in Milan, Italy)
• 1996	RADASKY, Michael J.		43	Automobile accident (in Texas)
• 1996	REGAN, Phil		89	Died in Santa Barbara, CA
• 1996	# RETTIG, Tommy		54	Natural causes (at his home in Marina Del Rey, CA)
• 1996	RICHARDS, E. Claude		72	Leukemia (at the VA Hospital in The Bronx, NY)
• 1996	RICHARDSON, Don		77	Heart failure (in Los Angeles, CA)
• 1996	# ROARKE, Adam		58	Heart attack (at his home in Euless, TX)
• 1996	ROCKETT, Norman		84	Heart failure (in Los Angeles, CA)
• 1996	ROSATTI, Gregory Joseph		43	Complications of A.I.D.S. (in Sherman Oaks, CA)
• 1996	SILLIPHANT, Stirling	★	78	Prostate cancer (in Bangkok, Thailand)
• 1996	SIMPSON, Don		52	Found dead of a probable heart attack (in his Bel-Air, CA, home)
• 1996	SNYDER, Jimmy "The Greek"		76	Heart failure (at a hospital in Las Vegas, NV)
• 1996	SOSNICK, Harry		89	After a long illness (at Calvary Hospital in New York)
• 1996	STAMENKOVIC, Stan		39	Head injuries from a fall in his home (in Titova Uzice, Serbia)
• 1996	STEVENS, Chuck		64	Massive heart attack (in Las Vegas, NV)
• 1996	STEVENSON, McLean		66	Heart attack (at a hospital in Los Angeles, CA)
• 1996	SULLIVAN, Fred G. Jr.		50	Heart failure (in Saranac Lake, NY)
• 1996	TAKEMITSU, Toru		65	Pneumonia while undergoing cancer treatments (in Tokyo, Japan)
• 1996	TALBOT, Lyle		94	Natural causes (at his home in San Francisco, CA)
• 1996	UYS, Jamie		74	Died at his home in Johannesburg, South Africa
• 1996	WEI, Lo		76	Heart failure (in a Hong Kong hospital)
• 1996	WESTON, Jack		71	After a 6 yr. bout with lymphoma (at Lenox Hill Hosp. in New York)
• 1996	WILLIAMS, Palmer		79	Prostate cancer

MONTGOMERY CLIFT

2

DEATHS OF MOVIE AND TELEVISION PERSONALITIES – BY NAME

DEATHS OF MOVIE AND TELEVISION PERSONALITIES — BY NAME

YEAR	NAME		AGE	CAUSE AND/OR PLACE OF DEATH
	A			
1988	AAMES, Angela		32	*Died in West Hills, CA*
• 1952	ABBEY, May		80	*Fell or jumped from a building (in New York, NY)*
1974	#+ ABBOTT, Bud		78	*Cancer (in Woodland Hills, CA)*
• 1968	ABBOTT, Dorothy		?	
• 1957	ABBOTT, Frank		77	*Died in Los Angeles, CA*
• 1995	ABBOTT, George		107	*Stroke (at his home in Miami Beach, FL)*
• 1952	ABBOTT, Gypsy		57	*Died in Hollywood, CA*
• 1937	ABBOTT, Marion		69	*Pneumonia (in Philadelphia, PA)*
• 1977	ABBOTT, Merriel		84	*Died in Chicago, IL*
• 1937	ABEL, Alfred		57	
1987	ABEL, Walter		88	*Heart attack (in Essex, CT)*
• 1919	ABELES, Edward		49	*Pneumonia (in New York, NY)*
1990	ABERNATHY, Ralph		64	
1992	ABRAHAMS, Gary		48	*A.I.D.S.*
• 1982	ACE, Goodman		83	
• 1974	ACE, Jane		74	
1978	+ ACKER, Jean (Valentino)		85	*Died in Los Angeles, CA*
1991	+ ACKERMAN, Harry		78	*Pulmonary failure (in Burbank, CA)*
1991	ACKERMAN, Jack		59	*Brain tumor (in Los Angeles, CA)*
• 1938	ACKERMAN, Walter		57	*Died in Hollywood, CA*
1986	# ACKLES, Kenneth		70	*Stroke (in Pasadena, TX)*
1931	+ ACORD, Art		39	*Suicide (arsenic) in Chihuahua, Mexico*
1974	ACOSTA, Rudolfo		53	*Cancer (in Woodland Hills, CA)*
1956	ACUFF, Eddie		48	*Heart attack (in Hollywood, CA)*
1992	+ ACUFF, Roy		89	*Congestive heart failure*
1940	ADAIR, Jack		46	*Died in Hollywood, CA*
1953	ADAIR, Jean		80	*Died in New York*
1952	ADAIR, John		66	*Died in New York*
1954	ADAIR, Robert		54	*Died in London, England*
1979	ADAM, Ronald		83	*Died in London, England*
1978	ADAMS, Claire		78	*Died in Melbourne, Australia*
• 1960	+ ADAMS, Constance (DeMille)		67	*Died in Hollywood, CA*
1988	ADAMS, Dorothy		88	*Died in Woodland Hills, CA*
1947	ADAMS, Ernest S.		62	*After a long illness (in Hollywood, CA)*
1936	ADAMS, Howard		27	*Airplane crash (in Chicago, IL)*
• 1933	# ADAMS, Jimmy		43	*Heart attack (in Glendale, CA)*
1959	ADAMS, Kathryn		64	*Heart attack (in Hollywood, CA)*
• 1952	ADAMS, Lionel		86	*Died in New York, NY*
1953	#+ ADAMS, Maude		80	*Heart attack (in Tannersville, NY)*
1968	#+ ADAMS, Nick	☆	35	*Drug overdose (in Beverly Hills, CA)*
1987	ADAMS, Peter		69	*Cancer (in Beverly Hills, CA)*
• 1958	ADAMS, Sam		86	
1977	ADAMS, Stanley		62	*Suicide (gunshot) in Santa Monica, CA*
• 1961	ADAMS, Stella		?	
• 1972	ADAMS, William Perry		85	*Died in New York*
• 1995	ADAMSON, Al		66	*Found murdered and buried under his house (in Indio, CA)*
• 1956	# ADAMSON, James		59	*Heart attack (in Los Angeles, CA)*
1972	# ADAMSON, Victor		82	*Died in Hollywood, CA*
1985	ADDAMS, Dawn		55	*Cancer*
1977	ADDINSELL, Richard		73	*Died in London, England*
1992	ADES, Daniel		59	*Causes unreported (in Los Angeles, CA)*
1960	#+ ADLER, Buddy		51	*Lung cancer (in Hollywood, CA)*
• 1979	# ADLER, Celia		88	*Died in The Bronx, NY*
1993	ADLER, Clyde		67	*After a long illness (in Petasky, Michigan)*
1978	ADLER, Jay		82	*After a long illness (in Woodland Hills, CA)*
1984	ADLER, Luther		81	*Died in Kutztown, PA*
1992	ADLER, Stella		91	*Died in her sleep of heart failure (in Los Angeles, CA)*
1947	ADLON, Louis		40	*Heart attack (in Los Angeles, CA)*
1933	ADOLFI, John G.		45	*Cerebral hemorrhage (while on a hunting trip in Canada)*
1933	#+ ADOREE, Renée		35	*Tuberculosis (in Tujunga, CA)*
1959	#+ Adrian		56	*Suicide (in New York)*
1994	# ADRIAN, Iris		81	*Complications from earthquake injuries (in Northridge, CA)*
1991	# ADRIAN, Louis		93	*Died in Lakeport, CA*
1973	# ADRIAN, Max		70	*Died in Wilford, England*

• New entry.   # Original name (Pt. 7).   + Interment (Pt. 5).   ☆ Oscar nominee, ★ Oscar winner (Pt. 10)

...DEATHS OF MOVIE AND TELEVISION PERSONALITIES — BY NAME...

YEAR	NAME	AGE	CAUSE AND/OR PLACE OF DEATH
1948	AGAR, Jane	59	Died in Lakewood, OH
• 1955	AGEE, James	45	Heart attack (in New York, NY)
1991	AGMON, Ami	43	After a long bout with cancer
1984	AGNEW, Robert "Bobby"	84	Kidney failure (in Palm Springs, CA)
1970	AGUGLIA, Mimi	85	Died in Woodland Hills, CA
1993	AGUILAR, Thomas J.	41	A.I.D.S. (in Honolulu, Hawaii)
1969	AHEARNE, Tom	63	Influenza (in New York)
1986	AHERNE, Brian ☆	83	Heart failure (in Venice, FL)
1992	# AHERNE, Gladys	?	After a brief illness
1970	AHERNE, Patrick	69	Cancer (in Hollywood, CA)
1954	AHLM, Philip E.	49	Murdered (shot) in Hollywood, CA
1978	AHN, Philip	66	Lung cancer (in Los Angeles, CA)
1993	+ AIDMAN, Charles	68	Cancer (in Beverly Hills, CA)
1992	AIKEN, Bill	34	After a 1-year bout with cancer
1989	AILEY, Alvin	58	Dyscrasia (a blood disorder) in New York
1945	AINLEY, Henry H.	66	Died in London, England
1967	# AINLEY, Richard	56	Died in London, England
1948	AINSLEY, Norman	67	After a year's illness (at a private sanitarium in Hollywood, CA)
1922	# AINSWORTH, Sidney	50	After an illness of several months (in Madison, WI)
1933	AITKEN, Frank "Spottiswoode"	64	After a lingering illness (in Los Angeles, CA)
1955	AKED, Muriel	68	Died in Settle, England
1973	+ AKEMAN, David "Stringbean"	57	Shot to death by burglars in his home
1994	+ AKINS, Claude	67	Cancer (in Altadena, CA)
1970	# Aladdin	57	Found dead at home of apparent heart attack (in Van Nuys, CA)
1962	ALBERNI, Luis	74	Died in Hollywood, CA
1960	ALBERS, Hans	67	Died in Munchen, Germany
1964	+ ALBERTSON, Frank	55	Died in Santa Monica, CA
1981	+ ALBERTSON, Jack ★	74	Cancer (in Hollywood Hills, CA)
1982	ALBERTSON, Mabel	81	Complications from numerous illnesses (in Santa Monica, CA)
1994	ALBIN, Andy	86	After a long illness (in Woodland Hills, CA)
1971	# ALBRIGHT, Hardie	67	Heart failure and pneumonia (in Mission Viejo, CA)
1986	#+ ALDA, Robert	72	Effects of a stroke (in Los Angeles, CA)
1946	# ALDEN, Mary	63	Died in Woodland Hills, CA
1987	ALDERMAN, John	53	Apparent heart attack (in Hollywood, CA)
1957	ALDERSON, Erville	74	Died in Glendale, CA
1980	# ALDERSON, Floyd Taliaferro	84	Pneumonia after suffering a stroke (in Mt. Sheridan, WY)
1983	ALDRICH, Robert	65	Kidney failure (in Los Angeles, CA)
• 1995	ALDRIDGE, Kay (Tucker)	77	Died in Camden, Maine
1994	ALDRIDGE, Michael	73	Died in London, England
• 1996	ALEA, Tomas Gutierrez	69	Lung cancer (in Havana, Cuba)
1990	ALEX, Robert	30	Gunshot wounds during a robbery at his home (in Silver Lake, CA)
1969	# ALEXANDER, Ben	58	Natural causes (in Westchester, CA)
1982	+ ALEXANDER, John	85	
1981	ALEXANDER, Katherine	79	Died in Florida
1989	ALEXANDER, Richard	86	Pulmonary edema (in Woodland Hills, CA)
1937	+ ALEXANDER, Ross	29	Suicide (gunshot) in Los Angeles, CA
1992	ALEXANDER, Tom	29	A.I.D.S. (in Hollywood, CA)
1983	ALEXANDROV, Grigori	80	Died in Moscow, Russia
1990	ALINDER, Dallas	58	Heart failure following a liver transplant
1992	ALISON, Dorothy	66	Causes unreported (in London, England)
1990	ALLAN, Elizabeth	80	Died in London, England
1979	ALLBRITTON, Louise	58	Cancer
1987	ALLEGRET, Yves	79	Heart attack (in France)
1970	ALLEN, A. A.	?	Found dead in a San Francisco hotel room
1993	ALLEN, Adrianne	86	After suffering from cancer (in Montreux, Switzerland)
• 1947	ALLEN, Alfred	80	
1974	ALLEN, Barbara Jo "Vera Vague"	70	Died in Santa Barbara, CA
1984	ALLEN, Chet	44	Suicide (in Columbus, OH)
• 1995	ALLEN, Dennis	55	Lung cancer (in Kansas City, Missouri)
• 1970	ALLEN, Dorothy	74	Died in New York
1956	#+ ALLEN, Fred	62	Heart attack (in New York, NY)
1964	#+ ALLEN, Gracie	58	Heart attack (in Los Angeles, CA)
• 1951	ALLEN, Harry R.	68	
1987	ALLEN, Irving	82	After a long illness (in Encino, CA)
1991	+ ALLEN, Irwin ★	75	After suffering a heart attack (in Santa Monica, CA)

YEAR	NAME		AGE	CAUSE AND/OR PLACE OF DEATH
• 1962	ALLEN, Joseph Jr.		44	*Died in Patchogue, NY*
1949	ALLEN, Lester		58	*Struck and killed by an automobile (in Hollywood, CA)*
1992	ALLEN, Peter	★	48	*An A.I.D.S.-related illness (in San Diego, CA)*
• 1995	ALLEN, Randy		38	*A.I.D.S.*
1991	ALLEN, Ronald		56	*Lung cancer (in Reading, England)*
1934	ALLEN, Sam		73	*Died in Los Angeles, CA*
1987	ALLEN, Vera		89	*Heart failure (at a retirement home in Croton-on-Hudson, NY)*
1966	ALLENBY, Peggy		65	*After a brief illness (in New York)*
1993	# ALLEY, Paul		87	*Died in Winter Park, Florida*
1950	+ ALLGOOD, Sara	☆	66	*Heart attack (in Woodland Hills, CA)*
1989	ALLISON, Fran		81	*Complications of a blood disorder (in Sherman Oaks, CA)*
1989	ALLISON, May		98	*Respiratory failure (in Bratenahl, OH)*
1970	# ALLISTER, Claud		76	*Cancer (in Santa Barbara, CA)*
1971	ALLMAN, Duane		24	*Motorcycle accident (in Macon, GA)*
1992	ALLMAN, Elvia		87	*Pneumonia (in Santa Monica, CA)*
1978	+ ALLWYN, Astrid		68	*Cancer (in Los Angeles, CA)*
1976	ALLYN, Alyce		?	*While hospitalized (in Santa Monica, CA)*
1992	ALMENDROS, Nestor	★	61	*Lymphoma (in New York)*
1967	# ALVARADO, Don		62	*Cancer (in Los Angeles, CA)*
1992	ALZADO, Lyle		43	*After suffering brain cancer (in Portland, OR)*
1959	AMBLER, Joss		59	*Died in England*
1993	#+ AMECHE, Don	★	85	*Prostate cancer (at his son's home in Scottsdale, AZ)*
1947	#+ AMES, Adrienne		43	*Cancer (in New York, NY)*
• 1933	AMES, Gerald		51	*Injuries from a fall (in London, England)*
• 1965	AMES, Jimmy		50	*Heart attack (in Hollywood, CA)*
1993	+ AMES, Leon		91	*Complications after a stroke (Laguna Beach, CA)*
1931	AMES, Robert		33	*Bladder hemorrhage (in New York)*
• 1996	AMOS, Beth		80	*Died in Toronto, Canada while attending a theatre*
1986	AMY, George J.		86	*After a long illness (in Los Angeles, CA)*
1992	AMYES, Julian		74	*Causes unreported (in London, England)*
• 1958	ANALLA, Isabel		37	*Cancer (in San Francisco, CA)*
1985	ANDEN, Matthew		42	*After a lengthy illness (in New York)*
1981	+ ANDERS, Glenn		92	*Died in Englewood, NJ*
1992	# ANDERS, Laurie		70	*Cancer (in Tarzana, CA)*
1964	# ANDERSON, Claire		68	
1977	+ ANDERSON, Eddie "Rochester"		71	*Heart attack*
1985	ANDERSON, Edward		70	
1971	#+ ANDERSON, G. M. "Broncho Billy"		88	
1994	ANDERSON, Herbert		77	*Died in his sleep 2-months after a stroke (in Palm Springs, CA)*
• 1969	ANDERSON, James "Jim"		48	*Died in Billings, MT*
1992	ANDERSON, John		69	*Heart attack*
1992	# ANDERSON, Judith	☆	93	*Pneumonia after suffering a brain tumor*
• 1939	ANDERSON, Lawrence		45	*Pneumonia (in London, England)*
1994	ANDERSON, Lindsay		71	*Heart attack (after swimming at a friend's pool in Nice, France)*
1993	ANDERSON, Marian		96	*Congestive heart failure following a stroke*
• 1996	ANDERSON, Thomas Charles		90	*After a long illness following a stroke (in Englewood, NJ)*
1976	ANDERSON, Warner		65	
1991	# ANDOR, Lotte Palfi		87	*After an illness*
1991	# ANDOR, Paul		90	*After a long illness*
1984	ANDRE, E. J.		76	*Cancer*
1959	#+ ANDRE, Gwili		51	*Burned to death when fire swept her apartment*
1986	ANDREWS, Ann		95	
1992	# ANDREWS, Dana		83	*Congestive heart failure & pneumonia*
1985	#+ ANDREWS, Edward		70	*Heart attack*
1989	ANDREWS, Harry		77	*Viral infection complicated by asthma*
1967	+ ANDREWS, LaVerne		51	*Cancer*
1968	# ANDREWS, Lois		44	
• 1995	ANDREWS, Maxine		79	*Heart attack (while vacationing in Hyannis, Cape Cod, MA)*
1989	ANDREWS, Nancy		68	*Heart attack*
1969	ANDREWS, Stanley		77	
1992	ANDREWS, Thomas		37	*A.I.D.S.*
1972	ANDREWS, Tod		52	*Heart attack*
1986	+ ANGEL, Heather		76	
1971	# ANGELI, Pier		39	*Suicide (overdose of barbiturates)*
1971	ANGOLD, Edit		76	*After an illness of several years*

YEAR	NAME		AGE	CAUSE AND/OR PLACE OF DEATH
•	1996	ANGUS, Robert	74	Pneumonia (in Fountain Valley, CA)
	1985	ANKERS, Evelyn	67	Cancer
	1964	# ANKRUM, Morris	67	Trichinosis
•	1968	ANSON, Laura	76	Died in Woodland Hills, CA
	1993	ANTHONY, Joseph	80	Died in Hyannis, MA
	1989	# ANTHONY, Rick	60	
	1967	ANTRIM, Harry	71	Heart attack
•	1961	AOKI, Tsuru	69	Acute peritonitis (in Tokyo, Japan)
	1938	APFEL, Oscar	?	Heart attack
	1990	APPLEBY, Dorothy	84	
	1950	APPLEBY, William C.	27	Coronary thrombosis
	1959	APPLEGATE, Hazel	73	
	1988	ARAGON, Jesse	32	Motorcycle accident
	1991	ARAVINDAM, Govindan	55	
•	1939	ARBUCKLE, Andrew	55	Died in Los Angeles, CA
	1931	ARBUCKLE, Maclyn	68	Died at his home in Waddington, NY
	1933	#+ ARBUCKLE, Roscoe "Fatty"	46	Heart attack
	1959	ARCHAINBAUD, George	68	Heart attack
	1990	#+ ARDEN, Eve ☆	83	Heart failure & cancer
	1992	ARDENT, Keith	38	A.I.D.S.
	1993	ARDOLINO, Emile ★	50	Complications from A.I.D.S. (in Bel-Air, CA)
	1991	ARKIN, David	49	
	1947	# ARLEDGE, John	41	
	1966	ARLEN, Betty	62	
	1986	ARLEN, Harold	81	
	1976	#+ ARLEN, Richard	75	Emphysema
	1989	ARLEN, Roxanne (Shafer)	57	Cancer
	1992	# Arletty	94	Died in Paris, France
	1950	ARLISS, Florence	?	Died in London, England
	1946	# ARLISS, George ★	77	Bronchial trouble
	1987	ARLISS, Leslie	86	
	1963	ARMENDARIZ, Pedro	51	Suicide (gunshot) after suffering with lymph cancer
	1945	+ ARMETTA, Henry	57	Heart attack
•	1924	ARMSTRONG, Billy	32	
	1986	+ ARMSTRONG, Herbert W.	93	Died in his sleep
	1971	#+ ARMSTRONG, Louis "Satchmo"	71	Heart ailment
	1973	+ ARMSTRONG, Robert	76	
	1987	# ARNAUD, Georges	69	
•	1958	ARNAUD, Yvonne	65	Died in London, England
	1986	#+ ARNAZ, Desi	69	Lung cancer
	1983	# ARNE, Peter	62	Murdered (battered to death)
	1955	ARNHEIM, Gus	55	Heart attack
	1975	# ARNO, Sig	80	Parkinson's disease
	1931	ARNOLD, Cecile	?	Influenza
•	1995	ARNOLD, Danny	70	Heart failure (in Los Angeles, CA)
	1956	#+ ARNOLD, Edward	66	Cerebral hemorrhage
	1992	ARNOLD, Jack	75	Arteriosclerosis
•	1971	# ARNOLD, Jessie	93	Heart attack (in Los Angeles, CA)
	1991	ARNOLD, Monroe	64	After a heart attack
	1968	ARNOLD, Phil	58	
	1940	ARNOLD, William R.	56	Streptococcus infection
	1974	#+ ARQUETTE, Cliff	69	Heart attack
	1991	ARRAU, Claudio	88	Complications after surgery for intestinal blockage
•	1948	ARTAUD, Antonin	52	Colon cancer (in Paris, France)
	1991	#+ ARTHUR, Jean ☆	89	Heart failure, following a paralyzing stroke
	1951	# ARTHUR, Johnny	68	Heart disease (in Woodland Hills, CA)
	1989	ARTHUR, Lee	49	Cancer
	1988	ARUNDELL, Dennis	90	
	1979	ARVAN, Jan	66	Heart attack
	1949	# ARVIDSON, Linda	65	Died in New York
	1979	ARZNER, Dorothy	82	
•	1974	# ASH, Russell	63	Cancer (in Los Angeles, CA)
•	1951	ASH, Samuel Howard	67	Died in Hollywood, CA
	1988	ASHBY, Hal ★	59	Liver cancer (in Malibu, CA)
	1991	# ASHCROFT, Peggy ★	83	After suffering a stroke

...DEATHS OF MOVIE AND TELEVISION PERSONALITIES – BY NAME...

YEAR	NAME		AGE	CAUSE AND/OR PLACE OF DEATH
1988	ASHCROFT, Ronnie		65	After a long illness
1993	+ ASHE, Arthur		49	A.I.D.S.-related pneumonia
1991	ASHE, Martin		80	Respiratory failure
1947	ASHE, Warren		44	Automobile accident
1957	ASHER, Max		76	
1977	# ASHLEY, Sylvia		73	Cancer
1991	ASHMAN, Howard	★	40	Complications from A.I.D.S.
1936	ASHTON, Dorrit		63	Died in Los Angeles, CA
1940	ASHTON, Sylvia		60	
1992	ASIMOV, Isaac		72	Heart and kidney failure
1940	ASKAM, Earl		41	After a heart attack while playing golf
1982	ASKEY, Arthur		82	
1982	# ASLAN, Gregoire		74	Heart attack
1981	#+ ASTAIRE, Adele		82	Stroke
1987	#+ ASTAIRE, Fred	☆	88	Pneumonia
1981	ASTHER, Nils		84	
1977	ASTOR, Gertrude		90	Stroke
1987	#+ ASTOR, Mary	★	81	Emphysema
1943	ATCHLEY, Hooper		56	Suicide (gunshot)
1962	+ ATES, Roscoe		70	Lung cancer
1963	ATKINSON, Frank		69	
1987	ATTAWAY, Ruth		77	Injuries from a fire in her apartment
1992	ATTERBURY, Malcolm		85	Died in Beverly Hills, CA
1986	ATWATER, Edith		74	Cancer
1946	+ ATWILL, Lionel		61	Bronchial cancer and pneumonia
1994	AUBREY, James T.		75	Heart attack (at UCLA Med. Ctr. emergency room)
1991	AUBUCHON, Jacques		67	Heart failure
1988	AUCLAIR, Michel		65	
1991	AUDLEY, Eleanor		86	Respiratory failure
1992	AUDLEY, Maxine		69	Heart attack
• 1995	# AUDLEY, Michael		82	Died at his home in New Orleans, LA
• 1962	AUER, Florence		81	Died in New York, NY
1967	# AUER, Mischa	☆	61	Heart attack
1984	AUERBACH, Leon		48	
1957	AUERBACK, Arthur "Mr. Kitzel"		54	Heart attack
1964	AUGUST, Edwin		81	
1951	# AULT, Marie		81	
1983	AURIC, Georges		84	
1953	AUSTIN, Albert		71	After a long illness
1972	#+ AUSTIN, Gene		71	Cancer (in Palm Springs, CA)
• 1927	AUSTIN, Jere		51	Cancer (in Hollywood, CA)
• 1957	AUSTIN, Lois		47	Cachexia (in Hollywood, CA)
• 1974	AUSTIN, Richard		33	Automobile accident (in Hawthorne, CA)
1951	AUSTIN, William		66	Stroke
• 1926	# AVERY, Charles		53	Died in Hollywood, CA
1973	AVERY, Patricia		71	
• 1980	#+ AVERY, Tex		71	Cancer (in Burbank, CA)
• 1973	AVERY, Tol		58	Heart attack (in CA)
• 1995	AVILES, Rick		41	Heart failure (in Los Angeles, CA)
1991	AXTHELM, Pete		47	Liver failure
• 1951	# AYE, Maryon		45	Suicide (poison) in Hollywood, CA
1946	AYLESWORTH, Arthur		61	
1964	AYLMER, David		31	Suicide
1979	# AYLMER, Felix		90	Died in a nursing home in England
1940	#+ AYRES, Agnes		42	Cerebral hemorrhage (while in a sanitarium for depression)
1968	AYRES, Robert		54	Heart attack
• 1916	AYRES, Sydney		?	Died in Oakland, CA
	B			
1992	# BABBITT, Art		85	Kidney failure
1992	BABIN, Vitya Vronsky		82	After a long illness
1969	BACCALONI, Salvatore		69	Following deterioration of a number of organs
• 1978	BACCHIOCCHI, Norman		34	
• 1941	BACH, Reginald		54	Pneumonia (in New York, NY)
1939	BACKUS, George		81	
1989	+ BACKUS, Jim "Mr. Magoo"		76	Pneumonia & Parkinson's disease

YEAR	NAME		AGE	CAUSE AND/OR PLACE OF DEATH
1974	BACLANOVA, Olga		75	
1943	# BACON, David		29	Stab wounds (in Los Angeles, CA)
1965	+ BACON, Irving		71	Died in Hollywood, CA
1955	+ BACON, Lloyd		65	Cerebral hemorrhage (in Burbank, CA)
1948	BACON, Rod		33	
1976	# BADDELEY, Angela		71	Flu and bronchitis (in London, England)
1986	BADDELEY, Hermione	☆	79	Stroke
1982	# BADEL, Alan		58	
1964	BADGER, Clarence		84	Following surgery
1986	+ BAER, Jacob "Buddy"		71	
1959	BAER, Max		50	Heart attack
1972	# BAGDASARIAN, Ross		52	Natural causes (in Beverly Hills, CA)
• 1960	BAGGETT, Lynne		31	Overdose of barbiturates (in Hollywood, CA)
1948	BAGGOTT, King		68	Stroke (in Los Angeles, CA)
• 1954	BAGNI, John		42	Heart attack (in Hollywood, CA)
1978	BAILEY, Bill		66	(Do not confuse with any of the 3 William Bailey's)
1989	BAILEY, John		73	
1990	+ BAILEY, Pearl		72	Heart failure following surgery to replace a knee
1980	BAILEY, Raymond		75	Heart attack (in Irvine, CA)
1983	BAILEY, Robert		70	
1987	BAILEY, Sherwood "Spud"		64	Cancer
• 1995	BAILEY, William		84	Died in San Francisco, CA (Do not confuse with Bill Bailey, d. 1978)
1990	BAILEY, William H.		72	(Do not confuse with actor Bill Bailey, d. 1978)
1962	BAILEY, William Norton		76	Died in Hollywood, CA (Do not confuse with Bill Bailey, d. 1978)
1968	+ BAINTER, Fay	★	76	Died in Los Angeles, CA
1992	BAIR, Ron		62	Cancer
1987	BAIRD, Bil		82	
1971	BAIRD, Leah		88	Anemia, after a long illness (in Hollywood, CA)
• 1947	BAIRD, Stewart		66	Heart attack (in New York, NY)
1966	+ BAKER, Art		68	Heart attack (in Los Angeles, CA)
1957	BAKER, Belle		60	Heart attack
1994	BAKER, Benny		87	Died at MPTF Hospital in Woodland Hills, CA
1975	# BAKER, Bob		74	Stroke (in Prescott, AZ)
1988	# BAKER, Chet		59	Fall from a 2nd floor window (in Amsterdam)
1992	BAKER, Dorothy Helen		78	Died in Los Angeles, CA
1968	# BAKER, Eddie		70	Died in Hollywood, CA
1980	BAKER, Frank		86	Died in Woodland Hills, CA
1993	BAKER, Howard		61	Cancer (in Hale, Cheshire, England)
1986	BAKER, Hylda		78	
1985	#+ BAKER, Kenny		72	Heart attack
1982	BAKER, Lenny		37	Cancer
1963	BAKER, Phil		67	After a long illness (in Copenhagen, Denmark)
1982	BAKER, Russell F.		66	After a brief illness
1982	BAKER, Sam		56	Heart attack
1976	BAKER, Stanley		48	Complications after a lung cancer operation (in Malaga, Spain)
1991	BAKER, Terence		52	
• 1995	BAKER, Tommie		70	
1986	BAKER-BERGEN, Stuart		40	Complications from A.I.D.S. (in New Orleans, LA)
1993	BAKEWELL, Billy		85	Leukemia (in Los Angeles, CA)
1983	+ BALANCHINE, George		79	Creutzfeld-Jakob disease
1982	BALDWIN, Bill		69	Cancer
1977	BALDWIN, Walter		89	Pneumonia (in Santa Monica, CA)
1990	BALFOUR, Katharine		69	
1990	BALIN, Ina		52	Pulmonary hypertension
1989	#+ BALL, Lucille		77	Ruptured aorta (after heart surgery)
1955	#+ BALL, Suzan (Long)		22	Cancer after knee surgery while filming in Sumatra
1991	BALL, William		60	
1976	BALLARD, Flo		33	Cardiac arrest from pills and alcohol (in Detroit, MI)
1988	BALLARD, Lucien		84	Bicycle accident
1993	BALLARD, Lucinda	☆	87	Cancer
1956	BALLIN, Hugo		76	
1958	BALLIN, Mabel		73	
• 1996	BALSAM, Martin	★	76	Heart attack (found dead in a hotel room in Rome, Italy)
• 1969	# BANCROFT, Charles		57	Cancer (in Woodland Hills, CA)
1956	+ BANCROFT, George	☆	74	After a brief illness (in Santa Monica, CA)

YEAR	NAME	AGE	CAUSE AND/OR PLACE OF DEATH
1986	BANDY, Way	45	A.I.D.S.
1990	BANEY, Joan Blazer	55	Brain tumor
1948	# BANJAMIN, Gladys	?	
1968	#+ BANKHEAD, Tallulah	66	Double pneumonia complicated by emphysema (in New York, NY)
1952	BANKS, Leslie	61	Died in London, England
1950	# BANKS, Monty	52	Heart attack
1991	#+ BANKY, Vilma	90	Died in a L.A. nursing home after a 10-yr. illness
1973	# BANNER, John	62	Intestinal hemorrhage (in Vienna, Austria)
1961	BANNISTER, Harry	71	
1989	BANZHAF, Peter G.	57	Arrhythmia
1990	BARA, Nina	66	Cancer
1955	#+ BARA, Theda (Brabin)	69	Abdominal cancer (in Los Angeles, CA)
1975	BARAGREY, John	57	Cerebral hemorrhage
1992	# BARBER, Red	84	Intestinal disorder
1945	BARBIER, George	83	Heart attack (in Los Angeles, CA)
• 1965	# BARBOUR, Dave	53	Hemorrhaged ulcer
1978	BARCENA, Catalina	82	Died in Spain
1975	# BARCLAY, Don	83	Died in Palm Springs, CA
• 1993	BARCLIFT, Edgar Nelson	76	After a lengthy illness (in Los Angeles, CA)
1969	# BARCROFT, Roy	67	Cancer (in Woodland Hills, CA)
1974	BARD, Ben	81	Cerebral thrombosis (in Los Angeles, CA)
1977	BARDETTE, Trevor	75	
1991	BAREFIELD, Eddie	81	Heart attack
1975	BARHARD, Lawrence "Slim"	71	Apparent heart failure
1989	# BARI, Lynn	73	After a long illness
1951	BARKER, Bradley	68	Died in New York, NY
1990	BARKER, Eric L.	78	
1973	# BARKER, Lex	53	Heart attack (in New York, NY)
1945	BARKER, Reginald	59	Following a heart attack (in Los Angeles, CA)
1972	BARLOW, Howard	80	Heart attack
1943	BARLOW, Reginald	76	Died in Hollywood, CA
1953	BARNARD, Ivor	66	
1949	BARNES, George	59	Following an operation for cancer
• 1965	BARNET, Boris	63	Suicide (despondent over his faltering career) in Moscow
1991	BARNET, Charlie	77	Alzheimer's disease & pneumonia
• 1947	BARNETT, Chester A.	62	Pneumonia (in Jefferson City, MO)
1958	BARNETT, Griff	72	Heart condition and pneumonia
1988	BARNETT, Nate	48	Heart attack
• 1988	BARNETT, Sanford H. ★	79	Following a stroke (in Oxnard, CA)
1977	# BARNETT, Vince	75	Heart ailment (in Encino, CA)
1985	BARNEY, Jay	72	Cancer
1980	# BARR, Leonard	77	After suffering a stroke
1985	BARR, Patrick	77	
1970	BARRAT, Robert	78	Died in Hollywood, CA
1994	BARRAULT, Jean-Louis	83	Died in his sleep of apparent heart attack (in Paris, France)
1977	BARRETT, Edith	64	Heart attack at a nursing home (in Albuquerque, N.M.)
1937	# BARRIE, James	77	Pneumonia complicated by heart trouble
• 1980	BARRIE, John	62	Died in York, England
1978	#+ BARRIE, Wendy	65	After a long illness (in Englewood, N.J.)
1964	+ BARRIER, Edgar	57	Heart attack (in Hollywood, CA)
1989	BARRIER, Ernestine	81	
1962	+ BARRIS, Harry	57	Cancer (in Burbank, CA)
1965	BARRISCALE, Bessie	81	Died in Kentfield, CA
1993	BARRON, Lee	78	Respiratory failure (in Omaha, Nebraska)
1993	BARROW, Bernard	65	Lung cancer (at Lennox Hill Hospital in NY)
• 1945	BARROWS, Henry A.	69	
1925	BARROWS, James O.	72	Heart attack
1980	#+ BARRY, Don "Red"	69	Suicide (gunshot) after a scuffle with his estranged wife
1990	BARRY, J. J.	58	Bronchial complications
1984	BARRY, Jack	66	Heart attack while jogging
1989	BARRY, Joan	87	
1931	# BARRY, Tom	47	Heart trouble
1960	#+ BARRYMORE, Diana	38	Natural causes (in New York, NY)
1959	#+ BARRYMORE, Ethel ★	79	Heart condition (in Beverly Hills, CA)
1942	#+ BARRYMORE, John	60	Cardiac condition and other ailments (in Los Angeles, CA)

YEAR	NAME	AGE	CAUSE AND/OR PLACE OF DEATH
1954	#+ BARRYMORE, Lionel ★	76	Heart attack (in Van Nuys, CA)
1988	+ BARSI, Judith	10	Murdered (shot by her father)
1991	BARTELL, Eddie	83	Aneurysm
1991	BARTELME, Joe	61	Cancer
1963	+ BARTHELMESS, Richard ☆	66	Cancer (in Southampton, NY)
1992	# BARTHOLOMEW, Freddie	67	Emphysema & heart failure
1994	# BARTLETT, Richard	70	Complications of diabetes (in Havre de Grace, MD)
1990	BARTLETT, Scott	47	Complications from a kidney & liver transplant
1981	BARTON, Charles T.	79	After two heart attacks
1962	+ BARTON, James	72	Heart attack
1990	BARTON, Larry	80	Following a stroke
1991	BARUCH, André	83	
1969	BARZELL, Wolfe	71	Heart attack
1984	+ BASEHART, Richard	70	Stroke
1986	BASELEON, Michael	61	
1984	#+ BASIE, William "Count"	79	Pancreatic cancer
1948	BASKETT, James	44	Heart ailment
1994	# BASQUETTE, Lina	87	Cancer (at her home in Wheeling, W. Va.)
1987	# BASS, Alfie	66	Heart attack
• 1996	BASS, Saul ★	75	Non-Hodgkin's lymphoma (at Cedars-Sinai Med. Ctr. in L.A., CA)
1952	BASSERMAN, Albert ☆	86	Heart attack (in Zurich, Switzerland)
• 1918	BASSETT, Russell	71	Brain hemorrhage (in New York, NY)
1989	BASTIN, Charles A.	68	Cardiopulmonary arrest
1991	BATCHELOR, Joy	77	
1985	BATE, Tom	85	
1969	#+ BATES, Barbara	43	Suicide (in Denver, CO)
1954	# BATES, Florence	65	Heart attack (in Burbank, CA)
1940	+ BATES, Granville	58	Heart attack (in Hollywood, CA)
• 1978	BATES, Michael	57	Cancer (in London, England)
1991	BATES, Ralph	50	Cancer
1990	# BATORS, Stiv	40	After being hit by a car
1993	BATTLE, Edwin Louis	33	Stroke (in Toronto, Canada)
1985	BAUER, Charita	62	Following a long illness
1987	BAUERSMITH, Paula	78	Cancer
1989	BAUM, Bobby	62	Following a brief illness
1960	# BAUM, Vicki	64	After a brief illness
• 1943	BAUR, Harry	63	Died mysteriously after being interrogated by the Gestapo in Paris
1980	BAVA, Mario	66	Heart attack
1989	BAVIER, Frances	86	Heart problems
1990	BAXLEY, Barbara	63	Apparent heart attack
1976	BAXTER, Alan	67	Cancer (in Woodland Hills, CA)
1985	BAXTER, Anne ★	62	Stroke
• 1996	BAXTER, Les	73	Heart attack due to kidney failure (in Newport Beach, CA)
• 1951	+ BAXTER, Warner ★	58	Pneumonia after lobotomy to ease pain (in Beverly Hills, CA)
• 1973	+ BAYLIS, Peter	63	
1982	BAYNE, Beverly	87	Natural causes
1989	BAZLEN, Brigid	44	
• 1996	BEACH, Scott	65	Died in San Francisco, CA
1990	BEAGLE, Edward H.	46	Natural causes
• 1934	BEAL, Frank	70	Died in Hollywood, CA
1969	BEAL, Royal	68	Cancer (in Keene, N.H.)
1973	BEAL, Scott	83	Cancer (in Hollywood, CA)
1989	BEAM, Alvin	61	Cardiopulmonary arrest
1981	+ BEARD, Matthew "Stymie" Jr.	56	Stroke (in Los Angeles, CA)
1980	BEATON, Cecil	78	
1965	+ BEATTY, Clyde	62	Cancer of the esophagus (in Ventura, CA)
1992	BEATTY, Robert	82	Pneumonia
1992	BEAUCHAMP, Clem	94	Natural causes
1970	+ BEAUDINE, William Sr.	78	Complications of uremic poisoning (in Canoga Park, CA)
1966	BEAUMONT, Harry ☆	78	Died in Santa Monica, CA
1982	BEAUMONT, Hugh	72	Apparent heart attack
1937	BEAUMONT, Lucy	63	Died in New York, NY
1962	BEAVERS, Louise "Beulah"	64	Heart attack (in Hollywood, CA)
1986	BECHER, John C.	71	Cancer
1993	BECK, John	83	Cancer (in Woodland Hills, CA)

	YEAR	NAME		AGE	CAUSE AND/OR PLACE OF DEATH
	1993	BECKER, Robert		47	Car accident (in Santa Clarita, CA)
•	1996	BECKER, Sandy		74	Heart attack
	1968	# BECKETT, Scotty		38	Following a serious beating (in Los Angeles, CA)
	1980	BECKLEY, Tony		50	Cancer
	1965	BECKWITH, Reginald		56	Died in Bourne End, England
	1991	BEDDOE, Don		102	
	1957	BEDOYA, Alfonso (Indio)		53	Died in Mexico City
	1955	# BEECHER, Janet		70	Died in Washington, CT
	1958	BEECROFT, Victor R.		71	Died in Newport News, VA
	1994	BEERY, Noah Jr.		81	After surgery for bleeding in his brain (nr. Tehachapi, CA)
	1946	+ BEERY, Noah Sr.		60	Heart attack (in Los Angeles, CA)
	1949	+ BEERY, Wallace	★	64	Heart attack (in Los Angeles, CA)
	1949	BEERY, William C.		70	
•	1995	BEGELMAN, David		73	Apparent suicide (gunshot) in a Los Angeles hotel room
	1970	+ BEGLEY, Ed	★	69	Heart attack (in Hollywood, CA)
	1931	#+ BEIDERBECKE, "Bix"		28	Lobar pneumonia and edema of the brain
	1988	BELASCO, Leon		86	Complications after a stroke
•	1943	BELCHER, Charles M.		71	Died in Hollywood, CA
	1969	BELGADO, Maria		63	After a 3-week illness
	1990	BELL, David		53	After a long illness (Do not confuse with David Scott Bell, d. 1980)
•	1980	BELL, David Scott		22	Murdered (shot) in North Hollywood, CA
	1991	BELL, Hal		65	After suffering a stroke
	1950	BELL, Henry "Hank"		58	Following a heart attack (in Hollywood, CA)
•	1973	BELL, James		81	
	1958	+ BELL, Monta		66	After a lengthy illness (in Hollywood, CA)
	1936	BELL, Ralph W.		53	Pneumonia (in San Francisco, CA)
	1962	#+ BELL, Rex		58	Coronary occlusion (in Las Vegas, NV)
•	1968	BELL, Rodney		52	
•	1933	BELL, Ruth		26	Suicide (poison) in Los Angeles, CA
•	1944	BELLAMY, George		78	
	1990	BELLAMY, Madge		89	Heart failure
	1991	+ BELLAMY, Ralph	★	87	Respiratory infection
	1993	BELLAVER, Harry		88	Pneumonia (in a Nyack, NY, hospital)
	1987	BELLIN, Olga		54	Cancer
	1994	BELLIN, Steve		43	A.I.D.S. complications
	1975	BELLINI, Laura		73	
	1953	BELMORE, Lionel		85	Died in Woodland Hills, CA
	1982	+ BELUSHI, John		33	After speedballing a mix of cocaine & heroin (in Hollywood, CA)
	1968	+ BENADARET, Bea		62	Cancer
	1945	BENCHLEY, Robert	★	56	Cerebral hemorrhage (in New York, NY)
	1969	# BENDER, Russell		59	Died in Woodland Hills, CA
	1964	+ BENDIX, William	☆	58	Lobar pneumonia and cancer (in Los Angeles, CA)
	1992	BENEDEK, Laslo		87	After a lengthy hospital stay
•	1968	BENEDICT, Brooks		?	
•	1951	BENEDICT, Kingsley		69	Died in Woodland Hills, CA
	1984	BENEDICT, Richard		64	Heart attack
	1982	BENET, Brenda		36	Suicide (gunshot)
•	1955	BENGE, Wilson		80	Died in Hollywood, CA
•	1969	BENHAM, Harry		83	Died in Sarasota, FL
	1990	BENNER, Richard		47	A.I.D.S.
	1987	BENNET, Spencer Gordon		94	
	1958	BENNETT, Barbara		52	
	1932	BENNETT, Belle		41	Following a long illness (in Los Angeles, CA)
•	1951	# BENNETT, Billie		75	Cerebral hemorrhage (in Los Angeles, CA)
•	1995	BENNETT, Charles		95	Natural causes (Do not confuse with Charles J. Bennett, d. 1943)
•	1943	BENNETT, Charles J.		51	Died in Hollywood (Do not confuse with Charles Bennett, d. 1995)
	1965	+ BENNETT, Constance		59	Cerebral hemorrhage (at Ft. Dix, N.J.)
	1969	BENNETT, Enid		74	Heart attack (in Malibu, CA)
•	1950	BENNETT, Hugh		57	Coronary thrombosis (at his home in Malibu, CA)
	1990	BENNETT, Jill		59	Suicide
	1990	BENNETT, Joan		80	Cardiac arrest
	1931	# BENNETT, Joe		35	Heart attack
	1982	BENNETT, Marjorie		87	Cancer
	1991	BENNETT, Matt		52	Brain tumor
•	1950	BENNETT, Mickey		35	Heart attack (in Hollywood, CA)

YEAR	NAME		AGE	CAUSE AND/OR PLACE OF DEATH
• 1957	BENNETT, Ray		62	*Heart attack (in Hollywood, CA)*
1944	+ BENNETT, Richard		71	*Heart attack (in Los Angeles, CA)*
1974	#+ BENNY, Jack		80	*Pancreatic cancer (in Holmby Hills, CA)*
• 1995	# BENSON, Court		80	*Heart failure (in Mount Kisco, NY)*
1989	BENSON, Joe		73	*Cancer*
1984	BENSON, Lucille		69	*Cancer*
1965	# BENTLEY, Irene		61	*Heart attack (in Palm Beach, FL)*
1958	BENTLEY, Robert		63	*Died in Benton Harbor, MI*
1944	BERESFORD, Harry		80	*After a long illness*
1966	+ BERG, Gertrude		66	*Heart failure*
1978	#+ BERGEN, Edgar		75	*Heart attack (in Las Vegas, NV)*
1969	BERGER, Ludwig		77	*Heart failure*
1974	BERGERE, Ouida		88	
1941	+ BERGERE, Ramona		39	*Died in Glendale, CA*
1990	BERGHOF, Herbert		81	*Heart ailment*
• 1917	BERGMAN, Henri		?	*Died in New York (Do not confuse with Henry Bergman, d. 1946)*
1946	BERGMAN, Henry		76	*Heart attack (Do not confuse with actor Henri Bergman, d. 1917)*
1982	+ BERGMAN, Ingrid ★		67	*Cancer*
1986	BERGNER, Elizabeth ☆		85	
1958	BERKE, William		54	
1976	#+ BERKELEY, Busby		80	
1992	BERKELEY, George		70	*Heart attack*
• 1951	# BERKES, John "Johnny"		54	*Died in Hollywood, CA*
1985	BERLE, Jack		80	
1965	BERLIN, Abby		58	*Died in his sleep*
1989	#+ BERLIN, Irving		101	*Died in his sleep*
1987	BERMAN, Dr. Edgar		68	
1932	+ BERN, Paul		42	*Suicide (gunshot)*
1986	+ BERNARDI, Herschel		62	*Heart attack*
1994	BERNARDI, Jack		85	*Heart attack*
1989	BERNAU, Christopher		49	
1981	BERNHARDT, Curtis (Kurt)		81	
1923	#+ BERNHARDT, Sarah		78	*Uremic poisoning/weak heart (in Paris, France)*
1943	BERNIE, Ben		52	*After a lingering illness*
1990	+ BERNSTEIN, Leonard		72	*Complications from lung cancer & emphysema*
• 1995	BERNSTEIN, Rick		51	*Pancreatic cancer (at his home in Los Angeles, CA)*
1991	BERNSTEIN, Sam		80	
1993	BERRY, Eric		80	*Cancer (in Laguna Beach, CA)*
1993	BERTHELSON, Larry		60	*Died in Santa Barbara, CA*
1991	BERTI, Dehl		70	*Heart attack*
1990	BERTO, Juliet		42	*Cancer*
1955	+ BERTRAND, Mary		73	
1988	+ BESSER, Joe		80	*Found dead in his home*
1934	BESSERER, Eugenie		64	*While planning her golden wedding anniversary*
1974	# BEST, Edna		74	*Died in Geneva, Switzerland*
1962	BEST, Willie		45	*Cancer (in Woodland Hills, CA)*
1978	BETZ, Carl		56	*Lung cancer (in Los Angeles, CA)*
1938	# BETZ, Matthew		56	*After a long illness (in Los Angeles, CA)*
1957	# BEVAN, William "Billy"		60	*Died in Escondido, CA*
1963	# BEVANS, Clem		83	*Died in Woodland Hills, CA*
1992	BEYERS, Bill		37	*A.I.D.S.*
1977	BIBERMAN, Abner		68	*Died in San Diego, CA*
1971	BIBERMAN, Herbert		71	*Bone cancer*
1967	+ BICKFORD, Charles ☆		78	*Emphysema (in Los Angeles, CA)*
1983	BIERNE, Michael		46	
1967	# BIG TREE, Chief John		92	
1933	BIGGERS, Earl Derr		48	*Heart attack*
1934	BILLINGS, George A.		63	*Died in West Los Angeles, CA*
1983	BILON, Michael "E. T."		35	*Complications from pneumonia*
1991	BINDER, Maurice		72	
1947	+ BING, Herman		57	*Suicide (gunshot) in Los Angeles, CA*
1990	BINGO, Joe		65	*Complications from a staph infection*
• 1957	BINNEY, Faire		57	*Pneumonia*
1990	BINNS, Edward		74	*Heart attack*
1918	BINNS, George H.		?	*Double pneumonia induced by influenza*

	YEAR	NAME	AGE	CAUSE AND/OR PLACE OF DEATH
	1978	BINYON, Claude	72	
	1969	BIRCH, Paul	61	
	1959	# BIRCH, Wyrley	75	
	1982	BISHOP, Ronald	59	
	1993	BISHOP, Wesdon	60	Liver ailment (in Nashville, TN)
	1959	BISHOP, William	42	Cancer (in Malibu, CA)
	1993	BISSELL, Jennifer Raine	60	Heart ailment (in Los Angeles, CA)
	1987	BISSELL, Patrick	30	Overdose of cocaine, codeine, methadone
•	1996	# BISSELL, Whit	86	Died in Los Angeles, CA
	1993	BITTNER, Jack	76	Heart attack (in New York)
	1993	+ BIXBY, Bill	59	Prostate cancer (in his Century City, CA, home)
	1960	BJOERLING, Jussi	49	Heart attack
	1993	BJORLING, Rolf	64	
	1986	# BJORNSTRAND, Gunnar	77	
	1985	BLACK, Dorothy	85	
•	1938	BLACK, Maurice	46	Died in Hollywood, CA
•	1995	BLACKBURN, Clarice	74	Cancer
	1994	BLACKBURN, Royce	69	Cancer (in New Ipswich, NH)
•	1937	BLACKFORD, Mary	23	Results of an automobile accident (in Santa Monica, CA)
•	1955	# BLACKLEY, Douglas	46	(See Robert Kent)
	1973	BLACKMER, Sidney	79	Cancer
•	1968	BLACKTON, James Stuart Jr.	71	
	1941	# BLACKTON, James Stuart Sr.	66	Fractured skull after being struck by a car (in Hollywood, CA)
	1994	BLACKTON, Jay	84	Heart attack (in Los Angeles, CA)
•	1973	# BLACKTON, Violet	60	
	1974	BLACKWELL, Carlyle Jr.	61	After a 6-month illness
	1955	BLACKWELL, Carlyle Sr.	71	
•	1995	BLACKWELL, Charles	65	Cancer
•	1996	BLACKWOOD, Caroline	64	Cancer (in New York)
	1992	BLACKWOOD, Christian	50	Lung cancer
	1971	BLAGOI, George	73	
•	1995	BLAINE, Vivian	74	Congestive heart failure and pneumonia (at a NYC hospital)
•	1995	BLAIR, Frank	79	Died on Hilton Head Island, S.C.
•	1983	# BLAIR, Randy	32	Cardiac and respiratory arrest while playing a charity basketball game
	1992	# BLAIRE, Sallie	68	Liver failure
	1930	BLAISDELL, Charles "Big Bill"	56	Died in Hollywood, CA
•	1931	BLAISDELL, William	?	Died in Brooklyn, NY
•	1966	# BLAKE, Al	89	Heart attack (in Los Angeles, CA)
	1989	# BLAKE, Amanda "Miss Kitty"	60	A.I.D.S.-related complications
•	1973	BLAKE, Anne	?	
	1985	# BLAKE, Arthur	70	Heart attack
	1983	# BLAKE, Eubie	100	
	1991	BLAKE, Katharine	62	
	1982	BLAKE, Larry J.	68	
	1969	BLAKE, Madge	68	Heart attack
	1978	# BLAKE, Marie	81	
	1987	# BLAKELY, Colin	56	Leukemia
	1987	BLAKELY, Gene	66	Bone cancer
•	1959	BLAKENEY, Olive	56	Died in Hollywood, CA
	1990	BLAKEY, Art	71	Lung cancer
	1989	#+ BLANC, Mel	81	Heart disease
	1970	BLANCHARD, Mari	43	Cancer (in Woodland Hills, CA)
	1962	+ BLANDICK, Clara	81	Suicide (took pills and pulled a plastic bag over her head)
•	1995	BLANE, Ralph ☆	81	After battling Parkinson's disease (in Broken Arrow, OK)
	1987	BLASETTI, Alessandro	86	
•	1995	BLASI, Silverio	73	Undisclosed causes (in Rome, Italy)
	1991	BLATT, Edward A.	88	Heart attack
	1992	BLATTNER, Robert	40	Airplane crash
•	1995	BLAUSTEIN, Julian	82	Cancer (in Beverly Hills, CA)
•	1943	BLEDSOE, Jules	44	Died in Hollywood, CA
	1992	BLETCHER, Arline	99	Natural causes
	1979	# BLETCHER, Billy	84	After a long illness
	1989	BLEYER, Archie	79	
	1989	BLIER, Bernard	73	
•	1941	BLINN, Benjamin F.	68	Died in Hollywood, CA

...DEATHS OF MOVIE AND TELEVISION PERSONALITIES — BY NAME...

YEAR	NAME	AGE	CAUSE AND/OR PLACE OF DEATH
• 1956	BLINN, Genevieve	?	Died in Ross, CA
• 1928	BLINN, Holbrook	56	After falling from a horse (in Crota, NY)
• 1980	BLISS, Lela	84	Died in Woodland Hills, CA
1982	+ BLOCH, Ray	79	Heart attack
1990	BLOCK, Eva Sully	88	Heart failure
1972	+ BLOCKER, Dan	43	Pulmonary embolus (in Hollywood, CA)
1979	#+ BLONDELL, Joan ☆	73	Leukemia (in Santa Monica, CA)
1936	BLOOD, Adele	50	Suicide (gunshot) in Yonkers, NY
• 1974	# BLOOM, Bobby	27	Murdered or suicide? (shot) in West Hollywood, CA
1989	BLOOM, George	95	
1959	BLORE, Eric	71	Heart attack (in Hollywood, CA)
1975	#+ BLUE, Ben	73	Died in Los Angeles, CA
1982	BLUE, David	41	Heart attack while jogging
1963	+ BLUE, Monte	73	Coronary attack (in Milwaukee, WI)
• 1945	BLUM, Sammy	56	Heart attack (in Hollywood, CA)
1975	# BLYDEN, Larry	49	Automobile accident (while vacationing in Agadir, Morocco)
1938	BLYSTONE, John G.	45	Heart attack (in Beverly Hills, CA)
1956	# BLYSTONE, Stanley	61	Heart attack (in Hollywood, CA)
1972	# BLYTHE, Betty ★	78	Died in Woodland Hills, CA
1991	BOARDMAN, Eleanor	93	Died in Santa Barbara, CA
1918	# BOARDMAN, True	36	Following a nervous breakdown (in Norwalk, CA)
1971	# BOARDMAN, Virginia True	81	Heart attack (in Hollywood, CA)
• 1990	+ BOCK-LEADER, Deborah Lyn	38	
• 1972	BOESEN, William	47	
1957	#+ BOGART, Humphrey ★	57	Cancer of the esophagus (in Los Angeles, CA)
• 1912	BOGGS, Francis	?	Murdered (shot at the Selig film studio by a disgruntled employee)
• 1978	BOHN, Merritt F.	73	Pneumonia following a stroke (in Torrence, CA)
• 1949	BOHNEN, Roman	54	Heart attack (in Hollywood, CA)
1991	BOIS, Curt	90	Died in Berlin, Germany
1935	BOLAND, Eddie	51	Heart attack (in Santa Monica, CA)
1987	BOLAND, Joseph S.	83	
1965	+ BOLAND, Mary	83	Died in New York, NY
• 1937	BOLDER, Robert "Bobbie"	78	Died in Beverly Hills, CA
1977	# BOLES, Jim	63	Apparent heart attack (in Sherman Oaks, CA)
1969	+ BOLES, John	73	Heart attack (in San Angelo, TX)
1937	+ BOLESLAWSKI, Richard	47	Apparent heart attack
1963	+ BOLEY, May	81	Cancer (in Hollywood, CA)
1987	#+ BOLGER, Ray	83	Cancer
• 1969	# BOLGER, Robert "Bo"	32	Killed while skydiving (in Oceanside, CA)
• 1995	# BOLT, Robert ★	70	Heart problems (at home nr. Petersfield, Hampshire, Eng.)
• 1996	BOMBECK, Erma	69	Complications from a kidney transplant (in San Francisco, CA)
1969	BONANOVA, Fortunio	73	Cerebral hemorrhage
• 1952	# BOND, Jack	52	Died in Hollywood, CA
• 1978	BOND, Johnny	63	Died in Burbank, CA
1991	BOND, Lilian	83	
• 1972	BOND, Lyle	54	Heart attack (in San Diego, CA)
1989	BOND, Raleigh	54	Lymphoma
1982	BOND, Rudy	66	Heart attack
1984	BOND, Sudie	56	Respiratory ailment
1960	+ BOND, Ward	57	Heart attack (in Dallas, TX)
1994	BONDARCHUK, Sergei	74	Cardio-vascular disease (in Moscow, Russia)
1981	# BONDI, Beulah ☆	88	Pulmonary complications
• 1980	# BONELLI, Richard	91	Died in Los Angeles, CA
1980	BONHAM, John	32	Choked to death after drinking 40 shots of vodka
• 1950	BONIFACE, Symona	56	Died in Woodland Hills, CA
1953	BONN, Walter	64	Died in Hollywood, CA
1986	BONNELL, Lee	67	Heart attack (in Santa Monica, CA)
1988	BONNER, Margerie	83	Following a stroke
• 1996	BONNER, Priscilla	97	Died in Los Angeles, CA
1984	BONNEY, Gail	83	
1978	BONOMO, Joe	75	Kidney ailment and pneumonia (in Hollywood, CA)
• 1969	BONUCCI, Alberto	49	Heart attack (in Rome, Italy)
1994	+ BOOKE, Sorrell "Boss Hogg"	64	Colon cancer (in Sherman Oaks, CA)
1987	BOOKER, Bernice Ingalls	91	
1981	+ BOONE, Richard	63	Cancer

• New entry. # Original name (Pt. 7). + Interment (Pt. 5).   142   ☆ Oscar nominee, ★ Oscar winner (Pt. 10)

	YEAR	NAME		AGE	CAUSE AND/OR PLACE OF DEATH
	1991	# BOOTH, Edwina		86	Died of heart failure, in Long Beach, CA
•	1915	BOOTH, Elmer		32	Automobile accident (in Los Angeles, CA)
•	1971	BOOTH, Helen		?	Died in England
	1994	BOOTH, Jim		48	Cancer (in Wellington, New Zealand)
	1992	# BOOTH, Shirley	★	94	Natural causes
	1937	BOOTH, Sydney Barton		60	Cerebral hemorrhage (in Stanford, CT)
	1993	# BOOTS, Tubby		59	After a blood clot traveled to his lungs
•	1995	BORBONI, Paola		95	After suffering a stroke (in Bodio Lomnago, Varese)
•	1950	# BORDEAUX, Joe		56	Died in Hollywood, CA
•	1955	BORDEN, Eddie		67	Died in Hollywood, CA
	1972	BORDEN, Eugene		75	
	1947	#+ BORDEN, Olive		40	Stomach ailment (in Los Angeles, CA)
	1953	BORDONI, Irene		59	Died in New York, NY
	1973	BORG, Veda Ann		58	Died in Hollywood, CA
•	1939	BORGATO, Agostino		67	Heart attack (in Hollywood, CA)
•	1948	BORLAND, Barlowe		71	Died in Woodland Hills, CA
	1994	BORLAND, Carroll		79	Pneumonia (in Arlington, VA)
	1951	BOROS, Ferike		70	Died in Hollywood, CA
•	1995	BORSOS, Phillip		41	Leukemia (in Vancouver, B.C.)
•	1975	BORZAGE, Daniel "Danny"		78	Died in Los Angeles, CA
	1962	+ BORZAGE, Frank	★	72	Cancer (in Hollywood, CA)
	1991	# BOSTWICK, Dorothy Davis		?	Cardiac arrest
	1976	+ BOSWELL, Connee		68	Stomach cancer (in New York, NY)
	1958	BOSWELL, Martha (Lloyd)		53	After a long illness (in Peekskill, NY)
	1988	# BOSWELL, Vet		77	
	1943	+ BOSWORTH, Hobart		76	Pneumonia (in Glendale, CA)
	1992	BOTAS, Juan Suarez		34	A.I.D.S.
	1943	BOTELER, Wade		52	Heart attack (in Hollywood, CA)
	1991	BOTTCHER, Ron		50	A.I.D.S.
	1977	BOUCHEY, Willis "Bill"		82	Died in Burbank, CA
	1989	BOUISE, Jean		60	Cancer
	1985	BOULTING, John		71	
•	1962	BOULTON, Matthew		69	
•	1978	BOURBON, Diana		77	Cancer (in Los Angeles, CA)
	1956	BOURNE, Hazel (Imboden)		?	After a 2-yr. illness (in Kansas City)
•	1972	BOURNE, William Payne		36	Suicide (gunshot) in Hollywood, CA
	1979	BOURNEUF, Philip		71	Found dead in his Santa Monica apartment
	1991	BOVASSO, Julie		61	Cancer
	1965	+ BOW, Clara		60	Heart attack while watching a movie on TV (in Los Angeles, CA)
	1988	BOW, Simmy		65	Complications after a stroke
	1991	BOWEN, Joe		56	Heart attack
•	1996	BOWEN, Roger		63	Heart attack (while vacationing in Florida)
	1936	BOWERS, John		36	Suicide (walked into the surf off Malibu Beach)
	1946	+ BOWES, Major Edward		71	Died at his summer home in Rumson, N.J.
•	1947	BOWKER, Aldrich		71	Arteriosclerosis (in Los Angeles, CA)
•	1981	#+ BOWLING, Alice		54	
	1979	BOWMAN, Lee		64	Heart attack (in Brentwood, CA)
	1991	BOX, Muriel		85	
	1992	BOXER, Warren Neal		34	A.I.D.S.
•	1971	BOYD, Betty		63	
•	1973	#+ BOYD, Jim		77	
•	1977	#+ BOYD, Stephen		48	Heart attack (in Northridge, CA)
	1972	+ BOYD, William "Hopalong Cassidy"		77	Parkinson's disease and heart failure (in South Laguna, CA)
	1978	+ BOYER, Charles	☆	78	Suicide (overdose of Seconal) 2 days after his wife died (in AZ)
	1994	BOYLAN, John		82	Lung cancer & pneumonia (at his home in Bellevue, Wash.)
	1984	BOYLAN, Mary		70	
•	1966	# BOYNE, Sunny		83	Died in Van Nuys, CA
	1993	BOZYK, Reizl		79	Died at St. Vincent's Hosp. Med. Ctr., NYC
	1957	+ BRABIN, Charles J.		75	Heart attack (in Santa Monica, CA)
	1942	BRACEY, Sidney		64	After a brief illness (in Hollywood, CA)
•	1936	BRADBURY, James Jr.		41	Suicide (burns) in Los Angeles, CA
•	1940	BRADBURY, James Sr.		83	Died in Clifton, Staten Island, NY
	1990	BRADDELL, Maurice		89	
	1993	BRADEN, Bernard		76	Heart attack (in London, England)
	1973	BRADFORD, Lane		50	Following a massive cerebral hemorrhage (in Honolulu, Hawaii)

YEAR	NAME		AGE	CAUSE AND/OR PLACE OF DEATH
• 1971	BRADFORD, Marshall		74	Heart attack (in Hollywood, CA)
• 1916	BRADLEY, Amanda		?	Automobile accident (in New York, NY)
• 1947	BRADLEY, Harry C.		78	Heart attack (in Hollywood, CA)
1974	+ BRADLEY, Truman		69	Died in Los Angeles, CA
1973	BRADSHAW, Eunice		80	
1939	+ BRADY, Alice	★	46	Cancer (in New York, NY)
• 1942	BRADY, Edward J.		53	Heart attack (in Hollywood, CA)
• 1961	# BRADY, Fred		49	Heart failure (in Los Angeles, CA)
1972	BRADY, Pat		57	Died while visiting friends in Green Mountain Falls, Colorado
1985	#+ BRADY, Scott		60	Respiratory failure
1993	BRAFA, Tony		72	Heart attack (in Los Angeles, CA)
• 1947	BRAHAM, Lionel		68	Heart attack (in Hollywood, CA)
1982	BRAHM, John		89	Died in his sleep at home
• 1948	BRAITHWAITE, Lilian		75	Heart attack (in London, England)
1985	BRAMBELL, Wilfrid		72	Cancer
1992	+ BRAND, Neville		71	Emphysema
1993	BRANDA, Richard		57	Colon cancer (in Los Angeles, CA)
1990	BRANDON, Henry		77	Apparent heart attack
1983	BRANDON, Peter		57	Apparent heart attack after jogging
1993	# BRANDT, Buzz		60	Heart failure
• 1924	BRANDT, Charles		60	Died in Philadelphia, PA
1987	BRANNUM, Hugh		77	Cancer
1980	#+ BRASSELLE, Keefe		57	Cirrhosis of the liver
1990	# BRAUER, Tiny		82	Heart condition
1990	BRAUNBERGER, Pierre		85	
1983	BRAY, Robert		65	Natural causes
1990	BRAY, Stephen		33	
1994	BRAZZI, Rossano		78	Viral infection (in Rome, Italy)
1973	BREAKSTON, George P.		53	Died in Paris, France
• 1943	BREAMER, Sylvia		40	Died in New York, NY
1946	BRECHER, Egon		66	After a heart attack (in Hollywood, CA)
• 1945	BRECKNER, Gary		49	Automobile accident (in Redlands, CA)
• 1977	BREEDEN, John Norton		73	Died in San Francisco, CA
1982	BREEDING, Larry		36	Killed when his car struck a pole in Hollywood
1918	BREEN, Harry		?	Drowned in Lake Elsinore
1936	+ BREESE, Edmund		64	Peritonitis (in New York, NY)
1990	BREM, Beppo		84	Heart failure
1986	BREMEN, Lennie		71	
• 1996	BREMER, Lucille		79	Heart attack (in San Diego, CA)
1964	# BRENDEL, El		74	Heart attack (in Hollywood, CA)
1953	BRENEMAN, Mark L.		54	Heart attack
1983	BRENGEL, George		69	Cancer
1974	+ BRENNAN, Walter	★	80	Emphysema (in Oxnard, CA)
• 1977	BRENNEN, Claire		43	Cancer (in Hollywood, CA)
1992	BRENNER, Glenn		44	Cerebral hemorrhage from a malignant brain tumor
1958	BRENON, Herbert	☆	78	
1975	# BRENT, Evelyn		75	Heart attack (in Los Angeles, CA)
1979	# BRENT, George		75	Natural causes (in Solana Beach, CA)
1976	# BRENT, Romney		74	
• 1995	BRESLO, Robert Paul		37	Complications of A.I.D.S. (at New York Hosp. in Manhattan)
1987	BRESSAN, Arthur J. Jr.		44	A.I.D.S.
1949	+ BRESSART, Felix		69	Leukemia (in Los Angeles, CA)
1969	BRETHERTON, Howard		73	
• 1995	BRETT, Jeremy		59	Died in his sleep of heart failure (at his London home)
1993	BRIAN, David		82	Cancer & heart failure (in Sherman Oaks, CA)
1951	#+ BRICE, Fanny		59	Cerebral hemorrhage (in Beverly Hills, CA)
• 1966	BRICE, Lew		72	Heart attack (in Hollywood, CA)
• 1957	BRIDGE, Alan "Al"		66	
1993	BRIDGES, James	☆	57	Intestinal cancer (in Los Angeles, CA)
1985	BRIGGS, Charles		53	
1986	BRIGGS, Donald P.		75	Cancer
• 1995	BRIGGS, Fred		63	Cancer (in Boston, MA)
1952	BRIGGS, Harlan		72	After a brief illness
1962	BRIGGS, Matt		79	
1990	BRIGGS, Richard R.		71	After a short illness

YEAR	NAME		AGE	CAUSE AND/OR PLACE OF DEATH
1992	BRIGHT, David		49	Automobile accident
1989	BRIGHT, John		81	Stroke
• 1995	BRINEGAR, Paul		77	Emphysema (in Los Angeles, CA)
1950	BRISCOE, Lottie		69	Died in New York, NY
1958	# BRISSON, Carl		64	Jaundice (in Copenhagen, Denmark)
1984	+ BRISSON, Frederick		71	After suffering a stroke
1989	BRISTER, John Tyler		38	A.I.D.S.
• 1972	# BRITT, Elton		59	Died in Connellsville, PA
1980	# BRITTON, Barbara		59	Cancer
• 1948	# BRITTON, Milt		53	Heart attack (in New York, NY)
1974	+ BRITTON, Pamela		51	Brain tumor (in Arlington Heights, IL)
1988	BROADBENT, George		83	
1993	BROCCO, Peter		89	Heart attack (in Los Angeles, CA)
• 1995	BROCK, Alan		85	Died at his home in Hastings-On-Hudson, NY
1989	BROCK, Heinie		89	Emphysema
1991	BROCK, Stanley		59	Heart attack
• 1924	BROCK, Tony		?	Auto accident while filming stunt in "The Great Circus Mystery" (NY)
• 1995	BROCKETT, Don		65	Apparent heart attack (in Pittsburgh, PA)
1929	BROCKWELL, Gladys		35	Peritonitis from car accident injuries (in Hollywood, CA)
1959	BRODERICK, Helen		68	Died in Beverly Hills, CA
1982	+ BRODERICK, James		55	Cancer
1992	BRODIE, Steve		72	Cancer
1990	BRODKIN, Herbert		77	Aneurysm
1986	BRODUS, Tex		81	Massive stroke
• 1944	# BRODY, Ann		59	Died in New York, NY
1991	BROIDY, Steve		86	Following a heart attack
• 1975	BROKAW, Charles		77	Died in New York City
1951	BROMBERG, J. Edward		47	Natural causes (in London, England)
1971	# BRONSON, Betty		63	Died in Pasadena, CA
1994	BRONSTON, Samuel		85	After a brief illness (in Sacramento, CA)
1974	# BROOK, Clive		87	Died in London, England
1962	BROOK-JONES, Elwyn		51	
• 1951	BROOKE, Clifford		79	After being struck by a car (in Santa Monica, CA)
• 1963	# BROOKE, Ralph		43	Died in Hollywood, CA
1943	# BROOKE, Tyler		52	Suicide (carbon monoxide in his car) in North Hollywood, CA
1921	# BROOKE, Van Dyke		62	Died in Saratoga Springs, NY
1986	BROOKE, Walter		71	Emphysema
1989	BROOKNER, Howard		34	A.I.D.S.
1992	# BROOKS, Beverley		63	Stroke
1977	# BROOKS, Geraldine		52	Cancer (in Riverhead, NY)
• 1944	BROOKS, Jesse Lee		50	Heart attack (in Hollywood, CA)
1985	BROOKS, Louise		78	Heart attack
• 1967	BROOKS, Pauline		54	Cancer (in Glendale, CA)
• 1995	BROOKS, Phyllis (Macdonald)		80	Died in Cape Neddick, Maine
1992	BROOKS, Richard	☆	79	Congestive heart failure
1960	#+ BROPHY, Ed		65	Died in Los Angeles, CA
1989	BROTHERSON, Eric		78	
1934	BROUGH, Mary		71	Heart ailment (in London, England)
1946	BROWER, Otto		50	Heart failure (in Hollywood, CA)
1988	BROWN, Alfredine "Alfie"		56	Heart failure from kidney disease
1975	BROWN, Barbara		68	
1978	BROWN, Barry		27	Suicide at home (self-inflicted wounds)
1948	BROWN, Charles D.		60	Heart ailment (in Hollywood, CA)
1987	+ BROWN, Clarence	☆	97	Kidney failure
1956	BROWN, Clifford		25	Automobile accident
1992	# BROWN, Georgia		57	Infection after surgery for an intestinal blockage
1986	BROWN, Harry		69	(Do not confuse with Harry Joe Brown, d. 1972)
1972	BROWN, Harry Joe		78	Apparent heart attack (Do not confuse with Harry Brown, d. 1986)
• 1974	BROWN, Helen "Mina"		58	Cancer (in CA)
1992	BROWN, James		72	Lung cancer
1973	#+ BROWN, Joe E.		80	After a long illness (in Brentwood, CA)
1957	+ BROWN, John H. "Digger O'Dell"		53	Following a heart attack
1974	+ BROWN, Johnny Mack		70	Cardiac condition (in Woodland Hills, CA)
1982	BROWN, Joseph		59	
1990	BROWN, Karl		93	

YEAR	NAME	AGE	CAUSE AND/OR PLACE OF DEATH
1992	# BROWN, Lucille E.	74	After a long illness
• 1939	BROWN, Raymond "Ray"	58	Died in Los Angeles, CA
1991	# BROWN, Reno	70	Cancer
1993	BROWN, Richard "Dick"	68	Cancer (in Los Angeles, CA)
1963	BROWN, Rowland	62	Heart attack
1964	BROWN, Russ	72	Died in Englewood, N.J.
1989	BROWN, Tally	64	After suffering a stroke
• 1996	BROWN, Terry James	48	Lupus (in Los Angeles, CA)
1990	# BROWN, Tom	75	Cancer
1961	BROWN, Wally	57	Died in Los Angeles, CA
1991	+ BROWNE, Coral	77	Breast cancer
1965	BROWNE, Irene	72	Cancer (in London, England)
1976	BROWNE, Lucile	69	
1962	+ BROWNING, Tod	82	Following an operation for cancer (in Hollywood, CA)
• 1948	BROWNLEE, Frank	73	
1993	BROX, Lorayne (Hall)	94	Unreported causes (in Los Angeles, CA)
1988	BROX, Patricia (Gerstenzang)	?	
1974	BRUCE, Betty	54	Cancer
1976	BRUCE, David	60	Heart attack (in Hollywood, CA)
1946	BRUCE, Kate	87	
1966	#+ BRUCE, Lenny	40	Overdose of narcotics (in Hollywood, CA)
1953	#+ BRUCE, Nigel	58	Heart attack (in Santa Monica, CA)
1982	# BRUCE, Virginia	72	After a long illness
1982	BRUCK, Bella	70	Heart attack
1987	BRUCK, Karl	81	Cancer
1955	+ BRUCKMAN, Clyde	60	Suicide (gunshot)
• 1967	BRUGGEMAN, George	62	Died in North Hollywood, CA
1989	BRUMER, Martin	28	Automobile accident
• 1939	BRUNDAGE, Mathilde	67	
• 1943	BRUNETTE, Fritzi	53	Died in Hollywood, CA
1992	BRUNI, Peter	60	Heart failure
1991	BRUNNER, Howard	51	A.I.D.S.
1993	BRUSATI, Franco	66	Leukemia (in Rome, Italy)
• 1959	BRYAN, Arthur Q.	60	Died in Hollywood, CA
1986	BRYAN, Ken	32	An A.I.D.S.-related illness
1992	BRYAN, William Donald Sr.	74	Cancer
1948	BRYANT, Charles	67	
1983	BRYANT, Hazel	44	Heart attack
1989	BRYANT, John	72	Cancer
1988	BRYANT, Margot	90	
• 1978	BRYANT, Marie	58	Cancer (in Los Angeles, CA)
1955	BRYANT, Nana	67	Died in Hollywood, CA
1985	# BRYNNER, Yul ★	65	Lung cancer
1986	# BUBBLES, John W.	84	Died in Los Angeles, CA
1979	#+ BUCHANAN, Edgar	76	Died in Palm Desert, CA
1957	BUCHANAN, Jack	66	Spinal arthritis (in London, England)
1975	BUCHMAN, Sidney	73	Cancer (in Cannes, France)
1989	BUCK, David	53	Cancer
1950	BUCK, Frank	62	Lung ailment (in Houston, TX)
1973	BUCK, Pearl S.	80	
1936	BUCKLER, Hugh	64	Drowned with his son in a car accident
1936	BUCKLER, John (Jack)	30	Drowned with his father in a car accident
1946	BUCQUET, Harold S.	54	
1989	BUETEL, Jack	74	After a long illness
1994	BULGAKOVA, Maya	62	Automobile accident (in Russia)
1984	BULL, Peter	72	Heart attack
1993	BULLOCK, Burdette III	38	Cancer
1985	BULOFF, Joseph	85	After a long illness
1966	BUNKER, Ralph	77	Stroke
1990	BUNNAGE, Avis	67	
1915	+ BUNNY, John	51	Bright's disease (in Brooklyn, NY)
1935	BUNSTON, Herbert	61	Heart attack
1983	BUNUEL, Luis	83	Cirrhosis of the liver
1982	+ BUONO, Victor	44	
1993	BURDETT, Winston	79	After a long illness (in Rome, Italy)

YEAR	NAME		AGE	CAUSE AND/OR PLACE OF DEATH
1985	BURGE, James C.		41	Respiratory failure (pneumonia)
• 1961	BURGESS, Dorothy		54	
1937	+ BURGESS, Helen		19	Lobar pneumonia (in Beverly Hills, CA)
1992	BURKE, Alan		69	Emphysema
1970	#+ BURKE, Billie	☆	84	Died in Los Angeles, CA
1968	# BURKE, James		81	Died in Los Angeles, CA
1980	BURKE, Kathleen		66	
1984	BURKE, Walter		75	Emphysema
1989	BURKS, Rick		26	Automobile accident
1993	BURKS, Stephen		36	Undisclosed causes (in Los Angeles, CA)
1949	BURNABY, Davy		68	Heart attack
1987	BURNELL, Peter		44	
1967	#+ BURNETTE, Smiley		55	Leukemia (in Los Angeles, CA)
1956	+ BURNS, Bob "Bazooka"		64	After a 3-yr. illness (at his home in San Fernando Valley, CA)
1971	BURNS, David		67	Heart attack (while performing on stage in Philadelphia, PA)
• 1996	#+ BURNS, George		100	Died at his home in Beverly Hills, CA
1948	BURNS, Harry		63	Following a heart attack (in Santa Monica, CA)
1967	BURNS, Paul E.		86	Heart attack (in Van Nuys, CA)
1990	BURNS, Stephan		35	A.I.D.S.
• 1940	BURR, Eugene "Gene"		?	Pulmonary edema (in Los Angeles, CA)
1993	#+ BURR, Raymond		76	Cancer of the liver (in Sonoma County, CA)
1950	+ BURROUGHS, Edgar Rice		74	Heart ailment
1985	# BURROWS, Abe		74	After a long illness
1990	BURRUD, Bill		65	Heart attack (while swimming in the ocean)
• 1939	BURTIS, James		46	Died in California
• 1933	BURTON, Clarence		51	Heart attack (in Hollywood, CA)
1957	BURTON, Frederick		86	After being hospitalized (in Woodland Hills, CA)
• 1955	BURTON, George H.		55	Heart attack (in Los Angeles, CA)
1984	BURTON, Margaret		60	Heart attack
1976	BURTON, Martin		71	After a lengthy illness
1984	#+ BURTON, Richard	☆	58	Cerebral hemorrhage
1964	BURTON, Robert		69	Lung cancer (in Woodland Hills, CA)
1946	+ BUSCH, Mae		55	After a 5-mo. illness (in a San Fernando Valley sanitarium)
1991	BUSCH, Niven		88	Heart failure
• 1969	BUSH, Pauline		83	Pneumonia (in San Diego, CA)
1991	BUSH, Warren V.		65	Cardiac arrest
1966	+ BUSHMAN, Francis X.		83	Heart attack due to fall (in Pacific Palisades, CA)
1978	# BUSHMAN, Ralph		74	Respiratory failure (in Los Angeles, CA)
• 1955	BUSSE, Henry		61	Heart attack (in Memphis, TN)
• 1965	# BUSTER, Budd		74	Heart attack (in Los Angeles, CA)
1994	BUTLER, Chris	☆	42	A.I.D.S. complications (in Los Angeles, CA)
1979	# BUTLER, David		84	Ruptured diverticulum, peritonitis and heart failure (in Arcadia, CA)
1929	# BUTLER, Fred		64	Kidney trouble (in Los Angeles, CA)
1993	BUTLER, John		74	Cancer (in New York)
1973	# BUTLER, Royal "Roy"		80	Died in Desert Hot Springs, CA
1991	BUTLER, Tim		36	A.I.D.S.
1989	BUTRICK, Merritt		29	A.I.D.S.
1988	BUTTERFIELD, Billy		71	
1987	BUTTERFIELD, Paul		44	
1946	BUTTERWORTH, Charles		49	Automobile accident (Suicide?) in Los Angeles, CA
1979	BUTTERWORTH, Peter		60	Heart attack (in Coventry, England)
1994	BUTTRAM, Pat		78	Kidney failure (at UCLA Medical Center)
1985	# BUZZELL, Eddie		89	
1971	+ BYINGTON, Spring	☆	84	Died in Hollywood, CA
1952	+ BYRD, Ralph M. "Dick Tracy"		43	Heart attack (in Tarzana, CA)
1993	BYRD, William D.		27	Heart failure (in Inglewood, CA)
1981	BYRNE, Eddie		70	
1943	+ BYRON, Arthur		71	After a long illness (in Hollywood, CA)
1959	BYRON, Paul		68	Heart attack (in San Diego, CA)
	◖ C			
1950	# CABANNE, William C.		62	Heart attack (in Philadelphia, PA)
1972	#+ CABOT, Bruce		68	Lung and throat cancer
1977	+ CABOT, Sebastian		59	Stroke (in Victoria, B.C., Canada)
1986	CABOT, Susan		59	Beaten to death in her home
1967	CADELL, Jean		83	Died in London, England

YEAR	NAME		AGE	CAUSE AND/OR PLACE OF DEATH
1992	CADY, Frank		74	Complications following heart surgery
1986	CAESAR, Adolph		52	Heart attack
1986	+ CAGNEY, James	★	86	Diabetes, heart & lung problems
1984	CAGNEY, Jeanne		65	Lung cancer
1988	CAGNEY, William J.		82	Heart attack
1991	CAHAN, George M.		72	Pneumonia
1963	CAHN, Edward L.		64	
1993	#+ CAHN, Sammy	★	79	Congestive heart failure
1954	CAIN, Robert		67	Died in New York, NY
1964	CAINE, Georgia		88	Died in Hollywood, CA
1993	CAINE, Howard		67	Heart attack (in Los Angeles, CA)
1983	CAINE, Joan-Ellen		57	Cancer
1986	CALDWELL, Don		51	A.I.D.S.
1956	#+ CALHERN, Louis	☆	61	Heart attack, brought on by alcohol and medicine (in Tokyo, Japan)
1966	# CALHOUN, Alice		65	Cancer (in Los Angeles, CA)
• 1995	CALLAGHAN, Jack		64	Heart attack (in Charlotte, N.C.)
1977	#+ CALLAS, Maria		53	Heart attack
1975	# CALLEIA, Joseph		78	Died in Malta
1993	CALLEN, Michael		38	A.I.D.S. (in Los Angeles, CA)
1992	# CALLENDER, Red		76	Thyroid cancer
1994	# CALLOWAY, Cab		86	Pneumonia following a stroke (in Hockessin, DE)
1990	CALLOWAY, Northern J.		41	After being taken to a psychiatric hospital
1940	CALTHROP, Donald		52	After a heart attack (in England)
1982	CALVE, Olga		82	Bronchial pneumonia
1941	# CALVERT, E. H.		78	Died in Hollywood, CA
1975	#+ CALVIN, Henry		57	
1976	+ CAMBRIDGE, Godfrey		43	Heart attack (in Burbank, CA)
1955	CAMERON, Donald		66	Died in West Cornwall, CT
1987	CAMERON, Donald A.		61	
1983	# CAMERON, Rod		73	Following a long illness
• 1958	CAMERON, Rudolph "Rudy"		63	Hemorrhage (in Los Angeles, CA)
• 1996	CAMMELL, Donald		57	Suicide (gunshot) at his home in Hollywood Hills, CA
1929	CAMP, Sheppard		47	From injuries during filming of "Song of Flame"
1988	CAMP, Wilson		74	Cancer
1993	+ CAMPANELLA, Roy		71	After a heart attack (in Woodland Hills, CA)
1963	CAMPBELL, Alan		58	Died in West Hollywood, CA
1987	CAMPBELL, Archie		72	Renal & heart failure
1966	CAMPBELL, Colin		83	Died in Woodland Hills, CA
1917	CAMPBELL, Eric		37	Automobile accident (in Los Angeles, CA)
1985	CAMPBELL, Kay		80	Injuries from automobile accident
• 1995	CAMPBELL, Mifflin James		89	Cancer (in Indianapolis, IN)
1986	CAMPBELL, Muriel		75	
1972	# CAMPBELL, Webster		79	
1943	CAMPEAU, Frank		79	Died in Woodland Hills, CA
1974	CAMPEAU, June Harrison		48	Cirrhosis of the liver
1985	CAMPOS, Rafael		49	Stomach cancer
1994	#+ CANDY, John		43	Heart attack in his sleep (on location in Durango, Mexico)
• 1973	CANE, Charles		74	Died in Woodland Hills, CA
1972	CANNON, Esma		76	
1983	#+ CANOVA, Judy		66	Cancer
1993	# Cantinflas		81	Lung cancer (died in Mexico City)
1964	#+ CANTOR, Eddie		72	Heart attack (in Beverly Hills, CA)
• 1962	# CANTOR, Ida		70	Heart attack (in Beverly Hills, CA)
1991	CANTOR, Michael (Max)		32	
1986	CANTY, Marietta		80	
1986	# CANUTT, Yakima		90	Natural causes
1984	+ CAPOTE, Truman		59	Died in his sleep (drug & alcohol mix)
1988	CAPPELLANO, Francesca (Piazza)		92	Pneumonia
1991	+ CAPRA, Frank	★	94	Died in his sleep of natural causes
1990	# Capucine		57	Suicide plunge from her 8th floor apartment (in Lausanne, Switz.)
• 1964	CARD, Kathryn		70	Heart attack (in Costa Mesa, CA)
• 1954	# CARDWELL, James		32	Suicide (gunshot) in Hollywood, CA
• 1995	CAREW, Peter		73	Heart attack (at his home in Paramus, NJ)
1937	CAREWE, Arthur Edmund		42	Suicide (gunshot)
1940	# CAREWE, Edwin		56	Heart attack (in Los Angeles, CA)

...DEATHS OF MOVIE AND TELEVISION PERSONALITIES – BY NAME...

YEAR	NAME		AGE	CAUSE AND/OR PLACE OF DEATH
1955	# CAREWE, Ora		62	Died in Los Angeles, CA
1986	CAREY, Denis		77	
1947	+ CAREY, Harry	☆	67	Coronary thrombosis, attributed to a bee sting (in Brentwood, CA)
1994	+ CAREY, Macdonald		81	Cancer (in his Beverly Hills, CA, home)
1990	CAREY, Mary Jane		66	
1988	CAREY, Olive (Golden)		92	
1994	+ CAREY, Timothy		65	After suffering a stroke (at Cedars-Sinai Med. Ctr. in L.A.)
1959	CARHART, Georgiana		93	
1985	CARIDEO, Eddie		72	
1992	CARISI, Johnny		70	Complications from heart surgery
1990	CARISTI, Vincent		42	Cancer
1941	# CARLE, Richard		69	Heart attack
1979	CARLETON, Claire		66	Cancer (in Northridge, CA)
1950	CARLETON, George		65	Heart attack (in Hollywood, CA)
1947	+ CARLETON, William P.		73	Automobile accident (in Hollywood, CA)
1991	CARLIN, Thomas A.		62	Heart failure
1993	CARLON, Fran		80	Cancer (at her home in Manhattan)
1977	+ CARLSON, Richard		65	Cerebral hemorrhage (in Encino, CA)
1942	• CARLYLE, Richard		63	Died in San Fernando, CA
1986	CARMEL, Roger		53	Drug overdose
1994	CARMET, Jean		73	Heart failure (at his home in Sèvres, France)
1981	#+ CARMICHAEL, Hoagy		82	Heart attack
1971	# CARMINATI, Tullio		77	Stroke (in Rome, Italy)
1989	CARMINE, Michael		30	Heart failure
1967	CARNERA, Primo		60	Liver ailment (in Sequals, Italy)
1973	# CARNEY, Alan		63	Heart attack (at the Hollywood Park racetrack)
1947	CARNEY, George		60	
1992	CARNOVSKY, Morris		94	Natural causes
1982	CAROL, Sue		73	(See Sue Carol Ladd)
1990	CARPENTER, Charles		77	Heart attack
1983	+ CARPENTER, Karen		32	Heart attack caused by anorexia nervosa (in Downey, CA)
1984	+ CARPENTER, Ken		84	After a brief illness (in Santa Monica, CA)
1964	• CARPENTER, Paul		42	Died in London, England
1991	CARR, Eric		41	Complications from cancer
1971	• CARR, Georgia		46	Stroke (in Los Angeles, CA)
1954	• CARR, Geraldine		37	Automobile accident (in Hollywood, CA)
1957	• # CARR, Jane		48	
1979	• # CARR, Joe "Fingers"		69	Automobile accident (in Camarillo, CA)
1973	# CARR, Mary K.		98	Died in Woodland Hills, CA
1944	#+ CARR, Nat		57	Died in Hollywood, CA
1946	• CARR, Trem		54	After a heart attack (while vacationing in San Diego, CA)
1937	• CARR, William (actor/director)		69	Do not confuse with other actors of the same name
1988	#+ CARRADINE, John		82	Heart attack after strenuous stair climbing (in Italy)
1995	• CARRARO, Tino		84	Cardiac arrest (in a Milan, Italy, hospital)
1990	CARRERAS, James		81	
1961	+ CARRILLO, Leo		80	Cancer (in Santa Monica, CA)
1992	# CARROL, Regina		49	Cancer
1994	CARROLL, Bob		76	After a long illness (at a hospital in Manhasset, L.I., NY)
1992	CARROLL, David		41	A.I.D.S.
1980	# CARROLL, Dee		54	Following corrective surgery after a stroke
1948	+ CARROLL, Earl		56	Airplane crash (in Mt. Carmel, PA)
1993	CARROLL, Janice		61	Cancer (in San Fernando Valley, CA)
1979	+ CARROLL, John		71	Leukemia (in Hollywood, CA)
1972	CARROLL, Leo G.		79	Died in Hollywood, CA
1987	CARROLL, Madeleine		81	Following a long illness
1965	# CARROLL, Nancy	☆	59	Natural causes (in New York, NY)
1928	• CARROLL, William A.		51	Cancer (in Glendale, CA)
1977	CARSON, Charles		91	
1963	+ CARSON, Jack		53	Cancer (in Encino, CA)
1994	CARSON, Ken		79	Amyotrophic lateral sclerosis (in Jacksonville, FL)
1979	CARSON, Robert		69	Stroke (in Atascadero, CA)
1990	# CARSON, Sunset "Kit"		67	Heart attack
1982	CARSON, Wayne		55	
1946	CARTER, Ben F.		35	(Do not confuse with musician Benny Carter)
1992	CARTER, Beverly		51	Cancer

• New entry. # Original name (Pt. 7). + Interment (Pt. 5).　　　　149　　　　☆ Oscar nominee, ★ Oscar winner (Pt. 10)

...DEATHS OF MOVIE AND TELEVISION PERSONALITIES — BY NAME...

YEAR	NAME		AGE	CAUSE AND/OR PLACE OF DEATH
1994	CARTER, Janis		80	Heart attack (in Durham, NC)
1957	CARTER, Louise		82	After a 4-month illness (in Hollywood, CA)
1985	CARTER, Lynne		60	Pneumonia complicated by A.I.D.S.
1978	+ CARTER, Maybelle		69	
1950	CARTER, Monte		66	
1994	CARTIER, Rudolph		90	Died in his sleep (in London, England)
1921	+ CARUSO, Enrico		48	Peritonitis
1987	# CARUSO, Enrico Jr.		82	Following a heart attack
1956	# CARVER, Louise		86	Died in Hollywood, CA
1955	# CARVER, Lynn		45	Suicide (in New York, NY)
1992	CASCELLA, John J.		45	Found dead in his car of apparent heart attack
1986	CASE, Allen		51	Heart attack
1945	# CASEY, Dolores		28	Died in Hollywood, CA
1965	CASEY, Kenneth		66	Heart ailment (in Newburg, NY)
• 1995	CASH, Rosalind		56	Cancer (at Cedars-Sinai Med. Ctr. in Los Angeles, CA)
• 1961	CASON, John L.		?	
1987	CASPARY, Vera		87	
1954	CASS, Maurice		69	Heart attack (in Hollywood, CA)
1989	+ CASSAVETES, John	☆	59	Cirrhosis of the liver
1992	CASSELL, W. Barry Jr.		74	Pneumonia
1968	CASSIDY, Ed		74	Died in Woodland Hills, CA
1976	#+ CASSIDY, Jack		49	Burned to death (in West Hollywood, CA)
1979	+ CASSIDY, Ted "Lurch"		46	During heart surgery (in Los Angeles, CA)
1991	CASSIDY, Tom		41	A.I.D.S.
1990	CASSON, Ann		74	
1988	CASTELLANO, Richard	☆	55	Heart failure
1963	CASTIGLIONI, Iphigene		62	Died in Hollywood, CA
1966	CASTLE, Don		47	Found dead from overdose of medication (in Hollywood, CA)
1969	#+ CASTLE, Irene		75	Died in Eureka Springs, Arkansas
1990	CASTLE, Lee		?	Heart attack
1959	CASTLE, Lillian		94	After a brief illness (in Los Angeles, CA)
1968	#+ CASTLE, Nick		58	Heart attack (in Los Angeles, CA)
1973	CASTLE, Peggy		46	Cirrhosis of the liver and heart condition (in Hollywood, CA)
1918	+ CASTLE, Vernon		30	Airplane crash (in Houston, TX)
• 1977	# CASTLE, William		63	Heart attack (in Los Angeles, CA)
• 1981	CASTLETON, Barbara		85	
1990	CATHEY, Dalton		44	A.I.D.S.
1960	CATLETT, Walter		71	Stroke (in Woodland Hills, CA)
1992	CATTANI, Rico		64	Respiratory disease from a chronic heart condition
1991	+ CAULFIELD, Joan		69	After surgery for cancer
1982	CAVALCANTI, Alberto		85	
1989	CAVALLARO, Carmen		76	Cancer
1964	CAVANAGH, Paul		68	Heart attack
1950	CAVANAUGH, Hobart		53	Following major surgery (in Woodland Hills, CA)
1963	CAVANNA, Elise		61	Cancer (in Hollywood, CA)
• 1941	CAVEN, Allan		60	Died in Hollywood, CA
• 1962	CAVENDER, Glen W.		77	Died in Hollywood, CA
• 1960	CAVENDISH, David		69	Heart attack (in Hollywood, CA)
• 1976	CAVENDISH, June		?	Leukemia (in Los Angeles, CA)
• 1962	# CAVENS, Fred		79	Uremia (in Woodland Hills, CA)
1949	CAWTHORNE, Joseph		81	Stroke (in Beverly Hills, CA)
1989	CAYATTE, André		80	
1978	CAZALE, John		42	Cancer (in New York, NY)
• 1940	CECIL, Edward		52	Died in Los Angeles, CA
1971	+ CERF, Bennett		73	Heart attack
1974	CERVI, Gino		72	Pulmonary stroke
1991	CHABEAU, Ray Edgar		49	
1940	CHADWICK, Helene		42	From injuries after a fall (in Los Angeles, CA)
1990	CHAFFEY, Don		72	Heart disease
1992	CHALIAPIN, Feodor Jr.		87	After a brief illness
• 1938	+ CHALIAPIN, Feodor Sr. "Felix"		65	
1989	CHALLEE, William		84	Alzheimer's disease
1966	CHALMERS, Thomas		82	Died in Greenwich, CT
1984	CHAMBERLIN, Howland		73	Complications of lung & liver disease
• 1917	CHAMBERLIN, Riley C.		62	Died in New Rochelle, NY

YEAR	NAME		AGE	CAUSE AND/OR PLACE OF DEATH
1958	CHAMBERS, J. Wheaton		69	Died in Hollywood, CA
1991	CHAMBERS, Kathy L.		41	Cancer
1980	CHAMPION, Gower		60	Waldenstrom's disease
1990	# CHAMPLIN, Irene		59	After a long illness
1965	CHANDET, Louis W.		81	After an illness of several years
1988	# CHANDLER, Chick		83	
• 1948	CHANDLER, Eddie		54	(Do not confuse with actor Edward S. Chandler)
1985	CHANDLER, George		82	Alzheimer's disease
1965	+ CHANDLER, Helen		59	After surgery for a bleeding ulcer (in Hollywood, CA)
1994	# CHANDLER, Janet		78	Heart failure after a stroke (at UCLA Med. Ctr., CA)
1961	#+ CHANDLER, Jeff	☆	42	Blood poisoning after spinal surgery (in Culver City, CA)
1988	CHANDLER, Jim		65	Lung cancer
1979	CHANDLER, Joan		55	
1972	# CHANDLER, Lane		73	Cardiovascular disease (in Hollywood, CA)
1989	CHANDLER, Marjorie Grossel		71	Cancer
1967	# CHANEY, Frances		78	Cerebral hemorrhage (in Sierra Madre, CA)
1973	# CHANEY, Lon Jr.		67	Heart attack, throat cancer, liver ailment (in San Clemente, CA)
1930	#+ CHANEY, Lon Sr.		47	Lung and throat cancer (in Los Angeles, CA)
1936	# CHANEY, Norman "Chubby"		18	After an operation for a glandular ailment (in Baltimore, MD)
1968	CHAPLIN, Charles Jr.		42	Blood clot (in Hollywood, CA)
1977	#+ CHAPLIN, Charlie	☆	88	Blood clot (in Corsiersur-vevey, Switzerland)
1991	CHAPLIN, Oona		66	Following cancer surgery
1965	# CHAPLIN, Sydney		80	Died in Nice, France
1991	CHAPMAN, Ben		83	Heart & kidney failure
1977	CHAPMAN, Edward		76	Heart attack (in Brighton, England)
1948	CHAPMAN, Edythe		85	Died in Glendale, CA
1989	CHAPMAN, Graham		48	Spinal cancer
1986	CHAPMAN, Ted		63	Natural causes
1987	CHARLES, Anthony		42	Heart attack
• 1979	CHARLES, Lewis		63	Cancer (in Los Angeles, CA)
1990	CHARLESON, Ian		40	A.I.D.S. (Septicemia)
• 1961	CHARLESON, Mary		68	Died in Woodland Hills, CA
• 1956	CHARLOT, Andre		73	Died in Woodland Hills, CA
1943	+ CHARTERS, Spencer		68	Suicide (pills and carbon monoxide) in Hollywood, CA
1940	#+ CHASE, Charley		47	Heart attack (in Hollywood, CA)
• 1937	# CHASE, Colin		50	Paralysis attack (in Los Angeles, CA)
1978	CHASE, Ilka		72	Internal hemorrhage from a fall (in Mexico City, Mexico)
1961	+ CHATTERTON, Ruth	☆	67	Died in Norwalk, CT
1966	CHATTON, Sydney		48	Coronary attack (in Berkeley, CA)
1934	CHAUTARD, Emile		69	Organic trouble (in Westwood, CA)
1981	#+ CHAYEFSKY, Paddy		58	Cancer
• 1971	# CHEATHAM, Jack		76	Heart failure (in La Mirada, CA)
1993	CHECCHI, Robert J.		67	After suffering a stroke (in Los Angeles, CA)
1983	CHECCO, Jessie		85	
• 1975	# CHEFEE, Jack		81	Died in Hollywood, CA
1955	CHEKHOV, Michael	☆	64	Died in Beverly Hills, CA
1982	CHEN, Renee Shinn		6	Killed by helicopter rotor while filming
1990	CHENAL, Pierre		86	
• 1995	CHERKASSKY, Shura		84	Respiratory complications (in London, England)
• 1995	CHEROT, Lewis		26	Automobile accident (in Los Angeles, CA)
1989	CHERRILL, Christine		71	
1959	# CHESEBRO, George		70	Arteriosclerosis (in Hermosa Beach, CA)
1968	+ CHESHIRE, Harry "Pappy"		76	
• 1949	CHESNEY, Arthur		67	Died in London, England
1972	#+ CHEVALIER, Maurice	☆	83	Heart attack after kidney surgery (in Paris, France)
1989	CHIARI, Mario		79	
1991	CHIARI, Walter		67	Heart attack
1964	CHILDERS, Naomi		70	After a long illness (in Hollywood, CA)
1986	CHILDRESS, Alvin		78	Parkinson's disease, diabetes, pneumonia
1989	CHING, William		75	Congestive heart failure
1977	CHITTY, Erik		70	
1988	CHODOROV, Edward		84	
1982	CHRISTI, Frank		52	Shot to death at his home
1992	CHRISTI, Panos		54	Complications from A.I.D.S.
1983	CHRISTIAN, Robert		42	Cancer

YEAR	NAME		AGE	CAUSE AND/OR PLACE OF DEATH
1994	# Christian-Jaque		89	Heart attack (in Boulogne-Billancourt, France)
1951	+ CHRISTIANS, Mady		51	Cerebral hemorrhage (in South Norwalk, CT)
1951	CHRISTIE, Al		69	Heart attack
1989	CHRISTIE, Audrey		79	Emphysema
1991	CHRISTMAS, Jason		49	Killed outside a NY comedy club by robbers
1983	CHRISTOPHER, Richard		37	Cancer
1987	CHRISTY, Ann		82	Heart attack
1992	CHRISTY, Howard		79	After a long illness
1949	CHRISTY, Ivan		61	After a heart attack (in Burbank, CA)
1990	# CHRISTY, June		64	Complications of kidney failure
1962	CHRISTY, Ken		67	Died in Hollywood, CA
1990	# CHRYSIS, International		38	Cancer
1940	CHURCHILL, Berton		63	Uremic poisoning (in New York, NY)
1991	CHURCHILL, Donald		60	Apparent heart attack
1982	CHURCHILL, Sarah		67	Following a long illness
1969	CIANNELLI, Eduardo		81	Cancer (in Rome, Italy)
1993	CINCOTTA, Carmine		41	Hodgkin's disease (in New York)
1967	CIOLLI, Augusta		65	
1989	CIRO, Steve		46	
1981	# CLAIR, René		82	
• 1928	CLAIRE, Gertrude		75	Died in Los Angeles, CA
• 1974	CLAIRE, Helen		67	Died in Birmingham, AL
1985	# CLAIRE, Ina		95	Lingering effects of a stroke
1990	CLAIRE, Ludi		70	After a long illness
1990	CLANCY, Tom		67	Stomach cancer
1970	CLARE, Mary		76	Died in London, England
1955	# CLARENCE, O. B.		85	
1960	#+ CLARK, Bobby		72	Heart attack (in New York, NY)
1949	#+ CLARK, Buddy		38	Airplane crash (in Beverly Hills, CA)
1953	CLARK, Cliff		59	Heart attack (in Hollywood, CA)
1990	CLARK, Dee		52	
1989	CLARK, Dort		71	Diabetes and cancer
1954	CLARK, Eddie		75	Heart attack (in Hollywood, CA)
1968	#+ CLARK, Fred		54	Liver ailment (in Santa Monica, CA)
1938	CLARK, Harvey		52	Following a heart attack (in Hollywood, CA)
1967	CLARK, Ivan-John		?	
• 1947	CLARK, John J.		69	Died in Hollywood, CA
• 1967	CLARK, Johnny		50	Heart attack (in Hollywood, CA)
1983	CLARK, Kendall		70	
1986	CLARK, Mamo		72	Cancer
1940	+ CLARK, Marguerite		53	Pneumonia after a cerebral hemorrhage (in New York, NY)
• 1978	CLARK, Roger W.		69	Stroke (in Los Angeles, CA)
• 1961	CLARK, Wallis		71	
1972	CLARKE, Gordon B.		65	After a heart attack (in New York, NY)
1992	# CLARKE, Mae		81	Cancer
1985	CLARKE, Philip Norman		81	
1987	CLARKE, Raymond		47	A.I.D.S.
1957	# CLARKE, Robert "Buddy"		61	
1989	CLARKE, T. E. B.		81	
1959	# CLARKE-SMITH, D. A.		71	
• 1931	CLARY, Charles		58	Died in Los Angeles, CA
1992	CLATWORTHY, William	☆	80	After a brief illness
1994	CLAVELL, James		69	Stroke after suffering from cancer (at home in Switzerland)
1991	# CLAYTON, Buck		80	
• 1966	CLAYTON, Ethel		82	Died in Oxnard, CA
• 1950	CLAYTON, Gilbert		89	
• 1995	CLAYTON, Jack		73	After a short illness (at a hosp. in Slough, Berkshire, Eng.)
1983	CLAYTON, Jan		66	Cancer
1950	# CLAYTON, Marguerite B.		50	Injuries from an automobile accident
1993	CLAYWORTH, June		80	Lymphoma (in Calabasas, CA)
1990	CLEMENT, Marc R.		39	Automobile accident
• 1996	CLEMENT, Rene	★	82	Following heart trouble (in Monte Carlo, France)
• 1972	# CLEMENTE, Roberto		38	Airplane crash (in San Juan, Puerto Rico)
1950	# CLEMENTO, Steve		64	Cerebral hemorrhage (in Los Angeles, CA)
1988	CLEMENTS, John		77	

...DEATHS OF MOVIE AND TELEVISION PERSONALITIES — BY NAME...

YEAR	NAME		AGE	CAUSE AND/OR PLACE OF DEATH
1981	CLEMENTS, Stanley		55	Emphysema
1957	+ CLEVELAND, George		74	Heart attack (in Burbank, CA)
1991	CLEVELAND, James		59	Respiratory problems & heart failure
1988	CLEWES, Howard		75	
1956	# CLIFFORD, Jack		76	
1962	CLIFFORD, Kathleen		74	Died in Hollywood, CA
1961	CLIFT, Denison		76	Heart ailment
1966	+ CLIFT, Montgomery	☆	45	Occlusive coronary artery disease (in New York, NY)
1949	+ CLIFTON, Elmer		59	Cerebral hemorrhage (in Los Angeles, CA)
1922	# CLIFTON, Emma Bell		47	Heart attack (in Los Angeles, CA)
1961	# CLINE, Eddie		68	Died in Hollywood, CA
1963	#+ CLINE, Patsy		30	Airplane crash (in a forest near the Tennessee River)
1937	#+ CLIVE, Colin		37	Tuberculosis complicated by alcoholism
1940	# CLIVE, E. E.		60	Heart attack (in North Hollywood, CA)
1960	# CLIVE, Henry		77	Lung cancer (in Hollywood, CA)
1990	CLOCHE, Maurice		82	Parkinson's disease
1992	CLORE, Leon		73	Cancer
1977	CLOUZOT, Henri Charles		70	
1956	CLUTE, Chester		64	Heart attack (in Woodland Hills, CA)
1985	CLUTE, Sidney		69	Cancer
1967	+ CLYDE, Andy		75	Died in Los Angeles, CA
1945	CLYDE, David		60	Died in San Fernando Valley, CA
1962	CLYDE, Jean		73	Died in Helensburgh, Scotland
1968	COATES, Paul		47	Heart attack (in West Hollywood, CA)
1994	+ COBAIN, Kurt		27	Suicide (gunshot) while high on heroin & valium
1991	COBB, Dita		68	After a long illness
1974	COBB, Edmund F.		82	Heart attack (in Woodland Hills, CA)
1944	+ COBB, Irvin S.		67	Died in New York, NY
1976	#+ COBB, Lee J.	☆	64	Heart attack (in Woodland Hills, CA)
1961	# COBB, Ty		74	Died in Atlanta, GA
1961	#+ COBURN, Charles	★	84	Heart ailment (in New York)
1960	+ COCHRAN, Eddie (singer)		21	Killed in a taxi crash at Bath, England
1994	COCHRAN, Ron		81	After a short illness (in Florida)
1965	# COCHRAN, Steve		48	Acute infectious edema of lung (off coast of Guatemala)
1987	COCO, James		56	Heart attack
1963	+ COCTEAU, Jean		74	Heart attack (in Milly-la-Foret, France)
1961	CODEE, Ann		70	Heart attack (in Hollywood, CA)
1948	# CODY, Bill Sr.		57	After an illness of several months (in Santa Monica, CA)
1960	# CODY, Emmett		40	
1991	CODY, Iron Eyes		?	
1934	# CODY, Lew		50	Heart disease (in Beverly Hills, CA)
1988	CODY, William "Wild Bill"		75	
1987	COE, Peter		58	Killed when his car collided with a van
1983	COFFIELD, Peter		37	
1990	COFFIN, Tristram "Tris"		80	Lung cancer
1942	+ COHAN, George M.		64	Cancer of the lower intestine (in New York, NY)
1986	COHEN, Myron		83	
1988	COHEN, Nat		82	
1938	COHL, Emil		81	Burns (after his beard caught fire from a candle)
1958	+ COHN, Harry		66	Heart attack
1996	COHN, Joseph Judson		100	Died in his sleep (at his home in Beverly Hills, CA)
1985	COLASANTO, Nicholas "Coach"		61	Heart ailment
1992	# COLBY, Anita		77	Lung disease
1952	COLCORD, Mabel		80	
1964	#+ COLE, Buddy		48	Heart attack
1985	COLE, Lester		81	
1965	#+ COLE, Nat "King"		45	Lung cancer (in Santa Monica, CA)
1951	COLEMAN, Charles		65	Stroke (in Woodland Hills, CA)
1986	COLERIDGE, Sylvia		76	
1992	COLES, Charles "Honi"		81	Died in his sleep of lung cancer
1989	COLEY, Thomas		75	Heart attack
1989	COLIN, Jean		83	
1993	COLLARD, Cyril		35	A.I.D.S. (in Paris, France)
1958	COLLEANO, Bonar		34	Automobile accident (in Liverpool, England)
1955	# COLLIER, Constance		77	Died in New York, NY

• New entry. # Original name (Pt. 7). + Interment (Pt. 5).   153   ☆ Oscar nominee, ★ Oscar winner (Pt. 10)

YEAR	NAME		AGE	CAUSE AND/OR PLACE OF DEATH
1987	# COLLIER, Patience		76	
1987	COLLIER, William "Buster" Jr.		86	Cardiac arrest
1944	+ COLLIER, William Sr.		77	Pneumonia (in Beverly Hills, CA)
1974	COLLINGE, Patricia	☆	81	Heart attack (in New York, NY)
1988	COLLINS, Brent		46	Apparent heart attack
1994	COLLINS, Christopher		44	After a brief illness (in Ventura, CA)
1994	# COLLINS, Dorothy		67	Heart failure (at her home in Watervliet, NY)
1959	COLLINS, G. Pat		64	Cancer (in Los Angeles, CA)
1918	COLLINS, John Hancock		28	Pleural pneumonia following influenza
1954	COLLINS, Lewis D.		55	Heart attack
1951	# COLLINS, Monty		52	Heart attack (in North Hollywood, CA)
1965	+ COLLINS, Ray		75	Emphysema (in Santa Monica, CA)
1965	COLLINS, Russell		68	Heart attack (in West Hollywood, CA)
1992	COLLOFF, Roger		46	Cancer
1969	+ COLLYER, Bud		61	
1968	# COLLYER, June		60	Bronchial pneumonia (in Los Angeles, CA)
1988	COLMAN, Ben		81	Septicemia
1975	COLMAN, Irene		60	Leukemia (in Santa Monica, CA)
1958	+ COLMAN, Ronald	★	67	Following operation for a lung infection (in Santa Barbara, CA)
1995	COLON, Alex		53	After an extended illness
1986	# COLONNA, Jerry		82	Kidney failure
1934	#+ COLUMBO, Russ		26	Accidentally shot by a friend while examining a pistol (in Hollywood)
1991	COLVIG, Vance		72	Cancer
1991	COLVIN, Michael		41	After suffering a head injury on a film set
1992	COMBS, Frederick		57	A.I.D.S.
1972	# COMINGORE, Dorothy		58	Died in Stonington, CT
1974	COMPSON, Betty		77	Died in Glendale, CA
1978	COMPTON, Fay		84	Died in England
1964	COMPTON, Francis		79	Died in Noroton, CT
1959	COMPTON, Walter		47	After a long illness
1977	CONDON, Jackie		59	Cancer (in Inglewood, CA)
1988	CONDOS, Nick		73	
1990	CONDOS, Steve		71	Heart attack
1990	CONIGLIARO, Tony		45	
1959	CONKLIN, Charles "Heinie"		79	Died in Hollywood, CA
1971	CONKLIN, Chester		83	Died in Woodland Hills, CA
1962	CONLIN, Jimmy		77	Cancer (in Encino, CA)
1993	CONN, Billy		75	Pneumonia (in Pittsburgh, PA)
1922	# CONNELLY, Bobby		13	Bronchitis and an enlarged heart (in Lynbrook, NY)
1988	CONNELLY, Christopher		47	Cancer
1928	CONNELLY, Edward J.		73	Influenza (in Hollywood, CA)
1931	CONNELLY, Erwin		57	Automobile accident (in Los Angeles, CA)
1940	CONNOLLY, Walter		53	Stroke (in Beverly Hills, CA)
1993	CONNOR, Kenneth		77	Cancer (in London, England)
1988	CONNOR, Whitfield		71	Complications following surgery
1992	#+ CONNORS, Chuck		71	Lung cancer
1983	CONRAD, Michael		58	Stomach cancer
1994	+ CONRAD, William		73	Heart attack (at the Medical Center of N. Hollywood)
1982	# CONRIED, Hans		64	Heart ailment
1964	CONROY, Frank		73	Heart ailment (in Paramus, NY)
1993	CONSTANTINE, Eddie		75	Heart attack (in Wiesbaden, Germany)
1975	#+ CONTE, Richard		59	Heart attack and stroke (in Los Angeles, CA)
1967	# CONTI, Albert		79	Stroke (in Hollywood, CA)
1991	+ CONVY, Bert		56	Cancer (brain tumor)
1974	CONWAY, Curt		59	After suffering a massive heart attack
1952	CONWAY, Jack (actor/director)		65	(Do not confuse with comedian/film actor Jack Conway, d. 1951)
1951	CONWAY, Jack (comedian/actor)		?	(Do not confuse with actor/director Jack Conway, d. 1952)
1981	CONWAY, Morgan		81	
1967	#+ CONWAY, Tom		63	Liver ailment (in Culver City, CA)
1994	CONWELL, John		72	Cancer (at his home in Santa Barbara, CA)
1935	# COOGAN, Jack Sr.		55	Automobile accident (nr. San Diego, CA)
1984	+ COOGAN, Jackie		69	Heart ailment
1978	COOGAN, Robert		53	
1981	COOK, Billy Boy		?	
1984	COOK, Clyde		92	Died in his sleep

YEAR	NAME		AGE	CAUSE AND/OR PLACE OF DEATH
1991	# COOK, Cookie		77	Kidney failure
1961	COOK, Donald		60	Heart attack (in New Haven, CT)
• 1995	COOK, Elisha Jr.		91	After suffering a stroke (in Big Pine, CA)
1959	# COOK, Joe		69	Died in Clinton Hollows, NY
1988	COOK, Nathan		38	Allergic reaction to penicillin
• 1995	COOK, Peter		57	Gastro-intestinal hemorrhage (in a London hospital)
1990	COOK, Roderick		58	
1953	COOKE, Baldwin G. "Baldy"		65	Died in Los Angeles, CA
1964	+ COOKE, Sam		29	Shot by motel manager while the actor was pursuing a girl (in L.A.)
1948	COOLEY, James R.		68	Died in Hollywood, CA
1969	# COOLEY, Spade		58	Massive heart attack (in Oakland, CA)
1967	COOLIDGE, Philip		58	Cancer (in Hollywood, CA)
1966	# COOMBE, Carol		55	Died in London, England
1989	COONAN, Sheila M.		66	Liver disease
1975	COOPER, Clancy		68	Heart attack while driving his car near his home (in Hollywood, CA)
1988	COOPER, Dorothy Jordan		82	
1981	COOPER, Dulcie		77	After a lengthy illness
1986	COOPER, Edna Mae		85	
1984	COOPER, Edwin		89	
1961	#+ COOPER, Gary	★	60	Cancer (in Hollywood, CA)
1971	+ COOPER, Gladys	☆	82	Died in her sleep from pneumonia (in England)
1973	+ COOPER, Melville G.		76	Cancer (in Woodland Hills, CA)
1973	COOPER, Merian C.		79	Cancer (in Coronado, CA)
1976	COOPER, Miriam		83	Stroke
1987	COOPER, Olive		94	Pneumonia
1992	COOPER, Ralph		?	Cancer
1982	COOTE, Robert		73	
1990	COPLAND, Aaron	★	90	Complications of 2 strokes & respiratory problems
1991	COPPOLA, Carmine	★	80	After suffering a stroke
1961	CORBETT, Ben		69	Died in Hollywood, CA
1993	CORBETT, Glenn		59	Lung cancer (in San Antonio, TX)
1982	CORBETT, Harry H.		57	Heart attack
1933	CORBETT, James J.		65	Cancer of the liver
1960	CORBETT, Leonora		52	Died in Vleuten, Holland
• 1974	CORBETT, Mary		47	
• 1942	CORBIN, Virginia Lee		31	Heart disease (in Winfield, IL)
1990	CORBUCCI, Sergio		62	Heart attack
1993	# CORDAY, Josephine Rich		79	Heart & kidney failure (in Los Angeles, CA)
1992	# CORDAY, Rita		68	Complications of diabetes after gall bladder surgery (in CA)
• 1954	CORDING, Harry		63	Died in Sun Valley, CA
• 1965	# CORDY, Henry		57	Heart ailment (in New York, NY)
1993	COREY, Dorian		56	A.I.D.S. (in a New York hospital)
• 1972	# COREY, Joseph		45	Heart attack (in Los Angeles, CA)
1968	+ COREY, Wendell		54	Liver ailment (in Woodland Hills, CA)
1974	+ CORNELL, Katharine		81	After a long illness (in Vineyard Haven, MA)
1972	+ CORRELL, Charles J. "Andy"		82	Heart attack (in Chicago, IL)
• 1945	CORRIGAN, D'Arcy		75	
• 1995	CORRIGAN, Douglas "Wrong Way"		88	Died in Orange, CA
• 1929	CORRIGAN, James		57	Died in Los Angeles, CA
1969	CORRIGAN, Lloyd		69	Died in Woodland Hills, CA
1976	# CORRIGAN, Ray "Crash"		74	Heart attack (in Brookings Harbor, OR)
• 1995	CORSAUT, Aneta		62	Cancer (in Studio City, CA)
1993	CORT, William		53	Cancer (in Los Angeles, CA)
1989	CORTEZ, Mildred		72	Cardiac arrest
1977	# CORTEZ, Ricardo		77	Died in New York, NY
1947	+ CORTHELL, Herbert		69	After a year's illness (in Hollywood, CA)
1988	CORTLAND, Nicholas		47	A.I.D.S.
1994	CORVO, Phil		67	After a long illness (in Los Angeles, CA)
1993	CORY, Ken		51	A.I.D.S.
• 1995	# COSELL, Howard		77	A heart embolism (at NYU Hospital in New York)
• 1949	COSGRAVE, Luke		86	Died in Woodland Hills, CA
1951	COSSART, Ernest		74	Died in New York, NY
1989	COSTA, Bob		66	
1983	COSTELLO, Anthony		42	
1987	COSTELLO, Carole		48	Stroke

• New entry.   # Original name (Pt. 7).   + Interment (Pt. 5).

☆ Oscar nominee, ★ Oscar winner (Pt. 10)

YEAR	NAME	AGE	CAUSE AND/OR PLACE OF DEATH
1979	COSTELLO, Delores	73	Died in Fallbrook, CA
1945	COSTELLO, Don	44	Died in his sleep (in Hollywood, CA)
1957	COSTELLO, Helene	53	Pneumonia, tuberculosis, narcotics (in Los Angeles, CA)
1959	#+ COSTELLO, Lou	52	Heart attack (in Los Angeles, CA)
1950	COSTELLO, Maurice	73	Heart ailment (in Hollywood, CA)
• 1971	COSTELLO, William A.	73	Died in San José, CA
1991	COSTON, Ann Sorg	62	After a short illness
1994	+ COTTEN, Joseph	88	Pneumonia (at his Los Angeles home)
1992	COTTLE, Graham D.	51	Congestive heart failure
• 1969	# COTTON, Billy	68	Heart attack (in London, England)
1916	COTTON, Richard	?	Run over by an automobile
1976	COUGHLIN, Kevin	29	Hit-and-run accident while cleaning his car windshield (in L.A., CA)
1989	COULOURIS, George	85	Heart attack
• 1918	COURTLEIGH, William Jr.	25	Pneumonia (in Philadelphia, PA)
• 1930	COURTLEIGH, William Sr.	61	Died in Rye, NY
1980	COURTNEIDGE, Cicely	87	Died in London, England
1975	COURTNEY, Inez	67	Died in Neptune, NJ
1986	COURTOT, Marguerite	88	
• 1933	COURTRIGHT, William "Uncle Billy"	84	Died in Ione, CA
1989	COVAN, Willie	92	
1993	COVINGTON, Fred	65	Cancer (in a Marietta, GA, hospital)
1972	#+ COWAN, Jerome	74	Died in Encino, CA
1973	#+ COWARD, Noel ★	73	Heart attack (in Port Maria, Jamaica)
• 1942	COWL, George	64	
1950	+ COWL, Jane	62	Cancer (in Santa Monica, CA)
1943	COWLES, Jules	65	Died in Hollywood, CA
1968	COX, Morgan	68	
1974	COX, Robert	79	Died in Phoenix, AZ
1973	#+ COX, Wally	48	Heart attack (in Los Angeles, CA)
• 1954	COXEN, Edward Albert	70	Died in Hollywood, CA
• 1974	COY, Walter	68	
• 1973	COYNE, Jeanne	50	
1983	# CRABBE, Larry "Buster"	75	Heart attack
1945	CRAIG, Alec	60	After a long illness (in Glendale, CA)
• 1940	# CRAIG, Blanche	74	Died in Los Angeles, CA
• 1970	CRAIG, Carolyn	?	
1979	CRAIG, Edith	71	After a long illness (Do not confuse with the English actress)
1986	CRAIG, Helen	74	Cardiac arrest
1985	#+ CRAIG, James	73	Lung cancer
1972	CRAIG, May	82	Died in Dublin, Ireland
1965	CRAIG, Nell	73	Died in Hollywood, CA
1933	# CRAIG, Richy Jr.	31	Heart failure after a lengthy illness
1960	# CRAMER, Rychard	71	Laennec's cirrhosis (in Los Angeles, CA)
1978	+ CRANE, Bob	48	Murdered (skull crushed by a blow while sleeping) in Scottsdale, AZ
1973	#+ CRANE, Norma	42	Cancer (in West Los Angeles, CA)
1969	+ CRANE, Richard O.	51	Heart attack (in San Fernando Valley, CA)
1928	CRANE, Ward	37	Pneumonia (in Saranac Lake, NY)
1994	CRAVAT, Nick	82	Lung cancer (in Woodland Hills, CA)
• 1960	CRAVAT, Noel	49	After surgery (in Hollywood, CA)
1991	# CRAVEN, Eddie	?	After an illness
1945	+ CRAVEN, Frank	70	Heart ailment (in Beverly Hills, CA)
• 1995	CRAVEN, John	79	Following a brief illness (in Salt Point, NY)
1991	CRAVENS, Kathryn	92	Cancer
• 1956	# CRAWFORD, Anne	35	Died in London, England
1986	#+ CRAWFORD, Broderick ★	74	Series of strokes
1969	# CRAWFORD, Howard Marion	55	An overdose of sleeping pills (in London, England)
1962	+ CRAWFORD, Jesse	66	Stroke (in Los Angeles, CA)
1977	#+ CRAWFORD, Joan ★	71	Cancer and acute coronary occlusion (in New York, NY)
• 1980	CRAWFORD, Kathryn	72	Cancer (in Pasadena, CA)
1944	#+ CREGAR, Laird	28	Following two heart attacks (in Los Angeles, CA)
1966	CREHAN, Joseph	79	Stroke (in Hollywood, CA)
1959	CREWS, Kay C.	58	
1942	+ CREWS, Laura Hope	62	After a month's illness (in New York, NY)
• 1945	# CRIMMONS, Daniel "Dan"	82	
• 1953	# CRIPPS, Kernan	67	

...DEATHS OF MOVIE AND TELEVISION PERSONALITIES — BY NAME...

YEAR	NAME		AGE	CAUSE AND/OR PLACE OF DEATH
1974	+ CRISP, Donald	★	93	After a series of strokes (in Van Nuys, CA)
1992	CRISTALDI, Franco	★	68	Heart attack
• 1938	CRITTENDEN, Throckwood Dwight		59	Murdered (gunshot) in Los Angeles, CA
1973	+ CROCE, Jim		30	Airplane crash (on takeoff from Natchitoches Municipal airport, LA)
• 1958	CROCKER, Harry		64	
• 1934	CROCKETT, Charles B.		62	Died in Los Angeles, CA
• 1979	# CROCKETT, Dick		63	Cancer (in Los Angeles, CA)
• 1922	CROCKETT, John		?	Died in Los Angeles, CA
• 1995	#+ CROGHAN, Joe		74	Cancer (at Manor Care Ruxton, Baltimore, MD)
1979	# CROMWELL, John		91	Pulmonary embolism (in Santa Barbara, CA)
1960	#+ CROMWELL, Richard		50	Died in Hollywood, CA
1992	CRONIN, Laurel		53	Cancer
1977	#+ CROSBY, Bing	★	73	Heart attack (in Madrid, Spain)
1993	CROSBY, Bob		79	Cancer (in La Jolla, CA)
1991	+ CROSBY, Dennis		56	Suicide (gunshot)
1952	#+ CROSBY, Dixie Lee		40	Cancer
• 1995	CROSBY, Gary		62	Complications of lung cancer (at St. Jos. Med Ctr, Burbank, CA)
1989	CROSBY, Lindsay		51	Suicide (gunshot)
1975	CROSBY, Wade		70	After a grand mal seizure aboard a yacht (in Newport Beach, CA)
1936	CROSLAND, Alan		42	Injuries after a car wreck
1944	CROSMAN, Henrietta		83	Died in Pelham Manor, NY
1975	CROSS, Milton		77	Apparent heart attack (in New York, NY)
1960	CROSSLEY, Syd		75	Died in Troon, England
1986	+ CROTHERS, Benjamin "Scatman"		76	Lung cancer
1985	CROTHERS, Joel		44	Cancer
• 1932	CROWELL, Josephine		?	Died in Amityville, NY
1988	CRUICKSHANK, Andrew		80	
1942	#+ CRUZE, James		58	Heart ailment (in Hollywood, CA)
1965	CRUZE, Mae		74	After a long illness (in Hollywood, CA)
1992	# CUEVAS, Joey		34	A.I.D.S.
1990	CUGAT, Xavier		90	Heart failure due to arterial sclerosis
1983	+ CUKOR, George	★	83	Heart failure
• 1996	CULHANE, Shamus		87	Congestive heart failure (in New York)
1990	# CULLEN, Bill		70	Heart failure from lung cancer
1982	CULLEN, Fred		48	Heart attack
• 1942	CULLEY, Frederick		63	
1950	CULLINANI, Ralph		68	
• 1995	CULLINGHAM, Mark		53	Complications of A.I.D.S. (in Los Angeles, CA)
1925	CULLINGTON, Margaret		34	After a 6-month illness
1987	# CULVER, Calvin		43	Pulmonary infection
1984	CULVER, Roland		83	Heart attack
• 1996	CUMMINGS, Irving Jr.		77	Cancer (in Van Nuys, CA)
1959	CUMMINGS, Irving Sr.	☆	70	Heart attack (in Hollywood, CA)
1989	CUMMINGS, Jack		84	Heart attack
1990	+ CUMMINGS, Robert "Bob"		80	Parkinson's disease, kidney failure & pneumonia
1984	CUMMINGS, Ruth Sinclair		90	
1982	# CUMMINGS, Sandy		68	Pneumonia while hospitalized for another illness
1983	# CUMMINS, Dorothy		80	
1967	# CUNARD, Grace		73	After a long bout with cancer (in Woodland Hills, CA)
1925	CUNEO, Lester		37	Suicide (gunshot) after his wife filed for divorce
1959	CUNNINGHAM, Cecil		70	Arteriosclerosis (in Woodland Hills, CA)
• 1943	# CUNNINGHAM, Joe		52	Coronary occlusion (in Los Angeles, CA)
1986	CUNNINGHAM, Sarah		67	Asthmatic attack
1967	CUNNINGHAM, Zamah		74	
1994	CUNY, Alain		85	Died at the Cochin Hospital in Paris, France
• 1960	CURLEY, Leo		82	Arteriosclerosis (in Woodland Hills, CA)
• 1941	CURRAN, Thomas A.		60	Pneumonia (in Hollywood, CA)
1968	# CURRIE, Finlay		90	Died in Gerrads Cross, England
1928	CURRIER, Frank		71	Blood poisoning after car door was shut on a finger (in Hollywood)
1990	CURRIN, Jay C.		34	Injuries from a 55-foot fall while filming
1994	CURRY, John		44	A.I.D.S.-related heart attack (at his home in England)
1953	# CURTIS, Alan		43	Following a kidney operation
1988	CURTIS, Billy		79	Heart attack
1952	CURTIS, Dick		49	Died in Hollywood, CA
• 1956	CURTIS, Jack		75	(Do not confuse with the child actor or Jack B. Curtis)

...DEATHS OF MOVIE AND TELEVISION PERSONALITIES — BY NAME...

YEAR	NAME		AGE	CAUSE AND/OR PLACE OF DEATH
1985	# CURTIS, Jackie		38	Drug overdose
1991	# CURTIS, Ken		74	
1970	CURTIS, Willa Pearl		74	Cerebral arteriosclerosis and diabetes
1962	#+ CURTIZ, Michael	★	73	Cancer
• 1976	CURZON, George		79	Died in London, England
1993	CUSACK, Cyril		82	Motor neuron disease (at his home in London)
1994	CUSHING, Peter		81	Cancer (in a Canterbury hospice, England)
1974	# CUSTER, Bob		76	Natural causes
1988	CUTHBERTSON, Allan		67	
• 1972	# CUTTING, Dick		59	Kidney disease and uremia (in Woodland Hills, CA)
1974	CUTTS, Patricia		48	Found dead at home from an overdose of pills
	D			
1989	DaCOSTA, Morton		74	Heart failure
1980	# DAGOVER, Lil		82	Died in West Germany
1978	+ DAILEY, Dan	☆	62	Anemia (in Hollywood, CA)
1986	# DAINTY, Billy		59	
• 1948	# D'ALBROOK, Sidney		62	Heart attack (in Los Angeles, CA)
1969	DALBY, Amy		81	
1991	# DALE, Bobby		92	Myocardial infarction
1971	# DALE, Charlie		90	Died in a Teaneck, N.J., nursing home
1957	DALE, Dorothy (Hyman)		74	Burned to death in her shack
1961	DALE, Esther		75	Died in Hollywood, CA
1972	DALE, Margaret		92	
1994	# DALE, Virginia		77	Complications of emphysema (in Burbank, CA)
1975	#+ DALEY, Cass		59	Neck pierced by glass in a fall at home (in Hollywood, CA)
1989	DALI, Salvador		84	Heart failure & pneumonia
1983	# DALIO, Marcel		83	
1971	# DALL, John	☆	52	Heart attack (in Beverly Hills, CA)
1973	DALLIMORE, Maurice		72	Laennec's cirrhosis (in Los Angeles, CA)
1989	DALRYMPLE, Ian		85	
1984	DALTON, Doris		82	Cardiac arrest
1972	DALTON, Dorothy		78	Died in Scarsdale, NY
1978	DALY, James		59	Heart attack (in Nyack, NY) — Do not confuse with James L. Daly
1933	DALY, James L.		81	Heart trouble (in Philadelphia, PA)
1991	# DALY, John		77	Cardiac arrest
1957	DALY, Mark		70	
1957	D'AMBRICOURT, Adrienne		69	Heart attack after her car struck another car (in Hollywood, CA)
1989	D'AMICO, Teresa Tirelli		81	Brain tumor
1994	#+ DAMITA, Lili		92	Alzheimer's disease (in Palm Beach, FL)
1987	DAMON, Cathryn		56	Cancer
1962	DAMON, Les		53	
1955	# DAMPIER, Claude		75	Pneumonia (in London, England)
• 1950	DAMROSCH, Walter		88	Died in New York, NY
1983	DANA, Leora		60	Cancer
1987	# DANA, Viola		90	Heart failure
1965	+ DANDRIDGE, Dorothy	☆	42	Overdose of Tofranil, an anti-depressant (in West Hollywood, CA)
1987	DANDRIDGE, Ruby		87	
1934	+ DANE, Karl		47	Suicide (gunshot) in Los Angeles, CA
• 1962	# DANIEL, Billy		49	Coronary attack (in Beverly Hills, CA)
1963	# DANIELL, Henry		69	Died in Santa Monica, CA
1971	#+ DANIELS, Bebe		70	Cerebral hemorrhage (in London, England)
1955	#+ DANIELS, Victor		66	Cancer (in Ventura, CA)
1988	DANIELS, William "Billy"		73	Stomach cancer
1994	DANO, Royal "Ted" Jr.		47	Liver failure (in Santa Monica, CA)
1994	DANO, Royal Sr.		71	Pulmonary fibrosis (at his home in Santa Monica, CA)
1992	DANOVA, Cesare		66	Heart attack
1982	+ DANTINE, Helmut		63	Massive coronary
1992	DANTON, Ray		61	After suffering from kidney disease
1992	+ DARBY, Ken	★	82	Died in Sherman Oaks, CA
• 1996	D'ARCY, Alexander		87	Heart failure (in West Hollywood, CA)
1969	# D'ARCY, Roy		75	Died in Redlands, CA
• 1995	DARDEN, Severn		65	Heart failure (at his home in Santa Fe, N.M.)
1955	DARIEN, Frank Jr.		?	Died in Hollywood, CA
1973	#+ DARIN, Bobby	☆	37	After heart surgery (in Hollywood, CA)
• 1971	DARK, Christopher		?	Heart attack (in Hollywood, CA)

...DEATHS OF MOVIE AND TELEVISION PERSONALITIES — BY NAME...

YEAR	NAME		AGE	CAUSE AND/OR PLACE OF DEATH
• 1974	# DARLING, Candy		25	Cancer and pneumonia (in New York)
• 1936	DARLING, Ida		60	Died in Hollywood, CA
1963	DARMOND, Grace		65	Lung ailment (in Los Angeles, CA)
1983	DARNAY, Toni		61	Lung cancer
1965	#+ DARNELL, Linda		43	Fire burns (in Chicago, IL)
1968	D'ARRAST, Harry		71	
1970	+ DARRELL, J. Stevan		65	Died in Hollywood, CA
1976	# DARRO, Frankie		58	Heart attack (in Huntington Beach, CA)
1974	DARVAS, Lili		72	Died at her Manhattan home
1971	# DARVI, Bella		42	Suicide (opened the gas jets on her apartment stove) in Monaco
1967	#+ DARWELL, Jane	★	87	Heart attack (in Woodland Hills, CA)
1974	# DASH, Pauly		55	After cancer treatment (at a hospital in Miami, FL)
1986	DaSILVA, Howard		76	
1980	+ DASSIN, Joseph "Joe"		42	Heart attack (in Papeete, Tahiti)
1963	+ DASTAGIR, Sabu			(See under Sabu, below)
1960	+ DASTAGIR, Sheik		47	
1959	# DAUBE, Belle		71	Died in Hollywood, CA
1993	DAUGHERTY, Herschel		82	Pneumonia
1978	# DAUPHIN, Claude		75	Intestinal occlusion
1936	#+ DAVENPORT, Alice		82	Died in Los Angeles, CA
1977	DAVENPORT, Dorothy		81	Died in Woodland Hills, CA
1949	DAVENPORT, Harry		83	Heart attack (in Los Angeles, CA)
1993	DAVENPORT, John		62	Diabetes
1977	#+ DAVES, Delmar		73	
1993	DAVID, Mack		81	Died in a hospital in Rancho Mirage, CA
1978	# DAVID, Thayer		51	Heart attack (in New York, NY)
1968	DAVIDSON, John		81	Heart failure (in Los Angeles, CA) — Do not confuse with the singer
1950	DAVIDSON, Max		75	After a long illness (in Woodland Hills, CA)
1947	DAVIDSON, William B.		59	Following an operation (in Santa Monica, CA)
1955	DAVIES, Betty Ann		44	Complications after appendectomy (in Manchester, England)
1961	#+ DAVIES, Marion		64	Cancer (in Hollywood, CA)
1994	DAVIES, Richard		80	Heart attack (in Weaverville, CA)
1976	DAVIES, Rupert		60	Cancer (in London, England)
1994	# DAVIS, Battle		42	Non-Hodgkins lymphoma
1989	#+ DAVIS, Bette	★	81	Breast cancer
1963	DAVIS, Boyd		77	Died in Hollywood, CA
1991	+ DAVIS, Brad		41	Complications from A.I.D.S.
• 1936	DAVIS, Edwards		64	Died in Hollywood, CA
• 1965	DAVIS, George		75	Cancer (in Woodland Hills, CA)
1982	DAVIS, Herbert H.		52	
1968	DAVIS, Jack		?	
1992	# DAVIS, Jackie		78	Respiratory failure
1991	DAVIS, Jerome L.		73	Stroke
1981	#+ DAVIS, Jim		65	Following surgery for a perforated ulcer (in Northridge, CA)
1961	+ DAVIS, Joan (Williams)		53	Heart attack (in Palm Springs, CA)
1983	DAVIS, Johnny "Scat"		73	Heart attack
• 1979	DAVIS, Karl "Killer"		72	Died in Chicago, IL
1969	DAVIS, Mildred		68	Heart attack (in Santa Monica, CA)
1991	#+ DAVIS, Miles		65	Pneumonia, respiratory failure & a stroke
1949	DAVIS, Owen Jr.		42	Drowned after falling overboard from a sloop (in L.I. South, NY)
1990	DAVIS, Patrick "Grampy"		87	Heart attack
1985	DAVIS, Rick		71	Heart failure
1993	DAVIS, Robert		76	Emphysema
1974	# DAVIS, Rufe		66	Died in Torrance, CA
1990	+ DAVIS, Sammy Jr.		64	Throat cancer
1970	# DAW, Evelyn		58	
1988	DAWN, Hazel		98	
1966	DAWN, Isabel		62	Pulmonary infection (in Woodland Hills, CA)
1950	DAWSON, Dorice		56	
• 1953	DAWSON, Frank		83	Died in Hollywood, CA
1987	DAWSON, Hal K.		90	Stroke
1985	DAWSON, Kurt		43	Complications from cancer
1984	DAWSON, Ronald		81	Pneumonia
1988	#+ DAY, Dennis		71	Amyotrophic lateral sclerosis
1978	DAY, Josette		63	

• New entry. # Original name (Pt. 7). + Interment (Pt. 5).   159   ☆ Oscar nominee, ★ Oscar winner (Pt. 10)

...DEATHS OF MOVIE AND TELEVISION PERSONALITIES – BY NAME...

YEAR	NAME		AGE	CAUSE AND/OR PLACE OF DEATH
1992	DEA, Marie		72	
1984	DEACON, Richard		62	Heart attack
1991	DeACUTIS, William		33	Brain lymphoma
1955	#+ DEAN, James	☆	24	Automobile accident (near Paso Robles, CA)
1952	DEAN, Julia		74	Died in Hollywood, CA
1988	DEAN, Priscilla		91	As a result of a fall
1990	# DEANE, Palmer		56	A.I.D.S.
1974	DEARING, Edgar		81	Lung cancer (in Woodland Hills, CA)
1969	DeAUBRY, Diane		79	Heart attack
1981	DeBANZIE, Brenda		66	Following surgery on a non-malignant tumor (in Sussex, England)
1948	DeBRULIER, Nigel		69	
1958	DEBUCOURT, Jean		64	Leukemia (in Paris, France)
1989	DeCARLO, Vinnie		54	Heart attack
1966	# DeCASALIS, Jeanne		70	
• 1996	DECKARD, James		58	Brain cancer (in Garden Grove, CA)
1919	DECKER, Kathryn Browne		?	Died in Columbo, Ceylon, while on a tour of the Orient
1977	DECKERS, Eugene		60	
1950	+ DeCORDOBA, Pedro		68	Found dead of a heart attack (at his home in Sunland, CA)
1973	# DeCORDOVA, Arturo		66	Died in Mexico City, Mexico
1973	DeCORSIA, Ted		69	Natural causes (in Encino, CA)
1988	DEENE, Lally		68	
1986	DEERING, Olive		67	Cancer
1993	+ DeFORE, Don		80	Cardiac arrest (in Santa Monica, CA)
1983	deFUNES, Louis		68	Heart attack
1940	DeGRASSE, Joseph		67	Heart attack (in Eagle Rock, CA)
1953	DeGRASSE, Sam		78	Heart attack (in Hollywood, CA)
• 1941	# DeGREY, Sydney		55	
1993	DeGROOT, Katherine Hynes		88	Complications from a stroke (in Englewood, NJ)
1990	DeGRUNWALD, Dimitri		76	
1979	DeHAVEN, Carter Jr.		68	After a brief illness (in Encino, CA)
1977	DeHAVEN, Carter Sr.		90	Died in Woodland Hills, CA
1992	# DEHNER, John		76	Emphysema & diabetes
1968	# DEKKER, Albert		63	Found dead (with S. and M. trappings) in his bath tub (in H'wood)
1981	DeKOVA, Frank		71	Found dead in his home (in Sepulveda, CA)
1988	DeKOVEN, Roger		81	Cancer
1950	DeLaMOTTE, Marguerite		47	Cerebral thrombosis (in San Francisco, CA)
• 1995	DELANEY, Bessie		104	Died in her sleep
1959	DELANEY, Charles		67	Died in Hollywood, CA
1992	DELAUDER, Doug		38	A.I.D.S.
1992	DeLAURENTIIS, Luigi		75	After a 3-year illness
1943	DeLEATH, Vaughn		42	Uremic poisoning and a heart condition
1992	DELERUE, Georges	★	67	After a brief illness
1975	DELEVANTI, Cyril		88	Lung cancer (in Hollywood, CA)
• 1969	DELGADO, Maria		60	Died in Hollywood, CA
• 1973	DELGADO, Roger		53	Automobile accident (in Turkey)
• 1977	DELL, Claudia		67	Died in Hollywood, CA
1934	DELL, Dorothy		19	Automobile accident (in Pasadena, CA)
1988	DELL, Gabriel		68	Leukemia
• 1959	# DEL MAR, Claire		57	Murdered (head and knife wounds) in her Carmel, CA home
1984	+ DELMAR, Kenny		73	Died in a Stamford, CT hospital
1983	# DEL RIO, Dolores		77	Natural causes
1961	DEL RUTH, Roy		66	Heart attack
• 1975	# DEL VAL, Jean		82	Heart attack (in Pacific Palisades, CA)
1988	DELVANDO, Amapola		78	
• 1954	# DEMAIN, Gordon		56	
1983	DEMAREST, William	☆	91	
1992	DEMAZIS, Orane		87	
1993	DeMILLE, Agnes		88	Stroke & heart failure in her sleep (at home in NY)
1959	#+ DeMILLE, Cecil B.	☆	77	Heart disease (in Los Angeles, CA)
• 1995	DeMILLE, Katherine (Quinn)		83	Alzheimer's disease (in Tucson, AZ)
1955	+ DeMILLE, William C.		76	Died in Playa del Rey, CA
1983	DEMPSEY, Jack		87	After an illness of several years
1947	DEMPSEY, Thomas		79	After a long illness (in Hollywood, CA)
1991	DEMPSTER, Carol		89	After a long illness
1987	DEMPSTER, Hugh		86	Heart failure

• New entry. # Original name (Pt. 7). + Interment (Pt. 5).　　160　　☆ Oscar nominee, ★ Oscar winner (Pt. 10)

...DEATHS OF MOVIE AND TELEVISION PERSONALITIES — BY NAME...

YEAR	NAME		AGE	CAUSE AND/OR PLACE OF DEATH
1990	DEMY, Jacques		59	Leukemia
1994	DENGEL, Jake		61	Cancer (at Group One Hospice in Sherman Oaks, CA)
• 1995	DENNER, Charles		69	Cancer (in Dreux, France)
1992	# DENNIS, Sandy	★	54	Ovarian cancer
1994	DENNY, C. Patterson		46	Cancer (in Glenbrook, IL)
1990	DENNY, Joe		61	Respiratory failure
1967	#+ DENNY, Reginald		75	Stroke (in Surrey, England)
1963	DENT, Vernon		63	Died in Hollywood, CA
1988	DENTLER, Mary Ann		96	Stroke
1988	dePAUL, Gene Vincent		68	
1988	DEPEW, Joseph D.		76	
• 1957	DEPP, Harry		70	Died in Hollywood, CA
1931	+ DePUTTI, Lya		31	Pneumonia after operation to remove chicken bone from her throat
1993	+ DeRITA, Joe		83	Pneumonia (in Woodland Hills, CA)
1952	# DeROACH, Charles		72	
1992	DERR, Richard		74	Pancreatic cancer & heart failure
1986	DeRUE, Carmen		78	Heart attack
1988	DeSALES, Francis		76	Cancer
1989	DeSANTIS, Joe		80	Congestive heart failure
1974	DeSICA, Vittorio	☆	73	Died in Paris, France
1993	# DESMOND, Florence		87	Unreported causes (in Guildford, England)
1985	+ DESMOND, Johnny		65	Cancer
1949	DESMOND, William		71	Heart attack (in Los Angeles, CA)
1963	DeSOTO, Henry		75	
1990	DeTREAUX, Tamara "E.T."		31	Respiratory & heart problems
1980	DEUTSCH, Adolph	★	82	
1991	DEUTSCH, David		65	Kidney failure
1969	DEUTSCH, Ernst		78	Heart attack (in Berlin, West Germany)
1992	DEUTSCH, Helen		85	Natural causes
1982	# DEVEAU, Jack		47	Cancer
1990	DeVEGA, José Jr.		56	A.I.D.S.
1918	DEVERE, Margaret		22	Pneumonia
1958	DEVEREAUX, Jack		76	
1977	#+ DEVINE, Andy		71	Leukemia (in Orange, CA)
1994	DEVINE, Jerry		85	Died in Santa Barbara, CA)
1990	DeVITO, Julia		85	
1991	# DEVLIN, J. G.		84	
1976	# DEVORE, Dorothy		77	Died in Woodland Hills, CA
1991	DEWHURST, Colleen		67	Cancer
1972	# DeWILDE, Brandon	☆	30	After his car skidded on wet pavement and hit a truck (in Denver)
• 1976	DEWITT, Alan "Boomie"		52	Heart attack (in Los Angeles, CA)
1990	DeWITT, Lew		53	Intestinal disorder
1974	#+ DeWOLFE, Billy		67	Cancer (in Los Angeles, CA)
1984	DEXTER, Alan		65	Heart attack
1941	DEXTER, Elliott		71	After several weeks illness (in Amityville, NY)
1991	DHIEGH, Khigh		75	Kidney & heart disease
1988	# DIAMOND, I. A. L.		67	Multiple myeloma (a form of cancer)
1985	+ DIAMOND, Selma		64	Cancer
• 1968	# DICKERSON, Henry		61	Cerebral thrombosis (in Lynwood, CA)
1945	DICKSON, Gloria		28	Asphyxiation from a fire
1935	DICKSON, W. K. Laurie		75	
1975	DIERKES, John		69	Emphysema
1972	# DIETERLE, William	☆	79	Died in Ottobrunn, West Germany
1992	#+ DIETRICH, Marlene	☆	90	Died in Paris, France
1983	DIETZ, Howard		86	
1989	DIFFRING, Anton		70	
1947	+ DIGGES, Dudley		68	Stroke (in New York, NY)
1979	DIGNAM, Basil		74	Died in England
1989	DIGNAM, Mark		80	
• 1995	DILLARD, William		83	Complications from lupus & pneumonia (in Manhattan)
1982	DILLAWAY, Donald P.		78	After a long illness
1933	DILLON, Edward "Eddie"		53	Heart attack (in Hollywood, CA)
1937	# DILLON, Jack		61	Pneumonia (in Los Angeles, CA)
1934	+ DILLON, John Francis		50	After suffering a heart attack at a dinner party (in Beverly Hills, CA)
1971	DILLON, Josephine		87	Died in Verdugo City, CA

YEAR	NAME		AGE	CAUSE AND/OR PLACE OF DEATH
• 1965	DILLON, Tim		77	Died in Burbank, CA
• 1962	# DILLON, Tom		66	Died in Hollywood, CA
1944	DILSON, John		53	
1944	#+ DINEHART, Alan Sr.		54	Heart attack (in Hollywood, CA)
1992	DINEHART, Alan Jr.		74	Emphysema
1956	DINGLE, Charles W.		68	After an illness of several months (in Worcester, MA)
• 1936	DIONE, Rose		60	Died in Los Angeles, CA
• 1954	DIONNE, Emelie		20	Epileptic seizure
• 1970	DIONNE, Marie		35	
• 1979	DIONNE, Oliva		71	Died in North Bay, Ontario, Canada
• 1971	+ DISNEY, Roy		77	
1966	#+ DISNEY, Walt		65	Circulatory collapse after lung surgery
1989	DITTMAN, Dean Gus		57	Heart failure
1988	#+ Divine		42	Heart disease
1982	DIX, Constance		60	
1970	DIX, Dorothy		77	
1949	#+ DIX, Richard	☆	55	Acute cardiac collapse (in Los Angeles, CA)
1992	DIXON, Adèle		83	Bronchial pneumonia
1972	# DIXON, Denver		82	Heart attack
1981	DIXON, Jean (actress)		84	After a long illness (in New York, NY)
1992	DIXON, Joan		61	Heart disease
1987	DOBSON, James		67	Heart attack
1966	DODD, (Rev.) Neal		88	After a long illness
1973	DODD, Claire		64	Cancer (in Beverly Hills, CA)
1964	DODD, Jimmie		54	Heart ailment (in Honolulu, Hawaii)
1994	DODSON, Jack		63	Heart failure after a year of failing health (in Encino, CA)
• 1964	# DODSWORTH, John		53	Suicide (asphyxiation) in Los Angeles, CA
1988	DOHERTY, Charla		41	Natural causes
• 1963	DOLENZ, George		55	Heart attack (in Hollywood, CA)
1941	#+ DOLLY, Jenny		48	Suicide (hanging) in Hollywood, CA
1970	#+ DOLLY, Rosie		77	Heart failure (in New York, NY)
1970	# DOMINGUEZ, Joe		76	Died in Woodland Hills, CA
1986	DOMINIQUE, Laurien		29	Embolism
1993	DONALD, James		76	Stomach cancer (at his home in Wiltshire, England)
1994	DONALDSON, Norma		68	Cancer (at Cedars-Sinai Med. Ctr. in Los Angeles, CA)
1958	DONAT, Robert	★	53	Asthma (in London, England)
1967	DONATH, Ludwig		67	Leukemia (in New York, NY)
1972	+ DONLEVY, Brian	☆	73	Throat cancer (in Woodland Hills, CA)
1991	DONN, Lee		96	Stroke
1988	# DONNELL, Jeff		66	Apparent heart attack
• 1937	DONNELLY, James		71	Died in Hollywood, CA
1982	DONNELLY, Ruth		86	
1987	# DONOVAN, Casey		43	Pulmonary infection
1987	DONOVAN, King		69	Cancer
1988	DONOVAN, Warde		72	
1958	DOONAN, Patric		33	Suicide (by gassing himself) in London, England
• 1967	DORLEAC, Francoise		25	After car skidded on wet road and burst into flames (Nice, France)
1975	#+ DORN, Philip		69	Heart attack (in Woodland Hills, CA)
1956	# DORO, Marie		74	Heart ailment (in New York, NY)
• 1980	# DORR, Harry		87	Pneumonia (in Los Angeles, CA)
1993	DORR, John		48	A.I.D.S.
1984	DORS, Diana		52	After two operations for ovarian cancer
1993	D'ORSA, Lonnie		96	Died in Beverly Hills, CA
1983	+ D'ORSAY, Fifi		79	Cancer
1957	#+ DORSEY, Jimmy		53	Cancer (in New York, NY)
1956	#+ DORSEY, Tommy		51	Choked while asleep (in Greenwich, CT)
• 1958	DOUCET, Catherine		82	Died in New York, NY
1994	DOUCETTE, John		73	Cancer (at his home in Cabazon, CA)
• 1938	DOUGHERTY, Virgil Jack		42	Suicide (carbon monoxide) in Hollywood, CA
1945	# DOUGLAS, Donald "Don"		40	Complications after appendectomy (in Los Angeles, CA)
1993	DOUGLAS, Gordon		85	Cancer (in Los Angeles, CA)
1993	DOUGLAS, Hugh		78	Heart attack (in Los Angeles, CA)
1994	DOUGLAS, Jack		72	Cancer (in Los Angeles, CA)
1981	# DOUGLAS, Melvyn	★	80	Pneumonia and cardiac complications (in New York, NY)
1959	+ DOUGLAS, Paul		52	Heart attack (in Hollywood, CA)

• New entry.   # Original name (Pt. 7).   + Interment (Pt. 5).

☆ Oscar nominee, ★ Oscar winner (Pt. 10)

YEAR	NAME		AGE	CAUSE AND/OR PLACE OF DEATH
1993	# DOUGLAS, Steve		55	Heart attack (during a studio recording session)
1978	DOUGLAS, Tom		82	Heart attack (in Cuernavaca, Mexico)
1966	# DOUGLASS, Kent		58	
• 1956	DOVZHENKO, Alexander		62	Heart attack
1992	DOWELL, Clifton		44	A.I.D.S.
1969	+ DOWLING, Constance		49	Cardiac arrest (in Los Angeles, CA)
1976	# DOWLING, Eddie		81	Died in Smithfield, RI
• 1954	DOWLING, Joan		26	Found dead in a gas-filled room (in London, England)
1928	DOWLING, Joseph J.		80	After a 2-year illness
1985	DOWNEY, Morton Sr.		83	Effects of a stroke
1978	DOWNS, Cathy		52	
1994	DOWNS, Johnny "Our Gang"		80	Cancer (at his home in Coronado, CA)
• 1995	DOYLE, Mary		63	Lung cancer (in New York)
1973	DOYLE, Maxine		58	Cancer (in Studio City, CA)
• 1975	DOYLE, Patricia		60	Cancer (in Los Angeles, CA)
1991	DOYLE, Roz		49	Breast cancer
1991	DOZIER, William		83	Stroke
1980	DRAGONETTE, Jessica		75	Heart attack (in New York City)
1992	# DRAKE, Alfred		77	Heart failure after a long bout with cancer
1994	DRAKE, Charles		79	After a lengthy illness (at his home in East Lyme, CT)
1989	DRAKE, Dona		69	Cancer
1990	DRAKE, Fabia		86	
1991	DRAKE, Oliver		88	After a long illness
1982	#+ DRAKE, Tom		64	Lung cancer
1989	DRANE, Gary		46	
1990	DRAPER, Don		62	A.I.D.S.
1956	DRAPER, Ruth		72	Apparent heart attack (in New York)
1949	DRAYTON, Alfred		68	
1981	DRAYTON, Noel		68	
1993	DREIFUSS, Arthur		85	After a bout with the flu (in Studio City, CA)
1965	# DRESSER, Louise	☆	86	Intestinal obstruction (in Woodland Hills, CA)
1934	#+ DRESSLER, Marie	★	65	Cancer (in Santa Barbara, CA)
1974	DREW, Ann		83	Died in a Miami nursing home
1993	DREW, Larry		73	After a long illness (in London, England)
1919	DREW, Sidney		54	Uremic poisoning and heart disease (in New York, NY)
1989	DRINKWATER, Terry		53	Cancer
1968	DRISCOLL, Bobby		31	Hardening of the arteries (in New York, NY)
1983	DRISCOLL, Robert Miller		55	
1986	DRIVAS, Robert		50	
• 1988	DRU, Jason		58	Emphysema-induced heart failure (in Van Nuys, CA)
1978	DRURY, Norma		?	
1989	DRYHURST, Edward		84	
1992	DUBMAN, Laura		69	Kidney failure (in New York)
1951	+ DUCHIN, Eddie		41	Leukemia (in New York, NY)
1955	DUDLEY, Robert Y.		80	Died in San Clemente, CA
1971	# DUEL, Peter		31	Apparent suicide (gunshot) in Hollywood, CA
1992	DUELL, Randall	☆	89	Stroke
1990	DUFF, Howard		72	Heart attack
1994	# DUFF-GRIFFIN, William		54	Prostate cancer (at the Manhattan home of his companion)
1993	DUFFY, John Paul		42	Apparent suicide (in W. Hollywood, CA)
1992	DUFINE, Herbert		61	Heart condition
1952	DUFKIN, Sam		61	
1958	# DUGAN, Tom		69	Automobile accident (in Redlands, CA)
1988	DUGGAN, Andrew		64	Cancer (in Westwood, CA)
1977	DUGGAN, Jan		?	Died in Los Angeles, CA
1982	DUKE, E. L. Tony		48	Heart attack
1994	DUKE, Edward		50	Cancer (in London, England)
1994	DULO, Jane		75	After cardiac surgery (at Cedars-Sinai Med. Ctr. in Los Angeles)
1989	DuMAURIER, Daphne		81	After a brief illness
1974	DUMBRILLE, Douglas		85	Heart attack (in Woodland Hills, CA)
1964	DUMKE, Ralph		64	Died in Sherman Oaks, CA
1965	#+ DUMONT, Margaret		75	Heart attack (in Los Angeles, CA)
• 1953	DUNBAR, David		60	Died in Woodland Hills, CA
1991	# DUNBAR, Dixie		72	After a series of heart attacks
1992	DUNBAR, Dorothy		90	

YEAR		NAME		AGE	CAUSE AND/OR PLACE OF DEATH
•	1933	DUNBAR, Helen		65	Died in Los Angeles, CA
	1960	DUNCAN, Bud		77	Circulatory failure (in Los Angeles, CA)
•	1972	DUNCAN, Evelyn		79	Died in Bellflower, CA
	1927	+ DUNCAN, Isadora		49	Strangled in her car by a scarf that caught in rear wheel (in France)
	1972	# DUNCAN, Kenne		69	Stroke (in Hollywood, CA)
	1993	DUNCAN, Mary (Sanford)		98	Natural causes
	1959	+ DUNCAN, Rosetta "Topsy"		58	Automobile accident (in Acero, IL)
	1986	+ DUNCAN, Vivian "Little Eva"		84	Alzheimer's disease
	1961	DUNCAN, William A.		80	Died in Hollywood, CA
	1953	DUNDEE, Jimmie		52	Leukemia (in Woodland Hills, CA)
•	1994	# DUNFEE, Nora		78	After a brief illness (in Manhattan, NY)
•	1972	# DUNHAM, Phil		87	Died in Los Angeles, CA
	1970	DUNLAP, Scott		77	
	1966	# DUNN, Bobby		74	Heart attack
	1987	DUNN, Clara Whips		90	Congestive heart failure
	1951	DUNN, Edward F. "Eddie"		55	Died in Hollywood, CA
	1966	DUNN, Emma		91	Died in Los Angeles, CA
	1967	#+ DUNN, James	★	65	Died in Santa Monica, CA
	1983	DUNN, Josephine		76	Cancer
	1976	DUNN, Liam		59	Emphysema and other medical complications
	1973	# DUNN, Michael	☆	39	Congenital chondrodystrophy (dwarfism) in London, England
	1990	DUNN, Patricia		60	Lung cancer
	1990	DUNN, Peter		68	Heart attack
•	1968	DUNN, Ralph		65	
•	1937	DUNN, Robert "Bobby"		45	Heart attack (in Hollywood, CA)
	1982	+ DUNNE, Dominique		23	Strangled by her boyfriend
	1990	#+ DUNNE, Irene	☆	88	Heart failure
	1992	DUNNE, Philip		84	Cancer
	1991	DUNNOCK, Mildred	☆	90	Died in Oak Bluffs, Martha's Vineyard, MA
	1956	DUPONT, E. A.		64	After a long bout with cancer
	1987	DuPRE, Jacqueline		42	Multiple sclerosis
	1984	DUPREZ, June		66	
	1984	DURANT, Jack		78	Cancer
	1980	#+ DURANTE, Jimmy		86	Pneumonitis (in Santa Monica, CA)
	1989	DURANTE, Vito		64	A.I.D.S.
	1975	+ DURFEE, Minta (Arbuckle)		85	Congestive heart failure (in Woodland Hills, CA)
	1935	#+ DURKIN, Junior		19	Automobile accident (near San Diego, CA)
	1991	+ DUROCHER, Leo		86	Natural causes (in Palm Springs, CA)
	1968	+ DURYEA, Dan		61	Cancer (in Los Angeles, CA)
	1963	# DURYEA, George		67	(See Tom Keene)
	1990	d'USSEAU, Arnaud		73	After surgery
	1967	DUVIVIER, Julien		71	After his car hit another car and tree (in Paris, France)
	1990	DUX, Pierre		82	
	1979	#+ DVORAK, Ann		67	Died in Honolulu, Hawaii
	1981	#+ DWAN, Alan		96	Heart failure (in Woodland Hills, CA)
•	1940	DWIRE, Earl		55	Died in Carmichael, CA
	1950	DYALL, Franklin		76	Died in Worthing, England
	1985	DYALL, Valentine		75	
•	1933	DYER, William J. "Billy"		52	
	1991	DYER-BENNETT, Richard		73	
		ⅇ			
	1929	+ EAGELS, Jeanne	☆	35	Alcohol and sleeping pills overdose (in New York, NY)
	1959	# EAGLE, Jimmy		52	Cirrhosis of the liver (in Los Angeles, CA)
•	1995	EAGLE, White		43	A.I.D.S. (in Sioux Falls, S.D.)
	1989	EAMES, John Matthew		64	
	1971	# EAMES, Virginia		81	(See Virginia True Boardman)
	1993	EARLE, Don (TV sportscaster)		64	
	1958	EARLE, Dorothy		?	
•	1972	EARLE, Edward		90	Died in Woodland Hills, CA
	1984	EARLE, Merie		95	Uremic poisoning after colon cancer surgery
	1985	# EARLES, Harry		83	
	1956	EASON, Reeves "Breezy"		69	Heart attack (in Sherman Oaks, CA)
	1990	EASTERLING, Gary Lamont		38	
	1970	EATON, Jay		70	Heart attack (in Hollywood, CA)
	1948	EATON, Mary		46	After a heart attack (in Hollywood, CA)

	YEAR		NAME		AGE	CAUSE AND/OR PLACE OF DEATH
	1979		EBERLE, Ray		60	Heart attack
	1981		EBERLY, Bob		65	After 4 heart attacks from cancer chemotherapy
	1960		EBURNE, Maude		85	Died in Hollywood, CA
	1986		ECCLES, Donald		77	Automobile crash
	1991		ECKHARDT, John		82	Heart failure
	1993		ECKSTINE, Billy		78	Cardiac arrest after suffering a stroke
•	1995		EDDINGTON, Paul		68	After suffering a rare form of skin cancer (in London, Eng.)
	1990		EDDY, Helen Jerome		92	Heart failure
	1967	#+	EDDY, Nelson		65	After suffering a stroke (while performing on stage in Miami Beach)
•	1970	+	EDENS, Roger	★	64	Cancer
	1931		EDESON, Robert		63	Hardening of the arteries (in Hollywood, CA)
	1971	+	EDWARDS, Cliff "Ukelele Ike"		76	Died in Hollywood, CA
	1990		EDWARDS, Douglas		73	Cancer of the bladder
	1967		EDWARDS, Edna Park		72	Died in Burbank, CA
	1991		EDWARDS, George		67	Cancer
	1988		EDWARDS, Gloria		43	Cancer
•	1945	#	EDWARDS, Gus		64	Died in Los Angeles, CA
	1986		EDWARDS, Guy		51	Heart attack
•	1952		EDWARDS, Henry		70	Died in Chobham, England
•	1925		EDWARDS, J. Gordon		57	
	1970		EDWARDS, James		58	Heart attack (in San Diego, CA)
	1988	#	EDWARDS, Jimmy		68	Bronchial pneumonia (Do not confuse with James Edwards, d. 1970)
•	1965	#	EDWARDS, Neely		75	Died in Woodland Hills, CA
	1965		EDWARDS, Sarah		81	Died in Hollywood, CA
	1937	+	EDWARDS, Snitz		75	Arthritis after a long illness (in Los Angeles, CA)
•	1996	#+	EDWARDS, Vince		67	Pancreatic cancer (in Los Angeles, CA)
•	1995		EGAN, Eddie		65	Cancer
	1987	+	EGAN, Richard		65	Prostate cancer
	1988		EGOROV, Youri		33	Complications of A.I.D.S.
	1990	#	EICHELBERGER, Ethyl		45	Suicide (cut wrists)
	1978	#+	EILERS, Sally		69	Heart attack (in Woodland Hills, CA)
•	1995		EISENSTAEDT, Alfred		96	Natural causes
	1948		EISENSTEIN, Sergei		50	Died in Moscow, Russia
	1992		EISLER, David		36	Pneumonia
	1950		ELDRIDGE, Anna Mae		56	
	1988	#	ELDRIDGE, Florence		86	Natural causes
	1961	#	ELDRIDGE, John		57	Heart attack (in Laguna Beach, CA)
•	1995	+	ELGART, Les		77	Heart attack (in Dallas, TX)
	1991		ELKINS, Lenore		77	Heart failure
	1992		ELLERBE, Harry		91	Died in Atlanta, GA
	1974	#+	ELLINGTON, Duke		75	Lung cancer and pneumonia (in New York, NY)
	1974	#+	ELLIOT, Cass		32	Heart attack, chronic obesity and exhaustion (in London, England)
	1992		ELLIOTT, Denholm	☆	70	AIDS-related tuberculosis
	1961	#	ELLIOTT, Dick		75	
•	1956		ELLIOTT, John H.		80	Heart attack (in Los Angeles, CA)
	1959		ELLIOTT, Lillian		83	Stroke (in Hollywood, CA)
	1951		ELLIOTT, Robert		72	
	1965	#	ELLIOTT, William "Wild Bill"		61	Cancer (in Las Vegas, NV)
	1983	#	ELLIOTT, William D.		49	(Do not confuse with William "Wild Bill" Elliott, d. 1965)
	1930		ELLIS, Diane		20	Died in Madras, India on her honeymoon
	1952		ELLIS, Edward		80	Died in Hollywood, CA
	1991		ELLIS, Karl		41	A.I.D.S.
	1970	#	ELLIS, Patricia		49	Cancer (in Kansas City, MO)
	1973		ELLIS, Robert "Bobby"		40	Kidney failure following an operation (in Los Angeles, CA)
•	1974		ELLIS, Robert Reel		82	Cardiac arrest (in Santa Monica, CA)
	1993	#	ELLISON, James		83	After breaking his neck in a fall (in Montecito, CA)
	1942		ELLSLER, Effie		87	Following a heart attack
	1985		ELLSWORTH, Stephen R.		77	Heart failure
•	1967		ELMAN, Mischa		76	Heart attack (in New York, NY)
	1945	#	ELMER, Billy		75	After a long illness (in Hollywood, CA)
	1981	#	ELSOM, Isobel		87	Died in Woodland Hills, CA
	1990		EMERSON, Elsie Mae		86	Complications from strokes
	1983		EMERSON, Faye		65	Stomach cancer
	1960	+	EMERSON, Hope	☆	61	Liver ailment
	1956	#	EMERSON, John		84	After a long illness

YEAR	NAME		AGE	CAUSE AND/OR PLACE OF DEATH
• 1944	# EMERTON, Roy		51	Died in England
1983	EMERY, Dick		65	
1945	# EMERY, Gilbert		70	
1964	EMERY, John		59	Died in New York, NY
1980	EMERY, Katherine		73	Pulmonary illnesses (in Portland, Maine)
1988	EMERY, Mary		91	
• 1994	EMHARDT, Robert		80	Died at his home in Ojai, CA
1946	+ EMMETT, Fern (Roquemore)		50	Died in Hollywood, CA
1980	EMNEY, Fred		79	
1991	EMR, Roland Jon		45	Murdered (shot)
• 1995	# ENDFIELD, Cy		80	Died in London, England
1981	ENGEL, Roy		67	Meningitis (in Burbank, CA)
• 1966	ENGLE, Billy		77	Heart attack (in Hollywood, CA)
1985	ENGLE, Darleen		48	Cancer
1969	# ENGLISH, John W.		66	
1993	ENGLUND, Kenneth		78	A recurring illness (in Woodland Hills, CA)
1992	ENRIGHT, Dan		74	After a brief illness
1965	ENRIGHT, Ray		69	Heart attack after a long illness
1990	ENRIQUEZ, Rene		58	Pancreatic cancer
1932	# ENTWISTLE, Peg		24	Suicide (jumped off the "Hollywood" Hills sign)
1992	EPHRON, Henry		81	
1992	EPPER, John		86	Prostate cancer
1992	# EPSTEIN, David S.		73	Heart attack
1991	# EPSTEIN, Jerry		69	Causes unreported (in London, England)
• 1995	# ERGAS, Joseph		72	Diabetes (in New York)
1986	# ERICKSON, Leif		72	
1951	+ ERROL, Leon		70	Heart attack (in Los Angeles, CA)
1990	Erté		97	
1985	ERVIN, (Senator) Sam		88	Kidney failure after gall bladder surgery
1965	ERWIN, June		47	Found dead in her home (in Carmichael, CA)
1967	+ ERWIN, Stuart	☆	65	Heart attack (in Beverly Hills, CA)
1992	# Esmeralda		65	Diabetes & complications
1990	ESMOND, Jill		82	
1973	ESSLER, Fred		77	After a long illness
• 1995	ESTABROOK, Ted		76	Died in New York
1943	ETHIER, Alphonse		68	After a long illness
1982	ETHRIDGE, Ella		88	
1978	+ ETTING, Ruth		81	Died in Colorado Springs, CO
1945	EVANS, Charles		88	
1985	EVANS, Clifford		73	
1968	EVANS, Douglas		64	
1976	EVANS, Edith	☆	88	After a brief illness (in Cranbrook, Kent, England)
1954	EVANS, Evan		53	
• 1952	EVANS, Herbert		68	Died in San Gabriel, CA
1950	EVANS, Jack		57	Heart attack (in Hollywood, CA)
1991	EVANS, John Morgan		49	After a long illness
1983	EVANS, Madge		73	Cancer (in Oakland, NJ)
1989	EVANS, Maurice		87	
1989	EVANS, Peter		38	Complications of A.I.D.S.
1969	EVANS, Rex		66	Following surgery (in Glendale, CA)
1987	EVANS, Wilbur W.		81	
1967	EVELYN, Judith		54	Cancer
1968	EVEREST, Barbara		77	Died in London, England
• 1996	EVERSON, William K.		67	Prostate cancer (in New York)
1948	EVERTON, Paul		79	Following a heart attack (in Woodland Hills, CA)
1994	EWART, John		66	Cancer (in Sydney, Australia)
1994	# EWELL, Tom		85	After a long series of illnesses (in Woodland Hills, CA)
1957	# EYTHE, William		38	Acute hepatitis (in Los Angeles, CA)
	F			
• 1996	FABREGAS, Manolo		75	After suffering a heart attack (in Mexico City)
1994	FABRI, Zoltan		77	Heart attack (at his home in Budapest, Hungary)
1990	FABRIZI, Aldo		84	Heart attack
• 1995	FABRIZI, Franco		79	Cancer (in Cortemaggiore, Italy)
• 1938	+ FACTOR, Max		61	Kidney and liver ailment (at his home in Beverly Hills, CA)
1980	FADDEN, Tom		84	

YEAR	NAME		AGE	CAUSE AND/OR PLACE OF DEATH
1989	FAIN, Sammy		87	
• 1957	FAIR, Elinor		53	Died in Seattle, WA
• 1948	FAIR, Virginia		49	Died in Hollywood, CA
1939	#+ FAIRBANKS, Douglas Sr.		56	Heart attack
• 1945	FAIRBANKS, William		50	Lobar pneumonia (in Los Angeles, CA)
1941	# FAIRBROTHER, Sydney		69	Died in London, England
1980	# FAIRE, Virginia Brown		75	Died in a hospital in Laguna Beach, CA
1976	+ FAITH, Percy		67	Cancer
1991	FALAT, Stephen J.		34	After a long illness
1993	FALCO, Louis		50	A.I.D.S. (in New York)
• 1971	# FARLEY, Dot		90	Died in South Pasadena, CA
1947	# FARLEY, Jim		65	After a long illness (in a Pacolma, CA, sanitarium)
1988	FARLEY, Morgan		90	
1970	+ FARMER, Frances		55	Cancer (in Indianapolis, IN)
1983	FARMER, Richard		67	Cancer
1988	# FARMER, Virginia		90	
1929	FARNUM, Dustin		53	Kidney trouble (in New York, NY)
1961	+ FARNUM, Franklyn		85	Cancer (in Hollywood, CA)
1953	+ FARNUM, William		76	Cancer (in Los Angeles, CA)
1986	FARR, Derek		74	
• 1995	FARRAR, David		87	Died in South Africa
1967	FARRAR, Geraldine		85	
1925	FARRAR, Margaret		24	After swallowing poison
1990	#+ FARRELL, Charles		89	Cardiac arrest
1971	+ FARRELL, Glenda		66	Died in New York, NY
1988	FARRELL, Jack		52	Cancer
1989	FARRELL, Timothy (Sperl)		66	Heart condition
1968	+ FARRELL, Virginia		72	
1963	+ FARROW, John	☆	56	Apparent heart attack
1982	FASSBINDER, Rainer Werner		36	Lethal combination of cocaine & sleeping pills
1987	FAULKNER, Ralph B.		95	After a brief illness
1939	FAWCETT, George D.		77	Heart trouble
1961	+ FAY, Frank		63	Died in Santa Monica, CA
1991	FAYE, Frances		?	Following a series of strokes
1980	FAYE, Herbie		81	Died in Las Vegas, NV
1966	FAYE, Julia		72	Cancer (in Santa Monica, CA)
1992	FAYE, Marty		70	Heart attack
1985	#+ FAYLEN, Frank		79	After a long illness
1962	+ FAZENDA, Louise		66	Cerebral hemorrhage (in Beverly Hills, CA)
1971	FEALY, Maude		90	After being hospitalized (in Woodland Hills, CA)
1994	FEDDERSON, Donald		81	After a series of heart problems (at Cedars-Sinai Hosp. in L.A.)
1965	FEIST, Felix E.		55	Cancer
1993	FELD, Fritz		93	After a lengthy illness (in Santa Monica, CA)
1972	FELDMAN, Andrea		?	Suicide (jumped from the 14th floor of 51 Fifth Ave, NY)
1982	+ FELDMAN, Marty		48	Heart attack
1991	FELDMAN, Phil		69	Cancer
1993	+ FELLINI, Federico	★	73	After suffering a stroke & heart attack (in Rome)
1950	FELLOWES, Rockcliffe		65	Heart attack (in Los Angeles, CA)
1992	FELLOWS, Arthur		74	Cancer
1966	FELTON, Verna		76	Stroke (in North Hollywood, CA)
1992	FENNELL, Willie		72	Apparent heart attack
1988	FENNELLY, Parker		96	
1957	# FENTON, Frank		51	After a brief illness (in Los Angeles, CA)
1978	# FENTON, Leslie C.		76	Died in Montecito, CA
• 1971	FERGUSON, Al		83	
1961	FERGUSON, Elsie		78	Died in New London, CT
1978	FERGUSON, Frank		78	Cancer (in Los Angeles, CA)
1944	FERGUSON, George S.		60	Died in Hollywood, CA
1977	FERGUSON, Helen		76	Died in Clearwater, FL
1971	#+ Fernandel		67	Lung cancer (in Paris, France)
1986	FERNANDEZ, Emilio		82	Heart attack
1992	# FERRER, José	★	80	After a brief illness
1985	# FETCHIT, Stepin		83	Pneumonia & heart failure
• 1965	# FETHERSTON, Eddie		?	Heart attack (in Yucca Valley, CA)
1985	FEURY, Peggy		?	Automobile accident

YEAR	NAME	AGE	CAUSE AND/OR PLACE OF DEATH
1948	FEYDER, Jacques	54	
1988	FIDLER, Jimmie	89	
1979	+ FIEDLER, Arthur	84	Heart failure
1973	FIELD, Betty	55	Stroke (in Hyannis, MA)
1991	FIELD, Filip J.	67	Heart failure
• 1925	FIELD, George	46	Tuberculosis (in CA)
1990	FIELD, Irene	59	
1989	FIELD, Ron	55	Neurological impairment due to brain lesions
1992	# FIELD, Virginia	74	Cancer
1976	FIELD, Walter	100	Died in Hollywood, CA
1945	FIELDING, Edward	65	Heart attack (while mowing his lawn in Beverly Hills, CA)
1992	FIELDING, Sol Baer	83	Following a long illness
1979	# FIELDS, Gracie	81	After a hospital stay for bronchial pneumonia (in Capri, Italy)
1941	# FIELDS, Stanley	57	Heart attack (in Los Angeles, CA)
1978	#+ FIELDS, Totie	48	Apparent heart failure
1946	#+ FIELDS, W. C.	66	Violent hemorrhage, dropsy and other ailments (in Pasadena, CA)
1964	FILAURI, Antonio	74	Emphysema (in San Gabriel, CA)
1940	+ FINCH, Flora	71	Streptococcus infection (in Los Angeles, CA)
• 1995	FINCH, Nigel	45	An A.I.D.S.-related illness (at his home in London, Eng.)
1977	#+ FINCH, Peter ★	60	Heart attack (in Beverly Hills, CA)
1975	#+ FINE, Larry	73	Stroke (in Woodland Hills, CA)
1994	FINK, Agnes	74	Died in Germany
1953	# FINLAYSON, James	66	Heart attack (in Los Angeles, CA)
1989	FINLEY, Evelyn	73	Heart attack
1920	FINLEY, Ned	50	Suicide (strychnine) in New York, NY
• 1995	FINNEY, Jack	84	Pneumonia
1971	FioRITO, Ted	70	Heart attack (in Scottsdale, AZ)
1994	FIRKUSNY, Rudolf	82	Cancer (in New York)
1991	FISHELSON, Stanley	66	Natural causes
1944	# FISKE, Richard	29	Killed in action (in World War 2)
• 1944	FISKE, Robert L.	54	Congestive heart failure (in Sunland, CA)
1961	# FITZGERALD, Barry ★	72	Died in Dublin, Ireland
1941	FITZGERALD, Cissy	68	Died in Ovingdean, England
1982	FITZGERALD, Neil	90	
1976	# FITZGERALD, Walter	80	Died in London, England
1940	+ FITZMAURICE, George	45	After a 2-month streptococcus infection (in Los Angeles, CA)
1980	FITZPATRICK, James A.	78	Stroke (in Cathedral City, CA)
1993	FITZSIMMONS, Bob	53	Heart attack (after collapsing in a NY restaurant)
1983	#+ FIX, Paul	82	Kidney failure
• 1995	FLACK, Tim	?	After a long battle with A.I.D.S. (in Los Angeles, CA)
1962	FLAGSTAD, Kirsten	67	
• 1970	FLAHERTY, Pat J. Sr.	67	Heart attack (in New York)
1951	FLAHERTY, Robert	67	
• 1995	FLANDERS, Ed	60	Suicide (shot himself in the head) in Denny, CA
1979	#+ FLATT, Lester	64	Heart attack (in Nashville, TN)
1990	FLAUM, Mayer	89	Pneumonia
1976	FLAVIN, James	69	Ruptured aorta (in Los Angeles, CA)
• 1995	FLEETWOOD, Susan	51	After a 10-yr. bout with cancer (in Salisbury, England)
1979	FLEISCHER, Dave	84	Stroke (in Woodland Hills, CA)
1985	FLEISCHER, Louis	94	
1966	+ FLEMING, Eric	41	Drowned in a river while filming in Peru
1969	# FLEMING, Ian (actor)	80	Died in London, England (Do not confuse with the writer)
1949	+ FLEMING, Victor ★	64	After a heart attack
1988	FLETCHER, Bramwell	84	
1990	FLETCHER, Jack	68	Heart failure
1967	FLINT, Helen	69	Struck by a car while crossing the street (in Washington, D.C.)
• 1980	FLINT, Sam	98	Died in Woodland Hills, CA
1971	+ FLIPPEN, Jay C.	72	Aneurysm (in Hollywood, CA)
1917	FLOOD, Pauline "Baby Sunshine"	1	Run over by a truck (in Los Angeles, CA)
1991	FLORANCE, Sheila	75	Cancer
1984	FLOWERS, Bess	85	
1988	# FLOWERS, Wayland	48	Cancer
1990	FLUELLEN, Joel	82	Apparent suicide (gunshot)
1959	#+ FLYNN, Errol	50	Heart attack (in Vancouver, B.C., Canada)
1974	#+ FLYNN, Joe	49	Accidental drowning (in Beverly Hills, CA)

YEAR	NAME		AGE	CAUSE AND/OR PLACE OF DEATH
1970	# FLYNN, Sean		29	Missing in Cambodia (presumed dead)
1990	FOGERTY, Tom		48	
1968	#+ FOLEY, Red		58	Acute pulmonary edema (in Fort Wayne, IN)
1988	FOLSEY, George		90	
1982	#+ FONDA, Henry	★	77	Heart failure
1987	FONG, Benson		70	Following a stroke
1978	+ FONTAINE, Frank		58	Heart attack
1990	FONTANA, Arlene		54	Cancer
1974	+ FONTANE, Tony		47	Cancer (in Canoga Park, CA)
1983	#+ FONTANNE, Lynn	☆	95	Pneumonia
1991	# FONTEYN, Margot		71	Cancer
1953	FOO, Wing		43	Heart attack
1979	# FORAN, Dick		69	Died in Panorama City, CA
1981	FORAN, Mary		61	Died in Los Angeles, CA
1964	FORBES, Mary		84	Heart attack (in Beaumont, CA)
1951	# FORBES, Ralph		54	Died at Montefiore Hospital in New York, NY
1993	FORD, Constance		69	Cancer (in New York)
• 1995	FORD, Derek		62	Heart attack (in Bromly, Kent, England)
1953	# FORD, Francis		71	After a long illness (in Los Angeles, CA)
1957	FORD, Harrison		63	Died in Woodland Hills, CA (Do not confuse with the younger actor)
1973	#+ FORD, John	★	78	Cancer (in Palm Desert, CA)
1991	FORD, Lloyd		79	Ventricular fibrillation
1977	#+ FORD, Mary		52	Complications of diabetes and pneumonia (in Arcadia, CA)
1976	#+ FORD, Paul		74	Died in Mineola, NY
1988	FORD, Ross		65	Cardiac arrest
1991	# FORD, "Tennessee" Ernie		72	Liver disease
1966	# FORD, Wallace		68	Heart ailment (in Woodland Hills, CA)
1984	FOREMAN, Carl		69	Brain cancer
• 1996	FOREMAN, Jack P.		71	Heart attack (at his home in Brentwood, CA)
1992	FOREMAN, John		67	Heart attack
1982	FORMAN, Joey		53	Complications from pulmonary fibrosis
1926	FORMAN, Tom		33	Suicide (shot himself through the heart) in Venice, CA
1961	# FORMBY, George		56	Died in Preston, Lancashire, England
• 1941	FORREST, Alan		51	Died in Detroit, MI
1989	FORREST, William H.		86	Natural causes
• 1995	FORRISTAL, John		37	Automobile accident (in Colorado)
1982	FORSTER, Peter		62	
1967	# FORTE, Joe		71	After a heart attack (in Hollywood, CA)
1987	# FOSSE, Bob	★	60	Massive heart attack
1985	FOSTER, Alan		80	Cancer
1973	FOSTER, Dudley		47	Suicide (in London, England)
1974	FOSTER, Lewis R.		75	Heart attack
1976	# FOSTER, Norman		76	Cancer (in Santa Monica, CA)
1985	# FOSTER, Phil		71	Heart attack
1970	+ FOSTER, Preston		69	Died in La Jolla, CA
1970	FOULGER, Byron K.		69	Heart condition (in Hollywood, CA)
1988	FOULGER, Dorothy Adams		88	
1942	FOWLER, Brenda		59	Following a short illness (in Los Angeles, CA)
1960	+ FOWLER, Gene		70	
1994	FOX, George S.		89	Congestive heart failure (in Los Angeles, CA)
• 1959	# FOX, Harry		77	Died in Woodland Hills, CA
1984	FOX, John		60	
1980	FOX, Virgil		68	Cancer
1982	FOX, Virginia (Zanuck)		79	Complications from stroke & emphysema
1958	+ FOX, Wallace		63	
1952	FOX, William		73	
1993	FOX, William J.		95	Died in Fillmore, CA
• 1973	FOXE, Earle A.		84	Died in Los Angeles, CA
1991	# FOXX, Redd		68	Heart attack during rehearsal for new TV show
1977	+ FOY, Bryon		82	Following a series of heart attacks
1983	# FOY, Eddie Jr.		78	Cancer of the pancreas
1928	#+ FOY, Eddie Sr.		71	Heart disease (in Kansas City, MO)
1977	# FRANCEN, Victor		89	Died in Aix-en-Provence, France
1991	FRANCESCATTI, Zino		89	
1992	# FRANCHI, Franco		70	Hemorrhage (in a hospital in Rome, Italy)

YEAR	NAME		AGE	CAUSE AND/OR PLACE OF DEATH
1990	FRANCHI, Sergio		64	Brain cancer
1934	FRANCIS, Alec B.		65	Following an emergency operation (in Hollywood, CA)
• 1973	FRANCIS, Coleman		53	Arteriosclerosis (in Hollywood, CA)
1986	FRANCIS, Ivor		68	
1968	# FRANCIS, Kay		65	Cancer (in New York, NY)
• 1959	FRANCIS, Noel		48	Died in Los Angeles, CA
• 1952	FRANCIS, Olin		59	Died in Hollywood, CA
1987	FRANCIS, Raymond		76	
1955	+ FRANCIS, Robert		25	Airplane crash (in Burbank, CA)
• 1981	# FRANCIS, Sandra		47	Results of a motorcycle accident (in Santa Monica, CA)
1991	# FRANCIS, Wilma		73	Complications after lung surgery
1950	FRANCISCO, Betty		50	Heart attack (at her ranch in El Cerito, CA)
1991	# FRANCISCUS, James		57	Emphysema
1990	FRANCK, Edward A.		70	Pneumonia
1940	# FRANEY, Billy		55	Influenza (in Hollywood, CA)
1987	FRANJU, Georges		75	
1990	FRANK, Ben		56	Heart attack
1988	FRANK, Melvin		75	Complications following open-heart surgery
• 1995	FRANK, Richard Edward		42	Complications of A.I.D.S. (in Los Angeles, CA)
1994	FRANKEL, Daniel		91	Natural causes (in Winchester, N.H.)
1976	FRANKLIN, Alberta		79	
• 1995	# FRANKLIN, Melvin		52	Heart failure after a series of seizures (in Los Angeles, CA)
1939	+ FRANKLIN, Rupert		77	Died in Los Angeles, CA
1918	FRANKLIN, Ruth Darling		22	Crushed by auto while waiting for a street car
1931	+ FRANKLIN, Sidney (actor)		61	After a long illness (Do not confuse with director, d. 1972)
1972	#+ FRANKLIN, Sidney (director)	☆	79	(Do not confuse with silent film actor of same name, d. 1931)
1992	# FRANKOVICH, Mike	★	82	Pneumonia & Alzheimer's disease
1983	FRANZ, Eduard		81	
1987	# FRASER, Bill		79	
• 1974	FRASER, Harry		84	Died in Pamona, CA
1992	FRASER, June Joyce Lewis		75	Complications of pneumonia
1992	FRASER, Tom		60	Heart failure after exercising at his gym
1966	+ FRAWLEY, William		79	Heart attack (in Los Angeles, CA)
1985	# FRAZEE, Jane		67	Pneumonia (following a stroke)
1944	FRAZER, Robert W.		53	Died in Los Angeles, CA
• 1939	FRAZIN, Gladys		37	Suicide (jumped from her apartment window) in New York, NY
1975	FRECHETTE, Mark		27	Crushed to death by a barbell while in jail
1933	# FREDERICI, Blanche		55	Heart attack enroute to a Christmas church service (in Visalia, CA)
1986	+ FREDERICK, Freddie Burke		65	Ventricular arrhythmia due to myocardial infarction
1994	FREDERICK, Lynne		39	Found dead in bed, apparently of natural causes (in Los Angeles)
1990	FREDERICK, Pauline (TV news)		84	Heart attack (Do not confuse with actress Pauline Frederick, d. 1938)
1938	#+ FREDERICK, Pauline (actress)		54	Asthma (in Los Angeles) Do not confuse with P. Frederick, d. 1990
1970	FREDERICKS, Charles		50	Heart attack
1973	#+ FREED, Arthur		78	Heart attack
1994	FREED, Bert		74	Heart attack (while on vacation in British Columbia)
1991	FREEMAN, Everett		79	Renal failure
1967	# FREEMAN, Howard		68	
• 1969	+ FREEMAN, Young Frank		78	
1987	FREGONESE, Hugo		78	Heart attack
• 1995	#+ FRELENG, Friz		89	Natural causes
1952	FRENCH, Charles K.		92	After a heart attack (in Hollywood, CA)
1961	+ FRENCH, George B.		78	Heart attack (in Hollywood, CA)
1989	FRENCH, Norma		47	Lymphoma
1990	FRENCH, Valerie		59	Leukemia
1989	FRENCH, Victor		54	Lung cancer
1977	FREND, Charles		68	
1975	# FRESNAY, Pierre		77	Respiratory ailment (in Neuilly-sur-Seine, France)
1969	FREUND, Karl		79	
1961	FREY, Arno		60	Blood clot (in Los Angeles, CA)
1988	FREY, Leonard	☆	49	A.I.D.S.
1988	FRIEBUS, Florida		79	
1981	FRIEDHOFER, Hugo	★	80	While hospitalized after a fall in his home
1955	FRIGANZA, Trixie		84	After being bedridden with arthritis (in Flintridge, CA)
1972	#+ FRIML, Rudolph		92	Brain hemorrhage
1958	# FRISCO, Joe		68	After a long illness

...DEATHS OF MOVIE AND TELEVISION PERSONALITIES — BY NAME...

YEAR	NAME		AGE	CAUSE AND/OR PLACE OF DEATH
• 1973	FRITSCH, Willy		72	Heart attack (in Hamburg, Germany)
1975	#+ FRIZZELL, Lefty		47	After suffering a stroke
1988	# FROEBE, Gert		75	Heart attack
1987	FROHLICH, Gustav		85	Following surgery
1980	FROMAN, Jane		71	Natural causes
1989	FROME, Milton		78	Heart failure
1992	FROMMER, Ben		78	
1993	FROST, Terry		86	Heart failure (in Los Angeles, Ca)
1994	FRYD, Joseph		89	Following a stroke (in Rome, Italy)
1943	+ FRYE, Dwight		44	Heart attack (in Los Angeles, CA)
1993	FUCCELLO, Tom		55	A.I.D.S. (in a Van Nuys, CA, convalescent home)
1993	FUCHS, Daniel	★	84	Heart failure (in Los Angeles, CA)
1983	FUJIKAWA, Jerry		71	Heart disease
• 1996	FULCI, Lucio		68	After a long battle with diabetes (at his home in Rome, Italy)
1961	FULLER, Clem		52	Cancer
1980	FULLER, Frances		73	
• 1948	FULLER, Leslie		58	Died in Margate, England
1973	+ FULLER, Mary		85	Massive pulmonary embolism
1950	+ FULTON, Maude		69	Died at the Motion Picture Country Home, CA
1945	FUNG, Willie		49	Coronary occlusion (in Los Angeles, CA)
• 1971	FUQUA, Charles		60	Died in New Haven, CT
• 1938	FUREY, Barney		49	Liver ailment (in Los Angeles, CA)
1994	# FURNESS, Betty		78	Stomach cancer (at Sloan-Kettering Memorial Hospital, NY)
1991	# FURST, Anton	★	47	Suicide (jumped from 8th level of parking garage)
1966	FURTHMAN, Jules		78	Stroke (while vacationing in Oxford, England)
1994	FUSCO, Nelly		85	Cancer (at St. Francis Hosp. in Poughkeepsie, NY)
• 1947	FYFFE, Will		36	Fall from his hotel window (in St. Andrews, Scotland)
	G			
1972	# GAAL, Franceska		68	
1986	GABEL, Martin		73	
1976	# GABIN, Jean		72	Heart attack (in Neuilly, France)
1960	#+ GABLE, Clark	★	59	Heart attack (in Los Angeles, CA)
• 1995	+ GABOR, Eva		74	Complications of pneumonia (at Cedars-Sinai Med. Ctr. in L.A.)
• 1981	GAFNI, Miklos		57	Massive heart attack (at Kennedy Airport, NY)
• 1978	GAGE, Ben		62	Died in Los Angeles, CA
1991	GAILLARD, Slim		74	Cancer
• 1975	GAINES, Richard H.		70	Heart attack (in North Hollywood, CA)
1991	GAINSBOURG, Serge		62	Heart trouble
1948	GALE, Marguerite H.		63	
1979	GALENTO, Tony "Twoton"		69	Heart attack
• 1953	GALLAGHER, Raymond "Ray"		67	Heart attack (in Camarillo, CA)
1955	# GALLAGHER, Skeets		64	Following a heart attack (in Santa Monica, CA)
1972	GALLIAN, Ketti		?	
1984	GALLO, Mario		61	
• 1960	# GALVANI, Dino		69	Died in London, England
1990	GAMBARELLI, Maria		89	Cerebral hemorrhage
1959	GAN, Chester		50	Died in San Francisco, CA
1981	GANCE, Abel		92	Lung ailment
1985	GANTRY, Donald		52	Cancer
1956	+ GANZHORN, John W.		75	
1959	GARAT, Henri		57	Died in Toulon, France
• 1977	GARBER, Jan		82	Died in Shreveport, LA
1990	#+ GARBO, Greta	☆	84	
• 1938	GARCIA, Allan		51	Died in Los Angeles, CA
1970	GARCIA, Henry		66	After a long illness (in a hospital in San Antonio, TX)
• 1995	#+ GARCIA, Jerry		53	Heart attack (at Serenity Knolls drug treatment center in CA)
1989	GARDE, Betty		84	
1967	GARDEN, Mary		92	
1992	# GARDENIA, Vincent	☆	71	Found dead in his hotel room of a heart attack
1980	+ GARDINER, Reginald		77	Heart attack
1990	#+ GARDNER, Ava	☆	67	Pneumonia
1968	# GARDNER, Helen		83	Died in Orlando, FL
1989	GARDNER, Hy		80	Pneumonia
1977	GARDNER, Jack		77	After a short illness
• 1994	GARFIELD, David		51	Heart attack

• New entry.   # Original name (Pt. 7).   + Interment (Pt. 5).

☆ Oscar nominee,   ★ Oscar winner (Pt. 10)

YEAR	NAME		AGE	CAUSE AND/OR PLACE OF DEATH
1952	#+ GARFIELD, John	☆	39	Heart attack (in New York, NY)
1964	GARGAN, Edward		63	Died in New York, NY
1983	GARGAN, Mary Elizabeth		76	Lung cancer
1979	GARGAN, William	☆	73	Heart attack (in San Diego, CA)
1969	#+ GARLAND, Judy	☆	47	Accidental drug overdose (in London, England)
1978	GARMES, Lee	★	80	
1977	GARNER, Erroll		53	
1984	GARNER, Peggy Ann		52	Cancer
1977	GARNETT, Tay		83	Leukemia
• 1965	# GARON, Pauline		63	
1981	# GARRALAGA, Martin		85	
1993	GARRETT, Joy		47	Liver failure (in Los Angeles, CA)
1982	GARROWAY, Dave		69	Apparent suicide (gunshot)
• 1996	GARSON, Greer	★	92	Heart failure (at Presbyterian Hospital in Dallas, TX)
1993	GARVARENTZ, George		61	Heart failure (in Aubagne, France)
1950	GARWOOD, William		66	Coronary occlusion (in Los Angeles, CA)
1963	GASNIER, Louis		87	
1977	GATESON, Marjorie		86	Pneumonia (in New York, NY)
1990	GATLIFF, Frank		62	
1992	# GAUDIO, Joe		79	Cancer
1960	GAUGE, Alexander		46	Heart attack (in Woking, Surrey, England)
1974	GAUGUIN, Lorraine		50	Died when fire destroyed her Los Angeles home
1988	GAUTHIER, Suzanne		61	Cancer
1962	GAWTHORNE, Peter		77	Died in London, England
1963	GAXTON, William		70	
1955	GAYE, Howard		?	Died in London, England
1984	#+ GAYE, Marvin		44	Murdered (shot by his father) in Los Angeles, CA
1984	#+ GAYNOR, Janet	★	77	Pneumonia
• 1995	# GAZZO, Michael V.	☆	71	Complications from a stroke (in Los Angeles, CA)
1946	# GEARY, Bud		47	Injuries from an automobile crash (in Hollywood, CA)
1987	GEARY, John		47	Apparent heart attack (while driving)
• 1919	GEBHARDT, George M.		39	Tuberculosis
• 1954	GEBUEHR, Otto		76	Died in Wiesbaden, West Germany
• 1995	GEE, Kevin John		40	Pneumonia (in New York City)
1989	GEER, Lenny		75	Heart failure
1978	#+ GEER, Will		76	Respiratory arrest (in Los Angeles, CA)
1941	#+ GEHRIG, Lou		37	Amyotrophic lateral sclerosis (in New York)
1992	GEIL, Joe "Corky"		64	After an illness
1988	GEISE, Tanya "Sugar"		71	After a brief illness
• 1935	GELDERT, Clarence		67	Heart attack (in Calabasas, CA)
1978	+ GELLER, Bruce		47	Airplane crash
1978	GENN, Leo	☆	72	Died in London, England
1958	GENTLE, Alice		69	
1989	GENTRY, Britt Nilsson		46	Cancer
1993	GENTRY, Minnie L.		77	Lung cancer (in New York)
1981	# GEORGE "Chief" Dan	☆	82	
1983	+ GEORGE, Christopher		54	Heart attack
1993	GEORGE, George L.	★	85	Heart failure (in New York)
1954	# GEORGE, Gladys	☆	54	Brain hemorrhage (in Los Angeles, CA)
1963	#+ GEORGE, Gorgeous		48	Heart attack (in Los Angeles, CA)
• 1946	# GEORGE, Heinrich		53	Died in a Soviet internment camp
• 1968	GEORGE, John		70	Emphysema (in Los Angeles, CA)
1992	GEORGE, Joseph L.		65	Cancer
1965	GEORGE, Muriel		82	Died in England
1966	GERAGHTY, Carmelita		65	Died in New York, NY
1987	GERAGHTY, Maurice		78	
1985	GERASIMOV, Sergei		79	
1973	# GERAY, Steven		75	
1977	GERING, Marion		73	
1950	# GERRARD, Douglas		69	After being found unconscious on the street (in Hollywood, CA)
1989	GERRINGER, Robert		63	After a series of strokes
• 1944	# GERRON, Kurt		?	Executed (in Auschwitz, Germany)
1991	GERRY, Toni		65	Cancer
1937	#+ GERSHWIN, George		38	Brain tumor
1983	+ GERSHWIN, Ira		86	

YEAR	NAME		AGE	CAUSE AND/OR PLACE OF DEATH
1992	# GERSON, Jeanne		87	Cancer & pneumonia
1957	GERSON, Paul		86	
1970	# GERSTLE, Frank		54	Cancer (in Santa Monica, CA)
1987	GESSNER, Adrienne		90	
1965	GEST, Inna		43	Hepatitis
1991	GETZ, Stan		64	After a 5-year battle with liver cancer
• 1995	GIANNETI, Alfredo		71	After suffering a stroke (in Rome, Italy)
1988	+ GIBB, Andy		30	Heart inflammation caused by a virus
• 1995	GIBBENS, Vince		46	Apparent heart attack (in Milwaukee, WI)
1994	GIBBERSON, William		74	Effects of a stroke (in New York)
1993	GIBBINS, Duncan		41	Burns (while trying to rescue a cat in a Malibu, CA, fire)
1988	GIBBS, Alan R.		47	Cancer
1986	GIBNEY, Louise		90	
• 1977	# GIBSON, Helen		85	Stroke and heart attack (in Roseburg, OR)
1962	#+ GIBSON, Hoot		70	Cancer (in Woodland Hills, CA)
1991	GIBSON, Marc		51	Apparent heart attack after a workout
1987	GIBSON, Wynne		82	Stroke
1989	GIFFORD, Alan		78	
1994	GIFFORD, Frances		72	Emphysema (in Pasadena, CA)
1971	+ GILBERT, Billy		77	Stroke (in North Hollywood, CA)
1991	GILBERT, Joan		84	
1979	GILBERT, Jody		62	Following an automobile accident (in Sherman Oaks, CA)
1959	GILBERT, Joe		56	
1936	#+ GILBERT, John		38	Heart attack (in Los Angeles, CA)
1978	GILBERT, Lou		69	Apparent heart attack
1947	GILBERT, Walter		60	Heart attack
• 1919	GILFETHER, Daniel		65	Kidney disease (in Long Beach, CA)
1990	# GILFORD, Jack	☆	81	Stomach cancer
• 1955	GILL, Basil		77	Died in Hove, England
1992	GILL, Ray		42	A.I.D.S.
• 1971	GILL, Tom		54	
1993	# GILLESPIE, Dizzy		75	Died in his sleep of pancreatic cancer (in Englewood, CA)
1932	+ GILLETT, King		77	
1994	GILLETTE, Ruth		89	Cancer (in Los Angeles, CA)
1994	GILLIAT, Sidney		85	Died at his home in Wiltshire, England)
1991	GILLIES, Carol		50	Cancer
1939	GILLINGWATER, Claude		69	Suicide (gunshot) in Beverly Hills, CA
1986	GILLMORE, Margalo		88	
1985	GILMAN, Sam		70	Cancer
1986	GILMORE, Virginia		66	Emphysema
1989	GIMPEL, Jakob		82	
1987	+ GINGOLD, Hermione		89	Pneumonia & cardiac disease
1992	# GIOVALE, Franco		44	After a car accident
1992	GIOVANNITTI, Len		71	Heart disease
1949	# GIRARD, Joe		78	
1939	GIRARDOT, Etienne		83	After a brief illness (in Hollywood, CA)
1978	GIRDLER, William		30	Helicopter crash (in the Philippines)
1968	#+ GISH, Dorothy		70	Bronchial pneumonia (in Rapallo, Italy)
1993	GISH, Lillian	☆	99	Cerebral hemorrhage and heart failure (in New York, NY)
1978	GIVNEY, Kathryn		80	
1984	GIVOT, George		81	
• 1966	GLASS, Everett		74	Died in Los Angeles, CA
1965	GLASS, Gaston J.		66	Died in Santa Monica, CA
1984	GLASS, Ned		78	
1989	# GLAUDI, Hap		77	Cancer
1970	GLAUM, Louise		70	Pneumonia
1987	+ GLEASON, Jackie	☆	71	Cancer of the liver & colon
1959	#+ GLEASON, James	☆	76	Asthma (in Woodland Hills, CA)
1947	# GLEASON, Lucille		59	Heart attack (in Brentwood, CA)
1946	GLEASON, Russell		37	Accidental fall from a 4th floor hotel window (in New York, NY)
1939	GLECKLER, Robert P.		49	Uremic poisoning (in Los Angeles, CA)
• 1937	GLENDON, Jonathan Frank		49	Died in Hollywood, CA
1974	# GLENN, Raymond		76	Natural causes
1971	GLENN, Roy Sr.		56	Apparent heart attack (in Los Angeles, CA)
• 1967	GLENNON, Bert	☆	72	

• New entry. # Original name (Pt. 7). + Interment (Pt. 5).   173   ☆ Oscar nominee, ★ Oscar winner (Pt. 10)

	YEAR	NAME		AGE	CAUSE AND/OR PLACE OF DEATH
	1990	GLIDDON, John		92	
	1992	GLIONA, Michael		45	Liver failure
•	1966	GLORI, Enrico		64	Died in Rome, Italy
•	1954	GLYNNE, Mary		56	Died in London, England
	1991	GOBEL, George		71	Complications after arterial leg surgery
•	1981	GODDARD, Alf		83	
	1990	# GODDARD, Paulette	☆	84	Heart failure
•	1955	GODDEN, Jimmy		75	
	1983	GODFREY, Arthur		79	Pneumonia & emphysema
	1970	GODFREY, Peter		70	After a long illness
	1975	+ GODOWSKY, Dagmar		78	
	1990	GODSELL, Vanda		70	
•	1995	GODUNOV, Alexander		45	Natural causes (found dead in his West Hollywood, CA, home)
•	1969	+ GOETZ, William		66	
•	1964	GOETZKE, Bernhard		79	Died in Berlin, Germany
	1991	GOLDEN, Murray		79	Complications after a stroke
•	1971	# GOLDIN, Pat		68	Heart attack (in Los Angeles, CA)
•	1955	GOLDNER, Charles		54	Died in London, England
	1991	GOLDRICH, Bert		84	
	1993	GOLDSTEIN, Elayne		59	Cancer
	1976	#+ GOLDWYN, Frances Howard		73	(See Frances Howard)
	1973	#+ GOLDWYN, Samuel		91	Cancer
	1973	GOMBELL, Minna		80	Died in Santa Monica, CA
	1971	+ GOMEZ, Thomas	☆	65	Died in Santa Monica, CA
•	1995	GONZALES, Pancho		67	
•	1918	GONZALEZ, Myrtle		27	Heart disease and pneumonia (in Los Angeles, CA)
	1971	# GOODE, Jack		63	Acute infectious hepatitis
	1976	GOODLIFFE, Michael		61	Suicide leap while in a hospital (in London, England)
	1986	+ GOODMAN, Benny		77	Heart attack
	1988	GOODMAN, Lee		64	Tuberculosis
	1984	GOODRICH, Frances		93	
	1992	+ GOODSON, Mark		77	Cancer
	1958	#+ GOODWIN, Bill		47	Heart attack (in Palm Springs, CA)
	1983	GOODWIN, Robert L.		55	
	1961	# GOODWIN, Ruby		?	
	1992	GOODWIN, Thomas Jr.		51	Prostate cancer
	1980	GOOLDEN, Richard		86	
	1955	GORCEY, Bernard		67	Injuries from an auto accident (in Hollywood, CA)
	1984	GORCEY, David		63	Diabetic coma
	1969	#+ GORCEY, Leo		53	Liver ailment (in Oakland, CA)
	1974	GORDON, Bert		76	After a long bout with cancer
	1940	# GORDON, C. Henry		57	Result of leg amputation (in Los Angeles, CA)
•	1972	GORDON, Colin		61	Died in Haslemere, England
	1990	GORDON, Dexter	☆	67	Kidney failure
•	1995	GORDON, Gale		89	Cancer (at Redwood Terrace Health Ctr. in Escondido, CA)
	1983	GORDON, Gavin		82	
•	1946	GORDON, Hal		52	
	1956	+ GORDON, Huntly		59	Heart attack (in Hollywood, CA)
	1941	GORDON, James		60	After an emergency operation (in Hollywood, CA)
	1933	GORDON, Julia Swayne		54	After a long illness (in Columbus, OH)
	1974	GORDON, Kitty		96	Died at a Brentwood, NY nursing home
	1960	+ GORDON, Leon		66	Heart ailment
	1963	GORDON, Mary		81	Died in Pasadena, CA
•	1940	GORDON, Maude Turner		71	Pneumonia (in Los Angeles, CA)
	1993	GORDON, Michael		83	Natural causes (at a hospital in Century City, CA)
	1985	GORDON, Noele		61	Cancer
	1971	# GORDON, Robert		76	
	1985	# GORDON, Ruth	★	88	Stroke
	1982	GORDON, Steve		44	Heart attack
	1948	GORDON, Vera		61	Died in Beverly Hills, CA
	1993	GORI, Mario Cecchi		73	Apparent heart attack (in Rome)
•	1982	GORIN, Igor		80	
	1988	GORMAN, Bobby		59	Following a long illness
	1966	GORSS, Saul		58	Heart attack
	1982	+ GOSDEN, Freeman "Amos"		83	Heart failure

...DEATHS OF MOVIE AND TELEVISION PERSONALITIES — BY NAME...

YEAR	NAME		AGE	CAUSE AND/OR PLACE OF DEATH
1964	GOSFIELD, Maurice		51	After being hospitalized for diabetes
1944	GOTT, Barbara		?	
1995	+ GOTTLIEB, Conrad I.		77	Congestive heart failure (at J. Hopkins Hosp. in Balt., MD)
1944	GOTTSCHALK, Ferdinand		75	Died in London, England
1985	GOUDAL, Jetta		86	
1968	GOUGH, John		70	Cancer (in Hollywood, CA)
1984	GOUGH, Lloyd		77	Aortic aneurysm
1982	+ GOULD, Glenn		50	Massive stroke
1996	GOULD, Morton		82	Died in Orlando, FL
1972	GOULDING, Alfred		76	Pneumonia
1959	GOULDING, Edmund		68	
1990	GOULDING, Ray		68	Kidney failure
1951	GOWLAND, Gibson		79	Died in London, England
1973	#+ GRABLE, Betty		56	Lung cancer (in Santa Monica, CA)
1967	GRAF, Louis C.		77	Heart attack
1994	GRAF, William		82	Heart failure complicated by pneumonia (in Los Angeles, CA)
1969	GRAFF, Wilton		65	Died in Pacific Palisades, CA
1991	# GRAHAM, Bill		60	Helicopter crash
1979	GRAHAM, Fred		61	Died in Scottsdale, AZ
1935	GRAHAM, Julia Ann		20	Suicide (gunshot) in Los Angeles, CA
1991	GRAHAM, Martha		96	Pneumonia & cardiac arrest
1949	# GRAHAM, Morland		57	Heart attack (in London, England)
1988	GRAHAM, Sheilah		84	Congestive heart failure
1981	# GRAHAME, Gloria	★	57	Cancer
1982	GRAHAME, Margot		70	Respiratory failure from chronic bronchitis
1932	GRAN, Albert		70	Injuries from an automobile accident (in Los Angeles, CA)
1945	GRANACH, Alexander		54	After a brief illness (in New York, NY)
1965	GRANBY, Joseph		80	Cerebral hemorrhage (in Hollywood, CA)
1988	GRANDIN, Ethel		94	
1991	GRANGE, Red		87	
1995	GRANGER, Dorothy		83	Cancer (at her home in Los Angeles, CA)
1993	GRANGER, John		69	Cerebral hemmorage (in Doylestown, PA)
1993	# GRANGER, Stewart		80	Prostate and bone cancer (in Santa Monica, CA)
1996	GRANGIER, Gilles		85	Died in Paris, France
1986	#+ GRANT, Cary	☆	82	Massive stroke
1970	+ GRANT, Earl		39	Automobile accident (near Lordsburg, N.M.)
1985	# GRANT, Kirby		74	Automobile accident
1952	GRANT, Lawrence		82	Died in Santa Barbara, CA
1984	# GRANT, Shauna		20	Suicide? Murdered? (gunshot)
1959	# GRANT, Tiny		45	
1988	+ GRANVILLE, Bonita (Wrather)	☆	65	
1968	GRANVILLE, Louise		73	Contracted Hong Kong flu after being hospitalized for asthma
1956	#+ GRAPEWIN, Charley		80	After a long illness (in Corona, CA)
1953	GRASSBY, Bertram		72	Died in Scottsdale, AZ
1978	GRAVERS, Steve		56	Lung cancer
1977	GRAVES, Ralph		77	Heart attack (in Santa Barbara, CA)
1970	# GRAVET, Fernand		64	Myocardial infarction (in Paris, France)
1954	GRAVINA, Cesare		96	Died in Italy
1975	GRAY, Alexander		73	
1959	#+ GRAY, Gilda		61	Found dead after food poisoning (in Hollywood, CA)
1963	# GRAY, Glen		63	Died in Plymouth, MA
1956	GRAY, Jack		76	After a long illness (in Woodland Hills, CA)
1970	GRAY, Lawrence		71	Died in Mexico City, Mexico
1981	GRAY, Mack		75	Following a prolonged illness
1994	GRAY, Nadia		70	Stroke (at New York Hospital in Manhattan)
1913	GRAYBILL, Joseph		26	Spinal meningitis (in New York, NY)
1995	GRAYSON, Arlene		45	Bone cancer (at her home in Los Angeles, CA)
1990	# GRAZIANO, Rocky		68	Cardiopulmonary failure
1973	# GREAZA, Walter		76	
1973	GREEN, Abel		72	Died in New York
1960	+ GREEN, Alfred E.		71	After a long illness
1963	GREEN, Dorothy		71	
1940	GREEN, Fred E.		50	
1984	GREEN, Gilbert		68	Died in Tarzana, CA
1958	# GREEN, Harry		66	Heart attack (in London, England)

• New entry. # Original name (Pt. 7). + Interment (Pt. 5).   175   ☆ Oscar nominee, ★ Oscar winner (Pt. 10)

...DEATHS OF MOVIE AND TELEVISION PERSONALITIES – BY NAME...

YEAR	NAME		AGE	CAUSE AND/OR PLACE OF DEATH
1989	GREEN, John		80	
1969	GREEN, Kenneth		61	Heart attack while operating heavy equipment
1991	GREEN, Lee		72	Automobile accident
1975	# GREEN, Martyn		75	Blood infection (in Hollywood, CA)
1969	# GREEN, Mitzi		48	Cancer (in Huntington Harbor, CA
1972	GREEN, Nigel		48	Found dead at his home (in Brighton, England)
1978	GREENE, Angela		55	Stroke (in Los Angeles, CA)
• 1973	GREENE, Billy M.		76	Heart attack (in Los Angeles, CA)
1991	GREENE, Graham		86	Leukemia
1945	GREENE, Harrison		61	After a lingering illness (in Hollywood, CA)
• 1995	GREENE, John L.		82	Died at UCLA Med. Ctr. in Los Angeles, CA
1987	+ GREENE, Lorne		72	Pneumonia following ulcer surgery (in Santa Monica, CA)
1985	GREENE, Richard		66	Cardiac arrest after a fall (in Norfolk, England)
1981	GREENE, Stanley		70	After a long illness (in New York City)
1971	GREENE, Victor Hugo		76	Died in Los Angeles, CA
1970	GREENE, William		43	Heart attack (in Cleveland Heights, OH)
1985	GREENFIELD, Calvin "Rusty"		58	Lung cancer (in Santa Monica, CA)
1963	GREENLEAF, Raymond		71	
1991	GREENSPAN, David		68	Lung cancer
1954	#+ GREENSTREET, Sydney	☆	74	After a long illness (in Los Angeles, CA)
1985	GREENWAY, Tom		75	Heart attack (in Los Angeles, CA)
1978	# GREENWOOD, Charlotte		84	Died in Beverly Hills, CA
1970	GREENWOOD, Ethel		82	Heart attack (in Hollywood, CA)
1987	GREENWOOD, Joan		65	Heart attack (in London, England)
• 1961	GREENWOOD, Winifred L.		69	Died in Los Angeles, CA
• 1939	GREET, Clare		67	Died in London, England
1959	GREGG, Everley		60	Died in Beaconsfield, England
1986	GREGG, Virginia		70	Cancer (in Encino, CA)
1990	GREGORY, Charles "Mr. Music"		89	Pneumonia
1993	GREGORY, Dennis		40	Pneumonia (in East Meadow, NY)
1992	GREGORY, Mercedes		56	Cancer
1975	GREGSON, John		55	Apparent heart attack on a woodland stroll (in Porlock Weir, Eng.)
1958	GREIG, Robert		77	Died in Hollywood, CA
1979	# GRENFELL, Joyce		69	Cancer (in London, England)
• 1996	GREY, Denise		99	Died in Paris, France
• 1947	GREY, Gloria		38	Died in Hollywood, CA
1993	# GREY, Nan		75	Heart failure (in her San Diego, CA, home)
• 1973	# GREY, Olga		75	Died in Los Angeles, CA
1934	# GREY, Robert H.		42	Died in Los Angeles, CA
1939	GREY, Zane		64	Died at his home in Altadena, CA
1965	# GRIBBON, Eddie		75	Cancer (in North Hollywood, CA)
1961	GRIBBON, Harry		76	After a long illness (in Los Angeles, CA)
1977	GRIES, Tom		54	Heart attack
1935	GRIEVES, Jack		33	Died in Burbank, CA
1975	# GRIFFIES, Ethel		97	Stroke (in London, England)
1989	GRIFFIN, Bessie		67	Cancer
1940	# GRIFFIN, Carlton E.		47	Heart attack
1956	GRIFFIN, Charles		67	Died in Hollywood, CA
1953	GRIFFIN, Frank L.		63	Heart attack (in Hollywood, CA)
1919	GRIFFIN, Gerald		65	Died in Venice, CA
1992	GRIFFIN, Rodney		46	A.I.D.S.
1979	# GRIFFITH, Corinne		84	Cardiac arrest (in Santa Monica, CA)
1948	#+ GRIFFITH, D. W.		73	Massive cerebral hemorrhage (in Los Angeles, CA)
1975	GRIFFITH, Edward H.		86	
1958	GRIFFITH, Gordon		51	Heart attack
1926	# GRIFFITH, Harry		59	Died in Pasadena, CA
1980	GRIFFITH, Hugh	★	67	Died in London, England
1921	# GRIFFITH, Katherine		45	Died in Los Angeles, CA
1948	GRIFFITH, Linda Arvidson		65	(See Linda Arvidson)
1957	GRIFFITH, Raymond		67	Heart attack (while dining in Hollywood, CA)
1960	GRIFFITH, William M.		62	Died in Hollywood, CA
1994	GRIGAS, John		71	Heart attack
• 1995	GRIMSBY, Roger		66	Lung cancer (at Lenox Hill Hospital, NYC)
• 1995	+ GRINKOV, Sergei		28	Massive heart attack while ice skating (in Lake Placid, NY)
• 1955	GROVES, Frederick "Fred"		74	

YEAR	NAME		AGE	CAUSE AND/OR PLACE OF DEATH
•	1996	GROVES, William "Bill"	74	Lung cancer (at his home in Morongo Valley, CA)
•	1995	GRUENBERG, Leonard S.	83	Natural causes (at his home in Rancho Mirage, CA)
•	1963	GRUNDGENS, Gustav	63	Suicide (in Manila, Philippine Islands)
	1993	GRUNDY, Bill	69	Died in Cheshire, England
	1961	# GUARD, Kit	67	Cancer (in Hollywood, CA)
•	1995	GUARDINO, Harry	69	Lung cancer (in Palm Springs, CA)
	1983	GUFFEY, Burnett	78	
	1943	GUHL, George	?	Died in Los Angeles, CA
	1989	GUIGLEY, Robert	76	Died in Los Angeles, CA
	1964	# GUILFOYLE, James	72	Heart attack (in Woodland Hills, CA)
	1961	GUILFOYLE, Paul	59	
	1933	#+ GUINAN, Mary "Texas"	48	After an operation for colitis (in Vancouver, B.C., Canada)
	1984	GUNEY, Yilmaz	47	Cancer
•	1918	GUNN, Charles E.	35	Spanish influenza (in Los Angeles, CA)
	1993	GUNN, Moses	64	Complications of asthma (in Guilford, CT)
	1969	# GURIE, Sigrid	58	Pulmonary embolism (in Mexico City, Mexico)
	1972	GURIN, Ellen	24	Suicide, after a nervous depression
	1991	GUTHRIE, A. B. Jr.	90	
	1967	#+ GUTHRIE, Woody	55	After a 13-yr. bout with Huntington's chorea
•	1968	GUY-BLANCHE, Alice	95	Natural causes (at her daughter's home in Mahwah, NJ)
	1991	GUZMAN, Pato	57	After a brief illness
	1959	#+ GWENN, Edmund ★	83	Died in Woodland Hills, CA
•	1976	GWYNN, Michael	59	Heart attack (in London, England)
	1993	# GWYNNE, Fred "Herman Munster"	66	Pancreatic cancer (in Taneytown, MD)
		H		
	1966	HAADE, William	63	
	1968	HAAS, Hugo	65	Asthmatic attack (in Vienna, Austria)
	1967	HACK, Herman	68	Heart attack (in Hollywood, CA)
	1973	HACK, Signe	73	Leukemia (in Hollywood, CA)
	1940	HACKATHORNE, George	44	After a long illness (in Los Angeles, CA)
	1959	HACKEL, A. W.	76	Heart attack (in Hollywood, CA)
	1994	HACKES, Peter	69	Heart attack (in Washington, D.C.)
•	1995	HACKETT, Albert	95	Pneumonia (at St. Lukes-Roosevelt Hosp. in Manhattan)
	1976	# HACKETT, Bobby	61	
	1954	HACKETT, Florence	72	Died in New York City
	1967	HACKETT, Hal	44	After a long illness
	1983	#+ HACKETT, Joan	49	Cancer (in Encino, CA)
	1948	# HACKETT, Karl	55	After a long illness (in Sawtelle, CA)
	1973	HACKETT, Lillian	76	Cerebral hemorrhage (in Hollywood, CA)
	1958	HACKETT, Raymond	55	Died in Hollywood, CA
	1981	# HADEN, Sara	82	Died in Woodland Hills, CA
	1974	# HADLEY, Reed	63	Heart attack (in Los Angeles, CA)
	1958	HAGEN, Charles F.	96	Died in Hollywood, CA
	1977	# HAGEN, Jean ☆	54	Cancer (in Woodland Hills, CA)
	1991	HAGERTY, Michael	39	A.I.D.S.
•	1973	# HAGNEY, Frank S.	79	Died in Los Angeles, CA
	1988	HAHN, Paul	67	After a short illness
	1989	HAIG, Jack	76	Cancer
	1942	HAINES, Donald	24	
	1964	HAINES, Rhea	69	
	1990	HAINES, Richard	43	After surgery for a brain tumor
	1973	+ HAINES, William	73	Cancer (in Santa Monica, CA)
	1990	HAKINS, Dick	87	
	1990	HALE, Alan Jr.	71	Cancer
	1950	#+ HALE, Alan Sr.	57	Liver ailment — virus infection (in Hollywood, CA)
	1965	# HALE, Creighton	83	Died in South Pasadena, CA
	1985	# HALE, Georgia	79	
	1966	# HALE, Jonathan	74	Suicide (gunshot) in Woodland Hills, CA
	1933	HALE, Louise Closser	60	Following an accident (in Los Angeles, CA)
	1981	HALE, Richard	87	Natural causes
	1959	# HALE, Sonnie	57	Myelofibrosis (a blood disease) in London, England
	1992	HALEY, Alex	70	Heart attack
	1979	#+ HALEY, Jack	80	Heart attack (in Los Angeles, CA)
	1968	HALL, Alexander ☆	74	Stroke
	1959	#+ HALL, Charlie	60	Died in North Hollywood, CA

YEAR	NAME		AGE	CAUSE AND/OR PLACE OF DEATH
1991	HALL, Ed		60	Cancer
• 1981	HALL, Ella		85	Died in Canoga Park, CA
1970	HALL, Geraldine		65	Heart attack while hospitalized
1985	HALL, Grayson	☆	58	Cancer
1940	# HALL, James		39	Liver ailment
1979	#+ HALL, Jon		64	Suicide after bladder cancer surgery (gunshot) in Sherman Oaks, CA
1968	HALL, Juanita		66	Diabetic complications
1991	HALL, Kevin Peter		35	Pneumonia
1953	# HALL, Porter		65	Heart attack (in Los Angeles, CA)
1990	HALL, Stuart		86	Complications from lung surgery
1958	HALL, Thurston		75	Heart attack (in Beverly Hills, CA)
• 1947	HALL, Winter		68	
• 1933	HALL-DAVIS, Lilian		32	Suicide (gas) in London, England
• 1942	HALLARD, C. M.		75	Died in Surrey, England
1966	HALLIDAY, Gardner		56	Suicide (sleeping pills) after suffering with cancer
1947	HALLIDAY, John		67	Heart ailment
1957	HALLIGAN, William		72	After a lingering illness (in Woodland Hills, CA)
1989	HALLIWELL, Leslie		59	Abdominal cancer
• 1944	HALLOR, Ray		44	Automobile accident (near Palm Springs, CA)
1967	HALLS, Ethel May		85	
1976	#+ HALOP, Billy		56	Died in Brentwood, CA
1986	HALOP, Florence		63	Cancer
1989	HALSTED, Fred		47	Overdose of barbiturates
1959	+ HALTON, Charles		83	Hepatitis (in Los Angeles, CA)
1989	HAMBLEN, Stuart		80	Brain cancer
1990	# HAMER, Rusty		42	Suicide (gunshot)
• 1995	HAMILTON, Anthony		42	A.I.D.S. pneumonia
1991	HAMILTON, Frank		66	Prostate cancer
1942	+ HAMILTON, Hale R.		62	Cerebral hemorrhage
1925	HAMILTON, Jack "Shorty"		37	Crushed after his car hit a steam shovel
1958	HAMILTON, John		71	Heart condition (in Hollywood) Do not confuse with J. H., d. 1985
1985	HAMILTON, John		?	Heart attack (Do not confuse with John Hamilton, d. 1958)
1935	HAMILTON, Lloyd		43	Following an operation for a stomach disorder (in Hollywood, CA)
• 1960	HAMILTON, Mahlon		77	Cancer (in Woodland Hills, CA)
1985	HAMILTON, Margaret		83	Heart attack
1986	HAMILTON, Murray		63	Cancer
1984	# HAMILTON, Neil		85	Complications from asthma
1993	HAMMER, Alvin		78	Died in New York
1990	+ HAMMER, Armand		92	
1987	HAMMER, Irene Wicker		86	
1993	HAMMER, Peter		54	Cancer (in New York)
1960	+ HAMMERSTEIN II, Oscar		65	Stomach cancer
1948	HAMMERSTEIN, Elaine		50	Automobile collision
1980	# HAMMOND, Kay		71	
1992	HAMMOND, Ruth		96	Died in her sleep
1972	HAMMOND, Virginia		78	
1955	#+ HAMPDEN, Walter		75	Stroke (in Hollywood, CA)
• 1963	# HAMPTON, Grace		87	Died in Woodland Hills, CA
1982	HAMPTON, Hope		84	Heart attack
1954	HAMPTON, Louise		72	Bronchial trouble (in London, England)
1992	+ HANCOCK, John		51	Found dead of a heart attack
1968	# HANCOCK, Tony		44	Suicide (overdose of sleeping pills) in Sydney, Australia
1987	HANDL, Irene		85	
• 1978	# HANDWORTH, Octavia		90	Died in Hemet, CA
1964	HANEY, Carol		30	Pneumonia and diabetes (in Saddle River, NJ)
1985	HANEY, David		44	Heart attack
1970	HANLEY, Jimmy		51	Cancer (in England)
• 1972	HANNEN, Nicholas		91	Died in London, England
1992	HANNES, Art		72	Respiratory failure
• 1947	HANRAY, Lawrence		73	
• 1961	HANSEN, Juanita		64	Heart attack (in Hollywood, CA)
1975	HANSEN, William		64	After a lengthy illness
1965	HANSON, Lars		78	Died in Stockholm, Sweden
• 1960	HARBAUGH, Carl		73	Died in Hollywood, CA
• 1941	HARBEN, Hubert		63	Died in London, England

YEAR	NAME	AGE	CAUSE AND/OR PLACE OF DEATH
1981	HARBURG, E. Y.	84	Killed in an automobile crash
• 1951	HARCOURT, James	77	
1973	HARDIE, Russell	69	After an illness of several years (in Clarence, NY)
1991	HARDIN, Ken	62	Cancer
1981	#+ HARDING, Ann ☆	79	After an illness of several months (in Sherman Oaks, CA)
1952	# HARDING, Lyn	85	
• 1962	HARDTMUTH, Paul	72	Fall from his apartment building (in London, England)
1964	HARDWICKE, Cedric	71	Lung ailment (in New York, NY)
1990	HARDY, Ian Dudley	79	Killed in a storm
1990	HARDY, Joseph	71	
1957	#+ HARDY, Oliver	65	Following a paralytic stroke (in North Hollywood, CA)
1935	+ HARDY, Sam	52	Intestinal problems (in Los Angeles, CA)
1964	HARE, F. Lumsden	89	Died in Hollywood, CA
1979	HARE, J. Robertson	87	Died in London, England
• 1996	HAREN, Christian	61	A.I.D.S. (in San Francisco, CA)
1984	HARGREAVES, Christine	43	Brain hemorrhage
• 1996	HARGREAVES, John	50	After a long illness (in Sydney, Australia)
1967	HARKER, Gordon	81	Died in London, England
1967	HARLAN, Kenneth	71	Aneurysm (in Sacramento, CA)
1940	HARLAN, Otis	75	Stroke (in Martinsville, IN)
1974	HARLAN, Russell B.	70	Died in Newport Beach, CA
1937	#+ HARLOW, Jean	26	Cerebral edema following uremic poisoning (in Los Angeles, CA)
1958	HARMON, Pat	70	Died in Riverside, CA
1990	HARMON, Tom	70	Heart attack
1974	# HAROLDE, Ralf	75	Pneumonia (in Santa Monica, CA)
1994	HARP, Bill	70	Heart attack (in Hollywood, CA)
1984	HARPER, Cecilia DeMille	75	
1994	HARPER, Pat (TV anchor)	59	Heart attack (at her home in Capiliera, Spain)
1989	HARRIGAN, Nedda	89	Lung cancer
1966	+ HARRIGAN, William	72	Following surgery
1978	HARRINGTON, Kate	74	Following a stroke
1991	HARRIS, Cassandra	39	Ovarian cancer
• 1994	HARRIS, Chris	51	Apparent heart attack (at his home in Newbury Park, CA)
1988	HARRIS, Fox	52	Lung cancer
1991	HARRIS, Lou	85	Natural causes
1944	HARRIS, Marion	38	Burns in bed from a cigarette fire
1944	HARRIS, Mildred	42	Pneumonia after an abdominal operation (in Los Angeles, CA)
• 1974	# HARRIS, Morris	59	
• 1995	HARRIS, Phil	91	Heart failure (at his home in Rancho Mirage, CA)
• 1995	HARRIS, Robert	95	After a brief illness
1981	HARRIS, Robert H.	72	Died in Los Angeles, CA (Do not confuse with British actor)
1990	+ HARRIS, Robin	36	Found dead in his hotel room
• 1973	HARRIS, Stacy B.	54	Heart attack (in Los Angeles, CA)
1991	HARRIS, Ted	52	Cancer
1992	HARRIS, William E.	37	Stabbed when he interrupted a burglary
• 1995	HARRISON, Henry M. Jr. (Rev.)	67	Stroke (in Pineville, N.C.)
1994	HARRISON, Joan	83	Died in London, England
1990	HARRISON, Rex	82	Pancreatic cancer
1920	# HARRON, Bobby	27	Accidentally shot (in New York, NY)
1939	HARRON, John	36	Died in Seattle, WA
1918	# HARRON, Tessie	22	Spanish Influenza (in Los Angeles, CA)
• 1940	HART, Albert	65	Died in Hollywood, CA
1943	+ HART, Lorenz	47	Pneumonia
1961	+ HART, Moss	57	
1949	# HART, Neal	70	Died in Woodland Hills, CA
1951	HART, Richard	35	Heart attack
1946	#+ HART, William S.	83	Stroke (in Los Angeles, CA)
1965	HARTE, Betty	81	Died in Sunland, CA
1984	HARTFORD, Karen Kadler	50	Cancer
• 1951	# HARTIGAN, Pat	69	Coronary attack (in Los Angeles, CA)
• 1994	HARTLEY, Neil	78	Heart failure (at his home in Los Angeles, CA)
1958	HARTMAN, Don	57	Died in his sleep of apparent heart attack
1987	HARTMAN, Elizabeth ☆	45	Suicide (jumped from her 5th-floor apartment)
1973	HARTMAN, Paul	69	Heart attack (in Los Angeles, CA)
• 1975	HARTNELL, William "Billy"	67	Died in London, England

• New entry.   # Original name (Pt. 7).   + Interment (Pt. 5).   179   ☆ Oscar nominee, ★ Oscar winner (Pt. 10)

YEAR	NAME		AGE	CAUSE AND/OR PLACE OF DEATH
1992	HARTOG, Simon		52	Leukemia
1963	HARVEY, Don C.		51	Apparent heart attack (in Studio City, CA)
1945	HARVEY, Forrester		65	Stroke (in Laguna Beach, CA)
1929	# HARVEY, Hank		?	Died at his home in Culver City, CA
• 1996	HARVEY, Harold A. "Herk"		71	Died in Lawrence, Kansas
1985	HARVEY, Harry Sr.		84	
1973	# HARVEY, Laurence	☆	45	Cancer (in London, England)
1968	# HARVEY, Lilian		61	Died in Antibes, France
1955	+ HARVEY, Paul (actor)		72	Coronary thrombosis (Do not confuse with radio commentator)
1993	HARVEY, Rick		43	Kidney failure (died in Memphis, TN)
1992	HARVEY, Rudy		60	Kidney failure after a series of strokes
1990	HARVUOT, Clifford		77	Pancreatic cancer
1984	HASKIN, Byron	☆	84	Cancer
1978	# HASSE, O. E.		75	Died in a hospital (in West Berlin, Germany)
• 1937	HASSELL, George		55	Heart attack (in Chatsworth, CA)
1985	+ HATHAWAY, Henry	☆	86	Heart attack
1971	# HATTON, Raymond		84	Heart attack (in Palmdale, CA)
• 1931	HATTON, Richard "Dick"		40	Traffic accident (in Los Angeles, CA)
1946	+ HATTON, Rondo		51	Heart attack (in Beverly Hills, CA)
1991	HAULMAN, Bob		49	Apparent heart attack
1931	HAUPT, Ullrich		43	Accidentally shot on a deer hunting trip (near Santa Maria, CA)
1985	HAUSER, Gayelord		89	Complications from pneumonia
1960	HAVER, Phyllis		61	Suicide (despondent over Mack Sennett's death) in Falls Village, CT
1994	HAWKINS, Corwin		29	Pneumonia (in Los Angeles, CA)
1973	HAWKINS, Jack		62	Cancer (in London, England)
1977	+ HAWKS, Howard	☆	81	Died in his sleep following a fall and concussion
• 1963	# HAWLEY, Wanda		67	Died in Los Angeles, CA
1993	HAWORTH, Ted	★	76	Heart failure
• 1942	HAWTHORNE, David		54	
1988	HAWTREY, Charles		72	Arterial disease
1957	HAY, Mary		55	Prolonged heart ailment
1949	HAY, Will		60	Died in London, England
1973	# HAYAKAWA, Sessue	☆	84	Cerebral thrombosis and pneumonia (in Tokyo, Japan)
1955	+ HAYDEN, Harry		72	Died in Los Angeles, CA
1981	#+ HAYDEN, Russell "Lucky"		68	Viral pneumonia (in Palm Springs, Ca.)
1986	# HAYDEN, Sterling		70	Cancer
1985	HAYDN, Richard		80	
1994	HAYDON, Julie		84	Abdominal cancer (in LaCrosse; WI)
1991	HAYDON, Tom		53	Cancer
• 1957	HAYE, Helen		83	Died in London, England
1977	# HAYES, Allison		47	Blood poisoning (in La Jolla, CA)
1987	HAYES, Bernadine		75	Heart attack
1991	HAYES, Christopher		?	Heart attack
1969	+ HAYES, George "Gabby"		83	Heart ailment (in Burbank, CA)
1989	HAYES, Grace		93	
1993	+ HAYES, Helen	★	92	Congestive heart failure (in Nyack, NY)
1977	# HAYES, Margaret		61	Cancer complicated by hepatitis (in Miami Beach, FL)
1958	# HAYES, Sam		53	Heart attack preparing his morning news program (in San Diego)
1988	HAYES, William S.		29	A.I.D.S.
• 1963	HAYLE, Grace		73	Died in Los Angeles, CA
1994	HAYMAN, Lillian		72	Heart attack (at her home in Hollis, NY)
1989	HAYMER, Johnny		69	Cancer
1980	#+ HAYMES, Dick		64	Lung cancer (in Los Angeles, CA)
1966	HAYNES, Arthur		52	Heart attack
1986	HAYNES, Hilda		72	
1987	HAYNES, Lloyd		52	Lung cancer
1994	HAYNES, Tiger		79	Cardiac arrest (at St. Vincent's Hospital in New York City)
1992	HAYS, Mickey		20	Progeria (a rare aging disorder)
1954	HAYS, Will H.		74	
1983	HAYTER, James		75	
1985	# HAYWARD, Louis		76	Lung cancer
1975	#+ HAYWARD, Susan	★	57	Brain tumor (in Beverly Hills, CA)
1987	#+ HAYWORTH, Rita		68	Alzheimer's disease
1994	HAZEN, Joseph		96	Died in his sleep (at home in Boca Raton, FL)
1981	+ HEAD, Edith		82	Died in Los Angeles, CA

...DEATHS OF MOVIE AND TELEVISION PERSONALITIES – BY NAME...

	YEAR	NAME		AGE	CAUSE AND/OR PLACE OF DEATH
•	1995	HEALY, David		64	Following a heart operation (in London, England)
	1937	#+ HEALY, Ted		41	Heart attack (in Los Angeles, CA)
	1963	# HEARN, Edward "Eddie"		74	
	1964	+ HEARN, Sam		75	Heart attack (in Los Angeles, CA)
	1993	HEARST, William Randolph Jr.		85	Heart attack (in New York)
	1991	HEATH, Gordon		72	
•	1937	HEATHERLEY, Clifford		48	Died in London, England
	1972	HEATTER, Gabriel		82	Pneumonia
	1964	HECHT, Ben		70	Heart attack
	1985	HECHT, Howard		77	
	1994	HEFLIN, Frances		71	Lung cancer (in New York, NY)
	1971	#+ HEFLIN, Van	★	60	After a massive stroke while swimming (in Hollywood, CA)
	1936	# HEGGIE, O. P.		59	Pneumonia (in Los Angeles, CA)
	1992	HEIDER, Frederick		75	
	1986	+ HEIDT, Horace		85	Pneumonia & heart trouble
	1987	HEIFETZ, Jascha		86	Following brain surgery (after a fall)
•	1972	HEINZ, Gerard		68	
	1979	+ HEISLER, Stuart R.		82	
	1918	+ HELD, Anna		45	Pernicious anemia and bronchial pneumonia
	1992	HELD, Martin		83	
	1947	+ HELLINGER, Mark		44	Heart attack
	1984	+ HELLMAN, Lillian		79	Heart disease
•	1995	HELMORE, Tom		91	Died in Longboat Key, FL
	1986	HELPMANN, Robert		76	
	1971	+ HELTON, Percy		76	Died in Hollywood, CA
	1981	# HEMING, Violet		86	Died in New York, NY
	1968	HEMSLEY, Estelle		70	After a brief illness
	1976	HENABERY, Joseph E.		88	
•	1967	HENCKLES, Paul		81	Died in Dusseldorf, Germany
	1956	# HENDERSON, Del		73	Died in Hollywood, CA
	1985	# HENDERSON, Dickie		62	Cancer
•	1978	HENDERSON, Douglas "Doug"		58	Suicide (carbon monoxide) in Studio City, CA
	1952	# HENDERSON, Fletch		54	Stroke
	1983	HENDERSON, Jack E.		88	
	1988	HENDERSON, Jo		54	Automobile accident
	1988	HENDLEY, Janet Stover		55	Cancer
	1938	HENDRICKS, Ben Jr.		44	Died in Los Angeles, CA
•	1930	HENDRICKS, Ben Sr.		67	Died in Hollywood, CA
•	1965	HENDRIKSON, Anders		69	Died in Sweden
	1970	#+ HENDRIX, Jimi		27	Inhalation of vomit after barbiturate intoxication (in London, Eng.)
	1981	#+ HENDRIX, Wanda		52	Double pneumonia (in Burbank, CA)
	1984	HENDRY, Ian		53	
	1969	+ HENIE, Sonja		57	Leukemia (on a private plane bound for Oslo, Norway)
	1964	HENLEY, Hobart		72	After a long illness (in Los Angeles, CA)
	1969	HENNECKE, Clarence R.		74	After a brief illness
	1973	HENNING, Pat		62	
	1992	# HENREID, Paul		84	Pneumonia after a stroke
	1980	# HENRY, Charlotte		65	Brain tumor (in La Jolla, CA)
•	1971	HENRY, Robert "Buzz"		40	Motorcycle accident (in Los Angeles, CA)
•	1980	# HENRY, Tom		?	Died in CA
	1989	HENSHAW, Wandalie		54	Parkinson's disease
	1990	HENSON, Basil		71	Stroke
	1990	HENSON, Jim		53	Streptococcus pneumonia
	1993	#+ HEPBURN, Audrey	★	63	Colon cancer (in Tolochenaz, Switzerland)
	1953	HEPWORTH, Cecil M.		78	Died in Greenford, Middlesex, England
	1956	#+ HERBERT, Holmes		74	Died in Hollywood, CA
	1952	+ HERBERT, Hugh		64	Heart attack (in North Hollywood, CA)
	1992	HERBERT, Percy		72	Heart attack
	1989	HERBERT, Pitt		74	Amyotrophic lateral sclerosis
	1927	HERBERT, Sidney		?	
	1986	HERBERT, Tim		71	Heart attack
	1924	+ HERBERT, Victor		65	Heart attack
	1987	#+ HERMAN, Woody		74	Congestive heart failure & emphysema
•	1945	# HERNANDEZ, Anna		77	Pneumonia (in Los Angeles, CA)
•	1922	HERNANDEZ, George F.		59	Died in Los Angeles, CA

YEAR	NAME		AGE	CAUSE AND/OR PLACE OF DEATH
1970	HERNANDEZ, Juan "Juano"		74	Cerebral hemorrhage (in San Juan, Puerto Rico)
1990	# HERNDON, Bill		54	A.I.D.S.
• 1995	# HERRIOT, James		78	Prostate cancer (at his home in Thirsk, England)
1975	HERRMANN, Bernard		64	Heart attack
1941	HERSHELL, Mayall		78	Cerebral hemorrhage
• 1995	HERSHMAN, Robert		41	A.I.D.S. (in Santa Monica, CA)
1956	+ HERSHOLT, Jean	★	69	Cancer (in Beverly Hills, CA)
1992	HERZBERGER, Jack L.		75	Following heart surgery
1989	HESLER, G. Christian		33	A.I.D.S.
1982	HESSEL, Edith Bell		58	Alzheimer's disease & exposure
• 1967	HESTERBERG, Trude		70	Died in Munich, Germany
1986	HEWITT, Alan		71	Cancer
• 1947	# HEWSTON, Alfred H.		66	
1984	HEXUM, Jon-Erik		26	Accidentally shot himself
1951	HEYBURN, Weldon		46	
1960	HEYDT, Louis Jean		54	Heart attack (in Boston, MA)
1993	HEYES, Douglas		73	Congestive heart failure (in Beverly Hills, CA)
1958	HEYES, Herbert		68	Died in North Hollywood, CA
1989	HEYWOOD, Eddie		73	Parkinson's & Alzheimer's disease
• 1964	HEYWOOD, Herbert		83	Coronary thrombosis (in Van Nuys, CA)
1994	# HIATT, Ruth		88	Congestive heart failure (in Montrose, CA)
1993	HIBBERT, Dora		77	Following an illness (in New York)
1985	HIBBS, Jesse		79	Alzheimer's disease
1986	HICKMAN, Bill		65	Cancer
1950	HICKMAN, Howard C.		69	Following a heart attack (in Los Angeles, CA)
1994	HICKS, Bill		32	Pancreatic cancer (in Little Rock, Ark.)
1957	# HICKS, Russell		61	Heart attack after a traffic accident (in Hollywood, CA)
1933	HIERS, Walter		39	Pneumonia (in Los Angeles, CA)
1986	HIGBE, Mary Jane		70	Stroke
1988	HIGGINS, Colin		47	A.I.D.S.
• 1976	# HILDEBRAND, Hilde		78	
• 1954	HILL, Al		62	(Do not confuse with stage actor of same name)
1992	#+ HILL, Benny		67	Heart ailment
1918	HILL, Dale P.		?	Spanish influenza
1934	# HILL, George W.		40	Suicide (gunshot)
1993	HILL, Jacqueline		68	Cancer (in London, England)
1994	HILL, James		75	Died in London, England
1990	HILL, Ken		49	A.I.D.S.
1993	HILL, Martin		80	Cancer (in Sherman Oaks, CA)
1966	HILL, Robert F.		79	After a long illness
1938	HILL, Thelma		32	Following a 3-month illness
1988	HILLAIRE, Marcel		79	Complications following surgery
1947	HILLIARD, Ernest		57	Following a heart attack (in Santa Monica, CA)
1966	HILLIARD, Harry S.		?	Complications after a fall (in St. Petersburg, FL)
1985	HILLPOT, William A.		79	Pneumonia
1979	# Hilo Hattie		78	Cancer following a stroke (in Honolulu, Hawaii)
1954	HILTON, James		54	Cancer of the liver
1947	HILYARD, Norman		74	
1948	HINDS, Samuel S.		73	After a brief illness (in Pasadena, CA)
1967	HINES, Harry		78	After suffering from emphysema (in Hollywood, CA)
1970	HINES, Johnny		73	Heart attack (in Los Angeles, CA)
1988	HINTERMANN, Carlo		64	Automobile accident
1958	HINTON, Ed		30	Airplane crash (on Catalina Island, CA)
1980	+ HITCHCOCK, Alfred	☆	80	Heart attack (in Los Angeles, CA)
1929	HITCHCOCK, Raymond		58	Heart trouble
• 1995	HIVELY, Jack B.		85	After a brief illness (at his home in Hollywood, CA)
1962	HOBBES, Halliwell		84	Heart attack (in Santa Monica, CA)
• 1968	HOBBS, Jack		74	Died in Brighton, England
1979	HOCH, Winton C.		73	Effects of a stroke
1979	HODGE, Al		66	Heart failure from chronic bronchitis and emphysema
• 1995	HODGES, Gill		80	
1961	HODGES, William C.		85	
1964	HODGINS, Earle		65	Heart attack (in Hollywood, CA)
1949	# HODGSON, Leland		55	Heart attack (at his home in Hollywood, CA)
1955	+ HODIAK, John		41	Coronary thrombosis (in Tarzana, CA)

...DEATHS OF MOVIE AND TELEVISION PERSONALITIES — BY NAME...

	YEAR	NAME		AGE	CAUSE AND/OR PLACE OF DEATH
•	1956	# HOEFLICH, Lucie		73	Heart attack (in Berlin, Germany)
	1981	HOERBIGER, Paul		87	Died in Vienna, Austria
	1960	# HOEY, Dennis		67	Died in Palm Beach, FL
	1992	HOFF, Louise		69	After an illness
	1989	HOFFMAN, Abbie		52	Suicide (massive drug overdose)
	1986	HOFFMAN, Beth Webb		89	
	1961	HOFFMAN, David		57	
•	1944	# HOFFMAN, Otto		65	Lung cancer (in Woodland Hills, CA)
	1993	HOGAN, Paul (of WMAQ-TV)		48	Apparent heart attack (Do not confuse with the actor)
	1964	HOHL, Arthur		74	Died in CA
	1987	HOLCOMBE, Harry		80	
	1973	#+ HOLDEN, Fay		77	Cancer (in Woodland Hills, CA)
	1981	#+ HOLDEN, William	★	63	Blood loss after head was cut in a fall (in Santa Monica, CA)
•	1929	HOLDING, Thomas		49	Heart disease (in New York, NY)
•	1974	# HOLDREN, Judd		58	Suicide (gunshot) in West Los Angeles, CA
	1990	HOLE, William J. Jr.		71	Respiratory failure
	1959	#+ HOLIDAY, Billie		44	Liver ailment and cardiac failure (in New York, NY)
	1988	HOLLAND, Anthony		60	Suicide (after suffering from A.I.D.S.)
	1993	HOLLAND, John		85	Respiratory failure and pneumonia (in Woodland Hills, CA)
•	1994	HOLLAND, Joseph		84	Heart failure (in Santa Fe, N.M.)
	1984	HOLLANDER, Adam		19	Struck by car while riding a bicycle
•	1950	# HOLLES, Antony		49	
	1984	HOLLIDAY, Bill		49	Apparent heart attack
	1948	HOLLIDAY, Frank Jr.		35	Suicide (hanged himself with a belt while in jail)
	1965	#+ HOLLIDAY, Judy	★	41	Throat cancer (in New York, NY)
	1969	HOLLIDAY, Marjorie		49	Brain hemorrhage
	1926	HOLLINGSWORTH, Alfred		52	After a brief illness
•	1973	HOLLISTER, Alice		86	Died in Costa Mesa, CA
	1982	HOLLOWAY, Stanley	☆	91	
	1992	HOLLOWAY, Sterling		87	Cardiac arrest
	1959	#+ HOLLY, Buddy		22	Airplane crash (northwest of Mason City, IA)
	1947	HOLMAN, Harry		73	After a heart attack (in his Hollywood, CA, home)
	1971	# HOLMAN, Libby "Peaches"		65	Died in North Stamford, CT
	1984	HOLMES, Billy		56	Cancer
	1958	HOLMES, Burton		88	Died in Hollywood, CA
	1950	HOLMES, Helen		58	Heart attack (in Burbank, CA)
	1988	HOLMES, John C.		43	Encephalitis as a result of A.I.D.S.
	1942	HOLMES, Phillips		33	Air collision of two RCAF planes (near Armstrong, Ont., Canada)
•	1945	HOLMES, Ralph		56	Natural causes (in New York, NY)
	1971	HOLMES, Stuart		84	Ruptured abdominal aortic (in Hollywood, CA)
	1959	HOLMES, Taylor		87	Died in Hollywood, CA
	1951	#+ HOLT, Jack		62	Coronary thrombosis (in Los Angeles, CA)
	1989	HOLT, Jason		39	A.I.D.S.
	1973	# HOLT, Tim		54	Brain cancer (in Shawnee, OK)
	1980	HOLTZ, Lou		87	Following open-heart surgery
	1947	HOMANS, Robert E.		72	Heart attack (in Los Angeles, CA)
	1978	HOMOLKA, Oscar	☆	79	Died in Sussex, England
	1993	HONDA, Ishiro		81	Died in Tokyo, Japan
•	1955	HONEGGER, Arthur		63	Heart disease
	1987	HONRI, Baynham		83	
	1979	#+ HOOD, Darla		47	Died in North Hollywood, CA
	1965	HOOD, Joseph B. Sr.		69	
•	1995	# HOON, Shannon		28	Drug overdose (on a tour bus in New Orleans, LA)
•	1972	# HOOVER, J. Edgar		77	Heart disease (in Washington, D.C.)
	1988	HOPE, Harry		62	Heart attack after playing in a basketball game
•	1963	HOPE, Vida		45	Automobile accident (in Chelmsford, England)
	1950	HOPKINS, Arthur		71	Heart ailment
	1972	# HOPKINS, Miriam	☆	69	Heart attack (in New York, NY)
	1946	HOPKINS, Sis			(See Rose Melville)
	1993	HOPKINS, Speed	☆	44	Viral infection (in Sparks, MD)
	1935	# HOPPER, De Wolf		77	Shortly after a radio broadcast (in Kansas City, MO)
	1967	HOPPER, E. Mason		82	
	1966	#+ HOPPER, Hedda		75	Double pneumonia and heart complications (in Los Angeles, CA)
	1988	HOPPER, Jerry		81	After suffering from heart problems
	1970	#+ HOPPER, William		55	Pneumonia (in Palm Springs, CA)

YEAR	NAME		AGE	CAUSE AND/OR PLACE OF DEATH
1945	# HOPTON, Russell "Russ"		45	Found dead of an overdose of sleeping pills (in N. Hollywood, CA)
• 1995	HORDERN, Michael		83	After a long illness (at an Oxford, England, hospital)
1994	HOREN, Robert		68	Cancer (in New York)
• 1970	HORNE, David		71	Died in London, England
1942	HORNE, James W.		60	Cerebral hemorrhage
• 1994	HORNER, Harry	★	84	Pneumonia (at his home in Pacific Palisades, CA)
1989	HORNEZ, André		84	
• 1995	HORNUNG, Richard		45	Complications from A.I.D.S. (in Los Angeles, CA)
1989	#+ HOROWITZ, Vladimir		85	Heart attack
1991	HORRALL, Craig		?	A.I.D.S.
1970	+ HORTON, Edward Everett		84	Cancer (in Encino, CA)
1978	# HORVATH, Charles		57	Died in Woodland Hills, CA
1980	# HOSKINS, Allen "Farina"		59	Cancer (in Oakland, CA)
• 1954	HOTELY, Mae		81	Died in Coronado, CA
1926	#+ HOUDINI, Harry		52	Peritonitis from a ruptured appendix (in Detroit, MI)
1989	HOULE, Daniel		41	A.I.D.S.
1961	HOUSE, Billy		71	Heart attack
1988	# HOUSEMAN, John	★	86	Spinal cancer
1942	#+ HOUSMAN, Arthur		52	Pneumonia (in Los Angeles, CA)
• 1993	HOUSTON, David		57	Brain aneurysm
1991	HOUSTON, Donald		67	
1944	HOUSTON, George F.		46	Heart attack
1980	# HOUSTON, Renée		77	Died in London, England
1981	HOVEN, Adrian		57	Heart attack (in West Germany)
1992	HOVING, Jane Pickens		83	Heart failure
1936	HOWARD, Booth		47	Run down by a car (in Los Angeles, CA)
1993	HOWARD, Cy		77	Heart failure (in Los Angeles, CA)
1941	HOWARD, David		45	Heart ailment
1965	HOWARD, Esther		72	Heart attack (in Hollywood, CA)
1965	HOWARD, Eugene		84	
1976	HOWARD, Frances		73	After a lengthy illness
1952	#+ HOWARD, Jerome "Curly"		48	Following several strokes (in San Gabriel, CA)
• 1995	HOWARD, John		82	Heart failure (at his home in Santa Rosa, CA)
1956	HOWARD, Kathleen		75	Died in Hollywood, CA
1943	#+ HOWARD, Leslie	☆	50	In a passenger plane shot down by a Nazi fighter (in Bay of Biscay)
1989	# HOWARD, Mary		76	After a brief illness
1975	#+ HOWARD, Moe		77	Cancer (in Hollywood, CA)
1955	#+ HOWARD, Shemp		55	Coronary occlusion (in Hollywood, CA)
1946	HOWARD, Sydney		61	
1988	HOWARD, Trevor	☆	71	Influenza, bronchitis & jaundice
1954	HOWARD, William K.		54	Throat cancer
1949	#+ HOWARD, Willie		61	After a brief illness (in New York, NY)
1991	HOWDEN, Victoria		27	Suicide (gunshot)
• 1976	#+ HOWE, James Wong		76	Cancer
• 1961	HOWELL, Alice		72	Died in Los Angeles, CA
1982	HOWELL, Lottice		84	
1993	# HOWELL, Wayne		72	Unreported causes (in Pompano Beach, FL)
1992	HOWERD, Frankie		70	Apparent heart attack
1964	# HOWES, Reed		64	Died in Woodland Hills, CA
1936	+ HOWLAND, Jobyna		56	Heart attack (in Los Angeles, CA)
1984	HOWLETT, Noel		82	
1959	# HOWLIN, Olin		63	Died in Hollywood, CA
1982	HOXIE, Al		80	
1965	HOXIE, Jack		75	Died in Keyes, OK
1983	HOYOS, Rudolfo Jr.		68	Cerebral hemorrhage
• 1980	HOYOS, Rudolfo Sr.		83	Results of a fall (in Los Angeles, CA)
1953	HOYT, Arthur		79	After a long illness (in Woodland Hills, CA)
1991	# HOYT, John		86	Lung cancer
1988	HUBBARD, John		65	
1993	HUBER, Gusti		78	Heart failure (in Mount Kisco, NY)
1959	HUBER, Harold		49	Died in New York, NY
• 1963	HUDD, Walter		64	Died in London, England
1991	HUDDLESTON, Floyd	☆	73	Following a heart attack
• 1964	HUDMAN, Wesley		47	Murdered (in Williams, AZ)
1992	#+ HUDNET, Bill		47	Liver disease

...DEATHS OF MOVIE AND TELEVISION PERSONALITIES — BY NAME...

YEAR	NAME		AGE	CAUSE AND/OR PLACE OF DEATH
1972	HUDSON, Rochelle		57	Died in Palm Desert, CA
1985	#+ HUDSON, Rock	☆	59	Complications from A.I.D.S.
1974	#+ HUDSON, William		49	Laennec's cirrhosis (in Woodland Hills, CA)
1973	HUFF, Louise		77	
1985	HUFFMAN, David		40	Murdered (stabbed to death)
1983	HUGHES, Arthur		89	Pneumonia
1965	HUGHES, Gareth		71	Died in Woodland Hills, CA
1976	+ HUGHES, Howard		70	Stroke (on a chartered airplane from Acapulco to Texas)
1970	HUGHES, Joseph Anthony		65	Acute alcohol and barbiturate mixture (in Pasadena, CA)
1995	HUGHES, Lillian H.		73	Cancer (at her Charlestown Retire. Ctr. home in Balt., MD)
1958	+ HUGHES, Lloyd		60	Died in Los Angeles, CA
1994	HUGO, Laurence		76	Alzheimer's disease (in Charlottesville, VA)
1974	HUGO, Mauritz		65	Heart ailment (in Woodland Hills, CA)
1964	HULBERT, Claude		63	Died in Sydney, Australia
1978	HULBERT, Jack		69	Died in London, England
1977	HULL, Henry		86	Died in Cornwall, England
1957	#+ HULL, Josephine	★	71	Cerebral hemorrhage (in New York, NY)
1974	# HULL, Warren		71	Heart failure (in Waterbury, CT)
1994	+ HUMANN, Helena Enize		52	After a long illness (in Dallas, Texas)
1984	+ HUMBERSTONE, Bruce H.		80	Stomach cancer & pneumonia
1963	HUMBERT, George		81	
1967	HUME, Benita		61	Died in Egerton, England
1926	HUMPHREY, Paul		22	Premature explosion of dynamite while filming
1942	# HUMPHREY, William		68	Coronary thrombosis (in West Hollywood, CA)
1979	HUNNICUTT, Arthur	☆	68	Cancer (in Woodland Hills, CA)
1993	HUNT, Frances		77	Complications following a stroke
1969	HUNT, Martita		68	Died in London, England
1992	HUNT, Richard		40	A.I.D.S.
1975	HUNTER, Ian		75	Died in England
1969	#+ HUNTER, Jeffrey		42	Head injuries from a fall in his home (Van Nuys, CA)
1996	# HUNTER, Ross	☆	75	Cancer (in Los Angeles, CA)
1974	+ HUNTLEY, Chet		61	Lung cancer (in Bozeman, MT)
1990	HUNTLEY, Raymond		86	
1995	HURD, Hugh		70	Complications of hypertension and kidney failure (in NY)
1974	#+ HUROK, Sol		85	Apparent heart attack
1986	HURST, B. D.		91	
1947	HURST, Brandon		80	Arteriosclerosis (in Burbank, CA)
1994	HURST, Margaret		75	Heart failure (at Sherman Oaks Med. Ctr., CA)
1953	HURST, Paul C.		64	Suicide (in Hollywood, CA)
1946	+ HURT, Marlin		40	Heart attack
1995	HURWITZ, Harry		57	Heart failure (in Los Angeles, CA)
1991	HURWITZ, Leo		81	
1987	+ HUSTON, John	★	81	Complications from emphysema
1950	#+ HUSTON, Walter	★	66	Aneurysm (in Beverly Hills, CA)
1991	HUTCHENRIDER, C. B.		83	
1976	HUTCHESON, David		71	
1945	HUTCHINS, Robert "Wheezer"		20	Killed in an Army training camp accident during World War 2
1967	HUTH, Harold		75	Died in London, England
1984	HUTTON, Ina Ray		65	
1979	#+ HUTTON, Jim		45	Cancer of the liver (in Los Angeles, CA)
1987	# HUTTON, Marion		67	Cancer
1994	# HUTTON, Robert		73	Died in Kingston, NY)
1977	HYAMS, Leila		72	
1992	HYDE, Jacquelyn		61	
1991	HYDE-WHITE, Wilfrid		87	Congestive heart failure
1977	HYLAND, Diana		41	Cancer
1995	+ HYMAN, Phyllis		45	Suicide (pills) found unconscious in her NYC apt.
1948	HYMER, Warren		42	After a long illness (alcoholism) in Los Angeles, CA
1955	HYTTEN, Olaf		67	After a heart attack (on the set of "Sir Walter Raleigh") in L.A.
1990	IBBS, Ronald		74	Cancer
1990	IDEN, Rosalind		82	
1972	+ IHNAT, Steve		37	Heart attack (in Cannes, France)
1987	ILINSKY, Igor		85	
1991	IMAI, Tadashi		79	

• New entry. # Original name (Pt. 7). + Interment (Pt. 5).　　185　　☆ Oscar nominee, ★ Oscar winner (Pt. 10)

...DEATHS OF MOVIE AND TELEVISION PERSONALITIES — BY NAME...

YEAR	NAME		AGE	CAUSE AND/OR PLACE OF DEATH
1974	IMBODEN, David C.		87	Died in Kansas City, Missouri
1958	IMHOF, Roger		83	Died in Hollywood, CA
1989	# IMMEDIATO, Al		72	Cancer
1947	# INCE, John E.		68	Pneumonia (in Hollywood, CA)
1937	# INCE, Ralph W.		49	Automobile accident (in London, England)
1938	INCE, Richard		23	Died in Oakland, CA
1924	INCE, Thomas H.		42	Heart failure (in Beverly Hills, CA)
1968	INDRISANO, John "Johnny"		62	Apparent suicide (hanged himself in his San Fernando Valley home)
1976	# INESCORT, Frieda		74	Multiple sclerosis (in Woodland Hills, CA)
1973	# INGE, William		60	Suicide (in Hollywood, CA)
1936	INGERSOLL, William		75	Acute indigestion (in Los Angeles, CA)
1993	INGLIS, Brian		76	Died in London, England
1956	INGRAHAM, Lloyd		81	Pneumonia (in Woodland Hills, CA)
1989	INGRAM, Bill		69	
1969	INGRAM, Jack		66	Heart attack (in Canoga Park, CA)
1969	+ INGRAM, Rex		73	Heart attack (in L.A.) — Do not confuse with Rex Ingram (Hitchcock)
1950	#+ INGRAM, Rex (Hitchcock)		57	Cerebral hemorrhage (in North Hollywood, CA)
1993	INNOCENT, Harold		60	After a short illness (in London)
1995	IPPOLITO, Joseph A.		39	Kidney failure (in Santa Monica, CA)
1990	+ IRELAND, Jill		54	Breast & lung cancer
1992	IRELAND, John	☆	78	Leukemia
1990	IRVING, Richard		73	After heart surgery
1943	IRVING, William J.		50	Died in Los Angeles, CA
1961	IRVING. George		87	Heart attack (in Hollywood, CA)
1956	IRWIN, Bobby		42	Died in Los Angeles, CA
1957	IRWIN, Boyd		76	Died in Woodland Hills, CA
1969	# IRWIN, Charles W.		81	Cancer (in Woodland Hills, CA)
1938	IRWIN, May		76	Bronchial pneumonia
1992	ISING, Rudolf "Rudy"	★	88	
1969	ITURBI, Amparo		70	
1980	+ ITURBI, José		84	Heart attack (in Los Angeles, CA)
1959	IVAN, Rosalind		75	
1989	IVENS, Joris		90	
1995	IVES, Burl		85	Mouth cancer & congestive heart failure (in Anacortes, WA)
1992	JABARA, Paul	★	44	Lymphoma from A.I.D.S.
1995	# JACK, Wolfman		57	Heart attack (at his home in Belvidere, N.C.)
1992	JACKSON, Felix		90	Congestive heart failure
1990	JACKSON, Freda		82	
1990	JACKSON, Gordon		66	Cancer
1972	+ JACKSON, Mahalia		60	Heart disease (in Evergreen Park, IL)
1991	#+ JACKSON, Mary Ann		68	
1971	# JACKSON, Selmer		82	Heart disease (in Burbank, CA)
1967	JACKSON, Thomas		81	Heart attack (in Hollywood, CA)
1950	JACKSON, Warren		57	After his car collided with a truck
1973	JACOBS, Arthur P.		51	Massive heart attack in his sleep
1992	JACOBS, Everett "Jake"		68	Cancer
1993	JACOBSON, Arthur		92	Died in Woodland Hills, CA
1988	JACOBSON, Henrietta		82	
1980	# JACQUES, Hattie		56	Heart attack (in London, England)
1991	JAFFA, Max		79	
1989	JAFFE, Allen		60	After a long illness
1974	JAFFE, Carl		71	Died in London, England
1992	JAFFE, Henry		85	Died in Beverly Hills, CA
1984	+ JAFFE, Sam	☆	93	Cancer
1991	JAGGER, Dean	★	87	Influenza
1986	JAMES, Claire		65	
1995	JAMES, Edward		86	Heart failure (in Escondido, CA)
1948	JAMES, Gladden		56	Leukemia (in Hollywood, CA)
1983	JAMES, Harry		67	Lymphatic cancer
1925	JAMES, Horace B.		72	After a long illness
1990	JAMES, Jessica		60	Cancer
1992	JAMES, Ralph		67	
1976	JAMES, Sidney "Sid"		62	Died in Sunderland, England
1946	JAMES, Walter		60	Heart attack (in Gardena, CA)

YEAR	NAME		AGE	CAUSE AND/OR PLACE OF DEATH
1987	JAMESON, Joyce		55	
1944	# JAMISON, Bud		50	Died in Hollywood, CA
1980	JANNEY, Leon		63	Cancer (in Guadalajara, Mexico)
1938	JANNEY, William "Bill"		34	After a short, serious setback while hospitalized
1950	# JANNINGS, Emil	★	63	Cancer (in Austria)
1980	#+ JANSSEN, David		48	Died of a massive heart attack (at his home in Malibu, CA)
1990	JANSSEN, Werner		91	
• 1958	# JAQUET, Frank		73	Heart attack (in Los Angeles, CA)
1990	JARAY, Hans		83	Heart failure
1994	JARMAN, Derek		52	Complications of A.I.D.S. (in London, England)
1987	# JARRETT, Art		81	Pneumonia
1970	JARVIS, Al		60	Heart attack
1933	JARVIS, Jean		30	After a lingering illness
1933	JARVIS, Laura E.		67	Injuries from hit-and-run driver
1993	JARVIS, Patience		56	Melanoma
1971	JARVIS, Robert C.		79	
1990	JARVIS, Scott		48	A.I.D.S.
1939	JARVIS, Sydney		58	Died in Hollywood, CA
1979	# JASON, Leigh		74	After a long illness
• 1940	JAUBERT, Maurice		40	Killed in action during World War 2
• 1995	JEAKINS, Dorothy	☆	81	Alzheimer's and Parkinson's diseases (in Santa Barbara, CA)
1985	JEANS, Isabel		93	
1973	# JEANS, Ursula		66	Died near London, England
1963	JEAVES, Allan		78	Heart attack (in London, England)
1932	JEFFERSON, Thomas		76	Following a brief illness (in Hollywood, CA)
1988	JEFFREY, Howard		53	A.I.D.S.
1987	JEFFRIES, Lang		55	Cancer
1991	JEFFRIES, Peter		62	Following open-heart surgery
1974	# JENKINS, Allen		74	Complications following surgery (in Santa Monica, CA)
1984	JENKINS, Gordon		73	Amyotrophic lateral sclerosis
1962	JENKS, Frank		60	Cancer (in Hollywood, CA)
1970	# JENKS, Si		93	Heart disease (in Woodland Hills, CA)
1961	JENNINGS, Al		97	Died in Tarzana, CA
1979	# JENNINGS, Claudia		29	Head-on collision with a truck (on Pacific Coast Hwy, CA)
1937	JENNINGS, De Witt		57	Died in Hollywood, CA
1932	# JENNINGS, S. E.		51	
1993	JENSEN, Lenore Kingston		79	Cancer (in Van Nuys, CA)
1986	# JEROME, Suzie		26	Cut wrists & exposure
• 1955	# JERROLD, Mary		77	Died in London, England
1981	+ JESSEL, George		83	Heart attack (in Los Angeles, CA)
1972	JEWELL, Isabel		61	Natural causes (in Hollywood, CA)
1966	JIMINEZ, Solodad		92	Following a stroke
1994	JOBIM, Antonio Carlos		67	Heart failure after minor surgery (in New York City)
1993	JOHANN, Zita		89	Pneumonia (in Nyack Hospital, Nyack, NY)
1991	JOHANSEN, Gunnar		85	Liver cancer
1916	JOHNSON, Arthur V.		39	Died in Philadelphia, PA
• 1996	JOHNSON, Ben	★	77	Apparent heart attack (in Mesa, AZ)
1981	JOHNSON, Brad		56	
1982	JOHNSON, Celia		73	Stroke
1962	#+ JOHNSON, Chic		70	Kidney ailment
• 1974	# JOHNSON, Chubby		71	Died in Hollywood, CA
1982	JOHNSON, Dan		38	
1984	JOHNSON, E. Lamont		29	
1960	JOHNSON, Emory		66	Critically burned when his bed caught fire
1957	# JOHNSON, Katie		79	
1975	# JOHNSON, Kay		71	
1937	JOHNSON, Martin		52	Airplane crash (in Los Angeles, CA)
1977	+ JOHNSON, Nunnally		80	
1953	JOHNSON, Osa		58	Heart attack (in New York, NY)
1965	JOHNSON, Rita		52	Brain hemorrhage (in Los Angeles, CA)
1984	JOHNSON, Sunny		30	Cerebral hemorrhage
1971	#+ JOHNSON, Tor		67	Heart condition (in San Fernando, CA)
• 1996	JOHNSTON, Johnny		80	Heart failure (in Cape Coral, FL)
1966	JOHNSTON, Oliver		78	
1978	JOLLEY, L. Stanford		78	Died in Woodland Hills, CA

YEAR	NAME		AGE	CAUSE AND/OR PLACE OF DEATH
1950	#+ JOLSON, Al		64	Heart attack (in San Francisco, CA)
1983	JONAH, Dolly		53	
1992	JONES, Allan		84	Lung cancer
1976	JONES, Anissa "Buffy"		18	Lethal mix of Quaaludes and alcohol (in Oceanside, CA)
1981	JONES, Barry		87	
• 1971	# JONES, Bobby		69	Died in Atlanta, GA
1969	#+ JONES, Brian		25	Drowned while under the influence of liquor and drugs (in England)
1942	#+ JONES, Buck		52	Burned to death while trying to save others in a fire (in Boston, MA)
1990	# JONES, Candy		64	Cancer
1983	+ JONES, Carolyn	☆	54	Cancer
1992	# JONES, Charlotte		76	Heart disease
1986	JONES, Darby		76	Cancer
1988	JONES, Duane		51	
1972	# JONES, Emrys		57	Heart attack
• 1930	JONES, F. Richard "Dick"		36	Heart disease
• 1963	JONES, Gordon		52	Heart attack (in Tarzana, CA)
1993	+ JONES, Ken		54	Cancer (in Los Angeles, CA)
1989	JONES, Reed		35	Liver cancer
1965	#+ JONES, Spike		53	Emphysema (in Beverly Hills, CA)
1971	# JONES, T. C.		50	Cancer (in Duarte, CA)
1985	JONES, Tyrone		29	Automobile accident
1992	JONSON, Kevin Joe		74	Cancer
1970	+ JOPLIN, Janis		27	Accidental drug overdose (heroin morphine) in Hollywood, CA
1988	JORDAN, Dorothy (Cooper)		82	
1991	JORDAN, Gerry		45	A.I.D.S.
1988	+ JORDAN, Jim "Fibber McGee"		91	Blood clot in brain (from a fall)
1984	JORDAN, John Duffield		81	
1961	#+ JORDAN, Marion "Molly McGee"		64	Cancer (in Encino, CA)
1993	# JORDAN, Richard		56	Brain tumor (at his home in Los Angles, CA)
1965	JORDAN, Robert "Bobby"		42	Liver ailment (in Los Angeles, CA)
1989	JORGENSEN, Christine (George)		62	Cancer of the bladder
1982	+ JORY, Victor		79	Apparent heart attack
1981	JOSLYN, Allyn		75	Cardiac failure (in Woodland Hills, CA)
• 1951	JOUVET, Louis		63	Heart attack (in Paris, France)
1985	# JOY, Leatrice		91	
1964	JOY, Nicholas		79	
1955	JOYCE, Alice "Vitagraph Girl"		65	Heart ailment (in Hollywood, CA)
1986	JOYCE, Anna		74	
1957	JOYCE, Peggy Hopkins		63	
1980	JOYCE, Yootha		53	Cirrhosis of the liver (in London, England)
• 1969	JUDEL, Charles		86	
1974	JUDGE, Arlene		62	Natural causes (in West Hollywood, CA)
1994	#+ JULIA, Raul		54	Complications of a stroke (at a hospital in Manhasset, NY)
1943	+ JULIAN, Rupert		54	Stroke
• 1943	JUNKERMANN, Hans		70	Died in Berlin, Germany
1982	JURGENS, Curt		69	Heart failure
• 1995	JURGENS, Dick		85	Cancer (in Sacramento, CA)
1993	JURIST, Ed		76	Died in Los Angeles, CA
1975	JUSTICE, James Robertson		70	Found dead in bed (in Winchester, Hampshire, England)
	K			
1994	# KABIBBLE, Ish		86	Respiratory failure due to emphysema (Joshua Tree, CA)
1979	KADAR, Jan		61	After being hospitalized (in Los Angeles, CA)
1968	KAHANAMOKU, Duke		77	After a heart attack (at the Waikiki Yacht Club in Honolulu, Hawaii)
• 1995	KAIDANOVSKY, Alexander		49	Heart attack (in Moscow)
• 1975	KALICH, Jacob		82	Cancer (in Lake Mahopac, NY)
• 1941	KALIZ, Armand		48	Heart attack (in Beverly Hills, CA)
• 1995	KALKIN, Gary		44	Complications from A.I.D.S. (at his home in L.A., CA)
1980	# KALLMAN, Dick		46	Murdered (in his Manhattan apartment)
1980	KAMINSKA, Ida	☆	80	
• 1950	KAMPERS, Fritz		59	Died in Germany
1992	KANE, Dennis		69	Cancer
1969	KANE, Eddie		79	Heart attack (in Hollywood, CA)
1966	+ KANE, Helen		58	After a 10-year bout with cancer (in Jackson Heights, NY)
1975	KANE, Joseph		81	Heart attack
1992	KANE, Paul		?	Heart attack

YEAR	NAME		AGE	CAUSE AND/OR PLACE OF DEATH
1993	KANIN, Michael		83	Died in Los Angeles, CA
1983	KAPER, Bronislau		81	Cancer
1984	KARAS, Anton		78	
1993	KARAS, Barry		49	Leukemia (in Boston, MA)
1993	KARIN, Rita		73	Following a bout with pneumonia (in New York)
1969	# KARLOFF, Boris		81	Respiratory ailment (in London, England)
1985	# KARLSON, Phil		77	Cancer
1979	KARNES, Robert		62	Heart failure (in Sherman Oaks, CA)
1970	+ KARNS, Roscoe		76	Died in Los Angeles, CA
• 1995	KAROL, Darcie		37	Breast cancer (in Boston, MA)
1990	KASHA, Lawrence		57	Brain cancer
1965	+ KASSEL, Art		69	
1984	KAST, Pierre		63	
1979	# KASZNAR, Kurt		65	Cancer (in Santa Monica, CA)
1958	# KATCH, Kurt		62	During surgery for cancer (in Los Angeles, CA)
1985	+ KATZ, Mickey		75	Natural causes
• 1996	KATZ, Oscar		82	After a bout with pneumonia (at his home in Los Angeles, CA)
1990	KATZKA, Gabriel		58	Heart attack
1984	+ KAUFMAN, Andy		35	Lung cancer (in Los Angeles, CA)
1915	KAUFMAN, Joseph		35	Pneumonia
1991	KAUFMAN, Robert	☆	60	Heart attack
1986	# KAY, Beatrice		79	After suffering several strokes
1987	#+ KAYE, Danny		74	Heart failure due to hepatitis
1987	+ KAYE, Nora (Ross)		67	Cancer
1987	KAYE, Sammy		77	
1991	KAYE, Sylvia Fine		78	Emphysema
• 1995	KAYE, Toni		49	Cancer (in Los Angeles, CA)
1989	KAYE-MARTIN, Edward		50	Lymphoma
• 1945	KAYSSLER, Friedrich		71	Died in Leinmachnow, Germany
1986	KEAN, Betty		69	After a brief illness
• 1959	KEANE, Edward		75	
1993	KEANE, Joe		69	Cancer (in Woodland Hills, CA)
1981	KEANE, Robert Emmett		96	Died in Hollywood, CA
1956	KEARNS, Allen B.		61	
• 1962	KEARNS, Joseph		54	
1961	KEATING, Fred		64	Heart attack
1964	KEATING, Larry		67	Leukemia (in Hollywood, CA)
1966	#+ KEATON, Buster		70	Lung cancer (in Woodland Hills, CA)
• 1946	KEATON, Joseph Sr.		78	Died in Hollywood, CA
• 1981	KEATON, Louise		78	Cancer (in Van Nuys, CA)
• 1955	KEATON, Myra		?	
1994	KEATS, Steven		48	Suicide (found dead in his Manhattan apartment)
1993	KEEGAN, Terry		59	Suicide (near Kingman, Arizona)
1993	+ KEELER, Ruby		83	Cancer (in Rancho Mirage, CA)
• 1970	KEEN, Malcolm		82	Died in England
1986	KEENAN, Paul		30	A.I.D.S.
1971	KEENE, Richard		80	
1963	# KEENE, Tom		64	Died in Woodland Hills, CA
1984	+ KEIGHLEY, William		94	Stroke
1960	# KEITH, Ian		61	Died in New York, NY
1966	KEITH, Robert		68	Died in Los Angeles, CA
1973	+ KELLAWAY, Cecil	☆	79	Died in West Los Angeles, CA
1987	KELLER, Harry		73	Heart complications
• 1968	KELLER, Helen		86	Died in Westport, CT
1975	KELLERMAN, Annette		87	
1991	KELLEY, Edward (Barry)		82	Congestive heart failure
1983	KELLIN, Mike		61	Lung cancer
• 1995	KELLIN, Sally Moffet		63	Lung cancer (in Nyack, NY)
1982	# KELLJAN, Robert		52	After a long bout with cancer
1976	KELLOGG, Ray		70	Cancer
1966	# KELLY, Dorothy		51	Died in a fire at her home in La Jolla, CA
1979	+ KELLY, Emmett		80	Heart attack
• 1996	# KELLY, Gene	★	83	Died in his sleep after suffering 2 strokes in 2 yrs. (in Beverly Hills)
1982	+ KELLY, Grace	★	52	Brain hemorrhage after a car crash
1992	KELLY, Jack		65	After suffering a stroke

• New entry.   # Original name (Pt. 7).   + Interment (Pt. 5).

189

☆ Oscar nominee, ★ Oscar winner (Pt. 10)

...DEATHS OF MOVIE AND TELEVISION PERSONALITIES — BY NAME...

YEAR	NAME		AGE	CAUSE AND/OR PLACE OF DEATH
• 1964	KELLY, James "Tiny"		49	Heart ailment (in Hollywood) Do not confuse with James T. Kelly
• 1933	KELLY, James T.		79	(Do not confuse with James "Tiny" Kelly, d. 1964)
1959	KELLY, Joe		57	Heart attack
1947	KELLY, John		46	
1968	KELLY, Kitty		66	Cancer
1944	KELLY, Lew		65	Died in Los Angeles, CA
• 1995	KELLY, Nancy	☆	73	Complications of diabetes (at her home in Bel Air, CA)
1981	#+ KELLY, Patsy		71	Cancer (in Woodland Hills, CA)
1956	#+ KELLY, Paul		57	Heart attack (in Los Angeles, CA)
1992	KELLY, Paula		72	After a long illness
1961	KELSEY, Fred A.		77	Died in Hollywood, CA
1946	KELSO, Mayme		79	Heart attack (in South Pasadena, CA)
1968	KELTON, Pert		60	Stroke
1940	KEMP, Hal		36	Pneumonia after auto injuries
1953	KEMP, Paul		54	Died in Bad Godesberg, West Germany
1950	KEMPER, Charles		49	Injuries from an automobile crash
1991	KEMPFF, Wilhelm		95	Parkinson's disease
1953	# KENDALL, Cy		55	Died in Woodland Hills, CA
1959	#+ KENDALL, Kay (Harrison)		32	Leukemia (in London, England)
1990	KENDRICK, Henry		56	Emphysema and pneumonia
1992	KENDRICKS, Eddie		52	Lung cancer
1985	KENIN, Alexa		23	
1990	KENNEDY, Arthur	☆	75	Brain tumor
1973	# KENNEDY, Douglas		58	Cancer (in Kailua, Hawaii)
1948	+ KENNEDY, Edgar		58	Throat cancer (in Woodland Hills, CA)
1958	# KENNEDY, Fred		48	A broken neck (after falling from his horse during filming)
1987	KENNEDY, Madge		96	Respiratory failure
1944	KENNEDY, Merna		35	Following a heart attack
1965	KENNEDY, Tom		81	Bone cancer (in Woodland Hills, CA)
1989	KENNER, Warren		64	Heart attack
1992	#+ KENNY, Herbert C.		77	Cancer
1923	KENT, Charles		70	After being hospitalized (in Brooklyn, NY)
1953	KENT, Craufurd		72	After a short illness (in Los Angeles, CA)
• 1955	# KENT, Robert		46	
1980	KENTON, Erle C.		83	Parkinson's disease & emphysema
1979	#+ KENTON, Stan		66	Stroke
1979	KENYON, Doris		81	Died in Beverly Hills, CA
1990	# KERMACK, Paul		57	Heart attack
1991	KERMAN, Sheppard		62	Lung cancer
1966	KERN, James V.		57	Pneumonia, after a short illness
1945	#+ KERN, Jerome		60	Cerebral hemorrhage
1968	KERR, Lorence "Larry"		?	
1994	# KERR, Stu		66	After 8-yr. battle with bone marrow cancer (in Balt., MD)
1947	#+ KERRIGAN, J. Warren		67	Bronchial pneumonia (1 of several actors with this name)
1964	KERRIGAN, Joseph M.		76	Died in Hollywood, CA
1956	# KERRY, Norman		66	Died in Hollywood, CA
1991	+ KERT, Larry		60	A.I.D.S.
• 1995	KETCHUM, Larry		49	Heart attack (in Sierra Vista, AZ)
1954	# KEY, Kathleen		47	
1985	KEYSER, Andy		33	Cancer
1987	KEZER, Glenn B.		63	Cancer
• 1995	KHEIFITS, Iosif		89	Died in St. Petersburg, Russia
1956	#+ KIBBEE, Guy		70	Parkinson's disease (in East Islip, NY)
1993	KIBBEE, Lois		71	Brain tumor (at Sloane-Kettering Cancer Ctr., NY)
• 1970	KIBBEE, Milton		73	Died in Simi Valley, CA
1987	KIDD, Jonathan (Kurt Richards)		73	After surgery for an aorta aneurysm
1990	KIELY, Pat		59	After a long illness
• 1966	KIEPURA, Jan		64	Heart ailment (in Harrison, NY)
• 1996	KIESLOWSKI, Krzysztof	☆	54	Heart attack
1991	KIKER, Douglas		61	Heart attack
• 1953	#+ Kiki		52	Natural causes (in Paris, France)
1972	KIKUME, Al		78	
1964	+ KILBRIDE, Percy		76	Brain injury from auto accident (in Los Angeles, CA)
1965	+ KILGALLEN, Dorothy		52	Accidental death? (Seconal and alcohol)
1991	# KILIAN, Pauline		83	Complications from diabetes

• New entry. # Original name (Pt. 7). + Interment (Pt. 5).   190   ☆ Oscar nominee, ★ Oscar winner (Pt. 10)

...DEATHS OF MOVIE AND TELEVISION PERSONALITIES — BY NAME...

YEAR	NAME		AGE	CAUSE AND/OR PLACE OF DEATH
1979	+ KILIAN, Victor		81	Killed by burglars (in his Hollywood apartment)
1938	KIMBALL, Edward M.		78	Died in Hollywood, CA
1996	KINDLE, Tom		47	Complications of A.I.D.S. (in Los Angeles, CA)
1963	KING, Anita		74	Heart attack
1944	KING, Charles		54	Pneumonia (in London) Do not confuse with Chas. L. King, d. 1957
1957	KING, Charles L. Sr.		58	Died in Hollywood, CA (Do not confuse with Charles King d. 1944)
1941	# KING, Claude E.		62	Died in Los Angeles, CA
1986	KING, Dennis Jr.		?	Heart attack
1971	# KING, Dennis Sr.		73	Heart condition (in New York, NY)
1982	+ KING, Henry	☆	86	Died in his sleep at home
1993	KING, Jean		76	Heart attack (in North Hollywood, CA)
1951	KING, Joe		68	Died in Woodland Hills, CA
1947	KING, Leslie		71	
1968	KING, Martin Luther Jr.		39	Murdered (shot)
1992	# KING, Michael		69	
1982	KING, Mollie		86	Following a stroke
1984	KING, Walter Woolf		84	Heart attack
1985	KING, Wayne		84	
1991	KINGHAM, Bernard		65	A stroke related to spinal cancer
1958	KINGSFORD, Walter		75	Heart attack (in North Hollywood, CA)
1995	# KINGSLEY, Sidney		88	Stroke (at his home in Oakland, N.J.)
1984	KINGSLEY, Susan		37	Died when her car was struck head-on by another
1993	KINGSTON, Lenore (Jensen)		79	Cancer (in Van Nuys, CA)
1967	KINGSTON, Winifred		?	
1992	KINISON, Sam		38	Internal injuries following a car crash
1988	KINNEAR, Roy		54	After falling from his horse during filming
1954	KINNELL, Murray		65	
1992	KINNEY, Jack		82	
1983	KINSER, Patrick		30	Pulmonary failure
1991	KINSKI, Klaus		65	Found dead, apparently of natural causes
1974	KINSOLVING, Lee		36	
1995	KIRBY, George		71	Parkinson's disease (at a nursing home in Las Vegas, NV)
1948	KIRK, Jack "Pappy"		53	Died in Alaska
1948	KIRK, John		86	After a heart attack
1990	KIRK, Lisa		62	Lung cancer
1971	KIRKLAND, Muriel		68	Emphysema and complications
1989	KIRKWOOD, James Jr.		64	Cancer
1963	KIRKWOOD, James Sr.		80	Died in Woodland Hills, CA
1992	KIRSTEN, Dorothy		82	Complications from a stroke
1988	KJELLIN, Alf		68	Heart attack
1983	KLEIN, Adelaide		82	Brain tumor
1973	KLEMPERER, Otto		88	Died in his sleep
1982	KLINGER, Ruth S.		59	Died in her sleep
1950	KLOEPFER, Eugen		64	Died in Wiesbaden, Germany
1993	KLOS, Elmar	★	83	Cause unreported (in Prague, Czechoslovakia)
1981	KNAPP, Evelyn		72	Died in West Hollywood, CA
1993	# KNIGHT, Bob		72	Heart attack (in New York)
1987	KNIGHT, Esmond		80	
1976	# KNIGHT, Fuzzy		74	Died in Hollywood, CA
1987	# KNIGHT, June		74	Complications after a stroke
1986	#+ KNIGHT, Ted		62	After surgery for a urinary tract growth
1981	KNOPF, Edwin H.		82	After a long illness
1955	KNOTT, Lydia		88	Died in Woodland Hills, CA
1995	# KNOWLES, Patric		84	Cerebral hemorrhage (in Los Angeles, CA)
1995	KNOX, Alexander		88	Bone cancer (at an infirmary in Northumberland, Eng.)
1974	KNOX, Teddy		78	Died in England
1991	KOBAL, John		51	Pneumonia
1995	KOCH, Howard	★	93	Pneumonia (in Kingston, NY) Do not confuse with producer
1938	KOHLER, Fred		49	Heart attack (in Los Angeles, CA)
1964	KOLB, Clarence		89	Stroke (in Los Angeles, CA)
1991	KOLB, Glenn		39	A.I.D.S.
1947	+ KOLKER, Henry		72	Injuries from a fall (in Los Angeles, CA)
1992	KOPLIN, Merton Y.		71	
1956	KORDA, Alexander		62	Heart attack
1961	KORDA, Zoltan		66	

• New entry. # Original name (Pt. 7). + Interment (Pt. 5).　　191　　☆ Oscar nominee, ★ Oscar winner (Pt. 10)

YEAR	NAME		AGE	CAUSE AND/OR PLACE OF DEATH
1944	KORFF, Arnold		73	Heart ailment
1980	+ KORJUS, Miliza	☆	73	Heart attack
1957	+ KORNGOLD, Erich Wolfgang		60	The aftermath of a cerebral thrombosis suffered a year earlier
1973	KORNMAN, Mary		56	Cancer (in Glendale, CA)
• 1967	KORTMAN, Robert F.		79	Cancer (in Long Beach, CA)
1970	KORTNER, Fritz		78	Leukemia (in Munich, Germany)
1994	KOSCINA, Sylva		61	After a long illness complicated by heart problems (in Rome)
1994	KOSLECK, Martin		89	After abdominal surgery (in Santa Monica, CA)
1956	KOSLOFF, Theodore		74	Died in Los Angeles, CA
1994	KOSTAL, Irwin	★	83	Heart attack (in Studio City, CA)
1980	+ KOSTELANETZ, Andre		79	
1988	KOSTER, Henry		83	
1962	+ KOVACS, Ernie		42	Automobile accident (in Beverly Hills, CA)
1993	KRAFT, David		35	Crohn's disease (in Los Angeles, CA)
• 1950	# KRAHLY, Hanns		65	Died in Los Angeles, CA
1989	KRAMER, Mandel J.		72	
1992	KRAMER, Sy		59	Cancer
1992	KRAMER, Tim		34	A.I.D.S.
• 1995	KRAMEROV, Savelly		60	Cancer (in San Francisco, CA)
1981	KRASKER, Robert		67	
1984	KRASNA, Norman	★	74	Heart attack
1959	KRAUSS, Werner		75	Died in Vienna, Austria
1991	KREBS, Nita		85	Apparent heart attack
1989	KREEL, Kenneth		48	A.I.D.S.
1962	+ KREISLER, Fritz		86	Following a heart attack
1994	KRIM, Arthur		84	After a long illness (at his home in New York City)
1991	KROEGER, Berry		78	Kidney failure
1990	KRUEGER, Michael		39	Cancer
1960	KRUGER, Alma		91	Died in Seattle, WA
1974	+ KRUGER, Otto		89	Stroke and cerebral vascular complications (in Woodland Hills, CA)
1992	KRUGMAN, Lou		78	Cancer
1973	+ KRUPA, Gene		64	Heart problems and leukemia (in Yonkers, NY)
1976	+ KUHLMAN, Kathryn		63	Pulmonary hypertension after open-heart surgery
1965	# KULKY, Henry "Hank"		53	Heart attack (in Oceanside, CA)
1993	KULLER, Sid Charles		83	Colon cancer (in Sherman Oaks, CA)
1983	KULLMAN, Charles		80	
1991	KULP, Nancy		69	Cancer of the jaw
1990	KULUVA, Will		78	Embolism
1963	KUPCINET, Karyn		22	Murdered (bound and strangled)
1992	KUSELL, Maurice L.		89	Pneumonia
• 1931	KUWA, George K.		46	
1982	KYDD, Sam		67	Respiratory ailment
1985	+ KYSER, Kay		79	Heart attack
	L			
1917	LaBADIE, Florence		29	Blood poisoning after being crushed when her car overturned (in NY)
1952	LaCAVA, Gregory	☆	59	Died at his home in Malibu Beach, CA
• 1979	LACEY, Catherine		75	Died in London, England
1991	LACEY, Ronald		55	Cancer
1975	LACHMAN, Harry		88	Heart attack
1968	LACKTEEN, Frank		73	Cerebral and respiratory illness (in Woodland Hills, CA)
1964	+ LADD, Alan		50	Accidental death (alcohol/drug mix) in Palm Springs, CA
1982	+ LADD, Sue Carol		73	Complications of heart attack
1979	LAEMMLE, Carl Jr.		71	Stroke (after a 16-yr. battle with multiple sclerosis)
1939	+ LAEMMLE, Carl Sr.		72	Heart attack
1967	#+ LAHR, Bert		72	Internal hemorrhage (in New York, NY)
• 1963	LAIDLAW, Ethan		63	
• 1936	LAIDLAW, Roy		52	Heart attack (in Hollywood, CA)
1991	+ LAIRD, Jack		69	Cancer
1967	LAKE, Alice		71	Heart attack (in Paradise, CA)
1987	#+ LAKE, Arthur "Dagwood"		81	Heart attack
1980	LAKE, Florence		75	Died in Woodland Hills, CA
1973	#+ LAKE, Veronica		51	Acute hepatitis (in Burlington, VT)
1985	LALLY, Michael Sr.		82	
1926	#+ LaMARR, Barbara		29	Over-dieting (in Altadena, CA)
1982	+ LAMAS, Fernando		67	Cancer

...DEATHS OF MOVIE AND TELEVISION PERSONALITIES — BY NAME...

YEAR	NAME		AGE	CAUSE AND/OR PLACE OF DEATH
1921	LAMBERT, Clara		?	
1986	LAMBERT, Douglas		50	A.I.D.S.
1950	# LAMBERTI, Professor		58	After a long illness
1993	LAMONT, Charles		98	Pneumonia (in Woodland Hills, CA)
1991	LAMONT, Deni		59	Lung cancer
1990	LAMONT, Estelle		82	Respiratory failure
1989	LAMPKIN, Charles		76	Natural causes
• 1919	LAMPTON, Dee		21	Appendicitis (in New York, NY)
1994	# LANCASTER, Burt		80	Heart attack after suffering a stroke (at his condo in L.A.)
1983	LANCASTER, Robert		70	
1986	#+ LANCHESTER, Elsa	☆	84	Bronchial pneumonia
1935	LANDAU, David		57	After a lingering illness
1993	LANDAU, Ely A.		73	Complications following a stroke (in Los Angeles, CA)
1993	LANDAU, Richard		79	Complications after surgery (in Century City, CA)
1991	LANDERS, Hal		63	After being hospitalized for cancer treatment
1962	LANDERS, Lew		61	Heart attack
1948	# LANDI, Elissa		43	Cancer (in Kingston, NY)
1973	LANDIN, Hope		79	
1948	#+ LANDIS, Carole		29	Suicide (sleeping pills) in Brentwood Heights, CA
1975	LANDIS, Cullen		77	Died in Bloomfield Hills, MI
1992	# LANDIS, David		42	A.I.D.S.
1972	LANDIS, Jessie Royce		67	Cancer (in Danbury, CT)
1986	LANDIS, Joseph P.		67	Cancer
1992	LANDIS, Walter James		65	After a long illness
1991	#+ LANDON, Michael		54	Cancer of the liver & pancreas
1959	LANDOWSKA, Wanda		80	Died at her home in Lakeville, CT
1973	#+ LANE, Allan "Rocky"		69	Bone marrow cancer (in Woodland Hills, CA)
1945	# LANE, Charles		76	Cancer
1993	LANE, David T.		52	Brain cancer (in Dallas, Texas)
1981	#+ LANE, Lola		75	Inflammation of the arteries (in Santa Barbara, CA)
1959	# LANE, Lupino "Nipper"		67	Died in London, England
1953	LANE, Pat		53	Heart attack
• 1995	# LANE, Priscilla		76	After a brief illness (in an Andover, MA, nursing home)
1982	LANE, Richard		83	
1974	#+ LANE, Rosemary		60	Diabetes and pulmonary obstruction (in Woodland Hills, CA)
• 1995	LANE, Ziggy		75	Congestive heart failure (at his home in Miami, FL)
1972	+ LANFIELD, Sidney		74	Heart attack
1976	+ LANG, Fritz		85	
• 1941	LANG, Howard		64	Died in Hollywood, CA
• 1948	LANG, Matheson		68	Died in Bridgeton, Barbados
1972	LANG, Walter	☆	73	Kidney failure
1991	LANGAN, Glenn		73	Complications from cancer
1944	LANGDON, Harry		60	Cerebral hemorrhage (in Los Angeles, CA)
1943	LANGDON, Lillian		?	Died in Santa Monica, CA
1972	LANGLEY, Faith		43	Died in New York, NY
1994	LANGTON, David		82	Heart attack (at Stratford-on-Avon, England)
1980	LANGTON, Paul		66	Heart attack (in Burbank, CA)
1991	LANHAM, Roy		68	Cancer
1991	LANIN, Howard		93	Pneumonia
1972	# LANSING, Joi		42	Cancer (in Santa Monica, CA)
1994	# LANSING, Robert		66	Cancer (at Calgary Hospice in the Bronx, NY)
1990	LANSON, Snooky		76	
1993	# LANTEAU, William		70	Complications after heart surgery (in Los Angeles)
1992	# LANTZ, Gracie		88	Spinal cancer
1994	+ LANTZ, Walter	★	93	Heart attack (in Burbank, CA)
1959	#+ LANZA, Mario		38	Heart attack after suffering pneumonia and phlebitis (in Rome, Italy)
• 1979	LaPLANCHE, Rosemary		54	Died in Glendale, CA
• 1945	LaRENO, Richard "Dick"		71	Died in Hollywood, CA
1974	LARGAY, Raymond J. "Ray"		88	Stroke (in Woodland Hills, CA)
• 1946	LARKIN, George		57	
1936	LARKIN, John		62	Pneumonia (in Los Angeles, CA)
1969	#+ LaROCQUE, Rod		70	Died in Beverly Hills, CA
1975	LARRIMORE, Francine		77	Pneumonia
1988	LARSON, Eric		83	
1990	LaRUE, Bart		57	Heart failure

• New entry. # Original name (Pt. 7). + Interment (Pt. 5).   **193**   ☆ Oscar nominee, ★ Oscar winner (Pt. 10)

...DEATHS OF MOVIE AND TELEVISION PERSONALITIES — BY NAME...

YEAR	NAME	AGE	CAUSE AND/OR PLACE OF DEATH
1960	# LaRUE, Frank H.	81	Died in Woodland Hills, CA
1984	#+ LaRUE, Jack	83	Heart attack
1988	LASKY, Jesse L. Jr.	77	
1958	+ LASKY, Jesse L. Sr.	77	Died in Beverly Hills, CA
1959	Lassie (original dog)	18	
1985	LATCHAW, Paul	38	Complications from A.I.D.S.
1967	# LATELL, Lyle	62	Heart attack (in Hollywood, CA)
1988	# LATZ, Elaine	71	
1984	LAU, Wesley	63	Heart failure
1980	LAUCK, Chester H. "Lum"	79	After a brief illness (in Hot Springs, AR)
• 1950	LAUDER, Harry	79	Kidney ailment (in Lenarkshire, Scotland)
1948	#+ LAUGHLIN, Billy "Froggy"	16	Motor scooter—truck accident (in Corvina, CA)
1962	+ LAUGHTON, Charles ★	63	Following surgery for spinal cancer (in Los Angeles, CA)
• 1952	LAUGHTON, Edward "Eddie"	49	Pneumonia (in Hollywood, CA)
1965	#+ LAUREL, Stan	74	Heart attack (in Santa Monica, CA)
1980	LAURIE, John	83	Emphysema & a lung ailment (in Chalfont St. Peter, England)
1990	LAUTER, Harry	76	Heart failure
1971	LAVA, William B.	59	
1991	LaVERE, Jane	87	Heart problems
1945	#+ LAVERNE, Lucille	72	After being hospitalized for a broken hip (in Culver City, CA)
1940	LAW, Walter	64	Died in Hollywood, CA
1960	LAWFORD, Betty	50	After a long illness (in NY)
• 1940	LAWFORD, Ernest	69	Died in New York, NY
• 1972	# LAWFORD, May	?	Died in Monterey Park, CA
1984	+ LAWFORD, Peter	61	Cardiac arrest, liver & kidney disease
• 1995	LAWRENCE, Bruno	54	Lung cancer (at his home on New Zealand's North Island)
• 1931	LAWRENCE, Eddy	?	Suicide (gas) in San Diego, CA
1938	+ LAWRENCE, Florence	50	Suicide (mixture of cough syrup and ant paste) in Beverly Hills, CA
• 1957	LAWRENCE, Gerald	84	Died in England
1952	#+ LAWRENCE, Gertrude	54	Cancer of the liver (in New York, NY)
1992	LAWRENCE, John	60	Apparent heart failure
1990	LAWRENCE, Keith	39	Pneumonia
1926	+ LAWRENCE, Lillian	66	Died at the home of her daughter in Beverly Hills, CA
1991	LAWRENCE, Mark (producer)	70	Prostate cancer (Do not confuse with actor Marc Lawrence)
1991	LAWRENCE, Mary	73	Respiratory failure following pneumonia
• 1995	LAWRENCE, Rodha	71	Pulmonary fibrosis (in Sherman Oaks, CA)
• 1961	+ LAWRENCE, Walter Smith	59	Died in Palm Dale, CA
1947	#+ LAWRENCE, William E. "Babe"	51	Died in Hollywood, CA
• 1966	# LAWSON, Wilfrid	66	Heart attack (in London, England)
1969	# LAWTON, Frank	64	Died in London, England
1994	LAYTON, Joe	64	After an extended illness (in Key West, FL)
1993	LAZARUS, Irma	80	Cancer (in Cincinnati, Ohio)
1990	LEACOCK, Philip	73	Collapsed lungs
1992	LEAMING, Chet	66	After a brief illness
1991	LEAMING, Jim	72	After a long illness
1991	LEAN, David	83	After a long illness
• 1981	# LEANDER, Zarah	74	Died near Stockholm, Sweden
1987	LEARN, Betsy	98	
1966	LEASE, Rex	64	Found dead (at his home in Hollywood, CA)
1953	+ LEBEDEFF, Ivan	53	Heart attack (in Hollywood, CA)
1990	LEBERMAN, Joseph	85	Cancer
1989	LeBORG, Reginald	86	Heart attack
1983	LeBOUVIER, Jean	62	
1984	LeCLAIR, Lucille	62	Diabetic infection
1992	LECLERC, Ginette	79	
1949	+ LEDBETTER, Huddie "Leadbelly"	60	Amyotrophic lateral sclerosis
1976	LEDERER, Charles	65	After a long illness (at UCLA Med. Ctr., CA)
1955	LEDERER, Gretchen	64	
1972	LEDERMAN, D. Ross	76	Kidney and heart condition
1992	LEDERMAN, Victoria Kellem	52	Amyloidosis
1993	LEDOUX, Fernand	96	Unreported causes (in Vilerville, France)
• 1941	LEE, Auriol	?	Automobile accident (in Hutchison, KS)
1961	LEE, Belinda	25	Automobile accident (in San Bernardino, CA)
1981	LEE, Bernard	73	Cancer (in London, England)
1989	# LEE, Billy	60	Heart failure

• New entry.   # Original name (Pt. 7).   + Interment (Pt. 5).

☆ Oscar nominee, ★ Oscar winner (Pt. 10)

YEAR		NAME		AGE	CAUSE AND/OR PLACE OF DEATH
1993	+	LEE, Brandon		27	Hit with a .44-caliber bullet in a filming accident (Wilmington, NC)
1989		LEE, Brian		36	Pneumonia
1973	#+	LEE, Bruce		32	Acute cerebral edema after taking prescribed pain-killer (Hong Kong)
1952	#+	LEE, Canada		45	Heart attack (in New York, NY)
1986		LEE, Carl		52	
1980		LEE, Chingwah		78	
1952	#	LEE, Dixie		40	Cancer (in Holmby Hills, CA)
1959		LEE, Duke R.		78	Died in Los Angeles, CA
1962		LEE, Florence		74	Died in Hollywood, CA
1961	#	LEE, Gwen		55	
1970	#+	LEE, Gypsy Rose		56	Cancer (in Los Angeles, CA)
1992		LEE, Irving Allen		43	A.I.D.S.
1965	#	LEE, Johnny "Calhoun"		67	Heart attack (in Los Angeles, CA)
1990		LEE, Larry		48	A.I.D.S.
1973	#	LEE, Lila		71	Stroke (in Saranac Lake, NY)
1982		LEE, My-ca Dinh		7	Killed by helicopter rotor while filming
1993	#	LEE, Pinky		85	Heart attack (in CA)
1974		LEE, Raymond		64	Died in a Los Angeles suburban hospital
1975		LEE, Rowland V.		84	Apparent heart attack (at his home)
1975	#	LEE, Ruth		79	After a long illness (in Woodland Hills, CA)
1992	#	LEE, Vanessa		71	Causes unreported (in London, England)
1982		LEE, Will		74	Heart attack
1984	#	LEEDS, Andrea	☆	70	
1993		LEETCH, Thomas		60	Leukemia (in Sherman Oaks, CA)
1991		LEFEVRE, René		93	
1991		LeGALLIENNE, Eva		92	Heart failure
1990		LEGATT, Alison		86	
1948		LEHAR, Franz		78	Stomach cancer
1993		LEHMAN, Gladys Collins		101	Pneumonia (in Newport Beach, CA)
1979		LEHMANN, Beatrix		76	
1990		LEHMANN, Carla		73	
1950		LEHR, Lew		54	Died at a sanitarium in Brookline, MA
1946	+	LEHRMAN, Henry		60	Following a heart attack
1992	+	LEHRMAN, Oscar S.		73	Prostate cancer
1949	+	LEIBER, Fritz		67	Heart attack (in Pacific Palisades, CA)
1976		LEIBERT, Richard "Dick"		73	
• 1948		LEIGH, Frank		?	Died in Hollywood, CA
1988		LEIGH, George		78	Heart disease & diabetes
1990		LEIGH, Megan		26	Apparent suicide
1967	#	LEIGH, Vivien	★	53	Tuberculosis (in London, England)
1956		LEIGHTON, Lillian		81	Died in Woodland Hills, CA
1976		LEIGHTON, Margaret	☆	53	Multiple sclerosis (in Chichester, England)
1991		LEIGHTON, Merrill		51	Automobile accident
1972		LEISEN, Mitchell		74	Coronary complications
1993		LeMASSENA, William		76	Lung cancer
1982	+	LEMBECK, Harvey		59	Heart attack
1983		LeMESURIER, John		71	Abdominal illness
1956	#	LeMOYNE, Charles		76	Died in Hollywood, CA
1929		LENI, Paul		44	Blood poisoning from a neglected ulcerated tooth
1980	+	LENNON, John		40	Murdered (shot) in New York, NY
1991		LENSKY, Leib		82	Liver cancer
1981	#	LENYA, Lotte	☆	83	Died in New York, NY
1994		LEONARD, Bill		78	Stroke (at Laurel Regional Hospital in Laurel, MD)
1939	#	LEONARD, Gus		83	After a long illness (in Los Angeles, CA)
1973	#	LEONARD, Jack E.		62	Diabetic complications (in New York, NY)
• 1956		LEONARD, Marion		75	Died in Woodland Hills, CA
1968	#+	LEONARD, Robert Z.	☆	78	Aneurysm (in Beverly Hills, CA)
1986		LEONE, Johnny		71	Stroke
1989		LEONE, Sergio		60	Heart attack
• 1979	#	LEONETTI, Tommy		50	Cancer (in Houston, TX)
1993		LEONTOVICH, Eugenie		93	Cardiac arrest and pneumonia (in Los Angeles, CA)
1993		LEOPOLD, Douglas		49	A.I.D.S.
1986		LERNER, Alan Jay		67	Lung cancer
1976		LERNER, Irving		67	Heart attack
• 1989	+	LERNER, Sam		86	

YEAR	NAME		AGE	CAUSE AND/OR PLACE OF DEATH
1985	# LeROY, Hal		71	Following heart surgery
1987	+ LeROY, Mervyn	☆	86	Heart failure
1940	LeSAINT, Edward J.		69	After a long illness (in Hollywood, CA)
1987	LESCOULIE, Jack		75	Colon cancer
• 1974	# LESLEY, Carole		38	Died in New Barnet, England
1991	LESLIE, Bob		64	
• 1953	# LESLIE, Gene		48	Died in Los Angeles, CA
• 1976	LESLIE, Gladys		77	Died in Boynton Beach, FL
• 1940	LESLIE, Lilie "Lila"		48	Died in Los Angeles, CA
1980	LESSER, Sol	★	90	
• 1947	LESSEY, George A.		?	Died in Westbrook, CT
• 1995	LESTER, Jerry		85	Complications of Alzheimer's disease (in Miami, FL)
1924	# LESTER, Kate		65	Burned as studio dressing room gas stove exploded
1963	# L'ESTRANGE, Dick		73	Died in Burbank, CA
1918	L'ESTRANGE, Julian		38	Spanish influenza (in New York, NY)
• 1955	LETONDAL, Henri		52	Heart attack (in Burbank, CA)
1975	LETTIERI, Al		47	After being hospitalized
1972	+ LEVANT, Oscar		65	Heart attack (in Beverly Hills, CA)
1980	# LEVENE, Sam		74	Heart attack (in New York, NY)
1980	# LEVENSON, Sam		68	
1989	LeVEQUE, Edward		92	
• 1955	LEVEY, Ethel		73	Heart attack (in New York, NY)
1975	LEVEY, Jules		78	Apparent heart attack (on a Manhattan street)
1980	LEVIN, Henry		70	Heart attack on the final day of filming
• 1996	LEVIN, Irving H.		74	Cancer (at his home in Brentwood, CA)
1987	LEVINE, Joseph E.		81	
1989	LEVINE, Nathan		89	
1992	LEVY, Franklin R.		43	Pulmonary embolism
1968	LEWIN, Albert		73	Pneumonia
1986	LEWIS, Buddy		62	Apparent heart attack
1968	LEWIS, Cathy		50	Cancer (in Hollywood Hills, CA)
1992	LEWIS, David		83	After a short illness
1993	# LEWIS, Edwina		42	Heart attack (in Augusta, Michigan)
1990	LEWIS, Elliott		73	Cardiac arrest
• 1977	LEWIS, Forrest		77	Heart attack (in Burbank, CA)
• 1996	# LEWIS, Henry		63	Heart attack (at his home in Manhattan)
1985	LEWIS, Jarma		54	Natural causes
1971	LEWIS, Joe E.		69	Liver and kidney ailments (in NYC) Do not confuse with the boxer
1993	LEWIS, Marlo		77	Heart failure (in Los Angeles, CA)
1956	+ LEWIS, Mitchell J.		76	Died in Woodland Hills, CA
1937	LEWIS, Ralph		65	Injuries from an automobile accident (in Los Angeles, CA)
1991	# LEWIS, Robert Q.		71	Emphysema
1982	LEWIS, Ronald		54	Suicide (sleeping pills) Do not confuse with R. "Raan" L., d. 1995
• 1995	#+ LEWIS, Ronald "Raan"		39	Complications from A.I.D.S. (Do not confuse with R. L., d. 1982)
1958	LEWIS, Sheldon		89	Died in San Gabriel, CA
1971	#+ LEWIS, Ted		80	Heart attack (in New York, NY)
1927	+ LEWIS, Tom		63	Following an operation for cancer
1956	LEWIS, Vera		72	Died at the Motion Picture Country Hospital near Los Angeles, CA
• 1932	LEWIS, Walter P.		60	
• 1948	LEYTON, George		84	Died in London, England
1978	L'HERBIER, Marcel		91	
1983	+ LIBERACE, George		71	Leukemia and heart disease
1987	#+ LIBERACE, Walter "Lee"		67	Complications from A.I.D.S.
1992	LIDDELL, Laura		83	Following a series of heart problems
• 1945	LIEDTKE, Harry		64	Died in Germany
1988	LIGHT, Ann Rork		79	
1971	LIGHTNER, Winnie		69	Heart attack (in Sherman Oaks, CA)
• 1965	# LIGON, Grover G.		79	Died in Hollywood, CA
1989	# LILLIE, Beatrice		94	
1952	#+ LINCOLN, Elmo		63	Heart attack (in Hollywood, CA)
• 1957	LINDER, Alfred		?	Died in Hollywood, CA
1925	# LINDER, Max		45	Suicided with his wife (cut wrists and took poison)
• 1995	LINDFORS, Viveca		74	Complications from rheumatoid arthritis (in Uppsala, Sweden)
• 1968	LINDO, Olga		68	Died in London, England
1993	LINDQUIST, Dan		65	Pneumonia (in Burbank, CA)

YEAR	NAME		AGE	CAUSE AND/OR PLACE OF DEATH
1968	LINDSAY, Howard		78	
• 1928	LINDSAY, James		59	
1981	#+ LINDSAY, Margaret		70	Emphysema (in Los Angeles, CA)
1988	LINDSAY, Phillip		64	Pneumonia
• 1978	# LINGEN, Theo		75	
1950	LINGHAM, Thomas J.		75	Died in Woodland Hills, CA
1985	LINTON, Mark		28	Heart failure & pneumonia
1989	LION, Margo		90	
1950	LIPATTI, Dinu		33	
1992	LISS, Ted		72	Heart attack
1985	LIST, Eugene		66	Found dead at home
• 1951	LISTER, Francis		52	Died in London, England
1970	# LISTON, Sonny		38	Died in Las Vegas, NV
• 1995	LISTYEV, Vladislav		?	Assassinated (at his home in Moscow)
1972	# LITEL, John		77	Died in Woodland Hills, CA
1984	LITTLE, Ann		93	
• 1967	# LITTLE, Billy		72	Stroke (in Hollywood, CA)
• 1952	# LITTLE, Bozo		45	Heart ailment (in Los Angeles, CA)
1992	LITTLE, Cleavon		53	Colon cancer
1965	#+ LITTLE, Malcolm "Malcolm X"		39	Assassinated (shot) in the Audubon Ballroom in Harlem, NY
1959	+ LITTLEFIELD, Lucien		64	Died in Hollywood, CA
1982	LITTLER, Susan		33	Cancer
1974	# LITVAK, Anatole	☆	72	
1961	LIVESEY, Jack		60	Aneurysm (in Burbank, CA)
1976	LIVESEY, Roger		69	Died in Watford, England
1936	LIVESEY, Sam		63	Following surgery (in London, England)
1985	LIVINGSTON, Margaret		89	
1988	# LIVINGSTON, Robert (Bob)		79	Emphysema
• 1994	LIVINGSTON, Valerie Cossart		87	Pneumonia (in New York)
1983	#+ LIVINGSTONE, Mary		77	Heart ailment
• 1941	LLEWELLYN, Fewlass		55	
1983	LLEWELLYN, Richard		76	Heart attack
• 1954	LLOYD, Art		58	Paralytic stroke (after filming the Bikini Atoll atom bomb test)
1948	LLOYD, Charles M.		78	Heart attack
1968	LLOYD, Doris		68	"Strained" heart (in Santa Barbara, CA)
1960	+ LLOYD, Frank	★	74	Died in Santa Monica, CA
• 1949	LLOYD, Frederick W.		69	Died in Hove, England
• 1971	LLOYD, Gladys		74	Stroke (in Culver City, CA)
1971	LLOYD, Harold Jr. "Duke"		39	Died in a sanitarium in North Hollywood, CA
1971	#+ LLOYD, Harold Sr.		77	Cancer (in Beverly Hills, CA)
1988	LLOYD, Paul Francis (Jimmy)		69	Liver disease
1938	LLOYD, Rollo		55	Died in Los Angeles, CA
1994	LOCCHI, Pino		69	After suffering two strokes (in Rome, Italy)
1977	LOCHARY, David		30	Drug overdose
1969	#+ LOCHER, Felix		86	Died in Sherman Oaks, CA
• 1995	LOCKE, Katherine		85	Brain tumor (at her home in Thousand Oaks, CA)
1990	+ LOCKER, Frances		79	
1957	#+ LOCKHART, Gene	☆	65	Coronary thrombosis (in Santa Monica, CA)
1978	# LOCKHART, Kathleen		83	Died in Los Angeles, CA
1920	+ LOCKLEAR, Omer		28	A plane crash filming accident
1990	# LOCKWOOD, Alexander		88	
1918	LOCKWOOD, Harold A.		29	Spanish influenza (in New York, NY)
1971	LOCKWOOD, King		73	Massive stroke (in Hollywood, CA)
1990	LOCKWOOD, Margaret		73	
1990	LOCKWOOD, Paul		51	Heart disease
1980	LODEN, Barbara		48	Cancer (in New York, NY)
1988	# LODER, John		90	
1985	LODGE, John Davis		82	Heart attack
1984	LOEB, Tony		76	Cancer
1969	+ LOESSER, Frank		59	Lung cancer (in New York, NY)
1927	+ LOEW, Marcus		57	Died in his sleep of heart failure
1988	LOEWE, Frederick		86	Heart failure
• 1957	LOFGREN, Marianne		47	Died in Sweden
1947	+ LOFT, Arthur		49	Died in Los Angeles, CA
1943	LOFTUS, Cecilia "Cissie"		66	Heart attack (in her New York City hotel room)

...DEATHS OF MOVIE AND TELEVISION PERSONALITIES – BY NAME...

YEAR	NAME		AGE	CAUSE AND/OR PLACE OF DEATH
1969	+ LOGAN, Ella		56	Died in San Mateo, CA
1983	LOGAN, Jacqueline		78	
1988	LOGAN, Joshua	☆	79	Supranuclear palsy
1953	LOGAN, Stanley		67	Died in New York
1975	LOHR, Marie		84	Died in London, England
1961	LOMAS, Herbert		73	Died in Devonshire, England
1942	#+ LOMBARD, Carole	☆	33	Airplane crash (southeast of Las Vegas, NV)
1991	LOMBARDI, Paul Michael		31	A.I.D.S.
• 1970	# LOMBARDI, Vince		57	Cancer
• 1971	LOMBARDO, Carmen		67	Cancer (in North Miami, FL)
1977	#+ LOMBARDO, Guy		75	Respiratory, kidney and heart failure (in Houston, TX)
1993	LOMBARDO, Lebert J.		88	Emphysema (in Fort Meyers, FL)
1985	LONDON, George		64	Following a heart attack
• 1980	LONDON, Jean "Babe"		79	
1993	LONDON, Roy		50	Lymphoma (in Los Angeles, CA)
1963	#+ LONDON, Tom		70	Died in North Hollywood, CA
1987	LONERGAN, Lenore		59	Cancer
1959	LONERGAN, Lester Jr.		65	After a long illness
1984	LONG, Avon		73	Cancer
• 1938	LONG, Jack		?	Motorcycle accident (in Los Angeles, CA)
• 1949	LONG, Nick Jr.		43	Results of an automobile accident (in New York, NY)
1974	+ LONG, Richard		47	Heart ailment (in Los Angeles, CA)
1952	LONG, Walter		73	Heart attack (in Los Angeles, CA)
• 1971	LONGDEN, John		70	
• 1923	LONSDALE, Harry G.		?	
• 1974	LONTOC, Leon		64	Died in Los Angeles, CA
1983	LOO, Richard		80	
1981	LOOS, Anita		93	Died in Manhattan, NY
1986	LOOS, Anne		70	
• 1954	LOOS, Theodor		70	Died in Stuttgart, West Germany
1986	LOPEZ, J. Victor		39	A.I.D.S.
1975	#+ LOPEZ, Vincent		76	Liver and pancreas failure (in Miami Beach, FL)
1947	LORCH, Theodore A.		74	After a long illness (in Hollywood, CA)
1942	LORD, Marion		59	Died in Hollywood, CA
1950	+ LORD, Pauline		60	Heart trouble (in Alamogordo, NM)
• 1973	LORDE, Athena		58	Cancer (in Van Nuys, CA)
1992	LORENTZ, Pare		86	Heart failure
• 1995	LORIMER, Louise		97	Following an extended illness (in Newton, MA)
1986	LORMER, Jon		80	
1968	# LORNE, Marion		80	Heart attack (in New York, NY)
1934	# LORRAINE, Harry		54	
1955	# LORRAINE, Lillian		63	Died in New York, NY
1981	# LORRAINE, Louise		79	After a long illness (in New York, NY)
1964	#+ LORRE, Peter		59	Stroke (in Hollywood, CA)
1975	# LOSCH, Tilly		70	Cancer
1937	LOSEE, Frank		81	Pulmonary embolism after an attack of arthritis (in Yonkers, NY)
1984	# LOSEY, Joseph		75	
1990	# LOSS, Joe		80	Kidney failure
1991	LOTT, Lawrence		40	A.I.D.S.
1948	LOUDEN, Thomas		73	After a stroke (in Hollywood, CA)
1981	#+ LOUIS, Joe "Brown Bomber"		66	Cardiac arrest (in Las Vegas, NV)
1926	LOUIS, Willard		40	After being ill with typhoid fever and pneumonia (in Glendale, CA)
1970	#+ LOUISE, Anita		55	Massive stroke (in West Los Angeles, CA)
1991	LOURIE, Eugene		89	Heart failure & complications from strokes
1986	# LOVE, Bessie	☆	87	
1991	LOVE, Edward M.		43	A.I.D.S.
1991	LOVE, Geoff		73	
1943	# LOVE, Montagu		62	Died in Beverly Hills, CA
1948	LOVE, Robert		34	Suicide (5-story leap from his doctor's office)
1962	+ LOVEJOY, Frank		48	Heart attack (in New York, NY)
1953	LOVELL, Raymond		53	Died in London, England
• 1980	# LOVELY, Louise		83	Died in Hobart, Australia
1988	LOW, Carl		71	Cancer
1958	LOW, Jack		60	After a 2-year illness
1989	LOW, Warren		83	Following a long illness

YEAR	NAME		AGE	CAUSE AND/OR PLACE OF DEATH
1982	LOWE, Arthur		67	Following a stroke
1971	+ LOWE, Edmund		81	Lung ailment (in Woodland Hills, CA)
1937	LOWELL, Helen		71	After a lingering illness
1992	LOWENSTEIN, Cary Scott		30	A.I.D.S.
1991	LOWENSTEIN, Lynn Gendron		30	An inoperable brain tumor
1971	# LOWERY, Robert		57	Heart attack (in Hollywood, CA)
1976	# LOWRY, Judith		86	Apparent heart attack (in New York, NY)
1988	LOWRY, Margerie Bonner		83	After suffering a stroke
1993	#+ LOY, Myrna	★	88	During surgery, after a lengthy illness (in New York)
• 1995	LOY, Nanni		69	Heart attack (while vacationing in Fregene nr. Rome, Italy)
• 1995	LUBIN, Arthur		96	Six months after a stroke (in a Glendale, CA, nursing home)
1947	+ LUBITSCH, Ernst	☆	55	Heart attack (in Los Angeles, CA)
1987	LUBOFF, Norman		70	Cancer
• 1954	# LUCAN, Arthur		67	Died in Hull, England
1990	LUCAS, Gail		37	Viral hemorrhagic pneumonia
1982	LUCAS, Nick		84	Following a stroke
1940	LUCAS, Wilfred		69	After an illness of 6-weeks (in Los Angeles, CA)
1989	LUCE, Claire		88	(Do not confuse with Clare Boothe Luce, d. 1987)
1987	# LUCE, Clare Boothe		84	Cancer (Do not confuse with Claire Luce, d. 1989)
1989	LUCKHAM, Cyril		81	
• 1945	LUCY, Arnold		80	
1981	LUDDEN, Allen		63	Cancer (in Los Angeles, CA)
1987	LUDLAM, Charles		44	Pneumonia complicated by A.I.D.S.
• 1996	LUDMIR, Joseph (Pepe)		64	Heart attack (in Woodland Hills, CA)
1982	LUDWIG, Edward		83	Stroke while hospitalized
• 1975	LUEDERS, Guenther		69	Cancer (in Duesseldorf, Germany)
• 1952	# LUFKIN, Sam		59	Uremia (in Los Angeles, CA)
1956	#+ LUGOSI, Bela		73	Heart attack (in Hollywood, CA)
• 1995	LUKAS, Karl		75	Died in Agoura Hills, CA
1971	# LUKAS, Paul	★	76	Heart attack (in Tangier, Morocco)
1991	+ LUKE, Keye		86	After a stroke
• 1970	LULLI, Folco		58	Heart attack (in Rome, Italy)
1988	LUMMIS, Dayton		84	
• 1947	# LUNCEFORD, Jimmy		45	Died in Seaside, OR
1990	LUND, Art		75	Liver cancer
1992	LUND, John		81	Found dead in his home; heart trouble
• 1960	LUND, Richard		75	Died in Sweden
1975	+ LUNDIGAN, William "Bill"		61	Lung and heart congestion (in Duarte, CA)
1977	+ LUNT, Alfred	☆	84	Cancer (in Chicago, IL)
• 1995	LUPINO, Ida		77	Colon cancer following a stroke (at her home in Burbank, CA)
• 1942	LUPINO, Stanley		48	Died in London, England
• 1961	# LUPINO, Wallace		63	Died in Ashford, England
1960	# LUTHER, Ann		67	Heart condition (in Hollywood, CA)
• 1960	LUTHER, Johnny		51	Drowned in a boating accident (in San Pedro, CA)
• 1962	LUTHER, Lester		73	Stroke (in Hollywood, CA)
1953	# LUTTRINGER, Al		74	Died in Hollywood, CA
1994	LUXFORD, Nola (Dolberg)		99	Died at a convalescent home in Pasadena, CA
1969	LYDECKER, Howard		58	
• 1972	LYEL, Viola		71	
• 1925	LYELL, Lottie		33	Died in Sydney, Australia
1957	+ LYMAN, Abe		59	Died in Los Angeles, CA
1994	LYNCH, Christopher		73	Heart attack (at his home in Worchestershire, England)
• 1965	LYNCH, Helen		64	Died in Miami Beach, FL
1990	LYNCH, Ken		79	Viral infection
1982	+ LYNDE, Paul		55	
1971	#+ LYNN, Diana		45	Brain hemorrhage (in Los Angeles, CA)
1994	LYNN, Donald		54	A.I.D.S. complications (at his home in Manhattan)
1958	LYNN, Emmett		61	Heart attack (in Hollywood, CA)
1967	LYNN, George M.		?	
1993	LYNN, Jack		67	Leukemia (in Albuquerque, NM)
• 1995	# LYNN, Jeffrey		89	Died at St. Joseph's Hospital in Burbank, CA
1988	LYNN, Mara		60	Cancer
• 1962	LYNN, Ralph		81	Died in London, England
1963	# LYNN, Sharon		58	Died in Hollywood, CA
1979	+ LYON, Ben		78	Heart attack (aboard a ship in the Pacific Ocean)

YEAR	NAME	AGE	CAUSE AND/OR PLACE OF DEATH
• 1961	LYON, Frank	59	Died in Gardner, MA
• 1995	LYON, Milton	72	Natural causes (at his home in Princeton, NJ)
• 1974	# LYONS, Cliff "Tex"	71	Died in Los Angeles, CA
• 1926	LYONS, Eddie	39	Died in Pasadena, CA
1921	# LYONS, Fred	?	After his car skidded and overturned
1986	# LYS, Lya	78	Heart ailment
1954	LYTELL, Bert	69	Following surgery (in New York, NY)
1954	LYTELL, Wilfred	62	After an illness of several weeks (in Salem, NY)
• 1924	LYTTON, L. Rogers	57	
	M		
1975	#+ MABLEY, Jackie "Moms"	78	Died in White Plains, NY
1956	MacARTHUR, Charles	60	
1957	MacBRIDE, Donald	67	After a long illness (in Los Angeles, CA)
1989	MACCARI, Ruggero	70	
1959	MacDONALD, Donald	61	
1951	MacDONALD, Edmund	43	Cerebral hemorrhage (in Los Angeles, CA)
1952	#+ MacDONALD, J. Farrell	77	Died in Hollywood, CA
1991	MacDONALD, James	84	Heart failure
1965	+ MacDONALD, Jeanette	57	Heart attack (in Houston, TX)
1956	MacDONALD, Katherine	62	After a 30-month illness
1978	MacDONALD, Wallace	87	Died in Santa Barbara, CA
1941	MacDOWELL, Melbourne	84	Blood clot on the brain (in Decoto, CA)
1917	# MACE, Fred	38	Apoplexy (found dead in his room at the Hotel Astor in NYC)
1983	MACE, Paul	33	Killed in a traffic accident
1967	MacFADDEN, Gertrude "Mickey"	67	Heart attack
1987	MacGIBBON, Harriet	81	After suffering from pulmonary & heart problems
1973	MacGOWRAN, Jack	54	After a bout with the flu (in his New York hotel room)
1992	MacGRATH, Leueen	77	Complications after a stroke
1948	MacGREGOR, Harman	70	
1963	MACHATY, Gustav	63	After a lengthy illness (in Munich, Germany)
• 1962	# MACK, Cactus	62	Heart attack (in Hollywood, CA)
1934	#+ MACK, Charles E.	46	Automobile accident (near Mesa, AZ) d.n.c. with C. Emmett Mack
1927	MACK, Charles Emmett	27	When another car struck and overturned his car (in Riverside, CA)
1986	# MACK, Helen	72	Cancer
• 1927	# MACK, Hughie	42	Heart disease (in Santa Monica, CA)
1948	MACK, James T.	77	
1989	# MACK, Marion	86	Heart failure
1927	+ MACK, Rose	61	Died in the Lenox Hill hospital in New York
1972	MACK, Russell	79	Stroke
1976	MACK, Ted	71	
1993	MACK, Wayne	68	Cancer (in New Orleans, LA)
1964	MACK, Wilbur	91	Died in Hollywood, CA
1990	MACKAILL, Dorothy	87	Kidney failure
1987	MACKAY, Fulton	64	
1940	MACKAYE, Dorothy	41	Injuries from an automobile accident (in San Fernando Valley, CA)
1968	MacKAYE, Norman	62	After a brief illness
1993	MACKENDRICK, Alexander	81	Pneumonia (in Los Angeles, CA)
1962	# MacKENNA, Kenneth	63	After a long bout with cancer
• 1966	MacKENZIE, Mary	44	Automobile accident (in London, England)
• 1973	MACKIN, Clara	?	Died in Santa Monica, CA
1969	+ MacLANE, Barton	68	Double pneumonia (in Santa Monica, CA)
1985	MacLAREN, Mary	85	Respiratory problems
1986	MacLAUGHLIN, Don	79	
1967	MacLEAN, Douglas	70	Stroke (in Beverly Hills, CA)
1991	MacMAHON, Aline ☆	92	Pneumonia
1954	MacMILLAN, Violet	66	
1991	#+ MacMURRAY, Fred	83	Pneumonia
1944	MacPHERSON, Aimee Semple	53	Heart attack in her sleep
1946	MacPHERSON, Jeanie	59	After a long illness (in Hollywood, CA)
1942	MacQUARRIE, Murdock	63	Died in Los Angeles, CA
• 1967	# MACRAE, Duncan	61	Died in Glasgow, Scotland (Do not confuse with Duncan McRae)
1986	MacRAE, Gordon	65	Cancer of the mouth & jaw
1973	+ MACREADY, George	63	Emphysema (in Los Angeles, CA)
1985	MacVEIGH, Earle	74	Cancer
• 1956	MACY, Jack	70	Heart attack (in Wyoming)

	YEAR	NAME		AGE	CAUSE AND/OR PLACE OF DEATH
	1983	MADDEN, Donald		49	
	1989	MADDEN, Jeanne		73	Heart trouble
	1976	MADDEN, Peter		71	
	1964	MADISON, Cleo		81	Heart attack (in Burbank, CA)
•	1996	# MADISON, Guy		74	Emphysema (at Desert Hospital Hospice in Palm Springs, CA)
	1975	# MADISON, Noel		77	Died in Fort Lauderdale, FL
•	1967	MAERTENS, Willy		74	Died in Hamburg, Germany
	1993	MAGALOFF, Nikita		80	After a long illness
	1982	MAGEE, Patrick		58	Natural causes
	1992	MAGERMAN, Les		46	A.I.D.S.
	1973	MAGNANI, Anna	★	64	Cancer (in Rome, Italy)
	1987	MAGNOTTA, Vic		43	Drowned during filming of a car stunt
	1952	MAGRILL, George		52	Died in Los Angeles, CA
	1989	MAGUIRE, Kathleen		64	Cancer
	1989	# MAHONEY, Jock		70	Stroke following an auto accident
	1991	MAIBAUM, Richard		81	After a short illness
	1937	# MAILES, Charles H.		66	Died in Los Angeles, CA
	1975	#+ MAIN, Marjorie	☆	85	Cancer (in Los Angeles, CA)
•	1929	MAITLAND, Lauderdale		51	
•	1961	# MAITLAND, Ruth		81	Died in Dorking, England
	1956	MAKEHAM, Eliot		73	Died in London, England
	1952	MALA, Ray		46	Heart attack (in Hollywood, CA)
	1952	MALATESTA, Fred		62	After a surgical operation (in Burbank, CA)
•	1995	MALEY, Alan	★	64	Heart attack (at his Belvedere, CA, home)
	1948	MALLALIEU, Aubrey		74	
•	1995	MALLE, Louis		63	Lymphoma complications (at his home in Beverly Hills, CA)
	1969	MALLESON, Miles		80	Died in London, England
	1958	MALLORY, Boots		45	
•	1978	MALONEY, James J. "Jim"		63	
	1929	MALONEY, Leo D.		41	Heart disease aggravated by alcoholism (in New York, NY)
	1963	# MALTBY, H. F.		82	Died in London, England
	1993	MALVERN, Paul		91	Died in Los Angeles, CA
	1961	# MALYON, Eily		81	Died in South Pasadena, CA
	1987	+ MAMOULIAN, Rouben		90	Natural causes
	1994	MANCINI, Henry	★	70	Complications from liver and pancreatic cancer (in Los Angeles)
	1946	# MANDER, Miles		57	Heart attack (in Hollywood, CA)
	1945	MANDY, Jerry		52	Following a heart attack (in Hollywood, CA)
	1989	MANES, Gina		94	
	1989	MANGANO, Silvano		59	Heart attack following a tumor operation
	1987	MANGER, Winifred Brison		94	Following a long illness
	1993	MANKIEWICZ, Francis		69	Cancer (in Montreal, Canada)
	1953	MANKIEWICZ, Herman J.		55	Uremic poisoning
	1993	# MANKIEWICZ, Joseph L.	★	83	Heart failure (in Bedford, NY)
	1958	MANKIEWICZ, Rose Stradner		45	Found dead at the family summer home
•	1996	MANLEY, Walter		?	Apparent asthma attack (in New York)
	1967	# MANN, Anthony		60	Heart attack
•	1974	# MANN, Billy		?	Died in New York, NY
	1991	# MANN, Daniel		79	Heart failure
	1977	MANN, George Kline		72	Cancer
	1971	# MANN, Hank		84	Died in South Pasadena, CA
	1987	MANN, Jerry		77	After a series of strokes that left him an invalid
•	1941	MANN, Margaret		72	Cancer (in Los Angeles, CA)
	1976	MANNHEIM, Lucie		81	Died in Braunlage, West Germany
•	1979	MANNI, Ettore		52	Accidental gun shot (in Rome, Italy)
	1946	MANNING, Aileen		60	Died in Hollywood, CA
	1980	MANNING, Knox		76	
	1993	MANOS, Gloria		69	Cancer (in Reno, Nevada)
	1967	#+ MANSFIELD, Jayne		35	Automobile accident (in New Orleans, LA)
	1988	MANSFIELD, Marian		83	Emphysema
	1923	# MANSFIELD, Martha		23	Burns when her dress accidentally ignited on location (San Antonio)
•	1995	+ MANTLE, Mickey		63	Cancer following a liver transplant (in Dallas, TX)
	1965	# MANTZ, Paul		61	When a makeshift aircraft crashed enroute to film set (in CA)
	1983	MANULIS, Katherine Bard		66	
	1984	MAPES, Ted		82	
	1988	MARAVICH, Pete		40	

YEAR	NAME		AGE	CAUSE AND/OR PLACE OF DEATH
1989	MARCH, Alex		68	Heart failure
• 1995	MARCH, Donald		53	Complications from A.I.D.S.
• 1974	MARCH, Eve		?	Cancer (in Hollywood, CA)
1975	#+ MARCH, Fredric	★	77	Cancer (in Los Angeles, CA)
1970	+ MARCH, Hal		49	Pneumonia and lung cancer (in Los Angeles, CA)
1969	#+ MARCIANO, Rocky		44	Airplane crash (near Des Moines, IA)
1937	MARCUS, James A.		69	Heart attack (in Hollywood, CA)
1967	MARCUSE, Theodore		47	When his car struck a truck on a Hollywood freeway
1978	MARDEN, Adrienne		69	Massive heart attack (in Los Angeles, CA)
1990	MARGLISS, Frances		76	Heart attack
1985	#+ Margo (Margo Albert)		68	
1993	MARGOLIN, Janet		50	Ovarian cancer (in Los Angeles, CA)
• 1946	MARIAN, Ferdinand		44	Automobile accident (near Durneck, Germany)
1988	MARICLE, Leona		81	Apparent heart attack
1951	MARIN, Edwin L.		50	After a 3-week illness
1973	MARION, Frances		85	Died in Los Angeles, CA
1945	MARION, George F. Sr.		85	Following a heart attack (in Carmel, CA)
1965	MARION, Sid		65	Heart attack
1985	MARIS, Roger		51	
1975	MARK, Michael		85	Heart failure (in Woodland Hills, CA)
1981	MARKEY, Enid		83	Natural causes
1981	MARKHAM, Dewey "Pigmeat"		77	Stroke
1991	MARKHAM, Marcella		68	Breast cancer
1991	MARKLE, Fletcher		70	Heart failure
• 1952	MARKS, Willis		87	Died in Los Angeles, CA
1993	MARLAND, Douglas		58	Complications following abdominal surgery (in Norwalk, CT)
• 1970	MARLE, Arnold		81	Died in London, England
1984	MARLEY, John	☆	77	Following open-heart surgery
1975	MARLOWE, Alan		40	Airplane crash
1964	MARLOWE, Frank		60	Heart attack (in Hollywood, CA)
1982	#+ MARLOWE, Hugh		71	Heart attack
1984	MARLOWE, June		81	
1991	MARLOWE, Louis J.		85	Kidney failure
1977	MARLOWE, Nora		?	After a long illness (in Los Angeles, CA)
1978	# MARLY, Florence		59	Heart attack (in Glendale, CA)
1977	MARMONT, Percy		93	Died in Denville Hall, England
1991	MAROFF, Robert		57	
1987	MARQUAND, Richard		49	Stroke
1990	MARQUARD, Yvonne Peattie		73	Natural causes
• 1979	MARQUET, Mary		84	Results of a fall (in Paris, France)
1989	MARQUISS, Ralph E. Jr.		34	Adrenal cancer
1990	MARR, Alice		89	
1991	MARRERO, Ralph		33	Automobile accident
• 1949	# MARRIOTT, Moore		64	
• 1962	MARRIOTT, Sandee		63	Heart attack (in Hollywood, CA)
• 1981	# MARSH, Garry		78	Natural causes (in London, England)
1990	MARSH, Lois R.		74	After a long illness
1968	# MARSH, Mae		72	Heart attack (in Hermosa Beach, CA)
• 1925	# MARSH, Marguerite		33	Bronchial pneumonia (in New York, NY)
1989	# MARSH, Tiger Joe		78	
1961	MARSHAL, Alan		52	Heart attack during live performance of "Sextette" (in Chicago, IL)
1989	MARSHALL, Andrew 3rd		52	Cancer
1950	MARSHALL, Boyd		65	Died in Jackson Heights, NY
• 1992	# MARSHALL, Brenda		77	Throat cancer (in Palm Springs, CA)
1975	+ MARSHALL, George E.		84	
1966	MARSHALL, Herbert		75	Heart attack (in Beverly Hills, CA)
1991	MARSHALL, Robert H.		67	After a brief illness
1943	#+ MARSHALL, Tully		78	Heart and lung ailment (in Encino, CA)
• 1939	# MARSON, Aileen		26	Childbirth (in London, England)
1990	MARSTON, Merlin		45	Non-Hodgkins lymphoma
• 1976	MARTEL, Alphonse		85	
1953	# MARTIN, Chris-Pin		59	Heart attack (in Montebello, CA)
• 1995	#+ MARTIN, Dean		78	Acute respiratory failure (at his home in Beverly Hills, CA)
1987	+ MARTIN, Dean Paul Jr.		35	Crash of his F-4C Phantom-II jet on a training flight
1984	MARTIN, D'urville		45	Heart attack

YEAR	NAME		AGE	CAUSE AND/OR PLACE OF DEATH
	1964	MARTIN, Edie	83	*Died in London, England*
•	1995	# MARTIN, Ernest H.	75	*Liver cancer (at his home in Los Angeles, CA)*
	1983	MARTIN, Freddy	76	*After a series of strokes*
	1990	MARTIN, Kiel	46	*Cardiovascular collapse caused by lung cancer*
	1959	MARTIN, Lock	?	
	1985	+ MARTIN, Marion	76	*Natural causes*
	1990	+ MARTIN, Mary	76	*Cancer*
	1994	MARTIN, Richard	75	*Leukemia (at Hoag Mem. Hospital, Newport Beach, CA)*
	1981	#+ MARTIN, Ross	61	*Heart attack*
	1980	+ MARTIN, Strother	61	*Heart attack*
	1987	MARTIN, Vivian	95	*After a long illness*
	1988	MARTIN-HARVEY, Muriel	97	
	1955	MARTINDEL, Edward B.	78	*Heart attack (in Woodland Hills, CA)*
	1993	MARTINEZ, José "Tun Tun"	61	*Following surgery for intestinal blockage (Mexico)*
	1976	MARTINI, Nino	72	*Heart attack*
	1992	# MARTON, Andrew	87	*Pneumonia*
	1987	+ MARVIN, Lee ★	63	*Heart attack*
	1961	#+ MARX, "Chico"	74	*Heart attack (in Beverly Hills, CA)*
	1977	#+ MARX, "Groucho"	86	*Pneumonia (in West Hollywood, CA)*
	1977	#+ MARX, "Gummo"	79	*Lung cancer*
	1964	#+ MARX, "Harpo"	75	*During heart surgery (in Los Angeles, CA)*
	1979	#+ MARX, "Zeppo"	78	*Cancer (in Palm Springs, CA)*
	1992	+ MARX, Samuel	90	*Congestive heart failure (Do not confuse with Samuel Marx, d. 1933)*
	1933	# MARX, Samuel "Frenchie"	72	*Heart and kidney failure (in Hollywood, CA)*
	1969	# MASCHWITZ, Eric	68	
	1994	+ MASINA, Giulietta (Fellini)	74	*Lung cancer (at the Columbus Clinic in Rome, Italy)*
•	1968	MASKELL, Virginia	31	*Exposure and overdose of drugs (in Stoke Mandeville, England)*
•	1975	MASON, Buddy	71	*Died in Woodland Hills, CA*
	1929	# MASON, Dan	76	*Following an attack of pneumonia (in Baersville, NY)*
•	1966	MASON, Haddon	68	*Died in London, England*
	1984	MASON, James ☆	75	*Massive heart attack*
	1947	MASON, LeRoy	44	*After a heart attack (while filming "California Firebrand") in L.A.*
	1959	MASON, Louis	71	*After a long illness*
•	1980	# MASON, Mary	69	*Cancer (in New York, NY)*
	1962	MASON, Reginald	80	
	1979	#+ MASON, Shirley (Lanfield)	78	*Cancer (in Los Angeles, CA)*
•	1976	MASON, Sydney	70	*Heart attack (in Los Angeles, CA)*
	1941	MASON, William C. "Smiling Billy"	52	*After a lengthy illness (in Orange, NJ)*
	1985	MASONER, Gene	41	*A.I.D.S.*
	1983	MASSENGALE, Joseph	66	*Suicide (gunshot)*
	1991	+ MASSEY, Curt	81	
	1984	+ MASSEY, Edith	65	*Cancer*
	1974	#+ MASSEY, Ilona	63	*Cancer (in Bethesda, MD)*
	1983	+ MASSEY, Raymond ☆	86	*Pneumonia*
	1969	MASTERS, Ruth	75	
	1964	MATE, Rudolph	66	*Following several heart attacks*
	1958	MATHER, Aubrey	72	*Died in London, England*
	1966	MATHER, Jack	58	*Heart attack (in Wauconda, IL)*
	1985	MATHESON, Murray	73	*Heart failure*
•	1995	MATHEWS, Carmen Sylva	84	*Natural causes (at her farm in W. Redding, CT)*
•	1975	MATHIESON, Muir	64	*Died in Oxford, England*
•	1932	MATIESEN, Otto	58	*Died in Safford, AZ*
	1978	MATRAY, Ernst	87	*Heart attack (in Los Angeles, CA)*
	1989	MATSUDA, Yusaku	40	*Bladder cancer*
	1960	# MATTHEWS, A. E. "Matty"	90	*Died in Bushey Heath, England*
	1977	+ MATTHEWS, Dorothy	54	*Stroke*
	1984	MATTHEWS, George	73	*Heart disease*
	1981	MATTHEWS, Jessie	74	*Cancer*
	1975	MATTHEWS, Lester	74	
•	1934	# MATTO, Sesto	39	*Automobile accident (in Los Angeles, CA)*
	1933	MATTOX, Martha	54	*Heart ailment (in Sidney, NY)*
•	1946	MATTRAW, Scott	61	*Died in Hollywood, CA*
	1989	MATUSZAK, John	38	*Heart failure from drug overdose*
	1951	MAUDE, Cyril	88	*Died in Torquay, England*
	1979	MAUDE, Margery	90	

...DEATHS OF MOVIE AND TELEVISION PERSONALITIES — BY NAME...

YEAR	NAME	AGE	CAUSE AND/OR PLACE OF DEATH
• 1965	# MAUGHAM, W. Somerset	91	Died in Nice, France
1964	MAUR, Meinhart	73	
1988	MAURA, Luis	38	A.I.D.S.
• 1918	# MAURICE, Mary "Mother"	73	
1980	MAX, Edwin "Ed"	71	
1963	MAXEY, Paul	54	Heart attack (in Pasadena, CA)
1948	MAXWELL, Edwin	62	Cerebral hemorrhage (in Falmouth, MA)
1963	+ MAXWELL, Elsa	80	Died in New York, NY
1990	MAXWELL, James	33	A.I.D.S.
1981	MAXWELL, Jenny	39	Shot to death outside her condo by possible robbers
• 1996	MAXWELL, Larry	43	Leukemia (at his home in Laurelville, OH)
1972	#+ MAXWELL, Marilyn	49	High blood pressure and pulmonary ailment (in Beverly Hills, CA)
1992	MAXWELL, Paul	70	
• 1980	MAY, Alyce	65	Heart attack (in Rosa Rito Beach, Baja, Mexico)
1984	MAY, Doris	82	Heart failure
1954	MAY, Joe	73	After a long illness
• 1980	MAY, Mia	96	Died in Los Angeles, CA
• 1995	MAYA, Frank	45	Heart failure due to complications of A.I.D.S. (in NYC)
1941	MAYALL, Hershell	78	Cerebral hemorrhage (in Detroit, MI)
1985	MAYER, Kenneth M. "Ken"	66	
1957	#+ MAYER, Louis B.	72	Leukemia (in Los Angeles, CA)
• 1948	MAYER, Ray	47	Heart attack (in Salt Lake City, UT)
• 1995	MAYER, Seymour R.	86	Heart failure (in New York City)
1973	+ MAYNARD, Ken	77	Died alone in his trailer of malnutrition (in Woodland Hills, CA)
1971	MAYNARD, Kermit	68	Heart attack (in Hollywood, CA)
1947	MAYNE, Eric	80	Died in Hollywood, CA
1968	+ MAYO, Archie	77	Cancer
• 1970	MAYO, Edna	76	Died in San Francisco, CA
1963	+ MAYO, Frank	77	Heart attack (in Laguna Beach, CA)
1994	MAYS, Joe	45	A.I.D.S. complications (in Little Rock, Ark.)
1992	MAYS, Wendell	72	Cancer
1990	# MAZURKI, Mike	82	
1989	McANALLY, Ray	63	
1984	McAVOY, May	82	
1992	McBATH, James H.	69	Heart attack
1990	McBEAN, Angus	86	
1993	McBEE, Keith W.	66	Cancer complicated by other illnesses
1976	McBRIDE, Mary Margaret	77	
1925	McCABE, Harry	44	After two operations
1994	McCALL, Barbara "Bobbie"	50	After a 3-yr. bout with cancer (in Beverly Hills, CA)
1938	McCALL, William	58	Died in Hollywood, CA
1991	McCALLION, James	72	Heart attack
• 1976	McCALLUM, Neil	45	Brain hemorrhage (in Reading, England)
1969	+ McCAREY, Leo ★	70	
1948	McCAREY, Ray	50	Died alone in his apartment
1986	McCARTHY, Frank	74	
1962	McCARTHY, John P.	78	Coronary thrombosis
1992	McCARTHY, Julia	64	Cancer
1980	McCARTY, Mary	56	
1919	McCAULEY, Edna	?	Typhoid fever
1993	McCLEOD, Mercer	86	Heart failure (in New York)
• 1995	McCLURE, Doug	59	Lung cancer (at his home in Sherman Oaks, CA)
1959	McCOMB, Kate	87	
• 1979	McCONNELL, Gladys	71	
• 1962	McCONNELL, Lulu	80	Cancer (in Hollywood, CA)
1945	+ McCORMACK, John	61	Died at his home in County Kildare, Ireland
1953	McCORMACK, William M.	62	Following a heart attack (in Hollywood, CA)
• 1953	# McCORMICK, Merrill	61	Heart attack (in Hollywood, CA)
1962	McCORMICK, Myron	54	Cancer (in New York, NY)
• 1995	McCOY, Dan	37	Complications of A.I.D.S. (at Roosevelt Hosp. in Manhattan)
1967	# McCOY, Gertrude	63	Died in Atlanta, GA
1937	McCOY, Harry	43	Heart attack (in Hollywood, CA)
1991	McCOY, Jack	72	
1978	#+ McCOY, Tim	86	Died in Huachuca, AZ
1988	McCRACKEN, James	61	Following two strokes

YEAR	NAME		AGE	CAUSE AND/OR PLACE OF DEATH
1990	# McCRAY, Helen Mary "Honey"		83	
• 1996	McCREA, Dusty Iron Wing		55	Diabetes (in Hondo, N.M.)
1990	McCREA, Joel		84	Pulmonary complications
1992	McCULLERS, Edward		64	Heart attack
1981	McCULLOUGH, Philo		90	Died in Burbank, CA
1991	McCULLOUGH, Stephen N.		48	Pulmonary hypertension
1946	McDANIEL, Etta		55	
1952	+ McDANIEL, Hattie ★		57	Breast cancer (in San Fernando Valley, CA)
• 1995	McDANIEL, Keith		38	Complications of A.I.D.S. (in Los Angeles, CA)
1962	# McDANIEL, Sam "Deacon"		76	Throat cancer (in Woodland Hills, CA)
• 1972	McDERMOTT, Hugh		63	Died in London, England
1929	McDERMOTT, Marc		47	During gall bladder surgery (in Glendale, CA)
• 1996	McDERMOTT, Tom		83	Complications of prostate cancer (at Beth Israel hosp. in NY)
1976	# McDEVITT, Ruth		80	Died in Hollywood, CA
1968	McDONALD, Francis J.		77	After a lengthy illness (in Hollywood, CA)
1980	McDONALD, Frank		80	
1965	#+ McDONALD, Marie		41	Accidental drug overdose (in Hidden Hills, CA)
1959	McDONALD, Ray		34	
1966	# McDOWELL, Claire		88	After a long illness (in Woodland Hills, CA)
1992	McEDWARD, Jack		94	
1942	McFADDEN, Charles Ivor		55	Cerebral hemorrhage (in Los Angeles, CA)
1993	+ McFARLAND, George "Spanky"		64	Unknown causes (in a Grapevine, TX, hospital)
1975	McFARLAND, Nan		58	Cancer
1977	McGANN, William H.		84	Died in his sleep
1975	# McGILL, Moyna		80	
1992	McGILL, Shaun		30	A.I.D.S.
1977	McGINN, Walter		38	After his car crashed into a parked truck (in Los Angeles, CA)
1990	McGIVENEY, Maura		51	Liver disease
1975	# McGIVER, John		61	Heart attack (in West Fulton, NY)
• 1951	McGLYNN, Frank		84	Died in Newburgh, NY
1977	# McGOWAN, J. P. "Jack"		81	(Screenplay writer)
1952	# McGOWAN, John P.		72	(Silent star/producer) Died in Hollywood, CA
1971	McGOWAN, Oliver F.		64	Died in his sleep
1955	McGOWAN, Robert F.		72	
1970	McGRAIL, Walter B.		70	
1967	McGRATH, Frank		64	Heart attack (in Beverly Hills, CA)
1978	McGRATH, Paul		74	Died in his sleep (in London, England)
1980	# McGRAW, Charles		66	After falling thru a glass shower door at home (in Studio City, CA)
1945	# McGREGOR, Malcolm		52	Burns (in Los Angeles, CA)
1971	McGUINN, Joseph Ford "Joe"		67	Heart attack one week after surgery (in Hollywood, CA)
1989	McGUIRE, Jon Brandon		34	Liver failure
1978	McGUIRE, Kathryn		73	Pancreatic cancer (in Los Angeles, CA)
1954	McGUIRE, Tom		80	Died in Hollywood, CA
1988	McGUIRE, Tucker		75	
1994	McHUGH, Burke		77	Heart failure & pnemonia (at Falmouth Hosp., MA)
• 1995	McHUGH, Dorothy		87	Stroke
1981	McHUGH, Frank		82	Died in Greenwich, CT
1983	# McHUGH, Jack		69	Heart attack
• 1969	McHUGH, Jimmy		74	Heart attack (in Beverly Hills, CA)
1971	# McHUGH, Matt		76	Heart attack (in Northridge, CA)
1991	McINTIRE, John Herrick		83	Emphysema & cancer
1986	McINTIRE, Tim		42	Heart failure
1942	McINTOSH, Burr		79	Following a heart attack (in Hollywood, CA)
1984	McINTYRE, Christine		69	
1959	McINTYRE, Hal		44	Burns after falling asleep while smoking
1953	# McINTYRE, Leila		70	After a long illness (in Los Angeles, CA)
1945	# McKAY, George W. "Red"		60	Died in Hollywood, CA
1987	McKAY, Scott		71	Kidney failure
• 1959	# McKEE, Lafe		87	Arteriosclerosis (in Temple City, CA)
• 1933	# McKEEN, Snookums		8	Blood poisoning (in Los Angeles, CA)
• 1967	McKEEVER, Mike		27	Brain injuries from an automobile accident (in Hollywood, CA)
1958	McKENNA, Henry T.		64	Heart attack
1986	McKENNA, Siobhan		63	
1987	McKENZIE, Ella		?	
1967	McKENZIE, Eva B.		78	

YEAR	NAME		AGE	CAUSE AND/OR PLACE OF DEATH
1986	McKENZIE, Ida Mae		?	
1949	McKENZIE, Robert B.		65	*Heart attack (in Rhode Island)*
1927	McKIM, Robert		39	*Cerebral hemorrhage (in Hollywood, CA)*
1975	McKINNEY, Florine		62	
• 1978	McKINNEY, Mira		?	
1967	McKINNEY, Nina Mae		54	
• 1978	McLAGLEN, Clifford		86	*Died in Huddersfield, Yorkshire, England*
1959	+ McLAGLEN, Victor	★	72	*Congestive heart failure (in Newport Beach, CA)*
1986	McLAUGHLIN, Don		79	*After a brief illness*
1991	McLAUGHLIN, Emily		61	*Cancer*
1960	McLAUGHLIN, Gibb		76	
• 1996	McLEAN, Barbara	★	92	*Died in Newport Beach, CA*
• 1995	McLEAN, David		73	*Lung cancer (at UCLA Med. Ctr. in Los Angeles, CA)*
1961	McLEOD, Gordon		71	
1964	# McLEOD, Norman Z.		65	*After suffering a stroke*
• 1973	# McLEOD, Tex		76	*Heart attack (in Brighton, England)*
1994	McLIAM, John		76	*Chronic bronchitis, Parkinson's disease and melanoma (in L.A.)*
1971	McMAHON, Horace		65	*Heart ailment*
1994	McMANUS, Mark		59	*Pneumonia (in Glasgow, Scotland)*
1989	McMILLAN, Kenneth		56	*Liver disease*
1984	McMURRAY, Richard		68	*Lung cancer*
1994	#+ McNALLY, Stephen		82	*Heart failure (at his home in Beverly Hills, CA)*
1944	McNAMARA, Edward C.		57	*Heart attack (on a Hollywood-bound train near Boston)*
1978	McNAMARA, Maggie		48	*Overdose of pills*
1928	McNAMARA, Ted		?	*Pneumonia (in Ventura, CA)*
• 1955	McNAUGHTON, Charles		77	
1969	# McNAUGHTON, Gus		85	*Died in Castor, England*
1967	McNAUGHTON, Harry		70	
1969	+ McNEAR, Howard		63	*After a long illness (in San Fernando Valley, CA)*
1993	McNEIL, Claudia		77	*Complications from diabetes (in Englewood, NJ)*
1944	McPHAIL, Douglas		30	*From the effects of poison*
• 1940	McPHERSON, Quinton		68	*Died in London, England*
1990	McPHILLIPS, Hugh		70	*Injuries from an automobile accident*
• 1995	#+ McQUEEN, "Butterfly"		84	*Burns (while lighting a kerosene heater in her home in GA)*
1980	#+ McQUEEN, Steve	☆	50	*Heart attack after cancer surgery*
1994	McRAE, Carmen		74	*Following a stroke (at her home in Beverly Hills, CA)*
• 1931	McRAE, Duncan		49	*Died in London, England (Do not confuse with Duncan Macrae)*
1944	McRAE, Henry		68	*Heart attack*
• 1964	McSHANE, Kitty		65	*Died in London, England*
• 1961	McTURK, Joe		62	*Heart attack (in Hollywood, CA)*
1925	# McVEY, Lucille		35	*Died at her home in Hollywood, CA*
1973	McVEY, Patrick		63	*After being hospitalized (in New York, NY)*
1943	McWADE, Edward		?	*After a brief illness*
• 1956	McWADE, Margaret		83	
1938	McWADE, Robert Jr.		55	*Heart attack (in Culver City, CA)*
1941	MEADE, Bill		?	*Fell from a horse onto his sword while filming*
1968	# MEADE, Claire		84	*Pneumonia (in Encino, CA)*
• 1963	MEADER, George		75	
• 1996	+ MEADOWS, Audrey		71	*Lung cancer (at Cedars-Sinai Med. Ctr. in Los Angeles, CA)*
1986	MEARS, Martha		78	*Complications from Alzheimer's disease*
1980	# MEDFORD, Kay	☆	59	
1946	+ MEEK, Donald		66	*Acute leukemia and heart attack (in Los Angeles, CA)*
1988	# MEEKER, Ralph		67	*Heart attack*
1988	MEGLIN, Ethel		98	
• 1995	MEGNA, John		42	*A.I.D.S. (in Los Angeles, CA)*
• 1981	# MEGOWAN, Don		59	*Throat cancer (in Panorama City, CA)*
• 1968	MEHAFFEY, Blanche		60	*Died in Los Angeles, CA*
• 1995	MEIGHAN, Howard S.		88	*Cardiac arrest (at New York Hospital in Manhattan)*
1936	MEIGHAN, Thomas		57	*Cancer (in Great Neck, NY)*
1989	MEILLON, John		55	
1940	# MEINS, Gus		45	*Suicide (after arrest on morals charges)*
1993	MEISER, Edith		95	*Heart attack (at Roosevelt Hospital in New York)*
• 1994	MEISNER, Gunter		66	*Heart failure (in Berlin, Germany)*
1973	# MELCHIOR, Lauritz		82	*After gall bladder operation (in Santa Monica, CA)*
1949	# MELESH, Alex		58	*Died in Hollywood, CA*

YEAR	NAME		AGE	CAUSE AND/OR PLACE OF DEATH
1961	MELFORD, George		84	Heart attack (in Hollywood, CA)
• 1938	MELIES, Georges		77	Died in Paris, France
• 1977	MELL, Joseph "Joe"		62	Heart condition (in Los Angeles, CA)
1992	# MELL, Marisa		53	Cancer
1962	MELLER, Raquel		74	
1930	MELLISH, Fuller Jr.		35	Cerebral hemorrhage (in Forest Hills, NY)
1936	MELLISH, Fuller Sr.		71	Heart attack (in New York, NY)
1951	MELTON, Frank		43	After a heart attack (in Hollywood, CA)
1961	MELTON, James		57	Pneumonia
1995	MELTZER, Lewis		84	Pneumonia (at his home in Albuquerque, N.M.)
1946	MELVILLE, Rose "Sis Hopkins"		73	Died at her home in Lake George, NY
1989	MELVILLE, Sam		52	Heart attack
1985	MEMMOLI, George T.		46	Heart failure
1963	MENAHAN, Jean		?	
1990	MENDENHALL, Jim		62	Brain cancer
1963	+ MENJOU, Adolphe	☆	73	Chronic hepatitis (in Beverly Hills, CA)
• 1956	# MENJOU, Henri		64	Died in West Los Angeles, CA
• 1966	MENKEN, Helen		63	Heart attack (in New York, NY)
1957	# MENZIES, William C.	★	60	
1975	# MERANDE, Doro		?	Following a massive stroke (in Miami, FL)
1939	+ MERCER, Beryl		56	Following a major operation (in Santa Monica, CA)
1984	MERCER, Jack		74	
1976	#+ MERCER, Johnny		66	After surgery for a brain tumor (in Bel Air, CA)
1982	MERCHANT, Vivien	☆	53	Jaundice & hemorrhage caused by alcoholism
1994	# MERCOURI, Melina		68	Complications of lung cancer (at a New York hospital)
1991	# MERCURY, Freddie		45	A.I.D.S.
1964	+ MEREDITH, Charles		70	Died in Los Angeles, CA
• 1964	MEREDITH, Cheerio		74	Died in Woodland Hills, CA
1980	# MEREDITH, Iris		64	Died in Los Angeles, CA
• 1969	# MEREDYTH, Bess		?	Died in Woodland Hills, CA
1990	MERIVALE, John		72	Pneumonia
1946	MERIVALE, Philip		65	Heart ailment (in Los Angeles, CA)
1986	MERKEL, Una	☆	82	
• 1976	MERLO, Anthony "Tony"		88	Died in Woodland Hills, CA
• 1984	# MERMAN, Ethel		75	Results of a brain tumor
1966	MERRILL, Frank		71	Died in Hollywood, CA
1990	MERRILL, Gary		74	Cancer
1992	MERRILL, Joan		74	Stroke & Alzheimer's disease
• 1977	MERRITT, George		86	Died in London, England
• 1947	# MERSON, Billy		66	Died in London, England
1959	# MERTON, John		58	Heart attack (in Los Angeles, CA)
1976	# MERVYN, William		64	Died in London, England
1965	# MESSENGER, Buddy		55	Died in Hollywood, CA
1950	METAXA, Georges		51	Heart ailment (in Monroe, LA)
1990	METCALFE, Gordon		43	A.I.D.S.
1960	METCALFE, James J.		53	
1951	METHOT, Mayo		47	Died in Portland, OR
1987	MEYER, Dorothy		62	Cancer
1987	+ MEYER, Emile G.		76	Alzheimer's disease
• 1965	MEYER, Greta		82	
1975	MEYER, Torben		90	Bronchial pneumonia (in Hollywood, CA)
• 1939	MEYERHOLD, Vsevolod		65	Tortured by Stalin's secret police on false charges of treason
1969	MEYERS, Sidney		63	
1989	MEYERS, Timothy		44	A.I.D.S.
1964	MICHAEL, Gertrude		53	Died in Beverly Hills, CA
1985	MICHAELIDES, George		66	Complications after heart surgery
1983	MICHAELS, Loretta R.		45	Cancer
• 1949	MIDDLEMASS, Robert M.		64	Died in Los Angeles, CA
1949	MIDDLETON, Charles B.		69	Heart attack (in Los Angeles, CA)
1973	# MIDDLETON, Guy		64	Died near London, England
• 1971	MIDDLETON, Josephine		87	Died in England
1984	MIDDLETON, Ray		77	Heart attack
1977	# MIDDLETON, Robert		66	Heart failure
• 1932	MIDGELY, Fannie		54	
1949	MIDGLEY, Florence		59	Died in Hollywood, CA

YEAR	NAME		AGE	CAUSE AND/OR PLACE OF DEATH
• 1948	MIKHOELS, Solomon		58	Murdered (run over by a truck) presumably on Stalin's orders
1989	MILANOV, Zinka		83	Stroke
1991	MILES, Bernard		83	
1980	#+ MILESTONE, Lewis	★	84	Following abdominal surgery
1991	# MILFORD, Gene	★	89	Pneumonia
1960	MILJAN, John		66	Died in Hollywood, CA
1986	# MILLAND, Ray	★	81	Cancer
1966	MILLAR, Marjie		?	
• 1931	MILLARDE, Harry		45	Heart attack (in Queens, NY)
1990	MILLER, Barbara		68	After a brain tumor operation
• 1979	# MILLER, Carl		85	Died in Honolulu, Hawaii
1955	MILLER, Charles B.		64	Suicide (gunshot) due to unemployment and ill health (Hollywood)
1986	MILLER, Court		34	Complications from A.I.D.S.
1992	MILLER, David		82	Cancer
1948	MILLER, Edward G.		65	
• 1971	MILLER, Flournoy E.		82	Heart failure (in Hollywood, CA)
1944	# MILLER, Glenn		40	Lost when his RAF plane, bound for Paris, disappeared
1992	MILLER, Hope		63	Breast cancer
1988	MILLER, Joan		78	
• 1978	# MILLER, Lorraine		49	
1936	#+ MILLER, Marilyn		37	Toxemia from a sinus infection (in New York, NY)
• 1969	# MILLER, Martin		70	Heart attack (in Austria)
1985	+ MILLER, Marvin		72	
• 1963	# MILLER, Max		68	Died in Brighton, England
• 1995	MILLER, Patsy Ruth		91	Heart failure (at her home in Palm Desert, CA)
• 1939	MILLER, Ranger Bill		61	Died in Los Angeles, CA
1992	MILLER, Roger		56	Cancer
• 1976	MILLER, Ruby		86	Died in Chichester, England
1981	MILLER, Ruth		78	
• 1922	# MILLER, W. Christy		79	Died in Staten Island, NY
1940	# MILLER, Walter C.		48	After collapsing on a Republic Pictures set (in Los Angeles, CA)
1993	MILLHOLLIN, James		77	Cancer (in Biloxi, Mississippi)
1955	MILLICAN, James		45	Died in Los Angeles, CA
1991	MILLIGAN, Andy		62	A.I.D.S.
• 1973	MILLS, Frank		82	Arteriosclerosis (in Los Angeles, CA)
1982	+ MILLS, Harry F.		68	Following a tumor operation
1989	MILLS, Herbert		77	
• 1936	MILLS, John Jr.		25	Tuberculosis (in Bellefontaine, OH)
• 1967	MILLS, John Sr.		78	Died in Ohio
• 1966	# MILOS, Milos		24	Suicide (gunshot) in Los Angeles, CA
1992	MILSTEIN, Nathan		88	Heart attack
1989	MILTON, Billy		83	
1956	MILTON, Robert D.		70	After a long illness and hospitalization
1962	MINCIOTTI, Esther		74	
1976	#+ MINEO, Sal	☆	37	Murdered (stabbed to death) in West Hollywood, CA
1982	# MINER, Tony		82	After being hospitalized the previous day
• 1964	MING, Moy Luke		101	Died in Grenada Hills, CA
1986	+ MINNELLI, Vincente	★	83	
1969	MINNER, Kathryn		77	Heart attack
1987	MINOR, Michael		46	A.I.D.S.
1990	MINOTIS, Alexis		90	Stroke
1984	#+ MINTER, Mary Miles		82	Heart failure
1988	# MINTZ, Eli		83	Pneumonia
1955	#+ MIRANDA, Carmen		51	Heart attack (in Beverly Hills, CA)
1982	MIRANDA, Isa		77	Infected bone fracture
• 1955	# Miroslava		29	Suicide (poison) in Mexico City, Mexico
• 1973	MISHIMA, Masao		67	Heart ailment (in Tokyo, Japan)
1979	MITCHELL, Belle		90	After a long illness (in Woodland Hills, CA)
1952	MITCHELL, Bruce		68	Anemia (in Hollywood, CA)
1994	MITCHELL, Cameron		75	Lung cancer (at his home in Pacific Palisades, CA)
1992	MITCHELL, Chuck		64	Cirrhosis of the liver
1992	MITCHELL, Coleman		48	After a sudden illness
1988	MITCHELL, Ewing Young		77	Following a stroke
1991	MITCHELL, Frank		?	Cardiac arrest
1949	MITCHELL, Geneva		42	Died in California

YEAR	NAME		AGE	CAUSE AND/OR PLACE OF DEATH
1957	MITCHELL, Grant		82	Following a stroke (in Los Angeles, CA)
• 1954	MITCHELL, Julien		65	
1949	+ MITCHELL, Margaret		46	Struck by a speeding automobile
1953	MITCHELL, Millard		53	Lung cancer (in Santa Monica, CA)
1957	MITCHELL, Rhea "Ginger"		52	Found strangled to death (at her home in Los Angeles, CA)
1962	+ MITCHELL, Thomas	★	70	Cancer (in Beverly Hills, CA)
1979	MITCHELL, Yvonne		53	Cancer
1988	MITRY, Jean		80	
1994	MITTY, Nomi		54	Cancer (at her home in Los Angeles, CA)
1940	#+ MIX, Tom		60	A broken neck after his car overturned (in Florence, AZ)
1988	MOBERLY, Robert		49	A.I.D.S.
1970	MODOT, Gaston		82	
• 1942	MOFFAT, Margaret		49	Pneumonia (in Los Angeles, CA)
1965	MOFFATT, Graham		46	Heart attack (in Bath, England)
• 1995	MOFFET, Sally		63	Lung cancer
1968	MOHR, Gerald		54	Heart attack (in Stockholm, Sweden)
1974	MOJICA, Don José		75	Heart ailment (in Lima, Peru)
1992	MOLINARI, Antoinette		63	Kidney failure
1986	MOLLISON, Clifford		89	
• 1938	# MONCRIES, Edward		78	Heart attack (in Hollywood, CA)
1991	MONDO, Peggy		50	Heart attack
1940	MONG, William V.		65	After a 2-years' illness (in Studio City, CA)
1991	MONICA, Maria A. G.		92	
1982	+ MONK, Thelonius		64	Following a stroke
1994	MONKS, James		81	Cancer (at St. Luke's-Roosevelt Hospital in New York City)
1962	#+ MONROE, Marilyn		36	Suicide? (drug overdose) in Brentwood, CA
1973	+ MONROE, Vaughn		62	
• 1919	MONTAGUE, Frederick		55	Acute intestinal obstruction (in Los Angeles, CA)
1959	# MONTAGUE, Walter "Monte"		67	Died in Burbank, CA
1991	MONTALBAN, Carlos		87	Heart failure
1950	# MONTANA, Lewis "Bull"		62	Coronary thrombosis (in Los Angeles, CA)
1991	#+ MONTAND, Yves		70	Stroke
1964	MONTEUX, Pierre		89	
1951	# MONTEZ, Maria		33	Heart seizure while bathing in her home (in France)
1966	# MONTGOMERY, Douglass		57	Died in Ridgefield, CT
1987	MONTGOMERY, Earl		65	Cancer
• 1995	MONTGOMERY, Elizabeth		62	Cancer after surgery to remove a tumor (Beverly Hills, CA)
1978	MONTGOMERY, Goodee		72	After a brief illness (in Hollywood, CA)
1981	#+ MONTGOMERY, Robert	☆	77	Cancer (in New York, NY)
1993	MONTI, Carlotta		86	After a long illness (in Woodland Hills, CA)
1980	MONTOVANI, Annunzio		75	
1970	MONTOYA, Alex P.		62	Congestive heart failure (in Los Angeles, CA)
1971	MOODY, Ralph		83	Heart attack following surgery (in Burbank, CA)
• 1967	MOON, George		80	Died in London, England
1978	MOON, Keith		31	Found dead from an overdose of heminevrin (in London, England)
1991	MOORCROFT, Judy		58	
1992	MOORE, Brian		59	Congestive heart failure
• 1977	MOORE, Carlyle Jr.		67	Died in Sun Valley, ID
1924	MOORE, Carlyle Sr.		?	Suicide (in his Milford, NJ, home)
1959	# MOORE, Clara		?	Murdered
1973	MOORE, Cleo		44	Died in Inglewood, CA
1988	# MOORE, Colleen		85	Following a long illness
1970	MOORE, Del		53	Apparent heart attack (at his home in Encino, CA)
1964	MOORE, Dennis		49	
1991	# MOORE, Eleanor		84	Complications from emphysema
• 1955	MOORE, Eva		85	
1993	# MOORE, Garry		78	Emphysema (at his home on Hilton Head Island)
1947	MOORE, Grace	☆	45	Airplane crash
1964	MOORE, Ida		81	
1993	MOORE, Irving		74	Heart attack (in Sherman Oaks, CA)
1983	MOORE, Kathryn		96	
1960	MOORE, Matt		72	Died in Hollywood, CA
1939	MOORE, Owen		52	Died in Beverly Hills, CA
• 1972	MOORE, Patti		71	Cancer (in Los Angeles, CA)
1984	MOORE, Robert (director)		56	After a brief illness

• New entry. # Original name (Pt. 7). + Interment (Pt. 5). 209 ☆ Oscar nominee, ★ Oscar winner (Pt. 10)

YEAR	NAME	AGE	CAUSE AND/OR PLACE OF DEATH
1955	MOORE, Tom	70	Cancer (in Santa Monica, CA)
1962	+ MOORE, Victor	86	Heart attack (in Long Island, NY)
1974	#+ MOOREHEAD, Agnes ☆	67	Lung cancer (in Rochester, MN)
1991	MORALI, Jacques	44	A.I.D.S.
1982	MORAN, Dolores	56	
• 1967	# MORAN, Frank	80	Heart attack (in Hollywood, CA)
1949	# MORAN, George	67	After suffering a stroke (in Oakland, CA)
1990	# MORAN, Jackie	67	Cancer
1961	MORAN, Lee	70	Heart ailment (in Woodland Hills, CA)
1990	# MORAN, Lois	81	Cancer
1968	MORAN, Patsy	63	Died in Hollywood, CA
• 1968	MORAN, Percy	?	
1952	# MORAN, Polly	68	Heart ailment (in Los Angeles, CA)
• 1964	MORANTE, Milburn	76	Heart disease (in Pacoima, CA)
1982	MORE, Kenneth	67	Parkinson's disease
• 1981	MORE, Unity	86	Died in London, England
1984	# MORECAMBE, Eric	58	Heart disease
1973	+ MORELAND, Mantan	72	Died in Hollywood, CA
1978	# MORELL, André	69	Died in London, England
1967	MORENO, Antonio	78	After a long illness (in Beverly Hills, CA)
• 1968	MORENO, Dario	47	Died in Istanbul, Turkey
• 1948	MORENO, Marguerite	77	Died in France
• 1938	MORENO, Thomas "Sky Ball"	43	Died in West Los Angeles, CA
1988	MORGAN, Boyd F. "Red"	72	
1994	# MORGAN, Dennis	85	Heart failure (at a hospital in Fresno, CA)
1993	MORGAN, Edward P.	82	Cancer
1987	MORGAN, Elizabeth	84	After a stroke
1949	#+ MORGAN, Frank ☆	59	Died at his home in Beverly Hills, CA
1940	# MORGAN, Gene	48	Heart attack (in Santa Monica, CA)
1991	MORGAN, George J.	77	Cancer
1941	+ MORGAN, Helen	41	Kidney and liver ailments (in Chicago, IL)
1994	# MORGAN, Henry	79	Lung cancer (at his home in Manhattan, NY)
• 1967	# MORGAN, Lee	64	Heart disease (in Los Angeles, CA)
1989	MORGAN, Mary	81	
1956	#+ MORGAN, Ralph	72	After a 3-yr. illness (in New York)
1975	MORGAN, Ray	?	Cancer
1989	MORGAN, Rex	67	Parkinson's disease
1969	+ MORGAN, Russ	65	Cerebral hemorrhage (in Las Vegas, NV)
1989	MORIN, Alberto	86	Stroke
1993	MORK, Erik	67	Died in Copenhagen, Denmark
• 1964	# MORLAY, Gaby	67	Died in Nice, France
1952	MORLEY, Robert ☆	60	(Do not confuse with Robert Morley, d. 1992)
1992	MORLEY, Robert	84	After suffering a stroke (Do not confuse with Robert Morley, d. 1952)
1948	MOROSCO, Walter	49	Stroke
1955	MORRELL, George	82	After a long illness (in Hollywood, CA)
1994	MORRILL, Priscilla	67	Kidney infection (in Los Angeles, CA)
1978	Morris (the original TV cat)	17	
1941	MORRIS, Adrian	38	Died in Los Angeles, CA
1994	MORRIS, Anita	50	Cancer (at her home in Los Angeles, CA)
• 1995	MORRIS, Charlotte	75	Multiple medical problems (at NY Hosp.–Cornell Med. Ctr.)
1970	# MORRIS, Chester ☆	69	Overdose of barbiturates (in New Hope, PA)
1974	MORRIS, Glenn	62	After a long illness
1990	MORRIS, Jack Julius	87	Natural causes
1969	# MORRIS, Johnny	83	Died in Hollywood, CA
• 1933	MORRIS, Lee	69	Died in California
• 1968	MORRIS, Margaret	64	(Do not confuse with choreographer of same name)
1988	MORRIS, Mary	72	
1949	# MORRIS, Philip	56	Died in Los Angeles, CA
• 1996	MORRIS, Richard	72	Cancer (in Los Angeles, CA)
1986	MORRIS, Rolland "Rusty"	63	Cancer
1959	#+ MORRIS, Wayne	45	Heart attack (aboard an aircraft carrier in the Pacific Ocean)
1978	MORRISON, Ann	62	After a lengthy illness
1950	MORRISON, Arthur	71	Died in Los Angeles, CA
1992	MORRISON, Barbara	84	Heart failure
• 1975	MORRISON, Chester A.	52	Died in Portland, OR

...DEATHS OF MOVIE AND TELEVISION PERSONALITIES — BY NAME...

YEAR	NAME		AGE	CAUSE AND/OR PLACE OF DEATH
1989	# MORRISON, Ernie		76	Cancer
1973	MORRISON, George "Pete"		81	Died in Los Angeles, CA
1993	MORRISON, Harold		62	Died in Springfield, Missouri
• 1974	# MORRISON, James		86	Died in New York, NY
1971	+ MORRISON, Jim		27	Heart attack in his bath tub (after heavy drinking) in Paris, France
• 1946	MORRISON, Louis "Lou"		80	Died in CA
1993	MORRISON, Michael D.		33	Accidental overdose of alcohol & illegal drugs
• 1944	# MORRISSEY, Betty		?	Died in New York, NY
1968	# MORROW, Doretta		41	Cancer
1993	MORROW, Jeff		86	After a long illness (in Canoga Park, CA)
1982	+ MORROW, Vic		50	Killed in a filming accident
1993	MORSE, Carleton		91	Died in Sacramento, CA
• 1964	MORTIMER, Charles		78	Died in London, England
1969	MORTON, Charles J.		70	Heart attack
• 1966	MORTON, Charles S.		59	Heart disease (in North Hollywood, CA)
1975	MORTON, Clive		71	Died in London, England
1942	MORTON, James C.		58	After a long illness (in Reseda, CA)
1940	# MOSCOVITCH, Maurice		68	Following abdominal surgery (in Los Angeles, CA)
• 1964	# MOSER, Hans		83	Cancer (in Vienna, Austria)
• 1995	MOSES, Gilbert		52	Multiple myeloma (in New York)
1983	MOSQUINI, Marie		84	
1989	MOSS, Arnold		80	Lung cancer
1977	# MOSTEL, Zero		62	Cardiac disorder (in Philadelphia, PA)
1969	+ MOWBRAY, Alan		72	Heart attack (in Hollywood, CA)
1965	MOWER, Jack		74	Died in Hollywood, CA
1989	MOWER, Margaret		93	
1965	# MUDIE, Leonard		81	Heart ailment (in Hollywood, CA)
1989	# MUELLER, Cookie		40	A.I.D.S.
1992	MUELLER, William A. ☆		92	Natural causes
• 1960	# MUELLER, Wolfgang		36	Airplane crash (in Lostallo, Switzerland)
• 1995	MUIR, Esther		92	Natural causes (in Mount Kisco, NY)
1972	MUIR, Gavin		64	Died in Fort Lauderdale, FL
• 1964	MULCASTER, George H.		72	Died in England
1979	MULHALL, Jack		87	Congestive heart failure (in Woodland Hills, CA)
1982	MULLANEY, Jack		51	Stroke
• 1979	MULLEN, Barbara		64	Heart attack (in London, England)
• 1937	# MULLER, Renate		30	Died in Berlin, Germany
1990	MULLINS, Ted		50	Heart attack
• 1974	MUMBY, Diana		51	Died in Westlake, CA
1939	MUNDIN, Herbert		40	Fractured skull from auto accident (in Van Nuys, CA)
1967	#+ MUNI, Paul ★		71	Heart trouble (in Montecito, CA)
1945	MUNIER, Ferdinand		55	After a heart attack (in Hollywood, CA)
• 1924	MUNRO, Douglas		?	Double pneumonia (in Birmingham, England)
1972	MUNRO, Janet		38	Choked to death while drinking tea (in London, England)
1992	MUNRO, Nan		87	
1970	MUNSHIN, Jules		54	Heart attack
1955	#+ MUNSON, Ona		51	Suicide (sleeping pills) in New York, NY
• 1968	MURAT, Jean		79	Coronary thrombosis (in Aix-en-Provence, France)
1990	MURDOCH, Richard B.		83	Apparent heart attack
• 1939	# MURDOCK, Ann		48	Died in Lucerne, Switzerland
1931	MURNAU, F. W.		42	Automobile accident
1971	#+ MURPHY, Audie		46	Airplane crash (near Roanoke, VA)
• 1974	# MURPHY, Edna		69	Died in Santa Monica, CA
1992	MURPHY, George		89	Leukemia
1961	MURPHY, Joseph J.		84	Died in San Jose, CA
1978	MURPHY, Maurice		65	Died in Los Angeles, CA
1993	MURPHY, Richard		81	Stroke (in Los Angeles, CA)
1988	MURPHY, Timothy Patrick		29	A.I.D.S.
1991	# MURRAY, Arthur		95	Pneumonia
• 1979	# MURRAY, Bobby		80	Died in Nashua, NH
1941	MURRAY, Charlie		69	Pneumonia (in Hollywood, CA)
1940	MURRAY, J. Harold		49	After treatment for a kidney ailment
1936	MURRAY, James		35	Drowned when he fell off a N.Y.C. pier
1957	MURRAY, John T.		71	Following a stroke (in Woodland Hills, CA)
1988	MURRAY, Ken		85	

YEAR	NAME	AGE	CAUSE AND/OR PLACE OF DEATH
1965	#+ MURRAY, Mae	75	Heart condition (in North Hollywood, CA)
1990	MURRAY, Mary Phillips	68	Cancer
1935	MURRAY, Tom	60	After a 1-year illness (in Hollywood, CA)
1989	# MURRAY-MAZWI, Mark	52	Heart attack
1965	+ MURROW, Edward R.	57	Lung cancer
1979	MUSE, Clarence	90	Cerebral hemorrhage (in Perris, CA)
• 1957	# Musidora	68	Died in Paris, France
1991	MUSILLI, John	55	Cancer
• 1996	MUSTARD, Jim	51	Bone cancer and A.I.D.S. (in Baltimore, MD)
1977	+ MUSTIN, Burt	94	Died in Glendale, CA
1990	MYDLAND, Brent	37	Overdose of morphine & cocaine
1980	+ MYERS, Carmel	79	After a heart attack (in Los Angeles, CA)
1938	MYERS, Harry	52	Pneumonia (in Los Angeles, CA)
1993	MYERS, Stanley	63	Cancer (in London, England)
• 1995	MYERS, William	74	Pneumonia (in New York City)
1992	MYHERS, John	70	Pneumonia
1984	MYLES, Mary	93	Congestive heart failure
1975	MYLONG, John	82	After a long illness
1978	MYRTILE, Odette	80	Stroke (in a hospital in Doylestown, PA)
	N		
1992	NABBIE, Jim	72	After double bypass heart surgery
1990	NADEL, Arthur H.	68	Diabetes
1966	# NAGEL, Anne	53	Cancer (in Los Angeles, CA)
1970	NAGEL, Conrad	72	Died in New York, NY
1973	#+ NAISH, J. Carrol ☆	73	Died in La Jolla, CA
1992	# NAISMITH, Laurence	83	After a short illness
1991	# NALDER, Reggie	80	Bone cancer
1961	#+ NALDI, Nita	61	Died in New York, NY
1988	# NAPIER, Alan	85	Natural causes
1974	NAPIER, Russell	64	Died in England
1990	NAPOLEAN, Phil	89	
• 1943	# NARES, Owen	54	Died in Brecon, Wales
1985	NASH, Clarence "Donald Duck"	80	Leukemia
1950	NASH, Florence	60	Heart ailment
1979	NASH, June	68	Died in Hampton Bays, L.I., NY
1976	# NASH, Mary	91	Died in Brentwood, CA
1942	NATHEAUX, Louis	44	Died in Los Angeles, CA
1990	NATWICK, Grim	100	Pneumonia & heart disease
1994	+ NATWICK, Mildred ☆	89	Cancer (at her home in New York City)
1992	NAUGHTON, Bill	81	
• 1976	NAUGHTON, Charlie	88	Died in London, England
1986	NAZARRO, Ray	83	
1945	#+ NAZIMOVA, Alla	66	Coronary thrombosis (in Los Angeles, CA)
• 1979	# NAZZARI, Amedeo	71	Cardiac arrest (in Rome, Italy)
1986	# NEAGLE, Anna	81	
1972	NEAL, Tom	58	Natural causes (in North Hollywood, CA)
1972	# NEDELL, Bernard	74	Died in Hollywood, CA
1947	+ NEGIN, Koliz	60	
1987	#+ NEGRI, Pola	87	Brain tumor, complicated by pneumonia
1993	+ NEGULESCO, Jean	93	Heart failure (in Marbella, Spain)
1989	NEIDORF, Ross Lee	34	A.I.D.S.
1958	NEILAN, Marshall	67	Cancer (in Woodland Hills, CA)
1931	+ NEILL, James	70	Heart trouble (in Glendale, CA)
1970	NEILL, Richard R.	94	Died at Motion Picture Country Hospital, Woodland Hills, CA
1946	NEILL, Roy William	59	After a heart attack, in London
1948	NELSON, Anne	37	
1979	NELSON, Billy	75	Following a heart attack
1988	NELSON, Christine	60	Lung cancer
1986	+ NELSON, Frank	75	Cancer
1994	#+ NELSON, Harriet	85	Congestive heart failure (at her home in Laguna Beach, CA)
1990	NELSON, Herbert	76	
1993	NELSON, Kenneth	60	An A.I.D.S.-related illness (in London)
1975	#+ NELSON, Ozzie	69	Cancer (in Hollywood, CA)
1987	NELSON, Ralph	71	Cancer
1985	#+ NELSON, Rick	45	Airplane crash (near DeKalb, TX) traces of cocaine found in his body

• New entry. # Original name (Pt. 7). + Interment (Pt. 5).   212   ☆ Oscar nominee, ★ Oscar winner (Pt. 10)

YEAR	NAME		AGE	CAUSE AND/OR PLACE OF DEATH
1992	NELSON, Ruth		87	Cancer complicated by a stroke & pneumonia
• 1975	# NERVO, Jimmy		85	Died in London, England
1982	NESBITT, Cathleen		93	
1990	# NESBITT, Frank M.		48	Cancer
1960	NESBITT, John		49	
• 1954	NESBITT, Miriam		80	Died in Hollywood, CA
1972	NESMITH, Ottola		83	Died in Hollywood, CA
1958	+ NEUMANN, Kurt		50	After emergency hospitalization in Hollywood
• 1995	NEVAREZ, Aramando		44	Complications of A.I.D.S. (in Los Angeles, CA)
1932	NEVILLE, George		66	Died in New York, NY
1937	NEWALL, Guy		51	Died in London, England
1969	NEWBURG, Frank		83	Died at Motion Picture Country Hospital, CA
1980	NEWELL, David (actor)		75	
1967	+ NEWELL, William "Billy"		72	Died in Hollywood, CA
1964	NEWFIELD, Sam		64	Cancer
1994	NEWINGTON, Peter		71	
1970	+ NEWMAN, Alfred	★	68	Emphysema and complications
• 1995	NEWMAN, Joseph		82	Lymphoma (in Washington, D.C.)
1989	+ NEWMAN, Lionel		73	Cardiac arrest
1978	# NEWMAN, Scott		28	Apparent accidental overdose of Valium and alcohol
1991	NEWMAN, Thomas		60	Heart attack
1993	NEWMAN, Walter Brown	☆	77	Cancer (at his home in Sherman Oaks, CA)
1926	NEWTON, Charles		?	
1965	+ NEWTON, Robert		50	Heart attack (in Beverly Hills, CA)
1981	# NEY, Marie		86	
• 1996	NGOR, Dr. Haing S.	★	55	Murdered (shot) outside his home in Los Angeles, CA
1948	#+ NIBLO, Fred Sr.		74	Pneumonia (in New Orleans, Louisiana)
• 1977	NICHOLLS, Anthony		69	Died in London, England
1976	# NICHOLS, Barbara		47	Liver ailment
1986	# NICHOLS, Dandy		78	
1960	NICHOLS, Dudley		64	While hospitalized (in Hollywood) for cancer
1939	+ NICHOLS, George Jr.		42	Automobile accident
1927	NICHOLS, George Sr.		62	Died at his home in Hollywood, CA
1965	#+ NICHOLS, Red		60	Heart attack (in Las Vegas, NV)
1991	NICHOLSON, Thomas D.		68	Cancer
1988	#+ Nico		49	Cerebral hemorrhage from bicycle fall
• 1972	# NIELSEN, Asta		89	Died in Copenhagen, Denmark
• 1967	NIELSEN, Hans		56	Died in Berlin, Germany
1975	NIESEN, Gertrude		62	Died in Kaiser-Permanente Hospital, Glendale, CA
1993	NIGH, Jane		68	Stroke (in Los Angeles, CA)
1989	NIGHTINGALE, Earl		68	After heart surgery
1992	NIGRO, Robert		45	A.I.D.S.
• 1995	NIJHOFF, Loudi		94	Died in Amsterdam, Holland
1950	+ NIJINSKY, Vaslav		62	Nephritis (in London, England)
1988	NILES, Ken		82	
1974	# NILSSON, Anna Q.		85	Natural causes (in Hemet, CA)
1994	#+ NILSSON, Harry		52	Following a heart attack (in Agoura Hills, CA)
1988	NISSEN, Greta		82	Parkinson's disease
1983	+ NIVEN, David	★	73	Amyotrophic lateral sclerosis
1983	NIXON, Marion		78	Complications following open-heart surgery
1993	#+ NIXON, Pat		81	Lung cancer
1994	NOBLE, Leighton		82	Died in Victoria, Canada
• 1978	NOBLE, Ray		70	Cancer (in London, England)
1980	+ NOLAN, Bob		72	Heart attack (in Newport Beach, CA)
1985	NOLAN, James		69	Lung cancer
1985	+ NOLAN, Lloyd		83	Lung cancer
1948	#+ NOLAN, Mary		42	Found dead at home (in Los Angeles, CA)
1968	# NOONAN, Tommy		45	After an operation for a malignant brain tumor (in Woodland Hills)
1988	NORDEN, Christine		63	Chest infection after heart surgery
• 1949	NORDEN, Cliff		26	Suicide (pills) in Hollywood, CA
1951	# NORMAN, Josephine		46	Died in Roslyn, NY
1993	NORMAN, Lester		81	Heart failure
1930	#+ NORMAND, Mabel		35	Tuberculosis (in Monrovia, CA)
1983	NORRIS, Kenneth		34	Injuries from a fall
1991	NORTH, Alex	☆	81	Pancreatic cancer

YEAR	NAME		AGE	CAUSE AND/OR PLACE OF DEATH
1990	NORTH, Edmund		79	
1945	# NORTH, Joe		71	
1935	NORTH, Wilfrid		82	After a brief illness (in Hollywood, CA)
• 1936	NORTHRUP, Harry S.		58	Died in Los Angeles, CA
1956	# NORTON, Barry		51	Heart attack (in Hollywood, CA)
• 1953	NORTON, Edgar		84	Died in Woodland Hills, CA
1958	# NORTON, Jack		69	Respiratory ailment (in Saranac Lake, NY)
• 1948	# NORWOOD, Eille		87	
1959	NORWORTH, Jack		80	Stroke and heart ailment (in Laguna Beach, CA)
1979	NOVAES, Guiomar		84	
1988	NOVAK, Eva		90	Pneumonia
1990	NOVAK, Jane		94	Complications caused by a stroke
1968	#+ NOVARRO, Ramon		69	Murdered (bludgeoned) in his Hollywood Hills home
1990	NOVELLI, Santo Alex		73	
1951	# NOVELLO, Ivor		58	Coronary thrombosis (in London, England)
1982	NOVELLO, Jay		78	
1992	NOVELLO, Roselle		95	
1994	NOVOTNA, Jarmila		86	Natural causes (at her home in Manhattan, NY)
1980	NUGENT, Elliott		80	Died in his sleep (in New York, NY)
1947	NUGENT, J. C.		72	Coronary thrombosis (at the Lambs Club in New York City)
1993	+ NUREYEV, Rudolph		54	Cardiac complications from A.I.D.S. (in Paris, France)
1993	NUSSBAUM, Raphael		61	Cancer (in Burbank, CA)
1991	NUTE, Don		56	A.I.D.S.
1982	NUTT, Rev. Grady		47	Airplane crash
1993	NYBY, Christian	☆	80	Natural causes (in Temecula, CA)
1974	NYE, Carroll		72	Heart attack and kidney failure (in North Hollywood, CA)
	◕			
1978	#+ OAKIE, Jack	☆	74	Aortic aneurysm (in Northridge, CA)
1983	OAKLAND, Simon		61	
1958	# OAKLAND, Vivien		63	Died in Hollywood, CA
1949	OAKMAN, Wheeler		59	Died in Van Nuys, CA
1982	OATES, Warren		53	Heart attack
1982	+ OBER, Philip		80	Heart failure
1950	OBER, Robert		68	Died in New York
1979	#+ OBERON, Merle	☆	68	Stroke (in Los Angeles, CA)
1987	OBOLER, Arch		78	Stroke
• 1969	# O'BRIEN, David "Dave"		57	Heart attack (on Catalina Island, CA)
1985	+ O'BRIEN, Edmond	★	69	Alzheimer's disease, after suffering heart problems
1987	O'BRIEN, Eloise Taylor		84	
1966	O'BRIEN, Eugene		83	Bronchial pneumonia (in Los Angeles, CA)
1985	O'BRIEN, George		85	Following a stroke
1985	O'BRIEN, Kenneth		49	Cancer
• 1996	O'BRIEN, Liam	☆	83	Heart failure (at his home in Los Angeles, CA)
1983	#+ O'BRIEN, Pat		83	Massive heart attack
1983	O'BRIEN, Richard		65	Cancer
1947	#+ O'BRIEN, Tom		55	Died in Los Angeles, CA
1979	O'BRIEN-MOORE, Erin		77	Cancer (in Los Angeles, CA)
1993	OCHS, Saul P.		82	Unreported causes (in N. Hollywood, CA)
1991	OCKO, Daniel		78	Respiratory failure
1981	O'CONNELL, Arthur	☆	73	Alzheimer's disease (in Woodland Hills, CA)
• 1996	O'CONNELL, David J.		79	Chronic lung disease (in Santa Monica, CA)
1993	+ O'CONNELL, Helen (Devol)		73	Cancer (at a hospice in San Diego, CA)
1943	O'CONNELL, Hugh		44	After a heart attack (in Hollywood, CA)
• 1932	O'CONNER, Edward		70	Died in New York, NY
1959	O'CONNOR, Frank (director/actor)		71	After a long illness (in Hollywood, CA)
1971	O'CONNOR, Harry M.		98	Pneumonia, complicated by cardiac trouble
• 1995	O'CONNOR, Hugh		33	Suicide (gunshot) after 16 yrs. of drug abuse (in Los Angeles)
1991	O'CONNOR, Kevin		56	Cancer
1962	O'CONNOR, Robert Emmett		77	Burns after his cigarette ignited his clothing (in Hollywood, CA)
1959	+ O'CONNOR, Una		78	After a long illness (in New York, NY)
1989	O'DAVOREN, Vesey		100	
1987	# O'DAY, Molly		64	Cancer
1989	O'DAY, Nell		79	Cardiac arrest
• 1955	ODEMAR, Fritz		65	Died in Munich, Germany
1963	+ ODETS, Clifford		57	Cancer

YEAR	NAME		AGE	CAUSE AND/OR PLACE OF DEATH
1970	# O'DONNELL, Cathy		44	Following a long illness (in Los Angeles, CA)
1992	O'DONNELL, Gene		81	Lung cancer
1996	O'DONNELL, Lynn		43	Ovarian cancer (in San Francisco, CA)
1963	OFFERMAN, George Jr.		45	Died in New York, NY
1992	OGAWA, Shinsuke		56	
1940	# OGLE, Charles		75	Died in Long Beach, CA
1989	# O'HANLON, George		76	Stroke
1979	+ O'HARA, Barry J.		53	
1993	O'HARA, Patrick J.		55	After a lengthy illness (in Burbank, CA)
1979	# O'HARA, Shirley		68	Cancer
1994	# O'HARE, Brad		43	Complications of A.I.D.S. (in Manhattan, NY)
1995	OKADA, Eiji		75	Died in Japan
1968	#+ O'KEEFE, Dennis		60	Lung cancer (in Santa Monica, CA)
1938	#+ OLAND, Warner		57	Bronchial pneumonia (in Stockholm, Sweden)
1949	OLCOTT, Sidney		76	After a long illness
1946	# OLDFIELD, Barney		68	Cerebral hemorrhage
1992	OLIVER, David		30	A.I.D.S.
1942	#+ OLIVER, Edna May	☆	59	Intestinal disorder (in Hollywood, CA)
1995	OLIVER, Gordon		84	Emphysema (at Cedars-Sinai Med. Ctr. in Los Angeles)
1932	OLIVER, Guy		54	After a long illness (in the Hollywood Hospital, CA)
1990	# OLIVER, Susan		53	Cancer
1988	# OLIVER, Sy		77	
1964	# OLIVER, Vic		66	
1988	OLIVER, Virgil		72	
1989	+ OLIVIER, Laurence	★	82	Died in his sleep (in London, England)
1995	OLLE, Andrew		47	Brain tumor (after collapsing in his Sydney, Australia home)
1975	# OLMSTEAD, Gertrude		70	Died at her Beverly Hills (Ca.) home
1954	+ OLSEN, Moroni		65	Natural causes (in Los Angeles, CA)
1963	#+ OLSEN, Ole		71	Kidney ailment
1985	OLSON, Johnny ("Come on down")		75	Brain hemorrhage
1951	O'MADIGAN, Isabel		78	Died in Los Angeles, CA
1985	O'MALLEY, J. Pat		80	Heart condition (Do not confuse with Pat O'Malley, d. 1966)
1966	# O'MALLEY, Pat		75	Died while eating dinner at home (in Van Nuys, CA)
1976	O'MALLEY, Rex		75	Died at the Mary Manning Walsh Home, NY
1983	O'MOORE, Patrick		74	Following surgery
1987	ONDRA, Anny		84	
1971	# O'NEAL, Anne		77	Pancreatitis (in Woodland Hills, CA)
1992	# O'NEAL, Frederick		86	After a long illness
1994	O'NEAL, Patrick		66	Respiratory failure, tuberculosis & cancer (in Manhattan, NY)
1980	O'NEIL, Barbara	☆	69	
1968	# O'NEIL, Sally		57	Pneumonia
1961	O'NEILL, Henry		69	Died in Hollywood, CA
1957	O'NEILL, Jack		74	
1945	O'NEILL, Peggy		21	Suicide after a lover's quarrel (sleeping pills) in Beverly Hills, CA
1996	OPATOSHU, David		78	After a long illness (in Los Angeles, CA)
1987	O'PHELAN, Sean		33	Cancer
1957	# OPHULS, Max		54	2-months after a heart attack (in Hamburg, Germany)
1988	+ ORBISON, Roy		52	Heart attack
1979	ORCHARD, Julian		49	Died in London, England
1957	ORLAMOND, William		89	
1987	# ORLANDO, Don		75	Heart attack (while playing golf in Glendale, CA)
1992	# ORLOFF, Thelma		76	Kidney failure
1985	ORMANDY, Eugene		85	
1994	ORMONT, David		79	Heart attack (at his W. Hollywood, CA, home)
1946	# O'ROURKE, Brefni		57	
1988	+ O'ROURKE, Heather		12	Septic shock, congenital bowel narrowing
1948	# ORTES, Armand F.		68	
1962	ORTH, Frank		82	Died in Hollywood, CA
1956	ORZAZEWSKI, Kasia		67	Rheumatic heart disease
1980	O'SHEA, Daniel T.		75	
1973	# O'SHEA, Michael		67	Heart attack (in Dallas, TX)
1958	#+ OSBORN, Lyn		32	Following brain surgery
1994	# OSBORNE, John	★	65	Heart attack (in a hospital in Shropshire, England)
1988	OSBORN, Paul		86	Died in New York, NY
1961	OSBORNE, Vivienne		64	

YEAR	NAME		AGE	CAUSE AND/OR PLACE OF DEATH
1932	# OSBOURNE, Jefferson		61	Stroke (in Hondo, CA)
1964	# OSBOURNE, Lennie "Bud"		82	Died in Hollywood, CA
1969	# OSCAR, Henry		78	Died in London, England
1994	OSIRIS, Wanda "Wandissima"		89	Cardiac arrest (at her home in Milan, Italy)
1960	O'SHEA, Oscar		78	Died in Hollywood, CA
• 1995	O'SHEA, Tessie		82	Died in Leesburg, Florida
1959	OSMOND, Hal		40	
1989	OSTRICHE, Muriel		93	
1989	OSWALD, Gerd		72	Cancer
• 1948	# OSWALDA, Ossi		49	Died in Prague, Czechoslovakia
1992	O'TOOLE, Ollie		79	After a long illness
1994	OTT, Dennis		36	A.I.D.S. (in Los Angeles, CA)
1942	OTTIANO, Rafaela		48	Heart attack (in Boston, MA)
1992	OULTON, Brian		84	
1949	+ OUSPENSKAYA, Maria	☆	73	Burned to death from a cigarette fire (in her L.A. apartment)
1950	OVERMAN, Jack		34	Following a heart attack (in Hollywood, CA)
1943	OVERMAN, Lynne		55	Following two heart attacks (in Santa Monica, CA)
1967	OVERTON, Frank		49	Heart attack (in Pacific Palisades, CA)
• 1951	OVEY, George		80	Died in Hollywood, CA
1965	OWEN, Catherine Dale		62	
1951	OWEN, Garry		48	Heart attack (in Hollywood, CA)
1980	OWEN, Malcolm		24	Overdose of heroin
1972	#+ OWEN, Reginald		85	Heart attack (in Boise, ID)
1966	# OWEN, Seena		70	After a brief illness (in Hollywood, CA)
• 1980	# OWENS, Jesse		66	Lung cancer (in Tucson, AZ)
1937	+ OWSLEY, Monroe		35	Heart attack (in Belmont, CA)
1989	OZERAY, Madeleine		78	
	P			
• 1967	PADDEN, Sarah		?	
• 1943	PADDOCK, Charles		42	Airplane crash (near Sitaka, Alaska)
• 1941	+ PADEREWSKI, Ignace		80	Pneumonia
1991	PADILLA, Ruben Dario Sr.		81	Cancer
• 1967	# PADULA, Vincent		66	Peritonitis (in Glendale, CA)
1991	PAGANO, Ronald F.		37	After a long illness
1983	# PAGE, Gale		72	Lung cancer
1987	PAGE, Geraldine	★	62	Heart attack
1990	# PAGE, Jean		95	
1974	# PAGE, Paul		70	Heart attack (in Hermosa Beach, CA)
1925	PAGET, Alfred		?	
• 1980	# PAGLIERO, Marcello		73	Died in Paris, France
• 1995	PAICH, Martin "Marty" Louis		70	Cancer (at his Santa Ynez, CA, home)
1954	PAIGE, Mabel		74	Died in Van Nuys, CA
1987	# PAIGE, Robert		76	
1966	PAIVA, Nestor		61	Died in Sherman Oaks, CA
1980	+ PAL, George		72	Heart attack
• 1962	PALANGE, Inez		73	Died in CA
1993	PALEY, Irving		77	Heart attack (in Los Angeles, CA)
1990	PALEY, William S.		89	Apparent heart attack brought on by pneumonia
1990	PALK, Anna		48	Cancer
• 1934	PALLENBERG, Max		57	Airplane crash (near Karlovy Vary, Czechoslovakia)
1954	PALLETTE, Eugene		65	After a long illness (in Los Angeles, CA)
1991	PALMER, John		75	After a short illness
1986	#+ PALMER, Lilli		71	Cancer
1981	PALMER, Maria		57	Cancer (in Los Angeles, CA)
1986	PALMER, Norman		65	
• 1964	# PALMER, Patricia		69	Died in Hollywood, CA
• 1987	#+ PAM, Anita		77	
1990	PAN, Hermes		80	Apparent stroke
1958	+ PANGBORN, Franklin		65	Died in Santa Monica, CA
• 1937	PANZER, Paul		70	Heart trouble (in NYC) Do not confuse with Paul Wolfgang Panzer
1958	#+ PANZER, Paul Wolfgang		86	Died in Hollywood, CA (Do not confuse with Paul Panzer, d. 1937)
• 1944	PAPE, Edward Lionel		77	Died in Woodland Hills, CA
1990	PARADJANOV, Sergei		66	
• 1955	PARDAVE, Joaquin		54	Died in Mexico City, Mexico
1984	PARFREY, Woodrow		61	Heart attack

YEAR	NAME		AGE	CAUSE AND/OR PLACE OF DEATH
1993	# PARHAM, Ernie		64	After a long illness (in Glen Falls, NY)
1991	# PARIS, Freddie		63	Cancer
1986	PARIS, Jerry		60	Complications from a brain tumor
• 1959	# PARIS, Manuel		65	Congestive heart failure (in Woodland Hills, CA)
• 1960	PARKE, Macdonald		68	Died in London, England
1992	PARKER, Al		40	A.I.D.S. (Do not confuse with Albert Parker, d. 1974)
1974	PARKER, Albert		87	(Do not confuse with Al Parker, d. 1992)
• 1941	# PARKER, Barnett		54	Died in Los Angeles, CA
1971	# PARKER, Cecil		73	Died in Brighton, England
1993	PARKER, Cecilia		79	Died in Ventura, CA
1955	+ PARKER, Charlie "Bird"		34	Heart attack (in the NY apartment of a female friend)
1985	PARKER, Dennis		38	
1990	PARKER, Ed		59	Following a heart attack
• 1960	PARKER, Edwin		59	Heart attack (in Sherman Oaks, CA)
• 1962	# PARKER, Frank "Pinky"		70	Heart attack (in Hollywood, CA)
1972	PARKER, Lew		64	Cancer (in New York, NY)
1993	PARKIN, Leonard		64	Cancer of the spine (in England)
1992	PARKS, Bert		77	Lung cancer (in La Jolla, CA)
1975	#+ PARKS, Larry	☆	60	Heart attack (in Studio City, CA)
1958	# Parkyakarkus		54	Heart attack (in Los Angeles, CA)
1979	PARNELL, Emory		85	Heart attack (in Woodland Hills, CA)
1961	PARNELL, James		38	Found dead in his automobile (in Hollywood, CA)
1959	PARRISH, Helen		34	After a long illness (in Hollywood, CA)
• 1995	PARRISH, Robert	★	79	Died at Southampton Hospital on Long Island, NY
1939	#+ PARROTT, James		46	Heart attack (in Hollywood, CA)
1985	PARRY, Harvey		85	Heart attack
1992	PARSONS, Lindsley Sr.		87	Heart failure
1972	#+ PARSONS, Louella (Martin)		91	Arteriosclerosis (in Santa Monica, CA)
• 1980	PARSONS, Milton		75	
• 1944	PARSONS, Percy		66	
1954	PASCAL, Gabriel		60	
1992	PASCAL, Jean-Claude		64	Following surgery
• 1933	PASHA, Kalla		56	Died in Talmage, CA
• 1975	PASOLINI, Pier Paolo		53	Murdered (beaten) near Ostia, Italy
1989	PASS, Lenny		37	
1991	PASTERNAK, Joe		89	Parkinson's disease and other ailments (in Beverly Hills, CA)
1992	PASTOR, Guy		55	Heart attack
1970	# PATCH, Wally		82	Died in London, England
1978	+ PATERSON, Pat		67	Cancer (in Phoenix, AZ)
1957	PATHE, Charles		93	Died in Monte Carlo
1950	PATON, Charles		64	
1944	PATON, Stuart		59	
1987	PATRICK, Dorothy		65	Cancer
1980	# PATRICK, Gail		69	Leukemia (in Hollywood, CA)
• 1923	PATRICK, Jerome		40	Heart disease (in New York)
1982	+ PATRICK, Lee (Wood)		76	Heart seizure
1981	# PATRICK, Nigel		68	Cancer (at a hospital in London, England)
1950	PATRICOLA, Tom		55	Following brain surgery (in Pasadena, CA)
• 1996	PATTEN, Luana		57	Respiratory failure (in Long Beach, CA)
1966	PATTERSON, Elizabeth		91	Died in Los Angeles, CA
1975	# PATTERSON, Hank		86	Bronchial pneumonia (in Woodland Hills, CA)
1991	PATTISON, Arthur		60	Cancer
1982	PATTON, Mary		66	Cancer
• 1951	PATTON, William "Bill"		57	
• 1962	PAUL, Val		75	Died in Hollywood, CA
• 1933	PAULIG, Albert		?	Heart trouble
• 1954	PAULSEN, Harald		59	Heart attack (in Hamburg, Germany)
1989	PAULSON, Al		67	Heart failure
• 1931	PAVLOVA, Anna		46	Died in The Hague, Netherlands
1936	PAWLE, Lennox		63	Cerebral hemorrhage (at a hospital in Hollywood, CA)
1988	PAWLEY, Edward		84	
1952	PAWLEY, William		46	Died in New York
1973	# PAXINOU, Katina	★	72	Cancer (in Athens, Greece)
• 1965	PAYNE, Douglas		90	Died in England
• 1953	PAYNE, Edna		61	Liver ailment (in Los Angeles, CA)

YEAR	NAME	AGE	CAUSE AND/OR PLACE OF DEATH
1989	PAYNE, John	77	Congestive heart failure
1953	# PAYNE, Lou	77	Died in Woodland Hills, CA
1964	PAYSON, Blanche	83	Died in Hollywood, CA
1967	PAYTON, Barbara	39	Natural causes (in San Diego, CA)
• 1955	# PAYTON, Claude	72	Died in Los Angeles, CA
1970	PEABODY, Eddie	58	Stroke (in Covington, KY)
• 1966	PEACOCK, Kim	65	Heart attack (in Emsworth, England)
• 1918	PEACOCK, Lillian	27	From previous filming injuries (in Los Angeles, CA)
1993	PEALE, (Rev.) Norman Vincent	95	Following a stroke (at his farm in Pawling, NY)
1966	PEARCE, Alice	46	Cancer (in Los Angeles, CA)
1940	# PEARCE, George C.	75	Died in Los Angeles, CA
1984	PEARCE, Muriel	85	After a long illness
• 1964	# PEARCE, Peggy	69	Died in Hollywood, CA
• 1966	PEARCE, Vera	69	Died in London, England
1993	PEARDON, Patricia	69	Pneumonia (at St. Luke's Hospital in Manhattan, NY)
• 1996	# PEARL, Minnie	83	Following a stroke (in Nashville, TN)
• 1969	# PEARSON, Drew	71	Died in Washington, D.C.
1966	PEARSON, Lloyd	68	Died in London, England
1958	PEARSON, Virginia	70	Uremic poisoning (in Los Angeles, CA)
1985	PEARY, Harold "Gildersleeve"	76	Heart attack
1992	PECK, Ed	75	Heart attack
1959	+ PECKHAM, Francis Miles	66	
1984	PECKINPAH, Sam	59	Following several heart attacks
1984	PEEPLES, Dennis	50	Heart attack
1984	PEERCE, Jan	80	Pneumonia and coma
• 1975	PEERS, Joan	64	
1962	# PEIL, Edward Jr.	54	After a 2-year illness
1958	# PEIL, Edward Sr.	70	Died in Hollywood, CA
1983	PELISH, Thelma	55	
1987	PELLER, Clara	86	Died in her sleep (at her home in Chicago, IL)
• 1977	PELT, Timothy "Tim"	39	Automobile accident (in Pacific Palisades, CA)
1950	PEMBERTON, Brock	64	After a heart attack at his home (in New York, NY)
• 1972	PENA, Julio	60	Heart attack (in Marbella, Spain)
1986	PENDER, Stephen	35	Complications from A.I.D.S.
1967	PENDLETON, Nat	68	Heart attack (in San Diego, CA)
1992	PENDRELL, Ernest	?	Cancer
• 1975	# PENN, Leonard	68	Heart attack (in Los Angeles, CA)
1941	#+ PENNER, Joe	35	Heart attack (in Philadelphia, PA)
1964	PENNICK, Jack	68	After a year's illness (in Hollywood, CA)
1971	PENNINGTON, Ann	78	Died in New York
• 1931	PENROD, Alexander G.	?	Killed in a ship explosion while on location in the Antarctic
• 1930	PENWARDEN, Duncan	50	Died in Jackson Heights, NY
1994	+ PEPPARD, George	65	Pneumonia (at UCLA Medical Center, CA)
1969	PEPPER, Barbara	53	Coronary (in Panorama City, CA)
1993	# PEPPER, Buddy	70	Heart failure
1993	+ PEPPLE, Sydney Chester	83	Died at Scripps Ocean View Hospital, Encinitas, CA
1934	# PERCIVAL, Walter C.	46	Died of complications (in Hollywood, CA)
1973	PERCY, Eileen	72	After an illness of many years (in Beverly Hills, CA)
1957	# PERCY, Esme	69	Died in Brighton, England
1993	PEREDES, Daniel	46	A.I.D.S. (in Los Angeles, CA)
• 1983	+ PEREIRA, Hal	?	
1978	+ PERFECT, Rose	82	
1994	PERILLI, Ivo	92	After suffering a stroke (in Rome, Italy)
1965	PERINAL, Georges	68	
1940	PERIOLAT, George	63	Suicide (arsenic) at his home in Los Angeles, CA
1992	PERKINS, Anthony ☆	60	Complications from A.I.D.S. (at his home in Hollywood, CA)
1986	# PERKINS, Marlin	81	Lymphatic cancer
1937	PERKINS, Osgood	45	Apparent heart attack after tonsilitis (in Washington, D.C.)
1977	PERKINS, Voltaire	80	Apparent heart attack (in Los Angeles, CA)
1967	PERRIN, Jack	71	Heart attack (in Hollywood, CA)
1989	PERRIN, Vic	73	Cancer
1962	PERRINS, Leslie	60	Died in Esher, England
• 1946	# PERRY, Antoinette	58	Heart attack (in New York, NY)
• 1995	PERRY, Frank	65	Prostate cancer (at Mem. Sloan-Kettering Cancer Ctr. in NY)
1962	PERRY, Robert E. "Bob"	82	Died in Hollywood, CA

YEAR	NAME		AGE	CAUSE AND/OR PLACE OF DEATH
• 1954	PERRY, Walter		85	*Died in CA*
1991	PERTWEE, Michael		74	
1994	PETERKOCH, Lydia		29	*Automobile accident (in Los Angeles, CA)*
• 1965	PETERS, Ann		45	*Heart attack (in Paris, France)*
1967	# PETERS, House Sr.		87	*Died at M.P.C. Hospital, Woodland Hills, CA*
1992	PETERS, Lennie		59	
1994	PETERS, Michael		46	*Complications from A.I.D.S. (in Los Angeles, CA)*
• 1916	PETERS, Page E.		?	*Drowned (at Hermosa Beach, CA)*
• 1959	PETERS, Ralph		56	*Died in Hollywood, CA*
1952	#+ PETERS, Susan	☆	31	*Bronchial pneumonia and chronic kidney infection (in Visalia, CA)*
• 1971	PETERS, Werner		51	*Died in Wiesbaden, West Germany*
• 1979	PETERSON, Dorothy		?	
• 1930	Petey ("Our Gang" dog)		7	*Arsenic poisoning (in Los Angeles, CA)*
1948	# PETRIE, Hay		53	
1968	PETRIE, Howard A.		61	*After a long illness (at a hospital in Keene, NH)*
• 1977	# PETROVA, Olga		91	*Died in Clearwater, FL*
1966	PETTINGELL, Frank		75	*Died in London, England*
• 1995	PETTIT, Tom		64	*Complications after surgery to repair a ruptured aorta (in NYC)*
1992	# PETTYJOHN, Angelique		48	*Cancer*
1918	PEYTON, Lawrence R. "Larry"		?	*Killed in action in France during World War I*
1992	PEYTON, Rev. Patrick		83	*Renal failure*
1993	PHELPS, Donald		61	*A.I.D.S. (in West Hollywood, CA)*
1953	PHELPS, Lee		58	*Died in Culver City, CA*
1993	PHILBIN, Mary		90	*Complications from Alzheimer's disease (in Huntington Beach, CA)*
1982	PHILBROOK, James		58	
1959	PHILIPPE, Gerard		36	*Heart attack (in Paris, France)*
1975	PHILIPS, Mary		74	*Cancer (in Santa Monica, CA)*
1982	# PHILLIPS, Barney		68	*After a brief illness*
• 1980	PHILLIPS, Dorothy		90	*Pneumonia (in Woodland Hills, CA)*
1965	PHILLIPS, Edward N.		65	*Killed by a car while crossing the street (in North Hollywood, CA)*
1915	# PHILLIPS, Edwin R.		?	*Died in the hospital of a complication of diseases*
1993	PHILLIPS, Linn III		45	*Heart attack (in Denver, Colorado)*
• 1963	PHILLIPS, Mina		77	*Heart ailment (in New Orleans, LA)*
• 1931	PHILLIPS, Norman Sr.		38	*Heart attack (in Culver City, CA)*
• 1930	PHILLIPS, Tubby		45	*Automobile accident (in London, England)*
1980	PHILLPOTTS, Ambrosine		68	*Died in Ascot, England*
1980	PHIPPS, Nicholas		66	*Died in London, England*
1978	# PHIPPS, Sally		67	*Died at Long Island College Hospital, NY*
1986	# PHOENIX, Pat		62	*Lung cancer*
1993	+ PHOENIX, River		23	*Acute multiple drug intoxication (at a niteclub in West Hollywood)*
1963	#+ PIAF, Edith		47	*Internal hemorrhage (in Plascassier, France)*
1976	+ PIATIGORSKY, Gregor		73	
1991	PIAZZA, Ben		58	*Cancer*
1973	PICASSO, Pablo		91	*Died in Mougins, France*
1954	PICHEL, Irving		63	*Following a heart attack (in Hollywood, CA)*
• 1931	PICK, Lupu		45	*Food poisoning*
1959	PICKARD, Helena		59	
1983	# PICKENS, Slim		64	*Pneumonia*
1933	#+ PICKFORD, Jack		36	*Multiple neuritis (in Paris, France)*
1936	#+ PICKFORD, Lottie		?	*Heart attack*
1979	#+ PICKFORD, Mary	★	86	*Cerebral hemorrhage (in Santa Monica, CA)*
• 1978	PICKLES, Wilfrid		73	*Died in Brighton, England*
1982	PICKMAN, Kathryn		60	*Cancer*
1992	PICON, Molly		94	*Died in her sleep following Alzheimer's disease (in Lancaster, PA)*
1984	+ PIDGEON, Walter	☆	87	*Series of strokes*
• 1963	PIEL, Harry		71	*Died in Munich, Germany*
1993	PIERCE, Edward		77	*Natural causes (in Jamesport, NY)*
1968	+ PIERCE, Jack P.		79	
1991	PIERCE, Webb		69	*Pancreatic cancer*
1955	+ PIERLOT, Francis		78	*Heart ailment (in Hollywood, CA)*
1975	PIERSON, Arthur		73	*Died at St. John's Hospital in Santa Monica, CA*
1962	PIGOTT, Tempe		78	*Died in Hollywood, CA*
• 1963	PILOTTO, Camillo		?	
1938	PINCHOT, Rosamond		33	*Suicide (carbon monoxide poisoning)*
1950	PINE, Ed		46	*Died at the Motion Picture Country Home, CA*

• New entry.   # Original name (Pt. 7).   + Interment (Pt. 5).

☆ Oscar nominee, ★ Oscar winner (Pt. 10)

...DEATHS OF MOVIE AND TELEVISION PERSONALITIES — BY NAME...

YEAR	NAME		AGE	CAUSE AND/OR PLACE OF DEATH
• 1934	PINERO, Arthur Wing		79	Died in London, England
1988	PINERO, Miguel		41	Cirrhosis of the liver
1957	#+ PINZA, Ezio		65	Following a series of strokes (in Stamford, CT)
• 1979	PIOUS, Minerva		75	
1979	PIPER, Frederick		77	
1990	PIPPIN, Nick		35	A.I.D.S.
• 1996	PISTILLI, Luigi		66	Suicide at his home before appearing on stage (in Milan, Italy)
• 1976	PISU, Mario		66	Cerebral hemorrhage (in Castelli Romani, Italy)
1990	PITOEFF, Sacha		70	Heart failure
1963	+ PITTS, Zasu (Woodall)		65	Cancer (in Hollywood, CA)
1993	PLAGE, Dieter		57	Died in a filming accident in the Sumatra rain forest
1974	PLATT, Edward C. "Ed"		58	Heart attack (in Santa Monica, CA)
• 1934	PLAYFAIR, Nigel		60	Died in London, England
• 1937	PLAYTER, Wellington		57	Died in Oakland, CA
• 1995	PLEASENCE, Donald		75	After surgery to replace a heart valve (at home in France)
• 1960	# PLUMB, E. Hay		77	
• 1928	PLUMER, Lincoln		51	Heart disease (in Hollywood, CA)
1980	POE, James ★		58	Heart attack (at his home in Malibu, CA)
• 1952	# POFF, Lon		82	
1979	# POHLMANN, Eric		66	
1992	POIRET, Jean		65	Heart attack
• 1976	POLANSKI, Goury		83	Cancer (in Hollywood, CA)
1987	POLK, David		55	Cancer
1993	POLK, Lee		69	Leukemia
1971	POLLACK, Ben		67	Suicide (hanged himself in his bathroom) in Palm Springs, CA
• 1978	# POLLARD, Daphne		87	Died in Los Angeles, CA
1934	+ POLLARD, Harry		55	After several weeks illness (Do not confuse with Harry "Snub" P.)
1962	#+ POLLARD, Harry "Snub"		75	Died in Burbank, CA (Do not confuse with Harry Pollard, d. 1934)
1961	# POLO, Eddie		86	Heart attack (in Hollywood, CA)
1966	POMMER, Erich		77	
1989	POMPEII, James S.		51	After a long illness
1990	POND, Barbara		?	Lung cancer
1976	# PONS, Lily		77	Cancer (in Dallas, TX)
1981	PONSELLE, Rosa		84	
• 1957	PONTO, Erich		71	Died in Stuttgart, Germany
1986	POOLE, Roy		62	
1991	POPKIN, Harry M.		85	Cancer
1992	+ PORCARO, Jeff		38	After an apparent allergic reaction to pesticides
1946	PORCASI, Paul		66	After a long illness (in Hollywood, CA)
• 1960	PORTEN, Henny		70	Died in Berlin, Germany
1964	+ PORTER, Cole		71	Following surgery for a kidney stone
• 1978	PORTER, Dick		45	Heart attack (in Sedalia, MO)
1941	+ PORTER, Edwin S.		71	
• 1995	PORTER, Eric		67	Colon cancer (at a hospital in north London, England)
1969	PORTMAN, Eric		66	Heart ailment (in St. Veep, England)
• 1952	POST, Charles A. "Buddy"		55	Died in CA
1968	POST, Guy Bates		92	Died in Hollywood, CA
1935	POST, Wiley		50	Airplane crash (near Barrow, Alaska)
1989	POST, William Jr.		88	Pulmonary disease
1994	# POTAMKIN, Luba		73	Alzheimer's disease (at her home in Miami, FL)
1947	POTEL, Victor "Vic"		57	Died in Hollywood, CA
• 1995	POTTER, Allan M.		75	Cancer (in Stuart, FL)
1994	POTTER, Dennis		59	Pancreatic & liver cancer (in Gloucestershire, England)
1977	# POTTER, H. C.		73	After a brief illness (in New York, NY)
1925	POWELL, David		39	Pneumonia after a nervous breakdown (in a NY Sanitarium)
1963	#+ POWELL, Dick		58	Cancer (in Hollywood, CA)
1982	+ POWELL, Eleanor		69	Cancer
1944	#+ POWELL, Lee B.		36	Killed in action in the S. Pacific, during W.W.II
1990	POWELL, Michael		84	
1937	+ POWELL, Richard		39	Fractured skull from auto accident
• 1950	# POWELL, Russ		75	Arteriosclerosis (in Woodland Hills, CA)
1984	+ POWELL, William ☆		91	Natural causes
1931	# POWER, F. Tyrone		62	Heart attack
1966	POWER, Hartley		71	After a long illness (in London, England)
• 1968	# POWER, Paul		65	Died in Hollywood, CA

• New entry. # Original name (Pt. 7). + Interment (Pt. 5).   220   ☆ Oscar nominee, ★ Oscar winner (Pt. 10)

YEAR	NAME		AGE	CAUSE AND/OR PLACE OF DEATH
1958	#+ POWER, Tyrone		44	Heart attack (in Madrid, Spain)
1991	POWERS, Tim		34	A.I.D.S.
1955	POWERS, Tom		65	Heart ailment (in Hollywood, CA)
1994	POZZI, Moana		33	Liver cancer (in Lyon, France)
• 1981	PRACK, Rudolf		77	Died in Vienna, Austria
1972	PRAGER, Stanley		55	While on a business trip (in Hollywood, CA)
• 1958	# PRATHER, Lee		67	During surgery (in Los Angeles, CA)
1991	PRATT, James C.		86	Pneumonia
1941	PRATT, Purnell B.		54	Died in Hollywood, CA
• 1995	PRECHT, Andrew		34	Cause unreported (in Grenada)
1984	PREISSER, June		61	Automobile collision
1979	PREJEAN, Albert		85	Died in Paris, France
1986	PREMINGER, Otto	☆	79	Cancer
1992	PRENTICE, Keith		52	Cancer
• 1979	PRENTISS, Eleanor		67	Died in New York, NY
1977	#+ PRESLEY, Elvis		42	Cardiac arrhythmia (possibly due to drug abuse) in Memphis, TN
1988	PRESSBURGER, Emeric		85	
1987	# PRESTON, Robert		68	Lung cancer
1992	PRESTON, Wayde		62	Cancer
• 1978	PRETTY, Arline		84	Died in Hollywood, CA
1993	PREVIN, Steve		68	Unreported causes (in Palm Desert, CA)
1937	# PREVOST, Marie		38	Acute alcoholism (in Los Angeles, CA)
• 1973	# PRICE, Dennis		58	Died in Guernsey, Channel Islands
1991	PRICE, Gilbert		48	Found dead in Vienna
• 1964	PRICE, Hal		77	
1943	# PRICE, Kate		70	After a long illness (in Woodland Hills, CA)
• 1987	PRICE, Kenny		?	
• 1970	# PRICE, Nancy		90	Died in Worthing, England
1955	PRICE, Stanley L.		55	Heart attack (in Hollywood, CA)
1993	+ PRICE, Vincent		82	Lung cancer (at his home in Hollywood Hills, CA)
• 1976	PRICKETT, Maudie		60	Uremic poisoning (in Pasadena, CA)
1993	PRIESTLY, Jack		66	Unreported causes (at his home in Los Angeles, CA)
1991	PRIM, Suzy		95	
1978	+ PRIMA, Louis		66	Pneumonia (in New Orleans, LA)
1989	# PRINGLE, Aileen		94	
• 1977	# PRINTEMPS, Yvonne		81	Died in Paris, France
1977	#+ PRINZE, Freddie		22	Suicide (gunshot) in Los Angeles, CA
• 1954	# PRIOR, Herbert		87	
1986	PROACH, Henry		66	
• 1974	PROHASKA, Janos		52	Airplane crash (in Inyo County, CA)
• 1953	+ PROKOFIEV, Sergei		62	Cerebral hemorrhage
1952	PROSSER, Hugh		46	Automobile crash (near Gallup, NM)
1956	PROUTY, Jed		77	After a brief illness (in New York)
1991	# PROVENZA, Sal		45	Lymphoma
1967	PRUD'HOMME, Cameron		75	After a long illness (in a New Jersey hospital)
• 1972	# PRUD'HOMME, George		71	Brain tumor (in Los Angeles, CA)
1974	PRYOR, Roger		72	Heart attack (while visiting in Puerta Vallarta, Mexico)
• 1953	PUDOVKIN, Vsevolod		60	Natural causes (in Moscow, Russia)
1975	PUGLIA, Frank		83	Died in South Pasadena, CA
• 1968	PUIG, Eva G.		74	Diabetes and heart failure (in Panorama City, CA)
1983	+ PULEO, Johnny		75	Respiratory failure
1972	PURCELL, Irene		70	Died at her home in Racine, WI
1985	PURCELL, Noel		84	
1944	PURCELL, Richard "Dick"		35	Heart attack after a car crash (in Los Angeles, CA)
1953	# PURDELL, Reginald		56	Died in London, England
1960	PURDY, Constance		75	Arteriosclerosis (in Los Angeles, CA)
1982	PURSELL, Robert		26	Apparent suicide (hung himself from a tree) in Levittown, PA
1958	+ PURVIANCE, Edna		63	After a long illness (in Woodland Hills, CA)
1970	PYNE, Joe		45	Lung cancer (in Los Angeles, CA)
	𝐐			
1987	# QUALEN, John		87	Heart failure
• 1958	QUARTERMAINE, Charles		80	
1989	QUAYLE, Anthony	☆	76	Cancer
1989	QUERTERMOUS, Charlie		41	Cancer
1964	QUIGLEY, Charles		58	Cirrhosis of the liver (in Los Angeles, CA)

	YEAR	NAME		AGE	CAUSE AND/OR PLACE OF DEATH
	1990	QUILLAN, Eddie		83	*Cancer*
	1989	QUINE, Richard		68	*Suicide (shot himself) in his California home*
	1919	QUINN, James		35	*Accidental (?) asphyxiation (gas) Do not confuse with Jimmie Quinn*
	1988	QUINN, Louis		73	*After a brief illness*
	1967	QUINN, Tony		67	*Died in London, England (Do not confuse with Anthony Quinn)*
	1926	QUIRK, William "Billy"		45	*Died at a Hollywood rest home after a 2-yr. illness*
		R			
	1993	# RA, Sun		79	*Circulatory problems after a series of strokes*
	1988	RAAB, Kurt		46	*A.I.D.S.*
•	1974	# RABAGLIATI, Alberto		67	*Cerebral thrombosis (in Rome, Italy)*
	1943	+ RACHMANINOFF, Sergei		69	*Cancer and pneumonia*
	1992	RACKMIL, Milton R.		89	*Stroke*
•	1996	RADASKY, Michael J.		43	*Automobile accident (in Texas)*
•	1976	RADD, Ronald		47	*Brain hemorrhage (in Toronto, Canada)*
	1952	RADFORD, Basil		55	*Heart attack (in London, England)*
	1989	+ RADNER, Gilda		42	*Ovarian cancer (in Los Angeles, CA)*
	1957	RAE, Jack		58	*Heart attack*
•	1976	# RAEBURN, Frances		?	*Heart failure (in CA)*
	1971	# RAFFERTY, Chips		62	*Heart attack (in Sydney, Australia)*
	1990	# RAFFETTO, Michael		91	*Natural causes*
	1980	#+ RAFT, George		85	*Leukemia (in Los Angeles, CA)*
	1946	# RAGLAND, John "Rags"		40	*Uremia (in Los Angeles, CA)*
	1991	RAGNI, Gerome		48	*Cancer*
•	1957	RAHM, Knute		81	*Heart disease (in Los Angeles, CA)*
•	1946	# RAIMU, Jules		62	*Heart attack (in Paris, France)*
	1979	RAINE, Jack		82	*Died in South Laguna, CA*
	1988	RAINES, Ella		66	*Throat cancer*
	1967	+ RAINS, Claude ☆		77	*Intestinal hemorrhage (in Laconia, NH)*
	1984	RAISCH, William		79	*Lung cancer*
•	1959	# RAKER, Lorin		68	*Cancer (in Woodland Hills, CA)*
•	1923	# RALEIGH, Saba		57	
	1944	# RALPH, Jessie		79	*After a lingering illness (in Gloucester, MA)*
	1994	RALSTON, Esther		91	*After a short illness (in Ventura, CA)*
	1992	RALSTON, Howard		?	*After an illness*
	1967	RALSTON, Jobyna		62	*Died in Woodland Hills, CA*
	1988	# RAMAGE, Cecil		93	
	1970	+ RAMBEAU, Marjorie ☆		80	*Died in Palm Springs, CA*
	1994	RAMBO, Dack		53	*A.I.D.S. (in Delano, CA)*
	1967	# RAMBO, Dirk		25	*Burned to death in a car accident*
•	1966	# RAMBOVA, Natacha		69	*Dietary complications (in Pasadena, CA)*
	1992	RAMOS, Lou		51	*After a brief illness*
	1988	RAMSEY, Anne ☆		59	*Throat cancer*
	1993	RAMSEY, Gordon		63	*Cancer (at his home in New York City)*
•	1929	# RAMSEY, John Nelson		65	*Heart disease (in London, England)*
•	1976	# RAMSEY-HILL, C. S.		84	*Died in Van Nuys, CA*
•	1940	RAND, John F.		67	*Died in Hollywood, CA*
	1979	#+ RAND, Sally		75	*Heart failure (in Glendora, CA)*
	1945	#+ RANDALL, Addison "Jack"		38	*Fell to his death from a horse, while filming (in Canoga Park, CA)*
	1984	RANDALL, Sue		49	*Cancer of the lungs & larynx*
	1967	+ RANDOLPH, Amanda		65	*Stroke (in Durate, CA)*
	1930	# RANDOLPH, Anders		60	*Following a relapse after a recent operation (in Hollywood, CA)*
	1993	RANDOLPH, Donald		87	*Pneumonia (in Los Angeles, CA)*
	1973	RANDOLPH, Isabel		82	*Died in Burbank, CA*
	1980	+ RANDOLPH, Lillian		65	*Cancer (in Los Angeles, CA)*
	1972	RANK, (Lord) J. Arthur		83	
	1947	# RANKIN, Arthur		46	*After a cerebral hemorrhage (in Hollywood, CA)*
	1946	RANKIN, Doris		66	*Died in Washington, D.C.*
•	1949	+ RAPF, Harry		67	*Heart attack*
	1991	RAPF, Matthew		71	*After an attack of the flu*
	1983	RAPHAELSON, Samson		87	
	1990	RAPPAPORT, David		38	*Apparent suicide (gunshot)*
	1921	+ RAPPE, Virginia		25	*Ruptured bladder (in San Francisco, CA)*
	1991	RASCEL, Renato		78	*Heart failure*
•	1976	# RASP, Fritz		85	*Died in Graefelfing, Germany*
	1991	RASULALA, Thalmus		55	*Heart attack after suffering from leukemia*

...DEATHS OF MOVIE AND TELEVISION PERSONALITIES — BY NAME...

YEAR	NAME		AGE	CAUSE AND/OR PLACE OF DEATH
1956	RASUMNY, Mikhail		65	
• 1948	# RATCLIFFE, E. J.		85	Died in Los Angeles, CA
1967	#+ RATHBONE, Basil	☆	75	Heart attack (in New York, NY)
1960	RATOFF, Gregory		63	Died in Solothurn, Switzerland
1925	# RATTENBERRY, Harry		65	Died at his home in Hollywood, CA
1977	RATTIGAN, Terence		66	Bone marrow cancer
1992	RAWLINGS, Richard Sr.		75	After a brief illness
1947	RAWLINS, Herbert		?	
1988	RAWLINS, Lester		63	Heart attack
1953	RAWLINSON, Herbert		67	Lung cancer (in Woodland Hills, CA)
1994	RAWSON, Ron		76	Cancer (at his home in Cohasset, Mass.)
1991	# RAY, Aldo		64	Complications from throat cancer & pneumonia
1955	RAY, Barbara		40	Leukemia
1943	#+ RAY, Charles		52	Throat infection from an infected tooth (in Los Angeles, CA)
1992	RAY, Harry Milton		45	Stroke
1975	RAY, Jack		58	Died in Montclair, CA
1990	RAY, Johnnie (pop singer)		63	Liver failure (Do not confuse with actor Johnny Ray, d. 1927)
1979	# RAY, Nicholas		67	Lung cancer (in New York, NY)
1993	# RAY, René		81	Unreported causes (in Jersey, the Channel Islands)
1992	RAY, Satyajit	★	70	Heart ailment
• 1977	# RAY, Ted		67	Died in London, England
1994	#+ RAYE, Martha		78	After a stroke and circulatory problems (in Los Angeles, CA)
1973	RAYMOND, Cyril		76	
1961	RAYMOND, Frances "Frankie"		92	Died in Hollywood, CA
1951	# RAYMOND, Jack		49	Heart attack (in Santa Monica) Do not confuse with British actor
• 1953	# RAYMOND, Jack		66	Died in London, England (Do not confuse with U.S. actor, d. 1951)
• 1949	# RAYMOND, Royal		33	Cancer (in Van Nuys, CA)
• 1941	RAYNER, Minnie		72	Died in London, England
• 1948	# RAZETTO, Stella		67	Died in Malibu, CA
• 1968	REA, Mabel Lillian		36	Automobile accident (in Charlotte, NC)
• 1963	READ, Barbara		45	
1992	READE, Charles A.		82	After a 2-year hospitalization for a stroke
1985	READICK, Robert		59	Automobile accident
1991	READING, Bertice		58	Stroke
1988	REARDON, John		58	Pneumonia
1991	REASONER, Harry		68	Complications and pneumonia after brain clot surgery
1994	RECTOR, Richard		69	After a brief illness (in San Rafael, CA)
1967	REDDING, Otis		26	Airplane crash (near Madison, WI)
• 1995	REDENBACHER, Orville		88	Drowned in his whirlpool spa after heart attack (Coronado, CA)
1976	REDFIELD, William "Billy"		49	Respiratory ailment complicated by leukemia (in New York, NY)
1985	REDGRAVE, Michael	☆	77	Parkinson's disease
1971	# REDWING, Rodd		66	Heart attack (while enroute by plane from London to Los Angeles)
1962	REECE, Brian		48	Bone disease
1977	# REED, Alan		69	After a long illness (in St. Vincent's hosp., West Los Angeles, CA)
1952	REED, Barbara		85	
• 1974	REED, Billy		59	Heart attack (in New York, NY)
1976	REED, Carol	★	69	Heart attack (Do not confuse with Carol Reed, d. 1970)
1970	# REED, Carol		44	Cancer (Do not confuse with Carol Reed, d. 1976)
• 1973	REED, Donald		70	
1986	#+ REED, Donna	★	64	Pancreatic cancer
1967	+ REED, Florence		86	
1990	REED, Gavin		59	Respiratory failure
1952	# REED, George H.		85	Arteriosclerosis (in Woodland Hills, CA)
1959	REED, J. Theodore "Ted"		72	Died in San Diego, CA
1961	REED, Luther		73	After a long illness
1980	REED, Marshall J.		62	Massive hemorrhage after suffering a brain tumor (in Los Angeles)
• 1974	REED, Maxwell		55	Died in England
1992	# REED, Robert		59	Colon lymphoma & A.I.D.S.
1987	REED, T. Michael		42	Complications from A.I.D.S.
1993	REED, Taylor		60	Heart attack (in New York)
1992	REED, Vernon William Sr.		73	After a long illness
1992	REESE, Robert		66	Natural causes
1985	REESE, Sammy Pharr		55	Massive stroke
1966	REEVE, Ada		91	
1990	REEVE, Scott		38	A.I.D.S.

• New entry.   # Original name (Pt. 7).   + Interment (Pt. 5).   223   ☆ Oscar nominee, ★ Oscar winner (Pt. 10)

YEAR	NAME		AGE	CAUSE AND/OR PLACE OF DEATH
1959	#+ REEVES, George "Superman"		45	Apparent suicide (gunshot) in Beverly Hills, CA
1964	#+ REEVES, Jim		40	Airplane crash (near Nashville, TN)
1971	REEVES, Kynaston		78	Died in London, England
• 1969	REEVES, Michael		25	Suicide (sleeping pills)
1967	#+ REEVES, Richard J.		54	Cirrhosis of the liver (in Northridge, CA)
• 1996	REGAN, Phil		89	Died in Santa Barbara, CA
1940	REGAS, George		50	Following an operation for a throat infection (in Los Angeles, CA)
1974	# REGAS, Pedro		92	Died in Hollywood, CA
1965	REICHER, Frank		89	Died in Playa del Rey, CA
1973	+ REID, Carl Benton		79	Died in Studio City, CA
• 1920	REID, Hal		46	
1993	REID, Kate		62	Cancer (in Stratford, Ontario)
• 1965	REID, Trevor		55	Died in London, England
1989	REID, Vivian		95	Natural causes
1923	+ REID, Wallace		31	Drug addiction (in Los Angeles, CA)
1991	REILLY, Howard		79	After a coronary bypass operation
1994	REINHARDT, Gottfried		80	Pancreatic cancer (in Los Angeles, CA)
1943	+ REINHARDT, Max		70	Pneumonia following paralysis
1993	REINHEART, Alice		83	Died in Avon, CT
1953	REIS, Irving		47	Following a cancer operation
1962	REISNER, Charles F. "Chuck"		75	Following a heart attack
1991	Rellys		85	
1960	RELPH, George		72	
1970	REMARQUE, Erich Maria		72	Heart collapse
1991	REMICK, Lee		55	Kidney & lung cancer
1992	REMME, John		56	A.I.D.S.
• 1967	REMY, Albert		54	Died in Paris, France
1980	# RENALDO, Duncan "Cisco Kid"		76	Lung cancer (in Goleta, CA)
1969	RENEVANT, George		74	After a long illness (in Guadalajara, Mexico)
1991	RENICK, Ralph		62	Hepatitis & liver cancer
1984	RENICK, Ruth		91	
1992	# Renie	★	90	Natural causes
1965	RENNIE, James		76	Died in New York, NY
1971	RENNIE, Michael		61	Died in Harrogate, Yorkshire, England
1979	RENOIR, Jean	☆	84	Parkinson's disease (in Beverly Hills, CA)
1952	RENOIR, Pierre		67	Died in Paris, France
1974	# REPP, Stafford		56	Heart attack (in Inglewood, CA)
• 1996	# RETTIG, Tommy		54	Natural causes (at his home in Marina Del Rey, CA)
1990	REVERE, Anne	★	87	Pneumonia
1993	# REVIER, Dorothy		89	Died at Queen of Angels–Hollywood Pres. Med. Ctr., CA
1982	REVILLE, Alma (Hitchcock)		82	
1987	+ REY, Alejandro		57	Cancer
1994	# REY, Fernando		76	Bladder cancer (in Madrid, Spain)
1961	REYNOLDS, Adeline De Walt		98	Died in Los Angeles, CA
1949	# REYNOLDS, Craig		42	Motorcycle/car crash (in Los Angeles, CA)
1983	+ REYNOLDS, Frank		59	Viral hepatitis
1990	REYNOLDS, Helen Fortescu		65	
1990	REYNOLDS, Jack		83	Natural causes
• 1927	+ REYNOLDS, Lynn		37	Suicide (gunshot) during a cocktail party
• 1975	REYNOLDS, Peter		48	Died in Australia
1965	REYNOLDS, Quentin		62	Cancer
1962	# REYNOLDS, Vera		62	Died in Woodland Hills, CA
1988	# RHODES, Billie		93	Died in Los Angeles, CA
1967	RHODES, Billy "Little Billy"		72	Stroke
1990	+ RHODES, Erik		84	Pneumonia
1987	RHODES, Grandon		82	After a long illness
1979	RHODES, Marjorie		76	Died in Hove, Sussex, England
1971	RIANO, Renie		71	After a long illness (in Woodland Hills, CA)
• 1976	RICCI, Nora		50	Liver ailment (in Rome, Italy)
1987	+ RICE, Adnia		64	Cancer
1990	RICE, Felix		46	A.I.D.S.
1974	RICE, Florence		63	Lung cancer (in Honolulu, Hawaii)
• 1936	# RICE, Frank		43	Nephritis and hepatitis (in Los Angeles, CA)
1954	RICE, Grantland	★	73	Following a heart attack (in New York)
• 1968	# RICE, Jack		75	Cancer (in Woodland Hills, CA)

YEAR	NAME		AGE	CAUSE AND/OR PLACE OF DEATH
1987	#+ RICH, Buddy		69	Heart attack (during brain tumor surgery)
• 1995	RICH, Charlie		62	Acute pulmonary embolism
• 1956	RICH, Freddie		58	Died in Beverly Hills, CA
1988	# RICH, Irene		96	Heart failure
1954	RICH, Lillian		53	Died at the Motion Picture Country Home, in Woodland Hills, CA
• 1957	RICH, Vivian		64	Automobile accident (in Hollywood, CA)
1964	#+ RICHARDS, Addison		61	Heart attack (in Los Angeles, CA)
1978	RICHARDS, Cully		68	Cancer (in Los Angeles, CA)
• 1996	RICHARDS, E. Claude		72	Leukemia (at the VA Hospital in The Bronx, NY)
1964	RICHARDS, Gordon		70	Died in Hollywood, CA
1963	RICHARDS, Grant		47	Leukemia (in Hollywood, CA)
1992	RICHARDS, Lloyd		89	Pneumonia
1974	RICHARDS, Paul		50	Cancer
• 1996	RICHARDSON, Don		77	Heart failure (in Los Angeles, CA)
1962	RICHARDSON, Frankie		63	Following a heart attack (in Philadelphia, PA)
1983	RICHARDSON, James G.		37	Injuries from a fall while skiing
• 1959	#+ RICHARDSON, Jiles "Big Bopper"		28	Airplane crash (along with Buddy Holly, near Mason City, IA)
1983	+ RICHARDSON, Ralph	☆	80	
• 1995	RICHARDSON, Ron		43	Complications from A.I.D.S. (in a Bronxville, NY, hospital)
1991	RICHARDSON, Tony	★	63	A.I.D.S.
1940	RICHMAN, Charles		75	After a brief illness (in a Bronx, NY nursing home)
• 1972	+ RICHMAN, Harry		77	
• 1973	# RICHMOND, Kane		66	
1948	RICHMOND, Warner		53	Coronary thrombosis (in Los Angeles, CA)
• 1976	RICHTER, Hans		87	Died in Locarno, Switzerland
• 1961	RICHTER, Paul		65	Died in Vienna, Austria
• 1929	# RICKARD, Tex		59	Peritonitis following appendectomy (in Miami Beach, FL)
• 1939	RICKETTS, Thomas "Tom"		85	Pneumonia (in Hollywood, CA)
• 1958	RICKSON, Joe		77	Died in CA
1985	+ RIDDLE, Nelson		64	Cardiac & kidney failure
1962	RIDGELY, Cleo		68	Died in Glendale, CA
1968	# RIDGELY, John		58	Heart ailment (in New York, NY)
1951	# RIDGES, Stanley		59	Died in Westbrook, CT
• 1959	RIEMANN, Johannes		72	Died in Konstanz, West Germany
• 1963	RIETTI, Victor		75	Heart ailment (in London, England)
1968	RIGA, Nadine		59	Cerebral hemorrhage
1951	# RIGBY, Edward		71	Died in London, England
• 1995	RIGGS, Bobby		77	Prostate cancer (at his home in Leucadia, CA)
1994	RIGGS, Marlon		37	A.I.D.S. complications (in Oakland, CA)
• 1981	RIGON, Paolo		22	Injuries from a filming accident (in Cortina d'Ampezzo, Italy)
1992	RILEY, Alice Mary		51	Cancer
1988	RILEY, Jay Flash		72	
1992	RILEY, Larry		39	A.I.D.S.
1932	Rin Tin Tin (original dog)		16	
1992	# RINALDO, Fred		78	Complications after an operation for a broken hip
• 1970	# RINDT, Jochen		28	Injuries from automobile crash (near Monza, Italy)
1961	RING, Blanche		84	Died in Santa Monica, CA
1967	RING, Cyril		74	Died in Hollywood, CA
1992	RINI, David		40	Brain cancer
1992	RIO, Joan Maloney		57	Cancer
1984	+ RIORDAN, Marjorie (Schlaff)		63	
1961	RIPLEY, Arthur		66	
1949	# RIPLEY, Robert L.		55	Heart attack (in New York, NY)
• 1979	+ RIPPERTON, Minnie		31	Cancer
1958	RISDON, Elisabeth		71	Brain hemorrhage (in Santa Monica, CA)
1955	RISKIN, Robert		58	After a long illness
1970	RISS, Dan		60	Heart attack (at his home in Hollywood, CA)
• 1977	RISSONI, Giuditta		80	Died in Rome, Italy
1977	#+ RITCHARD, Cyril		80	Cardiac arrest (in Chicago, IL)
1921	RITCHIE, Billie		42	After a 2-yr. illness caused by a filming injury
1918	RITCHIE, Franklin		?	Crushed beneath his overturned automobile (in Los Angeles, CA)
1918	RITCHIE, Perry V.		?	Suicide
1990	RITT, Martin	☆	76	Cardiac disease
1974	#+ RITTER, Tex		67	Heart attack (in Nashville, TN)
1969	RITTER, Thelma	☆	63	Heart attack (in New York, NY)

YEAR	NAME		AGE	CAUSE AND/OR PLACE OF DEATH
1965	#+ RITZ, Al		64	*Heart attack (in New Orleans, LA)*
1986	+ RITZ, Harry		78	*Cancer*
1985	+ RITZ, Jimmy		81	*Heart failure*
1976	RIVERO, Julian		84	*Died in Hollywood, CA*
1993	RIVERS, Al		65	*Cancer*
• 1977	RIVERS, Victor		29	*Injuries from performing a stunt (in Los Angeles, CA)*
1971	ROACH, Bert		79	
1972	+ ROACH, Hal Jr.		53	*Pneumonia*
1992	+ ROACH, Hal Sr.	★	100	*Pneumonia*
1996	# ROARKE, Adam		58	*Heart attack (at his home in Euless, TX)*
1963	+ ROBARDS, Jason Sr.		70	*Heart attack (in Sherman Oaks, CA)*
1992	ROBBINS, Duke		71	*Pneumonia*
1992	+ ROBBINS, Fred		73	*Lymphoma*
1980	ROBBINS, Gale		57	*Lung cancer (in Tarzana, CA)*
1982	+ ROBBINS, Marty		57	
1992	ROBBINS, Michael		62	
1985	ROBBINS, Randall		45	
1933	ROBBINS, Roy "Skeeter Bill"		?	*Killed by a truck while wiping snow from his car*
1952	ROBER, Richard		46	*Killed when his car went down an embankment due to fog*
1988	+ ROBERSON, Chuck		69	*Cancer*
1938	ROBERTI, Lyda		29	*Heart ailment (in Los Angeles, CA)*
1993	ROBERTS, Davis		76	*Emphysema (in Chicago, IL)*
1935	# ROBERTS, Edith		36	*Died following the birth of a son (in Los Angeles, CA)*
• 1962	ROBERTS, Evelyn		76	
1940	+ ROBERTS, Florence		79	*After a brief illness (in Hollywood) Do not confuse with F.R., d. 1927*
1992	ROBERTS, Howard		62	*Prostate cancer*
• 1961	ROBERTS, John H.		76	*Died in London, England*
• 1978	ROBERTS, Lenore		47	*Cancer (in Los Angeles, CA)*
1954	ROBERTS, Leona		73	*Died in Santa Monica, CA*
1978	#+ ROBERTS, Lynne (Mary Hart)		58	*An intracranial hemorrhage*
1992	ROBERTS, Meade		61	*Congestive heart failure*
1980	ROBERTS, Rachel	☆	53	*Suicide (acute barbiturate intoxication) in Los Angeles, CA*
• 1940	ROBERTS, Ralph Arthur		55	*Died in Berlin, Germany*
1975	+ ROBERTS, Roy (actor)		69	*Died suddenly in Los Angeles after complaining of back pain*
1936	ROBERTS, Stephen		41	*Heart attack*
1928	+ ROBERTS, Theodore		67	*Uremic poisoning after a flu attack (in Los Angeles, CA)*
1941	ROBERTSHAW, Jerrold		74	
1988	ROBERTSON, Hugh A.		55	*Cancer*
1964	ROBERTSON, John Stuart		86	*Died in Escondida, CA*
1948	ROBERTSON, Willard		62	
1976	#+ ROBESON, Paul		77	*Cerebral vascular disorder (stroke) in Philadelphia, PA*
1954	# ROBEY, George		85	*Died in Saltdean, Sussex, England*
1995	ROBIN, Dany		68	*Died in a fire (at her home in Paris, France)*
1986	ROBINS, Barry		41	
1986	ROBINSON, Bartlett "Bart"		73	*After a long bout with cancer*
1949	+ ROBINSON, Bill "Bojangles"		71	*Heart ailment (in New York)*
1992	ROBINSON, Cardew		75	*Following a bowel infection*
1988	+ ROBINSON, Dar Allen		39	*Motorcycle accident*
• 1995	ROBINSON, Darren		28	
1950	ROBINSON, Dewey		52	*After a heart attack (in Las Vegas, Nevada)*
1973	#+ ROBINSON, Edward G.	★	79	*Cancer (in Hollywood, CA)*
1974	+ ROBINSON, Edward G. Jr.		40	*Natural causes (found unconscious in his West Hollywood home)*
• 1971	# ROBINSON, Frances		55	*Heart attack (in Hollywood, CA)*
• 1962	ROBINSON, Gertrude R.		70	*Died in Hollywood, CA*
1957	ROBINSON, Inez Buck		67	
• 1972	# ROBINSON, Jackie		53	*Heart disease (in Stamford, CT)*
1988	ROBINSON, Max		49	*A.I.D.S.*
1989	+ ROBINSON, Sugar Ray		67	*Heart & Alzheimer's disease & diabetes*
1970	ROBLES, Rudy		60	*Died in Manila, Philippine Islands*
1984	+ ROBSON, Flora	☆	82	
1978	ROBSON, Mark		64	*Heart attack*
1942	#+ ROBSON, May	☆	84	*Neuritis (in Beverly Hills, CA)*
• 1995	ROCCA, Daniela		57	*Heart failure (at a rest home in Milo, Sicily)*
• 1934	ROCCARDI, Albert		70	
1952	ROCHE, John		56	*Stroke (in Los Angeles, CA)*

YEAR	NAME	AGE	CAUSE AND/OR PLACE OF DEATH
1981	ROCHELLE, Claire	72	Cancer (in La Jolla, CA)
• 1919	ROCK, Charles	53	Died in London, England
1984	ROCK, Joe	93	
• 1996	ROCKETT, Norman	84	Heart failure (in Los Angeles, CA)
• 1931	# ROCKNE, Knute	43	Airplane crash (near Bazaar, KS)
1991	RODDENBERRY, Gene	70	Cardiac arrest from a massive blood clot
1979	+ RODGERS, Richard	77	
1951	RODGERS, Walter	64	Following a stroke (in Los Angeles, CA)
1994	RODNEY, Red	66	Lung cancer (in Boynton Beach, FL)
• 1966	RODRIGUEZ, Estelita	52	
1958	RODZINSKI, Artur	64	Heart ailment
1994	ROEBLING, Paul	60	While vacationing on a Navajo Indian reservation in Arizona
1988	ROGELL, Albert S.	86	Cancer & diabetes
1919	ROGERS, Eugene	51	Found dead in bed of myocarditis and alcoholism (in Los Angeles)
• 1995	#+ ROGERS, Ginger	83	Natural causes (at her home in Rancho Mirage, CA)
1991	# ROGERS, Jean	74	Following surgery
1994	ROGERS, Milton "Shorty"	70	Died in Van Nuys, CA
• 1966	ROGERS, Rena	64	Died in Santa Monica, CA
1935	#+ ROGERS, Will	55	Airplane crash (near Barrow, Alaska)
1993	ROGERS, Will Jr.	81	Apparent suicide (gunshot) in Tubac, AZ
1991	ROGOT, Peter	37	Apparent heart attack
• 1995	ROKER, Roxie	66	Undisclosed causes
1994	# ROLAND, Gilbert "Cisco Kid"	88	Cancer (at his Beverly Hills, CA, home)
1937	+ ROLAND, Ruth	45	Cancer (in Los Angeles, CA)
• 1957	ROLF, Erik	?	
1993	ROLFE, Sam ☆	69	Heart attack while playing tennis (in Los Angeles)
1990	ROLFING, Tom	40	An A.I.D.S.-related illness
• 1995	# ROMAGNOLI, Margaret	73	Died in Mount Auburn hospital in Cambridge, MA
1991	ROMAN, Paul Reid	55	Cancer
1991	ROMANCE, Viviane	82	
1971	# ROMANOFF, Michael	78	Heart failure (in Los Angeles, CA)
1951	+ ROMBERG, Sigmund	64	Cerebral hemorrhage
1965	# ROME, Stewart	79	Died in Newbury, England
1994	+ ROMERO, Cesar	86	Complications from bronchitis and pneumonia (Santa Monica, CA)
1983	RONET, Maurice	55	After a long illness
• 1958	ROOKE, Irene	?	Died in England
1962	ROONEY, Pat, II	82	Died in New York, NY
• 1979	ROONEY, Pat, III	70	Died in Lake Blaisdell, NH
1961	ROOPE, Fay	68	Died in Port Jefferson, L.I., NY
1989	ROOS, Joanna	88	Ruptured aorta
• 1973	# ROOSEVELT, Buddy	75	Died in Meeker, CO
1991	ROOSEVELT, James	83	Complications from a stroke & Parkinson's disease
1966	#+ ROPER, Jack	62	Throat cancer (in Woodland Hills, CA)
1943	ROQUEMORE, Henry	55	Died at his home in Beverly Hills, CA
• 1973	ROQUEVERT, Noel	81	Died in Paris, France
1987	+ RORKE, Hayden	76	Cancer
• 1938	RORKE, Mary	80	Died in London, England
1996	ROSATTI, Gregory Joseph	43	Complications of A.I.D.S. (in Sherman Oaks, CA)
• 1974	# ROSAY, Françoise	82	Died in Paris, France
1933	# ROSCOE, Alan	45	After a lingering illness (in a Hollywood hospital)
1966	+ ROSE, Billy	67	
1953	# ROSE, Blanche	74	Died at her home in Hollywood, CA
1990	+ ROSE, David (pianist/composer)	80	Heart disease (Do not confuse with David E. Rose, d. 1992)
1992	ROSE, David E. (producer)	96	Died in Phoenix, AZ (Do not confuse with the pianist/composer)
1988	ROSE, George	68	Automobile accident
1979	ROSE, Jane	66	Cancer
1987	ROSE, William	67	
1966	ROSEMOND, Clinton C.	82	Pneumonia and stroke (in Los Angeles, CA)
1990	ROSEN, Al	80	
1951	# ROSEN, Phil	63	Died in Hollywood, CA
1992	ROSENBERG, Mark	44	Heart attack
1992	ROSENBERGER, James	84	Pneumonia
1991	ROSENBLATT, Martin	74	Heart attack
1976	#+ ROSENBLOOM, "Slapsie" Maxie	71	Paget's disease (in South Pasadena, CA)
• 1995	ROSENBLUM, Ralph	69	Heart failure (at his home in Manhattan)

...DEATHS OF MOVIE AND TELEVISION PERSONALITIES — BY NAME...

	YEAR	NAME		AGE	CAUSE AND/OR PLACE OF DEATH
	1953	ROSENTHAL, Harry		52	Heart attack (in Hollywood, CA)
	1942	#+ ROSING, Bodil		63	Heart attack (in Hollywood, CA)
	1937	ROSLEY, Adrian		47	Following a heart attack (in Hollywood, CA)
•	1971	# ROSMER, Milton		90	Died in Chesham, England
	1991	ROSQUI, Tom		62	Cancer
	1955	ROSS, Anthony		46	Died in New York
	1990	ROSS, Betsy King		66	
	1947	ROSS, Betty		67	Died at her home in Hollywood, CA
•	1995	ROSS, Bob		52	Cancer (at his home in Orlando, FL)
	1990	ROSS, Frank		85	After brain surgery
•	1995	ROSS, Gordon		65	Cancer (at his home in Studio City, CA)
	1985	ROSS, Jane		50	During surgery for cancer
	1982	+ ROSS, Joe E.		67	Apparent heart attack
	1988	# ROSS, Lanny		82	Following two strokes
	1976	# ROSS, Lenny		71	Cancer
	1975	# ROSS, Shirley		62	Cancer (at a hospital in Menlo Park, CA)
	1959	ROSS, Thomas W.		86	Died in Torrington, CT
	1977	ROSSELLINI, Roberto		71	
	1966	ROSSEN, Robert	☆	57	
	1990	ROSSIF, Frédéric		67	
	1984	ROSSITER, Leonard		57	Apparent heart attack
	1991	# ROSSITTO, Angelo		83	Complications from surgery
	1960	ROSSON, Arthur H.		73	
	1988	ROSSON, Harold "Hal"		93	Natural causes
	1953	+ ROSSON, Richard "Dick"		60	Suicide (carbon monoxide poisoning) in Los Angeles, CA
	1979	ROTA, Nino		68	Blood clot
•	1995	ROTH, David		72	Leukemia (in Leonia, NJ)
•	1976	# ROTH, Gene		73	Struck by a car (in Los Angeles, CA)
•	1980	#+ ROTH, Lillian		69	Stroke (in New York, NY)
	1984	ROTHA, Paul		76	
	1989	ROUD, Richard		59	Heart attack
•	1981	ROULEAU, Raymond		77	Died in Paris, France
	1983	ROUNDS, David		40	Cancer
	1974	# ROUNESVILLE, Robert		60	Heart attack (in New York City)
	1987	ROUSE, Russell		74	Heart failure
	1987	ROWAN, Dan		65	Lymphatic cancer
	1966	ROWAN, Donald W.		60	Cerebral hemorrhage (in Rocky Hill, CT)
	1988	# ROWE, Fanny		75	Died in London, England
•	1971	ROWLAND, Adele		?	
	1984	ROWLAND, Henry		70	
	1944	ROWLANDS, Art		46	Died in Hollywood, CA
•	1946	# ROYCE, Julian		76	
	1946	ROYCE, Lionel		55	Heart attack in Manilla while entertaining troops with the U.S.O.
	1971	ROYCE, Ruth		78	
	1983	ROYLE, Selena		78	After a brief illness
	1989	ROZAKIS, Gregory		46	A.I.D.S.
•	1995	ROZSA, Miklos	★	88	Pneumonia following a stroke (at Good Sam. Hosp. in L.A.)
•	1956	RUB, Christian		69	
	1942	RUBEN, J. Walter		43	Heart ailment
	1931	# RUBENS, Alma		33	Pneumonia (in Los Angeles, CA)
	1982	+ RUBENSTEIN, Artur		95	Natural causes
	1992	RUBENSTEIN, Phil		51	Heart attack
	1986	RUBIN, Benny		86	
	1991	RUDOLPH, Oscar		79	Following a stroke
	1994	RUEHMANN, Heinz		92	Died in Berg, Germany
	1991	RUFFIN, David		50	Apparent drug overdose
	1970	+ RUGGLES, Charles		84	Cancer (in Santa Monica, CA)
	1972	+ RUGGLES, Wesley	☆	82	After a stroke (in Santa Monica, CA)
	1974	RUICK, Barbara		41	Natural causes (in Reno, NV)
	1967	# RUMANN, Sig		82	Heart attack (in Julian, CA)
	1946	# RUNYON, Damon		62	After a long bout with cancer (in New York, NY)
•	1995	RUSHTON, Donald		70	Died in Indianapolis, IN
•	1995	RUSHTON, Matthew		43	Complications of A.I.D.S. (in Los Angeles, CA)
	1990	RUSINOW, Irving		75	Cancer
•	1976	RUSKIN, Shimen		69	Cancer (in Los Angeles, CA)

• New entry. # Original name (Pt. 7). + Interment (Pt. 5).   228   ☆ Oscar nominee, ★ Oscar winner (Pt. 10)

YEAR	NAME		AGE	CAUSE AND/OR PLACE OF DEATH
1929	RUSSELL, Albert		37	Pneumonia (in Los Angeles, CA)
1992	# RUSSELL, Andy		72	Complications from a stroke
1963	RUSSELL, Byron		79	After a brief illness (in New York)
1990	RUSSELL, Craig		42	A.I.D.S.
1981	# RUSSELL, Don		54	Heart attack
1961	+ RUSSELL, Gail (Moseley)		36	Found dead from alcohol overindulgence (in Los Angeles, CA)
1935	RUSSELL, J. Gordon		52	Heart attack (in Los Angeles, CA)
1991	RUSSELL, John		70	
1922	#+ RUSSELL, Lillian		61	Complications after a fall onboard ship
1976	+ RUSSELL, Rosalind (Brisson)	☆	65	Cancer complicated by arthritis (in Beverly Hills, CA)
1915	RUSSELL, William		?	(Do not confuse with William Russell, d. 1929)
1929	RUSSELL, William		42	Pneumonia (in Beverly Hills) Do not confuse with W. R., d. 1915
1948	#+ RUTH, Babe		53	Cancerous tumor
1982	RUTHERFORD, Jack "Buffalo Bill"		89	
1972	RUTHERFORD, Margaret	★	80	After breaking a hip in a fall (in Buckinghamshire, England)
1983	RUTTENBERG, Joseph		93	
• 1941	RUTTMAN, Walther		54	Killed while filming a newsreel of the Eastern Front during W.W.2
1960	RUYSDAEL, Basil		72	Died in Hollywood, CA
1969	RYAN, Dick		72	After a long illness (in Burbank, CA)
1984	RYAN, Edmond		79	Heart attack
1973	#+ RYAN, Irene		70	Stroke (in Santa Monica, CA)
• 1944	RYAN, Joe		57	
1985	RYAN, Kathleen		63	
1973	RYAN, Robert	☆	63	Lymphatic cancer (in New York, NY)
1975	# RYAN, Sheila		54	Lung ailment (in Woodland Hills, CA)
1956	RYAN, Tim		57	Heart attack (in Hollywood, CA)
1918	RYCKMAN, Chester		21	Spanish influenza
1985	RYSKIND, Morrie		89	Apparent stroke
1993	RYU, Chishu		88	Cancer (in Yokohama, Japan)
	🙞			
1993	SABATINO, Anthony		48	A.I.D.S. (in Los Angeles, CA)
1994	SABLON, Jean		87	After a 3-yr. illness (at Clinica Hosp. in Cannes-la-Bocca, France)
1963	#+ Sabu		39	Heart attack (in Chatsworth, CA)
1992	SACHA, Kenny		39	A.I.D.S.
1990	SACHS, Leonard		82	Kidney failure
1992	SACHS, Scotty		39	Murdered (multiple gunshot wounds)
1994	SACKS, Amy Jill		39	Complications from lupus (in Philadelphia, PA)
• 1964	SADO, Keiji		38	Automobile accident (in Japan)
1994	SADOFF, Fred		68	A.I.D.S. complications (in Los Angeles, CA)
• 1981	+ SAGAL, Boris		58	Automobile accident
• 1974	# SAGE, Willard		51	Died in Sherman Oaks, CA
• 1971	SAIS, Marin		81	Cerebral arteriosclerosis (in CA)
1955	#+ SAKALL, S. Z. "Cuddles"		71	Heart attack (in Los Angeles, CA)
1982	SAKATA, Harold		56	Cancer
1993	SALANT, Richard "Dick"		78	Heart failure (while giving a speech)
1990	SALCIDO, Michael A.		39	Liver failure
1936	#+ SALE, Chic		51	Pneumonia (in Los Angeles, CA)
1993	SALE, Richard		80	After suffering two strokes (in Los Angeles, CA)
1992	SALE-WREN, Virginia		92	Heart failure
1935	SALISBURY, Monroe		59	Skull fracture from a fall (in San Bernardino, CA)
1993	SALKIN, Leo	☆	80	Congestive heart failure (in Burbank, CA)
1990	SALMI, Albert		62	Apparent suicide (gunshot)
1993	SALMON, Scott		51	After an auto accident (in Northridge, CA)
• 1968	SALMONOVA, Lyda		79	Died in Prague, Czeckoslovakia
1987	SALT, Waldo		72	
1994	SALTER, Hans J.		98	Heart attack (in Los Angeles, CA)
• 1920	SALTER, Harry		?	Natural causes (in a New Jersey hospital)
1953	SALTER, Thelma		?	After a lingering illness (in Hollywood, CA)
1994	SALTZMAN, Harry		78	Died at the American Hospital in Neuilly-sur-Seine, France
1984	SALVIO, Robert		45	Complications from A.I.D.S.
1983	SAMPLES, Junior		56	Heart attack
1987	SAMPSON, Will		53	Following a heart-lung transplant
• 1963	SAMSON, Ivan		67	Died in London, England
1992	SAMUEL, Andrew		82	
1972	SANDE, Walter		65	Heart attack (while waiting for cab at O'Hare Airport in Chicago, IL)

YEAR	NAME		AGE	CAUSE AND/OR PLACE OF DEATH
• 1980	SANDERS, (Col.) Harland		90	Leukemia and pneumonia (in Louisville, KY)
• 1995	#+ SANDERS, Al		54	Lung cancer (at Johns Hopkins Hosp., Baltimore, MD)
1987	SANDERS, Denis		58	Died in his sleep
1972	SANDERS, George	★	65	Suicide (overdose of barbiturates) in Casteldelfels, Spain
1992	SANDERSON, Joan		79	After a lengthy illness
• 1961	# SANDFORD, Tiny		67	
1925	SANDOW, Eugene		58	After a blood vessel in his brain burst
1945	SANDRICH, Mark		44	Heart disease (at his home in Hollywood, CA)
• 1980	SANDRINI, Luis "Felipe"		75	Cerebral hemorrhage (in Buenos Aires, Argentina)
• 1937	SANDROCK, Adele		73	Died in Berlin, Germany
1984	+ SANDS, Billy		73	Lung cancer
1973	+ SANDS, Diana		39	Cancer (in New York, NY)
1990	Sandy (original "Annie" dog)		16	Died in his sleep
1963	SANFORD, Ralph		64	Heart ailment (in Van Nuys, CA)
• 1969	SANGER, Bert		75	Died in Blackpool, England
• 1978	SANO, Shuji		66	
1990	SANSBERRY, Hope		94	Natural causes
1981	# SANTELL, Alfred		86	After a lengthy illness & several strokes
• 1995	SANTI, Lionello "Nello"		77	After a long illness (in Rome, Italy)
1953	# SANTLEY, Fred		64	Died in Hollywood, CA
1971	# SANTLEY, Joseph		81	Died in his West Los Angeles home
1987	SANTORO, Dean		49	
1931	SANTSCHI, Tom		51	High blood pressure (in Hollywood, CA)
• 1980	# SAPPINGTON, Fay		82	Died in Englewood, NJ
1994	# SARGENT, Dick		64	Prostate cancer (at Cedars-Sinai Med. Ctr. in Los Angeles)
1993	SARGENT, Thornton		90	Died in Rancho Palos Verdes, CA
1953	SARNO, Hector V.		73	After a long illness (in Pasadena, CA)
1985	# SARONY, Leslie		88	
1992	SATZ, Wayne		47	Found dead in his home
1989	SAUERS, Patricia		49	Complications from diabetes
1943	SAUM, Clifford		60	Died in Glendale, CA
1954	SAUNDERS, Jackie		61	Died in Palm Springs, CA
1993	SAUTER, Carl		44	Undisclosed causes (in Los Angeles, CA)
1985	+ SAVALAS, George		60	Leukemia
1994	#+ SAVALAS, Telly "Kojak"	☆	70	Died in his sleep of prostate cancer (Universal City, CA)
1985	SAVILLE, Ruth		92	
1979	SAVILLE, Victor		82	Died in London, England
1983	SAVITCH, Jessica		35	Automobile accident
1982	# SAWYER, Joe		80	Liver cancer
1970	SAWYER, Laura		85	Died in a Matawan, N.J., nursing home
• 1935	# SAXE, Templar		69	Died in Cincinnati, OH
1945	SAXON, Hugh A.		76	Died at his home in Beverly Hills, CA
1989	SAYER, Philip		42	Abdominal cancer
1963	# SAYLOR, Syd		67	Heart attack (in Hollywood, CA)
• 1974	SAYRE, Jeffrey		73	Murdered (shot) in Los Angeles, CA
1972	#+ SCALA, Gia		38	Overdose of alcohol and medication (in Hollywood, CA)
• 1995	SCALI, John A.		77	Heart failure (in Washington, D.C.)
1994	SCANLAN, John		73	Congestive heart failure (at his home in Closter, NJ)
1954	SCARDON, Paul		75	Heart attack (in Fontana, CA)
1994	SCARFIOTTI, Ferdinando	★	53	After a brief illness (in Los Angeles, CA)
• 1968	SCARFIOTTI, Lodovico		34	Automobile crash (in Berchtesgaden, Germany)
1947	SCHABLE, Robert		74	Died in Hollywood, CA
• 1957	SCHAEFER, Ann		87	Died in Los Angeles, CA
1967	SCHAEFER, Armand L.		69	Died in Bridgeport, CA
1991	SCHAEFFER, Elizabeth		42	Cerebral hemorrhage
1989	+ SCHAEFFER, Rebecca		21	Murdered (shot)
1991	SCHAFER, Natalie		90	Cancer
1993	SCHAFFEL, Hal		78	Undisclosed causes
1989	+ SCHAFFNER, Franklin J.	★	69	Cancer
1989	SCHAKNE, Robert		63	Cancer
• 1963	# SCHARF, Herman "Boo-Boo"		61	Heart attack (in Hollywood, CA)
1980	SCHARY, Dore		74	
1941	+ SCHERTZINGER, Victor	☆	52	Died in Hollywood, CA
1964	+ SCHILDKRAUT, Joseph	★	67	Heart attack (in New York, NY)
1930	SCHILDKRAUT, Rudolf		65	Heart disease (in Los Angeles, CA)

...DEATHS OF MOVIE AND TELEVISION PERSONALITIES — BY NAME...

YEAR	NAME	AGE	CAUSE AND/OR PLACE OF DEATH
1957	# SCHILLING, Gus	48	Heart attack (in Hollywood, CA)
• 1948	# SCHINDELL, Cy	41	Died in Van Nuys, CA
• 1965	SCHIPA, Tito	76	Heart attack (in New York, NY)
1949	+ SCHLESINGER, Leon	66	Viral infection
• 1945	# SCHLETTOW, Hans Adelbert	57	Died in Berlin, Germany
1993	SCHMIECHEN, Richard	45	A.I.D.S. (died in Los Angeles, CA)
• 1955	SCHMITZ, Sybille	42	Suicide (pills) in Munich, Germany
1993	SCHNEIDER, Abe	87	Pneumonia & Alzheimer's disease complications
1993	SCHNEIDER, Alexander	84	Heart disease (in New York)
1994	SCHNEIDER, Harold	55	Heart attack
1967	SCHNEIDER, James	85	
1982	#+ SCHNEIDER, Romy	43	Found dead of cardiac arrest (at her apartment in Paris, France)
1975	SCHNEIDER, Stanley	45	Died in his hotel room
1990	SCHNUR, Jerome	66	Melanoma (skin cancer)
1993	SCHOENBRUN, Michael	54	Pancreatic cancer (in Tarzana, CA)
• 1978	SCHOENHALS, Albrecht	90	Died in Baden-Baden, West Germany
1961	SCHOFIELD, Johnnie	71	
1989	SCHORR, William	88	Respiratory failure
1980	SCHRAMM, Karla	88	Died in Los Angeles, CA
• 1936	SCHRECK, Max	57	Died in Munich, Germany
• 1995	SCHULMAN, Edward L.	79	Heart disease (at his daughter's home in Detroit, MI)
1935	# SCHULTZ, Harry	52	After a lengthy illness (in Hollywood, CA)
• 1972	SCHULZ, Fritz	75	Died in Zurich, Switzerland
1936	+ SCHUMANN-HEINK, Ernestine	75	Leukemia
1958	SCHUMANN-HEINK, Ferdinand	65	Heart attack (in Los Angeles, CA)
1990	SCHUMM, Hans	93	Heart failure
• 1954	SCHUNZEL, Reinhold	68	Heart ailment (in Munich, Germany)
1986	SCHUSTER, Harold	83	
1960	+ SCHWARTZ, Maurice	69	Heart attack (near Tel Aviv, Israel)
1992	SCHWARTZ, Sammy	86	Heart attack
1968	SCOBIE, James	?	
1993	SCORSESE, Luciano Charles	80	After a long illness (in New York)
1991	# SCOTT, Daniel Simon	71	Alzheimer's disease
1991	SCOTT, Dennis	51	After a long illness
• 1964	SCOTT, Harold	72	Died in London, England
1981	#+ SCOTT, Hazel	61	Cancer
1986	SCOTT, Ken	58	Emphysema & heart failure
1976	SCOTT, Mabel Julienne	82	Died at the Burlington Convalescent Hospital in Los Angeles, CA
• 1960	SCOTT, Mark	45	Heart attack (in Burbank, CA)
1987	# SCOTT, Randolph	89	Natural causes
1994	SCOTT, Terry	67	Cancer (in Godalming, England)
1988	SCOTT, Timothy	32	Complications from A.I.D.S. (Do not confuse with T. Scott, d. 1995)
• 1995	SCOTT, Timothy	57	Lung cancer (in Los Angeles) Do not confuse with T. Scott, d. 1988
1965	#+ SCOTT, Zachary	51	Brain tumor (in Austin, TX)
1985	SCOURBY, Alexander	71	
1973	SEABURY, Ynez	64	Internal complications (at her home in Sherman Oaks, CA)
1990	SEALES, Franklyn	37	A.I.D.S.
1921	# SEARLE, Kamuela	33	From injuries while filming "The Son of Tarzan"
1942	SEARS, Allan	55	After a long illness (in Los Angeles, CA)
1957	SEARS, Fred	44	Heart attack (in Hollywood, CA)
1960	# SEASTROM, Victor	80	
1979	SEATON, George ☆	68	Cancer
1968	SEATON, Scott	90	After a lengthy illness (in Hollywood, CA)
1992	SEAY, James	78	Died in Capitol Beach, CA
1957	+ SEBASTIAN, Dorothy	54	Died in Woodland Hills, CA
1979	#+ SEBERG, Jean	40	Suicide (drug overdose) found dead in her car in Paris, France
• 1969	# SEBRING, Jay	35	Murdered (in Los Angeles, CA)
1987	SECREST, James	51	Lymphoma of the brain
1982	SEDAN, Rolfe	86	
1968	#+ SEDDON, Margaret	95	Died in Philadelphia, PA
1971	#+ SEDGWICK, Edie	28	Acute barbitural intoxication (in Santa Barbara, CA)
1953	SEDGWICK, Edward Jr.	60	Following a heart attack (in North Hollywood, CA)
1991	SEDGWICK, Eileen	93	
1973	SEDGWICK, Josie	75	Stroke (in Santa Monica, CA)
1990	SEEGAR, Sara	76	Cerebral hemorrhage

• New entry.   # Original name (Pt. 7).   + Interment (Pt. 5).

☆ Oscar nominee, ★ Oscar winner (Pt. 10)

...DEATHS OF MOVIE AND TELEVISION PERSONALITIES — BY NAME...

YEAR	NAME		AGE	CAUSE AND/OR PLACE OF DEATH
1918	SEELOS, Annette		27	Spanish influenza
1992	SEGAL, Vivienne		95	Heart failure
• 1962	# SEGAR, Lucia		77	Died in New York, NY
1987	SEGOVIA, Andres		94	Heart failure
1964	SEITER, William A.		72	Heart attack (in his Beverly Hills home)
1944	SEITZ, George B.		56	Died in Hollywood, CA
1982	SEKA, Ron		48	Heart attack
1950	SELBIE, Evelyn		68	Heart ailment (in Hollywood, CA)
1940	SELBY, Norman "Kid McCoy"		66	Suicide (in a downtown hotel in Detroit, MI)
1980	SELBY, Sarah		73	Died in Los Angeles, CA
1948	# SELIG, William N.		84	
1980	+ SELLERS, Peter	☆	54	Heart attack (in London, England)
1937	SELLON, Charles		58	After a long illness (in La Crescenta, CA)
• 1939	# SELTEN, Morton		79	Died in London, England
1980	SELTZER, Daniel		47	Heart attack
1948	# SELWYN, Clarissa		62	Died in West Hollywood, CA
1944	SELWYN, Edgar		68	After a cerebral hemorrhage
1954	#+ SELWYN, Ruth		49	After a long illness (in Hollywood, CA)
1965	#+ SELZNICK, David O.		63	Acute coronary
1990	SELZNICK, Irene		83	Breast cancer
1944	+ SELZNICK, Myron		45	Following an attack of portal thrombosis
1946	SEMELS, Harry		58	Died in Los Angeles, CA
1928	SEMON, Larry		39	Pneumonia (near Victorville, CA)
1960	#+ SENNETT, Mack		80	Died in Hollywood, CA
1980	SEN YUNG, Victor		65	Apparent victim of a gas leak at his home in North Hollywood, CA
1989	# SERATO, Massimo		73	Heart attack
• 1965	SERDA, Julia		90	Died in Dresden, East Germany
1991	SERKIN, Rudolph		88	Cancer
1975	+ SERLING, Rod		50	Complications after heart surgery (in Rochester, NY)
1992	SERPE, Ralph B.		81	Cancer
• 1976	SERVAIS, Jean		65	Heart failure following surgery (in Paris, France)
1968	SERVOSS, Mary		80	Heart ailment (at her home in Los Angeles, CA)
1974	SESSIONS, Almira		86	Died in Los Angeles, CA
1969	SETON, Bruce		60	Died in London, England
1991	# SEUSS, Dr.		87	Respiratory & kidney problems
1992	SEVAREID, Eric		79	Stomach cancer
1990	SEYLER, Athene		101	
1988	SEYMOUR, Anne		79	Heart failure
1920	SEYMOUR, Clarine		19	Surgical complications (in New York, NY)
1993	+ SEYMOUR, Dan		78	Following a stroke (in Santa Monica, CA)
1967	SEYMOUR, Harry		77	Heart attack (in Hollywood, CA)
1956	# SEYMOUR, Jane		56	Died in New York, NY
1990	SEYRIG, Delphine		58	Lung disease
• 1956	SHADE, Jamesson		60	Heart attack (in Hollywood, CA)
1967	# SHAIFFER, Howard "Tiny"		48	Died in Burbank, CA
• 1957	SHANNON, Cora		88	Cancer (in Woodland Hills, CA)
1990	SHANNON, Del		50	Suicide
1954	SHANNON, Effie		87	Died in Bay Shore, L.I., NY
1951	SHANNON, Ethel		53	
1959	SHANNON, Frank Connolly		83	Died in Hollywood, CA
1964	SHANNON, Harry		74	Died in Hollywood, CA
1990	SHANNON, Paul		80	Cancer
1941	#+ SHANNON, Peggy		32	Acute alcoholism (in North Hollywood, CA)
1993	SHARAFF, Irene	★	83	Congestive heart failure (in New York)
1993	SHARITS, Paul		50	Heart attack (in Buffalo, NY)
1994	# SHARKEY, Jack		91	Respiratory arrest (at the Beverly, Mass., Hospital)
1993	SHARKEY, Ray		40	A.I.D.S. (in a Brooklyn, NY hospital)
1944	SHARLAND, Reginald		57	Died in Loma Linda, CA
1984	SHARP, Anthony		69	
1964	# SHARP, Henry		76	
1980	+ SHARPE, David H.		70	Parkinson's disease (in Altadena, CA)
1985	# SHAUGHNESSY, Mickey		64	Lung cancer
• 1968	SHAW, C. Montague		83	Died in Woodland Hills, CA
1971	SHAW, Denis		49	Heart attack (in London, England)
• 1950	SHAW, George Bernard		94	Bladder ailment and injuries from a fall (in Ayot St. Lawrence, Eng.)

• New entry. # Original name (Pt. 7). + Interment (Pt. 5).   232   ☆ Oscar nominee, ★ Oscar winner (Pt. 10)

YEAR	NAME		AGE	CAUSE AND/OR PLACE OF DEATH
• 1926	SHAW, Harold M.		47	Automobile accident
1982	+ SHAW, Reta		69	
1978	SHAW, Robert	☆	53	Heart attack (near Tourmakeady, Ireland)
1990	SHAW, Steve		25	Injuries from an automobile accident
• 1978	# SHAW, Susan		49	Died in Middlesex, England
1988	# SHAW, Victoria		53	Asthma
1982	# SHAW, Wini		72	
1987	# SHAWLEE, Joan		61	Cancer
1990	SHAWLEY, Robert		63	Pneumonia
1987	#+ SHAWN, Dick		63	Apparent heart attack (while appearing on stage)
1978	#+ SHAY, Dorothy		57	Following a massive stroke (in Santa Monica, CA)
1992	# SHAYNE, Robert		92	Lung cancer
1983	SHAYNE, Tamara		80	Following a heart attack
1982	SHDANOFF, Elsa Schreiber		81	Heart failure
• 1969	SHEA, Donald J. "Shorty"		?	Murdered (in Chatsworth, CA)
• 1953	# SHEA, Mervin		52	Died in Sacramento, CA
• 1918	# SHEA, William		?	Died in Brooklyn, NY
1949	# SHEAN, Al		81	Died in New York, NY
1979	SHEAR, Barry		?	Cancer
1971	SHEARER, Douglas		71	
1993	SHEARER, Jacqueline		46	Colon cancer (at her home in Cambridge, MA)
1983	#+ SHEARER, Norma	★	82	Bronchial pneumonia
1952	SHEEHAN, John J., Jr.		61	Died in Hollywood, CA
1945	SHEEHAN, Winfield		62	Following abdominal surgery
1979	+ SHEEN, (Bishop) Fulton J.		84	Heart trouble (in New York, NY)
• 1957	# SHEFFIELD, Reginald		56	Died in Pacific Palisades, CA
1939	SHELBY, Margaret		39	
1982	SHELDON, Gene		75	Heart attack
1962	SHELDON, Jerome		71	(Do not confuse with Jerry Sheldon)
1962	# SHELDON, Jerry		60	(Do not confuse with Jerome Sheldon)
1992	SHELDON, Richard		59	Cancer
1989	SHELLEY, Dave		58	Lung complications after heart surgery
1994	SHELTON, Anne		66	Apparent heart attack (at her home in Herstmonceux, Eng.)
1976	SHELTON, Don		64	Died in Los Angeles, CA
1971	SHELTON, George		86	Burns
1972	SHELTON, John		54	Natural causes (in Ceylon)
1989	SHENAR, Paul		53	A.I.D.S.
1993	SHEPARD, Bob		76	Heart attack (on a visit to Manhattan)
1961	# SHEPLEY, Michael		53	Died in London, England
1988	SHER, Jack		75	After a brief illness
1967	#+ SHERIDAN, Ann		51	Cancer (in Hollywood, CA)
1963	# SHERIDAN, Dan		46	Suicide (overdose of barbiturates)
1943	SHERIDAN, Frank		74	Died in Hollywood, CA
• 1973	+ SHERMAN, Allan		49	
1989	SHERMAN, Connie		72	Respiratory failure
1969	SHERMAN, Fred E.		64	After suffering a stroke in 1962
1991	SHERMAN, George		82	Heart & kidney failure
1952	SHERMAN, Harry		67	After two surgical operations
1989	SHERMAN, Hiram		81	Following a stroke
1934	+ SHERMAN, Lowell		49	Pneumonia (in Hollywood, CA)
1980	# SHERMAN, Mary		93	
1985	SHERMAN, Ransom		87	
1944	# SHERRY, J. Barney		71	Died in Philadelphia, PA
• 1990	SHERWOOD, Bill		?	A.I.D.S.
• 1981	# SHERWOOD, Bobby		65	Cancer (in Auburn, MA)
1989	SHERWOOD, Lydia		82	
1989	SHERWOOD, Madeline Hurlock		89	
• 1962	SHIELD, Leroy		68	Died in Fort Lauderdale, FL
1970	SHIELDS, Arthur		74	Emphysema (in Santa Barbara, CA)
1975	# SHIELDS, Frank		64	
1984	SHIELDS, John Webster		34	Cancer
1993	SHIELDS, Pat		70	Found dead in his car (in Death Valley)
1994	SHILTS, Randy		42	A.I.D.S. (in Guerneville, CA)
• 1981	SHIMODA, Yuki		58	Died in Los Angeles, CA
1982	SHIMURA, Takashi		76	Emphysema

...DEATHS OF MOVIE AND TELEVISION PERSONALITIES — BY NAME...

YEAR	NAME		AGE	CAUSE AND/OR PLACE OF DEATH
• 1977	SHINDO, Eitaro		78	Heart failure (in Tokyo, Japan)
• 1939	SHINE, Wilfred		75	Died in Kingston, England
• 1966	SHINER, Ronald		63	Died in London, England
1993	# SHIRLEY, Anne	☆	74	Lung cancer after a long illness (in Los Angeles)
1989	SHIRLEY, Bill		68	Lung cancer
1978	SHOEMAKER, Ann		87	Cancer (in Los Angeles, CA)
1988	SHOLOMIR, Jack		57	Heart attack
• 1966	Shooting Star		76	Stroke (in Hollywood, CA)
1994	#+ SHORE, Dinah		76	Cancer (in her Beverly Hills, CA, home)
1957	SHORES, Byron L.		50	Multiple sclerosis (in Kansas City, MO)
1992	SHORR, Lester	★	85	Cancer
1972	SHORT, Antrim		72	Emphysema (in Woodland Hills, CA)
1968	SHORT, Gertrude		66	After a brief illness (in Hollywood, CA)
1958	SHORT, Lewis W.		83	
• 1975	+ SHOSTAKOVICH, Dmitri		68	After a 9-yr. battle with heart disease
1934	SHOTWELL, Marie		?	Died in L.I., NY
1970	# SHRINER, Herb		51	Killed with his wife in a car crash (in Delray Beach, FL)
1937	SHUBERT, Eddie		38	After being stricken watching a golf tournament (in Los Angeles)
1985	SHUE, Larry		38	Airplane crash
• 1995	SHULMAN, Irving		82	Alzheimer's disease (in Sherman Oaks, CA)
1991	SHUMAN, Mort		52	
1973	+ SHUMAN, Roy		49	
1979	SHUMLIN, Herman E.		80	Heart failure complicated by emphysema
1959	# SHUMWAY, Lee		74	
• 1965	# SHUMWAY, Walter		80	Heart disease (in Woodland Hills, CA)
1976	SHUTTA, Ethel		79	Died at St. Clare's Hospital in New York
1945	SHY, Gus		51	After a long illness
1945	# SIDNEY, George (actor)		69	After a long illness (in Los Angeles, CA)
1993	SIDNEY, Sid		?	Parkinson's disease
1976	SIEBER, Rudolf		77	Following a long illness
• 1940	# SIEGEL, Bernard		72	Heart attack (in Los Angeles, CA)
1991	SIEGEL, Don		78	After a long illness
1928	SIEGMANN, George		45	Pernicious anemia (in Hollywood, CA)
1993	SIEGRIST, Jeremy		20	Killed in a hiking accident in the Calif. mountains
• 1963	SIERRA, Margarita		27	Following heart surgery (in Hollywood, CA)
1985	# SIGNORET, Simone	★	64	Cancer
1964	SILETTI, Mario G.		59	Automobile accident (in Los Angeles, CA)
• 1996	SILLIPHANT, Stirling	★	78	Prostate cancer (in Bangkok, Thailand)
1930	SILLS, Milton		48	Heart disease (in Santa Monica, CA)
• 1976	SILVA, David		58	Thrombosis (in Mexico City, Mexico)
1980	# SILVA, Mario		79	
• 1957	SILVA, Simone		29	Natural causes (in London, England)
1988	SILVA, Trinidad Jr.		38	Traffic accident
• 1964	SILVANI, Aldo		73	Died in Milan, Italy
1994	SILVANI, Jole		84	Died in her hometown of Trieste, Italy
1991	SILVER, Dave		72	Heart attack
1989	SILVER, Joe		66	Liver cancer
1970	SILVERA, Frank		56	Accidentally electrocuted in his home (in Pasadena, CA)
1980	#+ SILVERHEELS, Jay "Tonto"		62	Complications from pneumonia (in Woodland Hills, CA)
1989	SILVERMAN, Mark		36	A.I.D.S.
1985	#+ SILVERS, Phil		73	Natural causes
1976	SILVERS, Sid		72	
1976	SIM, Alastair		75	Cancer (in London, England)
1994	SIMEK, Vasek		66	Collapsed while playing at the Croatian Nat. Theatre (in Zagreb)
1994	SIMMS, Ginny		81	Heart attack (at Desert Hosp. in Palm Springs, CA)
1994	# SIMMS, Hilda		75	Pancreatic cancer (in Buffalo, NY)
• 1969	SIMON, Abe		56	Died in Queens, NY
• 1975	# SIMON, Michel		80	Heart failure (near Paris, France)
1992	SIMON, Robert F.		83	Heart attack
1951	+ SIMON, S. Sylvan		41	Heart attack
1986	# SIMPSON, Bill		54	
• 1996	SIMPSON, Don		52	Found dead of a probable heart attack (in his Bel-Air, CA, home)
1951	SIMPSON, Ivan		76	Died in New York, NY
1985	SIMPSON, Mickey		72	Heart attack
1959	SIMPSON, Russell		79	Died in Hollywood, CA

	YEAR	NAME		AGE	CAUSE AND/OR PLACE OF DEATH
•	1980	# SINATRA, Ray		76	Died in Las Vegas, NV
•	1951	# SINCLAIR, Arthur		68	Died in Belfast, Northern Ireland
•	1962	SINCLAIR, Hugh		59	Died in Slapton, England
•	1995	SINCLAIR, Madge		57	Leukemia (in Los Angeles, CA)
	1970	SINCLAIR, Robert B.		65	Stabbed to death by a burglar (in his California home)
	1992	SINCLAIR, Ronald		68	Respiratory failure
	1969	#+ SINGLETON, Catherine		65	Died in Ft. Worth, Texas
	1973	# SIODMAK, Robert	☆	73	Heart attack (in Switzerland)
	1928	SIPPERLY, Ralph		37	Died in Bangor, Maine
	1987	# SIRK, Douglas		86	Cancer
•	1975	SISSLE, Noble		86	Died in Tampa, FL
•	1954	SISSON, Vera		63	Died in Carmel, CA
	1994	SKALA, Lilia	☆	90s	Died at her home in Bay Shore, NY
	1934	# SKELLY, Hal		42	Killed by a train in a grade crossing accident (in West Cornwall, CT)
•	1976	# SKELTON, Georgia		54	Suicide (gunshot) in Rancho Mirage, CA
	1979	SKINNER, Cornelia Otis		78	Cerebral hemorrhage (in New York, NY)
	1968	SKINNER, Frank		69	Cancer
	1942	SKINNER, Otis		83	Died at his home in New York
	1952	# SKIPWORTH, Alison		88	Died in New York, NY
	1983	SKOLSKY, Sidney		78	Parkinson's disease
	1971	SKOURAS, Spyros		78	
•	1965	SLACK, Freddie		55	Natural causes (in Hollywood, CA)
	1989	SLATE, Jack		80	Heart attack
	1975	SLATER, John		58	Heart attack (in London, England)
	1987	SLATER, Patrick Scott		42	A.I.D.S.
•	1956	# SLAUGHTER, Tod		70	
	1983	SLEEPER, Martha		72	Heart attack
•	1946	SLEZAK, Leo		71	Died in Bavaria, Germany
	1983	SLEZAK, Walter		80	Suicide (gunshot)
	1990	SLOANE, Doreen		56	Cancer
	1965	SLOANE, Everett		55	Suicide (sleeping pills) in Brentwood, CA
	1963	SLOANE, Olive		66	Died in London, England
	1972	SLOMAN, Edward "Ted"		87	Died in Woodland Hills, CA
	1992	SLYTER, Fred		56	After a long illness
	1939	#+ SMALLEY, Phillips		63	Died in Hollywood, CA
	1993	SMANEY, June		71	An apparent suicide (in Los Angeles, CA)
	1960	SMART, J. Scott		57	Died in Springfield, IL
	1945	SMILEY, Joseph W.		64	Died in New York
•	1939	SMITH, Albert J.		44	Died in Hollywood, CA
	1993	# SMITH, Alexis		72	Cancer (at Cedars-Sinai Med. Ctr. in Los Angeles)
	1973	# SMITH, Art		73	Heart attack (in West Babylon, NY)
	1991	SMITH, Burleigh		70	Cancer
	1948	# SMITH, C. Aubrey		85	Double pneumonia (in Beverly Hills, CA)
	1988	SMITH, Charles "Dizzy"		67	Apparent heart attack
	1937	SMITH, Clifford S.		51	Peritonitis following a ruptured appendix
•	1963	SMITH, Cyril		70	Died in London, England
	1959	SMITH, G. Albert		61	After a brief illness (in New York, NY)
	1974	# SMITH, Gerald		77	After a short illness (in Woodland Hills, CA)
	1994	+ SMITH, Hal		77	Apparent heart attack (at his Santa Monica, CA, home)
	1968	SMITH, Howard I.		74	Heart attack (in Hollywood, Ca.)
	1989	SMITH, Jack		57	A.I.D.S. (Do not confuse with "Whispering" Jack Smith, d. 1950)
	1992	SMITH, Jacqueline		?	After a lengthy illness
•	1995	# SMITH, John		63	Cirrhosis & heart problems (at his home in L.A., CA)
	1981	# SMITH, Joseph		96	
	1986	SMITH, Justin		66	Complications from A.I.D.S.
	1986	#+ SMITH, Kate		79	After a long bout with diabetes & heart problems
	1985	SMITH, Kent		78	Congestive heart failure
•	1995	# SMITH, Michael C.		34	Died in Stoughton, MA)
	1985	SMITH, Muriel		61	
	1979	SMITH, Pete	★	86	Suicide (jumped from the roof of a nursing home) in Santa Monica
	1978	SMITH, Queenie		70	Cancer (in Burbank, CA)
	1991	SMITH, Ray		55	
	1985	SMITH, Samantha		13	Airplane crash after filming in England
	1988	SMITH, Tucker		52	Cancer of the neck and jaw
	1950	SMITH, "Whispering" Jack		51	Heart attack (in New York) Do not confuse with Jack Smith, d. 1989

YEAR	NAME		AGE	CAUSE AND/OR PLACE OF DEATH
1974	SNEGOFF, Leonid		90	Heart failure and arteriosclerosis (in Los Angeles, CA)
1958	SNOW, Marguerite		68	Kidney complications (in Hollywood, CA)
1982	SNOWDEN, Leigh		51	Cancer
• 1996	SNYDER, Jimmy "The Greek"		76	Heart failure (at a hospital in Las Vegas, NV)
1991	SOBEK, Allan		46	A.I.D.S.
1948	SODERLING, Walter		75	Died in Los Angeles, CA
1988	SOFAER, Abraham		91	Congestive heart failure
1954	# Sojin		63	Died in Tokyo, Japan
1962	SOKOLOFF, Vladimir		72	Stroke (in Hollywood, CA)
• 1961	SOLER, Domingo Jr.		59	Heart attack (in Acapulco, Mexico)
1985	SOLON, Ewen		62	
1983	SOMACK, Jack		64	Heart attack
• 1974	# SOMERSET, Pat		77	Arterial hemorrhage (in Apple Valley, CA)
1994	SOMES, Michael		77	Brain tumor (in London, England)
1990	SOMMER, Bert		42	Liver failure
• 1995	SONBERT, Warren		46	Complications of A.I.D.S.
1985	# SONDERGAARD, Gale	★	86	
1991	SONNTAG, Jack		77	After a long illness
1979	#+ SOO, Jack		63	Cancer of the esophagus (in Los Angeles, CA)
1948	SOREL, George S.		48	Died in Hollywood, CA
1989	SORM, Evald		57	
• 1996	SOSNICK, Harry		89	After a long illness (at Calvary Hospital in New York)
1947	# SOTHERN, Hugh		65	After an illness of 2 years (in Hollywood, CA)
1992	# SOUEZ, Ina		89	Stroke
1994	SOULE, Olan		84	Lung cancer (at his daughter's home in Corona, CA)
1932	+ SOUSA, John Philip		77	Heart attack
1975	SOUSSANIN, Nicholas		66	Cardiac arrest (in New York, NY)
1990	SOUTHARD, Stephen		30	A.I.D.S.
1991	# SOUTHERN, Jeri		64	Pneumonia
• 1995	SOUTHERN, Terry		71	
1983	SPACE, Arthur		74	Cancer
1940	SPACEY, John Graham		44	Suddenly, after attending a party (in Hollywood, CA)
• 1981	SPADARO, Umberto		77	Cancer (in Rome, Italy)
1983	SPAIN, Fay		50	Cancer
1957	# SPARKS, Ned		73	Intestinal block (in Apple Valley, CA)
1969	SPEAR, Harry		47	Died in Hollywood, CA
• 1995	SPENCE, Irven "Irv"		86	Natural causes (in Dallas, TX)
• 1949	SPENCE, Ralph		60	Heart attack (in Woodland Hills, CA)
1960	SPENCER, Douglas		50	Diabetic condition (in Hollywood, Ca.)
1992	SPENCER, Herbert	☆	87	
• 1988	+ SPERLING, Milton		76	
1990	SPEWACK, Bella		91	
1985	SPIEGEL, Sam		84	While vacationing in the Caribbean
1989	SPINELL, Joe		51	Heart attack
1990	# SPITALNY, Evelyn		79	
1970	SPITALNY, Phil		80	Cancer (in Miami Beach, FL)
1989	SPITZ, Hank		84	
1994	SPIVAK, Laurence		93	Congestive heart failure (in Washington, D.C.)
1971	# Spivy		64	Died at the Motion Picture Country Home, CA
1985	SPOLIANSKY, Mischa		86	
1953	SPOOR, George K.		81	
1958	# SQUIRE, Ronald		72	Died in London, England
1989	SQUIRE, William		72	
1992	STAFFORD, Grace		88	
1968	#+ STAFFORD, Hanley		69	Heart attack (in Hollywood, Ca.)
1950	+ STAHL, John M.		63	Heart attack
• 1961	STAINTON, Philip		53	
1990	STALKER, John		67	
• 1996	STAMENKOVIC, Stan		39	Head injuries from a fall in his home (in Titova Uzice, Serbia)
• 1946	STAMP-TAYLOR, Enid		41	Injuries from a fall (in London, England)
1994	+ STANDER, Lionel		86	Lung cancer (at his home in Brentwood, CA)
1937	STANDING, Guy		63	Following a heart attack
1955	STANDING, Herbert Jr.		71	Died in New York, NY
• 1917	STANDING, Jack		31	Died in Los Angeles, CA
• 1979	STANDING, Joan		75	Cancer (in Houston, TX)

YEAR	NAME		AGE	CAUSE AND/OR PLACE OF DEATH
• 1963	# STANDING, Wyndham		82	Died in Los Angeles, CA
• 1935	STANHOPE, Adeline		82	Died in Los Angeles, CA
• 1994	STANLEY, Anita		88	
1944	STANLEY, Edwin		64	Died in Hollywood, CA
• 1969	STANLEY, Forrest		80	Results of a fall (in Los Angeles, CA)
1990	# STANLEY, Helene		62	
1982	STANLEY, Louise		?	
• 1943	# STANMORE, Frank		65	
• 1978	# STANTON, Harry		76	Heart disease (in Los Angeles, CA)
1955	STANTON, Paul		70	
1969	# STANTON, Will		84	Bronchial pneumonia (in Santa Monica, CA)
1990	#+ STANWYCK, Barbara	☆	82	Congestive heart failure
• 1977	# STARK, Pauline		76	Died in Santa Monica, CA
• 1995	STARK, Wilbur		83	Cancer (at New York Hospital in Manhattan)
1990	STARR, Jimmy		86	
1950	STARR, Muriel		62	Heart attack
• 1970	# STARR, Randy		39	Died in Los Angeles, CA
1986	STARRETT, Charles		82	Cancer
1989	STARRETT, Jack		52	Kidney failure
1984	STAUDTE, Wolfgang		77	
1988	STAVRIDIS, Nicos		77	Heart failure
1952	ST. CLAIR, Malcolm		55	Died in Pasadena, CA.
• 1974	ST. CYR, Lillian "Red Wing"		100	Died in New York, NY
1968	#+ ST. DENIS, Ruth		90	Heart attack (in Hollywood, CA)
1993	STEADMAN, John		83	Pneumonia (in Montrose, CA)
• 1966	STEADMAN, Vera		66	Died in Long Beach, CA
1990	STEBER, Eleanor		76	Congestive heart failure
1948	STEDMAN, Lincoln		41	Died in Los Angeles, CA
1938	STEDMAN, Myrtle		48	Heart trouble (in Los Angeles, CA)
1992	STEEL, Pippa		44	Cancer
1988	#+ STEELE, Bob		82	Heart failure after a long illness (in Burbank, CA)
1955	STEELE, Vernon		72	Heart attack (in Los Angeles, Ca.)
• 1966	STEELE, William "Bill"		76	Died in Los Angeles, CA
1983	STEEN, Malcolm H.		55	
1951	# STEERS, Larry		69	Died in Woodland Hills, CA
1991	STEIN, Robert M.		40	Lung cancer
• 1965	STEINER, Elio		60	Died in Rome, Italy
1971	+ STEINER, Max		83	
• 1929	STEINRUCK, Albert		57	Died in Berlin, Germany
1993	# STEN, Anna		85	Cardiac arrest (at her home in Manhattan)
1980	STEPANEK, Karel		80	
1986	STEPHENS, Harvey		85	
• 1995	STEPHENS, Robert		64	After a liver and kidney transplant (in London, England)
1956	#+ STEPHENSON, Henry		85	After a brief illness (in San Francisco, CA)
1941	+ STEPHENSON, James	☆	53	Heart attack (in Pacific Palisades, CA)
1992	STEPHENSON, Skip		54	Following an apparent heart attack
• 1969	STEPPAT, Ilse		52	Died in West Berlin, Germany
1932	STEPPLING, John C.		62	After an extended illness (in Hollywood, CA)
1939	# STERLING, Ford		58	Thrombosis of veins and heart attack (in Los Angeles, CA)
1958	STERLING, Larry		23	A water-skiing accident
1959	STERLING, Richard		78	Heart attack
1971	STERN, Bill		64	Heart attack (in Rye, NY)
• 1964	STEVENS, Bert		59	Heart attack (in Hollywood, CA)
1964	STEVENS, Charles		71	Died in Hollywood, CA
• 1996	STEVENS, Chuck		64	Massive heart attack (in Las Vegas, NV)
1993	STEVENS, Dudley		57	A.I.D.S. (in Hove, England)
1923	STEVENS, Edwin		?	Pleurisy
1991	STEVENS, Fran		72	Cancer
1975	+ STEVENS, George Sr.	★	70	Heart attack (in Lancaster, CA)
1970	# STEVENS, Inger		35	After an overdose of barbiturates (enroute to a Hollywood hospital)
1994	# STEVENS, K. T.		74	Lung cancer (at her home in Brentwood, CA)
1940	#+ STEVENS, Landers		63	Heart attack following appendectomy (in Hollywood, CA)
1991	STEVENS, Mort		62	Pancreatic cancer
1977	# STEVENS, Onslow		74	Murdered (while in a convalescent home) in Van Nuys, CA
1986	STEVENS, Paul		65	Pneumonia

...DEATHS OF MOVIE AND TELEVISION PERSONALITIES — BY NAME...

YEAR	NAME	AGE	CAUSE AND/OR PLACE OF DEATH
1989	STEVENS, Robert	68	Heart attack
1953	STEVENSON, Houseley	74	Died at City of Hope Sanitarium, near Los Angeles, CA
• 1996	STEVENSON, McLean	66	Heart attack (at a hospital in Los Angeles, CA)
1986	STEVENSON, Robert (director)	81	After a long illness
1961	+ STEWART, Anita	66	Died in Beverly Hills, CA
• 1940	STEWART, Athole	61	Died in Buckinghamshire, England
1993	STEWART, Bill	67	Heart attack (at a London airport, after filming in Madeira)
• 1952	STEWART, Blanche	?	
1994	STEWART, Dennis	46	Heart problems & swelling of the brain
• 1966	STEWART, Donald	54	Died in Chertsey, England
1970	STEWART, Fred	63	Died at the Actors Studio in New York
• 1966	STEWART, Jack	51	Died in London, England
1986	STEWART, Paul	77	Heart attack
1938	STEWART, Richard	?	
1933	STEWART, Roy	43	Heart attack (in Los Angeles, Ca.)
• 1995	STEWART, Samuel Douglas	75	Parkinson's disease (at the Motion Picture Hospital)
• 1977	STEWART, Sophie	69	Died in London, England
1991	STIERLE, Edward	23	A.I.D.S.
1928	STILLER, Mauritz	?	Pleurisy
1990	# ST. JACQUES, Raymond	60	Lymphatic cancer
1988	ST. JOHN, Adela Rogers	94	
1963	# ST. JOHN, Al "Fuzzy"	69	Heart attack (in Vidalia, GA)
1974	ST. JOHN, Howard	68	Heart attack (in New York, NY)
1957	ST. JOHN, Jane Lee	45	After a long illness
1993	ST. JOSEPH, Ellis	82	Cancer (in Beverly Hills, CA)
1994	ST. JUST, Maria	?	Heart failure from severe rheumatoid arthritis (in London)
• 1959	ST. MAUR, Adele	70	Leukemia (in Sunnydale, CA)
1986	STOCK, Nigel	66	Heart attack
• 1953	# STOCKDALE, Carl	79	Heart attack (in Woodland Hills, CA)
• 1966	# STOCKFIELD, Betty	61	Cancer (in London, England)
• 1959	STOECKEL, Joe	65	Circulatory ailment (in Munich, Germany)
• 1966	# STOKER, H. G.	81	Died in England
1977	#+ STOKOWSKI, Leopold	95	Coronary attack (in Nether Wallop, Hampshire, England)
1985	STOLL, George	79	
1980	STOLOFF, Morris W. ★	85	
1940	STONE, Arthur	56	After a brief illness (in Hollywood, CA)
• 1995	STONE, Christopher	55	Heart attack
1994	STONE, Ezra "Henry Aldrich"	76	Automobile accident (near Perth Amboy, NJ)
1959	+ STONE, Fred	85	After a 2-year illness (in North Hollywood, CA)
1967	# STONE, George E.	63	Following a paralytic stroke (in Woodland Hills, CA)
1953	# STONE, Lewis ☆	74	Heart attack (while chasing 3 teen-aged vandals) in Los Angeles
1980	+ STONE, Milburn	75	Heart attack (in La Jolla, CA)
1986	STONE, Sidney	83	Heart failure
• 1995	STONEBURNER, Sam	66	Esophageal cancer (at his Manhattan home)
1941	STONEHOUSE, Ruth	47	Died in Hollywood, CA
• 1950	# STOOPNAGLE, Col. Lemuel Q.	52	
1988	STOPPA, Paolo	81	
1985	STORER, Conrad L.	55	Cancer
1992	# STOREY, June	73	Cancer
1993	STORRS, Tim	43	Found dead in his apartment after a fall
1973	STOSSEL, Ludwig	89	Died in Beverly Hills, CA
1949	STOTHART, Herbert	64	After an illness of several months
1989	STOUT, Bill	62	Cardiac arrest
1919	STOWELL, William H.	34	Killed in a train wreck (in Elizabethville, South Africa)
• 1946	# ST. POLIS, John	72	
1958	STRADNER, Rose	45	
1992	STRAIT, Ralph	56	Heart attack
• 1963	STRANDMARK, Erik	44	Died in Sweden
1992	STRANGE, Bill	62	Cancer
1973	#+ STRANGE, Glenn	74	Cancer (in Burbank, CA)
1952	STRANGE, Robert	70	Died in Hollywood, CA
1982	#+ STRASBERG, Lee ☆	80	Heart attack
• 1974	STRASSBERG, Morris	75	Died in South Laguna Beach, CA
1980	#+ STRATTEN, Dorothy	20	Murdered (shot by her husband) in West Los Angeles, CA
1970	STRATTON, Chester	57	Died at his Los Angeles home

YEAR	NAME		AGE	CAUSE AND/OR PLACE OF DEATH
1975	STRAUSS, Robert	☆	61	Complications following a stroke (in New York, NY)
1943	STRAUSS, William H.		58	After a heart attack (in Hollywood, Ca.)
1964	STRAYER, Frank R.		72	
• 1971	STREET, David		54	Died in Los Angeles, CA
1985	STRETTON, Ellen		71	Pneumonia
1938	STRICKLAND, Helen		74	Died at Mt. Sinai Hospital in New York, NY
1974	STRIKER, Joseph		74	Died in St. Barnabas Hospital, Livingston, NJ
1993	STRIVELLI, Jerry		61	Heart attack (in New York)
1994	STRODE, Woody		80	Died in his sleep after long bout with cancer (Glendora, CA)
1991	STROHM, Walter Clarence		86	Heart failure
1968	+ STROMBERG, Hunt		74	Massive stroke
1980	# STRONG, Leonard		71	Died in Glendale, CA
• 1980	STRONG, Michael		?	Cancer (in Los Angeles, CA)
1923	STRONG, Porter		44	Died in New York City
1993	STRONG, Robert B.		87	Natural causes (in Burbank, CA)
1985	STROUD, Claude		78	Throat cancer
1983	STRUDWICK, Shepperd		75	Cancer
1987	STRYKER, Christopher		27	A.I.D.S.
1944	STUART, Donald		45	Following a heart attack (in Hollywood, CA)
1936	STUART, Iris		33	
1978	# STUART, John		81	Died in London, England
1973	# STUART, Nick		68	Cancer (in Biloxi, MS)
• 1950	# STUBBS, Harry		75	Heart attack (in Woodland Hills, CA)
1986	STUCKER, Stephen		36	Complications from A.I.D.S.
• 1976	# STUEWE, Hans		75	Died in Berlin, Germany
1992	STURGES, John	☆	82	Heart attack and emphysema (at his home in San Luis Obispo, CA)
1959	#+ STURGES, Preston		60	Heart attack
• 1947	# STURGIS, Eddie		66	Heart disease (in Los Angeles, CA)
1990	STUSSY, Jan		68	Cancer
1994	STYNE, Jule		88	After open-heart surgery (at Mt. Sinai Med. Ctr., CA)
1991	SUBOTSKY, Milton		70	Heart disease
1970	SUDLOW, Joan		78	Results of a fall (in back of her Calif. hillside home)
• 1995	SUGHRUE, John		67	Lung cancer (in New York)
• 1957	SULKY, Leo		82	Died in CA
1960	#+ SULLAVAN, Margaret	☆	48	Suicide (sleeping pills) in New Haven, CT
1994	SULLIVAN, Barry		81	After a chronic respiratory ailment (Sherman Oaks, CA)
• 1969	# SULLIVAN, Brian		49	Died in Lake Geneva, Switzerland
1974	#+ SULLIVAN, Ed		72	Cancer of the esophagus (in New York, NY)
1974	SULLIVAN, Elliott (Elliot)		66	Heart attack (while visiting in Los Angeles, CA)
1956	# SULLIVAN, Francis L.		53	Died in New York, NY
• 1996	SULLIVAN, Fred G. Jr.		50	Heart failure (in Saranac Lake, NY)
1993	SULLIVAN, Jeremiah		58	An A.I.D.S.-related illness (in Hollywood, CA)
• 1995	SULLIVAN, Joseph H.		67	After suffering a heart attack (at his Baltimore, MD, home)
1992	SULLIVAN, Larry		46	Stroke
1991	SULLIVAN, Marie Madeline		80	After a brief illness
1987	SULLIVAN, Maxine		75	A seizure brought on by pneumonia
• 1933	SULLIVAN, Pat		46	Pneumonia brought on by alcoholism
• 1946	SULLIVAN, William A. "Billy"		54	Died in Great Neck, NY
1975	# SULLY, Frank		67	Died in Woodland Hills, CA
1979	SUMMERS, Hope		78	Heart failure (in Woodland Hills, CA)
1946	# SUMMERVILLE, Slim		53	Stroke (in Laguna Beach, CA)
• 1976	# SUNBEAUTY, Olga		78	
1987	SUNDBERG, Clinton		81	Heart failure
1989	SUNDIN, Michael		28	
• 1959	# SUNDMARK, Betty		45	Died in New York
• 1917	# SUNSHINE, Baby			(See Pauline Flood, d. 1917)
1963	# SUNSHINE, Marion		65	Died in New York, NY
1992	# Superman		54	Slain in combat with "Doomsday"
1962	SURATT, Valeska		79	
1987	SUSSKIND, David		66	Natural causes (heart attack?)
1934	SUTHERLAND, Dick		51	Died in Hollywood, CA
1973	# SUTHERLAND, Eddie		78	Following a long illness (in Palm Springs, CA)
1987	SUTHERLAND, Esther		54	Heart attack
1968	SUTHERLAND, Victor		79	Died in Los Angeles, CA
• 1995	SUTTER, Linda		54	Brain cancer (in Cambridge, MA)

...DEATHS OF MOVIE AND TELEVISION PERSONALITIES — BY NAME...

YEAR	NAME		AGE	CAUSE AND/OR PLACE OF DEATH
1974	SUTTON, Frank		50	Heart attack (in Shreveport, LA)
• 1995	# SUTTON, Grady		89	Natural causes (in Woodland Hills, CA)
1963	SUTTON, John		54	
1970	SUTTON, Paul		58	Muscular dystrophy (in Ferndale, MI)
1994	SWACKHAMER, E. W.		67	Ruptured aortic aneurysm (in Berlin, Germany)
1935	SWAIN, Mack		59	Apparent heart attack (in Tacoma, WA)
1983	# SWANSON, Gloria	☆	84	Following heart surgery
• 1968	SWANWICK, Peter		56	Died in London, England
1969	SWARTHOUT, Gladys		64	Died in Florence, Italy
1957	SWASEY, Bill		29	Automobile accident
• 1995	SWAYZE, John Cameron		89	Natural causes (at his home in Sarasota, FL)
1992	SWEENEY, Bob		73	Cancer
1950	SWEENEY, Jack		61	
1986	SWEET, Blanche		90	Stroke
1985	SWEET, Dolph		64	Cancer
1978	SWENSON, Karl		70	Apparent heart attack (while visiting relatives in Torrington, CT)
1940	SWICKARD, Joseph		74	After a long illness (in Hollywood, CA)
1994	+ SWIFT, Paul "Eggman"		60	A.I.D.S. (at Francis Scott Key Med. Ctr., Baltimore, MD)
1959	+ SWITZER, Carl "Alfalfa"		32	Murdered (shot over a $50. debt) in Sepulveda, CA
1943	SWOR, Bert		65	Found dead in his Tulsa, Oklahoma hotel room
1965	SWOR, John		82	Died in Dallas, Texas
• 1968	SYDNEY, Basil		73	Died in London, England
1989	SYDNOR, Earl		81	Lung cancer
• 1953	SYLVANI, Gladys		68	Died in Alexandria, VA
• 1980	SYLVIA, Gaby		60	Heart attack (in France)
• 1970	# Sylvie		87	Died in Paris, France
1992	SYMS, Sylvia		74	Apparent heart attack (while performing on stage in London, Eng.)
1993	SYRON, Brian		58	Leukemia (in Sydney, Australia)
1974	TABBERT, William		53	Apparent heart attack
1957	TABER, Richard		72	Died in New York
1953	# TABLER, P. Dempsey		79	Died in San Francisco, CA
1979	TAFLER, Sydney		63	Cancer (in London, England)
1989	TAFOYA, Alfonso		60	Massive heart attack
• 1973	TAFT, Sara		?	Heart attack (in Los Angeles, CA)
• 1947	TAGGART, Ben L.		58	Died in Santa Monica, CA
• 1995	TAGLIAVINI, Ferruccio		81	Respiratory problems after a long illness (in Reggio, Italy)
• 1996	TAKEMITSU, Toru		65	Pneumonia while undergoing cancer treatments (in Tokyo, Japan)
• 1996	TALBOT, Lyle		94	Natural causes (at his home in San Francisco, CA)
1979	TALIAFERRO, Mabel		89	Died in Honolulu, Hawaii
1991	TALLICHET, Margaret (Wyler)		77	Cancer
1973	+ TALMADGE, Constance		75	Pneumonia (in Los Angeles, CA)
1969	+ TALMADGE, Natalie		70	Died in Santa Monica, CA
1957	+ TALMADGE, Norma		64	Cerebral stroke and pneumonia (in Las Vegas, NV)
1981	# TALMADGE, Richard		88	Cancer (in Carmel, CA)
1968	+ TALMAN, William		53	Cancer (in Encino, CA)
1992	TALTON, Alix		72	After a long battle with lung cancer (in Burbank, CA)
• 1943	# Tamara		?	Airplane crash (near Lisbon, Portugal)
• 1980	TAMBERLANI, Carlo		81	Died in Subiaco, Italy
1972	TAMIROFF, Akim	☆	72	Died in Palm Springs, CA
• 1977	TANAKA, Kinuyo		67	Cerebral tumor
1994	TANDY, Jessica	★	85	Ovarian cancer (at her home in Easton, CT)
1947	+ TANGUAY, Eva		68	Heart attack and cerebral hemorrhage (in Los Angeles, CA)
1980	TANNEN, Charles D.		65	Heart attack (while vacationing in San Bernardino, CA)
1965	TANNEN, Julius		84	After suffering a stroke (in Hollywood, CA)
1976	TANNEN, William		65	Died in Woodland Hills, CA
1956	TAPLEY, Rose		72	Died at the Motion Picture Country Hospital in Woodland Hills, CA
1986	TARKOVSKY, Andrei		54	Cancer
1993	TARLETON, Diane R.		51	Breast cancer (at her home in Manhattan)
1992	TARLOW, Florence		70	Cancer (in New York)
1990	TARRON, Elsie		87	Heart failure
1972	TASHLIN, Frank		59	Heart attack
1934	TASHMAN, Lilyan		33	Tumorous condition and/or cancer (in New York, NY)
• 1955	TATE, Reginald		58	Died in London, England
1969	+ TATE, Sharon (Polanski)		26	Murdered by members of the Charles Manson cult

• New entry. # Original name (Pt. 7). + Interment (Pt. 5).　　　240　　　☆ Oscar nominee, ★ Oscar winner (Pt. 10)

YEAR	NAME		AGE	CAUSE AND/OR PLACE OF DEATH
1982	# TATI, Jacques		74	Pulmonary embolism
1956	+ TATUM, Art		46	Uremia
• 1967	+ TATUM, Reese "Goose"		45	
1948	#+ TAUBER, Richard		56	After an illness of several months (in a nursing home in London)
1981	TAUROG, Norman	★	82	
1992	TAVARES, Albert		39	A.I.D.S.
1990	+ TAYBACK, Vic "Mel"		60	Heart attack
• 1974	TAYLOR, Alma		79	Died in London, England
1966	TAYLOR, Deems		67	Stroke
1966	TAYLOR, Donald F.		47	Found dead at home from an overdose of seconal
1994	# TAYLOR, Dub		87	Congestive heart failure (at Westlake Med. Ctr., L.A., CA)
1958	TAYLOR, Estelle		58	Cancer (in Los Angeles, CA)
1961	TAYLOR, Ferris		68	Heart attack (in Hollywood, Ca.)
• 1965	TAYLOR, Forrest		80	
1982	TAYLOR, John		61	Heart attack
1987	#+ TAYLOR, Kent		80	Following several heart operations
1984	TAYLOR, Lance Sr.		69	Heart attack
1946	#+ TAYLOR, Laurette (Cooney)		62	Coronary thrombosis after several weeks of illness
1952	TAYLOR, Ray		63	Died in Hollywood, CA
1969	#+ TAYLOR, Robert		57	Lung cancer (in Santa Monica, CA)
1958	TAYLOR, Sam		62	Heart attack
1983	TAYLOR, Vaughn		72	Massive cerebral hemorrhage
1922	#+ TAYLOR, William Desmond		45	Murdered (shot) in Los Angeles, CA
1930	TAYLOR, William H. "Billy"		101	
1964	+ TEAGARDEN, Jack		57	Pneumonia (in New Orleans, LA)
1976	TEAL, Ray		74	After a long illness (in Santa Monica, CA)
1994	TEALE, Leonard		72	Heart attack (in Sydney, Australia)
1938	# TEARLE, Conway		60	Heart attack (in Los Angeles, CA)
1953	TEARLE, Godfrey		68	Died in London, England
1994	TEAS, William Ellis		80	Died at Fort Miley Veterans Hospital in San Francisco, CA
1987	TEASDALE, Verree		80	
1925	Teddy (dog)		14	(In Mack Sennett comedies)
1986	TEITEL, Carol		62	Complications after a car accident
1951	TELL, Olive		56	Died in New York, NY
1934	# TELLEGEN, Lou		52	Suicide (stabbed himself with a pair of scissors) in Los Angeles
• 1942	# TEMPEST, Marie		78	Died in London, England
1939	+ TEMPLETON, Fay		74	
1979	TEMPLETON, Olive		96	
• 1960	# TENBROOK, Harry		72	Lung cancer (in Woodland Hills, CA)
1973	TERHUNE, Max "Ábibe"		82	Heart attack and stroke (in Cottonwood, AZ)
• 1966	#+ TERRELL, Kenneth		61	
1989	TERRIS, Norma		87	After a brief illness
• 1971	# TERRISS, Ellaine		100	Died in London, England
1987	# TERRY, Alice (Alice Ingram)		88	
1988	# TERRY, Don		86	Stroke
1931	TERRY, Ethel Grey		48	After a year's illness (in Hollywood, CA)
• 1957	# TERRY, Sheila		46	
1985	# TERRY, Tex		82	
1990	# Terry-Thomas		78	Parkinson's disease
1994	TESSARI, Duccio		67	Cancer (in Rome, Italy)
1990	TESSIER, Robert		56	Cancer
1975	# TETLEY, Walter		60	
1977	TETZEL, Joan		56	Cancer
1992	THACKER, Jim		64	Stroke
1936	#+ THALBERG, Irving		37	Lobar pneumonia
• 1942	# THATCHER, Eva		80	Died in Los Angeles, CA
1987	THATCHER, Heather		90	
1981	# THATCHER, Torin		76	Cancer (in Thousand Oaks, CA)
1967	THAW, Evelyn Nesbit		82	Died in a Santa Monica, Ca. nursing home
1982	THEARD, Sam		78	
1961	THESIGER, Ernest		81	Died in London, England
1975	# THIELE, William J.		85	Died at the Motion Picture Country Home, CA
1992	THOM, Ruth Corbett		78	After a long illness
1982	THOMA, Michael		55	Cancer
1989	THOMAS, Ann		75	Lung cancer

YEAR	NAME		AGE	CAUSE AND/OR PLACE OF DEATH
1980	#+ THOMAS, Billy "Buckwheat"		49	Heart attack (in Los Angeles, CA)
1991	# THOMAS, Danny		79	After a heart attack
1981	THOMAS, David		73	
1989	THOMAS, Frank M.		100	
1993	THOMAS, Gerald		72	Died in Beaconsfield, England
1939	THOMAS, Jameson		49	Tuberculosis (in Sierra Madre, CA)
1960	THOMAS, John Charles		68	Intestinal cancer (in Apple Valley, CA)
1981	THOMAS, Lowell		89	Heart attack
1989	THOMAS, Madoline		99	Natural causes
1920	THOMAS, Olive		35	Suicide (mercury poisoning) in Paris, France
• 1995	THOMAS, Rachel		90	After a fall & long illness (at Cardiff Hosp. in London, Eng.)
1992	# THOMAS, Ted		88	Heart attack (in Van Nuys, CA)
1991	THOMAS, Wilfrid		87	
1988	THOMPKINS, Toney		33	A.I.D.S.
1990	# THOMPSON, Carlos		67	Suicide (gunshot)
1925	THOMPSON, Frederick A.		55	Heart disease
1992	# THOMPSON, Marshall		66	Congestive heart failure (in Royal Oak, MI)
1928	THOMSON, Fred		38	After an operation for gall stones (in Los Angeles, CA)
1967	THOMSON, Kenneth		68	Pulmonary emphysema and fibrosis (in Los Angeles, CA)
1989	THOR, Dan		34	A.I.D.S.
1993	THOR, Jerome		69	Cardiac arrest (in Westwood, CA)
• 1976	THOR, Larry		58	Heart attack (in Santa Monica, CA)
• 1967	THORBURN, June		36	Airplane crash (in Fernhurst, Sussex, England)
1978	THORDSEN, Kelly		61	Cancer
• 1972	THORNDIKE, Russell		?	Died in London, England
1976	THORNDIKE, Sybil		93	Heart attack (in London, England)
1953	THORPE, Jim		64	Heart attack (in Los Angeles, CA)
1991	# THORPE, Richard		95	
1989	THORPE-BATES, Peggy		75	
• 1994	THRING, Frank Jr.		68	Cancer (in Melbourne, Australia)
1955	#+ THUNDERCLOUD, Chief (1st)		66	Cancer (Do not confuse with 2nd Chief Thundercloud, d. 1967)
1967	# THUNDERCLOUD, Chief (2nd)		68	(Do not confuse with 1st Chief Thundercloud, d. 1955)
1925	THURMAN, Mary		31	Pneumonia (in New York, NY)
1977	THURSBY, David		88	Died in Hollywood, CA
1994	THURSTON, Ted		77	Stomach cancer (in East Hampton, NY)
1960	+ TIBBETT, Lawrence	☆	63	Following surgery for an old head injury (in New York, NY)
• 1960	TIEDTKE, Jakob		85	Died in Berlin, Germany
1991	TIERNEY, Gene	☆	70	Emphysema
1950	TILBURY, Zeffie		86	Died in Los Angeles, CA
1983	+ TINCHER, Fay		99	Natural causes
1992	TINDALL, Hilary		54	Cancer (in Selbourne, England)
1973	+ TINDALL, Loren		51	Heart attack
1979	+ TIOMKIN, Dimitri	★	80	Natural causes
1992	TIPPET, Clark		37	A.I.D.S.
1993	TIPPING, Tim "Tip"		34	While re-enacting a sky-diving accident for TV (in Alnwick, England)
1989	TIRELLI, Teresa		81	Brain tumor
• 1973	TISSIER, Jean		76	Died in Paris, France
1929	TITUS, Lydia Yeamans		63	2 yrs. after a paralytic stroke (in a hospital in Glendale, CA)
1980	TOBIAS, George		78	Cancer (in Los Angeles, CA)
1982	TOBIN, Dan		72	
• 1995	TOBIN, Genevieve		93	Died at Las Encinas Hospital in Pasadena, CA
1993	TODD, Ann		82	After a stroke (in a London hospital)
1992	# TODD, Christopher		30	A.I.D.S. (in New York, NY)
1958	#+ TODD, Mike		49	Airplane crash
1935	+ TODD, Thelma		30	Suicide? Murder? Accident? (carbon monoxide) in Santa Monica, CA
1990	TOGNAZZI, Ugo		68	Cerebral hemorrhage
1948	TOLAND, Gregg		44	Coronary thrombosis
1947	TOLER, Sidney		73	Died at his home in Beverly Hills, CA
1962	#+ TOMACK, Sid		55	Heart ailment (in Palm Springs, CA)
1987	TOMLIN, Pinky		80	Heart attack
1993	TOMLINSON, Kate		96	Died in New Jersey, cause unreported
1968	# TONE, Franchot	☆	63	Lung cancer (in New York, NY)
1969	TONG, Kam		62	Died in Costa Mesa, CA
1964	TONG, Sammee		63	Suicide at his home (in Culver City, CA)
• 1942	# Tony (Tom Mix's horse)		33	

	YEAR	NAME		AGE	CAUSE AND/OR PLACE OF DEATH
	1991	TOOMEY, Regis		93	
•	1957	TOREN, Marta		30	Rare brain disease (in Stockholm, Sweden)
•	1995	TORNBERG, Jeff		43	Complications of A.I.D.S. (in Los Angeles, CA)
	1951	# TORRENCE, David		87	
	1933	#+ TORRENCE, Ernest		54	After an operation for gall stones (in New York, NY)
	1987	+ TORRES, Raquel		78	Heart attack
	1983	TORS, Ivan		67	Massive heart attack
	1957	+ TOSCANINI, Arturo		89	Following a stroke
•	1967	# Toto		69	Died in Rome, Italy (Do not confuse with Toto the Clown, d. 1938)
•	1938	# Toto the Clown		50	Died in New York, NY (Do not confuse with Toto, d. 1967)
•	1995	TOTTEN, Robert		57	Heart attack (at his home in Sherman Oaks, CA)
	1992	TOUCHSTONE, John		59	Cirrhosis of the liver (in Sherman Oaks, CA)
	1977	TOURNEUR, Jacques		73	
	1961	# TOURNEUR, Maurice		85	
	1923	TOWNSEND, Anna		39	Died in Los Angeles, CA
•	1995	TOWNSEND, Claire		43	Cancer (at her parents' home in Los Angeles, CA)
•	1995	TOWNSEND, Dallas		76	Injuries from a fall (at Montclair, N.J., Community Hospital)
	1972	TOZERE, Frederic		71	Died in his New York apartment
•	1978	TOZZI, Fausto		57	Emphysema (in Rome, Italy)
	1992	TRACE, Christopher		59	Cancer
	1968	# TRACY, Lee	☆	70	Cancer of the liver (in Santa Monica, CA)
	1967	+ TRACY, Spencer	★	67	Heart attack (in Beverly Hills, CA)
	1986	TRACY, Steve		34	Complications from A.I.D.S.
	1967	TRACY, William		49	Died in Hollywood, CA
	1987	TRAEGER, Kim Patrick		36	Heart attack
	1987	# TRAEGER, Rick		74	Apparent heart attack two days after his son died
	1940	+ TRAINOR, Leonard		61	Heart attack
•	1918	TRASK, Wayland		31	Spanish influenza (in Los Angeles, CA)
	1983	TRAUBE, Shepard		76	Cancer
	1972	+ TRAUBEL, Helen		69	Heart attack (in Santa Monica, CA)
	1990	TRAUBERG, Leonid		88	
	1994	TRAVERS, Bill		72	Died in his sleep (at his home in Dorking, England)
	1965	#+ TRAVERS, Henry	☆	91	Arteriosclerosis (in Los Angeles, CA)
	1935	TRAVERS, Richard C.		45	Pneumonia (in San Pedro, CA)
	1964	TRAVERSE, Madlaine		88	Died in Cleveland, Ohio
	1989	TRAVIS, Richard		76	
	1989	TRAYLOR, William		60	After a long illness
	1975	# TREACHER, Arthur		81	Heart ailment (in Manhasset, NY)
•	1967	TREACY, Emerson		61	Died in Woodland Hills, CA
	1960	TREADWELL, Laura		81	Died in Hollywood, CA
	1992	# TREE, Dorothy		85	Heart failure (in Englewood, NJ)
	1937	# TREE, Lady		72	After an operation from which she did not rally
	1989	TREEN, Mary		82	Cancer
	1989	TREGOE, William		67	Cardiac arrest
	1990	TRENKER, Luis		97	
	1988	TREVELYAN, John		83	
	1978	# TREVOR, Austin		80	Died in London, England
	1933	TREVOR, Hugh		30	Three-weeks after an appendectomy (in Los Angeles, CA)
	1980	TRIESAULT, Ivan		79	Heart failure (in Los Angeles, CA)
	1965	+ Trigger (Roy Rogers' horse)		33	Natural causes
	1954	TRIMBLE, Lawrence		69	Died at the Motion Picture Country House in Ca.
	1994	TROISI, Massimo		41	Heart attack (in Ostia, near Rome, Italy)
	1992	TROP, Jack Dunn		92	Respiratory infection (in Miami, FL)
	1975	+ TROTTER, John Scott		67	Cancer
	1987	TROUGHTON, Patrick		67	
	1967	+ TROWBRIDGE, Charles		85	
	1994	TROY, Louise		60	Breast cancer (at her home in Manhattan)
	1985	TRUBSHAWE, Michael		80	
	1994	TRUEMAN, Paula		96	Died in New York Hospital
•	1941	TRUESDALE, Howard		80	Heart attack (in Los Angeles, CA)
	1973	+ TRUEX, Ernest		83	Heart attack (in Fallbrook, CA)
	1984	+ TRUFFAUT, François		52	Brain cancer
	1977	TRUMAN, Ralph		77	Died in Ipswich, England
	1993	TRUSCOTT, John	★	57	During emergency heart surgery (in Melbourne)
•	1970	TRYON, Glenn		70	

• New entry.   # Original name (Pt. 7).   + Interment (Pt. 5).   243   ☆ Oscar nominee, ★ Oscar winner (Pt. 10)

YEAR	NAME		AGE	CAUSE AND/OR PLACE OF DEATH
1991	# TRYON, Tom		65	Stomach cancer
• 1980	# TSCHECHOWA, Olga		83	
1971	TSIANG, H. T.		71	
1984	TUBB, Ernest		70	Emphysema
1986	+ TUCKER, Forrest		71	Throat cancer
1921	# TUCKER, George Loane		49	After a years' illness (in Los Angeles, CA)
• 1949	# TUCKER, Harland		?	Heart attack (in CA)
1989	TUCKER, Julius L.		92	
1991	TUCKER, Lem		52	Liver failure
1986	TUCKER, Lorenzo		79	Cancer
1942	TUCKER, Richard (actor)		58	Heart attack (in Woodland Hills, CA) Do not confuse with singer
1975	+ TUCKER, Richard (singer)		60	Heart attack (Do not confuse with actor, d. 1942)
1966	#+ TUCKER, Sophie		82	Lung and kidney ailment (in New York, NY)
1989	TUCKER, Tommy		86	
1970	# TUFTS, Sonny		57	Pneumonia (in Santa Monica, CA)
1991	TULLY, Lee		?	Cancer
1982	TULLY, Tom	☆	74	Complications after a long illness
1992	TUNBERG, Karl		83	
• 1978	# TUNNEY, Gene		80	Blood poisoning (in Greenwich, CT)
1990	TUPPER, Loretta		84	Cancer
1956	TURNBULL, John		75	
1946	TURNER, Florence		61	After a long illness (in Woodland Hills, CA)
1923	TURNER, Fred A.		?	
1987	TURNER, Jerry		60	Throat cancer (in Baltimore, MD)
• 1995	# TURNER, Lana		75	After a long battle with throat cancer
1918	TURNER, Otis "Daddy"		?	
1992	TURNER, Teddy		75	Died in Horsforth, England
1940	#+ TURPIN, Ben		65	Heart disease (in Santa Monica, CA)
1963	#+ TUTTLE, Frank		70	
1986	+ TUTTLE, Lurene		79	
1958	# TWELVETREES, Helen		49	Overdose of sleeping pills (in Harrisburg, PA)
1957	# TWITCHELL, A. R. "Archie"		50	Killed in a midair collision over Pacoima, CA
1993	# TWITTY, Conway		59	Surgery complications after a stomach aneurysm (Springfield, MO)
1961	TYLER, Harry		73	Cancer (in Hollywood, CA)
1957	# TYLER, Judy		24	Killed in an automobile crash
1954	# TYLER, Tom		50	Heart attack after suffering crippling arthritis (in Hamtramck, MI)
1967	TYNAN, Brandon		91	Died at Lynwood Nursing Home in New York, NY
• 1949	TYRELL, John E.		46	Died in CA
	U			
1972	ULMER, Edgar G.		68	After a long illness
1971	ULRIC, Lenore		78	After several years of hospitalization
• 1966	UNDERWOOD, Loyal		73	
1990	UNGER, Bertil		69	Liver disease
1978	UNSWORTH, Geoffrey	★	64	Heart attack
1975	URE, Mary	☆	42	Accidental mix of alcohol and tranquilizers (in London, England)
1966	# URECAL, Minerva		71	Heart attack (in Glendale, CA)
• 1979	URZI, Saro		66	Heart attack (in San Giuseppe Vesuviano, Italy)
1944	USHER, Guy		69	After a brief illness (at his ranch in San Diego, CA)
• 1996	UYS, Jamie		74	Died at his home in Johannesburg, South Africa
	▼			
1974	# VAGUE, Vera		70	Died in Santa Barbara, CA
1954	VAJDA, Ernest		67	Heart attack
1962	VAL, Paul		75	
• 1918	VALE, Louise		?	Died in Madison, WI
1959	#+ VALENS, Ritchie		17	Airplane crash (along with Buddy Holly, near Mason City, IA)
1926	#+ VALENTINO, Rudolph		31	Peritonitis from a perforated ulcer and ruptured appendix (in N.Y.)
1987	VALENTY, Lili		86	
1983	VALERIE, Joan		68	Automobile accident
1956	# VALK, Frederick		55	Died in London, England
1986	#+ VALLEE, Rudy		84	Heart attack
1993	VALLI, June		64	Cancer
• 1980	VALLI, Romolo		54	Automobile accident (in Rome, Italy)
1968	#+ VALLI, Virginia (Farrell)		68	Following a stroke (in Palm Springs, CA)
• 1977	VALLIN, Richard "Rick"		57	
• 1932	VALLIS, Robert "Bob"		?	Died in Brighton, England

YEAR	NAME		AGE	CAUSE AND/OR PLACE OF DEATH
1993	VALVANO, Jim		45	After a 1-year bout with cancer (in Durham, NC)
1980	#+ VAN, Bobby		49	After surgery to remove a brain tumor (in Los Angeles, CA)
1968	VAN, Gus		80	After two brain operations when hit by a car in Miami Beach, FL
• 1974	VAN, Wally		93	Died in Englewood, NJ
• 1949	# VANBRUGH, Irene		76	Died in London, England
1947	VanBUREN, Mabel		69	After a short illness (in Hollywood, CA)
1994	VANCE, Danitra		35	Breast cancer (at her grandfather's home in Markham, IL)
1979	+ VANCE, Vivian		66	Cancer (in Belvedere, CA)
1989	+ VanCLEEF, Lee		64	Heart attack
1984	VanDYKE, Truman		86	Heart failure
1944	#+ VanDYKE, W. S. "Woody"	☆	53	After a 6-months' illness
1986	VanDYKE, Willard		79	Heart attack (while driving from New Mexico to Mass.)
1940	VANE, Denton		50	Heart attack (while walking in Union Hill, N.J.)
1989	VANEL, Charles		96	
1969	VanEYCK, Peter		55	Died in Zurich, Switzerland
• 1995	VanEYSSEN, John		73	Cancer (at a hospital in London, England)
1990	VanHEUSEN, Jimmy		77	
1991	VANOFF, Nick		61	Cardiac arrest
1973	VanROOTEN, Luis		66	Died in Chatham, MA
1977	VanSICKEL, Dale		69	After a lengthy illness (at his home in Newport Beach, CA)
1964	VanSLOAN, Edward		81	Died in San Francisco, CA
1946	VanTASSELL, Marie		72	Died in Oakland, CA
1958	VanZANDT, Philip		53	Overdose of sleeping pills (in Hollywood, CA)
1977	VanZANT, Ronnie		28	
1976	# VARCONI, Victor		85	Heart attack (in Santa Barbara, CA)
1958	VARDEN, Evelyn		65	Died in New York, NY
1989	VARDEN, Norma		90	Heart failure
1982	VARELA, Nina		83	
1969	VARLEY, Beatrice		73	
1992	VARSI, Diane	☆	54	Respiratory problems and Lyme disease (in Los Angeles, CA)
1955	VAUGHAN, Dorothy		65	Cerebral hemorrhage (in Hollywood, CA)
1990	VAUGHAN, Sarah		66	Lung cancer
1989	VAUGHAN, Skeeter		66	Heart attack
1990	+ VAUGHAN, Stevie Ray		35	Helicopter crash
1991	+ VAUGHN, Billy		72	Cancer
1957	VAUGHN, Hilda		60	
1994	VAWTER, Ron		45	A.I.D.S.-related heart attack (on a plane bound to NY)
1984	VEAZIE, Carol Eberts		89	
1988	VEHR, Bill		48	A.I.D.S.
1943	+ VEIDT, Conrad		50	Heart attack (in Los Angeles, CA)
1943	VEILLER, Bayard		74	After an illness of 2-months
1990	VEJAR, Rudolph		57	Respiratory failure
1944	#+ VELEZ, Lupe		36	Suicide (sleeping pills) in Beverly Hills, CA
1993	VENABLE, Evelyn		80	Cancer (in Post Falls, Idaho)
1974	VENABLE, Reginald		48	Heart attack (in Hollywood, Ca.)
• 1960	VENESS, Amy		84	Died in Saltdean, England
1992	VENTURA, Charlie		75	Lung cancer
• 1995	VENUTA, Benay		84	Lung cancer (at her home in Manhattan)
1978	VENUTI, Joe		81	Died in Seattle, WA
1981	# Vera-Ellen		55	Cancer (in Los Angeles, CA)
1958	VERMILYEA, Harold		68	
1984	VERNAC, Denise		66	
1967	# VERNE, Kaaren		49	Died in Hollywood, CA
1975	VERNO, Jerry		79	
1939	+ VERNON, Bobby		42	Heart attack (in Hollywood, CA)
• 1970	# VERNON, Dorothy		94	Heart disease (in Grenada Hills, CA)
1987	VERNON, Jackie		62	Apparent heart attack
1970	VERNON, Wally		65	Killed by a hit-and-run driver (at a crosswalk in Van Nuys, CA)
• 1976	# VESOTA, Bruno		54	Heart attack (in Culver City, CA)
1982	VESTOFF, Virginia		42	
• 1939	VIBART, Henry		75	
1979	VICIOUS, Sid		21	Overdose of heroin
1971	# VICKERS, Martha		46	After a long illness (in Van Nuys, CA)
1965	# VICTOR, Charles		69	Died in London, England
1983	VICTOR, Dee		?	After a long illness

...DEATHS OF MOVIE AND TELEVISION PERSONALITIES – BY NAME...

YEAR	NAME		AGE	CAUSE AND/OR PLACE OF DEATH
1945	VICTOR, Henry		46	Brain tumor (in Hollywood, CA)
• 1959	VIDAL, Henri		40	Heart attack (in Paris, France)
1959	VIDOR, Charles		58	Apparent heart attack
1977	# VIDOR, Florence		82	Died in Pacific Palisades, CA
1982	VIDOR, King	☆	88	Heart ailment
1953	VIERTEL, Berthold		68	Heart ailment (in Vienna, Austria)
1953	VIGNOLA, Robert G.		71	Died in Hollywood, CA
• 1934	VIGO, Jean		29	Rheumatic septicemia
1986	VIGRAN, Herbert		76	Cancer
1994	VILLARD, Tom		40	Pneumonia complicated by A.I.D.S. (at a L.A. hospital)
• 1958	VILLARREAL, Julio		73	Died in Mexico City, Mexico
1993	VILLECHAIZE, Herve "Tatoo"		50	Suicide (gunshot) in his North Hollywood home
1991	# VINCENT, Chuck		51	Heart attack after a bout with pneumonia
1957	VINCENT, James		74	After a long illness (in New York)
1989	+ VINCENT, Romo		80	
• 1966	# VINCENT, Sailor Billy		70	Heart attack (in Toluca Lake, CA)
1992	VINE, Sam		69	Cancer
1963	# VINTON, Arthur		?	Died in Guadalajara, Mexico
1951	VISAROFF, Michael		58	Pneumonia (in Hollywood, CA)
1976	VISCONTI, Luchino		69	Influenza/cardiac ailment
1983	# VITTE, Ray		33	Stopped breathing after forcible police arrest
1991	# VITTO, G. L.		69	Heart attack
1961	VIVIAN, Percival		70	Arteriosclerosis
1983	+ VIVYAN, John		67	Heart failure
• 1969	# VOGAN, Emmett		76	Septicemia and pneumonia (in Woodland Hills, CA)
1942	VOGEDING, Fredrik		52	Following a heart attack (in Los Angeles, CA)
1925	VOGEL, Henry		60	Heart disease
• 1967	VOGEL, Rudolf		67	Died in Munich, Germany
1994	VOLONTE, Gian Maria		61	Heart attack (in Florina, Greece)
1962	VonBLOCK, Bela		73	
1946	# VonBRINCKEN, Wilhelm		54	Following a ruptured artery (in Los Angeles, CA)
1989	VonCZIFFRA, Geza		88	
1964	VonELTZ, Theodore		70	After a long illness (in Woodland Hills, CA)
• 1991	#+ VonERICH, Chris		21	
• 1984	#+ VonERICH, David		25	
• 1993	#+ VonERICH, Kerry		33	
• 1987	#+ VonERICH, Michael		23	
1989	VonKARAJAN, Herbert		81	Heart failure
• 1956	# VonMETER, Harry		85	Died in CA
1943	VonSEYFFERTITZ, Gustav		80	Died in Woodland Hills, CA
1969	#+ VonSTERNBERG, Josef	☆	75	Heart attack
1968	VonSTROHEIM, Erich Jr.		52	Cancer
1957	# VonSTROHEIM, Erich Sr.	☆	71	Spinal cancer (in Paris, France)
1988	VonSTROHEIM, Valerie		91	
1947	VonTRAPP, Baron Georg		57	
1987	VonTRAPP, Marie Augusta		82	Congestive heart failure
1958	# VonTWARDOWSKI, Hans		60	Died in New York, NY
• 1961	VonWINTERSTEIN, Eduard		90	Died in East Berlin, Germany
1981	VonZELL, Harry		75	Cancer (in Woodland Hills, CA)
1992	VonZERNECK, Peter		84	Complications after surgery (in Burbank, CA)
1989	VOORHEES, Donald		85	Pneumonia
1981	VOSKOVEC, George		76	
1976	# VYE, Murvyn		62	Natural causes (while vacationing in Pompano Beach, FL)
	W			
1974	WADSWORTH, Henry		72	
1950	WADSWORTH, William		77	Died at Queens General Hospital in New York
1979	+ WAGENHEIM, Charles		83	Murdered (bludgeoned) in Hollywood, CA
1984	WAGGNER, George		90	Natural causes
1963	+ WAGNER, "Gorgeous" George		48	Heart attack
1965	WAGNER, Jack		68	Died in Hollywood, CA
• 1975	WAGNER, Max		73	Heart attack (in West Los Angeles, CA)
1992	WAGNER, Roger		78	Cancer
1964	WAGNER, William		79	Died in Hollywood, CA
• 1949	# WAITE, Malcolm		56	Died in Los Angeles, CA
1951	WAKEFIELD, Douglas		51	

• New entry.   # Original name (Pt. 7).   + Interment (Pt. 5).

246

☆ Oscar nominee, ★ Oscar winner (Pt. 10)

	YEAR	NAME		AGE	CAUSE AND/OR PLACE OF DEATH
	1971	WAKEFIELD, Hugh		83	Died in London, England
	1982	WAKELY, Jimmy		68	Heart failure
	1969	WALBURN, Raymond		81	Died in New York, NY
	1962	WALD, Jerry		51	
	1974	WALDIS, Otto		68	Heart attack
•	1945	WALDMULLER, Lizzi		41	Killed during an air raid (in Vienna, Austria)
	1957	WALDRIGE, Harold		50	
	1946	+ WALDRON, Charles D.		71	Died in Hollywood, CA
•	1952	WALDRON, Charles K.		37	Airplane crash (in Los Angeles, CA)
	1952	WALES, Ethel		71	Died in Hollywood, CA
	1980	# WALES, Wally		83	Pneumonia, after suffering a stroke (in Sheridan, WY)
	1982	WALKER, Betty		54	
	1992	WALKER, Bill		95	Cancer (in Woodland Hills, CA)
	1958	WALKER, Charlotte		80	Died in Kerville, Texas
	1971	WALKER, Cheryl		49	
	1956	WALKER, Hal		60	
	1968	WALKER, Helen		47	Cancer (in North Hollywood, CA)
	1949	WALKER, Johnnie		53	Coronary thrombosis (in New York, NY)
	1966	+ WALKER, June		61	
•	1995	WALKER, Junior		57	Cancer
	1975	WALKER, Lillian "Dimples"		87	Died in Trinidad, West Indies (where she had a home)
	1992	# WALKER, Nancy		69	Following a 2-year battle with lung cancer (in Studio City, CA)
	1971	WALKER, Nella		85	Heart disease (in Los Angeles, CA)
	1980	WALKER, Ray W.		76	Heart failure (in Los Angeles, CA)
	1951	WALKER, Robert		32	Respiratory failure (Do not confuse with R. "Bob" Walker, d. 1954)
•	1954	WALKER, Robert "Bob"		65	(Do not confuse with actor Robert Walker, d. 1951)
	1941	WALKER, Stuart		53	After a heart attack (at his Hollywood home)
	1994	WALKER, Sydney		73	After a brief bout with cancer (in San Francisco, CA)
	1975	WALKER, Walter "Wally"		74	Stroke
	1992	WALKER, William Arlen		74	Died in Lancaster, CA
	1990	WALL, Max		82	
	1990	# WALLACE, Jean		66	After an internal hemorrhage
	1938	# WALLACE, May		61	Heart disease (in Los Angeles, Ca.)
	1953	WALLACE, Morgan		65	Died in Tarzana, CA
	1978	# WALLACE, Regina		86	Stroke (in Englewood, N.J.)
	1951	WALLACE, Richard		57	
•	1995	WALLACH, Ira	☆	83	Complications following a stroke (in New York City)
	1992	WALLACK, Roy Homer		64	Pneumonia (in Van Nuys, CA)
	1977	+ WALLER, Eddy C.		88	Stroke (in Los Angeles, CA)
	1943	+ WALLER, Thomas "Fats"		39	Influenza and bronchial pneumonia (in Kansas City, MO)
	1983	WALLGREN, Gunn		69	After a long illness
	1961	+ WALLING, Effie B.		81	
•	1932	WALLING, William "Will"		59	
	1986	+ WALLIS, Hal		88	Died in his sleep
•	1949	WALLS, Tom		66	Died in Edwell, England
	1981	WALSH, George		92	Complications from pneumonia (in Pamona, CA)
	1981	# WALSH, Raoul		93	Apparent heart attack (in Simi Valley, CA)
	1991	WALTERS, Casey		75	After an illness brought on by a stroke
	1982	WALTERS, Charles	☆	70	Lung cancer
	1940	WALTERS, Hal		48	Killed by a German bomb during a WW2 air raid (in England)
	1991	WALTERS, Thorley		78	
	1936	+ WALTHALL, Henry B.		58	Chronic illness (near Monrovia, CA)
•	1971	#+ WALTHALL, Wallace		89	
	1961	# WALTON, Douglas		52	Died in New York
	1936	# WALTON, Fred		71	Pneumonia (in Los Angeles, CA)
	1993	WALTON, Gladys (Herbel)		90	Cancer (at a nursing home in Morro Bay, CA)
	1993	WANAMAKER, Sam		74	After a 5-yr. bout with cancer (in London)
	1981	WARBURTON, John		78	Cancer
•	1926	# WARD, Carrie		63	Died in Hollywood, CA
	1952	WARD, Fannie		80	After suffering a cerebral hemorrhage
•	1995	WARD, Janet		70	Comp. from a heart attack (at Mt. Sinai Med. Ctr. in NYC)
	1952	WARD, Lucille		72	Died in Dayton, Ohio
•	1967	# WARD, Warwick		76	
	1975	WARDE, Anthony		66	Died in Hollywood, CA
•	1980	WARDE, Harlan		?	

YEAR	NAME	AGE	CAUSE AND/OR PLACE OF DEATH
1939	WARE, Helen	61	Throat infection (in Carmel, CA)
1951	+ WARFIELD, David	84	Died in New York
1991	# WARFIELD, Marjorie	88	Pneumonia
1987	+ WARHOL, Andy	59	Cardiac arrest (gall bladder surgery)
1984	WARING, Fred	84	Stroke
1993	WARING, Richard	82	Natural causes
1986	WARNER, Gertrude	68	Cancer
1958	#+ WARNER, H. B. ☆	82	Died in Los Angeles, CA
1958	+ WARNER, Harry M.	76	Cerebral occlusion
1978	WARNER, Jack L.	86	
1995	+ WARNER, Jack M.	79	Cancer (at Cedars-Sinai Med. Ctr. in Los Angeles, CA)
1927	+ WARNER, Sam	40	Sinus infection/brain abscess/pneumonia
1986	WARNERS, Robert	29	
1990	WARREN, Betty	83	
1971	# WARREN, C. Denier	82	Died in Torquay, England
1990	WARREN, Charles Marquis	77	Following surgery for a heart aneurysm
1940	WARREN, E. Alyn	64	Died in Los Angeles, CA
1983	WARREN, Flip	69	
1940	WARREN, Fred H.	60	Ruptured ulcer (in Hollywood, CA)
1981	#+ WARREN, Harry (songwriter) ★	87	Died at Cedars-Sinai Med. Ctr., Los Angeles, CA
1988	WARREN, Jerry	65	Lung cancer
1993	WARREN, Joseph	77	Respiratory failure (at Village Nursing Home, NY)
1995	WARRILOW, David	60	Complications of A.I.D.S. (in New York City)
1993	WARRISS, Ben	83	
1972	# WARWICK, John	67	Heart attack
1964	# WARWICK, Robert	85	Following a brief illness (in Los Angeles, CA)
1988	WASHBOURNE, Mona	84	
1929	WASHBURN, Alice	68	After an illness of several years (in Oshkosh, WI)
1960	WASHBURN, Bryant Jr.	?	
1963	WASHBURN, Bryant Sr.	74	Heart attack (in Hollywood, CA)
1963	# WASHINGTON, Dinah	39	Overdose of sleeping pills (in Detroit, MI)
1994	WASHINGTON, Fredi	91	
1919	WASHINGTON, Jesse	?	Drowned during a filming accident
1988	WASHINGTON, Vernon	64	
1995	WATERMAN, Willard	80	Bone marrow disease (at his home in Burlingame, CA)
1993	WATERS, Chuck	70	Died in Saginaw, Michigan
1990	WATERS, Elsie	95	
1977	+ WATERS, Ethel ☆	80	Heart ailment (in Chatsworth, CA)
1960	WATKIN, Pierre	70	Died in Hollywood, CA
1968	WATSON, Benjamin T. "Ben"	?	
1965	# WATSON, Bobby	77	Died in Hollywood, CA
1989	WATSON, Douglass	68	Heart attack
1962	WATSON, Lucile ☆	83	Died in New York, NY
1965	WATSON, Minor	75	Died in Alton, IL
1937	WATSON, Roy	61	
1966	# WATSON, Wylie	67	
1987	WATT, Harry	80	
1975	WATTIS, Richard	62	Heart attack (in London, England)
1966	WATTS, Charles	?	After a long illness (in Nashville, TN)
1990	WATTS, Jr., Leroy	72	
1980	WATTS, Queenie	52	Cancer (in London, England)
1967	#+ WAXMAN, Franz	60	Cancer
1985	WAYNE, Carol	42	Drowned
1995	# WAYNE, David	81	After a long bout with lung cancer (in Los Angeles, CA)
1979	#+ WAYNE, John ★	72	Lung and stomach cancer (in Los Angeles, CA)
1990	WAYNE, Johnny	72	Cancer
1970	WAYNE, Naunton	69	Died in Subiton, England
1959	WAYNE, Robert "Duke"	55	Following a heart attack
1989	WEAVER, Carl Earl	36	A.I.D.S.
1983	# WEAVER, Doodles	71	Apparent suicide (gunshot)
1992	WEAVER, Jackson	72	Heart & kidney failure
1982	WEBB, Alan	75	
1966	#+ WEBB, Clifton ☆	72	Heart attack (in Beverly Hills, CA)
1959	WEBB, Harry	63	Heart attack
1982	+ WEBB, Jack	62	Heart attack

...DEATHS OF MOVIE AND TELEVISION PERSONALITIES — BY NAME...

YEAR	NAME		AGE	CAUSE AND/OR PLACE OF DEATH
1935	WEBB, Millard		42	Intestinal ailment (in Los Angeles, CA)
1993	WEBB, Richard		77	Suicide (gunshot) after suffering a long illness (in Van Nuys, CA)
1990	WEBB, Robert D.		87	Following a long illness
1982	WEBB, Roy		94	Heart attack
1989	WEBBER, Robert		64	Amyotrophic lateral sclerosis
1942	#+ WEBER, Joe		74	After an illness of 2-months (in Los Angeles, CA)
1990	WEBER, Karl		74	Congestive feart failure
1939	WEBER, Lois		56	After a long illness (in Los Angeles, CA)
1918	# WEBER, Rex		29	Spanish influenza
1947	WEBSTER, Ben		82	Following an operation (in Hollywood, CA)
1991	WEBSTER, Byron		58	A.I.D.S.
1984	WEBSTER, Paul Francis		77	
1975	WEED, Leland T.		74	Stroke (in Prescott, Arizona)
1972	# WEEDE, Robert		69	After several months in a hospital
1993	WEEDIN, Harfield		77	Died in Boise, Idaho, of undisclosed causes
1954	WEEKS, Barbara		47	
1968	WEEKS, Marion		81	Died in New York
1963	WEEMS, Ted		62	Emphysema (in Tulsa, OK)
• 1948	WEGENER, Paul		74	Died in Berlin, Germany
• 1996	WEI, Lo		76	Heart failure (in a Hong Kong hospital)
1968	WEIDLER, Virginia		41	Heart attack
• 1951	WEIGEL, Paul		83	
1967	WEISBART, David		52	Stroke (while playing golf)
1987	WEISENBORN, Gordon		64	
1984	#+ WEISSMULLER, Johnny		79	Heart disease
1991	WEIST, Dwight		81	Heart attack
1960	WELCH, Joseph L.		69	
1976	WELCH, Niles		81	Died in Laguna Nigel, CA
1992	+ WELK, Lawrence		89	Pneumonia
1993	WELLES, Gwen		42	Cancer (at her home in Santa Monica, CA)
1985	# WELLES, Orson	☆	70	Heart attack
1946	WELLESLEY, Charles		71	Died at the Brunswick Home, Amityville, L.I., NY
1993	WELLINGTON, Valerie		33	Brain aneurysm (in Maywood, IL)
1975	#+ WELLMAN, William A.	☆	79	Leukemia
1994	WELLS, Frank		62	Helicopter crash (in central Nevada)
• 1946	WELLS, H. G.		80	Died in London, England
• 1949	WELLS, Marie		55	Suicide (sleeping pills) in Hollywood, CA
1992	+ WELLS, Mary		49	After a long bout with cancer
1947	WELLS, Ted		48	Heart attack
1985	WELSH, John		70	Cancer
• 1995	WELSH, Patricia		79	Pneumonia (in Green Valley, AZ)
1993	# WELSH, Ronnie		52	Brain cancer (in New York)
1946	# WELSH, William		76	Died in Los Angeles, CA
1974	# WENGRAF, John E.		76	
1974	# WENTWORTH, Martha		?	Died in Sherman Oaks, CA
1956	# WERBISECK, Gisela		81	After a 3-year illness
1984	# WERNER, Oskar	☆	61	Heart attack
• 1965	WERNICKE, Otto		72	Died in Munich, Germany
1965	# WESSEL, Dick		51	Heart attack (in Studio City, CA)
1945	# WESSELHOEFT, Eleanor		72	
1979	# WESSON, Dick		59	Suicide (gunshot) in Costa Mesa, CA
1975	# WEST, Billy		82	Heart attack (leaving Hollywood Park racetrack, CA)
1984	+ WEST, Brooks		67	Cerebral hemorrhage
1943	WEST, Charles H.		57	
1943	WEST, Claudine		59	
1991	# WEST, Dottie		58	Complications after an automobile accident
1989	WEST, Lockwood		83	Cancer
1985	WEST, Madge		93	
1980	#+ WEST, Mae		88	Complications following a stroke (in Hollywood, CA)
1944	# WEST, Pat		55	Died in Hollywood, CA
1952	WEST, Roland		65	Heart ailment (in Santa Monica, Ca.)
• 1918	WEST, William		?	Injuries from a fall (in New York, NY)
1935	WESTCOTT, Gordon		31	After falling from his horse in a polo game (in Hollywood, CA)
1971	WESTERFIELD, James		59	Heart attack
1942	# WESTLEY, Helen		67	

YEAR	NAME		AGE	CAUSE AND/OR PLACE OF DEATH
1970	WESTMAN, Nydia		68	Cancer (in Burbank, CA)
1973	# WESTMORE, Bud		55	Heart attack
1967	+ WESTMORE, Ernest		63	After a heart attack
1985	WESTMORE, Frank		62	After treatment for a cardiac condition
1940	WESTMORE, Monte		39	Heart condition after a tonsilectomy
1970	#+ WESTMORE, Perc		65	Coronary occlusion
1973	# WESTMORE, Wally		67	Stroke
1960	WESTON, Doris		42	Cancer (in New York, NY)
• 1996	WESTON, Jack		71	After a 6 yr. bout with lymphoma (at Lenox Hill Hosp. in New York)
1985	WESTON, Steve		45	Results of a fall from the roof of his home
1989	WETMORE, Joan		77	Cancer
1957	+ WHALE, James		60	Died in Hollywood, CA
1974	# WHALEN, Michael		72	Bronchial pneumonia (in Woodland Hills, CA)
1992	WHALEY, Jim		44	Heart attack
• 1963	# WHEAT, Lawrence "Larry"		87	
• 1966	# WHEATCROFT, Stanhope		77	Heart attack (in Woodland Hills, CA)
1991	WHEATLEY, Alan		84	Heart attack
1991	WHEDON, John Ogden		86	Pneumonia
1986	WHEEL, Patricia		61	
1968	#+ WHEELER, Bert		72	Emphysema (in New York, NY)
1990	WHEELER, Jerry B.		44	A.I.D.S.
1993	+ WHELAN, Arleen (Cagney)		78	Following a stroke (in Orange County, CA)
1993	WHELAN, Kenneth		72	Died in New York
1957	WHELAN, Tim		63	Died in Beverly Hills, CA
1975	WHIPPER, Leigh		97	
• 1960	WHITAKER, Charles "Slim"		66	Heart attack
1983	WHITE, Alice		78	Stroke
1991	WHITE, Carol		47	
1989	WHITE, Chrissie		94	
1990	WHITE, David		74	Run over by an automobile
1992	WHITE, Glenn		42	A.I.D.S.
• 1945	WHITE, J. Fisher		79	
1988	WHITE, John Sylvester		68	Pancreatic cancer
1985	WHITE, Jules J.		84	Alzheimer's disease
1990	WHITE, Larry		74	Heart attack
1949	# WHITE, Lee Roy "Lasses"		61	Died in Hollywood, CA
1948	WHITE, Leo		68	Died in Hollywood, CA
• 1955	WHITE, Lew		52	Died in New York
1935	WHITE, Marjorie		27	Automobile accident
1938	WHITE, Pearl		49	Liver ailment (in Paris, France)
1969	WHITE, Ruth		55	Cancer (in Perth Amboy, NJ)
• 1995	# WHITE, Slappy		74	Heart attack (at his home in Brigantine, N.J.)
1987	WHITE, Ward		60	Cancer
1962	WHITEHEAD, John		89	
1967	WHITEMAN, Paul		77	Heart attack
1961	WHITING, Jack		59	Died in New York
1984	WHITING, Napoleon		75	Heart attack
• 1958	# WHITLEY, Crane		?	
1989	WHITLEY, Keith		33	Alcohol poisoning
1979	WHITLEY, Ray		77	While on a fishing trip (in Mexico)
• 1966	WHITLOCK, T. Lloyd		75	
1954	WHITMAN, Ernest		61	Following a heart attack
1958	#+ WHITMAN, Gayne		68	Heart attack (in Hollywood, CA)
1969	WHITNEY, Claire		79	Died in Sylmar, CA
1982	WHITNEY, John Hay "Jock"		77	After a long illness
1983	WHITNEY, Michael		52	After a heart attack in a restaurant
1972	# WHITNEY, Peter		55	Heart attack (in Santa Barbara, CA)
• 1928	WHITNEY, Ralph		54	Injuries from a fall (in Los Angeles, CA)
1961	WHITTELL, Josephine		?	Died in Hollywood, CA
1948	WHITTY, May	☆	82	Died in Beverly Hills, CA
1966	WHORF, Richard		60	Heart attack after hospitalization for an ulcer (in Santa Monica, CA)
1987	WIARD, William		59	Lung cancer
• 1995	# WICKES, Mary		85	Complications from surgery (at UCLA Med. Ctr. in Los Angeles)
1994	WICKS, Mark Randall		43	A.I.D.S. complications (in Los Angeles, CA)
1986	WIECK, Dorothea		78	

...DEATHS OF MOVIE AND TELEVISION PERSONALITIES — BY NAME...

YEAR	NAME		AGE	CAUSE AND/OR PLACE OF DEATH
• 1938	WIENE, Robert		57	Cancer (in Paris, France)
1970	+ WIERE, Sylvester		60	Kidney ailment (in Hidden Hills, CA)
• 1968	WIFSTRAND, Naima		78	Died in Sweden
1994	WIGGINS, James		30	A.I.D.S. (in Goldsboro, NC)
1993	WILBERN, George E.		77	Emphysema (in Los Angeles, CA)
1973	WILBUR, Crane		83	Following a stroke (in North Hollywood, CA)
• 1974	WILCOX, Frank		66	Died in Northridge, CA
1964	WILCOX, Fred M.		59	Died at his Beverly Hills, Ca. home
1977	WILCOX, Herbert		85	Following a long illness
1955	WILCOX, Robert		45	Heart attack (on a train near Rochester, NY)
1984	WILCOXON, Henry		78	Congestive heart failure
1989	#+ WILDE, Cornel	☆	74	Leukemia
• 1995	# WILDER, Honeychile		76	Cancer (at Mem. Sloan-Kettering Cancer Ctr., NY)
1983	WILDER, Marie		53	
1915	WILDER, Marshall P.		56	Heart disease, aggravated by pneumonia
1979	WILDING, Michael		66	Injuries from a fall (at his home in Chichester, England)
1993	WILEY, Jan (Greene)		83	Cancer (in Rancho Palos Verdes, CA)
1971	WILKERSON, Guy		72	Cancer (in Hollywood, CA)
1993	WILKINSON, Kate		76	Bone cancer (in New York)
• 1968	WILLARD, Jess		86	Cerebral hemorrhage (in Los Angeles, CA)
1988	WILLES, Jean		65	Liver cancer
1948	# WILLIAM, Warren		52	Multiple myeloma and blood disease (in Encino, CA)
1922	# WILLIAMS, Bert		49	Pneumonia (in New York, NY)
1992	# WILLIAMS, Bill		77	Complications of a brain tumor (in Burbank, CA)
• 1961	WILLIAMS, Bramsby		91	Died in London, England
1990	WILLIAMS, Brenda		43	Cancer
1958	WILLIAMS, Charles B.		59	After a long illness (in Hollywood, CA)
1928	WILLIAMS, Clara		?	Following an operation (at her home in Los Angeles, CA)
1989	WILLIAMS, Clark		83	
1927	WILLIAMS, Cora		56	Heart trouble (in Los Angeles, CA)
1927	#+ WILLIAMS, Earle		47	Bronchial pneumonia (in Los Angeles, CA)
1987	WILLIAMS, Emlyn		81	Following cancer surgery
• 1995	WILLIAMS, Frances E.		89	Complications from a stroke (in Los Angeles, CA)
1985	WILLIAMS, Grant		54	Peritonitis
1962	WILLIAMS, Guinn "Big Boy"		63	Uremic poisoning (in Hollywood, CA)
1989	# WILLIAMS, Guy		65	Heart attack
1953	+ WILLIAMS, Hank Sr.		29	Heart attack from excessive drinking (in Oak Hill, WV)
• 1957	WILLIAMS, Harcourt		77	
1969	# WILLIAMS, Hugh		65	Died in London, England
1983	WILLIAMS, John		80	Following an aneurysm (Do not confuse with John J. Williams)
1918	WILLIAMS, John J.		62	Heart failure (Do not confuse with John Williams, d. 1983)
1960	WILLIAMS, Kathlyn		72	Died in Hollywood, CA
1988	WILLIAMS, Kenneth		62	Heart attack
1965	WILLIAMS, Mack		58	Heart attack (in Hollywood, CA)
1994	WILLIAMS, Marion		66	Vascular disease (in Philadelphia, PA)
• 1996	WILLIAMS, Palmer		79	Prostate cancer
• 1973	WILLIAMS, Paul		34	Suicide (sang with "The Temptations")
1969	+ WILLIAMS, Rhys		76	Died in Santa Monica, CA
1931	WILLIAMS, Robert		31	Peritonitis after an operation for appendicitis
1969	WILLIAMS, Spencer "Andy"		76	Kidney ailment (in Los Angeles, CA)
1983	+ WILLIAMS, Tennessee		71	After choking on a plastic bottle cap
1985	WILLIAMS, Tex		68	Cancer
1992	WILLIAMS, Tony		64	
1989	WILLINGER, Laszlo		80	
• 1995	WILLINGHAM, Calder		72	Lung cancer (at a hospital in Laconia, N.H.)
1989	# WILLIS, Matt		75	
1988	WILLMAN, Noel		70	Heart attack
1990	WILLOCK, Dave		81	Complications following a stroke
1963	WILLS, Beverly		29	Killed in a fire (in Palm Springs, CA)
1975	WILLS, Bob		70	Bronchial pneumonia (in Ft. Worth, TX)
1978	WILLS, Chill	☆	75	Died in Encino, CA
• 1951	WILLS, Drusilla		66	Died in London, England
1984	# WILLSON, Meredith		82	Heart failure
1991	WILSHIN, Sunday		86	
1930	WILSON, Benjamin F.		54	Heart ailment (in Glendale, CA)

...DEATHS OF MOVIE AND TELEVISION PERSONALITIES — BY NAME...

	YEAR	NAME		AGE	CAUSE AND/OR PLACE OF DEATH
	1994	WILSON, Billy		59	Complications from A.I.D.S. (in New York)
•	1948	WILSON, Charles Cahill		53	Esophagal hemorrhage
	1941	# WILSON, Clarence H.		64	Died in Hollywood, CA
	1983	WILSON, Dennis		39	Drowned
	1982	WILSON, Don		81	Stroke
	1953	WILSON, Dooley		59	Died in Los Angeles, CA
	1987	WILSON, Earl		79	After a long illness
	1981	# WILSON, Edith		83	Cerebral hemorrhage (in Chcago, IL)
•	1966	WILSON, Jack		49	Cerebral hemorrhage (in Los Angeles, CA)
	1990	WILSON, Josephine		86	Heart attack
	1993	WILSON, Lester		51	Heart attack (in Los Angeles, CA)
	1988	WILSON, Lois		93	Pneumonia
	1986	WILSON, Margery		89	
	1972	#+ WILSON, Marie		56	Cancer (in Hollywood Hills, CA)
	1991	WILSON, Richard		75	Pancreatic cancer
	1991	WILSON, Stu		87	
	1986	WILSON, Teddy		73	Following intestinal surgery
	1991	WILSON, Theodore		47	Stroke
•	1965	WILSON, Tom		84	Died in California
	1989	WILSON, Trey		40	Cerebral hemorrhage
	1964	WILSON, Whip		49	Heart attack (in Hollywood, CA)
	1957	WILTON, Eric		73	
	1972	+ WINCHELL, Walter		74	Died in Los Angeles, CA
	1989	WINCKLER, Robert		62	Stomach cancer
	1972	# WINDSOR, Claire		75	Heart attack (in Los Angeles, CA)
	1986	WINDSOR, Marie		64	
	1960	WINDUST, Bretaigne		54	Died in New York
•	1969	WING, Dan		46	Heart attack (in Fresno, CA)
	1957	WING, Paul R.		65	Following a heart attack
	1974	# WING, Red		90	
	1969	# WINNINGER, Charles		84	Died in Palm Springs, CA
	1991	WINSLOW, Dick		75	Complications from diabetes
	1991	WINTERS, Bernie		58	Cancer
	1989	WINTERS, Roland		84	Stroke
	1950	# WINTHROP, Joy		86	
	1980	WINTLE, Julian		67	
•	1958	WINTON, Jane		51	Died in New York
	1984	#+ WINWOOD, Estelle		101	Heart failure
	1959	#+ WITHERS, Grant		54	Suicide (sleeping pills) in Hollywood, CA
•	1968	WITHERS, Isabel		72	Died in Hollywood, CA
	1957	WITHERSPOON, Cora		67	Died in Las Crusas, NM
	1990	WITTENBERG, Marguerite N.		77	Cancer
	1990	WITTENBERG, Paul B.		63	Cancer
	1956	WIX, Florence E.		73	Cancer (in Woodland Hills, CA)
	1993	WOLF, Harry L.		85	Died at Cedars-Sinai Hospital, CA
	1994	WOLFBERG, Dennis		48	After a 2-yr. battle with melanoma (in Culver City, CA)
	1992	WOLFE, Ian		95	Natural causes (in Los Angeles, CA)
	1971	# WOLFF, Frank		43	Suicide (slashed his throat with a safety razor)
	1931	WOLHEIM, Louis		50	Stomach cancer (in Los Angeles, CA)
	1993	WONDER, Tommy		78	Complications from an ulcer (in New York City)
	1961	#+ WONG, Anna May		54	Heart attack (in Santa Monica, CA)
	1989	WONG, Iris		68	
•	1978	WONG, Joe		75	Heart condition
•	1940	# WONG, Mary		25	Suicide (hanging) in Los Angeles, CA
•	1960	WONTNER, Arthur		85	Died in London, England
	1965	WOOD, Britt		70	After a 6-month illness (in Hollywood, CA)
	1983	WOOD, Cindi		52	
	1966	WOOD, Douglas		85	Died in Woodland Hills, CA
•	1978	#+ WOOD, Ed		54	Heart attack brought on by acute alcoholism
	1956	WOOD, Freeman N.		59	After a short illness (in Hollywood, CA)
	1990	WOOD, George		56	Diabetes
	1981	#+ WOOD, Natalie	☆	43	Accidental drowning (off Catalina Island, CA)
	1978	WOOD, Peggy	☆	86	Died in Stamford, CT
	1949	+ WOOD, Sam	☆	66	Heart attack
•	1958	WOOD, Victor		44	Died in London, England

• New entry.   # Original name (Pt. 7).   + Interment (Pt. 5).

252

☆ Oscar nominee, ★ Oscar winner (Pt. 10)

...DEATHS OF MOVIE AND TELEVISION PERSONALITIES — BY NAME...

YEAR	NAME		AGE	CAUSE AND/OR PLACE OF DEATH
1973	WOODBRIDGE, George		66	
1989	WOODBURY, Joan		73	Respiratory failure
• 1995	WOODMAN, William		63	Cardiac arrest (in New York)
1980	WOODRUFF, Eleanor		89	
• 1942	WOODS, Arthur		38	Killed in action during World War 2
1968	# WOODS, Harry L. Sr.		79	Uremia (in Los Angeles, CA)
1983	WOODS, Maurice		45	Cancer
1972	WOODWARD, Robert "Bob"		63	Heart attack (in Hollywood, CA)
1989	WOOLAND, Norman		83	Following several strokes
1992	# WOOLERY, Ade		82	Cancer (in Santa Monica, CA)
1994	WOOLF, Charles		67	Cancer (in Sherman Oaks, CA)
1943	WOOLLCOTT, Alexander		56	Heart attack (while broadcasting at CBS in New York, NY)
1963	#+ WOOLLEY, Monty	☆	74	Kidney and heart ailment (in Albany, NY)
1938	+ WOOLSEY, Robert		48	Kidney ailment
1992	#+ WORDEN, Hank		91	Died in his sleep of natural causes (at his Brentwood, CA, home)
1973	WORLOCK, Frederick		87	Cerebral ischemia after a long illness (in Woodland Hills, CA)
1985	WORMS, Robert A. III		52	Heart failure
1991	WORSLEY, Wallace Jr.		82	Heart failure
• 1963	# WORTH, Constance		48	
• 1956	WORTH, Peggy		64	Died in New York, NY
• 1941	WORTHINGTON, William J.		68	Died in Beverly Hills, CA
• 1968	WRAY, Aloha		39	Died in Hollywood, CA
1940	# WRAY, John		52	After a long illness (in Los Angeles, CA)
1950	WRAY, Ted		41	Following a heart attack
1962	WREN, Sam		65	
1989	WRIGHT, Ben		74	Heart failure after heart surgery
• 1995	WRIGHT, Eric "Easy-E"		31	A.I.D.S.
• 1943	WRIGHT, Haidee		44	Died in London, England
• 1940	WRIGHT, Hugh E.		60	Died in Windsor, England
1965	WRIGHT, Mack V.		69	Died in Boulder City, Nevada
1962	WRIGHT, Will		71	Cancer (in Hollywood) Do not confuse with William Wright d. 1949
1949	WRIGHT, William		37	Cancer (in Ensenada, Mex.) Do not confuse with Will Wright d. 1962
1993	WRIGHTSON, Earl		77	Heart failure (in E. Norwich, CT)
1945	WU, Honorable		42	Died in Hollywood, CA
• 1958	WUEST, Ida		74	Died in Berlin, Germany
1925	WUNDERLEE, Frank		50	Apoplexy attack (while dining at the Green Room Club in NYC)
1990	WURSCHMIDT, Sigrid		37	Metastasized breast cancer
1992	WYATT, Allan Sr.		72	Cancer (in Burbank, CA)
1956	+ WYCHERLY, Margaret	☆	74	Died in New York
1988	WYCKOFF, Michael		69	After a stroke
1992	WYLER, Jorie		61	After a brief illness (in New York, NY)
1981	+ WYLER, William	★	79	
• 1970	+ WYMARK, Patrick		44	Found dead in his hotel room of natural causes (in Australia)
1966	#+ WYNN, Ed	☆	79	Cancer (in Los Angeles, CA)
1936	WYNN, Hugh		46	
1986	#+ WYNN, Keenan		70	Cancer
1971	WYNN, Nan		55	Cancer (in Santa Monica, CA)
1990	WYNNE, Paul		47	A.I.D.S.
1964	# WYNYARD, Diana	☆	58	Kidney ailment (in London, England)
	X			
1965	#+ X, Malcolm		39	(See Malcolm Little)
	Y			
1965	YACONELLI, Frank		67	Lung cancer (in Los Angeles, CA)
1986	YALE, Joseph		36	Complications from A.I.D.S.
1951	YARBOROUGH, Barton		51	Died in Hollywood, CA
• 1944	YARDE, Margaret		65	Died in London, England
1992	YARMY, Dick		59	Lung cancer (in Studio City, CA)
1991	YATES, Sterling		65	Cerebral hemorrhage
1928	YEARSLEY, Ralph		31	Suicide (at his home in Hollywood, CA)
1991	YELLEN, Jack		98	
1992	YEVSTIGNEEV, Yevgeny		66	Cardio-vascular problems (in London, England)
1969	YORK, Chick		83	
1992	YORK, Dick		63	Emphysema and degenerative spinal condition (Grand Rapids, MI)
1952	YORK, Duke		49	Suicide (found shot to death in his Hollywood home)
• 1934	# YORKE, Edith		?	

• New entry. # Original name (Pt. 7). + Interment (Pt. 5).   253   ☆ Oscar nominee, ★ Oscar winner (Pt. 10)

...DEATHS OF MOVIE AND TELEVISION PERSONALITIES — BY NAME...

YEAR	NAME		AGE	CAUSE AND/OR PLACE OF DEATH
1945	# YOST, Herbert A.		65	Died in New York, NY
1946	YOUMANS, Vincent		47	Tuberculosis
1971	YOUNG, Carleton G.		64	Cancer (in Hollywood, CA)
1960	YOUNG, Clara Kimball		69	Died in Woodland Hills, CA
1951	YOUNG, Clifton		34	Asphyxiation after falling asleep while smoking (in Los Angeles, CA)
• 1995	YOUNG, Donald Jr.		63	Coronary artery disease (at his home in Los Angeles, CA)
1978	#+ YOUNG, Gig	★	64	Suicide (gunshot) after shooting his 5th wife (in New York, NY)
1992	YOUNG, Jack Haydn		81	Neurological illness
1993	YOUNG, Marvin		90	Natural causes (in Los Angeles, CA)
1934	+ YOUNG, Mary		77	Following a 3-month illness
1958	YOUNG, Noah		?	
• 1940	YOUNG, Olive		33	Internal hemorrhages (in Bayonne, NJ)
1953	YOUNG, Roland	☆	65	Died at his home in New York, NY
1993	# YOUNG, Skip "Wally"		63	Found dead at his CA home of natural causes
1936	YOUNG, Tammany		49	Died in his sleep of a heart attack (in Hollywood, CA)
1994	YOUNG, Terence		79	Heart attack (at a hospital in Cannes, France)
• 1956	+ YOUNG, Victor	★	55	Cancer
1957	YOUNG, Walter		79	After a brief illness
• 1995	YOUNGERMAN, Joseph C.		89	Complications from a stroke (at Cedars-Sinai Med. Ctr. in L.A.)
1974	YOUNGSON, Robert		56	Died at St. Vincent's Hospital in New York
1966	# YOWLACHIE, Chief		74	Pneumonia
1950	+ YULE, Joe		55	Heart attack (in Hollywood, CA)
1974	#+ YURKA, Blanche		87	Arteriosclerosis
	Z			
1947	ZAHLER, Lee		53	
1994	ZAMORA, Pedro		22	Neurological complications from A.I.D.S. (in Miami, FL)
1991	ZAMPA, Luigi		86	After a long illness
1994	# ZANE, Bartine		96	Heart attack (in Burbank, CA)
1979	#+ ZANUCK, Darryl F.		77	Pulmonary embolism aggravated by pneumonia
1982	+ ZANUCK, Virginia Fox		83	
1993	#+ ZAPPA, Frank		52	Prostate cancer (in Los Angeles, CA)
1986	# ZAREMBA, Jack		77	Heart attack
1989	ZAVATTINA, Cesare		86	
1952	# ZEARS, Marjorie		41	
1989	ZEMAN, Karel		78	
1994	# ZETTERLING, Mai		68	Cancer (in London, England)
1932	+ ZIEGFELD, Florenz		63	Pleurisy and pneumonia
1975	# ZIMBALIST, Al		59	Heart attack
1985	ZIMBALIST, Efrem Sr.		95	
1958	ZIMBALIST, Sam		57	Heart attack
1991	ZORNOW, Edith		72	Cancer
• 1962	+ ZUCCO, Frances		?	Throat cancer following an overdose of radiation therapy
1960	+ ZUCCO, George		74	Pneumonia (at Monterey Sanitarium, S. San Gabriel, CA)
1976	ZUKOR, Adolph		103	
1994	ZUKOR, Eugene		97	Died at his home in Beverly Hills, CA
1991	ZWICKLER, Phil		36	Complications from A.I.D.S.

3

STATISTICAL
SUMMARY
OF DEATHS

STATISTICAL SUMMARY OF DEATHS

TOTAL NUMBER OF DEATHS LISTED

8,009

TOTAL NUMBER OF DEATHS LISTED — BY SEX

Males 5,947   Females 2,062

TOTAL NUMBER OF DEATHS LISTED — BY YEAR

Year		Year	
1912	1	1955	85
1913	1	1956	83
1915	6	1957	97
1916	5	1958	101
1917	8	1959	113
1918	30	1960	88
1919	14	1961	101
1920	7	1962	93
1921	9	1963	98
1922	9	1964	109
1923	11	1965	117
1924	9	1966	115
1925	22	1967	128
1926	15	1968	125
1927	14	1969	127
1928	20	1970	107
1929	21	1971	131
1930	16	1972	115
1931	32	1973	145
1932	21	1974	137
1933	38	1975	129
1934	34	1976	120
1935	28	1977	111
1936	42	1978	122
1937	50	1979	131
1938	43	1980	145
1939	43	1981	117
1940	73	1982	149
1941	49	1983	142
1942	45	1984	144
1943	55	1985	168
1944	57	1986	171
1945	61	1987	189
1946	67	1988	213
1947	69	1989	271
1948	86	1990	315
1949	64	1991	346
1950	82	1992	361
1951	71	1993	322
1952	72	1994	250
1953	77	1995	255
1954	66	1996	86

...STATISTICAL SUMMARY OF DEATHS...

TOTAL NUMBER OF DEATHS LISTED – BY AGE

Age	Count		Age	Count
Age 1	1		Age 58	131
Age 6	1		Age 59	141
Age 7	2		Age 60	166
Age 8	1		Age 61	130
Age 10	1		Age 62	148
Age 12	1		Age 63	157
Age 13	2		Age 64	185
Age 14	1		Age 65	192
Age 16	3		Age 66	175
Age 17	2		Age 67	195
Age 18	3		Age 68	195
Age 19	5		Age 69	203
Age 20	8		Age 70	195
Age 21	7		Age 71	201
Age 22	11		Age 72	208
Age 23	9		Age 73	205
Age 24	9		Age 74	196
Age 25	14		Age 75	209
Age 26	15		Age 76	178
Age 27	21		Age 77	213
Age 28	17		Age 78	176
Age 29	30		Age 79	176
Age 30	29		Age 80	181
Age 31	22		Age 81	172
Age 32	22		Age 82	184
Age 33	42		Age 83	176
Age 34	33		Age 84	148
Age 35	39		Age 85	132
Age 36	33		Age 86	131
Age 37	42		Age 87	102
Age 38	50		Age 88	81
Age 39	52		Age 89	83
Age 40	49		Age 90	71
Age 41	48		Age 91	48
Age 42	75		Age 92	39
Age 43	60		Age 93	44
Age 44	67		Age 94	30
Age 45	89		Age 95	30
Age 46	69		Age 96	27
Age 47	81		Age 97	10
Age 48	83		Age 98	12
Age 49	100		Age 99	6
Age 50	85		Age 100	10
Age 51	94		Age 101	6
Age 52	117		Age 102	1
Age 53	109		Age 103	1
Age 54	129		Age 104	1
Age 55	117		Age 107	1
Age 56	99		Age ?	173
Age 57	138			

...STATISTICAL SUMMARY OF DEATHS...

Heart Problems, including: | 1,742 | 28.86%
- Heart attack
- Heart failure
- Heart disease, etc.

Cancer, including: | 1,120 | 18.56%
- Leukemia
- Lung, breast, throat, brain, ovarian, etc.

Respiratory Problems, including: | 623 | 10.32%
- Asthma
- Emphysema
- Influenza
- Pneumonia
- Tuberculosis, etc.

Cause	Count	Percent
Accidents	326	5.40%
Following a Long Illness	290	4.80%
Stroke	279	4.62%
A.I.D.S.	213	3.53%
Suicide	155	2.57%
During or after surgery	147	2.44%
Hemorrhage	107	1.77%
After a Brief Illness	103	1.71%
Natural Causes	103	1.71%
Kidney Ailments	95	1.57%
Blood Disorders, including:	92	1.52%

- Anemia, etc.

Liver Ailments, including: | 89 | 1.47%
- Hepatitis
- Cirrhosis
- Jaundice, etc.

Cause	Count	Percent
Drug Overdose	80	1.33%
Murdered	68	1.13%
Pancreatic diseases, including:	57	0.94%

- Diabetes, etc.

Cause	Count	Percent
Tumor	42	0.70%
Sclerosis, including:	35	0.58%

- Amyotrophic lateral sclerosis, etc.

Cause	Count	Percent
Intestinal Disorders	34	0.56%
Alzheimer's Disease	27	0.45%
Parkinson's Disease	27	0.45%
Lymphatic Diseases	25	0.41%
Stomach Disorders	22	0.36%
Other infections	21	0.35%
Aneurysm	15	0.25%
Arthritis	8	0.13%
Spinal Diseases	8	0.13%
Ulcers	8	0.13%
Edema	7	0.12%
Gall Bladder Ailments	6	0.10%
All Other Causes	62	1.03%
	6,036	100%

GRAPHICAL SUMMARY OF
MOST FREQUENTLY LISTED CAUSES OF DEATH
(1912 – 1996)

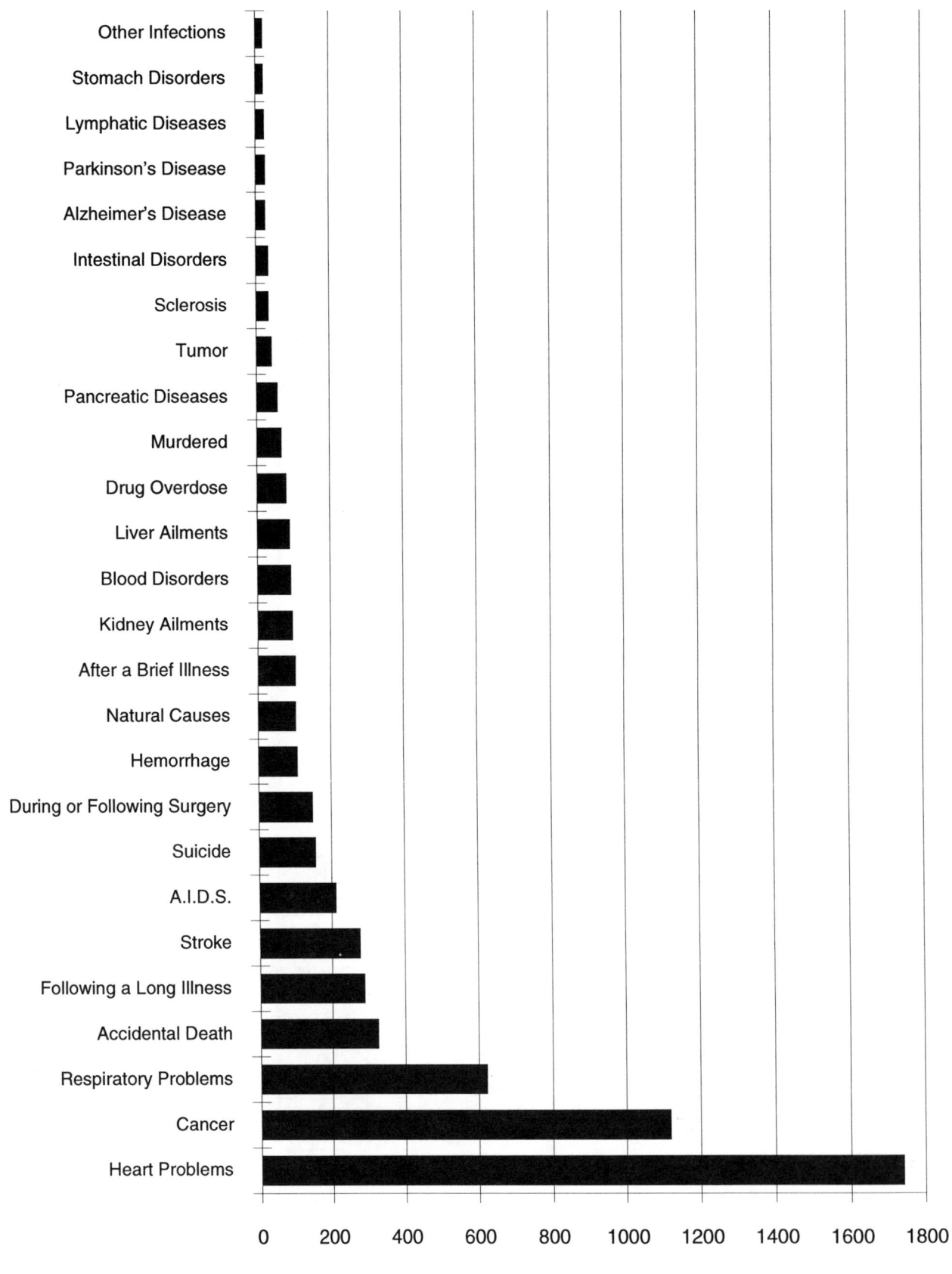

4

DIRECTORY

OF

CEMETERIES

STATE/CITY	CEMETERY	STREET	ZIP	PHONE
C				
◆ **CALIFORNIA**				
Altadena	Mountain View Cemetery	2400 N. Fair Oaks Ave.	91001	(818) 794-7133
Chatsworth	Oakwood Memorial Park	22601 Lassen	91311	(818) 341-0344
Coachella	Coachella Valley Cemetery	82925 Avenue 52	92238	(619) 398-3221
Compton	Woodlawn Memorial Park	1715 W. Greenleaf Blvd.	90220	(213) 636-1696
Covina	Forest Lawn—Covina Hills	21300 E. Via Verde Dr.	91724	(714) 599-1236
"	"	"	"	(818) 966-3671
Culver City	Holy Cross Cemetery and Maus.	5835 W. Slauson Ave.	90230	(213) 776-1855
Cypress	Forest Lawn Mem. Park, Cypress	4471 Lincoln Ave.	90630	(213) 431-2517
"	"	"	"	(714) 828-3131
Escondido	Oak Hill Cemetery	2640 Glen Ridge Rd.	92027	(619) 745-1781
Glendale	Forest Lawn Mem. Park, Glendale	1712 S. Glendale Ave.	91205	(213) 254-3131
"	"	"	"	(818) 241-4151
Glendale	Grand View Memorial Park	1341 Glenwood Rd.	91201	(818) 242-2697
Hollywood	Beth-Olam Cemetery and Maus.	900 Gower	90038	(213) 469-2322
Hollywood	Hollywood Memorial Park	6000 Santa Monica Blvd.	90038	(213) 469-1181
Inglewood	Inglewood Park Cemetery	720 E. Florence Ave.	90301	(310) 412-6500
La Jolla	El Camino Memorial Park	5600 Carroll Canyon Rd.	92037	(619) 453-2121
Long Beach	Forest Lawn—Sunnyside	1500 E. San Antonio Dr.	90807	(310) 424-1631
Los Angeles	Calvary Cemetery	4201 Whittier Blvd.	90023	(213) 261-3106
Los Angeles	Chapel of the Pines Crematory	1605 S. Catalina	90006	(Unpublished)
Los Angeles	Evergreen Cem. and Crematory	204 N. Evergreen Ave.	90033	(213) 268-6714
Los Angeles	Forest Lawn—Hollywood Hills	6300 Forest Lawn Dr.	90068	(213) 254-7251
"	"	"	"	(818) 984-1711
Los Angeles	Hillside Memorial Park	6001 W. Centinela Ave.	90045	(818) 502-8649
Los Angeles	Home of Peace Memorial Park	4334 Whittier Blvd.	90023	(213) 261-6135
Los Angeles	Los Angeles National Cemetery	950 Sepulveda Blvd.	90049	(310) 824-4311
Los Angeles	Mount Sinai Memorial-Park	5950 Forest Lawn Dr.	90068	(213) 469-6000
Los Angeles	Odd Fellows Cemetery	3640 Whittier Blvd.	90023	(213) 261-6156
Los Angeles	Rose Dale Cemetery	1831 W. Washington Blvd.	90007	(213) 734-3155
Los Angeles	Westwood Village Memorial Park	1218 Glendon Ave.	90024	(213) 474-1579
Newhall	Eternal Valley Memorial Park	23287 Sierra Hwy.	91321	(805) 259-0800
Newport Beach	Pacific View Memorial Park	3500 Pacific View Drive	92663	(714) 644-2700
North Hollywood	Valhalla Memorial Park	10621 Victory Blvd.	91606	(818) 763-9121
Oceanside	Eternal Hills Memorial Park	1999 El Camino Real	92054	(619) 757-2020
Palm Springs	Desert Memorial Park	69920 Ramon Rd.	92264	(619) 328-3316
Palm Springs	Welwood Murray Cemetery	100 S. Palm Canyon Dr.	92262	(619)323-8296
Red Bluff	Los Molinas Cemetery	Hwy 99-E at Taft St.	96055	(916) 384-1864
Sacramento	East Lawn Sierra Hills Mem. Park	5757 Greenback Lane	95841	(916) 732-2020
San Bruno	San Bruno/Golden Gate National	Sneath Lane (off Route 101)	94066	(415) 716-4616
San Diego	Catalina-Ft. Rose Crans Nat'l.	P.O. Box 6237	92166	(619) 553-2084
San Diego	Greenwood Memorial Park	Interstate 805 at Imperial Av.	92112	(619) 264-3131
San Fernando	Eden Memorial Park	11500 Sepulveda Blvd.	91345	(818) 361-7161
San Fernando	Glen Haven Memorial Park	13017 N. Lopez Canyon Rd.	91342	(818) 899-5211
San Fernando	San Fernando Mission Cemetery	11160 Stranwood Ave.	91345	(818) 361-7387
San Mateo	Holy Cross Cemetery	Menlo Park	94014	(415) 323-6375
Santa Barbara	Calvary Cemetery	199 Hope Ave.	93110	(805) 687-8811
Santa Barbara	Santa Barbara Cemetery	E. Cabrillo Blvd.	93108	(805) 969-3231
Santa Monica	Woodlawn Cemetery	1847 14th St.	90404	(310) 450-0781
Victorville	Roy Rogers-Dale Evans Museum	15650 Seneca Rd.	92392	(619) 243-4547
Westlake Village	Valley Oaks Memorial Park	5600 N. Lindero Canyon Rd.	91362	(818) 889-0902
Whittier	Rose Hills Memorial Park	3900 S. Workman Mill Rd.	90601	(213) 699-0921
◆ **COLORADO**				
Colorado Springs	Evergreen Cemetery	1005 S. Hancock Ave.	80903	(719) 578-6646
Denver	Fairmount Cemetery	430 S. Quebec St.	80231	(303) 399-0692
Lakewood	Crown Hill Cemetery and Mortuary	W. 29th Av. at Wadsworth Bl.	80218	(303) 233-4611

...DIRECTORY OF CEMETERIES — BY STATE AND CITY...

STATE/CITY	CEMETERY	STREET	ZIP	PHONE
CONNECTICUT				
Bridgeport	Mountain Grove Cemetery	2675 North Ave.	06604	(203) 336-3579
Greenwich	Putnam Cemetery	35 Parsonage Rd.	06830	(203) 869-4828
New Haven	Beaverdale Memorial Park	90 Pine Rock Ave.	06515	(203) 387-6601
Ridgefield	St. Mary's Cemetery			(Unpublished)
Stamford	Long Ridge Congregational Church			(203) 322-6975
Wethersfield	Emanuel Cemetery	1361 Berlin Turnpike	06109	(203) 236-1275
D.C.				
Washington	Congressional Cemetery, The	1801 East Street, S.E.	20003	(202) 543-0539
FLORIDA				
Ft. Lauderdale	Lauderdale Memorial Park	400 N.W. 27th Ave.	33310	(305) 761-5434
Gainesville	Evergreen Cemetery	Box 490 (1800 S.E. 4th St.)	32602	(904) 334-2160
Miami	Southern Memorial Park	15000 W. Dixie Hwy.	33181	(305) 947-3543
Stuart	Fernhill Memorial Gardens	1501 SE Kanner Hwy.	34997	(407) 283-6246
Tampa	American Legion Cemetery			
GEORGIA				
Carrollton	Our Lady of Perpetual Help Church	Center Point Rd.	30117	(404) 832-8977
Savannah	Bonaventure Cemetery	Bonaventure Rd.	31404	(912) 651-6843
IDAHO				
Boise	Morris Hill Cemetery	317 N. Latah	83706	(208) 384-4391
ILLINOIS				
Calumet City	Holy Cross Cemetery	Burnham at Michigan City Rd	60409	(312) 862-5398
Chicago	Graceland Cemetery	4001 N. Clark St.	60613	(708) 525-1105
Chicago (Forest Pk.)	Waldheim/Forest Home Cemetery	863 S. Desplaines St.	60607	(708) 366-4541
Worth	Holy Sepulchre Cemetery	6001 W. 111th St.	60482	(708) 422-3020
INDIANA				
Bloomington	Rosehill Cemetery and Mausoleum	5800 N. Ravenswood Ave.	46401	(317) 561-5940
Fairmount	Park Cemetery	111 W. Washington	46928	(317) 948-4040
Lafayette	Rest Haven Memorial Park	1200 Sagamore Pkwy., N.	47904	(317) 447-1797
Noblesville	Oak Lawn Memorial Gardens	9700 Allisonville Rd.	46250	(317) 849-3616
Peru	Mount Hope Cemetery	W. 12th Street	46970	(317) 472-2493
IOWA				
Davenport	Oakdale Cemetery	2501 Eastern Avenue	52803	(319) 324-5121
Ft. Dodge	Oakland Cemetery	15th Street		
KENTUCKY				
Crestwood	Mt. Tabor United Methodist Church	3301 W. Highway 22	40014	(502) 241-8811
LOUISIANA				
Metairie	Providence Memorial Park	8200 Airline Highway	70003	(504) 464-0541
New Orleans	Greenwood Cemetery	120 City Park Ave.	70119	(504) 482-3232
New Orleans	Metairie Cemetery	5100 Pontchartrain Blvd.	70179	(504) 486-6331
MAINE				
Westbrook	St. Hyacinth's Church Cemetery	Stroudwater St.		(207) 854-2003

...DIRECTORY OF CEMETERIES — BY STATE AND CITY...

STATE/CITY	CEMETERY	STREET	ZIP	PHONE
♦ MARYLAND				
Baltimore	Arbutus Memorial Park	1101 Sulphur Spring Rd.	21227	(410) 242-2700
Baltimore	Druid Ridge Cemetery	Park Hts. Ave. at Old Court Rd.	21208	(410) 486-5300
Baltimore	Hebrew Friendship Cemetery	3600 E. Baltimore, St.	21224	(410) 276-8025
Baltimore	Hebrew Young Men's Cemetery	5800 Windsor Mill Rd.	21207	(410) 764-6393
Baltimore	Holy Cross Cemetery and Mausoleum	6020 Gov. Ritchie Hwy.	21225	(410) 789-5400
Baltimore	Lorraine Park Cemetery and Maus.	5608 Dogwood Rd.	21207	(410) 298-8118
Baltimore	New Cathedral Cemetery	4300 Old Frederick Rd.	21229	(410) 566-7770
Cockeysville	Dulaney Valley Mem. Gardens	200 Padonia Road, East	21030	(410) 666-0490
Columbia	St. John the Evangelist RC Church	Wilde Lake	21044	(410) 964-1425
nr. Chestertown	Old St. Paul's Episcopal Church	Sandy Bottom Rd (off Rt. 20)	21620	(410) 778-1540
Silver Spring	Gate of Heaven Cemetery	13801 Georgia Ave.	20906	(301) 871-6500
Towson	Prospect Hill Cemetery	York Rd. at Joppa Rd.	21204	(410) 252-8462
♦ MASSACHUSETTS				
Becket	Becket Cemetery	Rt. 8, west of Rt. 20	01223	(413) 623-5236
Chilmark (M.V.)	Abel's Hill Cemetery	South Rd.	02535	(No phone)
Medford	Oak Grove Cemetery	165 Mystic Ave.	02155	(617) 396-7773
Newton	Newton Cemetery and Crematory	791 Walnut	02158	(617) 332-0047
Quincy	Mount Wollaston Cemetery	20 Sea St.	02169	(617) 376-1295
Southborough	Southborough Cemetery	Rt. 85, Cordaville Rd.	01772	(508) 485-1618
Tisbury (M.V.)	Village Cemetery	Franklin St. (Town Hall)	02568	(508) 696-4200
Upton	Upton Cemetery			
West Roxbury	St. Joseph Cemetery	990 La Grange St.	02132	(617) 327-1010
♦ MICHIGAN				
Dearborn	Northview Cemetery	600 Kensington St.	48128	(313) 565-0005
Saginaw	Mt. Olivet Cemetery and Mausoleum	3440 S. Washington	48601	(517) 752-7159
♦ MISSOURI				
Kansas City	Calvary Catholic Cemetery	6901 Troost	64131	(816) 523-2114
♦ MONTANA				
Helena	Forestdale Cemetery	490 Forestdale Rd, Box 5448	59604	(406) 458-5313
N				
♦ NEVADA				
Las Vegas	Palm Mortuary Mausoleum	1325 N. Main St.	89101	(702) 382-1340
♦ NEW HAMPSHIRE				
Moultonborough	Red Hill Cemetery	Bean Rd.	03254	(Unpublished)
♦ NEW JERSEY				
Paramus	Cedar Park Cemetery	Forest Ave.	07652	(201) 262-1100
♦ NEW MEXICO				
Carlsbad	Carlsbad Cemetery	1506 Boyd Drive at Juarez St.	88220	(505) 887-1191
♦ NEW YORK				
Brooklyn	Cypress Hills Cemetery	833 Jamaica Ave.	11208	(718) 277-2900
Brooklyn	Evergreen Cemetery	Bushwick at Conway Aves.	11207	(718) 455-5300
Brooklyn	Friends (Quaker) Cemetery	Prospect Park	11215	(718) 768-8298
Brooklyn	Green-Wood Cemetery	5th Ave. at 25th St.	11232	(718) 768-7300
Clovesville	Clovesville Cemetery	Rt. 28		(914) 254-5305
Cold Spring Harbor	St. John's Church Mem. Cemetery	P.O. Box 114	11724	(516) 692-6748
Elmira	Woodlawn Cemetery	1200 Walnut St.	14905	(607) 732-0151
Elmont (L.I.)	Beth David Cemetery	Elmont Road	11003	(516) 328-1300
Farmingdale (L.I.)	Long Island National Cemetery	Wellwood Ave.	11735	(516) 454-4949
Farmingdale (L.I.)	Pinelawn Memorial Park	Pinelawn Rd., P.O. Box 420	11735	(516) 249-6100
Flushing (Queens)	Flushing Cemetery	163-06 46th Ave.	11385	(718) 359-0100

STATE/CITY	CEMETERY	STREET	ZIP	PHONE
Flushing (Queens)	Mount Hebron Cemetery	130-04 Horace Harding Exp.	11367	(718) 939-9405
Glendale (Queens)	Mt. Lebanon Cemetery	7800 Myrtle Ave.	11385	(718) 821-0200
Hartsdale	Ferncliff Cemetery and Mausoleum	Secor Road	10530	(914) 693-4700
Hastings-on-Hudson	Mount Hope Cemetery	Saw Mill River Rd at Jackson	10706	(914) 478-1855
Hastings-on-Hudson	Temple Israel Cemetery	Saw Mill River Rd at Jackson	10706	(914) 478-1343
Hastings-on-Hudson	Westchester Hills Cemetery	400 Saw Mill River Rd.	10706	(914) 478-1767
Hawthorne	Cemetery of the Gate of Heaven	Stevens Ave.	10532	(914) 769-3672
Hawthorne	Mount Pleasant Cemetery	80 Commerce St.	10532	(914) 769-0397
Horsehead	Maple Grove Cemetery			
Johnstown	Ferndale Cemetery	545 N. Perry	13452	(518) 762-3922
Lake Ronkonkoma	Cenacle Convent (Retreat House)	310 Cenacle Rd. (L.I.)	11779	(516) 588-8366
Maspeth (Queens)	Mt. Zion Cemetery	59-63 54th Ave.	11378	(718) 335-2500
New Rochelle	Holy Sepulchre Cemetery	Shea Place	10801	(914) 636-6343
New York	St. Bartholomew's Episcopal Church	109 E. 50th St.	10022	(212) 751-1616
New York	St. Patrick's Cathedral	Fifth Ave. at 50th St.	10022	(212) 753-2261
N. Tarrytown	Sleepy Hollow Cemetery	540 N. Broadway	10591	(914) 631-0081
Port Jervis	Laurel Grove Cemetery		12771	(No phone)
Ridgewood (Queens)	Beth-El Cemetery	80-12 Cypress Hills St.	11385	(718) 366-3558
Ridgewood (Queens)	Machpelah Cemetery	82-30 Cypress Hills St.	11385	(718) 366-5959
Ridgewood (Queens)	Union Field Cemetery	8211 Cypress Ave.	11385	(718) 366-3748
Sag Harbor (L.I.)	Oakland Cemetery	Jermain Ave.	11963	(No phone)
Saratoga Springs	Greenridge Cemetery	17 Greenridge Place, S.W.	12866	(518) 584-5572
Southampton (L.I.)	Sacred Heart Cemetery	156 Hill St.	11968	(516) 283-0097
Staten Island	Silver Mount Cemetery	918 Victory Blvd.	10301	(718) 727-7020
The Bronx	St. Raymond's Cemetery	1140 Balcom Ave.	10465	(212) 792-1451
The Bronx	Woodlawn Cem. and Crematory	E. 233rd St. at Webster Ave.	10470	(212) 920-0500
Valhalla	Kensico Cemetery	Commerce at Lakeview Ave.	10595	(914) 949-0347
West Point	National Cemetery			(Unpublished)
Woodside (Queens)	Calvary Cemetery	4902 Laurel Hill Blvd.	11377	(718) 786-8000

◆ NORTH CAROLINA

Chapel Hill	Old Cemetery			(919) 968-2738
Smithfield	Sunset Memorial Park	State Highway 70	27577	(919) 934-0139
Waynesville	Green Hills Cemetery	315 S. Welsh St.	28786	(704) 452-4227

O
◆ OHIO

Circleville	Forest Cemetery	905 N. Court	43113	(614) 474-4401
Cleveland	Lake View Cemetery	12316 Euclid Ave.	44106	(216) 421-2665
Dayton	Dayton Memorial Park	8135 N. Dixie Dr.	45414	(513) 890-1831

◆ OKLAHOMA

Claremore	Will Rogers Memorial	P. O. Box 157	74018	(918) 341-0719
El Reno	El Reno Cemetery	E. Elm at Heritage Dr.	73036	(405) 422-2146
Oklahoma City	Memorial Park	13400 N. Kelley	73131	(405) 478-0556

P
◆ PENNSYLVANIA

Altoona	Rose Hill Cemetery	1207 12th Ave.	16601	(814) 942-1152
Berwick	SS. Cyril and Methodius Cemetery	706 N. Warren St.	18603	(717) 752-3172
Frazer	Haym Salomon Memorial Park	200 Moores Rd.	19355	(215) 877-1142
Kennett Square	Union Hill Cemetery	424 N. Union (Rt. 82)	19348	(215) 444-4554
Pen Argyl	Fairview Cemetery	U.S. Rt. 22	18072	
Philadelphia	Mt. Vernon Cemetery	Ridge at Lehigh Ave.	19132	(215) 229-6038
Pittsburgh	Allegheny Cemetery	4734 Butler St.	15201	(412) 682-1624

T
◆ TENNESSEE

Goodlettsville	Forest Lawn Memorial Park	1150 Dickerson Rd.	37072	(615) 859-5279
Hendersonville	Woodlawn Memorial Park East	353 Johnny Cash Pkwy.	37075	(615) 824-3855

...DIRECTORY OF CEMETERIES — BY STATE AND CITY...

STATE/CITY	CEMETERY	STREET	ZIP	PHONE
Madison	Spring Hill Cemetery and Mausoleum	5110 Gallatin Pike	37115	(615) 865-1101
Memphis	Graceland	3765 Elvis Presley Blvd.	38116	(901) 332-3322
Nashville	Woodlawn Memorial Park	660 Thompson Lane	37211	(615) 383-4754
Sparta	Crestlawn Cemetery	P.O. Box 825	38503	(615) 526-6384
◆ TEXAS				
Austin	Austin Memorial Park	2800 Hancock Drive	78731	(512) 453-2320
Beaumont	Forest Lawn Memorial Park	4955 Pine St.	77703	(409) 892-5912
Beeville	Glenwood Cemetery	Rt. 3, Box 120 (Lee Archer)		(512) 358-7238
Carthage	Jim Reeves Memorial Park	US Hwy 79, NE of Carthage	75633	(903) 693-6634
Dallas	Grove Hill Memorial Park	4118 Samuell Blvd.	75228	(214) 381-7118
Dallas	Hillcrest Memorial Park	7403 Northwest Hwy.	75225	(214) 363-5401
Dallas	Laurel Land Memorial Park	6000 S. R. L. Thornton Fwy.	75232	(214) 371-1336
Dallas	Restland Memorial Park	13005 Greenville Ave	75243	(214) 238-7111
DeKalb	Woodmen Cemetery	646 Front St. (US 82)	75559	(903) 667-3706
El Paso	Ft. Bliss National Cemetery	5200 Fred Wilson Hwy.	79906	(915) 564-0201
Fort Worth	Greenwood Memorial Park	3100 White Settlement Rd.	76107	(817) 336-0584
Fort Worth	Mount Olivet Cemetery	2301 N. Sylvania Ave.	76111	(817) 831-0511
Fort Worth	Oakwood Cemetery	701 Grand Ave.	76106	(817) 624-3531
Houston	Glenwood Cemetery			
Longview	Rosewood Park	Rt. 1844 (Seven Pines Rd.)	75601	(903) 757-0544
Lubbock	City of Lubbock Cemetery	2011 E. 31st St. at M.L.K. Blvd.	79404	(806) 767-2270
Port Neches	Oak Bluff Memorial Park	101 Block St.	77651	(409) 722-2114
▼				
◆ VIRGINIA				
Arlington	Arlington National Cemetery	Fort Myer	22211	(703) 545-6700
Lancaster	St. Mary's Whitechapel Trinity Church	Rt. 201 at Rt. 354	22507	(804) 462-7457
Petersburg	Blanford Cemetery			(804) 733-2397
Richmond	Woodland Cemetery	2300 Magnolia Rd.	23223	(804) 643-4702
Winchester	Shenandoah Memorial Park	1270 Front Royal Pike	22602	(703) 667-2012
W				
◆ WASHINGTON				
Renton	Greenwood Memorial Cemetery	350 Monroe, N.E.	98057	(206) 255-1511
Seattle	Lake View Cemetery	1554 15th Avenue, East	98112	(206) 322-1582
◆ WISCONSIN				
Milwaukee	Forest Home Cemetery	2405 W. Forest Home Ave.	53215	(414) 645-2632

...OTHER COUNTRIES...

COUNTRY/CITY	CEMETERY	STREET	ZIP	PHONE
B				
◆ BRAZIL				
Rio de Janeiro	Sao Joao Baptista Cemetery			
C				
◆ CANADA				
Toronto (Ontario)	Mount Pleasant Cem. and Mausoleum	375 Mount Pleasant		
E				
◆ ENGLAND				
Brighton	St. Nicholas Churchyard			
Cheltenham (Glou.)	Priory Road Cemetery	(In township of Prestbury)		
Harrogate (Yorkshire)	Harlow Hill Cemetery			
London	Brompton Cemetery	Old Brompton Rd.		
London (North)	Golders Green Cemetery	Hoop Rd.		

STATE/CITY	CEMETERY	STREET	ZIP	PHONE
London (North)	Hampstead Cemetery	Fortune Green Rd. nr. Finchley		
London (North)	Highgate Cemetery (West and East)	Swains Lane		
London (North)	St. John-at-Hampstead Cemetery	Church Row		
London (North)	St. Marylebone Cemetery	East End and North Circular Rd.		
London	Westminster Abbey	Victoria St.		
Shirley (Southampton)	Hollybrook Cemetery			
F				
◆ FRANCE				
nr. Paris	Boissy-Sans-Avoir			
Paris	Batignolles Cemetery	Avenue du Cimetière		
Paris	Montmartre Cemetery	Rue Rachel off Blvd. de Clichy		
Paris	Montparnasse Cemetery	Boulevard Edgar Quinet		
Paris	Passy Cemetery	Rue du Commandant Schloesing		
Paris	Père Lachaise Cemetery	Boulevard de Ménilmontant		
G				
◆ GERMANY				
Berlin	Friedenau Cemetery			
I				
◆ IRELAND				
Booterstown	Dean's Grange Cemetery			
◆ ITALY				
Milan	Cimitero Monumentale	Via Carlo Farini at Garibaldi Sta.		
Naples	Cimitero di Santa Maria del Pianto	Nuovo del Campo		
Rimini	Civico Cimitero	Via Popilia, on road to Ravenna		
◆ ISRAEL				
Jerusalem	(In a forest just outside the city)			
J				
◆ JAMAICA				
Grant's Town	"Firefly" (a private estate)			
M				
◆ MEXICO				
Mexico City	Pateon Dolores Cemetery			
P				
◆ POLAND				
Warsaw	St. John the Baptist Cathedral			
R				
◆ RUSSIA				
Moscow	Novodevichy Cemetery			
Moscow	Vagankovskoya Cemetery			
S				
◆ SWITZERLAND				
Vaud	Tolochenaz			
Vevey	Corsier-Sur-Vevey			

5

SPECIFIC
INTERMENT LOCATIONS
— BY NAME

NAME	YEAR	CEMETERY	INTERMENT SITE*
A			
• ABBOTT, Bud	1974	(Cremated—not interred)	Ashes scattered in the Pacific Ocean
ACKER, Jean (Valentino)	1978	Holy Cross Cem. and Maus., Culver City, CA	Section N, "Mother of Sorrows," Plot 542
ACKERMAN, Harry	1991	Forest Lawn—Hollywood Hills, Los Angeles, CA	Garden of Heritage, Plot #3019
ACORD, Art	1931	Forest Lawn Memorial-Park, Glendale, CA	
ACUFF, Roy	1992	Spring Hill Cemetery, Madison, TN	
• ADAMS, Constance (DeMille)	1960	Hollywood Memorial Park, Hollywood, CA	Section 8, in twin marble sarcophagi
ADAMS, Maude	1953	Cenacle Convent, Lake Ronkonkoma (L.I.), NY	
ADAMS, Nick (Adamshock)	1968	SS. Cyril and Methodius Cemetery, Berwick, PA	
ADLER, Buddy	1960	Forest Lawn Memorial-Park, Glendale, CA	Garden of Memory
ADOREE, Renée	1933	Hollywood Memorial Park, Hollywood, CA	Abbey of the Psalms, Foyer, Crypt 219
Adrian	1959	Hollywood Memorial Park, Hollywood, CA	Section 8, Lot 193
AIDMAN, Charles	1993	Westwood Village Mem. Park, Los Angeles, CA	Room of Prayer
AKEMAN, David	1973	Forest Lawn Memorial Park, Goodlettsville, TN	
AKINS, Claude	1994	(Cremated—not interred)	Ashes scattered
ALBERTSON, Frank	1964	Holy Cross Cem. and Maus., Culver City, CA	Section P, Grave 1, Lot 309
ALBERTSON, Jack	1981	(Cremated—not interred)	Ashes scattered at sea
ALDA, Robert	1986	Forest Lawn Memorial-Park, Glendale, CA	Ascension Garden
ALEXANDER, John	1982	Kensico Cemetery, Valhalla, NY	Actors Fund Plot
ALEXANDER, Ross	1937	Forest Lawn Memorial-Park, Glendale, CA	
ALLEN, Fred	1956	Cem. of the Gate of Heaven, Hawthorne, NY	
ALLEN, Gracie (Burns)	1964	Forest Lawn Memorial-Park, Glendale, CA	Freedom Maus., Sanctuary of Heritage
ALLEN, Irwin	1991	Mount Sinai Memorial-Park, Los Angeles, CA	In Maus. behind the Garden of Heritage
ALLGOOD, Sara	1950	Holy Cross Cem. and Maus., Culver City, CA	Section D, Sacred Heart
• ALLWYN, Astrid	1978	Forest Lawn Memorial-Park, Glendale, CA	Outside Freedom Mausoleum
AMECHE, Don	1993	(Cremated)	
AMES, Adrienne	1947	Oakwood Cemetery, Fort Worth, TX	Block 31, Lot 44 (nr. Avenue IX & B Street)
AMES, Leon	1993	Forest Lawn—Hollywood Hills, Los Angeles, CA	Col. of Valor, G-64429
ANDERS, Glenn	1981	Kensico Cemetery, Valhalla, NY	Actors Fund Plot
ANDERSON, Eddie	1977	Evergreen Cemetery, Los Angeles, CA	Section A, Lot 2504
ANDERSON, G. M.	1971	Chapel of the Pines Crematory, Los Angeles, CA	
• ANDRE, Gwili	1959	(Cremated)	Ashes in an urn in Copenhagen, Denmark
ANDREWS, Edward	1985	(Cremated—not interred)	Ashes scattered at sea
ANDREWS, LaVerne	1967	Forest Lawn Memorial-Park, Glendale, CA	Great Maus., Col. of Memory
ANGEL, Heather	1986	Santa Barbara Cemetery, Santa Barbara, CA	
ARBUCKLE, Roscoe "Fatty"	1933	(Cremated—not interred)	Ashes scattered at sea
ARDEN, Eve (West)	1990	Westwood Village Mem. Park, Los Angeles, CA	Section D, #81 (ashes interred)
ARLEN, Richard	1976	Holy Cross Cem. and Maus., Culver City, CA	Section T, Tier 57, Grave 130
ARMETTA, Henry	1945	Holy Cross Cem. and Maus., Culver City, CA	Section D
• ARMSTRONG, Herbert W.	1986	Mountain View Cemetery, Altadena, CA	
ARMSTRONG, Louis	1971	Flushing Cemetery, Flushing (Queens), NY	Sect. 8
ARMSTRONG, Robert	1973	Forest Lawn—Hollywood Hills, Los Angeles, CA	Murmuring Trees, Plot #7318, Space 1
ARNAZ, Desi	1986	(Cremated—not interred)	Ashes scattered
ARNOLD, Edward	1956	San Fernando Mission Cem., San Fernando, CA	Section D, Block 9, Lot 132
ARQUETTE, Cliff	1974	(Cremated—not interred)	Ashes scattered by the Telophase Society
ARTHUR, Jean	1991	(Cremated—not interred)	Ashes scattered at sea off Point Lobos, CA
• ASHE, Arthur	1993	Woodland Cemetery, Richmond, VA	
ASTAIRE, Adele (Douglas)	1981	Oakwood Memorial Park, Chatsworth, CA	
ASTAIRE, Fred	1987	Oakwood Memorial Park, Chatsworth, CA	
ASTOR, Mary	1987	Holy Cross Cem. and Maus., Culver City, CA	Section N, Lot 523, Grave 5
ATES, Roscoe	1962	Forest Lawn Memorial-Park, Glendale, CA	
ATWILL, Lionel	1946	Chapel of the Pines Crematory, Los Angeles, CA	
AUSTIN, Gene	1972	Forest Lawn Memorial-Park, Glendale, CA	Great Maus., Sanctuary of Sacred Promise
AVERY, Frederick B. "Tex"	1980	Forest Lawn—Hollywood Hills, Los Angeles, CA	Gentleness
AYRES, Agnes	1940	Hollywood Memorial Park, Hollywood, CA	Columbarium, Niche 3, T.3, Lower S. Wall
B			
BACKUS, Jim	1989	Westwood Village Mem. Park, Los Angeles, CA	Section D, #203
BACON, Irving	1965	Catalina-Ft. Rose Crans Cem., San Diego, CA	
BACON, Lloyd	1955	Forest Lawn—Hollywood Hills, Los Angeles, CA	
BAER, Jacob "Buddy"	1986	E. Lawn Sierra Hills Mem. Pk., Sacramento, CA	
• BAILEY, Pearl	1990	Rolling Green Memorial Park, Westchester, PA	
BAINTER, Fay	1968	Arlington National Cemetery, Arlington, VA	

NAME	YEAR	CEMETERY	INTERMENT SITE*
BAKER, Art	1966	Forest Lawn Memorial-Park, Glendale, CA	Great Maus., Col. of Memory
BAKER, Kenny	1985	Solvang, CA	Priv. inter. in Santa Barbara Co. nr. Solvang
BALANCHINE, George	1983	Oakland Cemetery, Sag Harbor (L.I.), NY	
BALL, Lucille (Morton)	1989	Forest Lawn—Hollywood Hills, Los Angeles, CA	Courts of Remem., Col. of Radiant Dawn
BALL, Suzan (Long)	1955	Forest Lawn Memorial-Park, Glendale, CA	Eventide, Plot #2922
BANCROFT, George	1956	Woodlawn Cemetery, Santa Monica, CA	In Mausoleum, 147-P-3
BANKHEAD, Tallulah	1968	Old St. Paul's Epis. Ch., nr. Chestertown, MD	Buried near woods, 100 yds. behind church
BANKY, Vilma	1991	(Cremated—not interred)	Ashes scattered at sea
BARA, Theda	1955	Forest Lawn Memorial-Park, Glendale, CA	Great Maus., Col. of Memory, Niche #19566
BARRIE, Wendy	1978	Kensico Cemetery, Valhalla, NY	Actors Fund Plot
BARRIER, Edgar	1964	Westwood Village Mem. Park, Los Angeles, CA	
BARRIS, Harry	1962	Forest Lawn—Hollywood Hills, Los Angeles, CA	
BARRY, Don "Red"	1980	Forest Lawn—Hollywood Hills, Los Angeles, CA	Court of Liberty, Plot #5442 (under tree)
BARRYMORE, Diana	1960	Woodlawn Cemetery, The Bronx, NY	Div. 20, bet. E. Border Ave and Chapel Hill
BARRYMORE, Ethel (Colt)	1959	Calvary Cemetery, Los Angeles, CA	Main Mausoleum, Block 60, Crypt 3F
BARRYMORE, John	1942	Mt. Vernon Cemetery, Philadelphia, PA	Cremated 1980, reburied from Calvary Cem.
BARRYMORE, Lionel	1954	Calvary Cemetery, Los Angeles, CA	Main Mausoleum, Block 352
BARSI, Judith	1988	Forest Lawn—Hollywood Hills, Los Angeles, CA	
BARTHELMESS, Richard	1963	Ferncliff Cemetery and Maus., Hartsdale, NY	Maus., Unit 8, Alcove BB, Col. B, Niche 1
BARTON, James	1962	St. John's Ch. Cem., Cold Spring Harbor, NY	
BASEHART, Richard	1984	Westwood Village Mem. Park, Los Angeles, CA	Urn Garden (3 down from top, on right)
• BASIE, William "Count"	1984	Pinelawn Mem. Park, Farmingdale (L.I.), NY	
BATES, Barbara	1969	Crown Hill Cemetery and Mort., Lakewood, CO	Section 2, Block 69, Lot 144, Unit A
BATES, Granville	1940	Graceland Cemetery, Chicago, IL	
BAXTER, Warner	1951	Forest Lawn Memorial-Park, Glendale, CA	Garden of Memory
• BAYLIS, Peter	1973	St. John-at-Hampstead Cem., London, England	At back of cemetery
BEARD, Matthew "Stymie"	1981	Evergreen Cemetery, Los Angeles, CA	
BEATTY, Clyde	1965	Forest Lawn—Hollywood Hills, Los Angeles, CA	Courts of Remem., 2175
BEAUDINE, William	1970	Hollywood Memorial Park, Hollywood, CA	
BEERY, Noah Sr.	1946	Forest Lawn—Hollywood Hills, Los Angeles, CA	Sheltering Hills
BEERY, Wallace	1949	Forest Lawn Memorial-Park, Glendale, CA	Vale of Memory
BEGLEY, Ed Sr.	1970	San Fernando Mission Cem., San Fernando, CA	Section C, Block 8, Lot 401
BEIDERBECKE, Leon "Bix"	1931	Oakdale Cemetery, Davenport, IA	
• BELL, Monta	1958	Hollywood Memorial Park, Hollywood, CA	Section 8, grave near Nelson Eddy
BELL, Rex	1962	Forest Lawn Memorial-Park, Glendale, CA	Freedom Maus., Sanctuary of Heritage
BELLAMY, Ralph	1991	Forest Lawn—Hollywood Hills, Los Angeles, CA	God's Acre, Plot #8687
BELUSHI, John	1982	Abel's Hill Cemetery, Chilmark (M.V.), MA	
BENADERET, Bea	1968	Valhalla Memorial Park, N. Hollywood, CA	Mausoleum of Hope, Row C, Crypt 34
BENDIX, William	1964	San Fernando Mission Cem., San Fernando, CA	Section D, at Curb No. 241, 14 rows in
BENNETT, Constance	1965	Arlington National Cemetery, Arlington, VA	
BENNETT, Richard	1944	Forest Lawn Memorial-Park, Glendale, CA	
BENNY, Jack	1974	Hillside Memorial Park, Los Angeles, CA	Mausoleum, Graciousness-Sarcophagus F
BERG, Gertrude	1966	Clovesville Cemetery, Clovesville, NY	In Jewish section
BERGEN, Edgar	1978	Inglewood Park Cemetery, Inglewood, CA	131 Miramar Plot, Grave #2
BERGERE, Ramona R.	1941	Forest Lawn Memorial-Park, Glendale, CA	
• BERGMAN, Ingrid	1982	(Cremated—not interred)	Ashes scattered off the coast of Sweden
BERKELEY, Busby	1976	Desert Memorial Park, Palm Springs, CA	Section A-14, Lot 74
BERLIN, Irving	1989	Woodlawn Cemetery, The Bronx, NY	F-4, Columbine
BERN, Paul	1932	Inglewood Park Cemetery, Inglewood, CA	Cremated in Mausoleum, Niche F96
BERNARDI, Herschel	1986	Mount Sinai Memorial-Park, Los Angeles, CA	Courts of Tanach, Crypt 52250
BERNHARDT, Sarah	1923	Père Lachaise Cemetery, Paris, France	Division 44
BERNSTEIN, Leonard	1990	Green-Wood Cemetery, Brooklyn, NY	
BERTRAND, Mary (Rall)	1955	Forest Lawn Memorial-Park, Glendale, CA	
BESSER, Joe	1988	Forest Lawn Memorial-Park, Glendale, CA	
BICKFORD, Charles	1967	Woodlawn Cemetery, Santa Monica, CA	Cremated
BING, Herman	1947	Hollywood Memorial Park, Hollywood, CA	Section 8, 20 ft. east of John Huston
BIXBY, Bill	1993	(Cremated—not interred)	Ashes scattered on his Hana, Maui estate
BLANC, Mel	1989	Hollywood Memorial Park, Hollywood, CA	Pineland Section
BLANDICK, Clara	1962	Forest Lawn Memorial-Park, Glendale, CA	
BLOCH, Ray	1982	Ferncliff Cemetery and Maus., Hartsdale, NY	St. Paul, Plot 184, Grave 2
BLOCKER, Dan	1972	Woodmen Cemetery, DeKalb, TX	
BLONDELL, Joan	1979	Forest Lawn Memorial-Park, Glendale, CA	Garden of Honor, Col. of the Evening Star

• New entry.

* Some cemeteries refuse to reveal specific locations.

NAME	YEAR	CEMETERY	INTERMENT SITE*
BLUE, Ben	1975	Hillside Memorial Park, Los Angeles, CA	Mausoleum, Col. of Graciousness-810
BLUE, Monte	1963	Forest Lawn Memorial-Park, Glendale, CA	
BOCK-LEADER, Deborah Lyn	1990	Dulaney Valley Mem. Gdns., Cockeysville, MD	Eternal Light Section
BOGART, Humphrey	1957	Forest Lawn Memorial-Park, Glendale, CA	Garden of Memory, Col. of Eternal Light
BOLAND, Mary	1965	Forest Lawn Memorial-Park, Glendale, CA	Great Maus., Sanctuary of Vespers
BOLES, John	1969	Westwood Village Mem. Park, Los Angeles, CA	Sanctuary of Serenity
BOLESLAWSKI, Richard	1937	Calvary Cemetery, Los Angeles, CA	In mausoleum
BOLEY, May	1963	Forest Lawn Memorial-Park, Glendale, CA	
BOLGER, Ray	1987	Holy Cross Cem. and Maus., Culver City, CA	Mausoleum, Block 35, Crypt F-2
BOND, Ward	1960	Forest Lawn Memorial-Park, Glendale, CA	
BOOKE, Sorrell	1994	Hillside Memorial Park, Los Angeles, CA	Garden of Memories, Dedication-272-4B
BOONE, Richard	1981	(Cremated—not interred)	Ashes scattered in the Hawaiian Islands
BORDEN, Olive	1947	Forest Lawn Memorial-Park, Glendale, CA	
BORZAGE, Frank	1962	Forest Lawn Memorial-Park, Glendale, CA	
BOSWELL, Connee	1976	Ferncliff Cemetery and Maus., Hartsdale, NY	Hillcrest J, Grave 227
BOSWORTH, Hobart	1943	Forest Lawn Memorial-Park, Glendale, CA	
BOW, Clara (Bell)	1965	Forest Lawn Memorial-Park, Glendale, CA	Freedom Maus., Sanctuary of Heritage
BOWES, Major Edward	1946	Sleepy Hollow Cemetery, N. Tarrytown, NY	Off Vernon Ave.
• BOWLING, Alice	1981	Rosewood Park, Longview, TX	Chapel Mausoleum
• BOYD, Jim	1973	Restland Memorial Park, Dallas, TX	
• BOYD, Stephen	1977	Oakwood Memorial Park, Chatsworth, CA	Outside mausoleum
BOYD, William	1972	Forest Lawn Memorial-Park, Glendale, CA	Great Maus., Sanctuary of Sacred Promise
BOYER, Charles	1978	Holy Cross Cem. and Maus., Culver City, CA	St. Ann's Garden, Tier 186, Grave 5
BRABIN, Charles J.	1957	Forest Lawn Memorial-Park, Glendale, CA	
BRADLEY, Truman	1974	Forest Lawn—Hollywood Hills, Los Angeles, CA	Enduring Faith, Plot #3718
BRADY, Alice	1939	Sleepy Hollow Cemetery, N. Tarrytown, NY	
BRADY, Scott	1985	Holy Cross Cem. and Maus., Culver City, CA	Mausoleum, Block 156, Crypt B-7 upper flr.
BRAND, Neville	1992	E. Lawn Sierra Hills Mem. Pk., Sacramento, CA	
BRASSELLE, Keefe	1980	Holy Cross Cem. and Maus., Culver City, CA	Section R, Tier 29, Grave 168
BREESE, Edmund	1936	Forest Lawn Memorial-Park, Glendale, CA	
BRENNAN, Walter	1974	San Fernando Mission Cem., San Fernando, CA	Section D at Curb 445, 8 rows in
BRESSART, Felix	1949	Hollywood Memorial Park, Hollywood, CA	Section 14, Row J, Grave 89
BRICE, Fanny	1951	Home of Peace Mem. Park, Los Angeles, CA	Chapel Maus., Har. and Benev., 57E #1109
BRISSON, Frederick	1984	Holy Cross Cem. and Maus., Culver City, CA	Section M, Lot 536, Grave 1
BRITTON, Pamela	1974	Forest Lawn—Hollywood Hills, Los Angeles, CA	Col. of Radiant Dawn, G61685
BRODERICK, James	1982	Holy Cross Cem. and Maus., Culver City, CA	Mausoleum, lower floor, top level
• BROPHY, Ed	1960	Woodlawn Cemetery, Santa Monica, CA	
BROWN, Clarence	1987	Forest Lawn Memorial-Park, Glendale, CA	Columbarium of Honor
BROWN, Joe E.	1973	Forest Lawn Memorial-Park, Glendale, CA	Sunrise Slope
BROWN, John H.	1957	Eden Memorial Park, San Fernando, CA	Akiba 17-55
BROWN, Johnny Mack	1974	Forest Lawn Memorial-Park, Glendale, CA	Columbarium of Heavenly Peace
BROWNE, Coral	1991	Hollywood Memorial Park, Hollywood, CA	Ashes scattered in the rose garden.
• BROWNING, Tod	1962	Chapel of the Pines Crematory, Los Angeles, CA	
BRUCE, Lenny	1966	Eden Memorial Park, San Fernando, CA	
BRUCE, Nigel	1953	Chapel of the Pines Crematory, Los Angeles, CA	Vault #35167
BRUCKMAN, Clyde	1955		Body donated to L.A. County Med. Asso.
BUCHANAN, Edgar	1979	Forest Lawn—Hollywood Hills, Los Angeles, CA	Morning Light, Plot #7780
BUNNY, John	1915	Evergreen Cemetery, Brooklyn, NY	
BUONO, Victor	1981	Greenwood Memorial Park, San Diego, CA	Unmarked grave nr. pond, next to his mom
BURGESS, Helen M.	1937	Forest Lawn Memorial-Park, Glendale, CA	
BURKE, Billie	1970	Kensico Cemetery, Valhalla, NY	
BURNETTE, Smiley	1967	Forest Lawn—Hollywood Hills, Los Angeles, CA	Sheltering Hills, Plot #266
BURNS, Bob	1956	Forest Lawn Memorial-Park, Glendale, CA	Great Maus., Col. of Adoration
• BURNS, George	1996	Forest Lawn Memorial-Park, Glendale, CA	Freedom Maus., Sanctuary of Heritage
• BURR, Raymond	1993	Frasier Cemetery, New Westminister, B.C.	
BURROUGHS, Edgar Rice	1950	18354 Ventura Blvd., Tarzana, CA	Ashes buried under walnut tree in front yd
BURTON, Richard	1984	Protestant Churchyard, Celigny, Switzerland	
BUSH, Mae	1946	Chapel of the Pines Crematory, Los Angeles, CA	Near front door, on left, at eye-level
BUSHMAN, Francis X.	1966	Forest Lawn Memorial-Park, Glendale, CA	Freedom Maus., Sanctuary of Gratitude
BYINGTON, Spring	1971		Body donated for medical research
BYRD, Ralph M.	1952	Forest Lawn Memorial-Park, Glendale, CA	Eventide (under the olive tree)
BYRON, Arthur William	1943	(Cremated at Forest Lawn, Glendale, CA)	Ashes sent back to Maine

NAME	YEAR	CEMETERY	INTERMENT SITE*
C			
CABOT, Bruce	1972	Carlsbad Cemetery, Carlsbad, NM	Division A, Block 48, Space 5 (E. Bujac, Jr.)
CABOT, Sebastian	1977	Westwood Village Mem. Park, Los Angeles, CA	Urn Garden East (top row, 9 from right)
CAGNEY, James	1986	Cem. of the Gate of Heaven, Hawthorne, NY	
CAHN, Sammy	1993	Westwood Village Mem. Park, Los Angeles, CA	Section D (near Donna Reed)
CALHERN, Louis	1956	Hollywood Memorial Park, Hollywood, CA	Abbey of Psalms, Foyer, Niche 308, Tier 3
• CALLAS, Maria	1977	Pere Lachaise Cemetery, Paris, France	
• CALVIN, Henry	1975	Grove Hill Memorial Park, Dallas, TX	60-3-16
CAMBRIDGE, Godfrey	1976	Forest Lawn—Hollywood Hills, Los Angeles, CA	Enduring Faith
• CAMPANELLA, Roy	1993	Forest Lawn—Hollywood Hills, Los Angeles, CA	
CANDY, John	1994	Holy Cross Cem. and Maus., Culver City, CA	Mausoleum, Room 7, Crypt B-1
CANOVA, Judy	1983	Forest Lawn Memorial-Park, Glendale, CA	Garden of Memory, Col. of Eternal Light
CANTOR, Eddie	1964	Hillside Memorial Park, Los Angeles, CA	Mausoleum, Graciousness-207
CAPOTE, Truman	1984	Westwood Village Mem. Park, Los Angeles, CA	New Mausoleum, 1st column, bottom
CAPRA, Frank	1991	Coachella Valley Cemetery, Coachella, CA	(near Indio)
CAREY, Harry	1947	Forest Lawn Memorial-Park, Glendale, CA	
CAREY, Macdonald	1994	Holy Cross Cem. and Maus., Culver City, CA	Section "Grotto," Lot 196, Grave 19
CAREY, Timothy	1994	Rose Hills Memorial Park, Whittier, CA	
• CARLETON, William P.	1947	Chapel of the Pines Crematory, Los Angeles, CA	Permanent storage vault
CARLSON, Richard	1977	Chapel of the Pines Crematory, Los Angeles, CA	
CARMICHAEL, Hoagy	1981	Rosehill Cemetery, Bloomington, IN	
CARPENTER, Karen	1983	Forest Lawn Memorial-Park, Cypress, CA	Ascension M. Maus., Sanct. of Compassion
CARPENTER, Ken	1984	Westwood Village Mem. Park, Los Angeles, CA	Sanctuary of Tenderness, on rear wall
CARR, Nathan C. "Nat"	1944	Forest Lawn Memorial-Park, Glendale, CA	
CARRADINE, John	1988		Buried at sea, in the Catalina Channel, CA
CARRILLO, Leo	1961	Woodlawn Cemetery, Santa Monica, CA	Section 2, (near 14th Street)
CARROLL, Earl	1948	Forest Lawn Memorial-Park, Glendale, CA	Garden of Memory
CARROLL, John	1979	Forest Lawn Memorial-Park, Glendale, CA	
CARSON, Jack	1963	Forest Lawn Memorial-Park, Glendale, CA	Great Maus., Col. of Memory
CARTER, Maybelle	1978	Woodlawn Mem. Park East, Hendersonville, TN	
• CARUSO, Enrico	1921	Cimitero di Santa Maria del Pianto, Naples, Italy	Down the hill on the left, in sarcophagus
CASSAVETES, John	1989	Westwood Village Mem. Park, Los Angeles, CA	Lot 308
CASSIDY, Jack	1976	(Cremated—not interred)	Ashes scattered at sea
• CASSIDY, Ted "Lurch"	1979	(Cremated)	Ashes buried in the front lawn of his home
CASTLE, Irene	1969	Woodlawn Cemetery, The Bronx, NY	Division 29, off Park View & Spruce Ave.
CASTLE, Nick	1968	Holy Cross Cem. and Maus., Culver City, CA	Section "Grotto," Lot 187, Grave 2
CASTLE, Vernon	1918	Woodlawn Cemetery, The Bronx, NY	Division 29, off Park View & Spruce Ave.
• CAULFIELD, Joan	1991	Forest Lawn—Hollywood Hills, Los Angeles, CA	
CERF, Bennett	1971	(Cremated—not interred)	Ashes scattered at his Mt. Kisco, NY, home
• CHALIAPIN, Feodor	1938	Batignolles Cemetery, Paris, France	Div. 25, rose granite mon. topped w/cross
• CHANDLER, Helen	1965	(Cremated—not interred)	Ashes have never been claimed
CHANDLER, Jeff (Ira Grossel)	1961	Hillside Memorial Park, Los Angeles, CA	Mausoleum, Graciousness-2nd. Floor-4015
CHANEY, Lon F. Sr.	1930	Forest Lawn Memorial-Park, Glendale, CA	
CHAPLIN, Charles	1977	Corsier-Sur-Vevey, Switzerland	
CHAPLIN, Charles Jr. (son)	1968	Hollywood Memorial Park, Hollywood, CA	Abbey of the Psalms, Crypt 1065, Corr E-2
CHARTERS, Spencer H.	1943	Forest Lawn Memorial-Park, Glendale, CA	
CHASE, Charley	1940	Forest Lawn Memorial-Park, Glendale, CA	Sunrise Slope, Lot 72, Grave 147
CHATTERTON, Ruth	1961	Mountain Grove Cemetery, Bridgeport, CT	
CHAYEFSKY, Paddy	1981	Kensico Cemetery, Valhalla, NY	Sharon Gardens section
CHESHIRE, Harry "Pappy"	1968	Forest Lawn—Hollywood Hills, Los Angeles, CA	Remembrance, Plot #323
CHEVALIER, Maurice	1972	Marnes-La-Coquette, France	(France)
CHRISTIANS, Mady	1951	Ferncliff Cemetery and Maus., Hartsdale, NY	
CLARK, Bobby	1960	Woodlawn Cemetery, The Bronx, NY	
CLARK, Buddy	1949	Forest Lawn Memorial-Park, Glendale, CA	
CLARK, Fred	1968	Chapel of the Pines Crematory, Los Angeles, CA	
CLARK, Marguerite	1940	Metairie Cemetery, New Orleans, LA	Section 97 (Frank Williams property)
CLEVELAND, George	1957	Forest Lawn Memorial-Park, Glendale, CA	
CLIFT, Montgomery	1966	Friends Cemetery, Brooklyn, NY	
CLIFTON, Elmer	1949	Forest Lawn Memorial-Park, Glendale, CA	
CLINE, Patsy	1963	Shenandoah Memorial Park, Winchester, VA	
• CLIVE, Colin	1937	(Cremated in Los Angeles, CA)	Ashes unclaimed
CLYDE, Andy	1967	Forest Lawn Memorial-Park, Glendale, CA	Whispering Pines

NAME	YEAR	CEMETERY	INTERMENT SITE*
• COBAIN, Kurt	1994	(Cremated—not interred)	Ashes given to his wife, Courtney Love
COBB, Irvin S.	1944	(Cremated—not interred)	Ashes fertilized a sapling in Paducah, KY
COBB, Lee J. (Leo Jacoby)	1976	Mount Sinai Memorial-Park, Los Angeles, CA	Garden of Sherrot, Lot 421
COBURN, Charles	1961	(Cremated—not interred)	Ashes scattered in Georgia, Mass. & N.Y.
COCHRAN, Eddie (singer)	1960	Forest Lawn Memorial-Park, Cypress, CA	Abiding Faith, Plot #2996
• COCTEAU, Jean	1963	Milly La Foret Cemetery, Milly La Foret, France	
COHAN, George M.	1942	Woodlawn Cemetery, The Bronx, NY	Division 31, off Park Ave.
COHN, Harry	1958	Hollywood Memorial Park, Hollywood, CA	Section 8, Lot 86
COLE, Edwin "Buddy"	1964	Forest Lawn—Hollywood Hills, Los Angeles, CA	Enduring Faith, Plot #3999
COLE, Nat "King"	1965	Forest Lawn Memorial-Park, Glendale, CA	Freedom Maus., Sanctuary of Heritage
COLLIER, William Sr.	1944	Forest Lawn Memorial-Park, Glendale, CA	
COLLINS, Ray	1965	Forest Lawn—Hollywood Hills, Los Angeles, CA	Garden of Heritage, Plot #909
COLLYER, Bud	1969	Putnam Cemetery, Greenwich, CT	
COLMAN, Ronald	1958	Santa Barbara Cemetery, Santa Barbara, CA	Ridge Oval Section, Lot 663
COLUMBO, Russ	1934	Forest Lawn Memorial-Park, Glendale, CA	Great Maus., Sanctuary of Vespers
• CONNORS, Chuck	1992	San Fernando Mission Cem., San Fernando, CA	
CONRAD, William	1994	Forest Lawn—Hollywood Hills, Los Angeles, CA	Lincoln Terrace, Plot #4448
CONTE, Richard	1975	Westwood Village Mem. Park, Los Angeles, CA	Section D, #62
CONVY, Bert	1991	Forest Lawn—Hollywood Hills, Los Angeles, CA	Court of Liberty, left of sidewalk
CONWAY, Tom	1967	Chapel of the Pines Crematory, Los Angeles, CA	
COOGAN, Jackie	1984	Holy Cross Cem. and Maus., Culver City, CA	Section F, Tier 56, Grave 47
COOKE, Sam	1964	Forest Lawn Memorial-Park, Glendale, CA	Garden of Honor
COOPER, Gary	1961	Sacred Heart Cemetery, Southampton (L.I.), NY	Reburied from L.A., under a 3-ton boulder
• COOPER, (Dame) Gladys	1971	Hampstead Cemetery, London, England	Nr. Public Footpath and 3rd path on right
COOPER, Melville	1973	Valhalla Memorial Park, N. Hollywood, CA	
COREY, Wendell	1968	Beckett Cemetery, Beckett, MA	
CORNELL, Katharine	1974	Village Cemetery, Tisbury (M.V.), MA	(Martha's Vineyard)
CORRELL, Charles "Andy"	1972	Holy Cross Cem. and Maus., Culver City, CA	
CORTHELL, Herbert	1947	Forest Lawn Memorial-Park, Glendale, CA	
COSTELLO, Lou	1959	Calvary Cemetery, Los Angeles, CA	Main Mausoleum, Block 354, Crypt B-1
COTTON, Joseph	1994	Blanford Cemetery, Petersburg, VA	
COWAN, Jerome	1972	Forest Lawn—Hollywood Hills, Los Angeles, CA	Col. of Remembrance
COWARD, Noel	1973	"Firefly Hill", Grant's Town, Jamaica	(his private estate)
COWL, Jane	1950	Valhalla Memorial Park, N. Hollywood, CA	
COX, Wally	1973	(Cremated—not interred)	Ashes scattered in the Atlantic Ocean
CRAIG, James	1985	Forest Lawn Memorial-Park, Glendale, CA	
CRANE, Bob	1978	Oakwood Memorial Park, Chatsworth, CA	
CRANE, Norma	1973	Westwood Village Mem. Park, Los Angeles, CA	Section D, #62
• CRANE, Richard	1969	Valhalla Memorial Park, N. Hollywood, CA	
CRAVEN, Frank	1945	Kensico Cemetery, Valhalla, NY	
CRAWFORD, Broderick	1986	Ferndale Cemetery, Johnstown, NY	
CRAWFORD, Jesse	1962	Ferncliff Cemetery and Maus., Hartsdale, NY	Maus., Unit 3, Alcove 4, Niche Arc.#21
CRAWFORD, Joan (Steele)	1977	Ferncliff Cemetery and Maus., Hartsdale, NY	Maus., Unit 8, Alcove E, Crypt 42
CREGAR, (Samuel) Laird	1944	Forest Lawn Memorial-Park, Glendale, CA	Eventide, Lot 37, Space 2
CREWS, Laura Hope	1942	Cypress Lawn Cemetery, Colma, CA	Rose Mound
CRISP, Donald	1974	Forest Lawn Memorial-Park, Glendale, CA	
CROCE, Jim	1973	Haym Salomon Memorial Park, Frazer, PA	
• CROGHAN, Joe	1995	New Cathedral Cemetery, Baltimore, MD	
CROMWELL, Richard	1960	Chapel of the Pines Crematory, Los Angeles, CA	
CROSBY, Dennis	1991	(Cremated—not interred)	Ashes strewn in the north CA Novato area
CROSBY, Harry "Bing"	1977	Holy Cross Cem. and Maus., Culver City, CA	Section "Grotto," Lot 119, Grave 1
CROSBY, Wilma "Dixie Lee"	1952	Holy Cross Cem. and Maus., Culver City, CA	Section "Grotto," Lot 119, Grave 2
CROTHERS, Ben "Scatman"	1986	Forest Lawn—Hollywood Hills, Los Angeles, CA	Lincoln Terrace, Plot #4545
CRUZE, James	1942	Hollywood Memorial Park, Hollywood, CA	Abbey of Psalms, Foyer, Niche 211, Tier 2
CUKOR, George	1983	Forest Lawn Memorial-Park, Glendale, CA	Court of Freedom
CUMMINGS, Robert	1990	Forest Lawn Memorial-Park, Glendale, CA	Great Maus., Col. of Sanctity
CURTIZ, Michael	1962	Forest Lawn Memorial-Park, Glendale, CA	
D			
DAILEY, Dan	1978	Forest Lawn Memorial-Park, Glendale, CA	Marker 7065, left of Statue of Immortality
DALEY, Cass (Katherine)	1975	Hollywood Memorial Park, Hollywood, CA	Section 8, near curb ("Williamson")
DAMITA, Lili (Loomis)	1994	Oakland Cemetery, Ft. Dodge, IA	
DANDRIDGE, Dorothy	1965	Forest Lawn Memorial-Park, Glendale, CA	Freedom Maus., Col. of Victory

NAME	YEAR	CEMETERY	INTERMENT SITE*
DANE, Karl	1934	Hollywood Memorial Park, Hollywood, CA	Section 13, Plot 303 (next to road)
DANIELS, Bebe	1971	Hollywood Memorial Park, Hollywood, CA	Col., Niche 7-8, T.3, Upper N. Wall
DANIELS, Victor	1955	Forest Lawn Memorial-Park, Glendale, CA	
DANTINE, Helmut	1982	Westwood Village Mem. Park, Los Angeles, CA	Section D, #130
DARBY, Ken	1992	Forest Lawn—Hollywood Hills, Los Angeles, CA	Lincoln Terrace, Plot #4246
DARIN, Bobby	1973	(No funeral)	Body donated to UCLA for med. research
DARNELL, Linda	1965	Union Hill Cemetery, Kennett Square, PA	
DARRELL, J. Stevan	1970	Westwood Village Mem. Park, Los Angeles, CA	
DARWELL, Jane	1967	Forest Lawn Memorial-Park, Glendale, CA	Whispering Pines, Plot #1817
DASSIN, Joe	1980	Hollywood Memorial Park, Hollywood, CA	Section 14, Grave 79, Row I
DASTAGIR, Sabu	1963	Forest Lawn—Hollywood Hills, Los Angeles, CA	Sheltering Hills, Plot #402
DASTAGIR, Sheik	1960	Forest Lawn—Hollywood Hills, Los Angeles, CA	Sheltering Hills, Plot #490
DAVENPORT, Alice	1936	Forest Lawn Memorial-Park, Glendale, CA	
• DAVES, Delmar	1977	Forest Lawn Memorial-Park, Glendale, CA	Great Maus., Col. of Memory
DAVIES, Marion	1961	Hollywood Memorial Park, Hollywood, CA	Douras Mausoleum, Section 8, Lot 261-264
DAVIS, Bette	1989	Forest Lawn—Hollywood Hills, Los Angeles, CA	Courts of Remem., near entrance
DAVIS, Brad	1991	Forest Lawn—Hollywood Hills, Los Angeles, CA	Col. of Valor, G64054
DAVIS, Jim	1981	Forest Lawn Memorial-Park, Glendale, CA	Great Maus., 3rd floor (cremated)
DAVIS, Joan (Williams)	1961	Holy Cross Cem. and Maus., Culver City, CA	Mausoleum, Block 46, Crypt D-1, rt. of altar
DAVIS, Miles	1991	Woodlawn Cemetery, The Bronx, NY	D-4, Alpine Hill
DAVIS, Sammy Jr.	1990	Forest Lawn Memorial-Park, Glendale, CA	Garden of Honor
DAY, Dennis	1988	Holy Cross Cem. and Maus., Culver City, CA	Section W, Tier 53, Grave 37
DEAN, James	1955	Park Cemetery, Fairmount, IN	
• DeCORDOBA, Pedro	1950	Holy Cross Cem. and Maus., Culver City, CA	Section G, Lot 258, Grave 1
DeFORE, Don	1993	Westwood Village Mem. Park, Los Angeles, CA	Rose Garden
DELMAR, Kenny	1984	Long Ridge Congregational Ch., Stamford, CT	
DeMILLE, Cecil B.	1959	Hollywood Memorial Park, Hollywood, CA	Section 8, in twin marble sarcophagi
DeMILLE, William C.	1955	Hollywood Memorial Park, Hollywood, CA	Abbey of the Psalms, Niche 2, T.6, Corr E-3
DENNY, Reginald	1967	Forest Lawn—Hollywood Hills, Los Angeles, CA	Morning Light, Plot #7451
DePUTTI, Lya	1931	Ferncliff Cemetery and Maus., Hartsdale, NY	Maus., Unit 1, Alcove E, Crypt 31
DeRITA, Joe	1993	Valhalla Memorial Park, N. Hollywood, CA	
DESMOND, Johnny	1985	Holy Cross Cem. and Maus., Culver City, CA	Section F, Tier 44, Grave 30
DEVINE, Andy	1977	(Cremated—not interred)	Ashes scattered at sea
DeWOLFE, Billy	1974	Mount Wollaston Cemetery, Quincy, MA	
DIAMOND, Selma	1985	Hillside Memorial Park, Los Angeles, CA	Courts of the Book, Jacob-I-4004
DIETRICH, Marlene	1992	Friedenau Cemetery, Berlin, Germany	Near her mother, Josefine von Losch
DIGGES, Dudley	1947	Cem. of the Gate of Heaven, Hawthorne, NY	
DINEHART, Mason Alan	1944	Forest Lawn Memorial-Park, Glendale, CA	
• DISNEY, Roy	1971	Forest Lawn—Hollywood Hills, Los Angeles, CA	Sheltering Hills
DISNEY, Walt	1966	Forest Lawn Memorial-Park, Glendale, CA	Freedom Maus., outside front left
Divine (Harris Glenn Milstead)	1988	Prospect Hill Cemetery, Towson, MD	
DIX, Richard	1949	Forest Lawn Memorial-Park, Glendale, CA	Whispering Pines, nr. "Finding of Moses"
DOLLY, Roszika "Rosie"	1970	Forest Lawn Memorial-Park, Glendale, CA	Great Maus., hall right side
DOLLY, Yansci "Jenny"	1941	Forest Lawn Memorial-Park, Glendale, CA	Great Maus., hall right side
DONLEVY, Brian	1972	(Cremated—not interred)	Ashes scattered at sea nr. Santa Monica, CA
DORN, Philip	1975	Westwood Village Mem. Park, Los Angeles, CA	Sanctuary of Tranquility, rear wall
D'ORSAY, Fifi	1983	Forest Lawn Memorial-Park, Glendale, CA	Devotion
• DORSEY, Jimmy	1957	Annunciation Cemetery, Shenandoah, PA	
DORSEY, Tommy	1956	Kensico Cemetery, Valhalla, NY	On Cherokee Ave.
DOUGLAS, Paul	1959	Chapel of the Pines Crematory, Los Angeles, CA	
DOWLING, Constance (Tors)	1969	Holy Cross Cem. and Maus., Culver City, CA	Section P, Grave 4, Lot 421
DRAKE, Tom	1982	Holy Cross Cem. and Maus., Culver City, CA	Section R, Tier 26, Grave 188
DRESSLER, Marie	1934	Forest Lawn Memorial-Park, Glendale, CA	Great Maus., Sanctuary of Benediction
DUCHIN, Eddie	1951	(Cremated—not interred)	Ashes scattered in the Atlantic Ocean
DUMONT, Margaret	1965	Chapel of the Pines Crematory, Los Angeles, CA	
DUNCAN, Isadora	1927	Père Lachaise Cemetery, Paris, France	Div. 87, ashes interred in the Columbarium
DUNCAN, Rosetta	1959	Forest Lawn Memorial-Park, Glendale, CA	
DUNCAN, Vivian	1986	Forest Lawn Memorial-Park, Glendale, CA	
DUNN, James	1967	(Cremated—not interred)	Ashes scattered at sea
DUNNE, Dominique	1982	Westwood Village Mem. Park, Los Angeles, CA	Section D, #189
DUNNE, Irene (Griffin)	1990	Calvary Cemetery, Los Angeles, CA	Left of altar in the Mausoleum church area
DURANTE, Jimmy	1980	Holy Cross Cem. and Maus., Culver City, CA	Section F, Tier 96, Grave 6

• New entry.

* Some cemeteries refuse to reveal specific locations.

NAME	YEAR	CEMETERY	INTERMENT SITE*
• DURFEE, Minta (Arbuckle)	1975	Forest Lawn Memorial-Park, Glendale, CA	Great Maus., Col. of Constancy #17743
DURKIN, Junior	1935	Forest Lawn Memorial-Park, Glendale, CA	
DUROCHER, Leo	1991	Forest Lawn—Hollywood Hills, Los Angeles, CA	Hillside, Plot #3211
DURYEA, Dan	1968	Forest Lawn—Hollywood Hills, Los Angeles, CA	Revelation, Plot #7347
DVORAK, Ann	1979	(Cremated—not interred)	Ashes scattered
DWAN, Allan	1981	San Fernando Mission Cem., San Fernando, CA	
E			
EAGELS, Jeanne	1929	Calvary Catholic Cemetery, Kansas City, MO	
EDDY, Nelson	1967	Hollywood Memorial Park, Hollywood, CA	Section 8, Lot 89
EDENS, Roger	1970	Westwood Village Mem. Park, Los Angeles, CA	Sanctuary of Remembrance
EDWARDS, Cliff	1971	Valhalla Memorial Park, N. Hollywood, CA	Section D, near Heritage Fountain
EDWARDS, Snitz	1937		Cremated
• EDWARDS, Vince (Zoine)	1996	Holy Cross Cem. and Maus., Culver City, CA	Section CC, Tier 64, Grave 29
• EGAN, Richard	1987	Holy Cross Cem. and Maus., Culver City, CA	Section AA, Tier 37, Grave 139 (unmarked)
EILERS, Sally	1978	Forest Lawn Memorial-Park, Glendale, CA	Freedom Maus., Columbarium
• ELGART, Les	1995	Hillcrest Memorial Park, Dallas, TX	Garden of Prayer, Block 10, Lot 27, Sp 2
ELLINGTON, Duke	1974	Woodlawn Cemetery, The Bronx, NY	Division 49, at Fir & Knollwood Aves.
ELLIOT, "Mama" Cass	1974	Mount Sinai Memorial-Park, Los Angeles, CA	Court of Tanach, Lot 5000, Grave 2F
EMERSON, Hope	1960	Grace Hills Cemetery, Hawarden, PA	
EMMETT, Fern (Roquemore)	1946	Forest Lawn Memorial-Park, Glendale, CA	Masonic Section
ERROL, Leon	1951	Forest Lawn Memorial-Park, Glendale, CA	
ERWIN, Stuart	1967	Chapel of the Pines Crematory, Los Angeles, CA	
ETTING, Ruth	1978	Evergreen Cemetery, Colorado Springs, CO	Shrine of Rest Mausoleum
F			
• FACTOR, Max	1938	Hillside Memorial Park, Los Angeles, CA	Courts of the Book, Isaiah-U-314
FAIRBANKS, Douglas Sr.	1939	Hollywood Memorial Park, Hollywood, CA	Section 11
FAITH, Percy	1976	Hillside Memorial Park, Los Angeles, CA	Garden of Memories, Honor, Lawn Crypt 407
FARMER, Frances	1970	Oak Lawn Memorial Gardens, Noblesville, IN	
FARNUM, Franklyn	1961	Chapel of the Pines Crematory, Los Angeles, CA	
FARNUM, William	1953	Forest Lawn Memorial-Park, Glendale, CA	
FARRELL, Charles	1990	Welwood Murray Cemetery, Palm Springs, CA	Section 10-3, Lot G
FARRELL, Glenda	1971	National Cemetery, West Point, NY	
FARRELL, Virginia Valli	1968	Welwood Murray Cemetery, Palm Springs, CA	Section 10-3, Lot F
FARROW, John	1963	Holy Cross Cem. and Maus., Culver City, CA	Section P, Holy Redeemer, Plot #342
FAY, Frank	1961	Calvary Cemetery, Los Angeles, CA	
FAYLEN, Frank	1985	San Fernando Mission Cem., San Fernando, CA	
FAZENDA, Louise	1962	Inglewood Park Cemetery, Inglewood, CA	
FELDMAN, Marty	1982	Forest Lawn—Hollywood Hills, Los Angeles, CA	Garden of Heritage, Plot #5420
FELLINI, Federico	1993	Civico Cimitero, Rimini, Italy	Section O, in a brown brick-like family vault
• Fernandel	1971	Passy Cemetery, Paris, France	Black stone tomb with a raised cross
FIEDLER, Arthur	1979	St. Joseph Cemetery, West Roxbury, MA	
FIELDS, Totie (Johnson)	1978	Mount Sinai Memorial-Park, Los Angeles, CA	Reinterred here 2/96 (from Las Vegas, NV)
FIELDS, W. C.	1946	Forest Lawn Memorial-Park, Glendale, CA	Great Maus., Hall of Inspiration
FINCH, Flora	1940	Hollywood Memorial Park, Hollywood, CA	Section 1, Grave 416
FINCH, Peter	1977	Hollywood Memorial Park, Hollywood, CA	H'wood Cath. Maus., Crypt 1224, off Corr A
FINE, Larry	1975	Forest Lawn Memorial-Park, Glendale, CA	Freedom Maus., Sanctuary of Liberation
FITZMAURICE, George F.	1940	Forest Lawn Memorial-Park, Glendale, CA	
• FIX, Paul	1983	Woodlawn Cemetery, Santa Monica, CA	Block 17
FLATT, Lester	1979	Crestlawn Cemetery, Sparta, TN	
• FLEMING, Eric	1966	(Cremated)	
FLEMING, Victor	1949	Hollywood Memorial Park, Hollywood, CA	Abbey of the Psalms, Crypt 2081, Corr G-2
FLIPPEN, Jay C.	1971	Westwood Village Mem. Park, Los Angeles, CA	Corridor of Memories
FLYNN, Errol	1959	Forest Lawn Memorial-Park, Glendale, CA	Garden of Everlasting Peace
FLYNN, Joseph A. "Joe"	1974	Holy Cross Cem. and Maus., Culver City, CA	Section W, Tier 20, Grave 75
FOLEY, Red	1968	Woodlawn Memorial Park, Nashville, TN	
FONDA, Henry	1982	Grand View Memorial Park, Glendale, CA	Cremated (Ashes given to his family)
FONTAINE, Frank	1978	Oak Grove Cemetery, Medford, MA	
FONTANE, Tony	1974	Forest Lawn—Hollywood Hills, Los Angeles, CA	Courts of Remem., 409
FONTANNE, Lynn	1983	Forest Home Cemetery, Milwaukee, WI	
FORD, John	1973	Holy Cross Cem. and Maus., Culver City, CA	Section M, Lot 304, Grave 5
FORD, Mary	1977	Forest Lawn—Covina Hills, Covina, CA	
FORD, Paul	1976	Forest Lawn Memorial-Park, Cypress, CA	

NAME	YEAR	CEMETERY	INTERMENT SITE*
FOSTER, Preston	1970	El Camino Memorial Park, La Jolla, CA	Sanctuary of Love (3), Crypt 4, Tier F
FOWLER, Gene	1960	Holy Cross Cem. and Maus., Culver City, CA	Section M, Lot 792, Grave 3
FOX, Wallace W.	1958	Forest Lawn Memorial-Park, Glendale, CA	
FOY, Bryan	1977	Calvary Cemetery, Los Angeles, CA	
FOY, Eddie Sr.	1928	Holy Sepulchre Cemetery, New Rochelle, NY	
FRANCIS, Robert	1955	Forest Lawn—Hollywood Hills, Los Angeles, CA	Hillside, Plot #4535
FRANKLIN, Rupert	1939	Forest Lawn Memorial-Park, Glendale, CA	
FRANKLIN, Sidney (actor)	1931	Hollywood Memorial Park, Hollywood, CA	Section 13, Lot #321
FRANKLIN, Sidney (director)	1972	Hollywood Memorial Park, Hollywood, CA	Section 8, grave next to palm tree
FRAWLEY, William	1966	San Fernando Mission Cem., San Fernando, CA	Section C, at Curb No. 64, 5 rows in
FREDERICK, Fred Burke	1986	Chapel of the Pines Crematory, Los Angeles, CA	Cremated
FREDERICK, Pauline	1938	Grand View Memorial Park, Glendale, CA	
FREED, Arthur	1973	Hillside Memorial Park, Los Angeles, CA	Garden of Memories, Honor, Lawn Crypt 418
• FREEMAN, Young Frank	1969	Westview Cemetery, Atlanta, GA	Section 10, Lot 277, Grave 10
• FRELENG, Isadore "Friz"	1995	Hillside Memorial Park, Los Angeles, CA	Canaan, Block E-249
FRENCH, George B.	1961	Forest Lawn Memorial-Park, Glendale, CA	
FRIML, Rudolph	1972	Forest Lawn Memorial-Park, Glendale, CA	Court of Last Supper
FRIZZELL, Lefty	1975	Forest Lawn Cemetery, Nashville, TN	
• FRYE, Dwight	1943	Forest Lawn Memorial-Park, Glendale, CA	
FULLER, Mary	1973	Congressional Cemetery, Washington, D.C.	
FULTON, Maude	1950	Forest Lawn Memorial-Park, Glendale, CA	
G			
GABLE, Clark	1960	Forest Lawn Memorial-Park, Glendale, CA	Great Maus., Sanctuary of Trust
• GABOR, Eva	1995	Westwood Village Mem. Park, Los Angeles, CA	Nr. Armand Hammer's Maus. (Right front)
GANZHORN, John W.	1956	Forest Lawn Memorial-Park, Glendale, CA	
GARBO, Greta	1990	(Cremated—not interred)	Ashes given to her niece, Gray Reisfield
• GARCIA, Jerry	1995	(Cremated)	Ashes scattered in the Ganges River, India
GARDINER, Reginald	1980	Forest Lawn—Hollywood Hills, Los Angeles, CA	Courts of Remem., Sanc. of Reflection, 3322
• GARDNER, Ava	1990	Sunset Memorial Park, Smithfield, NC	
GARFIELD, John	1952	Westchester Hills Cem, Hastings-on-Hudson, NY	
GARLAND, Judy	1969	Ferncliff Cemetery and Maus., Hartsdale, NY	Maus., Unit 9, Section HH, Crypt 31
GAYE, Marvin	1984	(Cremated—not interred)	Ashes scattered from a ship at sea
GAYNOR, Janet (Gregory)	1984	Hollywood Memorial Park, Hollywood, CA	Section 8, Lot 193
GEER, Will	1978	(Cremated—not interred)	Ashes scattered in San Fernando Valley, CA
GEHRIG, Lou	1941	Kensico Cemetery, Valhalla, NY	Ashes in family vault
GELLER, Bruce	1978	Mount Sinai Memorial-Park, Los Angeles, CA	
GEORGE, Christopher	1983	Westwood Village Mem. Park, Los Angeles, CA	Sanctuary of Tranquility
GEORGE, Gorgeous	1963	(See WAGNER, "Gorgeous" George)	
GERSHWIN, George	1937	Mount Hope Cem., Hastings-on-Hudson, NY	
GERSHWIN, Ira	1983	Mount Hope Cem., Hastings-on-Hudson, NY	
GIBB, Andy	1988	Forest Lawn—Hollywood Hills, Los Angeles, CA	Courts of Remem., 2534
GIBSON, Hoot	1962	Inglewood Park Cemetery, Inglewood, CA	Lot 92, Grave #6, Magnolia Plot
GILBERT, Billy	1971	Odd Fellows Cemetery, Los Angeles, CA	
GILBERT, John	1936	Forest Lawn Memorial-Park, Glendale, CA	Whispering Pines
GILLETT, King	1932	Forest Lawn Memorial-Park, Glendale, CA	Great Maus., Begonia Corridor
GINGOLD, Hermione	1987	Forest Lawn Memorial-Park, Glendale, CA	Great Maus., Sanctuary of the Holy Spirit
GISH, Dorothy	1968	St. Bartholomew's Epis. Ch., New York, NY	
• GLEASON, Jackie	1987	Our Lady of Mercies Cemetery, Miami, FL	
GLEASON, James	1959	Holy Cross Cem. and Maus., Culver City, CA	Section D, Sacred Heart
GODOWSKY, Dagmar	1975	Mount Hope Cem., Hastings-on-Hudson, NY	
• GOETZ, William	1969	Hillside Memorial Park, Los Angeles, CA	Garden of Memories, Devotion, Sarcoph. B
GOLDWYN, Frances Howard	1976	Forest Lawn Memorial-Park, Glendale, CA	
GOLDWYN, Samuel	1973	Forest Lawn Memorial-Park, Glendale, CA	Garden of Honor, first garden on right
GOMEZ, Thomas	1971	Westwood Village Mem. Park, Los Angeles, CA	
GOODMAN, Benny	1986	Long Ridge Cemetery, Stamford, CT	
GOODSON, Mark	1992	Hillside Memorial Park, Los Angeles, CA	Mausoleum, Gdn. of Abraham-Sarcoph. B
GOODWIN, Bill	1958	Desert Memorial Park, Palm Springs, CA	Section B-1, Lot 17
GORCEY, Leo	1969	Los Molinas Cemetery, Red Bluff, CA	
GORDON, Huntly	1956	Forest Lawn Memorial-Park, Glendale, CA	
GORDON, Leon	1960	Forest Lawn Memorial-Park, Glendale, CA	
GOSDEN, Freeman	1982	Forest Lawn—Hollywood Hills, Los Angeles, CA	
• GOTTLIEB, Conrad I.	1995	Hebrew Young Men's Cem., Baltimore, MD	

NAME	YEAR	CEMETERY	INTERMENT SITE*
GOULD, Glenn	1982	Mount Pleasant Cem., Toronto (Ont.), Canada	
GRABLE, Betty (James)	1973	Inglewood Park Cemetery, Inglewood, CA	Golden West Maus., A78, Sanc. of Dawn
• GRANT, Cary	1986	(Cremated)	
GRANT, Earl	1970	Forest Lawn—Hollywood Hills, Los Angeles, CA	Lincoln Terrace, Plot #226
GRANVILLE, Bonita (Wrather)	1988	Holy Cross Cem. and Maus., Culver City, CA	Section "Grotto," Lot 196, Grave 12
GRAPEWIN, Charles	1956	Forest Lawn Memorial-Park, Glendale, CA	Great Maus., Col. of Inspiration
GRAY, Gilda	1959	Holy Cross Cem. and Maus., Culver City, CA	
• GREEN, Alfred E.	1960	Forest Lawn Memorial-Park, Glendale, CA	Great Maus., Sanc. of Refuge, Crypt #5089
GREENE, Lorne	1987	Hillside Memorial Park, Los Angeles, CA	Courts of the Book, Lawn Crypt-5-800-8B
GREENSTREET, Sydney	1954	Forest Lawn Memorial-Park, Glendale, CA	Ashes in a utility room (not open to public)
GRIFFITH, David Wark	1948	Mt. Tabor United Meth. Ch., Crestwood, KY	
• GRINKOV, Sergei	1995	Vagankovskoye Cem., Moscow, Russia	
GUINAN, Mary L. "Texas"	1933	Calvary Cemetery, Woodside (Queens), NY	Section 47
GUTHRIE, Woody	1967	(Cremated—not interred)	Ashes cast into the ocean at Coney Is., NY
GWENN, Edmund	1959	Chapel of the Pines Crematory, Los Angeles, CA	In basement holding vault, not on view
H			
HACKETT, Joan	1983	Hollywood Memorial Park, Hollywood, CA	Abbey of the Psalms, Crypt 2314, Corr D-3
HAINES, William	1973	Woodlawn Cemetery, Santa Monica, CA	
HALE, Alan Sr.	1950	Forest Lawn Memorial-Park, Glendale, CA	Whispering Pines
HALEY, Jack	1979	Holy Cross Cem. and Maus., Culver City, CA	Section "Grotto," Lot 100, Grave 2
HALL, Charlie	1959	Forest Lawn Memorial-Park, Glendale, CA	Eventide, Lot 1928
HALL, Jon	1979	Forest Lawn—Hollywood Hills, Los Angeles, CA	Court of Liberty, same row w/Buster Keaton
HALOP, Billy	1976	Mount Sinai Memorial-Park, Los Angeles, CA	Garden of Sherrot, Crypt 64181 along wall
HALTON, Charles	1959	Forest Lawn Memorial-Park, Glendale, CA	
HAMILTON, Hale Rice	1942	Forest Lawn Memorial-Park, Glendale, CA	
HAMMER, Armand	1990	Westwood Village Mem. Park, Los Angeles, CA	In family mausoleum, near entrance
HAMMERSTEIN, Oscar II	1960	Ferncliff Cemetery and Maus., Hartsdale, NY	Ashes buried
HAMPDEN, Walter	1955	Restland Memorial Park, Burbank, CA	
HANCOCK, John	1992	Forest Lawn—Hollywood Hills, Los Angeles, CA	Devotion, Plot #8018
HARDING, Ann	1981	Forest Lawn Memorial-Park, Glendale, CA	Cremated
HARDY, Oliver	1957	Valhalla Memorial Park, N. Hollywood, CA	Gdn. of Hope, 2nd wall to rt. of Her. Fount.
HARDY, Sam	1935	Forest Lawn Memorial-Park, Glendale, CA	
HARLOW, Jean	1937	Forest Lawn Memorial-Park, Glendale, CA	Great Maus., Sanctuary of Benediction
HARRIGAN, William	1966	Arlington National Cemetery, Arlington, VA	
HARRIS, Robin	1990	Inglewood Park Cemetery, Inglewood, CA	Chap. of Freedom, Manchester Maus. #D5
HART, Lorenz	1943	Mt. Zion Cemetery, Maspeth, NY	
HART, Moss	1961	Ferncliff Cemetery and Maus., Hartsdale, NY	Maus., Unit 8 Alcove EE-FF, Col. D Niche 4
HART, William S.	1946	Green-Wood Cemetery, Brooklyn, NY	
HARVEY, Paul (actor)	1955	Forest Lawn Memorial-Park, Glendale, CA	
HATHAWAY, Henry	1985	Holy Cross Cem. and Maus., Culver City, CA	Mausoleum, left of the altar
• HATTON, Rondo	1946	American Legion Cemetery, Tampa, FL	
HAWKS, Howard	1977	(Cremated—not interred)	Ashes scattered
HAYDEN, Harry	1955	Forest Lawn Memorial-Park, Glendale, CA	
HAYDEN, Russell	1981	Oakwood Memorial Park, Chatsworth, CA	
HAYES, George "Gabby"	1969	Forest Lawn—Hollywood Hills, Los Angeles, CA	Hillside, Plot #4972
• HAYES, Helen	1993	Oak Hill Cememtery, Nyack, NY	
HAYMES, Dick	1980	(Cremated—not interred)	Ashes given to family
HAYWARD, Susan	1975	Our Lady of Perpetual Help Ch., Carrollton, GA	
HAYWORTH, Rita	1987	Holy Cross Cem. and Maus., Culver City, CA	Section "Grotto", Lot 196, Grave 6
HEAD, Edith	1981	Forest Lawn Memorial-Park, Glendale, CA	Cathedral slope, Plot 1675, at the top of hill
HEALY, Ted	1937	Calvary Cemetery, Los Angeles, CA	Section F, Lot 1693, Grave 14
HEARN, Sam	1964	Forest Lawn Memorial-Park, Glendale, CA	
HEFLIN, Van	1971	Chapel of the Pines Crematory, Los Angeles, CA	
HEIDT, Horace	1986	Forest Lawn—Hollywood Hills, Los Angeles, CA	Enduring Faith
HEISLER, Stuart	1979	Eternal Hills Memorial Park, Oceanside, CA	
HELD, Anna	1918	Cem. of the Gate of Heaven, Hawthorne, NY	
HELLINGER, Mark	1947	Kensico Cemetery, Valhalla, NY	
• HELLMAN, Lillian	1984	Abels Hill Cemetery, Chilmark (M.V.), MA	
HELTON, Percy	1971	Westwood Village Mem. Park, Los Angeles, CA	Sanctuary of Remembrance
HENDRIX, Jimi	1970	Greenwood Memorial Cemetery, Renton, WA	
HENDRIX, Wanda	1981	Forest Lawn—Hollywood Hills, Los Angeles, CA	Courts of Remem., 4349
• HENIE, Sonja	1969	Henie-Onstad Art Center, Oslo, Norway	

• New entry.

* Some cemeteries refuse to reveal specific locations.

NAME	YEAR	CEMETERY	INTERMENT SITE*
HEPBURN, Audrey	1993	Tolochenaz, Vaud, Switzerland	
HERBERT, Holmes	1956	Forest Lawn Memorial-Park, Glendale, CA	
HERBERT, Hugh	1952	Holy Cross Cem. and Maus., Culver City, CA	Section D, Lot 267, Grave 11
HERBERT, Victor	1924	Woodlawn Cemetery, The Bronx, NY	Div. 42, in maus. at Border and Linden Ave.
HERMAN, Woody	1987	Hollywood Memorial Park, Hollywood, CA	Grounds, Crypt 6689, Unit 10
HERSHOLT, Jean	1956	Forest Lawn Memorial-Park, Glendale, CA	Great Maus., monument opp. entrance
HILL, Benny	1992	Hollybrook Cem., Shirley, Southampton, Eng.	
HITCHCOCK, (Sir) Alfred	1980	(Cremated—not interred)	Ashes scattered
HODIAK, John	1955	Calvary Cemetery, Los Angeles, CA	Main Mausoleum, next to Mabel Normand
HOLDEN, Fay	1973	Forest Lawn Memorial-Park, Glendale, CA	Whispering Pines
HOLDEN, William	1981	(Cremated—not interred)	Ashes scattered in the Pacific Ocean
HOLIDAY, Billie	1959	St. Raymond's Cemetery, The Bronx, NY	
HOLLIDAY, Judy	1965	Westchester Hills Cem, Hastings-on-Hudson, NY	
HOLLY, Buddy	1959	City of Lubbock Cemetery, Lubbock, TX	Block 44 at Azalea Ave. (nr. path)
HOLT, Jack	1951	Los Angeles National Cemetery, Los Angeles, CA	Section 107
HOOD, Darla	1979	Hollywood Memorial Park, Hollywood, CA	Abbey of the Psalms, Crypt 7213, Corr G-4
HOPPER, Hedda	1966	Rose Hill Cemetery, Altoona, PA	Ashes buried
• HOPPER, William	1970	Rose Hills Memorial Park, Whittier, CA	Memorial Urn Garden, Space 210
• HOROWITZ, Vladimir	1989	Cimitero Monumentale, Milan, Italy	Toscanini family mausoleum
HORTON, Edward Everett	1970	Forest Lawn Memorial-Park, Glendale, CA	
HOUDINI, Harry	1926	Machpelah Cemetery, Ridgewood, (Queens), NY	
HOUSMAN, Arthur	1942	Los Angeles National Cemetery, Los Angeles, CA	
HOWARD, Jerome "Curly"	1952	Home of Peace Mem. Park, Los Angeles, CA	Western Jewish Institute, SW Corner, Plot 1
HOWARD, Leslie	1943		Body never recovered from Atlantic Ocean
HOWARD, Moe	1975	Hillside Memorial Park, Los Angeles, CA	Garden of Memories, Alcove of Love C233
HOWARD, Shemp	1955	Home of Peace Mem. Park, Los Angeles, CA	Chapel Maus., Eternal Light Corr., EW215
HOWARD, Willie	1949	Cedar Park Cemetery, Paramus, NJ	
HOWE, James Wong	1976	Westwood Village Mem. Park, Los Angeles, CA	Sanctuary of Tranquility, rear wall
HOWLAND, Jobyna	1936	Forest Lawn Memorial-Park, Glendale, CA	
HUDNET, William H. "Bill"	1992	Holy Cross Cemetery, Baltimore, MD	
HUDSON, Rock	1985	(Cremated—not interred)	Ashes scattered at sea
HUDSON, William Woodson Jr.	1974	Westwood Village Mem. Park, Los Angeles, CA	
• HUGHES, Howard	1976	Glenwood Cemetery, Houston, TX	
HUGHES, Lloyd	1958	Forest Lawn Memorial-Park, Glendale, CA	
HULL, Josephine	1957	Newton Cemetery, Newton, MA	
• HUMANN, Helena	1994	Restland Memorial Park, Dallas, TX	Chapel Gardens, Crypt 5 S-130
HUMBERSTONE, Bruce H.	1984	Hollywood Memorial Park, Hollywood, CA	
HUNTER, Jeffrey	1969	Glen Haven Memorial Park, San Fernando, CA	
• HUNTLEY, Chet	1974	Sunset Hills Cemetery, Bozeman, ID	
HUROK, Sol	1974	Mount Hope Cem., Hastings-on-Hudson, NY	
HURT, Marlin	1946	Forest Lawn Memorial-Park, Glendale, CA	
HUSTON, John	1987	Hollywood Memorial Park, Hollywood, CA	Section 8, Lot 8
HUSTON, Walter	1950	(Cremated at Chapel of the Pines, L. A., CA)	Ashes given to his family
HUTTON, Jim	1979	Westwood Village Mem. Park, Los Angeles, CA	
• HYMAN, Phyllis	1995	(Cremated)	Ashes sent to her family in Pittsburgh, PA
I			
IHNAT, Steve	1972	Westwood Village Mem. Park, Los Angeles, CA	Corridor of Memories
INGRAM, Rex (actor)	1969	Forest Lawn—Hollywood Hills, Los Angeles, CA	Court of Liberty, Plot #822
INGRAM, Rex (director)	1950	Forest Lawn Memorial-Park, Glendale, CA	Great Maus., Col. of Memory, under window
• IRELAND, Jill	1990	Forest Lawn Memorial-Park, Glendale, CA	
ITURBI, José	1980	Holy Cross Cem. and Maus., Culver City, CA	Mausoleum, Block 16, Crypt E-1
J			
JACKSON, Mahalia	1972	Providence Memorial Park, Metairie, LA	Section E, on east side of Mausoleum
JACKSON, Mary Ann	1991	Lake View Cemetery, Cleveland, OH.	Section 43, Lot 678
JAFFE. Sam	1984	Eden Memorial Park, San Fernando, CA	Top of outside wall, at top of hill
JANSSEN, David	1980	Hillside Memorial Park, Los Angeles, CA	Mausoleum, Memorial Court-516
JESSEL, George	1981	Hillside Memorial Park, Los Angeles, CA	Mausoleum, Memorial Court-516
JOHNSON, Chic	1962	Palm Mortuary Mausoleum, Las Vegas, NV	Ground burial
JOHNSON, Nunnally	1977	Westwood Village Mem. Park, Los Angeles, CA	Sanctuary of Tranquility, rear wall
• JOHNSON, Tor	1971	Eternal Valley Memorial Park, Newhall, CA	
JOLSON, Al	1950	Hillside Memorial Park, Los Angeles, CA	In Al Jolson Memorial (at top of waterfall)
JONES, Brian	1969	Priory Road Cemetery, Cheltenham, England	(In Prestbury)

NAME	YEAR	CEMETERY	INTERMENT SITE*
JONES, Buck	1942	(Cremated—not interred)	Ashes scattered at sea
JONES, Carolyn	1983	Forest Lawn Memorial-Park, Glendale, CA	Great Maus., Col. of Memory
JONES, Ken	1993	Inglewood Park Cemetery, Inglewood, CA	Lot 932, Grave E, Pineview Plot
JONES, Lindley "Spike"	1965	Holy Cross Cem. and Maus., Culver City, CA	Mausoleum, Block 70, Crypt A-7
JOPLIN, Janis	1970	(Cremated—not interred)	Ashes strewn along coast of Northern CA
JORDAN, Jim	1988	Holy Cross Cem. and Maus., Culver City, CA	St. Ann's Garden, Tier 153, Grave 1
JORDAN, Marion	1961	Holy Cross Cem. and Maus., Culver City, CA	St. Ann's Garden, Tier 153, Grave 2
JORY, Victor	1982	Westwood Village Mem. Park, Los Angeles, CA	
JULIA, Raul	1994	San Juan, Puerto Rico	
JULIAN, Rupert	1943	Forest Lawn Memorial-Park, Glendale, CA	
K			
KANE, Helen	1966	Long Island Nat'l Cem., Farmingdale (L.I.), NY	
KARNS, Roscoe	1970	Hollywood Memorial Park, Hollywood, CA	
KASSEL, Art	1965	Forest Lawn—Hollywood Hills, Los Angeles, CA	Col. of Remembrance, 6098
• KATZ, Mickey	1985	Hillside Memorial Park, Los Angeles, CA	Valley of Remembrance, Block 1-196-2
KAUFMAN, Andy	1984	Beth David Cemetery, Elmont (L.I.), NY	
KAYE, Danny	1987	Kensico Cemetery, Valhalla, NY	Valhalla Plot
KAYE, Nora (Ross)	1987	Westwood Village Mem. Park, Los Angeles, CA	Section D, #36
KEATON, Buster	1966	Forest Lawn—Hollywood Hills, Los Angeles, CA	Court of Liberty, nr. G. Washington statue
KEELER, Ruby	1993	Holy Sepulchre Cemetery, Orange, CA	"Ruby K. Lowe," Sect. N, Tier 21, Grave 46
KEIGHLEY, William	1984	Forest Lawn Memorial-Park, Glendale, CA	Great Maus., Col. of Memory
KELLAWAY, Cecil	1973	Westwood Village Mem. Park, Los Angeles, CA	Sanctuary of Remembrance
KELLY, Emmett	1979	Rest Haven Memorial Park, Lafayette, IN	Sunset Terr. sect., bet. entr. and exit drives
KELLY, Grace	1982	Cathedral of St. Nicholas, Monte Carlo, Monaco	Grimaldi family vault
KELLY, Patsy	1981	Calvary Cemetery, Woodside (Queens), NY	
KELLY, Paul	1956	Holy Cross Cem. and Maus., Culver City, CA	Sect. D, Sacred Heart, 1 row above Plot 61
• KENDALL, Kay (Harrison)	1959	St. John-at-Hampstead Cem., London, England	Near front fence
KENNEDY, Edgar	1948	Holy Cross Cem. and Maus., Culver City, CA	Section D, Sacred Heart, Grave 7, Lot 193
KENNY, Herbert C.	1992	St. John the Evangelist RC Ch., Columbia, MD	
KENTON, Stan	1979	Westwood Village Mem. Park, Los Angeles, CA	Rose Garden
KERN, Jerome	1945	Ferncliff Cemetery and Maus., Hartsdale, NY	Maus., Unit 4 Alcove C, Pvt. Niche Mem. 1
KERRIGAN, J. Warren	1947	Forest Lawn Memorial-Park, Glendale, CA	
KERT, Larry	1991	(Cremated—not interred)	
KIBBEE, Guy	1956	Kensico Cemetery, Valhalla, NY	Actors Fund Plot
• Kiki	1953	Montparnasse Cemetery, Paris, France	
KILBRIDE, Percy	1964	San B./Golden Gate Nat'l Cem., San Bruno, CA	Section 2-B, nr. chain link fence by freeway
KILGALLEN, Dorothy	1965	Cem. of the Gate of Heaven, Hawthorne, NY	
KILIAN, Victor	1979	Westwood Village Mem. Park, Los Angeles, CA	Ashes scattered in the Rose Garden
KING, Henry	1982	Holy Cross Cem. and Maus., Culver City, CA	
KNIGHT, Ted	1986	Forest Lawn Memorial-Park, Glendale, CA	Ascension Garden (left side)
KOLKER, Joseph Henry	1947	Forest Lawn Memorial-Park, Glendale, CA	
KORJUS, Miliza	1980	Westwood Village Mem. Park, Los Angeles, CA	Sanctuary of Tranquility, rear wall
KORNGOLD, Erich Wolfgang	1957	Hollywood Memorial Park, Hollywood, CA	Section 8, Lot 15
KOSTELANETZ, Andre	1980	(Cremated—not interred)	Ashes scattered at sea, off Kauai, Hawaii
KOVACS, Ernie	1962	Forest Lawn—Hollywood Hills, Los Angeles, CA	Across Vista Ln., facing Courts of Remem.
KREISLER, Fritz	1962	Woodlawn Cemetery, The Bronx, NY	Division 31, in mausoleum off Filbert Ave.
KRUGER, Otto	1974	Forest Lawn—Hollywood Hills, Los Angeles, CA	Churchyard, Plot #4266
KRUPA, Gene	1973	Holy Cross Cemetery, Calumet City, IL	Immaculata Section
KUHLMAN, Kathryn	1976	Forest Lawn Memorial-Park, Glendale, CA	Garden of Memory
KYSER, Kay	1985	Old Cemetery, Chapel Hill, NC	
L			
LADD, Alan	1964	Forest Lawn Memorial-Park, Glendale, CA	Freedom Maus., Sanctuary of Heritage
LADD, Sue Carol	1982	Forest Lawn Memorial-Park, Glendale, CA	Freedom Maus., Sanctuary of Heritage
LAEMMLE, Carl	1939	Home of Peace Mem. Park, Los Angeles, CA	Chapel Maus., in the Laemmle family room
LAHR, Bert	1967	Union Field Cem., Ridgewood (Queens), NY	
• LAIRD, Jack	1991	Hollywood Memorial Park, Hollywood, CA	Section 8
LAKE, Arthur	1987	Hollywood Memorial Park, Hollywood, CA	Douras Mausoleum, Section 8, Lot 261-264
LAKE, Veronica	1973	(Cremated—not interred)	Ashes scattered at sea in Virgin Islands
LaMARR, Barbara	1926	Hollywood Memorial Park, Hollywood, CA	H'wood Cath. Maus.
LAMAS, Fernando	1982	Rose Dale Cemetery, Los Angeles, CA	
LANCHESTER, Elsa	1986	(Cremated—not interred)	Ashes scattered at sea
LANDIS, Carole	1948	Forest Lawn Memorial-Park, Glendale, CA	Everlasting Love, Lot 968, Gr. 8 next to curb

NAME	YEAR	CEMETERY	INTERMENT SITE*
LANDON, Michael	1991	Hillside Memorial Park, Los Angeles, CA	Ashes in private room with clear glass door
LANE, Allan "Rocky"	1973	Inglewood Park Cemetery, Inglewood, CA	Inside Grave A, Lot 70, Rosehill Plot
LANE, Lola	1981	Calvary Cemetery, Santa Barbara, CA	Sect. M, Tier 17, Gr 97 (Lola Lane Hanlon)
LANE, Rosemary	1974	Forest Lawn Memorial-Park, Glendale, CA	No headstone
LANFIELD, Sidney	1972	Westwood Village Mem. Park, Los Angeles, CA	Sanctuary of Remembrance
LANG, Fritz	1976	Forest Lawn—Hollywood Hills, Los Angeles, CA	Murmuring Trees, Plot #3818
LANTZ, Walter	1994	Forest Lawn—Hollywood Hills, Los Angeles, CA	Col. of Radiant Light
LANZA, Mario	1959	Holy Cross Cem. and Maus., Culver City, CA	Mausoleum, Crypt D-2, Block 46
LaROCQUE, Rod	1969	(Cremated—not interred)	Ashes scattered at sea
LaRUE, Jack	1984	Holy Cross Cem. and Maus., Culver City, CA	Mausoleum, Block 69, Crypt E-3
LASKY, Jesse L. Sr.	1958	Hollywood Memorial Park, Hollywood, CA	Abbey of the Psalms, Crypt 2196, Corr G-3
LAUGHLIN, Billy "Froggy"	1948	Rose Hills Memorial Park, Whittier, CA	Older section
LAUGHTON, Charles	1962	Forest Lawn—Hollywood Hills, Los Angeles, CA	Courts of Remem., in black marble vault
LAUREL, Stanley	1965	Forest Lawn—Hollywood Hills, Los Angeles, CA	Ashes in Garden of Heritage at garden wall
LAVERNE, Lucille	1945	Inglewood Park Cemetery, Inglewood, CA	Center Grave D, Lot 236, Palm Plot
LAWFORD, Peter	1984	(Cremated—not interred)	Ashes scattered at sea
LAWRENCE, Florence	1938	Hollywood Memorial Park, Hollywood, CA	Section 2, buried in an unmarked grave
LAWRENCE, Gertrude	1952	Upton Cemetery, Upton, MA	
• LAWRENCE, Lillian	1926	Hollywood Memorial Park, Hollywood, CA	H'wood Cath. Maus.
• LAWRENCE, Walter Smith	1961	Glenwood Cemetery, Beeville, TX	
• LAWRENCE, William E.	1947	Maple Grove Cemetery, Horsehead, NY	
LEBEDEFF, Ivan	1953	Forest Lawn Memorial-Park, Glendale, CA	
LEDBETTER, Huddie	1949	Shiloh Church Cemetery, Shreveport, LA	
LEE, Brandon	1993	Lake View Cemetery, Seattle, WA	Buried next to his father, Bruce Lee
LEE, Bruce	1973	Lake View Cemetery, Seattle, WA	
LEE, Canada	1952	Woodlawn Cemetery, The Bronx, NY	
LEE, Gypsy Rose	1970	Inglewood Park Cemetery, Inglewood, CA	Lot 1087, Grave #8, Pinecrest Plot
LEHRMAN, Henry	1946	Hollywood Memorial Park, Hollywood, CA	Section 8, Lot 257 (next to Virginia Rappe)
LEHRMAN, Oscar S.	1992	Westwood Village Mem. Park, Los Angeles, CA	Section D, #81
LEIBER, Fritz	1949	Forest Lawn—Hollywood Hills, Los Angeles, CA	Everlasting Love, Plot #864, Grave 13
LEMBECK, Harvey	1982	Eden Memorial Park, San Fernando, CA	
LENNON, John	1980	(Cremated—not interred)	Ashes given to his wife, Yoko Ono
• LEONARD, Robert Z.	1968	Forest Lawn Memorial-Park, Glendale, CA	Great Maus., Sanctuary of Vespers
• LERNER, Sam	1989	Hillside Memorial Park, Los Angeles, CA	Laurel Gardens, Block 18-177-3A
LeROY, Mervyn	1987	Forest Lawn Memorial-Park, Glendale, CA	Garden of Memory
LEVANT, Oscar	1972	Westwood Village Mem. Park, Los Angeles, CA	Sanctuary of Love, bottom right
LEWIS, Mitchell	1956	Forest Lawn Memorial-Park, Glendale, CA	
• LEWIS, Ronald "Raan"	1995	Laurel Land Memorial Park, Dallas, TX	Field of Honor, Lot 125 B/C
LEWIS, Ted	1971	Forest Cemetery, Circleville, OH	
LEWIS, Tom	1927	Calvary Cemetery, Woodside (Queens), NY	
Liberace	1987	Forest Lawn—Hollywood Hills, Los Angeles, CA	Courts of Remem., in white sarcophagus
LIBERACE, George	1983	Forest Lawn—Hollywood Hills, Los Angeles, CA	Courts of Remem., in white sarcophagus
LINCOLN, Elmo	1952	Hollywood Memorial Park, Hollywood, CA	
LINDSAY, Margaret	1981	Holy Cross Cem. and Maus., Culver City, CA	Section P, Holy Redeemer, rt. of Plot 432
LITTLE, Malcolm "Malcolm X"	1965	Ferncliff Cemetery and Maus., Hartsdale, NY	Pinewood B, Grave 150
LITTLEFIELD, Lucien	1959	Forest Lawn Memorial-Park, Glendale, CA	Whispering Pines, Plot #1720
LIVINGSTONE, Mary (Benny)	1983	Hillside Memorial Park, Los Angeles, CA	Mausoleum, Graciousness, Sarcophagus F
LLOYD, Frank	1960	Forest Lawn Memorial-Park, Glendale, CA	
LLOYD, Harold Sr.	1971	Forest Lawn Memorial-Park, Glendale, CA	Great Maus., Begonia corridor #771
LOCHER, Felix	1969	Forest Lawn—Hollywood Hills, Los Angeles, CA	Court of Liberty
LOCKER, Frances	1990	Hollywood Memorial Park, Hollywood, CA	Abbey of the Psalms
LOCKHART, Gene	1957	Holy Cross Cem. and Maus., Culver City, CA	Section D, Lot 279, Grave 6
LOCKLEAR, Omer	1920	Greenwood Cemetery, Fort Worth, TX	89 - 9E
LOESSER, Frank	1969	(Cremated—not interred)	Ashes scattered at sea
LOEW, Marcus	1927	Cypress Hills Cemetery, Brooklyn, NY	
LOFT, Arthur	1947	Forest Lawn Memorial-Park, Glendale, CA	
LOGAN, Ella	1969	Holy Cross Cemetery, San Mateo, CA	
LOMBARD, Carole (Gable)	1942	Forest Lawn Memorial-Park, Glendale, CA	Great Maus., Sanctuary of Trust
LOMBARDO, Guy	1977	Pinelawn Mem. Park, Farmingdale (L.I.), NY	
LONDON, Tom	1963	Forest Lawn Memorial-Park, Glendale, CA	
LONG, Richard	1974	Grand View Memorial Park, Glendale, CA	
LOPEZ, Vincent	1975	Southern Memorial Park, Miami, FL	

• New entry.

* Some cemeteries refuse to reveal specific locations.

NAME	YEAR	CEMETERY	INTERMENT SITE*
LORD, Pauline	1950	Kensico Cemetery, Valhalla, NY	
LORRE, Peter	1964	Hollywood Memorial Park, Hollywood, CA	H'wood Cath. Maus., Niche 5, T-1, Corr C
• LOUIS, Joe	1981	Arlington National Cemetery, Arlington, VA	
LOUISE, Anita (Marks)	1970	Forest Lawn Memorial-Park, Glendale, CA	Next to her husband, Buddy Adler
LOVEJOY, Frank	1962	Holy Cross Cem. and Maus., Culver City, CA	Section P, Lot 306, Grave 5
LOWE, Edmund	1971	San Fernando Mission Cem., San Fernando, CA	Section B, Block 7, Lot 1113
LOY, Myrna	1993	Forestdale Cemetery, Helena, MT	Ashes buried alongside her parents
LUBITSCH, Ernst	1947	Forest Lawn Memorial-Park, Glendale, CA	
LUGOSI, Bela	1956	Holy Cross Cem. and Maus., Culver City, CA	Section "Grotto," Tier 120, Grave 1
LUKE, Keye	1991	Rose Hills Memorial Park, Whittier, CA	
LUNDIGAN, William	1975	Holy Cross Cem. and Maus., Culver City, CA	Section D, Lot 269, Grave 3
LUNT, Alfred	1977	Forest Home Cemetery, Milwaukee, WI	
LYMAN, Abe	1957	Forest Lawn Memorial-Park, Glendale, CA	
LYNDE, Paul	1982	(Cremated)	Ashes buried in Mount Vernon, Ohio
LYNN, Diana	1971	Chapel of the Pines Crematory, Los Angeles, CA	
LYON, Ben	1979	Hollywood Memorial Park, Hollywood, CA	Col., Niche 7-8, T.3, Upper No. Wall
M			
MABLEY, Jackie "Moms"	1975	Ferncliff Cemetery and Maus., Hartsdale, NY	Knollwood Garden I, Row 14, Grave 4
MacDONALD, Jeanette	1965	Forest Lawn Memorial-Park, Glendale, CA	Freedom Maus., Sanctuary of Heritage
• MacDONALD, Joseph Farrell	1952	Chapel of the Pines Crematory, Los Angeles, CA	Memory Hall, Section K, B-2
MACK, Charles E.	1934	Forest Lawn Memorial-Park, Glendale, CA	
• MACK, Rose	1927	In the family plot in Holyoke, MA	Buried with her husband, Joseph Lester
MacLANE, Barton	1969	Valhalla Memorial Park, N. Hollywood, CA	
MacMURRAY, Fred	1991	Holy Cross Cem. and Maus., Culver City, CA	Mausoleum, Room 7, Crypt D-1
MACREADY, George	1973		Body given to UCLA Medical School
MAIN, Marjorie	1975	Forest Lawn—Hollywood Hills, Los Angeles, CA	Enduring Faith, Plot #2083
MAMOULIAN, Rouben	1987	Forest Lawn Memorial-Park, Glendale, CA	Ascension Garden
MANSFIELD, Jayne	1967	Fairview Cemetery, Pen Argyl, PA	Grave is near entrance
• MANTLE, Mickey	1995	Hillcrest Memorial Park, Dallas, TX	Mausoleum St. Mark NE-N-C-13
• MARCH, Fredric	1975	New Milford, CT	Buried on his farm
• MARCH, Hal	1970	Hillside Memorial Park, Los Angeles, CA	Mount Sholom, Block 4-144-6
• MARCIANO, "Rocky"	1969	Lauderdale Memorial Park, Ft. Lauderdale, FL	
Margo (Albert)	1985	Westwood Village Mem. Park, Los Angeles, CA	Section D, #61
MARLOWE, Hugh	1982	Ferncliff Cemetery and Maus., Hartsdale, NY	Maus., Unit 10, Alcove BB-CC, Niche 9A
MARSHALL, George E.	1975	Holy Cross Cem. and Maus., Culver City, CA	Mausoleum
• MARSHALL, Tully	1943	Hollywood Memorial Park, Hollywood, CA	Section 8, grave is beneath a tree
• MARTIN, Dean	1995	Westwood Village Mem. Park, Los Angeles, CA	Sanctuary of Love
• MARTIN, Dean Paul Jr.	1987	Los Angeles National Cemetery, Los Angeles, CA	
MARTIN, Marion	1985	Holy Cross Cem. and Maus., Culver City, CA	
MARTIN, Mary	1990	Old Greenwood Cemetery, Weatherford, TX	Has iron fence surrounding gravesite
MARTIN, Ross	1981	Mount Sinai Memorial-Park, Los Angeles, CA	Temple Beth Hillel, Plot #3628
MARTIN, Strother	1980	Forest Lawn—Hollywood Hills, Los Angeles, CA	Courts of Remem., G62420
MARVIN, Lee	1987	Arlington National Cemetery, Arlington, VA	Section 7A, Grave 176
MARX, Arthur "Harpo"	1964	Forest Lawn Memorial-Park, Glendale, CA	
MARX, Herbert "Zeppo"	1979	(Cremated—not interred)	Ashes scattered at sea
MARX, Julius "Groucho"	1977	Eden Memorial Park, San Fernando, CA	In the Mausoleum, across from entrance
MARX, Leonard "Chico"	1961	Forest Lawn Memorial-Park, Glendale, CA	Freedom Maus., Sanctuary of Worship
MARX, Milton "Gummo"	1977	Forest Lawn Memorial-Park, Glendale, CA	Freedom Maus., Sanct. of Brotherhood
MARX, Samuel	1992	Westwood Village Mem. Park, Los Angeles, CA	Urn Garden (southeast)
• MASINA, Giulietta (Fellini)	1994	Civico Cimitero, Rimini, Italy	Section O, in the brown Fellini family vault
MASON, Shirley (Lanfield)	1979	Westwood Village Mem. Park, Los Angeles, CA	Sanctuary of Remembrance
MASSEY, Curt	1991	Westwood Village Mem. Park, Los Angeles, CA	Room of Prayer
MASSEY, Edith	1984	Westwood Village Mem. Park, Los Angeles, CA	Ashes scattered in the Rose Garden
MASSEY, Ilona (Dawson)	1974	Arlington National Cemetery, Arlington, VA	
MASSEY, Raymond	1983	Beaverdale Memorial Park, New Haven, CT	
MATHIS, June	1927	Hollywood Memorial Park, Hollywood, CA	H'wood Cath. Maus., Crypt 1199, Corr A
MATTHEWS, Dorothy (Davis)	1977	Westwood Village Mem. Park, Los Angeles, CA	
MAXWELL, Elsa	1963	Ferncliff Cemetery and Maus., Hartsdale, NY	Rosewood 2, Grave 1132
MAXWELL, Marilyn	1972	(Cremated at Chapel of the Pines, L.A., CA)	Ashes scattered at sea
MAYER, Louis B.	1957	Home of Peace Mem. Park, Los Angeles, CA	Chapel Maus., Corr. of Immortality, SW 405
MAYNARD, Ken	1973	Forest Lawn Memorial-Park, Cypress, CA	
• MAYO, Archie	1968	Beth-Olam Cemetery, Hollywood, CA	Mausoleum

...SPECIFIC INTERMENT LOCATIONS — BY NAME...

NAME	YEAR	CEMETERY	INTERMENT SITE*
MAYO, Frank	1963	Forest Lawn—Hollywood Hills, Los Angeles, CA	Col. of Remembrance, on left, 60450
McCAREY, Leo	1969	Holy Cross Cem. and Maus., Culver City, CA	
McCORMACK, John	1945	Dean's Grange Cemetery, Booterstown, Ireland	
McCOY, Tim	1978	Mt. Olivet Cemetery, Saginaw, MI	
McDANIEL, Hattie	1952	Rose Dale Cemetery, Los Angeles, CA	Section D, across from the office
McDONALD, Marie	1965	Forest Lawn Memorial-Park, Glendale, CA	Freedom Maus., Sanctuary of Heritage
McFARLAND, George	1993	(Cremated)	Ashes given to his family
McLAGLEN, Victor	1959	Forest Lawn Memorial-Park, Glendale, CA	Garden of Memory, Col. of Eternal Light
McNALLY, Stephen	1994	Holy Cross Cem. and Maus., Culver City, CA	Section Y, St. Francis, Plot 35
McNEAR, Howard	1969	Los Angeles National Cemetery, L.A., CA	Columbarium
• McQUEEN, "Butterfly"	1995	Body willed to the Medical College of Georgia	
McQUEEN, Steve	1980	(Cremated—not interred)	Ashes scattered in Santa Paula Valley, CA
• MEADOWS, Audrey (Six)	1996	Holy Cross Cem. and Maus., Culver City, CA	Section F, Tier 29, Grave 57
MEEK, Donald	1946	Fairmount Cemetery, Denver, CO	In Maus., Sect. 392, Tier BB, Main floor
MENJOU, Adolphe	1963	Hollywood Memorial Park, Hollywood, CA	Section 8, Lot 11
MERCER, Beryl	1939	Forest Lawn Memorial-Park, Glendale, CA	Sunrise Slope 337
MERCER, Johnny	1976	Bonaventure Cemetery, Savannah, GA	
MEREDITH, Charles	1964	Westwood Village Mem. Park, Los Angeles, CA	
MEYER, Emile G.	1987	Greenwood Cemetery, New Orleans, LA	
MILESTONE, Lewis	1980	Westwood Village Mem. Park, Los Angeles, CA	Sanctuary of Tranquility
MILLER, Marilyn	1936	Woodlawn Cemetery, The Bronx, NY	Division 50, Heather and Whitewood Ave
MILLER, Marvin E.	1985	Westwood Village Mem. Park, Los Angeles, CA	Sanctuary of Tenderness
MILLS, Harry F.	1982	Forest Lawn—Hollywood Hills, Los Angeles, CA	Courts of Remem., 3446
MINEO, Sal	1976	Cem. of the Gate of Heaven, Hawthorne, NY	Division 2
MINNELLI, Vincente	1986	Forest Lawn Memorial-Park, Glendale, CA	Small priv. garden in Triumphant Faith Terr.
MINTER, Mary Miles	1984	(Cremated—not interred)	Ashes scattered
MIRANDA, Carmen	1955	Sao Joao Baptista Cem., Rio de Janeiro, Brazil	
• MITCHELL, Margaret	1949	Oakland Cemetery, Atlanta, GA	
MITCHELL, Thomas	1962	Chapel of the Pines Crematory, Los Angeles, CA	
MIX, Tom	1940	Forest Lawn Memorial-Park, Glendale, CA	Whispering Pines, Grave 986
MONK, Thelonius	1982	Ferncliff Cemetery and Maus., Hartsdale, NY	Hillcrest I, Grave 405
MONROE, Marilyn	1962	Westwood Village Mem. Park, Los Angeles, CA	Corridor of Memories, #24
MONROE, Vaughn	1973	Fernhill Memorial Gardens, Stuart, FL	
• MONTAND, Yves	1991	Pere Lachaise Cemetery, Paris, France	
MONTGOMERY, Robert	1981	(Cremated—not interred)	Ashes given to family
MOORE, Victor	1962	Cypress Hills Cemetery, Brooklyn, NY	
MOOREHEAD, Agnes	1974	Dayton Memorial Park, Dayton, OH	
MORELAND, Mantan	1973	Valhalla Memorial Park, N. Hollywood, CA	
MORGAN, Frank	1949	Green-Wood Cemetery, Brooklyn, NY	
MORGAN, Helen	1941	Holy Sepulchre Cemetery, Worth, IL	
MORGAN, Ralph	1956	Green-Wood Cemetery, Brooklyn, NY	The Wupperman lot
MORGAN, Russ	1969	Palm Mortuary Mausoleum, Las Vegas, NV	
MORRIS, Wayne	1959	Arlington National Cemetery, Arlington, VA	
MORRISON, Jim	1971	Père Lachaise Cemetery, Paris, France	Division 6
MORROW, Vic	1982	Hillside Memorial Park, Los Angeles, CA	Mount of Olives, Block 5-80-1
MOWBRAY, Alan	1969	Holy Cross Cem. and Maus., Culver City, CA	
MUNI, Paul	1967	Hollywood Memorial Park, Hollywood, CA	Section 14, Row 00, Grave 57
MUNSON, Ona	1955	Ferncliff Cemetery and Maus., Hartsdale, NY	Maus., Unit 8, Tier Y, Col. G, Niche 5
MURPHY, Audie	1971	Arlington National Cemetery, Arlington, VA	Near the Battleship Maine memorial
MURRAY, Mae	1965	Valhalla Memorial Park, N. Hollywood, CA	Section G, Block 6328, Lot 6
MURROW, Edward R.	1965	Green-Wood Cemetery, Brooklyn, NY	Ashes buried
MUSTIN, Burt	1977	Forest Lawn—Hollywood Hills, Los Angeles, CA	Loving Kindness, Plot #7844
MYERS, Carmel	1980	(Cremated—not interred)	Ashes strewn in Rose Garden at Pickfair
N			
NAISH, J. Carrol	1973	Calvary Cemetery, Los Angeles, CA	Section G, Lot 1098, Grave 22
NALDI, Nita	1961	Calvary Cemetery, Woodside (Queens), NY	
NATWICK, Mildred	1994	Lorraine Park Cemetery, Baltimore, MD	
NAZIMOVA, Madame Alla	1945	Forest Lawn Memorial-Park, Glendale, CA	Whispering Pines
NEGIN, Koliz	1947	Forest Lawn Memorial-Park, Glendale, CA	
NEGRI, Pola	1987	Calvary Cemetery, Los Angeles, CA	In Maus., St. Paul Corr, Blk 56, Crypt E19
NEGULESCO, Jean	1993	Marbella, Spain	
NEILL, James	1931	Bonaventure Cemetery, Savannah, GA	Section E, Lot 171

• New entry.

284

* Some cemeteries refuse to reveal specific locations.

NAME	YEAR	CEMETERY	INTERMENT SITE*
NELSON, Frank	1986	Forest Lawn Memorial-Park, Glendale, CA	Garden of Honor
NELSON, Harriet	1994	Forest Lawn—Hollywood Hills, Los Angeles, CA	Revelation
NELSON, Ozzie	1975	Forest Lawn—Hollywood Hills, Los Angeles, CA	Revelation
NELSON, Rick	1985	Forest Lawn—Hollywood Hills, Los Angeles, CA	Revelation
NEUMANN, Kurt	1958	Home of Peace Mem. Park, Los Angeles, CA	Chapel Maus., Corr. of Eternal Life
NEWELL, William Most	1967	Westwood Village Mem. Park, Los Angeles, CA	
NEWMAN, Alfred	1970	Forest Lawn Memorial-Park, Glendale, CA	Great Maus., Sanctuary of Eternal Prayer
NEWMAN, Lionel	1989	Westwood Village Mem. Park, Los Angeles, CA	
NEWTON, Robert	1965	Chapel of the Pines Crematory, Los Angeles, CA	
NIBLO, Fred L. Sr.	1948	Forest Lawn Memorial-Park, Glendale, CA	
NICHOLS, Ernest "Red"	1965	Forest Lawn—Hollywood Hills, Los Angeles, CA	Col. of Remembrance, on right, 60780
NICHOLS, George Jr.	1942	Forest Lawn Memorial-Park, Glendale, CA	
• Nico (Christa Paffgen)	1988	Grunewald-Forst Cemetery, Berlin, Germany	
• NIJINSKY, Vaslav	1950	Montmartre Cemetery, Paris, France	Division 22
NILSSON, Harry	1994	Valley Oaks Mem. Park, Westlake Village, CA	
• NIVEN, David	1983	Village Churchyard, Chateau DOex, Switzerland	
NIXON, Pat	1993	Nixon Presidential Library, Yorba Linda, CA	Interred in the garden of the library
NOLAN, Bob	1980	(Cremated)	
NOLAN, Lloyd	1985	Westwood Village Mem. Park, Los Angeles, CA	Section D, #84
NOLAN, Mary	1948	Hollywood Memorial Park, Hollywood, CA	
NORMAND, Mabel (Cody)	1930	Calvary Cemetery, Los Angeles, CA	Main Mausoleum, in a main hallway
NOVARRO, Ramon	1968	Calvary Cemetery, Los Angeles, CA	Section C, Lot 586, Grave 5
• NUREYEV, Rudolph	1993	Ste. Genevieve-Des-Bois, Paris, France	(Essone District)
O			
OAKIE, Jack	1978	Forest Lawn Memorial-Park, Glendale, CA	Whispering Pines #1066 hilltop nr Cath. Dr.
OBER, Philip	1982	Chapel of the Pines Crematory, Los Angeles, CA	
OBERON, Merle (Wolders)	1979	Forest Lawn Memorial-Park, Glendale, CA	Garden of Remembrance
O'BRIEN, Edmond	1985	Holy Cross Cem. and Maus., Culver City, CA	Section F, Tier 54, Grave 50
O'BRIEN, Pat	1983	Holy Cross Cem. and Maus., Culver City, CA	Section F, Tier 56, Grave 62
O'BRIEN, Thomas Everett	1947	Forest Lawn Memorial-Park, Glendale, CA	
O'CONNELL, Helen (Devol)	1993	Holy Cross Cem. and Maus., Culver City, CA	Section CC, Tier 56, Grave 55
O'CONNOR, Una	1959	Calvary Cemetery, Woodside (Queens), NY	
ODETS, Clifford	1963	Forest Lawn Memorial-Park, Glendale, CA	Columbarium of Honor
• O'HARA, Barry J.	1979	Cremated	Ashes given to his wife, Helen
O'KEEFE, Dennis	1968	(Cremated—not interred)	Ashes scattered at sea
OLAND, Warner	1938	Southborough Cemetery, Southborough, MA	
OLDFIELD, Barney	1946	Holy Cross Cem. and Maus., Culver City, CA	Section D, Lot 290, Grave 11
OLIVER, David	1992	Forest Lawn—Hollywood Hills, Los Angeles, CA	
OLIVER, Edna May	1942	Forest Lawn Memorial-Park, Glendale, CA	
• OLIVIER, Laurence	1989	Westminster Abbey, London, England	Poets' Corner
OLSEN, Moroni	1954	Forest Lawn Memorial-Park, Glendale, CA	
OLSEN, Ole	1963	Palm Mortuary Mausoleum, Las Vegas, NV	Ground burial
ORBISON, Roy	1988	Westwood Village Mem. Park, Los Angeles, CA	Section D, #97 (unmarked) nr. water spigot
O'ROURKE, Heather	1988	Westwood Village Mem. Park, Los Angeles, CA	New Mausoleum, 1st column, bottom
OSBORN, Lyn	1958	Forest Lawn Memorial-Park, Glendale, CA	
OUSPENSKAYA, Maria	1949	Chapel of the Pines Crematory, Los Angeles, CA	
OWEN, Reginald	1972	Morris Hill Cemetery, Boise, ID	
OWSLEY, Monroe Righter	1937	Forest Lawn Memorial-Park, Glendale, CA	
P			
PADEREWSKI, Ignace Jan	1941	St. John the Baptist Cathedral, Warsaw, Poland	Originally buried in Arlington Nat'l. Cem.
"			His heart is entombed at the Shrine of
"			Our Lady of Czestochowa, Doylestown, PA
"			Reburied in free Poland in 1992.
PAL, George	1980	Holy Cross Cem. and Maus., Culver City, CA	
PALMER, Lilli (Thompson)	1986	Forest Lawn Memorial-Park, Glendale, CA	Freedom Courtyard
• PAM, Anita	1987	Greenwood Memorial Park, Fort Worth, TX	Maus.-Westminster area (Valutage) (NM)
PAN, Hermes	1990	Holy Cross Cem. and Maus., Culver City, CA	Mausoleum, Block 127, Crypt D-5
PANGBORN, Franklin	1958	Forest Lawn Memorial-Park, Glendale, CA	
PANZER, Paul	1958	Forest Lawn—Hollywood Hills, Los Angeles, CA	
• PARKER, Charlie "Bird"	1955	Lincoln Cemetery, Kansas City, KS	
PARKS, Larry	1975	(Cremated)	Ashes buried at his Studio City, CA, home
PARROTT, James	1939	Forest Lawn Memorial-Park, Glendale, CA	Devotion

NAME	YEAR	CEMETERY	INTERMENT SITE*
PARSONS, Louella (Martin)	1972	Holy Cross Cem. and Maus., Culver City, CA	Section D, Lot 235, Grave 8
PATERSON, Pat (Boyer)	1978	Holy Cross Cem. and Maus., Culver City, CA	St. Ann's Garden, Grave 6, Tier 186
PATRICK, Lee (Wood)	1982	Westwood Village Mem. Park, Los Angeles, CA	Room of Prayer
PECKHAM, Francis Miles	1959	Lake View Cemetery, Cleveland, OH	
PENNER, Joe	1941	Forest Lawn Memorial-Park, Glendale, CA	
• PEPPARD, George	1994	Northview Cemetery, Dearborn, MI	
PEPPLE, Sydney Chester	1993	All Saints Episcopal Cemetery, San Luis Rey, CA	Cremated—ashes interred
PEREIRA, Hal	1983	Westwood Village Mem. Park, Los Angeles, CA	
PERFECT, Rose	1978	Westwood Village Mem. Park, Los Angeles, CA	
PETERS, Susan	1952	Forest Lawn Memorial-Park, Glendale, CA	Whispering Pines, at "Finding of Moses"
PHOENIX, River	1993	Evergreen Cemetery, Gainesville, FL	
PIAF, Edith	1963	Père Lachaise Cemetery, Paris, France	Black tomb in Division 97
PIATIGORSKY, Gregor	1976	Westwood Village Mem. Park, Los Angeles, CA	Section D, #154
PICKFORD, Jack	1933	Forest Lawn Memorial-Park, Glendale, CA	Garden of Memory
PICKFORD, Lottie	1936	Forest Lawn Memorial-Park, Glendale, CA	Garden of Memory
PICKFORD, Mary	1979	Forest Lawn Memorial-Park, Glendale, CA	Garden of Memory
PIDGEON, Walter	1984	(No funeral)	Body donated to UCLA for med. research
PIERCE, Jack P.	1968	Forest Lawn Memorial-Park, Glendale, CA	Whispering Pines, nr. "Finding of Moses"
PIERLOT, Francis	1955	Forest Lawn Memorial-Park, Glendale, CA	
PINZA, Ezio	1957	Putnam Cemetery, Greenwich, CT	Section L-1
PITTS, Zazu (Woodall)	1963	Holy Cross Cem. and Maus., Culver City, CA	Section "Grotto," Lot 195, Grave 1
POLLARD, Harry A.	1934	Forest Lawn Memorial-Park, Glendale, CA	
POLLARD, Harry "Snub"	1962	Forest Lawn—Hollywood Hills, Los Angeles, CA	Sheltering Hills
PORCARO, Jeff	1992	Forest Lawn—Hollywood Hills, Los Angeles, CA	Lincoln Terrace, Plot #120
PORTER, Cole	1964	Mount Hope Cemetery, Peru, IN	
PORTER, Edwin S.	1941	Kensico Cemetery, Valhalla, NY	
POWELL, Dick	1963	Forest Lawn Memorial-Park, Glendale, CA	Garden of Memory, Col. of Honor
POWELL, Eleanor	1982	Hollywood Memorial Park, Hollywood, CA	H. C. Maus., Niche 432, T3, Foyer E/W
POWELL, Lee	1944		Missing in action in the Marianas Islands
POWELL, Richard	1937	Forest Lawn Memorial-Park, Glendale, CA	
POWELL, William	1984	Desert Memorial Park, Palm Springs, CA	Ashes interred in Section B-10, Lot 20
POWER, Tyrone	1958	Hollywood Memorial Park, Hollywood, CA	Section 8, near the Marion Davies Maus.
PRESLEY, Elvis	1977	Graceland, Memphis, TN	
PRICE, Vincent	1993	(Cremated—not interred)	
PRIMA, Louis	1978	Metairie Cemetery, New Orleans, LA	Section 88
PRINZE, Freddie (Preutzel)	1977	Forest Lawn—Hollywood Hills, Los Angeles, CA	Courts of Remem., Sanctuary of Light
• PROKOFIEV, Sergei	1953	Novodevichy Cemetery, Moscow, Russia	
PULEO, Johnny	1983	Gate of Heaven Cemetery, Silver Spring, MD	
PURVIANCE, Edna	1958	Forest Lawn Memorial-Park, Glendale, CA	
R			
RACHMANINOFF, Sergei	1943	Kensico Cemetery, Valhalla, NY	
RADNER, Gilda	1989	Long Ridge Cemetery, Stamford, CT	
RAFT, George	1980	Forest Lawn—Hollywood Hills, Los Angeles, CA	Courts of Remem., Sanctuary of Light
RAINS, Claude	1967	Red Hill Cemetery, Moultonborough, NH	Black marble headstone
RAMBEAU, Marjorie	1970	Desert Memorial Park, Palm Springs, CA	
RAND, Sally	1979	Oakdale Cemetery, Glendora, CA	ELM, Lot 34, Space 10
RANDALL, Addison Owen	1945	Forest Lawn Memorial-Park, Glendale, CA	
RANDOLPH, Amanda	1967	Forest Lawn—Hollywood Hills, Los Angeles, CA	Gentleness, under a tree
RANDOLPH, Lillian	1980	Forest Lawn—Hollywood Hills, Los Angeles, CA	Gentleness, under a tree
• RAPF, Harry	1949	Home of Peace Mem. Park, Los Angeles, CA	Chapel Maus., Corr. of Immortality
RAPPE, Virginia	1921	Hollywood Memorial Park, Hollywood, CA	Section 8, Lot 257
RATHBONE, Basil	1967	Ferncliff Cemetery and Maus., Hartsdale, NY	Shrine of Mem. Maus., Unit 1, T-K, #117
RAY, Charles	1943	Forest Lawn Memorial-Park, Glendale, CA	
RAYE, Martha	1994	Fort Bragg Military Cemetery, NC	
REED, Donna	1986	Westwood Village Mem. Park, Los Angeles, CA	Section D, #142
REED, Florence	1967	Kensico Cemetery, Valhalla, NY	Actors Fund Plot
REEVES, George	1959	Mountain View Cemetery, Altadena, CA	Ashes, Pasadena Maus. Sunrise Cor. #3555
REEVES, Jim	1964	Jim Reeves Memorial Park, Carthage, TX	On US Highway 79, 4 miles NE of Carthage
• REEVES, Richard J.	1967	Oakwood Memorial Park, Chatsworth, CA	Section Elm, Lot 209, Grave 4
REID, Carl Benton	1973	Forest Lawn—Hollywood Hills, Los Angeles, CA	Enduring Faith, Plot #3722
REID, Wallace	1923	Forest Lawn Memorial-Park, Glendale, CA	Great Maus., Azalea Columbarium
REINHARDT, Max	1943	Westchester Hills Cem, Hastings-on-Hudson, NY	

NAME	YEAR	CEMETERY	INTERMENT SITE*
REY, Alejandro	1987	Holy Cross Cem. and Maus., Culver City, CA	Section L, Lot 403, Grave 1
• REYNOLDS, Frank	1983	Arlington National Cemetery, Arlington, VA	
• REYNOLDS, Lynn	1927	Hollywood Memorial Park, Hollywood, CA	Section 8
RHODES, Erik	1990	El Reno Cemetery, El Reno, OK	Ashes buried New Add., Blk 14, Lot 24-A
RICE, Adnia	1987	Rose Hill Cemetery, Fayetteville, TN	
RICH, Buddy	1987	Westwood Village Mem. Park, Los Angeles, CA	Sanc. of Tranquility, 2nd column, bottom
RICHARDS, Addison	1964	Forest Lawn Memorial-Park, Glendale, CA	
• RICHARDSON, Jiles	1959	Forest Lawn Memorial Park, Beaumont, TX	Block C, Lot 31, Space 3
• RICHARDSON, (Sir) Ralph	1983	Highgate East Cemetery, London, England	Near Main Road
• RICHMAN, Harry	1972	Hillside Memorial Park, Los Angeles, CA	Garden of Memories, Alcove of Love B319
RIDDLE, Nelson	1985	Hollywood Memorial Park, Hollywood, CA	T-Bldg., Niche 702, Tier 7, Corr T-1
RIORDAN, Marjorie (Schlaff)	1984	Westwood Village Mem. Park, Los Angeles, CA	Section D, #1
• RIPPERTON, Minnie	1979	Westwood Village Mem. Park, Los Angeles, CA	
RITCHARD, Cyril	1977	St. Mary's Cemetery, Ridgefield, CT	
RITCHIE, Billie	1921	Forest Lawn—Hollywood Hills, Los Angeles, CA	
RITTER, Tex	1974	Oak Bluff Memorial Park, Port Neches, TX	Section 8
RITZ, Al	1965	Hollywood Memorial Park, Hollywood, CA	T-Bldg., T-4, Bottom row, right side
RITZ, Harry	1986	Hollywood Memorial Park, Hollywood, CA	T-Bldg., 3rd floor
RITZ, Jimmy	1985	Hollywood Memorial Park, Hollywood, CA	T-Bldg., T-5
ROACH, Hal Jr.	1972	Calvary Cemetery, Los Angeles, CA	Block 14, Crypt 11 (at top)
• ROACH, Hal Sr.	1992	Woodlawn Cemetery, Elmira, NY	Just inside the Walnut St. gate, 1st turn rt.
ROBARDS, Jason Sr.	1963	Forest Lawn—Hollywood Hills, Los Angeles, CA	Remembrance, Grave 975 (at curb)
ROBBINS, Fred	1992	Hebrew Friendship Cemetery, Baltimore, MD	
ROBBINS, Marty	1982	Woodlawn Memorial Park, Nashville, TN	
• ROBERSON, C. H. "Chuck"	1988	Forest Lawn—Hollywood Hills, Los Angeles, CA	
ROBERTS, Florence	1940	Forest Lawn Memorial-Park, Glendale, CA	
ROBERTS, Lynne (Mary Hart)	1978	Forest Lawn—Hollywood Hills, Los Angeles, CA	Buried beside her mother
ROBERTS, Roy	1975	Greenwood Memorial Park, Fort Worth, TX	314 - 42
ROBERTS, Theodore	1928	Hollywood Memorial Park, Hollywood, CA	Pineland section
ROBESON, Paul	1976	Ferncliff Cemetery and Maus., Hartsdale, NY	Hillcrest A, Grave 1511
ROBINSON, Bill "Bojangles"	1949	Evergreen Cemetery, Brooklyn, NY	
• ROBINSON, Dar Allen	1988	Forest Lawn—Hollywood Hills, Los Angeles, CA	
ROBINSON, Edward G.	1973	Beth-El Cemetery, Ridgewood (Queens), NY	
ROBINSON, Edward G. Jr.	1973	Hollywood Memorial Park, Hollywood, CA	Abbey of the Psalms, Crypt 4386, Corr E-4
ROBINSON, Sugar Ray	1989	Inglewood Park Cemetery, Inglewood, CA	Lot 24, Pinecrest Addition (top of hill)
ROBSON, (Dame) Flora	1984	St. Nicholas Churchyard, Brighton, England	
ROBSON, May	1942	Flushing Cemetery, Flushing (Queens), NY	Sect. 9, plain stone has fam. name 'Brown'
RODGERS, Richard	1979	(Cremated—not interred)	Ashes scattered
• ROGERS, Ginger	1995	Oakwood Memorial Park, Chatsworth, CA	Section E, Lot 303
ROGERS, Will	1935	Will Rogers Memorial, Claremore, OK	Reinterred in 1944 from Forest Lawn, CA
ROLAND, Ruth M.	1937	Forest Lawn Memorial-Park, Glendale, CA	Great Mausoleum, Azalea Columbarium
ROMBERG, Sigmund	1951	Ferncliff Cemetery and Maus., Hartsdale, NY	Maus., Unit 1, Sect. BC-1, Crypt 5
• ROMERO, Cesar	1994	Inglewood Park Cemetery, Inglewood, CA	Niche
ROPER, Jack	1966	Cremated	Ashes given to his wife
• RORKE, Hayden	1987	Holy Cross Cem. and Maus., Culver City, CA	
ROSE, Billy	1966	Westchester Hills Cem, Hastings-on-Hudson, NY	
ROSE, David	1990	Mount Sinai Memorial-Park, Los Angeles, CA	In Maus. behind the Garden of Heritage
ROSENBLOOM, Maxie	1976	Valhalla Memorial Park, N. Hollywood, CA	Section J, Block 9820, Space 3
ROSING, Bodil Ann	1942	Forest Lawn Memorial-Park, Glendale, CA	
ROSS, Joe E.	1982	Forest Lawn—Hollywood Hills, Los Angeles, CA	SummerLand, Plot #148
ROSSON, Richard	1953	Hollywood Memorial Park, Hollywood, CA	Section 8, near Cecil B. DeMille
ROTH, Lillian	1980	Mount Pleasant Cemetery, Hawthorne, NY	
RUBENSTEIN, Artur	1982	Jerusalem, Israel	Buried in a special plot in forest outside city
RUGGLES, Charlie	1970	Forest Lawn Memorial-Park, Glendale, CA	Garden of Memory
RUGGLES, Wesley	1972	Forest Lawn Memorial-Park, Glendale, CA	Garden of Memory
RUSSELL, Gail (Moseley)	1961	Valhalla Memorial Park, N. Hollywood, CA	Evergreen Section, Curb #4795
RUSSELL, Lillian	1922	Allegheny Cemetery, Pittsburgh, PA	In Mausoleum, Section 40, Space 5
RUSSELL, Rosalind (Brisson)	1976	Holy Cross Cem. and Maus., Culver City, CA	Section M, Lot 536, Grave 2
RUTH, George Herman "Babe"	1948	Cem. of the Gate of Heaven, Hawthorne, NY	Sect. 25 (at 10-ft. tall gray granite marker)
RYAN, Irene	1973	Woodlawn Cemetery, Santa Monica, CA	In Mausoleum, 109-C-1
Sabu	1963	(See DASTAGIR, Sabu)	

• New entry.

* Some cemeteries refuse to reveal specific locations.

NAME	YEAR	CEMETERY	INTERMENT SITE*
• SAGAL, Boris	1981	Forest Lawn—Hollywood Hills, Los Angeles, CA	Sheltering Hills
SAKALL, S. Z. "Cuddles"	1955	Forest Lawn Memorial-Park, Glendale, CA	Garden of Memory, as 'Szoke Szakall'
SALE, Charles P. "Chic"	1936	Forest Lawn Memorial-Park, Glendale, CA	
• SANDERS, Al	1995	Arbutus Memorial Park, Baltimore, MD	
SANDS, Billy	1984	Holy Cross Cem. and Maus., Culver City, CA	Mausoleum
SANDS, Diana	1973	Ferncliff Cemetery and Maus., Hartsdale, NY	Ashewood, Grave 545
SAVALAS, George	1985	Forest Lawn—Hollywood Hills, Los Angeles, CA	Lincoln Terrace, Plot #4596
SAVALAS, Telly	1994	Forest Lawn—Hollywood Hills, Los Angeles, CA	Garden of Heritage, Plot #1281
SCALA, Gia	1972	Holy Cross Cem. and Maus., Culver City, CA	Section M, 3 spaces left of Plot 581
SCHAEFFER, Rebecca	1989	Ahavai Sholom Cemetery, Portland, OR	
SCHAFFNER, Franklin J.	1989	Westwood Village Mem. Park, Los Angeles, CA	Lot 236
SCHERTZINGER, Victor	1941	Forest Lawn Memorial-Park, Glendale, CA	
SCHILDKRAUT, Joseph	1964	Hollywood Memorial Park, Hollywood, CA	Beth Olam Mausoleum, Niche 43
• SCHLESINGER, Leon	1949	Beth-Olam Cemetery, Hollywood, CA	Mausoleum, ashes in vault
SCHNEIDER, Romy	1982	Boissy-Sans-Avoir (nr. Paris), France	
SCHUMANN-HEINK, Ernestine	1936	Greenwood Memorial Park, San Diego, CA	Cathedral Mausoleum, Corr. of Sunshine
SCHWARTZ, Maurice	1960	Mount Hebron Cem., Flushing (Queens), NY	
SCOTT, Hazel	1981	Flushing Cemetery, Flushing (Queens), NY	Sect. 9, next to ex-husb. Adam C. Powell Sr.
SCOTT, Zachary	1965	Austin Memorial Park, Austin, TX	Block 4, Lot 187A, Space 12
• SEBASTIAN, Dorothy	1957	Holy Cross Cem. and Maus., Culver City, CA	
SEBERG, Jean	1979	Montparnasse Cemetery, Paris, France	Division 13
SEDDON, Margaret	1968	Greenmount Cemetery, Baltimore, MD	
• SEDGWICK, Edie	1971	Oak Hill Cemetery, Ballard, CA	
• SELLERS, Peter	1980	Golders Green Cemetery, London, England	
SELWYN, Ruth (Warburton)	1954	Forest Lawn Memorial-Park, Glendale, CA	
SELZNICK, David O.	1965	Forest Lawn Memorial-Park, Glendale, CA	Great Maus., Sanctuary of Trust
• SELZNICK, Myron	1944	Forest Lawn Memorial-Park, Glendale, CA	
SENNETT, Mack	1960	Holy Cross Cem. and Maus., Culver City, CA	Section N, Lot 490, Grave 1
• SERLING, Rod	1975	Interlaken Cemetery, Interlaken, NY	
• SEYMOUR, Dan	1993	Hillside Memorial Park, Los Angeles, CA	Mount of Olives, Block 7-175-1
SHANNON, Peggy	1941	Hollywood Memorial Park, Hollywood, CA	Section 5, Plot 43 (two rows in from road)
SHARPE, David H.	1980	(Cremated)	
SHAW, Reta	1982	Forest Lawn—Hollywood Hills, Los Angeles, CA	Col. of Remembrance, on left, 60402
SHAWN, Dick	1987	Hillside Memorial Park, Los Angeles, CA	Mausoleum, Memorial Court-734
SHAY, Dorothy	1978	Westwood Village Mem. Park, Los Angeles, CA	
SHEARER, Norma (Thalberg)	1983	Forest Lawn Memorial-Park, Glendale, CA	Great Maus., Sanctuary of Benediction
SHEEN, (Bishop) Fulton J.	1979	St. Patrick's Cathedral, New York, NY	In a crypt below the altar
SHERIDAN, Ann	1967	Chapel of the Pines Crematory, Los Angeles, CA	In vault #57542, not avail. for viewing
• SHERMAN, Allan	1973	Hillside Memorial Park, Los Angeles, CA	Mausoleum, Columbarium of Hope-513
SHERMAN, Lowell	1934	Forest Lawn Memorial-Park, Glendale, CA	Great Maus., Sanctuary of Trust
SHORE, Dinah	1994	Hillside Memorial Park, Los Angeles, CA	Courts of the Book, Isaiah-V-247
• SHOSTAKOVICH, Dimitri	1975	Novodevichy Cemetery, Moscow, Russia	
SHUMAN, Roy	1973	Kensico Cemetery, Valhalla, NY	Actors Fund Plot
SILVERHEELS, Jay	1980	(Cremated at Chapel of the Pines, L.A., CA)	Ashes returned to his native Ontario, Can.
SILVERS, Phil	1985	Mount Sinai Memorial-Park, Los Angeles, CA	Garden of Heritage, Vault 1004
• SIMON, S. Sylvan	1951	Forest Lawn Memorial-Park, Glendale, CA	Great Maus., Col. of Memory, Niche #20174
• SINGLETON, Catherine M.	1969	Mount Olivet Cemetery, Fort Worth, TX	Garden of Our Lady of Peace D, 136-B
SMALLEY, W. Phillips	1939	Forest Lawn—Hollywood Hills, Los Angeles, CA	Col. of Remembrance, on right, 60750
SMITH, Hal	1994	Woodlawn Cemetery, Santa Monica, CA	
SMITH, Kate	1986	Lake Placid Cemetery, North Elba, NY	In a small private mausoleum
SOO, Jack	1979	Forest Lawn—Hollywood Hills, Los Angeles, CA	Eternal Love, Plot #3980
SOUSA, John Philip	1932	Congressional Cemetery, Washington, D.C.	
• SPERLING, Milton	1988	Mount Sinai Memorial-Park, Los Angeles, CA	
STAFFORD, Hanley	1968	Forest Lawn Memorial-Park, Glendale, CA	
STAHL, John M.	1950	Forest Lawn Memorial-Park, Glendale, CA	
• STANDER, Lionel	1994	Forest Lawn Memorial-Park, Glendale, CA	Outside Freedom Maus. (front)
• STANWYCK, Barbara	1990	(Cremated—not interred)	Ashes scattered over Lone Pine, CA
ST. DENIS, Ruth	1968	Forest Lawn—Hollywood Hills, Los Angeles, CA	Courts of Remem.
STEELE, Bob	1988	Forest Lawn—Hollywood Hills, Los Angeles, CA	Col. of Remembrance, on right, 60722
STEINER, Max	1971	Forest Lawn Memorial-Park, Glendale, CA	Great Maus., Sanctuary of Sacred Promise
STEPHENSON, Henry	1956	Kensico Cemetery, Valhalla, NY	Actors Fund Plot
STEPHENSON, James	1941	Forest Lawn Memorial-Park, Glendale, CA	

NAME	YEAR	CEMETERY	INTERMENT SITE*
• STEVENS, George	1975	Forest Lawn—Hollywood Hills, Los Angeles, CA	Morning Light
STEVENS, John Landers	1940	Forest Lawn Memorial-Park, Glendale, CA	
STEWART, Anita (Converse)	1961	Forest Lawn Memorial-Park, Glendale, CA	
• STOKOWSKI, Leopold	1977	St. Marylebone Cemetery, London, England	East Avenue at Rosemary
STONE, Fred	1959	Forest Lawn—Hollywood Hills, Los Angeles, CA	
STONE, Milburn	1980	El Camino Memorial Park, La Jolla, CA	Vista del Lago, 401-D
STRANGE, Glenn	1973	Forest Lawn—Hollywood Hills, Los Angeles, CA	Churchyard, Plot #4295
STRASBERG, Lee	1982	Westchester Hills Cem, Hastings-on-Hudson, NY	
STRATTEN, Dorothy	1980	Westwood Village Mem. Park, Los Angeles, CA	Section D, #170
STROMBERG, Hunt	1968	Calvary Cemetery, Los Angeles, CA	Section H, Lot 416 (by tree)
STURGES, Preston	1959	Ferncliff Cemetery and Maus., Hartsdale, NY	Maplewood R, Garden Grave 74
SULLAVAN, Margaret	1960	St. Mary's Whitechapel Church, Lancaster, PA	In churchyard, near curve in path
SULLIVAN, Ed	1974	Ferncliff Cemetery and Maus., Hartsdale, NY	Maus., Unit 8, Alcove G, Side Comp. 122
SWIFT, Paul "Eggman"	1994	New Cathedral Cemetery, Baltimore, MD	
SWITZER, Carl "Alfalfa"	1959	Hollywood Memorial Park, Hollywood, CA	Section 6, Lot 26, Grave 6
T			
TALMADGE, Constance	1973	Hollywood Memorial Park, Hollywood, CA	Abbey of the Psalms, Family Rm, Corr G-7
TALMADGE, Natalie	1969	Hollywood Memorial Park, Hollywood, CA	Abbey of the Psalms, Family Rm, Corr G-7
TALMADGE, Norma	1957	Hollywood Memorial Park, Hollywood, CA	Abbey of the Psalms, Family Rm, Corr G-7
TALMAN, William	1968	Forest Lawn—Hollywood Hills, Los Angeles, CA	Garden of Heritage, Garden Crypt 633
TANGUAY, Eva	1947	Hollywood Memorial Park, Hollywood, CA	Abbey of the Psalms, Crypt 0558, Corr. D-1
TATE, Sharon (Polanski)	1969	Holy Cross Cem. and Maus., Culver City, CA	St. Ann's Garden, Grave 6, Tier 152
TATUM, Art	1956	Rose Dale Cemetery, Los Angeles, CA	Section 5, in Row 178
• TATUM, Reece "Goose"	1967	Ft. Bliss National Cemetery, El Paso, TX	Section D, Grave 2668
• TAUBER, Richard	1948	Brompton Cemetery, London, England	First sect. left of center path (nr. entrance)
TAYBACK, Victor	1990	Forest Lawn—Hollywood Hills, Los Angeles, CA	Sheltering Hills, Plot #3813
TAYLOR, Kent	1987	Westwood Village Mem. Park, Los Angeles, CA	Sanctuary of Remembrance
TAYLOR, Laurette (Cooney)	1946	Woodlawn Cemetery, The Bronx, NY	
TAYLOR, Robert	1969	Forest Lawn Memorial-Park, Glendale, CA	Garden of Honor, Col. of the Evening Star
TAYLOR, William Desmond	1922	Hollywood Memorial Park, Hollywood, CA	H'wood Cath. Maus., Crypt 594
TEAGARDEN, Jack	1964	Forest Lawn—Hollywood Hills, Los Angeles, CA	
TEMPLETON, Fay	1939	Kensico Cemetery, Valhalla, NY	Actors Fund Plot
• TERRELL, Kenneth	1966	Oakwood Memorial Park, Chatsworth, CA	Section Hollypoint, Lot 327
THALBERG, Irving Grant	1936	Forest Lawn Memorial-Park, Glendale, CA	Great Maus., Sanctuary of Benediction
THOMAS, William "Buckwheat"	1980	Inglewood Park Cemetery, Inglewood, CA	777 Acacia Slope, Grave 1
THUNDERCLOUD, Chief	1955	Forest Lawn Memorial-Park, Glendale, CA	Great Maus., Corridor of Mercy
TIBBETT, Lawrence	1960	Forest Lawn Memorial-Park, Glendale, CA	
TINCHER, Fay	1983	Silver Mount Cemetery, Staten Island, NY	
TINDALL, Loren	1973	Memorial Park, Oklahoma City, OK	Section 18, Lot 61, Space 6
TIOMKIN, Dimitri	1979	Forest Lawn Memorial-Park, Glendale, CA	Great Maus., Col. of Memory, Niche #19425
TODD, Mike	1958	Waldheim/Forest Home Cem., Chicago (F.P.), IL	
• TODD, Thelma	1935	Forest Lawn Memorial-Park, Glendale, CA	
TOMACK, Sid	1962	Desert Memorial Park, Palm Springs, CA	Section A-9, Lot 14
TORRENCE, Ernest	1933	Forest Lawn Memorial-Park, Glendale, CA	Great Maus., Col. of Prayer, Niche #10677
TORRES, Raquel	1987	Forest Lawn Memorial-Park, Glendale, CA	Great Maus., Hall of Celestial Peace
• TOSCANINI, Arturo	1957	Cimitero Monumentale, Milan, Italy	In the family's white marble mausoleum
TRACY, Spencer	1967	Forest Lawn Memorial-Park, Glendale, CA	Garden of Everlasting Peace
TRAINOR, Leonard E.	1940	Forest Lawn Memorial-Park, Glendale, CA	
TRAUBEL, Helen (Bass)	1972	Westwood Village Mem. Park, Los Angeles, CA	Sanctuary of Remembrance
TRAVERS, Henry	1965	Forest Lawn Memorial-Park, Glendale, CA	Great Maus., Hall of Inspiration
Trigger	1965	Roy Rogers–Dale Evans Museum, Victorville, CA	On display in the museum
TROTTER, John Scott	1975	Sharon Cemetery, Charlotte, NC	
TROWBRIDGE, Charles	1967	Forest Lawn—Hollywood Hills, Los Angeles, CA	Remembrance, Plot #233
TRUEX, Ernest	1973	Flushing Cemetery, Flushing (Queens), NY	
• TRUFFAUT, François	1984	Montmartre Cemetery, Paris, France	Div. 21, near entrance, on Ave. Berlioz
TUCKER, Forrest	1986	Forest Lawn—Hollywood Hills, Los Angeles, CA	Courts of Remem., Col. of Radiant Dawn
TUCKER, Richard	1975	Mt. Lebanon Cemetery, Glendale (Queens), NY	
TUCKER, Sophie	1966	Emanuel Cemetery, Wethersfield, CT	
TURPIN, Ben	1940	Forest Lawn Memorial-Park, Glendale, CA	Great Mausoleum, Azalea Columbarium
TUTTLE, Frank W.	1963	Westwood Village Mem. Park, Los Angeles, CA	Section D, #105
TUTTLE, Lurene	1986	Forest Lawn Memorial-Park, Glendale, CA	Whispering Pines, Lot #1570

NAME	YEAR	CEMETERY	INTERMENT SITE*
▼			
VALENS, Ritchie	1959	San Fernando Mission Cem., San Fernando, CA	Section C, at Curb No. 247, 3 rows in
VALENTINO, Rudolph	1926	Hollywood Memorial Park, Hollywood, CA	H'wood Cath. Maus., #1205, off Corr A
VALLEE, Rudy	1986	St. Hyacinth's Church Cemetery, Westbrook, ME	
VAN, Bobby	1980	Mount Sinai Memorial-Park, Los Angeles, CA	Maimonides, Plot #3728
• VANCE, Vivian	1979	(Cremated)	
VanCLEEF, Lee	1989	Forest Lawn—Hollywood Hills, Los Angeles, CA	Serenity, 5 plots to right of marker 129
Van DYKE, Woody S. II	1944	Forest Lawn Memorial-Park, Glendale, CA	
VAUGHAN, Stevie Ray	1990	Laurel Land Memorial Park, Dallas, TX	Section 25, Lot 194, Space 4
VAUGHN, Billy	1991	Oak Hill Cemetery, Escondido, CA	
VEIDT, Conrad	1943	Ferncliff Cemetery and Maus., Hartsdale, NY	
VELEZ, Lupe	1944	Pateon Delores Cemetery, Mexico City, Mexico	
VERNON, Bobby	1939	Forest Lawn Memorial-Park, Glendale, CA	
VIDOR, Charles	1959	Home of Peace Mem. Park, Los Angeles, CA	Warner Maus. (was Harry's son-in-law)
• VINCENT, Romo	1989	Westwood Village Mem. Park, Los Angeles, CA	Sanc. of Tranquility, on right, 4 bays up
VIVYAN, John	1983	Westwood Village Mem. Park, Los Angeles, CA	Room of Prayer
• VonERICH, Chris	1991	Grove Hill Memorial Park, Dallas, TX	Hilltop Lot 535, Space 4
• VonERICH, David	1984	Grove Hill Memorial Park, Dallas, TX	Hilltop Lot 535
• VonERICH, Kerry	1993	Grove Hill Memorial Park, Dallas, TX	Hilltop near Lot 535
• VonERICH, Michael	1987	Grove Hill Memorial Park, Dallas, TX	Hilltop Lot 535
VonSTERNBERG, Josef	1969	Westwood Village Mem. Park, Los Angeles, CA	Sanctuary of Remembrance
▼			
WAGENHEIM, Charles	1979	Westwood Village Mem. Park, Los Angeles, CA	
WAGNER, "Gorgeous" George	1963	Valhalla Memorial Park, N. Hollywood, CA	Section G, Block 6659, Sp. 2, next to mother
WALDRON, Charles D.	1946	Forest Lawn Memorial-Park, Glendale, CA	
WALKER, June	1966	Westwood Village Mem. Park, Los Angeles, CA	
WALLER, Eddy	1977	Forest Lawn—Hollywood Hills, Los Angeles, CA	Col. of Remembrance, on left, #60409
• WALLER, Thomas "Fats"	1943	(Cremated—not interred)	Ashes scattered over Harlem, NY
WALLING, Effie Bond	1961	Forest Lawn Memorial-Park, Glendale, CA	
WALLIS, Hal	1986	Forest Lawn Memorial-Park, Glendale, CA	Great Mausoleum
• WALTHALL, Henry B.	1936	Hollywood Memorial Park, Hollywood, CA	Abbey of the Psalms
• WALTHALL, Wallace	1971	Restland Memorial Park, Dallas, TX	Acacia 288, Grave 2-3
WARFIELD, David	1951	Ferncliff Cemetery and Maus., Hartsdale, NY	St. Paul, Plot 180, Grave 1
• WARHOL, Andy	1987	St, John the Baptist Byzantine Cem, Bethel, PA	
WARNER, Harry B.	1958	Home of Peace Mem. Park, Los Angeles, CA	Warner Maus., Section D, Plot 16
WARNER, Harry M.	1958	Home of Peace Mem. Park, Los Angeles, CA	
WARNER, Jack L.	1978	Home of Peace Mem. Park, Los Angeles, CA	Undergrd crypt, 50 yd. from Warner Maus.
• WARNER, Jack M.	1995	Hillside Memorial Park, Los Angeles, CA	
WARNER, Sam	1927	Home of Peace Mem. Park, Los Angeles, CA	In Mausoleum
WARREN, Harry	1981	Westwood Village Mem. Park, Los Angeles, CA	Sanctuary of Tenderness, 5th col. bottom
WATERS, Ethel	1977	Forest Lawn Memorial-Park, Glendale, CA	Ascension Garden (center)
• WAXMAN, Franz	1967	Beth-Olam Cemetery, Hollywood, CA	Mausoleum, ashes in urn at 2nd entrance
WAYNE, John	1979	Pacific View Mem. Park, Newport Beach, CA	On a hill in an unmarked grave
WEBB, Clifton	1966	Hollywood Memorial Park, Hollywood, CA	Abbey of the Psalms, Crypt 2350, Corr G-6
WEBB, Jack	1982	Forest Lawn—Hollywood Hills, Los Angeles, CA	Sheltering Hills, Plot #1999
WEBER, Joe	1942	Hollywood Memorial Park, Hollywood, CA	Cremated; remains placed in a vault
• WEISSMULLER, Johnny	1984	Valley of Light Cemetery, Acapulco, Mexico	
• WELK, Lawrence	1992	Holy Cross Cem. and Maus., Culver City, CA	Section Y, Tier 9, Grave 110
• WELLMAN, William A.	1975	(Cremated—not interred)	Ashes scattered from a WWI fighter plane
WELLS, Mary	1992	Forest Lawn Memorial-Park, Glendale, CA	Freedom Maus., Columbarium of Patriots
WEST, Brooks	1984	Westwood Village Mem. Park, Los Angeles, CA	Section D, #81
WEST, Mae	1980	Cypress Hills Cemetery, Brooklyn, NY	
WESTMORE, Ernest	1967	Hollywood Memorial Park, Hollywood, CA	Section 8, three-in from the road
WESTMORE, Perc	1970	Forest Lawn Memorial-Park, Glendale, CA	Garden of Remem., #1751, 3-in from walk
• WHALE, James	1957	Forest Lawn Memorial-Park, Glendale, CA	Great Maus., Col. of Memory, Niche #20076
WHEELER, Bert	1968	Calvary Cemetery, Woodside (Queens), NY	Sect. 47, Catholic Actors Guild of America
WHELAN, Arleen (Cagney)	1993	Holy Cross Cem. and Maus., Culver City, CA	
WHITMAN, Gayne	1958	Forest Lawn Memorial-Park, Glendale, CA	
WIERE, Sylvester	1970	Westwood Village Mem. Park, Los Angeles, CA	
WILDE, Cornel	1989	Westwood Village Mem. Park, Los Angeles, CA	Urn Garden
WILLIAMS, Earle	1927	Forest Lawn Memorial-Park, Glendale, CA	
• WILLIAMS, Hank Sr.	1953	Oakwood Cemetery Annex, Montgomery, AL	

NAME	YEAR	CEMETERY	INTERMENT SITE*
WILLIAMS, Rhys	1969	Forest Lawn—Hollywood Hills, Los Angeles, CA	Col. of Remembrance, on right, #60467
• WILLIAMS, Tennessee	1983	Calvary Cemetery, St. Louis, MO	
WILSON, Marie	1972	Forest Lawn—Hollywood Hills, Los Angeles, CA	Col. of Remembrance, Vault 61274
• WINCHELL, Walter	1972	Greenwood Memorial Park, Phoenix, AZ	
WINWOOD, Estelle	1984	Westwood Village Mem. Park, Los Angeles, CA	
WITHERS, Grant	1959	Forest Lawn Memorial-Park, Glendale, CA	
WONG, Anna May	1961	Rose Dale Cemetery, Los Angeles, CA	Section 5
• WOOD, Ed	1978	(Cremated—not interred)	Ashes scattered at sea
WOOD, Natalie (Wagner)	1981	Westwood Village Mem. Park, Los Angeles, CA	Section D, #60
WOOD, Sam	1949	Forest Lawn Memorial-Park, Glendale, CA	
WOOLLEY, Monty	1963	Greenridge Cemetery, Saratoga Springs, NY	
WOOLSEY, Robert R.	1938	Forest Lawn Memorial-Park, Glendale, CA	
WORDEN, Hank	1994	Forest Lawn Memorial-Park, Glendale, CA	
WRATHER, Jack	1984	Holy Cross Cem. and Maus., Culver City, CA	Section "Grotto," Lot 196
WYCHERLY, Margaret	1956	Bepton Mid-Hurst Cemetery, Bepton, England	(Margaret Wycherly Veiller)
WYLER, William	1981	Forest Lawn Memorial-Park, Glendale, CA	Eventide, Plot #2998
• WYMARK, Patrick	1970	Highgate West Cemetery, London, England	Near Chapel and Swains Lane
WYNN, Ed	1966	Forest Lawn Memorial-Park, Glendale, CA	Great Maus., Col. of Dawn
WYNN, Keenan	1986	Forest Lawn Memorial-Park, Glendale, CA	Great Maus., Col. of Dawn
X			
X, Malcolm	1965	(See LITTLE, Malcolm)	
Y			
YOUNG, Gig	1978	Green Hills Cemetery, Waynesville, NC	Ashes interred under the name "Byron Barr"
YOUNG, Mary	1934	Forest Lawn Memorial-Park, Glendale, CA	
• YOUNG, Victor	1956	Beth-Olam Cemetery, Hollywood, CA	Mausoleum, main foyer
YULE, Joe	1950	Forest Lawn Memorial-Park, Glendale, CA	
YURKA, Blanche	1974	Kensico Cemetery, Valhalla, NY	Actors Fund Plot
Z			
ZANUCK, Darryl F.	1979	Westwood Village Mem. Park, Los Angeles, CA	Section D, #41
ZANUCK, Virginia Fox	1982	Westwood Village Mem. Park, Los Angeles, CA	Section D, #41
ZAPPA, Frank	1993	Westwood Village Mem. Park, Los Angeles, CA	Section D, #100 (unmarked) Next to Guild
ZIEGFELD, Florenz	1932	Kensico Cemetery, Valhalla, NY	
• ZUCCO, Frances	1962	Forest Lawn—Hollywood Hills, Los Angeles, CA	
• ZUCCO, George	1960	Forest Lawn—Hollywood Hills, Los Angeles, CA	Cremated

• New entry.

* Some cemeteries refuse to reveal specific locations.

INGRID BERGMAN

6

SPECIFIC
INTERMENT LOCATIONS
— BY CEMETERY

CEMETERY	YEAR	NAME	INTERMENT SITE*
A			
Abel's Hill Cemetery, Chilmark (M.V.), MA	1982	BELUSHI, John	
"	1984	HELLMAN, Lillian	
Ahavai Sholom Cemetery, Portland, OR	1989	SCHAEFFER, Rebecca	
Allegheny Cemetery, Pittsburgh, PA	1922	RUSSELL, Lillian	In Mausoleum, Section 40, Space 5
All Saints Episcopal Cemetery, San Luis Rey, CA	1993	PEPPLE, Sydney Chester	Cremated—ashes interred
American Legion Cemetery, Tampa, FL	1946	HATTON, Rondo	
Annunciation Cemetery, Shenandoah, PA	1957	DORSEY, Jimmy	
Arbutus Memorial Park, Baltimore, MD	1995	SANDERS, Al	
Arlington National Cemetery, Arlington, VA	1971	MURPHY, Audie	Near the Battleship Maine memorial
"	1987	MARVIN, Lee	Section 7A, Grave 176
"	1968	BAINTER, Fay	
"	1965	BENNETT, Constance	
"	1966	HARRIGAN, William	
"	1981	LOUIS, Joe	
"	1974	MASSEY, Ilona (Dawson)	
"	1959	MORRIS, Wayne	
"	1983	REYNOLDS, Frank	
Austin Memorial Park, Austin, TX	1965	SCOTT, Zachary	Block 4, Lot 187A, Space 12
B			
Batignolles Cemetery, Paris, France	1938	CHALIAPIN, Feodor	Div. 25, rose granite mon. topped w/cross
Beaverdale Memorial Park, New Haven, CT	1983	MASSEY, Raymond	
Beckett Cemetery, Beckett, MA	1968	COREY, Wendell	
Bepton Mid-Hurst Cemetery, Bepton, England	1956	WYCHERLY, Margaret	(Margaret Wycherly Veiller)
Beth David Cemetery, Elmont (L.I.), NY	1984	KAUFMAN, Andy	
Beth-El Cemetery, Ridgewood (Queens), NY	1973	ROBINSON, Edward G.	
Blanford Cemetery, Petersburg, VA	1994	COTTON, Joseph	
Boissy-Sans-Avoir (nr. Paris), France	1982	SCHNEIDER, Romy	
Bonaventure Cemetery, Savannah, GA	1931	NEILL, James	Section E, Lot 171
"	1976	MERCER, Johnny	
Brompton Cemetery, London, England	1948	TAUBER, Richard	First sect. left of center path, near entrance
C			
Calvary Catholic Cemetery, Kansas City, MO	1929	EAGELS, Jeanne	
Calvary Cemetery, Los Angeles, CA	1972	ROACH, Hal Jr.	Block 14, Crypt 11 (at top)
"	1987	NEGRI, Pola	In Maus., St. Paul Corr, Blk 56, Crypt E19
"	1937	BOLESLAWSKI, Richard	In mausoleum
"	1990	DUNNE, Irene (Griffin)	Left of altar in the Mausoleum church area
"	1954	BARRYMORE, Lionel	Main Mausoleum, Block 352
"	1959	COSTELLO, Lou	Main Mausoleum, Block 354, Crypt B-1
"	1959	BARRYMORE, Ethel (Colt)	Main Mausoleum, Block 60, Crypt 3F
"	1930	NORMAND, Mabel (Cody)	Main Mausoleum, in a main hallway
"	1955	HODIAK, John	Main Mausoleum, next to Mabel Normand
"	1968	NOVARRO, Ramon	Section C, Lot 586, Grave 5
"	1937	HEALY, Ted	Section F, Lot 1693, Grave 14
"	1973	NAISH, J. Carrol	Section G, Lot 1098, Grave 22
"	1968	STROMBERG, Hunt	Section H, Lot 416 (by tree)
"	1961	FAY, Frank	
"	1977	FOY, Bryan	
Calvary Cemetery, Santa Barbara, CA	1981	LANE, Lola	Sect. M, Tier 17, Gr 97 (Lola Lane Hanlon)
Calvary Cemetery, St. Louis, MO	1983	WILLIAMS, Tennessee	
Calvary Cemetery, Woodside (Queens), NY	1933	GUINAN, Mary L. "Texas"	Section 47
"	1968	WHEELER, Bert	Sect. 47, Catholic Actors Guild of America
"	1981	KELLY, Patsy	
"	1927	LEWIS, Tom	
"	1961	NALDI, Nita	
"	1959	O'CONNOR, Una	
Carlsbad Cemetery, Carlsbad, NM	1972	CABOT, Bruce	Division A, Block 48, Space 5 (E. Bujac, Jr.)
Catalina-Ft. Rose Crans Cem., San Diego, CA	1965	BACON, Irving	
Cathedral of St. Nicholas, Monte Carlo, Monaco	1982	KELLY, Grace	Grimaldi family vault
Cedar Park Cemetery, Paramus, NJ	1949	HOWARD, Willie	
Cem. of the Gate of Heaven, Hawthorne, NY	1976	MINEO, Sal	Division 2
"	1948	RUTH, George Herman "Babe"	Sect. 25 (at 10-ft. tall gray granite marker)

• New entry.

* Some cemeteries refuse to reveal specific locations.

CEMETERY	YEAR	NAME	INTERMENT SITE*
Cem. of the Gate of Heaven, Hawthorne, NY	1956	ALLEN, Fred	
"	1986	CAGNEY, James	
"	1947	DIGGES, Dudley	
"	1918	HELD, Anna	
"	1965	KILGALLEN, Dorothy	
Cenacle Convent, Lake Ronkonkoma (L.I.), NY	1953	ADAMS, Maude	
Chapel of the Pines Crematory, Los Angeles, CA	1986	FREDERICK, Fred Burke	Cremated
"	1959	GWENN, Edmund	In basement holding vault, not on view
• "	1947	CARLETON, William P.	Permanent storage vault
"	1967	SHERIDAN, Ann	In vault #57542, not avail. for viewing
• "	1952	MacDONALD, Joseph Farrell	Memory Hall, Section K, B-2
"	1946	BUSH, Mae	Near front door, on left, at eye-level
"	1953	BRUCE, Nigel	Vault #35167
"	1971	ANDERSON, G. M.	
• "	1946	ATWILL, Lionel	
"	1962	BROWNING, Tod	
"	1977	CARLSON, Richard	
"	1968	CLARK, Fred	
"	1967	CONWAY, Tom	
"	1960	CROMWELL, Richard	
"	1959	DOUGLAS, Paul	
"	1965	DUMONT, Margaret	
"	1967	ERWIN, Stuart	
"	1961	FARNUM, Franklyn	
"	1971	HEFLIN, Van	
"	1971	LYNN, Diana	
"	1962	MITCHELL, Thomas	
"	1965	NEWTON, Robert	
"	1982	OBER, Philip	
"	1949	OUSPENSKAYA, Maria	
• Cimitero di Santa Maria del Pianto, Naples, Italy	1921	CARUSO, Enrico	Down the hill on the left, in sarcophagus
• Cimitero Monumentale, Milan, Italy	1989	HOROWITZ, Vladimir	Toscanini family mausoleum
• "	1957	TOSCANINI, Arturo	In the family's white marble mausoleum
City of Lubbock Cemetery, Lubbock, TX	1959	HOLLY, Buddy	Block 44 at Azalea Ave. (nr. path)
• Civico Cimitero, Rimini, Italy	1993	FELLINI, Federico	Section O, in brown brick-like family vault
• "	1994	MASINA, Giulietta (Fellini)	Section O, in the brown Fellini family vault
Clovesville Cemetery, Clovesville, NY	1966	BERG, Gertrude	In Jewish section
Coachella Valley Cemetery, Coachella, CA	1991	CAPRA, Frank	(near Indio)
Congressional Cemetery, Washington, D.C.	1973	FULLER, Mary	
"	1932	SOUSA, John Philip	
Corsier-Sur-Vevey, Switzerland	1977	CHAPLIN, Charles	
Crestlawn Cemetery, Sparta, TN	1979	FLATT, Lester	
Crown Hill Cemetery and Mort., Lakewood, CO	1969	BATES, Barbara	Section 2, Block 69, Lot 144, Unit A
Cypress Hills Cemetery, Brooklyn, NY	1927	LOEW, Marcus	
"	1962	MOORE, Victor	
"	1980	WEST, Mae	
Cypress Lawn Cemetery, Colma, CA	1942	CREWS, Laura Hope	Rose Mound
D			
Dayton Memorial Park, Dayton, OH	1974	MOOREHEAD, Agnes	
Dean's Grange Cemetery, Booterstown, Ireland	1945	McCORMACK, John	
Desert Memorial Park, Palm Springs, CA	1984	POWELL, William	Ashes interred in Section B-10, Lot 20
"	1962	TOMACK, Sid	Section A-9, Lot 14
"	1976	BERKELEY, Busby	Section A-14, Lot 74
"	1958	GOODWIN, Bill	Section B-1, Lot 17
"	1970	RAMBEAU, Marjorie	
Dulaney Valley Mem. Gdns., Cockeysville, MD	1990	BOCK-LEADER, Deborah Lyn	Eternal Light Section
E			
Eden Memorial Park, San Fernando, CA	1957	BROWN, John H.	Akiba 17-55
"	1977	MARX, Julius "Groucho"	In the Mausoleum, across from entrance
"	1984	JAFFE. Sam	Top of outside wall, at top of hill
"	1966	BRUCE, Lenny	
"	1982	LEMBECK, Harvey	

CEMETERY	YEAR	NAME	INTERMENT SITE*
E. Lawn Sierra Hills Mem. Pk., Sacramento, CA	1986	BAER, Jacob "Buddy"	
"	1992	BRAND, Neville	
El Camino Memorial Park, La Jolla, CA	1970	FOSTER, Preston	Sanctuary of Love (3), Crypt 4, Tier F
"	1980	STONE, Milburn	Vista del Lago, 401-D
El Reno Cemetery, El Reno, OK	1990	RHODES, Erik	Ashes buried New Add., Blk 14, Lot 24-A
Emanuel Cemetery, Wethersfield, CT	1966	TUCKER, Sophie	
Eternal Hills Memorial Park, Oceanside, CA	1979	HEISLER, Stuart	
• Eternal Valley Memorial Park, Newhall, CA	1971	JOHNSON, Tor	
Evergreen Cemetery, Brooklyn, NY	1915	BUNNY, John	
"	1949	ROBINSON, Bill "Bojangles"	
Evergreen Cemetery, Colorado Springs, CO	1978	ETTING, Ruth	Shrine of Rest Mausoleum
Evergreen Cemetery, Gainesville, FL	1993	PHOENIX, River	
Evergreen Cemetery, Los Angeles, CA	1977	ANDERSON, Eddie	Section A, Lot 2504
"	1981	BEARD, Matthew "Stymie"	
F			
Fairmount Cemetery, Denver, CO	1946	MEEK, Donald	In Maus., Sect. 392, Tier BB, Main floor
Fairview Cemetery, Pen Argyl, PA	1967	MANSFIELD, Jayne	Grave is near entrance
Ferncliff Cemetery and Maus., Hartsdale, NY	1960	HAMMERSTEIN, Oscar II	Ashes buried
"	1973	SANDS, Diana	Ashewood, Grave 545
"	1955	ARLEN, Harold	Hickory, Grave 1666
"	1976	ROBESON, Paul	Hillcrest A, Grave 1511
"	1982	MONK, Thelonius	Hillcrest I, Grave 405
"	1976	BOSWELL, Connee	Hillcrest J, Grave 227
"	1975	MABLEY, Jackie "Moms"	Knollwood Garden I, Row 14, Grave 4
"	1959	STURGES, Preston	Maplewood R, Garden Grave 74
"	1931	De PUTTI, Lya	Maus., Unit 1, Alcove E, Crypt 31
"	1951	ROMBERG, Sigmund	Maus., Unit 1, Sect. BC-1, Crypt 5
"	1962	CRAWFORD, Jesse	Maus., Unit 3, Alcove 4, Niche Arc.#21
"	1945	KERN, Jerome	Maus., Unit 4 Alcove C, Pvt. Niche Mem. 1
"	1963	BARTHELMESS, Richard	Maus., Unit 8, Alcove BB, Col. B, Niche 1
"	1977	CRAWFORD, Joan (Steele)	Maus., Unit 8, Alcove E, Crypt 42
"	1961	HART, Moss	Maus., Unit 8 Alcove EE-FF, Col. D Niche 4
"	1974	SULLIVAN, Ed	Maus., Unit 8, Alcove G, Side Comp. 122
"	1955	MUNSON, Ona	Maus., Unit 8, Tier Y, Col. G, Niche 5
"	1969	GARLAND, Judy	Maus., Unit 9, Section HH, Crypt 31
"	1982	MARLOWE, Hugh	Maus., Unit 10, Alcove BB-CC, Niche 9A
"	1965	LITTLE, Malcom	Pinewood B, Grave 150
"	1965	Malcolm X.	Pinewood B, Grave 150
"	1963	MAXWELL, Elsa	Rosewood 2, Grave 1132
"	1967	RATHBONE, Basil	Shrine of Mem. Maus., Unit 1, T-K, #117
"	1951	WARFIELD, David	St. Paul, Plot 180, Grave 1
"	1982	BLOCH, Ray	St. Paul, Plot 184, Grave 2
"	1951	CHRISTIANS, Mady	
"	1943	VEIDT, Conrad	
Ferndale Cemetery, Johnstown, NY	1986	CRAWFORD, Broderick	
Fernhill Memorial Gardens, Stuart, FL	1973	MONROE, Vaughn	
"Firefly Hill", Grant's Town, Jamaica	1973	COWARD, Noel	(his private estate)
Flushing Cemetery, Flushing (Queens), NY	1971	ARMSTRONG, Louis	Sect. 8
"	1981	SCOTT, Hazel	Sect. 9, next to ex-husb. Adam C. Powell Sr.
"	1942	ROBSON, May	Sect. 9, plain stone has fam. name 'Brown'
"	1973	TRUEX, Ernest	
Forest Cemetery, Circleville, OH	1971	LEWIS, Ted	
Forestdale Cemetery, Helena, MT	1993	LOY, Myrna	Ashes buried alongside her parents
Forest Home Cemetery, Milwaukee, WI	1983	FONTANNE, Lynn	
"	1977	LUNT, Alfred	
Forest Lawn Cemetery, Nashville, TN	1975	FRIZZELL, Lefty	
Forest Lawn—Covina Hills, Covina, CA	1977	FORD, Mary	
Forest Lawn—Cypress, Cypress, CA	1983	CARPENTER, Karen	Ascension M. Maus., Sanct. of Compassion
"	1960	COCHRAN, Eddie (singer)	Abiding Faith, Plot #2996
"	1976	FORD, Paul	
"	1973	MAYNARD, Ken	
Forest Lawn—Glendale, Glendale, CA	1986	ALDA, Robert	Ascension Garden

CEMETERY	YEAR	NAME	INTERMENT SITE*
Forest Lawn—Glendale, Glendale, CA	1986	KNIGHT, Ted	Ascension Garden (left side)
"	1987	MAMOULIAN, Rouben	Ascension Garden
"	1977	WATERS, Ethel	Ascension Garden (center)
"	1954	GREENSTREET, Sydney	Ashes in a utility room (not open to public)
"	1981	HEAD, Edith	Cathedral slope, Plot 1675, at the top of hill
"	1974	BROWN, Johnny Mack	Columbarium of Heavenly Peace
"	1987	BROWN, Clarence	Columbarium of Honor
"	1963	ODETS, Clifford	Columbarium of Honor
"	1983	CUKOR, George	Court of Freedom
"	1972	FRIML, Rudolph	Court of Last Supper
"	1981	HARDING, Ann	Cremated
"	1983	D'ORSAY, Fifi	Devotion
"	1939	PARROTT, James	Devotion
"	1952	BYRD, Ralph M.	Eventide (under the olive tree)
"	1955	BALL, Suzan (Long)	Eventide, Plot #2922
"	1944	CREGAR, (Samuel) Laird	Eventide, Lot 37, Space 2
"	1959	HALL, Charlie	Eventide, Lot 1928
"	1981	WYLER, William	Eventide, Plot #2998
"	1948	LANDIS, Carole	Everlasting Love, Lot 968, Gr. 8 next to curb
"	1986	PALMER, Lilli (Thompson)	Freedom Courtyard
"	1965	DANDRIDGE, Dorothy	Freedom Maus., Col. of Victory
"	1978	EILERS, Sally	Freedom Maus., Columbarium
"	1992	WELLS, Mary	Freedom Maus., Columbarium of Patriots
"	1966	DISNEY, Walt	Freedom Maus., outside front left
"	1977	MARX, Milton "Gummo"	Freedom Maus., Sanct. of Brotherhood
"	1966	BUSHMAN, Francis X.	Freedom Maus., Sanctuary of Gratitude
"	1964	ALLEN, Gracie (Burns)	Freedom Maus., Sanctuary of Heritage
"	1962	BELL, Rex	Freedom Maus., Sanctuary of Heritage
"	1965	BOW, Clara (Bell)	Freedom Maus., Sanctuary of Heritage
"	1996	BURNS, George	Freedom Maus., Sanctuary of Heritage
"	1965	COLE, Nat "King"	Freedom Maus., Sanctuary of Heritage
"	1964	LADD, Alan	Freedom Maus., Sanctuary of Heritage
"	1982	LADD, Sue Carol	Freedom Maus., Sanctuary of Heritage
"	1965	MacDONALD, Jeanette	Freedom Maus., Sanctuary of Heritage
"	1965	McDONALD, Marie	Freedom Maus., Sanctuary of Heritage
"	1975	FINE, Larry	Freedom Maus., Sanctuary of Liberation
"	1961	MARX, Leonard "Chico"	Freedom Maus., Sanctuary of Worship
"	1959	FLYNN, Errol	Garden of Everlasting Peace
"	1967	TRACY, Spencer	Garden of Everlasting Peace
"	1964	COOKE, Sam	Garden of Honor
"	1990	DAVIS, Sammy Jr.	Garden of Honor
"	1986	NELSON, Frank	Garden of Honor
"	1979	BLONDELL, Joan	Garden of Honor, Col. of the Evening Star
"	1969	TAYLOR, Robert	Garden of Honor, Col. of the Evening Star
"	1973	GOLDWYN, Samuel	Garden of Honor, first garden on right
"	1960	ADLER, Buddy	Garden of Memory
"	1951	BAXTER, Warner	Garden of Memory
"	1948	CARROLL, Earl	Garden of Memory
"	1976	KUHLMAN, Kathryn	Garden of Memory
"	1987	LeROY, Mervyn	Garden of Memory
"	1933	PICKFORD, Jack	Garden of Memory
"	1936	PICKFORD, Lottie	Garden of Memory
"	1979	PICKFORD, Mary	Garden of Memory
"	1970	RUGGLES, Charlie	Garden of Memory
"	1972	RUGGLES, Wesley	Garden of Memory
"	1955	SAKALL, S. Z. "Cuddles"	Garden of Memory, as 'Szoke Szakall'
"	1957	BOGART, Humphrey	Garden of Memory, Col. of Eternal Light
"	1983	CANOVA, Judy	Garden of Memory, Col. of Eternal Light
"	1959	McLAGLEN, Victor	Garden of Memory, Col. of Eternal Light
"	1963	POWELL, Dick	Garden of Memory, Col. of Honor
"	1970	WESTMORE, Perc	Garden of Remem., #1751, 3-in from walk
"	1979	OBERON, Merle (Wolders)	Garden of Remembrance

CEMETERY	YEAR	NAME	INTERMENT SITE*
Forest Lawn—Glendale, Glendale, CA	1986	WALLIS, Hal	Great Mausoleum
"	1923	REID, Wallace	Great Maus., Azalea Columbarium
"	1937	ROLAND, Ruth M.	Great Maus., Azalea Columbarium
"	1940	TURPIN, Ben	Great Maus., Azalea Columbarium
"	1932	GILLETT, King	Great Maus., Begonia Corridor
"	1971	LLOYD, Harold Sr.	Great Maus., Begonia corridor #771
"	1956	BURNS, Bob	Great Maus., Col. of Adoration
• "	1975	DURFEE, Minta (Arbuckle)	Great Maus., Col. of Constancy #17743
"	1966	WYNN, Ed	Great Maus., Col. of Dawn
"	1986	WYNN, Keenan	Great Maus., Col. of Dawn
"	1956	GRAPEWIN, Charles	Great Maus., Col. of Inspiration
"	1967	ANDREWS, LaVerne	Great Maus., Col. of Memory
"	1966	BAKER, Art	Great Maus., Col. of Memory
"	1955	BARA, Theda	Great Maus., Col. of Memory, Niche #19566
"	1963	CARSON, Jack	Great Maus., Col. of Memory
• "	1977	DAVES, Delmar	Great Maus., Col. of Memory
"	1950	INGRAM, Rex (director)	Great Maus., Col. of Memory, under window
"	1983	JONES, Carolyn	Great Maus., Col. of Memory
"	1984	KEIGHLEY, William	Great Maus., Col. of Memory
• "	1951	SIMON, S. Sylvan	Great Maus., Col. of Memory, Niche #20174
"	1979	TIOMKIN, Dimitri	Great Maus., Col. of Memory, Niche #19425
• "	1957	WHALE, James	Great Maus., Col. of Memory, Niche #20076
"	1933	TORRENCE, Ernest	Great Maus., Col. of Prayer, Niche #10677
"	1990	CUMMINGS, Robert	Great Maus., Col. of Sanctity
"	1955	THUNDERCLOUD, Chief	Great Maus., Corridor of Mercy
"	1987	TORRES, Raquel	Great Maus., Hall of Celestial Peace
"	1946	FIELDS, W. C.	Great Maus., Hall of Inspiration
"	1965	TRAVERS, Henry	Great Maus., Hall of Inspiration
"	1970	DOLLY, Roszika "Rosie"	Great Maus., hall right side
"	1941	DOLLY, Yansci "Jenny"	Great Maus., hall right side
"	1956	HERSHOLT, Jean	Great Maus., monument opp. entrance
"	1934	DRESSLER, Marie	Great Maus., Sanctuary of Benediction
"	1937	HARLOW, Jean	Great Maus., Sanctuary of Benediction
"	1983	SHEARER, Norma (Thalberg)	Great Maus., Sanctuary of Benediction
"	1936	THALBERG, Irving Grant	Great Maus., Sanctuary of Benediction
"	1970	NEWMAN, Alfred	Great Maus., Sanctuary of Eternal Prayer
• "	1960	GREEN, Alfred E.	Great Maus., Sanc. of Refuge, Crypt #5089
"	1972	AUSTIN, Gene	Great Maus., Sanctuary of Sacred Promise
"	1972	BOYD, William	Great Maus., Sanctuary of Sacred Promise
"	1971	STEINER, Max	Great Maus., Sanctuary of Sacred Promise
"	1987	GINGOLD, Hermione	Great Maus., Sanctuary of the Holy Spirit
"	1960	GABLE, Clark	Great Maus., Sanctuary of Trust
"	1942	LOMBARD, Carole (Gable)	Great Maus., Sanctuary of Trust
"	1965	SELZNICK, David O.	Great Maus., Sanctuary of Trust
"	1934	SHERMAN, Lowell	Great Maus., Sanctuary of Trust
"	1965	BOLAND, Mary	Great Maus., Sanctuary of Vespers
"	1934	COLUMBO, Russ	Great Maus., Sanctuary of Vespers
• "	1968	LEONARD, Robert Z.	Great Maus., Sanctuary of Vespers
"	1981	DAVIS, Jim	Great Maus., 3rd floor (cremated)
"	1978	DAILEY, Dan	Marker 7065, left of Statue of Immortality
"	1946	EMMETT, Fern (Roquemore)	Masonic Section
"	1970	LOUISE, Anita (Marks)	Next to her husband, Buddy Adler
"	1974	LANE, Rosemary	No headstone
• "	1994	STANDER, Lionel	Outside Freedom Maus. (front)
"	1986	MINNELLI, Vincente	Small priv. garden in Triumphant Faith Terr.
"	1973	BROWN, Joe E.	Sunrise Slope
"	1940	CHASE, Charley	Sunrise Slope, Lot 72, Grave 147
"	1939	MERCER, Beryl	Sunrise Slope 337
"	1949	BEERY, Wallace	Vale of Memory
"	1967	CLYDE, Andy	Whispering Pines
"	1936	GILBERT, John	Whispering Pines
"	1950	HALE, Alan Sr.	Whispering Pines

• New entry.

299

* Some cemeteries refuse to reveal specific locations.

CEMETERY	YEAR	NAME	INTERMENT SITE*
Forest Lawn—Glendale, Glendale, CA	1973	HOLDEN, Fay	Whispering Pines
"	1945	NAZIMOVA, Madame Alla	Whispering Pines
"	1978	OAKIE, Jack	Whispering Pines #1066 hilltop nr Cath. Dr.
"	1952	PETERS, Susan	Whispering Pines, at "Finding of Moses"
"	1940	MIX, Tom	Whispering Pines, Grave 986
"	1986	TUTTLE, Lurene	Whispering Pines, Lot #1570
"	1949	DIX, Richard	Whispering Pines, nr. "Finding of Moses"
"	1968	PIERCE, Jack P.	Whispering Pines, nr. "Finding of Moses"
"	1959	LITTLEFIELD, Lucien	Whispering Pines, Plot #1720
"	1967	DARWELL, Jane	Whispering Pines, Plot #1817
"	1931	ACORD, Art	
"	1937	ALEXANDER, Ross	
"	1978	ALLWYN, Astrid	
"	1962	ATES, Roscoe	
"	1944	BENNETT, Richard	
"	1941	BERGERE, Ramona R.	
"	1955	BERTRAND, Mary (Rall)	
"	1988	BESSER, Joe	
"	1962	BLANDICK, Clara	
"	1963	BLUE, Monte	
"	1963	BOLEY, May	
"	1960	BOND, Ward	
"	1947	BORDEN, Olive	
"	1962	BORZAGE, Frank	
"	1943	BOSWORTH, Hobart	
"	1957	BRABIN, Charles J.	
"	1936	BREESE, Edmund	
"	1937	BURGESS, Helen M.	
"	1947	CAREY, Harry	
"	1944	CARR, Nathan C. "Nat"	
"	1979	CARROLL, John	
"	1930	CHANEY, Lon F. Sr.	
"	1943	CHARTERS, Spencer H.	
"	1949	CLARK, Buddy	
"	1957	CLEVELAND, George	
"	1949	CLIFTON, Elmer	
"	1944	COLLIER, William Sr.	
"	1947	CORTHELL, Herbert	
"	1985	CRAIG, James	
"	1974	CRISP, Donald	
"	1962	CURTIZ, Michael	
"	1955	DANIELS, Victor	
"	1936	DAVENPORT, Alice	
"	1944	DINEHART, Mason Alan	
"	1959	DUNCAN, Rosetta	
"	1986	DUNCAN, Vivian	
"	1935	DURKIN, Junior	
"	1951	ERROL, Leon	
"	1953	FARNUM, William	
"	1940	FITZMAURICE, George F.	
"	1958	FOX, Wallace W.	
"	1939	FRANKLIN, Rupert	
"	1961	FRENCH, George B.	
"	1943	FRYE, Dwight	
"	1950	FULTON, Maude	
"	1956	GANZHORN, John W.	
"	1976	GOLDWYN, Frances Howard	
"	1956	GORDON, Huntly	
"	1960	GORDON, Leon	
"	1959	HALTON, Charles	
"	1942	HAMILTON, Hale Rice	
"	1935	HARDY, Sam	

CEMETERY	YEAR	NAME	INTERMENT SITE*
Forest Lawn—Glendale, Glendale, CA	1955	HARVEY, Paul (actor)	
"	1955	HAYDEN, Harry	
"	1964	HEARN, Sam	
"	1956	HERBERT, Holmes	
"	1970	HORTON, Edward Everett	
"	1936	HOWLAND, Jobyna	
"	1958	HUGHES, Lloyd	
"	1946	HURT, Marlin	
"	1990	IRELAND, Jill	
"	1943	JULIAN, Rupert	
"	1947	KERRIGAN, J. Warren	
"	1947	KOLKER, Joseph Henry	
"	1953	LEBEDEFF, Ivan	
"	1956	LEWIS, Mitchell	
"	1960	LLOYD, Frank	
"	1947	LOFT, Arthur	
"	1963	LONDON, Tom	
"	1947	LUBITSCH, Ernst	
"	1957	LYMAN, Abe	
"	1934	MACK, Charles E.	
"	1964	MARX, Arthur "Harpo"	
"	1947	NEGIN, Koliz	
"	1948	NIBLO, Fred L. Sr.	
"	1942	NICHOLS, George Jr.	
"	1947	O'BRIEN, Thomas Everett	
"	1942	OLIVER, Edna May	
"	1954	OLSEN, Moroni	
"	1958	OSBORN, Lyn	
"	1937	OWSLEY, Monroe Righter	
"	1958	PANGBORN, Franklin	
"	1941	PENNER, Joe	
"	1955	PIERLOT, Francis	
"	1934	POLLARD, Harry A.	
"	1937	POWELL, Richard	
"	1958	PURVIANCE, Edna	
"	1945	RANDALL, Addison Owen	
"	1943	RAY, Charles	
"	1964	RICHARDS, Addison	
"	1940	ROBERTS, Florence	
"	1942	ROSING, Bodil Ann	
"	1936	SALE, Charles P. "Chic"	
"	1941	SCHERTZINGER, Victor	
"	1954	SELWYN, Ruth (Warburton)	
"	1944	SELZNICK, Myron	
"	1968	STAFFORD, Hanley	
"	1950	STAHL, John M.	
"	1941	STEPHENSON, James	
"	1940	STEVENS, John Landers	
"	1961	STEWART, Anita (Converse)	
"	1960	TIBBETT, Lawrence	
"	1935	TODD, Thelma	
"	1940	TRAINOR, Leonard E.	
"	1944	Van DYKE, Woody S. II	
"	1939	VERNON, Bobby	
"	1946	WALDRON, Charles D.	
"	1961	WALLING, Effie Bond	
"	1958	WHITMAN, Gayne	
"	1927	WILLIAMS, Earle	
"	1959	WITHERS, Grant	
"	1949	WOOD, Sam	
"	1938	WOOLSEY, Robert R.	
"	1994	WORDEN, Hank	

...SPECIFIC INTERMENT LOCATIONS — BY CEMETERY...

CEMETERY	YEAR	NAME	INTERMENT SITE*
Forest Lawn—Glendale, Glendale, CA	1934	YOUNG, Mary	
"	1950	YULE, Joe	
Forest Lawn—Hollywood Hills, Los Angeles, CA	1965	LAUREL, Stanley	Ashes in Garden of Heritage at garden wall
"	1978	ROBERTS, Lynne (Mary Hart)	Buried beside her mother
"	1974	KRUGER, Otto	Churchyard, Plot #4266
"	1973	STRANGE, Glenn	Churchyard, Plot #4295
"	1974	BRITTON, Pamela	Col. of Radiant Dawn, G61685
"	1994	LANTZ, Walter	Col. of Radiant Light
"	1972	COWAN, Jerome	Col. of Remembrance
"	1965	KASSEL, Art	Col. of Remembrance, 6098
"	1977	WALLER, Eddy	Col. of Remembrance, on left, #60409
"	1982	SHAW, Reta	Col. of Remembrance, on left, 60402
"	1963	MAYO, Frank	Col. of Remembrance, on left, 60450
"	1969	WILLIAMS, Rhys	Col. of Remembrance, on right, #60467
"	1988	STEELE, Bob	Col. of Remembrance, on right, 60722
"	1939	SMALLEY, W. Phillips	Col. of Remembrance, on right, 60750
"	1965	NICHOLS, Ernest "Red"	Col. of Remembrance, on right, 60780
"	1972	WILSON, Marie	Col. of Remembrance, Vault 61274
"	1993	AMES, Leon	Col. of Valor, G-64429
"	1991	DAVIS, Brad	Col. of Valor, G64054
"	1969	LOCHER, Felix	Court of Liberty
"	1991	CONVY, Bert	Court of Liberty, left of sidewalk
"	1980	BARRY, Don "Red"	Court of Liberty, Plot #5442 (under tree)
"	1969	INGRAM, Rex (actor)	Court of Liberty, Plot #822
"	1979	HALL, Jon	Court of Liberty, same row w/Buster Keaton
"	1966	KEATON, Buster	Court of Liberty, nr. G. Washington statue
"	1989	BALL, Lucille (Morton)	Courts of Remem., Col. of Radiant Dawn
"	1986	TUCKER, Forrest	Courts of Remem., Col. of Radiant Dawn
"	1962	LAUGHTON, Charles	Courts of Remem., in black marble vault
"	1987	Liberace	Courts of Remem., in white sarcophagus
"	1983	LIBERACE, George	Courts of Remem., in white sarcophagus
"	1980	GARDINER, Reginald	Courts of Remem., Sanc. of Reflection, 3322
"	1968	ST. DENIS, Ruth	Courts of Remem.
"	1974	FONTANE, Tony	Courts of Remem., 409
"	1965	BEATTY, Clyde	Courts of Remem., 2175
"	1988	GIBB, Andy	Courts of Remem., 2534
"	1982	MILLS, Harry F.	Courts of Remem., 3446
"	1981	HENDRIX, Wanda	Courts of Remem., 4349
"	1980	MARTIN, Strother	Courts of Remem., G62420
"	1989	DAVIS, Bette	Courts of Remem., near entrance
"	1977	PRINZE, Freddie (Preutzel)	Courts of Remem., Sanctuary of Light
"	1980	RAFT, George	Courts of Remem., Sanctuary of Light
"	1992	HANCOCK, John	Devotion, Plot #8018
"	1976	CAMBRIDGE, Godfrey	Enduring Faith
"	1986	HEIDT, Horace	Enduring Faith
"	1975	MAIN, Marjorie	Enduring Faith, Plot #2083
"	1974	BRADLEY, Truman	Enduring Faith, Plot #3718
"	1973	REID, Carl Benton	Enduring Faith, Plot #3722
"	1964	COLE, Edwin "Buddy"	Enduring Faith, Plot #3999
"	1979	SOO, Jack	Eternal Love, Plot #3980
"	1949	LEIBER, Fritz	Everlasting Love, Plot #864, Grave 13
"	1968	TALMAN, William	Garden of Heritage, Garden Crypt 633
"	1965	COLLINS, Ray	Garden of Heritage, Plot #909
"	1994	SAVALAS, Telly	Garden of Heritage, Plot #1281
"	1991	ACKERMAN, Harry	Garden of Heritage, Plot #3019
"	1982	FELDMAN, Marty	Garden of Heritage, Plot #5420
"	1980	AVERY, Frederick B. "Tex"	Gentleness
"	1967	RANDOLPH, Amanda	Gentleness, under a tree
"	1980	RANDOLPH, Lillian	Gentleness, under a tree
"	1991	BELLAMY, Ralph	God's Acre, Plot #8687
"	1991	DUROCHER, Leo	Hillside, Plot #3211
"	1955	FRANCIS, Robert	Hillside, Plot #4535

...SPECIFIC INTERMENT LOCATIONS — BY CEMETERY...

CEMETERY	YEAR	NAME	INTERMENT SITE*
Forest Lawn—Hollywood Hills, Los Angeles, CA	1969	HAYES, George "Gabby"	Hillside, Plot #4972
"	1992	PORCARO, Jeff	Lincoln Terrace, Plot #120
"	1970	GRANT, Earl	Lincoln Terrace, Plot #226
"	1992	DARBY, Ken	Lincoln Terrace, Plot #4246
"	1994	CONRAD, William	Lincoln Terrace, Plot #4448
"	1986	CROTHERS, Ben "Scatman"	Lincoln Terrace, Plot #4545
"	1985	SAVALAS, George	Lincoln Terrace, Plot #4596
"	1977	MUSTIN, Burt	Loving Kindness, Plot #7844
• "	1975	STEVENS, George	Morning Light
"	1967	DENNY, Reginald	Morning Light, Plot #7451
"	1979	BUCHANAN, Edgar	Morning Light, Plot #7780
"	1976	LANG, Fritz	Murmuring Trees, Plot #3818
"	1973	ARMSTRONG, Robert	Murmuring Trees, Plot #7318, Space 1
"	1968	CHESHIRE, Harry "Pappy"	Remembrance, Plot #323
"	1962	KOVACS, Ernie	Remembrance
"	1963	ROBARDS, Jason Sr.	Remembrance, Grave 975 (at curb)
"	1967	TROWBRIDGE, Charles	Remembrance, Plot #233
"	1994	NELSON, Harriet	Revelation
"	1975	NELSON, Ozzie	Revelation
"	1985	NELSON, Rick	Revelation
"	1968	DURYEA, Dan	Revelation, Plot #7347
"	1989	VanCLEEF, Lee	Serenity, 5 plots to right of marker 129
"	1946	BEERY, Noah Sr.	Sheltering Hills
"	1967	BURNETTE, Smiley	Sheltering Hills, Plot #266
"	1963	DASTAGIR, Sabu	Sheltering Hills, Plot #402
"	1960	DASTAGIR, Sheik	Sheltering Hills, Plot #490
• "	1971	DISNEY, Roy	Sheltering Hills
"	1962	POLLARD, Harry "Snub"	Sheltering Hills
• "	1981	SAGAL, Boris	Sheltering Hills
"	1990	TAYBACK, Victor	Sheltering Hills, Plot #3813
"	1982	WEBB, Jack	Sheltering Hills, Plot #1999
"	1982	ROSS, Joe E.	SummerLand, Plot #148
"	1955	BACON, Lloyd	
"	1962	BARRIS, Harry	
"	1988	BARSI, Judith	
• "	1993	CAMPANELLA, Roy	
• "	1991	CAULFIELD, Joan	
"	1982	GOSDEN, Freeman	
"	1992	OLIVER, David	
"	1958	PANZER, Paul	
"	1921	RITCHIE, Billie	
• "	1988	ROBERSON, C. H. "Chuck"	
• "	1988	ROBINSON, Dar Allen	
"	1959	STONE, Fred	
"	1964	TEAGARDEN, Jack	
• "	1962	ZUCCO, Frances	
• "	1960	ZUCCO, George	Cremated
• Forest Lawn Memorial Park, Beaumont, TX	1959	RICHARDSON, Jiles	Block C, Lot 31, Space 3
Forest Lawn Memorial Park, Goodlettsville, TN	1973	AKEMAN, David	
Fort Bragg Military Cemetery, NC	1994	RAYE, Martha	
• Frasier Cemetery, New Westminister, B.C.	1993	BURR, Raymond	
Friedenau Cemetery, Berlin, Germany	1992	DIETRICH, Marlene	Near her mother, Josefine von Losch
Friends Cemetery, Brooklyn, NY	1966	CLIFT, Montgomery	
• Ft. Bliss National Cemetery, El Paso, TX	1967	TATUM, Reece "Goose"	Section D, Grave 2668
G			
Gate of Heaven Cemetery, Silver Spring, MD	1983	PULEO, Johnny	
Glen Haven Memorial Park, San Fernando, CA	1969	HUNTER, Jeffrey	
• Glenwood Cemetery, Beeville, TX	1961	LAWRENCE, Walter Smith	
• Glenwood Cemetery, Houston, TX	1976	HUGHES, Howard	
• Golders Green Cemetery, London, England	1980	SELLERS, Peter	
Grace Hills Cemetery, Hawarden, PA	1960	EMERSON, Hope	
Graceland Cemetery, Chicago, IL	1940	BATES, Granville	

• New entry.   * Some cemeteries refuse to reveal specific locations.

CEMETERY	YEAR	NAME	INTERMENT SITE*
Graceland, Memphis, TN	1977	PRESLEY, Elvis	
Grand View Memorial Park, Glendale, CA	1982	FONDA, Henry	Cremated (Ashes given to his family)
"	1938	FREDERICK, Pauline	
"	1974	LONG, Richard	
• Green Hills Cemetery, Asheville, NC	1978	YOUNG, Gig	Ashes interred under the name "Byron Barr"
Greenmount Cemetery, Baltimore, MD	1968	SEDDON, Margaret	
Greenridge Cemetery, Saratoga Springs, NY	1963	WOOLLEY, Monty	
Green-Wood Cemetery, Brooklyn, NY	1965	MURROW, Edward R.	Ashes buried
"	1956	MORGAN, Ralph	The Wupperman lot
"	1990	BERNSTEIN, Leonard	
"	1946	HART, William S.	
"	1949	MORGAN, Frank	
Greenwood Cemetery, Fort Worth, TX	1975	ROBERTS, Roy	314 - 42
"	1920	LOCKLEAR, Omer	89 - 9E
Greenwood Cemetery, New Orleans, LA	1987	MEYER, Emile G.	
Greenwood Memorial Cemetery, Renton, WA	1970	HENDRIX, Jimi	
• Greenwood Memorial Park, Fort Worth, TX	1987	PAM, Anita	Maus.-Westminster area (Valutage) (NM)
• Greenwood Memorial Park, Phoenix, AZ	1972	WINCHELL, Walter	
Greenwood Memorial Park, San Diego, CA	1936	SCHUMANN-HEINK, Ernestine	Cathedral Mausoleum, Corr. of Sunshine
"	1981	BUONO, Victor	Unmarked grave nr. pond, next to his mom
• Grove Hill Memorial Park, Dallas, TX	1975	CALVIN, Henry	60-3-16
• "	1991	VonERICH, Chris	Hilltop Lot 535, Space 4
• "	1984	VonERICH, David	Hilltop Lot 535
• "	1993	VonERICH, Kerry	Hilltop near Lot 535
• "	1987	VonERICH, Michael	Hilltop Lot 535
• Grunewald-Forst Cemetery, Berlin, Germany	1988	Nico (Christa Paffgen)	
H			
• Hampstead Cemetery, London, England	1971	COOPER, (Dame) Gladys	Near Public Footpath and 3rd path on right
Haym Salomon Memorial Park, Frazer, PA	1973	CROCE, Jim	
Hebrew Friendship Cemetery, Baltimore, MD	1992	ROBBINS, Fred	
• Hebrew Young Men's Cem., Baltimore, MD	1995	GOTTLIEB, Conrad I.	
• Henie-Onstad Art Center, Oslo, Norway	1969	HENIE, Sonja	
• Highgate East Cemetery, London, England	1983	RICHARDSON, (Sir) Ralph	Near Main Rd.
• Highgate West Cemetery, London, England	1970	WYMARK, Patrick	Near Chapel and Swains Lane
• Hillcrest Memorial Park, Dallas, TX	1995	MANTLE, Mickey	Mausoleum St. Mark NE-N-C-13
• "	1995	ELGART, Les	Garden of Prayer, Block 10, Lot 27, Sp 2
Hillside Memorial Park, Los Angeles, CA	1991	LANDON, Michael	Ashes in private room with clear glass door
• "	1995	FRELENG, Isadore "Friz"	Canaan, Block E-249
• "	1938	FACTOR, Max	Courts of the Book, Isaiah, U-314
"	1994	SHORE, Dinah	Courts of the Book, Isaiah, V-247
"	1985	DIAMOND, Selma	Courts of the Book, Jacob, I-4004
"	1987	GREENE, Lorne	Courts of the Book, Lawn Crypt, 5-800-8B
• "	1975	HOWARD, Moe	Garden of Memories, Alcove of Love C233
"	1972	RICHMAN, Harry	Garden of Memories, Alcove of Love B319
"	1994	BOOKE, Sorrell	Garden of Memories, Dedication, 272-4B
• "	1969	GOETZ, William	Garden of Memories, Devotion, Sarcoph. B
"	1976	FAITH, Percy	Garden of Memories, Honor, Lawn Crypt 407
"	1973	FREED, Arthur	Garden of Memories, Honor, Lawn Crypt 418
"	1950	JOLSON, Al	In Al Jolson Memorial (at top of waterfall)
• "	1989	LERNER, Sam	Laurel Gardens, Block 18-177-3A
"	1975	BLUE, Ben	Mausoleum, Col. of Graciousness, 810
• "	1973	SHERMAN, Allan	Mausoleum, Col. of Hope, 513
"	1992	GOODSON, Mark	Mausoleum, Gdn. of Abraham, Sarcoph. B
"	1974	BENNY, Jack	Mausoleum, Graciousness, Sarcophagus F
"	1983	LIVINGSTONE, Mary (Benny)	Mausoleum, Graciousness, Sarcophagus F
"	1961	CHANDLER, Jeff (Ira Grossel)	Mausoleum, Graciousness, 2nd Floor, 4015
"	1964	CANTOR, Eddie	Mausoleum, Graciousness, 207
"	1980	JANSSEN, David	Mausoleum, Memorial Court, 516
"	1981	JESSEL, George	Mausoleum, Memorial Court, 516
"	1987	SHAWN, Dick	Mausoleum, Memorial Court, 734
• "	1982	MORROW, Vic	Mount of Olives, Block 5-80-1
• "	1993	SEYMOUR, Dan	Mount of Olives, Block 7-175-1

CEMETERY	YEAR	NAME	INTERMENT SITE*
• Hillside Memorial Park, Los Angeles, CA	1970	MARCH, Hal	Mount Sholom, Block 4-144-6
• "	1985	KATZ, Mickey	Valley of Remembrance, Block 1-196-2
• "	1995	WARNER, Jack M.	
Hollybrook Cem., Shirley, Southampton, Eng.	1992	HILL, Benny	
• Hollywood Memorial Park, Hollywood, CA	1934	DILLON, John Francis	Abbey of the Psalms
• "	1990	LOCKER, Frances	Abbey of the Psalms
• "	1975	LACHMAN, Harry	Abbey of the Psalms
• "	1936	WALTHALL, Henry B.	Abbey of the Psalms
"	1947	TANGUAY, Eva	Abbey of the Psalms, Crypt 0558, Corr. D-1
"	1968	CHAPLIN, Charles Jr. (son)	Abbey of the Psalms, Crypt 1065, Corr E-2
"	1949	FLEMING, Victor	Abbey of the Psalms, Crypt 2081, Corr G-2
"	1958	LASKY, Jesse L. Sr.	Abbey of the Psalms, Crypt 2196, Corr G-3
"	1983	HACKETT, Joan	Abbey of the Psalms, Crypt 2314, Corr D-3
"	1966	WEBB, Clifton	Abbey of the Psalms, Crypt 2350, Corr G-6
"	1973	ROBINSON, Edward G. Jr.	Abbey of the Psalms, Crypt 4386, Corr E-4
"	1979	HOOD, Darla	Abbey of the Psalms, Crypt 7213, Corr G-4
"	1973	TALMADGE, Constance	Abbey of the Psalms, Family Rm, Corr G-7
"	1969	TALMADGE, Natalie	Abbey of the Psalms, Family Rm, Corr G-7
"	1957	TALMADGE, Norma	Abbey of the Psalms, Family Rm, Corr G-7
"	1933	ADOREE, Renée	Abbey of the Psalms, Foyer, Crypt 219
"	1942	CRUZE, James	Abbey of Psalms, Foyer, Niche 211, Tier 2
"	1956	CALHERN, Louis	Abbey of Psalms, Foyer, Niche 308, Tier 3
"	1955	DeMILLE, William C.	Abbey of the Psalms, Niche 2, T.6, Corr E-3
"	1991	BROWNE, Coral	Ashes scattered in the rose garden.
• "	1968	MAYO, Archie	Beth Olam Mausoleum
• "	1949	SCHLESINGER, Leon	Beth Olam Mausoleum, ashes in vault
• "	1967	WAXMAN, Franz	Beth Olam Maus., ashes in urn at 2nd ent.
• "	1956	YOUNG, Victor	Beth Olam Mausoleum, main foyer
"	1964	SCHILDKRAUT, Joseph	Beth Olam Mausoleum, Niche 43
"	1971	DANIELS, Bebe	Col., Niche 7-8, T.3, Upper N. Wall
"	1979	LYON, Ben	Col., Niche 7-8, T.3, Upper No. Wall
"	1940	AYRES, Agnes	Columbarium, Niche 3, T.3, Lower S. Wall
"	1942	WEBER, Joe	Cremated; remains placed in a vault
"	1961	DAVIES, Marion	Douras Mausoleum, Section 8, Lot 261-264
"	1987	LAKE, Arthur	Douras Mausoleum, Section 8, Lot 261-264
"	1987	HERMAN, Woody	Grounds, Crypt 6689, Unit 10
"	1926	LaMARR, Barbara	H'wood Cath. Maus.
"	1926	LAWRENCE, Lillian	H'wood Cath. Maus.
"	1922	TAYLOR, William Desmond	H'wood Cath. Maus., Crypt 594
"	1927	MATHIS, June	H'wood Cath. Maus., Crypt 1199, Corr A
"	1926	VALENTINO, Rudolph	H'wood Cath. Maus., #1205, off Corr A
"	1977	FINCH, Peter	H'wood Cath. Maus., Crypt 1224, off Corr A
"	1964	LORRE, Peter	H'wood Cath. Maus., Niche 5, T-1, Corr C
"	1982	POWELL, Eleanor	H. C. Maus., Niche 432, T-3, Foyer E/W
"	1989	BLANC, Mel	Pineland section
"	1928	ROBERTS, Theodore	Pineland section
"	1940	FINCH, Flora	Section 1, Grave 416
"	1938	LAWRENCE, Florence	Section 2, buried in an unmarked grave
"	1941	SHANNON, Peggy	Section 5, Plot 43 (two rows in from road)
"	1959	SWITZER, Carl "Alfalfa"	Section 6, Lot 26, Grave 6
"	1959	DeMILLE, Cecil B.	Section 8
• "	1991	LAIRD, Jack	Section 8
• "	1927	REYNOLDS, Lynn	Section 8
• "	1943	MARSHALL, Tully	Section 8, grave beneath a tree
• "	1972	FRANKLIN, Sidney (director)	Section 8, grave next to palm tree
"	1947	BING, Herman	Section 8, 20 ft. east of John Huston
"	1963	MENJOU, Adolphe	Section 8, Lot 11
"	1957	KORNGOLD, Erich Wolfgang	Section 8, Lot 15
"	1959	Adrian	Section 8, Lot 193
"	1984	GAYNOR, Janet (Gregory)	Section 8, Lot 193
"	1921	RAPPE, Virginia	Section 8, Lot 257
"	1946	LEHRMAN, Henry	Section 8, Lot 257 (next to Virginia Rappe)

CEMETERY	YEAR	NAME	INTERMENT SITE*
Hollywood Memorial Park, Hollywood, CA	1987	HUSTON, John	Section 8, Lot 8
"	1958	COHN, Harry	Section 8, Lot 86
"	1967	EDDY, Nelson	Section 8, Lot 89
"	1953	ROSSON, Richard	Section 8, near Cecil B. DeMille
"	1975	DALEY, Cass (Katherine)	Section 8, near curb ("Williamson")
"	1958	BELL, Monta	Section 8, near Nelson Eddy
"	1958	POWER, Tyrone	Section 8, near the Marion Davies Maus.
"	1967	WESTMORE, Ernest	Section 8, three-in from the road
"	1939	FAIRBANKS, Douglas Sr.	Section 11
"	1931	FRANKLIN, Sidney (actor)	Section 13, Lot #321
"	1934	DANE, Karl	Section 13, Plot 303 (next to road)
"	1980	DASSIN, Joe	Section 14, Grave 79, Row I
"	1967	MUNI, Paul	Section 14, Row 00, Grave 57
"	1949	BRESSART, Felix	Section 14, Row J, Grave 89
"	1986	RITZ, Harry	T-Bldg., 3rd floor
"	1985	RIDDLE, Nelson	T-Bldg., Niche 702, Tier 7, Corr T-1
"	1965	RITZ, Al	T-Bldg., T-4, Bottom row, right side
"	1985	RITZ, Jimmy	T-Bldg., T-5
"	1970	BEAUDINE, William	
"	1984	HUMBERSTONE, Bruce H.	
"	1970	KARNS, Roscoe	
"	1952	LINCOLN, Elmo	
"	1948	NOLAN, Mary	
Holy Cross Cem. and Maus., Culver City, CA	1975	MARSHALL, George E.	Mausoleum
"	1984	SANDS, Billy	Mausoleum
"	1980	ITURBI, José	Mausoleum, Block 16, Crypt E-1
"	1987	BOLGER, Ray	Mausoleum, Block 35, Crypt F-2
"	1961	DAVIS, Joan (Williams)	Mausoleum, Block 46, Crypt D-1, rt. of altar
"	1959	LANZA, Mario	Mausoleum, Block 46, Crypt D-2
"	1984	LaRUE, Jack	Mausoleum, Block 69, Crypt E-3
"	1965	JONES, Lindley "Spike"	Mausoleum, Block 70, Crypt A-7
"	1990	PAN, Hermes	Mausoleum, Block 127, Crypt D-5
"	1985	BRADY, Scott	Mausoleum, Block 156, Crypt B-7 upper floor
"	1985	HATHAWAY, Henry	Mausoleum, left of the altar
"	1982	BRODERICK, James	Mausoleum, lower floor, top level
"	1994	CANDY, John	Mausoleum, Room 7, Crypt B-1
"	1991	MacMURRAY, Fred	Mausoleum, Room 7, Crypt D-1
"	1979	HALEY, Jack	Section "Grotto," Lot 100, Grave 2
"	1977	CROSBY, Harry "Bing"	Section "Grotto," Lot 119, Grave 1
"	1952	CROSBY, Wilma "Dixie Lee"	Section "Grotto," Lot 119, Grave 2
"	1956	LUGOSI, Bela	Section "Grotto," Lot 120, Grave 1
"	1968	CASTLE, Nick	Section "Grotto," Lot 187, Grave 2
"	1963	PITTS, Zazu (Woodall)	Section "Grotto," Lot 195, Grave 1
"	1984	WRATHER, Jack	Section "Grotto," Lot 196
"	1988	GRANVILLE, Bonita (Wrather)	Section "Grotto," Lot 196, Grave 12
"	1994	CAREY, Macdonald	Section "Grotto," Lot 196, Grave 19
"	1987	HAYWORTH, Rita	Section "Grotto," Lot 196, Grave 6
"	1987	EGAN, Richard	Section AA, Tier 37, Grave 139 (unmarked)
"	1993	O'CONNELL, Helen (Devol)	Section CC, Tier 56, Grave 55
"	1996	EDWARDS, Vince (Zoine)	Section CC, Tier 64, Grave 29
"	1950	ALLGOOD, Sara	Section D "Sacred Heart"
"	1945	ARMETTA, Henry	Section D "Sacred Heart"
"	1959	GLEASON, James	Section D "Sacred Heart"
"	1956	KELLY, Paul	Section D, 1 row above Lot 61
"	1952	HERBERT, Hugh	Section D, Lot 267, Grave 11
"	1975	LUNDIGAN, William	Section D, Lot 269, Grave 3
"	1946	OLDFIELD, Barney	Section D, Lot 290, Grave 11
"	1948	KENNEDY, Edgar	Section D, Lot 193, Grave 7
"	1972	PARSONS, Louella (Martin)	Section D, Lot 235, Grave 8
"	1957	LOCKHART, Gene	Section D, Lot 279, Grave 6
"	1996	MEADOWS, Audrey (Six)	Section F, Tier 29, Grave 57
"	1985	DESMOND, Johnny	Section F, Tier 44, Grave 30

CEMETERY	YEAR	NAME	INTERMENT SITE*
Holy Cross Cem. and Maus., Culver City, CA	1985	O'BRIEN, Edmond	Section F, Tier 54, Grave 50
"	1984	COOGAN, Jackie	Section F, Tier 56, Grave 47
"	1983	O'BRIEN, Pat	Section F, Tier 56, Grave 62
"	1980	DURANTE, Jimmy	Section F, Tier 96, Grave 6
"	1950	DeCORDOBA, Pedro	Section G, Lot 258, Grave 1
"	1987	REY, Alejandro	Section L, Lot 403, Grave 1
"	1973	FORD, John	Section M, Lot 304, Grave 5
"	1984	BRISSON, Frederick	Section M, Lot 536 (below the big cross)
"	1976	RUSSELL, Rosalind (Brisson)	Section M, Lot 536, Grave 2
"	1972	SCALA, Gia	Section M, 3 spaces left of Lot 581
"	1960	FOWLER, Gene	Section M, Lot 792, Grave 3
"	1960	SENNETT, Mack	Section N, Lot 490, Grave 1
"	1987	ASTOR, Mary	Section N, Lot 523, Grave 5
"	1978	ACKER, Jean (Valentino)	Section N, Lot 542
"	1962	LOVEJOY, Frank	Section P, Lot 306, Grave 5
"	1964	ALBERTSON, Frank	Section P, Lot 309, Grave 1
"	1963	FARROW, John	Section P, Lot 342
"	1969	DOWLING, Constance (Tors)	Section P, Lot 421, Grave 4
"	1981	LINDSAY, Margaret	Section P, rt. of Lot 432
"	1982	DRAKE, Tom	Section R, Tier 26, Grave 188
"	1980	BRASSELLE, Keefe	Section R, Tier 29, Grave 168
"	1976	ARLEN, Richard	Section T, Tier 57, Grave 130
"	1988	DAY, Dennis	Section W, Tier 53, Grave 37
"	1974	FLYNN, Joseph A. "Joe"	Section W, Tier 20, Grave 75
"	1992	WELK, Lawrence	Section Y, Tier 9, Grave 110
"	1994	McNALLY, Stephen	Section Y, Lot 35
"	1969	TATE, Sharon (Polanski)	St. Ann's Garden, Tier 152, Grave 6
"	1988	JORDAN, Jim	St. Ann's Garden, Tier 153, Grave 1
"	1961	JORDAN, Marion	St. Ann's Garden, Tier 153, Grave 2
"	1978	BOYER, Charles	St. Ann's Garden, Tier 186, Grave 5
"	1978	PATERSON, Pat (Boyer)	St. Ann's Garden, Tier 186, Grave 6
"	1972	CORRELL, Charles "Andy"	
"	1959	GRAY, Gilda	
"	1982	KING, Henry	
"	1985	MARTIN, Marion	
"	1969	McCAREY, Leo	
"	1969	MOWBRAY, Alan	
"	1980	PAL, George	
"	1987	RORKE, Hayden	
"	1957	SEBASTIAN, Dorothy	
"	1993	WHELAN, Arleen (Cagney)	
Holy Cross Cemetery, Baltimore, MD	1992	HUDNET, William H. "Bill"	
Holy Cross Cemetery, Calumet City, IL	1973	KRUPA, Gene	Immaculata Section
Holy Cross Cemetery, San Mateo, CA	1969	LOGAN, Ella	
Holy Sepulchre Cemetery, New Rochelle, NY	1928	FOY, Eddie Sr.	
Holy Sepulchre Cemetery, Orange, CA	1993	KEELER, Ruby	"Ruby K. Lowe," Sect. N, Tier 21, Grave 46
Holy Sepulchre Cemetery, Worth, IL	1941	MORGAN, Helen	
Home of Peace Mem. Park, Los Angeles, CA	1955	HOWARD, Shemp	Chapel Maus., Eternal Light Corr., EW215
"	1958	NEUMANN, Kurt	Chapel Maus., Corr. of Eternal Life
"	1957	MAYER, Louis B.	Chapel Maus., Corr. of Immortality, SW 405
"	1949	RAPF, Harry	Chapel Maus., Corr. of Immortality
"	1951	BRICE, Fanny	Chapel Maus., Har. and Benev., 57E #1109
"	1939	LAEMMLE, Carl	Chapel Maus., in the Laemmle family room
"	1927	WARNER, Sam	In Mausoleum
"	1978	WARNER, Jack L.	Undergrd crypt, 50 yd. from Warner Maus.
"	1959	VIDOR, Charles	Warner Maus. (was Harry's son-in-law)
"	1958	WARNER, Harry B.	Warner Maus., Section D, Plot 16
"	1952	HOWARD, Jerome "Curly"	Western Jewish Institute, SW Corner, Plot 1
"	1958	WARNER, Harry M.	
Inglewood Park Cemetery, Inglewood, CA	1978	BERGEN, Edgar	131 Miramar Plot, Grave #2
"	1980	THOMAS, William "Buckwheat"	777 Acacia Slope, Grave 1

CEMETERY	YEAR	NAME	INTERMENT SITE*
Inglewood Park Cemetery, Inglewood, CA	1945	LAVERNE, Lucille	Center Grave D, Lot 236, Palm Plot
"	1990	HARRIS, Robin	Chap. of Freedom, Manchester Maus. #D5
"	1932	BERN, Paul	Cremated in Mausoleum, Niche F96
"	1973	GRABLE, Betty (James)	Golden West Maus., A78, Sanc. of Dawn
"	1973	LANE, Allan "Rocky"	Inside Grave A, Lot 70, Rosehill Plot
"	1970	LEE, Gypsy Rose	Lot 1087, Grave #8, Pinecrest Plot
"	1989	ROBINSON, Sugar Ray	Lot 24, Pinecrest Addition (top of hill)
"	1993	JONES, Ken	Lot 932, Grave E, Pineview Plot
"	1962	GIBSON, Hoot	Lot 92, Grave #6, Magnolia Plot
• "	1994	ROMERO, Cesar	Niche
"	1962	FAZENDA, Louise	
• Interlaken Cemetery, Interlaken, NY	1975	SERLING, Rod	
J			
Jerusalem, Israel	1982	RUBENSTEIN, Artur	Buried in a special plot in forest outside city
Jim Reeves Memorial Park, Carthage, TX	1964	REEVES, Jim	On US Highway 79, 4 miles NE of Carthage
K			
Kensico Cemetery, Valhalla, NY	1982	ALEXANDER, John	Actors Fund Plot
"	1981	ANDERS, Glenn	Actors Fund Plot
"	1978	BARRIE, Wendy	Actors Fund Plot
"	1956	KIBBEE, Guy	Actors Fund Plot
"	1967	REED, Florence	Actors Fund Plot
"	1973	SHUMAN, Roy	Actors Fund Plot
"	1956	STEPHENSON, Henry	Actors Fund Plot
"	1939	TEMPLETON, Fay	Actors Fund Plot
"	1974	YURKA, Blanche	Actors Fund Plot
"	1941	GEHRIG, Lou	Ashes in family vault
"	1956	DORSEY, Tommy	On Cherokee Ave.
"	1981	CHAYEFSKY, Paddy	Sharon Gardens section
"	1970	BURKE, Billie	
"	1945	CRAVEN, Frank	
"	1947	HELLINGER, Mark	
"	1987	KAYE, Danny	
"	1950	LORD, Pauline	
"	1941	PORTER, Edwin S.	
"	1943	RACHMANINOFF, Sergei	
"	1932	ZIEGFELD, Florenz	
L			
Lake Placid Cemetery, North Elba, NY	1986	SMITH, Kate	In a small private mausoleum
Lake View Cemetery, Cleveland, OH	1959	PECKHAM, Francis Miles	
"	1991	JACKSON, Mary Ann	Section 43, Lot 678
Lake View Cemetery, Seattle, WA	1993	LEE, Brandon	Buried next to his father, Bruce Lee
"	1973	LEE, Bruce	
Lauderdale Memorial Park, Ft. Lauderdale, FL	1969	MARCIANO, "Rocky"	
Laurel Grove Cemetery, Port Jervis, NY	1968	DEAN, Julia	Grave unmarked
• Laurel Land Memorial Park, Dallas, TX	1995	LEWIS, Ronald "Raan"	Field of Honor, Lot 125 B/C
"	1990	VAUGHAN, Stevie Ray	Section 25, Lot 194, Space 4
• Lincoln Cemetery, Kansas City, KS	1955	PARKER, Charlie "Bird"	
Long Island Nat'l Cem., Farmingdale (L.I.), NY	1966	KANE, Helen	
Long Ridge Cemetery, Stamford, CT	1986	GOODMAN, Benny	
"	1989	RADNER, Gilda	
Long Ridge Congregational Ch., Stamford, CT	1984	DELMAR, Kenny	
Lorraine Park Cemetery, Baltimore, MD	1994	NATWICK, Mildred	
• Los Angeles National Cemetery, L.A., CA	1987	MARTIN, Dean Paul Jr.	
"	1969	McNEAR, Howard	Columbarium
"	1951	HOLT, Jack	Section 107
"	1942	HOUSMAN, Arthur	
Los Molinas Cemetery, Red Bluff, CA	1969	GORCEY, Leo	
M			
Machpelah Cemetery, Ridgewood (Queens), NY	1926	HOUDINI, Harry	
• Maple Grove Cemetery, Horsehead, NY	1947	LAWRENCE, William E.	
Marbella, Spain	1993	NEGULESCO, Jean	
Marnes-La-Coquette, France	1972	CHEVALIER, Maurice	(France)

CEMETERY	YEAR	NAME	INTERMENT SITE*
Memorial Park, Oklahoma City, OK	1973	TINDALL, Loren	Section 18, Lot 61, Space 6
Metairie Cemetery, New Orleans, LA	1978	PRIMA, Louis	Section 88
"	1940	CLARK, Marguerite	Section 97 (Frank Williams property)
• Milly La Foret Cemetery, Milly La Foret, France	1963	COCTEAU, Jean	
• Montmartre Cemetery, Paris, France	1984	TRUFFAUT, François	Division 21, near entrance, on Ave. Berlioz
• "	1950	NIJINSKY, Vaslav	Division 22
• Montparnasse Cemetery, Paris, France	1953	Kiki	
"	1979	SEBERG, Jean	Division 13
Morris Hill Cemetery, Boise, ID	1972	OWEN, Reginald	
Mountain Grove Cemetery, Bridgeport, CT	1961	CHATTERTON, Ruth	
Mountain View Cemetery, Altadena, CA	1959	REEVES, George	Ashes, Pasadena Maus. Sunrise Cor. #3555
• "	1986	ARMSTRONG, Herbert W.	
Mount Hebron Cem., Flushing (Queens), NY	1960	SCHWARTZ, Maurice	
Mount Hope Cem., Hastings-on-Hudson, NY	1937	GERSHWIN, George	
"	1983	GERSHWIN, Ira	
"	1975	GODOWSKY, Dagmar	
"	1974	HUROK, Sol	
Mount Hope Cemetery, Peru, IN	1964	PORTER, Cole	
• Mount Olivet Cemetery, Fort Worth, TX	1969	SINGLETON, Catherine M.	Garden of Our Lady of Peace D, 136-B
Mount Pleasant Cem., Toronto (Ont.), Canada	1982	GOULD, Glenn	
Mount Pleasant Cemetery, Hawthorne, NY	1980	ROTH, Lillian	
Mount Sinai Memorial-Park, Los Angeles, CA	1986	BERNARDI, Herschel	Courts of Tanach, Crypt 52250
"	1985	SILVERS, Phil	Garden of Heritage, Vault 1004
"	1976	HALOP, Billy	Garden of Sherrot, Crypt 64181 along wall
"	1976	COBB, Lee J. (Leo Jacoby)	Garden of Sherrot, Lot 421
"	1991	ALLEN, Irwin	In Maus. behind the Garden of Heritage
"	1990	ROSE, David	In Maus. behind the Garden of Heritage
"	1980	VAN, Bobby	Maimonides, Plot #3728
"	1981	MARTIN, Ross	Temple Beth Hillel, Plot #3628
"	1974	ELLIOT, "Mama" Cass	Court of Tanach, Lot 5000, Grave 2F
• "	1978	FIELDS, Totie (Johnson)	Reinterred here 2/96 (from Las Vegas, NV)
"	1978	GELLER, Bruce	
• "	1988	SPERLING, Milton	
Mount Wollaston Cemetery, Quincy, MA	1974	DeWOLFE, Billy	
Mt. Lebanon Cemetery, Glendale (Queens), NY	1975	TUCKER, Richard	
Mt. Olivet Cemetery, Saginaw, MI	1978	McCOY, Tim	
Mt. Tabor United Meth. Ch., Crestwood, KY	1948	GRIFFITH, David Wark	
Mt. Vernon Cemetery, Philadelphia, PA	1942	BARRYMORE, John	Cremated 1980, reburied from Calvary Cem.
Mt. Zion Cemetery, Maspeth, NY	1943	HART, Lorenz	
N			
National Cemetery, West Point, NY	1971	FARRELL, Glenda	
• New Cathedral Cemetery, Baltimore, MD	1995	CROGHAN, Joe	
"	1994	SWIFT, Paul "Eggman"	
New Milford, CT	1975	MARCH, Fredric	Buried on his farm
Newton Cemetery, Newton, MA	1957	HULL, Josephine	
Nixon Presidential Library, Yorba Linda, CA	1993	NIXON, Pat	Interred in the garden of the library
• Northview Cemetery, Dearborn, MI	1994	PEPPARD, George	
• Novodevichy Cemetery, Moscow, Russia	1953	PROKOFIEV, Sergei	
• "	1975	SHOSTAKOVICH, Dmitri	
O			
Oak Bluff Memorial Park, Port Neches, TX	1974	RITTER, Tex	Section 8
Oakdale Cemetery, Davenport, IA	1931	BEIDERBECKE, Leon "Bix"	
Oakdale Cemetery, Glendora, CA	1979	RAND, Sally	ELM, Lot 34, Space 10
Oak Grove Cemetery, Medford, MA	1978	FONTAINE, Frank	
• Oak Hill Cememtery, Nyack, NY	1993	HAYES, Helen	
• Oak Hill Cemetery, Ballard, CA	1971	SEDGWICK, Edie	
Oak Hill Cemetery, Escondido, CA	1991	VAUGHN, Billy	
• Oakland Cemetery, Atlanta, GA	1949	MITCHELL, Margaret	
Oakland Cemetery, Ft. Dodge, IA	1994	DAMITA, Lili (Loomis)	
Oakland Cemetery, Sag Harbor (L.I.), NY	1983	BALANCHINE, George	
Oak Lawn Memorial Gardens, Noblesville, IN	1970	FARMER, Frances	
• Oakwood Cemetery Annex, Montgomery, AL	1953	WILLIAMS, Hank Sr.	

CEMETERY	YEAR	° NAME	INTERMENT SITE*
Oakwood Cemetery, Fort Worth, TX	1947	AMES, Adrienne	Block 31, Lot 44 (nr. Avenue IX & B Street)
• Oakwood Memorial Park, Chatsworth, CA	1967	REEVES, Richard J.	Section Elm, Lot 209, Grave 4
• "	1995	ROGERS, Ginger	Section E, Lot 303
• "	1966	TERRELL, Kenneth	Section Hollypoint, Lot 327
"	1981	ASTAIRE, Adele (Douglas)	
"	1987	ASTAIRE, Fred	
• "	1977	BOYD, Stephen	Outside mausoleum
"	1978	CRANE, Bob	
"	1981	HAYDEN, Russell	
Odd Fellows Cemetery, Los Angeles, CA	1971	GILBERT, Billy	
Old Cemetery, Chapel Hill, NC	1985	KYSER, Kay	
Old Greenwood Cemetery, Weatherford, TX	1990	MARTIN, Mary	Has iron fence surrounding gravesite
Old St. Paul's Epis. Ch., nr. Chestertown, MD	1968	BANKHEAD, Tallulah	Buried near woods, 100 yds. behind church
• Our Lady of Mercies Cemetery, Miami, FL	1987	GLEASON, Jackie	
Our Lady of Perpetual Help Ch., Carrollton, GA	1975	HAYWARD, Susan	
P			
Pacific View Mem. Park, Newport Beach, CA	1979	WAYNE, John	On a hill in an unmarked grave
Palm Mortuary Mausoleum, Las Vegas, NV	1962	JOHNSON, Chic	Ground burial
"	1963	OLSEN, Ole	Ground burial
"	1969	MORGAN, Russ	
Park Cemetery, Fairmount, IN	1955	DEAN, James	
• Passy Cemetery, Paris, France	1971	Fernandel	Black stone tomb with a raised cross
Pateon Delores Cemetery, Mexico City, Mexico	1944	VELEZ, Lupe	
Père Lachaise Cemetery, Paris, France	1923	BERNHARDT, Sarah	Division 44
• "	1977	CALLAS, Maria	
"	1927	DUNCAN, Isadora	Div. 87, ashes interred in the Columbarium
• "	1991	MONTAND, Yves	
"	1971	MORRISON, Jim	Division 6
"	1963	PIAF, Edith	Black tomb in Division 97
Pinelawn Mem. Park, Farmingdale (L.I.), NY	1977	LOMBARDO, Guy	
• "	1984	BASIE, William "Count"	
Priory Road Cemetery, Cheltenham, England	1969	JONES, Brian	(In Prestbury)
Prospect Hill Cemetery, Towson, MD	1988	Divine (Harris Glenn Milstead)	
Protestant Churchyard, Celigny, Switzerland	1984	BURTON, Richard	
Providence Memorial Park, Metairie, LA	1972	JACKSON, Mahalia	Section E, on east side of Mausoleum
Putnam Cemetery, Greenwich, CT	1957	PINZA, Ezio	Section L-1
"	1969	COLLYER, Bud	
R			
Red Hill Cemetery, Moultonborough, NH	1967	RAINS, Claude	Black marble headstone
Rest Haven Memorial Park, Lafayette, IN	1979	KELLY, Emmett	Sunset Terr. sect., bet. entr. and exit drives
Restland Memorial Park, Burbank, CA	1955	HAMPDEN, Walter	
• Restland Memorial Park, Dallas, TX	1971	WALTHALL, Wallace	Acacia 288, Grave 2-3
• "	1994	HUMANN, Helena	Chapel Gardens, Crypt 5 S-130
• "	1973	BOYD, Jim	
Rimini, Italy	1993	FELLINI, Federico	Buried in a family vault
• Rolling Green Memorial Park, Westchester, PA	1990	BAILEY, Pearl	
Rose Dale Cemetery, Los Angeles, CA	1961	WONG, Anna May	Section 5
"	1956	TATUM, Art	Section 5, in Row 178
"	1952	McDANIEL, Hattie	Section D, across from the office
"	1982	LAMAS, Fernando	
Rose Hill Cemetery, Altoona, PA	1966	HOPPER, Hedda	Ashes buried
Rosehill Cemetery, Bloomington, IN	1981	CARMICHAEL, Hoagy	
Rose Hill Cemetery, Fayetteville, TN	1987	RICE, Adnia	
• Rose Hills Memorial Park, Whittier, CA	1970	HOPPER, William	Memorial Urn Garden, Space 210
"	1948	LAUGHLIN, Billy "Froggy"	Older section
"	1994	CAREY, Timothy	
"	1991	LUKE, Keye	
• Rosewood Park, Longview, TX	1981	BOWLING, Alice	Chapel Mausoleum
Roy Rogers–Dale Evans Museum, Victorville, CA	1965	Trigger	On display in the museum
S			
Sacred Heart Cemetery, Southampton (L.I.), NY	1961	COOPER, Gary	Reburied from L.A., under a 3-ton boulder
San B./Golden Gate Nat'l Cem., San Bruno, CA	1964	KILBRIDE, Percy	Section 2-B, nr. chain link fence by freeway

CEMETERY	YEAR	NAME	INTERMENT SITE*
San Fernando Mission Cem., San Fernando, CA	1971	LOWE, Edmund	Section B, Block 7, Lot 1113
"	1959	VALENS, Ritchie	Section C, at Curb No. 247, 3 rows in
"	1966	FRAWLEY, William	Section C, at Curb No. 64, 5 rows in
"	1970	BEGLEY, Ed Sr.	Section C, Block 8, Lot 401
"	1974	BRENNAN, Walter	Section D at Curb 445, 8 rows in
"	1964	BENDIX, William	Section D, at Curb No. 241, 14 rows in
"	1956	ARNOLD, Edward	Section D, Block 9, Lot 132
"	1992	CONNORS, Chuck	
"	1981	DWAN, Allan	
"	1985	FAYLEN, Frank	
San Juan, Puerto Rico	1994	JULIA, Raul	
Santa Barbara Cemetery, Santa Barbara, CA	1958	COLMAN, Ronald	Ridge Oval Section, Lot 663
"	1986	ANGEL, Heather	
Sao Joao Baptista Cem., Rio de Janeiro, Brazil	1955	MIRANDA, Carmen	
Sharon Cemetery, Charlotte, NC	1975	TROTTER, John Scott	
Shenandoah Memorial Park, Winchester, VA	1963	CLINE, Patsy	
Shiloh Church Cemetery, Shreveport, LA	1949	LEDBETTER, Huddie	
Silver Mount Cemetery, Staten Island, NY	1983	TINCHER, Fay	
Sleepy Hollow Cemetery, N. Tarrytown, NY	1946	BOWES, Major Edward	Off Vernon Ave.
"	1939	BRADY, Alice	
Solvang, CA	1985	BAKER, Kenny	Priv. inter. in Santa Barbara Co. nr. Solvang
Southborough Cemetery, Southborough, MA	1938	OLAND, Warner	
Southern Memorial Park, Miami, FL	1975	LOPEZ, Vincent	
Spring Hill Cemetery, Madison, TN	1992	ACUFF, Roy	
SS. Cyril and Methodius Cemetery, Berwick, PA	1968	ADAMS, Nick (Adamshock)	
St. Bartholomew's Epis. Ch., New York, NY	1968	GISH, Dorothy	
St. Hyacinth's Church Cemetery, Westbrook, ME	1986	VALLEE, Rudy	
• St. John-at-Hampstead Cem., London, England	1973	BAYLIS, Peter	At back of cemetery
• "	1959	KENDALL, Kay (Harrison)	Near front fence
• St. John the Baptist Byzantine Cem., Bethel, PA	1987	WARHOL, Andy	
St. John the Baptist Cathedral, Warsaw, Poland	1941	PADEREWSKI, Ignace Jan	Originally buried in Arlington Nat'l. Cem.
"		"	His heart is entombed at the Shrine of
"		"	Our Lady of Czestochowa, Doylestown, PA
"		"	Reburied in free Poland in 1992.
St. John the Evangelist RC Ch., Columbia, MD	1992	KENNY, Herbert C.	
St. John's Ch. Cem., Cold Spring Harbor, NY	1962	BARTON, James	
St. Joseph Cemetery, West Roxbury, MA	1979	FIEDLER, Arthur	
• St. Marylebone Cemetery, London, England	1977	STOKOWSKI, Leopold	East Ave. at Rosemary
St. Mary's Cemetery, Ridgefield, CT	1977	RITCHARD, Cyril	
St. Mary's Whitechapel Church, Lancaster, PA	1960	SULLAVAN, Margaret	In churchyard, near curve in path
St. Nicholas Churchyard, Brighton, England	1984	ROBSON, (Dame) Flora	
St. Patrick's Cathedral, New York, NY	1979	SHEEN, (Bishop) Fulton J.	In a crypt below the altar
St. Raymond's Cemetery, The Bronx, NY	1959	HOLIDAY, Billie	
• Ste. Genevieve-Des-Bois, Paris, France	1993	NUREYEV, Rudolph	(Essone District)
• Sunset Hills Cemetery, Bozeman, ID	1974	HUNTLEY, Chet	
• Sunset Memorial Park, Smithfield, NC	1990	GARDNER, Ava	
T			
Tolochenaz, Vaud, Switzerland	1993	HEPBURN, Audrey	
U			
Union Field Cem., Ridgewood (Queens), NY	1967	LAHR, Bert	
Union Hill Cemetery, Kennett Square, PA	1965	DARNELL, Linda	
Upton Cemetery, Upton, MA	1952	LAWRENCE, Gertrude	
V			
• Vagankovskoye Cem., Moscow, Russia	1995	GRINKOV, Sergei	
Valhalla Memorial Park, N. Hollywood, CA	1961	RUSSELL, Gail (Moseley)	Evergreen Section, Curb #4795
"	1957	HARDY, Oliver	Gdn. of Hope, 2nd wall to rt. of Her. Fount.
"	1968	BENADERET, Bea	Mausoleum of Hope, Row C, Crypt 34
"	1971	EDWARDS, Cliff	Section D, near Heritage Fountain
"	1965	MURRAY, Mae	Section G, Block 6328, Lot 6
"	1963	WAGNER, "Gorgeous" George	Section G, Block 6659, Sp. 2, next to mother
"	1976	ROSENBLOOM, Maxie	Section J, Block 9820, Space 3
"	1973	COOPER, Melville	

CEMETERY	YEAR	NAME	INTERMENT SITE*
Valhalla Memorial Park, N. Hollywood, CA	1950	COWL, Jane	
"	1969	CRANE, Richard	
"	1993	DeRITA, Joe	
"	1969	MacLANE, Barton	
"	1973	MORELAND, Mantan	
Valley Oaks Mem. Park, Westlake Village, CA	1994	NILSSON, Harry	
• Valley of Light Cemetery, Acapulco, Mexico	1984	WEISSMULLER, Johnny	
Village Cemetery, Tisbury (M.V.), MA	1974	CORNELL, Katharine	(Martha's Vineyard)
• Village Churchyard, Chateau DOex, Switzerland	1983	NIVEN, David	
W			
Waldheim/Forest Home Cem., Chicago (F.P.), IL	1958	TODD, Mike	
Welwood Murray Cemetery, Palm Springs, CA	1968	FARRELL, Virginia Valli	Section 10-3, Lot F
	1990	FARRELL, Charles	Section 10-3, Lot G
Westchester Hills Cem, Hastings-on-Hudson, NY	1952	GARFIELD, John	
"	1965	HOLLIDAY, Judy	
"	1943	REINHARDT, Max	
"	1966	ROSE, Billy	
"	1982	STRASBERG, Lee	
• Westminster Abbey, London, England	1989	OLIVIER, Laurence	Poets' Corner
• Westview Cemetery, Atlanta, GA	1969	FREEMAN, Young Frank	Section 10, Lot 277, Grave 10
Westwood Village Mem. Park, Los Angeles, CA	1979	KILIAN, Victor	Ashes scattered in the Rose Garden
"	1984	MASSEY, Edith	Ashes scattered in the Rose Garden
"	1971	FLIPPEN, Jay C.	Corridor of Memories
"	1972	IHNAT, Steve	Corridor of Memories
"	1962	MONROE, Marilyn	Corridor of Memories, #24
"	1990	HAMMER, Armand	In family mausoleum, near entrance
"	1989	SCHAFFNER, Franklin J.	Lot 236
"	1989	CASSAVETES, John	Lot 308
"	1984	CAPOTE, Truman	New Mausoleum, 1st column, bottom
"	1988	O'ROURKE, Heather	New Mausoleum, 1st column, bottom
• "	1995	GABOR, Eva	Nr. Armand Hammer's Maus. (Right front)
"	1993	AIDMAN, Charles	Room of Prayer
"	1991	MASSEY, Curt	Room of Prayer
"	1982	PATRICK, Lee (Wood)	Room of Prayer
"	1983	VIVYAN, John	Room of Prayer
"	1993	DeFORE, Don	Rose Garden
"	1979	KENTON, Stan	Rose Garden
"	1972	LEVANT, Oscar	Sanctuary of Love, bottom right
• "	1995	MARTIN, Dean	Sanctuary of Love
"	1970	EDENS, Roger	Sanctuary of Remembrance
"	1971	HELTON, Percy	Sanctuary of Remembrance
"	1973	KELLAWAY, Cecil	Sanctuary of Remembrance
"	1972	LANFIELD, Sidney	Sanctuary of Remembrance
"	1979	MASON, Shirley (Lanfield)	Sanctuary of Remembrance
"	1987	TAYLOR, Kent	Sanctuary of Remembrance
"	1972	TRAUBEL, Helen (Bass)	Sanctuary of Remembrance
"	1969	VonSTERNBERG, Josef	Sanctuary of Remembrance
"	1969	BOLES, John	Sanctuary of Serenity
"	1984	CARPENTER, Ken	Sanctuary of Tenderness, rear wall
"	1985	MILLER, Marvin E.	Sanctuary of Tenderness
"	1981	WARREN, Harry	Sanctuary of Tenderness, 5th col., bottom
"	1975	DORN, Philip	Sanctuary of Tranquility, rear wall
"	1983	GEORGE, Christopher	Sanctuary of Tranquility
"	1976	HOWE, James Wong	Sanctuary of Tranquility, rear wall
"	1977	JOHNSON, Nunnally	Sanctuary of Tranquility, rear wall
"	1980	KORJUS, Miliza	Sanctuary of Tranquility, rear wall
"	1980	MILESTONE, Lewis	Sanctuary of Tranquility
"	1987	RICH, Buddy	Sanctuary of Tranquility, 2nd col., bottom
• "	1989	VINCENT, Romo	Sanctuary of Tranquility, right, 4 bays up
"	1993	CAHN, Sammy	Section D (near Donna Reed)
"	1984	RIORDAN, Marjorie (Schlaff)	Section D, #1
"	1987	KAYE, Nora (Ross)	Section D, #36

• New entry.

* Some cemeteries refuse to reveal specific locations.

CEMETERY	YEAR	NAME	INTERMENT SITE*
Westwood Village Mem. Park, Los Angeles, CA	1979	ZANUCK, Darryl F.	Section D, #41
"	1982	ZANUCK, Virginia Fox	Section D, #41
"	1981	WOOD, Natalie (Wagner)	Section D, #60
"	1985	Margo (Albert)	Section D, #61
"	1975	CONTE, Richard	Section D, #62
"	1973	CRANE, Norma	Section D, #62
"	1992	LEHRMAN, Oscar S.	Section D, #81
"	1984	WEST, Brooks	Section D, #81
"	1990	ARDEN, Eve (West)	Section D, #81 (ashes interred)
"	1985	NOLAN, Lloyd	Section D, #84
"	1988	ORBISON, Roy	Section D, #97 (unmarked) Nr. water spigot
"	1993	ZAPPA, Frank	Section D, #100 (unmarked) Next to Guild
"	1963	TUTTLE, Frank W.	Section D, #105
"	1982	DANTINE, Helmut	Section D, #130
"	1986	REED, Donna	Section D, #142
"	1976	PIATIGORSKY, Gregor	Section D, #154
"	1980	STRATTEN, Dorothy	Section D, #170
"	1982	DUNNE, Dominique	Section D, #189
"	1989	BACKUS, Jim	Section D, #203
"	1984	BASEHART, Richard	Urn Garden (3 down from top, on right)
"	1989	WILDE, Cornel	Urn Garden
"	1992	MARX, Samuel	Urn Garden (southeast)
"	1977	CABOT, Sebastian	Urn Garden East (top row, 9 from right)
"	1964	BARRIER, Edgar	
"	1970	DARRELL, J. Stevan	
"	1971	GOMEZ, Thomas	
"	1974	HUDSON, William Woodson Jr.	
"	1979	HUTTON, Jim	
"	1982	JORY, Victor	
"	1977	MATTHEWS, Dorothy (Davis)	
"	1964	MEREDITH, Charles	
"	1967	NEWELL, William Most	
"	1989	NEWMAN, Lionel	
"	1983	PEREIRA, Hal	
"	1978	PERFECT, Rose	
"	1979	RIPPERTON, Minnie	
"	1978	SHAY, Dorothy	
"	1979	WAGENHEIM, Charles	
"	1966	WALKER, June	
"	1970	WIERE, Sylvester	
"	1984	WINWOOD, Estelle	
Will Rogers Memorial, Claremore, OK	1935	ROGERS, Will	Reinterred in 1944 from Forest Lawn, CA
• Woodlawn Cemetery, Elmira, NY	1992	ROACH, Hal Sr.	Just inside the Walnut St. gate, 1st turn rt.
• Woodlawn Cemetery, Santa Monica, CA	1983	FIX, Paul	Block 17
"	1967	BICKFORD, Charles	Cremated
"	1973	RYAN, Irene	In Mausoleum, 109-C-1
"	1956	BANCROFT, George	In Mausoleum, 147-P-3
"	1961	CARRILLO, Leo	Section 2, (near 14th Street)
"	1960	BROPHY, Ed	
"	1973	HAINES, William	
"	1994	SMITH, Hal	
Woodlawn Cemetery, The Bronx, NY	1960	BARRYMORE, Diana	Div. 20, bet. E. Border Ave and Chapel Hill
"	1969	CASTLE, Irene	Division 29, off Park View & Spruce Ave.
"	1918	CASTLE, Vernon	Division 29, off Park View & Spruce Ave.
"	1962	KREISLER, Fritz	Division 31, in mausoleum off Filbert Ave.
"	1942	COHAN, George M.	Division 31, off Park Ave.
"	1924	HERBERT, Victor	Div. 42, in maus. at Border and Linden Ave.
"	1974	ELLINGTON, Duke	Division 49, at Fir & Knollwood Aves.
"	1936	MILLER, Marilyn	Division 50, Heather and Whitewood Ave
"	1989	BERLIN, Irving	
"	1960	CLARK, Bobby	
"	1991	DAVIS, Miles	

CEMETERY	YEAR	NAME	INTERMENT SITE*
Woodlawn Cemetery, The Bronx, NY	1952	LEE, Canada	
"	1946	TAYLOR, Laurette (Cooney)	
Woodlawn Mem. Park East, Hendersonville, TN	1978	CARTER, Maybelle	
Woodlawn Memorial Park, Nashville, TN	1968	FOLEY, Red	
"	1982	ROBBINS, Marty	
Woodmen Cemetery, DeKalb, TX	1972	BLOCKER, Dan	

7

ORIGINAL
NAMES
OF THE STARS

ORIGINAL NAMES OF THE STARS

A

PROFESSIONAL NAME*	BIRTH, LEGAL OR FORMER NAME**
ABBOTT, Bud	*William Abbott*
ACKLES, Kenneth	*Kenneth Vincent Ackles*
Acromaniacs, The	*Italo (Al) Immediato*
"	*Hugo Immediato*
"	*Nino (Nick) Immediato*
ADAMS, Don	*Don Yarmy*
ADAMS, Edie	*Elizabeth Edith Enke*
• ADAMS, Jimmy	*James B. Adams*
ADAMS, Maude	*Maude Kiskadden*
ADAMS, Nick	*Nicholas Aloysius Adamschock*
• ADAMSON, James	*William James Adamson*
ADAMSON, Victor	*(aka Denver Dixon)*
ADLER, Buddy	*Maurice E. Adler*
• ADLER, Celia	*Celia Feinman Adler*
ADOREE, Renée	*Jeanne de la Fonte*
Adrian	*Adrian Adolph Greenberg (aka Gilbert Adrian)*
ADRIAN, Iris	*Iris Adrian Hosletter*
ADRIAN, Louis	*Louis Methenitis*
ADRIAN, Max	*Max Bor (aka Max Cavendish)*
AHERNE, Gladys	*Gladys Reese*
AINLEY, Richard	*(aka Richard Riddle)*
AINSWORTH, Sidney	*(aka Sydney Ainsworth)*
Aladdin	*Aladdin Abdullah Achmed Anthony Pallante*
ALBERT, Eddie	*Edward Albert Heimberger*
ALBRIGHT, Hardie	*Hardy Albrecht*
ALBRIGHT, Wally	*Walton Albright, Jr.*
ALDA, Robert	*Alphonso d'Abruzzo*
• ALDEN, Mary	*Mary Maguire Alden*
ALDERSON, Floyd Taliaferro	*(aka Hal Taliaferro and Wally Wales)*
ALEXANDER, Ben	*Nicholas Benton Alexander*
ALEXANDER, Jane	*Jane Quigley*
Alfalfa (of "Our Gang")	*Carl Switzer*
ALLEN, Fred	*John F. Sullivan*
ALLEN, Gracie	*Grace Ethel Cecile Rosale*
ALLEN, Woody	*Allen Stewart Konigsberg*
ALLEY, Paul	*Paul Richter Alley*
ALLISTER, Claud	*Claud Palmer*
ALLYSON, June	*Jan Allyson*
ALVARADO, Don	*José Page*
AMECHE, Don	*Dominic Felix Amici*
• AMES, Adrienne	*Ruth Adrienne Ames*
AMES, Leon	*Leon Wycoff*
Amos (of "Amos & Andy")	*Freeman F. Gosden*
ANDERS, Laurie	*Laurie Raddatz*
ANDERSON, Claire	*Claire Mathes Anderson*
ANDERSON, (Dame) Judith	*Frances Margaret Anderson*
ANDERSON, G. M.	*Max Aronson (aka Gilbert M. Anderson)*
ANDOR, Lotte Palfi	*Lotte Mosbacher*
ANDOR, Paul	*Wolfgang Zilzer*
• ANDRE, Gwili	*Gurli Andresen*
Andrews Sisters, The	*LaVerne Andrews*
"	*Maxine Andrews*
"	*Patti Andrews*
ANDREWS, Dana	*Carver Dana Andrews*
ANDREWS, Edward	*Edward Bryan Andrews, Jr.*
ANDREWS, Julie	*Julia Elizabeth Wells*
ANDREWS, Lois	*Lorraine Gourley*
Andy (of "Amos & Andy")	*Charles J. Correll*
ANGELI, Pier	*Anna Maria Pierangeli*
• ANKRUM, Morris	*Morris Nussbaum (aka Stephen Morris)*
Ann-Margret	*Ann-Margaret Olson*
Annabella	*Suzanne Charpentier*
ANTHONY, Rick	*Enrico Cipriani*
ARBUCKLE, Roscoe "Fatty"	*Roscoe Conklin Arbuckle*

...ORIGINAL NAMES OF THE STARS...

PROFESSIONAL NAME*	BIRTH, LEGAL OR FORMER NAME**
ARCHER, John	Ralph Bowman
ARDEN, Eve	Eunice Quedens
ARLEDGE, John	Johnson Lundy Arledge
ARLEN, Richard	Richard van Mattimore
Arletty	Léonie Bathiat
ARLISS, George	George Augustus Andrews
ARMSTRONG, Louis	Louis Daniel Armstrong
ARNAUD, Georges	Henri Giraud
ARNAZ, Desi	Desiderio Arnaz
ARNE, Peter	Peter Arne Albrecht
ARNESS, James	James Aurness
ARNO, Sig	Siegfried Arno
ARNOLD, Edward	Guenther Schneider
• ARNOLD, Jessie	Jessie Gertrude Arnold
ARQUETTE, Cliff	aka Charley Weaver
ARTHUR, Beatrice (Bea)	Bernice Frankel
ARTHUR, Jean	Gladys Georgianna Greene
ARTHUR, Johnny	John Williams
ARTHUR, Robert	Robert Arthaud
• ARVIDSON, Linda	Linda Johnson
• ASH, Russell	Russell Harvey Ash
ASHCROFT, (Dame) Peggy	Edith Margaret Emily Ashcroft
ASHLEY, (Lady) Sylvia	Sylvia Hawkes
ASLAN, Gregoire	Krikor Aslanian
ASTAIRE, Adele	Adele Marie Austerlitz
ASTAIRE, Fred	Frederick Austerlitz
ASTOR, Mary	Lucile Langhanke
• AUDLEY, Michael	Michael Audley Keck
AUER, Mischa	Mischa Ounskowsky
AULT, Marie	Marie Cragg
AUMONT, Jean-Pierre	Jean-Pierre Salomons
• AUSTIN, Gene	Eugene Lucas
AVALON, Frankie	Francis Avallone
• AVERY, Charles	Charles Bradford Avery
• AYE, Maryon	(aka Marion Aye)
AYERS, Agnes	Agnes Hinkle
AYERS, Lew	Lewis Ayer
AYLMER, (Sir) Felix	Felix Edward Aylmer Jones
B	
BABBITT, Art	Arthur Babitsky
Baby Jane	Juanita Quigley
Baby Sandy	Sandra Lea Henville
Baby Sunshine	Pauline Flood
BACALL, Lauren	Betty Jean Perske
• BACON, David	David Gaspar Griswold Bacon
BADDELEY, Angela	Madeleine Angela Clinton-Baddeley
BADEL, Alan	Alan Fernand Badel
BAER, Buddy	Jacob Henry Baer
• BAGDASARIAN, Ross	(aka David Seville)
BAKER, Bob	Leland T. Weed
BAKER, Chet	Chesney Baker
BAKER, Eddie	Edward King
BAKER, Kenny	Kenneth Lawrence Baker
BAKER-BERGEN, Stuart	Stuart Bergen, Jr.
• BALANCHINE, George	Georgi Melitonovich Balanchivadze
BALDWIN, Alec	Alexander Rae Baldwin. III
BALL, Lucille	Dianne Belmont
BALL, Susan	Suzan Ball
BALLARD, Kaye	Catherine Gloria Balotta
BANCROFT, Anne	Anna Maria Italiano
• BANCROFT, Charles	Fred Bently
BANJAMIN, Gladys	Gladys Lanphere
BANKHEAD, Tallulah	Tallulah Brockman Bankhead
BANKS, Monty	Mario Bianchi
BANKY, Vilma	Vilma Lonchit

...ORIGINAL NAMES OF THE STARS...

PROFESSIONAL NAME*	BIRTH, LEGAL OR FORMER NAME**
BANNER, John	*Johann Banner*
BARA, Theda	*Theodosia Goodman*
BARBER, Red	*Walter Lanier Barber*
• BARBOUR, Dave	*David Michael Barbour*
• BARCLAY, Don	*Don Van Tassel Barclay*
BARCROFT, Roy	*Howard Ravenscroft*
BARDOT, Brigitte	*Camille Javal*
BARI, Lynn	*Marjorie Bitzer*
BARKER, Lex	*Alexander Crichlow Barker, Jr.*
BARNETT, Vince	*Vincent Barnett*
BARR, Leonard	*Leonard Barri*
BARRIE, (Sir) James	*James Matthew Barrie*
BARRIE, Wendy	*Wendy Jenkins*
BARRY, Don "Red"	*Donald Barry d'Acosta*
BARRY, Gene	*Eugene Klass*
BARRY, Tom	*Hal Donahue*
• BARRY, Viola	*(aka Peggy Pearce)*
BARRYMORE, Diana	*Diana Blanche Barrymore Blythe*
BARRYMORE, Ethel	*Ethel Mae Blythe*
BARRYMORE, John	*John Blythe*
BARRYMORE, John Jr.	*John Drew Barrymore*
BARRYMORE, Lionel	*Lionel Blythe*
BARTHOLOMEW, Freddie	*Frederick Llewellyn (Bartholomew was aunt's name)*
BARTLETT, Richard	*Richard Norris*
BASIE, Count	*William Basie*
BASQUETTE, Lina	*Lina Baskette*
BASS, Alfie	*Alfred Bass*
BATES, Barbara	*Barbara Jane Bates*
BATES, Florence	*Florence Rabe*
BATORS, Stiv	*Steve Bator*
BAUM, Vicki	*Hedwig Baum*
BEAL, John	*James Alexander Bliedung*
BEAN, Orson	*Dallas Burrows*
• Beatles, The	*Ringo Starr (Richard Starkey)*
• "	*John Lennon*
• "	*Paul McCartney*
• "	*George Harrison*
BEATTY, Warren	*Warren Beaty*
BECKETT, Scotty	*Scott Hastings Beckett*
BEDDOE, Don	*Donald T. Beddoe*
• BEECHER, Janet	*Janet Beecher Meysenburg*
Bee Gees, The	*Robin, Barry and Maurice Gibb*
BEIDERBECKE, Bix	*Leon Bismark Beiderbecke*
BEL GEDDES, Barbara	*Barbara Geddes Schrewer*
Belita	*Maria Belita Gladys Lyne Jepson-Turner*
BELL, Rex	*George Francis Beldam*
BENATAR, Pat	*Patricia Andrzejewski*
• BENDER, Russell "Russ"	*Richard Bender Jr.*
• BENNETT, Billie	*Emily Haynie*
BENEDICT, Billy	*William Benedict*
BENNETT, Bruce	*Herman Brix*
BENNETT, Joe	*Joseph Bennett Aldert*
BENNETT, Tony	*Anthony Dominick Benedetto*
BENNY, Jack	*Benjamin Kubelsky*
• BENSON, Court	*Courtenay E. Benson*
BENSON, Robbie	*Robin David Segal*
• BENTLEY, Irene	*Alexina Bentley*
BERANGER, George	*George Andre Beranger*
BERGEN, Edgar	*Edgar John Berggren*
BERKELEY, Busby	*William Berkeley Enos, Jr.*
• BERKES, John	*John Patrick Berkes*
BERLE, Milton	*Milton Berlinger*
BERLIN, Irving	*Israel Isidore Baline*
BERNHARDT, Sarah	*Henrietta Rosine Bernard*
BERRY, Chuck	*Charles Edward Anderson Berry*

• New entry.   * Includes both living & deceased persons.   ** Sources do not always agree on spelling.

...ORIGINAL NAMES OF THE STARS...

PROFESSIONAL NAME*	BIRTH, LEGAL OR FORMER NAME**
• BEST, Edna	Edna Hove
• BETZ, Matthew	Matthew Von Betz
Beulah	Louise Beavers
• BEVAN, William "Billy"	William Bevan Harris
BEVANS, Clem	Clem Blevins
BEY, Turhan	Turhan Selahattin Sahultavy Bey
• Big Bopper	(See RICHARDSON, Jiles)
Big Boy	Guinn Williams
BIG TREE, Chief John	Isaac Johnny John
Biograph Girl	Florence Lawrence
BIRCH, Wyrley	Ernest Wyrley Birch
BISHOP, Joey	Joseph Abraham Gottlieb
BISHOP, Julie	Jacqueline Wells-Brown (aka Diane Duval)
BISSELL, Whit	Whitner Bissell
BJORNSTRAND, Gunnar	Knut Gunnar Björnstrand
• BLACKLEY, Douglas	(See Robert Kent)
• BLACKTON, J. Stuart	James Stuart Blackton
• BLACKTON, Violet	Violet Virginia Blackton
BLAINE, Vivian	Vivienne S. Stapleton
BLAIR, Betsy	Elizabeth Winifred Boger
BLAIR, Randy	William Randall Blair
BLAIRE, Sallie	Sara Hutchins (aka Sallie Blair)
• BLAKE, Al	Alva D. Blake (aka A. D. Blake)
BLAKE, Amanda	Beverly Louise Neill
BLAKE, Arthur	Arthur Blakely Clark
BLAKE, Eubie	James Hubert Blake
BLAKE, Marie	Edith Blossom MacDonald
BLAKE, Robert	Michael James Vijencio Gubitosi (aka Mickey Gubitosi)
BLAKELY, Colin	Colin George Edward Blakely
BLANC, Mel	Melvin Jerome Blanc
BLETCHER, Billy	William Bletcher
• BLONDELL, Joan	Rose Joan Blondell
Blondie (Bumstead)	(see SINGLETON, Penny)
• BLOOM, Bobby	Robert Martin Bloom
BLUE, Ben	Benjamin Bernstein
• BLYDEN, Larry	Ivan Lawrence Blieden
• BLYSTONE, Stanley	William Stanley Blystone
BLYTHE, Betty	Elizabeth Blythe Slaughter
BOARDMAN, True	William True Boardman
BOARDMAN, Virginia True	Virginia Eames
BOGARDE, Dirk	Derek Jules Gaspard Ulric Niven van den Bogaerde
BOGART, Humphrey	Humphrey DeForest Bogart
• BOLES, Jim	James Boles, Jr.
BOLGER, Ray	Raymond Wallace Bulcao
• BOLGER, Robert	Robert Erin Bolger
• BOLT, Robert	Robert Oxton Bolt
• BOND, Jack	Alfred Welch
BONDI, Beulah	Beulah Bondy
• BONELLI, Richard	Richard Bunn
Bono (U2 lead singer)	Paul Hewson
BONO, Sonny	Salvatore Philip Bono
BOONE, Pat	Charles Eugene Patrick Boone
BOOTH, Edwina	Josephine Constance Woodruff
BOOTH, Shirley	Thelma Booth Ford
BOOTS, Tubby	Charles Andrew Booth
• BORDEAUX, Joe	(aka Joe Bordeau)
BORDEN, Olive	Sybil Trinkle
BORGE, Victor	Borge Rosenbaum
BOSTWICK, Dorothy Davis	Dorothy Gompert (aka Dorothy Royce)
BOSWELL, Vet	Helvetia Boswell
• Bowery Boys, The	Leo Gorcey
• "	Huntz Hall
• "	Bobby Jordan
• "	Gabriel Dell
• "	Bernard Gorcey

• New entry. * Includes both living & deceased persons. ** Sources do not always agree on spelling.

...ORIGINAL NAMES OF THE STARS...

PROFESSIONAL NAME*	BIRTH, LEGAL OR FORMER NAME**
• Bowery Boys, The (cont'd)	David Gorcey
• "	Billy Benedict
• "	Bennie Bartlett
BOWIE, David	David Robert Hayward-Jones
• BOWLING, Alice	Alice Lon Bowling
• BOYD, Jim	James A. Boyd
BOYD, Stephen	William Stephen Millar
• BOYNE, Sunny	Hazel Boyne
• BRADY, Fred	Frederick Kress
BRADY, Scott	Gerald Kenneth Tierney
BRANDON, Henry	Henry Kleinbach
BRAUER, Tiny	Harold G. Brauer
BRENDEL, El	Elmer Goodfellow Brendel
BRENT, Evelyn	Mary Elizabeth Riggs
BRENT, George	George Nolan
BRENT, Romney	Romulo Larralde
BRIAN, Mary	Louise Dantzler
BRICE, Fanny	Fannie Borach
• BRISSON, Carl	Carl Brisson Peterson
• BRITT, Elton	James Britt Baker
BRITT, May	Maybritt Wilkens
BRITTANY, Morgan	Suzanne Cupito
BRITTEN, Barbara	Barbara Brantingham
• BRITTON, Milt	Milton Levy
BRODIE, Steve	John Stevens
• BRODY, Ann	Ann Brody Goldstein
BROMFIELD, John	Farron Bromfield
Broncho Billy	G. M. Anderson
• BRONSON, Betty	Elizabeth Ada Bronson
BRONSON, Charles	Charles Buchinsky
BROOK, Clive	Clifford Brook
• BROOKE, Ralph	Ralph Tweer Brooks
• BROOKE, Tyler	Victor Huge de Biere
BROOKE, Van Dyke	Stewart McKerrow
BROOKS, Albert	Albert Einstein
BROOKS, Beverley	(aka Viscountess Rothermere)
BROOKS, Geraldine	Geraldine Stroock
BROOKS, Mel	Melvin Kaminsky
BROPHY, Ed	Edward S. Brophy
Brown Bomber	Joe Louis
BROWN, Georgia	Lillian Klot
BROWN, Joe E.	Joseph Evans Brown
BROWN, Reno	Ruth Clarke
BROWN, Tom	Thomas E. Brown
BROWN, Vanessa	Smylla Brind
BRUCE, David	Marden McBroom
BRUCE, Lenny	Leonard Alfred Schneider
BRUCE, Nigel	William Nigel Bruce
BRUCE, Virginia	Helen Virginia Briggs
BRYNNER, Yul	Taidje Khan
BUBBLES, John W.	John W. Sublett
BUCHANAN, Edgar	William Edgar Buchanan
Buckwheat (of "Our Gang")	William (Billy) Henry Thomas, Jr.
Buffalo Bill	William Frederick Cody
Bull	Lewis Montana
BURKE, Billie	Mary William Ethelbert Appleton Burke
BURKE, Chris	Christopher Joseph Burke
BURNETTE, Smiley	Lester Alvin Burnette
BURNS, Bazooka	Bob Burns
• BURNS, Edmund J.	(aka Edward Burns and Ed Burns)
BURNS, George	Nathan Birnbaum
BURR, Raymond	Raymond William Stacy Burr
BURROWS, Abe	Abram Solman Borowitz
BURSTYN, Ellen	Edna Gilhooley
BURTON, LeVar	Levardis Robert Martyn Burton, Jr.

• New entry.   * Includes both living & deceased persons.   ** Sources do not always agree on spelling.

PROFESSIONAL NAME*	BIRTH, LEGAL OR FORMER NAME**
BURTON, Richard	Richard Jenkins
BUSHMAN, Francis X.	Francis Xavier Bushman
• BUSTER, Budd	Budd Leland Buster (aka Bud Buster and George Selk)
Butch (of "Our Gang")	Tommy Bond
BUTLER, David	David Wayne Butler
BUTLER, Fred	Alfred Joline Butler
• BUTLER, Royal	Royal Edwin Butler
BUTTONS, Red	Aaron Chwatt
BUZZELL, Eddie	Edward Buzzell
C	
CABANNE, William	William Christy Cabanne
CABOT, Bruce	Etienne de Pelissier Bujac, Jr.
CAGE, Nicolas	Nicholas Coppola
CAINE, Michael	Maurice J. Micklewhite
CALHERN, Louis	Carl Henry Vogt
CALHOUN, Alice	Alice Calhoun Chotiner
CALHOUN, Rory	Francis Timothy Durgin
CALLAS, Maria	Maria Calogeropoulas
CALLAWAY, Cab	Cabell Calloway III
CALLEIA, Joseph	Joseph Spurin-Calleja
CALLENDER, Red	George Sylvester Callender
CALLOWAY, Cab	Cabell Calloway
CALVERT, E. H.	Elisha Helm
CALVERT, Phyllis	Phyllis Bickle
CALVET, Corinne	Corinne Dibos
CALVIN, Henry	Wimberly Calvin Goodman, Jr.
CAMERON, Rod	Rod Cox
CAMPBELL, Webster	William Webster Campbell
CANDY, John	John Franklin Candy
CANOVA, Judy	Juliet Canova
CANTINFLAS	Mario Moreno
CANTOR, Eddie	Edward Israel Iskowitz
• CANTOR, Ida	Ida Tobias
CANUTT, Yakima	Enos Edward Canutt
Capucine	Germaine Lefebvre
• CARDWELL, James	Albert James Cardwell
CAREWE, Edwin	Jay Fox
• CAREWE, Ora	Ora Whytock
CAREY, Joyce	Joyce Lawrence
CARLE, Richard	Charles Nicholas Carleton
CARLISLE, Kitty	Catherine Holzman
CARMICHAEL, Hoagy	Hoaglund Howard Carmichael
CARMINATI, Tullio	Count Tullio Carminati de Brambilla
• CARNEY, Alan	David Bougal
• CARR, Jane	Rita Brunstrom
• CARR, Joe "Fingers"	Louis Busch
CARR, Mary K.	Mary Kennevan
CARR, Nat	Nathan C. Carr
CARRADINE, John	Richmond Reed Carradine
CARROL, Regina	Regina Gelfan
CARROLL, Dee	Betty Jean Marsh
CARROLL, Diahann	Carol Diahann Johnson
CARROLL, John	Julian la Faye
CARROLL, Nancy	Ann Veronica LaHiff
CARSON, Sunset "Kit"	Michael Harrison
CARTER, Helena	Helen Rickerts
CARTER, Janis	Janis Dremann
• CARVER, Louise	Louise Spilger Murray
• CARVER, Lynn	Virginia Reid Sampson
CASEY, Dolores	Margaret Dolores Katherine Casey
CASSIDY, Hopalong	William Boyd
CASSIDY, Jack	John Edward Joseph Cassidy
CASTLE, Irene	Irene Foote
• CASTLE, William	William Schloss
• CAVENS, Fred	Frederic Adolphe Cavens

...ORIGINAL NAMES OF THE STARS...

PROFESSIONAL NAME*	BIRTH, LEGAL OR FORMER NAME**
CHAMPLIN, Irene	*Irene Field*
CHANDLER, Jeff	*Ira Grossel*
CHANDLER, Janet	*Lillian Guenther (aka Lillian Barrett)*
CHANDLER, Lane	*Robert L. Oakes*
CHANEY, Frances	*Frances Cleveland Bush (aka Cleva Creighton)*
CHANEY, Lon (Jr.)	*Creighton T. Chaney*
CHANEY, Lon (Sr.)	*Alonso Chaney*
CHANEY, Norman "Chubby"	*Norman Myers Chaney*
CHAPLIN, Charlie	*Charles Spencer Chaplin*
CHAPLIN, Sydney	*Sydney Hawkes (half-brother of Charles)*
CHARISSE, Cyd	*Tula Finklea*
CHARLES, Ray	*Ray Charles Robinson*
CHASE, Charley	*Charles Parrott*
CHASE, Chevy	*Cornelius Crane Chase*
• CHASE, Colin	*Colin Collings*
CHASE, Stephen	*Stephen Alden Chase*
CHAYEFSKY, Paddy	*Sidney Chayefsky*
• CHEATHAM, Jack	*John Preston Cheatham*
CHECKER, Chubby	*Ernest Evans*
• CHEFEE, Jack	*(aka Jack Chefe)*
Cher	*Cherilyn Sarkisian LePierre*
• CHESEBRO, George	*George Newell Chesebro*
• CHEVALIER, Maurice	*Maurice Auguste Chevalier*
Chief Thundercloud (later)	*Scott T. Williams*
Chief Thundercloud (original)	*Victor Daniels*
Chief Yowlachie	*Daniel Simmons*
Christian-Jaque	*Christian Maudet*
CHRISTIAN, Linda	*Blanca Rosa Welter*
CHRISTY, June	*Shirley Luter*
CHRYSIS, International	*Billy Schumacher (became a transexual)*
Chubby (of "Our Gang")	*Norman Myers Chaney*
Cisco Kid	*Duncan Renaldo*
CLAIR, René	*René-Lucien Chomette*
CLAIRE, Ina	*Ina Fagan*
CLARENCE, O. B.	*Oliver B. Clarence*
CLARK, Bobby	*Robert Edwin Clark*
CLARK, Buddy	*Samuel Goldberg (Do not confuse with B. Clarke, d. 1957)*
CLARK, Dane	*Bernard Zanville*
CLARK, Fred	*Frederic Leonard Clark*
CLARKE, Buddy	*Robert Clarke (Do not confuse with Buddy Clark, d. 1949)*
CLARKE, Mae	*Mary Klotz*
CLARKE-SMITH, D. A.	*Douglas A. Clarke-Smith*
CLAYTON, Buck	*Wilbur Dorsey Clayton*
CLAYTON, Marguerite	*(aka Marguerite Bitter)*
• CLEMENTE, Roberto	*Roberto Walker Clemente*
CLEMENTO, Steve	*aka Steve Clemente and Steve Clements*
CLIBURN, Van	*Harvey Lavan Cliburn, Jr.*
• CLIFFORD, Jack	*Virgil James Montani*
• CLIFTON, Emma Bell	*Emma MacGrew*
• CLINE, Eddie	*Edward Francis Cline*
CLINE, Patsy	*Virginia Patterson Hensley*
CLIVE, Colin	*Clive Greig*
CLIVE, E. E.	*Edward E. Clive*
• CLIVE, Henry	*Henry Clive O'Hara*
COBB, Lee J.	*Leo Jacoby*
• COBB, Ty	*Tyrus Raymond Cobb*
• COBURN, Charles	*Charles Douville Coburn*
COBURN, Doddie	*Dorothy Coburn*
COCHRAN, Steve	*Robert Alexander Cochran*
• CODY, Bill Sr.	*William Frederick Cody*
CODY, Emmett	*Emmett Francis Cody*
CODY, Lew	*Louis Joseph Coté*
COGHLAN, Junior	*Frank Coghlan*
COLBERT, Claudette	*Lily Chauchoin*
COLBY, Anita	*Anita Counihan*

...ORIGINAL NAMES OF THE STARS...

PROFESSIONAL NAME*	BIRTH, LEGAL OR FORMER NAME**
COLE, Buddy	Edwin Lamar Cole
COLE, Nat King	Nathaniel Adams Coles
COLLIER, Constance	Laura Constance Hardie
COLLIER, Patience	René Ritcher
COLLINS, Dorothy	Marjorie Chandler
• COLLINS, Monty	Monte Francis Collins, Jr.
COLONNA, Jerry	Gerald Colonna
COLUMBO, Russ	Ruggerio Eugenio di Rudolpho Colombo
• COMINGORE, Dorothy	Linda Winters
COMO, Perry	Pierino Como
• CONNELLY, Bobby	Robert J. Connelly
CONNORS, Chuck	Kevin Joseph Connor
CONNORS, Michael	Krekor Ohanian
CONRAD, Robert	Conrad Robert Falk
CONRIED, Hans	Frank Foster Conried
CONTE, Richard	Nicholas Conte
• CONTI, Albert	Albert De Conti Cadassamare
CONWAY, Tom	Thomas Sanders
• COOGAN, Jack Sr.	John Coogan
COOK, Cookie	Charles Cook
• COOK, Joe	Joseph Lopez
COOKE, Alistair	Alfred Alistair Cooke
COOLEY, Spade	Donell Clyde Cooley
COOMBE, Carol	Gwendoline Alice Coombe
COOPER, Albert	Albert Raymond Cooper
COOPER, Alice	Vincent Furnier
COOPER, Gary	Frank James Cooper
COOPER, Jackie	John Cooperman, Jr.
COPPERFIELD, David	David Seth Kotkin
CORDAY, Josephine Rich	(aka Josie Rich)
CORDAY, Rita	Jeanne Paule Teipotemarga
"	(aka Paula Corday and Paula Croset)
• CORDY, Henry	Henry Korn
• COREY, Joseph	Joseph Martorano
• CORRIGAN, Ray "Crash"	Raymond Benard (aka Ray Benard)
CORTEZ, Ricardo	Jacob (Jake) Krantz (Kranze)
COSELL, Howard	Howard William Cohen
COSTELLO, Elvis	Declan Patrick McManus
COSTELLO, Lou	Louis Francis Cristillo
• COTTON, Billy	William Edward Cotton
COWAN, Jerome	Jerome Palmer Cowan
• COWARD, (Sir) Noel	Noel Pierce Coward
• COX, Wally	Wallace Maynard Cox
CRABBE, Larry "Buster"	Clarence Linden Crabbe
• CRAIG, Blanche	Blanche Sanderson
CRAIG, James	John Henry Meador
CRAIG, Michael	Michael Gregson
• CRAMER, Rychard	Rychard Earl Cramer (aka Richard Cramer)
CRANE, Norma	Norma Anna Bella Zuckerman
CRAVEN, Eddie	John Edward Craven
CRAVEN, John E.	John Edward Craven
• CRAWFORD, Anne	Imelda Crawford
CRAWFORD, Broderick	William Broderick Crawford
CRAWFORD, Howard Marion	(aka Howard Marion)
CRAWFORD, Joan	Lucille LeSueur
CREGAR, Laird	Samuel Laird Cregar
• CRIMMONS, Daniel	Alexander M. Lyons
• CRIPPS, Kernan	John Kernan Cripps
• CROCKETT, Dick	Richard Crockett
• CROGHAN, Joe	Joseph Michael Croghan
• CROMWELL, John	Elwood Dager Cromwell
CROMWELL, Richard	Roy Radebaugh
CRONYN, Hume	Hume Cronyn Blake
CROSBY, Bing	Harry Lillis Crosby
CROSBY, Dixie Lee	Dixie Lee Harriman

...ORIGINAL NAMES OF THE STARS...

|---|---|
CRUISE, Tom	*Thomas Cruise Mapother, IV*
CRUZE, James	*Jens Cruz Bosen*
Cuddles (S. Z. Sakall)	*Eugene Gero Szakall*
CUEVAS, Joey	*José Luis Cuevas*
CULVER, Cal	*John Calvin Culver (aka Casey Donovan)*
CUMMINGS, Constance	*Constance Halverstadt*
CUMMINGS, Robert	*Clarence Orville Cummings*
CUMMINGS, Sandy	*Sanford B. Cummings*
CUMMINS, Dorothy	*Dorothy Louise Cassil (aka Dorothy Cassil)*
• CUNARD, Grace	*Harriet Mildred Jefferies*
• CUNNINGHAM, Joe	*Joseph A. Cunningham*
Curly (of "3 Stooges")	*Jerome Howard (Horowitz)*
CURRIE, Finlay	*Finley Jefferson*
CURTIS, Alan	*Harold Neberroth*
CURTIS, Jackie	*John Holder, Jr.*
CURTIS, Ken	*Curtis Gates*
CURTIS, Tony	*Bernard Schwartz*
CURTIZ, Michael	*Mihaly Kertesz*
CUSTER, Bob	*Raymond Glenn*
• CUTTING, Dick	*Richard H. Cutting*
D	
DAGOVER, Lil	*Marta Maria Liletts*
Dagwood (Bumstead)	*(see LAKE, Arthur)*
DAINTY, Billy	*William Dainty*
• D'ALBROOK, Sidney	*(aka Sidney Dalbrook)*
DALE, Bobby	*Robert Flatley*
DALE, Charlie	*Charlie Marks*
DALE, Virginia	*Virginia Paxton*
DALEY, Cass	*Catherine Dailey*
DALIO, Marcel	*Israel Bleuschild*
DALL, John	*John Jenner Thompson*
DALY, John	*John Charles Daly*
DAMITA, Lili	*Liliane Marie Madeleine Carré (aka Liliane Loomis)*
DAMONE, Vic	*Vito Farinola*
DAMPIER, Claude	*Claude Cowan*
DANA, Viola	*Virginia Flugrath*
DANGERFIELD, Rodney	*Jacob Cohen*
• DANIEL, Billy	*William Baker*
DANIELL, Henry	*Charles Henry Daniell*
DANIELS, Bebe	*Virginia Daniels*
DANIELS, Mickey	*Richard Daniels, Jr.*
DANIELS, Victor	*(aka Chief Thundercloud)*
• D'ARCY, Roy	*Roy F. Guisti*
DARIN, Bobby	*Robert Walden Cassotto*
Darla (of "Our Gang")	*Darla Jean Hood*
• DARLING, Candy	*James Slattery*
DARLING, Jean	*Dorothy Jean LeVake*
DARNELL, Linda	*Manetta Eloisa Darnell*
DARREN, James	*James Ercolani*
DARRO, Frankie	*Frank Johnson*
DARVI, Bella	*Bayla Wegier*
DARWELL, Jane	*Patti Woodward*
DASH, Pauly	*Paul Walter Dashiff*
DAUBE, Belle	*(aka Harda Daube)*
DAUPHIN, Claude	*Claude Legrand*
DAVENPORT, Alice	*Alice Shepard*
DAVES, Delmar	*Delmar Lawrence Daves*
DAVID, Thayer	*Thayer David Hersey*
DAVIES, Marion	*Marion Douras*
DAVIS, Battle	*Thomas Battle Davis*
DAVIS, Bette	*Ruth Elizabeth Davis*
DAVIS, Jackie	*John H. Davis*
• DAVIS, Jim	*James Davis*
DAVIS, Miles	*Miles Dewey Davis III*
DAVIS, Rufe	*Rufus Davidson*

...ORIGINAL NAMES OF THE STARS...

PROFESSIONAL NAME*	BIRTH, LEGAL OR FORMER NAME**
DAW, Evelyn	Evelyn Daw Smith
DAY, Dennis	Eugene Dennis McNulty
DAY, Doris	Doris von Kappelhoff
DAY, Laraine	Laraine Johnson
• Dead End Kids, The	Leo Gorcey
• "	Huntz Hall
• "	Billy Halop
• "	Bobby Jordan
• "	Bernard Punsley
DEAN, Eddie	Edgar D. Glossup
DEAN, James	James Byron Dean
DEANE, Palmer	Palmer Deane Whitted, Jr.
DeCARLO, Yvonne	Peggy Yvonne Middleton
DeCASALIS, Jeanne	Jeanne de Casalis de Pury
DeCORDOVA, Arturo	Arturo Garcia
DEE, Frances	Jean Dee
DEE, Sandra	Alexandra Zuck (or Sandra Douvain)
• DeGREY, Sydney	Sidney de Gray
DEHNER, John	John Forkum
• DEKKER, Albert	Albert Ecke
• DEL MAR, Claire	Clara Eloise Mohr (married name)
DEL RIO, Dolores	Lolita Dolores de Martinez
• DEL VAL, Jean	Jean Gauthier
• DEMAIN, Gordon	(aka Gordon D. Wood)
DeMILLE, Cecil B.	Cecil Blount DeMille
DENNING, Richard	Louis A. Denninger
DENNIS, Sandy	Sandra Dale Dennis
DENNY, Reginald	Reginald Leigh Daymore
DENVER, John	Henry John Deutschendorf, Jr.
DEREK, Bo	Mary Cathleen Collins
DEREK, John	Derek Harris
DeROACH, Charles	Charles deRochefort
DESMOND, Florence	Florence Dawson
DEVEAU, Jack	John R. Deveau
• DEVINE, Andy	Andrew Devine
DeVITO, Danny	Daniel Michael DeVito
DEVLIN, J. G.	James G. Devlin
DEVORE, Dorothy	Alma Inez Williams
• DeWILDE, Brandon	Andre Brandon de Wilde
DeWOLFE, Billy	William Andrew Jones
DEXTER, Anthony	Walter Fleischmann
DIAMOND, I. A. L.	Itek Dommnici (aka Isadore Diamond)
• DICKERSON, Henry	Dudley Henry Dickerson
DICKINSON, Angie	Angeline Brown
DIETERLE, William	Wilhelm Dieterle
DIETRICH, Marlene	Maria Magdalene von Losch
DILLER, Phyllis	Phyllis Driver
DILLON, Jack	John T. Dillon
• DILLON, Tom	Thomas Patrick Dillon
DISNEY, Walt	Walter Elias Disney
Divine	Harris Glenn Milstead
DIX, Richard	Ernest Carlton Brimmer
DIXON, Denver	Victor Adamson
• DODSWORTH, John	John Cecil Dodsworth
DOLBERG, Nola	Nola Luxford
DOLLY, Jenny	Janszieka Deutsch
DOLLY, Rosie	Roszicka Deutsch
• DOMINGUEZ, Joe	José J. Dominguez
DONAHUE, Troy	Merle Johnson
DONNELL, Jeff	Jean Marie Donnell
DONOVAN, Casey	John Calvin Culver
DORN, Philip	Fritz van Dungen
DORO, Marie	Marie K. Stewart
• DORR, Harry	Harry Lester Dorr (aka Lester Dorr)
DORS, Diana	Diana Fluck

• New entry.   * Includes both living & deceased persons.   ** Sources do not always agree on spelling.

...ORIGINAL NAMES OF THE STARS...

PROFESSIONAL NAME*	BIRTH, LEGAL OR FORMER NAME**
• DORSEY, Jimmy	James Francis Dorsey
• DORSEY, Tommy	Thomas Francis Dorsey
DOUGLAS, Donald	Douglas Kinleyside
DOUGLAS, Kirk	Issur Danielovitch Demsky
DOUGLAS, Melvyn	Melvyn Hesselberg
DOUGLAS, Robert	Robert Douglas Finlayson
DOUGLAS, Steve	Steven Kreisman
DOUGLASS, Kent	Douglass Montgomery
DOVE, Billie	Lilian Bohny
DOW, Peggy	Peggy Varnadow
DOWLING, Eddie	Joseph Nelson Goucher
DOWNS, Johnny	John Morey Downs
DRAKE, Alfred	Alfred Capurro
DRAKE, Charles	Charles Ruppert
DRAKE, Dona	Rita Novella
DRAKE, Tom	Alfred Alderdice
DRESSER, Louise	Louise Kerlin
DRESSLER, Marie	Leila Koerber
DREW, Ellen	Terry Ray
• Dr. Kildare	Joel McCrea (1937)
• "	Lew Ayres (1938-42)
• "	Van Johnson (1942-44) — tried to replace Lew Ayres
• "	Philip Dorn (1942) — tried to replace Lew Ayres
• "	Keye Luke (1942-47) — tried to replace Lew Ayres
• "	Richard Quine (1942) — tried to replace Lew Ayres
• "	James Craig (1947) — new protégé of Dr. Gillespie
• "	Richard Chamberlain (1960-65) — Dr. Kildare on TV
DRU, Joanne	Joanne la Cock
DUEL, Peter	Peter Deuel
DUFF-GRIFFIN, William	William Joseph Duffy
• DUGAN, Tom	Thomas J. Dugan
DUKE, Patty	Anna Marie Duke
DUMONT, Margaret	Daisy Baker
DUNBAR, Dixie	Christine Elizabeth Dunbar
DUNCAN, Kenne	Kenneth Duncan
Duncan Sisters, The	Rosetta Duncan ("Topsy")
"	Vivian Duncan ("Little Eva")
• DUNFEE, Nora	Marjorie Dean Dunfee
• DUNHAM, Phil	Phillip Gray Dunham
DUNN, Bobby	Robert Dunn
• DUNN, James	James Howard Dunn
DUNN, Michael	Gary Neil Miller
DUNNE, Irene	Irene Marie Dunn
Durango Kid, The	Charles Starrett
• DURANTE, Jimmy	James Francis Durante
DURBIN, Deanna	Edna Mae Durbin
DURKIN, Junior	Trent Junior Durkin
DURYEA, George	(aka Tom Keene)
DVORAK, Ann	Ann McKim
DWAN, Allan	Joseph Aloysius Dwan
DYLAN, Bob	Robert Zimmerman
◨▶	
EAGLE, Jimmy	James Eagle
EAMES, Virginia	(aka Virginia True Boardman)
EARLES, Harry	Kurt Schneider (aka Harry Doll)
EBSEN, Buddy	Christian Rudolf Ebsen
EDDY, Nelson	Nelson Ackerman Eddy
EDEN, Barbara	Barbara Huffman
• EDWARDS, Gus	Gus Simon
EDWARDS, Jimmy	James Keith O'Neill Edwards
• EDWARDS, Neely	Cornelius Limbach
• EDWARDS, Vince	Vincent Edward Zoine, III
EICHELBERGER, Ethyl	James Roy Eichelberger
• EILERS, Sally	Dorothea Sally Eilers
ELDRIDGE, Florence	Florence McKechnie

• New entry.   * Includes both living & deceased persons.   ** Sources do not always agree on spelling.

...ORIGINAL NAMES OF THE STARS...

PROFESSIONAL NAME*	BIRTH, LEGAL OR FORMER NAME**
• ELDRIDGE, John	John Eldredge
ELLINGTON, Duke	Edward Kennedy Ellington
ELLIOT, Cass	Ellen Naomi Cohen (aka Mama Cass)
ELLIOTT, Dick	Richard Damon Elliott
ELLIOTT, William "Wild Bill"	Gordon Nance
ELLIOTT, William D.	William David Elliott
ELLIS, Patricia	Patricia Gene O'Brien
ELLISON, James	James Ellison Smith
ELMER, Billy	William E. Johns
ELSOM, Isobel	Isobel Reed (aka Isobel Harbord)
ELY, Ron	Ronald Pierce
EMERSON, John	Clifton Paden
• EMERTON, Roy	Hugh Fitzroy Emerton
EMERY, Gilbert	Gilbert Emery Pottle
• ENDFIELD, Cy	Cyril Raker Endfield
ENGLISH, John W.	John Wilkinson English
ENTWISTLE, Peg	Lillian Millicent Entwistle
EPSTEIN, David S.	David Schaffer Epstein
• EPSTEIN, Jerry	Jerome Epstein
ERICKSON, Leif	William Anderson
ERICSON, John	Joseph Meibes
• ERGAS, Joseph	(aka Brutus Peck)
Esmeralda	Alma Graciela Haro Cabello (aka Haro Cabello)
ESMOND, Carl	Willy Eichberger
EVANS, Dale	Frances Butts
EVANS, Joan	Joan Eunson
EVERETT, Chad	Raymond Lee Cramton
EWELL, Tom	S. Yewell Tompkins
EYTHE, William	John Joseph Eythe
F	
Fabian	Fabian Anthony Forte-Bonaparte
Fabio	Fabio Lanzoni
FABRAY, Nanette	Ruby Bernadette Nanette Theresa Fabares
FAIRBANKS, Douglas Jr.	Douglas Elton Ullman, Jr.
FAIRBANKS, Douglas Sr.	Douglas Elton Thomas Ullman
FAIRBROTHER, Sydney	Sydney Tapping
FAIRCHILD, Morgan	Patsy McClenny
FAITH, Adam	Terence Nelhams
FALK, Peter	Peter Michael Falk
FALKENBERG, Jinx	Euginia Falkenburg
FARENTINO, James	Ferdinand Anthony Ferrandino
Farina (of "Our Gang")	Allen Clayton Hoskins, Jr.
• FARLEY, Dot	Dorothea Farley
FARLEY, Jim	James Lee Farley
FARMER, Frances	Frances Elena Farmer
FARMER, Virginia	Mary Virginia Farmer
FARROW, Mia	Maria de Lourdes Villiers
FAWCETT, Farrah	Mary Farrah Leni Fawcett
FAYE, Alice	Alice Jeanne Leppert
FAYLEN, Frank	Frank Ruf
FELDMAN, Marty	Martin Alan Feldman
• FENTON, Frank	Frank Fenton-Morgan
• FENTON, Leslie C.	Leslie Carter Fenton
Fernandel	Fernand Joseph Désiré Contandin
FERRER, José	José Vincente Ferrery de Otero y Cintron
FERRER, Mel	Melchior Gaston Ferrer
FETCHIT, Stepin	Lincoln Theodore Monroe Andrew Skeeter Perry
• FETHERSTON, Eddie	(aka Eddie Featherstone)
Fibber McGee	Jim Jordan
FIELD, Virginia	Margaret Cynthia Field
FIELDS, Gracie	Grace Stansfield
FIELDS, Stanley	Walter L. Agnew
FIELDS, Totie	Sophie Feldman
FIELDS, W. C.	William Claude Dukenfield
FINCH, Peter	Peter George Frederick Ingle-Finch

...ORIGINAL NAMES OF THE STARS...

PROFESSIONAL NAME*	BIRTH, LEGAL OR FORMER NAME**
FINE, Larry	*Laurence Feinberg*
FINLAYSON, James	*James Henderson Finlayson*
FISHER, Carrie	*Carrie Frances Fisher*
FISHER, Eddie	*Edwin Jack Fisher*
• FISKE, Richard	*Thomas Richard Potts*
FISKE, Robert	*Robert L. Fiske*
FITZGERALD, Barry	*William Joseph Shields*
FITZGERALD, Walter	*Walter Bond*
FIX, Paul	*Paul Fix Morrison*
FLATT, Lester	*Lester Raymond Flatt*
FLEISCHER, Max	*Maximilian Fleischer*
FLEMING, Ian	*Ian Mac Farlane*
FLEMING, Rhonda	*Marilyn Louis*
FLOWERS, Wayland	*Wayland Parrott Flowers, Jr.*
FLYNN, Errol	*Errol Leslie Thompson Flynn*
FLYNN, Joe	*Joseph Flynn*
FLYNN, Sean	*Sean Leslie Flynn*
FOCH, Nina	*Nina Consuelo Maud Fock*
FOLEY, Red	*Clyde Julian Foley*
FONDA, Henry	*Henri Jaynes Fonda*
FONDA, Jane	*Jane Seymour Fonda*
FONDA, Peter	*Peter Henry Fonda*
FONTAINE, Joan	*Joan de Beauvoir de Havilland*
FONTANNE, Lynn	*Lillie Louise Fontanne*
FONTEYN, (Dame) Margot	*Peggy Hookham*
FORAN, Dick	*John Nicholas Foran*
FORBES, Ralph	*Ralph Taylor*
• FORD, Francis	*Francis O'Fearna*
FORD, Glenn	*Gwyllyn Samuel Newton Ford*
FORD, John	*Sean Aloyius O'Fearna*
• FORD, Mary	*Colleen Summers*
FORD, Paul	*Paul Ford Weaver*
FORD, "Tennessee" Ernie	*Ernest Jennings Ford*
FORD, Wallace	*Samuel Jones Grundy*
• FORMBY, George	*(aka George Hoy)*
FORREST, Mark	*Lou Degni*
FORREST, Sally	*Katherine Sally Feeney*
FORREST, Steve	*William Forrest Andrews*
FORSYTHE, John	*John Lincoln Freund*
FORTE, Joe	*Josef Forte*
FOSSE, Bob	*Robert Louis Fosse*
FOSTER, Dianne	*Dianne Laruska*
FOSTER, Jodie	*Ariane Alicia Christian Foster*
FOSTER, Norman	*Norman Hoeffer*
FOSTER, Phil	*Fivel Feldman*
FOSTER, Susanna	*Suzanne DeLee Flanders Larsen*
• FOX, Harry	*Arthur Carringford*
FOX, Michael J.	*Michael Andrew Fox*
FOXX, Redd	*John Elroy Sanford*
FOY, Eddie Jr.	*Edward Fitzgerald, Jr.*
FOY, Eddie Sr.	*Edward Fitzgerald*
FRANCEN, Victor	*Victor Franssen*
FRANCHI, Franco	*Francesco Benenato*
FRANCIOSA, Anthony	*Anthony George Papaleo*
FRANCIS, Ann	*Frances S. Roberts*
FRANCIS, Arlene	*Arlene Francis Kazanjian*
FRANCIS, Connie	*Concetta Maria Rosa Franconero*
FRANCIS, Kay	*Katherine Edwina Gibbs*
FRANCIS, Robert	*Robert Charles Francis*
• FRANCIS, Sandra	*Sandra Francis Dian Bawdin (aka Sandra Donat)*
FRANCIS, Wilma	*Wilma Sareussen*
FRANCISCUS, James	*James Grover Franciscus*
FRANEY, Billy	*William Franey*
• FRANKLIN, Melvin	*David English*
FRANKLIN, Sidney	*Sidney Arnold Franklin*

PROFESSIONAL NAME*	BIRTH, LEGAL OR FORMER NAME**
FRANKOVICH, Mike	Mitchell J. Frankovich
FRASER, Bill	William Fraser
FRAZEE, Jane	Mary Jane Frahse
• FREDERICI, Blanche	Blanche Friderici Campbell (aka Blanche Friderici)
• FREDERICK, Pauline (actress)	Pauline Libbey
FREED, Arthur	Arthur Grossman
FREEMAN, Howard	Howard Schoppe Freeman
FREEMAN, Mona	Monica Elizabeth Freeman
• FRELENG, Friz	Isadore Freleng
Frenchie	Samuel Marx
FRESNAY, Pierre	Pierre Jules Louis Laudenbach
FRIGANZA, Trixie	Brigid O'Callaghan
FRIML, Rudolf	Charles Rudolf Friml
FRISCO, Joe	Lewis W. Joseph
FRIZZELL, Lefty	William Orville Frizzell
FROEBE, Gert	Karl-Gerhard Frober
Froggy (of "Our Gang")	Billy McLaughlin
FURNESS, Betty	Elizabeth Mary Furness
FURST, Anton	Anthony Francis Furst
G	
GAAL, Franceska	Fanny Zilveritch
Gabby	George Hayes
GABIN, Jean	Jean-Alexis Moncourge
GABLE, Clark	William Clark Gable
GABOR, Zsa Zsa	Sari Gabor
GALLAGHER, Skeets	Richard Gallagher
• GALVANI, Dino	(aka Dino Galvanoni)
GARBO, Greta	Greta Gustafsson
GARCIA, Andy	Andres Arturo Garcia-Menendez
• GARCIA, Jerry	Jerome John Garcia
GARDENIA, Vincent	Vincent Scognamiglio
• GARDINER, Reginald	William Reginald Gardiner
GARDNER, Ava	Ava Lavinia Gardner
GARDNER, Helen	Helen Louise Gardner
GARFIELD, John	Julius Garfinkle
GARLAND, Beverly	Beverly Campbell
GARLAND, Judy	Frances Gumm
GARNER, James	James Baumgarner
• GARON, Pauline	Marie Pauline Garon
GARRALAGA, Martin	Martin Gorralaag
GAUDIO, Joe	Joseph E. Gaudio
GAYE, Marvin	Marvin Gay, Jr.
GAYLE, Crystal	Brenda Gayle Webb
GAYNOR, Janet	Laura Gainer
GAYNOR, Mitzi	Francesca Mitzi Marlene de Charney von Gerber
• GAZZO, Michael	Michael Vincente Gazzo
• GEARY, Bud	S. Maine Geary
GEER, Will	Will Ghere
• GEHRIG, Lou	Henry Louis Gehrig
GENTRY, Minnie L.	Minnie Lee Watson
GEORGE, Boy	George Alan O'Dowd
GEORGE, "Chief" Dan	Geswanouth Slahoot
GEORGE, Gladys	Gladys Clare
GEORGE, Gorgeous	George Raymond Wagner
• GEORGE, Heinrich	Heinz Georg Schulz
GERAY, Steve	Stefan Gyergay
• GERRARD, Douglas	Douglas Gerrard McMurrogh-Kavanagh (aka Douglas Gerard)
• GERRON, Kurt	Kurt Gerson
GERSHWIN, George	George Gershvin (Gershovitz or Gershwine)
GERSON, Jeanne	Jeanne Aleshnick
• GERSTLE, Frank	Frank Morris Gerstle
• GIBSON, Helen	Rose August Wenger (aka Rose Gibson)
GIBSON, Hoot	Edmund Richard Gibson
GIBSON, Mel	Mel Columcille Gibson
GILBERT, John	John Pringle

...ORIGINAL NAMES OF THE STARS...

PROFESSIONAL NAME*	BIRTH, LEGAL OR FORMER NAME**
GILFORD, Jack	Jacob Gellmann
GILLESPIE, Dizzy	John Birks Gillespie
GILLIS, Ann	Alma O'Connor
GIOVALE, Franco	Francesco Giovale
GISH, Dorothy	Dorothy de Guiche
GISH, Lillian	Lillian de Guiche
GLAUDI, Hap	Lloyd Glaudi
• GLEASON, James	James Austin Gleason
GLEASON, Lucille	Lucille Webster
GLENN, Raymond	(aka Bob Custer)
GODDARD, Paulette	Marion Levy
GOLDBERG, Whoopi	Karen Johnson
• GOLDIN, Pat	(aka Pat Golden)
GOLDWYN, Frances Howard	Frances McLaughlin (aka Frances Howard)
GOLDWYN, Samuel	Samuel Goldfish
GOODE, Jack	Irwin Thomas Whittridge
GOODWIN, Bill	William Nettles Goodwin
GOODWIN, Ruby	Ruby Berkley Goodwin
GORCEY, Leo	Leo Bernard Gorcey
• GORDON, C. Henry	Henry Racke
GORDON, Robert	Robert Gordon Duncan
GORDON, Ruth	Ruth Jones
GORME, Eydie	Edith Gormezano
GRABLE, Betty	Ruth Elizabeth Grable
GRAHAM, Bill	Wolfgang Grajonca
• GRAHAM, Morland	(aka Moreland Graham)
GRAHAME, Gloria	Gloria Hallward
GRANGER, Stewart	James Lablanche Stewart
GRANT, Cary	Archibald Alexander Leach
GRANT, Kathryn	Katherine Grandstaff
GRANT, Kirby	Kirby G. Horn
GRANT, Lee	Lyova Haskell Rosenthal
GRANT, Shauna	Colleen Marie Applegate
GRANT, Tiny	Ralph Grant Matthiessen
GRAPEWIN, Charley	Charles Grapewin
GRAVES, Peter	Peter Arness
GRAVET, Fernand	Fernand Mertens (aka Fernand Gravey)
GRAY, Charles	Donald M. Gray
GRAY, Coleen	Doris Jensen
GRAY, Dulcie	Dulcie Bailey
GRAY, Gilda	Marianna Michalska
GRAY, Glen	Glen Gray Knoblaugh
GRAYSON, Kathryn	Zelma Hedrick
GRAZIANO, Rocky	Rocco Barbella
• Greatful Dead, The	Jerry Garcia
• "	Mickey Hart
• "	Bill Kreutzmann
• "	Phil Lesh
• "	Bob Weir
• "	Vince Welnick
Great Gildersleeve	Harold Peary
GREAZA, Walter	Walter Noel Greaza
GREEN, Harry	Harry Blitzer
GREEN, Martyn	William Martyn Green
GREEN, Mitzi	Elizabeth Keno
GREENE, Herbert	Herbert Stanton Greene
GREENSTREET, Sydney	Sydney Hughes Greenstreet
GREENWOOD, Charlotte	Frances Charlotte Greenwood
• GRENFELL, Joyce	Joyce Irene Phipps
GREY, Joel	Joel Katz
GREY, Nan	Eschol Loleet Miller
• GREY, Olga	Anna Zachak
GREY, Robert H.	Henry Virtue Goerner
GRIBBON, Eddie	Edward T. Gribbon
GRIFFIES, Ethel	Ethel Woods

• New entry.   * Includes both living & deceased persons.   ** Sources do not always agree on spelling.

...ORIGINAL NAMES OF THE STARS...

PROFESSIONAL NAME*	BIRTH, LEGAL OR FORMER NAME**
GRIFFIN, Carlton	Carlton Elliott Griffin
GRIFFITH, Corinne	Corinne Scott
GRIFFITH, D. W.	David Llewelyn Wark Griffith
GRIFFITH, Harry	Harry Sutherland Griffith
GRIFFITH, Katherine	Katherine Kierman
GUARD, Kit	Christen Klitgaard
GUBITOSI, Mickey	(See Robert BLAKE)
GUILFOYLE, James	James Ancel Guilfoyle
GUINAN, Texas	Mary Louise Cecelie Guinan
GURIE, Sigrid	Sigrid Gurie Haukelid
GUTHRIE, Woody	Woodrow Wilson Guthrie
GWENN, Edmund	Edmund Kellaway, Jr.
GWYNNE, Anne	Marguerite Gwynne-Trice
GWYNNE, Fred	Frederick Hubbard Gwynne
H	
HACKETT, Bobby	Robert Leo Hackett
HACKETT, Buddy	Leonard Hacker
HACKETT, Joan	Joan Ann Hackett
HACKETT, Karl	Karl Ellsworth Germain
HADEN, Sara	Sara Hadden
HADLEY, Reed	Reed Bert Herring
HAGEN, Jean	Jean Shirley Verhagen
• HAGNEY, Frank S.	(aka Frank Hagny)
HALE, Alan	Rufus Alan McKanan
HALE, Creighton	Patrick Fitzgerald
HALE, Georgia	Georgette Theodora Hale
HALE, Jonathan	Jonathan Hatley
HALE, Sonnie	John Robert Hale Munro
HALEY, Jack	John Joseph Haley
HALL, Charlie	Charles D. Hall
HALL, Huntz	Henry Hall
HALL, James	James Brown
HALL, Jon	Charles H. Locher (aka Lloyd Crane)
HALL, Porter	Clifford Porter Hall
HALOP, Billy	William Halop
HAMER, Rusty	Russell Craig Hamer
HAMILTON, Neil	James Neal Hamilton
Hammer	Stanley Kirk Burrell
HAMMOND, Kay	Dorothy Katharine Standing
HAMPDEN, Walter	Walter Hampden Daugherty
• HAMPTON, Grace	(aka Grayce Hampton)
• HANCOCK, Tony	Anthony Hancock
• HANDWORTH, Octavia	Octavia Boas
HARDING, Ann	Dorothy Gatley
HARDING, Lyn	David Llewellyn Harding
HARDY, Oliver	Oliver Norvelle Hardy
HARLOW, Jean	Harlean Carpenter
HAROLDE, Ralf	Ralf Harolde Wigger
HARRELSON, Woody	Woodrow Tracy Harrelson
• HARRIS, Morris	Morris Oliver Harris
• HARRIS, Robert H.	Robert Harris Hurwitz
HARRISON, Rex	Reginald Carey
HARRON, Bobby	Robert Harron
• HARRON, Tessie	Anna Theresa Harron
• HART, Neal	Cornelius A. Hart, Jr.
HART, William S.	William Surrey Hart
• HARTIGAN, Pat	Patrick C. Hartigan
HARTLEY, Mariette	Mary Loretta Hartley
HARVEY, Hank	Herman Heacker
HARVEY, Laurence	Larushka Skikne
• HARVEY, Lilian	Lilian Muriel Helen Harvey
HASSE, O. E.	Otto Eduard
HASSO, Signe	Signe Larsson
• HATTON, Raymond	Raymond William Hatton
HAVER, June	June Stovenour

...ORIGINAL NAMES OF THE STARS...

PROFESSIONAL NAME*	BIRTH, LEGAL OR FORMER NAME**
HAVOC, June	Ellen Hovick
• HAWLEY, Wanda	(aka Wanda Petit)
HAYAKAWA, Sessue	Kintaro Hayakawa
HAYDEN, Russell "Lucky"	Pate Lucid
HAYDEN, Sterling	Sterling Relyea Walter
HAYES, Allison	Mary Jane Hayes
HAYES, Helen	Helen Hayes Brown
• HAYES, Margaret "Maggie"	Lorette Ottenheimer
• HAYES, Sam	Samuel Stewart Hayes
HAYMES, Dick	Richard Benjamin Haymes
HAYWARD, Louis	Seafield Grant
HAYWARD, Susan	Edythe Marreanner
HAYWORTH, Rita	Margarita Cansino
• HEALY, Ted	Charles Earnest Lee Nash
HEARN, Eddie	Guy Edward Hearn
HEFLIN, Van	Emmett Evan Heflin
HEGGIE, O. P.	Otto Peters Heggie
• HEMING, Violet	Violet Hemming
HENDERSON, Del	George Delbert Henderson
HENDERSON, Dickie	Richard Henderson
HENDERSON, Fletch	Fletcher Henderson
HENDRIX, Jimi	James Marshall Hendrix
HENDRIX, Wanda	Dixie Wanda Hendrix
HENRIED, Paul	Paul George Julius Henreid Ritter von Wasel Waldingau
HENRY, Charlotte	(aka Charlotte Virginia Henry)
• HENRY, Tom	Thomas Browne Henry
HEPBURN, Audrey	Edda Kathleen Hepburn van Heemstra
HERBERT, Holmes	Edward Sanger
HERLIE, Eileen	Eileen Herlihy
HERMAN, Pee-wee	Paul Reubenfeld (aka Paul Reubens)
HERMAN, Woody	Woodrow Wilson Herman
• HERNANDEZ, Anna	Anna Dodge
HERNDON, Bill	William E. Herndon
• HERRIOT, James	James Alfred Wight
HERSHEY, Barbara	Barbara Herzstine
HERVEY, Irene	Irene Herwick
• HEWSTON, Alfred H.	(aka Alfred Heuston)
HIATT, Ruth	Ruth Redfern
• HICKS, Russell	Edward Russell Hicks
• HILDEBRAND, Hilde	Emma Minna Hildebrand
Hildegarde	Hildegarde Loretta Sell
HILL, Benny	Alfred Hawthorn Hill
HILL, George W.	George William Hill
Hilo Hattie	Clara Nelson
HOBART, Rose	Rose Keefer
• HODGSON, Leland	(aka Leyland Hodgson)
• HOEFLICH, Lucie	Helene Lucie von Holwede
HOEY, Dennis	Samuel David Hyams
• HOFFMAN, Otto	Otto Frederick Hoffman
HOLDEN, Fay	Fay Hammerton
HOLDEN, William	William Beedle
• HOLDREN, Judd	Judd Clifton Holdren
HOLIDAY, Billie	Eleanor Gough McKay
• HOLLES, Antony	(aka Anthony Holles)
HOLLIDAY, Judy	Judith Tuvim
HOLLIMAN, Earl	Anthony Numkena
HOLLY, Buddy	Charles Hardin Holly
• HOLMAN, Libby "Peaches"	Elizabeth Holzman
HOLT, Jack	Charles John Holt
HOLT, Tim	John Charles Holt, III
HOLT, Ula	Ula Vale
HOMEIER, Skip	George Homeier
• HOOD, Darla	Darla Jean Hood
• HOON, Shannon	Richard Shannon Hoon
• HOOVER, J. Edgar	John Edgar Hoover

...ORIGINAL NAMES OF THE STARS...

PROFESSIONAL NAME*	BIRTH, LEGAL OR FORMER NAME**
Hopalong Cassidy	*William Boyd*
HOPE, Bob	*Leslie Townes Hope*
HOPKINS, Miriam	*Ellen Miriam Hopkins*
• HOPPER, De Wolf	*William DeWolf Hopper*
HOPPER, Hedda	*Elda Furry*
• HOPPER, William	*William DeWolf Hopper, Jr.*
HOPTON, Russell	*Harry Russell Hopton*
HOROWITZ, Vladimir	*Vladimir Gorowicz*
HORTON, Robert	*Mead Howard Horton*
• HORVATH, Charles	*Charles Frank Horvath*
• HOSKINS, Allen "Farina"	*Allen Clayton Hoskins, Jr.*
HOUDINI, Harry	*Ehrich Weiss*
HOUSEMAN, John	*Jacques Haussmann*
• HOUSMAN, Arthur	*(aka Arthur Houseman)*
• HOUSTON, Renée	*Katherine Houston Gribbin*
• HOWARD, Jerome "Curly"	*Jerome Lester Horowitz*
HOWARD, John	*John Cox*
HOWARD, Leslie	*Leslie Howard Stainer*
HOWARD, Mary	*Mary Rogers Brooks*
HOWARD, Moe	*Moses Horowitz*
HOWARD, Shemp	*Samuel Horowitz*
• HOWARD, Willie	*William Levkowitz*
HOWELL, Wayne	*Wayne Chappelle*
• HOWES, Reed	*Herman Reed Howes*
HOWLIN, Olin	*(aka Olin Howland)*
HOYT, John	*John Hoysradt*
HUDNET, Bill	*William H. Hudnet*
HUDSON, Rock	*Roy Scherer, Jr. (later Roy Fitzgerald)*
HUDSON, William	*William Woodson Hudson, Jr.*
HULL, Josephine	*Josephine Sherwood*
• HULL, Warren	*John Warren Hull*
HUMPERDINCK, Engelbert	*Arnold Dorsey*
• HUMPHREY, William	*William Jonathan Humphrey*
HUNT, Marsha	*Marcia Hunt*
HUNTER, Jeffrey	*Henry Herman McKinnies*
HUNTER, Kim	*Janet Cole*
HUNTER, Ross	*Martin Fuss*
HUNTER, Tab	*Arthur Gelien*
HUNTLEY, Chet	*Chester Robert Huntley*
HUROK, Sol	*Solomon Hurok*
HURT, Mary Beth	*Mary Supinger*
HUSTON, Walter	*Walter Houghston*
HUTTON, Betty	*Betty Jane Thornburg*
HUTTON, Jim	*Dana James Hutton*
HUTTON, Marion	*Marion Thornburg*
HUTTON, Robert	*Robert Bruce Winne*
I	
Ice-T	*Tracy Marrow*
ICE, Vanilla	*Robert Van Winkle*
IDOL, Billy	*William Michael Broad*
IMMEDIATO, Al	*Italo Immediato*
IMMEDIATO, Nick	*Nino Immediato*
INCE, John E.	*John Edward Ince*
INCE, Ralph W.	*Ralph Waldo Ince*
INESCORT, Frieda	*Frieda Wightman*
INGE, William	*(aka Walter Gage)*
INGRAM, Rex (Hitchcock)	*Reginald Ingram Montgomery Hitchcock*
"	*(aka Rex Hitchcock)*
"	*(Do not confuse with the black actor named Rex Ingram)*
Ink Spots, The	*Herbert C. Kenny (replaced Orville "Hoppy" Jones in 1944)*
"	*Bill Kenny*
"	*Charlie Fuqua*
"	*Billy Bowen*
IRWIN, Charles	*Charles Wesley Irwin*
"It" Girl, The	*Clara Bow*

• New entry. * Includes both living & deceased persons. ** Sources do not always agree on spelling.

PROFESSIONAL NAME*	BIRTH, LEGAL OR FORMER NAME**
IVES, Burl	*Burl Icle Ivanhoe*
J	
• JACK, Wolfman	*Bob Smith*
JACKSON, Mary Ann	*Gloria Pressman (aka Mildred Jackson)*
JACKSON, Selmer	*Selmer Adolph Jackson*
Jackson's, The	*Maureen "Rebbie" Jackson (Eldest)*
"	*Sigmund Esco "Jackie" Jackson*
"	*Toriano Adaryll "Tito" Jackson*
"	*Jermaine LaJaune Jackson*
"	*LaToya Yvonne Jackson*
"	*Marion David Jackson*
"	*Michael Joe Jackson*
"	*Steven Randall "Randy" Jackson*
"	*Janet Dameta Jackson (Youngest)*
JACQUES, Hattie	*Josephine Jacques*
JAMISON, Bud	*William Jamison (or Jamieson)*
JANNINGS, Emil	*Theodor Emil Janenz*
JANSSEN, David	*David Harold Meyer*
• JAQUET, Frank	*Frank Garnier Jaquet*
JARRETT, Art	*Arthur Jarrett*
JASON, Leigh	*Leigh Jacobson*
JEAN, Gloria	*Gloria Jean Schoonover*
• JEANS, Ursula	*Ursula McMinn*
JENKINS, Allen	*Alfred McGonegal*
JENKS, Si	*Howard H. Jenkins*
JENNINGS, Claudia	*Mimi Chesterton*
JENNINGS, S. E.	*Sylvester Ennis Jennings*
JEROME, Suzie	*Susan Willis*
• JERROLD, Mary	*Mary Allen*
JOEL, Billy	*William Martin Joel*
JOHN, Elton	*Reginald Kenneth Dwight*
JOHNSON, Chic	*Harold Ogden Johnson*
• JOHNSON, Chubby	*Charles Randolph Johnson*
JOHNSON, Don	*Donald Wayne*
JOHNSON, Katie	*Katherine Johnson*
JOHNSON, Kay	*Catherine Townsend*
JOHNSON, Tor	*Tor Johansson*
JOHNSON, Van	*Charles Van Johnson*
JOLSON, Al	*Asa Yoelson*
• JONES, Bobby	*Robert Tyre Jones, Jr.*
JONES, Brian	*Lewis Brian Hopkins-Jones*
JONES, Buck	*Charles Frederick Gebhardt*
JONES, Candy	*Jessica Arline Wilcox*
JONES, Charlotte	*Charlotte Nathanson*
JONES, Charlotte	*Charlotte Nathanson*
JONES, Emrys	*Emrys Whittaker-Jones*
JONES, Jennifer	*Phyllis Isley*
JONES, Spike	*Lindley Armstrong Jones*
JONES, T. C.	*Thomas Craig Jones*
JONES, Tom	*Thomas Woodward*
• JORDAN, Marion "Molly McGee"	*Marion Driscoll*
JORDAN, Richard	*Robert Anson Jordan*
JOSLYN, Allyn	*Allyn Morgan Joslyn*
JOURDAN, Louis	*Louis Gendre*
JOY, Leatrice	*Leatrice Joy Zeidler*
JOYCE, Brenda	*Betty Leabo*
JULIA, Raul	*Raul Rafael Carlos Julia y Arcelay*
JURADO, Katy	*Maria Jurado Garcia*
JUSTIN, John	*John Ledsma*
K	
KABIBBLE, Ish	*Merwyn Bogue*
KARINA, Anna	*Hanne Karin Bayer*
KARLOFF, Boris	*William Henry Pratt*
KARLSON, Phil	*Philip Karlstein*
• KASZNAR, Kurt	*Kurt Serwicher*

...ORIGINAL NAMES OF THE STARS...

PROFESSIONAL NAME*	BIRTH, LEGAL OR FORMER NAME**
KATCH, Kurt	Isser Kac
KAY, Beatrice	Hannah Beatrice Kuper
KAYE, Danny	David Daniel Kominski
KAYE, Darwood "Waldo"	Darwood Kenneth Smith
KAZAN, Elia	Elia Kazanjoglous
KEACH, Stacy	Walter Stacy Keach, Jr.
KEATON, Buster	Joseph Francis Keaton
KEATON, Diane	Diane Hall
KEATON, Michael	Michael Douglas
KEEL, Howard	Harold Leek
KEELER, Ruby	Ethel Keeler
KEENE, Tom	George Duryea (aka Richard Powers)
KEITH, Brian	Robert Brian Keith, Jr.
KEITH, Ian	Keith Ross
KELLJAN, Robert	Robert Kelljchian
KELLY, Dorothy	Dorothy Helen Kelly
KELLY, Gene	Eugene Curran Kelly
KELLY, Patsy	Sarah Kelly
KELLY, Paul	Paul Michael Kelly
• KENDALL, Cy	Cyrus W. Kendall
KENDALL, Kay	Justine Kendall McCarthy
KENNEDY, Arthur	John Arthur Kennedy
• KENNEDY, Douglas	Douglas Richards Kennedy (aka Keith Douglas)
KENNEDY, Fred	Frederick O. Kennedy
KENNY, Herbert C.	Herbert Cornelius Kenny
KENT, Jean	Joan Summerfield (aka Jean Carr)
• KENT, Robert	Douglas Blackley
KENTON, Stan	Stanley Newcombe Kenton
KERMACK, Paul	Stewart Auchinleck
KERN, Jerome	Jerome David Kern
KERR, Deborah	Deborah Kerr-Trimmer
KERR, Frederick	Frederick Keen
KERR, Stu	Thomas Stewart Kerr (aka Prof. Kool and Bozo the Clown)
KERRIGAN, J. Warren	Jack Warren Kerrigan
KERRY, Norman	Arnold Kaiser
• Kettles, The	Marjorie Main (Ma)
• "	Percy Kilbride (Pa)
KEY, Kathleen	Kitty Lanahan
• Keystone Kops, The	Charles Avery
• "	Eddie Baker
• "	Bobby Dunn
• "	Georgie Jesky
• "	Edgar Kennedy
• "	Grover Ligon
• "	Hank Mann
• "	Victor Potel
• "	Mack Riley
• "	Slim Summerville
KHAN, Chaka	Yvette Stevens
• KIBBEE, Guy	Guy Bridges Kibbee
KIDDER, Margot	Margaret Kidder
• Kiki	Alice Prin (aka Kiki du Montparnasse)
KILIAN, Pauline	(aka Pauline Hopkins and Pauline Stone)
KING, Andrea	Georgetta Barry
KING, Carole	Carole Klein
• KING, Claude E.	Claude Ewart King
KING, Dennis	Dennis Pratt
KING, Michael	Richard C. Wegener
KINGSLEY, Ben	Krishna Banji
• KINGSLEY, Sidney	Sidney Kirshner
KINSKI, Klaus	Nikolaus Gunther Nakszynski
KINSKI, Nastassja	Nastassja Nakszynski (aka Nastassia Kinski)
KIRK, Phyllis	Phyllis Kirkegaard
KNIEVEL, Evel	Robert Craig
KNIGHT, Bob	Robert Honold

• New entry.   * Includes both living & deceased persons.   ** Sources do not always agree on spelling.

...ORIGINAL NAMES OF THE STARS...

PROFESSIONAL NAME*	BIRTH, LEGAL OR FORMER NAME**
KNIGHT, Fuzzy	J. Forrest Knight
KNIGHT, June	Margaret Rose Vallikett
KNIGHT, Ted	Tadeus Wladyslaw Konopka
KNOWLES, Patric	Reginald Lawrence Knowles
"Kodak" Girl, The	Eleanor Boardman
KORVIN, Charles	Geza Karpathi
KOSLECK, Martin	Nicolai Yoshkin
KOSTER, Henry	Hermann Kosterlitz
• KRAHLY, Hanns	(aka Hans Kraly)
• KULKY, Henry	(aka Bomber Kulkavich)
L	
LADD, Cheryl	Cheryl Stoppelmoor
LAHR, Bert	Irving Lahrheim
LAINE, Frankie	Frank Paul Lo Vecchio
LAKE, Arthur	Arthur Silverlake
LAKE, Veronica	Constance Ockleman
LaMARR, Barbara	Reatha Watson
LAMARR, Hedy	Hedwig Kiesler
LAMBERTI, Professor	Michael Lamberti
LAMOUR, Dorothy	Mary Dorothy Stanton
LANCASTER, Burt	Burton Stephen Lancaster
LANCHESTER, Elsa	Elizabeth Sullivan
LANDERS, Ann	Esther "Eppie" Pauline Friedman
LANDI, Elissa	Elisabeth-Marie-Christine Kuhnelt
LANDIS, Carole	Frances Ridste
LANDIS, David	David Landis Fritz
LANDON, Michael	Eugene Maurice Orowitz
LANE, Allan "Rocky"	Harry L. Albershart
LANE, Charles	Charles Willis Lane
LANE, Lola	Lola Mullican
• LANE, Lupino	Henry George Lupino
LANE, Priscilla	Priscilla Mullican
LANE, Rosemary	Rosemary Mullican
LANG, June	June Vlasek
lang, k.d.	Katherine Dawn Lang
LANSING, Joi	Joyce Wassmansdoff
LANSING, Robert	Robert Brown
LANTEAU, William	William Lanctot
LANTZ, Gracie	Grace Stafford
LANZA, Mario	Alfredo Arnold Cocozza
LaROCQUE, Rod	Rodrique la Rocque de la Rour
• LaRUE, Frank H.	Frank Herman La Rue
LaRUE, Jack	Gaspare Biondolillo
• LATELL, Lyle	Lyle Zeiem
LATIMORE, Frank	Frank Kline
LATZ, Elaine	Elaine Sandra Latz
LAUGHLIN, Billy "Froggy"	(aka Billy McLaughlin)
LAUREL, Stan	Arthur Stanley Jefferson
LAURIE, Piper	Rosetta Jacobs
LAVERNE, Lucille	(aka Lucille Q. Scott)
• LAWFORD, (Lady) May	May Summerville
LAWRENCE, Gertrude	Alexandre Dagmar Lawrence-Klasen
LAWRENCE, Jody	Josephine Lawrence Goddard
LAWRENCE, Steve	Sidney Leibowitz
LAWSON, Wilfrid	Wilfred Worsnop
LAWTON, Frank	Frank Lawton Mokeley
• LEANDER, Zarah	Zarah Stina Hedberg
LEE, Anna	Joanna Winnifrith
LEE, Billy	Billy Lee Schlensker
LEE, Brenda	Brenda Mae Tarpley
LEE, Bruce	Li Yuen Kam (aka Li Siu-lung)
LEE, Canada	Leonard Lionel Cornelius Canegata
LEE, Dixie	Wilma Wyatt
• LEE, Gwen	Gwendolyn Le Pinski
LEE, Gypsy Rose	Rose Louise Hovick

• New entry.   * Includes both living & deceased persons.   ** Sources do not always agree on spelling.

PROFESSIONAL NAME*	BIRTH, LEGAL OR FORMER NAME**
• LEE, Johnny "Calhoun"	John Dotson Lee, Jr.
• LEE, Lila	Augusta Appel
LEE, Michelle	Michelle Dusiak
LEE, Peggy	Norma Egstrom
• LEE, Ruth	Ruth Rhodes
LEE, Vanessa	Winifred Ruby Moule
LEEDS, Andrea	Antoinette Lees
LEIGH, Janet	Jeanette Morrison
LEIGH, Vivien	Vivien Mary Hartley
LeMOYNE, Charles	Charles J. Lemon
LENYA, Lotte	Karoline Blamauer
• LEONARD, Gus	Gustav Lerond
• LEONARD, Jack E.	Leonard Lebitsky
• LEONARD, Robert Z.	Robert Zigler Leonard
LEONARD, Sheldon	Sheldon Bershad
• LEONETTI, Tommy	Nicola Tomaso Leonetti
LE ROY, Baby	Le Roy Winnebrenner
LE ROY, Hal	John LeRoy Schotte
• LESLEY, Carole	Maureen Rippingale
• LESLIE, Gene	Leslie Eugene Halverson
LESLIE, Joan	Joan Brodell
LESTER, Bruce	Bruce Lister
LESTER, Kate	Sarah Cody
L'ESTRANGE, Dick	Gunther van Strensch
"	(aka Richard LaStrange and Dick LeStrange)
• LEVENE, Sam	Samuel Levine
LEVENSON, Sam	Samuel Levenson
LEWIS, Buddy	Morgan Lewis, Jr.
LEWIS, Edwina	Margaret Klenck
• LEWIS, Henry	Henry Jay Lewis
LEWIS, Huey	Hugh Cregg
LEWIS, Jerry	Joseph Levitch
LEWIS, Joe	Joe Lewis Barrow
LEWIS, Robert Q.	Robert Lewis (he added the "Q." at age 22)
• LEWIS, Ronald "Raan"	Ronald Dean Lewis
• LEWIS, Ted	Theodore Leopold Friedman
LEXY, Edward	Edward Gerald Little
Liberace	Wladziu Valentin Liberace (aka Walter "Lee" Liberace)
LIGHTNER, Winnie	Winifred Hanson
• LIGON, Grover G.	(aka Grover Liggon and G. G. Ligon)
LILLIE, Beatrice	Constance Sylvia Munston (Lady Peel)
LINCOLN, Elmo	Otto Elmo Linkenhelt
LINDEN, Hal	Harold Lipshitz
LINDER, Max	Gabriel Louville
LINDFORS, Viveca	Elsa Viveca Tortensdotter
LINDSAY, Margaret	Margaret Kies
• LINGEN, Theo	Franz Theodor Schmitz
• LISTON, Sonny	Charles Liston
• LITEL, John	John Beach Litel
• LITTLE, Billy	Billy Rhodes
• LITTLE, Bozo	John F. Pizzo
Little Rascals, The	(see "Our Gang")
LITVAK, Anatole	Michael Anatole Litvak
LIVINGSTON, Robert (Bob)	Robert Randall
LIVINGSTONE, Mary	Sadye Marks
• LLOYD, Harold	Harold Clayton Lloyd
• LOCHER, Felix	Felix Maurice Locher
LOCKHART, Kathleen	Kathleen Arthur
LOCKWOOD, Alexander	Aleksander Wyrwicz
LOCKWOOD, Margaret	Margaret Day
LODER, John	John Lowe
LOM, Herbert	Herbert Charles Angelo Kuchacevich ze Schluderpacheru
LOMBARD, Carole	Jane Alice Peters
• LOMBARDI, Vince	Vincent Thomas Lombardi
LOMBARDO, Guy	Gaetano Albert Lombardo

...ORIGINAL NAMES OF THE STARS...

PROFESSIONAL NAME*	BIRTH, LEGAL OR FORMER NAME**
LONDON, Julie	Julie Peck
LONDON, Tom	Leonard Clapham
• LOPEZ, Vincent	Vincent Joseph Lopez
LORD, Jack	John Joseph Ryan
• LORDS, Traci	Nora Louise Kuzma
LOREN, Sophia	Sofia Scicolone
• LORNE, Marion	Marion Lorne MacDougal
LORRAINE, Harry	Harry Wolf
LORRAINE, Lillian	Mary Ann Brennan
• LORRAINE, Louise	Louise Escovar
LORRE, Peter	Laszlo Loewenstein
LORRING, Joan	Magdalen Ellis
LOSCH, Tilly	Ottila Losch
LOSEY, Joseph	Joseph Walton Losey
LOSS, Joe	Joshua Alexander Loss
• LOUIS, Joe "Brown Bomber"	Joseph Lewis Barrow
LOUISE, Anita	Anita Louise Fremault
LOVE, Bessie	Juanita Horton
LOVE, Montagu	(aka Montague Love)
• LOVELY, Louise	Louise Corbasse
LOWERY, Robert	Robert Lowery Hanke
LOWRY, Judith	Judith Ives
LOY, Myrna	Myrna Williams
• LUCAN, Arthur	Arthur Towle
LUCE, Clare Boothe	Ann Clare Boothe
• LUFKIN, Sam	Samuel William Lufkin
LUGOSI, Bela	Bela Lugosi Blasko
LUKAS, Paul	Pal Lukacs
• LUNCEFORD, Jimmy	James Melvin Lunceford
• LUPINO, Wallace	(aka Wallace Lane)
• LUTHER, Ann	(aka Anna Luther)
LUTTRINGER, Al	Alfonse Luttringer
LYEL, Viola	Violet Watson
LYNN, Diana	Dolly Loehr
LYNN, Jeffrey	Ragnar Godfrey Lind
• LYNN, Sharon	D'Auvergne Sharon Lindsay
• LYNN, (Dame) Vera	Vera Welch
LYONS, Fred	Fred F. Leyva
LYS, Lya	Natalia Lyecht
M	
• MABLEY, Jackie "Moms"	Loretta Mary Aiken
MacGRAW, Ali	Alice MacGraw
• MACK, Cactus	Thomas McPheeters
MACK, Charles E.	Charles E. Sellers
MACK, Helen	Helen McDougall
• MACK, Hughie	Hugh McGowan
MACK, Marion	Joey McCreery
MacKENNA, Kenneth	Leo Mielziner, Jr.
MacKENZIE, Gisele	Marie Marguerite Louise Gisele LaFleche
MacLAINE, Shirley	Shirley Maclean Beaty
MacMURRAY, Fred	Frederick Martin MacMurray
• MACRAE, Duncan	John Duncan Graham Macrae
MADISON, Guy	Robert Ozell Moseley
MADISON, Noel	Nathaniel Moscovitch
Madonna	Madonna Louise Veronica Ciccone
MAHONEY, Jock	Jacques O'Mahoney
MAILES, Charles H.	Charles Hill Mailes
MAIN, Marjorie	Mary Tomlinson (Krebs)
• MAITLAND, Ruth	Ruth Erskine
MAJORS, Lee	Harvey Lee Yeary, 2nd
MALDEN, Karl	Mladen Sekulovich
MALONE, Dorothy	Dorothy Maloney
MALTBY, H. F.	Henry F. Maltby
MALYON, Eily	Eily Sophie Lees-Craston
MANDER, Miles	Lionel Mander

• New entry.   * Includes both living & deceased persons.   ** Sources do not always agree on spelling.

PROFESSIONAL NAME*	BIRTH, LEGAL OR FORMER NAME**
MANKIEWICZ, Joseph L.	Joseph Leo Mankiewicz
MANN, Anthony	Emil Bundsmann
• MANN, Billy	William B. Mann
MANN, Daniel	Daniel Chugerman
MANN, Hank	David W. Lieberman
MANNERS, David	Rauff de Ryther Duan Acklom
MANNING, Irene	Inez Harvet
MANSFIELD, Jayne	Vera Jane Palmer
MANSFIELD, Martha	Martha Ehrlich
MANTZ, Paul	Albert Paul Mantz
MARA, Adele	Adelaida Delgado
MARCH, Fredric	Ernest Frederick McIntyre Bickel
MARCIANO, "Rocky"	Rocco Francis Marchegiano
Margo	Maria Marguerita Guadelupe Boldao y Castilla
MARLOWE, Hugh	Hugh Hipple
MARLY, Florence	Hana Smekalova
MARRIOTT, Moore	George Thomas Moore-Marriott
MARSH, Carol	Norma Simpson
MARSH, Garry	Leslie March Gerahty
MARSH, Mae	Mary Warne Marsh
• MARSH, Marguerite	Margaret Marsh (aka Marguerite Loveridge)
MARSH, Marion	Violet Krauth
MARSH, Tiger Joe	Joseph Marusich
MARSHALL, Brenda	Ardis Ankerson Gaines
MARSHALL, E. G.	Everett G. Marshall
MARSHALL, Peter	Pierre LaCock
MARSHALL, Tully	Tully Marshall Phillips
• MARSON, Aileen	Aileen Pitt Marson
MARTIN, Chris-Pin	Ysabel Chris-Pin Martin Piaz
MARTIN, Dean	Dino Paul Crocetti
• MARTIN, Ernest H.	Ernest Markowitz
MARTIN, Ross	Martin Rosenblatt
MARTIN, Tony	Alvin Maris
MARTON, Andrew	Endre Marton
MARTON, Andrew	Endre Marton
Marx Brothers, The	Leonard "Chico" Marx (eldest)
"	Adolph (aka Arthur) "Harpo" Marx
"	Milton "Gummo" Marx
"	Julius "Groucho" Marx
"	Herbert "Zeppo" Marx (youngest)
• MARX, Samuel "Frenchie"	Simon Marx
MASCHWITZ, Eric	Holt Marvell
MASON, Dan	Dan Grassman
• MASON, Mary	Betty Ann Jenks
• MASON, Shirley	Leonie Flugrath
MASSEY, Ilona	Ilona Hajmassy
MATTHAU, Walter	Walter Matuschanskayasky
• MATTHEWS, A. E.	Alfred Edward Matthews
• MATTO, Sesto	Sisto Mata
• MAUGHAM, W. Somerset	William Somerset Maugham
• MAURICE, Mary "Mother"	Mary Birch
MAXWELL, Lois	Lois Hooker
MAXWELL, Marilyn	Marvel Maxwell
MAY, Joe	Joseph Mandel
MAYER, Louis B.	Louis Burt Mayer
MAYO, Virginia	Virginia Jones
MAZURKI, Mike	Mikhail Mazuruski (Mazurski)
McCALLISTER, Lon	Herbert Alonzo McCallister
McCAMBRIDGE, Mercedes	Carlotta Mercedes McCambridge
McCLURE, Greg	Dale Easton
• McCORMICK, Merrill	William Merrill McCormick
• McCOY, Gertrude	Gertrude Lyon
McCOY, Tim	Timothy J. McCoy
McCRAY, Helen Mary	Helen Mary Keating
• McDANIEL, Sam "Deacon"	Samuel Rufus McDaniel

...ORIGINAL NAMES OF THE STARS...

PROFESSIONAL NAME*	BIRTH, LEGAL OR FORMER NAME**
McDEVITT, Ruth	Ruth Thane Shoecraft
McDONALD, Marie	Marie Frye
McDOWALL, Roddy	Andrew Roderick McDowall
• McDOWELL, Claire	(aka Claire MacDowell)
McGEE, Fibber	Jim Jordan
McGEE, Molly	Marion Jordan
McGILL, Moyna	Moyna McIldowie
• McGIVER, John	George Morris
McGOWAN, J. P. "Jack"	John P. McGowan
• McGRAW, Charles	Charles Butters
• McGREGOR, Malcolm	(aka Malcolm MacGregor)
McHUGH, Jack	John McHugh
McHUGH, Matt	Mathew O. McHugh
McKAY, George W.	George W. Reuben
• McKEE, Lafe	Lafayette Stocking McKee
McLEOD, Norman Z.	Norman Zenos McLeod
• McLEOD, Tex	Alexander D'Avila McLeod
McNALLY, Stephen	Horace Vincent McNally
McNAUGHTON, Gus	Augustus Howard
• McQUEEN, "Butterfly"	Thelma McQueen
McQUEEN, Steve	Terence Stephen McQueen
• McVEY, Lucille	(aka Mrs. Sidney Drew and June Morrow)
MEADE, Claire	Marguerite Fields
MEDFORD, Kay	Kathleen Patricia Regan
MEEKER, Ralph	Ralph Rathgeber
• MEGOWAN, Don	(aka Dan Megowan)
MEINS, Gus	Gustave Meins
MELCHIOR, Lauritz	Lebrecht Hommel
• MELESH, Alex	Alexander Melesher
MELL, Marisa	Marlies Moitzi
• MENJOU, Henri	Henry Arthur Menjou
MENZIES, William	William Cameron Menzies
MERANDE, Doro	Dora Matthews
MERCER, Johnny	John Herndon Mercer
MERCOURI, Melina	Maria Amalia Mercouri
MERCURY, Freddie	Frederick Bulsara
MEREDITH, Iris	Iris Meredith Berlin
• MEREDYTH, Bess	Helen MacGlashan
MERLO, Tony	Anthony Merlo
MERMAN, Ethel	Ethel Zimmerman
MERRALL, Mary	Mary Lloyd
• MERSON, Billy	William Henry Thompson
MERTON, John	John Merton La Varre
MERVYN, William	William Mervyn Pickwood
• MESSENGER, Buddy	Melvin Joe Messinger
MICHAEL, Ralph	Ralph Champion Shotter
MIDDLETON, Guy	Guy Middleton-Powell
MIDDLETON, Robert	Samuel G. Messer
MILES, Vera	Vera Ralston
MILFORD, Gene	Arthur Eugene Milford
MILLAND, Ray	Reginald Truscott-Jones
MILLER, Ann	Lucille Ann Collier
• MILLER, Carl	Carlton Miller
MILLER, Glenn	Alton Glenn Miller
• MILLER, Lorraine	(aka Lorraine Young)
MILLER, Marilyn	Mary Lynn Reynolds
• MILLER, Martin	Rudolph Muller
• MILLER, Max	Thomas Sargent
• MILLER, Walter C.	Walter Corwin Miller
• MILLER, W. Christy	William Christy Miller
• Mills Brothers, The	Herbert Mills
• "	Harry Mills
• "	Donald Mills
• "	John Mills, Jr.
• MILOS, Milos	Milos Milosevic

• New entry. * Includes both living & deceased persons. ** Sources do not always agree on spelling.

...ORIGINAL NAMES OF THE STARS...

PROFESSIONAL NAME*	BIRTH, LEGAL OR FORMER NAME**
MINEO, Sal	Salvatore Mineo, Jr.
MINER, Tony	Worthington C. Miner
MINTER, Mary Miles	Juliet Shelby
MINTZ, Eli	Edward Satz
MIRANDA, Carmen	Maria de Carmo Miranda de Cunha
• Miroslava	Miroslava Stern
MITCHELL, Joni	Roberta Joan Anderson
MIX, Tom	Thomas Edwin Mix
Moe (3 Stooges)	Moses Howard (Horowitz)
Molly McGee	Marion Jordan
Moms	Jackie Mabley
• MONCRIES, Edward	(aka Edward Moncrief)
MONROE, Marilyn	Norma Jean Mortenson (later Baker)
MONTAGUE, Monte	Walter Montague
• MONTANA, Lewis "Bull"	Luigi Montagna
MONTAND, Yves	Yvo Livi (aka Ivo Livi)
MONTEZ, Lola	Eliza Gilbert
MONTEZ, Maria	Maria Africa Antonia Gracia Vidal da Santo Silas
MONTGOMERY, Douglass	Robert Douglass Montgomery
MONTGOMERY, George	George Montgomery Letz
MONTGOMERY, Robert	Henry Montgomery
MOODY, Ron	Ronald Moodnick
MOORE, Clara	Clara Eloise Moore
MOORE, Colleen	Kathleen Morrison
MOORE, Demi	Demi Guynes
MOORE, Dickie	John Richard Moore
MOORE, Eleanor	(aka Eleanor Merry)
MOORE, Garry	Thomas Garrison Morfit
MOORE, Terry	Helen Koford
• MOOREHEAD, Agnes	Agnes Robertson Moorehead
• MORAN, Frank	Frank Charles Moran
• MORAN, George	George Searcy
MORAN, Jackie	John E. Moran
MORAN, Lois	Lois Darlington Dowling
• MORAN, Polly	Pauline Theresa Moran
MORECAMBE, Eric	John Eric Bartholemew
MORELL, André	André Mesritz
MORENO, Rita	Rosita Dolores Alverio
MORGAN, Dennis	Stanley Morner
MORGAN, Frank	Francis Wupperman
MORGAN, Gene	Eugene Schwartzkopf
MORGAN, Harry	Harry Bratsburg
MORGAN, Henry	Henry Lerner von Ost, Jr.
• MORGAN, Lee	Raymond Lee Morgan
MORGAN, Ralph	Raphael Kuhner Wupperman
MORISON, Patricia	Eileen Morrison
• MORLAY, Gaby	Blanche Fumoleau
MORLEY, Karen	Mildred Linton
MORRIS, Chester	John Chester Morris
• MORRIS, Johnny	John Morris Erickson
MORRIS, Philip	Francis Charles Philip Morris
MORRIS, Wayne	Bert de Wayne Morris
MORRISON, Ernie	Frederic Ernest Morrison
• MORRISON, James	James Woods Morrison
MORRISON, Lou	Louis Morrison
• MORRISSEY, Betty	(aka Betty Morrisey)
MORROS, Boris	Boris Milhailovitch
MORROW, Doretta	Doretta Marano
MOSCOVITCH, Maurice	Morris Maaskoff
• MOSER, Hans	Jean Juliet
MOSTEL, Zero	Samuel Joel Mostel
Mr. Green Jeans	Hugh Brannum
Mr. Magoo	voice by Jim Backus
• MUDIE, Leonard	Leonard Mudie Cheetham
MUELLER, Cookie	Dorothy Mueller

...ORIGINAL NAMES OF THE STARS...

PROFESSIONAL NAME*	BIRTH, LEGAL OR FORMER NAME**
• MUELLER, Wolfgang	(aka Wolfgang Muller)
• MULLER, Renate	(aka Renate Mueller)
MUNI, Paul	Muni Weisenfreund
MUNSON, Ona	Ona Wolcott
• MURDOCK, Ann	Irene Coleman
MURPHY, Audie	Audie Leon Murphy
• MURPHY, Edna	Elizabeth Edna Murphy
MURRAY, Arthur	Moses Teichman
• MURRAY, Bobby	Robert Hayes Murray
MURRAY, Jan	Murray Janofsky
MURRAY, Mae	Marie Adrienne Koenig
MURRAY-MAZWI, Mark	Ralph Holland Murray
• Musidora	Jeanne Roques
N	
NAGEL, Anne	Ann Dolan
NAISH, J. Carrol	Joseph Carrol Naish
NAISMITH, Laurence	Laurence Johnson
NALDER, Reggie	Alfred Reginald Natzler
NALDI, Nita	Anita Donna Dooley
NAPIER, Alan	Alan Napier-Clavering
NAPIER, Diana	Molly Ellis
NARES, Owen	Owen Nares Ramsay
• NASH, Mary	Mary Ryan
• NAZIMOVA, Alla	Alla Lavendera
• NAZZARI, Amedeo	Salvatore Amedeo Buffa
NEAGLE, Anna	Marjorie Robertson
• NEDELL, Bernard	Bernard Jay Nedell
NEFF, Hildegarde	Hildegarde Knef
NEGRI, Pola	Apolina Mathias-Chalupec
NELSON, Gene	Gene Berg
NELSON, Harriet	Harriet Louise Snyder
	(aka Peggy Lou Snyder and Harriet Hilliard)
NELSON, Ozzie	Oswald Nelson
NELSON, Rick (Ricky)	Eric Hilliard Nelson
• NERVO, Jimmy	James Nervo
NESBITT, Frank M.	Frank McCormick Nesbitt
New Kids On The Block	Jonathan Knight
"	Jordan Knight
"	Joe McIntyre
"	Donnie Wahlberg
"	Danny Wood
NEWMAN, Scott	Allan Scott Newman (aka William Scott)
NEY, Marie	Marie Fix
NIBLO, Fred	Federico Nobile
NICHOLS, Barbara	Barbara Marie Nicheraeur
NICHOLS, Dandy	Daisy Nichols
NICHOLS, Mike	Michael Igor Peschowsky
NICHOLS, Red	Ernest Loring Nichols
Nico	Christa Paffgen (aka Christa Pavlovski and Nico Ozsak)
• NIELSEN, Asta	(aka Die Asta)
NILSSON, Anna Q.	Anna Querentia Nilsson
NILSSON, Harry	Harry Edward Nelson, III
NIXON, Pat	Thelma Catherine Ryan
NOLAN, Mary	Mary Imogene Robertson
NOONAN, Tommy	Tommy Noon
NORMAN, Josephine	Josephine Arrich
NORMAND, Mabel	Mabel Fortescue
NORRIS, Chuck	Carlos Ray
NORTH, Joe	Joseph B. North
NORTH, Sheree	Dawn Bethel
• NORTON, Barry	Alfredo Biraben
NORTON, Jack	Mortimer J. Naughton
• NORWOOD, Eille	Anthony Brett
NOVAK, Kim	Marilyn Novak
NOVARRO, Ramon	Jose Ramon Samaniegos

• New entry. * Includes both living & deceased persons.   ** Sources do not always agree on spelling.

PROFESSIONAL NAME*	BIRTH, LEGAL OR FORMER NAME**
NOVELLO, Ivor	*David Ivor Novello*
O	
OAKIE, Jack	*Lewis Delaney Offield*
OAKLAND, Vivien	*Vivian Anderson*
OBERON, Merle	*Estelle Merle O'Brien Thompson*
O'BRIAN, Hugh	*Hugh Krampke*
O'BRIEN, Dave	*David Barclay*
O'BRIEN, Margaret	*Angela Maxine O'Brien*
O'BRIEN, Pat	*William Joseph O'Brien, Jr.*
O'BRIEN, Tom	*Thomas Everett O'Brien*
O'DAY, Molly	*Laverne Williamson*
O'DONNELL, Cathy	*Ann Steeley*
• OGLE, Charles	*Charles Stanton Ogle*
O'HANLON, George	*George Rice*
O'HARA, Maureen	*Maureen Fitzsimons*
O'HARA, Shirley	*Shirley O'Hara-Nolan*
O'HARE, Brad	*Steven Bradford O'Hare*
O'KEEFE, Dennis	*Edward 'Bud' Flanagan*
O'KEEFE, Win	*James Winston O'Keefe*
OLAND, Werner	*Wernur Olund*
OLCOTT, Sidney	*John S. Alcott*
• OLDFIELD, Barney	*Berna Eli*
OLIVER, Edna May	*Edna May Cox Nutter*
OLIVER, Susan	*Charlotte Gercke*
OLIVER, Sy	*Melvin James Oliver*
OLIVER, Vic	*Victor von Samek*
OLMSTEAD, Gertrude	*Gertrude Olmsted*
OLSEN, Ole	*John Sigvard Olsen*
• O'MALLEY, Pat	*Patrick H. O'Malley, Jr.*
O'NEAL, Anne	*Patsy Ann Epperson*
O'NEAL, Frederick	*Frederick Douglass O'Neal*
O'NEAL, Ryan	*Patrick Ryan O'Neal*
O'NEIL, Sally	*Virginia Louise Noonan (aka Chotsie Noonan)*
O'NEILL, Maire	*Maire Allgood*
Oomph Girl, The	*Ann Sheridan*
OPHULS, Max	*Max Oppenheimer*
ORLANDO, Don	*Orlando Biogio Ferrara*
ORLANDO, Tony	*Michael Anthony Orlando Cassavitis*
ORLOFF, Thelma	*Thelma Joel*
• O'ROURKE, Brefni	*(aka Brefni O'Rorke)*
ORTES, Armand	*Armand Francis Ortes*
OSBORN, Lyn	*Clair Lynn Osborn*
OSBORNE, John	*John James Osborne*
OSBOURNE, Jefferson	*Jefferson W. Schroeder*
• OSBOURNE, Lennie "Bud"	*(aka Miles Osborne)*
OSCAR, Henry	*Henry Oscar Wale*
O'SHEA, Michael	*Edward Michael O'Shea*
• Osmond Brothers	*Alan Osmond*
• "	*Wayne Osmond*
• "	*Merrill Osmond*
• "	*Jay Osmond*
• OSWALDA, Ossi	*Oswalda Staglich*
Our Gang (aka "The Little Rascals" on TV)	*Alfalfa (Carl Switzer)*
"	*Baby Patsy*
"	*Buckwheat (William Henry Thomas, Jr.)*
"	*Butch (Tommy Bond)*
"	*Chubby (Norman Chaney)*
"	*Darla Hood*
"	*Dickie Moore (John Richard Moore)*
"	*Echo (Dorothy Betty Jean DeBorba)*
"	*Farina (Allen Clayton Hoskins, Jr.)*
"	*Froggy (Billy Laughlin)*
"	*Harold Switzer*
"	*Harry Spear*
"	*Jackie Condon*

...ORIGINAL NAMES OF THE STARS...

PROFESSIONAL NAME*	BIRTH, LEGAL OR FORMER NAME**
Our Gang (Cont'd)	Jackie Cooper
"	Jackie Davis (John H. Davis)
"	Jay R. Smith
"	Jean Darling (Dorothy Jean LeVake)
"	Joe Cobb (Joe Frank Cobb)
"	Johnny Downs (John Morey Downs)
"	Mary Ann Jackson
"	Mary Kornman
"	Mickey Daniels (Richard Daniels, Jr.)
"	Mickey Gubitosi (now Robert Blake)
"	Mildred Jean Kornman
"	Pete, the Pup
"	Porky Lee (Eugene Lee)
"	Scotty Beckett
"	Shirley Jean Rickert
"	Spanky (George McFarland)
"	Stymie (Matthew Beard, Jr.)
"	Sunshine Sammy (Ernie Morrison)
"	Waldo (Darwood Kenneth Smith)
"	Wally Albright (Walton Albright, Jr.)
"	Wheezer (Bobby Hutchins)
OWEN, Bill	Bill Rowbotham
OWEN, Reginald	John Reginald Owen
• OWEN, Seena	Signe Auen
• OWENS, Jesse	James Cleveland Owens
P	
PACINO, Al	Alfredo Pacino
• PADULA, Vincent	Vincente Padula
PAGE, Gale	Sally Rutter
PAGE, Jean	Lucile Beatrice O'Hair
PAGE, Patti	Clara Ann Fowler
PAGE, Paul	Campbell U. Hicks
PAGET, Debra	Debralee Griffin
• PAGLIERO, Marcello	(aka Marcel Pagliero)
PAIGE, Janis	Donna Mae Tjaden
PAIGE, Robert	John Arthur Page
PALANCE, Jack	Vladimir (later, Walter) Palaniuk
PALMER, Gregg	Palmer Lee
PALMER, Lilli	Lilli Peiser
• PALMER, Patricia	(aka Margaret Gibson)
• PAM, Anita	Anita Friedheim Davidson
PANZER, Paul Wolfgang	Paul Panzerbeiter
PARHAM, Ernie	Ernest R. Parham
PARIS, Freddie	Freddie Paris-Smith
• PARIS, Manuel	Manuel R. Conesa
• PARKER, Barnett	William Barnett Parker
PARKER, Cecil	Cecil Schwabe
• PARKER, Frank "Pinky"	Franklin Parker
PARKER, Jean	Lois Mae Greene
PARKER, Suzy	Cecelia Parker
PARKS, Bert	Bert Jacobson
PARKS, Larry	Samuel Kleusman Lawrence Parks
Parkyakarkus	Harry Einstein
PARROTT, James	James Gibbons Parrott
• PARSONS, Louella	Louella Oettinger
PATCH, Wally	Walter Vinicombe
PATRICK, Gail	Margaret Fitzpatrick
• PATRICK, Nigel	Nigel Wemyss
PATTERSON, Hank	Elmer C. Patterson
PAUL, Les	Lester Polsfuss
PAVAN, Marisa	Marisa Pierangeli
• PAXINOU, Katina	Katina Konstantopoulou
PAYNE, Lou	William Lou Payne
• PAYTON, Claude	Claude Duval Payton (aka Claude Peyton)
Peaches	Libby Holman

...ORIGINAL NAMES OF THE STARS...

PROFESSIONAL NAME*	BIRTH, LEGAL OR FORMER NAME**
• PEARCE, George C.	(aka George Pierce)
• PEARCE, Peggy	(aka Viola Barry)
PEARL, Minnie	Sarah Ophelia Colley Cannon
• PEARSON, Drew	Andrew Russell Pearson
PECK, Gregory	Eldred Gregory Peck
PEIL, Edward Jr.	Charles Edward Peil, Jr. (aka Johnny Jones)
• PEIL, Edward Sr.	Charles Edward Peil, Sr.
• PENN, Leonard	Leonard Monson Penn
PENNER, Joe	Joe Pinter
PEPPER, Buddy	Jack R. Starkey
PERCIVAL, Walter C.	Charles David Lingenfelter
PERKINS, Marlin	Richard Marlin Perkins
PERKINS, Tony	Anthony Perkins
PERREAU, Gigi	Ghislaine Perreau-Saussine
• PERRY, Antoinette	(aka Annette Perry)
PETERS, Bernadette	Bernadette Lazzaro
PETERS, Roberta	Roberta Peterman
PETERS, Susan	Suzanne Carnahan
PETRIE, Hay	David Hay Petrie
PETROVA, Olga	(aka Muriel Harding)
PETTYJOHN, Angelique	(aka Heaven St. John and Angelique)
PHILLIPS, Barney	Bernard Phillips
PHIPPS, Sally	Byrnece Beutler
PHOENIX, Pat	Patricia Mansfield
PIAF, Edith	Edith Gassion
PICKENS, Slim	Louis Bert Lindley
PICKFORD, Jack	Jack Smith
PICKFORD, Lottie	Lottie Smith
PICKFORD, Mary	Gladys Mary Smith
PIERCE, Big Jim	James H. Pierce
PINZA, Ezio	Fortunato Pinza
• PLUMB, E. Hay	Edward Hay Plumb
• POFF, Lon	Alonzo M. Poff
POHLMANN, Eric	Erich Pohlmann
POLLAR, Gene	Joseph C. Pohler
• POLLARD, Daphne	Daphne Trott
POLLARD, Harry "Snub"	Harold Fraser
• POLO, Eddie	Edward P. Polo
PONS, Lily	Alice Josephine Pons
Porky (of "Our Gang")	Eugene Lee
POTAMKIN, Luba	Luba Chaiken
POTTER, H. C.	Henry Codman Potter
• POWELL, Dick	Richard E. Powell
POWELL, Jane	Suzanne Burce
POWELL, Lee B.	Lee Berrian Powell
POWELL, Russ	Russell J. Powell
POWER, F. Tyrone	Frederick Tyrone Power
• POWER, Paul	Luther Vestergard
POWER, Tyrone	Tyrone Edmund Power
POWERS, Mala	Mary Ellen Powers
POWERS, Stefanie	Stefania Zofia Ferderkievicz
• PRATHER, Lee	Oscar Lee Prather
PRENTISS, Paula	Paula Ragusa
PRESLEY, Elvis	Elvis Aron Presley
PRESTON, Robert	Robert Preston Meservey
PREVOST, Marie	Marie Bickford Dunn
PRICE, Dennis	Dennistoun Franklyn John Rose-Price
• PRICE, Kate	Kate Duffy
• PRICE, Nancy	Lillian Nancy Maude
Prince	Prince Rogers Nelson
PRINGLE, Aileen	Aileen Bisbee
• PRINTEMPS, Yvonne	Yvonne Wigniolle
PRINZE, Freddie	Freddie Preutzel
• PRIOR, Herbert	(aka Herbert Pryor)
PROVENZA, Sal	Salvatore D. Provenza

• New entry.   * Includes both living & deceased persons.   ** Sources do not always agree on spelling.

PROFESSIONAL NAME*	BIRTH, LEGAL OR FORMER NAME**
PRUD'HOMME, George	(aka George Pembroke)
PURDELL, Reginald	Reginald Grasdorf
Q	
QUALEN, John	John Oleson
Queen:	Brian May (guitar)
"	Roger Taylor (drums)
"	John Deacon (bass)
"	Freddie Mercury (vocal)
R	
RA, Sun	(aka Herman "Sonny" Blount and Sonny Bourke)
• RABAGLIATI, Alberto	Alberto Rabagliati-Vinata
• RAEBURN, Frances	Frances Hedrick Kurstin
RAFFERTY, Chips	John Goffage
RAFFETTO, Michael	Elwyn Creighton Raffetto
• RAFT, George	George Ranft
RAGLAND, Rags	John Ragland
• RAIMU, Jules	Jules Muraire
• RAKER, Lorin	(aka Lorrin Raker)
• RALEIGH, Saba	(aka Isabel Ellissen)
RALPH, Jessie	Jessie Ralph Chambers
RAMAGE, Cecil	Cecil Beresford Ramage
RAMBO, Dirk	Orman Ray Rambo
• RAMBOVA, Natacha	Winifred Shaunessy (aka Winifred Hudnut)
• RAMSEY, John Nelson	(aka Neilson Ramsey)
• RAMSEY-HILL, C. S.	(aka Ramsey Hill)
• RAND, Sally	Helen Gould Beck
RANDALL, Addison "Jack"	Addison Owen Randall
RANDALL, Tony	Leonard Rosenberg
RANDLE, Frank	Arthur McEvoy
RANDOLPH, Anders	Anders Randolf
RANKIN, Arthur	Arthur Davenport
• RASP, Fritz	Heinrich Rasp
• RATCLIFFE, E. J.	(aka E. J. Radcliffe)
RATHBONE, Basil	Philip St. John Basil Rathbone
• RATTENBERRY, Harry	(aka Harry Rattenbury)
RAY, Aldo	Aldo daRe
• RAY, Charles	Charles Edgar Alfred Ray
RAY, Nicholas	Raymond N. Kienzle
RAY, Rene	Irene Creese
RAY, Ted	Charles Olden
RAYE, Carol	Kathleen Corkrey
RAYE, Martha	Margaret Yvonne Reed
RAYMOND, Gene	Raymond Guion
• RAYMOND, Jack (d. 1951)	George Feder (U.S. actor/director)
• RAYMOND, Jack (d. 1953)	John Caines (British actor/director/producer)
RAYMOND, Paula	Paula Ramona Wright
• RAYMOND, Royal	Royal Aaron Raymond
• RAZETTO, Stella	(aka Stella Le Saint)
Red	Boyd F. Morgan
REDFORD, Robert	Charles Robert Redford, Jr.
REDWING, Rodd	Roderick Redwing
REED, Alan	(aka Teddy Bergman)
REED, Carol	Mary Walther
REED, Donna	Donna Belle Mullenger
• REED, George H.	George Henry Reed
REED, Robert	John Robert Rietz, Jr.
REESE, Della	Delloreese Patricia Early
REEVES, George	George Besselo
REEVES, Jim	James Travis Reeves
REGAS, Pedro	Panagiotis Regas
RENALDO, Duncan	Renault Renaldo Duncan
Renie	Irene Brouillet
• REPP, Stafford	Stafford Alois Repp
• RETTIG, Tommy	Thomas Noel Rettig
REVIER, Dorothy	Doris Velegra

...ORIGINAL NAMES OF THE STARS...

PROFESSIONAL NAME*	BIRTH, LEGAL OR FORMER NAME**
REY, Fernando	*Fernando Casado Arambillet*
REYNOLDS, Burt	*Burton M. Reynolds, Jr.*
• REYNOLDS, Craig	*Hugh Enfield*
REYNOLDS, Debbie	*Marie Frances Reynolds*
REYNOLDS, Marjorie	*Marjorie Goodspeed*
REYNOLDS, Peter	*Peter Horrocks*
• REYNOLDS, Vera	*Vera Norma Reynolds*
RHODES, Billie	*Levita Axlerod*
• RICE, Frank	*Frank Thomas Rice*
• RICE, Jack	*Jack Clifford Rice*
RICH, Buddy	*Bernard Rich*
RICH, Irene	*Irene Luther*
RICHARD, Cliff	*Harold Webb*
• RICHARDS, Addison	*Addison Whitaker Richards, Jr.*
RICHARDS, Kurt	*Jonathan Kidd*
• RICHARDSON, Jiles	*Jiles Perry Richardson (aka "The Big Bopper")*
RICHETTS, Tom	*Thomas Richetts*
RICHMOND, Kane	*Frederick W. Bowditch*
• RICKARD, Tex	*George L. Rickard*
RIDGELEY, John	*John Huntingdon Rea*
RIDGES, Stanley	*Stanley Charles Ridges*
RIGBY, Edward	*Edward Coke*
RINALDO, Fred	*Frederic I. Rinaldo*
• RINDT, Jochen	*Karl Jochen Rindt*
RIPLEY, Robert L.	*Robert LeRoy Ripley*
RISDON, Elizabeth	*Elizabeth Evans*
• RITCHARD, Cyril	*Cyril Trimnell-Ritchard*
RITTER, John	*Jonathan Ritter*
RITTER, Tex	*Maurice Woodward Ritter*
Ritz Brothers, The	*Al Joachim (aka Al Ritz)*
"	*Jimmy Joachim (aka Jimmy Ritz)*
"	*Harry Joachim (aka Harry Ritz)*
RIVERA, Chita	*Delores Conchita Figuero del Rivero*
RIVERA, Geraldo	*Miguel Rivera*
RIVERS, Joan	*Joan Sandra Molinsky*
• ROBERTS, Edith	*Edith Josephine Roberts*
ROBERTS, Lynne	*Theda Mae Roberts (aka Mary Hart)*
ROBERTS, Oral	*Granville Oral Roberts*
ROBEY, George	*George Edward Wade*
ROBINSON, Edward G.	*Emmanuel Goldenberg*
• ROBINSON, Frances	*Marion Frances Ladd*
• ROBINSON, Jackie	*Jack Roosevelt Robinson*
ROBSON, May	*Mary Robison*
ROC, Patricia	*Felicia Riese*
Rochester	*Eddie Anderson*
• ROCKNE, Knute	*Knute Kenneth Rockne*
ROGERS, Buddy	*Charles Rogers*
ROGERS, Ginger	*Virginia Katherine McMath*
ROGERS, Jean	*Eleanor Lovegren*
ROGERS, Roy	*Leonard Slye*
ROGERS, Will	*William Penn Adair Rogers*
ROLAND, Gilbert	*Luis Antonio Damaso de Alonso*
• ROMAGNOLI, Margaret	*Margaret O'Neill*
ROMANOFF, Michael	*Prince Michael Alexandrovich Dimitri Oblensky*
ROME, Stewart	*Septimus William Ryott*
ROMNEY, Edana	*Edana Rubenstein*
ROONEY, Mickey	*Joe Yule, Jr.*
• ROOSEVELT, Buddy	*Kenneth Sanderson*
• ROSAY, Françoise	*Françoise Bandy de Naleche*
• ROSCOE, Alan	*Albert Roscoe*
ROSE, Blanche	*Blanche Starr*
ROSEN, Phil	*Philip E. Rosen*
ROSENBLOOM, Maxie	*Maxie Rosenblum*
ROSING, Bodil	*Bodil Hammerich*
ROSMER, Milton	*Arthur Milton Lunt*

...ORIGINAL NAMES OF THE STARS...

PROFESSIONAL NAME*	BIRTH, LEGAL OR FORMER NAME**
ROSS, Lanny	*Lancelot Patrick Ross*
ROSS, Lenny	*Leonardo Del Rossi*
ROSS, Shirley	*Shirley Dolan Blum*
ROSSITTO, Angelo	*Angelo Salvatore Rossitto*
• ROTH, Gene	*(aka Gene Stutenroth)*
• ROTH, Lillian	*Lillian Rustein*
ROUNESVILLE, Robert	*(aka Robert Field)*
ROURKE, Mickey	*Philip André Rourke*
ROWE, Fanny	*Frances Rowe*
ROWLANDS, Gena	*Virginia Rowlands*
• ROYCE, Julian	*Julian Gardener*
• RUBENS, Alma	*Alma Smith*
• RUGGLES, Charles	*Charles Sherman Ruggles*
RUMANN, Sig	*Siegfried Albon Rumann*
• RUNYON, Damon	*Alfred Damon Runyon*
RUSSELL, Andy	*Andres Rabago*
RUSSELL, Don	*Samuel H. Borgesi*
RUSSELL, Jane	*Ernestine Jane Russell*
RUSSELL, Lillian	*Helen Leonard*
RUTH, Babe	*George Herman Ruth*
RYAN, Irene	*Irene Nablett*
RYAN, Sheila	*Katherine Elizabeth McLaughlin*
RYDER, Winona	*Winona Laura Horowitz*
🖚	
Sabu	*Sabu Dastagir*
• SAGE, Willard	*James Willard Sage*
SAKALL, S. Z.	*Eugene Gero Szakall*
SALE, Chic	*Charles Sale*
SALES, Soupy	*Milton Hines*
• SANDERS, Al	*Albert W. Gay, Jr.*
• SANDFORD, Tiny	*Stanley J. Sandford*
SANTELL, Alfred	*Alfred Allen Santell*
SANTLEY, Fred	*Frederic Santley*
SANTLEY, Joseph	*Joseph Mansfield*
• SAPPINGTON, Fay	*Harriet Richardson*
SARANDON, Susan	*Susan Tomaling*
SARGENT, Dick	*Richard Cox*
SARONY, Leslie	*Leslie Frye*
Satchmo	*Louis Armstrong*
SAVALAS, Telly	*Aristotle Savalas*
SAWYER, Joe	*Joseph Sauer (aka Joseph Sawyer)*
• SAXE, Templar	*Templer William Edward Edevein*
SAXON, John	*Carmen Orrico*
• SAYLOR, Syd	*Leo Sailor*
SCALA, Gia	*Giovanna Scoglio*
Scat	*Johnny Davis*
Scatman	*Benjamin Crothers*
• SCHARF, Herman	*(aka Herman Scharff)*
SCHILLING, Gus	*August E. Schilling*
• SCHINDELL, Cy	*Seymore Schindell*
• SCHLETTOW, Hans Adelbert	*(aka Hans von Schlettow)*
SCHNEIDER, Romy	*Rosemarie Magdalena Albach-Retty*
SCHULTZ, Harry	*Alexander Heinberg*
SCOTT, Daniel Simon	*Daniel Dale Simon*
SCOTT, Gordon	*Gordon M. Werschkull*
SCOTT, Hazel	*Dorothy Scott*
SCOTT, Lizabeth	*Emma Matzo*
SCOTT, Randolph	*George Randolph Crane Scott*
SCOTT, Zachary	*Zachary Thompson Scott, Jr.*
SEASTROM, Victor	*Victor Sjostrom*
SEBERG, Jean	*Jean Dorothy Seberg*
• SEBRING, Jay	*Thomas Jay Kummer*
SEDDON, Margaret	*Marguerite Hungerford Whiteley*
SEDGWICK, Edie	*Edith Minturn Sedgwick*
• SEGAR, Lucia	*(aka Lucia Seger and Lucia Bacus)*

...ORIGINAL NAMES OF THE STARS...

PROFESSIONAL NAME*	BIRTH, LEGAL OR FORMER NAME**
SELIG, William N.	William Nicholas Selig
SELTEN, Morton	Morton Stubbs
SELWYN, Clarissa	Clarissa Schultz
• SELWYN, Ruth	Ruth Wilcox
SELZNICK, David O.	David Oliver Selznick
SENNETT, Mack	Mickall Sinott (aka Michael Sinnott)
SERATO, Massimo	Giuseppe Segato
SEUSS, Dr.	Theodor Seuss Geisel
SEYMOUR, Jane	Joyce Frankenberg
SHAIFFER, Howard "Tiny"	Howard Charles Shaiffer
• SHANNON, Peggy	Winona Sammon
SHARKEY, Jack	Joseph Paul Cukoschay
SHARIF, Omar	Michel Shalhouz
SHARP, Henry	Henry Schacht
SHAUGHNESSY, Mickey	Joseph Shaughnessy
SHAW, Artie	Arthur Arshawsky
SHAW, Susan	Patsy Sloots
SHAW, Victoria	Jeanette Elphick
SHAW, Wini	Winifred Shaw
SHAWLEE, Joan	Joan Fulton
SHAWN, Dick	Richard Schulefand
SHAY, Dorothy	Dorothy Sims
SHAYNE, Robert	Robert Shaen Dawe
• SHEA, Mervin	Mervin David John Shea
• SHEA, William	William James Shea
SHEAN, Al	Alfred Schoenberg
SHEARER, Moira	Moira King
SHEARER, Norma	Edith Norma Fisher
SHEEN, Charlie	Carlos Irwin Estevez
SHEEN, Martin	Ramon Estevez
• SHEFFIELD, Reginald	Reginald Sheffield Casson
SHELDON, Jerry	Charles H. Patton (Do not confuse with Jerome Sheldon)
Shemp (3 Stooges)	Samuel Howard (Horowitz)
SHEPARD, Sam	Samuel Shepard Rogers
SHEPLEY, Michael	Michael Shepley-Smith
SHERIDAN, Ann	Clara Lou Sheridan
SHERIDAN, Dan	Daniel Marvin Sheridan
SHERMAN, Mary	Ida Sherman
SHERRY, J. Barney	J. Barney Sherry Reeves
• SHERWOOD, Bobby	Robert J. Sherwood, Jr.
SHIELDS, Frank	Francis X. Shields
SHIRE, Talia	Talia Coppola
SHIRLEY, Anne	Dawn Paris
SHORE, Dinah	Frances (Fanny) Rose Shore
SHRINER, Herb	Herbert Schiner
• SHUMWAY, Lee	Leonard C. Shumway
• SHUMWAY, Walter	Walter George Shumway
SIDNEY, George (actor)	Sammy Greenfield
SIDNEY, Sylvia	Sophia Kosow
• SIEGEL, Bernard	(aka Bernard Segal)
SIGNORET, Simone	Simone Kaminker
SILLS, Beverly	Belle Silverman
SILVA, Mario	(aka Murray Smith)
SILVERHEELS, Jay	Harold J. Smith
SILVERS, Phil	Philip Silversmith
SIMMONS, Daniel	(aka Chief Yowlachie)
SIMMS, Hilda	Hilda Moses (aka Julie Riccardo)
• SIMON, Michel	François Simon
SIMPSON, Bill	William Simpson
SINATRA, Frank	Francis Albert Sinatra
• SINATRA, Ray	Raymond Dominic Sinatra
• SINCLAIR, Arthur	Arthur McDonnell
• SINGLETON, Catherine	Catherine Moylan Singleton
SINGLETON, Penny	Dorothy McNulty
SIODMAK, Robert	Robert Siodmark

• New entry.   * Includes both living & deceased persons.   350   ** Sources do not always agree on spelling.

...ORIGINAL NAMES OF THE STARS...

PROFESSIONAL NAME*	BIRTH, LEGAL OR FORMER NAME**
SIRK, Douglas	*Detlef Sierck*
SKELLY, Hal	*Joseph Harold Skelly*
• SKELTON, Georgia	*Georgia Maureen Davis*
SKELTON, Red	*Richard Skelton*
SKIPWORTH, Alison	*Alison Groom*
• SLAUGHTER, Tod	*N. Carter Slaughter*
SMALLEY, Phillips	*Wendell Phillips Smalley*
SMITH, Alexis	*Gladys Smith*
SMITH, Art	*Arthur Gordon Smith*
• SMITH, Gerald	*Gerland Oliver Smith*
SMITH, John	*Robert Earl Van Orden*
SMITH, Joseph	*Joseph Sultzer*
SMITH, Kate	*Kathryn Elizabeth Smith*
SMITH, (Sir) C. Aubrey	*Charles Aubrey Smith*
Sojin	*Sojin Kamiyama*
SOMERS, Suzanne	*Suzanne Mahoney*
• SOMERSET, Pat	*Patrick Holme-Somerset*
SOMMER, Elke	*Elke Schletz*
SONDERGAARD, Gale	*Edith Holm Sondergaard*
SOO, Jack	*Goro Suzuki*
SOTHERN, Ann	*Harriette Lake*
SOTHERN, Hugh	*Roy Sutherland*
SOUEZ, Ina	*Ina Rains*
SOUTHERN, Jeri	*Genevieve Hering*
SPACEK, Sissy	*Mary Elizabeth Spacek*
Spanky (of "Our Gang")	*George Robert Phillips McFarland*
SPARKS, Ned	*Edward A. Sparkman*
SPITALNY, Evelyn	*Evelyn Klein*
Spivy	*Spivy Le Voe*
SQUIRE, Ronald	*Ronald Squirl*
STACY, James	*Maurice Elias*
• STAFFORD, Hanley	*John Austin*
• STANDING, Wyndham	*Charles Wyndham Standing*
STANLEY, Helene	*Delores Diane Freymouth (aka Delores Diane)*
• STANMORE, Frank	*Francis Henry Pink*
• STANTON, Harry	*Harry Isaacs Stanton*
STANTON, Will	*William Sidney Stanton*
STANWYCK, Barbara	*Ruby Stevens*
STAPLETON, Jean	*Jeanne Murray*
• STARK, Pauline	*Pauline Starke*
• STARR, Randy	*Joseph Randall*
STARR, Ringo	*Richard Starkey*
• ST. DENIS, Ruth	*Ruth Dennis*
STEELE, Bob	*Robert North Bradbury, Jr.*
STEELE, Tommy	*Tommy Hicks*
STEERS, Larry	*Lawrence Steers*
STEN, Anna	*Annel (or Anjuschka) Stenskaya Sudakevich*
STEPHENSON, Henry	*Henry S. Garroway*
Stepin Fetchit	*Lincoln Perry*
STERLING, Ford	*George F. Stitch*
STERLING, Jan	*Jane Sterling Adriance*
STERLING, Robert	*William Sterling Hart*
STEVENS, Cat	*Stephen Demetri Georgiou (aka Yusef Islam)*
STEVENS, Connie	*Concetta Ingolia*
STEVENS, Craig	*Gail Shikles*
STEVENS, Inger	*Inger Stensland*
STEVENS, K. T.	*Gloria Wood (aka Katherine Stevens)*
STEVENS, Landers	*John Landers Stevens*
STEVENS, Onslow	*Onslow Ford Stevenson*
STEVENS, Risé	*Risé Steenburg*
STEVENS, Stella	*Estelle Eggleston*
STEWART, James	*James Maitland Stewart*
• STEWART, Jon	*Jon Stewart Liebowitz*
Sting	*Gordon Matthew Sumner*
ST. JACQUES, Raymond	*James Arthur Johnson*

• New entry.   * Includes both living & deceased persons.   ** Sources do not always agree on spelling.

...ORIGINAL NAMES OF THE STARS...

PROFESSIONAL NAME*	BIRTH, LEGAL OR FORMER NAME**
ST. JAMES, Susan	*Susan Miller*
ST. JOHN, Betta	*Betty Streidler*
ST. JOHN, Fuzzy	*Al St. John*
ST. JOHN, Jill	*Jill Oppenheim*
• STOCKDALE, Carl	*Carlton Stockdale*
• STOCKFIELD, Betty	*(aka Betty Stockfeld)*
STOCKWELL, Dean	*Robert Dean Stockwell*
• STOKER, H. G.	*Hew Gordon Dacre Stoker (aka Hew Gordon)*
STOKOWSKI, Leopold	*Leopold Stokes (or Boleslowowicz)*
STONE, George E.	*George Stein*
STONE, Lewis	*Louis Shepherd Stone*
Stooges, The Three	*Moses "Moe" Howard (Horowitz)*
"	*Larry Fine*
"	*Jerome "Curly" Howard (Horowitz)*
" (after Curly's death):	*Samuel "Shemp" Howard (Horowitz)*
" (after June 1959):	*Joe DeRita*
" (after Shemp's death):	*Joe Besser*
• STOOPNAGLE, Col. Lemuel Q.	*F. Chase Taylor*
STOREY, June	*Mary June Storey*
STORM, Gale	*Josephine Cottle*
• ST. POLIS, John	*(aka John Sainpolis)*
STRANGE, Glenn	*George Glenn Strange*
STRASBERG, Lee	*Israel Strassberg*
STRATTEN, Dorothy R.	*Dorothy Hoogstraten*
STREEP, Meryl	*Mary Louise Streep*
STREISAND, Barbra	*Barbara Streisand*
• STRONG, Leonard	*Leonard Clarence Strong*
STUART, Gloria	*Gloria Stuart Finch*
STUART, John	*John Croall*
• STUART, Nick	*Nicholas Pratza*
• STUBBS, Harry	*Harry Oakes Stubbs*
• STUEWE, Hans	*(aka Hans Stuwe)*
STURGES, Preston	*Edmond P. Biden*
• STURGIS, Eddie	*Josef Edwin Sturgis*
STYNE, Jule	*Jules Styne*
Sugar	*Tanya Geise*
SULLAVAN, Margaret	*Margaret Brooke Sullavan*
SULLIVAN, Barry	*Patrick Barry*
• SULLIVAN, Brian	*Harry Joseph Sullivan*
• SULLIVAN, Ed	*Edward Vincent Sullivan*
SULLIVAN, Francis L.	*Francis Loftus Sullivan*
SULLY, Frank	*Frank Sullivan*
SUMMERS, Donna	*LaDonna Gaines*
SUMMERVILLE, Slim	*George J. Summerville*
• SUNBEAUTY, Olga	*(aka Olga Solbelli)*
• SUNDMARK, Betty	*Elizabeth S. Shannon*
• SUNSHINE, Baby	*Pauline Flood*
Sunshine Sammy (of "Our Gang")	*Frederic Ernest Morrison*
SUNSHINE, Marion	*Mary Tunstall Ijames*
Superman	*(aka Clark Kent)*
SUTHERLAND, Eddie	*A. Edward Sutherland*
• SUTTON, Grady	*Grady Harwell Sutton*
SWANSON, Gloria	*Gloria Swenson*
• Sylvie	*Louise Sylvain*
T	
TABLER, P. Dempsey	*Perce Dempsey Tabler*
TALBOT, Lyle	*Lisle Henderson*
TALMADGE, Richard	*Sylvester Metzetti*
• Tamara	*Tamara Swann*
TAMBLYN, Russ	*Russell Tamblyn*
Tarzan (the Ape Man)	*Elmo Lincoln (1918, 21)*
"	*Gene Pollar (1920)*
"	*P. Dempsey Tabler (1920-21)*
"	*Big Jim Pierce (1927)*
"	*Frank Merrill (1928, 30)*

• New entry.   * Includes both living & deceased persons.   ** Sources do not always agree on spelling.

...ORIGINAL NAMES OF THE STARS...

Professional Name	Birth, Legal or Former Name
Tarzan (Cont'd)	Johnny Weissmuller (1932, 34, 36, 39, 41-43, 45-48)
"	Buster Crabbe (1933)
"	Herman Brix (1935)
"	Glenn Morris (1938)
"	Lex Barker (1949-53)
"	Gordon Scott (1955, 57-60)
"	Dennis Miller (1959)
"	Jock Mahoney (1962-63)
"	Mike Henry (1966-68)
"	Ron Ely (1970)
"	Miles O'Keefe (1981)
"	Christopher Lambert (1984)
"	Joe Lara (1989 TV movie)
TATI, Jacques	Jacques Tatischeff
TAUBER, Richard	Ernst Seifert
TAYLOR, Billy	William H. Taylor
TAYLOR, Dub	Walter Clarence Taylor, 2nd
TAYLOR, Jackie Lynn	Jacqueline Lynn Taylor
TAYLOR, Kent	Louis Weiss
TAYLOR, Laurette	Laura Cooney (aka LaBelle Laurette)
TAYLOR, Robert	Spangler Arlington Brugh
TAYLOR, Rod	Robert Taylor
TAYLOR, William Desmond	William Deane-Tanner
TEARLE, Conway	Frederick Levy
• TELLEGEN, Lou	Isidor Louis Bernard Von Dammeir
• TEMPEST, (Dame) Marie	Marie Susan Etherington
• TENBROOK, Harry	Henry Olaf Hansen
• TERRISS, Ellaine	Ellaine Lewin
TERRY, Alice	Alice Frances Taafe
TERRY, Don	Don Loker
TERRY, Ruth	Ruth Mae McMahon
• TERRY, Sheila	Kay Clark
TERRY, Tex	Edward Earl Terry
Terry-Thomas	Thomas Terry Hoar-Stevens
TETLEY, Walter	Walter Campbell Tetley
THALBERG, Irving	Irving Grant Thalberg
• THATCHER, Eva	Evelyn Thatcher
THATCHER, Torin	Torren Thatcher
THIELE, William J.	Wilhelm J. Thiele
• THOMAS, Billy "Buckwheat"	William Henry Thomas, Jr.
THOMAS, Danny	Muzyad Yaghoob (aka Amos Jacobs)
THOMAS, Ted	Theodore Hertzl Thomashefsky
THOMPSON, Carlos	Juan Carlos Mundin Schafter
THOMPSON, Marshall	James Marshall Thompson
THORPE, Richard	Rollo Smolt Thorpe
THUNDERCLOUD, Chief (later)	Scott T. Williams
THUNDERCLOUD, Chief (original)	Victor Daniels
TIM, Tiny	Herbert Khaury
TODD, Ann	Ann Todd Mayfield
TODD, Christopher	Todd Wangberg
TODD, Mike	Avrom Hirsh Goldenborgen (Goldbogen)
TOMACK, Sid	Sidney Tomack
TONE, Franchot	Stanislas Franchot Tone
Tonto	Jay Silverheels
• Tony (Tom Mix's horse)	(aka Tony The Wonder Horse)
• TORRENCE, David	David Thoyson
• TORRENCE, Ernest	Ernest Thoyson
TORN, Rip	Elmore Torn
• Toto	Antonio Furst de Curtis-Gagliardi
• Toto the Clown	Armando Novello
TOURNEUR, Maurice	Maurice Thomas
TRACY, Lee	William Lee Tracy
TRAEGER, Rick	Richard A. Traeger
TRAVERS, Henry	Travers Heagerty
TRAVERS, Linden	Florence Lindon-Travers

PROFESSIONAL NAME*	BIRTH, LEGAL OR FORMER NAME**
TRAVIS, Richard	*William Justice*
TREACHER, Arthur	*Arthur Veary*
TREE, Dorothy	*Dorothy Estelle Triebitz*
TREE, Lady	*Helen Maude Holt*
TREVOR, Austin	*Austin Schilsky*
TREVOR, Claire	*Claire Wemlinger*
TRYON, Tom	*Thomas Tryon*
• TSCHECHOWA, Olga	*Olga von Knipper-Dolling*
TUCKER, George L.	*George Loane Tucker*
• TUCKER, Harland	*(aka Harlan Tucker)*
TUCKER, Sophie	*Sonia Kalish*
TUFTS, Sonny	*Bowen Charleton Tufts, III*
• TUNNEY, Gene	*James Joseph Tunney*
TURNER, Lana	*Julia Jean Mildred Frances Turner*
TURNER, Tina	*Annie Mae Bullock*
TURPIN, Ben	*Bernard Turpin*
TUTTLE, Frank	*Frank Wright Tuttle*
TWELVETREES, Helen	*Helen Jurgens*
Twiggy	*Leslie Hornby*
• TWITCHELL, A. R. "Archie"	*Michael Brandon*
TWITTY, Conway	*Harold Lloyd Jenkins*
Twoton	*Tony Galento*
TYLER, Judy	*Judith Mae Hess*
TYLER, Tom	*Vincent Markowski (aka Vincent Marko)*
U	
URECAL, Minerva	*Minerva Holzer*
V	
VADIM, Roger	*Roger Vadim Plemiannikow*
VAGUE, Vera	*Barbara Jo Allen*
• VALE, Jerry	*Genaro Louis Vitaliano*
VALENTINO, Rudolph	*Rudolfo Alfonzo Raffaelo Pierre Filibert Guglielmi di Valentina d'Antonguolla*
"	*Fritz Valk*
VALK, Frederick	*Fritz Valk*
VALLEE, Rudy	*Hubert Prior Vallee*
VALLI, Alida	*Alida Maria Altenburger*
VALLI, Frankie	*Frank Castelluccio*
VALLI, Virginia	*Virginia McSweeney*
VALLIN, Rick	*Richard Vallin*
VAN, Bobby	*Robert Jack Stein*
• VANBRUGH, (Dame) Irene	*Irene Barnes*
VanBUREN, Abigail	*Pauline "Popo" Esther Friedman*
VanDAMME, Jean-Claude	*Jean-Claude Van Varenberg*
VAN DOREN, Mamie	*Joan Lucille Olander*
Van DYKE, W. S.	*Woodbridge Strong Van Dyke II*
VARCONI, Victor	*Mihaly Varkonyi*
VELEZ, Lupe	*Guadelupe Velez de Villalobos*
Vera-Ellen	*Vera-Ellen Westmeyr Rohe*
VERNE, Kaaren	*Ingaborg Katrina Marie Rose Klinckerfuss*
VERNON, Anne	*Edith Vignaud*
• VERNON, Dorothy	*(aka Dorothy Baird and Dorothy Burns)*
VERSOIS, Odile	*Militza de Poliakoff-Baidarov*
• VESOTA, Bruno	*Bruno William VeSota*
VICKERS, Martha	*Martha MacVicar*
VICTOR, Charles	*Charles Victor Harvey*
• VIDOR, Florence	*Florence Cobb*
VIDOR, King	*King Wallis Vidor*
• Village People, The	*Victor Willis (1977-79) — cop and lead vocal*
• "	*Ray Simpson (1979-present) — cop and lead vocal*
• "	*Alex Briley — military man*
• "	*David Hodo — construction worker*
• "	*Glenn M. Hughes — biker*
• "	*Randy Jones — cowboy*
• "	*Felipe Rose — Indian chief*
VINCENT, Chuck	*Charles Vincent Dingley*
• VINCENT, Sailor Billy	*William J. Vincent*

...ORIGINAL NAMES OF THE STARS...

PROFESSIONAL NAME*	BIRTH, LEGAL OR FORMER NAME**
VINSON, Helen	Helen Rulfs
• VINTON, Arthur	Arthur Rolfe Vinton
"Vitagraph" Girl, The	Alice Joyce
VITTE, Ray	Raymond Anthony Vitte
VITTO, G. L.	Lawrence Vitto
VLADY, Marina	Marina de Poliakoff-Baidarov
• VOGAN, Emmett	Charles Emmet Vogan
Von BRINCKEN, Wilhelm	(aka Roger Beckwith)
• Von ERICH, Chris	Chris Barton Adkisson
• Von ERICH, David	David Adkisson
• Von ERICH, Kerry	Kerry Gene Adkisson
• Von ERICH, Michael	Michael Adkisson
• Von METER, Harry	(aka Harry Van Meter)
Von STERNBERG, Josef	(aka Jo Sternberg and Joe Stern)
Von STROHEIM, Erich	Hans Erich Maria Stroheim von Nordenwall
Von SYDOW, Max	Carl Von Sydow
Von TWARDOWSKI, Hans	Hans Heinrich von Twardowski
VYE, Murvyn	Murvyn Wesley Vye, Jr.

W

• WAITE, Malcolm	Malcolm Ivan Waite
WALBROOK, Anton	Adolf Wohlbruck
Waldo (of "Our Gang")	Darwood Kenneth Smith
WALES, Wally	Floyd Taliaferro Alderson
WALKEN, Christopher	Ronald Walken
WALKER, Clint	Norman Walker
WALKER, Nancy	Anna Myrtle Swoyer
WALLACE, Jean	Jean Wallasek
WALLACE, May	May Maddox
WALLACE, Regina	Regina Katherine Wallace
• WALSH, Raoul	Albert Edward Walsh
• WALTHALL, Wallace	Wallace Wales Walthall
WALTON, Douglas	J. Douglas Duder
WALTON, Fred	Frederick Heming
• WARD, Carrie	Carrie Clarke-Ward
WARD, Polly	Byno Poluski
• WARD, Warwick	Warwick Mannon
WARFIELD, Marjorie	Marjorie Warfield Chase
WARNER, H. B.	Henry Bryan Warner Lickford
WARREN, C. Denier	Charles Denier Warren (aka Denier Warren)
WARREN, Harry	Salvatore Guaragna
WARWICK, John	John Beattie
WARWICK, Robert	Robert Taylor Bien
• WASHINGTON, Dinah	Ruth Jones
WATSON, Bobby	Robert Watson Knucher
WATSON, Wylie	John Wylie Robertson
• WAYNE, David	Wayne James McMeekan
WAXMAN, Franz	Franz Wachsmann
WAYNE, David	Wayne David McMeekan
WAYNE, John	Marion Michael Morrison
WEAVER, "Doodles"	Winstead Sheffield Glendenning Dixon Weaver
WEAVER, Charley	Cliff Arquette
WEAVER, Sigourney	Susan Alexandra Weaver
WEBB, Clifton	Webb Parmalee Hollenbeck
• WEBER, Joe	Morris Weber
WEBER, Rex	Frederick Webber
WEIR, Peter	Peter Lindsay Weir
WEISSMULLER, Johnny	Peter John Weissmuller
WELCH, Raquel	Teresa Jo Tejada
WELD, Tuesday	Susan Ker Weld
WELLES, Orson	George Orson Welles
WELLMAN, William A.	William Augustus Wellman
WELLS, H. G.	Herbert George Wells
WELLS, Jacqueline	(aka Julie Bishop)
WELSH, William	William Joseph Welsh (aka William Welch)
WENDELL, Howard D.	Howard David Wendell

• New entry.   * Includes both living & deceased persons.   ** Sources do not always agree on spelling.

...ORIGINAL NAMES OF THE STARS...

PROFESSIONAL NAME*	BIRTH, LEGAL OR FORMER NAME**
WENGRAF, John E.	Johannes E. Wenngraft
WENTWORTH, Martha	Verna Martha Wentworth
WERBISECK, Gisela	Gisela Werbezirk
WERNER, Oskar	Oskar Josel Boschliessmayer
• WESSEL, Dick	Richard Wessel
WESSELHOEFT, Eleanor	Elinor Wesselhoeft
WESSON, Dick	Richard Lewis Wesson
• WEST, Billy	Roy B. Weisberg
WEST, Dottie	Dorothy Marie Marsh
WEST, Mae	Mae Cohen
WEST, Pat	Arthur Pat West
WESTCOTT, Helen	Myrthas Helen Hickman
WESTLEY, Helen	Henrietta Remson Meserole Manney
WESTMORE, Bud	Hamilton Adolph Westmore
"	(aka George Hamilton Westmore)
WESTMORE, Perc	Percy Westmore
WESTMORE, Wally	Walter J. Westmore
WHALEN, Michael	Joseph Kenneth Shovlin
WHEAT, Larry	Lawrence Wheat (aka Laurence Wheat)
• WHEATCROFT, Stanhope	Stanhope Nelson Wheatcroft
• WHEELER, Bert	Albert Jerome Wheeler
Wheezer (of "Our Gang")	Bobby Hutchins
WHITE, Jesse	Jesse Wiedenfeld
WHITE, Lasses	Lee Roy White
• WHITE, Slappy	Melvin White
• WHITLEY, Crane	Clem Wilenchick
• WHITMAN, Gayne	(aka Alfred Vosburgh)
WHITNEY, Peter	Peter King Engle
WICKES, Mary	Mary Isabelle Wickenhausen
Wild Bill	William Cody
WILDE, Cornel	Cornelius Louis Wilde
WILDER, Gene	Jerome Silberman
• WILDER, Honeychile	Patricia Wilder (aka Princess Alexander Hohenlohe and
• "	Princess Honeychile)
WILLES, Jean	Jean Donahue
WILLIAM, Warren	Warren William Krech
WILLIAMS, Bert	Egbert Austins Williams
WILLIAMS, Bill	William H. Katt, Sr.
• WILLIAMS, Earle	Earle Rafael Williams
WILLIAMS, Guy	Armand Catalano
WILLIAMS, Hank Sr.	Hiram Williams
• WILLIAMS, Hugh	Brian Williams
WILLIAMS, Scott T.	(aka Chief Thundercloud)
WILLIAMS, Treat	Richard Williams
WILLIS, Matt	Marion Willis, 3rd
WILLSON, Meredith	Robert Meredith Reiniger
WILSON, Clarence	Clarence Hummel Wilson
WILSON, Edith	Edith Woodall
WILSON, Marie	Katherine Elizabeth White
WINDSOR, Claire	Claire Viola Cronk
WINDSOR, Marie	Emily Marie Bertelson
WING, Red	Princess Lillian Red Wing St. Cyr
WING, Toby	Martha Virginia Wing
WINNINGER, Charles	Karl Winninger
WINSLOW, George 'Foghorn'	George Wenzlaff
WINTERS, Shelly	Shirley Schrift
WINTHROP, Joy	Josephine Williams
WINWOOD, Estelle	Estelle Goodwin
WITHERS, Googie	Georgette Withers
WITHERS, Grant	Granville G. Withers
WOLFF, Frank	Frank Hermann
WONDER, Stevie	Stevland Morris
WONG, Anna May	Wong Liu Tsong
• WONG, Mary	Mary Liu H. Wong
WOOD, Natalie	Natasha Gurdin

...ORIGINAL NAMES OF THE STARS...

PROFESSIONAL NAME*	BIRTH, LEGAL OR FORMER NAME**
• WOODS, Harry L. Sr.	Harry Lewis Woods
WOOLERY, Ade	Adrian Woolery
WOOLLEY, Monty	Edgar Montillion Woolley
WORDEN, Hank	Norton Earl Worden
• WORTH, Constance	Jocelyn Howarth
WRAY, John	John Griffith Wray
WYMAN, Jane	Sarah Jane Fulks
WYNN, Ed	Isaiah Edwin Leopold
WYNN, Keenan	Francis Keenan Wynn
WYNTER, Dana	Dagmar Wynter
WYNYARD, Diana	Dorothy Isobel Cox
X	
X, Malcolm	Malcolm Little (Muslim name: Hajj-Malik El-Shabazz)
Y	
• YORKE, Edith	Edithe Byard (aka Edithe Yorke)
YORKIN, Bud	Alan Yorkin
• YOST, Herbert A.	(aka Barry O'Moore)
YOUNG, Alan	Angus Young
YOUNG, Bobby	(aka Clifton Young)
YOUNG, Gig	Byron Ellsworth Barr (aka Bryant Fleming)
YOUNG, Loretta	Gretchen Young
YOWLACHIE, Chief	Daniel Simmons
YURKA, Blanche	Blanche Jurka
Z	
ZANE, Bartine	(aka Bartine Burkette)
ZANUCK, Darryl F.	Darryl Frank Zanuck
ZANUCK, Richard D.	Richard Darryl Zanuck
ZAPPA, Frank	Francis Vincent Zappa
ZAREMBA, Jack	John C. Zaremba
ZEARS, Marjorie	Marjorie Page
ZETTERLING, Mai	Mai Elizabeth Zetterling
ZIMBALIST, Al	Alfred N. Zimbalist
ZORINA, Vera	Eva Brigitta Hartwig

LANA TURNER

8

WHO IS RELATED TO WHOM — OFF SCREEN?

WHO IS RELATED TO WHOM — OFF SCREEN?*

HUSBAND	SHOW-BIZ WIVES**	WIFE	SHOW-BIZ HUSBANDS**
A		**A**	
Harry Ackerman	Elinor Donahue	May Abbey	George Lessey
Art Acord	Louise Lorraine	Gypsy Abbott	Henry King
William Perry Adams	Eleanor Wells	Paula Abdul	Emilio Estevez
Al Adamson	Regina Carrol	Jean Acker	Rudolph Valentino
Wesley Addy	Celeste Holm	Constance Adams	Cecil B. DeMille
Buddy Adler	Anita Louise	Edie Adams	Ernie Kovacs
Luther Adler	Sylvia Sidney	Renee Adoree	Tom Moore
John Agar	Shirley Temple	Lola Albright	Jack Carson
Brian Aherne	Joan Fontaine	Mari Aldon	Tay Garnett
Eddie Albert	Margo	Elizabeth Allan	Robert Montgomery
Ross Alexander	Anne Nagel	Adrianne Allen	Raymond Massey
Peter Allen	Liza Minnelli	Gracie Allen	George Burns
Steve Allen	Jayne Meadows	Kirstie Alley	Parker Stevenson
Robert Ames	Vivienne Segal	Astrid Allwyn	Robert Kent
Paul Andor	Lotte Palfi Andor	June Allyson	Dick Powell
Fatty Arbuckle	Minta Durfee	Loni Anderson	Burt Reynolds
Richard Arlen	Jobyna Ralston	Lotte Palfi Andor	Paul Andor
George Arliss	Florence Arliss	Ursula Andress	John Derek
Tom Arnold	Roseanne Barr	Julie Andrews	Blake Edwards
Desi Arnaz	Lucille Ball	Lois Andrews	George Jessel
William Asher	Elizabeth Montgomery	Pier Angeli	Vic Damone
Nils Asther	Vivian Duncan	Annabella	Tyrone Power
Roscoe Ates	Barbara Ray	Ann-Margret	Roger Smith
James T. Aubrey	Phyllis Thaxter	Laura Anson	Philo McCullough
Jean Pierre Aumont	Maria Montez	Tsuru Aoki	Sessue Hayakawa
"	Marisa Pavan	Zeudi Araya	Franco Cristaldi
Dan Aykroyd	Donna Dixon	Eve Arden	Brooks West
Lew Ayres	Lola Lane	Florence Arliss	George Arliss
"	Ginger Rogers	Lucie Arnaz	Laurence Luckinbill
		Patricia Arquette	Nicholas Cage
B		Jean Arthur	Frank Ross
Kevin Bacon	Kyra Sedgwick	Linda Arvidson	David W. Griffith
Max Baer	Dorothy Dunbar	Elizabeth Ashley	George Peppard (twice)
Alec Baldwin	Kim Bassinger	Dorrit Ashton	Charles Newton
Lucien Ballard	Merle Oberon	**B**	
Antonio Banderas	Melanie Griffith	Lauren Bacall	Humphrey Bogart
Monty Banks	Gladys Frazin	Barbara Bach	Ringo Starr
"	Gracie Fields	Olga Baclanova	Nicholas Soussanin
Harry Bannister	Ann Harding	Lynne Baggett	Sam Spiegel
Dave Barbour	Peggy Lee	Lucille Ball	Desi Arnaz
Ben Bard	Ruth Roland	Suzan Ball	Richard Long
Jess Barker	Susan Hayward	Anne Bancroft	Mel Brooks
Lex Barker	Arlene Dahl	Tallulah Bankhead	John Emery
"	Lana Turner	Vilma Banky	Rod La Rocque
Reginald Barker	Clara Williams	Theda Bara	Charles J. Brabin
John Barrymore	Delores Costello	Brigitte Bardot	Roger Vadim
Lionel Barrymore	Doris Rankin	Binnie Barnes	Mike Frankovich
Richard Barthelmess	Mary Hay	Roseanne Barr	Tom Arnold
Frank Beal	Louise Lester	Edith Barrett	Vincent Price
Royal Beal	Edna Bennett	Linda Barrett	Victor Sutherland
Wallace Beery	Gloria Swanson	Majel Barrett	Gene Roddenberry
Edward Begley	Martha Raye	Dusty Bartlett	Jeffrey Hunter
Monta Bell	Betty Lawford	Lina Basquette	Sam Warner
Rex Bell	Clara Bow	Kim Bassinger	Alec Baldwin
Ralph Bellamy	Catherine Willard	Anne Baxter	John Hodiak
"	Ethel Smith (organist)	Meredith Baxter	David Birney
Brian Benben	Madeleine Stowe	Jennifer Beals	Alexander Rockwell
Charles J. Bennett	Boots Mallory	Helen Beck	Peter Cushing
Richard Bennett	Adrianne Morrison	Olga Bellin	Paul Roebling
Jack Benny	Mary Livingstone		

* Includes only show-biz personalities.

** Spouses may not be current.

... WHO IS RELATED TO WHOM — OFF SCREEN?* ...

HUSBAND	SHOW-BIZ WIVES**	WIFE	SHOW-BIZ HUSBANDS**
Jacques Bergerac	Ginger Rogers	Constance Bennett	Gilbert Roland
Busby Berkeley	Esther Muir	Edna Bennett	Royal Beal
Paul Bern	Jean Harlow	Enid Bennett	Fred Niblo, Sr.
Herbert Biberman	Gale Sondergaard	Joan Bennett	Walter Wanger
David Birney	Meredith Baxter	Candice Bergen	Louis Malle
Bill Bixby	Brenda Benet	Ingrid Bergman	Roberto Rossellini
Clint Black	Lisa Hartman	Valerie Bertinelli	Eddie Van Halen
Larry Blyden	Carol Haney	Edna Best	Herbert Marshall
True Boardman	Virginia Eames	Josie Bissett	Rob Estes
Humphrey Bogart	Helen Menken	Betsy Blair	Gene Kelly
"	Mary Philips	Janet Blair	Joe "Fingers" Carr
"	Mayo Methot	Joan Blondell	Dick Powell
"	Lauren Bacall	"	Mike Todd
Robert Bolt	Sarah Miles (twice)	Claire Bloom	Rod Steiger
Sonny Bono	Cher	Betty Blythe	Paul Scardon
Ernest Borgnine	Ethel Merman	Eleanor Boardman	King Vidor
Frank Borzage	Rena Rogers	"	Harry d'Abbadie d'Arrast
Phillip Bourneuf	Frances Reid	Lillian Boardman	Howard I. Smith
John Bowers	Marguerite de la Motte	Adrian Booth	David Brian
Bruce Boxleitner	Melissa Gilbert	Shirley Booth	Archie Gardner
William Boyd	Elinor Fair	Veda Ann Borg	Andrew McLaglen
"	Dorothy Sebastian	Hazel Bourne	David C. Imboden
"	Grace Bradley	Clara Bow	Rex Bell
Charles Boyer	Pat Paterson	Grace Bradley	William Boyd
Charles J. Brabin	Theda Bara	Evelyn Brent	Harry Fox
Kenneth Branagh	Emma Thompson	Christie Brinkley	Billy Joel
George Brent	Ruth Chatterton	May Britt	Sammy Davis, Jr.
"	Helen Nolan	Helen Broderick	Lester Crawford
"	Constance Worth	Coral Browne	Vincent Price
"	Ann Sheridan	Lucile Browne	James Flavin
Jeremy Brett	Anna Massey	Lorayne Brox	Henry Busse
"	Joan Wilson	Virginia Bruce	John Gilbert
David Brian	Adrian Booth	Billie Burke	Florenz Ziegfeld
Jack Briggs	Giner Rogers	Delta Burke	Gerald McRaney
Frederick Brisson	Rosalind Russell	Olivia Burwell	John Gilbert
Mel Brooks	Anne Bancroft	Pauline Bush	Alan Dwan
Charles Bronson	Jill Ireland	**C**	
Pierce Brosnan	Cassandra Harris	Lily Cahill	Brandon Tynan
Georg Stanford Brown	Tyne Daly	Dyan Cannon	Cary Grant
Yul Brynner	Virginia Gilmore	Ida (Tobias) Cantor	Eddie Cantor
George Burns	Gracie Allen	Claudia Cardinale	Franco Cristaldi
Richard Burton	Elizabeth Taylor (twice)	Judy Carne	Burt Reynolds
Niven Busch	Teresa Wright	Sue Carol	Nick Stuart
Henry Busse	Lorayne Brox	"	Alan Ladd
Eddie Buzzell	Ona Munson	Regina Carrol	Al Adamson
C		Diahann Carroll	Vic Damone
Nicholas Cage	Patricia Arquette	Madeleine Carroll	Sterling Hayden
Louis Calhern	Natalie Schafer	Dixie Carter	Hal Holbrook
Kirk Cameron	Chelsea Noble	Irene Castle	Vernon Castle
Webster Campbell	Corinne Griffith	Phoebe Cates	Kevin Kline
Eddie Cantor	Ida (Tobias) Cantor	Joan Caulfield	Frank Ross
Thomas A. Carlin	Frances Sternhagen	Helene Chadwick	William Wellman
Joe "Fingers" Carr	Janet Blair	Marge (Belcher) Champion	Gower Champion
"	Margaret Whiting	Oona Chaplin	Charlie Chaplin
Keith Carradine	Sandra Will	Cyd Charisse	Tony Martin
Jack Carson	Lola Albright	Mary Charleson	Henry B. Walthall
Johnny Cash	June Carter	Charo	Xavier Cugat
Jack Cassidy	Shirley Jones	Ruth Chatterton	George Brent
Shaun Cassidy	Susan Diol	"	Ralph Forbes
Oleg Cassini	Gene Tierney	Cher	Sonny Bono

HUSBAND	SHOW-BIZ WIVES**	WIFE	SHOW-BIZ HUSBANDS**
Vernon Castle	*Irene Castle*	Linda Christian	*Tyrone Power*
William Chalee	*Ruth Nelson*	Connie Chung	*Maury Povich*
Gower Champion	*Marge (Belcher) Champion*	Marguerite Churchill	*George O'Brien*
Charlie Chaplin	*Mildred Harris*	Ina Claire	*John Gilbert*
"	*Paulette Goddard*	Ludi Claire	*John Claire*
"	*Oona Chaplin*	"	*Lawrence Hugo*
Arthur Chesney	*Estelle Winwood*	Ethel Clayton	*Ian Keith*
Donald Churchill	*Pauline Yates*	Rosemary Clooney	*José Ferrer (twice)*
John Claire	*Ludi Claire*	Imogene Coca	*King Donovan*
Stanley Clements	*Gloria Grahame*	Ann Codee	*Frank Orth*
Andy Clyde	*Elsie Tarron*	Claudette Colbert	*Norman Foster*
David Clyde	*Fay Holden*	Natalie Cole	*André Fischer*
Lew Cody	*Mabel Normand*	Constance Collier	*Julian L'Estrange*
"	*Dorothy Dalton*	Joan Collins	*Maxwell Reed*
William A. Colleran	*Lee Remick*	"	*Anthony Newley*
Gary Collins	*Mary Ann Mobley*	Lisa Collins	*Billy Zane*
G. Pat Collins	*Billie Rhodes*	June Collyer	*Stuart Erwin*
Ronald Colman	*Benita Hume*	Betty Compson	*James Cruze*
Nick Condos	*Martha Raye*	Sheilah Connolly	*Guy Madison*
Walter Connolly	*Nedda Harrigan*	Mara Corday	*Richard Long*
Jack Coogan Sr.	*Lillian Dolliver*	Rita Corday	*Harold Nebenzal*
Jackie Coogan	*Betty Grable*	Delores Costello	*John Barrymore*
Tom Corrigan	*Mabel Taliaferro*	Helen Costello	*Lowell Sherman*
Norman Corwin	*Katherine Locke*	Jeanne Coyne	*Gene Kelly*
Joseph Cotten	*Patricia Medina*	Edith Craig	*Richey Craig, Jr.*
William Courtleigh, Jr.	*Ethel Flemming*	Cindy Crawford	*Richard Gere*
Richy Craig, Jr.	*Edith Craig*	Joan Crawford	*Douglas Fairbanks Jr.*
Les Crane	*Tina Louise*	"	*Franchot Tone*
Lester Crawford	*Helen Broderick*	"	*Philip Terry*
Franco Cristaldi	*Claudia Cardinale*		
"	*Zeudi Araya*	**D**	
John Cromwell	*Ruth Nelson*	Arlene Dahl	*Fernando Lamas*
Richard Cromwell	*Angela Lansbury*	"	*Lex Barker*
Hume Cronyn	*Jessica Tandy*	Dorothy Dalton	*Lew Cody*
Bing Crosby	*Dixie Lee*	Tyne Daly	*Georg Stanford Brown*
"	*Kathryn Grant*	Lili Damita	*Errol Flynn*
Tom Cruise	*Mimi Rogers*	Bebe Daniels	*Ben Lyon*
"	*Nicole Kidman*	Dorothy Davenport	*Wallace Reid*
James Cruze	*Marguerite Snow*	Fanny Davenport	*Melbourne MacDowell*
"	*Betty Compson*	Bette Davis	*Gary Merrill*
Xavier Cugat	*Charo*	Geena Davis	*Jeff Goldblum*
Alan Curtis	*Ilona Massey*	Mildred Davis	*Harold Lloyd*
"	*Betty Sundmark*	Nancy Davis	*Ronald Reagan*
Dick Curtis	*Ruth Sullivan*	Frances Dee	*Joel McCrea*
Tony Curtis	*Janet Leigh*	Sandra Dee	*Bobby Darin*
Peter Cushing	*Helen Beck*	Gloria de Haven	*John Payne*
D		Marguerite de la Motte	*John Bowers*
Grover Dale	*Anita Morris*	Lorella De Luca	*Duccio Tessari*
Vic Damone	*Pier Angeli*	Katherine DeMille	*Anthony Quinn*
"	*Diahann Carroll*	Bo Derek	*John Derek*
Ted Danson	*Mary Steenburgen*	Colleen Dewhurst	*James Vickery*
Bobby Darin	*Sandra Dee*	"	*George C. Scott (twice)*
Frankie Darro	*Aloha Wray*	Susan Diol	*Shaun Cassidy*
Jules Dassin	*Melina Mercouri*	Donna Dixon	*Dan Aykroyd*
Thayer David	*Valerie French*	Shannen Doherty	*Ashley Hamilton*
Miles Davis	*Frances Taylor*	Lillian Dolliver	*Jack Coogan Sr.*
"	*Betty Mabry*	Jenny Dolly	*Harry Fox*
"	*Cicely Tyson*	Faith Domergue	*Hugo Fregonese*
Sammy Davis, Jr.	*May Britt*	Elinor Donahue	*Harry Ackerman*
Roy Del Ruth	*Winnie Lightner*	Jeff Donnell	*Aldo Ray*
		Cathy Downs	*Joe Kirkwood, Jr.*

... WHO IS RELATED TO WHOM — OFF SCREEN?* ...

HUSBAND	SHOW-BIZ WIVES**	WIFE	SHOW-BIZ HUSBANDS**
Gordon Demain	Octavia Handworth	Patricia Doyle	Robert Wise
Cecil B. DeMille	Constance Adams	Ethel Drew	Wilfrid Hyde-White
John Derek	Patti Behrs	Joanne Dru	Dick Haymes
"	Ursula Andress	"	John Ireland
"	Linda Evans	Dorothy Dunbar	Max Baer
"	Bo Derek	Vivian Duncan	Nils Asther
Bruce Dern	Dianne Ladd	Deanna Durbin	Felix Jackson
Vittorio de Sica	Giuditta Rissoni	Minta Durfee	Fatty Arbuckle
Danny DeVito	Rhea Perlman	Ann Dvorak	Leslie C. Fenton
Bradford Dillman	Suzy Parker	**E**	
Joe DiMaggio	Marilyn Monroe	Virginia Eames	True Boardman
Alan Dobie	Rachel Roberts	Dorothy Earle	George "Gabby" Hayes
Troy Donahue	Suzanne Pleshette	Nora Eddington	Errol Flynn
King Donovan	Imogene Coca	Sally Eilers	Hoot Gibson
Virgil Jack Dougherty	Barbara Lamar	Florence Eldridge	Fredric March
Paul Douglas	Jan Sterling	Vera Engels	Ivan Lebedeff
William Dozier	Ann Rutherford	Jill Esmond	Laurence Olivier
"	Joan Fontaine	Dale Evans	Roy Rogers
Sydney Drew	Lucille McVey	Linda Evans	John Derek
Howard Duff	Ida Lupino	**F**	
Douglas Dumbrille	Patricia Mowbray	Shelley Fabares	Mike Farrell
James Dunn	Frances Gifford	Elinor Fair	William Boyd
Charles Dutton	Debbie Morgan	Frances Farmer	Leif Erikson
Alan Dwan	Pauline Bush	Mia Farrow	Frank Sinatra
E		"	André Previn
Clint Eastwood	Dina Ruiz	Farrah Fawcett	Lee Majors
Blake Edwards	Julie Andrews	Alice Faye	Tony Martin
Neely Edwards	Marguerite Snow	"	Phil Harris
Denholm Elliott	Virginia McKenna	Elsie Ferguson	Frederick Worlock
"	Susan Robinson	Helen Ferguson	William Russell (d. 1929)
William D. Elliott	Dionne Warwick	Debra Feuer	Mickey Rourke
Robert Ellis	Vera Reynolds	Gracie Fields	Monty Banks
John Emerson	Anita Loos	Rhonda Fleming	Lang Jeffries
John Emery	Tallulah Bankhead	Ethel Flemming	William Courtleigh, Jr.
Leif Erikson	Frances Farmer	Jane Fonda	Roger Vadim
Stuart Erwin	June Collyer	"	Ted Turner
Rob Estes	Josie Bissett	Joan Fontaine	Brian Aherne
Emilio Estevez	Paula Abdul	"	William Dozier
Wilbur Evans	Susanna Foster	Lynn Fontanne	Alfred Lunt
Charles Eyton	Kathlyn Williams	Mary Ford	Les Paul
F		Susanna Foster	Wilbur Evans
Douglas Fairbanks, Jr.	Joan Crawford	Lynne Frederick	Peter Sellers
Douglas Fairbanks, Sr.	Mary Pickford	"	David Frost
Dustin Farnum	Winifred Kingston	Valerie French	Thayer David
Charles Farrell	Virginia Valli	**G**	
Mike Farrell	Shelley Fabares	Magda Gabor	George Sanders
John Farrow	Maureen O'Sullivan	Zsa Zsa Gabor	George Sanders
Frank Fay	Barbara Stanwyck	Ava Gardner	Mickey Rooney
Federico Fellini	Giulietta Masina	"	Artie Shaw
Leslie C. Fenton	Ann Dvorak	"	Frank Sinatra
José Ferrer	Rosemary Clooney (twice)	Judy Garland	David Rose
"	Uta Hagen	"	Vincente Minnelli
Mel Ferrer	Audrey Hepburn	Pauline Garon	Lowell Sherman
André Fischer	Natalie Cole	Greer Garson	Richard Ney
Eddie Fisher	Debbie Reynolds	Gladys George	Leonard Penn
"	Elizabeth Taylor	Frances Gifford	James Dunn
James Flavin	Lucile Browne	Melissa Gilbert	Bruce Boxleitner
Errol Flynn	Nora Eddington	Virginia Gilmore	Yul Brynner
"	Lili Damita	Dorothy Gish	James Rennie
"	Patrice Wymore	Lucille (Webster) Gleason	James Gleason

* Includes only show-biz personalities.   ** Spouses may not be current.

... WHO IS RELATED TO WHOM — OFF SCREEN?*...

HUSBAND	SHOW-BIZ WIVES**	WIFE	SHOW-BIZ HUSBANDS**
Henry Fonda	Margaret Sullavan	Paulette Goddard	Charlie Chaplin
Ralph Forbes	Ruth Chatterton	"	Burgess Meredith
Glenn Ford	Eleanor Powell	Dagmar Godowsky	Frank Mayo
Dudley Foster	Eileen Kenally	Frances Goodrich	Albert Hackett
Norman Foster	Claudette Colbert	Yekaterina Gordeeva	Sergei Grinkov
Harry Fox	Jenny Dolly	Betty Grable	Jackie Coogan
"	Evelyn Brent	"	Harry James
Robert Foxworth	Elizabeth Montgomery	Gloria Grahame	Stanley Clements
Anthony Franciosa	Shelley Winters	"	Nicholas Ray
Mike Frankovich	Binnie Barnes	"	Cy Howard
Hugo Fregonese	Faith Domergue	Kathryn Grant	Bing Crosby
Eugene Frenke	Anna Sten	Mary Grant	Vincent Price
David Frost	Lynne Frederick	Bonita Granville	Jack Wrather
G		Jane Greer	Rudy Vallee
Clark Gable	Carole Lombard	Mercedes Gregory	André Gregory
"	Josephine Dillon	Nan Grey	Frankie Laine
Ben Gage	Esther Williams	Corinne Griffith	Webster Campbell
Richard "Skeets" Gallagher	Pauline Mason	Melanie Griffith	Antonio Banderas
Archie Gardner	Shirley Booth	**H**	
Tay Garnett	Patsy Ruth Miller	Florence Hackett	Arthur V. Johnson
"	Mari Aldon	Uta Hagen	José Ferrer
Vittorio Gassman	Shelley Winters	Barbara Hale	Bill Williams
Richard Gere	Cindy Crawford	Geraldine Hall	Porter Hall
Hoot Gibson	Sally Eilers	Octavia Handworth	Harry Handworth
Frank Gifford	Kathie Lee	"	Gordon Demain
Billy Gilbert	Lally McKenzie	Carol Haney	Larry Blyden
John Gilbert	Olivia Burwell	Joan Harben	Clive Morton
"	Leatrice Joy	Ann Harding	Harry Bannister
"	Ina Claire	"	Werner Janssen
"	Virginia Bruce	Jean Harlow	Paul Bern
James Gleason	Lucille (Webster) Gleason	"	Harold Rosson
Jeff Goldblum	Geena Davis	Nedda Harrigan	Walter Connolly
Samuel Goldwyn	Frances Howard	"	Joshua Logan
James Gordon	Mabel Van Buren	Cassandra Harris	Pierce Brosnan
Kip Gowans	Lee Remick	Mildred Harris	Charles Chaplin
Stewart Granger	Elspeth March	Mary Hart	Burt Sugarman
"	Jean Simmons	Lisa Hartman	Clint Black
Cary Grant	Dyan Cannon	Teri Hatcher	Jon Tenney
Peter Graves	Vanessa Lee	June Haver	Fred MacMurray
Alfred E. Green	Vivian Reid	Mary Hay	Richard Barthelmess
André Gregory	Mercedes Gregory	Helen Hayes	Charles MacArthur
David W. Griffith	Linda Arvidson	Susan Hayward	Jess Barker
Raymond Griffith	Bertha Mann	Rita Hayworth	Dick Haymes
Sergei Grinkov	Yekaterina Gordeeva	"	Orson Welles
H		"	James Hill
Albert Hackett	Frances Goodrich	Amy Heckerling	Neal Israel
Raymond Hackett	Myra Hampton	Wanda Hendrix	Audie Murphy
"	Blanche Sweet	Audrey Hepburn	Mel Ferrer
John Hall	Frances Langford	Anna (Dodge) Hernandez	George F. Hernandez
Porter Hall	Geraldine Hall	Harriet Hilliard	Ozzie Nelson
Ashley Hamilton	Shannen Doherty	Alma Reville Hitchcock	(Sir) Alfred Hitchcock
Harry Handworth	Octavia (Boas) Handworth	Lucie Hoeflich	Emil Jannings
Tom Hanks	Rita Wilson	Fay Holden	David Clyde
Mickey Hargitay	Jayne Mansfield	Marjorie Holliday	Michael St. Angel
Kenneth Harlan	Marie Prevost	Celeste Holm	Wesley Addy
Tom Harmon	Elyse Knox	Miriam Hopkins	Anatole Litvak
Ed Harris	Amy Madigan	Hedda (Furry) Hopper	De Wolf Hopper
Phil Harris	Alice Faye	Marilyn Horne	Henry Lewis
Gregory Harrison	Randi Oakes	Frances Howard	Samuel Goldwyn
Rex Harrison	Lilli Palmer	Benita Hume	Ronald Colman

... WHO IS RELATED TO WHOM — OFF SCREEN?* ...

HUSBAND	SHOW-BIZ WIVES**	WIFE	SHOW-BIZ HUSBANDS**
Rex Harrison	*Rachel Roberts*	Benita Hume	*Goerge Sanders*
Laurence Harvey	*Margaret Leighton*	Martha Hyer	*Hal Wallis*
Sessue Hayakawa	*Tsuru Aoki*	**I**	
Russell "Lucky" Hayden	*Lillian Porter*	Jill Ireland	*Charles Bronson*
Sterling Hayden	*Madeleine Carroll*	Amy Irving	*Steven Spielberg*
George "Gabby" Hayes	*Dorothy Earle*	Elaine Irwin	*John Mellencamp*
Dick Haymes	*Rita Hayworth*	**J**	
"	*Joanne Dru*	Anne Jackson	*Eli Wallach*
Leland Hayward	*Margaret Sullavan*	Isabel Jeans	*Claude Rains*
Louis Hayward	*Ida Lupino*	Ursula Jeans	*Robin Irvine*
Jascha Heifetz	*Florence Vidor*	"	*Roger Livesey*
Del Henderson	*Florence Lee*	Anne Jeffries	*Robert Sterling*
Hugh Herbert	*Anita Pam*	Jennifer Jones	*Robert Walker*
George F. Hernandez	*Anna (Dodge) Hernandez*	"	*David O. Selznick*
Weldon Heyburn	*Greta Nissen*	Shirley Jones	*Jack Cassidy*
George F. Hill	*Frances Marion*	"	*Marty Ingels*
(Sir) Alfred Hitchcock	*Alma Reville Hitchcock*	Marion Jordan	*Jim "Fibber McGee" Jordan*
Henry M. Hobart	*Olive Tell*	Leatrice Joy	*John Gilbert*
John Hodiak	*Anne Baxter*	Alice Joyce	*Tom Moore*
Paul Hogan	*Linda Kozlowski*	Elaine Joyce	*Bobby Van*
Hal Holbrook	*Dixie Carter*	Arlene Judge	*Wesley Ruggles*
William Holden	*Brenda Marshall*	**K**	
Oscar Homolka	*Joan Tetzel*	Sylvia Fine Kaye	*Danny Kaye*
Arthur Hornblow, Jr.	*Myrna Loy*	Myra Keaton	*Joseph Keaton, Sr.*
James Horne	*Cleo Ridgely*	Ruby Keeler	*Al Jolson*
De Wolf Hopper	*Hedda (Furry) Hopper*	Nancy Kelly	*Edmond O'Brien*
Peter Horton	*Michelle Pfeiffer*	Eileen Kenally	*Dudley Foster*
Cy Howard	*Gloria Grahame*	Linda Kerridge	*Corey Parker*
Lawrence Hugo	*Ludi Claire*	Evelyn Keyes	*John Huston*
Jeffrey Hunter	*Barbara Rush*	"	*Artie Shaw*
"	*Dusty Bartlett*	Nicole Kidman	*Tom Cruise*
"	*Emily McLaughlin*	Winifred Kingston	*Dustin Farnum*
John Huston	*Evelyn Keyes*	Kathleen Kinmont	*Lorenzo Lamas*
Timothy Hutton	*Debra Winger*	Nastassja Kinski	*Ibraham Moussa*
Wilfrid Hyde-White	*Ethel Drew*	Patricia Knight	*Cornel Wilde*
I		Elyse Knox	*Tom Harmon*
David C. Imboden	*Hazel Bourne*	Linda Kozlowski	*Paul Hogan*
Marty Ingels	*Shirley Jones*	Lorraine Krueger	*Stu Wilson*
John Ireland	*Elaine Rosen*	**L**	
"	*Joanne Dru*	Dianne Ladd	*Bruce Dern*
Robin Irvine	*Ursula Jeans*	Barbara Lamar	*Virgil Jack Dougherty*
Neal Israel	*Amy Heckerling*	Hedy Lamarr	*John Loder*
J		Lillian La Monte	*Fred MacMurray*
Felix Jackson	*Deanna Durbin*	Elsa Lanchester	*Charles Laughton*
Henry Jaffe	*Jean Muir*	Diane Lane	*Christopher Lambert*
Harry James	*Betty Grable*	Lola Lane	*Lew Ayres*
Emil Jannings	*Lucie Hoeflich*	Hope Lange	*Don Murray*
Werner Janssen	*Ann Harding*	Frances Langford	*John Hall*
Lang Jeffries	*Rhonda Fleming*	Angela Lansbury	*Richard Cromwell*
George Jessel	*Norma Talmadge*	Betty Lawford	*Monta Bell*
"	*Lois Andrews*	Evelyn Laye	*Frank Lawton*
Billy Joel	*Christie Brinkley*	Zarah Leander (Hedberg)	*Nils Leander*
Arthur V. Johnson	*Florence Hackett*	Kelly LeBrock	*Steven Seagal*
Al Jolson	*Ruby Keeler*	Gretchen Lederer	*Otto Lederer*
Jim "Fibber McGee" Jordan	*Marion Jordan*	Dixie Lee	*Bing Crosby*
Richard Jordan	*Kathleen Widdoes*	Florence Lee	*Del Henderson*
K		Kathie Lee	*Frank Gifford*
Jacob Kalich	*Molly Picon*	Peggy Lee	*Dave Barbour*
Edward Kaufman	*Thelma Salter*	Vanessa Lee	*Peter Graves*
Danny Kaye	*Sylvia Fine Kaye*	Janet Leigh	*Tony Curtis*

* Includes only show-biz personalities.

** Spouses may not be current.

HUSBAND	SHOW-BIZ WIVES**	WIFE	SHOW-BIZ HUSBANDS**
James Keach	Jane Seymour	Vivien Leigh	Laurence Olivier
Robert Emmett Keane	Claire Whitney	Margaret Leighton	Laurence Harvey
Buster Keaton	Natalie Talmadge	"	Michael Wilding
Joseph Keaton, Sr.	Myra Keaton	Louise Lester	Frank Beal
Don Keefer	Catherine McLeod	Diana Lewis	William Powell
Ian Keith	Ethel Clayton	Winnie Lightner	Roy Del Ruth
David Kelley	Michelle Pfeiffer	Viveca Lindfors	Don Siegel
Gene Kelly	Jeanne Coyne	Mary Livingstone	Jack Benny
"	Betsy Blair	Gladys Lloyd	Edward G. Robinson
Paul Kelly	Dorothy Mackaye	Katherine Locke	Norman Corwin
Robert Kent	Astrid Allwyn	Kathleen (Arthur) Lockhart	Gene Lockhart
Val Kilmer	Joanne Whalley	Heather Locklear	Richie Sambora
Henry King	Gypsy Abbott	Carole Lombard	William Powell
James Kirkwood	Gertrude R. Robinson	"	Clark Gable
Joe Kirkwood, Jr.	Cathy Downs	Anita Loos	John Emerson
Werner Klemperer	Louise Troy	Sophia Loren	Carlo Ponti
Kevin Kline	Phoebe Cates	Louise Lorraine	Art Acord
Alexander Korda	Merle Oberon	Anita Louise	Buddy Adler
Ernie Kovacs	Edie Adams	Tina Louise	Les Crane
L		Judith Lowry	Rudd Lowry
Alan Ladd	Sue Carol	Margerie Bonner Lowry	Malcolm Lowry
Frankie Laine	Nan Grey	Myrna Loy	Arthur Hornblow, Jr.
Fernando Lamas	Arlene Dahl	"	Gene Markey
"	Esther Williams	Ida Lupino	Louis Hayward
Lorenzo Lamas	Kathleen Kinmont	"	Howard Duff
Christopher Lambert	Diane Lane	**M**	
Sidney Lanfield	Shirley Mason	Jeanette MacDonald	Gene Raymond
David Lansbury	Ally Sheedy	Ali MacGraw	Steve McQueen
Rod La Rocque	Vilma Banky	Rose Mack	Joseph Lester
Matt Lattanzi	Olivia Newton-John	Dorothy Mackaye	Paul Kelly
Charles Laughton	Elsa Lanchester	Amy Madigan	Ed Harris
Frank Lawton	Evelyn Laye	Madonna	Sean Penn
David Lean	Ann Todd	Boots Mallory	Charles J. Bennett
Nils Leander	Zarah (Hedberg) Leander	Bertha Mann	Raymond Griffith
Ivan Lebedeff	Vera Engels	Jayne Mansfield	Mickey Hargitay
Otto Lederer	Gretchen Lederer	Elspeth March	Stewart Granger
Robert Z. Leonard	Gertrude Olmstead	Margo	Eddie Albert
Mervyn Le Roy	Edna Murphy	Frances Marion	Fred Thomson
Edward J. LeSaint	Stella Razetto	"	George F. Hill
George Lessey	May Abbey	Brenda Marshall	William Holden
Joseph Lester	Rose Mack	Giulietta Masina	Federico Fellini
Julian L'Estrange	Constance Collier	Pauline Mason	Richard "Skeets" Gallagher
Henry Lewis	Marilyn Horne	Shirley Mason	Sidney Lanfield
Sheldon Lewis	Virginia Pearson	Anna Massey	Jeremy Brett
Anatole Litvak	Miriam Hopkins	Ilona Massey	Alan Curtis
Roger Livesey	Ursula Jeans	Virginia Mayo	Michael O'Shea
Harold Lloyd	Mildred Davis	Gertrude McCoy	Duncan McRae
Gene Lockhart	Kathleen (Arthur) Lockhart	Marie McDonald	Donald F. Taylor
John Loder	Hedy Lamarr	Claire McDowell	Charles H. Mailes
Joshua Logan	Nedda Harrigan	Virginia McKenna	Bill Travers
Richard Long	Suzan Ball	"	Denholm Elliott
"	Mara Corday	Eva B. McKenzie	Robert B. McKenzie
Lyle Lovett	Julia Roberts	Lally McKenzie	Billy Gilbert
Edmund Lowe	Lilyan Tashman	Emily McLaughlin	Jeffrey Hunter
Robert Lowery	Jean Parker	Catherine McLeod	Don Keefer
Malcolm Lowry	Margerie Bonner Lowry	Lucille McVey	Sydney Drew
Rudd Lowry	Judith Lowry	Margaret McWade	Edward McWade
Laurence Luckinbill	Lucie Arnaz	Jayne Meadows	Steve Allen
Allen Ludden	Betty White	Anne Meara	Jerry Stiller
Alfred Lunt	Lynn Fontanne	Patricia Medina	Joseph Cotten

HUSBAND	SHOW-BIZ WIVES**	WIFE	SHOW-BIZ HUSBANDS**
Ben Lyon	*Bebe Daniels*	Helen Menken	*Humphrey Bogart*
"	*Marion Nixon*	Melina Mercouri	*Jules Dassin*
M		Ethel Merman	*Ernest Borgnine*
Charles MacArthur	*Helen Hayes*	Dina Merrill	*Cliff Robertson*
Melbourne MacDowell	*Fanny Davenport*	Mayo Methot	*Humphrey Bogart*
Wilbur Mack	*Gertrude Purdy*	Sarah Miles	*Robert Bolt (twice)*
Fred MacMurray	*Lillian La Monte*	Patsy Ruth Miller	*Tay Garnett*
	June Haver	Liza Minnelli	*Peter Allen*
Guy Madison	*Gail Russell*	Mary Ann Mobley	*Gary Collins*
"	*Sheilah Connolly*	Marilyn Monroe	*Joe DiMaggio*
John Lee Mahin	*Patsy Ruth Miller*	Maria Montez	*Jean Pierre Aumont*
Charles H. Mailes	*Claire McDowell*	Elizabeth Montgomery	*Gig Young*
Lee Majors	*Farrah Fawcett*	"	*William Asher*
Louis Malle	*Candice Bergen*	"	*Robert Foxworth*
Henry Mancini	*Ginny O'Connor*	Goodee Montgomery	*Frank McDonald*
Fredric March	*Florence Eldridge*	Demi Moore	*Bruce Willis*
Gene Markey	*Myrna Loy*	Eleanor Moore	*Thomas J. Moore*
Hugh Marlowe	*K. T. Stevens*	Debbie Morgan	*Charles Dutton*
Herbert Marshall	*Edna Best*	Anita Morris	*Grover Dale*
William Marshall	*Ginger Rogers*	Adrianne Morrison	*Richard Bennett*
Steve Martin	*Victoria Tennant*	Patricia Mowbray	*Douglas Dumbrille*
Tony Martin	*Alice Faye*	Esther Muir	*Busby Berkeley*
"	*Cyd Charisse*	Jean Muir	*Henry Jaffe*
Raymond Massey	*Adrianne Allen*	Ona Munson	*Eddie Buzzell*
Frank Mayo	*Dagmar Godowsky*	Edna Murphy	*Mervyn Le Roy*
John McCallum	*Googie Withers*	**N**	
Joel McCrea	*Frances Dee*	Anne Nagel	*Ross Alexander*
Philo McCullough	*Laura Anson*	Diana Napier	*Richard Tauber*
Frank McDonald	*Goodee Montgomery*	Ruth Nelson	*John Cromwell*
Malcolm McDowell	*Mary Steenburgen*	"	*William Chalee*
John McEnroe	*Tatum O'Neal*	Olivia Newton-John	*Matt Lattanzi*
Paul McGrath	*Anne Sargent*	Lisa Niemi	*Patrick Swayze*
John McIntire	*Jeanette Nolan*	Greta Nissen	*Weldon Heyburn*
David McKay	*Joan Chandler*	Marion Nixon	*Ben Lyon*
Scott McKay	*Ann Sheridan*	Chelsea Noble	*Kirk Cameron*
Robert B. McKenzie	*Eva B. McKenzie*	Helen Nolan	*George Brent*
Andrew McLaglen	*Veda Ann Borg*	Jeanette Nolan	*John McIntire*
Steve McQueen	*Ali MacGraw*	Josephine Norman	*Herbert Rawlins*
Duncan McRae	*Gertrude McCoy*	Mabel Normand	*Lew Cody*
Gerald McRaney	*Delta Burke*	**O**	
Edward McWade	*Margaret McWade*	Vivien Oakland	*John T. Murray*
John Mellencamp	*Elaine Irwin*	Merle Oberon	*Alexander Korda*
Adolphe Menjou	*Veree Teasdale*	Eloise Taylor O'Brien	*Pat O'Brien*
Burgess Meredith	*Paulette Goddard*	Ginny O'Connor	*Henry Mancini*
Gary Merrill	*Bette Davis*	Gertrude Olmstead	*Robert Z. Leonard*
Vincente Minnelli	*Judy Garland*	Tatum O'Neal	*John McEnroe*
Ricardo Montalban	*Georgiana Young*	Maureen O'Sullivan	*John Farrow*
Yves Montand	*Simone Signoret*	Carré Otis	*Mickey Rourke*
George Montgomery	*Dinah Shore*	**P**	
Robert Montgomery	*Elizabeth Allan*	Geraldine Page	*Rip Torn*
Owen Moore	*Mary Pickford*	Jean Page	*Albert Edward Smith*
Thomas J. Moore	*Eleanor Moore*	Debra Paget	*David Street*
Tom Moore	*Alice Joyce*	Lilli Palmer	*Rex Harrison*
"	*Renee Adoree*	"	*Carlos Thompson*
Clive Morton	*Joan Harben*	Anita Pam	*Hugh Herbert*
"	*Fanny Rowe*	Jean Parker	*Robert Lowery*
Ibraham Moussa	*Nastassja Kinski*	Suzy Parker	*Bradford Dillman*
Audie Murphy	*Wanda Hendrix*	Pat Paterson	*Charles Boyer*
Don Murray	*Hope Lange*	Marisa Pavan	*Jean-Pierre Aumont*
John T. Murray	*Vivien Oakland*	Barbara Payton	*Franchot Tone*

368

... WHO IS RELATED TO WHOM — OFF SCREEN?* ...

HUSBAND	SHOW-BIZ WIVES**	WIFE	SHOW-BIZ HUSBANDS**
N		Virginia Pearson	Sheldon Lewis
Harold Nebenzal	Rita Corday	Barbara Pepper	Craig Reynolds
Liam Neeson	Natasha Richardson	Rhea Perlman	Danny DeVito
Ozzie Nelson	Harriet Hilliard	Susan Peters	Richard Quine
Anthony Newley	Joan Collins	Michelle Pfeiffer	Peter Horton
Paul Newman	Joanne Woodward	"	David Kelley
Charles Newton	Dorrit Ashton	Mary Philips	Humphrey Bogart
Richard Ney	Greer Garson	Mary Pickford	Owen Moore
Fred Niblo, Sr.	Enid Bennett	"	Douglas Fairbanks, Sr.
Edward Norris	Ann Sheridan	"	Buddy Rogers
O		Molly Picon	Jacob Kalich
Philip Ober	Vivian Vance	Suzanne Pleshette	Troy Donahue
Robert Ober	Mabel Taliaferro	Lillian Porter	Russell "Lucky" Hayden
Edmond O'Brien	Nancy Kelly	Eleanor Powell	Glenn Ford
"	Olga San Juan	Priscilla Presley	Elvis Presley
"	Anne Sargent	Kelly Preston	John Travolta
George O'Brien	Marguerite Churchill	Marie Prevost	Kenneth Harlan
Pat O'Brien	Eloise Taylor O'Brien	Gertrude Purdy	Wilbur Mack
Clifford Odets	Luise Rainer	**R**	
Michael O'Keefe	Bonnie Raitt	Gilda Radner	Gene Wilder
Gary Oldman	Uma Thurman	Luise Rainer	Clifford Odets
Laurence Olivier	Jill Esmond	Bonnie Raitt	Michael O'Keefe
"	Vivien Leigh	Jobyna Ralston	Richard Arlen
Frank Orth	Ann Codee	Vera Hruba Ralston	Herbert Y. Yates
Michael O'Shea	Virginia Mayo	Natacha Rambova	Rudolph Valentino
P		Doris Rankin	Lionel Barrymore
Corey Parker	Linda Kerridge	Barbara Ray	Roscoe Ates
Les Paul	Mary Ford	Martha Raye	Bud Westmore
John Payne	Gloria de Haven	"	David Rose
"	Anne Shirley	"	Nick Condos
Tony Peck	Cheryl Tiegs	"	Ed Begley
Leonard Penn	Gladys George	"	Mark Harris
Sean Penn	Madonna	Stella Razetto	Edward J. LeSaint
George Peppard	Elizabeth Ashley (twice)	Barbara Read	William Talman
Jack Pickford	Olive Thomas	Vanessa Redgrave	Tony Richardson
Roman Polanski	Sharon Tate	Frances Reid	Phillip Bourneuf
Carlo Ponti	Sophia Loren	Vivian Reid	Alfred E. Green
Maury Povich	Connie Chung	Lee Remick	William A. Colleran
Dick Powell	Joan Blondell	"	Kip Gowans
"	June Allyson	Dorothy (Velegra) Revier	Harry J. Revier
William Powell	Carole Lombard	Debbie Reynolds	Eddie Fisher
"	Diana Lewis	Vera Reynolds	Robert Ellis
Tyrone Power	Annabella	Billie Rhodes	G. Pat Collins
"	Linda Christian	Florence Rice	Robert Wilcox
Elvis Presley	Priscilla Presley	Natasha Richardson	Liam Neeson
André Previn	Mia Farrow	Cleo Ridgely	James Horne
Vincent Price	Edith Barrett	Blanche Ring	Charles Winninger
"	Mary Grant	Elisabeth Risdon	George Loane Tucker
"	Coral Browne	Giuditta Rissoni	Vittorio de Sica
Roger Pryor	Ann Sothern	Julia Roberts	Lyle Lovett
Q		Rachel Roberts	Alan Dobie
Dennis Quaid	Meg Ryan	"	Rex Harrison
Richard Quine	Susan Peters	Gertrude R. Robinson	James Kirkwood
Anthony Quinn	Katherine DeMille	Susan Robinson	Denholm Elliott
R		Estelita Rodriguez	Grant Withers
Claude Rains	Isabel Jeans	Ginger Rogers	Lew Ayres
Herbert Rawlins	Josephine Norman	"	Jack Briggs
Aldo Ray	Jeff Donnell	"	Jacques Bergerac
Nicholas Ray	Gloria Grahame	"	William Marshall
Gene Raymond	Jeanette MacDonald	Mimi Rogers	Tom Cruise

* Includes only show-biz personalities.   ** Spouses may not be current.

HUSBAND	SHOW-BIZ WIVES**
Ronald Reagan	Jane Wyman
"	Nancy Davis
Maxwell Reed	Joan Collins
Wallace Reid	Dorothy Davenport
James Rennie	Dorothy Gish
Harry J. Revier	Dorothy (Velegra) Revier
Burt Reynolds	Judy Carne
	Loni Anderson
Craig Reynolds	Barbara Pepper
Tony Richardson	Vanessa Redgrave
Tim Robbins	Susan Sarandon
Cliff Robertson	Dina Merrill
Edward G. Robinson	Gladys Lloyd
Alexander Rockwell	Jennifer Beals
Gene Roddenberry	Majel Barrett
Paul Roebling	Olga Bellin
Buddy Rogers	Mary Pickford
Roy Rogers	Dale Evans
Gilbert Roland	Constance Bennett
Erik Rolf	Ruth Warwick
Mickey Rooney	Ava Gardner
"	Martha Vickers
David Rose	Judy Garland
"	Martha Raye
Frank Ross	Jean Arthur
"	Joan Caulfield
Roberto Rossellini	Ingrid Bergman
Mickey Rourke	Carré Otis
	Debra Feuer
Charles Ruggles	Adele Rowland
Wesley Ruggles	Arlene Judge
William Russell (d. 1929)	Helen Ferguson
☞	
Richie Sambora	Heather Locklear
George Sanders	Benita Hume
"	Magda Gabor
"	Zsa Zsa Gabor
Tommy Sands	Nancy Sinatra
Paul Scardon	Betty Blythe
George C. Scott	Colleen Dewhurst
Steven Seagal	Kelly LeBrock
Douglas Seale	Louise Troy
Peter Sellers	Lynne Frederick
Edgar Selwyn	Ruth Wilcox Selwyn
David O. Selznick	Jennifer Jones
Artie Shaw	Lana Turner
"	Ava Gardner
"	Evelyn Keyes
Lowell Sherman	Pauline Garon
"	Helen Costello
Don Siegel	Viveca Lindfors
Frank Sinatra	Ava Gardner
"	Mia Farrow
Wendell Phillips Smalley	Lois Weber
Albert Edward Smith	Jean Page
Howard I. Smith	Lillian Boardman
Roger Smith	Ann-Margret
Nicholas Soussanin	Olga Baclanova
Sam Spiegel	Lynne Baggett
Steven Spielberg	Amy Irving

WIFE	SHOW-BIZ HUSBANDS**
Rena Rogers	Frank Borzage
Ruth Roland	Ben Bard
Elaine Rosen	John Ireland
Fanny Rowe	Clive Morton
Adele Rowland	Charles Ruggles
"	Conway Tearle
Dina Ruiz	Clint Eastwood
Barbara Rush	Jeffrey Hunter
Gail Russell	Guy Madison
Rosalind Russell	Frederick Brisson
Ann Rutherford	William Dozier
Meg Ryan	Dennis Quaid
☞	
Virginia Sale	Sam Wren
Thelma Salter	Edward Kaufman
Olga San Juan	Edmond O'Brien
Susan Sarandon	Tim Robbins
Anne Sargent	Edmond O'Brien
"	Paul McGrath
Natalie Schafer	Louis Calhern
Kim Schmidt	Gig Young
Patti Scialfa	Bruce Springsteen
Sydna Scott	Jerome Thor
Dorothy Sebastian	William Boyd
Kyra Sedgwick	Kevin Bacon
Sara Seegar	Ezra Stone
Vivienne Segal	Robert Ames
Ruth Wilcox Selwyn	Edgar Selwyn
Jane Seymour	James Keach
Norma Shearer	Irving Thalberg
Ally Sheedy	David Lansbury
Ann Sheridan	George Brent
"	Edward Norris
"	Scott McKay
Talia Shire	Jack Swartzman
Anne Shirley	John Payne
Ann Shoemaker	Henry Stephenson
Dinah Shore	George Montgomery
Sylvia Sidney	Luther Adler
Simone Signoret	Yves Montand
Jean Simmons	Stewart Granger
"	Richard Brooks
Nancy Sinatra	Tommy Sands
Alexis Smith	Craig Stevens
Ethel Smith	Ralph Bellamy
Maggie Smith	(Sir) Robert Stephens
Marguerite Snow	James Cruze
"	Neely Edwards
Gale Sondergaard	Herbert Biberman
Ann Sothern	Roger Pryor
"	Robert Sterling
Evelyn Klein Spitalny	Phil Spitalny
Jill St. John	Robert Wagner
Barbara Stanwyck	Frank Fay
"	Robert Taylor
Myrtle Stedman	Marshall Stedman
Mary Steenburgen	Malcolm McDowell
"	Ted Danson
Anna Sten	Eugene Frenke
Jan Sterling	Paul Douglas

370

HUSBAND	SHOW-BIZ WIVES**	WIFE	SHOW-BIZ HUSBANDS**
Phil Spitalny	*Evelyn Klein Spitalny*	Frances Sternhagen	*Thomas A. Carlin*
Bruce Springsteen	*Patti Scialfa*	Connie Stevens	*James Stacy*
James Stacy	*Connie Stevens*	K. T. Stevens	*Hugh Marlowe*
Michael St. Angel	*Marjorie Holliday*	Madeleine Stowe	*Brian Benben*
Ringo Starr	*Barbara Bach*	Margaret Sullavan	*Henry Fonda*
Marshall Stedman	*Myrtle Stedman*	"	*William Wyler*
Rod Steiger	*Claire Bloom*	"	*Leland Hayward*
(Sir) Robert Stephens	*Maggie Smith*	Ruth Sullivan	*Dick Curtis*
Henry Stephenson	*Ann Shoemaker*	Betty Sundmark	*Alan Curtis*
Robert Sterling	*Ann Sothern*	Gloria Swanson	*Wallace Beery*
"	*Anne Jeffreys*	**T**	
Craig Stevens	*Alexis Smith*	Mabel Taliaferro	*Tom Corrigan*
Parker Stevenson	*Kirstie Alley*	"	*Robert Ober*
Jerry Stiller	*Anne Meara*	Margaret Tallichet	*William Wyler*
Ezra Stone	*Sara Seegar*	Natalie Talmadge	*Buster Keaton*
David Street	*Debra Paget*	Norma Talmadge	*George Jessel*
Nick Stuart	*Sue Carol*	Jessica Tandy	*Hume Cronyn*
Burt Sugarman	*Mary Hart*	Elsie Tarron	*Andy Clyde*
Victor Sutherland	*Pearl White*	Lilyan Tashman	*Edmund Lowe*
"	*Linda Barrett*	Sharon Tate	*Roman Polanski*
Jack Swartzman	*Talia Shire*	Elizabeth Taylor	*Michael Wilding*
Patrick Swayze	*Lisa Niemi*	"	*Mike Todd*
T		"	*Eddie Fisher*
William Talman	*Barbara Read*	"	*Richard Burton (twice)*
Richard Tauber	*Diana Napier*	Veree Teasdale	*Adolphe Menjou*
Donald F. Taylor	*Marie McDonald*	Olive Tell	*Henry M. Hobart*
Robert Taylor	*Barbara Stanwyck*	Shirley Temple	*John Agar*
Conway Tearle	*Adele Rowland*	Victoria Tennant	*Steve Martin*
Jon Tenney	*Teri Hatcher*	Joan Tetzel	*Oscar Homolka*
Philip Terry	*Joan Crawford*	Phyllis Thaxter	*James T. Aubrey*
Duccio Tessari	*Lorella De Luca*	Olive Thomas	*Jack Pickford*
Irving Thalberg	*Norma Shearer*	Emma Thompson	*Kenneth Branagh*
Carlos Thompson	*Lilli Palmer*	Uma Thurman	*Gary Oldman*
Fred Thomson	*Frances Marion*	Cheryl Tiegs	*Tony Peck*
Jerome Thor	*Sydna Scott*	Gene Tierney	*Oleg Cassini*
Mike Todd	*Joan Blondell*	Ann Todd	*David Lean*
"	*Elizabeth Taylor*	Louise Treadwell	*Spencer Tracy*
Franchot Tone	*Joan Crawford*	Dorothy Tree	*Michael Uris*
"	*Jean Wallace*	Louise Troy	*Werner Klemperer*
"	*Barbara Payton*	"	*Douglas Seale*
Rip Torn	*Geraldine Page*	Lana Turner	*Artie Shaw*
Spencer Tracy	*Louise Treadwell*	"	*Lex Barker*
Bill Travers	*Virginia McKenna*	"	*Stephen Crane (twice)*
John Travolta	*Kelly Preston*	Cicely Tyson	*Miles Davis*
George Loane Tucker	*Elisabeth Risdon*	**V**	
Ted Turner	*Jane Fonda*	Virginia Valli	*Charles Farrell*
Brandon Tynan	*Lily Cahill*	Mabel Van Buren	*James Gordon*
U		Vivian Vance	*Philip Ober*
Michael Uris	*Dorothy Tree*	Lupe Velez	*Johnny Weismuller*
V		Martha Vickers	*Mickey Rooney*
Roger Vadim	*Annette Vadim*	Florence (Cobb) Vidor	*King Vidor*
"	*Brigitte Bardot*	"	*Jascha Heifitz*
"	*Jane Fonda*	**W**	
Rudolph Valentino	*Jean Acker*	Marcy Walker	*Billy Warlock*
"	*Natacha Rambova*	Jean Wallace	*Franchot Tone*
Rudy Vallee	*Jane Greer*	"	*Cornel Wilde*
Bobby Van	*Elaine Joyce*	Dionne Warwick	*William D. Elliott*
Eddie Van Halen	*Valerie Bertinelli*	Ruth Warwick	*Erik Rolf*
King Vidor	*Eleanor Boardman*	Lois Weber	*Wendell Phillips Smalley*
"	*Florence (Cobb) Vidor*	Eleanor Wells	*William Perry Adams*

HUSBAND	SHOW-BIZ WIVES**	WIFE	SHOW-BIZ HUSBANDS**
W		Gwen Welles	Harris Yulin
Robert Wagner	Natalie Wood (twice)	Joanne Whalley	Val Kilmer
"	Jill St. John	Betty White	Allen Ludden
Robert Walker	Jennifer Jones	Pearl White	Victor Sutherland
Eli Wallach	Anne Jackson	Margaret Whiting	Joe "Fingers" Carr
Hal Wallis	Martha Hyer	Claire Whitney	Robert Emmett Keane
Henry B. Walthall	Mary Charleson	Josephine Whittell	Robert Warwick
Walter Wanger	Joan Bennett	(Dame) May Whitty	Ben Webster
Billy Warlock	Marcy Walker	Kathleen Widdoes	Richard Jordan
Sam Warner	Lina Basquette	Sandra Will	Keith Carradine
Robert Warwick	Josephine Whittell	Catherine Willard	Ralph Bellamy
Ben Webster	(Dame) May Whitty	Clara Williams	Reginald Barker
Johnny Weismuller	Lupe Velez	Esther Williams	Ben Gage
Orson Welles	Rita Hayworth	"	Fernando Lamas
William Wellman	Helene Chadwick	Kathlyn Williams	Charles Eyton
Brooks West	Eve Arden	Joan Wilson	Jeremy Brett
Bud Westmore	Martha Raye	Rita Wilson	Tom Hanks
Robert Wilcox	Florence Rice	Debra Winger	Timothy Hutton
Cornel Wilde	Patricia Knight	Shelley Winters	Vittorio Gassman
"	Jean Wallace	"	Anthony Franciosa
Gene Wilder	Gilda Radner	Estelle Winwood	Arthur Chesney
Michael Wilding	Elizabeth Taylor	Googie Withers	John McCallum
"	Margaret Leighton	Natalie Wood	Robert Wagner
Bill Williams	Barbara Hale	Joanne Woodward	Paul Newman
Bruce Willis	Demi Moore	Constance Worth	George Brent
Stu Wilson	Lorraine Krueger	Aloha Wray	Frankie Darro
Charles Winninger	Blanche Ring	Teresa Wright	Niven Busch
Robert Wise	Patricia Doyle	Jane Wyman	Ronald Reagan
Grant Withers	Loretta Young	Patrice Wymore	Errol Flynn
"	Estelita Rodriguez	**Y**	
Frederick Worlock	Elsie Ferguson	Pauline Yates	Donald Churchill
Jack Wrather	Bonita Granville	Georgiana Young	Ricardo Montalban
Sam Wren	Virginia Sale	Loretta Young	Grant Withers
William Wyler	Margaret Sullavan		
"	Margaret Tallichet		
Y			
Herbert Y. Yates	Vera Hruba Ralston		
Gig Young	Elizabeth Montgomery		
"	Kim Schmidt		
Harris Yulin	Gwen Welles		
Z			
Billy Zane	Lisa Collins		
Florenz Ziegfeld	Billie Burke		

FATHER	SHOW-BIZ SONS	FATHER	SHOW-BIZ DAUGHTERS
A		**A**	
Henry H. Ainley	Richard Ainley	Desi Arnaz	Lucie Arnaz
Eddie Albert	Edward Albert, Jr.	**B**	
Robert Alda	Alan Alda	Martin Balsam	Talia Balsam
"	Antony Alda	George Bancroft	Ann Bancroft
Alan Arkin	Adam Arkin	John Barrymore	Diana Barrymore
Pedro Armendariz	Pedro Armendariz, Jr.	Maurice Barrymore	Ethel Barrymore
Herbert W. Armstrong	Garner "Ted" Armstrong	Frank Beal	Dolly Beal
Felix Aylmer	David Aylmer	Richard Bennett	Barbara Bennett
B		"	Constance Bennett
Maurice Barrymore	John Barrymore	"	Joan Bennett
"	Lionel Barrymore	Edgar Bergen	Candice Bergen
Frank Beal	Scott Beal	Pat Boone	Debbie Boone
Noah Beery, Sr.	Noah Beery, Jr.		

... WHO IS RELATED TO WHOM – OFF SCREEN?*...

FATHER	SHOW-BIZ SONS
Ed Begley	Ed Begley, Jr.
Jussi Bjorling	Rolf Bjorling
Dan Blocker	Dirk Blocker
Lloyd Bridges	Beau Bridges
Ca.l Brisson	Frederick Brisson
James Broderick	Matthew Broderick
Joe E. Brown	Mike Frankovich (adopted)
Francis X. Bushman	Francis X. Bushman, Jr.
"	(aka Ralph Bushman)
Fred Butler	David Butler
C	
Frank Capra	Tom Capra
John Carradine	David Carradine
"	Keith Carradine
"	Robert Carradine
Enrico Caruso	Enrico Caruso, Jr.
Jack Cassidy	David Cassidy
"	Shaun Cassidy
Lon Chaney	Lon Chaney, Jr.
Emile Chautard (step-father)	George Archainbaud
Nick Clooney	George Clooney
Jack Coogan Sr.	Jackie Coogan
Carmine Coppola	Francis Ford Coppola
William Courtleigh, Sr.	William Courtleigh, Jr.
Frank Craven	John Craven
Bing Crosby	Gary Crosby
"	Dennis Crosby
"	Lindsay Crosby
"	Philip Crosby
D	
James Daly	Timothy Daly
Jules Dassin	Joe Dassin
Harry Davenport	Arthur Rankin
Frank Davis	Battle Davis
Carter DeHaven, Sr.	Carter DeHaven, Jr.
Dom DeLuise	Peter DeLuise
"	Michael DeLuise
Gerard Depardieu	Guillaume Depardieu
Kirk Douglas	Michael Douglas
Morton Downey	Morton Downey, Jr.
Eddie Duchin	Peter Duchin
Franklin Dyall	Valentine Dyall
E	
Bob Elliott	Chris Elliott
F	
Douglas Fairbanks	Douglas Fairbanks, Jr.
Errol Flynn	Sean Flynn
Henry Fonda	Peter Fonda
Eddie Foy, Sr.	Eddie Foy, Jr.
"	Bryan Foy
G	
John Garfield	David Garfield
James Gleason	Russell Gleason
Bernard Gorcey	Leo Gorcey
"	David Gorcey
Woody Guthrie	Arlo Guthrie
H	
Alan Hale	Alan Hale, Jr.
George Hamilton	Ashley Hamilton
Ben Henricks, Sr.	Ben Hendricks, Jr.

FATHER	SHOW-BIZ DAUGHTERS
C	
Charlie Chaplin	Geraldine Chaplin
"	Josephine Chaplin
Nat "King" Cole	Natalie Cole
Carmine Coppola	Talia Shire
Francis Ford Coppola	Sofia Coppola
Ernest Cossart	Valerie Cossart Livingston
Lou Costello	Carol Costello
Maurice Costello	Dolores Costello
"	Helene Costello
Hume Cronyn	Tandy Cronyn
Tony Curtis	Jamie Lee Curtis
D	
James Daly	Tyne Daly
Harry Davenport	Dorothy Davenport
Carter DeHaven, Sr.	Gloria DeHaven
Cecil B. DeMille	Katherine DeMille (adopted)
Bruce Dern	Laura Dern
Oliva Dionne	Emelie Dionne
"	Marie Dionne
Maurice Dorléac	Catherine Deneuve
"	Françoise Dorléac
F	
John Farrow	Mia Farrow
Eddie Fisher	Carrie Fisher
Henry Fonda	Jane Fonda
Peter Fonda	Bridget Fonda
G	
Joel Gray	Jennifer Gray
H	
Jack Holt	Jennifer Holt
John Huston	Anjelica Huston
I	
Jules Irving	Amy Irving
K	
Edward M. Kimball	Clara Kimball Young
Klaus Kinski	Nastassja Kinski
L	
Michael Landon	Leslie Landon
Ernest Lawford	Betty Lawford
Gene Lockhart	June Lockhart
M	
Raymond Massey	Anna Massey
Marcello Mastroianni	Chiara Mastroianni
Cyril Maude	Margery Maude
Robert B. McKenzie	Ida Mae McKenzie
"	Lally McKenzie
"	Fay McKenzie
John Mills	Hayley Mills
Vincente Minnelli	Liza Minnelli
Robert Montgomery	Elizabeth Montgomery
Vic Morrow	Jennifer Jason Leigh
Alan Mowbray	Patricia Mowbray
O	
Ryan O'Neal	Tatum O'Neal
P	
Sidney Poitier	Pam Poitier
Richard Pryor	Rain Pryor
R	
John Raitt	Bonnie Raitt

... WHO IS RELATED TO WHOM — OFF SCREEN?*...

FATHER	SHOW-BIZ SONS
Jim Henson	Brian Henson
Taylor Holmes	Ralph Holmes
"	Phillips Holmes
Jack Holt	Tim Holt
"	David Holt
De Wolf Hopper	William Hopper
Rudolfo Hoyos, Sr.	Rudolfo Hoyos, Jr.
Jim Hutton	Timothy Hutton
I	
Thomas H. Ince	Richard Ince
John Ireland	John Ireland, Jr.
K	
Robert Kaufman	Christopher Kaufman
Dennis King, Sr.	Dennis King, Jr.
Sam Kydd	Jonathan Kydd
L	
Michael Landon	Michael Landon, Jr.
Bruce Lee	Brandon Lee
Duke R. Lee	Duke Lee, Jr.
"	John Lee
Jack Lemmon	Chris Lemmon
John Lennon	Julian Lennon
Sam Livesey	Jack Livesey
"	Roger Livesey
Felix Locher	Jon Hall
M	
Charles MacArthur	James MacArthur (adopted)
Bob Marley	Ziggy Marley
Dean Martin	Dean Paul Martin, Jr.
Samuel "Frenchie" Marx	"Chico" Marx
"	"Harpo" Marx
"	"Gummo" Marx
"	"Groucho" Marx
"	"Zeppo" Marx
Raymond Massey	Daniel Massey
John McIntire	Tim McIntire
Steve McQueen	Chad McQueen
Fuller Mellish, Sr.	Fuller Mellish, Jr.
John Merton	Lane Bradford
John Mills, Sr.	Herbert Mills
"	Harry Mills
"	Donald Mills
"	John Mills, Jr.
Maurice Moskovitch	Noel Madison
N	
Tom Neal	Tom Neal, Jr.
Ozzie Nelson	David Nelson
"	Rick Nelson
Rick Nelson	Matthew Nelson
"	Gunnar Nelson
Paul Newman	Scott Newman
George Nichols, Sr.	George Nichols, Jr.
Christian Nyby	Christian Nyby II
O	
Carroll O'Connor	Hugh O'Connor
Ryan O'Neal	Griffin O'Neal
P	
Emory Parnell	James Parnell
Tony Pastor	Guy Pastor
Gregory Peck	Tony Peck

FATHER	SHOW-BIZ DAUGHTERS
Michael Redgrave	Lynn Redgrave
"	Vanessa Redgrave
Grantland Rice	Florence Rice
Tony Richardson	Natasha Richardson
"	Joely Richardson
S	
Boris Sagal	Katey Sagal
"	Jean Sagal
"	Liz Sagal
Edward Sedgwick	Josie Sedgwick
Frank Sinatra	Nancy Sinatra
Otis Skinner	Cornelia Otis Skinner
(Sir) Guy Standing	Kay Hammond
	(aka Dorothy Standing)
Houseley Stevenson, Sr.	Onslow Stevens
Jerry Stiller	Amy Stiller
Lee Strasberg	Susan Strasberg
T	
Danny Thomas	Marlo Thomas
W	
Sam Wood	K. T. Stevens
"	(aka Gloria Wood)
Z	
Efrem Zimbalist, Jr.	Stephanie Zimbalist
George Zucco	Frances Zucco

FATHER	SHOW-BIZ SONS	FATHER	SHOW-BIZ DAUGHTERS
Edward Peil, Sr.	*Edward Peil, Jr.*		
Osgood Perkins	*Anthony Perkins*		
Norman Phillips Sr.	*Norman Phillips Jr.*		
F. Tyrone Power	*Tyrone Power*		
Tyrone Power	*Tyrone Power, Jr. (IV)*		
R			
Hal Reid	*Wallace Reid*		
Wallace Reid	*Wallace Reid, Jr.*		
Carl Reiner	*Rob Reiner*		
Max Reinhardt	*Gottfried Reinhardt*		
George Relph	*Michael Relph*		
Jason Robards, Sr.	*Jason Robards, Jr.*		
Will Rogers	*Will Rogers, Jr.*		
Pat Rooney, II	*Pat Rooney, III*		
Oscar Rudolph	*Alan Rudolph*		
S			
Rudolph Schildkraut	*Joseph Schildkraut*		
George C. Scott	*Campbell Scott*		
Edward Sedgwick	*Edward M. Sedgwick*		
Al Shean	*Larry Shean*		
Martin Sheen	*Emilio Estevez*		
"	*Charlie Sheen*		
Frank Sinatra	*Frank Sinatra, Jr.*		
Jack Sonntag	*Robert Sonntag*		
Sylvester Stallone	*Sage Stallone*		
Marshall Stedman	*Lincoln Stedman*		
Houseley Stevenson	*Onslow Stevenson*		
Jerry Stiller	*Ben Stiller*		
Donald Sutherland	*Kiefer Sutherland*		
T			
Julius Tannen	*Charles D. Tannen*		
"	*William Tannen*		
Dub Taylor	*Buck Taylor*		
Maurice Tourneur	*Jacques Tourneur*		
V			
Roger Vadim	*Christian Vadim*		
Dick Van Patten	*Nels Van Patten*		
"	*Jimmy Van Patten*		
"	*Vince Van Patten*		
Melvin Van Peebles	*Mario Van Peebles*		
W			
Charles D. Waldron	*Charles K. Waldron*		
Robert Walker	*Robert Walker, Jr.*		
Jack L. Warner	*Jack M. Warner*		
Bryant Washburn Sr.	*Bryant Washburn Jr.*		
John Wayne	*Patrick Wayne*		
Bill Williams	*William Katt*		
Ed Wynn	*Keenan Wynn*		
Y			
Joe Yule	*Mickey Rooney*		
Z			
Darryl F. Zanuck	*Richard D. Zanuck*		
Adolph Zukor	*Eugene Zukor*		

MOTHER	SHOW-BIZ SONS	MOTHER	SHOW-BIZ DAUGHTERS
B		**B**	
Fay Bainter	*Reginald Venable*	Dorothy Helen Baker	*Diane Baker*
Helen Broderick	*Broderick Crawford*	Lucille Ball	*Lucie Arnaz*

* Includes only show-biz personalities.

... WHO IS RELATED TO WHOM — OFF SCREEN?*...

MOTHER	SHOW-BIZ SONS
C	
Jeanne Cooper	Corbin Bernsen
Delores Costello	John Blythe Barrymore, Jr.
Dixie Lee Crosby	Gary Crosby
"	Dennis Crosby
"	Philip Crosby
"	Lindsay Crosby
D	
Arlene Dahl	Lorenzo Lamas
Lili Damita	Sean Flynn
Dorothy Davenport	Wallace Reid, Jr.
Mildred Davis	Harold Lloyd, Jr.
Catherine Deneuve	Christian Vadim
Julia De Vito	Danny De Vito
Colleen Dewhurst	Campbell Scott
E	
Lillian Eliott	Lloyd Corrigan
F	
Mary Forbes	Ralph Forbes
G	
Lucille Gleason	Russell Gleason
H	
Florence Hackett	Raymond Hackett
Barbara Hale	William Katt
Kay Hammond	John Standing
Helen Hayes	James MacArthur
Harriet Hilliard	David Nelson
"	Rick Nelson
Hedda Hopper	William Hopper
J	
Shirley Jones	Shaun Cassidy
"	David Cassidy (stepson)
L	
Lady May Lawford	Peter Lawford
Louise Lester	Scott Beal
M	
Brenda Marshall	Scott Holden
Anne Meara	Ben Stiller
N	
Harriet Hilliard Nelson	David Nelson
"	Rick Nelson
O	
Peggy O'Neill	Michael Landon
S	
Myrtle Stedman	Lincoln Stedman
Fanny Schiller	Manolo Fabregas
Adeline Stanhope	Stanhope Wheatcroft
Stella Stevens	Andrew Stevens
Barbra Streisand	Jason Gould
V	
Dorothy Vernon	Bobby Vernon
W	
Joanne Woodward	Scott Newman (stepson)

MOTHER	SHOW-BIZ DAUGHTERS
Adele Blood	Dawn Hope
C	
Maybelle Carter	June Carter (Cash)
Oona Chaplin	Geraldine Chaplin
"	Josephine Chaplin
D	
Abby Dalton	Kathleen Kinmont
Ruby Dandridge	Dorothy Dandridge
Alice Davenport	Dorothy Davenport
Joan Davis	Beverly Wills
Catherine Deneuve	Chiara Mastroianni
Renée Deneuve	Catherine Deneuve
"	Françoise Dorléac
G	
Judy Garland	Liza Minnelli
J	
Naomi Judd	Ashley Judd
"	Wynonna Judd
L	
Dianne Ladd	Laura Dern
Lillian Lawrence	Ethel Grey Terry
Louise Lester	Dolly Beal
M	
Moyna McGill	Angela Lansbury
Leila McIntyre	Leila Hyams
Eva B. McKenzie	Lally McKenzie
"	Fay McKenzie
Anne Meara	Amy Stiller
Jean Menahan	Eileen Brennan
Elizabeth Allen Montgomery	Elizabeth Montgomery
Adrianne Morrison	Barbara Bennett
"	Constance Bennett
"	Joan Bennett
O	
Maureen O'Sullivan	Mia Farrow
P	
Priscilla Pointer	Amy Irving
R	
Vanessa Redgrave	Natasha Richardson
Debbie Reynolds	Carrie Fisher
Joan Rivers	Melissa Rivers
S	
Dorothy Hammond Standing	Kay Hammond
T	
Jessica Tandy	Tandy Cronyn

SHOW-BIZ BROTHERS

A	
Alan Alda	Antony Alda
Don Ameche	Jim Ameche
Dana Andrews	Steve Forrest

SHOW-BIZ SISTERS

A	
LaVerne Andrews	Patti Andrews
"	Maxine Andrews
Pier Angeli	Marisa Pavan

SHOW-BIZ BROTHERS	
James Arness	Peter Graves
B	
Max Baer	Jacob "Buddy" Baer
Alec Baldwin	William Baldwin
"	Daniel Baldwin
"	Stephen Baldwin
John Barrymore	Lionel Barrymore
Wallace Beery	Noah Beery, Sr.
John Belushi	Jim Belushi
Herschel Bernardi	Jack Bernardi
Royce Blackburn	Ramon Blackburn (twins)
Frank Borzage	Daniel Borzage
Scott Brady	Lawrence Tierney
C	
Jack Carson	Robert Carson
Charlie Chaplin	Sydney Chaplin
Charley Chase	James Parrott
Andy Clyde	David Clyde
Gary Crosby	Dennis Crosby
"	Philip Crosby
"	Lindsay Crosby
D	
Sabu (Dastagir)	Sheik Dastagir
Dino DeLaurentiis	Luigi DeLaurentiis
Peter DeLuise	Michael DeLuise
Cecil B. DeMille	William C. DeMille
Jack Dillon	Edward Dillon
Walt Disney	Roy O. Disney
Jimmy Dorsey	Tommy Dorsey
E	
Les Elgart	Larry Elgart
F	
William Farnum	Dustin Farnum
Barry Fitzgerald	Arthur Shields
Dave Fleischer	Louis Fleischer
G	
William Gargan	Edward Gargan
George Gershwin	Ira Gershwin
Andy Gibb	Barry Gibb
"	Robin Gibb
"	Maurice Gibb
Leo Gorcey	David Gorcey
Eddie Gribbon	Harry Gribbon
Edmund Gwenn	Arthur Chesney
H	
Bobby Harron	John Harron
Phillips Holmes	Ralph Holmes
Donald Houston	Glyn Houston
Eugene Howard	Willie Howard
Jerome "Curly" Howard	Moe Howard
"	Shemp Howard
All Hoxie	Jack Hoxie
Jack Hulbert	Claude Hulbert
I	
Al Immediato	Hugo Immediato
"	Nino "Nick" Immediato
John E. Ince	Ralph W. Ince
"	Richard Ince
J	
Michael Jackson	Sigmund "Jackie" Jackson

SHOW-BIZ SISTERS	
B	
Hermione Baddeley	Angela Baddeley
Joan Bennett	Constance Bennett
C	
Dolores Costello	Helene Costello
D	
Catherine Deneuve	Françoise Dorléac
F	
Joan Fontaine	Olivia de Havilland
G	
Zsa Zsa Gabor	Magda Gabor
"	Eva Gabor
Lillian Gish	Dorothy Gish
Kathryn Grayson	Frances Raeburn
I	
May Irwin	Flo Irwin
J	
Ashley Judd	Wynonna Judd
L	
Priscilla Lane	Rosemary Lane
"	Lola Lane
M	
Jeanette MacDonald	Blossom Rock
Barbara Mandrell	Irlene Mandrell
"	Louise Mandrell
Hattie McDaniel	Etta McDaniel
Audrey Meadows	Jayne Meadows
Mary Miles Minter	Margaret Shelby
N	
Florence Nash	Mary Nash
O	
Ashley Olsen	Mary-Kate Olsen
P	Molly O'Day
P	
Paula Prentiss	Ann Prentiss
Michelle Pfeiffer	DeDee Pfeiffer
R	
Lillian Randolph	Amanda Randolph
Vanessa Redgrave	Lynn Redgrave
S	
Katey Sagal	Jean Sagal
"	Liz Sagal
Marguerite Shaw	Reta Shaw
T	
Norma Talmadge	Constance Talmadge
"	Natalie Talmadge
Nicholle Tom	Heather Tom
V	
Odile Versois	Marina Vlady
Marina Vlady	Odile Versois
Y	
Loretta Young	Georgianna Young
"	Sally Young
"	Polly Ann Young

SHOW-BIZ BROTHERS		SHOW-BIZ SISTERS	
Michael Jackson	Toriano "Tito" Jackson		
"	Marion David Jackson		
"	Michael Joe Jackson		
"	Steven "Randy" Jackson		
K			
Lawrence Kasha	Al Kasha		
Stacy Keach	James Keach		
Edgar Kennedy	Tom Kennedy		
Zoltan Korda	(Sir) Alexander Korda		
L			
Walter "Lee" Liberace	George Liberace		
Jack Livesey	Roger Livesey		
Guy Lombardo	Carmen Lombardo		
"	Lebert Lombardo		
Bert Lytell	Wilfred Lytell		
M			
"Groucho" Marx	"Chico" Marx		
"	"Harpo" Marx		
"	"Zeppo" Marx		
"	"Gummo" Marx		
Ken Maynard	Kermit Maynard		
Frank McHugh	Matt McHugh		
Lewis Meltzer	Sid Melton		
Adolphe Menjou	Henri Menjou		
Ricardo Montalban	Carlos Montalban		
Tom Moore	Matt Moore		
"	Owen Moore		
Frank Morgan	Ralph Morgan		
Chester Morris	Adrian Morris		
N			
Tommy Noonan	Michael Noon		
"	John Ireland (half-brother)		
P			
House Peters	Page E. Peters		
River Phoenix	Joaquin "Leaf" Phoenix		
Jeff Porcaro	Steve Porcaro		
"	Mike Porcaro		
André Previn	Steve Previn		
R			
Pedro Regas	George Regas		
Jean Renoir	Pierre Renoir		
Al Ritz	Harry Ritz		
"	Jimmy Ritz		
Mark Rosenberg	Alan Rosenberg		
Charles Ruggles	Wesley Ruggles		
William Russell (d. 1929)	Albert Russell		
S			
Terry Sanders	Denis Sanders		
Fred Santley	Joseph Santley		
David O. Selznick	Myron Selznick		
"	Howard Selznick		
Charlie Sheen	Emilio Estevez		
Rider Strong	Shiloh Strong		
T			
Charles D. Tannen	William Tannen		
(Sir) Godfrey Tearle	Conway Tearle (half-brother)		
David Torrence	Ernest Torrence		
V			
Dick Van Dyke	Jerry Van Dyke		

... WHO IS ~~RELATED~~ TO WHOM — OFF ~~SCREEN~~?*...

SHOW-BIZ BROTHERS	
W	
Raoul Walsh	*George Walsh*
Henry B. Walthall	*Wallace W. Walthall*
Jack L. Warner	*Harry M. Warner*
James Woolf	*John Woolf*

BROTHER	SHOW-BIZ SISTERS
A	
Fred Astaire	*Adele Astaire*
B	
Bill Bailey	*Pearl Bailey*
John Barrymore	*Ethel Barrymore*
Lionel Barrymore	*Ethel Barrymore*
Warren Beatty	*Shirley MacLaine*
Billy Bletcher	*Arline Bletcher*
Marlon Brando	*Jocelyn Brando*
Lew Brice	*Fanny Brice*
C	
James Cagney	*Jeanne Cagney*
Kirk Cameron	*Candace Cameron*
Richard Carpenter	*Karen Carpenter*
Andy Clyde	*Jean Clyde*
David Clyde	*"*
Bud Collyer	*June Collyer*
Francis Ford Coppola	*Talia Shire*
D	
Timothy Daly	*Tyne Daly*
Carter DeHaven, Jr.	*Gloria DeHaven*
F	
Peter Fonda	*Jane Fonda*
Ralph Forbes	*Brenda Forbes*
Mick Fleetwood	*Susan Fleetwood*
G	
Maurice Geraghty	*Carmelita Geraghty*
H	
Billy Halop	*Florence Halop*
Bobby Harron	*Tessie Harron*
John Harron	*"*

UNCLE	SHOW-BIZ NEPHEWS
B	
Wallace Beery	*Noah Beery, Jr.*
C	
Francis Ford Coppola	*Nicolas Cage*
Frank Craven	*Eddie Craven*

UNCLE	SHOW-BIZ NIECES
Cecil B. De Mille	*Agnes De Mille*

SHOW-BIZ COUSINS	
L	
Lupino Lane	*Ida Lupino*
Peter Lawford	*Betty Lawford*

SHOW-BIZ SISTERS	

BROTHER	SHOW-BIZ SISTERS
I	
David Irving	*Amy Irving*
José Iturbi	*Amparo Iturbi*
J	
Michael Jackson	*La Toya Jackson*
"	*Maureen Jackson*
"	*Jermaine Jackson*
"	*Janet Jackson*
K	
Jack Kelly	*Nancy Kelly*
L	
Arthur Lake	*Florence Lake*
M	
Louis J. Marlowe	*June Marlowe*
Sam "Deacon" McDaniel	*Hattie McDaniel*
"	*Etta McDaniel*
John Megna	*Connie Stevens (half-sister)*
P	
Jack Pickford	*Mary Pickford*
"	*Lottie Pickford*
R	
Howard Ralston	*Esther Ralston*
Cyril Ring	*Blanche Ring*
Eric Roberts	*Julia Roberts*
S	
Douglas Shearer	*Norma Shearer*
Andrew Shue	*Elisabeth Shue*
Chuck Stevens	*Connie Stevens*

AUNT	SHOW-BIZ NEPHEWS
C	
Rosemary Clooney	*George Clooney*
Olive Cooper	*George Stevens*
L	
Angela Lansbury	*David Lansbury*
S	
Talia Shire	*Nicholas Cage*

AUNT	SHOW-BIZ NIECES
Nanette Fabray	*Shelley Fabares*

BROTHER-IN-LAW	SHOW-BIZ SISTER-IN-LAWS
Dick Foran	*Mary Foran*

... WHO IS RELATED TO WHOM — OFF SCREEN?*...

SHOW-BIZ COUSINS	
M	
Henry Morgan	*Alan Jay Lerner*
R	
Bonnie Raitt	*James Raitt*
S	
Edie Sedgwick	*Kyra Sedgwick*
V	
Dee Victor	*James Arness, Peter Graves*

GRANDFATHER	SHOW-BIZ GRANDSONS
Carmine Coppola	*Nicholas Cage*

FATHER-IN-LAW	SHOW-BIZ SON-IN-LAWS
Arturo Toscanini	*Vladimir Horowitz*

GRANDMOTHER	SHOW-BIZ GRANDSONS
Virginia Fabregas	*Manolo Fabregas*

9

STUDIOS OF THE STARS

COLUMBIA

Robert Allen
Jean Arthur*
Lucille Ball*
James Blakeley
Johnny Mack Brown*
Jack Buckler*
Nancy Carroll*
Walter Connolly*
Donald Cook*
Inez Courtney*
Richard Cromwell*
Allyn Drake
Douglas Dumbrille*
Wallace Ford*
John Gilbert*
Arthur Hohl*

Jack Holt*
Victor Jory*
Fred Keating*
Peter Lorre*
Marian Marsh
Tim McCoy*
Geneva Mitchell*
Grace Moore*
George Murphy*
Gene Raymond
Florence Rice*
Billie Seward
Ann Sothern
Raymond Walburn*
Fay Wray

FOX

Frank Albertson*
Astrid Allwyn*
Rosemary Ames
Lew Ayres
Catalina Barcena*
Mona Barrie
Warner Baxter*
John Boles*
John Bradford
Frances Carlon*
Madeleine Carroll*
Dave Chasen*
Tito Coral
Jane Darwell*
Alan Dinehart*
James Dunn*
Jack Durant*
Alice Faye
Peggy Fears
Stepin Fetchit*
Dick Foran*
Norman Foster*
Ketti Gallian*
Janet Gaynor*
Harry Green*
Sterling Holloway*
Rochelle Hudson*
Roger Imhof*

Walter Johnson
Walter Woolf King*
June Lang
Edmund Lowe*
Victor McLaglen*
Frank Melton*
Frank Mitchell*
Conchita Montenegro
Rosita Moreno
Herbert Mundin*
Warner Oland*
Valentin Parera
Pat Paterson*
Ruth Peterson
John Qualen*
Will Rogers*
Gilbert Roland*
Raul Roulien
Siegfried Rumann*
Albert Shean*
Berta Singerman
Shirley Temple
Spencer Tracy*
Claire Trevor
Helen Twelvetrees*
Bianca Vischer
Henry B. Walthall*
Hugh Williams*

METRO-GOLDWYN-MAYER

Brian Aherne*
Katharine Alexander*
Elizabeth Allan*
Lionel Barrymore*
Wallace Beery*
Constance Bennett*

Virginia Bruce*
Ralph Bushman*
Charles Butterworth*
Mary Carlisle
Leo Carrillo*
Ruth Channing

Maurice Chevalier*
Mady Christians*
Constance Collier*
Jackie Cooper
Joan Crawford*
Jimmy Durante*
Nelson Eddy*
Stuart Erwin*
Madge Evans*
Muriel Evans
Louise Fazenda*
Preston Foster*
Betty Furness*
Clark Gable*
Greta Garbo*
Gladys George*
C. Henry Gordon*
Ruth Gordon*
Russell Hardie*
Jean Harlow*
Helen Hayes*
Louise Henry
William Henry
Jean Hersholt*
Irene Hervey
Isabel Jewell*
Barbara Kent
June Knight*
Otto Kruger*
Elsa Lanchester*
Evelyn Laye
Myrna Loy*

Jeanette MacDonald*
Una Merkel*
Robert Montgomery*
Frank Morgan*
Karen Morley
Ramon Novarro*
Maureen O'Sullivan
Cecil Parker*
Jean Parker
Nat Pendleton*
Rosamond Pinchot*
William Powell*
May Robson*
Shirley Ross*
Rosalind Russell*
Maurice Schwartz*
Norma Shearer*
Frank Shields*
Sid Silvers*
Martha Sleeper*
Harvey Stephens*
Lewis Stone*
Gloria Swanson*
William Tannen*
Robert Taylor*
Franchot Tone*
Henry Wadsworth*
Lucile Watson*
Johnny Weissmuller*
Diana Wynyard*
Robert Young

PARAMOUNT

Iris Adrian*
Gracie Allen*
Max Baer*
George Barbier*
Ben Bernie*
Douglas Blackley*
Mary Boland*
Grace Bradley
Lorraine Bridges
Carl Brisson*
Mary Ellen Brown
Kathleen Burke*
George Burns*
Alan Campbell*
Kitty Carlisle
Dolores Casey*
Claudette Colbert
Gary Cooper*
Jack Cox
Buster Crabbe*
Eddie Craven*
Bing Crosby*
Katherine DeMille*

Marlene Dietrich*
Frances Drake
Mary Ellis
W. C. Fields*
William Frawley*
Paul Gerrits
Cary Grant*
David Holt
Dean Jagger*
Roscoe Karns*
Lois Kent
Elissa Landi*
Charles Laughton*
Billy Lee*
Baby LeRoy
Carole Lombard*
Pauline Lord*
Ida Lupino*
Helen Mack*
Fred MacMurray*
Marian Mansfield*
Herbert Marshall*
Gertrude Michael*

* Known to be deceased, as of 5-3-96.

c. 1935

Ray Milland*	Ann Sheridan*
Joe Morrison	Sylvia Sidney
Lloyd Nolan*	Alison Skipworth*
Jack Oakie*	Queenie Smith*
Lynne Overman*	Sir Guy Standing*
Gail Patrick*	Colin Tapley
Joe Penner*	Kent Taylor*
George Raft*	Lee Tracy*
Lyda Roberti*	Virginia Weidler*
Lanny Ross*	Mae West*
Jean Rouverol	Henry Wilcoxon*
Charlie Ruggles*	Howard Wilson
Randolph Scott*	Toby Wing

RKO-RADIO PICTURES

Glenn Anders*	Katharine Hepburn
Fred Astaire*	Pert Kelton*
John Beal	Francis Lederer
Willie Best*	Gene Lockhart*
Eric Blore*	Joel McCrea*
Alice Brady*	Raymond Middleton*
Helen Broderick*	Polly Moran*
Bruce Cabot*	June Preston
Chic Chandler*	Gregory Ratoff*
Richard Dix*	Virginia Reid
Steffi Duna	Erik Rhodes*
Irene Dunne*	Barbara Robbins
Hazel Forbes	Ginger Rogers*
Skeets Gallagher*	Anne Shirley*
Wynne Gibson*	Frank Thomas, Jr.
Alan Hale*	Thelma Todd*
Margaret Hamilton*	Bert Wheeler*
Ann Harding*	Robert Woolsey*

UNIVERSAL

Heather Angel*	Boris Karloff*
Henry Armetta*	Frank Lawton*
Binnie Barnes	Bela Lugosi*
Noah Beery, Jr.*	Paul Lukas*
Dean Benton	Florine McKinney*
Mary Brooks	Douglass Montgomery*
Willy Castello	Victor Moore*
June Clayworth*	Chester Morris*
Carol Coombe*	Hugh O'Connell*
Philip Dakin	Roger Pryor*
Ann Darling	Claude Rains*
Andy Devine*	Onslow Stevens*
Sally Eilers*	Gloria Stuart
Valerie Hobson	Margaret Sullavan*
Henry Hull*	Francis L. Sullivan*
G. P. Huntley, Jr.	Polly Walters
Baby Jane	Alice White*
Lois January	Clark Williams*
Buck Jones*	Jane Wyatt

HAL ROACH

Don Barclay*	Patsy Kelly*
Billy Bletcher*	Stan Laurel*
Charley Chase*	Billy Nelson*
Billy Gilbert*	Our Gang
Oliver Hardy*	Douglas Wakefield*

20TH CENTURY

George Arliss*	Fredric March*
Ronald Colman*	Loretta Young

UNITED ARTISTS

Eddie Cantor*	Miriam Hopkins*
Charles Chaplin*	Mary Pickford*
Douglas Fairbanks*	Anna Sten*

WARNERS-FIRST NATIONAL

Ross Alexander*	Josephine Hutchinson
Johnnie Allen	Allen Jenkins*
Mary Astor*	Al Jolson*
Arthur Aylesworth*	Olive Jones
Robert Barrat*	Ruby Keeler*
Joan Blondell*	Guy Kibbee*
Glen Boles	Robert Light
George Brent*	Margaret Lindsay*
Joe E. Brown*	Anita Louise*
James Cagney*	Helen Lowell*
Enrico Caruso, Jr.*	Aline MacMahon*
Hobart Cavanaugh*	Everett Marshall
Joseph Cawthorn*	Frank McHugh*
Colin Clive*	James Melton*
Ricardo Cortez*	Jean Muir
Dorothy Dare*	Paul Muni*
Marion Davies*	Pat O'Brien*
Bette Davis*	Henry O'Neill*
Dolores Del Rio*	Dick Powell*
Claire Dodd*	Phillip Reed
Ruth Donnelly*	Philip Regan
Maxine Doyle*	Edward G. Robinson*
Ann Dvorak*	Winifred Shaw*
John Eldredge*	Barbara Stanwyck*
Patricia Ellis*	Lyle Talbot*
Florence Fair	Verree Teasdale*
Glenda Farrell*	Genevieve Tobin*
Errol Flynn*	Dorothy Tree*
Kay Francis*	Mary Treen*
William Gargan*	Harry Tyler*
Hugh Herbert*	Rudy Vallee*
Russell Hicks*	Gordon Westcott*
Leslie Howard*	Warren William*
Ian Hunter*	Donald Woods

10

MAJOR
ACADEMY
AWARDS

PLEASE NOTE

This section includes the names of Academy Award nominees and winners within only the following five categories:
- Best Actor
- Best Actress
- Best Supporting Actor
- Best Supporting Actress
- Best Director

If a person listed in Parts 1 and 2 is shown to be an Oscar winner but their name is missing from Part 10, it is because their category of award was other than one of the five identified above.

ANNUAL MAJOR ACADEMY AWARDS

YEAR	BEST PICTURE	BEST ACTOR	BEST ACTRESS
1927-28	"Wings"	Emil Jannings, *"The Way of All Flesh"*	Janet Gaynor, *"Seventh Heaven"*
1928-29	"Broadway Melody"	Warner Baxter, *"In Old Arizona"*	Mary Pickford, *"Coquette"*
1929-30	"All Quiet On The Western Front"	George Arliss, *"Disraeli"*	Norma Shearer, *"The Divorcee"*
1930-31	"Cimarron"	Lionel Barrymore, *"Free Soul"*	Marie Dressler, *"Min and Bill"*
1931-32	"Grand Hotel"	Fredric March, *"Dr. Jekyll and Mr. Hyde"* (tie) Wallace Berry, *"The Champ"* (tie)	Helen Hayes, *"The Sin of Madelon Claudet"*
1932-33	"Cavalcade"	Charles Laughton, *"The Private Life of Henry VIII"*	Katharine Hepburn, *"Morning Glory"*
1934	"It Happened One Night"	Clark Gable, *"It Happened One Night"*	Claudette Colbert, *"It Happened One Night"*
1935	"Mutiny On The Bounty"	Victor McLaglen, *"The Informer"*	Bette Davis, *"Dangerous"*
1936	"The Great Ziegfeld"	Paul Muni, *"The Story of Louis Pasteur"*	Luise Rainer, *"The Great Ziegfeld"*
1937	"The Life Of Emile Zola"	Spencer Tracy, *"Captains Courageous"*	Luise Rainer, *"The Good Earth"*
1938	"You Can't Take It With You"	Spencer Tracy *"Boys Town"*	Bette Davis, *"Jezebel"*
1939	"Gone With The Wind"	Robert Donat, *"Goodbye, Mr. Chips"*	Vivien Leigh, *"Gone With the Wind"*
1940	"Rebecca"	James Stewart, *"The Philadelphia Story"*	Ginger Rogers, *"Kitty Foyle"*
1941	"How Green Was My Valley"	Gary Cooper, *"Sergeant York"*	Joan Fontaine, *"Suspicion"*
1942	"Mrs. Miniver"	James Cagney, *"Yankee Doodle Dandy"*	Greer Garson, *"Mrs. Miniver"*
1943	"Casablanca"	Paul Lucas, *"Watch On the Rhine"*	Jennifer Jones, *"The Song of Bernadette"*
1944	"Going My Way"	Bing Crosby, *"Going My Way"*	Ingrid Bergman, *"Gaslight"*
1945	"The Lost Weekend"	Ray Milland, *"The Lost Weekend"*	Joan Crawford, *"Mildred Pierce"*
1946	"The Best Years Of Our Lives"	Fredric March, *"The Best Years of Our Lives"*	Olivia de Havilland, *"To Each His Own"*
1947	"Gentlemen's Agreement"	Ronald Colman, *"A Double Life"*	Loretta Young, *"The Farmer's Daughter"*
1948	"Hamlet"	Laurence Olivier, *"Hamlet"*	Jane Wyman, *"Johnny Belinda"*
1949	"All The King's Men"	Broderick Crawford, *"All the King's Men"*	Olivia de Havilland, *"The Heiress"*
1950	"All About Eve"	José Ferrer, *"Cyrano de Bergerac"*	Judy Holliday, *"Born Yesterday"*
1951	"An American In Paris"	Humphrey Bogart, *"The African Queen"*	Vivien Leigh, *"A Streetcar Named Desire"*
1952	"The Greatest Show On Earth"	Gary Cooper, *"High Noon"*	Shirley Booth, *"Come Back, Little Sheba"*
1953	"From Here To Eternity"	William Holden, *"Stalag 17"*	Audrey Hepburn, *"Roman Holiday"*
1954	"On The Waterfront"	Marlon Brando, *"On the Waterfront"*	Grace Kelly, *"The Country Girl"*
1955	"Marty"	Ernest Borgnine, *"Marty"*	Anna Magnani, *"The Rose Tatoo"*
1956	"Around The World In 80 Days"	Yul Brynner, *"The King and I"*	Ingrid Bergman, *"Anastasia"*
1957	"The Bridge On The River Kwai"	Alec Guiness, *"The Bridge On the River Kwai"*	Joanne Woodward, *"The Three Faces of Eve"*
1958	"Gigi"	David Niven, *"Separate Tables"*	Susan Hayward, *"I Want to Live"*

...ANNUAL MAJOR ACADEMY AWARDS...

YEAR	BEST PICTURE	BEST ACTOR	BEST ACTRESS
1959	"Ben-Hur"	Charlton Heston, *"Ben-Hur"*	Simone Signoret, *"Room At the Top"*
1960	"The Apartment"	Burt Lancaster, *"Elmer Gantry"*	Elizabeth Taylor, *"Butterfield 8"*
1961	"West Side Story"	Maximillian Schell, *"Judgment at Nuremberg"*	Sophia Loren, *"Two Women"*
1962	"Lawrence Of Arabia"	Gregory Peck, *"To Kill a Mockingbird"*	Anne Bancroft, *"The Miracle Worker"*
1963	"Tom Jones"	Sidney Poitier, *"Lillies of the Field"*	Patricia Neal, *"Hud"*
1964	"My Fair Lady"	Rex Harrison, *"My Fair Lady"*	Julie Andrews, *"Mary Poppins"*
1965	"The Sound Of Music"	Lee Marvin, *"Cat Ballou"*	Julie Christie, *"Darling"*
1966	"A Man For All Seasons"	Paul Scofield, *"A Man for All Seasons"*	Elizabeth Taylor, *"Who's Afraid of Virginia Woolf?"*
1967	"In The Heat Of The Night"	Rod Steiger, *"In the Heat of the Night"*	Katharine Hepburn, *"Guess Who's Coming to Dinner"*
1968	"Oliver"	Cliff Robertson, *"Charly"*	Katharine Hepburn, *"The Lion in Winter"* (tie) Barbra Streisand, *"Funny Girl"* (tie)
1969	"Midnight Cowboy"	John Wayne, *"True Grit"*	Maggie Smith, *"The Prime of Miss Jean Brodie"*
1970	"Patton"	George C. Scott, *"Patton"* (refused)	Glenda Jackson, *"Women in Love"*
1971	"The French Connection"	Gene Hackman, *"The French Connection"*	Jane Fonda, *"Klute"*
1972	"The Godfather"	Marlon Brando, *"The Godfather"* (refused)	Liza Minnelli, *"Cabaret"*
1973	"The Sting"	Jack Lemmon, *"Save the Tiger"*	Glenda Jackson, *"A Touch of Class"*
1974	"The Godfather Part II"	Art Carney, *"Harry and Tonto"*	Ellen Burstyn, *"Alice Doesn't Live Here Anymore"*
1975	"One Flew Over The Cuckoo's Nest"	Jack Nicholson, *"One Flew Over the Cuckoo's Nest"*	Louise Fletcher, *"One Flew Over the Cuckoo's Nest"*
1976	"Rocky"	Peter Finch, *"Network"*	Faye Dunaway, *"Network"*
1977	"Annie Hall"	Richard Dreyfuss, *"The Goodbye Girl"*	Diane Keaton, *"Annie Hall"*
1978	"The Deer Hunter"	Jon Voight, *"Coming Home"*	Jane Fonda, *"Coming Home"*
1979	"Kramer vs. Kramer"	Dustin Hoffman, *"Kramer vs. Kramer"*	Sally Field, *"Norma Rae"*
1980	"Ordinary People"	Robert De Niro, *"Raging Bull"*	Sissy Spacek, *"Coal Miner's Daughter"*
1981	"Chariots Of Fire"	Henry Fonda, *"On Golden Pond"*	Katharine Hepburn, *"On Golden Pond"*
1982	"Gandhi"	Ben Kingsley, *"Gandhi"*	Meryl Streep, *"Sophie's Choice"*
1983	"Terms Of Endearment"	Robert Duvall, *"Tender Mercies"*	Shirley MacLaine, *"Terms of Endearment"*
1984	"Amadeus"	F. Murray Abraham, *"Amadeus"*	Sally Field, *"Places in the Heart"*
1985	"Out Of Africa"	William Hurt, *"Kiss of the Spider Woman"*	Geraldine Page, *"The Trip to Bountiful"*
1986	"Platoon"	Paul Newman, *"The Color of Money"*	Marlee Matlin, *"Children of a Lesser God"*
1987	"The Last Emperor"	Michael Douglas, *"Wall Street"*	Cher, *"Moonstruck"*
1988	"Rain Man"	Dustin Hoffman, *"Rain Man"*	Jodie Foster, *"The Accused"*
1989	"Driving Miss Daisy"	Daniel Day-Lewis, *"My Left Foot"*	Jessica Tandy, *"Driving Miss Daisy"*

...ANNUAL MAJOR ACADEMY AWARDS...

YEAR	BEST PICTURE	BEST ACTOR	BEST ACTRESS
1990	"Dances With Wolves"	Jeremy Irons, *"Reversal of Fortune"*	Kathy Bates, *"Misery"*
1991	"The Silence Of The Lambs"	Anthony Hopkins, *"The Silence of the Lambs"*	Jodie Foster, *"The Silence of the Lambs"*
1992	"Unforgiven"	Al Pacino, *"Scent of a Woman"*	Emma Thompson, *"Howards End"*
1993	"Schindler's List"	Tom Hanks, *"Philadelphia"*	Holly Hunter, *"The Piano"*
1994	"Forrest Gump"	Tom Hanks, *"Forrest Gump"*	Jessica Lange, *"Blue Sky"*
1995	"Braveheart"	Nicolas Cage, *"Leaving Las Vegas"*	Susan Sarandon, *"Dead Man Walking"*

YEAR	BEST SUPPORTING ACTOR	BEST SUPPORTING ACTRESS	BEST DIRECTOR
1927-28	(No award)	(No award)	Frank Borzage, "Seventh Heaven"
1928-29	(No award)	(No award)	Frank Lloyd, "The Divine Lady"
1929-30	(No award)	(No award)	Lewis Milestone, "All Quiet On the Western Front"
1930-31	(No award)	(No award)	Norman Taurog, "Skippy"
1931-32	(No award)	(No award)	Frank Borzage, "Bad Girl"
1932-33	(No award)	(No award)	Frank Lloyd, "Cavalcade"
1934	(No award)	(No award)	Frank Capra, "It Happened One Night"
1935	(No award)	(No award)	John Ford, "The Informer"
1936	Walter Brennan, "Come and Get It"	Gale Sondergaard, "Anthony Adverse"	Frank Capra, "Mr. Deeds Goes to Town"
1937	Joseph Schildkraut, "The Life of Emile Zola"	Alice Brady, "In Old Chicago"	Leo McCarey, "The Awful Truth"
1938	Walter Brennan, "Kentucky"	Fay Bainter, "Jezebel"	Frank Capra, "You Can't Take It With You"
1939	Thomas Mitchell, "Stagecoach"	Hattie McDaniel, "Gone With the Wind"	Victor Fleming, "Gone With the Wind"
1940	Walter Brennan, "The Westerner"	Jane Darwell, "The Grapes of Wrath"	John Ford, "The Grapes of Wrath"
1941	Donald Crisp, "How Green Was My Valley"	Mary Astor, "The Great Lie"	John Ford, "How Green Was My Valley"
1942	Van Heflin, "Johnny Eager"	Teresa Wright, "Mrs. Miniver"	William Wyler, "Mrs. Miniver"
1943	Charles Coburn, "The More the Merrier"	Katina Paxinou, "For Whom the Bell Tolls"	Michael Curtiz, "Casablanca"
1944	Barry Fitzgerald, "Going My Way"	Ethel Barrymore, "None But the Lonely Heart"	Leo McCarey, "Going My Way"
1945	James Dunn, "A Tree Grows in Brooklyn"	Anne Revere, "National Velvet"	Billy Wilder, "The Lost Weekend"
1946	Harold Russell, "The Best Years of Our Lives"	Anne Baxter, "The Razor's Edge"	William Wyler, "The Best Years of Our Lives"
1947	Edmund Gwenn, "Miracle On 34th Street"	Celeste Holm, "Gentleman's Agreement"	Elia Kazan, "Gentleman's Agreement"
1948	Walter Huston, "Treasure of Sierra Madre"	Claire Trevor, "Key Largo"	John Huston, "Treasure of Sierra Madre"
1949	Dean Jagger, "Twelve O'Clock High"	Mercedes McCambridge, "All the King's Men"	Joseph L. Mankiewicz, "A Letter to Three Wives"
1950	George Sanders, "All About Eve"	Josephine Hull, "Harvey"	Joseph L. Mankiewicz, "All About Eve"
1951	Karl Malden, "A Streetcar Named Desire"	Kim Hunter, "A Streetcar Named Desire"	George Stevens, "A Place in the Sun"
1952	Anthony Quinn, "Viva Zapata"	Gloria Grahame, "The Bad and the Beautiful"	John Ford, "The Quiet Man"
1953	Frank Sinatra, "From Here to Eternity"	Donna Reed, "From Here to Eternity"	Fred Zinnemann, "From Here to Eternity"
1954	Edmund O'Brien, "The Barefoot Contessa"	Eva Marie Saint, "On the Waterfront"	Elia Kazan, "On the Waterfront"
1955	Jack Lemmon, "Mr. Roberts"	Jo Van Fleet, "East of Eden"	Delbert Mann, "Marty"
1956	Anthony Quinn, "Lust for Life"	Dorothy Malone, "Written On the Wind"	George Stevens, "Giant"
1957	Red Buttons, "Sayonara"	Miyoshi Umeki, "Sayonara"	David Lean, "The Bridge On the River Kwai"
1958	Burl Ives, "The Big Country"	Wendy Hiller, "Separate Tables"	Vincente Minnelli, "Gigi"
1959	Hugh Griffith, "Ben-Hur"	Shelley Winters, "The Diary of Anne Frank"	William Wyler, "Ben-Hur"

...ANNUAL MAJOR ACADEMY AWARDS...

YEAR	BEST SUPPORTING ACTOR	BEST SUPPORTING ACTRESS	BEST DIRECTOR
1960	Peter Ustinov, "Spartacus"	Shirley Jones, "Elmer Gantry"	Billy Wilder, "The Apartment"
1961	George Chakiris, "West Side Story"	Rita Moreno, "West Side Story"	Robert Wise & Jerome Robbins, "West Side Story"
1962	Ed Begley, "Sweet Bird of Youth"	Patty Duke, "The Miracle Worker"	David Lean, "Lawrence of Arabia"
1963	Melvyn Douglas, "Hud"	Margaret Rutherford, "The V.I.P.s"	Tony Richardson, "Tom Jones"
1964	Peter Ustinov, "Topkapi"	Lila Kedrova, "Zorba the Greek"	George Cukor, "My Fair Lady"
1965	Martin Balsam, "A Thousand Clowns"	Shelley Winters, "A Patch of Blue"	Robert Wise, "The Sound of Music"
1966	Walter Matthau, "The Fortune Cookie"	Sandy Dennis, "Who's Afraid of Virginia Woolf?"	Fred Zinnemann, "A Man For All Seasons"
1967	George Kennedy, "Cool Hand Luke"	Estelle Parsons, "Bonnie & Clyde"	Mike Nichols, "The Graduate"
1968	Jack Albertson, "The Subject Was Roses"	Ruth Gordon, "Rosemary's Baby"	Carol Reed, "Oliver!"
1969	Gig Young, "They Shoot Horses, Don't They?"	Goldie Hawn, "Cactus Flower"	John Schlesinger, "Midnight Cowboy"
1970	John Mills, "Ryan's Daughter"	Helen Hayes, "Airport"	Franklin J. Schaffner, "Patton"
1971	Ben Johnson, "The Last Picture Show"	Cloris Leachman, "The Last Picture Show"	William Friedkin, "The French Connection"
1972	Joel Grey, "Cabaret"	Eileen Heckart, "Butterflies Are Free"	Bob Fosse, "Cabaret"
1973	John Houseman, "The Paper Chase"	Tatum O'Neal, "Paper Moon"	George Roy Hill, "The Sting"
1974	Robert De Niro, "The Godfather, Part II"	Ingrid Bergman, "Murder On the Orient Express"	Francis Ford Coppola, "The Godfather, Part II"
1975	George Burns, "The Sunshine Boys"	Lee Grant, "Shampoo"	Milos Forman, "One Flew Over the Cuckoo's Nest"
1976	Jason Robards, "All the President's Men"	Beatrice Straight, "Network"	John Avildsen, "Rocky"
1977	Jason Robards, "Julia"	Vanessa Redgrave, "Julia"	Woody Allen, "Annie Hall"
1978	Christopher Walken, "The Deer Hunter"	Maggie Smith, "California Suite"	Michael Cimino, "The Deer Hunter"
1979	Melvyn Douglas, "Being There"	Meryl Streep, "Kramer vs. Kramer"	Robert Benton, "Kramer vs. Kramer"
1980	Timothy Hutton, "Ordinary People"	Mary Steenburgen, "Melvin and Howard"	Robert Redford, "Ordinary People"
1981	John Gielgud, "Arthur"	Maureen Stapleton, "Reds"	Warren Beatty, "Reds"
1982	Louis Gossett, Jr., "An Officer and a Gentleman"	Jessica Lange, "Tootsie"	Richard Attenborough, "Gandhi"
1983	Jack Nicholson, "Terms of Endearment"	Linda Hunt, "The Year of Living Dangerously"	James L. Brooks, "Terms of Endearment"
1984	Dr. Haing S. Ngor, "The Killing Fields"	Dame Peggy Ashcroft, "A Passage to India"	Milos Forman, "Amadeus"
1985	Don Ameche, "Cocoon"	Anjelica Huston, "Prizzi's Honor"	Sydney Pollack, "Out of Africa"
1986	Michael Caine, "Hannah and Her Sisters"	Dianne Wiest, "Hannah and Her Sisters"	Oliver Stone, "Platoon"
1987	Sean Connery, "The Untouchables"	Olympia Dukakis, "Moonstruck"	Bernardo Bertolucci, "The Last Emperor"
1988	Kevin Kline, "A Fish Called Wanda"	Geena Davis, "The Accidental Tourist"	Barry Levinson, "Rain Man"
1989	Denzel Washington, "Glory"	Brenda Fricker, "My Left Foot"	Oliver Stone, "Born On the Fourth of July"
1990	Joe Pesci, "GoodFellas"	Whoopi Goldberg, "Ghost"	Kevin Costner, "Dances With Wolves"
1991	Jack Palance, "City Slickers"	Mercedes Ruehl, "The Fisher King"	Jonathan Demme, "The Silence of the Lambs"

...ANNUAL MAJOR ACADEMY AWARDS...

YEAR	BEST SUPPORTING ACTOR	BEST SUPPORTING ACTRESS	BEST DIRECTOR
1992	Gene Hackman, *"Unforgiven"*	Marisa Tomei, *"My Cousin Vinny"*	Clint Eastwood, *"Unforgiven"*
1993	Tommy Lee Jones, *"The Fugitive"*	Anna Paquin, *"The Piano"*	Steven Spielberg, *"Schindler's List"*
1994	Martin Landau, *"Ed Wood"*	Dianne Wiest, *"Bullets Over Broadway"*	Robert Zemeckis, *"Forrest Gump"*
1995	Kevin Spacey, *"The Usual Suspects"*	Mira Sorvino, *"Mighty Aphrodite"*	Mel Gibson *"Braveheart"*

MAJOR ACADEMY AWARD WINNERS AND NOMINEES — BY NAME

NAME*	CATEGORY	YEARS WON	YEARS NOMINATED **
A			
ABRAHAM, F. Murray	Best Actor	1984	
ADAMS, Nick	Best Supp. Actor		1963
ADJANI, Isabelle	Best Actress		1975, 1989
AHERNE, Brian	Best Supp. Actor		1939
AIELLO, Danny	Best Supp. Actor		1989
AIMEE, Anouk	Best Actress		1966
ALBERT, Eddie	Best Supp. Actor		1953, 1972
ALBERTSON, Jack	Best Supp. Actor	1968	
ALEXANDER, Jane	Best Actress		1970, 1983
"	Best Supp. Actress		1976, 1979
ALEXANDRO, Norma	Best Supp. Actress		1987
ALLEN, Joan	Best Supp. Actress		1995
ALLEN, Woody	Best Actor		1977
"	Best Director	1977	1978, 1984, 1986, 1989, 1994
ALLGOOD, Sara	Best Supp. Actress		1941
ALTMAN, Robert	Best Director		1970, 1975, 1993
AMECHE, Don	Best Supp. Actor	1985	
ANDERSON, Judith	Best Supp. Actress		1940
ANDERSON, Michael	Best Director		1956
ANDREWS, Julie	Best Actress	1964	1965, 1982
Ann-Margret	Best Supp. Actress		1971
"	Best Actress		1975
ANTONIONI, Michelangelo	Best Director		1966
ARCHER, Anne	Best Supp. Actress		1987
ARDEN, Eve	Best Supp. Actress		1945
ARKIN, Alan	Best Actor		1966, 1968
ARLISS, George	Best Actor	1929-30	1929-30
ARTHUR, Jean	Best Actress		1943
ASHBY, Hal	Best Director		1978
ASHCROFT, Dame Peggy	Best Supp. Actress	1984	
ASTAIRE, Fred	Best Supp. Actor		1974
ASTOR, Mary	Best Supp. Actress	1941	
ATTENBOROUGH, Richard	Best Director	1982	
AUER, Mischa	Best Supp. Actor		1936
AVERY, Margaret	Best Supp. Actress		1985
AVILDSEN, John	Best Director	1976	
AYKROYD, Dan	Best Supp. Actor		1989
AYRES, Lew	Best Actor		1948
B			
BABENCO, Hector	Best Director		1985
BADDELEY, Hermione	Best Supp. Actress		1959
BADHAM, Mary	Best Supp. Actress		1962
BAINTER, Fay	Best Actress		1938
"	Best Supp. Actress	1938	1961
BAKER, Carroll	Best Actress		1956
BALSAM, Martin	Best Supp. Actor	1965	
BANCROFT, Anne	Best Actress	1962	1964, 1967, 1977, 1985
BANCROFT, George	Best Actor		1928-29
BANNEN, Ian	Best Supp. Actor		1965
BARRAULT, Marie-Christine	Best Actress		1976
BARRIE, Barbara	Best Supp. Actress		1979
BARRYMORE, Ethel	Best Supp. Actress	1944	1946, 1947, 1949
BARRYMORE, Lionel	Best Director		1928-29
"	Best Actor	1930-31	
BARTHELMESS, Richard	Best Actor		1927-28
BARYSHNIKOV, Mikhail	Best Supp. Actor		1977
BASSERMAN, Albert	Best Supp. Actor		1940
BASSETT, Angela	Best Actress		1993
BATES, Alan	Best Actor		1968

* Includes only actors, actresses and directors.   ** Other than years won.

NAME*	CATEGORY	YEARS WON	YEARS NOMINATED **
BATES, Kathy	Best Actress	1990	
BATES, Alan	Best Actor		1968
BATES, Kathy	Best Actress	1990	
BAXTER, Anne	Best Actress		1950
"	Best Supp. Actress	1946	
BAXTER, Warner	Best Actor	1928-29	
BEATTY, Ned	Best Supp. Actor		1976
BEATTY, Warren	Best Actor	1981	1967, 1978
"	Best Director		1978, 1981
BEAUMONT, Harry	Best Director		1928-29
BEERY, Wallace	Best Actor	1931-32	1929-30
BEGLEY, Ed	Best Supp. Actor	1962	
BEL GEDDES, Barbara	Best Supp. Actress		1948
BENDIX, William	Best Supp. Actor		1942
BENING, Annette	Best Supp. Actress		1990
BENTON, Robert	Best Director	1979	1984
BERENGER, Tom	Best Supp. Actor		1986
BERESFORD, Bruce	Best Director		1983
BERGEN, Candice	Best Supp. Actress		1979
BERGMAN, Ingmar	Best Director		1973, 1976, 1983
BERGMAN, Ingrid	Best Actress	1944, 1956, 1974	1943, 1945, 1948, 1978
BERGNER, Elizabeth	Best Actress		1935
BERLIN, Jeannie	Best Supp. Actress		1972
BERTOLUCCI, Bernardo	Best Director	1987	1973
BICKFORD, Charles	Best Supp. Actor		1943, 1947, 1948
BIKEL, Theodore	Best Supp. Actor		1958
BLACK, Karen	Best Supp. Actress		1970
BLAIR, Betsy	Best Supp. Actress		1955
BLAIR, Linda	Best Supp. Actress		1973
BLAKELY, Ronee	Best Supp. Actress		1975
BLONDELL, Joan	Best Supp. Actress		1951
BLYTH, Ann	Best Supp. Actress		1945
BOGART, Humphrey	Best Actor	1951	1943, 1954
BOGDANOVICH, Peter	Best Director		1971
BONDI, Beulah	Best Supp. Actress		1936, 1938
BOORMAN, John	Best Director		1972, 1987
BOOTH, Shirley	Best Actress	1952	
BORGNINE, Ernest	Best Actor	1955	
BORZAGE, Frank	Best Director	1927-28, 1931-32	
BOYER, Charles	Best Actor		1937, 1938, 1944, 1961
BRACCO, Lorraine	Best Supp. Actress		1990
BRADY, Alice	Best Supp. Actress	1937	1936
BRANAGH, Kenneth	Best Actor		1989
BRANDAUER, Klaus Maria	Best Supp. Actor		1985
BRANDO, Marlon	Best Actor	1954, 1972	1951, 1952, 1953, 1957, 1973
"	Best Supp. Actor		1989
BRENNAN, Walter	Best Supp. Actor	1936, 1938, 1940	1941
BRENON, Herbert	Best Director		1927-28
BRIDGES, Jeff	Best Supp. Actor		1971, 1974
"	Best Actor		1984
BROOKS, Albert	Best Supp. Actor		1987
BROOKS, James L.	Best Director	1983	
BROOKS, Richard	Best Director		1958, 1966, 1967
BROWN, Clarence	Best Director		1929-30 (2), 1930-31, 1943, 1945, 1946
BROWNE, Leslie	Best Supp. Actress		1977
BRYNNER, Yul	Best Actor	1956	
BUJOLD, Genevieve	Best Actress		1969
BUONO, Victor	Best Supp. Actor		1962
BURKE, Billie	Best Supp. Actress		1938
BURNS, Catherine	Best Supp. Actress		1969

NAME*	CATEGORY	YEARS WON	YEARS NOMINATED **
BURNS, George	Best Supp. Actor	1975	
BURSTYN, Ellen	Best Supp. Actress		1971
"	Best Actress	1974	1973, 1978, 1980
BURTON, Richard	Best Supp. Actor		1952
"	Best Actor		1953, 1964, 1965, 1966, 1969, 1977
BUSEY, Gary	Best Actor		1978
BUTTONS, Red	Best Supp. Actor	1957	
BYINGTON, Spring	Best Supp. Actress		1938
C			
CAAN, James	Best Supp. Actor		1972
CACOYANNIS, Michael	Best Director		1964
CAESAR, Adolph	Best Supp. Actor		1984
CAGE, Nicolas	Best Actor	1995	
CAGNEY, James	Best Actor	1942	1938, 1955
CAINE, Michael	Best Actor	1986	1966, 1972, 1983
CALHERN, Louis	Best Actor		1950
CAMPION, Jane	Best Director		1993
CANNON, Dyan	Best Supp. Actress		1969, 1978
CAPRA, Frank	Best Director	1934, 1936, 1938	1932-33, 1939, 1946
CARDIFF, Jack	Best Director		1960
CAREY, Harry	Best Supp. Actor		1939
CARLIN, Lynn	Best Supp. Actress		1968
CARNEY, Art	Best Actor	1974	
CARON, Leslie	Best Actress		1953, 1963
CARROLL, Diahann	Best Actress		1974
CARROLL, Nancy	Best Actress		1929-30
CASS, Peggy	Best Supp. Actress		1958
CASSAVETES, John	Best Supp. Actor		1967
"	Best Director		1974
CASSEL, Seymour	Best Supp. Actor		1968
CASTELLANO, Richard	Best Supp. Actor		1970
CHAKIRIS, George	Best Supp. Actor	1961	
CHANDLER, Jeff	Best Supp. Actor		1950
CHANNING, Carol	Best Supp. Actress		1967
CHANNING, Stockard	Best Actress		1993
CHAPLIN, Charles	Best Director		1927-28
"	Best Actor		1940
CHATTERTON, Ruth	Best Actress		1928-29, 1929-30
CHEKHOV, Michael	Best Supp. Actor		1945
Cher	Best Supp. Actress		1983
"	Best Actress	1987	
CHEVALIER, Maurice	Best Actor		1929-30
CHRISTIE, Julie	Best Actress	1965	1971
CILENTO, Diane	Best Supp. Actress		1963
CIMINO, Michael	Best Director	1978	
CLARK, Candy	Best Supp. Actress		1973
CLAYBURGH, Jill	Best Actress		1978, 1979
CLAYTON, Jack	Best Director		1959
CLIFT, Montgomery	Best Supp. Actor		1961
"	Best Actor		1948, 1951, 1953
CLOSE, Glenn	Best Supp. Actress		1983, 1984
"	Best Actress		1987, 1988
COBB, Lee J.	Best Supp. Actor		1954, 1958
COBURN, Charles	Best Supp. Actor	1943	1941, 1946
COLBERT, Claudette	Best Actress	1934	1935, 1944
COLLINGE, Patricia	Best Supp. Actress		1941
COLLINS, Pauline	Best Actress		1989
COLMAN, Ronald	Best Actor	1947	1929-30, 1942
COMPSON, Betty	Best Actress		1928-29
CONNERY, Sean	Best Supp. Actor	1987	

NAME*	CATEGORY	YEARS WON	YEARS NOMINATED **
CONTI, Tom	Best Actor		1983
COOPER, Gary	Best Actor	1941, 1952	1936, 1942, 1943
COOPER, Gladys	Best Supp. Actress		1942, 1943, 1964
COOPER, Jackie	Best Actor		1930-31
COPPOLA, Francis Ford	Best Director	1974	1972, 1979, 1990
CORBY, Ellen	Best Supp. Actress		1948
CORTESE, Valentina	Best Supp. Actress		1974
COSTA-GAVRAS	Best Director		1969
COSTNER, Kevin	Best Actor		1990
"	Best Director	1990	
COURTENAY, Tom	Best Supp. Actor		1965
"	Best Actor		1983
CRAIN, Jeanne	Best Actress		1949
CRAWFORD, Broderick	Best Actor	1949	
CRAWFORD, Joan	Best Actress	1945	1947, 1952
CRICHTON, Charles	Best Director		1988
CRISP, Donald	Best Supp. Actor	1941	
CROMWELL, James	Best Supp. Actor		1995
CRONYN, Hume	Best Supp. Actor		1944
CROSBY, Bing	Best Actor	1944	1945, 1954
CROSSE, Rupert	Best Supp. Actor		1969
CROUSE, Lindsay	Best Supp. Actress		1984
CRUISE, Tom	Best Actor		1989
CUKOR, George	Best Director	1964	1932-33, 1940, 1947, 1950
CUMMINGS, Irving	Best Director		1928-29
CUMMINGS, Quinn	Best Supp. Actress		1977
CURTIS, Tony	Best Actor		1958
CURTIZ, Michael	Best Director	1943	1938 (2), 1942
CUSACK, Joan	Best Supp. Actress		1988
D			
DAFOE, Willem	Best Supp. Actor		1986
DAILEY, Dan	Best Actor		1948
DALL, John	Best Supp. Actor		1945
DANDRIDGE, Dorothy	Best Actress		1954
DARIN, Bobby	Best Supp. Actor		1963
DARWELL, Jane	Best Supp. Actress	1940	
DASSIN, Jules	Best Director		1960
DAVIS, Bette	Best Actress	1935, 1938	1939, 1940, 1941, 1942, 1944, 1950, 1952, 1962
DAVIS, Geena	Best Supp. Actress	1988	
DAVIS, Judy	Best Actress		1984
DAVISON, Bruce	Best Supp. Actor		1990
DAY, Doris	Best Actress		1959
DAY-LEWIS, Daniel	Best Actor	1989	1993
DEAN, James	Best Actor		1955, 1956
De HAVILLAND, Olivia	Best Supp. Actress		1939
"	Best Actress	1946, 1949	1941, 1948
DEMAREST, William	Best Supp. Actor		1946
DeMILLE, Cecil B.	Best Director		1952
DEMME, Jonathan	Best Director	1991	
De NIRO, Robert	Best Supp. Actor	1974	
"	Best Actor	1980	1976, 1978, 1990
DENNIS, Sandy	Best Supp. Actress	1966	
DEPARDIEU, Gerard	Best Actor		1990
DERN, Bruce	Best Supp. Actor		1978
De SICA, Vittorio	Best Supp. Actor		1957
De WILDE, Brandon	Best Supp. Actor		1953
DiCAPRIO, Leonardo	Best Supp. Actor		1993
DIETERLE, William	Best Director		1937
DIETRICH, Marlene	Best Actress		1930-31

* Includes only actors, actresses and directors.

** Other than years won.

NAME*	CATEGORY	YEARS WON	YEARS NOMINATED **
DILLON, Melinda	Best Supp. Actress		1977
DIX, Richard	Best Actor		1930-31
DMYTRYK, Edward	Best Director		1947
DONAT, Robert	Best Actor	1939	1938
DONLEVY, Brian	Best Supp. Actor		1939
DOUGLAS, Kirk	Best Actor		1949, 1952, 1956
DOUGLAS, Melvyn	Best Supp. Actor	1963, 1979	
"	Best Actor		1970
DOUGLAS, Michael	Best Actor	1987	
DOURIF, Brad	Best Supp. Actor		1975
DRESSER, Louise	Best Actress		1927-28
DRESSLER, Marie	Best Actress	1930-31	1931-32
DREYFUSS, Richard	Best Actor	1977	1995
DUKAKIS, Olympia	Best Supp. Actress	1987	
DUKE, Patty	Best Supp. Actress	1962	
DUNAWAY, Faye	Best Actress	1976	1967, 1974
DUNN, James	Best Supp. Actor	1945	
DUNN, Michael	Best Supp. Actor		1965
DUNNE, Irene	Best Actress		1930-31, 1936, 1937, 1939, 1948
DUNNOCK, Mildred	Best Supp. Actress		1951, 1956
DURNING, Charles	Best Supp. Actor		1983
DUVALL, Robert	Best Supp. Actor		1972, 1979
"	Best Actor	1983	1980
E			
EAGELS, Jeanne	Best Actress		1928-29
EASTWOOD, Clint	Best Director	1992	
EGGAR, Samantha	Best Actress		1965
ELLIOTT, Denholm	Best Supp. Actor		1986
EMERSON, Hope	Best Supp. Actress		1950
ERWIN, Stuart	Best Supp. Actor		1936
EVANS, Dame Edith	Best Supp. Actress		1963, 1964
"	Best Actress		1967
F			
FALK, Peter	Best Supp. Actor		1960, 1961
FARNSWORTH, Richard	Best Supp. Actor		1978
FARROW, John	Best Director		1942
FELLINI, Federico	Best Director		1961, 1963, 1970, 1975
FERRER, Jose	Best Actor	1950	1952
"	Best Supp. Actor		1948
FIELD, Sally	Best Actress	1979, 1984	
FIENNES, Ralph	Best Supp. Actor		1993
FIGGIS, Mike	Best Director		1995
FINCH, Peter	Best Actor	1976	1971
FINLAY, Frank	Best Supp. Actor		1965
FINNEY, Albert	Best Actor		1963, 1974, 1983, 1984
FIRTH, Peter	Best Supp. Actor		1977
FISHBURNE, Laurence	Best Actor		1993
FITZGERALD, Barry	Best Supp. Actor	1944	
"	Best Actor		1944
FITZGERALD, Geraldine	Best Supp. Actress		1939
FLEMING, Victor	Best Director	1939	
FLETCHER, Louise	Best Actress	1975	
FOCH, Nina	Best Supp. Actress		1954
FONDA, Henry	Best Actor	1981	1940
FONDA, Jane	Best Actress	1971, 1978	1969, 1977, 1979, 1986
FONTAINE, Joan	Best Actress	1941	1940, 1943
FONTANNE, Lynne	Best Actress		1931-32
FORD, Harrison	Best Actor		1985
FORD, John	Best Director	1935, 1940, 1941, 1952	1939
FORMAN, Milos	Best Director	1975, 1984	

NAME*	CATEGORY	YEARS WON	YEARS NOMINATED **
FORREST, Frederic	Best Supp. Actor		1979
FOSSE, Bob	Best Director	1972	1974, 1979
FOSTER, Jodie	Best Supp. Actress		1976, 1994
FOSTER, Jodie	Best Actress	1988, 1991	
FRANCIOSA, Anthony	Best Actor		1957
FRANKLIN, Sidney	Best Director		1937
FREARS, Stephen	Best Director		1990
FREEMAN, Morgan	Best Supp. Actor		1987
"	Best Actor		1989, 1994
FREY, Leonard	Best Supp. Actor		1971
FRICKER, Brenda	Best Supp. Actress	1989	
FRIEDKIN, William	Best Director	1971	1973
G			
GABLE, Clark	Best Actor	1934	1935, 1939
GARBO, Greta	Best Actress		1929-30, 1937, 1939
GARCIA, Andy	Best Supp. Actor		1990
GARDENIA, Vincent	Best Supp. Actor		1973, 1987
GARDNER, Ava	Best Actress		1953
GARFIELD, John	Best Supp. Actor		1938
"	Best Actor		1947
GARGAN, William	Best Supp. Actor		1940
GARLAND, Judy	Best Actress		1954
"	Best Supp. Actress		1961
GARNER, James	Best Actor		1985
GARSON, Greer	Best Actress	1942	1939, 1941, 1943, 1944, 1945, 1960
GAYNOR, Janet	Best Actress	1927-28	1937
GAZZO, Michael V.	Best Supp. Actor		1974
GENN, Leo	Best Supp. Actor		1951
GEORGE, Chief Dan	Best Supp. Actor		1970
GEORGE, Gladys	Best Actress		1936
GERMI, Pietro	Best Director		1962
GIANNINI, Giancarlo	Best Actor		1976
GIBSON, Mel	Best Director	1995	
GIELGUD, John	Best Supp. Actor	1981	1964
GILFORD, Jack	Best Supp. Actor		1973
GISH, Lillian	Best Supp. Actress		1946
GLEASON, Jackie	Best Supp. Actor		1961
GLEASON, James	Best Supp. Actor		1941
GLENVILLE, Peter	Best Director		1964
GODDARD, Paulette	Best Supp. Actress		1943
GOLDBERG, Whoopi	Best Actress		1985
"	Best Supp. Actress	1990	
GOMEZ, Thomas	Best Supp. Actor		1947
GORDON, Dexter	Best Actor		1986
GORDON, Ruth	Best Supp. Actress	1968	1965
GOSSETT, Louis Jr.	Best Supp. Actor	1982	
GOULD, Elliott	Best Supp. Actor		1969
GRAHAME, Gloria	Best Supp. Actress	1952	1947
GRANT, Cary	Best Actor		1941, 1944
GRANT, Lee	Best Supp. Actress	1975	1951, 1970, 1976
GRANVILLE, Bonita	Best Supp. Actress		1936
GREENE, Graham	Best Supp. Actor		1990
GREENSTREET, Sydney	Best Supp. Actor		1941
GREY, Joel	Best Supp. Actor	1972	
GRIFFITH, Hugh	Best Supp. Actor	1959	1963
GRIFFITH, Melanie	Best Actress		1988
GUINNESS, Alec	Best Actor	1957	1952
"	Best Supp. Actor		1977, 1988
GWENN, Edmund	Best Supp. Actor	1947	1950

...MAJOR ACADEMY AWARD WINNERS AND NOMINEES — BY NAME...

NAME*	CATEGORY	YEARS WON	YEARS NOMINATED **
H			
HACKMAN, Gene	Best Supp. Actor	1992	1967, 1970
"	Best Actor	1971	1988
HAGEN, Jean	Best Supp. Actress		1952
HALL, Alexander	Best Director		1941
HALL, Grayson	Best Supp. Actress		1964
HALLSTROM, Lasse	Best Director		1987
HANKS, Tom	Best Actor	1993, 1994	1988
HARDING, Ann	Best Actress		1930-31
HARPER, Tess	Best Supp. Actress		1986
HARRIS, Barbara	Best Supp. Actress		1971
HARRIS, Ed	Best Supp. Actor		1995
HARRIS, Julie	Best Actress		1952
HARRIS, Richard	Best Actor		1963, 1990
HARRIS, Rosemary	Best Supp. Actress		1994
HARRISON, Rex	Best Actor	1964	1963
HARTMAN, Elizabeth	Best Actress		1965
HARVEY, Anthony	Best Director		1968
HARVEY, Laurence	Best Actor		1959
HATHAWAY, Henry	Best Director		1935
HAWKS, Howard	Best Director		1941
HAWN, Goldie	Best Supp. Actress	1969	
"	Best Actress		1980
HAWTHORNE, Nigel	Best Actor		1994
HAYAKAWA, Sessue	Best Supp. Actor		1957
HAYES, Helen	Best Actress	1931-32	
"	Best Supp. Actress	1970	
HAYWARD, Susan	Best Actress	1958	1947, 1949, 1952, 1955
HECKART, Eileen	Best Supp. Actress	1972	1956
HEFLIN, Van	Best Supp. Actor	1942	
HEMINGWAY, Mariel	Best Supp. Actress		1979
HENRY, Buck	Best Director		1978
HENRY, Justin	Best Supp. Actor		1979
HEPBURN, Audrey	Best Actress	1953	1954, 1959, 1961, 1967
HEPBURN, Katharine	Best Actress	1932-33, 1967, 1968, 1981	1935, 1940, 1942, 1951, 1955, 1956, 1959, 1962
HESTON, Charlton	Best Actor	1959	
HICKEY, William	Best Supp. Actor		1985
HILL, George Roy	Best Director	1973	1969
HILLER, Arthur	Best Director		1970
HILLER, Wendy	Best Actress		1938
"	Best Supp. Actress	1958	1966
HITCHCOCK, Alfred	Best Director		1940, 1944, 1945, 1954, 1960
HOFFMAN, Dustin	Best Actor	1979, 1988	1967, 1969, 1974, 1982
HOLDEN, William	Best Actor	1953	1950, 1976
HOLLIDAY, Judy	Best Actress	1950	
HOLLOWAY, Stanley	Best Supp. Actor		1964
HOLM, Celeste	Best Supp. Actress	1947	1949, 1950
HOMOLKA, Oscar	Best Supp. Actor		1948
HOPKINS, Anthony	Best Actor	1991	1993, 1995
HOPKINS, Miriam	Best Actress		1935
HOPPER, Dennis	Best Supp. Actor		1986
HOSKINS, Bob	Best Actor		1986
HOUSEMAN, John	Best Supp. Actor	1973	
HOWARD, Leslie	Best Actor		1932-33, 1938
HOWARD, Trevor	Best Actor		1960
HUDSON, Rock	Best Actor		1956
HULCE, Tom	Best Actor		1984
HULL, Josephine	Best Supp. Actress	1950	
HUNNICUTT, Arthur	Best Supp. Actor		1952

* Includes only actors, actresses and directors.   399   ** Other than years won.

NAME*	CATEGORY	YEARS WON	YEARS NOMINATED **
HUNT, Linda	Best Supp. Actress	1983	
HUNTER, Holly	Best Actress	1993	1987, 1993
HUNTER, Kim	Best Supp. Actress	1951	
HURT, John	Best Supp. Actor		1978
"	Best Actor		1980
HURT, William	Best Actor	1985	1986, 1987
HUSSEY, Ruth	Best Supp. Actress		1940
HUSTON, Anjelica	Best Supp. Actress	1985	1989
HUSTON, Anjelica	Best Actress		1990
HUSTON, John	Best Director	1948	1950, 1951, 1952, 1985
HUSTON, John	Best Supp. Actor		1963
HUSTON, Walter	Best Actor	1948	1936, 1941, 1942
HUTTON, Timothy	Best Supp. Actor	1980	
HYER, Martha	Best Supp. Actress		1958
I			
IRELAND, John	Best Supp. Actor		1949
IRONS, Jeremy	Best Actor	1990	
IRVING, Amy	Best Supp. Actress		1983
IVES, Burl	Best Supp. Actor	1958	
IVORY, James	Best Director		1986, 1993
J			
JACKSON, Glenda	Best Actress	1970, 1973	1971, 1975
JACKSON, Samuel L.	Best Supp. Actor		1994
JAECKEL, Richard	Best Supp. Actor		1971
JAFFE, Sam	Best Supp. Actor		1950
JAGGER, Dean	Best Supp. Actor	1949	
JANNINGS, Emil	Best Actor	1927-28	
JEWISON, Norman	Best Director		1967, 1971, 1987
JOFFE, Roland	Best Director		1984, 1986
JOHNS, Glynis	Best Supp. Actress		1960
JOHNSON, Ben	Best Supp. Actor	1971	
JOHNSON, Celia	Best Actress		1946
JONES, Carolyn	Best Supp. Actress		1957
JONES, James Earl	Best Actor		1970
JONES, Jennifer	Best Actress	1943	1945, 1946, 1955
"	Best Supp. Actress		1944
JONES, Shirley	Best Supp. Actress	1960	
JONES, Tommy Lee	Best Supp. Actor	1993	
JURADO, Katy	Best Supp. Actress		1954
K			
KAHN, Madeline	Best Supp. Actress		1973, 1974
KAMINSKA, Ida	Best Actress		1966
KANE, Carol	Best Actress		1975
KAZAN, Elia	Best Director	1947	1951, 1955, 1963
KEATON, Diane	Best Actress	1977	1981
KEDROVA, Lila	Best Supp. Actress	1964	
KELLAWAY, Cecil	Best Supp. Actor		1948, 1967
KELLERMAN, Sally	Best Supp. Actress		1970
KELLY, Gene	Best Actor		1945
KELLY, Grace	Best Supp. Actress		1953
"	Best Actress	1954	
KELLY, Nancy	Best Actress		1956
KENNEDY, Arthur	Best Supp. Actor		1949, 1955, 1957, 1958
"	Best Actor		1951
KENNEDY, George	Best Supp. Actor	1967	
KERR, Deborah	Best Actress		1949, 1953, 1956, 1957, 1958, 1960
KIESLOWSKI, Krzysztof	Best Director		1994
KING, Henry	Best Director		1943, 1944
KINGSLEY, Ben	Best Actor	1982	
KIRKLAND, Sally	Best Actress		1987

* Includes only actors, actresses and directors.

400

** Other than years won.

NAME*	CATEGORY	YEARS WON	YEARS NOMINATED **
KLINE, Kevin	Best Supp. Actor	1988	
KNIGHT, Shirley	Best Supp. Actress		1960, 1962
KNOX, Alexander	Best Actor		1944
KOHNER, Susan	Best Supp. Actress		1959
KORJUS, Miliza	Best Supp. Actress		1938
KOSTER, Henry	Best Director		1947
KRAMER, Stanley	Best Director		1958, 1961, 1967
KRUSCHEN, Jack	Best Supp. Actor		1960
KUBRICK, Stanley	Best Director		1964, 1968, 1971, 1975
KUROSAWA, Akira	Best Director		1985
L			
La CAVA, Gregory	Best Director		1936, 1937
LADD, Diane	Best Supp. Actress		1974, 1990
La GARDE, Jocelyne	Best Supp. Actress		1966
LAHTI, Christine	Best Supp. Actress		1984
LANCASTER, Burt	Best Actor	1960	1953, 1962, 1981
LANCHESTER, Elsa	Best Supp. Actress		1949, 1957
LANDAU, Martin	Best Supp. Actor	1994	1988, 1989
LANG, Walter	Best Director		1956
LANGE, Hope	Best Supp. Actress		1957
LANGE, Jessica	Best Supp. Actress	1982	
"	Best Actress	1994	1982, 1984, 1985, 1989
LANSBURY, Angela	Best Supp. Actress		1944, 1945, 1962
LAUGHTON, Charles	Best Actor	1932-33	1935, 1957
LAURIE, Piper	Best Actress		1961
"	Best Supp. Actress		1976, 1986
LEACHMAN, Cloris	Best Supp. Actress	1971	
LEAN, David	Best Director	1957, 1962	1946, 1947, 1955, 1965, 1984
LEE, Peggy	Best Supp. Actress		1955
LEEDS, Andrea	Best Supp. Actress		1937
LEIGH, Janet	Best Supp. Actress		1960
LEIGH, Vivien	Best Actress	1939, 1951	
LEIGHTON, Margaret	Best Supp. Actress		1971
Le LOUCH, Claude	Best Director		1966
LEMMON, Jack	Best Supp. Actor	1955	
"	Best Actor	1973	1959, 1960, 1962, 1979, 1980, 1982
LENYA, Lotte	Best Supp. Actress		1961
LEONARD, Robert Z.	Best Director		1929-30, 1936
Le ROY, Mervyn	Best Director		1942
LEVINSON, Barry	Best Director	1988	
LITHGOW, John	Best Supp. Actor		1983
LITVAK, Anatole	Best Director		1948
LLOYD, Frank	Best Director	1928-29, 1932-33	1928-29 (2), 1935
LOCKE, Sondra	Best Supp. Actress		1968
LOCKHART, Gene	Best Supp. Actor		1938
LOGAN, Joshua	Best Director		1955, 1957
LOGGIA, Robert	Best Supp. Actor		1985
LOMBARD, Carole	Best Actress		1936
LOREN, Sophia	Best Actress	1961	1964
LORRING, Joan	Best Supp. Actress		1945
LOVE, Bessie	Best Actress		1928-29
LUBITSCH, Ernst	Best Director		1928-29, 1929-30, 1943
LUCAS, George	Best Director		1973, 1977
LUKAS, Paul	Best Actor	1943	
LUMET, Sidney	Best Director		1957, 1975, 1976
LUNT, Alfred	Best Actor		1931-32
LYNCH, David	Best Director		1986
LYNNE, Adrian	Best Director		1987
M			
MacGRAW, Ali	Best Actress		1970

NAME*	CATEGORY	YEARS WON	YEARS NOMINATED **
MacLAINE, Shirley	Best Actress	1983	1958, 1960, 1963, 1977
MacMAHON, Aline	Best Supp. Actress		1944
MADIGAN, Amy	Best Supp. Actress		1985
MAGNANI, Anna	Best Actress	1955	1957
MAIN, Marjorie	Best Supp. Actress		1947
MAKO	Best Supp. Actor		1966
MALDEN, Karl	Best Supp. Actor	1951	1954
MALKOVICH, John	Best Supp. Actor		1984, 1993
MALONE, Dorothy	Best Supp. Actress	1956	
MANKIEWICZ, Joseph L.	Best Director	1949, 1950	1952, 1972
MANN, Delbert	Best Director	1955	
MANTELL, Joe	Best Supp. Actor		1955
MARCH, Fredric	Best Actor	1931-32, 1946	1930-31, 1937, 1951
MARCHAND, Colette	Best Supp. Actress		1952
MARLEY, John	Best Supp. Actor		1970
MARVIN, Lee	Best Actor	1965	
MASON, James	Best Actor		1954
"	Best Supp. Actor		1966
MASON, Marsha	Best Actress		1973, 1977, 1979, 1981
MASSEY, Daniel	Best Supp. Actor		1968
MASSEY, Raymond	Best Actor		1940
MASTRANTONIO, Mary Elizabeth	Best Supp. Actress		1986
MASTROIANNI, Marcello	Best Actor		1962, 1977, 1987
MATLIN, Marlee	Best Actress	1986	
MATTHAU, Walter	Best Supp. Actor	1966	
"	Best Actor		1971, 1975
McCAMBRIDGE, Mercedes	Best Supp. Actress	1949	1956
McCAREY, Leo	Best Director	1937, 1944	1945
McCARTHY, Kevin	Best Supp. Actor		1951
McCORMACK, Patty	Best Supp. Actress		1956
McDANIEL. Hattie	Best Supp. Actress	1939	
McDONNELL, Mary	Best Supp. Actress		1990
McDORMAND, Frances	Best Supp. Actress		1988
McGUIRE, Dorothy	Best Actress		1947
McLAGLEN, Victor	Best Actor	1935	1952
McNAMARA, Maggie	Best Actress		1953
McQUEEN, Steve	Best Actor		1966
MEDFORD, Kay	Best Supp. Actress		1968
MENJOU, Adolphe	Best Actor		1930-31
MERCHANT, Vivien	Best Supp. Actress		1966
MERCOURI, Melina	Best Actress		1960
MEREDITH, Burgess	Best Supp. Actor		1975, 1976
MERKEL, Una	Best Supp. Actress		1961
MIDLER, Bette	Best Actress		1979
MILES, Sarah	Best Actress		1970
MILES, Sylvia	Best Supp. Actress		1969, 1975
MILESTONE, Lewis	Best Director	1929-30	1927-28, 1930-31
MILFORD, Penelope	Best Supp. Actress		1978
MILLAND, Ray	Best Actor	1945	
MILLER, Jason	Best Supp. Actor		1973
MILLS, John	Best Supp. Actor	1970	
MINEO, Sal	Best Supp. Actor		1955, 1960
MINNELLI, Liza	Best Actress	1972	1969
MINNELLI, Vincente	Best Director	1958	1951
MIRREN, Helen	Best Supp. Actress		1994
MITCHELL, Thomas	Best Supp. Actor	1939	1937
MITCHUM, Robert	Best Supp. Actor		1945
MOLINARO, Edouard	Best Director		1979
MONTGOMERY, Robert	Best Actor		1937, 1941
MOODY, Ron	Best Actor		1968

NAME*	CATEGORY	YEARS WON	YEARS NOMINATED **
MOORE, Dudley	Best Actor		1981
MOORE, Grace	Best Actress		1934
MOORE, Juanita	Best Supp. Actress		1959
MOORE, Mary Tyler	Best Actress		1980
MOORE, Terry	Best Supp. Actress		1952
MOOREHEAD, Agnes	Best Supp. Actress		1942, 1944, 1948, 1964
MORENO, Rita	Best Supp. Actress	1961	
MORGAN, Frank	Best Actor		1934
"	Best Supp. Actor		1942
MORITA, Noriyuki "Pat"	Best Supp. Actor		1984
MORLEY, Robert	Best Supp. Actor		1938
MORRIS, Chester	Best Actor		1928-29
MULLIGAN, Robert	Best Director		1962
MUNI, Paul	Best Actor	1936	1928-29, 1932-33, 1937, 1959
MURRAY, Don	Best Supp. Actor		1956
N			
NAISH, J. Carrol	Best Supp. Actor		1943, 1945
NATWICK, Mildred	Best Supp. Actress		1967
NEAL, Patricia	Best Actress	1963	1968
NEESON, Liam	Best Actor		1993
NEGULESCO, Jean	Best Director		1948
NEWMAN, Paul	Best Actor	1986	1958, 1961, 1963, 1967, 1981, 1982, 1994
NGOR, Dr. Haing S.	Best Supp. Actor	1984	
NICHOLS, Mike	Best Director	1967	1966, 1983, 1988
NICHOLSON, Jack	Best Supp. Actor	1983	1969
"	Best Actor	1975	1970, 1973, 1974, 1985, 1987
NIVEN, David	Best Actor	1958	
NOONAN, Chris	Best Director		1995
O			
OAKIE, Jack	Best Supp. Actor		1940
OBERON, Merle	Best Actress		1935
O'BRIEN, Edmond	Best Supp. Actor	1954	1964
O'CONNELL, Arthur	Best Supp. Actor		1955, 1959
O'HERLIHY, Dan	Best Actor		1954
OLIN, Lena	Best Supp. Actress		1989
OLIVER, Edna May	Best Supp. Actress		1939
OLIVIER, Laurence	Best Actor	1948	1939, 1940, 1946, 1956, 1960, 1965, 1972, 1976, 1978
"	Best Director		1948
OLMOS, Edward James	Best Actor		1988
OLSON, Nancy	Best Supp. Actress		1950
O'NEAL, Ryan	Best Actor		1970
O'NEAL, Tatum	Best Supp. Actress	1973	
O'NEIL, Barbara	Best Supp. Actress		1940
O'TOOLE, Peter	Best Actor		1962, 1964, 1968, 1969, 1972, 1980, 1982
OUSPENSKAYA, Maria	Best Supp. Actress		1936, 1939
P			
PACINO, Al	Best Supp. Actor		1972, 1990
"	Best Actor	1992	1973, 1974, 1975, 1979
PAGE, Geraldine	Best Supp. Actress		1953, 1966, 1972, 1984
"	Best Actress	1985	1961, 1962, 1978
PAKULA, Alan J.	Best Director		1976
PALANCE, Jack	Best Supp. Actor	1991	1952, 1953
PALMINTERI, Chazz	Best Supp. Actor		1994
PAQUIN, Anna	Best Supp. Actress	1993	
PARKER, Alan	Best Director		1978, 1988
PARKER, Eleanor	Best Actress		1950, 1951, 1955
PARKS, Larry	Best Actor		1946

NAME*	CATEGORY	YEARS WON	YEARS NOMINATED **
PARSONS, Estelle	Best Supp. Actress	1967	1968
PAVAN, Marisa	Best Supp. Actress		1955
PAXINOU, Katina	Best Supp. Actress	1943	
PECK, Gregory	Best Actor	1962	1945, 1946, 1947, 1949
PENN, Arthur	Best Director		1962, 1967, 1969
PENN, Sean	Best Actor		1995
PEREZ, Rosie	Best Supp. Actress		1993
PERKINS, Anthony	Best Supp. Actor		1956
PERRINE, Valerie	Best Actress		1974
PERRY, Frank	Best Director		1962
PESCI, Joe	Best Supp. Actor	1990	
PETERS, Susan	Best Supp. Actress		1942
PFEIFFER, Michelle	Best Supp. Actress		1988
"	Best Actress		1989
PHOENIX, River	Best Supp. Actor		1988
PICKFORD, Mary	Best Actress	1928-29	
PIDGEON, Walter	Best Actor		1942, 1943
PITT, Brad	Best Supp. Actor		1995
POITIER, Sidney	Best Actor	1963	1958
POLANSKI, Roman	Best Director		1974
POLLACK, Sydney	Best Director	1985	1969
POLLARD, Michael J.	Best Supp. Actor		1967
PONTECORVO, Gillo	Best Director		1968
POSTLETHWAITE, Pete	Best Supp. Actor		1993
POWELL, William	Best Actor		1934, 1936, 1947
PREMINGER, Otto	Best Director		1944, 1963
Q			
QUAID, Randy	Best Supp. Actor		1973
QUAYLE, Anthony	Best Supp. Actor		1969
QUINLAN, Kathleen	Best Supp. Actress		1995
QUINN, Anthony	Best Supp. Actor	1952, 1956	
"	Best Actor		1957, 1964
R			
RADFORD, Michael	Best Director		1995
RAINER, Luise	Best Actress	1936, 1937	
RAINS, Claude	Best Supp. Actor		1939, 1943, 1944, 1946
RAMBEAU, Marjorie	Best Supp. Actress		1940, 1953
RAMSEY, Anne	Best Supp. Actress		1987
RATHBONE, Basil	Best Supp. Actor		1936, 1938
REDFORD, Robert	Best Actor		1973
"	Best Director	1980	1994
REDGRAVE, Lynn	Best Actress		1966
REDGRAVE, Michael	Best Actor		1947
REDGRAVE, Vanessa	Best Actress		1966, 1968, 1971, 1984
"	Best Supp. Actress	1977	
REDMAN, Joyce	Best Supp. Actress		1963, 1965
REED, Carol	Best Director	1968	1949, 1950
REED, Donna	Best Supp. Actress	1953	
REMICK, Lee	Best Actress		1962
RENOIR, Jean	Best Director		1945
REVERE, Anne	Best Supp. Actress	1945	1943, 1947
REYNOLDS, Debbie	Best Actress		1964
RICHARDS, Beah	Best Supp. Actress		1967
RICHARDSON, Miranda	Best Actress		1994
RICHARDSON, Ralph	Best Supp. Actor		1949, 1984
RICHARDSON, Tony	Best Director	1963	
RITT, Martin	Best Director		1963
RITTER, Thelma	Best Supp. Actress		1950, 1951, 1952, 1953, 1959, 1962
ROBARDS, Jr., Jason	Best Supp. Actor	1976, 1977	
ROBBINS, Jerome	Best Director	1961	

NAME*	CATEGORY	YEARS WON	YEARS NOMINATED **
ROBBINS, Tim	Best Director		1995
ROBERTS, Eric	Best Supp. Actor		1985
ROBERTS, Julia	Best Supp. Actress		1989
"	Best Actress		1990
ROBERTS, Rachel	Best Actress		1963
ROBERTSON, Cliff	Best Actor	1968	
ROBSON, Flora	Best Supp. Actress		1946
ROBSON, Mark	Best Director		1957, 1958
ROBSON, May	Best Actress		1932-33
ROGERS, Ginger	Best Actress	1940	
ROONEY, Mickey	Best Actor		1939, 1943
"	Best Supp. Actor		1956, 1979
ROSS, Diana	Best Actress		1972
ROSS, Herbert	Best Director		1977
ROSS, Katharine	Best Supp. Actress		1967
ROSSEN, Robert	Best Director		1949, 1961
ROTH, Tim	Best Supp. Actor		1995
ROWLANDS, Gena	Best Actress		1974, 1980
RUEHL, Mercedes	Best Supp. Actress	1991	
RUGGLES, Wesley	Best Director		1930-31
RUSSELL, Harold	Best Supp. Actor	1946	
RUSSELL, Ken	Best Director		1970
RUSSELL, Rosalind	Best Actress		1942, 1946, 1947, 1958
RUTHERFORD, Margaret	Best Supp. Actress	1963	
RYAN, Robert	Best Supp. Actor		1947
RYDER, Winona	Best Supp. Actress		1993
RYDER, Winona	Best Actress		1994
SAINT, Eva Marie	Best Supp. Actress	1954	
SANDERS, George	Best Supp. Actor	1950	
SARANDON, Chris	Best Supp. Actor		1975
SARANDON, Susan	Best Actress	1995	1981, 1991, 1992, 1994
SAVALAS, Telly	Best Supp. Actor		1962
SCHAFFNER, Franklin J.	Best Director	1970	
SCHEIDER, Roy	Best Supp. Actor		1971
"	Best Actor		1979
SCHELL, Maximilian	Best Actor	1961	1975
SCHELL, Maximilian	Best Supp. Actor		1977
SCHERTZINGER, Victor	Best Director		1934
SCHILDKRAUT, Joseph	Best Supp. Actor	1937	
SCHLESINGER, John	Best Director	1969	1965, 1971
SCHROEDER, Barbet	Best Director		1990
SCOFIELD, Paul	Best Actor	1966	
SCOFIELD, Paul	Best Supp. Actor		1994
SCORSESE, Martin	Best Director		1988, 1990
SCOTT, George C.	Best Supp. Actor		1959, 1961
"	Best Actor	1970	1971
SCOTT, Martha	Best Actress		1940
SEATON, George	Best Director		1954
SEGAL, George	Best Supp. Actor		1966
SELLERS, Peter	Best Actor		1964, 1979
SHARIF, Omar	Best Supp. Actor		1962
SHAW, Robert	Best Supp. Actor		1966
SHEARER, Norma	Best Actress	1929-30	1929-30, 1930-31, 1934, 1936, 1938
SHEPARD, Sam	Best Supp. Actor		1983
SHERIDAN, Jim	Best Director		1989, 1993
SHIRE, Talia	Best Supp. Actress		1974
"	Best Actress		1976
SHIRLEY, Anne	Best Supp. Actress		1937
SHUE, Elisabeth	Best Actress		1995

* Includes only actors, actresses and directors.

** Other than years won.

NAME*	CATEGORY	YEARS WON	YEARS NOMINATED **
SIDNEY, Sylvia	Best Supp. Actress		1973
SIGNORET, Simone	Best Actress	1959	1965
SIMMONS, Jean	Best Supp. Actress		1948
"	Best Actress		1969
SINATRA, Frank	Best Supp. Actor	1953	
"	Best Actor		1955
SINISE, Gary	Best Supp. Actor		1994
SIODMAK, Robert	Best Director		1946
SKALA, Lilia	Best Supp. Actress		1963
SMITH, Maggie	Best Supp. Actress	1978	1965, 1986
"	Best Actress	1969	1972
SNODGRESS, Carrie	Best Actress		1970
SONDERGAARD, Gale	Best Supp. Actress	1936	1946
SORVINO, Mira	Best Supp. Actress	1995	
SOTHERN, Ann	Best Supp. Actress		1987
SPACEK, Sissy	Best Actress	1980	1976, 1982, 1984, 1986
SPACEY, Kevin	Best Supp. Actor	1995	
SPIELBERG, Steven	Best Director	1993	1977
STACK, Robert	Best Supp. Actor		1956
STALLONE, Sylvester	Best Actor		1976
STAMP, Terence	Best Supp. Actor		1962
STANLEY, Kim	Best Actress		1964
STANWYCK, Barbara	Best Actress		1937, 1941, 1944, 1948
STAPLETON, Maureen	Best Supp. Actress	1981	1958, 1970, 1978
STEENBURGEN, Mary	Best Supp. Actress	1980	
STEIGER, Rod	Best Supp. Actor		1954
"	Best Actor	1967	1965
STEPHENSON, James	Best Supp. Actor		1940
STERLING, Jan	Best Supp. Actress		1954
STEVENS, George	Best Director	1951, 1956	1943, 1953, 1959
STEVENSON, Robert	Best Director		1964
STEWART, James	Best Actor	1940	1939, 1946, 1950, 1959
STOCKWELL, Dean	Best Supp. Actor		1988
STONE, Lewis	Best Actor		1928-29
STONE, Oliver	Best Director	1986, 1989	
STONE, Sharon	Best Actress		1995
STRAIGHT, Beatrice	Best Supp. Actress	1976	
STRASBERG, Lee	Best Supp. Actor		1974
STRAUSS, Robert	Best Supp. Actor		1953
STREEP, Meryl	Best Supp. Actress	1979	1978
"	Best Actress	1982	1981, 1983, 1985, 1987, 1988, 1990, 1995
STREISAND, Barbra	Best Actress	1968	1973
STURGES, John	Best Director		1955
SULLAVAN, Margaret	Best Actress		1938
SUZMAN, Janet	Best Actress		1971
SWANSON, Gloria	Best Actress		1927-28, 1929-30, 1950
T			
TAMBLYN, Russ	Best Supp. Actor		1957
TAMIROFF, Akim	Best Supp. Actor		1936, 1943
TANDY, Jessica	Best Actress	1989	
TARANTINO, Quentin	Best Director		1994
TAUROG, Norman	Best Director	1930-31	1938
TAYLOR, Elizabeth	Best Actress	1960, 1966	1957, 1958, 1959
TESHIGAHARA, Hiroshi	Best Director		1965
THOMPSON, Emma	Best Actress	1992	1993, 1995
"	Best Supp. Actress		1993
THOMPSON, J. Lee	Best Director		1961
THURMAN, Uma	Best Supp. Actress		1994
TIBBETT, Lawrence	Best Actor		1929-30
TIERNEY, Gene	Best Actress		1945

...MAJOR ACADEMY AWARD WINNERS AND NOMINEES — BY NAME...

NAME*	CATEGORY	YEARS WON	YEARS NOMINATED **
TILLY, Jennifer	Best Supp. Actress		1994
TILLY, Meg	Best Supp. Actress		1985
TODD, Richard	Best Actor		1949
TOMEI, Marisa	Best Supp. Actress	1992	
TOMLIN, Lily	Best Supp. Actress		1975
TONE, Franchot	Best Actor		1935
TOPOL	Best Actor		1971
TORN, Rip	Best Supp. Actor		1983
TRACY, Lee	Best Supp. Actor		1964
TRACY, Spencer	Best Actor	1937, 1938	1936, 1950, 1955, 1958, 1960, 1961,
"			1967
TRAVERS, Henry	Best Supp. Actor		1942
TRAVOLTA, John	Best Actor		1977, 1994
TREVOR, Claire	Best Supp. Actress	1948	1937, 1954
TROELL, Jan	Best Director		1972
TROISI, Massimo	Best Actor		1995
TRUFFANT, Francois	Best Director		1974
TULLY, Tom	Best Supp. Actor		1954
TURNER, Kathleen	Best Actress		1986
TURNER, Lana	Best Actress		1957
TYRRELL, Susan	Best Supp. Actress		1972
TYSON, Cicely	Best Actress		1972
U			
ULLMANN, Liv	Best Actress		1972, 1976
UMEKI, Miyoshi	Best Supp. Actress	1957	
URE, Mary	Best Supp. Actress		1960
USTINOV, Peter	Best Supp. Actor	1960, 1964	1951
V			
VACCARO, Brenda	Best Supp. Actress		1975
Van DYKE, W. S.	Best Director		1934, 1936
Van FLEET, Jo	Best Supp. Actress	1955	
VARSI, Diane	Best Supp. Actress		1957
VAUGHN, Robert	Best Supp. Actor		1959
VIDOR, King	Best Director		1927-28, 1929-30, 1931-32, 1938, 1956
VOIGHT, Jon	Best Actor	1978	1969, 1985
Von STERNBERG, Josef	Best Director		1930-31, 1931-32
Von STROHEIM, Erich	Best Supp. Actor		1950
Von SYDOW, Max	Best Actor		1988
W			
WALKEN, Christopher	Best Supp. Actor	1978	
WALTERS, Charles	Best Director		1953
WALTERS, Julie	Best Actress		1983
WARDEN, Jack	Best Supp. Actor		1975, 1978
WARNER, H. B.	Best Supp. Actor		1937
WASHINGTON, Denzel	Best Supp. Actor	1989	
WATERS, Ethel	Best Supp. Actress		1949
WATERSTON, Sam	Best Actor		1984
WATSON, Lucile	Best Supp. Actress		1943
WAYNE, John	Best Actor	1969	1949
WEAVER, Sigourney	Best Actress		1986, 1988
"	Best Supp. Actress		1988
WEBB, Clifton	Best Supp. Actor		1944, 1946
"	Best Actor		1948
WEIR, Peter	Best Director		1985, 1989
WELD, Tuesday	Best Supp. Actress		1977
WELLES, Orson	Best Actor		1941
"	Best Director		1941
WELLMAN, William A.	Best Director		1937, 1949, 1954
WERNER, Oskar	Best Actor		1965
WERTMULLER, Lina	Best Director		1976

* Includes only actors, actresses and directors. 407 ** Other than years won.

NAME*	CATEGORY	YEARS WON	YEARS NOMINATED **
WHITMAN, Stuart	Best Actor		1961
WHITMORE, James	Best Supp. Actor		1949
"	Best Actor		1975
WHITTY, Dame May	Best Supp. Actress		1937, 1942
WIDMARK, Richard	Best Supp. Actor		1947
WIEST, Dianne	Best Supp. Actress	1986, 1994	1989
WILD, Jack	Best Supp. Actor		1968
WILDE, Cornel	Best Actor		1945
WILDE, Ted	Best Director		1927-28
WILDER, Billy	Best Director	1945, 1960	1944, 1950, 1953, 1954, 1957, 1959
WILDER, Gene	Best Supp. Actor		1968
WILLIAMS, Cara	Best Supp. Actress		1958
WILLIAMS, Robin	Best Actor		1987, 1989
WILLS, Chill	Best Supp. Actor		1960
WINFIELD, Paul	Best Actor		1972
WINFREY, Oprah	Best Supp. Actress		1985
WINGER, Debra	Best Actress		1982, 1983, 1993
WINNINGHAM, Mare	Best Supp. Actress		1995
WINSLET, Kate	Best Supp. Actress		1995
WINTERS, Shelley	Best Actress		1951
"	Best Supp. Actress	1959, 1965	1972
WISE, Robert	Best Director	1961, 1965	1958
WOOD, Natalie	Best Supp. Actress		1955
"	Best Actress		1961, 1963
WOOD, Peggy	Best Supp. Actress		1965
WOOD, Sam	Best Director		1939, 1940, 1942
WOODARD, Alfre	Best Supp. Actress		1983
WOODS, James	Best Actor		1986
WOODWARD, Joanne	Best Actress	1957	1968, 1973, 1990
WOOLLEY, Monty	Best Actor		1942
"	Best Supp. Actor		1944
WRIGHT, Teresa	Best Supp. Actress	1942	1941
"	Best Actress		1942
WYCHERLY, Margaret	Best Supp. Actress		1941
WYLER, William	Best Director	1942, 1946, 1959	1936, 1939, 1940, 1941, 1949, 1951,
WYLER, William	Best Director		1953, 1956, 1965
WYMAN, Jane	Best Actress	1948	1946, 1951, 1954
WYNN, Ed	Best Supp. Actor		1959
WYNYARD, Diana	Best Actress		1932-33
Y			
YATES, Peter	Best Director		1979, 1983
YORK, Susannah	Best Supp. Actress		1969
YOUNG, Burt	Best Supp. Actor		1976
YOUNG, Gig	Best Supp. Actor	1969	1951, 1958
YOUNG, Loretta	Best Actress	1947	1949
YOUNG, Roland	Best Supp. Actor		1937
Z			
ZEFFIRELLI, Franco	Best Director		1968
ZEMECKIS, Robert	Best Director	1994	
ZINNEMANN, Fred	Best Director	1953, 1966	1948, 1952, 1959, 1960, 1977

SUGGESTED BIBLIOGRAPHY

▣ CELEBRITY DIRECTORY, 6th Ed. 1996. Published by Axiom Information Resources, P. O. Box 8015, Ann Arbor, MI 48107 ($39.95)

▣ CEMETERIES OF THE UNITED STATES by Deborah M. Burek, 1994 (Published by Gale) $155.

▣ THE 1995 FAN CLUB DIRECTORY, Issue #19. Published annually by the National Association of Fan Clubs, P.O. Box 7487, Burbank, CA 91510, (Telephone: 1-818-763-3280); Printed by "Not Just Printing," 4532 Telephone Rd., #102, Ventura, CA 93003, (Telephone: 1-805-644-3245)

▣ THE ILLUSTRATED WHO'S WHO OF HOLLYWOOD DIRECTORS by Michael Barson (Published by The Noonday Press, 19 Union Square West, New York, NY 10003) $27.50

▣ PERMANENT CALIFORNIANS (An Illustrated Guide to the Cemeteries of California) by Judi Culbertson and Tom Randall, 1989 (Published by Chelsea Green Pub. Co., Chelsea, Vermont) $16.95

▣ PERMANENT ITALIANS (An Illustrated Guide to the Cemeteries of Italy) by Judi Culbertson and Tom Randall, 1989 (Published in U.S. by Walker Pub. Co., 435 Hudson St., New York, NY 10014) $16.95

▣ PERMANENT LONDONERS (An Illustrated Guide to the Cemeteries of London) by Judi Culbertson and Tom Randall, 1991 (Published in U.S. by Walker Pub. Co., 435 Hudson St., New York, NY 10014) $16.95

▣ PERMANENT NEW YORKERS (An Illustrated Guide to the Cemeteries of New York) by Judi Culbertson and Tom Randall, 1989 (Published by Chelsea Green Pub. Co., Chelsea, Vermont) $16.95

▣ PERMANENT PARISIANS (An Illustrated Guide to the Cemeteries of Paris) by Judi Culbertson and Tom Randall, 1986 (Published in U.S. by Walker Pub. Co., 435 Hudson St., New York, NY 10014) $16.95

▣ STAR GUIDE (Movie Star Home Address Book), 1996-97. Published by Axiom Information Resources, P. O. Box 8015, Ann Arbor, MI 48107 ($12.95 + $1.95 S&H)

▣ TOO YOUNG TO DIE by Patricia Fox-Sheinwold, 1991 (Published by Crescent Books, distributed by Outlet Book Co., Inc., a Random House Co., New York, NY)

▣ VARIETY OBITUARIES (1905 to 1994) in 11 volumes + 4 Bi-annual Yearbooks (Garland Publishers, Inc., New York and London)

▣ VARIETY (Weekly) Newspaper (Subscription Dept., P.O. Box 6400, Torrance, CA 90504-9867)

▣ WHO WAS WHO ON SCREEN by Evelyn Mack Truitt, 3rd Ed. 1983 (Published by R. R. Bowker Co., 205 East 42nd St., New York, NY 10017). A condensed, softcover 1984 "Illustrated Edition" is available @ $29.95

JAMES DEAN   410

ABOUT THE AUTHOR

- master of science (business management information systems)
  University of Baltimore
- bachelor of science (education)
  Towson State University
- associate in arts (business data processing)
  Baltimore Community College
- certificate in piano
  Peabody Conservatory of Music, Preparatory Department
- certificate in personnel management supervision
  U.S. Army Adjutant General's School
- training instructor's certificate
  Sperry-UNIVAC, Washington, D.C.
- honorably discharged veteran (Korean War)
  United States Army, Corps of Engineers
- college preparatory diploma
  Baltimore Polytechnic Institute
- retired college professor
  Computer Information Systems
- founder, owner and general manager
  Wisdom for Youth Publishers
- former systems analyst and branch education administrator
  Sperry-UNIVAC (now UNISYS)
- author of 38 published books
  (including ten editions of four computer programming texts for college students; eight editions of Final Curtain/Deaths of Noted Movie and Television Personalities; Family Record; The Mystery Of The Gospel; Think On These Things; Wisdom For Youth; The Real Cause and Cure of A.I.D.S.; A Wolf In Sheep's Clothing—Confronting the Religious Bias Against Same-Sex Relationships)
- father of five and grandfather of twelve